Promise and Performance of American Democracy

With an In-depth Analysis of the 1984 Presidential Contest

5th ed.

Promise and Performance of American Democracy

RICHARD A. WATSON
University of Missouri-Columbia

John Wiley & Sons
New York Chichester Brisbane Toronto Singapore

Cover photo by George Gardner.
Cover and book design by Rafael Hernandez.
Copy Editor, Michele Millon.
Photo Editor, Elyse Rieder.
Production Supervisor, David Smith.

Library of Congress Cataloging in Publication Data:

Watson, Richard Abernethy, 1923-
Promise and performance of American democracy, with an in-depth analysis of the 1984 presidential contest.

Includes bibliographies and index.
1. United States—Politics and government. I. Title.
JK274.W33 1985 320.473 84-25691

ISBN 0-471-81371-0 (brief)
ISBN 0-471-81372-9 (national)

Printed in the United States of America.

10 9 8 7 6 5 4 3 2

To GEORGE A. PEEK, JR.
who first stimulated my interest in the basic course
and to my students who have sustained it.

About the Author

RICHARD A. WATSON is a native of Pennsylvania. He graduated from Bucknell University and the University of Michigan Law School, and after practicing law in Denver, returned to Michigan from which he received his Ph.D. in Political Science. He has taught at the University of Missouri-Columbia for the past 25 years.

Watson's other books include *The Politics of Urban Change* (1963), *The Politics of the Bench and the Bar* (with Rondal G. Downing, 1969), *The Presidential Contest* (1980 and 1984) and *The Politics of the Presidency* (with Norman C. Thomas, 1983). He is presently working on a study of presidential vetoes and national policy-making.

Active in professional life, he has served on the editorial boards of *The American Political Science Review* and the *Midwest Journal of Political Science,* and as Vice President of the Midwest Political Science Association. He has received grants from the American Historical and Political Science Associations, the Ford Foundation, and the Social Science Research Council; been a Fellow at the Center for Advanced Study in the Behavioral Sciences; and a Guest Scholar at the Brookings Institution and the University of Denver Law School.

When not teaching, writing, arguing politics, or agonizing over the Pittsburgh Pirates, he can be found hacking around the golf course or hitting tennis balls into the net.

Preface to the Fifth Edition

This fifth edition bears the particular imprint of Ronald Reagan. Chapters 7, 8, and 9—dealing with, respectively, the nomination, election, and voting for candidates—draw heavily upon his successful campaign against Jimmy Carter in 1980. Appendix A contains an in-depth analysis of the 1984 contest between Ronald Reagan and his Democratic challenger, Walter Mondale, and the voters' reactions to that contest.

All the pertinent chapters of this new edition have also been updated to take account of the myriad effects of "Reaganism" between those two elections. The "Public Policies" section of the National Edition contains an entirely new chapter "Social Policies" (Chapter 18) that analyzes the "attack on the welfare state." Also discussed is "Reaganomics"—tax and domestic budget cuts, "supply-side" economics, and the deregulation of business (Chapter 17), as well as the rapid military build-up initiated by President Reagan (Chapter 19).

Other effects of Reaganism are treated in both the Brief and National Editions. Included are topics such as his "New Federalism" (Chapter 3); the techniques the "Great Communicator" has utilized in wooing interest groups, the general public, the media, and Congress (Chapter 11); his attempts to tame the federal bureaucracy (Chapter 12); his appointment of the first woman Justice, Sandra Day O'Connor, to the Supreme Court (Chapter 13); and his reconstitution of the Civil Rights Commission (Chapter 15).

This fifth edition also treats other recent changes in our political system that are not *directly* attributable to President Reagan (he has, however, been affected by some of them). Included are the rise of the New Christian Right in interest-group politics (Chapter 5); the increased role played by Political Action

Committees (PACs) in congressional elections (Chapter 8); the development of a more "individualistic" Senate (Chapter 10); the Supreme Court's striking down of the legislative veto (Chapter 12); its recent decisions relaxing the wall between church and state and restrictions on the use of illegally-seized evidence (Chapter 14), together with its controversial opinions relating to abortion (Chapter 14) and "affirmative action" (Chapter 15).

Two other broad developments—the increased influence of blacks, women, and Hispanics in American society, and the augmented role the mass media play in American politics—are also highlighted in this edition. Since their effects are felt throughout the American political system, these developments are treated in many parts of the book rather than in a single chapter.

Despite these extensive revisions, I have tried to retain what faculty and students alike have told me are desirable features of previous editions: a comparison of the actual performance of American democracy with its theoretical promises; clarity and readability of style and objectivity of treatment; and chapter openings and concluding assessments that distinguish the book from other American government texts.

I have been assisted with this edition by many persons. I obtained helpful ideas on how to improve the book from a survey of users of the previous edition and from James Anderson of the University of Houston who reviewed two of the key chapters dealing with public policies. My colleagues at the University of Missouri and elsewhere alerted me to new literature, and June DeWeese, Barbara Francis, and John Wesselman of the Social Science Division of the University of Missouri Library helped me track down information from many sources. Finally, the entire Wiley team—Patricia Brecht, Butch Cooper, Rafael Hernandez, Carol Luitjens, Michele Millon, Mark Mochary, Tina Papatsos, Elyse Rieder, David Smith, and Susan Winick—facilitated the completion of this fifth edition.

As always, my wife, Joan, helped to edit and type the book, and along with my children, Suzy and John (Tom is now in Washington doing political writing of his own), put up with a husband–father who seems always to be closeted in his carrel in the university library.

September 18, 1984 RICHARD A. WATSON

Contents

PART 2
POPULAR CONTROL 97

PART 3
OFFICIAL DECISION-MAKING 301

CHAPTER 13
The Courts **435**

PART 4
INDIVIDUAL FREEDOMS **467**

CHAPTER 14
Civil Liberties **469**

CHAPTER 15
Civil Rights **509**

PART 5
PUBLIC POLICIES **553**

CHAPTER 16
Fundamentals of Public Policy **555**

CHAPTER 17
Economic Policies **575**

CHAPTER 18
Social Policies **623**

CHAPTER 19
Foreign and Military Policies **649**

Appendixes

Promise and Performance of American Democracy

CHAPTER 1

The Promise of Democracy

On Saturday morning, April 3, 1982, some 14 months after his inauguration, President Ronald Reagan began a series of weekly radio broadcasts to the American people. (In doing so, the president was returning to the medium in which he had begun his career half a century ago as a sports announcer for University of Iowa football and Chicago Cubs' baseball.) He explained to reporters that the presidential broadcasts were part of an administration effort to overcome ". . . all the confusion and all the conflicting things that come out of Washington . . ." by bringing ". . . the facts to the people as simply as I can and as much as I can in five minutes."

The first broadcast, from the Oval Office of the White House, was devoted to the president's tax and budget cuts (tabbed *Reaganomics*) and their effect on the nation's economy. In an attempt to justify a recent downturn in the economy, Reagan explained, "You've been told our program hasn't worked. Well, of course, it hasn't. It hasn't really started yet." He then went on to say, "Now I know you've been told by some that we should do away with the tax cuts in order to reduce the deficit. That's like trying to pull a game out of the fourth quarter by punting on the third down."

The networks provided equal time for the Democrats' reply to the president. House Majority Leader Jim Wright of Texas said that Democrats, ". . . believe that there has to be a better way . . ." than the Reagan economic program and that the budget should not be balanced ". . . without a serious consideration of the one-sided tax cuts of last year," which go "mostly to the wealthiest" and provide a "tax bonanza" for "the very largest corporations."

Another five-minute presidential talk and Democratic reply were broadcast a week later. Speaking from Barbados where he was spending a working vacation, President Reagan defended his budget proposals on the student-aid program. "We haven't cut loans. We've cut the costs to taxpayers of making those loans available." Senator Carl Levin of Michigan responded for the Democrats from depression-wracked Detroit. He invited the president to visit there after his tropical vacation to view the "pain and suffering" his economic program was causing. Senator Levin stated, "The President created an impression today—I think a wrong impression—that these are only administrative cuts."

The Saturday morning broadcasts continued in the following weeks. The President focused on a variety of topics: the nuclear freeze movement, interest rates, unemployment, the state of the armed forces, the federal budget, and other major public issues. On October 30, 1982, the last broadcast before the 1982 congressional elections, President Reagan once again urged Americans to be patient with his economic policies. Responding from the home of an unemployed auto worker in Worcester, Massachusetts, Senator Edward Kennedy asked, "How could the president possibly ask this family to 'stay the course'?"

The president resumed the broadcasts on January 15, 1983. He paid tribute to slain black leader Martin Luther King, whose fifty-fourth birthday was marked by remembrance ceremonies across the nation. Black Congressman Charles Rangel of New York retorted that the president's "fine words" are ". . . in conflict with those actions that his administration has taken regarding the civil and human rights of many in this country." On September 3, 1983, the president used a Labor Day theme to stress that the ". . . economy is gaining strength and that is good for all of us." Democratic Representative William Ford of Michigan replied that it is "ironic" that President Reagan is taking credit for reducing the unemployment rate. In effect, "he is saying that he is reducing the suffering he caused in the first place."

Thus, President Reagan—called by many the "Great Communicator"—sought to convey his administration's programs to the American people. However, all radio stations did not carry the presidential broadcasts and many (if not most) Americans did not tune in those that did. Moreover, the process was one way: listeners could not comment on the president's remarks or ask him questions about them.

These broadcasts point up the practical difficulties in trying to establish meaningful communication between political office-holders and a large, diverse population. The broadcasts also demonstrate another important characteristic of a modern democratic society: political institutions that enable elected representatives to act for the general populace. Thus, Democratic members of the Senate and House of Representatives who responded to President Reagan's broadcasts were able to make comments and raise questions about his administration's programs that citizens themselves could not. The dialogue between the incumbent president and spokespersons for the opposition party also enabled Americans to judge which of their respective ideas were best for them personally, as well as for the country as a whole.

In this first chapter, we will examine two models of government designed to keep political leaders responsible to the people: **direct democracy,** epitomized by Athens, a Greek city-state, and **representative democracy,** the type of government used in countries like Great Britain, Switzerland, and the United States. We will focus on the political techniques and institutions of direct and representative democracy as well as on the values and assumptions about human nature on which these two forms of government are based.

The initial sections of this chapter are

President Reagan's Saturday morning chat.

concerned with the "theory" of democracy—how it *ought to operate* if the expectations of those who developed the concept of democratic government are to be met. We thus focus on the "promise" of democracy—a standard by which our government can be judged.

Evaluating the way American democracy *actually works in practice*—that is, its "performance"—is a matter we will be concerned with throughout this book. Towards the end of this chapter we consider some of the major challenges and problems of our government today: the sheer size of our country, its geographical and social diversity, major changes occurring among its people and the complexities with which they must deal, our private economy, and the world community. We then summarize two overviews of our political system—one that suggests that it has for the most part met these and other challenges and lived up to the promise of democracy, and another that argues that we have not dealt effectively with our problems and that the performance of American government falls far short of democratic ideals.

The purpose of this first chapter, then, is to provide you with some general standards for judging our institutions, an appreciation of the kinds of challenges American democracy faces today, and some understanding of the supposed strengths and weaknesses of our political system. However, you should ultimately make your own judgments on American democracy. Others can provide ideas of what to look for and facts and interpretations to consider, but they should not be allowed to decide such matters for you.

THE GENERAL NATURE OF DEMOCRACY

The word *democracy* is derived from two Greek roots—*demos*, which means "people," and *kratia*, which connotes "rule."

Thus **democracy** literally means "rule by the people." For a society to be democratic, a large number of its people must enjoy the right to have some say over important decisions that seriously affect their lives. To put it another way, democratic government is based on the consent of the governed. Viewed thus, democracy is concerned with *how* political decisions are made, the *procedure* by which ordinary people participate in the making of such decisions.

While democracy is most often defined in terms of *how* governmental decisions are made, it is also associated with the *content* of those decisions. In other words, democracy involves not only the *process* of making public policies but also the *results* of the process. Democratic governments by definition produce policies that foster certain basic democratic *values* such as **liberty, equality,** and **justice.**

The underlying idea, of course, is that if a large number of people participate in governmental decisions, those decisions will produce liberty, equality, and justice for the great bulk of citizens. Therefore democracy is also based on certain *assumptions about human nature,* namely, that the ordinary person is rational enough to use his or her political influence for the purpose of fostering democratic values.

While there is agreement on these general features and beliefs of democracy, there are differences of opinion on the specifics. For example, what constitutes participation or some say over governmental decisions by ordinary citizens? Is it sufficient that they be able to choose public officials to make decisions or must the citizens have an even more direct influence over the content of policies? If so, how much influence and in what manner is it to be exercised? What is meant by *equality*? Are we talking about political equality, legal equality, economic equality, or what? How far does the rationality of the average person go? Must an individual be able to determine what kind of policy is needed to bring more liberty or equality in a society? Or is it sufficient to judge between policies suggested by others?

There are no definite answers to any of these questions; reasonable people equally committed to democracy differ over them. In this respect there is one general theory of democracy, but there are many theories about the specific procedures, ideals, and assumptions associated with a democratic society. Nonetheless it is possible to distinguish certain general types of democracy that have prevailed in various countries in different historical eras.

ATHENIAN DIRECT DEMOCRACY

Athens, an ancient Greek city-state with some 300,000 inhabitants, is known as the cradle of democracy. There in the fifth century B.C., it developed institutions and beliefs that were clearly democratic. Today we would refer to the Athenian system as **direct democracy** because all adult male citizens (women, slaves, foreigners, and free men under 20 years of age were excluded) were permitted to play an important role in the governance of the community. In fact, a significant number of eligible citizens actually did play such a role.

Political Techniques and Institutions

All adult, male citizens in Athens belonged to the Assembly, a town-meeting type of gathering that met 10 times a year to conduct public business. This body, however, was too large and met too infrequently to handle all the political problems of the city-state; much of the real governance was in the hands of a 500-man Council that in turn divided itself into 10 committees to expedite the consideration of problems. In addition, there were large juries composed of citizens who decided legal controversies.

The system was not the pure, direct democracy in which the average citizen participates in each and every political decision; nonetheless, each citizen played a significant part in many of them. Although the Council and its committees initially handled many problems, major issues came back to the Assembly for final disposition. That body, for example, gave its approval to declarations of war and negotiations of peace, the forming of alliances, the levying of direct taxes, and the like.

Officeholding by ordinary citizens was widespread. The 500-member Council was drawn by lot from persons elected by small geographical units, *demes*, the equivalent of our wards, townships, or parishes. Service on the Council and in most other political posts was typically for one year, so positions rotated from one person to another quickly. The large juries, ranging in size from 200 to 500 persons, were also drawn by lot from a panel of 6000 citizens selected each year. Because different juries were assigned to sit in particular courts, many juries were operating simultaneously. Such a system clearly called for broad participation by citizens: about one in six held some political office in any given year.

The operating principles of Athenian democracy were also distinctly democratic. The give-and-take of spirited debate and extensive discussions was the prevailing means of exploring and clarifying public problems. The final decisions in both the Assembly and the juries were reached by majority vote.

Statesman Pericles addresses fellow Athenians.

Values and Assumptions

Underlying the political institutions and operating principles of Athenian society were certain values that expressed what its citizens felt were the important things in life. Foremost of these was the belief that a citizen could achieve happiness and personal development only through *participation in the life of the community.* He was expected to attend to family and business affairs, but these were not to interfere with his duties to the broader community. His loyalty to the city-state was expected to supersede his private concerns and his attachments to less inclusive groups.

Political equality was another ideal of Athenian democracy. All citizens, regardless of their social station or financial situation, were given equal opportunity to participate in the political life of the community. To ensure that the poor could afford to take part in political affairs, most offices were paid; in some instances, individuals were even compensated for attending sessions of the Assembly.

Along with political equality went a *respect for the law.* The Athenian had great faith in the procedures by which the Assembly, Council, and popular juries reached their decisions, and he was inclined to follow those decisions once they were made. For the Athenian, the rule of law was distinctly Greek as contrasted to the edicts of arbitrary rulers under which barbarians were forced to live.

The whole political system was predicated on a great faith in the essential *rationality* of the ordinary citizen. Athenians attributed no special political competence to persons of higher social or economic standing in the community. Nor did they have particular regard for the expert; they rather extolled the virtues of the "happy versatility" of the average citizen—what we would term today the ability of the "amateur." Although Athenians did not expect everyone to originate public policies, they considered each man a sound judge of policies. The belief in man's rationality was also reflected in the discussions and debates that characterized the Athenian political process. The faith that a wise law or good institution could bear the scrutiny of many minds was a basic assumption under which this democracy operated.

Athenian government was thus a direct democracy in which a large sample of citizens participated in decisions of the Assembly while also exercising control over actions of the Council through the Assembly. At the same time a great number of citizens served on the Council and even more sat as members of the large juries.

Such political institutions have had little application throughout history. In the long period following the decline of Athens (which fell largely as a result of military encounters with its neighbors), people were governed by kings, merchant-princes, generals, religious leaders, aristocrats, or nobles. When democracy was revived in the form of direct citizen involvement in decision-making, it was confined to small units like Swiss cantons and New England town meetings.

The governance of large countries such as Great Britain and the United States required a different form of democracy. The general type of government that developed in these nations in recent centuries serves as the major example of democracy in the modern world. It is known by many names: **Western democracy** for the geographical location of the countries in which it originated;

for its emphasis on limiting government through legal means; **liberal democracy** for its concern with the liberty of the individual. Here it is referred to simply as **Western representative democracy,** both for its source and the basic technique it utilizes to implement the ideal of government by the people.

WESTERN REPRESENTATIVE DEMOCRACY

Representative democracy is a system of government in which ordinary citizens do not make governmental decisions themselves but instead choose public officials to make decisions for them. In modern nations encompassing millions of people, only a relatively few persons hold public positions, especially in the national government. Thus, each member of the United States House of Representatives represents some half-million people.

Democratic representative government as we know it today first developed in three Western nations: Great Britain, Switzerland, and the United States. In these countries in the late eighteenth and early nineteenth centuries a large number of people first began to select their political leaders. From this narrow base, democracy spread to other Western European nations and the British Commonwealth. Representative democracy, then, is a form of government that is restricted to a relatively small group of nations in recent centuries.

In fact, if full democracy requires that the majority of the population have the right to affect governmental decisions by choosing its leaders, then this type of government is an even more recent phenomenon. Great Britain and the United States did not provide for universal manhood suffrage until the latter part of the nineteenth century, and women were not permitted to vote in national elections until the 1920s. Switzerland did not fully extend the suffrage to women until nearly 50 years later.

Political Techniques and Institutions

As we have already seen, in a representative democracy ordinary citizens do not govern; rather they choose those who do. Aristotle referred to such a system as the "... rule of the few watched

The British House of Commons in the eighteenth century.

by the many." The crucial part of the phrase is not "rule by the few," since under all political systems a small minority of the populace holds major political office. The key idea is *the many watching those few.*

Representative democracy, however, requires more than mere watching; the many must also be able to implement their observations through political action. The system has to give the people control over their leaders, so that the latter can be held responsible for their actions. If the general populace is unable to exercise such control, then the government does not differ from an **oligarchy,** in which political authority is vested in a few persons who are not accountable to the people.

The particular mechanism that representative democracies have developed to keep their political leaders responsible to the general populace is *elections.* Indeed, democratic societies deliberately create insecurity of tenure for major office-holders, who are periodically required to go before the people to have their terms of office renewed. As Walter Lippmann, a perceptive writer and columnist, once put it, those "outside" the government pass judgment on those "inside."

If the citizens in a democracy are displeased with what those in public office are doing about major problems, the remedy is to replace them. Thus a democratic system of government must provide the electorate with competing groups of political leaders. The power of the people is effective only if they have the opportunity *to choose* one group over another.

All democratic societies, then, must develop some means of providing political leaders for the consideration of the populace. The institution that typically fills this need is the **political party,** which puts forward candidates for public office. In order to provide the element of choice for the voters, there must be at least two competing parties that propose candidates. A voter can then choose a candidate from Party A over one from Party B because he feels that the former will do the more satisfactory job in making political decisions that affect his interests. Since there must be at least two parties, it is entirely consistent with the theory of democracy that three or four (or more) parties should offer potential leaders to the voters.

Because no political party in a democracy can be permitted to be the sole provider of candidates for public office, each party must recognize the right of others to compete. The parties must accept one another's existence as a necessity; beyond that, they must be willing to coexist peacefully. Accordingly, the party (or parties) presently in control of a government must allow the opposition party (or parties) to criticize what the leaders are doing and to propose alternative courses of action for the voters' consideration. Moreover, the incumbents must hold elections in which they can be replaced by members of the opposition. Thus, today's majority must be prepared for the possibility of becoming tomorrow's minority.

It is precisely this spirit of tolerance and willingness to allow themselves to be voted out of office that presents the most difficulty for leaders of nations that are first experimenting with democracy. There is a natural tendency for those in political power to consider those who question their policies—indeed their very right to remain in control of the government—as subversive. We are familiar today with this attitude among leaders of emerging nations like South Korea, but, as we shall see later, a similar attitude existed among the early party leaders of our own country. The idea of a "loyal opposition" presupposes a considerable amount of maturity and sophistication in the ways of democracy. It is perhaps best exemplified today by the British system of government, which not only tolerates opposition but actually fosters it by including a post known as "Her Majesty's loyal opposition." That position, which is occupied by the leader of the party out of power, carries the right to use funds provided by the government to criticize the party in power.

The minority party (or parties) has more than the responsibility of criticizing the policies of the majority and of suggesting alternatives; it also has the obligation to accept the verdict at the polls and to permit the majority party to remain in office until the next election. One of the most eloquent statements of the proper attitude of a losing candidate in a democracy was made by Adlai Stevenson on the occasion of his defeat by Dwight Eisenhower in 1956. (Stevenson also lost the presidency to Eisenhower in 1952; the margin of loss was wider in the second election than in the first.)

> *To you who are disappointed tonight, let me confess that I am too! But we must not be downhearted. . . . For here in America, the people have made their choice in a vigorous partisan contest that has affirmed again the vitality of the democratic process. And I say God bless partisanship, for this is democracy's life blood.*
>
> *But beyond the seas, in much of the world, in Russia, in China, in Hungary, in all the trembling satellites, partisan controversy is forbidden and dissent suppressed.*
>
> *So I say to you, my dear and loyal friends, take heart—there are things more precious than political victory; there is the right to political contest.*

Democracy provides the electoral machinery whereby competing groups of leaders contest for political office by vying for the votes of the public. The winners take responsibility for developing policies to deal with the major problems of society; the losers have the obligation to criticize those policies and the right to use their criticism as a means of attracting enough supporters at the next election to assume political office themselves. The majority of the general populace has the responsibility of deciding which of the competing minorities will be permitted to govern until the next election.

Democracy not only requires competition between minorities who seek to govern with the consent of the people; individuals, too, must be permitted to become candidates for public office themselves and, if elected, to serve. The system must thus be open to everyone regardless of a person's social or economic status.

Beyond elections, which occur periodically, a democratic society must provide continuous communication between the leaders and the general populace so that personal views on public issues can be transmitted to those who make major political decisions. There is no obligation for those in political power to carry the suggestions into effect, but citizens must be entitled to have their viewpoints heard.

Although individuals can express their attitudes on various matters, to be effective they must join with other like-minded persons to form groups that can communicate their demands to decision-makers. The institution that has emerged in democracies to transmit demands to those in political power is called an **interest group.** Even these groups are likely to contain only a small proportion of the total population, but they enable a public officeholder to gain some understanding of how a number of people in a common situation—say, businessmen, laborers, or farmers—feel about such matters as taxes, wages, or farm prices. Moreover because communication is a two-way process, interest groups not only press **demands** on decision-makers but also transmit pro-

Adlai Stevenson conceding defeat

"Gray Power" rally at U.S. Capitol.

posals by political leaders to their memberships, who serve as potential sources of **support** for the proposals.

Just as parties compete in a democratic society to place their candidates in public office, so interest groups vie with one another to influence public policy. If the system is operating properly, they check and balance one another's efforts so that no one group or small number of groups dominates the political process. All kinds of groups representing persons with different social and economic backgrounds and concerns should be able to make themselves heard effectively by officials who make crucial governmental decisions.

The public officials who make the decisions in representative democracies are more diverse and specialized in training than those who held office in Athenian democracy. Although members of the general public still serve on juries in courtroom controversies, they decide on the facts of the case only; judges with extensive legal training rule on questions of law. Specialists also serve in the executive arm of the government. Only the legislature remains as the branch of the political "amateur," and, as in the Greek Assembly, decisions are typically made by majority vote.

While representative democracy supports majority rule, at the same time it protects the rights of minorities. Representatives of minority viewpoints are permitted to be heard and to criticize the opinions of the majority. Moreover, the system provides the opportunity for present minorities to become future majorities.

Minorities in a democracy, however, enjoy other rights besides that of eventually turning themselves into a majority. As we shall see below, certain fundamental rights are protected from infringement by public officials even when they are acting with the support of the majority. The protection comes through constitutions and courts that limit what the government can do. It also derives from attitudes and political customs that determine the proper way for the majority to act towards minorities.

So far we have considered how representative democracies go about making political decisions. But democracy is more than a set of procedures; it also involves values that the procedures are designed to foster and protect.

Values

The single most significant idea in democratic thought is the belief in the *basic integrity of the individual.* This overriding concern is best expressed in the command of philosopher Immanuel Kant to ". . . treat all individuals not merely as a means to an end, but as an end in and of themselves." In this view all persons are entitled to consideration simply because they are human beings. As such, they possess dignity and moral worth that everyone is obliged to respect.

One of the consequences of this concern is the belief that the government or the state exists for the individual, not the individual for the state. This idea is captured in the Declaration of Independence, which proclaims that people ". . . are endowed by their Creator with certain unalienable rights . . ." and that ". . . to secure these rights, Governments are instituted among Men, deriving their just powers from the consent of the governed." Government does not create these rights; rather *it* is created by individuals to safeguard their natural rights.

This idea of the proper relationship between the individual and government may seem too idealistic, yet it continues to be an important part of the democratic creed. David Lilienthal, the first director of the Tennessee Valley Authority and one of the nation's outstanding public servants, with a wealth of experience in practical, everyday affairs, expressed the same basic thought in testimony before a Senate committee:

> *I believe, and I conceive the Constitution of the United States to rest, as does religion, upon the fundamental proposition of the integrity of the individual, and that all government, and all private institutions, must be designed to promote and protect and defend the integrity of the individual.*

Another major value of democracy is *liberty.* Liberty involves a person's freedom to select his or her own purposes in life together with the means to accomplish them. Obviously neither of these liberties is absolute. Society, acting through the government, will impose reasonable restrictions; it will not permit a person, for example, to choose to become the world's most skillful thief. Or even if he selects a lofty aim for himself—say, the presidency of a great corporation—he will not be allowed to deal violently with rivals who stand in his path. There is a difference between liberty and *licence,* which is the *unrestricted* freedom to choose one's purposes and methods. Society will not let anyone "do his thing" if it interferes with the rights of others or even, in some cases, if it harms himself. Nonetheless in the ideal democratic society such restrictions are minimal, and citizens retain the liberty to develop themselves to the fullest extent of their capacities.

Liberty carries with it the idea of *privacy,* the freedom to be left alone. Individuals have the right to their own thoughts and their own property, and the government cannot force them to share such personal attributes with other citizens or with the government itself. Again, of course, privacy is not absolute; for example, an individual will be required to pay a proportionate share of taxes to provide government services—military and police protection, education, and the like. Still, democracy maintains as many private preserves for the individual as possible. Democracy thus involves freedom *from* (arbitrary government) as well as freedom *to* (participate in government).

Another major value of democracy is *equality*. There are, however, many kinds of equality. The one that is most often accepted as part of the democratic creed is **political equality.** This involves the right of all adult citizens to vote for their political officials with each vote counting as one and only one. Everyone is also equally entitled to seek and, if successful, to serve in public office. Political equality applies to other, nonelectoral activities as well, such as the opportunity to form interest groups or to discuss and debate political issues.

Equality not only relates to participation in influencing or making governmental decisions; it also involves being subject to those decisions. Thus everyone is entitled to **equality under the law.** The law is to be applied impartially without regard to the identity or status of the individual involved. Few persons quarrel with this concept.

Somewhat more controversial than political and legal equality is the concept of **social equality.** Its basis is the idea that people should be free of class or social barriers and discrimination. While many agree on the desirability of this ideal, they disagree on what, if anything, the government should do to require individuals to abide by it. The long battle over racial equality described in Chapter 15 reflects different attitudes on this basic question.

Economic equality is the most controversial of all democratic concepts, primarily because people attribute different meanings to it. Under a strict interpretation each person would receive the same amount of worldly goods regardless of his or her contribution to society. This is what Karl Marx had in mind when he wrote, "From each according to his abilities [society should take from the individual what he is able to contribute]; to each according to his needs [he should receive from society what he must have to get along in life]." If everyone's needs are basically the same, then each person should receive the same amount of economic wealth.

Although Western democracies have generally favored a fairly wide distribution of wealth, they have not construed economic equality to mean that everyone must obtain the same amount of material possessions. Rather, all persons should have **equality of opportunity,** the chance to develop themselves to the fullest extent of their capacities. But even that concept has different interpretations. Does it mean merely formal opportunity in the sense that positions should be open to everyone on the basis of capability? Or does it require that material conditions be equalized by universally providing basic services (good health care, education, and the like) that are vital to individual self-development? This latter position suggests that, although a democratic society need not ensure equality at the end of the developmental process, it should see to it that people are made equal at the beginning of it.

One of the reasons Western democracies such as Great Britain and the United States favor the equal opportunity concept is that it permits them to reconcile the two values of liberty and equality. If individuals differ in ability, then to give every person the liberty to develop to the fullest extent of his or her capacities will result in some acquiring more goods than others. In other words, Western democracy gives individuals the *equal opportunity to become unequal.*

Assumptions about Human Nature

Advocates of representative democracy urge the participation of the average person in government because they believe that people are, for the most part, rational and capable of deciding what is

Inequality, American style.

good for them personally. Even if their judgments are not always correct, they are more likely to be so than if an elite makes decisions for them. The democrat assumes that no elite group is wise enough or unselfish enough to rule in the interests of all members of society. The only way to ensure that the interests of everyone will be taken into account is to give the bulk of the population the right to influence the basic decisions that affect their lives.

The greatest influence most people have on these decisions is exerted through their choice of candidates for public office. Representative democracy does not, therefore, require that the average person himself make decisions about public problems; it only asks him to determine whether political leaders who do make such decisions are doing so satisfactorily. The populace thus acts as a "consumer" of public policy decisions produced by others. As one student of democratic theory, A. D. Lindsay, has suggested, "Only the ordinary man can tell whether the shoes pinch and where." In other words, only the individuals subject to rules and regulations know how they are personally affected by them. To determine this, the average person does not have to know how to make governmental decisions any more than he has to be a shoemaker to know that certain shoes hurt his feet.

The democrat is skeptical about the possibility of knowing what is absolutely "good" or "true" when dealing with worldly problems. He or she takes issue with belief in an objective truth that can be discovered by a special group of individuals set apart from the rest of the populace by intelligence and training. The democrat assumes either that no such absolutes exist or that, even if they do, they cannot be discovered by mortals, however intelligent or educated they may be. For all practical purposes, the truth is a relative matter. As Supreme Court Justice Oliver Wendell Holmes put it, ". . . the best test of truth is the power of the thought to get itself accepted in the competition of the market. . . ." By this he meant that in a democracy a variety of ideas and viewpoints can be expressed, and what emerges as the choice of the people is the closest thing to truth that can be achieved.

This lack of certainty about truth renders possible another assumption of democracy, namely, that individuals can *tolerate* viewpoints that differ from their own. Since no one has a private pipeline to eternal political verities, a person ought to be able to face up to the possibility that he or she *may* be wrong about a given matter and that the other person may be right. The adherent of democracy assumes that a spirit of give-and-take and a willingness to *compromise* will develop among individuals, enabling them to resolve their differences in a peaceful manner.

The democrat also takes the position that decisions made by a large number of people are more likely to be good ones than are those made by a few. E. B. White, an American writer, expresses this idea in his statement that "Democracy is the recurrent suspicion that more than half of the people are right more than half of the time." In other words, a majority is more likely than a minority to decide the correct thing to do. But White's statement underscores the tentative nature of democratic faith in the majority.

In fact, the proponent of democracy does not always trust the majority and consequently is not willing to allow it to decide all matters that affect peoples' lives. Minority rights must also be respected. Democracy evolved in Western Europe and America in the eighteenth and nineteenth centuries from an earlier concept known as **constitutionalism,** which had as a major principle the idea that government should be limited. For example, in the United States and Great Britain it makes no difference that more than half the population is Protestant; they are not permitted to tell persons of the Catholic, Jewish, or other faiths how to worship. Likewise, in Western democratic nations the individual's right to private property is respected, and his personal goods cannot be taken from him even for a public use (as, for example, when a university takes private land to expand its operations) without just compensation.* It is precisely this limitation on the scope of gov-

* It should be understood that some democracies have a socialistic economic system in which the basic means of production are owned by the government. However, such democracies compensate private owners whose property is appropriated and placed under government

ernment—based on a concern for privacy as well as on limited faith in majority rule—that distinguishes a democratic society from a totalitarian one.

Democracy presupposes neither a wholly optimistic, nor a wholly pessimistic view of human nature. It does not rest on the faith that people are innately good or cooperative, nor on the assumption made by some advocates of totalitarianism that the average person is depraved. The democrat's ambivalence toward human nature is aptly expressed in the comment of the late theologian Reinhold Niebuhr that ". . . man's capacity for justice makes democracy possible; but man's inclination to injustice makes democracy necessary."

This combination of political techniques and institutions, values, and assumptions regarding human nature underlies Western representative democracy. While such attributes are associated today with the political systems of certain European countries, Japan, and countries in the British Commonwealth, they have particular application to our own country.

Three distinguished foreign scholars who observed and wrote about American democracy, Alexis de Tocqueville (a Frenchman), James Bryce (an Englishman), and Gunnar Myrdal (a Swede), all noted the centrality of democratic ideals in the American way of life. De Tocqueville, who visited here in the 1830s, noted that ". . . from the Missouri to the Atlantic Ocean, the people are held to be the source of all legitimate power. The same notions are entertained respecting liberty and equality, the liberty of the press, the right of association, the jury, and the responsibility of the agents of governments." Bryce, who came here a half-century later, also saw the same major elements of the American Creed: the rights of the individual, the people as the source of political power, the wisdom of the majority compared to the minority, and the necessity of limiting the government by law. Myrdal, writing in the 1940s, echoed the same observation: "Americans of all national origins, classes, regions, creeds, and colors, have something in common: a social ethos, a political creed."

Our special lady.

control. Democracy is thus a *political system, not an economic one*; it can coexist with either a private-enterprise economy, such as we have in the United States, or with more socialistic economies, such as in Great Britain, France, and Sweden.

There is general agreement that these central elements of the American Creed have persisted over time. American political sociologist, Seymour Martin Lipset, concluded in 1963 that "... there is more continuity than change with respect to the main elements in the national value system."

Yet it should be understood that these principles are general in nature and often conflict with one another: liberty versus equality; majority rule versus minority rights; the liberty of the press versus the protection of the accused in a criminal proceeding. Throughout this book we will be examining the nature of such basic conflicts and the ways they have been resolved.

Not only have American democratic values persisted, but so have our basic techniques and political institutions for implementing them. But as also indicated in the chapters that follow, those techniques and institutions have had to adapt to changing conditions in American society. In the next section we identify some of those conditions that have constituted important challenges to American democracy.

CHALLENGES TO AMERICAN DEMOCRACY

The United States has changed greatly over the course of more than two centuries of existence. As a result, the conditions that political officials face today are radically different from those with which the Founders were familiar when they devised our basic system of government in the late 1780s. Moreover, the pace of change has accelerated in recent years: the United States is significantly different from what it was in the 1960s when most of the readers of this text were born. The alterations in American life are many and varied; here we focus on only a few of the major examples.

Size: Area and Population

The first census of the United States, taken in 1790, indicated that the territory included within the 13 original colonies covered less than 900,000 square miles. As Figure 1.1 indicates, the nation and the territories under its jurisdiction have been expanded on several occasions since 1803, when we bought the Louisiana Territory from France, until we purchased the Virgin Islands from Denmark in 1917. Today the 50 states, covering all of continental United States, Alaska, and Hawaii, include over 3,600,000 square miles. Thus the area included within our country (not counting its overseas territories) has quadrupled since its founding.

The increase in our population has been even more significant. The 1790 census showed that fewer than 4 million persons were included in our nation; at the outbreak of the War of 1812, that figure had doubled; by the turn of the twentieth century, it stood at 76 million. As Figure 1.2 indicates, the turn-of-the-century population almost doubled by mid-century and virtually tripled by the three-quarter mark. The population growth over the total period of our nation's history thus increased more than fifty times, from 4 million in 1790 to 227 million in 1980.

Diversity: Geographical and Social

Our nation is not only large but also diverse. The states run the gamut from tiny Rhode Island with 1200 square miles of area to mammoth Alaska with 566,000. In population the latter state is the smallest, with just over 400,000 residents in 1980, whereas California, the nation's most populous state, has almost 24 million people. Moreover, the various regions of the country are experiencing disparate rates of growth. As shown by Figure 1.3, the West and South had great population increases in the period from 1960 to 1980, while the numbers of people living in the North-

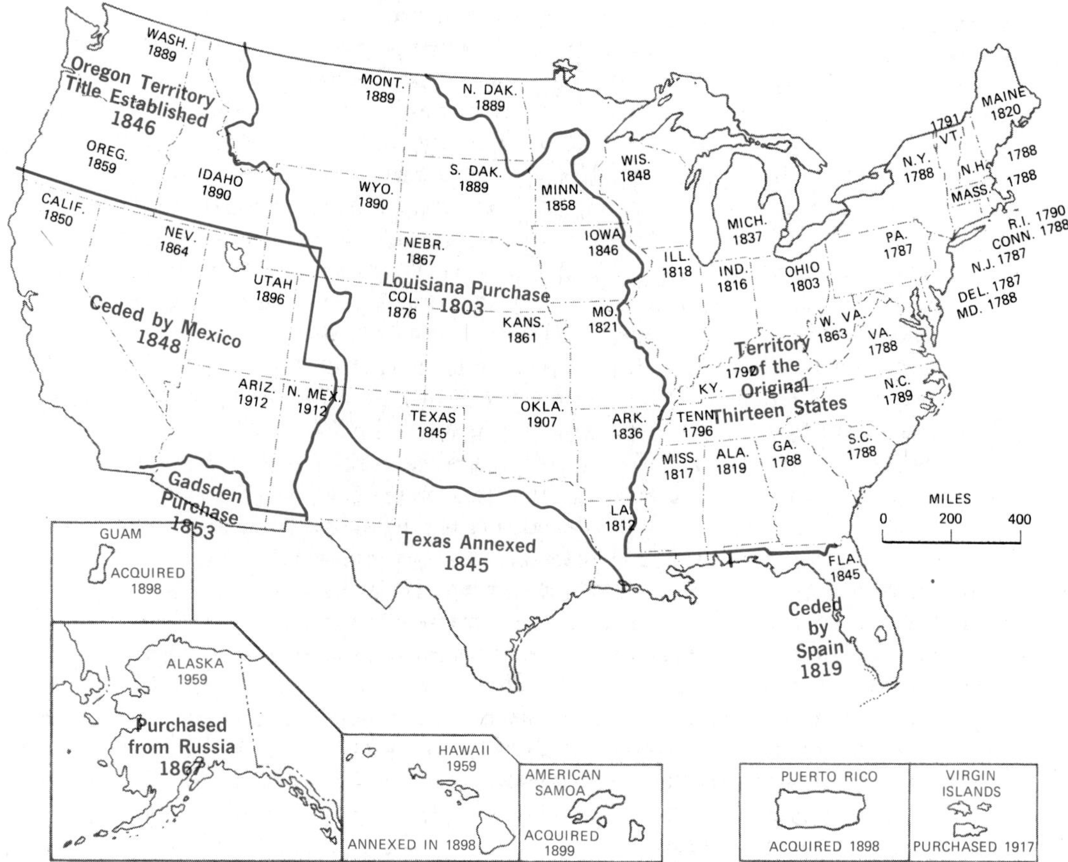

Figure 1.1 Territorial Expansion of the United States and Acquisitions of Other Principal Areas.
SOURCE: U.S. Bureau of the Census.

Figure 1.2 U.S. Population Growth (1900–1980).
SOURCE: U.S. Bureau of the Census.

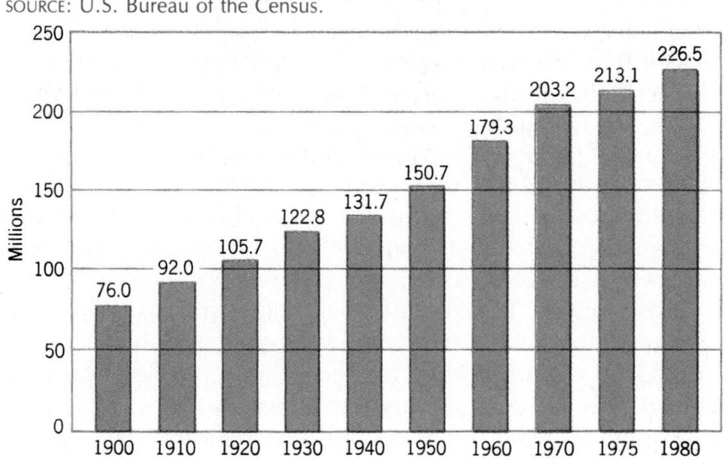

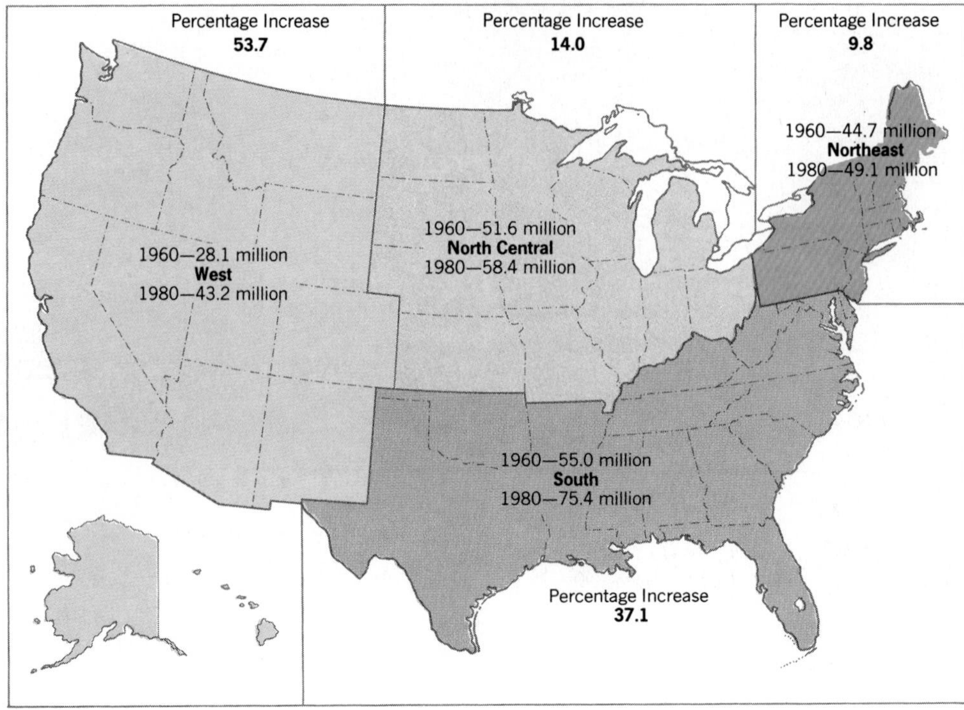

Figure 1.3 Population Change (1960–1980).
SOURCE: U.S. Bureau of the Census.

east and North Central regions remained fairly stable.

Another dominant population trend has been the movement of persons off the farms into urban areas. The first wave of this migration into the cities was due to the job opportunities fostered by the Industrial Revolution, which began in the mid-nineteenth century. By the third decade of the twentieth century, however, a new phase of the process began to assert itself as many persons began to move out of the cities into the surrounding suburbs. Automobiles, improved roads, and electrical interurban railroads served as vehicles and avenues of escape from the crowded cities. In increasing numbers persons gravitated towards the new promised land of lower rents and what was generally thought to be the better life of the suburbs, while continuing to maintain economic and social ties with the city.

The end result of these two population trends has been the development of metropolitan areas—urban communities composed of central cities surrounded by suburbs. In 1950 the Census Bureau designated such areas as **standard metropolitan** areas (the term was later changed to **standard metropolitan statistical areas**) (SMSAS), which included any central city with a population of 50,000, together with the county in which that city was located and any other counties that were economically and socially integrated with the county of the central city. With some minor modifications, that same definition has been used to describe such areas since 1950.

Since mid-century there has been a

Friday afternoon exodus.

great increase in the number of persons living in our metropolitan areas. In 1950, 56 percent of Americans resided in 168 SMSAs; in 1980, 75 percent lived in 318 SMSAs. The largest metropolitan area in 1980 was the New York–New Jersey area with a total population of 9.1 million, followed by Los Angeles–Long Beach with 7.5 million and Chicago with 7.1 million residents. Within such areas, the dominant trend has been the loss of population by many central cities (particularly older ones located in the Northeast and North Central regions) and a flourishing of suburban communities.

As far as particular social groups are concerned, the most significant population trend in recent years has been the movement of blacks from the South to the North and from rural to urban areas. In 1940, 77 percent of blacks lived in the South and only 22 percent in the Northeast and North Central regions; by 1980 barely over half—53 percent—of all blacks still lived in the South and 38 percent in the two northern regions.* (Meanwhile, the population of blacks residing in the West rose from 1 to 9 percent.) As Figure 1.4 shows, since 1950 within the urban communities blacks have settled primarily in the central cities. In contrast, few whites were added to the nation's central cities between 1960 and 1970 and central city whites actually declined between 1970 and 1978. On the other hand, suburban growth since 1950 has been overwhelmingly white.

Along with the migration of blacks from southern rural areas to northern central cities, there has been another major social development in recent years: the movement of women out of the home into the job market. In 1950, 31 percent of women of working age

* It should be noted, however, that during the 1970s, there was some movement of blacks back to the South from the Northeast and North Central states.

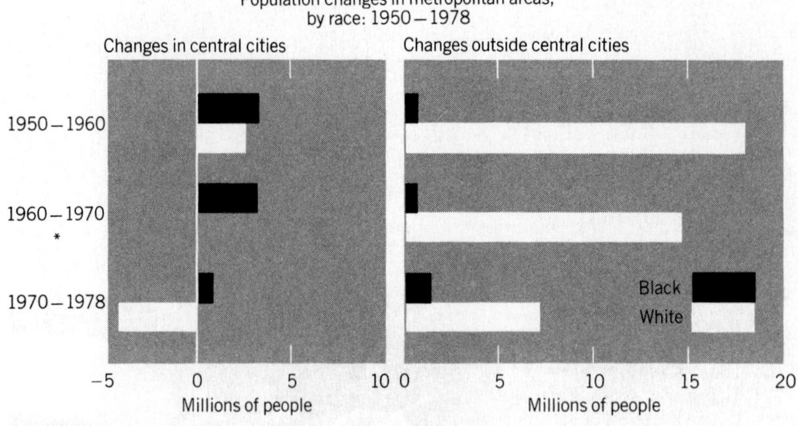

Figure 1.4 Population Changes in Metropolitan Areas by Race (1950–1978).
SOURCE: U.S. Bureau of the Census.

were in the work force; by 1980, that figure had climbed to 51 percent. Increasingly included in that work force were women with young children: in 1960, only about one-fifth of women with children under six were employed outside the home; by 1981, almost half were. The kinds of positions that women filled also have changed. For example, between 1972 and 1982 the proportion of women lawyers and judges almost quadrupled—from 3.8 to 14.1 percent. Women also began to hold jobs traditionally filled by men, such as security guards, construction workers, welders, and telephone repair persons. It should be noted, however, that despite such developments, in the early 1980s almost four out of five women remained in traditional "pink-collar" occupations, such as office clerks and secretaries.

Still another major social movement occurred in the United States in the 1970s: the arrival of a new wave of immigrants, particularly from Asia and from nations in this hemisphere. Included in the former category were Koreans (who increased over 400 percent between 1970 and 1980); Chinese (who replaced Japanese as the largest Asian group in the United States); Filipinos (who became the second-largest such group); and Vietnamese (who fled their country after the fall of South Vietnam). Hispanics dominated the immigration from the Americas; by 1980 our population included almost 9 million persons originally from Mexico, 2 million from Puerto Rico, and just over 800,000 from Cuba.

Complexities: The Economy and the World Community

Unlike many other countries in which the government owns the manufacturing industries (like steel and oil), financial institutions (banks and insurance companies), and transportation facilities (railroads and airlines), these great economic ventures are privately owned and operated in the United States. Moreover, such ownership is widespread. In 1980 there were 12.7 million proprietorships (businesses owned by one person) in the United States, 1.4 million partnerships, and 2.7 million corporations. All together, almost 17 million

Her Honor.

New Americans celebrate yuletide.

businesses had receipts of over 7 trillion and a net income of 302 billion.

At the same time, there is a considerable concentration of that private wealth. Of the 302 billion in net income earned by the three major kinds of businesses in 1980, 239 billion belonged to corporations. Moreover, a great concentration occurs within the corporate category of businesses. For example, in 1977, of the total assets held by manufacturing corporations, 46 percent were in the hands of 100 of them. There has also been a tendency towards greater concentration of corporate wealth in recent years: in 1950 the 100 largest companies owned a somewhat smaller share of total corporate assets—40 percent.

Along with big business has come big labor in the United States. As Figure 1.5 reveals, over the period from 1972 through 1981 the total labor force climbed from almost 90 million to some 113 million persons. Also presenting a problem for government was the fluctuating rate of unemployment over the period. After remaining at about 6 percent for the early part of the period, the unemployment rate rose to almost 9 percent in 1975 and after declining slightly after that, rose to almost 10 percent by mid-1982.

Another major economic challenge for American democracy in recent years has been the rise in prices that consumers must pay for goods and services. Using the cost of items in 1967 as the index of 100, Figure 1.6 shows a constant rise in prices for food, fuel, and utilities, and medical care over the period through 1981. To take an example, if we make the index of 100 in the base year, 1967, equal to $1.00, in 1981 a consumer had to spend about $2.75 for

Figure 1.5 Trends in the Labor Force (1972–1982).
SOURCE: U.S. Bureau of the Census.

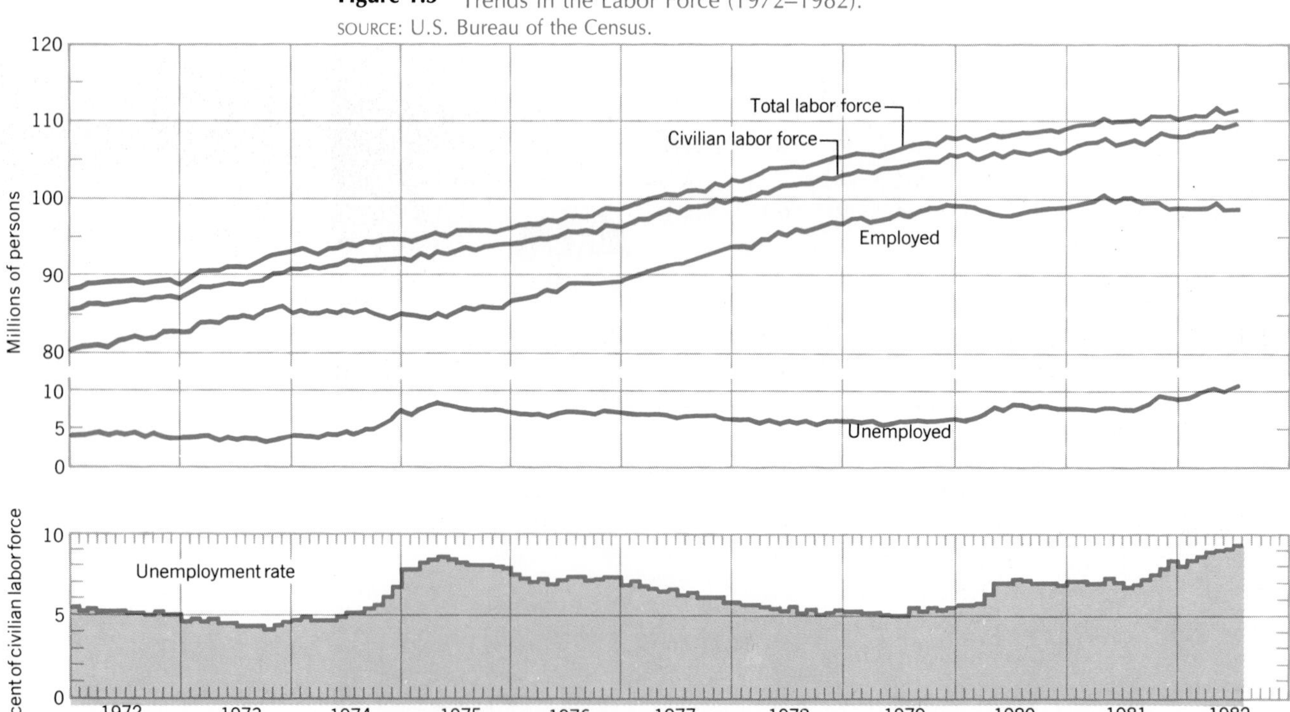

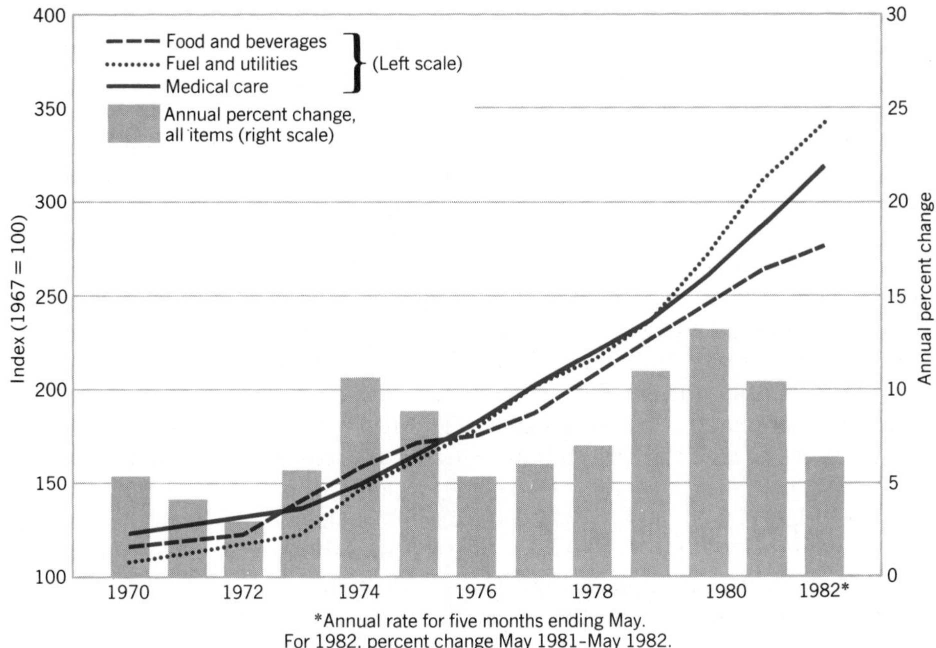

Figure 1.6 Consumer Price Indexes (1970–1982).
SOURCE: U.S. Bureau of the Census.

food and beverage items that could have been bought for $1.00 in 1967. Rising even more dramatically after 1973 was the cost of medical care and fuel and utilities. For those items, consumers had to spend more than $3.00 for every $1.00 they spent in 1967.

A final major challenge to the American political system comes in the area of international affairs. We are members of a world community composed of over 150 nations with a total population of 4 billion. The sovereign countries that belong to the United Nations range in area from tiny Maldives with 115 square miles to the Union of Soviet Socialist Republics with 8.6 million square miles, and in population from Sao Tome and Principe with 78,000 residents to the People's Republic of China with 814 million. Figure 1.7 indicates how the area and population of the United States compare with those of some of the other leading nations of the world.*

In various chapters of this book we will analyze the ways American democracy has been affected by these and other challenges. For example, Chapter 8 discusses how the apportionment of the House of Representatives and the number of votes in the electoral college for choosing the president have been adjusted to meet the expansion of our nation's area and population. Chapter 5 analyzes how business and labor have organized to protect their economic interests. Chapter 15 describes the ways blacks, women, and Hispanics have used

* Not shown in the figure is Canada, which ranks second among the nations in area with 3.9 million square miles; however, its 1974 population was only 22.5 million.

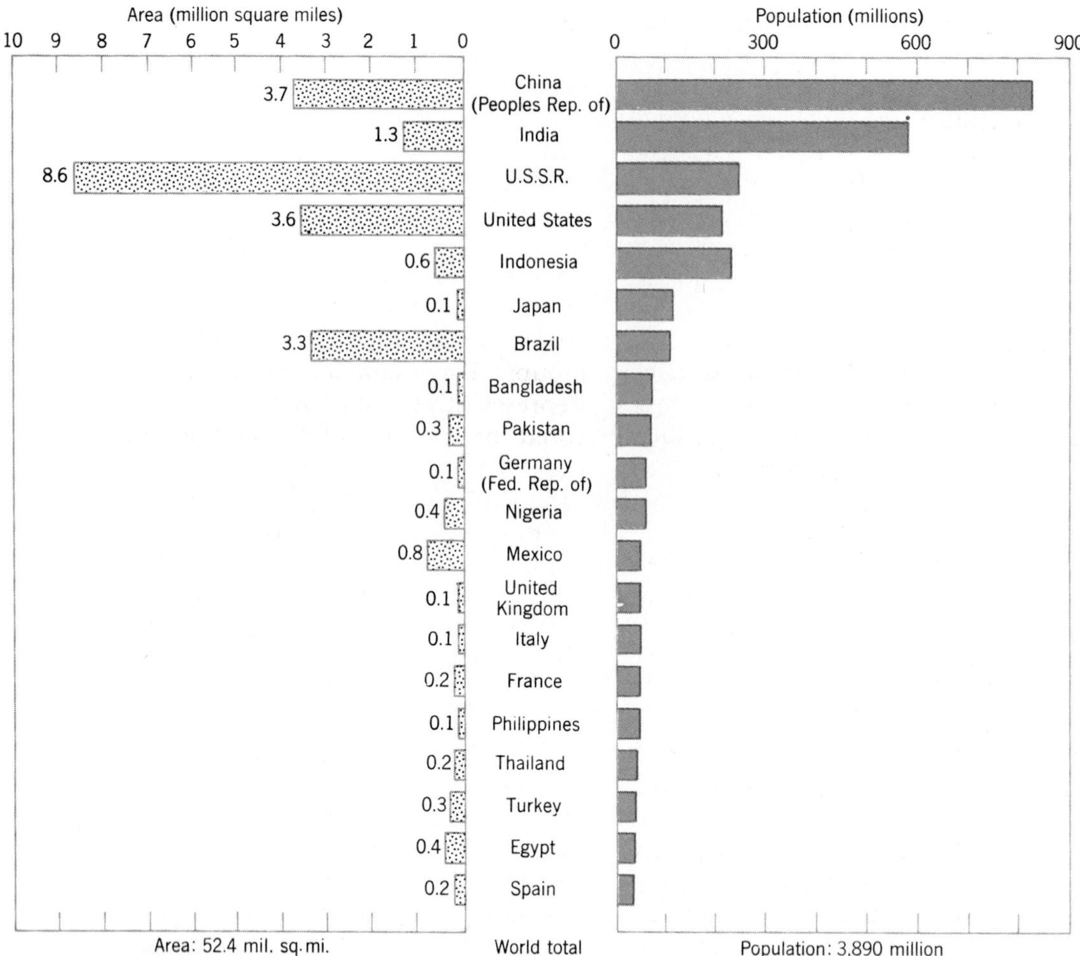

Figure 1.7 Area and Population of the United States and Leading Countries (1974).
SOURCE: U.S. Bureau of the Census; Data from the Statistical Office of the United Nations.

the political process to further their interests. However, before turning to a detailed analysis of the establishment of American democracy and how it has changed over the years, we shall examine two conflicting interpretations of how successful our political system has been in meeting major challenges and still retaining its democratic character.

CONFLICTING VIEWS OF AMERICAN DEMOCRACY

No institutions established by human beings ever entirely live up to their ideals. Political scientist Samuel Huntington suggests that there is an "Iv.I gap" that exists between political ideals and political institutions, or what we refer to in this book as the difference between the theoretical "promise" of American democracy and the actual "performance" of our democratic form of government.

Students of our political system differ fundamentally on the basic nature of American democracy today. While conceding that it is not perfect (and cannot be), some observers view it as a successful, if not the most successful, example of democracy in the world, one that has to a considerable extent lived up to its ideals or promises. Others feel, however, that the performance of American democracy falls far short of its promises and that some of those promises themselves need to be reinterpreted.

The Case for American Democracy

The case for American democracy rests on the assessment that our political techniques and institutions operate for the most part according to democratic principles. The leaders of the Republican and Democratic parties compete for the support of the voters by tailoring their proposals to appeal to the wishes of a wide variety of groups that make up the electorate. The winning party, representing a broad coalition of such groups, must continue to keep the preferences of many groups in mind after it assumes office. If it fails to do so, it can and will be replaced by the opposition party. The fact that the Republican and Democratic parties are so competitive (seldom does the losing party draw less than 40 percent of the vote in a presidential election) means that overturns in party control are frequent, and even when they do not actually occur, the possibility that they will keeps the majority party responsive to public preferences.

Between elections public policy is primarily influenced by the activities of concerned minorities who work through interest groups to make demands on decision-makers. Again, the system is competitive because groups such as business and labor take different views on public concerns and frustrate each other's ambitions. Therefore no one group or small number of groups dominates the American political process.

American governmental institutions also ensure that a wide variety of interests will be taken into account when political decisions are made. Public officials in different parts of the governmental system are responsive to different groups. For example, the House of Representatives has traditionally favored the concerns of people who live in rural areas and small towns, while the president generally has been receptive to ethnic groups in the large industrial states. Groups whose interests are not met by the national government can turn to state officials for help. As political scientist Robert Dahl puts it, "The normal American political process is one in which there is a high probability that an active and legitimate group in the population can make itself heard effectively at some crucial stage in the process of decision."

The American political system is, in this view, a highly **pluralistic** one in which power is distributed widely among many individuals and groups—businessmen, laborers, farmers, blacks, and white-collar workers among them. Although some groups have more political assets in the form of money, numbers, and campaign and propaganda skills than others, all have some political resources—at the minimum, the vote.

The American political system is also open in the sense that people from various ethnic, racial, sexual, and social backgrounds can become politically active. Indeed some groups, notably the Irish, have worked their way up the social and economic ladder by using the political process to further their interests. Eventually one of them may win the highest position in the American political system, the presidency—as John

San Francisco Mayor Diane Feinstein.

Chicago Mayor Harold Washington.

New York Mayor Ed Koch.

San Antonio Mayor Henry Cisneros.

F. Kennedy did. This process continues as Italians, Jews, and—most recently—blacks, women, and Hispanics are elected to more and more political offices.

Those with a favorable view of American democracy generally recognize that the successful operation of our political system depends primarily on persons who are interested and concerned about political matters. Referred to by various names—political "elites," "activists," or "influentials"—they are the citizens who offer themselves or others as candidates and who campaign for election, who fill the major appointive positions in the government, who propose policies for dealing with major problems, and who work through the political process to get their proposals enacted into law. They include not only individuals who hold public office but also those who are outside the formal structure of government in leadership posts in political parties, interest groups, private corporations, and labor unions, as well as newspaper editors, college teachers, and others who are in a position to help shape the political opinions of the average citizen.

It is the political moves and countermoves of this broad variety of political elites that make the American political system work as it does. While they compete vigorously with each other, at the same time they appreciate and abide by the democratic "rules of the game" regarding the right of freedom of speech and the press for those who oppose them. They are also personally committed to the major values of a democratic society—the liberty of the individual, the right of privacy, religious freedom, and justice under the law. It is these political activists who are the major carriers of the American Creed; they can be counted on to defend it when other less politically aware and educated individuals are willing to deny basic rights to unpopular minorities.

In the final analysis, supporters of American pluralistic democracy feel that it serves well the interests of a wide variety of individuals and groups in our society. Competing elites take the initiative in public affairs, but at the same time they must take into account the interests of ordinary citizens, on whom they ultimately depend for support of their policies as well as for their tenure in public office. The entire process, which takes place within prescribed democratic procedures, has moderated differences among our diverse people and brought the nation social peace as well as social progress.

Major Criticisms of American Democracy

Although most students of American democracy over the years have tended to support our system, it has also had its share of critics. Particularly in recent years, with the emergence of major problems—racial tensions, inflation and unemployment (particularly of the young), the war in Vietnam, and difficulties in the Mideast and Central America—and the decline in the credibility of public officials, critics have increasingly called into question the operation, ideals, and assumptions of our political system.

One of the major criticisms directed at American democracy is that it simply does not operate as its supporters claim it does. Rather than shape their actions in accordance with the wishes of the voters, candidates and officeholders manipulate the attitudes of the populace by clever public-relations techniques and the skillful use of the mass media. Republican and Democratic candidates, it is charged, stand for essentially the same policies, which means that voters have no significant choice between them. Moreover significant minorities—blacks, women,* Hispanics, Native Americans, the poor, and the young—are not represented or served by either of the two major parties.

Critics view the making of public policy between elections in essentially the same light. None of the above-mentioned minorities is nearly as effectively organized as are more dominant, affluent groups. As political scientist E. E. Schattschneider has suggested, "The flaw in the pluralist heaven is that the heavenly chorus sings with a strong upperclass accent. Probably about 90 percent of the people cannot get into the pressure system." Moreover the minorities that are organized do not actually check and balance one another as is generally claimed. Rather, each concentrates on getting what it wants from government: businessmen are served by the Department of Commerce, organized working people by the Department of Labor, and farmers by the Department of Agriculture. Instead of regulating such groups in the public interest, public officials grant them favors at the expense of the general taxpayer or each other.

Nor do the critics feel that the system is equally open or responsive to all kinds of individuals and groups. Few if any women, blacks, laborers, or members of the lower economic classes sit in Congress, in the executive departments, or on the Supreme Court. Middle- and upper-class persons dominate all three branches of our national government and those at the state level as well. Moreover, the increasing costs of political campaigns may make it even more difficult for those of limited means to hold elective office in the future, especially in the national government.

For such critics the American system is not pluralistic but **elitist** in the sense that organized minorities—checked neither by each other, nor by the general populace—dominate the political process. Their privileged status in the society at large, together with their uneven representation in the government itself, enables them to set the "public agenda," that is, to determine which matters become legitimate issues of governmental concern and action, and which remain "nonissues," ignored by public officials. The end result is a biased political system favoring the status quo, that is, established groups over unorganized ones and stability over change in American life.

As proof of their contentions critics point to the **public policies** of American government, which they feel do not really implement democratic ideals. We have done little to develop equality in American life, whether it be social

* While women are not actually a minority (they constitute over half of our population), they may be considered a minority in the sense that traditionally they have been both economically and politically disadvantaged compared to men.

equality for such groups as the blacks, women, or Hispanics; economic equality for those same groups and others of the poor as well; or equal justice under the law for all our disadvantaged citizens. Thus critics contend it is not sufficient to provide individuals with the mere opportunity to participate politically or to have the law applied impartially to them. We should see to it that all Americans are provided with the education, training, and necessary resources to make their participation effective—and with unobstructed access to legal aid and justice to ensure that their legal rights are fully protected.

Critics of American democracy also charge that we have been far too willing to accept the view that political elites should run the political system because "average" people are apathetic about public affairs and are not committed to the democratic rules of the game. According to this view, that position underestimates the possibility of educating the average citizen to appreciate his own political rights as well as the right of others to oppose his views. Moreover, an important reason that the average person does not participate politically is that he considers it futile; make the system more responsive to his needs and he will take a greater interest in its operation. Thus, we should not accept political apathy as endemic to human nature but rather as a condition that can be changed.

In fact, some critics suggest that we introduce more democracy into American life by utilizing its values and methods in other institutions besides the government. According to this view, corporations should not trade with South Africa because of its racist policies, boards of directors should include representatives of consumers and workers, and students should participate in the making of decisions that vitally affect their lives. Such actions would make these private organizations more humane; moreover, habits and experiences that citizens acquired in this way would carry over into the functioning of our governmental institutions as well.

Finally, critics charge that we have been far too ready to judge American democracy on the basis of the stability it has provided for our society and its success in reconciling conflicts among selfish interests. In the process we have lost track of the fundamental purpose for which democracy was originally established: the full development of the individual's personality through participation in the life of the community. Such a line of thought reflects a desire to return to the kinds of values and assumptions that underlay direct Athenian democracy. Thus, today's mottoes of **"participatory democracy"** and the "new politics" have much in common with the Greek precept that the individual should involve himself in public affairs, that he must think not only of his own private interests but also of those of the community at large.

These then represent two "overviews" of American democracy. Although they differ substantially, neither is absolute. Political scientist Robert Dahl, a leading representative of the pluralist line of thinking, has taken pains recently to explain that while all groups have the right to make themselves "heard effectively" by political decision-makers, that does not mean that "every group has equal control over the outcome" (of such decisions). "Neither individuals or groups are political equals." Similarly, the late sociologist, C. Wright Mills, a leading proponent of the elitist school of thought, concludes that while economic, social, and political elites control major decisions in our society (especially those involving foreign and military affairs), they do not control *all decisions* made by our political leaders.

GENERAL APPROACH AND ORGANIZATION OF THIS BOOK

With these models of democracy and conflicting views about the current state of the American political system in mind, we turn to a detailed analysis of that system in the chapters that follow. In the first section of each chapter, key concepts are treated (e.g., a constitution is defined and its purposes explained), and concepts are also distinguished from related ones (e.g., a political party from an interest group). The aim is to enable you to see important relationships and grasp essentials rather than to get bogged down in factual material unrelated to major ideas.

Many chapters also provide basic information on how our political system has evolved over time. Particular attention is focused on the nation's struggle to establish its political institutions and on periods of rapid change in our society. A student needs to understand how evolving forces mold and change political institutions; moreover, history provides an excellent basis of comparison. In evaluating our political system today, it is important to compare it not only with other models of democracy but with its own past accomplishments and failures.

With concepts and some historical perspective in mind, one is better able to appreciate the way our political system functions and how successful it is in dealing with current developments and problems in American society. An effort has been made to provide the factual information needed to judge how closely the performance of American democracy lives up to its promise. At the end of most chapters, the author gives his personal view of how the particular institution under study should be assessed. You are not necessarily expected to agree with this evaluation, but perhaps it will stimulate thought and controversy.

Part 1 of this book, and Chapter 2 in particular, analyze the *constitutional framework* of American government, together with the values and assumptions underlying that framework. Chapter 3 focuses on one major element of that framework, the principles of federalism that are utilized to divide political power between the national government and the states.*

Part 2 treats the general subject of *popular control*, that is, how citizens hold those in political power responsible for their actions. Chapter 4 explores the general nature of the political views of our citizens, how they are acquired, and the various outlets that exist for expressing such attitudes through the political process. Chapter 5 focuses on the major organization for expressing such views between elections—the interest group. Chapters 6, 7, 8, and 9 examine the role that political parties and the electoral process play in conveying public preferences to political officials.

Part 3 focuses on the institutions involved in *official decision-making* in our political system, including the Congress (Chapter 10), the presidency (Chapter 11), the bureaucracy (Chapter 12), and the courts (Chapter 13). These institutions are examined in terms of the kinds of persons who serve in them, their general structure, and the procedures that each utilizes to carry on its activities.

* Some instructors may also want to include as part of the constitutional framework, Chapter 14, which treats the civil liberties which all of us enjoy against infringement by national or state governments. (In the first three editions of this text, I utilized that sequence.) I have, however, placed that chapter immediately after the one on the courts (Chapter 13) because I think readers will better appreciate the nature of those liberties if they first understand the role of judicial review in our political system. I also believe that discussing civil liberties and civil rights in successive chapters (as I have done in Chapters 14 and 15) facilitates a better comparison of these two types of basic freedoms.

Also analyzed are the relationships that exist among the officials of these separate institutions.

Part 4 concentrates on basic, *individual freedoms.* Chapter 14 focuses on the liberties that all citizens enjoy over and against both national and state officials. Chapter 15 analyzes the quest for equality pursued by particular groups in our society—blacks, women, and Hispanics.

The National (contrasted to the Brief) edition of this book also contains Section Five, which treats *what governments do*, that is, the *public policies* that are enacted to try to mitigate various problems in our society. Chapter 16 analyzes the general nature of public-policy-making—types of policies, and the stages in which such policies are enacted and carried out. Chapter 17 focuses on economic policies and 18 on social policies. Chapter 19 concentrates on foreign and military policies.

The appendices in both the Brief and National editions contain important supplemental information. Included are an in-depth analysis of the 1984 presidential election, a glossary of all terms used in the book, and copies of the Constitution of the United States and the Declaration of Independence.

SELECTED READINGS

A classic study of the rise of modern democracy is A. D. Lindsay, *The Modern Democratic State* (New York: Oxford University Press, 1962). An extended treatment of the historical evolution and general nature of democracy is Leslie Lipson, *The Democratic Civilization* (New York: Oxford University Press, 1964).

Two excellent treatments of democratic theory are Henry Mayo, *An Introduction to Democratic Theory* (New York: Oxford University Press, 1960) and Giovanni Sartori, *Democratic Theory* (New York: Praeger Publishers, 1965). For a critique of the excessive optimism concerning human nature underlying some theories of democracy, see Reinhold Niebuhr, *The Children of Light and The Children of Darkness* (New York: Charles Scribner's Sons, 1944).

For a penetrating analysis of the gap that exists between American democratic ideals and the actual operation of our political institutions, see Samuel Huntington, *American Politics: The Promise of Disharmony* (Cambridge: The Belknap Press, 1981).

The case for pluralist American democracy is set forth by Robert Dahl in several studies. Included are *A Preface to Democratic Theory* (Chicago: University of Chicago Press, 1956), *Who Governs?* (New Haven: Yale University Press, 1961); and *Pluralist Democracy in the United States* (Chicago: Rand McNally, 1967). Other books expressing this same general viewpoint include Seymour Lipset, *Political Man* (Garden City, N.Y.: Doubleday & Co., 1960); and V. O. Key, *Public Opinion and American Democracy* (New York: Alfred A. Knopf, 1961). More recently, Dahl has analyzed some of the major problems inherent in pluralist democracy in his *Dilemmas of Pluralist Democracy: Autonomy vs. Control* (New Haven: Yale University Press, 1982).

An excellent criticism of Dahl's theory is by Jack Walker, "A Critique of the Elitist Theory of Democracy," *The American Political Science Review* 60 (1966): 285–95. For a more extended analysis of the same subject, see Peter Bachrach, *Theory of Democratic Elitism: A Critique* (Boston: Little, Brown, 1967). The leading example of an elitist interpretation of American society is C. Wright Mills, *The Power-Elite* (New York: Oxford University Press, 1956).

PART 1

The Constitutional Framework

CHAPTER 2

The American Constitution

During the summer of 1787, 55 delegates met in convention in Philadelphia to frame a new constitution for a young nation. Many of the leading public figures of the day were in the group: revered wartime commander, George Washington, a "Vesuvius of a man" who, despite his famed temper, presided over the four-month deliberations with fairness and dignity; beloved Benjamin Franklin, the nation's elder statesman (age 81), admired like Washington not only in his own country but also in the capitals of Europe; youthful Alexander Hamilton, brilliant prime-mover of the events that led to the calling of the Constitutional Convention; and diminutive James Madison—"no bigger," someone remarked, "than half a cake of soap," yet ultimately judged by historians the Convention's "giant."

Political history knows no more revered heroes than this assemblage of distinguished men. Americans of many generations have endowed the Constitution and its framers with almost divine qualities. Thomas Jefferson called his contemporaries ". . . an assembly of demigods . . ."; one of the more recent authors to chronicle these exciting days, Catherine Drinker Bowen, entitles her book, *The Miracle at Philadelphia.* Nor has the adulation been restricted to our own citizens: William Gladstone, four-time prime minister of Great Britain, once described the Constitution as ". . . the most wonderful work ever struck off at a given time by the brain and purpose of man."

Not all Americans, however, have joined in such veneration of our fundamental document. One outspoken opposition delegate at the Massachusetts ratifying convention, Amos Singletry, had this to say about Jefferson's demigods:

> *These lawyers and men of learning, and monied men that talk so finely, and gloss over matters so smoothly, to make us poor illiterate*

The radicals: Henry and Samuel Adams.

Independence Hall, Philadelphia.

people swallow down the pill, expect to get in the Congress themselves . . . get all the power . . . and then they will swallow up us little fellows, . . . just as the whale swallowed up Jonah.

Less partisan men than "plain-folks" spokesman Singletry have also questioned the purity of the Founders' motives. Scholars Vernon Parrington and J. Allen Smith viewed the Convention as a reaction against the era of the common man that followed the Revolutionary War. They thus regard the Convention as a "counterrevolution," an overturn of political power (although a peaceful one this time) by which the conservative, propertied classes recaptured control of the country from radicals like Samuel Adams and Patrick Henry, who dominated politics in the Revolutionary and immediate postwar eras. A similar stream of thought flows through historian Charles Beard's classic study, *An Economic Interpretation of the Constitution of the United States*, which suggests that the Founders wrote the Constitution primarily to protect their own property interests. Although written in 1913, Beard's work remains the most controversial analysis of the Constitution, as scholars continue to attack, defend, and qualify his thesis.

We shall assess these conflicting interpretations in the concluding portion of the chapter. First, however, we need to examine the circumstances that led to the calling of the Convention and the type of constitution that the proceedings produced.

THE PRECONSTITUTION PERIOD

The constitution of a democratic nation provides the basic principles that determine the conduct of its political affairs. These principles relate to three fundamental aspects of the political system. One aspect has to do with the *functions* of the government—the kinds of activities within public contrasted to private control. The second bears on *procedures*—the manner in which the government carries out the activities entrusted to it. Closely related is the third aspect, *structure*—the particular mechanisms used to execute public functions. Together these elements constitute the "rules of the game" by which political authority is exercised in the society.

Public officials make binding decisions in the form of legal regulations that determine what private individuals and groups may and may not do and how they shall conduct themselves toward other citizens and groups. A constitution performs a similar function in relation to the public officials themselves, because it determines what *they* can and cannot do and what their relationships shall be not only with other officeholders but also with the general populace. Reciprocity thus characterizes a constitutional form of government: the people grant public officials the power to enact laws and decrees that vitally affect their lives, but at the same time they control the manner in which that power is exercised.

A constitution, then, establishes legal relationships between leaders and the led; even more basically, it is at the heart of a nation's political process. On the one hand, it shapes that process by determining the rules to be followed in competing for and wielding political power. On the other, a constitution is itself shaped by the political process as groups struggle to write the rules of the game to favor their own particular interests.

To understand the background of the United States Constitution, we need to appreciate two factors or elements that preceded it and that led to its being written. The first is the earlier frames of government—the national Articles of Confederation and the state constitutions. The second is the economic conditions that created dissatisfaction with these earlier arrangements, which led some groups to seek a reshaping of the nation's governmental framework.

Frames of Government

The **Articles of Confederation** and the early state constitutions reflected American experiences during the colonial period. Because the colonists attributed their particular troubles to the heavy hand of the London government, they feared centralized political power. As a result, they declared themselves independent not only of the mother country but, in essence, of one another as well. The Articles of Confederation specifically provided that "Each state retains its sovereignty, freedom and independence, and every Power, Jurisdiction and Right" not "expressly delegated to the United States, in Congress assembled."

The functions so delegated to the national Congress were restricted primarily to matters of war and peace (raising an army and navy, entering into treaties and alliances, sending and receiving diplomatic representatives) that wartime experience indicated should be vested in the nation. Missing, for example, was Congress's power to regulate interstate and foreign commerce; the Confederation's framers associated this power with the abuses of the Acts of Trade and Navigation passed by the centralized authority of Parliament. A similar fear of the tyranny of taxation as practiced by the British resulted in denying the national government the power to tax. Although it had authority to requisition funds from the states for its expenses, the taxes to pay these requisitions had to be levied by the states themselves. National troops also had to be furnished by the states. Lacking authority both to require the states to meet their obligations (which many did not) and to tax or conscript individuals itself, the national government was denied the means to carry out the few functions entrusted to it. Moreover, the Articles provided little opportunity for changing these arrangements, since all 13 states had to consent to any alteration of the document.

Their experience with British rule colored the attitude of the Confederation's framers not only toward the distribution of authority between the nation and the states but also toward which particular branch of government should be entrusted with important political powers. Memories of George III and his emissaries, the colonial governors, led Americans of the Revolutionary period to identify tyranny with the executive. At the same time, they associated liberty with the legislature, the arm of colonial government that had represented their interests in battles with the king's agent, the governor. They had little use for the judiciary, which had been populated by representatives of the Crown.

These attitudes toward the various branches of government are directly reflected in the structures of both national and state governments in the post-Revolutionary period. The Articles of Confederation provided for a legislative body with a single house in which each state had an equal vote. There was no provision at all for independent executive and judiciary branches. In the states, too, the legislature was the dominant branch, even to the point of choosing most of the governors; only four states had a chief executive elected by the people. The state judiciaries were also generally weak, frequently appointed by the legislature, and usually given limited powers.

Beyond their particular fears of the national government and the executive, Americans in the Revolutionary era also had a profound distrust of political power in general. The Articles of Confederation and state constitutions provided checks on even the favored legislative bodies of the day. Terms of legislators were short—only one year in

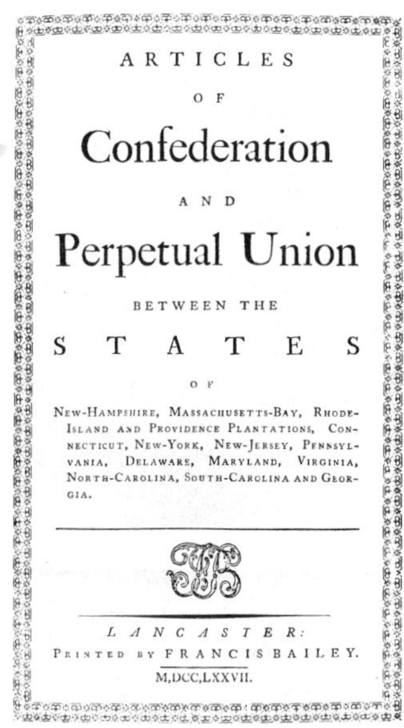

ARTICLES

OF

Confederation

AND

Perpetual Union

BETWEEN THE

STATES

OF

NEW-HAMPSHIRE, MASSACHUSETTS-BAY, RHODE-ISLAND AND PROVIDENCE PLANTATIONS, CONNECTICUT, NEW-YORK, NEW-JERSEY, PENNSYLVANIA, DELAWARE, MARYLAND, VIRGINIA, NORTH-CAROLINA, SOUTH-CAROLINA AND GEORGIA.

LANCASTER:

PRINTED BY FRANCIS BAILEY.

M,DCC,LXXVII.

the national Congress and most of the states; Rhode Islanders were even more wary of officeholders, allowing their representatives only six months before elections. For the popular legislator, there was an additional limitation in the form of forced rotation—for example, under the Articles of Confederation no person was ". . . capable of being a delegate for more than three years in any term of six years"; similar provisions plagued ambitious state legislators. As for the unpopular delegate, the voters need not endure him even during his short term, for the national Articles and many state constitutions gave the electorate the power of recall at any time. As a final check on arbitrary government, state constitutions established bills of rights ensuring fundamental liberties like freedom of speech and conscience and trial by jury.

In time a reaction set in against this legislative, semidirect democracy. The simple necessities of executive government required the national Congress to create departments of diplomacy, war, and finance, and to appoint eminent men like Robert Livingston, John Jay, and Robert Morris to head their activities. British occupation of New York required that state to develop a strong governorship free of legislative dominance in order to handle its military and civilian affairs. In Massachusetts the voters adopted a constitution that departed radically from the strong legislative–democratic model. Conceived by John Adams, who favored a **"mixed" government** representing various social interests, it provided for a popularly elected house of representatives and an "aristocratic" senate apportioned on the basis not of population but taxable wealth. Moreover, it included provision both for a popularly elected governor (eligible to succeed himself) with substantial powers, including that of vetoing legislative acts, and for an independent judiciary. The New York and Massachusetts constitutions were important not only for their influence on other states but also because they constituted alternative models to which the Founders would ultimately turn in their deliberations at the Constitutional Convention.

While alterations were thus being made in the structures of both the national and the state governments in the pre-Constitution period, attempts to change the distribution of powers between nation and state were continually frustrated. Before all the states had even signed the Articles of Confederation, Congress submitted an amendment to the states allowing it to levy a duty of five percent on imported goods; the amendment was not adopted because one state, Rhode Island, refused to ratify. Similar efforts to grant Congress authority to regulate foreign and interstate commerce as well as authority to require states to comply with requisitions of men or money owed to the national government ran afoul of the unanimous-consent requirement for amending the Articles. Financial affairs of the national government had reached such a sad state that its total income in 1786 was less than a third of the interest due on the national debt. Meanwhile seven states exercised the power to issue money, with the result that the new nation lacked a common currency; nine states even retained their own navies. Thus the United States in the pre-Constitution period lacked authority over what are fundamental concerns of any viable, sovereign nation—finances, commerce, and external affairs. Yet as we are about to see, it was precisely these matters that were of greatest concern to many Americans of that time.

Economic Conditions

Like many of the newly emerging nations in today's world, the United States in the 1780s faced a major period of adjustment following the successful revolt against Great Britain. Within a few years after the close of the Revolutionary War in 1781, Americans were experiencing an economic depression. Accounts differ about how serious it was; some historians suggest that the young nation was quite close to an economic disaster that threatened its very existence; others claim that the critical period was very brief and that the United States was well on the way to recovery by the time the Convention met in Philadelphia in mid-1787. There is general agreement, however, that the economic downturn did not affect all groups in the same way. Small farmers and the few hired laborers of the day bore little of the impact, while persons in commerce and finance were hit the hardest.

One of the ironies of the success of the Revolution was that while it brought relief from burdensome taxes imposed by the mother country, it also ended the favorable position of American businessmen in international commerce. After the war, in place of the preferential trade treatment and the assured markets they had enjoyed in the British Empire, merchants faced an economic threat from British manufacturers who dumped their goods on the American market. Infant businesses naturally found it very difficult to compete with the products of well-developed British industries; moreover, under the Articles of Confederation the national government lacked the authority to levy import duties on British merchants to protect the domestic market. Having thrown off the political yoke of Great Britain, the United States was threatened with being shackled by the economic power of the mother country.

Nor was the commercial competition faced by American merchants restricted to foreign sources alone. Domestic rivalries also developed as states levied duties, not only to raise needed revenue but also to protect local interests against out-of-state competitors. Particularly disadvantaged by such duties were those states with no seaports of their own. Madison suggested that "New Jersey between Philadelphia and New York was like a cask tapped at both ends, and North Carolina between Virginia and South Carolina was like a patient bleeding at both arms." Lacking the authority to levy duties on imports or to regulate interstate commerce, the national government was thus powerless either to erect a tariff barrier to protect American industries against the British or to break up the obstacles to free trade within the nation.

Another major group adversely affected in the postwar period was the creditors who financed both private and public ventures in the young nation. Debtors could use the political process at the state level to lighten the burden of their debt in various ways. One technique involved enacting "stay" laws to postpone the due date of promissory notes. Another similar type of legislation permitted a debtor to declare bankruptcy, pay off his obligation at less than the face value, and begin his financial life anew with a clean slate. Yet another advantage for debtors—and disadvantage for creditors—was the issuance of cheap paper money by state legislatures. This inflationary practice allowed obligations to be paid off with money that was worth far less in purchasing power than the currency originally borrowed.

Even more financially frustrated than private creditors were those who had lent the nation money to fight the Revolutionary War. No method existed for collecting on public securities issued by a government that lacked the financial ability to pay off its debts. Similarly affected were wartime veterans who lent not money but a more precious commodity, their services, for which they were to be later compensated by proceeds from government bonds.

Although the United States had theoretically achieved an independent sta-

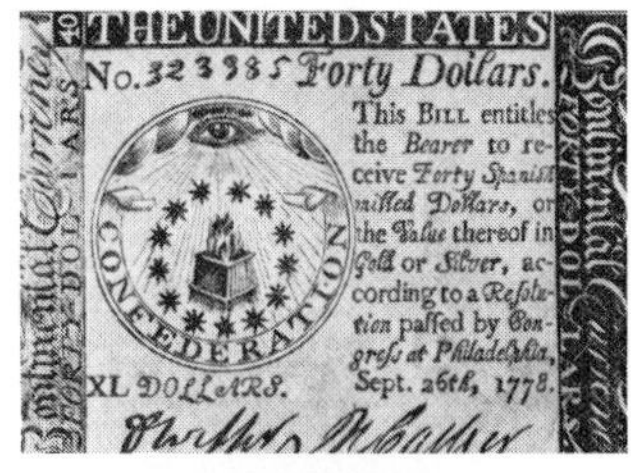

Currency of the pre-Constitution period.

tus in the family of nations as a result of the war, in fact numerous challenges to sovereignty persisted after the conclusion of hostilities. Unfriendly American Indian tribes continued to inhabit lands in the West, so that veterans found their claims to these lands no more realizable than the worthless bonds they were issued for their wartime services. Beyond this, the Spanish closed the mouth of the Mississippi to all shipping, and the supposedly vanquished British troops refused to withdraw from certain northwestern forts until claims of British creditors were honored.

Group Rivalries and the Movement for a Convention

In the situation described above, the groups particularly aggrieved by the postwar situation were those involved in commerce and finance—manufacturers, merchants, shipowners, and public and private creditors. The professional classes—lawyers, doctors, newspaper editors—viewed matters from the perspective of their clientele, and that perspective was shared by former soldiers who felt cheated out of their rightful claims for services rendered in the cause of nationhood. All in all, these groups comprised a potent array of people longing for a change in the unfortunate circumstances in which they found themselves. Later, after the Constitution had been framed, these disparate elements were to come together as an effective group working for its adoption under the name of **"Federalists."**

Although these groups were for the most part concentrated in the cities, some rural Americans also found their interests jeopardized by the postwar conditions. These were the commercial farmers who produced a surplus of crops that they wanted to dispose of in interstate and foreign markets. Typically large holders of fertile lands with slave labor and locations on river arteries that linked them to the outside world, they found common cause with merchants whose futures were also linked to commerce.

Arrayed against the emergent Federalists in the economic and political rivalries of the day were those Americans who were not dependent on trade for their livelihood. The small subsistence farmers, scratching out a living on poor soil remote from river valleys, who produced crops entirely for their own families or who marketed their small surpluses in nearby localities, formed the core of the group that was basically satisfied with life in the postwar period. Also included in its ranks were small businessmen, artisans, mechanics (the small laboring class of that time), and debtors who welcomed government assistance in their perennial struggle to keep one step ahead of their creditors. It was this coalition of interests, labeled **"anti-Federalists,"** that eventually led the fight to defeat the ratification of the Constitution.

The Federalists as a group were wealthier and better educated and held higher status occupations than their antagonists, who tended to be lower-class, obscure men of modest means. Although the leadership of the anti-Federalists included such prominent Americans as George Mason, Richard Henry Lee, Patrick Henry, and George Clinton, they could not match either in numbers or fame those who, like Washington, Hamilton, and Madison, lent their skill and prestige to the Federalists' cause. There were also major differences between the two groups of leaders: the anti-Federalists were "locals"—persons with interests and influence in their own states—while the Federalists were "cosmopolitans"—individuals with national reputations who were oriented to the world beyond their immediate communities. The latter enjoyed friendships across the breadth of the young nation, many bred by the camaraderie of common wartime experiences. A number of rich Federalists also acquired their wealth late compared to the established anti-Federalists like George Mason who, hailing from an old Virginia family, regarded George Washington as something of an upstart. Washington and Hamilton, by propelling themselves up the social and economic ladder through astute marriages, contributed to the nouveau-riche image entertained by local anti-Federalist notables.

These, then, were the opposing leaders and interests that were to vie over the writing and ratification of the Constitution. The future anti-Federalists were essentially satisfied with existing governmental arrangements, while those who were later to become Federalists sought to overturn these arrangements in favor of a constitutional system that would provide relief from their mounting problems.

Two events converged in the fall of 1786 that enabled the Federalists to convert their desires into successful action. One was a meeting at Annapolis, Maryland convened to discuss problems of interstate trade and the possibility of adopting a uniform system of commercial regulations. When only five states showed up, Hamilton and Madison seized the opportunity to issue a report to the Continental Congress suggesting that a commission be assembled the following May to ". . . render the constitution of the federal government adequate to the exigencies of the Union." The other event was the outbreak of an armed revolt in western Massachusetts; farmers there took to arms in response to an effort by the state to seize their property for failure to pay taxes and debts in the "hard" money of the time. Although Shays' Rebellion (named for its leader, Daniel Shays) was put down, it badly frightened many Americans who regarded it as a threat to the very existence of the government. Among such men was the most popular American of them all, George Washington. Appalled by the news that a former officer in his army had brought the state of Massachusetts to the brink of civil war, Washington lent his great prestige to the movement for the Convention. The following February the Congress called on the states to send delegates ". . . for the sole and express purpose of revising the Articles of Confederation." All except ever-recalcitrant Rhode Island—where debtor interests completely controlled the state—eventually responded, although the North Carolina delegation did not arrive until July of 1787, some two months after the deliberations began.

THE CONSTITUTIONAL CONVENTION

Personnel: The Founders

In terms of the economic, social, and political divisions described above, the most important feature of the Constitutional Convention was that the overwhelming proportion of the delegates were would-be Federalists. Even though the anti-Federalists matched or even exceeded their opponents in numbers among the general populace, they sent only a few of their men to the deliberations. This failure is puzzling since the state legislatures of the day, which in many instances were under the control of the debtor forces, were also entrusted with selecting delegates to the Convention; they could have packed their delegations with anti-Federalists. That they did not do so is most probably attributable to two causes. One is that some of the anti-Federalists did not want to dignify the constitutional assembly with their presence; a case in point was Patrick Henry, who stayed away because he "smelt a rat." The other is that they thought it was not important to attend, since the Convention was restricted to revising the Articles of Confederation; moreover, they could always ultimately

Anti-Federalists: Luther Martin, George Mason, and Eldridge Gerry.

block any undesirable changes in the Articles because such changes had to be approved by all the states. In any event, several persons who later opposed the Constitution refused their commissions to the Convention, a decision lamented by one of them, Richard Henry Lee, who wrote, "The nonattendance of eight or nine men who were appointed members of the convention, I shall ever consider as a very unfortunate event to the United States."

A sprinkling of future anti-Federalists did attend the Convention (including George Mason of Virginia, Elbridge Gerry of Massachusetts, Luther Martin of Maryland, and Robert Yates and John Lansing of New York), but they were badly outnumbered by their opponents, and even they belonged to the elite element of their group. The nation's subsistence farmers, who constituted the rank-and-file support of the anti-Federalist cause, were represented by only one delegate, a backwoods yeoman from Georgia. Since such farmers were the most numerous economic group in the nation at that time, the Convention's delegates were decidedly not a cross section of American life.

In fact, an analysis of the backgrounds of the members of the Convention indicates that they were definitely an elite group. Of the 55 delegates, 34 were lawyers; most of them held college degrees, 9 of them from universities abroad. To their educational attainments they added a wealth of practical political experience. Over three-fourths of them had served in the Continental Congress; many had participated in the writing of the Declaration of Independence and were active in state politics of the period. Learned men, seasoned in political struggles in the past, they represented the cream of the young nation. Some foreign political leaders of the day, not normally given to praising this newest member of the family of nations, conceded that the group matched in talents any that the most advanced European nation could muster.

Although almost all the 55 delegates took an active role in the proceedings, certain individuals naturally stood out as the major leaders of the Convention. By far the most influential delegate was James Madison. Like a schoolboy preparing for an important examination, Madison spent the months preceding the Convention poring over treatises on government, including accounts of the constitutions of the republics of Greece and Rome sent to him from Paris by Thomas Jefferson. These labors of the Convention's "egghead" were not in vain; his grasp of historical materials in addition to the practical experience he had enjoyed in state and national politics enabled him to play a creative role in the deliberations. As the author of the **Virginia Plan**—the first major proposal to be presented to the Convention—Madison became the leader of the movement to draft a constitutional scheme that would break radically with the principles of the Articles of Confederation. At the same time Madison was a man of large enough character to compromise his ideas in the interests of solidarity. Madison's contributions to the Constitution transcended the Convention itself; he was a key figure in both the pre- and post-Convention maneuverings, and his diary constitutes the major historical source of information on the four-month-long proceedings. By any standard Madison well deserves the epithet, "Father of the Constitution."

Next in importance to the giant from Virginia were the two delegates from Pennsylvania, James Wilson and Gouverneur Morris. Both in physical appearance and personal style they were poles apart: Wilson, a solid Scotsman of 44 years and a shrewd lawyer with a penetrating, logical turn of mind, earned the title of "unsung hero of the convention"; Morris, 11 years younger, a tall glamorous figure (considered by the ladies of the day as "very handsome, very bold, and very impudent"), possessor of a biting wit, became the convention's marathon talker, speaking on more occasions than any other single delegate. Their views on human nature also diverged sharply: Wilson placed great faith in the common people, whereas Morris regarded them with an aristocrat's mistrust and disdain. But despite such differences they had more vital matters in common: both were advocates of a strong national government headed by a potent chief executive and both were major figures on key committees of the Convention—Wilson on Detail and Morris on Style and Postponed Matters. Their convergence of views and positions of power at the Convention permitted them to shape both the contents and the phraseology of the document that ultimately emerged.

Two other figures, George Washington and Benjamin Franklin, contributed in an entirely different way to the eventual success of the Constitution. Neither had the slightest effect on its substance. Not until the final day did Washington address the Convention, but he did not miss a single session in his capacity as presiding officer; Catherine Drinker Bowen suggestively writes that ". . . the spirit of compromise sat on his shoulder like a dove." The assumption that Washington would be the nation's first chief executive gave the delegates the confidence to create an office with great legal and political potentialities; his mere presence at the Convention made Americans in general feel easier about the entire affair. The aged Franklin had long since passed the peak of a political creativity that had formulated the Albany Plan of Union more than 30 years before the Convention. Moreover, few of his junior colleagues were inclined to adopt his Convention proposals because they considered him to be something of a radical, too naive in his enthusiasm for the good sense of the common people. But his famed wit cooled tempers during the course of the heated debates, and he closed the proceedings on a benedictory note. Looking at the president's chair, Franklin observed that during many points in the long deliberations he had been unable to decide about the course of the sun that the chair bore as a decoration. "But now," he pronounced, "I have the happiness to know it is a rising and not a setting sun." In the ratification campaign that followed, no two Americans contributed more toward speeding the adoption of the Constitution than the young nation's greatest heroes, Washington and Franklin.

As with most human events, the Convention also had its failures. Most disappointing was Alexander Hamilton. Outnumbered in his own New York delegation by Yates and Lansing (sent to the Convention by anti-Federalist Governor George Clinton to keep an eye on Hamilton), he was also out of political step with the bulk of the delegates. His support for a life-tenured chief executive and senate smacked too much of the British model of king and House of Lords with which the late colonists were all too familiar. Thus the conservative ideas of the youthful Hamilton were as uncongenial to the Convention's thinking as the radical proposals of the aged Franklin. At one point Hamilton left the Convention in frustration; for all he had accomplished, he might just as well never have showed up at all. Ultimately he was to atone for his failure by joining Madison, his partner in the pre-Convention maneuverings, in successfully campaigning for the subsequent adoption of the Constitution.

Agreement and Disagreement at the Convention

Accounts of the great debates of the Constitutional Convention frequently obscure the substantial agreement that existed among the delegates on a num-

The Father of the Constitution: James Madison.

Key Convention committeemen: James Wilson and Gouverneur Morris.

The Convention conciliators: George Washington and Benjamin Franklin.

ber of features of the new government. The authority of the national government to raise revenue by taxing imports and to regulate interstate and foreign commerce was accepted by the delegates, even by the anti-Federalists. The Convention proposal that reflected the attitudes of that group, the **New Jersey Plan,** vested such vital functions (along with those previously provided for in the Articles) in the national government. The same plan permitted Congress to act against states that failed to honor financial requisitions; it also granted the federal executive the authority to "... call forth the powers of the confederated States ..." to enforce national laws and treaties against resistant states. Thus the very issues that had raised such difficulties between the nation and the states under the Articles of Confederation presented no serious conflicts at the Convention. Of course, the absence of the most independent and anti-union state of the 13, Rhode Island, undoubtedly contributed to this harmonious state of affairs.

Nor were there serious differences at the Convention over the general structure of the national government. Most delegates concurred in Jefferson's assessment of the Virginia experience with legislative supremacy that "... 173 despots could be as oppressive as one ..." and that "... concentrating all powers in the same hands was precisely the definition of despotic government." They were also mindful of the fact that under the Articles of Confederation the Congress had been forced to develop crude substitutes for the missing executive and judicial arms of the national government. The delegates thus agreed on the necessity for creating a government with three separate branches.

The greatest single cause of agreement among the delegates was the general issue of nation–state relations. The conflicting proposals for dealing with this basic issue and the way compromise was eventually reached will be discussed in detail in Chapter 3 (on federalism).

Closely connected to the issue of nation–state relations was the question of how the states would be represented in Congress. The Virginia Plan provided for a two-branch legislature—the first branch to be elected by the people, and the second to be chosen by the first from persons nominated by the state legislatures. The representation of a state in both branches was to be based on its financial contributions or population. Thus the plan would have been advantageous to the large, wealthy states, from which it drew its major supporters. In contrast, the New Jersey Plan would have retained the Confederation's one-house legislative body with its equality of state representation. It was backed by delegates who wanted essentially to retain the confederation system as well as by those who favored a strong national government but did not want to see it dominated by the large states. Ultimately the Convention adopted a bicameral legislature—one house representing the States by population, the other the states on an equal basis—as the best solution to the representation dilemma. Labeled the **"Connecticut Compromise"** because the delegates from that medium-sized state worked so diligently for its acceptance, it became the most famous of the accommodations developed to bridge the differences among the various delegates. (We shall see in the following chapter that the compromise also paved the way for the resolution of a number of issues bearing on the relationship between the national government and the states in the new constitutional system.)

The Convention eventually compromised on a series of issues that divided its members. Just as crucial as representation for the new government was the composition and method of selection of the executive branch. As we shall see in detail in Chapter 11, the presidential office that ultimately emerged from the deliberations differed greatly from that contemplated in early Convention proposals.

The divergent views of the North and South on slavery were also compromised on, with the Convention deciding to permit the continuation of the slave trade until 1808 and to count slaves as three-fifths of a free person for purposes of determining both the representation of a state in the lower house of the Congress and its share of direct taxes based on population. In addition, the desire of Southerners for free trade (as producers of raw materials like cotton they wanted to ship goods to Britain in return for finished products) led them to advocate requiring a two-thirds vote for navigation acts as a means of protecting themselves against tariffs favored by Northern manufacturers. While the Convention was unwilling to go this far in deferring to Southern interests, it did agree to a prohibition against export taxes.

This give-and-take process of the Convention led one close student of the subject, Max Farrand, to label the Constitution a "bundle of compromises." A number of factors contributed to the willingness of the delegates to search for, and achieve accommodations of their differences. Many genuinely believed that the new nation was on the brink of a dissolution that would divide the country into three separate parts—northern, middle, and southern; to fail in their purpose was thus to return the United States to chaos and eventual extinction. Moreover, since most of the delegates were Federalists, they agreed on the essential structure of the national government and the necessity for making radical changes in nation–state relations. Their consensus on fundamental principles thus permitted the delegates to reach compromises on the particular application of those principles. Compromise was also fostered by the delegates' early decision to keep the proceedings secret: operating free of public scrutiny and pressures permitted them to change their minds and modify their stands in the process of groping for answers to the nation's difficult problems.

But the very conditions that promoted agreement at the Convention itself were precisely the same ones that threatened to make the subsequent ratification process so difficult. Far from seeing the nation as about to disintegrate, the anti-Federalists viewed difficulties under the Articles of Confederation as both manageable and temporary. While the anti-Federalists were generally absent from the constitutional deliberations, they were well represented in the general population and the state legislatures. The very secrecy that promoted cooperation among the delegates themselves occasioned resentment and suspicion among those denied information about the proceedings. Thus the delegates who worked so hard to create a new constitutional framework faced major obstacles in getting the rest of the nation to accept the product of their labors.

THE RATIFICATION CAMPAIGN

Before the delegates left the Convention in mid-September 1787, they made decisions designed to facilitate the adoption of the proposed Constitution. They chose to ignore the unanimous-consent requirement for amending the Articles; instead they provided that ratification by nine states would be sufficient for the Constitution's adoption. In this way they avoided the possibility that a state like Rhode Island—which had refused even to send delegates to the Convention—could block their efforts. The fear that state legislatures would refuse to accept a constitution that reduced their powers also prompted the delegates to substitute elected state conventions as the ratifying bodies. Such a procedure provided the Federalists with at least an opportunity for victory, since they could influence the selection of the delegates to the state conventions as well as the course of the deliberations. Cloaking their real purposes in the rhetoric of democracy, the framers claimed that such a ratification process would more directly involve the people than would the use of state legislatures. Surprisingly, the old Continental Congress, which had much to lose under the new constitutional system, forwarded the Convention's instructions to the states for action.

Having written the rules of the ratification game to favor the Constitution's adoption, the Federalists set out to transform their opportunities into realities. They worked to get themselves and their sympathizers elected as state-convention delegates (25 of the 39 delegates to the Constitutional Convention who signed the document were so chosen), developed strategies for convention proceedings, and set out to sell the general public on the virtues of the new Constitution. In all of this, the Federalists were able to trade on a number of political advantages they held over their opponents: prestigious leaders like Washington and Franklin, whose endorsement alone was worth thousands of votes; continental figures, whose contacts across states and regions provided a communications link for the various state and local campaigns; the bulk of the nation's phrasemakers—newspaper editors, lawyers, teachers, ministers—who could spread the Federalist propaganda by word of mouth and printed page. In addition, they had one vital asset that their opponents lacked completely: a positive program to sell. Placed in the difficult position of favoring some changes in the Articles of Confederation, but having no concrete plan to substitute for it, the anti-Federalists were forced to adopt a negative, defensive stance in the ratification battle. Meanwhile, the Federalists argued that rejection of the Constitution would mean a return to the chaotic situation under the Articles.

Having written the ratification rules and rallied their resources, the Federalists turned to the practical problem of winning support for the Constitution in the nine states necessary for ratification. Some, like Delaware and New Jersey, burdened with heavy tax and debt loads or plagued by interstate duties, could be counted on for ready support, as could vulnerable Georgia, described by Washington as having ". . . Indians on its back and Spaniards on its flank." Others, notably Rhode Island, offered little hope for the Federalists. Four states were particularly important because of their size and political strength: Massachusetts, New York, Pennsylvania, and Virginia. Should any of these major states fail to ratify, even a legally constituted union of nine or more states would be a shaky one.

The activities of the Federalists in these four crucial states reveal the variety of tactics they used in order to win state convention support for the Constitution. Threatened with the loss of control of the Pennsylvania legislature in the upcoming elections, they pressed for immediate action by calling for delegate elections. When anti-Federalists tried to thwart this move by absenting themselves so as to deny a legislative quorum, they were unceremoniously dragged back to the chamber by the Federalists, thrust into their seats, and declared present for the crucial vote. The Federalists won two-thirds of the convention seats, and although they failed to convert a single anti-Federalist in the deliberations that followed, their margin held intact in the final convention vote. This early victory (only Delaware acted sooner than Pennsylvania) in the nation's second most populous state helped to start the campaign bandwagon rolling.

Five states had ratified the Constitution by the time the Massachusetts convention was held. When an early straw vote of the delegates indicated that the Federalists were in the minority, they set out to win over two of the state's favorite sons to their cause—Samuel Adams and John Hancock. Ultimately it was necessary to make a political deal with Hancock; in return for his endorsement of the Constitution, the Federalists promised to support him for the vice-presidency under Washington or, in the event that Virginia failed to ratify, the presidency itself. The Bay State Federalists also made an important concession on the content of the Constitution: a promise to have the first Congress initiate amendments to add a Bill of Rights to the document. Massachusetts's ratification of the Constitution with a specific recommendation to this effect established a precedent that other states would follow.

The ratification battle in Virginia was crucial, even though the necessary nine states had approved the Constitution by the time the Dominion State convention met. For the first time, the Federalists faced anti-Federalist delegates capable of matching wits with them. Madison, with the able assistance of young John Marshall (later to become chief justice of the Supreme Court), defended the Constitution against the criticisms of anti-Federalists Patrick Henry, George Mason, and future president James Monroe. The most influential Virginian of them all, George Washington, was not at the convention, but his known support of the Constitution (he even converted to the Federalist cause Governor Edmund Randolph, who had refused to sign the document at the national convention) swayed enough of the uncommitted delegates so that the result was a vote of 89–79.

Like Virginia, New York had its share of able anti-Federalist leaders, including Constitutional Convention delegates Lansing and Yates, and Governor George Clinton. But the recent Virginia decision; the series of newspaper articles authored by Hamilton, Madison, and John Jay under the title, ***The Federalist Papers,*** explaining and defending the Constitution; Hamilton's threat that New York City would secede from the state to join the Union if the state failed to ratify; and, perhaps most important of all, the prestige of Washington and Franklin—all these brought the Federalists a narrow convention victory (30–27) and New York into the fold in late July 1788 as the eleventh state to ratify. North Carolina and eventually even reluctant Rhode Island (which also feared the secession of its major city, Providence) were later to make ratification unanimous. The pangs of the formation and adoption struggle were over; a new nation was born.

The above analysis of the political and economic conditions of the pre-Constitution period, the groups favoring and opposing the Constitution, and the process by which it was formulated and adopted provide some important clues to the intentions and motives of the men who established our constitutional framework. Before we can fully assess them or the Constitution itself, however, we must examine the political beliefs of the Founders and the techniques and institutions they chose to implement those beliefs.

Madison's collaborators on the Federalist papers: Alexander Hamilton and John Jay.

THE POLITICAL PHILOSOPHY OF THE FOUNDERS

The 55 individuals at the Convention spanned the political spectrum from elitists to admirers of the common man. Yet the greater part of the group was committed to the same general scheme of values and made similar assumptions about the nature of man. The delegate who most clearly articulated the common view was James Madison. In 30 of the 85 Federalist papers attributed to him, and in Number 10 in particular, Madison set forth in plain and succinct terms the fundamental theory of the Constitution. Even though *The Federalist* was written in 1788 as a political document for the ratification campaign in New York State, it remains to this day the best single source for researching the Founders' philosophy.

As one reads *The Federalist*, it becomes obvious that the democratic value that Madison cherished most was liberty—an individual's being able to choose reasonable goals for himself and the means to reach those goals. He assumed that one such goal would be the acquisition of private property. However because of what he termed "... the diversity in the faculties of men ..."—that is, the differences in their individual abilities—Madison reasoned that some persons would be more successful in acquiring wordly goods than others. This being the case, government must protect property interests because they reflect innate differences in individual capacities. Madison thus embraced the view of English political philosopher John Locke that, because individual intelligence and effort are involved in gaining property, property represents an extension of the human personality.

For Madison, property was not only a value to be protected but also a factor to be appreciated if one were to understand the basis for natural divisions among mankind. In Federalist paper 10 he suggested that society is divided into various **factions,** which he defined as "... a number of citizens, whether amounting to a majority or a minority of the whole, who are united and actuated by some common impulse of passion, or of interest, adverse to the rights of other citizens, or to the permanent and aggregate interests of the community." While conceding that the causes of factions are numerous, including differences of opinion over religion and government, Madison stated that "... the most common and durable source of factions is the unequal distribution of property. Those who hold and those who are without property have ever formed distinct interests in society. Those who are creditors and those who are debtors, fall under a like discrimination."

Thus Madison's idea that property ownership was the major source of divisions in society paralleled Karl Marx's analysis more than a half-century later. Unlike Marx, however, Madison had no desire to remove divisions by converting private property to common ownership among individuals because such differences reflect "... the diversity in the faculties of men." Moreover, the government was not to wither away as it does in Marxist theory; instead, for Madison it was the major institution to referee the natural conflicts that develop among various factions in society. In fact, the government provides the legal framework within which factions may compete politically in such a way that no major interest can extinguish another.

Since removing the *causes* of factions would be both unwise (factions are desirable because they reflect diversity among individuals) and impossible (they are also rooted in human nature), Madison set out to construct a system of government that would control the harmful *effects* of factions. As he viewed the matter, minority factions presented no difficulty since the majority of society could always protect itself through voting down their "sinister views." The real problem arises when one faction constitutes a majority of the population. As Madison himself put the issue: "To secure the public good and private rights against the danger of such a faction, and at the same time to preserve the spirit and form of popular government, is then the great object to which our inquiries are directed."

CONSTITUTIONAL PRINCIPLES OF THE FOUNDERS

Given the human impulse to pursue selfish interests, Madison saw little hope in either morals or religion as an effective check on the appetites of men. Since ". . . men are not angels," society itself must create a series of obstacles to blunt and divert the opinions and wishes of the majority that threaten private rights and the public good. This aim can best be accomplished through a republican form of government, in which the people elect representatives to make binding decisions, contrasted to a pure democracy, in which they make such decisions themselves. Republican government is preferable for two reasons. First, a representative government provides for a ". . . refinement and enlargement of public views . . ." by passing them through a chosen body of citizens whose knowledge of the public good is superior to that of the general populace. Second, because representative government permits effective rule to be exercised over a larger and more populous territory than town-meeting government, it brings under its control a greater variety of people and interests than pure democracy does. This system thus makes it difficult to construct a majority from a large number of groups: because of communication problems, such interests are often unaware of their common motives, and even if they are, they find it difficult to work together politically to exercise their will over minorities or the general public.

But Madison was not willing to trust general principles of republicanism alone to contain the majority. He wanted to build additional controls within the governmental framework itself to protect minority rights. Reflecting his view of human nature, he suggested that ". . . ambition must be made to counteract ambition." In other words, selfish persons occupying different po-

"IS THE CONSTITUTION THE ONE THAT BEGINS, 'WHEN IN THE COURSE OF HUMAN EVENTS', OR IS IT THE ONE THAT BEGINS, 'WE THE PEOPLE OF THE UNITED STATES, IN ORDER TO FORM A MORE PERFECT UNION'?..."

litical positions must be deliberately pitted against one another in the struggle for power. In the course of frustrating one another's ambitions, they indirectly protect the liberties of minorities and the general public.

Separation of Powers

A major feature of Madison's scheme to make "ambition counteract ambition" was the doctrine of the **separation of powers**, which he borrowed from the French political philosopher, Charles Montesquieu. In his monumental *L'Esprit des lois* ("The Spirit of Laws"; 1748), Montesquieu concludes that the liberties then enjoyed by the English people were attributable to the fact that political power under their constitutional system was not centralized in the hands of one person or clique but was distributed among the legislative, executive, and—to a lesser degree—the judicial branches of the national government. Thus Montesquieu associated tyranny with the concentration of political power and liberty with its dispersal.

The separation of powers might more accurately be termed a *separation of processes.* That is, each of the three branches or arms of the government carries on a separate portion of the total political process: the legislature has the primary responsibility for making the laws, the executive for putting them into effect, and the judiciary for interpreting them. This distinction is similar to Aristotle's idea of the deliberative, administrative, and adjudicative processes used in making political decisions.

The doctrine, however, does not call for a *total* separation of processes. Although each of the three branches has the *major* responsibility for one of these processes—that is, making, executing, or interpreting laws—each participates to some degree in the principal activities of the others. For example, under our system of government, the Congress has the primary responsibility for enacting legislation, but the president is authorized both to recommend measures to the Congress and to veto laws actually passed by that body. Similarly, the Senate can affect the president's execution of the laws by failing to approve his nominees for major positions in the executive branch. Likewise, Congress can affect the courts' interpretations of the laws by determining their jurisdiction, that is, the kinds of cases they are entitled to hear.

By participating in one another's processes, the three branches are in a position to **check and balance** each other's influence and political power. A branch can assert and protect its own rights by withholding its support for the essential activities of a coordinate arm of the government. Thus the president may threaten to veto a piece of legislation as a means of preventing Congress from interfering with the operations of the executive branch. But since the three branches are dependent on one another, the system of shared processes ultimately forces them to cooperate in their mutual activities.

The two principles—separation of processes and checks and balances—complement each other to achieve the desired effect in the political system. The first provides that no branch can usurp an activity that is the *primary* responsibility of another; the second allows the three arms of the government to counteract one another's influence. The end result is a decentralization of political power. Figure 2.1 illustrates the relationships among the governmental branches.

But more than a partial separation of process is necessary to make Montesquieu's principle operate effectively. He also called for a *complete* separation of government *personnel.* In other words, the same persons who occupy the legislative seats of government cannot also serve in the executive or judicial branches. (Our system does not permit congressmen to hold executive or judicial positions, and executives and judges are also similarly restricted.) To allow such a practice would permit the concentration of all political powers in the same hands, the very definition of tyranny.

Another aspect of the doctrine reflected in the American system is the separation of **constituency.** That is, essentially different groups of people choose the personnel of the three branches. As originally conceived, the president, for instance, was to be selected by the electoral college, an independent group of electors, none of whom were to be congressmen; senators were chosen by state legislatures; representatives were elected by smaller local publics. Although members of the national courts were to be nominated by the president and confirmed by the Senate, no one branch was to choose them; moreover, once appointed and confirmed, they were to enjoy life tenure. Thus the personnel of the three branches had largely separate and independent bases of political support and power.

Mixed Government

There is good reason to believe that the Founders provided separate constituencies not only because they wished the branches of the national government to be independent of one another but because they wanted them to represent different kinds of social and economic interests.

The idea of **"mixed" government**—that is, one representing both property and number of people—was favored by John Adams, who succeeded in having the concept incorporated into the Massachusetts state constitution. Although he was in London at the time of the national Constitutional Convention, ideas expressed in the Federalist papers, as well as the similarities between the structure of the national government and that of Massachusetts, indicate that as a political thinker, Adams influenced the Constitution.

Although the Constitution nowhere provides for property qualifications for either officeholders or voters, it is significant that originally the House of Representatives was the only political body directly elected by the people. (The direct election of senators was not authorized until the ratification of the Seventeenth Amendment in 1913.) The other major offices were somewhat insulated from the general populace. As Figure 2.2 indicates, according to the original document, members of the Senate were two, the president three, and the Supreme Court four steps removed from direct control of the people. (It should also be noted that the Founders gave the House of Representatives no role in choosing members of the Supreme Court.) In addition, the longer terms of senators (six years), the president (four years), and Supreme Court members (life) would make them less subject to public pressures than members of the House of Representatives. Because fewer persons were to be chosen for the other three political bodies, positions in these would be more prestigious than seats in the lower house of the national legislature. This in turn would have the effect of attracting more able persons to these bodies, and since property ownership was considered reflective of natural ability (Adams and Madison agreed on this point), the men chosen would be those of economic substance from the upper social classes.

In all probability the Founders expected the House of Representatives to represent the interests of the many in society, the common people who owned no private property of any consequence. It would be the democratic, popular branch of the government. On the other hand, the Senate, with a smaller, more prestigious membership, insulated somewhat from popular control

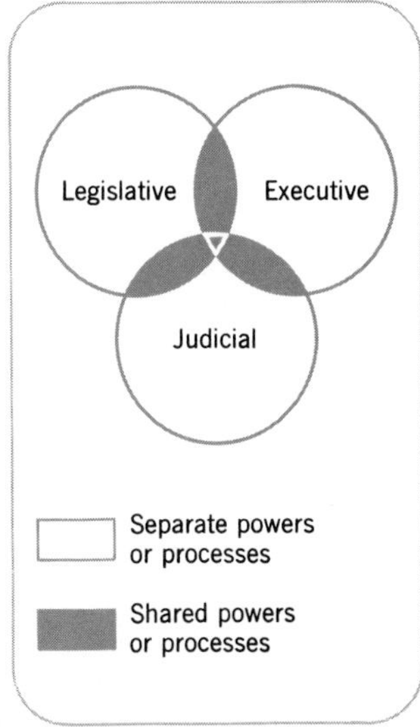

Figure 2.1 Governmental Arrangements under the Separation-of-Powers Doctrine.

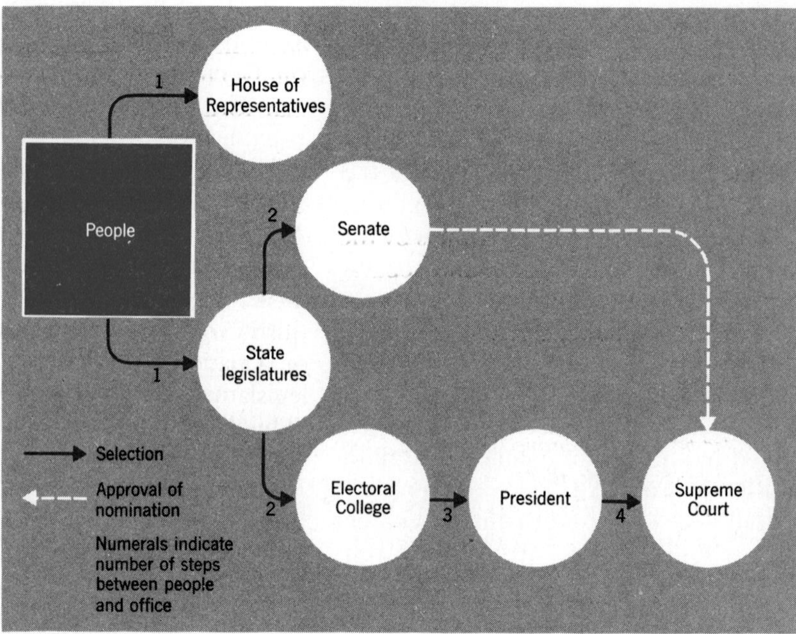

Figure 2.2 Relationship Between the People and the Selection of Various Officeholders of the Nation Under the Original Constitution.

both by its (then) indirect method of selection and its longer term of office, would represent the few in society with substantial possessions. It would constitute the oligarchic division of the legislative body.

It is somewhat more difficult to discern the exact intentions of the Founders concerning the kinds of interests the president and the Supreme Court were to represent in the governmental system. One interpretation calls for their standing above the many/few conflict as guardians of the general interest, promoting unity and justice in society. Another suggests that they were expected to join forces with the Senate to protect the interests of the propertied few against the excesses of the popular legislature. Given Madison's concern with safeguarding both the general interest and minority rights against the evils of a majority faction, it is probable that the president and the Supreme Court were expected to serve both purposes.

The Division of Powers

Madison conceived of one final check on the majority, which we will examine in detail in the next chapter—the **division of powers** between the national government and the states. His major concern is reflected in Federalist paper 10: "The influence of factious leaders may kindle a flame within the particular states, but they will be unable to spread a conflagration through the other states."

Thus Madison's system for checking the evils of faction was to create a series of dikes to interfere with the free flow of majority will. First, majority interests are *filtered* by the actions of their elected representatives, who have more refined views of the public good than the voters themselves. Second, the wishes of the majority are *diluted* because republicanism allows the expansion of the sphere of government to take in a wide variety of interests. Moreover, the distribution of power between the national government and the state governments under federalism *contains* or *segregates* the evil effects of a faction. Finally, the majority will is *diverted* into many channels by the joint effects of the division and separation of powers. As Madison himself put it in Federalist paper 51:

> *In the compound republic of America, the power surrendered by the people is first divided between two distinct governments, and then the portion allotted to each subdivided among distinct and separate departments. Hence a double security arises to the rights of the people. The different governments will control each other, at the same time each will be controlled by itself.*

This, then, was the type of political system the Founders had in mind for the new nation. As the next section shows, however, vast changes have since occurred in our constitutional framework.

CHANGING THE AMERICAN CONSTITUTION

A constitution necessarily reflects the interests and values of those groups responsible for its original formulation. In time, however, new groups arise that are dissatisfied with the status quo, the existing distribution of values, and quite often they seek to rewrite the rules of the democratic game to change that distribution. The press of events and the emergence of different attitudes on the part of leaders and the populace in general also require alterations in a nation's fundamental framework. Every democratic system of government must provide methods for bringing about such modifications peacefully or risk the danger that frustrated individuals and groups will turn to violence to accomplish their ends. Thus the question is not whether a democratic constitution will be changed, but rather what particular form such change will take.

Formal Amendments

One important method of changing the American Constitution has been the formal amendment process. Amendments can be proposed either by a two-thirds vote in both houses of Congress or a national convention called by the legislatures of two-thirds of the states. (This latter method has never actually been used).* Amendments so initiated must then be ratified either by three-fourths of the state legislatures or conventions held in three-fourths of the states, with Congress determining which ratification method is to be used. (Only the Twenty-first Amendment has been adopted by the latter procedure.) By 1980 Americans made 26 changes to the original document by the formal amendment process. (As discussed in Chapter 15, a twenty-seventh, the Equal Rights Amendment, failed on two separate occasions to be ratified by the 38 states required for its adoption.)

In analyzing the formal amendments it is helpful to understand the particular types of alterations they made in constitutional principles—that is, whether they affected the functions, procedures, or structure of the government—and which level or levels—national or state—were involved. Even more important is an appreciation of the particular groups involved in the amendment process and the kinds of values they sought to implement through a change in the rules of the game.

The anti-Federalists, who were pri-

---

* However, as discussed in Chapter 5, the call for a constitutional convention to propose an amendment to require the national government to operate under a balanced budget presently lacks only the votes of a few of the 34 states necessary to take that action.

Some amendments to the Constitution were the result of a long arduous struggle. The women's suffrage movement began in 1848; in 1914 these suffragists were still soliciting support; the efforts were not successful until the passage of the Nineteenth Amendment in 1920.

marily responsible for adding the first 10 amendments to the Constitution, were concerned with **civil liberties**—protecting individuals against arbitrary government action affecting their rights of speech, press, and religion, or the taking of their lives, freedom, or property in criminal proceedings. The first nine amendments place limits on the procedures that the national government may use in such matters. The Tenth Amendment reflects the anti-Federalists' preoccupation with preserving the powers of the states against encroachment by the national government. The amendments thus reflect political concerns that are much different from those of the Founders, who were preoccupied with guarding property rights against the actions of state governments.

Many of the remaining amendments reflect still another major value of a democratic society: equality. The Thirteenth, Fourteenth, and Fifteenth relate to race, while the Nineteenth, Twenty-third, Twenty-fourth, and Twenty-sixth govern the voting rights of, respectively, women, residents of the District of Columbia, persons who live in jurisdictions that levy a poll tax as a condition for voting, and young people between the ages of 18 and 21. They are thus designed to allow formerly disadvantaged groups to participate in the political process and, through the Thirteenth and Fourteenth amendments, the social and economic life of American society. It should be noted that this group of amendments primarily affects the states, not the national government.

Two other amendments, the Seventeenth and the Twenty-second, also relate to political participation. However, they affect the suffrage rights of all qualified voters, not particular groups. The former amendment, dealing with the direct election of senators, extends the rights of voters to choose members of the upper house of the national legislature; the latter, which affects the length of the president's term, prevents voters from choosing the same person more than twice. The two amendments are based on somewhat different assumptions about human capacities: the

Seventeenth expresses faith in the electorate's ability to choose good senators; the Twenty-second evidences a fear that the voters may fall victim to the entreaties of a demagogue.

Four of the amendments—the Eleventh, Twelfth, Twentieth, and Twenty-fifth—bear no particular imprint of group influence or political philosophy. They rather relate to changes brought about by the press of particular historical events and affect primarily the structure and procedures of all three branches of the national government.

The one other amendment, the Sixteenth (the Eighteenth and Twenty-first, dealing with alcoholic beverages, cancel each other out), establishes the procedures that the national government is permitted to follow in levying an income tax. It provides that the government may do so without allocating the tax on the basis of population of the individual states, a factor that prevented taxing persons residing in different states at the same rate. Although the amendment does not specifically favor or disadvantage any group, the revenue measures developed by the Congress have some potential for economic leveling since the wealthy are taxed at a higher rate than the poor.

Other Methods of Constitutional Change

Although important changes have been made in the American Constitution by means of formal amendments, only 26 have made it past the extramajority* hurdles created by the amendment process, and 10 of these came at once. Thus in a period of almost two centuries (ignoring the Eighteenth and Twenty-first, which counterbalance each other), formal alterations in the Constitution have been made on only 16 occasions.

But the formal amendment process does not begin to tell the full story of the vast changes that have occurred in the functions, procedures, and structure of the American political system over that period. The final document's brevity (it is much shorter than most of our state constitutions), as well as the

* A majority is one over half. An extramajority is greater than that proportion, typically two-thirds or three-fourths.

Celebrating the repeal.

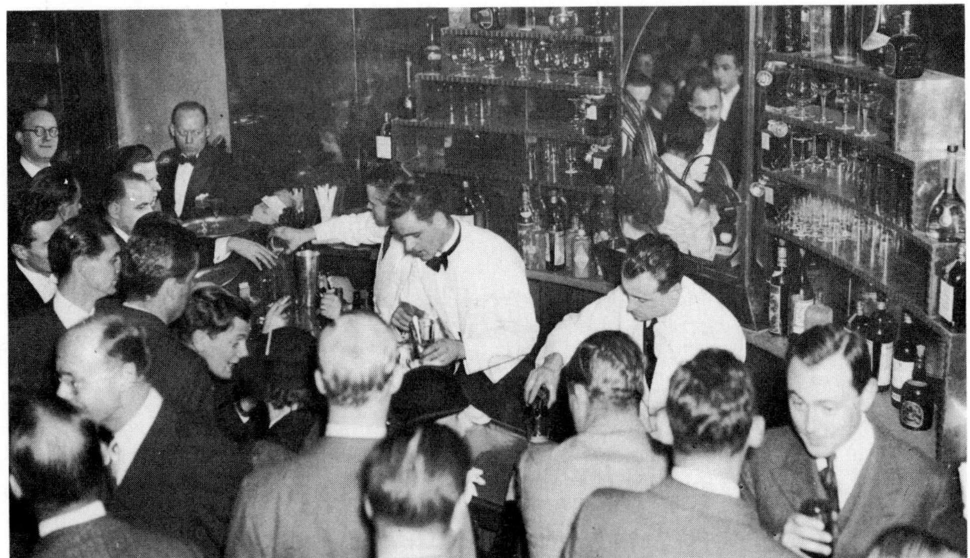

vagueness of many of its provisions, have also led to changes through its *interpretation* by officials of the three branches of the national government. For example, the formal document says nothing at all about the removal of officials of the executive branch; can the president do so on his own or must he receive the Senate's consent to such an action? As we shall see in Chapter 13, that issue surfaced as a major factor in the impeachment action taken against President Andrew Johnson by the House of Representatives and the Senate shortly after the Civil War and eventually led to important Supreme Court decisions on the matter after Presidents Woodrow Wilson and Franklin Roosevelt also removed key executive officials. Moreover, as we shall see in Chapters 8 and 15, within the last few decades shifts in the Supreme Court's interpretations of the **"equal protection of the laws"** clause of the Fourteenth Amendment have altered the composition of both the House of Representatives and the state legislatures and revolutionized race relations in this nation. Thus changes in the direction of more political and social equality in American life have come through judicial interpretation of the Constitution as well as by formal amendment.

Moreover, *custom and usage* have also contributed to changes in the American constitutional system. Article II, Section 3 states that the president ". . . shall from time to time give to the Congress information of the state of the Union and recommend to their consideration such measures as he shall judge necessary and expedient." We shall see in Chapter 11 that the generality of the language has enabled various presidents to utilize the power in different ways: some chief executives have delivered the message to Congress in writing, while others have done so in person; some have been satisfied to deliver the one message, while others have followed it with a series of special messages on particular topics of concern and even suggested specific legislation to deal with them.

Thus the American constitution has contributed to both the stability and the flexibility of the American political system. The relative difficulty of the formal amendment process has helped ensure that fundamental aspects of our governmental functions, procedures, and structure will not be easily altered. At the same time, the conciseness and ambiguity of many parts of the document have enabled our constitutional system to change through interpretation and custom and usage, and thus keep up with the necessities of the times.

ASSESSMENT

As we piece together the various bits of evidence on the intentions of the Founders—the economic and social conditions of the day, the major provisions of the new Constitution, and the philosophy articulated in the Federalist papers—it becomes clear that two concerns were paramount in their thinking. One was national unity, the necessity for drawing together, through an effective political union, the states that threatened to go their separate ways in the period immediately preceding the Constitutional Convention. In this respect the United States was faced with the same major problem that preoccupies the leaders of emerging nations today, namely, providing some sense of national identity for a people divided along lines of economic interests or regional loyalties. Such divisions, or "factions" as Madison called them, threatened the very existence of the American political system.

The other major concern of the Founders was the protection of private property against the incursion of majority rule. For property ownership was linked with their most cherished value, liberty, the right of each person to develop himself to the fullest extent of his capacities and to be free from arbitrary government action. It is significant that while the preamble of the Constitution refers to the "blessings of liberty," it nowhere mentions "equality." In fact, the Federalist papers specifically refer to "the equal division of property" as a "malady" and express concern over the "leveling spirit" of men. (As political scientist Martin Diamond suggests, the only concept of equality that the Founders would have approved is the right to equal political liberty.)

Debates over which of these concerns—national unity or property rights—was most important to the Founders are meaningless, since the two issues were inexorably linked in their thinking. They felt that a young nation could not survive in a situation of interstate commercial rivalries, uncertainties involving the collection of debts, and a worthless currency. Similarly, attempts to determine whether their prime motivation in writing the Constitution was to protect their own personal property interests or to promote the public good miss the point that for the Founders there was no real difference between the two inducements. They believed that the ownership of property gave men a "stake" in society and hence made them better citizens; moreover, like most people, they tended to identify their own interests with that of society as a whole.

The constitutional movement therefore represented a reaction against some of the democratic values and assumptions of the Revolutionary period. Ironically, the same political philosopher, John Locke, provided some of the major ideas for both. But whereas the earlier era espoused Locke's concepts of majority rule and legislative supremacy, the Founders rather stressed his concern with property rights and his recognition of executive prerogatives. Thus different aspects of Locke's philosophy were borrowed for dealing with different conditions in the two periods of national development.

The events of the pre-Constitution period tempered the essential optimism concerning human nature that characterized the earlier era. Even such a great admirer of the common man and the legislature as Thomas Jefferson referred to the "173 despots" in the Virginia legislature. It was thus experience, rather than a radical shift in leadership, that brought about a change in the dominant thinking of the two eras. For essentially the same men were involved in both. Jefferson and Adams, the major architects of the Declaration of Independence, both heartily approved the new Constitution, while James Wilson, a major figure at the Convention, had signed the Declaration. Moreover, some of the Founders had endorsed the Articles of Confederation or served in its national legislature. Although some new leaders emerged in the constitutional period, no genuine "counterrevolution" occurred whereby one group of Americans completely replaced another. Rather, some of the key men changed their minds about the kinds of political institutions that were needed to channel human weaknesses (as well as virtues) to achieve the public good.

In place of the legislatively dominated governments of the Articles of Confederation period, closely tied to the public by short terms, forced rotation in office, and recall, the Founders sought to substitute the concept of a political system with three rival branches, removed in different stages from direct public control. They favored a "mixed" government that would reflect the interests of both the few with property and the many without. Although they did not embrace the principles of semidirect democracy, they turned their backs on both monarchy and oligarchical control of society by members of the upper class. They created the most democratic system of the day, as evidenced by the refusal of Catherine the Great of Russia to recognize the new government because of its radical nature.

An analysis of the American constitutional system thus indicates that the original rules of the game were written primarily by groups interested in protecting property rights and avoiding what they considered the harmful effects of direct democracy. Their most cherished value was that of liberty. The major changes that have been made in the original constitutional system over the years have come from groups particularly solicitous of civil liberties as compared to property rights, and from those persons who desire to open up the democratic process to additional groups in society. In place of the liberty that was so valued by our nation's Founders, equality has become the dominant concern in our recent constitutional development.

SELECTED READINGS

The classic study of the Constitutional Convention is Max Farrand, *The Framing of the Constitution of the United States* (New Haven: Yale University Press, 1913). A more recent account of the event written in a journalistic style is Catherine Drinker Bowen, *Miracle at Philadelphia* (Boston: Little, Brown, 1966). Another excellent analysis, Clinton Rossiter, *1787: The Grand Convention* (New York: The Macmillan Co., 1966), also contains valuable background information on the events leading up to the calling of the Convention that is not present in the above selections.

In addition to Rossiter, other good sources on the economic, social, and political conditions that surrounded the calling of the Convention are David Smith, *The Convention and the Constitution* (New York: St. Martin's Press, 1965) and Alpheus T. Mason's edited work with commentaries, *The States' Rights Debate* (Englewood Cliffs, N.J.: Prentice–Hall, 1964). The latter work, along with Jackson Turner Main, *The Antifederalists: Critics of the Constitution, 1781–1788* (Chicago: Quadrangle Books, 1961), contains valuable information on the opponents of the Constitution. Bowen, Rossiter, Mason, and Main also touch on the campaign for the ratification of the Constitution.

The most controversial interpretation of the motives of the Founders is Charles Beard's classic study, *An Economic Interpretation of the Constitution of the United States* (originally published 1913; reissued, New York: Free Press, 1965), which suggests that they wrote the Constitution primarily to protect their own property interests. Two criticisms of Beard's work are Robert Brown, *Charles Beard and the Constitution* (Princeton: Princeton University Press, 1956) and Forest McDonald, *We the People* (Chicago: University of Chicago Press, 1958). Main, in his work cited above, basically defends the Beard thesis.

There are a number of good sources on the political philosophy of the Founders. Included are Hamilton, Jay, and Madison, *The Federalist*; Smith's book cited above; and

Paul Eidelberg, *The Philosophy of the Constitution* (New York: Free Press, 1968). Another work that touches on the subject as part of a larger historical study of values in American society is Seymour Lipset, *The First New Nation* (New York: Basic Books, 1963). An excellent recent analysis of the political philosophy of the framers of the Constitution written at the time of the nation's bicentennial is Martin Diamond, "The Declaration and the Constitution: Liberty, Democracy, and the Founders," in Nathan Glaser and Irving Kristol, eds., *The American Commonwealth* (New York: Basic Books, 1976).

CHAPTER 3

Federalism

In his State of the Union message to Congress on January 26, 1982, President Reagan presented a bold, new program designed "... to make government again accountable to the people, to make our system of federalism work again." The President blamed "... the overpowering growth of federal-grants-in-aid programs ..." (participated in jointly by national, state, and local governments) for creating "... a maze of interlocking jurisdictions and levels of government ..." that prevents citizens from knowing "... where to turn for answers, who to hold accountable, who to praise, who to blame, who to vote for or against." Such grants, he charged, have distorted the vital functions of government: the national government should be worrying about "... arms control, not potholes."

To remedy this situation, President Reagan proposed a *New Federalism* program (so tabbed by some administration officials; the President prefers the term, *federalism initiatives**) with two major features. One was a "swap" of existing programs. Beginning in fiscal year 1984, the federal government would assume full financial responsibility for the Medicaid health program for the "medically needy," relieving states of the portion of its costs to which they presently contribute. In return, the states would assume full responsibility for the Aid to Families with Dependent Children (AFDC) program (which they now share with the federal government) and also take over the Food Stamp program (now financed entirely by the federal government).

The second major feature of the President's New Federalism program involved a "turnback" of some 44 federal grants-in-aid programs to the states. Beginning in fiscal 1984 and last-

* One possible reason for that preference is that President Nixon previously used the term *New Federalism* to describe his proposals relating to nation-state relations.

President Reagan addresses Congress.

ing until fiscal 1987, states would be entitled to draw from a "trust fund" amounting to some $28 billion. The trust fund was to be composed of moneys raised by federal excise taxes on oil companies' "windfall" profits, tobacco, and telephones, as well as a portion of the federal tax on gasoline. The states could use these funds in one of two ways: (1) to continue various existing social, transportation, and community development programs by reimbursing the federal agencies that gave them grants for such programs; or (2) to take the federal funds in the form of a single grant, to be spent for any purpose the states desired. However, the president's proposal placed one major limitation on the latter alternative: some of the moneys drawn by the states from the federal trust fund would have to be "passed through" to local governments.

Beginning in fiscal 1988, the President's proposed turnback program would enter a new phase. Each year for the next four years, the federal trust fund would be reduced by 25 percent until it disappeared completely after fiscal 1991. In the interim, states would be free to raise their own taxes to make up the difference in lost federal funds. They would be entirely on their own after 1991, when all the federal excise taxes would be eliminated. At that time, full responsibility for the 44 previous federal grants-in-aid programs would belong to the individual states to be continued, modified, or eliminated as each saw fit.

As might be expected, the president's program drew great opposition. Many congressmen accused Reagan of trying to divert the public's attention from the nation's real problems—massive unemployment and huge budgetary deficits—which the New Federalism did not address at all. Some persons, particularly liberal Democrats, also charged that the president's real purpose was not to transfer the 44 federal grants-in-aid programs to the states—which could not or would not assume them—but rather to eliminate all government responsibility for such programs, a result consistent with Reagan's antagonism towards social programs developed since the New Deal.

Many governors also expressed reservations about the New Federalism; Republican Lamar Alexander of Tennessee said that most of the governors would prefer to have the federal government take over all those programs involved in the "swap"—AFDC, food stamps, and Medicaid—and give the states ". . . an even amount in programs of a more everyday concern like sewers." Some governors also expressed concern that the poorer states could not afford to eventually assume all the costs of the 44 federal grants-in-aid programs involved in the "turnback" feature of Reagan's New Federalism. Some local officials also expressed doubts that their interests would be protected: New York City's Mayor, Edward Koch, described the provision for the states "passing-through" moneys to the cities as "inadequate."

In the months following the President's State of the Union address, officials of the Reagan administration met with state and local officials to try and come to some agreement about the terms of the New Federalism. As a result, some changes were made in the President's original proposal. It was decided that the Food Stamp program would not be a part of the swap between federal and state governments; rather, it would remain the sole responsibility of the national government. Proceeds from the federal tax on oil companies' windfall profits would also be dropped from the trust fund program (and other financing substituted) because only a few states with significant oil production would be in a position to substitute a tax of their own when the federal tax expired. However, despite such concessions, the Reagan administration was unable to get needed political support for its New Federalism program, and ultimately decided not to even introduce the legislation in Congress.

While it was unsuccessful, President Reagan's New Federalism proposal does raise some basic issues about the nature of American federalism today that we will discuss later in the chapter. To understand such issues, however, we must first analyze the basic concept of a division of powers that underlies a federal system of government, and then rexamine how that concept has been applied to the American experience over the years.

MODELS OF DIVIDING POLITICAL POWER

Although societies employ a variety of methods to divide political power among governmental levels, it is possible to group the arrangements into three general categories—**confederative, unitary,** and **federal** systems. In order to understand what federalism is, it is helpful first to analyze what it is *not*, that is, to see how it differs from the other two models of divided political authority.

Confederation

The confederative system was employed by name under the Articles of Confederation. Assuming the people to be the ultimate source of political authority, one can illustrate the allocation of powers under a confederation as in Figure 3.1. The figure indicates that in a confederation the people grant political power over certain concerns to the gov-

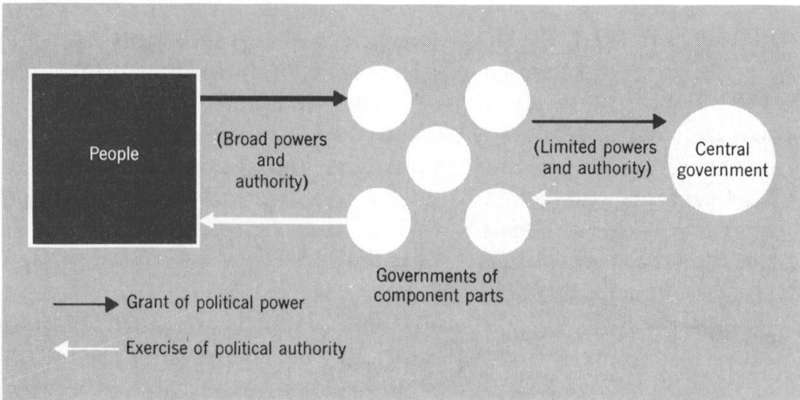

Figure 3.1 Confederation.

ernments of the component parts of the political system. These governments as a group in turn delegate power over certain of these concerns to the central government. In a confederation the scope of powers granted to the governments of the component parts is generally broad and covers all those activities that people feel should come under the control of public rather than private authorities. In contrast, the scope of powers of the central government is narrow and is restricted to only those matters that the component parts feel must be handled by the large and geographically more inclusive unit of government. For example, under the Articles of Confederation the functions of the national government were restricted to concerns of war and peace, while the state governments exercised broad authority over the remaining activities entrusted to political authorities.

Under a confederation the people grant no political power directly to the central government; thus that government cannot exercise direct legal control over the people. As Figure 3.1 suggests, the central government must depend on the governments of the component parts to enforce its authority over even the few concerns entrusted to it. Thus under the Articles of Confederation the national government had the power to raise an army and levy certain taxes. Yet it could not exercise direct control over people to enforce that authority; rather it was dependent on the state governments to provide money and troops. The national government also had to depend primarily on state courts to enforce its laws.

Two other features are usually associated with a confederation. One is the right of a component government to withdraw voluntarily from the larger union when it feels that its interests are not being served by the more inclusive unit of government. The other is the requirement that all the component parts of the union consent to any change in the division of powers between the two levels of government. Thus under the Articles of Confederation the national government could not be granted the power to levy import taxes because a single state (Rhode Island) refused to consent to an amendment granting this power to the central government.

A modern-day example of a confederation is the United Nations. In this body, of course, the nation–states (e.g., the United States or the Soviet Union) are the component governments, while the United Nations itself is the central political unit. The organization possesses the basic features of a confeder-

United Nation's General Assembly.

ation: the UN exercises only those powers granted to it by its members; its governmental authority is narrow compared to that retained by the nation–states; it depends on voluntary contributions of money and military forces by individual countries for its operations; it cannot impose its provisions on individual members; and nations are free to withdraw from it at any time (as Indonesia did temporarily some years ago). Although the consent of two-thirds of the member nations is sufficient to ratify proposed changes in the charter of the organization, that two-thirds must include all the permanent members of the Security Council (United States, Soviet Union, United Kingdom, France, and China).

Unitary Governments

Diametrically opposed to a confederation as a means of dividing political power between levels of government is a *unitary* system. As Figure 3.2 indicates, the people grant power over their activities to the central government, which in turn delegates authority over some of these activities to the component parts. The powers retained by the central unit are usually more extensive or more important than those it grants to the lower political units. Moreover, the governments of the component parts may impose their decrees on individuals only if they are authorized to do so by the central government.

A historical example of a unitary system of government is the British Empire in the period prior to the Revolutionary War. Initially the mother country allowed the colonists the right to tax themselves and raise their own troops. However, dissatisfaction with the inability of some colonies to provide adequate military forces during the French and Indian War led the British to decide, once the war was over, to use

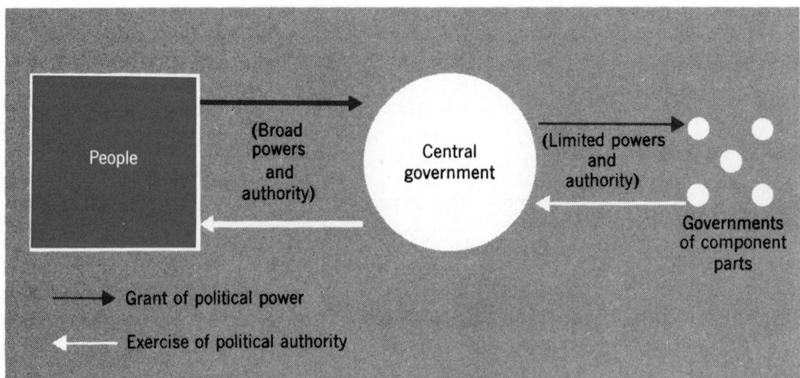

Figure 3.2 Unitary System.

their own troops to provide order in the colonies and to make the residents pay their share of the costs of such forces. In the view of the mother country, this decision to reassert her authority over colonial financial and military affairs did not require the consent of the colonies. Moreover, the colonists continued to depend on London for authority to enforce laws governing even those functions that remained in their jurisdiction. Finally, the British did not recognize the right of the colonies to declare themselves independent of the empire. Instead, the Revolutionary War was fought by Great Britain for the purpose of compelling Americans to remain under that authority.

Most countries in the world today have unitary governments. So do the individual states of our own nation: the arrangements between state government and its lesser units are essentially unitary. The state determines what functions will be granted to local governments (counties, cities, villages) and decides whether these political entities can create their own agencies or must rely on those of the states to control individuals. Neither can the lower units generally block changes in state–local relationships or legally withdraw from the jurisdiction of the state government.

Federalism

The American federal system evolved at the Constitutional Convention as a means to avoid either the excessive decentralization of the Articles of Confederation or the extreme centralism of the British Empire. A basic disagreement between the delegates occurred over the very basis of authority of the government: should the states remain as sovereign units possessing ultimate authority, or should the government represent the people of the whole nation? Fortunately the Connecticut Compromise, which resolved the small state versus large state controversy over representation in the national legislature,* also met the sovereignty issue. As Madison explained in *The Federalist*, the new government depended ". . . partly upon the states and partly on the people."

In using the term *federalism*, a political scientist refers to a system in which political power is divided between the central government of a country and the governments of its component parts

* The Senate, with equality of state representation benefited the small states; the House of Representatives, whose representation was based on population, benefited the large ones.

so that each level is legally independent of the other within its own sphere of activity. In the American system neither the national government, nor the government of an individual state, depends on the other for its source of political power. The same is true of other federations in the world. Although the names of the component parts of given nations differ, the principle is the same: provinces of Canada, cantons of Switzerland, and länder in West Germany all have bases of power independent of their national governments. Figure 3.3 indicates the relationships that exist under a federal political system.

Thus under a federal system each level of government is legally independent of the other. Each receives its grant of powers directly from the people. Each in turn has the concomitant right to exercise political authority over the people within its own sphere of activities without depending on the consent of the other level of government.

A federal system also has two other essential characteristics. First, both levels of government must participate in decisions to change the division of powers between them. Thus in the American system both the Congress and the states are involved in amending the federal Constitution. Second, the component parts are not free to leave the union voluntarily as may parts of a confederation. The major legal issue that precipitated the American Civil War was precisely that—the Southern states took the position that they had the right to secede from the Union; Lincoln and the Northern states disagreed. The issue was settled militarily on the battlefield, and subsequently the Supreme Court gave its legal blessing to the result by stating that ". . . the Constitution, in all its provisions, looks to an indestructible Union composed of indestructible States." In the late 1960s a similar state of affairs developed in Nigeria: Biafra sought to pull out of the federation, and the central authorities used force to prevent it from doing so.

It should be emphasized that differences between confederative, unitary, and federal forms of government are legal in nature. A division of political power occurs in all three. Moreover, considerable variations in the allocation of powers are possible within each of the major systems. As weak as the na-

Figure 3.3 Federation.

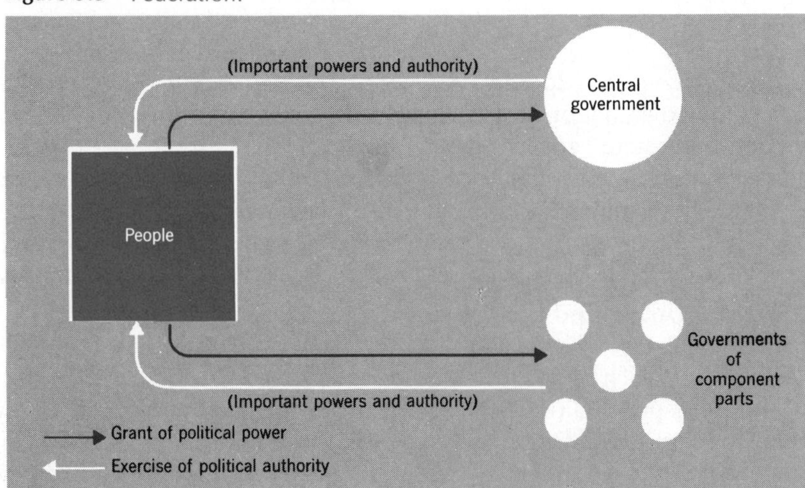

tional government was under the Articles of Confederation, it was granted more political power than the United Nations has today. Both France and Great Britain have unitary governments, but counties and towns exercise more important powers in the latter because of the British tradition of local self-government, compared to the historic patterns of centralism in France. Nevertheless, the powers that central authorities in London grant local governments in Britain today can be legally withdrawn tomorrow. Such a possibility is not present in a federation. In fact, federations utilize a series of institutions to safeguard the independence of both levels of the governmental system.

INSTITUTIONAL SAFEGUARDS OF FEDERALISM

The give-and-take process at the Convention led to the establishment of a number of institutional methods and practices that have come to be associated with a federal system of government because they are designed to protect both political levels in the system. Many such methods have been consciously borrowed (with some modifications, of course) by other nations, such as Canada and Australia, that have created federations similar to the one developed by the United States.

The basic method used by the Founders to distribute powers in the American system was a *formal written constitution.* Because they feared political power, they sought to curb its possible excesses by distributing it among different levels of government, each of which was assigned definite responsibilities in the constitutional system. By spelling out in some detail the respective spheres of authority of the national government and the states, they hoped to protect the domain of each from encroachment by the other. Other nations seeking to benefit from the American federal experience have likewise used written constitutions to distribute political powers among the central government and the component parts.

Federations can and do differ, however, on the particular methods they use to divide political power. The American approach is to assign certain specific powers to the national government and to reserve all remaining powers for the states. (The details of this division of power will be discussed later in this chapter.) Canada uses precisely the opposite technique of delegating particular powers to its provinces and permitting the Dominion (national government) to enjoy the remaining authority. Still other federations—for instance, West Germany—assign certain specific powers to one level of government and other specific powers to the other level. Whatever approach is used, the emphasis in all federations is on dividing political power so that important responsibilities are granted to both levels of government.

Since the two levels receive their respective powers from the written constitution, another practice logically follows in a federal system: *both* levels must participate in the formal process of altering that constitution. Otherwise, one of the governmental levels could change the original division of power in its favor. As discussed in the last chapter, under the American Constitution the Congress initiates amendments, either by a two-thirds vote of both houses or in response to a call from two-thirds of the state legislatures for a convention to consider proposed amendments. (This latter procedure has not been used to date.*) Three-fourths of the states in turn must ratify amendments through

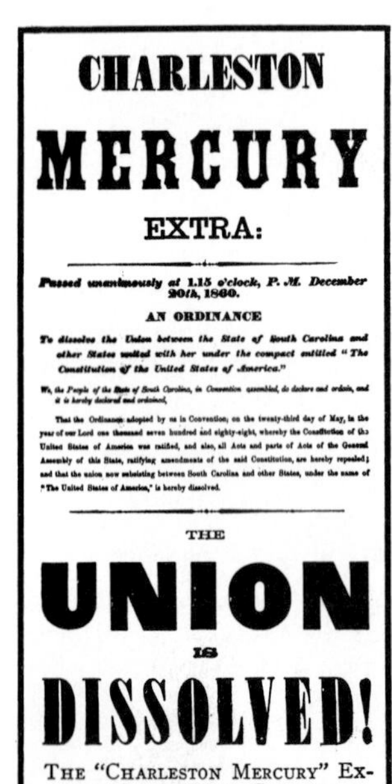

CHARLESTON

MERCURY

EXTRA:

Passed unanimously at 1.15 o'clock, P. M. December 20th, 1860.

AN ORDINANCE

To dissolve the Union between the State of South Carolina and other States united with her under the compact entitled "The Constitution of the United States of America."

We, the People of the State of South Carolina, in Convention assembled, do declare and ordain, and it is hereby declared and ordained,

That the Ordinance adopted by us in Convention, on the twenty-third day of May, in the year of our Lord one thousand seven hundred and eighty-eight, whereby the Constitution of the United States of America was ratified, and also, all Acts and parts of Acts of the General Assembly of this State, ratifying amendments of the said Constitution, are hereby repealed; and that the union now subsisting between South Carolina and other States, under the name of "The United States of America," is hereby dissolved.

THE

UNION

IS

DISSOLVED!

The "Charleston Mercury" Extra Announcing Secession

Canadian parliament building.

their legislatures or by conventions before they become effective. Similarly, in Australia and Switzerland the component parts (states and cantons, respectively) must approve amendments to their formal constitutions.

Another institution generally associated with a federal system is an *umpire* to settle disputes that inevitably arise between the two levels of government. No matter how carefully the language of a constitution is drawn, situations arise in which it is not clear from the division of powers which level of government is entitled to undertake a particular activity. In many instances, of course, the difficulty is unavoidable: constitution-framers cannot be expected to foresee all future developments, such as the rise of the modern corporation or the invention of television, and to provide for them accordingly. Thus some agency must be provided for allocating new governmental responsibilities between the central unit and the component parts. In a typical federal system the ultimate authority for settling such nation–state disputes rests with the highest court in the land, such as United States Supreme Court. (Switzerland, however, refers such issues to the people.)

Most federations also provide some protection for the states in the political process, generally a special house of the national legislature in which the component parts are represented as units. The purest form of this practice is absolute equality of representation as in the American and Australian senates.

* As previously indicated, in the late 1970s a number of state legislatures called for the assembling of a constitutional convention to propose an amendment requiring a balanced federal budget. Should the necessary 34 states call for such a convention, a number of legal issues would have to be decided, including whether Congress could limit the scope and authority of such a convention and how its delegates would be selected and apportioned among the states.

Other federations such as Canada give larger provinces more representation in their senates than smaller ones, but the disparity is not as great as it would be if population alone were the sole criterion.

Typically, federations create two separate sets of political institutions to carry on the constitutional responsibilities of the central government and its component parts. Each has its own legislative, executive, and judicial branches of government operating directly on individual citizens, and these two sets of institutions generally function independently of one another. Also, under a federal system, neither level of government can appoint or remove officials of the other.

By creating general governmental institutions like those described above, federal nations seek to maintain a balance between the central government and the parts. Whether such a balance is actually preserved depends on how such institutions work out in practice.

LEGAL SAFEGUARDS OF AMERICAN FEDERALISM

The operation of legal safeguards in the American federal system has been affected by two major factors: first, the method by which powers are divided in the Constitution between the national government and the states; second, how the Supreme Court has interpreted this division of powers in major cases.

The Division of Powers Under the National Constitution

Article I, Section 8 of the Constitution delegates certain specific, enumerated powers to the Congress. Its jurisdiction includes such varied functions as regulating interstate and foreign commerce, raising an army and navy, controlling the currency, and establishing post offices and roads. Congress is also granted the power to levy taxes to pay national debts and provide for the defense and general welfare of the nation, as well as the authority to borrow money on the credit of the United States. At the very end of Article I, Section 8 there appears an important clause granting Congress the power ". . . to make all laws which shall be necessary and proper for carrying into execution the foregoing powers. . . ." With this statement the Founders sought to expand the authority of the national government beyond those matters specifically listed in that section. In other words, they wanted the national government to have **implied** as well as **expressed powers.**

The Constitution makes no specific grant of powers to the states. In fact, in its original form the document made no mention at all of state prerogatives. By implication, the framers intended that all powers not granted to the national government would remain in the states. However, uneasiness among anti-Federalists over leaving states' rights to implication alone led to the adoption of the Tenth Amendment, which expressly provides that "The powers not delegated to the United States by the Constitution, nor prohibited by it to the States, are reserved to the States respectively, or to the people."

The general source of political powers of the American states are their own constitutions. Although their powers (and limitations) vary somewhat, the states in general possess **"police power,"** which enables them to pass laws for the "health, safety, and morals" of their people. This broad grant of political authority means that unlike the national government, a state government does not need to depend on a specific grant of power authorizing a particular function; unless an activity is specifically forbidden by the national or its own state constitution, or is considered by state courts to be an "unreasonable" use of the police power (such as permitting men, but not women, to drive motor vehicles), a state is free to legislate on it.

The resulting division of powers—whereby the national government can exercise specific enumerated powers, as well as powers implied from them, while the states are free to take advantage of the general police power—results in a broad area of **concurrent powers.** For example, both the national and the state governments are entitled to raise taxes to finance their activities. At the same time, the Constitution provides for settling possible conflicts that may arise between federal and state operations. Article VI, paragraph 2 declares that if state laws or constitutional provisions are at variance with the national Constitution, laws, or treaties, the latter prevail because they are considered "supreme."

This, then, is the basic method of distributing governmental powers in the American federal system. Since the constitutional language is broad and general, however, and since new situations have arisen that the framers could not possibly have foreseen, the Supreme Court has had to act as an umpire in legal disputes involving specific nation–state relationships. In deciding these disputes, the Court has had to interpret the meaning of certain key clauses of the Constitution.

The Supreme Court as Interpreter of the Division of Powers

The Court has had occasion to define a number of powers granted to the national government by the Constitution, three of which have been particularly crucial in shaping governmental jurisdiction: the "necessary and proper" clause, the power over interstate commerce, and the authority to tax and spend for the general welfare. In addition, the Court's interpretation of the Tenth Amendment has affected nation–state relationships.

The "Necessary and Proper" Clause. The national government was organized for only a year when Secretary of the Treasury Alexander Hamilton submitted a broad economic program to Congress proposing the establishment of a national bank. Because he had some doubts about its constitutionality, President Washington turned for legal advice to two perennial antagonists in his cabinet, Hamilton himself and Thomas Jefferson. The former maintained that although the national government was granted no specific authority to establish a bank, "the necessary and proper" clause of Article I, Section 8 gave it the implied power to do so. Pointing out that Congress was authorized to raise money by taxation or borrowing, Hamilton reasoned that the creation of a bank was a "convenient" means for keeping such moneys. He thus interpreted *necessary* to mean "convenient" or "appropriate." Jefferson took the opposite position: *necessary* should be strictly construed to mean "indispensable." Since the establishment of a national bank was not indispensable to the safeguarding of federal funds (they could be deposited in state banks, for instance), it lay beyond the authority of the national government.

Ultimately, Washington accepted Hamilton's arguments over Jefferson's and signed the national bank bill into law. About a quarter-century later the bank again became a constitutional issue. The state of Maryland taxed a branch of the national bank within its borders; on the instructions of the bank's officials, its cashier, James McCulloch, refused to pay the tax on the grounds that this constituted state interference with a legitimate activity of the national government. When the Maryland Supreme Court decided in favor of the state, the ruling was appealed to

Cruisin' down the Mississippi.

the United States Supreme Court. The case, *McCulloch* v. *Maryland* (1819), raised the basic issue of federalism first argued in the Washington administration: does the national government have the right to create a bank?

A battery of famous lawyers of the day argued the case before the Court. The major figure representing the United States was Daniel Webster; his courtroom opponent was the well-regarded Luther Martin of Maryland. The legal arguments were essentially the same as those made previously by Hamilton and Jefferson. Chief Justice John Marshall, a staunch Federalist and friend of a vigorous national government, not surprisingly wrote the Court's opinion in favor of that government. In

Answering the call.

Handsome Abe.

It couldn't be closed!

The National Bank.

doing so, he adopted Hamilton's interpretation of the necessary and proper clause. *Necessary* meant "appropriate," not "indispensable" or "absolutely necessary" as Jefferson and Martin maintained. The national government had the authority to create a bank because it was an appropriate means for exercising its power to raise moneys.

This early judicial test of the powers of the national government resulted in a liberal interpretation of its authority and opened the door to the expansion of its activities through the use of implied, as compared to expressed, powers. Yet two specific powers expressly granted to Congress—authority over interstate commerce and the right to tax and spend for the general welfare—have proved to be even more important bases for national power.

Interstate-Commerce Power. The constitutional issue concerning the interstate-commerce power is essentially the same as that of the "necessary and proper" clause: how liberal or strict an interpretation to give the phrase. The same John Marshall who interpreted the latter clause liberally in the historic *McCulloch* v. *Maryland* case used essentially the same approach for the commerce clause five years later in the landmark case of *Gibbons* v. *Ogden* (1824). In that instance he ruled that the national government had the authority to license the operation of boats on New York State waters because these passenger vessels were involved in interstate commerce, which he construed broadly to cover all "intercourse" between the states. In so doing, Marshall rejected the argument that the definition of interstate commerce should be limited to "traffic" involving only the buying and selling of goods.

Over the course of American constitutional history, justices of the Supreme Court have differed over which activities should be considered interstate commerce. When Congress began to use the powers increasingly to regulate (rather than to promote) the operations of American business, members of the Court who were opposed to government intervention in economic affairs narrowed the scope of such regulation by holding that only those activities directly involved in interstate commerce—such as transportation and communication—were subject to the jurisdiction of Congress. Such a strict construction of the interstate-commerce power meant that that body could not regulate the manufacturing and mining of products or their local sale or distribution. This interpretation of the commerce clause was dominant from the waning years of the last century into the third decade of the present one. In the 1940s, however, the Court changed the test from whether an activity is *involved* in interstate commerce to whether it economically *affects* such commerce. Using this approach, the Court in *Wickard* v. *Filburn* (1942) even justified the national government's regulating what a farmer fed his chickens on the reasoning that this activity economically affected the interstate market for wheat. This decision and others that followed have led students of constitutional law to conclude that, given the interdependent nature of American society today, there is almost no activity that the Court will consider beyond the scope of the commerce power.*

The Power to Tax and Spend for the General Welfare. Like the "necessary and proper" clause, the power of the national government to tax and spend for the general welfare provoked an early debate between two of the nation's prominent leaders, this time Hamilton and Madison. Both, of course, were supporters of a strong national government at the Convention and together they wrote the bulk of the *Federalist* papers. Yet Madison subsequently parted company with his co-author on the proper interpretation of the taxing and spending power. Madison considered that function to be subsidiary to the enumerated powers of the Congress, that is, the national government can tax and spend only for those activities over which it was given specific authority. Hamilton argued that the power was in addition to, and hence independent of, the enumerated ones; in other words, Congress can tax and spend moneys for functions that it could not otherwise control. The issue was ultimately resolved by the Supreme Court in favor of Hamilton's view.

A series of other constitutional questions relating to the taxing and spending power have also been decided in favor of the national government. The Supreme Court will no longer inquire into the motive behind the enactment of a tax; thus Congress can use it as an indirect method of regulating an activity (such as a tax on gambling) as well as for raising revenue. Moreover, the Court will not make a judgment about whether Congress' use of the taxing and spending power in particular instances is in "the general welfare," nor will it interfere with the right of Congress to establish the conditions under which the moneys it appropriates can be spent. The result is that the taxing and spending power of Congress has been converted into a kind of national police power (power to enact laws for the "health, safety, and morals" of the people), since most government activity involves the expenditure of money.

Thus the two powers that the Founders thought most crucial to the operation of a national government—interstate commerce and taxation—have been the major bases for the constitu-

* A recent exception to the rule was the Court's decision in *National League of Cities, National Governors' Conference et al.* v. *Usury* (1976) that the 1974 Fair Labor Standards Act amendments extending federal minimum wage protection to state and local employees were unconstitutional because they violated the concept of state sovereignty guaranteed in the Tenth Amendment.

"Hi, Mr. Tepper. This is the I.R.S. Say, back in April, when you paid your tax, we had no idea of the sort of bills Uncle Sam would be running up, and—well, the long and the short of it is that we have to soak you again."

Drawing by Handelsman. © The New Yorker Magazine, Inc.

tional expansion of national activities. At the same time, another key constitutional question of that early era—the relationship between national and state powers spelled out in the Tenth Amendment—has also played a major part in the continuous struggle over the division of political authority in the American system.

The Tenth Amendment. Constitutional questions raised by the Tenth Amendment concern its effect on the scope of national powers. Those friendly to an energetic central government have maintained that the Tenth Amendment is redundant—it merely expresses what was implied in the original document: that the states enjoy constitutional authority over any matter neither delegated to the national government, nor forbidden to the states. The amendment in no way diminishes or restricts the functions of the national government that are based on its expressed or implied powers. Those opposed to strong centralism contend that the amendment limits the scope of national power by preventing the central government from exercising its otherwise legitimate powers if they impinge on matters of state and local concern. Some Supreme Court justices have also been inclined to read the word *expressly* into the amendment ("... not *expressly* delegated ...") with respect to delegated powers (no such word appears in the Constitution although it does in the Articles of Confederation) so as to negate any idea of implied powers of the national government. Since the 1930s, however, this position has lost favor among the justices, so that the Tenth Amendment is now considered the redundancy that the early friends of a strong government maintained it was.

The effect of these judicial interpretations has been legal support for almost any activity in which the national government chooses to become involved. This support, coupled with judicial checks over state actions that affect matters of national concern (states may not, for example, "burden" commerce through regulations that curtail interstate business activities, nor may they tax the operations of the national government) is evidence that the Supreme Court has had a *nationalizing* influence on American federalism. The legal checks provided by federalism have thus *not* operated (at least in recent years) to maintain a balance in our political system; they have rather favored the interests of the national government over those of the states.

Some advocates of states' rights have ascribed this favoritism to the nonneutrality of the Supreme Court in federal–state disputes. Rather than an umpire in such conflicts, it is a member of the national team. To counteract this advantage the Council of State Governments (an organization of state officials) some years ago proposed a constitutional amendment creating a Court of the Union to be composed of the chief justices of the highest courts of the 50 states, with authority to overrule the decisions of the United States Supreme Court on nation–state issues. Nothing serious came of the proposal or a companion measure permitting state legislatures to amend the national Constitution without the concurrence of Congress. Fortunately for the states and their supporters, other safeguards have operated to protect their interests in the American federal system.

POLITICAL SAFEGUARDS OF AMERICAN FEDERALISM

Although the actions of the United States Supreme Court in recent decades have expanded the legal powers of the national government, the interests of the states have nonetheless been protected by our political processes. One reason for this development is the fact that, as lesser geographical units, the states are represented in the national government. Beyond equal state representation in the Senate, the Constitution requires that members of the House of Representatives be residents of the states they serve. (By political custom they are also residents of the congressional district they represent.) These provisions, plus the legal control that states exercise over the nomination and election of their senators and representatives (we shall explore how this control operates in Chapters 7 and 8), mean that the states possess considerable potential influence over the national legislature.

This potential is converted into actual influence by the realities of the American political-party system. One of the cardinal facts about our parties (the general subject will be treated in Chapter 6) is that they are highly decentralized; power resides at the state and local rather than the national level. The choice of candidates for the House and Senate is determined not by the national committees of the parties but by state and local party organizations and personal organizations formed by the candidates themselves. Moreover, most of the money for political campaigns comes not from the treasury of national organizations but from the contributions of state and local groups and individuals.

Since representatives and senators are familiar with these basic facts of political life, their concern lies with the interests of the districts and states that they represent. This is reflected in their wish to see national legislation either positively benefit their areas or at least not harm them. Thus members of Congress from urban districts and states typically seek aid for the cities, while those from areas whose businesses are threatened by foreign trade (such as states with automobile factories and steel mills) push for tariffs or quotas on the importation of competitive goods from abroad. This concern of individual legislators for state and local interests is further buttressed by important organizational features of the Congress: informal arrangements and understandings provide for committee seats to be assigned to representatives of the areas most vitally concerned with the work of the committee. Thus congressmen from working-class districts populate the committees concerned with labor legislation, while those from farming areas sit on the agricultural committees of the House and Senate.

Nor is the concern of congressmen for states and localities restricted to the legislative process. As overseers and financial providers of the activities of the executive branch (treated fully in Chapter 12), members of Congress are in an excellent position to ensure that the interests of their districts and states are taken into account. Thus key congressional leaders and committee chairmen can exercise considerable control over where a military base is located. It is no accident that so many defense and space installations were located in Texas and Georgia during the years that Texans Lyndon Johnson and Sam Rayburn (as Senate majority leader and Speaker of the House, respectively) and Georgians Walter George and Carl Vinson (chairmen of the Senate and House Armed Services committees, respectively) were influential, benefiting their state and local economies. (Recently some legislators have exerted the opposite kind of pressure, working to prevent the location of missile sites in their districts and states out of fear that such complex weapons might malfunction or make their areas prime targets for enemy nuclear attacks.) All members of Congress also spend a considerable portion of their time acting as liaison agents between individual constituents and executive agencies to see to it that "their" people are treated fairly.

Thus the two legislative houses of the national government, which reflect state and local interests, counterbalance the nationalizing influence of the Supreme Court in the American federal system. At times the legal and political processes come into direct conflict, as they did in the 1950s over the issue of tidelands oil. Both the national government and the states involved claimed title to valuable oil deposits located in submerged lands off the shores of Texas, Louisiana, California, and other coastal areas. After a lengthy period of litigation the Supreme Court ruled that the national government owned the disputed lands. The Congress, however, ultimately resolved the issue in favor of the states by passing legislation that deeded the valuable lands to them. On an earlier occasion in the 1940s the Supreme Court ruled that the national government had authority over insurance companies because of the interstate nature of their business transactions; Congress subsequently passed legislation permitting the states to continue to regulate insurance companies.

The legal aspects of American federalism thus permit the Congress to undertake almost any activity it wishes, but political forces tend to make it receptive to the interests of states and local areas. Together these factors have shaped the nature of the political system that has evolved in the United States.

THE GROWTH OF LOCAL, STATE, AND NATIONAL GOVERNMENT

An analysis of governmental developments points to one overriding pattern: the growth of activities at all levels of our political system. Local, state, and national governments are doing more today in providing services and regulating the actions of their citizens than they have ever done in the past; their total expenditures rose from under $2 billion in 1902 to over $1 trillion in 1982, the last year for which figures are available. Therefore, any assessment of American federalism must be based on the *relative* activity of the various levels, that is, how much the national government is doing in public affairs at a given time compared to state and local political units. A good measure of the relative activity is the proportion of total expenditures made by the three political levels. Table 3.1 shows such figures for various years of this century.

The most striking overall trend shown by the table is the comparative increase in the activities of the national government during the first half of the century. This development is most noticeable in three historical periods: 1913–1922 (World War I and its aftermath), 1932–1938 (the period of the New Deal response to the Great Depression), and finally the most dramatic change of all, the period from 1938—the beginning of the military buildup for World War II—to 1948, the first full postwar year for which expenditures are available. All told, the federal proportion of all government expenditures doubled in the period from 1902 to 1954.

These increases in the activities of the federal government are related to certain key factors during the first half of this century, particularly war and depression. Military matters have, of course, always been the primary concern of the national government rather than the states, so it is not surprising that wars should augment federal activities. The Great Depression, however, resulted in a change in traditional public attitudes against having the national government assume an active role

Table 3.1
Proportions of Total Government Expenditures: Selected Years (1902–1982)*

Levels of Government	*1902*	*1913*	*1922*	*1927*	*1932*	*1938*	*1948*	*1954*	*1962*	*1969*	*1974*	*1979*	*1982*
Federal	34	30	40	31	33	44	62	67	58	59	56	57	63
State	8	9	11	12	16	16	13	11	14	15	17	17	15
Local	58	61	49	57	51	40	25	22	28	26	27	26	22

* Federal, state, and local; 1982 is an estimate.

SOURCE: Frederick C. Moser and Orville F. Poland, *The Costs of American Government* (New York: Dodd, Mead, 1964), Table 3.2. The figures for 1969, 1974, 1979, and 1982 are derived from *Significant Features of Fiscal Federalism*, 1981–82 ed. (Washington, D.C.: Advisory Commission on Intergovernmental Relations, 1982), Table 2, p. 14.

in economic crises. As conditions worsened, neither private enterprise nor local and state governments proved capable of dealing with the unemployment problem; therefore people turned to the national government to get the country back on its feet. Armed with power over the currency, the banking system, the regulation of interstate economic activities; supported by a good tax base (the Sixteenth Amendment, ratified in 1913, enabled the Congress to tap an excellent source of revenue—incomes of individuals);* and guided by the powerful political leadership of President Franklin Roosevelt, the national government in the 1930s embarked on a series of new programs designed to lead the country to recovery. Thus the felt needs revealed by the military and economic crises in the first half of this century plus the fiscal and political capacity of the national government to meet these needs altered the division of governmental activities so as to favor the national government.

Table 3.1 also indicates that the comparative increase in government spending at the national level has been accompanied by a sharp decline in local expenditures. The latter stood at almost three-fifths of total government outlays in 1902; in 1954 they constituted slightly more than only one-fifth of the composite figure. The level of government least affected by overall trends has been the states: although their share of total expenditures increased somewhat during this century, state governments have continued to run a distant third to both the national and local governments in the spending of public funds.

* Prior to the amendment, the tax had to be apportioned among the states on the basis of population, and since income is not directly related to population, individuals residing in different states might be taxed at different rates, even though they had the same income.

Table 3.1 demonstrates another basic fact of American federalism: the comparative activities of the three governmental levels have stabilized considerably since the end of World War II. The military demands of the Korean conflict resulted in an increase in federal spending between 1948 and 1954, but this increase was not nearly so marked as those associated with the two world wars. In the period when the country became increasingly involved in the hostilities in Vietnam (1962–69), no substantial change occurred in the basic pattern of American federalism.

The overall balance in American federalism since World War II has resulted from increased spending by the national government, particularly for national defense, offset by mounting state and local expenditures for major domestic programs such as education, highways, welfare, and health. From 1948 to 1979 federal spending for defense-related matters rose from $28 billion to $156 billion before rising dramatically to $252 billion by 1982 (a result of President Reagan's emphasis on increasing our national security forces). In the same period, state and local governments increased their expenditures drastically to meet pressing domestic needs—from $20 billion in 1948 to $323 billion in 1979, before slowing somewhat to $405 billion by 1982 as many states and localities experienced citizens' revolts against increased taxes and spending.

This account of governmental expenditures reveals the basic dimensions of American federalism in the twentieth century: an overall growth in federal activities, especially relating to military and economic crises, accompanied by the continuing vitality of state and local units undertaking increased responsibilities for the nation's domestic needs. But we cannot justifiably conclude from these gross figures that the division of

Off we go!

functions in our political system has been simple, with the national government concerned almost entirely with military and foreign policy, while the states and local units go their own ways, raising public money and spending it on matters of exclusive concern to themselves. Instead, as the following section indicates, the governmental process of American federalism has been far more complex, involving close relationships among the various levels.

COOPERATIVE FEDERALISM

Students of American federalism frequently refer to recent developments in the system as a "new" federalism or, sometimes, a **"cooperative" federalism.** By this they mean that we no longer have three separate levels of government that undertake distinct functions and operate independently of one another; instead, they all share in carrying out various public functions.* Another dimension of the New Federalism is that the various political levels no longer view each other as "rivals" for public support and the exercise of political power; rather, they regard themselves as "partners" in the great enterprise of government.

Cooperative federalism may have become more prominent in the United States in recent years, but it is not entirely "new." Even before the Constitutional Convention, the Congress in 1785 passed a statute, supplemented by the

* The late political scientist Morton Grodzins likened our system not to a layer cake but to a "marble" one characterized by an intermingling of colors in vertical and diagonal strands representing the mixing of functions at all levels.

Joining the Santa Fe and Frisco.

Northwest Ordinance of 1787, that granted designated sections of public lands to the states for educational purposes. Thus the national government financially assisted the states in establishing primary and secondary schools, long considered in the United States to be one of the most basic local functions. Subsequently, Congress provided funds to both state and local governments to develop internal improvements such as roads, canals, rivers, and railroads. During the Civil War a national law was enacted that had a major impact on higher education in the United States: the Morrill Act donated lands to the states, the proceeds of which were to be used to establish colleges devoted to instruction in agriculture and mechanics. The "A & M" colleges, prominent in the Middle

Texas A & M University.

and Far West, thus owe their existence to the willingness of the national government to concern itself with traditional state matters.

These early grants involved a resource that the national government had in abundance: land. Toward the end of the nineteenth century a shift from land to cash occurred in the substance of grants. Moreover, the nature of the grants changed from once-only affairs to continuing appropriations made on an annual basis. This new form of subsidy is the **grant-in-aid,** familiar to the student of modern federalism in the United States.

Traditional Federal Grants-In-Aid

Development. Although a few federal grants-in-aid were established before 1900 (for example, in 1887 Congress provided the first continuing cash grant to assist states in establishing agricultural experiment stations), they are primarily a twentieth-century phenomenon. The grants are closely linked with a major fiscal development: the enactment of the income tax amendment in 1913. With the major new source of revenue available to the national government, and a president (Woodrow Wilson) and Congress willing and able to involve the national government more extensively in the economy, federal grant-in-aid expenditures increased from some $5 million in 1912 to almost $34 million in 1920. Not only were familiar objects of nineteenth-century subsidies favored (the Smith–Lever Act of 1914 established the agricultural extension program; vocational education and highways also drew major financial support), but the Congress provided the beginnings of modern assistance programs with provisions for maternal and child health.

The Republican administrations of the 1920s and early 1930s continued and improved the existing federal grant-in-aid programs. However, no significant new starts were made during the 12 years between the Wilson and Roosevelt terms. In contrast, the New Deal ushered in a different era in grant-in-aid programs. Ignoring the advice of many of his advisers to let the national government itself administer burgeoning new programs in welfare, health, employment security, and public housing, President Roosevelt chose instead to funnel such expenditures through lesser political units. As a result, during the period from 1932 to 1939 grant-in-aid expenditures swelled from some $200 million to almost $3 billion. Two significant departures from the Wilson years were also apparent: a shift in emphasis in the programs from rural to urban needs and the channeling of some of the assistance directly from the national government to local units, bypassing the states in the process. For example, cities became the direct recipients of federal aid in public housing.

The outbreak of World War II brought a temporary decline in federal grant-in-aid programs as the national government conserved its resources for military necessities. Beginning in 1948 grant expenditures began to rise again, but it was not until 1954 that they reached their prewar level of $3 billion. During the remainder of the Eisenhower administration grant moneys increased as the Republicans sought to counter the centralization of domestic programs in Washington. Also, consistent with that party's philosophy, the administration was careful not to bypass the states in favor of direct grants to cities.

The 1960s and early 1970s witnessed a major surge in federal-aid programs similar to that of the 1930s. A considerable increase occurred in the Johnson administration (some two-dozen new "Great Society" programs were inau-

Head Start class in Madison Georgia.

gurated in 1964–65 alone) and continued during the Nixon and Ford administrations, when nearly 100 additional grant programs were created. Programs tended to concentrate on the problems of the large metropolitan areas of the nation (central cities and suburbs) and ranged broadly in welfare, economic development, education, and race relations. They brought still another feature to the evolution of federal grants-in-aid: some, such as the Community Action Program in the antipoverty field, bypassed not only the states but even local governments in favor of private groups that received funds and, in some cases, helped administer the programs.

The development of the federal grant-in-aid program has thus had a major impact on governmental expenditures and revenues during this century. Federal outlays mushroomed from $3 million in 1903 to almost $95 billion in fiscal 1981, the last year of the Carter administration. By 1981 federal grants-in-aid financed almost 25 percent of all state and local expenditures.

However, the nature of cooperative Federalism began to change greatly with the advent of the Reagan administration. The size of federal grants-in-aid actually declined from $95 billion in fiscal 1981 to some $91 billion in fiscal 1982. President Reagan continued to propose further cuts in such aid; his 1983 budget called for expenditures of $81 billion, an 11 percent decline in one year alone. Moreover, his bold New Federalism Plan outlined at the beginning of this chapter would reduce the federal-aid share of state and local expenditures to about 4 percent by 1991.

Characteristics. As we have already seen, one of the distinguishing features of federal grants-in-aid is that they generally involve cash payments (one exception is the surplus agricultural commodities used in the school-lunch and social–welfare programs) authorized by Congress on a continuing basis or for a specific period of years. The distinction between continuous- and specific-term grants has tended to be a legal one, however; over the years Congress normally has extended the short-term grants when their original authorization period has expired, so in actual fact they

Breaking ground for senior citizen center.

too are continuous. In other words, once enacted, relatively few grant-in-aid programs have been terminated. Groups favored by such grants have used their political influence to prevent that termination. Thus the number of grant programs has swelled as new ones have been added to old ones.*

The new programs have seldom been integrated with those already in existence; instead, they have developed as separate programs. The outcome of this process is a proliferation of programs, each of which is designed for fairly narrow purposes. For example, until recently there were various categories of public-assistance programs: those for the aged, the blind, and the disabled, each of which operated independently of the others. An estimate of federal-aid programs in existence by the end of the Carter administration indicated that there were some 500 administered by departments and bureaus of the national government.

Categorical grants vary considerably in method of distribution to state and local governments. A few are "flat" grants, allocated in equal or minimum amounts to political units without any financial contributions by the units themselves. Most grants-in-aid, however, require states or localities to "match" federal funds by furnishing some of their own money for the program. But even in matching grants there are various formulas for determining the specific allocation of funds between levels of government and the amount of money to which each political unit is entitled. Some are based purely on population, while others take into account the financial needs and capabilities of the recipient governments. In

* That general situation changed when the Reagan administration took office: over 60 federal-aid programs were eliminated from the federal grants catalog on the grounds that no more moneys would be provided for them.

New York City food line.

the latter instance the federal share of the grant is higher for political units with a large number of citizens requiring assistance and those with limited tax resources than it is for those without such handicaps. A few programs are "open-ended" in that the federal government provides a certain percentage of the state contribution. This arrangement has a built-in incentive: the more a state spends on a program, the more federal moneys it receives.

Federal grant-in-aid programs also typically impose other conditions for states or localities besides a financial contribution, such as the establishment of a single state agency to administer a given program or the use of a merit system for the employees of all agencies receiving federal money. Furthermore, the federal government agency administering a grant program is generally entitled to review and supervise the work of the recipient agency and to audit its expenditures.

One additional feature of some grant-in-aid programs is that they are of the **"project"** type; that is, they are not automatically provided to states or localities but require the specific approval of federal officials. For example, while any community may be entitled to apply for a grant to build a waste-treatment plant, the total funds available may not be sufficient to cover all the requests, which means that federal officials must choose among them. One close student of the subject, political scientist Deil Wright, estimates that in recent years about four of every five grant-in-aid programs have been the project type.

Administrative Problems and Changes. As the grant-in-aid programs have multiplied in recent years, they have produced major problems of coordination and control for all parties involved in their administration. Some of these problems center on a single level of government; the administration of the wide variety of aid programs located in the myriad departments and bureaus of the national executive branch is a case in point. The compartmentalization of grants into so many agencies sometimes means that the federal left hand does not know what the federal right hand is doing: the Department of Transportation develops highways in urban areas that displace low-income groups that are a major concern to federal officials in the Department of Housing and Urban Development. A similar confusion arises in agencies at the state and local level, since each agency has its closest relationships not with other state and local agencies but with the corresponding *federal* bureau in the same program area—health, education, welfare, and so on. The end result is that officials entrusted with viewing overall public needs—legislators (senators and representatives, their state counterparts, and city councilmen) and executives (the president, governors, mayors, and city managers)—have difficulty controlling the activities of specialized agencies and establishing priorities among them.

The other major type of administrative problem involves relationships among the three levels of government. State officials complain that they are not properly informed and consulted by their federal counterparts in the formulation of administrative rules and practices relating to grant-in-aid programs and that the red tape and delay in the forwarding of federal funds hampers their operations and prevents them from executing their programs as efficiently as they might. State governors, legislators, and administrators also oppose the recent trend in some grant-in-aid programs to bypass the states in favor of direct relationships with local governments. Political officials at all levels are concerned about an even more recent development noted above: dispensing grants to private persons and groups that also play a major role in the administration of these programs.

A growing recognition of such problems by supporters as well as critics of federal grants-in-aid has led to concerted efforts in recent years to confront these problems. Lyndon Johnson's emphasis on what he termed "creative federalism"—that is, working out better relationships among officials at all levels of the federal system—resulted in some changes in the administration of federal grants-in-aid. The Congress sought to improve the coordination of federal urban programs by providing, in the Demonstration Cities and Metropolitan Development Act of 1966, that a metropolitan-wide planning agency screen all applications for federal grants relating to urban development projects in its metropolitan area. Richard Nixon's New Federalism also involved some administrative improvements, including the creation of Federal Regional Councils, through which a number of federal departments coordinate their activities with the cooperation of state and local officials. Jimmy Carter's first memorandum to his department heads stated his desire for state and local involvement in his administration's decision-making and assigned high priority to the formation of a policy group on urban and regional development.

Recent developments also reflect a particular concern for problems of state governments. The Intergovernmental Cooperation Act of 1968 directed federal agencies to speed up the dispersal of funds to state agencies; it also required federal officials, upon request, to furnish the governor or legislature of a state with information on the amount and purpose of each grant to that state or its localities. The Intergovernmental Personnel Act of 1970 provided grants to state (as well as local) governments for improving their personnel administration and training programs and permits their employees to work at another level of government for two years without losing any benefits (retirement, sick leave, and the like). The Grant and Cooperative Agreement Act of 1977 provided fewer conditions and restrictions for grants not requiring "substantial involvement" by the national government in the administration of the grant. In 1983 the Reagan administration turned over to the states the opportunity to shape state and local consultations with federal agencies on grant applications.

Block Grants

The most basic administrative reform sought in the federal grant-in-aid programs in recent years is the **"block" grant.** This approach has two major purposes: to channel federal grants-in-aid through state governments rather than directly to local governments or private groups, and to permit state officials to allocate funds for some broad purpose—such as health, education, or welfare—rather than have the federal government delineate specific limited purposes for grants. The block-grant approach was first utilized by Congress in such fields as health care, juvenile delinquency, and law enforcement. Typically, under such legislation a state agency develops a comprehensive plan for spending moneys under the broad purposes of the governing act.

The block grant has become a controversial topic among persons interested in federal grant-in-aid programs. It has drawn particular support from state governors and legislators as well as Republican officials at the national level. Big-city mayors and administrators of the present categorical grant system, along with Democrats who have supported that system over the years, generally oppose the approach on the grounds that state officials siphon away funds that should go to urban areas and spend the grants for the wrong purposes. The battle between these contending groups became particularly evident in the administration of the 1968 Omnibus Crime Control and Safe Streets Act; critics charged state officials with distributing too much money to suburban police departments instead of to high-crime areas of the cities and failing to allocate sufficient moneys for courts and correctional institutions. When the act was renewed in 1970, it provided that no state plan be approved for funding by federal officials unless it allocated an adequate share for areas of high-crime incidence; moreover, it earmarked 20 percent of the funds for corrections.

In the 1970s the battle over block grants continued with President Nixon advocating the consolidation of some 100 categorical grant-in-aid programs into six broad-purpose ones. The Democratic Congress resisted such a major change in the grant-in-aid program, but eventually approved block grants in manpower and employment training (1973), social services (1974), and community development (1974). By 1980 some 11 percent of federal grant-in-aid moneys were devoted to block grants.

The Reagan administration brought further changes in federal block grants. In his first budget, the new president proposed that 83 categorical grants be consolidated into six block ones; the Congress responded by eventually collapsing 57 categorical programs into nine block grants. The next year the president proposed further consolidations. However, Reagan's New Federalism suggestions differed greatly from Nixon's. The latter's proposals provided additional funds for block grants as "sweeteners" designed to win Democratic support for their enactment. In contrast, Reagan's proposals called for cuts in earlier Nixon consolidations and in the funding for grants Reagan himself had consolidated. Moreover, under Reagan's New Federalism program, all federal block grants would ultimately be eliminated.

Revenue Sharing

Development. Some students of American federalism concluded a number of years ago that there were fundamental defects in the grant-in-aid program that could not be remedied by the administrative changes outlined above, even those as drastic as the block-grant approach. Instead of using the various aid programs to channel federal moneys to states and localities to help them solve their domestic problems, they proposed distributing the national government's funds directly to these units and letting them decide how to spend the moneys themselves. One device developed to accomplish this purpose became known as **revenue sharing.**

Supporters of revenue sharing pointed to two major advantages that it provided over the previous system. First, states and localities would not have to depend on congressional action to receive funds: the receipt of funds would be automatic. Second, under the principle of **general revenue-sharing,** these units would have complete discretion in spending the funds and would not be limited by even the broad purposes spelled out in block-grant legislation.*

Over the years, the idea of revenue sharing won wide support in both parties. Proposed originally in 1958 by a Republican representative from Wisconsin, Melvin Laird, it was advocated in the early 1960s by Walter Heller, chairman of John Kennedy's Council of Economic Advisers. It was subsequently espoused by the conservative Republican senator from Arizona, Barry Goldwater, as well as by Hubert Humphrey, the liberal Democratic senator from Minnesota. In 1967 Gerald Ford, then minority leader of the House Republicans, declared that ". . . tax-sharing would restore the needed vitality and diversity to our federal system." Moreover the concept received an important political boost from President Nixon, who went before Congress in August 1969 with a dramatic message: "After a third of a century of power flowing from the people and the states to Washington, it is time for a New Federalism in which power, funds, and responsibility will flow from Washington to the states and to the people." To enable the states to assume greater responsibility for solving (not avoiding) problems, the president recommended that a set portion of the revenues from federal income taxes be remitted to the states. He also suggested that few restrictions be placed on how the dollars be used and that a proportion of them be channeled for the use of local governments. Terming such revenue sharing a ". . . gesture of faith in American states and localities and the principle of democratic self-government," Nixon said it would also help to create an effective, responsive government with not only one center of power, but many.

While the president's proposed measure was favored by leading figures in both political parties, the astronomical costs of the Vietnam war delayed congressional action as did disagreements on exactly how the money should be divided among the states and localities of the nation. Ultimately, the State and Local Fiscal Assistance Act of 1972 was passed, authorizing the return of $30.2 billion to state and local governments over a five-year period, two-thirds of the funds to be allocated to local govern-

* The term **special revenue sharing** is used synonymously with block grants (such as those proposed in recent years by President Nixon).

ments and one-third to the states. As the president requested, relatively few strings were attached to the moneys: states could use them almost as they pleased, while local governments could spend their funds for a wide variety of functions including public safety, environmental protection, public transportation, health, recreation, libraries, social services for the poor and aged, and financial administration.

Soon after its passage in late 1972, the machinery of the act went into operation. The Office of Revenue Sharing of the Treasury Department allocated funds to more than 38,000 units of state and local government, and each unit began to make decisions on how it would spend its new-found moneys. Public hearings were held (particularly at the local level), in which individuals and groups argued for their pet projects.

Effects of Revenue Sharing. Official reports filed with the Office of Revenue Sharing showed some definite patterns of expenditures of federal revenue-sharing funds. During fiscal 1974 states claimed to have spent 52 percent of their shared revenue for *education*, with such other functions as public transportation, health, governmental administration, and social services trailing far behind the educational expenditures. Local governments (which were forbidden by the 1972 act from using such funds for education) reported spending 36 percent of their shared revenues for *police* and *fire protection*, followed by public transportation, government administration, environmental protection, health, and recreation.

Some close students of the subject, however, discounted such claims on the grounds that states and localities frequently mixed the shared revenue with other funds and thus lost track of how their federal moneys were really being spent. Some academic studies of spending patterns of states and localities concluded that many of these governments were using the federal funds primarily to reduce taxes or prevent such taxes from going up. Thus, rather than using federal revenues to expand government services, states and localities were utilizing them as a means of reducing pressures on their own financial resources.

While most state and local officials welcomed the new source of revenue as "having Santa Claus come four times a year," there were complaints about the operation of the new program. Some critics charged that Presidents Nixon and Ford reduced or eliminated many categorical aid programs, so that states and localities had not more, but actually less money with which to attack their problems. Moreover, there were indications that health and social-service programs benefiting low-income and socially disadvantaged groups were not receiving a significant proportion of general revenue-sharing funds. Finally, charges were made that some state and local governments used federal funds in programs that discriminated against blacks and other minorities.

Extension of Revenue Sharing. Despite the objections outlined above, revenue sharing was extended in the fall of 1976 shortly before the original legislation was scheduled to expire. This time Congress placed the program on a fiscal-year basis, providing for a total of $25.5 billion dollars to be distributed over a 45-month period from 1 January 1977 through 30 September 1980. Many of the basic features of the 1972 act were retained, including the allocation of one-third of the funds to states and two-thirds to local units of government.

Some changes in the original program were made, however, to meet the criticisms expressed above. Civil rights groups were accommodated by new stipulations making the antidiscrimination provisions applicable to any activity of state or local governments unless

"A HUNDRED FOR YOU, A HUNDRED FOR YOU AND A HUNDRED FOR ME. A HUNDRED FOR YOU... SAY, THIS REVENUE-SHARING IS BETTER THAN I EXPECTED..."

these jurisdictions could show by clear and convincing evidence that such activities had not been funded directly or indirectly through revenue sharing. Moreover, the antidiscrimination provisions that originally covered race, color, national origin, or sex were expanded to include age, handicapped status, and religion.

The new legislation also reflected the wishes of other groups. State and local officials won their battle to remove all restrictions on the kinds of programs that could be funded with shared revenues, and to allow such funds to be used to match federal grants received under other programs. Groups demanding that there be more citizen participation in decisions on how shared revenues should be spent were appeased by requirements for full and specific information on how state and local governments intended to spend the funds, as well as for well-publicized public hearings before final decisions on such matters were made.

In August, 1980, the Carter administration proposed an extension of general revenue-sharing but suggested that it be restricted to local governments. Two reasons were given for excluding states—many of them were enjoying budget surpluses, and the federal government needed to restrain its spending so that it could balance its own budget in order to deal with inflation. Vigorous lobbying by supporters of the states led to a compromise: they would be eliminated from federal revenue-sharing in fiscal 1981 but would be entitled to participate in 1982 and 1983. However, unlike local governments that were automatically entitled to such moneys, states would receive them only if Congress actually appropriated such funds and if it did, states accepting them would have to give up an equivalent amount of categorical grant money to which they were entitled. As a matter of fact, no state requested funds under that law and none were appropriated by Congress. Local governments received $4.6 billion annually under the terms of the 1980 act.

In 1983, the Reagan administration supported another extension of general revenue-sharing at the same yearly $4.6 billion level, with states being completely eliminated from the program. The Democratically controlled House passed legislation increasing that figure to $5 billion annually, but the Senate bill provided for only the figure approved by the president. Under threat of a presidential veto, the House backed down and revenue-sharing was renewed for three more years at the $4.6 billion level.

Conflict and Competition in Cooperative Federalism

While recent developments in American federalism have tended to stress the federal–state–local partnership, it should be recognized that conflict and competition continue to exist in our political system. One of the major rivalries in what has been referred to as **picket-fence federalism** has developed between the specialists in the various public policy areas outlined in Figure 3.4 on the one hand, and policy generalists such as the president and members of Congress, state governors and legislators, and mayors, managers, and representatives of counties and cities on the other.* The former are professionals committed to enlarging programs in their specialized areas of expertise; the latter are politicians who must coordinate and establish priorities among the claims of these specialists for scarce public resources. Each group has its own type of organization to represent its interests: the specialists work through national associations of highway commissioners, social workers, teachers, and the like; while, as Figure 3.4 reveals, the generalists are organized into other kinds of associations—for example, the National Governors Conference and the Council of State Governments—collectively known as the "Big Seven." Moreover, the two groups prefer different mechanisms for distributing federal aid; the specialists favor the traditional categorical grant, while the generalists are partial to block grants and general revenue-sharing.

Of course, picket-fence federalism may also occasion competition and conflict among the specialists themselves. Each of the professional groups working in a particular functional area naturally thinks its own programs are more valuable than those carried on by other professionals: teachers believe that educating children and adults should have the highest priority among public needs, while social workers believe that caring for the disadvantaged persons in society is the most important activity for government to undertake. Thus specialists must compete with each other in trying to obtain adequate public funding for their programs.

Nor is competition in cooperative

* As shown by Figure 3.4, the pickets represent the vertical relationships among officials at all three levels who work in the same functional area (highways, welfare), while the crossrails depict the horizontal relationship between executive and legislative officials within the same level of government.

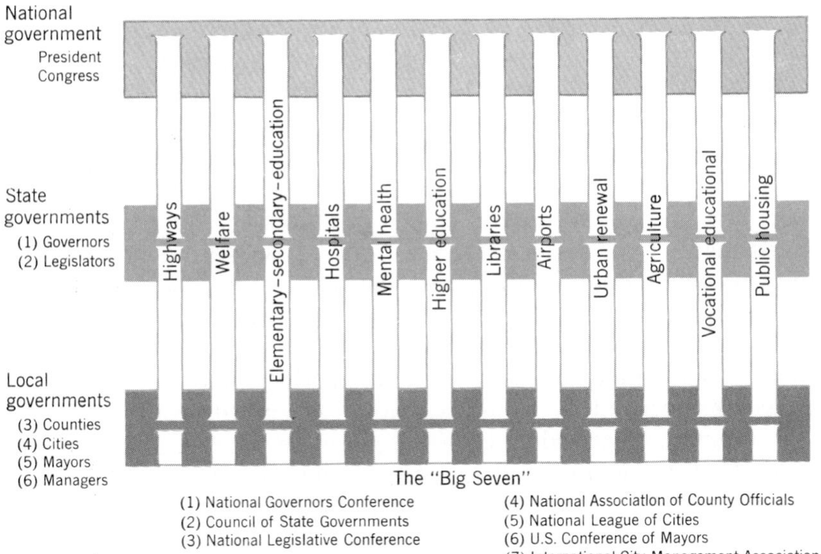

Figure 3.4 Picket-Fence Federalism: A Schematic Representation.
SOURCE: © 1974 Deil S. Wright.

federalism restricted to specialists: generalists serving at different levels of government have dissimilar views on the terms of the cooperation. There is a natural desire to want another level of government to be responsible for programs that are expensive and generally unpopular with the voters. As indicated at the beginning of the chapter, President Reagan proposed turning back to the states both the Aid to Families with Dependent Children and the Food Stamp programs, but many governors wanted to see them remain at the national level. State and local officials also come into conflict with one another. The former want federal aid to be funneled to them to use as they see fit (hence, their support for block grants); the latter desire a direct federal–local relationship, or if that is not possible, some protection in the form of "pass-through" provisions designed to ensure that at least a portion of the aid that reaches localities be used for programs that they think are most important for their citizens. State–local conflict was also evident in the general revenue-sharing program: the legislation passed in 1972 and 1976 provided for distribution of moneys to both state and local governments but the 1980 and 1983 extensions effectively eliminated the former as recipients.*

Behind the conflicts in cooperative federalism lie basic political interests and perceptions. Interest groups with good access to the national government naturally want to see it responsible for matters of concern to them; thus labor unions and welfare groups continue to support federal social programs. Those who oppose such programs, such as President Reagan, prefer to see them returned to the states because they calculate that such programs will not fare

* It is interesting to note that in 1980 the National League of Cities changed its position from being favorable to including states in general revenue-sharing to a neutral position on the issue.

well at that level.* Methods of financing governmental programs also affect views as to where they should be located. Traditionally many political liberals have preferred that the national government finance such programs because of the more progressive nature of the federal individual and corporate income tax (however, this progressive feature declined significantly in the 1980s), while many conservatives have favored state responsibility because of the more regressive nature of state sales taxes.†

Thus many types of conflicts occur within the context of cooperative federalism. National officials generally believe that they have a broader and more enlightened perspective on the nation's problems than their more parochial state and local counterparts; the latter complain that people in Washington do not appreciate the special circumstances and conditions of their particular areas. Moreover, struggles continue over the specific arrangement of the partnership: what policies will be established with respect to government programs, how will they be financed, and who will have the major control over their operation.

While conflicts over the nature of cooperative federalism continue, it appears to be accepted as a general principle. President Reagan's 1982 proposal of "swaps" and "turnbacks" designed to sort out public functions by level of government (and thus to return to the traditional "layer-cake" rather than the present "marble-cake" concept of federalism) drew relatively little political support and was eventually abandoned. At the same time, cooperative federalism is subject to change. While the president was unable to get his radical proposal accepted, his cutbacks in federal assistance to state and local governments and shifts from categorical to block grants have already had a major effect on American federalism and promise to have even more profound consequences in the future.

* The President is reported to have told the Republican members of the House Appropriations Committee that it is far easier for people to come to Washington for social programs because of their connections there and that it would be tougher for them if such programs were diffused and sent back to the states.

† A progressive tax is one that provides for an increase in rate as the taxable income increases, while a regressive tax provides for no such increase in rate.

ASSESSMENT

If majority rule is the most important feature of democracy, there is no doubt that our federal system possesses an undemocratic feature. It permits interests that are nationally in a minority on some issue, but in the majority in some individual states, to have their way on a matter, at least for a period of time. As political scientist William Riker has pointed out, the classic instance is the way in which southerners utilized the rationale of states' rights to pursue their own policies on race relations over the years.

Yet the federal system has not given the states a permanent veto on any issue. Since the 1950s, the South has been unable to prevent all three branches of the national government from pursuing policies favoring blacks and having these policies applied in the states. The legal powers of the national government, in addition to its revenue sources, are such that almost no issue is beyond its scope, provided national officials have the political will to deal with it.

A federal system also reflects a conflict between two other basic democratic values: liberty versus equality. When states undertake governmental activities, each is free to pursue its own approach to a problem. Indeed, an argument in favor of federalism is that states become "laboratories" so that successful governmental experiments by one state can be borrowed by another. However, because states vary widely in financial resources, some are in a position to provide much better governmental services than others. As a result, the quality of the services citizens receive varies widely and depends upon the particular state in which they reside.

One of the advantages of federal grant-in-aid programs is that they permit states to operate their own programs but stimulate state efforts and ensure that some minimum level of services will be provided to citizens wherever they live in the United States. In addition, the federal government has recently acted to force states into adequate regulation of matters that some have slighted too long. For instance, congressional legislation in air pollution, meat inspection, and disclosure of full credit information to consumers requires states to bring their controls up to national standards by a certain date or face the consequences of a federal takeover of those problems. The legislation thus attempts to protect citizens in all states.

Of course, federalism can sometimes serve the ulterior purposes of those who seek to prevent action on a given problem. For example, in recent years some individuals and groups unfavorable to certain social programs have opposed making them national ones on the grounds that the states should handle them, knowing full well that the states would not or could not make the financial sacrifice necessary to resolve the issues. Thus a basic principle of federalism—in this case, that problems at the state level should be handled at that level—can be used to masquerade the real motives of those who invoke the rhetoric of federalism, preventing *any* level of government from taking a course of action that they oppose.

Although federalism can lead to a failure of public officials to act on social problems, recent experiences in the United States also indicate that it can have precisely the opposite effect. Groups unable to get one level of government to handle a problem can shift their efforts to another. This tactic has been successfully pursued since the 1930s by those who have persuaded the Congress to undertake urban problems that state governments refuse to act on. At times groups have used both political levels to advantage. A case in point is public welfare legislation: having persuaded Congress to establish welfare programs, interested persons subsequently persuaded states to supplement and expand federal services in this field.

The charge that federalism is inherently negative is refuted by the rapid expansion of public activities at all levels of the American system. Moreover, developments in cooperative federalism indicate that a system of divided powers can operate in a positive fashion to meet public needs. Increasingly, our federation has evolved into a system wherein the national government appropriates moneys and establishes broad guidelines for certain basic programs that the states and localities administer on a day-to-day basis. A similar pattern is becoming prevalent within the states as they provide increased financing for locally administered, key programs (as in education).

SELECTED READINGS

For a general discussion of the issues involved in dividing political power in a society, see Arthur Maass, *Area and Power: A Theory of Local Government* (New York: Free Press, 1950). This book is particularly valuable in providing an analytical and theoretical treatment of the subject.

The classic study of the general principles of a federal system of government, together with the institutions and social, economic, and political conditions associated with such a form of government, is K. C. Wheare, *Federal Government* (London: Oxford University Press, 1953). Two other edited works that treat many facets of federalism in various nations of the world are Arthur MacMahon, *Federalism, Mature and Emergent* (Garden City, N.Y.: Doubleday & Co., 1955) and Valerie Earle, *Federalism: Infinite Variety in Theory and Practice* (Itasca, Ill.: F. E. Peacock Publications, 1968). A particularly valuable essay in the latter book is that by William S. Livingston, "Canada, Australia, and the United States: Variations on a Theme." For a provocative, critical analysis of federalism, see William Riker, *Federalism: Origin, Operation, Significance* (Boston: Little, Brown, 1964).

For analyses of the role of the Supreme Court in settling legal disputes of American federalism, see, in Earle, cited above, "The Role of the Court" by Alpheus Mason, and Samuel Krislov, *The Supreme Court in the Political Process* (New York: The Macmillan Co. 1965), pp. 80–95.

A broad treatment of federalism in the United States is Morton Grodzins, *The American System: A New View of Governments in the United States* (Chicago: Rand McNally, 1966). This book was edited by one of his former students, Daniel Elazar, after Grodzins' death. Subsequently, Elazar wrote his own general treatment of American federalism, *American Federalism: A View from the States* (New York: Thomas Y. Crowell, 2nd ed., 1972). Both books treat a wide variety of topics and are particularly strong on the historical dimensions and political aspects of American federalism. The best recent book that treats all aspects of American federalism is Deil Wright, *Understanding Intergovernmental Relations* (Monterey, Cal.: Brooks/Cole, 2nd ed., 1982).

A very good broad analysis of the New Federalism published during the Nixon administration is Michael Reagan's book, *New Federalism* (New York: Oxford University Press, 1972). Recent treatments of President Reagan's New Federalism include George Peterson, "The State and Local Sector," in John Palmer and Isabel Sawhill, eds., *The Reagan Experiment* (Washington, D.C.: Urban Institute Press, 1982); Edward Gramlich and Deborah Lauren, "The New Federalism," in Joseph Pechman, ed., *Setting National Priorities: The 1983 Budget* (Washington, D.C.: The Brookings Institution, 1982); and Robert Hawkins, Jr., ed., *American Federalism: A New Partnership for the Republic* (San Francisco: Institute for Contemporary Studies, 1982).

Finally, there are many good studies by public agencies of specific problems of federalism. One series of reports was issued in the 1950s by the Commission on Intergovernmental Relations appointed by President Eisenhower. Another series of very helpful reports has been published over the years by the Advisory Commission on Intergovernmental Relations, an agency established in 1959 to make continuous analyses of the problems of American federalism.

PART 2

Popular Control

CHAPTER 4

Political Attitudes, Socialization, and Participation

In mid-summer 1979, President Jimmy Carter, beset by inflation, the threat of recession, and an energy crisis, delivered a dramatic television address in which he pictured the nation's major problem as a "malaise of the spirit" and a "crisis of confidence" of the American people in the country and its institutions. White House staffers attributed the president's gloomy assessment to the findings of pollster Patrick Caddell, whose firm, Cambridge Survey Research, provided periodic readings of the nation's mood. Caddell and other polling organizations* showed that Americans had become increasingly pessimistic about the long-term outlook for the nation and their personal lives, and the short-term prospects of the economy and their assessment of the competence, responsiveness, and trustworthiness of government. While conceding that Jimmy Carter had made mistakes, Caddell attributed this decline in public confidence not primarily to presidential performance, but to ". . . a decade of shocks—Watergate, Vietnam, double-digit inflation, a near-stagnant rate of economic growth, and the energy crunch." Whatever the reasons for such a decline in public confidence, Caddell regarded it as serious enough to constitute a "crisis" and a "fundamental threat to American democracy."

Caddell's assessment of the nation's crisis of confidence brought a series of

* Such surveys, based on personal interviews with a cross section of Americans (usually about 1500), employ a technique known as *random sampling*, which permits information to be obtained from a small number of persons (the sample); information thus gathered is considered representative of the views of a larger group (the population). The important statistical principle involved is that each person in the population must have an equal chance of being chosen in the sample.

objections from other students of public attitudes. Warren Miller, a veteran survey-taker at the University of Michigan, countered that his studies showed no significant change in public confidence in government between 1976 and 1978; he further pointed out that during the same period confidence in the responsiveness of government actually increased among Democrats and conservative Republicans. Seymour Lipset of Stanford University differed with Caddell's analysis that the decline in public confidence was due to a series of shocks over the course of a decade; instead, Lipset attributed the nation's gloom to the performance of the Carter administration. Finally, there was disagreement over the seriousness of the situation: Miller contended that the degree of voter alienation had been grossly exaggerated and that ". . . there is no massive and personal disaffection from society or government."

Disagreements concerning the basic attitudes of the American people continued in the early 1980s. A series of surveys conducted by the Harris poll and the National Opinion Research Center led Seymour Lipset and William Schneider of the Hoover Institution at Stanford University to conclude that the decline in public confidence in persons running basic American economic, political, and social institutions that began in the mid-1960s had continued to the 1980s, actually growing worse between 1980 and 1983. In contrast, however, Arthur Miller of the University of Michigan reported that its studies showed that after a long downturn, the public confidence in the federal government rebounded somewhat between 1980 and 1982. More people in the latter rather than the former year were inclined to say that they ". . . trusted the government to do what is right . . . ," that ". . . government was run for the benefit of all . . . ," and that ". . . public officials cared about what they thought."

Despite these differences of opinion, all agreed on the importance of one element—the relation of public attitudes to the functioning of the American political system. As was seen in Chapter 1, the most distinctive feature of democratic government is that citizens have a major voice in determining the public decisions that vitally affect their lives. In pure, direct democracy people arrive at those decisions themselves; however in modern political units that encompass millions of individuals, responsibility for lawmaking must be vested in a small minority of the population, the political office-holders. The fundamental issue in a representative democracy thus concerns the amount and kind of influence that the general populace exercises over the policy-making of public officials.

One possible approach would be to maximize the influence of the mass over political decisions. In effect, the duty of those in public office would be to find out what the majority of the people wanted to do about a public issue—such as whether or not to raise income taxes—and then enact their wishes into law. Representatives would thus act as the agents of the people by converting their sentiments into public policy. Such a process would require the average person to take an interest in and be informed about political matters and also to be rational enough to know what course of action should be taken to deal with the problems of society. Given that condition, such a person's wishes would be respected—and indeed courted—by those in public office.

At the opposite extreme the public could play a minimal role in the enactment of governmental policy. Essentially the people in a democracy would have only one task: to elect public officials and let them make major political decisions without being hamstrung by the opinions of the general populace. This view is predicated on the belief that the mass of people have neither the interest, nor the capacity to deal with political problems in any meaningful way. Therefore those who have the interest and capacity—the ones who hold political office—should have no obligation to heed their desires.

Neither view fits the realities of the situation in the United States. Communication between the people and those who hold office is in fact a two-way process: the public presses certain demands on political decision-makers and provides support for the decision-makers and their actions; in turn, those in office respond to the demands of the people in some respects while also seeking public support for initiatives of their own on public policy matters.

This chapter and the following five explore the nature of public attitudes on political issues and how such attitudes are channeled to political decision-makers. This chapter analyzes the general substance of the political views of citizens, how they are acquired, and the various outlets that exist for expressing attitudes through the political process. Chapter 5 focuses on the major means for expressing views between elections: the interest group. Chapters 6, 7, 8, and 9 examine the role that political parties and the electoral process play in conveying public preferences to political officials.

THE NATURE OF POLITICAL ATTITUDES

Viewed in the broadest sense, attitudes exist on a variety of matters that affect the operation of a political system. Most fundamental of all are the feelings that citizens have toward their country and their sense of identity with it. For example, a problem frequently encountered by new nations is the difficulty its members may find in giving up their primary loyalty to tribes, regions, or religious groups. Until a substantial portion of persons in a society feel a sense of community with their fellow citizens and believe that they should be part of the same overall political system, the delicate act of governing them will be difficult if not impossible.

Closely allied to this sentiment of national identity are basic attitudes persons have toward their political system, that is, whether they consider it the legitimate vehicle for making the decisions that will affect their lives. This in turn depends on their attitudes towards the constitutional order—the functions, procedures, and structures of their government—or what we have been calling the rules of the game. Important here are not only formal rules set forth in legal documents but informal agreements and understandings concerning what is proper and improper in the realm of politics.

The feelings people have toward government officials themselves also determine whether the public will accept their decrees as legitimate and binding. Again, public support, active or passive, of such decrees must exist if the political process is to be effective in a society. In a democracy like the United States, the selection of major public officials through free elections in which the mass of people participate and the ease of removing and replacing the officials at reasonable intervals provide a basis for general acceptance of their rule.

The basic attitudes that people hold towards their political system have been termed by political scientist Gabriel Almond a nation's **political culture,** which he defines as "... a particular pattern of orientation to political actions." More specifically, political culture refers to such fundamental beliefs as (1) the ends or purposes of political activity, (2) the general nature of the political process, and (3) the part that individual citizens play in the process. The term is frequently used to include citizens' attitudes on how these basic elements of a political system *should* operate as well as their perception of how they work *in fact.* Viewed this way, political culture is concerned with the "promise" and the "performance" of a political system as viewed by the people that live under that system.*

Below the level of political culture—that is, the basic beliefs concerning the nation, the rules of the political game, and government leaders—there also exist public views toward matters that affect the day-to-day operation of the political system. In particular, people have ideas concerning the most important issues facing the nation and what policies the government should follow in dealing with these issues. They react to the personalities of candidates for office. They may also identify psychologically with particular groups, such as political parties or social, economic, or geographical divisions in the population and shape their attitudes on issues and candidates accordingly. These views, which are generally assumed to be less stable and enduring than political culture beliefs, are often referred to by political scientists as matters of **public opinion.**

Whether one is speaking of political culture or public opinion, the important point is that these are attitudes of the general populace, not political leaders, who often have strongly differing political views. (Such attitudes are referred to as **elite political culture** or **elite opinion.**) Of course, the number of persons having a view depends on the particular matter involved: most have basic attitudes concerning their nation and its political system, but fewer have definite opinions on what, if anything, the United States should do about the Arab–Israeli conflict. It would thus be more accurate to speak of not one "public" but a series of "publics"—separate groups of people with views on different political matters.

But if the public does not include all citizens, it must involve enough persons to have an impact on the political process. Yet a public is not composed of any precise minimum number of opinion-holding individuals, because the effectiveness of opinions depends on how intensely they are held and the political resources and skills of those who hold them. The definition of political scientist V. O. Key that public opinions are ". . . those opinions held by private persons which governments find it prudent to heed . . ." comes close to expressing the basic elements of the concept because it focuses on the influence of public attitudes on official decision-making.

Ultimately, of course, the importance of "publics" in the political process depends not only on their size and resources but also on the ways in which they channel their views to those in positions of political authority. Before turning to that topic, however, we need to examine the substance of individual political attitudes and the methods by which they are acquired.

THE FORMATION OF POLITICAL ATTITUDES

Teaching citizens proper attitudes and information about their government has long been a concern of political philosophers, as evidenced by Plato's views on the importance of civic education in the Greek city–state. Only very recently, however, have scholars begun to con-

* It should be understood that political culture refers to the *overall views of the general public*; there are often distinctive political attitudes held by blacks, Hispanics, southerners, easterners, and the like, which are often referred to as **political subcultures.**

Families of Iranian hostages meet the President and First Lady.

duct empirical examinations into the ways in which individuals actually come to acquire their political attitudes. This learning process is called **political socialization.**

Like political culture, political socialization is given different meanings. Some persons equate it with the study of how children acquire their political attitudes. Others restrict political socialization to the acquisition of the prevailing values and beliefs of the society, not deviations from them. In other words, they focus on how leaders instill a respect for the status quo in citizens. Here, however, we will interpret political socialization more broadly to mean the process by which individuals acquire all kinds of political attitudes (unfavorable as well as favorable to the existing political system) over a period of time that includes adulthood as well as childhood. Moreover, we will look at not only the individual who acquires political attitudes but also the agencies that shape those attitudes.

The Development of Political Attitudes

Guided by theories of psychologists, psychiatrists, and sociologists that emphasize the crucial importance of the formative years in molding a person's attitudes and beliefs, students of political socialization have focused most of their attention on the development of political opinions in children. They find that people begin to develop some awareness of the political world when they are quite young.* This earliest political orientation generally takes the form of strong patriotic feelings, as children react favorably toward symbols like the flag. The political system itself is personified for them primarily by the major officials. They first become aware of government executives at the top and bottom levels of the system—at the na-

* Most studies deal with school-age children, but some have discovered the beginnings of political attitude in preschoolers.

tional level, the president; at the local level, the mayor or the policeman. These identifications of such officials with the government, as with the nation itself, are generally positive; that is, children by and large look upon the president, mayor, or police chief as a "good" person who "helps" people and "gets things done." They also feel that they should respect and obey such persons. Thus a child's early orientation to the political system is essentially one of allegiance and support.

Young children are also inclined to find their own particular place in the political world. In particular they seek to identify with a group, to associate themselves with some persons in society, and to distinguish themselves from others. They may form an early psychological attachment to a political party. Indeed, children as young as seven already regard themselves as Republicans or Democrats; they also come to think of themselves as white or black, rich or poor, Protestant or Catholic or Jew. These identifications with social and economic groupings, like those with political parties and the nation and its political system, have deep emotional underpinnings, and therefore they tend to persist throughout subsequent stages of a person's political life.

Upon entering the teen years, the average person's conception of the political world begins to change. The young person does more critical thinking and is less likely to believe that the president, mayor, or police chief is all-benevolent and all-powerful. These figures no longer personify the young person's view of the political system as they once did; for example, the older child is able to disapprove of a particular individual serving as president without necessarily losing respect for the office itself. There is also an awareness that presidents and mayors share the running of the government with other groups, such as the Congress, the Supreme Court, and the local city council. Young people also add the state level of government to their view of the political system. Furthermore, they begin to develop some notion of what concepts like "democracy" and "communism" mean, although typically their views on such matters are superficial or, in many instances, erroneous.

Towards the end of childhood an individual becomes even more politically sophisticated. The young adult begins to see the differences between being a Republican and a Democrat, particularly in terms of the social and economic groups (business, labor, rich, poor, black, white) that each party favors. Reactions to political personalities also develop. Moreover, public policy issues and events—particularly those of a general nature, like race relations and international conflicts—become matters of concern to young adults. In addition, they may have ideas on how such problems should be handled by those in public office. They may also develop a better understanding of democracy and its procedures—majority rule, minority rights, and the like.

Information on the political socialization of adults is sparse. We have no studies of particular individuals over a long period of time that enable us to spell out in any detail how political attitudes of persons change after they reach maturity. What evidence is available indicates that political learning continues as persons are exposed to new experiences in life, such as getting a job, raising a family, moving to other areas of the country, or associating with different people and groups.

Thus political socialization is a developmental process. In the early years a person's political orientation is general, mostly positive, and based on strong emotional attachments toward nation, government, and officials. Later on, as persons become more knowledgeable and discriminating, they may develop

There She is girls!

expectations of what public officials should do about particular social issues. In short, their attitude toward political leaders changes from offering unqualified support to making demands.

This is not to suggest, however, that all persons follow this pattern. For example, studies have found that black and Hispanic children, as well as white children from Appalachia—a region characterized by poverty and physical isolation—are less favorably disposed toward the nation's political leaders than middle-class white children from affluent suburban areas. Moreover, people do not acquire political attitudes at the same pace: children from wealthier and better-educated families are more knowledgeable and discriminating about political matters than those of a similar age from poorer circumstances. As a rule, boys develop political interests and sophistication faster than girls; young people of both sexes with high IQs politically outdistance their lower-ranking classmates. Nor are people's eventual level of development the same. Some never proceed past the early stage of generalized emotional attitudes towards the political system, while others develop a keen interest in trying to analyze political issues and events objectively.

It is difficult to determine the precise reasons for differences in the development of political opinions of various individuals. One obvious factor, however, is the variation in associations with the key social groups that shape political orientations.

Agencies Affecting Political Opinions

A vast number of influences affect a person's political opinions. Some of them, like the family, are felt early in life, while others, such as work groups, affect political orientation as an adult. Some of the agencies of political socialization are primary groups, in which a person has close face-to-face relationships with the same individuals over a considerable length of time; again, the family is the prime example. Others are secondary groups like labor unions or employers' associations, in which contacts among members are more limited and frequently involve a range of different persons over time.

Family. By far the most potent group in shaping individual political attitudes is the family. It exercises its major effect on a person during the most impressionable years; one has one's closest emotional ties with it and it influences one's political attitudes during the time when other agencies have not yet begun to affect them. The family enjoys a near-monopoly over a person's political attention during the early years of life.

The family shapes the most basic aspects of a person's political opinions. Children who respect their parents are inclined to transfer this feeling to other authorities outside the family, such as the president. They will also imitate their parents' political opinions and behavior: if parents think and speak well of the president, children too will tend to favor him. Parents who do not hold the chief executive in high regard may keep their adverse feelings to themselves to avoid undercutting their children's respect for authority. If so, the children also will develop a favorable image of the president.

Parents also affect another basic feature of the child's early political attitudes: identification with a political party, as well as with social and economic groups. Young children are likely to identify with the same political party as their parents, particularly if the parents share strong partisan attachments. If there is a difference of opinion between the two parents about political parties, then their children may avoid the delicate problem of choosing between the mother's and father's views by declaring themselves political independents. Children also acquire from their parents a sense of identity with religious, racial, or social groups and so learn to think of themselves as Jews, blacks, or working-class people.

While parents have a strong influence on the political attitudes of their children, a major study of high-school seniors by political scientists M. Kent Jennings and Richard Niemi points out the limitations of that influence. Many parents do not consciously try to shape the views of their offspring and are often unaware of their children's views. The degree of transfer of political attitudes from one generation to another depends on the particular object of such attitudes: concrete matters like partisan affiliation, which are also meaningful for most persons on a constant, long-term basis, are more likely to be successfully transmitted than more abstract ideas such as the characteristics of a good citizen or a transient political issue like prayer in the public schools. Moreover, even the transfer of partisan affiliation suffers when the two parents have different party preferences. Finally, as children grow older, other influences begin to shape their views on political matters.

Public Schools. Another major institution that shapes political attitudes is the public school, which like the family has its major impact during the early years of a person's life. One of the major reasons why societies establish schools is to transmit values to the young; therefore teachers generally instill in students favorable attitudes toward their country and government. Thus symbolic exercises like saluting the flag, singing patriotic songs, and honoring the nation's heroes engender positive feelings toward the nation and its system of government. Teachers, like parents, try to develop a respect for authority, and children are inclined to transfer their respect for classroom supervisors to political leaders.

"My grandson, needless to say, is also pro-Reagan."

There are, however, some major differences in the shaping of political attitudes between the home and school. In the interests of maintaining good relationships with all kinds of parents, teachers are generally careful not to appear to favor one political party over another. If the schools are to fulfill the function of promoting harmony among children from various kinds of economic and social backgrounds (as many people feel they should), then teachers must strive to avoid partiality toward any one group. Thus unlike the family, schools do not generally shape a child's orientation toward his particular niche in the political world.

In the secondary and high schools the curriculum typically contains instruction in civics or the problems of democracy. Yet such courses often have relatively little impact on the political opinions of most students, partly because by the time a student takes such courses his basic political attitudes are already formed and most of the material presented in such courses is repetitious. Even so, children who have not been exposed to political matters in the home (most likely those from minority groups, and the poor and uneducated in general) may be influenced about their duty to vote and to respect the rules of the democratic game regarding the toleration of opposing viewpoints, and about how to make their wishes known to those in positions of authority.

Other factors besides the curriculum

shape students' political attitudes. Teaching techniques employed by particular instructors may have an impact: students acquire an understanding of the democratic process from the instructor who encourages debate and questioning in the classroom, in contrast to the authoritarian taskmaster who runs his classes with an iron hand. Extracurricular activities also influence political attitudes of students as they learn to govern themselves in clubs and organizations. The way that principals and other school authorities treat children and the kinds of rules and regulations developed by school boards regarding attire and personal appearance affect students' attitudes toward authority in particular. The nature of the student body is also important: students from lower-class backgrounds are sometimes affected by the attitudes of their middle-class classmates on such matters as the importance of personal liberty and the duty to vote, as well as on the necessity of using other means besides voting to affect the political process. Thus the total social setting of the public school shapes political attitudes.

College. Many young people who go on to college (12.3 million were enrolled in American institutions of higher learning in the fall of 1982) experience a marked change in political attitudes. Colleges generally encourage a critical approach to problems, and courses are much less likely to defend the status quo than those taught in the public schools. College faculties, particularly those in the social sciences, tend to be liberal in their political orientation (that is, they favor greater public concern with social problems in general and the plight of disadvantaged groups—blacks and the poor—in particular), and some students who come from politically conservative families are influenced by their values.

Other factors may be even more important in changing the political attitudes of college students. Leaving home is a major social dislocation for many students, because it involves breaking with families and the values learned

from them and becoming exposed to ideas of other persons with backgrounds quite different from their own. Particularly important at this point is the influence of their **peers,** that is, their contemporaries. While peers, of course, shape students' political attitudes earlier than during the college years, classmates are particularly influential at this time because students live together and are in constant association with one another. This common situation of breaking with the past and close physical proximity, in addition to easy communication among college students, is conducive to their forming distinct attitudes and values, including ways of looking at the political world.

Other Peer Groups. As they become adults, people's political attitudes may be influenced by other peer groups, such as churches, clubs, and ethnic groups. The extent of that influence depends on a number of factors: how important political concerns are to the group; how closely its members agree on such matters; whether the individual thinks it is proper for the organization to be involved in political issues (some persons, for example, feel that churches should not take political stands); and how closely the individual identifies with the group. Thus a person who belongs to a politically active labor union composed of like-minded members, who approves of the activities and whose self-image is that of a "union" person is likely to be strongly affected by the political beliefs of fellow union members.

It is also possible for individuals to have their political attitudes shaped by groups to which they do *not* belong. For example, a white liberal who is sympathetic with the plight of the underdog in society may identify with the National Association for the Advancement of Colored People or black groups in general and come to favor government programs that aid blacks without ever personally benefiting from them. Such groups are called **reference groups** or sometimes **reference symbols,** because they provide guideposts from which individuals take their social and psychological bearings. Of course, reference groups or reference symbols can be negative as well as positive: the self-made businessman may be against a proposal that he believes will benefit labor unions or social welfare organizations because he has unfavorable images of such groups.

The Mass Media. Another agency in our society with a considerable potential for shaping political opinions is the mass media: television, radio, newspapers, and magazines. Television, in particular, is an important influence, since it is the primary source of political information for most Americans. In fact, for many individuals, particularly those of lower social and economic status, television is the *only* source of such information. Persons who are unwilling to make the effort to read the printed page view television news inadvertently, that is, because it comes on after some other program or the news is on while they are waiting for the next program.

Many students of the subject stress the importance of the mass media in *defining social reality* for the public. There is so much going on in the world that if most of us had to assimilate it all, we would be overwhelmed by the sheer volume and complexity of events. This enables the mass media to play an important role in *selecting* those events that they feel are most meaningful and giving some *structure* to the information. Moreover, the fact that most of us have a rather narrow range of experience means that the media are in a position to provide us with information that we are not able to learn personally.

Political scientist Michael Robinson goes further in suggesting that television news creates what he calls, "video malaise," feelings of political distrust and cynicism. He attributes such feelings in part to the fact that television journalism tends to be essentially negative in character because "bad news is news." He also contends that the electronic media emphasize conflict and violence because they are visually exciting and that they often express an "anti-institutional theme," that is, they tend to attack established institutions in American society and to give favorable treatment to groups such as militants who are in conflict with such institutions. Robinson also suggests that the television networks imply ". . . that things were once better than they are now, that the government and the society and its members performed or behaved better in the good old days."

There are, however, a number of built-in limits on the long-term influence of the media on political attitudes. One such factor is the nature of the messages carried by the media. Most television programs, for example, are nonpolitical. Advertisers who pay the high costs of television time want the maximum audience for their dollar; since most people are far more interested in being entertained than they are in being informed on public affairs, few programs with political content are sponsored by private companies or groups. Under regulations of the Federal Communications Commission, networks and individual stations themselves carry a certain amount of "public affairs" programming, but many of these are not controversial (such as visits of foreign dignitaries or religious leaders like the pope) because the owners of the stations do not want to antagonize viewers and they have an obligation to provide free "equal time" to those with opposing viewpoints. For these reasons few stations have taken advantage of the opportunity provided by regulations of the Federal Communications Commission to carry editorial comments.

Of course, as previously indicated, the media do carry regular news programs, which include political developments. However, such programs typically constitute only a half-hour's programming per day—in fact, twenty-two minutes if the time for commercials is deducted. Moreover, as political scientist Doris Graber points out, the average news story lasts only a little over a minute and fifteen seconds, hardly adequate to cover complex political events and issues.

While the print media do not suffer from the same limitations as television, much of the content of newspapers is also nonpolitical, because editors seek to avoid antagonizing their readers and advertisers. Although editorial pages print controversial viewpoints, relatively few readers examine these columns. (The comics, sports, social, and financial sections are more likely to capture interest.) Some news magazines, notably *Time, Newsweek,* and *U. S. News and*

On the basis of these returns we predict!

World Report, carry a great deal of political information, but the readership of such publications is fairly limited.

Even the political content of the mass media has less effect on many people than may be supposed. Communication depends, after all, not only on the messages sent but also on the messages received. Some persons screen out political information entirely because they have no interest in it; a television viewer, for instance, may turn off the set or turn his attention to other matters when political comments are carried on the air. Others select only the messages they want to hear: thus the liberal may read the *New Republic*, and the conservative the *Chicago Tribune*. Still others actually misperceive what they hear or read; they interpret an editorial or other political comment to mean what they want it to mean, not what the conveyer of the message is trying to say.

Students of the mass media have discovered something else that bears on their impact on political attitudes: there is often a "two-step flow" or "multi-step flow" in the communication process. That is, many messages, especially those that appear in the print media, do not reach the average citizen directly because he is not interested enough to expose himself to them; instead they are transmitted to him indirectly via "opinion leaders" (party and interest-group officers or local "influentials" such as lawyers, doctors, bankers, and teachers) who are especially attentive to the print media and who discuss their content with less-informed persons. In the process, of course, these transmitters alter the messages in keeping with their views and biases.

Despite such limitations, however, there is little question that the mass media do play a major role in shaping political attitudes. As we shall see in later chapters, the media particularly affect reactions that people have towards the personality and character of political candidates, and persons who actually serve in public office.

Political Events and Experiences. We are aware by now that the developmental approach to political socialization focuses on the effects of various phases of the life cycle of an individual. In other words, one's political attitudes evolve as one progresses from an initial association—primarily with the family—to associations involving teachers and fellow students in schools and colleges, and ultimately to adult contacts with fellow workers and other peers. However, this conception of the political socialization process leaves out another major influence in the formation of political views: political events and experiences.

There are indications that even the fundamental political beliefs of children are affected by what is happening in the general political world. A study by political scientist F. Christopher Arterton of three groups of children in the third through sixth grades of elementary school—the first group in school in 1962, the second in 1973, and the third in 1975—showed a great variation in their attitudes towards the American president. The first group, who were in the primary grades when John Kennedy was in the White House, expressed the traditional attitude that the chief executive is a benevolent figure who would help them if they needed it and that he would also protect them. The second group, who were in school in 1973 at the time of Nixon's Watergate troubles, were much less inclined to think that the chief executive would take such helpful actions. The third group, who were students after Gerald Ford had succeeded to the presidential office, held an intermediate position on the issue: they were not as sure of the president's benevolence as the 1962 students, but not as skeptical about it as the 1973 primary graders.

Another study by Roberta Siegel and Marilyn Brooks analyzed the political attitudes of students when they were in the fourth, sixth, and eighth grades in 1966, and then again in 1968, when they had advanced to the sixth, eighth, and tenth grades, respectively. Interviews with the students indicated that during the two-year interval several dramatic events, including the war in Vietnam, the assassination of Martin Luther King Jr., and the riots in Detroit (the area in which the study was conducted), were matters of great concern to them. The study found that individual students in 1968 were less inclined to think that the government, and particularly the president, was responsive and helpful to people than they had been two years earlier, a result that could be attributed to their additional maturity and/or the events described above. Moreover, a comparison of different groups of students who were in the fourth and sixth grades in 1966 and 1968, respectively, showed the same results, which more clearly demonstrated the impact of the above-mentioned events, since the student groups in each of the two years were the same ages (the fourth-graders were nine years old and the sixth-graders eleven). Interestingly enough, however, while students were more critical of government and the president in 1968 than they were in 1966, they were also more politically involved; that is, they spoke about politics with friends and their family more in 1968 than in 1966. Thus political concern can affect political participation, a matter that we will explore in the last section of this chapter.

Besides the influence they exert in the early childhood years, political events have a marked effect on individuals during pre- and early adulthood (usually considered ages 17 through 25). Political scientists and sociologists refer to age *cohorts* (groupings) that share prominent and significant political experiences during those impressionable years as constituting a **political generation.** Thus persons who were between 17 and 25 years of age during the period of economic distress from 1929 to 1935 are frequently referred to as the "Depression" generation. Similar generations are identified with other dramatic events, such as the Vietnam War and the Watergate scandal. Such experiences are thought to have lasting effects on the persons who live through them. Thus persons who grew up in the 1930s are especially sensitive to economic problems and tend to vote Democratic because they associate the Depression with Herbert Hoover and the Republican party, and credit Democrat Franklin Roosevelt with leading the United States out of those difficulties. It remains to be seen whether the Vietnam and Watergate experiences will have similar long-term effects on the attitudes of the political generations associated with them.

Finally, even though the political attitudes of adults are generally considered more established and stable than those of young children and young adults, persons over age 25 are also affected by political events and experiences. As we shall see later in this chapter, the confidence of Americans in their political leaders declined significantly during the Vietnam and Watergate eras. Thus political attitudes of adult citizens concerning even such basic matters as the state of the nation and its major political officials are subject to change as a result of dramatic and significant political events.

Political events vary in the extent to which they affect the political attitudes of persons of different ages. A major study by political scientists Kent Jennings and Richard Niemi of the political views of high-school seniors, on the one hand, and their parents on the other, over the period from 1965 to 1973 revealed that some events affected the two generations similarly, while others had a different impact. For example, both groups reacted similarly to the issue of the role of the federal government in school desegregation: they were less likely in 1973 than they had been in 1965 to think that the federal government should help to integrate the schools, an attitude that the authors attribute mainly to the busing controversy. On the other hand, the views of the two generations differed on whether prayers should be allowed in the public schools: the seniors were more inclined than their parents to say no in 1965, and the differences between the two generations on that issue were even more pronounced eight years later. Jennings and Niemi attribute this difference to the fact that the high-school seniors were socialized in a more secular era than that in which their parents came of political age.

Thus political attitudes of individuals are shaped by three major factors. One is **life cycle,** the various stages of life—early family relations, school, college, work—through which one passes. Another is **political generation influences,** the outstanding political events experienced during the pre- and young adult years. The third is **period effects,** events that have a similar impact on persons of all ages. Together these factors mold the political attitudes of all of us.

POLITICAL ATTITUDES OF AMERICAN CITIZENS

Although it is difficult to determine with any precision how political views change over the course of an entire lifetime, we can analyze the general nature of the views held by Americans. As we have already noted, attitudes exist on a variety of political subjects, including basic orientations toward the nation and to the government and public officials that are vital to the very existence of a political system. Public reactions to the vital issues of the day also shape the public policies political leaders develop to meet them. The remainder of this chapter and all of Chapter 5 treat those aspects of public opinion that affect the everyday operation of our government. Attitudes toward political parties, social and economic groups, and political personalities that relate closely to the periodic electoral process are discussed in later chapters.

Attitudes Toward the Nation

The strong sense of loyalty to the nation that children in the United States develop very early in their lives persists in adulthood. A 70 nation survey conducted in 1976 under the joint auspices of the Gallup International Research Institute and the Kettering Foundation indicated that, when questioned, only 8 percent of Americans would like to settle permanently in another country. (In comparison, 22 percent of residents of the United Kingdom, 14 percent of Australians, and 12 percent of those living in continental European countries would like to emigrate.) In a 1981 survey by Civic Services Inc., 90 percent of the persons questioned agreed that America is still the best place in the world to live.

Attitudes Toward the American Political System

Surveys of public attitudes taken in the United States, Great Britain, West Germany, Italy, and Mexico during 1959 and 1960 by political scientists Gabriel Almond and Sidney Verba also reflect the favorable opinion Americans have of their government. When asked of what things about their country they were most proud, 85 percent of those questioned in the United States cited some feature of their political system, such as the Constitution, political freedom, or democracy. By way of comparison, only 46 percent of the Britons, 7 percent of the Germans, 3 percent of the Italians, and 30 percent of the Mexicans prized aspects of their government or political tradition. As Table 4.1 shows, citizens of these nations were more inclined to emphasize other aspects of their national life.

A Gallup Poll taken in mid-1973 confirmed the American attitude. When asked what they would tell foreign visitors was the "best thing about the United States," Americans responded by citing features related to democracy and freedom as their main preferences. Moreover, our people believe that political factors will continue to be a source of national pride. In a 1979 survey undertaken by ABC News and the Harris organization, 78 percent of the respondents said that ". . . a government that responds to the people's needs . . ." would be a major factor in making America great in the next 25 years.

The general attitudes evinced toward our political system raise a related concern: to what extent does the American public subscribe to the basic tenets of democracy discussed in Chapter 1? Are there any differences among our citizens in such matters?

"And don't waste your time canvassing the whole building, young man. We all think alike."

Table 4.1
Sources of National Pride (Expressed in Percentages)

	Nation				
Characteristic	U.S.	U.K.	Germany	Italy	Mexico
Governmental, political institutions	85	46	7	3	30
Social legislation	13	18	6	1	2
Position in international affairs	5	11	5	2	3
Economic system	23	10	33	3	24
Characteristics of people	7	18	36	11	15
Spiritual virtues and religion	3	1	3	6	8
Contributions to the arts	1	6	11	16	9
Contributions to science	3	7	12	3	1
Physical attributes of country	5	10	17	25	22
Nothing or don't know	4	10	15	27	16
Other	9	11	3	21	14
Total percentage of responses*	158	148	148	118	144
Total percentage of respondents	100	100	100	100	100
Total number of cases	970	963	955	995	1,007

* Percentages exceed 100 because of multiple responses.

SOURCE: Gabriel Almond and Sidney Verba, *The Civil Culture* (Princeton: Princeton University Press, 1963), p. 102.

Attitudes Toward Democratic Principles and Values

It will be recalled that democracy is based on certain operating principles. In particular, as it has developed in Western nations like the United States, democracy employs certain techniques and procedures of governance, among which are the concepts of majority rule and minority rights. Thus the question arises whether American citizens really believe in these two basic principles.

We have limited information on the subject, but one study of citizen attitudes in two cities—Ann Arbor, Michigan and Tallahassee, Florida—made a number of years ago by political scientists James Prothro and Charles Grigg indicates overwhelming public support for both principles. A sample of registered voters in each of these communities were asked whether every citizen should have an equal chance to influence public policy; they were also questioned whether they agreed with the statements that the minority should be free to try to win majority support for their opinions. The rate of agreement on these statements ranged from 94.7 to 98 percent.

Agreeing on abstract principles is one thing; applying the principles to particular situations is another. When the citizens of the two cities were asked their opinion toward a number of concrete questions that required them to make such an application, the responses shown in Table 4.2 resulted. The table shows that on none of the 10 statements does agreement on the democratic responses reach the 90 percent figure that was associated with the four more abstract principles pertaining to majority rule and minority rights. On only three statements (3, 7, and 9) do three-fourths or more of the respondents agree on the democratic response.

At the same time the table indicates that the responses of the voters to the questions vary with education and in-

Table 4.2

Democratic Responses to Basic Principles of Democracy Among Selected Population Groups (Expressed in Percentages)

Statements	Total N = 244	Education† High N = 137	Education† Low N = 106	Ann Arbor N = 144	Tallahassee N = 100	Income‡ High N = 136	Income‡ Low N = 99
Majority Rule							
1. Only informed vote*	49.0	61.7	34.7	56.3	38.4	56.6	40.8
2. Only taxpayers vote*	21.0	22.7	18.6	20.8	21.2	20.7	21.0
3. Bar Negro from office*	80.6	89.7	68.6	88.5	66.7	83.2	77.8
4. Bar Communist from office*	46.3	56.1	34.0	46.9	45.5	48.9	43.0
5. AMA right to bloc voting**	45.0	49.6	39.2	44.8	45.5	45.5	44.4
Minority Rights							
6. Allow antireligious speech**	63.0	77.4	46.5	67.4	56.6	72.8	52.1
7. Allow socialist speech**	79.4	90.2	65.7	81.3	76.8	83.8	73.7
8. Allow Communist speech**	44.0	62.9	23.5	51.4	33.3	52.2	36.7
9. Bar Negro from candidacy*	75.5	86.5	60.2	85.6	58.0	78.6	71.1
10. Bar Communist from candidacy*	41.7	48.1	30.3	44.1	38.2	44.8	34.4

* For this statement disagreement is recorded as the "democratic" response.

** For this statement agreement is recorded as the "democratic" response.

† "High education" means more than 12 years of schooling; "low education," 12 years or less.

‡ "High income" means an annual family income of $6000 or more; "low income," less than $6000.

SOURCE: James Prothro and Charles Grigg, "Fundamental Principles of Democracy: Bases of Agreement and Disagreement," *Journal of Politics* 22 (1960): 285.

come as well as their community. Persons with more education and income in both cities tended to give more democratic responses than less educated and less affluent persons, as did residents of the northern city as a whole compared with those in the southern community. Of the three factors education was the most important in differentiating between respondents. Yet even the more highly educated voters achieved the 90 percent figure on only one statement (7), and on three propositions (2, 5, and 10) less than half gave the democratic response.

A nationwide survey undertaken in 1971 by the National Opinion Research Center showed a considerable degree of public tolerance for two forms of freedom of expression that have become important in the United States—the right to demonstrate and the right to petition. Political scientist David Lawrence's analysis of the survey data (see Table 4.3) shows that the majority of the population was willing to approve petitioning by a variety of groups on a range of issues. The same is true of demonstrations with the exception of the legalization of marijuana, which is approved by about two-fifths of the respondents.

The Lawrence study does agree with one major finding of the earlier one by Prothro and Grigg: educated persons are more likely to be tolerant than those with less schooling. This is particularly true of actions involving what Lawrence terms "hard" issues. Thus some 64 percent of the college-educated respondents approved of demonstrations for the least tolerated issue shown in Table 4.3—the legalization of marijuana.

Thus Americans generally support basic procedural rules of democracy. However, there is less consensus on the application of general democratic principles to specific situations. Finally, there are differences among our citizens, the well-educated ones being more likely to support democratic principles.

Attitudes Toward Political Leaders

Traditionally, Americans have tended to maintain the faith in public officials that they originally acquired in childhood. For example, 83 percent of the Americans questioned in the 1959–60 five-nation survey mentioned above expected to be treated as well as anyone else if they had to take a tax-regulation or housing problem to the government office concerned. The same question drew the following percentages of similarly favorable responses from the citizens of the other four countries: Great Britain, 83; Germany, 65; Italy, 53; and Mexico, 42. Thus only the British expressed as much confidence in their public officials.

However, public polls taken in the 1960s and 1970s showed an erosion in the confidence and trust that Americans had in their political leaders. As indicated by Table 4.4, surveys conducted by the Institute for Social Research at the University of Michigan reveal that Americans became progressively disillusioned with governmental performance during the period from 1964 to 1980. However, in the period between 1980 and 1982 the process reversed itself with our citizens evidencing somewhat more confidence and trust in its political leaders. Nonetheless, the lack of confidence and mistrust remains high, much higher than it was in the 1960s and early 1970s.

Another measure of confidence—that shown by citizens in a variety of economic, political, and social institutions rather than the federal government alone—fails to show that public confidence grew in the early 1980s. As indicated at the beginning of the chapter, surveys taken by the Harris poll and the National Opinion Research Center revealed that confidence in such institutions actually declined between 1980 and 1983. Table 4.5, which is based on data from another poll—one conducted by the Gallup organization—tends to generally confirm the Harris and NORC findings. Between 1979 and 1983 public confidence in all 10 institutions declined. However, if the comparison is made between 1981 and 1983, confidence rose in four of the in-

Table 4.3
Percentage Permitting Demonstrating and Petitioning on Various Issues and by Various Groups

	Demonstrate	*Petition*
Because they were concerned about crime in their community	80.7%	94.6%
By a group of your neighbors	80.7%	94.6%
To ask the government to stop a factory from polluting the air	79.5%	93.2%
By a group of black militants	60.7%	69.0%
By a group of radical students	59.9%	71.9%
Calling for the legalization of marijuana	41.3%	52.0%
Calling for the government to make sure that blacks can buy and rent homes in white neighborhoods (whites only)	55.2%	69.9%

SOURCE: David Lawrence, "Procedural Norms and Tolerance: A Reassessment," *The American Political Science Review* 70 (March 1976): 88.

Table 4.4
Individual Confidence in Government Items (1964–1982)

Question: How much of the time do you think you can trust the government in Washington to do what is right—just about always, most of the time, or only some of the time?

	1964	1966	1968	1970	1972	1974	1976	1978	1980	1982
None of the time*	0%	3%	0%	0%	1%	1%	1%	4%	4%	2%
Some of the time*	22	28	36	44	44	61	62	64	69	62
Most of the time	62	48	54	47	48	34	30	27	23	31
Always	14	17	7	7	5	3	3	3	2	2
Don't know	2	4	2	2	2	2	3	3	2	3
PDI†	55	34	25	9	8	−26	−30	−39	−48	−31

Question: Would you say the government is pretty much run by a few big interests looking out for themselves or that it is run for the benefit of all people?

	1964	1966	1968	1970	1972	1974	1976	1978	1980	1982
Few big interests*	29%	33%	40%	50%	53%	66%	66%	67%	69%	61%
Benefit of all	64	53	51	41	38	25	24	24	21	29
Don't know	8	14	9	9	9	9	10	9	10	10
PDI	35	20	12	−9	−16	−42	−42	−42	−48	−32

Question: Do you think that people in the government waste a lot of money we pay in taxes, waste some of it, or don't waste very much of it?

	1964	1966	1968	1970	1972	1974	1976	1978	1980	1982
A lot*	47%	**	59%	69%	66%	74%	74%	77%	78%	66%
Some	44	**	34	26	30	22	20	19	17	29
Not much	7	**	4	4	2	1	3	2	2	2
Don't know	2	**	3	1	2	2	3	2	3	3
PDI	4	**	−21	−39	−33	−50	−51	−57	−59	−35

Question: I don't think public officials care much what people like me think.

	1964	1966	1968	1970	1972	1974	1976	1978	1980	1982
Agree*	35%	34%	43%	47%	49%	50%	51%	51%	52%	46%
Disagree	62	57	55	50	49	46	44	45	44	49
Don't know	2	9	2	3	2	5	4	5	4	5
PDI	26	22	12	2	0	−4	−7	−6	−8	+3

* Indicates cynical response.
** Data not available.
† The Percentage Difference Index is calculated by subtracting the percentage giving a cynical response from the percentage giving a trusting response.
SOURCE: Surveys by the University of Michigan, Institute for Social Research as reproduced in *Public Opinion* (June–July 1983): p. 17.

stitutions—the military, banks and banking, big business, and newspapers. The fact that the first three were favorably regarded by President Reagan may have played some role in increasing their esteem with the American public.

Table 4.5
Confidence in Institutions (1973–1983)

	Percent Saying "Great Deal" or "Quite a Lot"					
	1973	1975	1977	1979	1981	1983
Church or organized religion	66%	68%	64%	65%	64%	62%
Military	NA	58	57	54	50	53
Banks and banking	NA	NA	NA	60	46	51
U. S. Supreme Court	44	49	46	45	46	42
Public schools	58	NA	54	53	42	39
Newspapers	39	NA	NA	51	35	38
Congress	42	40	40	34	29	28
Big business	26	34	33	32	20	28
Organized labor	30	38	39	36	28	26
Television	37	NA	NA	38	25	25

NA—Not asked.
SOURCE: *Gallup Report* (October 1983): 4.

Attitudes on Policy Issues and Personalities

Among political attitudes, those on policy issues and personalities change most rapidly. For example, a survey taken in 1964 by the Institute for International Social Research showed that the five matters of greatest concern to Americans were: (1) keeping the country out of war, (2) combating world communism, (3) keeping our military defense strong, (4) controlling the use of nuclear weapons, and (5) maintaining respect for the United States in other countries. It should be noted that all of these matters concerned foreign and military policy; none involved a domestic problem.

Since 1964 public perceptions of issues facing the American people have changed considerably. By 1968 surveys by the same institute showed that concern with domestic issues had increased, so that two major problems—maintenance of law and order, and inflation and the cost of living—were among the five issues that most bothered Americans. In mid-1972 a study by Potomac Associates indicated that the four matters of greatest concern to Americans—rising prices and the cost of living, violence, drugs, and crime—were all domestic ones. (Vietnam rated in fifth place in the survey.) A 1976 Gallup poll that asked Americans what the biggest problem facing our nation was found that nine domestic matters (headed by the high cost of living and unemployment) bothered Americans more than defense spending, the foreign-policy issue that evoked the greatest concern. In the latter part of the 1970s similar polls revealed that inflation, energy, and unemployment most concerned our citizens. In the early 1980s, energy disappeared from the list of major problems facing the nation, and by 1983 "fear of war" moved into second place behind unemployment. Meanwhile, inflation continued to concern many Americans.

Dramatic events can change public perceptions even more rapidly. Surveys conducted by Louis Harris Associates in 1972 and again a year later showed that the percentage of Americans naming "integrity in government" as one of the two or three biggest problems facing the country jumped from 5 to 43 percent; meanwhile "taxes" as an issue fell from

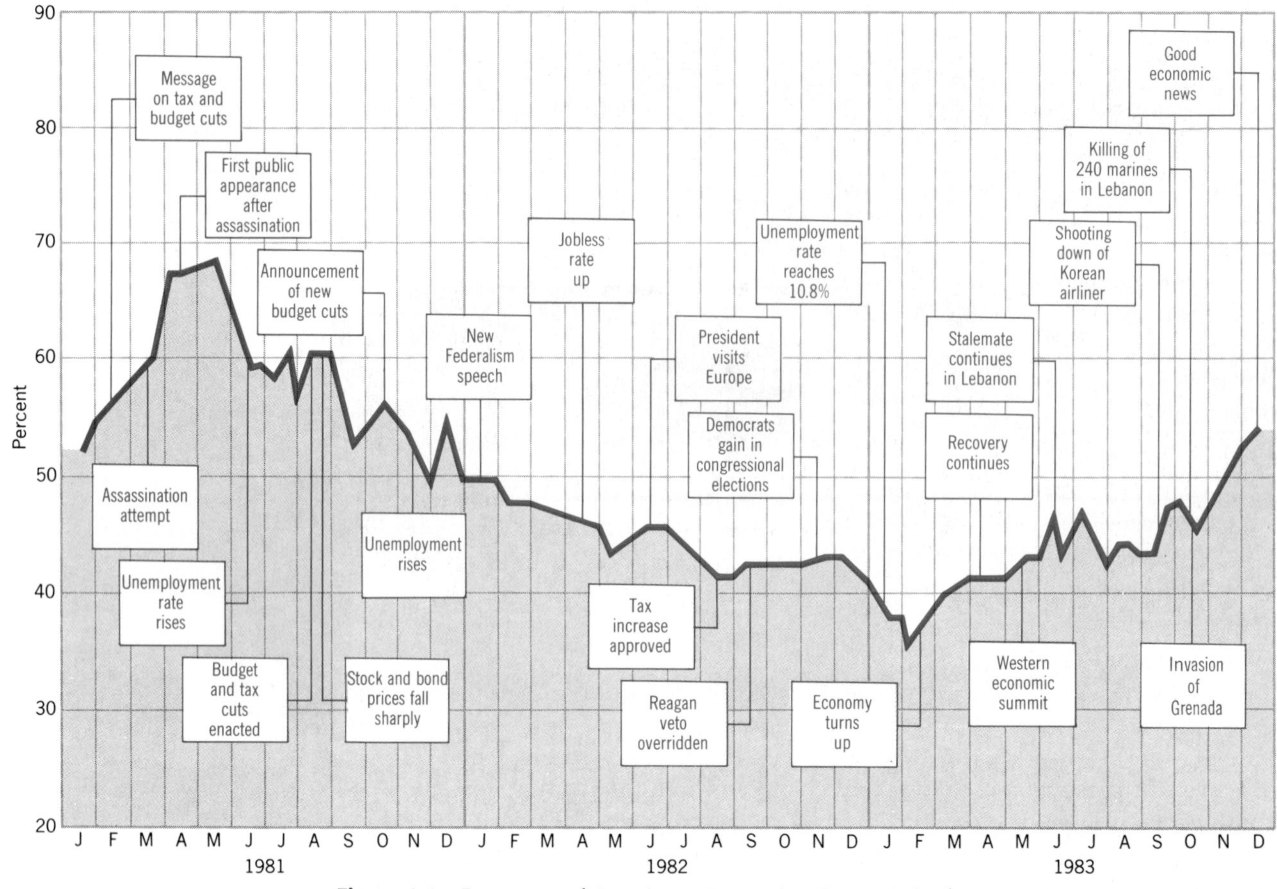

Figure 4.1 Percentge of Americans Approving Reagan's Performance as President (1981–1983).
SOURCE: The Gallup Report, December 1983, p. 19.

40 to 11 percent and "the war in Indo-China" from 29 to 4 percent. Even more dramatic was the alteration in public concern with the energy problem: it rose from none to 10 percent between the first and second Harris surveys, and in a Gallup poll taken in early 1974 it was named by almost half of all Americans as the most important problem facing the country.

The public's response to President Reagan's performance in office was also variable. As indicated by Figure 4.1, the president's popularity rose rapidly after he was inaugurated, a trend that accelerated after the unsuccessful attempt on his life. However, as the economic situation worsened, his approval rate generally declined and did not begin to rise again until the economy began to turn up in early 1983. He ended 1983 on a high note as the public reacted favorably to the successful invasion of Grenada and the good economic news.

These, then, represent the kinds of public attitudes that exist in the United States on a broad range of political matters. However, having an attitude on a matter is one thing; doing something about it politically is another. As the following section indicates, some people undertake a variety of political activities, while others take little or no part in public affairs.

Korean-Americans protest Soviet downing of Korean Airliner.

Rescuers in Lebanon speed wounded marine for treatment.

U.S. Troops invade Grenada.

POLITICAL PARTICIPATION

In a sense everyone participates in the political process since each is subject to laws and commands of political officials that may require such things as payment of taxes, performance of jury duty, or service in the armed forces. However, political *participation* is generally used by political scientists to include, as Herbert McClosky suggests, ". . . those voluntary activities by which members of a society share in the selection of rulers and, directly or indirectly, in the formation of public policy."

Forms of Political Participation

Political involvement may take many forms. Two students of the subject, Sidney Verba and Norman Nie, divide citizen participation into four major types of acts, or what they term *modes*: (1) *voting*, which is the most widespread and regularized activity, (2) other kinds of *campaign activities*, such as working for or contributing money to a party or candidate, (3) *citizen-initiated contacts* with government officials, in which a person acts on a matter of individual concern, and (4) *cooperative activities*, which involve group or organizational activity by citizens to deal with social and political problems.

Verba and Nie also point out that these four basic modes of political activity have different characteristics. For example, voting involves political conflict in the sense of a choice between competing candidates, seeks some collective outcome such as broad social policies for dealing with problems of concern to many persons, and requires little initiative on the part of the citizen. In contrast, citizen-initiated contacts typically do not involve conflict with other citizens, may seek a particularized outcome such as the repair of a sidewalk, and generally require much initiative on the part of the citizen.

Using these four basic modes of involvement to analyze political activities of American citizens as reported in a 1967 national survey (a joint venture of the Survey Research Center of the Uni-

Table 4.6
Americans Professing to Have Participated in Various Political Activities, 1952–1980 (Expressed in Percentages)

Activity	1952	1956	1960	1964	1968	1972	1976	1980
Work for political party	3	3	6	5	5	5	4	4
Attend political rally or meeting	7	10	8	9	9	9	6	8
Contribute money to campaign	4	10	12	11	9	9	9	6
Use political sticker or button	*	16	21	16	15	14	8	7
Give political opinions	27	28	33	31	30	31	28	36

* Not asked.

SOURCE: John P. Robinson, Jerrold G. Rusk, and Kendra B. Head, *Measures of Political Attitudes* (Ann Arbor: Center for Political Studies, 1968) p. 591; data for 1968, 1972, 1976, and 1980 from the Center's election studies made available through the Interuniversity Consortium on Political and Social Research.

versity of California, Berkeley, and the National Opinion Research Center at the University of Chicago), Verba and Nie develop six basic categories of participators. The **inactives,** some 22 percent of our citizenry, do not take part in political life in any form. Another 21 percent, termed the **voting specialists,** vote in presidential elections and always or almost always in local elections; but this is the extent of their political involvement. A very small group—some 4 percent of Americans, called the **parochial participants**—are average voters, do not engage in campaign or communal activities, but do initiate particularized contacts with government officials on matters that affect their personal lives. Another 20 percent of the population, the **communalists,** are active in cooperative ventures in community affairs but avoid the conflict of political campaigns; while still another group, the **campaigners** (some 15 percent of the populace), concentrate their efforts in this mode of participation and have little to do with communal activities. Finally some 11 percent of Americans are **complete activists** who engage in all types of political activities with great frequency. Thus Americans vary greatly in their political involvement: some avoid all forms of activity; others tend to concentrate their efforts in different kinds of participation, and a few have the time and energy to engage in a broad range of political acts.

Other recent surveys on political participation provide information on specific activities undertaken by citizens. Table 4.6, based on data gathered by the Center for Political Studies at the University of Michigan, indicates the percentage of Americans who have participated in activities associated with eight recent presidential elections. As the table shows, different proportions of persons participate in the various campaign activities analyzed. However, the percentage of Americans who involve themselves in each of these actions has remained fairly constant over the 28-year period.*

Data from a 1973 study of public attitudes toward government conducted by Louis Harris Associates for the U. S. Senate provide some basic information on certain *nonelectoral* activities of the American public. Table 4.7 shows a hierarchy of activities ranging from participation in a violent demonstration to the signing of a political petition.

Thus there are important distinctions among the various forms of political

* The major exception to that tendency is the marked decline in the use of political buttons and bumper stickers in 1976, as discussed in Chapter 8. This development continued in 1980.

Table 4.7
Involvement of Public in Various Kinds of Political Activities (Expressed in Percentages)

Activity	%
Took part in a demonstration where violence occurred	2
Picketed or took part in a street demonstration	11
Visited or talked in person with their senator	11
Visited state legislator in the state capital	14
Written a letter to a local government official	19
Visited or talked in person with their congressman	22
Written a letter to their senator	25
Participated in a school board discussion	27
Written a letter to their congressman	33
Actively defended the action of a public official in private discussion	56
Signed a petition	69

SOURCE: U. S. Congress, Senate Subcommittee on Intergovernmental Relations of the Committee on Governmental Operations, *Confidence and Concern: Citizens View American Government: A Survey of Public Attitudes*, 93rd Cong., 1st sess. (3 December 1973), pt. 1:83–84.

participation. There are also important differences among the kinds of persons who involve themselves extensively in public affairs compared to those who participate little or not at all in such matters.

Factors Affecting Political Participation

There are no easy answers to the question of what disposes some people to participate in politics and others to avoid such activities. Nonetheless, students of the subject have been able to identify certain basic factors associated with both participation and nonparticipation. These include (1) the social background and position a person occupies in society, (2) one's psychological attributes and attitudes, and (3) the general political setting in which participation takes place.

The factor that correlates most closely with political participation is **social-class status.** Well-educated persons are likely to be highly conscious of political matters and to possess the self-confidence to deal with them; the affluent see a financial stake in politics; and lawyers and teachers have important intellectual and social skills that are transferable to the political arena. Besides such individual attributes the general social situation of persons of high status gives them advantages: they are likely to receive political information and stimulation from persons with whom they associate; that is, they are most likely to be in the political center rather than on the periphery of the world of politics. Moreover, persons from the middle and upper classes are more likely than members of the lower classes to feel that they have the civic duty to participate in political affairs, even if they are not personally interested in such matters.

Other social circumstances also affect participation. Verba and Nie report that participation in voluntary associations as well as political parties tends to increase the political activities of citizens. Moreover, the heightened group consciousness of blacks in recent years has led to their greater involvement in political concerns and to a narrowing of the traditional gap between their participation and that of white citizens.

Some of the *psychological* attributes associated with participation have already been suggested as reasons why persons in positions of high social status become politically involved: they have a sense of confidence in their abilities and may also

Political participation takes many forms.

Registering voters.

Getting out the vote.

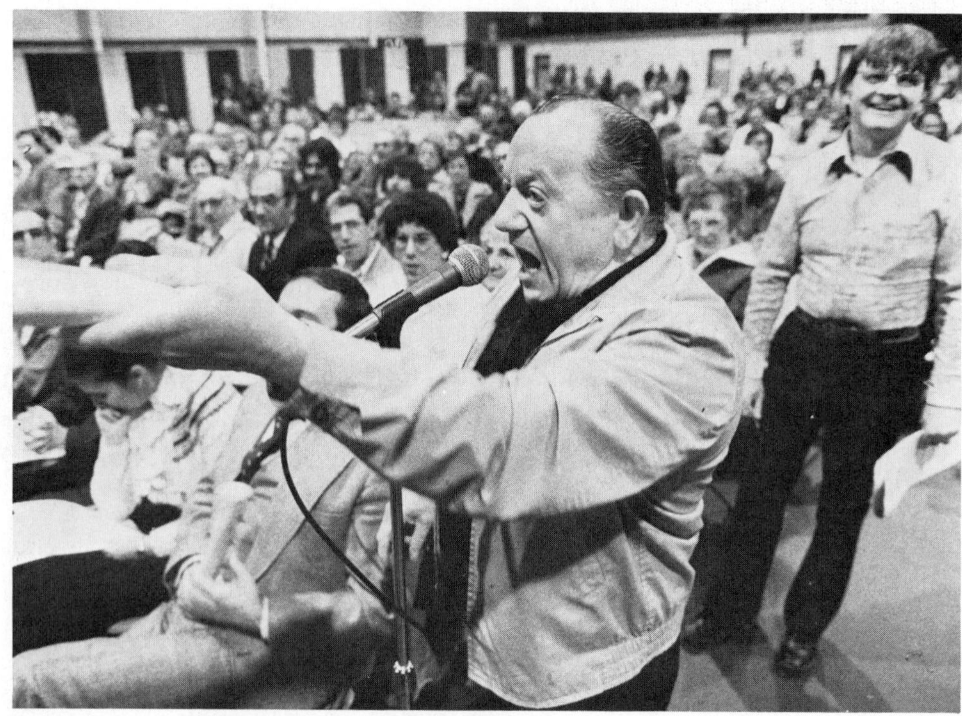

Speaking up at a town meeting.

Gathering signatures on petition.

Displaying opinions.

think that they have a duty to participate. Participants tend to feel politically effective; that is, they believe that government officials will respect their views and do something about them. Psychological motives associated with political involvement are of two general types: (1) **instrumental,** in which persons seek a specific goal such as a victory for a particular candidate or the passage of a bill, or (2) **expressive,** in which persons seek personal satisfaction at having done the "right" thing, even though they may see no real chance that their candidate will be elected or a favored bill enacted.

There are also different psychological reasons why people do *not* participate in political matters. One is sheer *indifference*; that is, some persons simply find politics dull and so prefer to devote their time and efforts to matters that they find more rewarding such as sports, entertainment, business activities, volunteer service, and the like. Others are not disinterested in politics, but they feel a sense of *powerlessness* in their personal ability to affect the political process or a general *cynicism* or *mistrust* of politicians, who they think are unfair and/or dishonest.

There is no general consensus among political scientists concerning the relative importance of these various reasons for nonparticipation in politics. Certainly the evidence on the point is not clear. For example, in the 1973 Harris study 60 percent of the American people admitted that they were not up-to-date on events in the federal government. One possible reason for this lack of knowledge was a general feeling of alienation and powerlessness. Yet when asked in the same survey what they could do to change things they didn't like about government, 94 percent said that they would vote against a public official, 84 percent would write their congressional representative, and 79 percent would work through a group, all responses that would seem to indicate a belief that the political process is responsive to American citizens and that their lack of interest in politics is due to indifference rather than disillusionment.

Finally, the **political setting** affects participation, a topic that we will explore in depth in Chapter 8 relative to voting in presidential and congressional elections. For now it is sufficient to note that different kinds of political races draw more interest than others; for example, more people vote for the president than for members of Congress. Moreover, people who live in areas where politics has traditionally been an important activity or where political contests are close tend to be drawn into the campaign process more actively than people who reside in areas of low political interest and competition. Verba and Nie also report that the type of community in which persons live affects participation: as communities grow in size and lose the characteristics of "boundedness" that distinguish the independent city from the suburb, participation declines.

ASSESSMENT

Traditionally most Americans have supported our nation, its major institutions, and its public officials. However, surveys show that beginning in the mid-1960s, citizen trust and confidence in the persons in charge of these institutions eroded. There is some disagreement as to whether that erosion has continued or whether some restoration in trust and confidence began to develop in the early 1980s. In any case, the polls show greater dissatisfaction with the performance of the persons who operate such institutions than with the structure of the basic institutions themselves.

Studies of political attitudes and participation indicate that the average American hardly meets the model of the Athenian citizen, highly interested and actively involved in political affairs. The American citizen tends to be an apathetic or passive spectator of the political process. Thus few persons become active in political campaigns or are interested or knowledgeable about major political issues.

There are, however, a minority of people in the United States who are concerned about public issues and take the time and effort to participate in the campaign process. The factor that is most closely related to both political interest and political participation is social-class background, particularly the amount of formal education a person has. The well-educated not only participate more but also have a greater appreciation of the rules of the game and the values of democracy.

There are certain advantages in the fact that persons who know little about issues and do not understand the democratic rules of the game do not participate more in the political process. Otherwise, uninformed opinions would be transmitted to political officials. There is also a danger that the rights of minorities and democratic values in general would not be protected. Viewed in this light, democracy is best protected by the present system, whereby the political activists bring their knowledge and understanding of democratic procedures to bear on the problems of governing our nation.

Yet there is also danger in the present situation. There is no assurance that the politically apathetic will always remain so: they may, for example, become excited over a controversial issue such as communism or race relations and suddenly enter the political arena in support of leaders and policies that may be highly undemocratic. Also there is no guarantee that upper-class activists will always take into account the interests of lower-class apathetics.

An ideal solution to the problem would be to politically educate individuals to protect their own interests and understand the democratic rules of the game. Political-socialization studies provide some evidence that disadvantaged persons can be given a greater appreciation of democratic procedures and values in high-school civics courses. Yet it would be naive to assume that such courses can accomplish miracles. It is much more realistic to think that political socialization must take place through many social institutions and at various stages of a person's life. Moreover, we must face the fact that some persons will never become politically interested and involved, however much we may want them to be.

There are some signs, however, that changes in our society may result in increased political interest and participation (especially in ways besides voting). Significantly, the conditions most closely associated with political understanding and involvement are also those that are becoming more prevalent in the United States. Thus a greater proportion of citizens today are attending college, going into the professions, and becoming part of the middle class. Also, with all their limitations, the mass media—particularly television—are providing political information to persons who have never before been exposed to it. It is also encouraging to find that blacks have begun to close the participation gap that has traditionally existed between them and white Americans.

Another factor also bears on political participation: the extent to which our political institutions effectively channel the concerns of citizens to public officials. It is to this general subject that we now turn.

SELECTED READINGS

The concept of political culture is utilized in Gabriel Almond and Sidney Verba, *The Civic Culture* (Boston: Little, Brown, 1963). A study that emphasizes a high degree of political consensus in our society is Donald Devine, *The Political Culture of the United States* (Boston: Little, Brown, 1972).

An excellent analysis of the role that public opinion plays in the United States is V. O. Key Jr., *Public Opinion and American Democracy* (New York: Alfred A. Knopf, 1961). A good recent treatment of the subject is Robert Erikson and Norman Luttbeg, *American Public Opinion: Its Origins, Content and Impact*, 2nd ed. (New York: John Wiley and Sons, 1980).

An analysis of the political socialization of elementary school children that pointed the way for other studies is Fred Greenstein, *Children and Politics* (New Haven: Yale University Press, 1965). Other major works in the field are Robert Hess and Judy Torney, *The Development of Political Attitudes in Children* (Chicago: Aldine Publishing Co., 1967), which focuses on the psychological aspects of political development; and David Easton and Jack Dennis, *Children in the Political System* (New York: McGraw-Hill Book Co., 1969), which emphasizes the way political attitudes learned early in life contribute to the stability of the American political system. An excellent general treatment of the subject that synthesizes the findings of a number of studies and places them within a meaningful analytical framework is Richard Dawson, Kenneth Prewitt, and Karen Dawson, *Political Socialization* (Boston: Little, Brown, 2nd ed., 1977). Two recent treatments of the political role of the media are Doris Graber, *Mass Media and American Politics* (Washington, D.C.: Congressional Quarterly Press, 1980) and another study edited by her entitled, *Media Power in Politics* (Washington, D.C.: Congressional Quarterly, Inc., 1984). Michael Robinson's views on "video malaise" appear in "Public Affairs Television and the Growth of Political Malaise: The Case of the Selling of the Pentagon," *The American Political Science Review* 70(1976): 409–432. Kent Jennings and Richard Niemi collaborated on two major works on the political attitudes of high-school students and their parents, entitled *The Political Character of Adolescence: The Influence of Families and Schools* (Princeton University Press, 1974) and *Generations and Politics: A Panel Study of Young Adults and Their Parents* (Princeton: Princeton University Press, 1981).

A pioneering study of political attitudes of citizens in the United States, Great Britain, West Germany, Italy, and Mexico is the Almond and Verba study cited above. Based on survey data, the analysis focuses on basic orientations of people in these five countries toward their government and the role that they expect to play in its operation.

A recent analysis of attitudes towards our basic institutions is Seymour Lipset and William Schneider, *The Confidence Gap: Business, Labor, and Government in the Public Mind* (New York: The Free Press, 1983).

The best empirical study of political participation is Sidney Verba and Norman Nie, *Participation in America: Political Democracy and Society Equality* (New York: Harper & Row, 1972).

NO NUKES!

CHAPTER 5

Interest Groups

In the early 1980s a wide variety of organizations joined forces to work for arms control. Leading the way were specialists—scientists, academics, professionals—who had long been active on the issue. Other specialists included Washington lobbyists for the Council for a Livable World, the Coalition for a New Foreign and Military Policy, SANE (a citizen's organization for a sane world), and the Union of Concerned Scientists, all of which met each Monday at lunch to plan actions to stop proposed additions to the nation's nuclear arsenal. Also participating were representatives of the Friends of the Earth, an environmental group that became interested in arms control because of its view that the MX missile is a threat to the Western United States.

Meanwhile, outside Washington a "grass-roots" movement began to try to get Congress to enact a "freeze" on the further development of nuclear weapons. Particularly prominent in the movement were two citizen-based organizations—Ground Zero and the Nuclear Weapons Freeze Campaign. The former group—named after the point of detonation of a nuclear weapon—operated through its 200 local affiliates to educate citizens and involve them in national election campaigns. The Nuclear Weapons Freeze Campaign concentrated on getting representatives from their individual districts to vote for a congressional resolution calling for a halt in the arms race and negotiations for a nuclear freeze with the Soviet Union.

Also joining the veteran arms-control specialists and the grass-roots "peace" groups in the attempt to halt the nuclear-arms race were two general-interest groups—Common Cause and the National Education Association (NEA). Common Cause, best-known for its activity on behalf of campaign finance and "good government" reforms, got involved in the arms-control issue when a

1982 poll of its 200,000 members showed it to be their most urgent concern. The Common Cause membership supported their concern through a $400,000 highly successful fund drive. Once involved, the organization joined the Washington Monday lunch group and conducted workshops to assist persons interested in trying to stop the nuclear-arms race. The 1.7-million member NEA, in turn, helped inaugurate a Citizen's Against Nuclear War grassroots campaign.

The efforts of the above groups (and others) soon had an effect on the arms-control debate. In August 1982, a resolution calling for a nuclear freeze failed by two votes in the House of Representatives but was passed the following May by a 278–149 vote after an amendment was added that the freeze agreement would be voided unless it led to arms reduction by both the United States and the Soviet Union within a specified period of time. In October 1983, a freeze proposal failed to pass in the Republican-controlled Senate but proponents took consolation in the fact that all senators were forced to go on the public record on the issue before the 1984 elections.

While all the groups agreed on the nuclear freeze, there were some differences as to how to proceed further on the general issue of arms control. Some, particularly those representing the veteran arms-control experts, continued to work against the approval of individual weapons systems (such as the MX missile), reasoning that it was inconsistent to support the freeze and then to vote for funds for weapons that would be limited by the freeze. Others, such as the grass-roots peace group, Nuclear Weapons Freeze Campaign, hesitated to go beyond supporting a mutual verifiable freeze on the grounds that fighting for selective-arms cuts could be construed as support for a unilateral freeze on the part of the United States alone.

The arms-control campaign illustrates a number of matters we will explore in this chapter, including the variety of groups that operate in the United States, as well as the kinds of techniques they employ to accomplish their purposes. It also shows the political advantages that accrue when groups join together to form a coalition on a particular issue, as well as potential problems that develop over the best strategy for reaching the common goal. Before examining such matters further, it will be helpful to consider a fundamental question: What do all interest groups have in common?

NATURE OF INTEREST GROUPS

An *interest group* is *any collection of persons with a shared attitude on some matter that makes certain claims or demands on others in society with respect to that matter.* It should be noted that not every group fits this description. People who have red hair, or who earn $10,000 or more a year, or who are members of the Baptist faith share something, have certain characteristics in common. (Sociologists call these *categorical groups.*) But these common characteristics may or may not produce a common viewpoint.

Shared attitudes develop among people who have a common interest in a particular subject; typically, they interact with one another over it. Thus people who like symphonic music may meet as a group to listen to records or attend concerts. Or they may work together to sponsor the visit of a touring orchestra. Such a group does not qualify as an interest group, however, unless it meets the second requirement of the definition: that it makes some claim on other people. If it demands that a local radio station stop playing only rock music and devote certain hours to classical concerts, it is acting as an interest group.

In many instances the claims that interest groups make on others do not involve the political process. If the symphony-lovers merely try to influence radio-station owners to play their preferred music, they do not qualify as a political interest group. But if the group demands that the Federal Communications Commission (an agency of the national government that grants licenses to radio stations) force every station to devote a certain percentage of air time to symphonic music under pain of losing its license, it is acting as a political interest group. This is the kind of interest group that is of primary concern to the student of government.

Typically, symphony-lovers in the United States do not turn to the political process to further their interests, but there would be obvious advantages if they did. A radio-station owner that refused to cooperate voluntarily might do so under threat of losing his license. Moreover, symphony-lovers might persuade their city council to subsidize a local orchestra by using public funds to make up any deficit the group might incur. In doing so, they would be taking advantage of the government's ability to take money from people who do not necessarily like orchestral music and use it for the enjoyment of those who do. Thus public officials are particularly helpful to groups because they can do what private individuals cannot: issue commands that people will have to consider legitimate and utilize the taxing and spending power to benefit some persons at the expense of others.

Political interest groups have available two basic approaches for attempting to influence public officials. They may seek *positive benefits*, such as requiring radio stations to play symphonic music or convincing city councils to subsidize a local symphony orchestra. Or they may try to *prevent* the government from taking an action; for instance, those who do not appreciate symphonic music may try as an interest group to stop public officials from pursuing either of the above policies. Groups that are generally satisfied with the present distribution of values attempt to preserve the status quo by taking defensive actions in the political arena. The two approaches are not mutually exclusive, however, and groups frequently pursue both simultaneously: at the same time that music-lovers are attempting to influence the city council to subsidize a local symphony, they may try to prevent the use of public money to support a baseball team.

Interest groups also attempt to accomplish their purposes through private channels. Although labor unions exert extensive influence in government, they also make demands on employers and the general public through strikes and picketing. Other groups also seek to satisfy their demands by dealing directly with private individuals and organizations; students have sought to bring about major changes in universities through negotiation, as well as confrontation, with school officials.

Thus interest groups attempt to achieve some of their objectives by private means and others through political channels. This is one of the characteristics that distinguish an interest group from a *political party*, which focuses its activities almost entirely on political processes. In addition, the primary methods by which interest groups and political parties attempt to accomplish their purposes differ. Political parties seek to staff governmental positions by running candidates for office; interest groups typically attempt to influence the actions of whatever officials are already in office.

This distinction is a matter of emphasis only; the division of political labor between the two kinds of organizations is not complete. As we shall see in Chapter 6, some persons who participate in political party activities are concerned with issues and support a party or its candidates primarily because of their stands on those issues. Conversely, some interest groups try to influence the selection of political officeholders because they believe that certain persons will be more likely than others to pursue sympathetic courses of action. Yet the primary purposes of the two types of organizations differ. Political parties *always* run candidates for office, and frequently issues are not a major factor in campaigns. Interest groups typically try to influence public officials on issues in which the groups are concerned; quite often they make no attempt to determine who is chosen; they *never* (at least in the United States) run a candidate for office under the label of their own organization.

A final note is in order on the name **pressure group,** an older term for interest group, often used in disapproval by persons who think of such groups as selfish, irresponsible organizations seeking privileges for their members. Yet some groups have members who devote themselves to causes that benefit others; many white persons, for instance, belong to the National Association for the Advancement of Colored People (NAACP) because they sympathize with the problems of blacks. The word *pressure* implies that such groups use improper means—force, bribery, threats—to achieve their purposes. But as this chapter will show, the techniques by which interest groups attempt to wield political influence vary greatly and include methods like conveying factual information to political officials, which can hardly be said to constitute pressure in the normal sense of the term. To avoid any emotional connotation or inaccurate characterization of what the groups under discussion actually are or do, the more neutral and descriptive term *interest group* is used here.

"Senator, according to this report, you've been marked for defeat by the A.D.A., the National Rifle Association, the A.F.L.-C.I.O., the N.A.M., the Sierra Club, Planned Parenthood, the World Student Christian Federation, the Clamshell Alliance . . ."

INCENTIVES FOR JOINING INTEREST GROUPS

People join interest groups for a variety of reasons. Political scientists Peter Clark and James Wilson suggest that these reasons may be grouped into three general categories. One is the **material benefits** that may derive from membership. Another is the **solidary benefits** that accrue to members of a group. The third is what Clark and Wilson refer to as **purposive benefits** from organizational membership.

Material benefits are tangible rewards that persons seek to gain through membership in an interest group. These may be monetary, such as higher wages that workers believe a labor union can achieve for them through negotiating a new contract with their employers. Material benefits may also be nonmonetary, such as safety provisions for coal miners through congressional laws requiring that mine owners use certain equipment and take particular precautions to prevent mine cave-ins or explosions.

Solidary incentives are basically intangible in nature. As Clark and Wilson suggest, they include rewards such as "... socializing, congeniality, the sense of group membership and identification, the status resulting from membership, fun and conviviality..." and the like. Thus a person may join a farm organization primarily because he and his family enjoy the opportunity to escape the isolation of their daily work and socialize with other persons involved in agricultural work.

Purposive incentives are those that transcend an individual's own material or solidary interests; they are benefits directed at other persons. As we shall see in Chapter 15, whites who established the NAACP were motivated to improve not their own situation but that of blacks in the United States. Some persons have even broader goals in mind: changes that will benefit society as a whole. Individuals who belong to **public interest groups** like Common Cause (to be discussed later) are primarily concerned with purposive incentives.

It should be understood that material, solidary, and purposive incentives are not mutually exclusive: the same organization may provide all three kinds of benefits. Thus the United Automobile Workers (UAW) furnishes material benefits to members in the form of wages obtained through contracts with management. At the same time, the UAW sponsors recreational and other activities with social appeal. Moreover, the organization in recent years has sought broad social and economic reforms to benefit disadvantaged groups as well as society in general. Thus the UAW provides divergent kinds of incentives that appeal to different people or in some cases to the same person.

One of the problems of many interest groups is that frequently the benefits that they help to secure are "collective" in the sense that they cannot be restricted to their members alone. For example, a union may negotiate a contract for increased wages that covers *all* the workers in a plant whether or not they belong to the organization, or a veteran may receive government benefits even though he is not a member of the American Legion or Veterans of Foreign Wars, which helped to get the legislation through Congress.

As economist Mancur Olson suggests, under these circumstances it is irrational to expect an individual to belong to an interest group the collective benefits of which he can enjoy without having to invest his time or money in its activities. He can simply let others win those benefits for him. However, groups have several ways of overcoming this problem. One is to get legislation passed providing for compulsory membership in an organization. Thus some states require a worker to join a union within a specified period of time if a majority of the total work force has voted to let the union represent them;* also, membership in the state bar association is required of all attorneys in some states. Moreover, as Olson suggests, groups can utilize "selective benefits" as incentives to induce persons to join their organization. These benefits, which are restricted to members alone, include low-cost life insurance and health plans for workers, malpractice insurance for doctors, the distribution of profits of cooperatives to farmers, technical information for businessmen, and the like. Finally members can use social pressure to persuade persons to do their part in achieving group goals by joining and contributing to the organization; they can threaten to ostracize those that do not.

While conceding that some persons join interest groups primarily because of economic selective benefits, political scientist Terry Moe feels that Olson overestimates the information available to members on how much their time and effort is needed in order to allow the organization to achieve its political goal of winning collective benefits. Moe's study of the members of five Minnesota economic interest groups showed that 60 to 70 percent of them thought their contribution made a difference in the group's political success. Moe also contends that Olson exaggerates the extent to which persons are motivated by their own economic self-interest and that, in fact, many of them are more interested

* Such an arrangement, referred to as a *union shop*, is permitted by the Taft–Hartley Act if a state passes legislation providing for it. However, federal law also permits states to have an *open shop*, which does not require a worker to join a union favored by his or her fellow employees. Organized labor has attempted unsuccessfully over the years to have the Taft–Hartley Act changed so as to require all states to have a union shop.

in the purposive and social benefits of group membership.

Thus individuals are induced to join an interest group for many reasons. As political scientist Robert Salisbury suggests, the formation of such groups is often dependent on *entrepreneur* organizers who provide a variety of the benefits discussed above to members in exchange for their dues,* and the time and effort some individuals invest in the activities of the organization. If the arrangement proves not to be worthwhile, members will probably leave the organization and perhaps join a similar one. Moreover, if the organizer fails in one venture, he or she may apply his or her entrepreneurial skills to the establishment of another organization, usually of the same general type (farm, business, good "cause"). The result of this process is the development of a wide variety of interest groups in the United States.

INTEREST GROUPS IN AMERICAN SOCIETY

Americans have long been known as joiners. Alexis de Tocqueville, a young French nobleman who came to America in the 1830s and wrote a perceptive analysis of American society, *Democracy in America*, had this to say on the subject:

> *The Americans of all ages, all conditions and all dispositions constantly form associations. They have not only commercial and manufacturing companies in which all take part, but associations of a thousand other kinds, religious, moral, serious, futile, restricted, enormous or diminutive. The Americans make associations to give entertainment, to found establishments for education, to send missionaries to the antipodes. Wherever at the head of some new undertaking you see the government of France or a man of rank in England, in the United States you will be sure to find an association.*

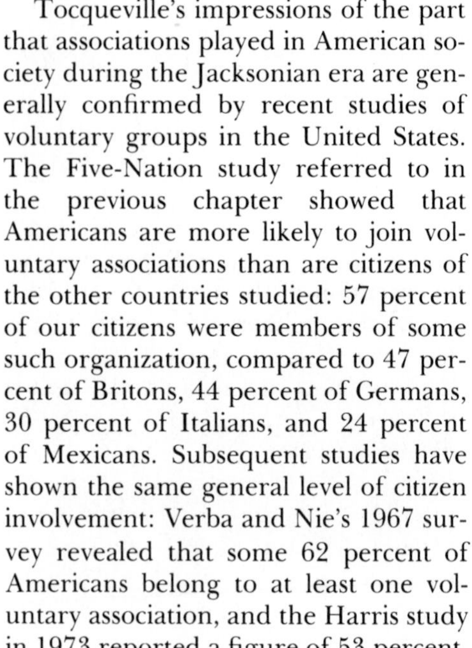

Tocqueville's impressions of the part that associations played in American society during the Jacksonian era are generally confirmed by recent studies of voluntary groups in the United States. The Five-Nation study referred to in the previous chapter showed that Americans are more likely to join voluntary associations than are citizens of the other countries studied: 57 percent of our citizens were members of some such organization, compared to 47 percent of Britons, 44 percent of Germans, 30 percent of Italians, and 24 percent of Mexicans. Subsequent studies have shown the same general level of citizen involvement: Verba and Nie's 1967 survey revealed that some 62 percent of Americans belong to at least one voluntary association, and the Harris study in 1973 reported a figure of 53 percent.

At the same time Tocqueville's statement is undoubtedly too sweeping. Not *all* Americans today (and, in all probability, not in his time either) belong to voluntary associations; in fact, almost half do not belong to even one. Moreover, there are marked differences in membership among people of different "conditions." The Verba–Nie study showed that fewer than one-half of those who were not high-school graduates belonged to a voluntary organization compared to almost four-fifths of those who had done some college work. Education also affected the degree of involvement of group members: only about one-quarter of the non-high-school graduates were active in at least one organization, but about three in five persons who had attended college were.

The student of government is of course particularly interested in political associations, specifically those that turn to the political process to accomplish at least some of their purposes. There are no precise statistics on how many of the more than 17,700 voluntary groups reported in the 1984 edition of the *Encyclopedia of Associations* are political in na-

* As political scientist Jack Walker has recently pointed out, in addition to dues, many interest groups, especially citizens' and nonprofit sector organizations, receive financial support from private foundations, wealthy individual contributors, government grants, and fees derived from publications, conferences, and training sessions.

ture, but the Verba–Nie study provides information on the extent to which organizations mentioned by respondents become involved in community affairs and/or participate in political discussions.

Table 5.1 indicates that there is a fairly high level of involvement in community affairs among all groups with the exception of those devoted to literary pursuits, hobbies, and sports. There are more organizations that tend to avoid political discussions, including youth and church-related groups, as well as fraternal associations, trade unions, school fraternities and sororities, and hobby and sports clubs. Perhaps the most surprising finding is the relative infrequency of political discussions in trade unions compared to service clubs and professional associations; this disparity probably relates to the higher social-class composition of members of the latter two groups.

Of course, discussing politics is one thing; doing something about a political problem is another. Groups that take political action differ in the extent that they do so. Some become politically involved only on rare occasions, while others do so almost constantly. Groups also vary with respect to the scope of their political activities. Some turn to government to accomplish a broad range of purposes; others restrict political involvement to a major issue.

Historically, economic groups have been most frequently involved politically in a broad range of issues. Commercial cliques (major manufacturers, merchants, ship owners, and big farmers) and noncommercial ones (small businessmen and farmers, artisans, and mechanics) contended over the writing of the Constitution; James Madison himself considered the major differences among men to be based on the distribution of property. Over the years these same kinds of groups, operating under the broad constellations of interests known as business, agriculture, and labor, have been most prominently involved in the American political process. The discussion that immediately follows focuses on the activities of these three major economic groupings.

Recently, however, other groups have emerged as important forces in American politics. Later in this section we examine four such groups: those representing public employees, those dedicated to pursuing the "public interest," those that concentrate on only one issue, and those that are ideological in nature. First, however, let us examine those groups that have traditionally been active in the political arena.

Business Interest Groups

The first national organization representing a variety of businesses was established in 1895 in response to an economic depression. Taking the name The National Association of Manufacturers (NAM), the group initially had the positive goal of promoting trade and commerce but soon shifted to the negative aim of counteracting the growing strength of organized labor. During the 1930s the NAM came under the control of large firms; it remains the major spokesman for big business today. Its 12,000 members consist of firms engaged in manufacturing; it also has "cooperating" members (financial institutions and transportation companies with close relationships to manufacturers) that contribute financially to the organization. Its major policy goals are counteracting the power of organized labor (although the organization now accepts the general principle of labor unions), lowering individual and corporate taxes, preventing extensive government regulation of business activities, and promoting free enterprise not only in the United States but also in other nations of the world.

The NAM never claimed to represent state and local chambers of com-

Table 5.1
Organizations by Type, Membership, and Kinds of Involvement and Activity

Type of Organization	Percentage of the Population Who Report Membership	Percentage of Members Who Report that Their Organizations Are Involved in Community Affairs	Percentage of Members Who Report that Political Discussions Take Place in the Organization
Political groups such as Democratic or Republican clubs and political action groups such as voters' leagues	8	85	97
School service groups such as the PTA or school alumni groups	17	82	54
Service clubs such as the Lions, Rotary, Zonta, or the Jr. Chamber of Commerce	6	81	64
Youth groups, such as the Boy Scouts, or Girl Scouts	7	77	36
Veterans' groups such as the American Legion	7	77	56
Farm organizations such as the Farmer's Union, Farm Bureau, or the Grange	4	74	61
Nationality groups such as the Sons of Norway or the Hibernian Society	2	73	57
Church-related groups such as a Bible study group or the Holy Name Society	6	73	40
Fraternal groups such as the Elks, Eagles, Masons, and their women's auxiliaries	15	69	33
Professional or academic societies such as the American Dental Association or Phi Beta Kappa	7	60	57
Trade Unions	17	59	44
School fraternities and sororities such as Sigma Chi or Delta Gamma	3	53	37
Literary, art, discussion, or study clubs such as book-review clubs or theater groups	4	40	56
Hobby or garden clubs such as stamp or coin clubs, flower clubs, or pet clubs	5	40	35
Sports clubs, bowling leagues, etc.	12	28	30

SOURCE: Sidney Verba and Norman Nie, *Participation in America: Political Democracy and Social Equality* (New York: Harper and Row, 1972), pp. 178–179.

merce or a large number of trade associations operating at the regional and national level. In 1912 the Taft administration sponsored a meeting of such groups from various parts of the nation to establish an organization that would legitimately speak for the general business community. At the meeting the Chamber of Commerce of the United States was born. Today it consists of 4,000 chambers of commerce and trade associations plus 250,000 business firms. Since its membership is broader than the NAM, its officials can speak more legitimately for the entire business community; however, because the Chamber represents such a wide range of businesses, it frequently cannot take stands on certain important issues. For example, it has avoided enunciating a definite position on reciprocal trade (exchanging goods between countries with little or no duty) because some members fear competition from companies abroad whereas others want to export goods free of foreign duties. The general political goals of the Chamber parallel those of the NAM: counteracting the power of organized labor, reducing taxes and government regulation, and promoting the virtues of a free economy.

A third business interest group, composed of businessmen and professional economists with somewhat different policy goals than those of the NAM and the national Chamber, is the Committee for Economic Development (CED). Founded in 1942 by persons who felt that business groups had been too negative toward the New Deal without developing positive economic programs of their own, the organization played a major role in the enactment of the Full Employment Act of 1946, under which the national government assumed the responsibility of promoting high employment, high production, and economic growth in the American economy. In keeping with this greater appreciation of the role of government in the affairs of the nation, several of the major leaders of the CED have occupied top positions in Washington. Most notably one of the founders of the organization, Paul Hoffman, served as the first director of the Economic Cooperation Association, which dispensed financial aid through the Marshall Plan to European nations after World War II. Favoring greater economic cooperation with other nations, the CED also played a major part in the establishment of the International Monetary Fund and the World Bank. In recent years, the organization has also turned its attention toward the management of the federal government as well as to economic and political problems of states and urban areas.

For much of American history, business groups dominated the political system. The depression of 1929, however, shook public confidence in the business community, which failed to prevent the passage of major New Deal legislation. The general prosperity after World War II restored some of that confidence so that business organizations once again became more politically effective. In recent years, however, they have become concerned with a lack of unity within the business community. In 1974 the NAM moved its headquarters from New York to Washington and began a concerted effort to work more closely with the U. S. Chamber of Commerce, the National Industrial Council (an NAM-supported umbrella organization of some 150 national, state, and local manufacturing and commercial associations), and the Business Roundtable, a group of Washington representatives of major corporations.

Agricultural Interest Groups

Today American farmers are represented by a variety of organizations. The largest, with a membership of over 3 million, is the American Farm Bureau

Federation. Established in 1919, the organization has traditionally had close ties with extension agents of the Department of Agriculture, who demonstrate new agricultural techniques to farmers, as well as with state land-grant colleges that carry on programs in agricultural research. During the 1920s and early 1930s the Federation worked with other farm groups to get the national government to guarantee farmers a fair price for their products. Since the end of the 1930s, however, the organization has opposed a price-support program for basic crops and now favors a reduced role for government in agriculture and a free market for determining the level of food prices. The Federation's change in attitude is due to its having come increasingly under the control of wealthy, large farmers in the Midwest corn and hog belt and cotton planters in the South. Such farmers, who benefit from the economics of large-scale farming, can now compete effectively in a free market; moreover, withdrawing price supports from small farmers forces many of them out of agriculture, thus removing the economic rivals of the large-farmer clientele of the Farm Bureau.

The primary voice of the less-advantaged farmer today is the National Farmers' Union,* founded in 1902 and with a current membership of 300,000. This group, which draws its support from wheat farmers of the Plains states—who are particularly vulnerable to vagaries of the weather (particularly droughts)—favors a high level of government support for farm products and the provision of cheap credit. In recent years, the NFU has also fought for legislation to protect migratory farm workers. The organization proclaims itself the champion of the dirt farmer, the person who devotes his or her life to farming as a way of life, rather than what the NFU calls the corporation farmer (represented by the Farm Bureau) who looks at farming strictly as a business.

Located somewhere between the Farm Bureau and the NFU in terms of clientele and general goals is the National Grange, the oldest of the farm organizations (founded in 1867). Today, with a membership of 425,000, the organization has its major base of support among dairy farmers in the New England, Middle Atlantic, and Pacific states. Traditionally concerned with providing social activities for farmers and less militant than the other two farm organizations, the Grange has moved closer politically in recent years to the NFU, primarily because it opposes the Farm Bureau's ultimate goal of abandoning government farm support programs.

Like labor, agriculture is experiencing a decline in its organizational potential because of technological developments. Mechanization and improved fertilizers mean that fewer farmers are needed to raise the nation's food supply. As a result, more and more people have left the farm in recent years to seek employment in the cities. (In 1960 our farm population was between 15 and 16 million; by 1969, it had fallen to between 10 and 11 million; by 1982 it stood at less than 7 million.) Furthermore, farmers are not much inclined to join interest groups. Today only about one in four farmers belongs to any of the major farm organizations.†

* This assessment is not shared by all farmers; those who belong to the American Agricultural Movement (AAM)—a loose organization of state groups—consider the NFU a part of the agricultural "establishment."

† A fourth general agricultural interest group, established in 1955, is the National Farmers' Organization. Concentrated primarily in Missouri and Iowa, it has tried unsuccessfully to withhold products from the market until a satisfactory price is received from food processors and purchasers. The group does not publish its membership size.

Labor Interest Groups

The first successful national organization, the American Federation of Labor (AFL), was established in 1886. Representing primarily skilled craftsmen, such as carpenters and bricklayers, the economic goals of the AFL were essentially conservative: using the governmental process in a negative way, primarily to seek protection against court orders forbidding strikes rather than for positive benefits in the form of minimum wages, public housing, or social security for its members. (In 1932, three years after the beginning of the Great Depression, the AFL still opposed unemployment insurance for workers on the grounds that such payments constituted governmental interference in concerns that should be left to management and labor.) The group's political tactics were similarly cautious: following the advice of the organization's founder, Samuel Gompers, to ". . . defeat labor's enemies and reward its friends . . . ," the union avoided blanket endorsements of candidates of either major political party.

The growth of mass industries (coal, steel, and automobiles) in the 1920s and 1930s created unskilled rather than skilled jobs. The appropriate organizational units for the new giant concerns were industry-wide unions joining all steelworkers, all autoworkers, and the like. The AFL leadership, however, was not eager to bring a flood of unskilled workers into the organization to threaten the dominance of skilled craftsmen and so refused to permit workers in the mass industries to be organized permanently along industrial lines. This decision led John L. Lewis, head of the United Mine Workers (UMW), to leave the organization and form a new national union known as the Congress of Industrial Organizations (CIO). Unlike its parent group, the CIO sought positive political goals such as public housing for low-income groups, social security, and minimum wages. The new organization also departed from the cautious political techniques of the AFL by establishing a Political Action Committee in 1944 to work for the re-election of Franklin Roosevelt.

This division in labor's ranks contributed to the movement's inability to prevent the passage in 1947 of the Taft–Hartley Act, a law placing restrictions on union activities. Eventually this outside threat from labor's traditional enemy—big business—forced the craft and industrial unions together in 1955 in a merger known as the AFL–CIO. However, tensions developed between the organization's new president, George Meany (former head of the AFL), and Walter Reuther, president of the Industrial Union Department of the new organization, who previously headed the United Auto Workers of the CIO. Besides the personal power struggle between the two men, there was also a difference in policy: Reuther charged that the organization was not involving itself in broad social causes, such as ending racial segregation in all areas of American life (including the construction industry, which AFL unions dominate). Differences in style between Meany, a cautious man with limited verbal abilities, and Reuther, called by many the "Billy Graham of Labor," also created personality clashes between them.

The break came in 1968 when Reuther's union, the United Auto Workers, left the AFL–CIO and shortly thereafter joined forces with another major ex-CIO union, the Teamsters (this union, led by Jimmy Hoffa, had been expelled in 1957 for alleged ties with gangsters and a misuse of union funds by its officers), to form a new group called the Alliance for Labor Action. Soon a third body, the International Chemical Workers Union, joined the organization. Boasting a membership of some four million, the new group ded-

icated itself to a Reuther-inspired program calling for broad social and economic reforms and an effort to forge links with the youth of America and the intellectual community. However, the organization lasted only a few years: the Chemical Workers returned to the AFL–CIO, while the UAW and Teamsters reverted to the status of independent unions.*

The result of these developments is a weakened labor movement. The nation's largest individual union—the Teamsters with 2-million members—lies outside the AFL-CIO as do other important elements of labor such as railroad workers, the National Education Association (NEA), with 1.7-million members, and miners. Thus labor speaks with a divided voice. Moreover, all labor organizations together today represent only about one-fifth of the civilian work force.

Crosscurrents are operating in the labor movement today. Automation has eliminated many of the blue-collar industrial employees who have traditionally joined unions. On the other hand, unions are now turning their attention to persons who have generally remained outside their ranks, such as migrant farm workers, service employees (such as hospital workers), and employees of the flourishing new industries of the South and Southwest. Moreover, they have experienced great success in recent years in organizing an increasingly important group in the nation's work force: public employees.

Public Employee Interest Groups

Historically, public officials have opposed the unionization of public employees on the grounds that allowing them to share in decisions regarding

* Recently, the UAW rejoined the AFL–CIO.

Cesar Chavez and United Farm Workers union.

compensation and working conditions would compromise the concept of governmental sovereignty: public officials should decide such matters themselves. In addition, unions have been associated with strikes, a weapon considered dangerous to vital public services such as education and transportation. However, a change of attitude began at both the state and national level in the early 1960s. Between 1962 and 1973 the number of states in which public employees had the right to enter into a formal relationship with their employers rose from 2 to 27. In 1962 President Kennedy issued an executive order that granted official recognition to federal employee unions and provided machinery for voting on exclusive bargaining agents for such employees. Subsequently, President Nixon issued additional executive orders permitting employees to have union dues deducted from their paychecks and providing for binding arbitration of employee grievances should they not be settled amicably with government officials.

This new legal climate for the organization of public employees soon resulted in a dramatic growth in union membership. In 1968 (the first year for which full figures on membership are available from the Bureau of Labor Statistics), 2.5-million persons belonged to state and local organizations; by 1977 this figure increased to 4.7 million, a rise of 88 percent. Meanwhile, union membership of federal employees went from 1.4 million in 1968 to 1.7 million in 1972, a gain of over 20 percent. In contrast, during the period from 1970 to 1976, membership in unions in the private sector of the economy rose only 2.1 percent. By 1976 more than one-fifth of all union members in the United States were public employees.

Today a number of organizations represent persons employed in the public sector. Two of the major ones—the American Federation of State, County and Municipal Employees (AFSCME) and the American Federation of Teachers (AFT)—are members of the AFL–CIO's Public Employee Department. However, the largest single public employee organization (with a 1984 membership of 1.7 million) is an independent one, the National Education Association (NEA). In addition, the Teamsters Union* represents some 200,000 public employees, primarily in the field of law enforcement.

These public employee unions not only have grown dramatically in size but have experienced a great change in their essential character. Starting as primarily social and professional organizations, they have become more militant in their dealings with employers. Led by aggressive leaders like Albert Shanker of the AFT, public employee unions have pressed hard for wage increases and have resorted increasingly to strikes (some of which have been illegal) to achieve their purposes. Moreover, the NEA has become increasingly active on the political front, spending large sums of money in federal, state, and local election campaigns in recent years.

Thus organizations providing primarily material benefits for their members have been among the most important interest groups in American society. However, as we shall see, those with essentially "purposive" goals have become more prominent in the United States in recent years.

Public Interest Groups

While citizens' associations and taxpayers' groups have been involved in American politics for a number of years, their effective organizations at the national level can be traced primarily to the late 1960s and early 1970s. Con-

* Officially known as the International Brotherhood of Teamsters, Chauffeurs, Warehousemen and Helpers of America.

sumer advocate Ralph Nader, made famous by his book *Unsafe at Any Speed* (an exposé of safety devices in automobiles), launched a series of investigations into foods and drugs, air and water pollution, nursing homes, banking, pesticides, and other aspects of American life. Staffed initially by idealistic law students and some practicing lawyers (called "Nader's Raiders"), an organization called Public Citizen, Inc. was eventually established to solicit funds in nominal amounts (usually $15) to finance major activities in which Nader and his associates were interested: investigating, exposing, recommending, and, when necessary, litigating, in order to bring about needed changes to protect consumer interests. (Although not a membership organization, Public Citizen, which is headed today by Joan Claybrook, is supported by an estimated 200,000 contributors annually.) Nader was also instrumental in helping to establish Public Interest Research groups on college and university campuses through which students petition to have a portion of the fees paid to their school allocated to the support of representatives to engage in citizen action.

Nader—Public advocate number 1.

Another organization at the forefront of the public interest group movement is Common Cause. Established in 1970 by former Secretary of Health, Education, and Welfare, John Gardner, this association soon gathered substantial contributions from foundations and corporations and a dues-paying membership to finance its activities. Within six months the organization reached its initial goal of 100,000 members; spurred by the public reaction to the Watergate scandal, by early 1974 more than 300,000 Americans joined the organization, whose budget exceeded $6 million. After that crisis subsided, the membership of Common Cause declined somewhat, and the organization, under Fred Wertheimer, is currently maintaining it at a level of 225,000 people.

Common Cause has placed its major emphasis on opening up the political process and making public officials more accountable to the general public. To that end, it has supported disclosure of the sources of campaign financing, the lobbying activities of interest groups, and the personal finances of officeholders. It has also called for "open" meetings of public leaders and the end of closed sessions of legislative committees and secret voting on the floor of Congress. Common Cause has also helped to organize offices in state capitals to pursue the same kinds of reforms in state and local government.

The major focus of Public Citizen has differed from that of Common Cause. Nader's groups have been more inclined than Gardner's to get involved in substantive matters, particularly economic, consumer, and environmental issues. While Common Cause has concentrated most of its activities on Congress and state legislatures, Public Citizen has been very active in supporting the claims of citizen groups in the courts and before executive agencies.

Despite differences in the basic emphasis of the two organizations, the division of labor between them has not been complete, particularly in recent years. Common Cause has supported substantive issues, such as ending the war in Indochina, working for nuclear-arms control, opposing the supersonic transport plane (SST), and more recently, the B-1 bomber; it also has become increasingly active in monitoring executive agencies and litigating in both federal and state courts. On the other hand, Nader and his associates undertook Congress Project, which profiled every member of that body running for re-election in 1972, and one of his current groups, Congress Watch, focuses on issues before the national legislature. In fact, the two organizations occasionally join forces, as they have done recently on tax reform and environmental issues.

Single-Issue Interest Groups

Unlike the previously discussed groups, "single-issue" interest groups focus their activities on one particular problem. While these groups are not new to American politics—witness the actions of such historic organizations as the Anti-Saloon League—they have become particularly assertive in recent years. Many of them are involved in highly controversial social issues such as abortion, busing, and gun control.

Some of the single-issue interest groups are involved not only in controversial issues but also in those involving basic constitutional rights. Frequently, groups that fail to get the Congress, executive agencies, and the courts to support their policy preferences attempt to have the Constitution amended to accomplish their purposes. We shall see later (Chapters 14 and 15) that those opposing court decisions on abortion and busing—as well as women's groups interested in obtaining equal rights with men—have all pursued that strategy.

Moreover, one group—the National Taxpayers Union (NTU)—has sought to have a constitutional convention called to amend the Constitution to require the federal government to operate under a balanced budget.* Established in 1969, the group gained momentum after the passage of "Proposition 13," a California state constitutional amendment passed in 1978 that sharply reduced property taxes in the nation's largest state. Working to get state legislatures to petition Congress for a constitutional convention to enact a budget-balancing amendment, by 1982 the NTU saw 31 of the necessary 34 states taking that action.†

* As we have seen in Chapter 2, that process has never been successfully used so far to initiate a constitutional amendment.

† An alternative to the constitutional convention, of course, would be to have the House and Senate initiate an amendment to accomplish the same purpose. This approach would actually be better for the NTU since it is possible that a constitutional convention might not restrict itself to the budget-balancing issue alone. Pressure from the NTU was in fact calculated to make Congress act on its own precisely to avoid the necessity for calling a convention.

Single-Issue groups.

Ideological Groups

Ideological groups, that is, those based on a concern with fundamental moral and philosophical values, have long been active in the American political scene, for example, the activities of the Women's Christian Temperance Union (WCTU) in support of Prohibition. In the latter part of the 1970s a new conservative force—The "New Christian Right"—first made its influence felt in national politics. Spearheading the movement were a group of fundamentalist Protestant ministers who rallied millions of evangelicals—persons who believe in the literal interpretation of the Bible and its application to everyday living, many of whom report being "born again"—on behalf of moral standards, traditional family values, and "Americanism."

The Christian Right included three major organizations. Christian Voice, started in January 1979 by ministers in California concerned with the "gay" life style and pornography, utilized television minister Pat Robertson's daily "700 Club" to reach listeners, particularly in the West and Southwest. A second group, the Moral Majority, founded in July of that same year by Reverend Jerry Falwell of Falls Church, Virginia, was especially popular with Southern Baptists and Presbyterians in the Sunbelt states. The third group, the Religious Roundtable, was established by Edward McAteer, a field organizer for the Conservative Caucus (a secular political group) to appeal to conservative clergymen who did not feel comfortable with either the Christian Voice or Moral Majority. While there were some differences among the three groups, their "electronic church" used television and radio to reach their supporters, many of whom donated money to these organizations.

A number of political developments led these groups to enter the political arena. Some, such as the possibility of the Federal Communication Commission's banning further licenses for Christian TV and radio stations, and inquiries by the Internal Revenue Service into the fund-raising activities of some of the electronic ministers, constituted direct threats to the Christian Right's own institutional interests. Others related to developments that these groups felt jeopardized basic moral values—the Supreme Court's approval of abortion and disapproval of prayer in the public schools.

The Christian Right found sympathetic allies in battles to protect its own interests, as well as those of society at large. Secular "New Right" activists such as Richard Viguerie, Howard Phillips, and Paul Weinrich helped the ministers organize for political action and trained them in the use of direct-mail techniques to rally their constituencies and raise money. Also helpful were conservative congressional allies such as Republican Senator Jesse Helms of North Carolina who introduced and supported measures in which the New Christian Right were interested.

In 1980 members of the New Christian Right supported the Republican presidential candidate, Ronald Reagan, deserting President Carter, whom many had supported in the 1976 election. They also joined forces with the secular New Right to help defeat several liberal Democratic senators such as George McGovern of South Dakota, Frank Church of Idaho, Birch Bayh of Indiana, John Culver of Iowa, Gaylord Nelson of Wisconsin, and Warren Magnuson of Washington. However, the major items on the Christian Right's social-issues agenda for the Reagan administration, such as the abolition of abortion and the restoration of prayer in the public schools, failed to garner sufficient congressional support. Moreover, the Christian Right and its allies were generally unsuccessful in their ventures into the 1982 congressional elections.

Thus a variety of interest groups in American society pursue different goals through different means. We will examine the nature of these means later in this chapter. First, however, we need to look at another important matter that affects the operation of interest groups: the relationship between the leaders and the regular members of such organizations.

Reverend Jerry Falwell of The Moral Majority.

INTERNAL OPERATION OF INTEREST GROUPS

In theory, at least, interest groups are internally democratic in the sense that the rank-and-file members have a say over policy decisions and the selection of officers.* A small voluntary group operating at the local level takes the form of direct democracy, with its periodic meetings the equivalent of the Greek Assembly or the New England town meeting. Officers serve the group by presiding over such meetings and carrying on the group's activities between them. Interest groups that are important in national politics, however, encompass thousands or even millions of members organized on a nationwide basis. Given their size, these organizations use institutions and procedures of representative democracy that permit a relatively few persons to act for the entire membership.

Most national interest groups have similar means for governing themselves. A national convention attended by delegates chosen at the state and local level usually meets once a year to pass on major policy matters and select the persons responsible for carrying on the activities of the organization between conventions. The latter group generally consists of an executive body composed of elected officials that meets periodically to discuss group affairs. (This body, in turn, often selects a permanent staff headed by an executive secretary, who carries on the day-to-day activities of the organization.) Thus the operating principles of an interest group are democratic in form, and the few who handle the organization's affairs are held responsible to the many through representative institutions and procedures.

As a matter of fact, however, internal governance in most interest groups works in precisely the opposite way: an active minority runs the organization and the rank-and-file members exercise relatively little control over their activities. Conventions held once a year attended by persons who have a limited knowledge of the details of the group's operations can hardly be expected to serve as a meaningful check on the actions of the group's leadership. Typically the convention adopts the leaders' policy proposals with relatively little debate. Elections at the conventions also generally result in acceptance of the leadership's nominees for office. In fact, it is not uncommon for the same persons to be elected year after year without significant opposition. The United Mine Workers, for instance, had no seriously contested election for its presidency for almost half a century—from 1926 until 1969, when the incumbent president, Tony Boyle, beat off a challenge to his leadership by another official of the organization, Joseph Yablonski.† The late George Meany served as president of the AFL–CIO from the time of its establishment in 1955 until he retired in 1979 at the age of 85; he handed over the reins of leadership to another insider, Lane Kirkland, the secretary–treasurer of the organization.

A number of factors contribute to this internal situation. For one thing, the active minority has certain advantages in dealing with the rank-and-file membership. Besides an extensive

* An exception exists in the form of "staff" organizations that have few members or none at all. This is particularly true of public interest groups to which persons contribute financially to support their causes and policies but do not want or expect to participate in their decisions.

† Boyle ultimately lost his presidency in 1973, but only after he was implicated in the murder of Yablonski, which occurred three weeks after the 1969 election; moreover, the federal government stepped in and conducted the 1973 election, which resulted in a victory for Arnold Miller, a candidate of the rank-and-file members of the union.

knowledge of the group's affairs, the experience the leaders gain in office helps them develop managerial and political skills that few regular members can match. They are also in a position to dominate the group's affairs in various ways: by appointing the "right" persons to key committees; by determining what views will be carried in the organization's newspaper (referred to generally as the *house organ*); and by seeing to it that the group's finances are used for the proper purposes. Thus power over personnel, the pen, and the purse enables the officers and staff of most interest groups to control their organization's activities.

Also contributing to the active minority's dominance is the fact that checks and balances are not built into the internal governance of most interest groups. Generally, no organized opposition (like a political party) exists to field a slate of candidates against the incumbent leadership and to criticize what they are doing. (Some groups have regulations forbidding members from conducting campaigns or holding behind-the-scenes meetings to line up support for elected officials; others have an informal understanding that such activities will not occur.) Nor is there a contending group of permanent officeholders present (such as a legislative body) to counter the ambitions of the ruling clique. Thus the concept of competing elites that operates in public democratic bodies is generally absent in private interest groups.

The situation described above characterizes *most* interest groups in the United States, but of course the active minority cannot always control all organizations: the International Typographical Union, for instance, has had two separate groups (or parties) vying for leadership within the organization for years. Moreover, splits sometimes occur within a group's leadership: David McDonald, for many years the president of the Steel Workers of America, ultimately lost his post to another officer of the organization, Walter Abel. Also, an official who threatens the autonomy of local units may also lose his top-level post: James Carey, longtime president of the International Union of Electrical, Radio, and Machine Workers, is reported to have been defeated on that issue in a crucial election.* Nor does the leadership of an interest group succeed entirely in imposing its policies on the rank-and-file membership: not all doctors subscribe to the AMA's fears concerning socialized medicine, for example.

Most interest groups, however, are able to reach substantial agreement on the organization's political goals and policies. The following section discusses the techniques they utilize to try to influence public officials to adopt those policies.

INFLUENCING PUBLIC POLICY

In order to accomplish its primary purpose of influencing public policy, a political interest group seeks **"access"** to official decision-makers; that is, the opportunity to present its point of view to them. For an interest group, however, access means more than mere contact with decision-makers; it also connotes a willingness to consider the group's views, whether or not the official ultimately decides to adopt them.

The process by which interest groups seek access to public officials is called **lobbying.** The term originated in the practice common to interest group rep-

* Carey sought to have union dues deducted from employees' paychecks sent directly to the central organization rather than to the local. Such a procedure would have denied locals the weapon of withholding dues from the central organization if they disagreed with its policies or procedures.

resentatives of frequenting the lobbies of government buildings in order to contact officials. Those who did so were referred to as *lobbyists* and the activity itself became known as *lobbying*.

Political scientist Lester Milbrath, a close student of the subject, defines lobbying as a process by which someone (the lobbyist) communicates with a governmental decision-maker* to try to influence what he or she does (or does *not* do) about a particular matter. Milbrath confines lobbying to communications made on behalf of someone else: a citizen who acts solely in his or her own interest concerning some public policy is not usually considered a lobbyist.

Lobbyists

As Milbrath suggests, interest groups make various arrangements to have their views presented to national officials. Large trade associations and corporations that have offices in Washington typically use their own executive officials as lobbyists, as do national labor unions that are headquartered there. Groups with offices elsewhere must depend on a "Washington representative" to handle their lobbying; the representative normally handles the political affairs of a number of organizations. Some law firms located in Washington not only carry on a standard legal practice before the courts but also represent clients on essentially political matters before legislative and executive officials. In addition, individual "lobbyist–entrepreneurs," who specialize in particular matters not requiring legal expertise, farm out their services to groups on a fee basis. Many founders and leaders of groups with purposive goals (eliminating hand guns, for example) serve as lobbyists for their organization. In 1983, more than 10,000 Washington lobbyists worked to influence governmental policies.

Whatever the arrangement, interest groups look for persons who possess information and skills that make them effective lobbyists. Ex-senators and former members of the House of Representatives (along with former members of their staffs) are knowledgeable about particular legislation, understand the complexities of the legislative process, and enjoy contacts with former colleagues and congressional staff. As former legislators, they have the right to go on the floor of the legislative chambers, a privilege that supposedly gives them an advantage in influencing legislation, particularly at the crucial time of a vote.† Despite these advantages, however, more lobbyists come from the executive than the legislative branch in Washington. The executive has a far larger number of former employees than the latter to draw from, and as we shall see in Chapter 12, more and more crucial decisions are made by administrative officials. Therefore, persons knowledgeable about a given government agency are invaluable to organizations with business before it.

The skills of two professions—law and journalism—are particularly helpful to lobbyists. Lawyers are able to analyze the provisions of legislation as well as executive regulations. Persons trained in writing and public-relations work can utilize those skills effectively to communicate with decision-makers, members of their own organizations,

* Although interest groups seek access to all three branches of government, the means by which they try to influence judges are very different from those they use on legislators and executive officials. We will examine the techniques they utilize with respect to the courts in Chapter 13.

† Former House members, however, are forbidden under a chamber rule to go on the floor if they are in the employ of an organization that is interested in the particular legislation under consideration. By custom, a similar restriction operates in the Senate.

and the general public—all targets of lobbying activities, as we shall see below.

Lobbying is not a profession for which people specifically prepare themselves. Most go into the work by happenstance. Serving a stint as a lobbyist for a business organization is often part of the broad training of executives. Labor lobbyists are typically people who have previously demonstrated their political and verbal skills in union activities. Former employees of the legislative and executive branches are often sought as lobbyists by interest groups that have observed them in their previous capacities.

Even though lobbyists do not specifically prepare themselves for that career, most of them enjoy the work. Particularly rewarding is the sense of accomplishing something for their organization, the opportunity to interact with other people, and the challenge involved in preparing and defending an argument supporting their group's point of view. Pay is also good, particularly for those lobbyists who represent business and professional groups. However, there is a rapid turnover in Washington lobbyists because of the long hours, high pressure, and low prestige associated with their work.

Types of Lobbying

Lobbyists utilize a variety of approaches in communicating viewpoints to decision-makers. Some involve direct contacts with public officials; others utilize intermediaries to try to influence such officials. The former method is called *direct* lobbying, the latter *indirect* lobbying.

Direct Lobbying. Lobbyists who are trying to influence Congress have a variety of options open to them. Since, as we shall see in Chapter 10, the fate of legislative proposals largely depends on the congressional committees that initially consider them, lobbyists appear

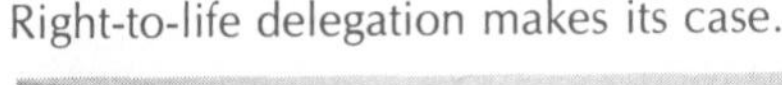

Right-to-life delegation makes its case.

before those committees to express their group's viewpoint on pending legislation. This approach permits the lobbyist to reach a number of influential legislators at one time. It also allows the lobbyist's group to get its views on record, since a transcript of committee hearings is made and distributed to concerned parties (including members of the interest group, who are thus furnished with proof that their lobbyist is working on their behalf).

Lobbyists, however, rate direct personal communications with individual representatives or senators as a more effective technique of persuasion than appearances before committees. Members of Congress are frequently absent from committee meetings, or they have their minds on other matters while testimony is being taken. A personal visit to a legislator ensures attention and is more likely to convey the impression that the lobbyist thinks the individual legislator is important enough to warrant special consultation.

The above techniques are applicable to direct communications with officials of the executive branch, before whom more and more lobbying takes place. Government agencies also hold official hearings to take the testimony of private groups, and lobbyists frequently call on executive officials to discuss the problems of their clients.

Indirect Lobbying. Lobbyists work through intermediaries to try to influence decision-makers. Members of Congress and top executive officials with busy schedules depend heavily on their assistants to keep them briefed on legislative and executive matters. Therefore, lobbyists who are able to persuade staff members of the merits of a client's point of view may be able to reach a

One-on-one lobbying by Common Cause.

major public official through the official's trusted employees.

Lobbyists often find it advantageous to work through other persons who enjoy special relationships with a decision-maker they hope to influence. Personal friends of officials, of course, may provide an entrée, but even more helpful in reaching senators and representatives are their constituents, particularly those who are in a position to affect their political careers. If a lobbyist is able to get a heavy contributor to a legislator's campaign or a newspaper editor who supported that legislator for election to adopt the interest group's point of view and convey it to the elected official, the lobbyist is virtually assured that it will be well received.

Lobbyists frequently use intermediaries to contact members of Congress and executive officials who are not generally sympathetic to their organization's political goals. By working through neutral persons, not only do they avoid rebuffs but they also hope to counteract any prejudice that might prevent their group's case from being examined by public officials on its merits. Lobbyists also use intermediaries as a means of increasing the number of people concerned with a particular issue. By widening their public they seek to increase the political support for (or opposition against) a program of concern to their group.

One natural source of political support for lobbyists is the membership of the organization they represent. Individual members are often unaware of the stands that their lobbyist takes in Washington, but they can be made aware of them through letters from the leadership or the organization's newspaper.* Thus the American Medical Association (AMA) ran stories in its weekly journal for years against "socialized medicine."

Lobbyists frequently enlist the aid of members of groups that they represent to try to influence public officials. One technique is to get persons to write to their legislators or the executive officials involved expressing their views. A flood of mail can serve to alert a decision-maker to the importance an issue has for some segments of the American public. At the same time, the experienced public official is able to detect a contrived letter-writing campaign by such clues as letters with identical wording, those sent on the same day, as well as those coming in disproportionate numbers from a particular area of the country. Wise lobbyists advise members of their organizations to express their views in their own words, and they seek to solicit letters written at different times from various parts of the nation.

Besides letter writing, other possibilities for using group members include getting them to talk to representatives and senators when the latter are back home campaigning or visiting, having individual members call on their legislators when they are in Washington,† and—perhaps most effective of all—calling a conference in the nation's capital to let the lawmakers know firsthand how concerned individuals and groups feel on a particular issue. In some instances these visits to Washington involve dramatic demonstrations: a variety of civil rights and antiwar groups used this tactic in the 1960s as did members of the American Agricultural Movement in the 1970s.

A further broadening of the public

* Many groups also provide their rank-and-file members with information on the extent to which individual legislators vote to support or oppose their positions on legislation in which they are particularly interested.

† A recent technological development with many of the advantages of such a Washington visit is the Chamber of Commerce's "Biznet" telecommunications system that enables subscribing companies to set up a two-way televised meeting with a member of Congress.

involves getting diverse interest groups to join forces in an effort to influence legislators and executive officials on a particular matter. This approach indicates to politicians that an issue is of concern to more than an isolated segment of the public. Groups that join political forces in this way are frequently drawn together as natural economic allies: General Motors, Ford, and Chrysler officials worked together with leaders of the United Auto Workers to delay the imposition of emission standards because, despite their differences over labor–management problems, all of them feared that they would be harmed economically by having to meet the timetable favored by the environmentalists. The range of groups working on arms control that was described at the beginning of the chapter indicates that political coalitions are also important on noneconomic issues.

Beyond immediate interests that lead groups to join forces on a particular issue, there is an increasing tendency for certain organizations with divergent interests to adopt each other's political causes. Thus the Chamber of Commerce of the United States typically sides with the American Farm Bureau Federation on agricultural policy questions, while the latter takes the Chamber's side on business issues before Congress. Similarly, the AFL–CIO and the National Farmers' Union tend to end up on the same side of most political issues. This form of **logrolling,*** or exchange of support has obvious political advantages for all parties concerned, but the practice also develops because members of various interest groups share certain fundamental values and political attitudes. Thus "liberal" organizations like the United Auto Workers, the National Farmers' Union, the Americans for Democratic Action (ADA), and the Federal Council of Churches generally advocate that the national government develop programs to help the disadvantaged. "Conservative" groups such as the National Association of Manufacturers, the American Farm Bureau Federation, the American Legion, and the Young Americans for Freedom prefer that the poor and deprived help themselves, or, if outside assistance is necessary, that it comes from private groups or state and local governments. Such opposing ideologies frequently result in two general constellations of interests—those that support and those that oppose government programs to change the status quo in favor of underdog groups in American society.

Besides rallying the support of members of their own organizations and forming alliances with like-minded groups, lobbyists in recent years have turned their attention to an even more inviting target for indirect lobbying: the general public. If an interest group can make enough people sympathetic to its desires and persuade them to convey their sentiments to those in public office, then it has achieved a major strategic objective: getting other people to lobby for it.

The effort to shape public attitudes on issues takes different forms and involves various strategies and groups. Frequently, lobbyists use members of their own organizations to influence the general public. In the fight against "socialized medicine" some years ago, the leadership of the American Medical Association got doctors to distribute literature and to talk to their patients about the matter. The organization capitalized on the layman's tendency to respect his own physician and to regard him as an expert on health issues. As another technique, the testimony of independent authorities can be presented to

* This term is usually used to describe the practice whereby legislators back each other's bills to their mutual advantage.

persuade the public of the merits of a particular view. Some years ago, when the development of an Antiballistic Missile (ABM) system to be placed around the nation's cities was under consideration, both the pro- and anti-ABM forces used this technique; the American Security Council published a booklet signed by a Nobel-prize-winning chemist supporting the weapon, while the other side countered with a publication by a former science adviser to President Kennedy setting forth his objections to it.

Yet another tactic is to operate through an organization whose name conceals the true identity of its supporters. Some years ago a group called the Small Business Economic Foundation was formed purportedly to speak for the views of the modest entrepreneur. On investigation it was determined that among the small businesses behind the organization were United States Steel, Goodyear Tire and Rubber, the Texas Company (Texaco), and a number of other firms of comparable size. This same attempt to capitalize on symbols to which the public responds favorably* is reflected in the title of an organization called the Committee for Constitutional Government, which was backed primarily by a number of conservative business groups in the United States. It had a counterpart, the Public Affairs Institute, through which liberal groups, particularly certain labor unions, conveyed their views to the public.

Interest groups also use the mass media to transmit ideas in ways that camouflage their true source: letters-to-the-editor columns of newspapers frequently carry statements signed by individuals that in actuality are drafted by lobbyists. A similar practice is the preparation of "canned" editorials. The harried editor of a weekly newspaper who has to handle all aspects of the paper's operation may welcome prepared statements on public issues that make it unnecessary to write original editorials—especially when the material expresses the editor's own viewpoint and is better organized and written than anything his or her busy schedule would permit. (Both parties benefit from such an arrangement: the editor is made to look like a perceptive and critical analyst of public issues, and the interest group gets its views purveyed without the public's knowing their real source.)

Television is another natural outlet for interest groups that seek to shape public attitudes on controversial issues. When President Kennedy outlined his program on medical care for the aged on national networks, a representative from the American Medical Association responded shortly thereafter with the physicians' case against the program. Standing alone in a bare studio, the AMA spokesman sought to convey the image of the solitary citizen battling to preserve his liberties against the organized forces of the national government and the awesome power of the presidency.

Thus lobbying has become increasingly complex and sophisticated over the years as interest-group representatives have directed their efforts at a broader array of targets and utilized a greater variety of techniques in their quest to influence public policy. Whereas communications were once directed essentially to legislators, lobbyists have now broadened their efforts, directing them to the executive branch of government, where more and more key decisions affecting private groups are now being made. At the same time, they have expanded their activities to take in

* An additional advantage in using such titles is the possibility that the organization will be considered an "educational" group by the government, thus qualifying it for certain tax advantages or exempting it from registering under federal legislation regulating lobbying.

"I underestimated the power of the highway lobby in this state."

various intermediaries—including the general public itself—that can assist them in their lobbying efforts. Their techniques have also undergone change as interest groups employ modern methods in influencing public attitudes through mass media.

Along with such changes has come a supplementary activity: keeping communication channels open to decision-makers so that future lobbying will be effective. In other words, lobbyists seek to create good relationships with legislative and executive officials to ensure that their messages will be well-received. They also strive to develop a generally favorable impression with the American people so that they may benefit from that impression when they later try to exert influence on behalf of their group.

Opening Communication Channels

In a democratic society the relationship between public officials and interest groups is a two-way process: private groups not only press demands on officials; they also serve as potential bases of support for such officials. Thus lobbyists can keep communication channels open to lawmakers and members of the executive branch by undertaking activities of value to them.

The most basic support that an interest group can provide any public official is to help him or her get into office in the first place. If the candidate seeks an appointive office, the group's representatives can use whatever political influence they have to see to it that persons responsible for the appointment are made aware of the person's qualifications and the high esteem in which he or she is held by that organization. As we shall see in Chapters 12 and 13, many interest groups become involved in appointments to major executive posts and seats on the federal bench; in the process, they try to persuade the president, who makes the nominations, and the Senate, which must confirm his nominees, to choose those who will be receptive to their organizations' views.

Interest groups are also in a position to provide important political support for a person running for an elected office. This support can take many forms: making financial contributions to the campaign; providing information or writers for political speeches, along with audiences for them; running favorable publicity for the candidate in the house organ, besides endorsing him or her publicly; or helping to get voters registered and to the polls to vote for the candidates. In these respects, an interest group can help the officeseeker in the nomination and/or the general election (analyzed in Chapters 7 and 8). The earlier the group provides a person political support and the more extensive that support, the more likely he or she is to grant access to the representatives of that organization.

Yet there are also political dangers involved for the interest group that commits itself to a would-be official. If he or she fails to be appointed or elected, it is not likely that the group will have access to the opponent. Moreover, it is by no means certain that an organization can deliver its members' votes in an electoral contest: despite organized labor's endorsement of Democratic presidential candidate Jimmy Carter in 1980, many rank-and-file workers voted for his opponent, Ronald Reagan. Or even if a group can persuade its members to support a particular candidate, they may be so widely scattered geographically that they have little impact on the election. The group must also consider the possibility that if it throws its active political support one way, its political enemies may be stimulated to enter the contest on the other side. Thus an organization's representatives must weigh the advantages and disadvantages of active political involvement in support of a particular political party or candidate.*

Whether or not an interest group decides to try to play a role in the selection of public officials, it typically performs important services for those who are already in office. These include the furnishing of factual information and, if the officials desire it, the writing of speeches to be given before their constituents. Lobbyists can also provide officials with ready-made audiences through their own membership and can rally their support for measures favored by the officials. Such services are designed to make public officials grateful and to incline them to be receptive to future lobbying.

Another technique for keeping channels open to public officials is entertainment or the "social lobby." Frequently, the general public is treated to newspaper exposés that play up such socializing as though it were the only form of lobbying. Undoubtedly this tactic is successful with some national officials, yet most of them are so busy that they reserve the few moments they can spare from the pressures of their job for their family and close friends. The social lobby may be more successful in state capitals, where legislators are away from their families during the week and hence have more time for (and less family scrutiny of) social activities.

Lobbyists are frequently pictured as stealthy figures with little black satchels stuffed with money that they disperse as bribes to win favorable decisions from members of Congress and officials of the executive branch. There is little question that bribery does occur at times. In 1956 lobbyists for an oil company were accused of offering Republican Senator Francis Case of South Dakota a $2500 campaign contribution (which he rejected) to influence his vote on a natural-gas bill. Moreover, allegations were made that dairy interests contributed to the 1972 Nixon campaign in return for an administration decision to increase milk prices, and that the International Telephone and Telegraph Corporation (ITT) made a pledge of financial support for the proposed Republican National Convention in 1972 in San Diego (later changed to Miami) in exchange for a favorable settlement of a government antitrust suit against the multinational conglomerate. More recently, Korean businessmen were accused of providing gifts and financial contributions to members of Congress in order to influence governmental decisions regarding their economic interests, and F.B.I. agents, posing as Arab businessmen, were alleged to have bribed several national legislators. However, such instances are the exception rather than the rule; lobbyists who engage in activities of this nature

* One technique employed by some groups is to contribute financially to more than one candidate or to have various leaders or members support different would-be officials. Then, presumably, no matter who wins, the organization has access.

Accused "Abscam" Senator Williams leaves hearing.

run the risk that exposure will ruin their professional reputation as well as damage the interests of their client.

Lobbyists also try to keep communication channels open to the American public in order to shape basic attitudes that are favorable to their respective groups. One approach is to work through the schools to promote particular textbooks; business prefers those that support the free-enterprise system, while labor looks with favor on books that emphasize the dignity of work and the contributions that unions have made to American life. Groups from both camps frequently send materials to teachers for use in the classrooms. Some have gone so far as to subsidize the writing of textbooks favorable to their general point of view on public issues. Another technique is **advocacy advertising,** which seeks to sell a political point of view as well as a commercial product. A recent example of this approach is the advertisement printed on the next page and recently run in the media.

A more subtle way of keeping channels open to the American people is through publicizing activities that reflect credit on a group. A number of years ago certain chain stores in California faced the possibility that a tax on their operations passed by the legislature would be approved in a referendum set for a year later.* A public-relations firm determined that their unfavorable public image could dispose the voters to support the tax. With the assistance of the firm, the stores launched a campaign publicizing a plan to improve their employees' wages and working conditions. They also cooperated with peach growers in helping to absorb an unforeseen surplus of their crop. In addition the chains offered to close their businesses on Sundays if independent stores would do likewise. A poll taken immediately before the referendum indicated a change in public attitude toward the chain stores, and the electorate subsequently voted down the proposed tax decisively.

* Laws passed by legislatures in most states can be referred to the voters for approval or rejection in referendum elections.

An occupational hazard

What promises to be a landmark case in the field of libel law began unfolding in the Federal District Court in New York recently. General William C. Westmoreland, who commanded U.S. forces in Vietnam from 1964 to 1968, is suing CBS for $120 million (which he will donate to charity if he wins), charging he was libeled by the CBS documentary, "The Uncounted Enemy: A Vietnam Deception," shown on January 23, 1982. Other defendants, in addition to CBS, are Mike Wallace, the interviewer on the show; George Crile, the producer; and Samuel A. Adams, a former Central Intelligence Agency analyst who served as a consultant.

We don't know whether CBS and the individuals involved did indeed libel General Westmoreland, nor do we intend to comment on the details of the case. Rather, our concern is with a seemingly ancillary issue we feel actually transcends in importance the case itself—the right of an individual like General Westmoreland to have his day in court, and to be able to present his case fairly without undue legal obstacles to his success.

General Westmoreland had a distinguished 36-year military career. He was an infantry officer in World War II; in Korea he led paratroops, and at 42 was the youngest major general in the Army. He was superintendent of West Point at 46, and wound up his career, after his Vietnam command, as Army Chief of Staff. His service to this country won him the Distinguished Service Medal, Bronze Star, Legion of Merit, and Air Medal. It also won him, during his career, the status of a "public official." What it did not win him was great wealth. Army officers seldom get rich.

So General Westmoreland, feeling that the reputation he had established during 36 years of public service had been left in tatters by the telecast, turned to the courts for redress. In doing so, he faced two major hurdles:

- The U.S. Supreme Court has ruled that public officials and public figures (generals, mayors, congressmen, prominent businessmen and actors have been held to fit these categories) must prove, in libel cases, that the statements made about them were false. They must also prove that the parties defaming them did so knowing the statements were false or made "with reckless disregard" of whether they were false or not. This is a much greater burden of proof than the ordinary citizen has, who is only required to prove negligent falsity.
- The General's second obstacle was the nature of his opponent—a major corporation with deep pockets (presumably including libel insurance) well able to afford teams of lawyers and other counsel. Legal expenses in the case have so far totaled almost $4 million.

Representing General Westmoreland is the Capital Legal Foundation, a public-interest law firm supported largely by grants from foundations and individuals. We don't know if their resources are adequate to provide General Westmoreland with the kind of representation to which he—and any other citizen—is entitled. We understand that private citizens, Vietnam veterans' organizations (with which General Westmoreland is not associated), and foundations have contributed to the Capital Legal Foundation's efforts on his behalf. If you wish to join this effort, send a check to the foundation at 700 E Street, S.E., Washington, D.C. 20003.

But what about other public officials, some of whom serve in relatively humble posts? Their positions may make them ready targets for libel, but the heavy burden of proof they face makes them second-class citizens.

How to make justice more readily attainable? In the best of all possible worlds, the U.S. Supreme Court would redefine the standards it applies to public officials and public figures. Other industrialized nations, such as the United Kingdom, don't apply such heavy burdens of proof in libel cases. But in the practical world, why not simply recognize that public officials face an occupational hazard—libel? And why not deal with it just as we deal with so many other hazards of the workplace?

Employers now provide medical insurance, dental insurance, workmen's compensation insurance, and disability insurance. We believe all public officials—generals, admirals, firemen, police officers, rubbish collectors—should be covered by insurance to allow them to sue for libel. Perhaps the employers should pay the premium (we at Mobil have taken out such insurance on behalf of key employees). Or perhaps the system should be government-financed, since the government, through its judicial arm, has stripped public officials of some of their civil rights.

No one should have the rights of citizenship diminished because he plays an active role in the system. That should be the lasting lesson of the Westmoreland case.

Mobil

Many interest groups today do not wait for an issue to develop before attempting to shape public attitudes; they rather work constantly to create a reservoir of goodwill toward their organizations from which they can draw when the occasion arises. Public-relations personnel see to it that favorable publicity about a group's members is released: when business executives and labor leaders head Red Cross drives and United Fund campaigns or offer their services voluntarily in building a Boy Scout camp or fixing up a church, news of their philanthropic activities is not hidden under a bushel but is displayed widely to the American people. Thus groups seek to keep the channels open to the general public as a means of ensuring that when they want to lobby on issues that concern them, their communications will fall on receptive ears.

Legal Regulation of Lobbying

Lobbying is regarded in the United States as a legitimate method for influencing public policy. It has been granted constitutional sanction as coming within the basic rights of free speech and petition guaranteed by the First and Fourteenth amendments to the Constitution. Congress has, however, placed two types of restriction on lobbying: (1) certain limits on the kinds of activities interest groups may engage in and (2) requirements that lobbyists and organizations disclose their identity as well as certain basic facts about their operations.

One type of lobbying that is clearly considered beyond the rules of the game is bribery. Federal laws make it a crime for people to offer a member of Congress "anything of value" for the purpose of buying a vote or otherwise trying to influence his or her official actions. Legislators who accept such offers are also subject to criminal charges. The difficulty with enforcing the law is that it is almost impossible to prove that a favor was tendered for the purpose forbidden by the act. (For example, it does not constitute bribery for a lobbyist to promise a member of Congress future political support in order to influence his or her vote on legislation.) Most students of the subject consider this legislation ineffective in preventing questionable dealings between interest-group representatives and members of Congress.

The role of lobbies in making financial contributions to political campaigns is limited by law. We will explore the subject of campaign finance in Chapters 7 and 8, provisions affecting both the nomination and election of candidates. It is sufficient for the present to note that certain organizations (foreign governments, for instance) are prohibited from making campaign contributions in federal elections and other groups face limitations on the amount of their contributions.

With these exceptions, interest groups are free to lobby at will. But Congress has taken the position that its members, as well as the American people, have the right to know who is supporting and opposing legislation and that financial arrangements of lobbyists and interest groups with business before the national legislature ought to be a matter of public record. Thus lobbying activities are not prohibited but illuminated.

Although lobbyists for certain groups were singled out by Congress in the 1930s and made to disclose information about themselves and their clients (included were lobbyists for public-utility holding companies and shipping firms as well as those representing foreign governments), it was not until 1946 that a law was passed requiring similar information of lobbyists and interest groups in general. Enacted as part of a broad statute dealing with the reorganization of Congress, the Federal Regulation of Lobbying Act requires any person (or group) hired by someone else for the "principal purpose" of influencing congressional legislation to register with the Secretary of the Senate and the Clerk of the House and file quarterly reports—on receipts and expenditures for lobbying—with the House Clerk. Organizations that collect money to engage in such activities but do not hire themselves out as lobbyists for someone else are required to file similar financial information with the Clerk of the House.

It is generally agreed that the law contains so many loopholes that it has not been effective. Groups ostensibly affected by the act avoid its application by arguing either that they spend their own funds for lobbying rather than soliciting them from outside sources or that the outside funds they collect are not raised for the "principal purpose" of influencing Congress. Lobbying directed to executive agencies or the general public is not covered by the law, nor is testifying before legislative committees.

The law also leaves it up to groups themselves to determine the portion of their total lobbying expenditures that needs to be reported; as a result, organizations with large financial outlays claim to spend very little, arguing that most of it goes for research and public information (which are not covered by the statute) rather than direct personal contact with legislators. Finally even the information that is reported is almost worthless, since no agency is empowered either to investigate its truthfulness or to ensure that violations of the law are enforced. Until such time as these deficiencies are rectified (to date, Congress has been unwilling to correct them),* the act will fail to accomplish its major objective—disclosure of activities of major lobbyists and interest groups in the United States.

Despite the lack of effective legal regulation of lobbying, however, Washington observers agree that most persons tend to respect certain informal rules of the game. Aside from matters of individual conscience, lobbyists naturally desire to protect their reputations with their colleagues and, even more importantly, with public officials. Lobbyists who provide false information to officials and are found out will certainly lose the very thing they work so hard to achieve: access to those officials. In all probability the officials will also tell others of their unfortunate experience, so that such lobbyists will find themselves cut off from a number of important persons who make vital decisions affecting their groups. Thus the denial of access is a powerful deterrent to lobbyists who may be tempted to engage in improper activities in seeking to influence public decisions.

* Both houses of Congress passed bills in 1976 to revise the 1946 law, but the session adjourned before they could agree on the specifics of the proposed legislation. (Only Common Cause, Nader's Congress Watch, and the AFL–CIO among the major interest groups supported the revision.) Subsequent attempts to change the law have also failed.

ASSESSMENT

Interest groups clearly make a valuable contribution to the American political system. By channeling citizens' demands to those in positions of public authority, they inform leaders on what people in various segments of our society think about important public issues. They also educate officials by providing them with factual information and arguments relating to vital issues. Although each interest group naturally presents its own side, legislative and executive officials are able to examine a wide range of views and can balance the merits of one against another in making decisions.

One major weakness in American interest groups is that not everyone benefits equally from them. Well-educated persons from the upper social classes are more inclined to join organizations than the less educated and the poor. Beyond the matter of representation, business and professional organizations have more financial resources to spend on lobbying than other interest groups. They also benefit from their prestige and the deference accorded their members by officeholders and the general public as well. The result is that upper- and middle-class Americans are more likely to have their demands satisfied than less-advantaged persons.

Yet the have-nots in American society are better organized today than they were in the past. A number of interest groups representing blacks, Hispanics, welfare mothers, tenants, and the like have been formed in recent years—a development that has helped to close the organizational gap between the advantaged and the disadvantaged. What these groups lack in the way of financial resources is at least partly compensated for by their numbers and the efficacy of direct-action techniques such as political protest marches and sit-ins. Moreover, these groups have been aided by the sympathy that many people in public office, as well as significant elements of the American public, have for their claims. (Also, many Americans have worked actively with such groups to help them organize for political action.) The outcome has been the enactment of a number of laws benefiting socially and economically disadvantaged persons.

Another encouraging development is the rise of public interest groups such as Public Citizen, Inc. and Common Cause. These groups have succeeded in involving many citizens who have not been politically active in the past. They have also been well received by the public: 49 percent of the respondents in a 1973 Harris poll expressed the view that ". . . groups of citizens and organizations are having more effect in getting government to get things done, compared with five years ago." It remains to be seen how much staying power public interest groups demonstrate, but despite a high turnover in the memberships of both Public Citizen, Inc. and Common Cause, both organizations have generally been able through effective recruiting campaigns to replace departing members with new persons willing to support their activities. By aiming their efforts at a limited number of issues, both groups have been able to develop more political muscle than many veteran observers of the Washington scene thought was possible for citizens' lobbies.

Single-issue interest groups articulate the particular concerns that trouble a growing number of Americans. In doing so, they help to implement the First Amendment freedom of people to petition the government for the redress of their grievances. At the same time, such groups present major problems of governance for public officials who must work out accommodations among the controversial demands made by persons who are unwilling to compromise their stands on a highly emotional issue and who judge such officials solely by how they vote on that one issue.

Another major aspect of interest groups that deserves comment is their internal operation. The form of their governance is democratic but the practice is oligarchical. Members typically have little control over their leaders, and competing internal elites do not frustrate one another's ambitions.

There are, of course, certain political advantages in that situation. Long-term leaders who are knowledgeable and experienced about group affairs are able to represent the interests of the members in the political arena effectively. Being cohesive and disciplined also assists an organization in combating its political rivals and in speaking with a united voice.

The danger in the internal situation, however, is that group leaders will pursue their own interests rather than those of the general membership. This has happened, for example, in certain labor unions where officers have misused moneys (especially in the administration of pension funds) and have also made arrangements with employers that benefited them but not the rank-and-file members. In some instances, moreover, group leaders promote political goals that have little appeal for the general membership.

Describing the problem of the internal governance of interest groups is much easier than figuring out ways to improve it. It seems unrealistic to expect such organizations to develop opposition candidates, together with other institutions and techniques that operate in public bodies; almost none has done so to date. Government regulation of certain aspects of internal governance—such as requiring disclosure of financial affairs and ensuring that elections of officers are honest—has been utilized, especially with respect to labor unions. Even so, there are limits to how much public authorities should intervene in the affairs of private organizations in a democracy.

There are, however, some mitigating circumstances. Rival organizations do exist in some instances, so that those who are not satisfied that the leadership of one organization is adequately representing their interests can join another. Furthermore, as the following chapters indicate, demands and preferences can be channeled to decision-makers through agencies and means besides interest groups, such as political parties and elections.

SELECTED READINGS

An excellent analysis of the arms-control lobby appears in *Spring 1983 Guide to Current American Government* (Washington, D.C.: Congressional Quarterly Inc., 1983), p. 68*f*.

A classic study of interest groups is David Truman, *The Governmental Process: Political Interests and Public Opinion* (New York: Alfred A. Knopf, 1951). Three very good recent treatments of the subject are Jeffrey Berry, *The Interest Group Society* (Boston: Little, Brown, 1984); Allan Cigler and Burdett Loomis (eds.), *Interest Group Politics* (Washington, D.C.: Congressional Quarterly Inc., 1983); and Ronald Hrebenar and Ruth Scott, *Interest Group Politics in America* (Englewood Cliffs, N.J.: Prentice–Hall, 1982).

Peter Clark and James Q. Wilson discuss the basic inducements for joining organizations in "Incentive Systems: A Theory of Organizations," *Administrative Science Quarterly* (1961): 129–66; Robert Salisbury attributes the formation of many interest groups to the entrepreneurial activities of their founders in "An Exchange Theory of Interest Groups," *Midwest Journal of Political Science* 13 (1969): 1–32. Other good general treatments of the subject include Terry Moe, *The Organization of Interests: Incentives and Internal Dynamics of Political Interest Groups* (Chicago: University of Chicago Press, 1980); Mancur Olson, *The Logic of Collective Action* (Cambridge: Harvard University Press, 1965); and James Q. Wilson, *Political Organizations*, (New York: Basic Books, 1973).

For an excellent account of the New Christian Right, see James Guth, "The Politics of the Christian Right," which appears as Chapter 3 in the volume edited by Cigler and Loomis cited above.

For an analysis of the internal operation of interest groups in terms of democratic theory, see Grant McConnell, "The Spirit of Private Government," *The American Political Science Review* 52 (1958): 754–70. Two excellent studies of the internal operation of specific interest groups are Oliver Garceau, *The Political Life of the American Medical Association* (Cambridge: Harvard University Press, 1941), and Seymour Martin Lipset, Martin Trow, and James S. Coleman, *Union Democracy: The Internal Politics of the International Typographical Union* (New York: Free Press, 1956). The former discusses the methods by which the leadership of the American Medical Association dominates its affairs; the latter examines the unusual "two-party" system of the ITU that offers the rank-and-file membership a choice between two groups of leaders.

The best empirical study of the characteristics of lobbyists who operate in the nation's capital and the means they use to communicate their desires to members of Congress is Lester W. Milbrath, *The Washington Lobbyists* (Chicago: Rand McNally, 1963). A good analysis of group activities in the nation's capital that includes some interesting case studies of lobbying on recent issues is *The Washington Lobby* (Washington, D.C.: Congressional Quarterly Inc., 4th ed., 1982). Another inside look at the practical aspects of lobbying in Washington is Lewis Dexter's *How Organizations are Represented in Washington* (Indianapolis: Bobbs–Merrill, 1969).

Two books that stress the contributions of interest groups to American democracy are those by Truman and Milbrath cited above. Critical of the narrow perspectives of such groups are E. E. Schattschneider, *The Semisovereign People: A Realist's View of Democracy in America* (New York: Holt, Rinehart and Winston, 1960), Grant McConnell, *Private Power and American Democracy* (New York: Alfred A. Knopf, 1966), and Theodore Lowi, *The End of Liberalism: Ideology, Policy, and the Crisis of Public Authority* (New York: W. W. Norton, 1969).

Ford '76
OUR 38th PRESIDENT
AUGUST 9th, 1974
President Ford
NORCROSS for U.S. SENATE
BETTY'S HUSBAND FOR PRESIDENT in '76
AVALON, N.J.

CHAPTER 6

Political Parties

In September 1796, six months before the end of his second term as president, George Washington announced to the American people his decision to eliminate himself as a candidate in the upcoming election. His famous Farewell Address set forth his hopes and fears for the young republic. What troubled Washington most was the possibility that it would be destroyed by the " . . . baneful effects of the spirit of party." For he saw parties, particularly those based on geographical divisions, as a threat to both national unity and popular government.

Almost two centuries later, at the end of the turbulent 1960s, a Gallup poll of American college students revealed the same mistrust of political parties. As Table 6.1 indicates, political parties ranked lowest of nine major American institutions in the estimation of the students. Statistically, not even one student in five rated political parties excellent or good, compared to two out of three who were favorably disposed towards universities. For a college generation not known for its satisfaction with institutions of higher learning, the poll pointed up how critical students were of political parties.

Nor did unfavorable student attitudes towards political parties disappear when American politics became calmer in the mid-1970s. In a Gallup poll published in September 1975, only 15 percent of college students were "highly favorable" to the Democratic party. Their attitude towards the Republican party was even more negative. Only 7 percent of the students were "highly favorable" to the GOP compared to 10 percent that were "highly unfavorable" to it; moreover, of the 11 basic American institutions and groups about which they were questioned, only one, the Students for a Democratic Society, ranked below the Republican party. Even the Pentagon was regarded more favorably than the GOP! The negative attitudes of the college students towards both parties were

Table 6.1
How Students Rate American Institutions

Institutions	Responses (in Percentages)		
	Excellent	Good	Total Favorable
Universities	12	56	68
Family	23	35	58
Business	12	44	56
Congress	7	49	56
Courts	6	40	46
Police	6	34	40
High schools	4	33	37
Organized religion	7	26	33
Political parties	2	16	18

SOURCE: The Newsweek Poll—The Gallup Organization, *Newsweek* (29 December, 1969), p. 43.

reflected in the fact that over half of them—52 percent—declared themselves to be Independents.

That vocal and critical young people of the 1960s and 1970s* would find themselves in agreement on a key political matter with the nation's chief father figure—a charter member of the American Establishment—is perhaps ironical. What is even more ironical is that despite Washington's attitude, the first democratic political parties in the world developed right here in the United States. In fact, they were already in existence at the time of the Farewell Address. Moreover, they have persisted: the Democratic party, indeed, is the world's oldest political party. Further, as Chapter 9 reveals, most Americans today identify with either the Republican or the Democratic party.

Such conflicting attitudes indicate that the national experience with parties has been ambivalent. Americans created a major political institution that exists in all democratic societies in the world, yet many Americans have great misgivings about its value. Why this is so is not clear, but exploring a number of questions may help to explain the situation: what is a political party and what part should it play in the governance of a free society? what are the major characteristics of political parties in the United States? what have they actually contributed to the political system and American society in general?

* While there were no comparable Gallup polls in the early 1980s of attitudes of college students as such, one taken in March 1981 showed that among college-educated persons, only 15 percent were "very favorable" towards the Democratic party while 14 percent felt the same about the Republican party.

THE NATURE OF POLITICAL PARTIES

Students of government have experienced as much difficulty in defining a *political party* as they have had explaining what is meant by *political culture*. Particularly confusing is the failure of political scientists to identify the specific features of a political party that distinguish it from other political agencies linking the general public to political officials.

Political Parties, Interest Groups, and Factions

The writings of some of the Founders illustrate the same problems of definition. In Federalist paper No. 10, Madison uses three separate terms to describe divisions in society. One is *faction*, a concept we explored in some detail in Chapter 2. Another is *interest*, which he calls the most durable source of factions, using as illustrations a manufacturing interest, a mercantile interest, and the like. Elsewhere in the same selection the Father of the Constitution refers to the conflict of rival *parties*. Washington's Farewell Address is similarly vague: his condemnation of the "spirit of party" seems to reflect an unhappiness with the general state of divisiveness and bickering among citizens rather than an attempt to single out a particular kind of political agency—the party—for criticism.

A student of government today has different things in mind when he or she uses these three terms. A political party is a group of persons that run candidates for public office under a label. It is this activity that distinguishes a party from an "interest," or what we today call an *interest group*. Members of the latter care about who holds office and may try to influence voters' decisions: business groups tend to support Republican candidates who they feel are generally sympathetic to their policies, while labor unions favor Democratic ones for the same reason. But neither group offers its name to persons seeking office: no one runs under the banner of the United States Chamber of Commerce or the AFL–CIO.

Frequently, if inaccurately, political parties are distinguished from interest groups on other grounds, such as the number of persons associated with each. Typically, political parties attract more supporters than interest groups: far more people identify with either the Republican or the Democratic party in the United States than belong to the Chamber of Commerce or the AFL–CIO. But the same is not true of minor political parties. Only about 13,300 people voted for the Workers' World presidential candidate in 1980 compared with the more than 14-million Americans who belonged to the nation's largest labor organization that year.

Nor can political parties necessarily be distinguished from interest groups on the basis of their *purposes*. Not all political parties have the capture of public office as their primary goal. Witness the succession of minor parties that have appeared from time to time in American politics. Although some members of these parties undoubtedly thought that their candidates had a chance to win, most members have worked through these organizations as a means of registering their political demands. They have reasoned that even if their party could not win, because of the publicity given its goals during the course of the campaign or the electoral threat posed to the two major parties, their demands might receive more attention than if they worked only through interest groups. As we shall see, many of the policy proposals of minor parties have eventually been adopted by officeholders and the major parties, evidence that the political calculations of minor-party backers have been vindicated.

On the other hand, not everyone who supports a political party does so because of its policies. Many people develop a psychological attachment to a particular party at an early age and, as discussed in Chapter 9, back its candidates without regard to their stand on issues. Some persons participate in party activities because they expect to be rewarded with some concrete benefit, such as a job or other political favor. Others enjoy the excitement of party activities or the social contacts.

In brief, the crucial factor that distinguishes a political party from an interest group is neither its size nor its purpose; it is rather the *method* each chooses to make its influence felt in the political arena—a political party is the only organization that runs candidates for office under its label.

It is also necessary to distinguish a political party from a *faction*. Historically, factions preceded political parties; they were groups of persons who joined together on an ad hoc basis to win some political advantage for themselves. Thus certain people in England worked as a group to influence the king or control Parliament. After the advent of elections to choose public officials, factions formed around particular persons or families (such as the Clintons in New York State). In the days of a restricted electorate and relatively few elective offices, these factions were able to control elections fairly effectively. However, as a greater number of people gained the right to vote, and more and more offices became elective, and the political arena was broadened to include a greater diversity of social groups, it became necessary to organize electoral efforts more extensively and to place them on a more permanent basis. Particularly important was the task of identifying candidates so that voters could tell who represented which group. It was then that factions took the crucial step that turned them into political parties: running candidates for office under a common label.

The term *faction* is still used today, primarily to designate groups that are part of a larger political entity. Sometimes it is employed to describe portions of an interest group, such as the two groups vying for control of the International Typographical Union described in the last chapter. More often, the term is used to designate some group within a political party based on a particular personality, philosophy, or geographical region. Thus we speak of the Daley faction of the Illinois Democratic party (after the late powerful mayor of Chicago), the conservative faction of the Republican party, or the southern faction of the Democratic party. In this sense *faction* is synonymous with *division* or *wing*.

A faction typically centers on some political personality, local political elite, or occasionally a particular political issue. Factions generally lack the features of a major political party—a permanent, well-organized structure and a symbolic relationship with their followers—that enable parties to transcend particular personalities or issues. For this reason factions are less likely to persist over a series of elections than are parties.* They also frequently operate behind the scenes rather than out in the open because they lack the legitimacy of political parties in that people are not willing to grant them the right to run candidates for office. In any event, they do not run candidates for public office under a given label—the hallmark of a political party.

Membership in American Political Parties

Another difficulty in dealing with political parties is the problem of identifying its members. Most Americans do not go through the formality of joining a political party and paying dues as is common in interest groups and many European political parties. Thus the Socialist party of France or the American Farm Bureau Federation of the United States can state that it has so many members, but the Republican and Democratic parties cannot. When we speak of those who belong to our two major parties, whom are we talking about?

One way to decide who should be considered a member of a party is to

* Exceptions do exist, however, particularly in certain Southern states. For instance, former senators Harry Byrd of Virginia and Huey Long of Louisiana dominated the politics of their states for years; even after they died, their respective followers continued to be associated as members of the Byrd and Long factions.

determine the ways in which various individuals are involved in the kinds of party activities discussed in Chapter 4. We could start with the following general categories:

1. *Party leaders.* Those who hold major positions in the party, such as the chairperson and members of the national, state, or local committee.

2. *Activists.* Those who work extensively in party affairs, raising money, recruiting candidates, making speeches for candidates, attending rallies, and canvassing voters.

3. *Supporters.* Those who support the organization by donating money to the party or its candidates and displaying labels, buttons, and bumper stickers.

4. *Voters and Identifiers.* Those who regularly vote for the party's candidates in elections or who, when asked, say that they consider themselves Republicans or Democrats.

Although this approach does make some important distinctions, it has some major limitations. First, the somewhat arbitrary categories may not reflect the actual influence various persons have in party affairs. Many activists, for example, swing more actual weight in party matters than those in formal party positions. Second, the realities of political life are such that no one remains in a category on a permanent basis: a person may become an activist in one election because of his or her interest in a particular candidate or issue, whereas in the next contest the same person may be merely a supporter or an ordinary voter. In which group should this person then be placed? Finally the categories do not include everyone who is associated with a party. The prime example is a senator, representative, state legislator, or executive official. Although a person in one of those positions does not hold an official party post, he or she is elected under the party label or is appointed to his or her position primarily because of his or her relationship to a particular party. Moreover, in the course of official activities this person is expected to reflect the views of his or her party. The person may thus be considered a party representative.

Aware of such difficulties, V. O. Key and Frank Sorauf identify three major divisions of political parties associated with different activities and different people who participate in them. They are:

1. The **party organization**. Those who are active in party affairs, whether they hold an official party post or not. These are the individuals who carry on the major campaign activities of the party, contributing their time, money, skills, and effort.

2. The **party in the government**. Those who hold official positions in the legislative and executive branches and, as indicated above, are considered to be party representatives.

3. The **party in the electorate**. Those who have a more casual relationship with the party—the supporters, voters, and identifiers.

These categories point up a major characteristic of political parties: they are broad-based and undertake a variety of activities. As the next section indicates, they also appeal to individuals for a variety of reasons.

INCENTIVES FOR JOINING POLITICAL PARTIES

The general incentives for belonging to political parties are similar to those previously described for interest groups: *material benefits, solidary benefits, and purposive benefits*. Political scientist James Q. Wilson has divided those participating

One of the last of the political professionals: Mayor Richard Daley.

The Kingfish: Huey Long.

in political party activities into two major categories: those whose incentives are primarily material and social in nature are known as **professionals,** while those who primarily pursue purposive goals are called **amateurs.** As indicated below, these two types of party activists also differ on other matters, such as the role of compromise in political disputes, whether or not political patronage should be used to reward those who help the party, and how political parties should be governed internally.

Party *professionals* are primarily in politics because they want something tangible for themselves such as a patronage job or a government contract, or because they like to exercise control over other persons' lives, or enjoy the deference paid to them by others because of the position they hold or the power they wield. They also tend to enjoy the game of politics for its own sake—the quest of victory, the maneuvering for advantage, and the camaraderie of working and socializing with other people in the political party.

The major goal of professionals is to win elections rather than to see to it that political programs or policies, such as better health care, environmental protection, and racial integration, are enacted into law. They may personally favor a particular program, but they evaluate it primarily in terms of its attracting political support; if such a program threatens to cost the party an electoral victory, professionals will not hesitate to change the program to meet objections or abandon it altogether. Professionals understand the importance of compromise in political affairs and are tolerant toward those who differ with them on political matters. As far as the internal affairs of the political party are concerned, professionals expect it to be oligarchical in nature, with the people in top positions in the organization deciding how it should be run.

The prototype of a party organization run by professionals was the old-time political **"machine"** dominated by a "boss," such as James Curley of Boston, Ed Crump of Memphis, Frank Hague of Jersey City, Tom Pendergast of Kansas City, Huey Long of Louisiana, and Gene Talmadge of Georgia. The arrangement between the boss and the people who supported him was reciprocal. The boss used his influence to see to it that his supporters or members of their families or friends were given public jobs or lucrative government contracts, that they received loans or gifts when they were in financial difficulties, a turkey at Thanksgiving or Christmas, or help when they got into trouble with the police. The political organization also sponsored picnics, beer parties, and other events for their supporters, many of whom were immigrants looking for new friends and outlets for their social interests. In return, the boss received votes from the recipients of his largesse, political contributions from those on the public payroll (usually a certain percentage of their salary, known as a "**lug**"), and **"kickbacks"** from those with government contracts.

In contrast, as Wilson suggests, political *amateurs* are persons who find politics intrinsically interesting because it expresses a concept of the public interest. They are thus concerned not with using political parties to further their own interests, but to help other individuals or groups or society in general. They believe in certain principles and values (such as racial equality or free enterprise), and are dedicated to seeing to it that those principles and values are implemented by public programs and policies.

This devotion to principle means that winning elections is not the primary goal of political amateurs. While they would, of course, prefer to be on the winning side, they will only back candidates who stand for the "right" things; it is better to support a loser who espouses their principles than a winner who does not. Unlike professionals, amateurs will not compromise their principles or even their favorite programs; rather, as political scientists Nelson Polsby and Aaron Wildavsky suggest, they are "purists" who believe that purism outside office is better than power inside government.

Amateurs also differ from professionals in other respects. Their purism makes them intolerant of persons who differ with them on political matters. Even if parties or candidates agree with political amateurs on most issues, that is not sufficient; they must prove themselves on *every* issue in order to be worthy of support. Moreover, political amateurs are very much opposed to patronage; they believe that people should participate in party activities out of a concern for the public interest, not for the sake of personal benefits. Finally, amateurs believe in internal party democracy; they are suspicious of strong party leaders and want rank-and-file members to have a major voice in the operations of political parties.

Wilson traces the development of organizations of amateurs to the political clubs formed in New York City, Chicago, and Los Angeles in the 1950s. Although these clubs operated at the city level, many of the persons that helped to establish them were drawn into politics originally by the presidential candidacy of Adlai Stevenson in 1952; moreover, many of the issues in which these amateurs were interested were national rather than local in nature. Since then political amateurs have been closely associated with presidential candidates in both parties, including liberals who worked for Democrats Eugene McCarthy in 1968 and George McGovern in 1972, and conservatives who backed Republicans Barry Goldwater in 1964 and Ronald Reagan in 1976 and 1980. Thus political amateurs represent both ends of the political spectrum.

It should be realized, however, that the political professional and the political amateur are "pure" or "ideal" types, and it is doubtful whether any individual or organization fits either category completely.* Few so-called professionals are totally disinterested in political programs, and few amateurs will refuse to compromise on any occasion. Also, a person's motivations for participating in political parties can change over time; studies indicate that some who first become politically active as amateurs eventually adopt the goals and techniques of political professionals. Nonetheless, it is possible to distinguish the major political orientation of many persons or organizations as essentially professional or amateur in nature. Moreover, as indicated at the end of this chapter, assessments of American political parties often turn on whether they are judged by the standards of a political professional or an amateur.

FUNCTIONS OF POLITICAL PARTIES

What do parties do? Some of their functions are specific and observable, such as recruiting candidates. Other functions are general and intangible, such as contributing to the peaceful settlement of disputes in society. A party's action may have a very specific intention, as when it runs a candidate with a particular ethnic background for office in order to attract the votes of members of that ethnic group. Yet a given action may also have a significant byproduct—

* It should be noted that the traditional political machine, epitomizing the "professional" organization, has largely disappeared in the United States in recent years, the exception being the Daley organization in Chicago. It remains to be seen whether Daley's successors can retain control over the politics of that community.

in this example, giving members of the minority group a feeling of importance, a sense of belonging to the society, and an allegiance to its government. In talking about party functions we must also distinguish between things that parties *should* do, if they operate according to democratic theory (as discussed in Chapter 1), and the things that they *actually succeed in accomplishing*. We must also delineate those functions that are characteristic of all parties compared to those that are peculiar to only some.

One function that all parties perform is running candidates for public office under their label. Sometimes party leaders themselves actually go out and induce people to become candidates. Political candidates are also recruited in other ways, however. A person may be approached by an interest group, another officeholder, or acquaintances to seek public office. Or one may be a self-starter, deciding on his own to become a candidate. Ultimately, however, one must run under some party label if one hopes for any success, at least in national and most state elections.*

In addition to providing political leaders, parties take the initiative in policy matters. The dominant party in particular helps to identify the major problems—social, economic, and political—that require the attention of the citizens of a society. As President Kennedy stated, it is the responsibility of these party leaders to lay the unfinished business of America before its people for

* Many local elections are nonpartisan in the sense that no label appears on the ballot. Judges in some states and state legislators in Nebraska are also elected in this way. The rationale behind nonpartisan elections is that by removing party labels from the ballot, "politics" is removed from the selection process. Studies indicate, however, that the political affiliations of the candidates are known by many voters anyway; moreover, removing party labels from the ballot does not eliminate politics—it merely *changes* the politics so that interest groups and newspapers (rather than the traditional parties) become influential in recruiting and backing candidates.

discussion and action. Besides setting an agenda, party leaders have the obligation of recommending specific programs to help mitigate the problems that they have identified.

Leaders of the party in the government also have the responsibility of using their influence to see that policies are implemented. The majority party organizes the legislative and executive branches of government so that the programs it favors can be enacted into law. The minority party has the function of criticizing the programs of the majority and proposing alternative solutions to problems.

Thus the major functions of political parties relate to three aspects of the political process: providing leadership through participation in elections; identifying problems and proposing programs to deal with them; and organizing and managing the government. There is little question that, of the three, the first is paramount. It is also the function on which American political parties have concentrated. Our two major political parties have been somewhat less concerned than European political parties, for example, with developing concrete social programs; they have also been less successful in organizing the legislative and executive branches of government to enact party programs into law.

Minor American political parties have also been deficient in regard to these latter two aspects of the political process. Although a variety of them have developed specific proposals for dealing with particular problems (witness their plans for outlawing alcoholic beverages, dealing with currency problems, giving relief to the farmer, and controlling the trusts),* they have not dealt with the broad range of issues demanding public attention. Nor have third parties performed the governing function. They have lacked the power to organize the political branches, and in most cases, their representation has been so limited that they have not even been able to effectively criticize the proposals of the major parties.

These activities of political parties produce certain side effects that benefit individuals, groups, and the entire society of a democratic nation. The party helps to structure the voting choice of many citizens. As we shall see in Chapter 9, many persons are unwilling to put in the time and effort to study the issues and the candidates' stands on them. Nor are they generally familiar with the background and abilities of the aspirants for public office. Lacking such information, some voters find it difficult to cast their ballots. For them the party serves as a point of reference, a guide to the best-qualified candidate and the one most likely to approach problems from their own general point of view. As imprecise as such guidelines are, they nonetheless provide clues for distinguishing the "good guys" from the "bad guys" in a large number of American electoral races.

For some the party serves as more than a point of reference in voting; it also helps to meet their economic, po-

First Republican convention at Jackson, Michigan, July 6, 1854.

* One 1980 presidential candidate ran on a "Down with Lawyers" ticket and received 1718 votes!

litical, and social needs. The classic case is the previously mentioned American political machine of the latter part of the last century and early years of the present century; whatever else can be said of it, the machine helped assimilate immigrants into American society by furnishing them with the necessities of life, finding them jobs, educating and socializing them in the ways of our political system, and sponsoring social activities for them. Few persons today in the United States are so dependent on party organizations or receive so many benefits from them; nonetheless, many continue to derive substantial satisfactions—psychological, social, and economic—from participating in party affairs.

Like interest groups, political parties also channel the views and demands of individuals and groups to public officials. Rather than *articulate* particular desires as interest groups do, major political parties *aggregate* multiple demands, that is, combine them and accommodate their differences. Parties do so because if they hope to win power at the polls (some minor parties may not), they must develop broad-based programs that appeal to a wide variety of groups. Working out accommodations among diverse—and at times conflicting—demands of various groups enables the party to satisfy enough people to win control of key governmental positions.

Finally, the activities of political parties contribute to the stability of the political system and the larger society. A personal identification with and commitment to a political party helps create a sense of allegiance to the government. The process whereby parties reconcile and accommodate a broad spectrum of views and demands assists in the settlement of conflicts in society and the development of significant areas of agreement among citizens of various backgrounds and perspectives. The creation of such a consensus, in turn, permits political parties to provide and citizens to accept the most basic feature of a democratic society: the pursuit and maintenance of political power by peaceful means and, when the populace desires it, the transfer of that power into other hands.

These, then, are the functions of political parties. We cannot say that all parties discharge them equally well; in fact some parties do not perform a number of these functions at all. Nor are political parties the only organizations that carry on such activities: interest groups, factions, and ad hoc groups also participate in recruiting candidates, organizing campaigns, and proposing public policies. It is even conceivable that a democratic society might not need political parties at all or that other institutions might be developed instead. The fact remains, however, that no democratic nation has ever done so; all have depended on political parties to perform these vital functions. The remainder of this chapter focuses on the oldest party system in the world: our own.

THE DEVELOPMENT OF AMERICAN POLITICAL PARTIES

If there was any one matter on which the political leaders discussed in Chapter 2 agreed, it was that the nation should not divide itself into warring political camps. Madison and Washington were particularly concerned lest divisions imperil the national unity at a time when the young republic was fighting for its very existence against disruptive forces of geographic and economic rivalries. Hamilton, who had little faith in the common man (at one time he told Jefferson that the "people" were a "great beast"), quite naturally had no use for political organizations that would enable the public at large to influence decisions that he felt were better

This Federalist cartoon of 1793 shows the Republicans as a band of lawless cutthroats keeping company with the Devil. Jefferson is shown standing on a bench and ranting wildly.

left to persons of superior intellect and training. Even Jefferson, who did place great trust in the masses and their ability to be educated politically, did not regard parties favorably: he declared in 1789 that "If I could not go to heaven but with a party, I would not go there at all." Instead he assumed that political officials would respond to currents of public opinion without the necessity of channeling public attitudes through political parties. Yet within less than a decade after the creation of the national government under the Constitution that they all favored, all four became key figures in the establishment of rival political parties.

What precipitated the formation of the two parties was the economic program that Hamilton, as the first Secretary of the Treasury in the Washington administration, proposed to the Congress in 1790. Designed to promote manufacturing and commerce and to place the new government on a sound financial basis, the plan called for a number of controversial measures, including the assumption by the national government of debts owed by the states as well as the creation of a national bank. Madison, who was serving in the Congress, opposed the assumption of debts on the grounds that many southern states had already paid theirs off and should not be taxed to help satisfy the obligations of northern states. Jefferson, who was serving in the Washington administration as Secretary of State, worked out a political compromise whereby the debts would be assumed by the national government in return for the location of the capital in the South (what was to become Washington, D. C.). But Jefferson was unwilling to consent to the creation of a national bank (he regarded it as a dangerous monopoly that would benefit only mercantile interests, not the farmers for whom he had great admiration) and joined forces with Madison in trying to defeat the proposal in the Congress. Hamilton's supporters prevailed, however, and the bank was authorized in 1791.

A number of other domestic issues contributed to the growing split between the former political allies. Hamilton's economic program called for financial measures that clearly favored the industrial sections of the nation: a tax on foreign goods (a tariff) was levied not only to raise revenue for the national government but to protect American manufacturers and merchants from foreign competition. Farmers who purchased manufactured goods bore the brunt of the tax since prices on foreign commodities were raised to cover the amount of the tariff. Even more vexing to them was the excise tax on liquor. While Eastern distillers could pass on the tax to their consumers, it was a direct levy on farmers who made liquor for their own use. Some frontiersmen in western Pennsylvania refused to pay the tax, intimidated government collectors, and dealt drastically with those who assisted revenue officers. Ultimately, an insurrection known as the Whiskey Rebellion broke out there in 1794, and Washington sent a military force over the Alleghenies to put down this threat to the legitimacy of the new government.

While domestic economic concerns thus contributed to a growing split between the contending forces, ideology and foreign policy widened the cleavage. The eruption of the French Revolution in 1789, coupled with the outbreak of hostilities between the new revolutionary regime and Great Britain some four years later, polarized Americans. The followers of Jefferson viewed the French Revolution as a logical extension of our own, with the common people of both nations removing the political yoke of the upper classes. Hamiltonians agreed with the British statesman Edmund Burke that the stability of society was threatened by the excesses of the French mob. Hamilton's belief that the affairs of state should be entrusted to the national aristocracy was completely at odds with Jefferson's faith in the basic equality of man and his disdain for the nobility.

Injected into this general ideological climate was the highly controversial agreement negotiated with the British in 1794 by the Washington administration. Although the Jay treaty (so-named because John Jay was the American negotiator) settled some major controversies with the British (they agreed, for example, to withdraw troops from forts in the Northwest), it failed to satisfy two basic American grievances: the lack of compensation for slaves that the British had carried away during the Revolution and the impressment into British service of American sailors who were serving on ships that the British seized for trading with the French. Overnight the treaty became the target of bitter attacks by the anti-Hamiltonians (their favorite curse was "Damn John Jay! Damn everyone who won't damn John Jay! Damn everyone who won't put out lights in his windows and sit up all night damning John Jay!"), and it was necessary to throw the great prestige of Washington into the political battle to win its approval in 1795.

Out of this series of controversies over domestic issues, ideology, and foreign policy, the Federalist and Republican parties were born. The former, with Hamilton as the initiator of policies and Washington as the popular leader around whom men could be rallied, had formed by the early 1790s and soon had candidates running for Congress under its label and voting in the legislature in favor of the Hamiltonian programs. Jefferson's resignation from the Washington administration at the end of 1793 over the national bank issue paved the way for the establishment of the opposition, who came to be known as the Republicans. Although Jefferson returned to his home in Monticello, Madison remained in the Congress and organized the party so well that by the middle of the decade an anti-administration block in the Congress was voting together consistently; soon congressional candidates were being identified with the party as well. With the retirement of Washington at the end of his second term, the party rivalry spread to presidential politics when Adams, the Federalist candidate, narrowly defeated Jefferson, the Republican, in 1796.

During the next four years the partisan battle became even more intense. Direct taxes were levied on the three major property sources of farmers who supported the Republican party—land, houses, and slaves. The passage of the Alien and Sedition laws and their partisan application against Republicans (particularly newspaper editors) by Federalist judges served to deepen the partisan schism in the young nation. The stage was thus set for the crucial presidential election of 1800, in which the Republican ticket of Jefferson and Burr decisively defeated the Federalist team of Adams and Charles Pinckney at the polls; and the Republicans gained control of both the Senate and the House of Representatives.

Thus, within a decade, the United States had gone through crucial stages of political development. Many had viewed Washington as a "patriot king" who would rule in the interests of all the people, but it soon became apparent that there were major differences among groups that could not be settled by a neutral political figure, no matter how fair-minded or popular. It also soon became apparent that traditional electoral organizations—factions based on local or state political personalities—would not be sufficient to capture control of the Congress and the presidency: to sponsor and help identify candidates for the growing electorate, permanent, visible, and broadly based organizations would have to be created. So the world's first democratic political parties were established in the United States. When the Federalists, however grudgingly, relinquished control of the national government to the Republicans in 1800, another political first was achieved: the peaceful transfer of power from one party to another. Orderly, nonviolent competition has continued to characterize the American party system ever since.

GENERAL NATURE OF PARTY COMPETITION

Political scientists distinguish three types of electoral situations: one-party, two-party, and multiparty. In the first, representatives of one political party hold all or almost all the major offices in the government. This condition may prevail where only one party is legally permitted to run candidates—as in Nazi Germany and Fascist Italy between the two world wars and the People's Republic of China and the Soviet Union today—or where opposition parties are legally recognized but, for one reason or another, only one party is successful in election contests—as in Mexico, where the Institutional Revolutionary party has won election after election for some 50 years despite the fact that other groups like the National Action party run opposition candidates. In the United States the Democratic party held a similar monopoly in most Southern states from the end of the Reconstruction period following the Civil War until recently. In a one-party system, if electoral competition exists, it involves only factions within the dominant party.

Under a two-party system, two and only two political parties have a reasonable chance of controlling major political offices. Both parties seek total political power, but neither is able to eliminate its rival at the ballot box. Each party is capable of capturing enough public positions to govern, but the opposition party continues to draw a sufficiently large vote to threaten the party in power. The result is that those in control of the various governments must take public wishes and sentiments into account lest they lose out to the opposition party at the next election. Moreover, the system works best if the opposition threat is realized from time to time, so that the two parties alternate in governing at reasonable intervals of time. According to Leon Epstein, a student of comparative political parties, only six nations have two-party systems: Australia, Austria, Canada, Great Britain, New Zealand, and the United States.

Under a multiparty system, three or more parties compete effectively for political offices, and none of them expects to win control of the government on its own. Rather, representatives of a combination of parties share the major positions of public authority. Generally, multiparty systems operate in countries with a parliamentary form of government, where the legislative body chooses the major leaders of the executive branch. Typically, a coalition is formed of parties that together control a majority of the seats in the legislature; these parties in turn divide up the cabinet seats among people from their respective organizations. Examples of nations with a multiparty system are France and Italy.

Only the one- and two-party systems have operated to any significant extent in the United States. Minor or **"third" parties*** have appeared from time to

---

* This is the term typically used for minor American parties, but it would be more precise to designate them as "third," "fourth," or "fifth" parties, depending on their relative electoral strength.

time, but they have had relatively little success in winning political office, particularly at the national level. Yet, as the discussion later in this chapter indicates, they have nonetheless had some important political effects in the United States.

French Socialist Party Leader Francois Mitterand.

AMERICAN PARTY COMPETITION AT THE NATIONAL LEVEL

The Historical Record

As we have seen, the United States had an operating two-party system within a few years of its establishment. Although the Federalist Adams edged out the Republican Jefferson for the presidency in 1796 and his party also managed to win control of the House of Representatives (at that time senators were chosen by state legislatures), the Republicans swept them from power in both branches in 1800. After that crucial election, the Federalist party continued to operate nationally for the next decade and a half, but it never again gained control of either the presidency or the House. The demise of the party has been ascribed to a number of causes: the split in the party organization created by differences between Adams and Hamilton; an elitist political philosophy

The Republican candidate of 1872.

The Republican campaign of 1888.

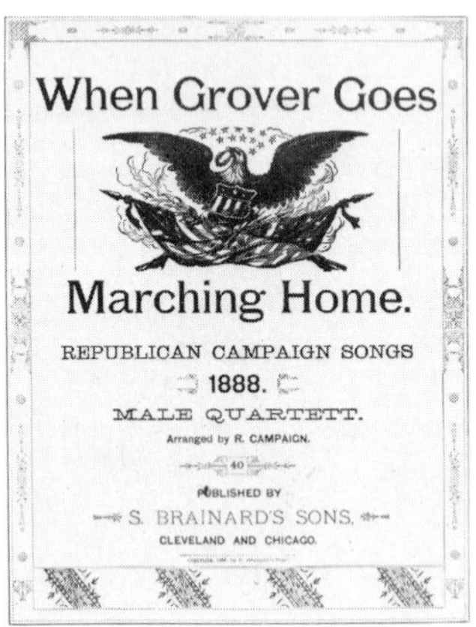

that prevented Federalist leaders from expanding membership to less-advantaged persons and organizing at the grass-roots level; the pro-British attitude of many Federalists (particularly in New England) during the War of 1812, which served to associate the party with disloyalty to the nation. The party disappeared completely from the national scene around 1816.

There then followed a period of one-party government. This so-called "era of good feeling" culminated in James Monroe's almost unanimous election as president in 1820. After that, however, competition broke out within the Republican party as "factions" formed around John Quincy Adams and Andrew Jackson. Gradually these factions developed into genuine parties: the followers of Adams became known as the National Republicans and those of Jackson as the Democratic Republicans. In the late 1830s, the National Republican party was replaced by the Whigs; when in 1840 the Whig candidate, William Henry Harrison, defeated the incumbent President Martin Van Buren (who ran under the label of the Democratic, rather than Democratic Republican party), true two-party competition returned. It continued into the middle 1850s when the Whig party disappeared, only to be succeeded by another group, the Republican party, which ran its first presidential candidate, General John Fremont, in 1856. Since that date, the Democratic and Republican parties have dominated American politics in the oldest continuous two-party competition in the world.

The Republican and Democratic rivalry over the years clearly meets the requirements of a two-party system. In the period from 1856 through 1982, the Republicans were successful in 19 presidential elections and the Democrats in 13. The competition every two years for control of the House of Representatives has also been relatively close: the Democrats have won 38 elections and the Republicans 26. In this century alone, the results are also fairly close: through 1980, the Republicans captured the White House on 11 occasions and the Democrats on 10; in the same period the Democrats enjoyed a 29–13 edge in contests for the control of the lower branch of Congress. Thus both Republicans and Democrats have been able to win political power in both the executive and legislative branches of the government.

Besides winning control of the national government, both parties have managed in defeat to win a substantial portion of the popular vote. "Landslide" presidential elections—those in which the winning candidate gets more than 60 percent of the vote—have occurred only four times in this century: Warren Harding's victory in 1920, Franklin Roosevelt's in 1936, Lyndon Johnson's in 1964, and Richard Nixon's in 1972. Contests for the House of Representatives since 1900 have been even closer. Only twice has the losing party received less than 40 percent of the vote—the Democrats in 1920 and the Republicans in 1936.

As for the alternation of parties in power, the record has been mixed. In their century-long rivalry, the Republicans and Democrats have generally been able to oust each other from office at fairly frequent intervals, although there have been some notable eras of one-party dominance. The newly formed Republican party controlled the presidency from Lincoln's election in 1860 until Cleveland won the office for the Democrats in 1884. The latter party, in turn, held the office over a 20-year span from 1933 until 1953, with Franklin Roosevelt's four consecutive victories followed by Truman's upset victory in 1948.

There have also been several periods of one-party control of the House of Representatives. The Republicans maintained extended majorities on three separate occasions: 1859–1875; 1895–1911; and 1917–1931. In turn, the Democrats have dominated the chamber in recent years, from 1933–1947 and again since 1955; in fact, they have been in control of the House for 48 of the 50 years from 1933 to 1983, being out of power from only 1947 to 1949 and 1953 to 1955. Thus if one were to focus only on the recent situation in the House of Representatives from the standpoint of party control of that chamber (the same general condition has prevailed in the Senate during this period, although the Republicans did control the Senate in 1980 and 1982), it would be proper to refer to the congressional electoral system as a one-party Democratic one.

However, on balance, the American system at the national level must be considered a two-party affair. The near-equality of Republican and Democratic victories over many years' time, the fairly close division of the popular votes, and the considerable degree of alternation in power—particularly for the presidency—place the system in the two-party category.

Reasons for the National Two-Party System

Political scientists have long puzzled over the question of why a given country has a one-, two-, or multiparty system. There is no ready answer because it is difficult, if not impossible, to demonstrate that certain social, economic, or political conditions actually "cause" the formation and operation of a given party arrangement. Yet it is possible to investigate the kinds of conditions that are associated with particular party systems and to deduce logical reasons for these associations.

Historical Factors. One reason for the original formation of the system was the early division into two general groups over political issues facing the young nation. As we saw in Chapter 2, two broad constellations of interests appeared in the battle over the Constitution: the Federalists representing the manufacturers, merchants, shipowners, and commercial farmers—all of whom were dependent on trade for their livelihood; the anti-Federalists speaking for the subsistence farmers, artisans, and mechanics—who were not dependent. This same general split persisted over the Hamiltonian economic program, with the commercial classes rallying to its support and agricultural interests generally opposing it.* This basic breach widened further when the large landowners (who supported the Constitution and Hamilton's early program) subsequently became disenchanted with the Federalists because the Jay treaty provided them with no compensation for the slaves the British carried away during the Revolution. Thus the two parties, the Federalists and the Republicans, represented two disparate groups: the former, the business and commercial elements of the nation that tended to be concentrated in the North, particularly along the coasts; the latter, the agricultural interests that predominated in the South and the interior along the "frontier."

Two broad constellations of interests have continued to characterize our party division. In the period of Jacksonian democracy, the Western-frontier forces were allied against Eastern monied interests. As the slavery issue became more salient, the East–West schism was replaced by a new sectionalism arising from conflicts between the

* Not all individuals, however, followed this pattern: Madison and Jefferson supported the Constitution, but founded the Republican party. Still, most proconstitutionalist leaders supported the Federalist party, while the anticonstitutionalists typically became Republicans.

The Republican campaign of 1900.

The Democratic campaign of 1932.

Promotional display for Republican campaign of 1932.

The Democratic campaign of 1952.

North and South. This cleavage, based on the different economies of the two regions (the industrial Northeast versus the more rural South), the memories of the Civil War, and the problems of race, persisted through the first third of this century. In fact, the period from the Civil War until the 1920s was characterized by *sectional* politics—the Republican party based in the Northeast and the Democrats in the South, with both vying for the support of the West and Midwest, which held the balance of political power.

Beginning in the late 1920s a new dimension was introduced into American politics by increasing urbanization. This development caused a breakup of sectional unity as industry increasingly located in the West and South. The result was the development of *class* politics, as the Republicans gathered the support of the upper and upper-middle economic groups, while the working class, together with ethnic groups (especially immigrants from central and southern Europe and their children) and blacks (who had traditionally been wedded to the Republicans since the Civil War), increasingly moved into the Democratic camp. The pattern continues to prevail today, but it is further complicated by the re-emergence of race as a major issue in American politics: more Southerners, together with some working-class whites and ethnics, have begun to cast their votes in presidential elections for Republican candidates (whom they perceive as being less pro-black than Northeastern and Western Democrats).

This historical sketch of party divisions is admittedly simplified (we will examine the nuances and complexities of voting patterns in more depth in Chapter 9), but it does indicate that the two parties have been able to develop broad coalitions and that between them they have managed to absorb and aggregate the major interests in our society. Unlike many European nations, we have not developed a number of major parties, each representing a fairly narrow range of groups and concerns.

Consensus. Another factor that has contributed to the American two-party system is the considerable consensus that has existed on the fundamental goals of our society and the major means of reaching these goals. Most Americans have shared the views of Locke and Madison on the importance of individual self-development, including the right to acquire private property. There has been little sentiment for vesting the ownership of the means of production in public ownership, a common goal elsewhere. This being so, the dispute between the parties has focused not on whether there should be private property or not, but on how it should be distributed. The Republicans have tended to represent the interests of the haves and the Democrats the have-nots who want to become haves. Certainly this division has not been absolute, but as historian Charles Beard expressed the idea some years ago, "The center of gravity of wealth is on the Republican side, while the center of poverty is on the Democratic side."

Agreement on fundamentals extends beyond economic matters to political and social concerns as well. Thus Americans are committed not only to the private enterprise system but also to our basic political institutions. No sizable group has ever advocated another form of government, such as monarchy, which many Frenchmen have proposed over the years. Because a feudal system never existed in the United States, there has been no aristocratic social class to establish an oligarchy in order to protect its privileges, as happened in other countries. Finally, the religious divisions that have plagued many societies and spawned a variety of parties have not played a meaningful role in American politics.* As will be discussed in Chapter 14, the early decision to separate matters of church and state has generally prevented that result here.

This agreement on fundamentals has meant that American society has not been rent by the variety of basic cleavages—economic, political, and social—around which multiple parties have clustered in other nations. Keeping religion generally out of politics, for example, has meant the absence of Catholic and Protestant parties or groups supporting and opposing the subsidizing of religious institutions, an issue that has divided parties in France and Italy. Nor have we had significant monarchist or socialist parties. Instead American parties have generally split on only one significant issue—how economic goods and privileges should be allocated among the population—and two parties have been sufficient to represent most of the views on that issue.

The economic nature of party differences has also made compromise possible in the American political system. Although individuals may not see eye to eye on the matter of who should have how much of the good things of life, conflicts in viewpoint are not irreconcilable. The issue is not an either-or proposition; everyone can receive something in terms of material comforts. Our great natural resources and expanding economy have made it possible to distribute economic benefits to ever more people without threatening the interests of those who already have considerable possessions. Few major groups have found it necessary to go outside our two major parties to protect their economic interests.

Very recently, however, some of the basic consensus in American society has begun to erode as issues have expanded beyond economic matters to racial and cultural concerns as well. As we shall see in Chapter 9, these developments have left our traditional two-party situation in a highly uncertain state at the present time.

Electoral Rules. The rules of the democratic game are seldom, if ever, neutral; they tend to favor some interests over others. One factor that has permitted the American two-party system to survive—and, indeed, to flourish—is that certain features of our electoral system give the major parties advantages over third parties. We will examine the electoral process in detail in Chapter 8; for the moment it will be sufficient to note the points most relevant to our party system.

The way we elect our president favors a two-party system. In nations with a parliamentary form of government under which the chief executive (the prime minister or premier) is chosen by the national legislative body, a minority party can become a part of a coalition that controls a majority of the legislative seats and may have one of its leaders chosen for the post. As will be explained in detail in Chapter 8, however, to win the American presidency a candidate must win a majority of the electoral votes, which means that he must have a large proportion of the popular vote. Third parties do not achieve that success; consequently they have not survived. A party that cannot capture control of the highest office—the presidency—cannot be a major force in the nation's politics.

Our method of electing representatives also favors the two major parties. Although most states elect several representatives to the House of Representatives (in the 1980s only Alaska, Delaware, Vermont, and Wyoming sent one), they are not chosen under a sys-

The campaign of 1960.

* While religion has sometimes been injected into political campaigns, particular churches and parties have not generally been closely linked.

"The old labels just don't seem to mean much anymore."

The Republican campaign of 1964.

tem of multimember constituencies and proportional representation as in many European countries. Under that electoral system, voters select a number of representatives, and the seats are allocated to the parties on the basis of their share of the popular vote. If, for example, Indiana, which is entitled to 10 members in the House of Representatives, used such a system, a minor party that won 20 percent of the popular vote would have two of its candidates sitting in Washington. Under the single-member district method used by Indiana and other states, it is divided into 10 separate House districts and voters cast their ballots only for the representative of their particular area. The winner is the contestant who gains a plurality of the votes (that is, more than any other candidate) for that district. Under this arrangement a minor party whose candidate draws 20 percent of the popular vote in any or all the 10 districts does not gain any representation in Washington, since under our two-party system that proportion would not constitute a plurality of votes. As with the presidential contest, our single-member-district-plurality method for choosing representatives operates under a winner-take-all principle; thus losing minor parties receive no electoral rewards for their efforts.

Two other types of electoral rules favor major parties over minor ones. Candidates from the former automatically appear on the ballot while those representing the latter must satisfy state laws that typically require that they file for office by a certain time prior to the election and that they obtain signatures of voters on their candidacy petition. In addition, as discussed in Chapter 8, presidential nominees of the two major parties receive full financing of their general election campaign while those representing minor parties receive only partial financing or none at all.

Natural Perpetuation of the Two-Party System. One final factor that supports the two-party system in the United States is that certain built-in mechanisms tend to make it self-perpetuating. As we saw in Chapter 4, children develop an attachment to a political party at an early age. This psychological identification, which they acquire primarily from their parents, tends to deepen during their adult lives. In a society where the two major political parties have been dominant for over a century, the citizens in overwhelming proportion naturally learn to think of themselves as Republican and Democratic. In other words, traditional party patterns, plus the political–socialization process by which attitudes are passed on from one generation to another, combine to perpetuate the two-party system in the United States.

Our two-party system also serves to concentrate the political leadership of the nation in the Republican and Democratic parties. Persons aspiring to political positions know that unless they can use one of these labels, they have little chance of succeeding in their quest for public office. Thus political talent is attracted towards the two major parties and away from minor parties, which typically back losing candidates.

The two-party system also perpetuates itself by channeling political conflict into two major outlets, the organization in power and the one out of power. Support for and opposition to the government and what it is doing tends to polarize around two distinct (party) groups. Under this arrangement citizens who are unhappy about the current state of affairs not only vote against the present officeholders but give their support to candidates of the other major party, which serves as the only real political alternative to the party in power.

But while the American national party system is clearly a two-party one, minor parties continue to exist in the United States. Although they have never captured a significant number of national offices, they have nonetheless had considerable impact on American politics—enough so that it is worthwhile to consider their record in some detail.

Campaign memorabilia: 1968.

The Democratic campaign of 1972.

MINOR AMERICAN PARTIES

There has been a wide variety of minor or third parties in American history. Some, like the Anti-Masonic party of the 1830s, contested a single presidential election and disappeared almost immediately from the political landscape. Others, like the Socialist party, have fielded candidates in a hopeless electoral cause over a number of years. Some, such as the Independent candidacy of John Anderson in 1980, are vehicles for individuals who run for the presidency; others, such as the Progressives of the early part of this century, seek offices at various levels of our political system. The Prohibition party has zeroed in on what members regard as the tragic flaw in the national well-being, while the Communist party has sought to overhaul the entire economic and political structure of a basically "decadent" society. The Progressives of the early part of this century genuinely expected to capture key offices and succeeded to some extent; the leaders of the Vegetarian party have accepted political realities and run presidential candidates for publicity. But despite these differences, minor parties have one thing in common: a feeling that certain values and interests are not being properly represented by the two major parties.

Campaign poster of the Greenback Party.

Goals and Types of Minor Parties

Some of the minor parties have promoted ideologies that are entirely foreign to the nation's traditional beliefs—notably the parties that were introduced into the United States from Europe but failed to adapt to our essentially free-enterprise economic environment. Included in this general category are the Socialist party, which advocates public ownership of basic industries but is satisfied with moving toward its goal gradually through the workings of parliamentary democracy; the Socialist Labor party, which also seeks to eliminate the capitalist system through essentially peaceful, but not too clearly defined, means; and the American Communist party, with traditionally close ties to the Soviet Union, which has not ruled out violence as a method to bring about a classless society.

Of the three, the Socialist Labor party has been the most long-lived, running presidential and vice-presidential candidates in every election from 1896 through 1976. On the other hand, the Socialist party has been by far the greatest vote-getter, polling close to a million votes in 1912, the first election in which it competed, and combining with the Progressive party in 1924 to give their joint candidate, Robert La Follette, almost 5 million votes. After 1932, however, it never again commanded a significant electoral following and ceased running presidential candidates regularly from 1956 to 1976, when it once again began to field candidates. Meanwhile, the forays of the Communist party into American electoral politics has been both sporadic and uniformly hopeless.*

* The party ran presidential candidates from 1924 through 1940 and again since 1968. Its highest vote total was 100,000 in 1932 (compared to Franklin Roosevelt's 23,000,000); in 1980 its supporters numbered some 45,000.

The most successful minor parties in the United States have, like the Marxist ones, protested economic injustices. Rather than tracing their origins and ideologies to foreign sources, however, they have been indigenous and proposed programs that remain within the American consensus of a free-enterprise system. Included in this category are two groups of the past century: the Greenback party, which ran candidates in the 1870s, and the Populists, which came into prominence in the 1890s. The former called for assistance to debtor farmers by issuing more cheap paper money; the latter proposed an expansion of the money supply in the form of free and unlimited coinage of silver along with gold at a ratio of 16:1, as well as a graduated income tax, the public ownership of railroads, and other measures designed to break the financial hold of the industrial East over the producers of raw materials in the West and South.

Twentieth-century minor parties have continued this tradition of sounding the call for reform while staying within basic institutions to achieve them. In 1912 former Republican president Theodore Roosevelt headed the Progressive party, which attacked abuses of both economic and political power in the United States. To correct the former, the party proposed governmental control of monopolies; for the latter, it urged adoption of such "direct democracy" devices as the **initiative** (allowing citizens to propose legislation), the **referendum** (referring laws to the voters for an ultimate decision), and the **recall** (permitting citizens to oust unsatisfactory officeholders between elections). Later on, as we have seen, another minor party adopted the label of the Progressives and joined the Socialists in backing Robert La Follette for president in 1924. This group's concern for the problems of the farmer paralleled that of the Populist party a quarter-century

Form of Sample Ballot containing the names of the Presidential Electors, as they will appear on the Official Ballot that each voter will receive on Election Day

In order to vote for HARDING and COOLIDGE, MARK THE OFFICIAL BALLOT PRECISELY AS THIS BALLOT IS MARKED, with a cross X mark in the CIRCLE under the EMBLEM OF THE REPUBLICAN PARTY.

You need make no other mark. Mark only with a pencil having BLACK LEAD.

If you tear, or deface, or wrongly mark the ballot handed you in your polling place on Election Day, RETURN IT AND OBTAIN ANOTHER.

Do this and vote out of power the inefficient, extravagant and autocratic Wilson Administration.

REMEMBER THAT YOU WILL BE HANDED THREE BALLOTS ON ELECTION DAY, one ballot containing the names of your STATE AND LOCAL CANDIDATES; another the PRESIDENTIAL ELECTORS, and A SEPARATE BALLOT FOR THE PROPOSED CONSTITUTIONAL AMENDMENTS

				INDEPENDENT NOMINATIONS.	INDEPENDENT NOMINATIONS.	BLANK COLUMN.
						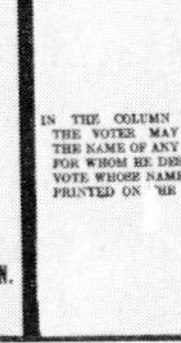 IN THE COLUMN BELOW, THE VOTER MAY WRITE THE NAME OF ANY PERSON FOR WHOM HE DESIRES TO VOTE WHOSE NAME IS NOT PRINTED ON THE BALLOT.
○	(X)	○	○	○	○	
DEMOCRATIC PARTY. For President, JAMES M. COX. For Vice-President, FRANKLIN D. ROOSEVELT.	REPUBLICAN PARTY. For President, WARREN G. HARDING. For Vice-President, CALVIN COOLIDGE.	SOCIALIST PARTY. For President, EUGENE VICTOR DEBS. For Vice-President, SEYMOUR STEDMAN.	PROHIBITION PARTY. For President, AARON S. WATKINS For Vice-President, D. LEIGH COLVIN.	SOCIAL LABOR PARTY. For President WILLIAM W. COX. For Vice-President, AUGUST GILLHAUS.	FARMER-LABOR PARTY. For President, PARLEY P. CHRISTENSEN. For Vice-President, MAX S. HAYES.	

earlier, but in addition it spoke for the laboring person who wanted the right to organize. Thus the two Progressive parties of the first quarter of this century* expanded economic protest beyond the rural areas of the West and South to the urban areas of the Northeast.

The race issue has also recently spawned some new developments in party competition. In 1948 a group of dissident Southern Democrats walked out of their party's presidential nominating convention over the issue of civil rights, formed a States' Rights Democratic party (Dixiecrat party), and nominated J. Strom Thurmond of South Carolina and Fielding Wright of Mississippi as president and vice president. Rather than use that label on the ballot for the selection of presidential electors (this matter will be explained in detail in Chapter 8), they chose instead to offer them as the "official" Democratic nominees in Alabama, Louisiana, Mississippi, and South Carolina, a tactic that paid off with victories in those four states. Twenty years later a third party with similar views on the race issue headed by George Wallace ran candidates under the label of the American Independent party. Although its candidates, Wallace and vice-presidential nominee Curtis LeMay, appeared on the ballot in all 50 states, they prevailed in only five—Alabama, Arkansas, Georgia, Louisiana, and Mississippi.

* Still another party using this name ran Henry Wallace for president in 1948. Its major emphasis, however, was on foreign affairs—in particular, a more conciliatory policy toward the Soviet Union.

Socialist party campaign poster of 1904.

THE FACTORS OF THE GREENBACK-LABOR-SOCIALIST-WOMAN-SUFFRAGE PARTY.

Effects of Minor Parties

At first blush one might conclude that third parties have been of little significance in American politics. Judged by the major criterion for evaluating parties—namely, their electoral victories—the record of such parties could hardly be less impressive. None has won the major prize in the American political system, the presidency, and few have even managed to capture much in the way of other national political offices (the most successful, the Populists, won a few seats in the House). Generally speaking, they fail to win any electoral votes at all in the presidential election (the most earned was Roosevelt's 88 in the 1912 election). Since the Civil War only four have gained more than 10 percent of the popular vote for President: the Populists in 1892, the Progressives in 1912, the Progressives in 1924, and the American Independent party in 1968.

The significance of minor parties, however, is greater if they are viewed from another perspective: the effect

1912 Progressive Party Candidate, Teddy Roosevelt.

they have had on the two major parties in the United States. In some instances, such as the presidential election of 1912, their presence on the ballot contributed to taking victory from one party and giving it to another. Even though this may not have been the only reason for Taft's defeat in 1912, it certainly was a major factor in bringing a Democratic candidate into the White House for the first time since the early 1890s. In other instances minor parties have made a difference in individual states where the vote between the candidates of the two leading parties was close. Richard Nixon's popular-vote margin over Hubert Humphrey was less than the size of the vote for George Wallace in no fewer than 17 states in 1968. In 1976 votes cast for third-party candidates (primarily Eugene McCarthy) were greater than the winning candidate's plurality in ten states. (Of the ten, Ford prevailed in eight and Carter in two.) Many observers also believe that if McCarthy had succeeded in getting on the ballot in New York State, he would have drained away enough votes from Carter to have given the state to Ford. Had that happened and the state's 41 electoral votes been cast for Ford instead of Carter, the incumbent president would have won the election.

Besides affecting the division of the vote at election time, minor parties frequently have an impact on the general policy orientation of the major parties. One of the two may clearly borrow the ideas of a third party—as in 1896 when the Democrats under William Jennings Bryan took over the position of the Populists on free and unlimited coinage of silver. In the process the Democratic party was pushed to the left and its dif-

1924 Progressive Party Candidate, Robert LaFollette.

ferences with the "sound-money," gold-standard policies of the Republican party became more apparent. A similar phenomenon occurred in the aftermath of the Progressives' show of strength in 1912 and 1924; the Democratic party absorbed some of the basic ideas of Roosevelt and La Follette (such as the regulation of large corporations and the promotion of labor interests) for which the Republicans had little concern. Similar shifts occur in the other direction: the Republican party under Richard Nixon adopted some of Wallace's American Independent party's civil rights policies and thereby distinguished itself more clearly from the general approach to the race issue taken by the Democratic party. It is precisely this kind of process that has led to the demise of many minor parties, because they find their programs and followers siphoned away by one of the two major parties. Many third-party supporters are not distressed by this result, however, since it means that the rationale for the party's formation no longer exists; values and interests that were formerly ignored are now represented.

Third parties also play a role in the composition of the two major parties. When the Henry Wallace Progressives of 1948 fielded candidates who advocated a more conciliatory policy with the Soviet Union, they drained away from the Democratic party some of its supporters who agreed with that position. At the same time, they pushed back into the party fold some traditional Democrats, particularly Catholics, who had been alienated by the nation's close relationship with Russia during the Democratic administrations in World War II years. Thus differences among the various factions of the principal parties—in particular, the majority party, which wins elections because it represents such a wide variety of interests*—may result in the defection of a group that feels it is losing out in basic conflicts over key issues within the national party. This analysis would help explain the formation of the Progressive party from the ranks of the Republicans in 1912, and the Dixiecrats and the American Independent party from the Democrats in 1948 and 1968, respectively. Moreover, the process may eventually lead to the migration of such groups to the other major party, with the minor organization serving as a halfway house en route to the new party home. Recent cases in point are former Dixiecrats, including political leaders like Strom Thurmond, who have now affiliated themselves with the Republican party.

* Journalist Samuel Lubell has suggested that ". . . the key to the political warfare of any particular period will be found in the conflict among the clashing elements in the majority party."

Finally, third parties serve vital interests of American democracy. Political scientists Austin Ranney and Wilmoore Kendall suggest that they act as ". . . safety valves for discontent . . . ," allowing voters to register a protest without threatening the constitutional order. Political scientists Steven Rosenstone, Roy Behr, and Edward Lazarus also contend that third parties serve as a check on the major parties, that is, they constitute a weapon citizens can use to force those parties to be more accountable.

ASSESSMENT

Generally speaking, the historical record of American political parties has been a good one. Established in the very early years of the republic, they became the world's first permanent electoral organizations and models for other democratic countries. Another measure of their success is the persistence of our party system for almost two centuries.

The success of American political parties has been due in large part to the favorable environment. A general American consensus on basic social, economic, and political values and institutions has spared our parties the problem of trying to represent and reconcile deep cleavages on such matters, cleavages that have plagued party leaders in other societies. Our expanding economy has also made it possible for a wide variety of groups to satisfy their demands through the rival parties without an all-out, do-or-die struggle.

American political parties, in turn, have contributed to the successful operation of our democratic institutions. They have recruited and backed many able men and women for public office. In addition, the close competition that has existed between the two major parties over the years, together with their representation of different economic and social interests, has provided voters with significant choices of personnel and policies.

On the other hand, American political parties have also had some notable failures. Their inability to deal with the race issue resulted in a bloody civil war. That issue and the memory of that war have continued to confuse party divisions over the years and spawned one-party politics in many areas, thereby denying the voters a meaningful choice between rival candidates and policies. As we shall see in Chapter 9, the race issue also confuses the American electoral scene at the national level today.

In recent years a number of political scientists have criticized our existing parties. One group associates itself with a 1950 report of the Committee on Political Parties of the American Political Science Association entitled, "Towards a More Responsible Two-Party System." This report advocates that our parties present alternative policy programs in their platforms and then use the discipline exercised by a strong national party organization over its members in Congress to get such programs enacted into law. Besides this "responsible party government" group, Austin Ranney also identifies another that favors "representative party structures"—that is, parties that represent more accurately the views and interests of rank-and-file members of the party. It should be noted that these are the same "programmatic" and "internal democracy" goals that were previously described as being associated with political "amateurs."

Not all political scientists, however, agree with the advocates of responsible party government. In fact, defenders of the existing party system attack the reformers on three separate grounds. One is that their goals are undesirable: if the two major parties did present highly different programs to Americans and the winning party then proceeded immediately to carry out these programs, the result would be a heightening of political conflict because the losers would resist implementation of public policies that threatened their basic values and interests. Also, more intraparty democracy would mean that decisions on the selection of candidates and the adoption of policies would be made by rank-and-file party members who are not as knowledgeable and skilled with respect to such matters as more experienced party leaders. Second, even if the goals of the reformers are desirable, they cannot be attained: it is unrealistic to expect programmatic national parties to develop in the United States with its federal system of government and tradition of pragmatism and protecting minorities' rights; also, rank-and-file members of parties will not take the time and effort to participate actively in party affairs. Third, the charges the reformers level against the American party system are untrue: as a matter of fact, our parties do present alternative programs in their platforms, and the party members in Congress actually see to it that such programs are enacted into law; moreover, rank-and-file members of parties do play a major role in helping to select candidates and adopt policies.

It would be premature at this point to assess which of the above groups and their various arguments is correct, but the student should keep them in mind as we examine the part that American political parties play in various aspects of American politics. In Chapters 7, 8, and 9, we focus on their role in the electoral process. In subsequent chapters we analyze the part that the party in the government plays in the making of public policy.

SELECTED READINGS

Particularly helpful for discussions of the nature of a political party and how it differs from other groups linking the general populace to political leaders are Chapter 1 of Leon Epstein, *Political Parties in Western Democracies* (New York: Praeger Publishers, 1967), and Austin Ranney's selection, "The Concept of 'Party,' " that appears in Oliver Garceau, ed., *Political Research and Political Theory* (Cambridge: Harvard University Press, 1968). The best theoretical treatment of the relationship of parties to democracy is Austin Ranney and Wilmoore Kendall, *Democracy and The American Party System* (New York: Harcourt, Brace, 1951).

Classic studies of political machines include Harold Gosnell, *Machine Politics, Chicago Style* (Chicago: University of Chicago Press, 1937), and Dayton McKean, *Boss: The Hague Machine in Action* (Boston: Houghton–Mifflin, 1940). For an excellent journalistic account of the lives of six bosses—Hague, Curley, Crump, Long, Talmadge, and Pendergast—see Alfred Steinberg, *The Bosses* (New York: New American Library, 1972). The best study of a modern political machine is Milton Rakove's analysis of the Daley organization, *Don't Make No Waves, Don't Back No Losers* (Bloomington: Indiana University Press, 1975).

James Q. Wilson draws the distinction between amateurs and professionals in *The Amateur Democrat* (Chicago: University of Chicago Press, 1962); Nelson Polsby and Aaron Wildavsky made the same distinction between professionals and "purists" in their *Presidential Elections* (New York: Charles Scribner's Sons, 4th ed., 1976).

The best treatment of the original establishment of political parties in the United States is William Chambers, *Political Parties in a New Nation: The American Experience* (New York: Oxford University Press, 1963). A good series of selections dealing with various stages in the growth of American parties is contained in a book edited by William Chambers and Walter Burnham, *The American Party System: Stages of Political Growth* (New York: Oxford University Press, 2nd ed., 1975). For more recent developments in American parties, see Samuel Lubell, *The Future of American Politics* (New York: Harper and Row, 1965).

Epstein's book cited above has an excellent discussion of various types of party competition, as does an article by Hugh McDowell Clokie, "The Modern Party State," *The Canadian Journal of Economics and Political Science* (May 1949): 139–57. Good discussions of two-party competition at the national level in the United States, including the reasons associated with that particular type of party system, are included in V. O. Key, Jr., *Politics, Parties, and Pressure Groups* (New York: Thomas Y. Crowell, 5th ed., 1964); Frank Sorauf, *Party Politics in America* (Boston: Little, Brown, 5th ed., 1984).

Chapter 10 of Key, cited above, has an excellent analysis of minor parties in the United States. A good recent treatment of the subject is Steven Rosenstone, Roy Behr, and Edward Lazarus, *Third Parties in America: Citizen Response to Major Party Failure* (Princeton, N.J. : Princeton University Press, 1984).

E. E. Schattschneider's book *Party Government* (New York: Holt, Rinehart, and Winston, 1942) makes the case for responsible party government, as does a Report of the Committee on Political Parties of the American Political Science Association chaired by Schattschneider, entitled "Towards a More Responsible Two-Party System," published as a supplement to the September 1950 issue of *The American Political Science Review*. More recent books supporting this general position are James MacGregor Burns, *The Deadlock of Democracy* (Englewood Cliffs, N.J.: Prentice–Hall, 1963), and David Broder, *The Party's Over* (New York: Harper and Row, 1972). A classic defense of the American party system is Pendleton Herring, *The Politics of Democracy* (New York: W. W. Norton, 1965—reprint of the 1940 edition); a recent example of a book with the same point of view is Polsby and Wildavsky, cited above. Austin Ranney has two books analyzing the general subject of party reform, *The Doctrine of Responsible Party Government* (Urbana: University of Illinois Press, 1954) and *Curing the Mischiefs of Faction* (Berkeley: University of California Press, 1975).

CHAPTER 7

The Nomination of Candidates

As the Democrats looked forward to the 1984 presidential contest, there was no shortage of potential nominees of their party. Leading the pack in terms of experience and voter-recognition was former vice president and Minnesota senator, Walter Mondale, who began organizing for the 1984 race soon after incumbent President Jimmy Carter's and his defeat by the Republican Reagan–Bush ticket in 1980. A political protegé of the late Hubert Humphrey, politically liberal Mondale benefitted from close ties with organized labor, minorities, Jews, Catholics, and blue-collar ethnics; he was also favored by many Democratic party leaders in Congress and at the state and local level. Another prominent candidate was Ohio Senator John Glenn, the first American to orbit the earth, a political "centrist" who was expected to do well with the business community, Southerners, middle-class Americans, and conservative elements of the Democratic party. Glenn's candidacy was also supported by some Democrats who believed he had the best chance of defeating President Reagan in the 1984 general election.

Four other less well-known candidates also sought the nomination. California Senator Alan Cranston, who was expected to compete with Mondale for the liberal vote, made the passage of a nuclear freeze the major issue of his campaign. Colorado Senator Gary Hart, George McGovern's campaign manager in the 1972 presidential contest, stressed the importance of "new" ideas and sought to appeal in particular to young people, women, environmentalists, and persons who supported Senator Edward Kennedy of Massachusetts prior to his withdrawal from the 1984 race. South Carolina Senator Ernest Hollings offered himself as a middle-of-the-road candidate, more favorable to a strong national defense than the other Democratic candidates and willing to freeze government expenditures across the

Glenn Joins the Race for Presidential Nomination

By HOWELL RAINES

Special to The New York Times

NEW CONCORD, Ohio, April 21 — Senator John Glenn declared his candidacy for the Democratic Presidential nomination today in a speech that sounded patriotic themes like those used three years ago by Ronald Reagan in seeking the Republican nomination.

Senator Glenn, however, accused President Reagan of abandoning the vision of America that he offered as a candidate. "During his 1980 campaign, President Reagan often spoke of a shining city on a hill," Senator Glenn told a cheering hometown crowd of 2,000 people. "It is no shining city that denies education, destroys jobs and diminishes opportunities."

Mr. Glenn said he planned to base his campaign on the "small town" values he learned here as a boy, "the values of excellence, honesty, fairness and compassion."

The Reagan Administration "likes to [illegible]

Jesse Jackson Says He'll Seek Presidency

By DAVID TREADWELL, *Times Staff Writer*

WASHINGTON—Civil rights leader Jesse Jackson, ending months of speculation over whether he would heed the call of his supporters to "Run, Jesse, Run," disclosed Sunday that he has decided to seek the 1984 Democratic presidential nomination.

Jackson, in an interview with correspondent Mike Wallace on CBS-TV's "60 Minutes," said he will formally announce his candidacy Thursday at Washington's new convention center.

"I'm concerned about our measurement for greatness," Jackson said, when asked why he was seeking the presidency. "Our great-

board as a means of helping to bring the nation's huge budget deficits under control. Finally, there was former Florida Governor Reuben Askew, who also served as a trade representative in the Carter administration, a moderate by Southern Democrats' standards but whose views on issues such as abortion (he opposes it except when necessary to protect the mother's health, or when incest or rape is involved) led many persons to view him as the most conservative of the Democratic candidates.

The fall of 1983 brought two late entrants into the race, neither of whom expected to win the nomination. George McGovern, the soundly defeated Democratic candidate of 1972 and now a private citizen because of his loss of his Senate seat in the 1980 election, offered his candidacy as a means of injecting a deep concern for nuclear disarmament and feeding the hungry into the campaign debate. Black minister and political activist, Jesse Jackson, offered himself " . . . as a vehicle to give a voice to voiceless, representation to the unrepresented, and hope to the downtrodden."

As the time neared for the official beginning of the nomination race (the Iowa caucuses were held on February 20, 1984), important developments began to affect the contest. Jackson made a personal visit to Syria and secured the release of captured U. S. airman, Lieutenant Robert Goodman, an event that brought the candidate much favorable publicity. However, Walter Mondale emerged as the clear frontrunner for the nomination as a result of endorsements in late 1983 from the AFL–CIO, the National Education Association (NEA), and the National Organization of Women (NOW). He also scored a victory in a Maine "straw poll" (unofficial survey) of party activists and won out over Jackson in a contest for the support of the black wing of the Alabama Democratic party. Mondale also garnered endorsements from the Democratic Speaker of the House, "Tip" O'Neill, and former Democratic National Committee chairman, Robert Strauss.

In early 1984, caucuses held by the Democratic members of the House of Representatives to pick their "superdelegates" to the Democratic National Convention (such persons, constituting some 14 percent of the total delegates, consist of national and state elected and party officials chosen by such officials themselves) revealed overwhelming sentiment for Mondale—even though such delegates were officially "unpledged." Public-opinion polls also showed Mondale pulling far ahead of Glenn as the favored Democratic candidate. In the eight-candidate debate held in mid-January at Dartmouth College, most of the participants seemed to recognize Mondale's frontrunner status by directing attacks on him, while he chose to focus on President Reagan. By the time of the Iowa caucuses, many political pundits were convinced that the Democratic contest was in fact already decided, and that on March 13, 1984—tabbed "Super-Tuesday" because nine states held primaries or caucuses that day—Mondale would win big and, as a result, force all his rivals from the race.

The results of the first round of the Iowa caucuses (February 20, 1984) seemed to confirm the above prediction. Mondale won almost half of the delegates. The remaining six candidates (Hollings did not enter) trailed far behind, with Hart nosing out McGovern for second place—15 to 12 percent. Most shocking was the abysmal showing of Glenn—he finished sixth (behind "uncommitted") with only 5 percent of the delegates.

There then occurred one of the biggest upsets in the history of presidential nomination contests. One week later, on February 27, Gary Hart defeated Mondale in the New Hampshire primary by

Opening Debate of 1984 Democratic Nomination Contest.

a 37–28 percent margin, with Glenn coming in a poor third with 12 percent of the votes. Three other candidates—Hollings, Cranston, and Askew—received 3, 2, and 1 percent of the vote, respectively, and withdrew from the presidential contest.

Virtually overnight Hart went from a blip on the public-opinion charts to the top, outdistancing both Mondale *and* President Reagan in popularity. Riding a media blitz and a psychological bandwagon, within a week Hart followed up his New Hampshire upset with a victory in the Maine caucuses (for which Mondale was very well-organized) and overwhelmed the former vice president in the Vermont primary as well. Six days later he scored another impressive victory in the Wyoming caucuses. Many political observers were then predicting that Mondale was finished politically, and that Hart wins in the "Super-Tuesday" primaries and caucuses would force the former vice president out of the race.

The heated-up nomination contest then took a new turn. Mondale stopped focusing on President Reagan and began to sharply attack Hart on the issues. He also accused the Colorado senator of having no substance to his supposedly "new" ideas, using the popular Wendy's commercial line, "Where's the beef?", to make his point during a televised debate. The media also began to focus more critically on Hart: it turned up information that he had changed his family name from Hartpence; that there were differing accounts of his actual age (46 or 47); and that he had obtained a naval commission at age 41, allegedly in order to assist him in his 1980 Senate race, which he won by a narrow margin.

"Super-Tuesday" turned out to have mixed results. Hart won three primaries in Florida, Massachusetts, and Rhode Island and captured caucuses in Washington, Oklahoma, and Nevada. Meanwhile, Mondale scored victories in the Alabama and Georgia primaries and in

62 THE WALL STREET JOURNAL, Thursday, March 15, 1984

Two-Man Race

Can Mondale Trip a Fast Hart?

By DENNIS FARNEY and JANE MAYER
Staff Reporters of THE WALL STREET JOURNAL

WASHINGTON – The Democratic presidential nomination is pretty much Sen. Gary Hart's to win—or to lose.

He carried the day on "Super Tuesday" with impressive victories in three primaries, including Massachusetts and Florida, and two Western caucuses. Walter Mondale managed to dodge the Hart bullet, winning in Alabama and Georgia, so he could live to fight another day.

The fight for the nomination is now a two-man race.

What Mr. Hart has to demonstrate is that he can hang on to what he has gained and continue to build support as the campaign picks up speed.

the Hawaii caucuses as well. Thus while Hart won most of the contests, he did not succeed in eliminating Mondale, who used his victories, especially in Alabama and Georgia, to revive his campaign. Meanwhile, Jackson made his most impressive showings to date in Georgia and Alabama where he drew about one-fifth of the votes. Both Glenn and McGovern did very poorly on "Super-Tuesday" and withdrew from the race, leaving just three candidates to contest for the nomination.

The campaign then entered a Mondale-comeback phase, in which he scored victories in a number of large states located in the industrial "Frost Belt," a tier of Middle Atlantic and Midwestern states with smokestack industries and high rates of unemployment. Included were primary victories in Illinois, New York, and Pennsylvania, along with caucus wins in Michigan and Wisconsin. While Hart did score some victories, particularly in Western and New England states, Mondale wins in the larger states allowed him to increase his margin over Hart in the important delegate count. When Mondale scored an impressive win in the caucuses in another large state, Texas, on May 5th, victory predictions again swung in his favor. Meanwhile, Jackson remained in the race, winning primaries in the District of Columbia and Louisiana, showing strength in several Southern-state caucuses, and drawing impressive support in urban areas with a large black population.

Results from the four primaries held on May 9 did not end the contest in Mondale's favor as many had anticipated. He did secure victories in Maryland and North Carolina but lost to Hart by narrow margins in Ohio and Indiana, two Frost Belt states that were supposed to be Mondale's favorite type of political territory. Hart then continued his winning ways during the remainder of May, picking up victories in five Western states. This set the stage for the final five primaries on June 5: Mondale predicted that victories in several of those states would bring him the necessary 1967 delegates required for the nomination. Hart contended that the nomination was now going his way and that Mondale defeats would convince party leaders and Democratic voters that he would be more electable in November than the former vice president.

Again, the results were inconclusive. Mondale won handily in New Jersey and West Virginia but Hart triumphed in California, New Mexico, and South Dakota. The vice president and key supporters then got on the phone and soon had pledges of support from several key party figures, including Atlanta's black mayor, Andrew Young, Senator Howard Metzenbaum of Ohio, Alabama governor, George Wallace, and most important, Gillis Long, chairman of the House Democratic Caucus and originally inclined toward Hart, who announced that the race was now over and that bickering must stop if the Democrats were to have a chance of defeating Reagan in November. With these and other previously unpledged delegates in his camp, Mondale went on television at noon on June 6, to announce that he had the required number of delegates needed to secure the nomination. Meanwhile, Hart vowed to fight on to

"For you, Jerry. Mondale."

the convention itself, and Jackson threatened to continue his battle to have the Democratic party change its nomination contest rules, which he contended gave him fewer delegates than he deserved. Thus after 57 primaries and caucuses held over 76 days, involving over 18-million participants, a dozen candidate debates, and the expenditure of about $50 million, the state-contest phase of the Democratic nomination race ended on a confused and sour note. The participants and Democratic party leaders would have to work to pull the party back together again at the national convention scheduled for mid-July.*

The situation in the Republican party was exactly the opposite of the prolonged, competitive Democratic race. Ronald Reagan became the first incumbent Republican president to run unopposed for his party's nomination since Eisenhower in 1956. While the Democratic contenders were savaging each other and exhausting themselves in the process, the president played the role of the ceremonial chief-of-state: visiting China, laying a wreath at the tomb of an unknown soldier of the Vietnamese War, visiting the Normandy beaches on the fortieth anniversary of the allied invasion of Europe, meeting with our European allies at an economic summit, and commemorating Olympic games for the disabled. When asked how he proposed to deal with his Democratic opposition, he replied, "Pretend they aren't there."

While candidates for other public offices do not experience the special rigors of a presidential contest, they must all pass through the crucible of the electoral process. To top it off, the procedure involves two separate tests of political strength. As we shall see first in this chapter, a candidate must win his party's nomination; then he must emerge victorious in the general election, a subject examined in the next chapter.

* Because of the early 1985 publication date of this book, it was not possible in this chapter to cover the 1984 contest beyond the end of the primaries in June 1984. However, the remainder of the 1984 presidential contest, including both national conventions, the fall campaign, and the results of the election are analyzed in Appendix A.

PURPOSE AND IMPORTANCE OF THE NOMINATION PROCESS

As we saw in Chapter 6, one of the major functions of political parties is to present alternative groups of candidates for the electorate's consideration, thereby structuring the voter's choice and making that choice more manageable. To do so, however, each party must itself have some method of deciding which person will wear its label for each office. That method is the nomination process.†

Although the selection of a candidate by political parties is important in all democratic political systems, it is particularly so in the United States. For one thing, we elect far more officials to public office than any other nation in the world (a recent estimate set the number at about a half-million), not only because our population is large but because Americans have been little disposed toward appointive political positions. The "Jacksonian Revolution" (associated with President Andrew Jackson), which swept the nation in the 1830s and 1840s and left lasting marks on politics, was based on faith in the common person and in his or her ability

Andrew Jackson

† Even in nonpartisan elections, some method is generally used to narrow the number of candidates. Typically, if no person receives the majority (one over half) of the votes in the initial election, a second election is held involving the two top runners.

Democratic Convention.

to choose political leaders wisely. As a result, we traditionally *elect* many officials, particularly at the state and local levels, who are *appointed* in other democracies.

Another basic feature of our politics that contributes to the importance of the nominating procedure is the large number of one-party areas in the United States. One of the two major

parties wins most political offices in about one-half of our states and in an overwhelming proportion of the nation's 3000 counties as well as municipalities that use partisan ballots to choose their officials. In such constituencies the significant competition involves opposing candidates and factions within the dominant party; the locus of the struggle is thus not the general elec-

tion but the process by which the party chooses its candidates.

Finally, the nomination process is important even where genuine two-party competition exists because our parties provide the voter with such a limited choice—between Republicans and Democrats—unless he or she is willing to back a third-party candidate, who, the voter knows, will rarely be successful in American politics. By way of contrast, in a multiparty system a range of can-

Republican Convention.

didates is available for consideration in the general election. Thus American citizens have a special incentive for taking an interest in the nomination process in order to avoid being presented with an undesirable choice in the general election.

As the following section shows, this problem has been a matter of concern over the course of the nation's political history as citizens have continued to seek improvements in the operation of the nomination process.

EVOLUTION OF THE NOMINATION PROCESS

Political parties appeared early in the history of the United States and so did the need to develop some means of choosing candidates to run under their labels. Races for local offices as well as for state legislatures and the House of Representatives presented no real difficulty, since they involved a limited number of voters. Therefore parties simply held caucuses, that is, meetings of their most active supporters to nominate candidates.

Selecting candidates for statewide offices presented more problems, however. Given the transportation of the day, it was difficult to assemble politicians from all over a state to choose a party's candidate for governor. Moreover, even if such a group could be convened, it would be too large and unwieldy to function efficiently. Of course, nominating the president and vice president, with their national constituency, presented the same problems in greater compass.

The Legislative Caucus

The parties soon moved to a more appropriate method of choosing nominees for state and nationwide offices: the **legislative caucus.** Under this method a party's members in state legislatures and the House of Representatives assembled to choose, respectively, candidates for statewide office, president, and vice president. By the end of the eighteenth century this procedure, popularly known as *King Caucus,* was in general use at both the state and national level.

The legislative caucus made a lot of sense in the early stages of party development. State legislators and members of Congress were already convened in one location, and since they were few in number, the nominating task was manageable. Moreover, legislators were likely to be highly knowledgeable about potential candidates from all parts of the political unit in question. Thus members of the party in the government were logical agents to choose candidates representing large constituencies.

There were, however, obvious defects in King Caucus. For one thing, it violated the separation-of-powers principle of the Constitution to have members of the legislative body play a key role in determining the occupants of major executive positions. The provisions of the Virginia and New Jersey plans to allow Congress to choose the president had been rejected by the Constitutional Convention. Yet now the legislative caucus threatened to bring the parliamentary system in the back door via the nomination process. This possibility eventually became near-actuality when the Republican legislative caucus in effect chose Madison and Monroe as presidents of the United States during the era of one-party politics.

The legislative caucus also proved to be deficient in representing various party elements. For example, when a party lost an election in a legislative district, state or congressional, that area was not represented in the decisions of the party's legislative caucus. Although this defect was eventually remedied by permitting local party leaders from such areas to sit in the caucus, a more fundamental flaw remained: interested and knowledgeable citizens who participated in party activities at the grass-roots level (especially in campaigns) had no direct say in nominations. The legislative caucus thus became too limited and centralized a group to make key decisions for parties that were increasingly local in organization and increasingly dependent for political victories on active members who did not hold legislative posts.

The fate of the legislative caucus is exemplified by what happened to the 1824 Republican congressional caucus to choose its party's presidential candidate. No fewer than five candidates emerged that year with support from various elements of the party. Only one-fourth of the Republican legislators attended the caucus, and in the general election that followed, no candidate received a majority of the electoral votes. As a result, the presidential election was thrown into the House of Representatives; to make matters worse, that body chose not Andrew Jackson—the candidate with the greatest number of popular and electoral votes—but John Quincy Adams. Adams benefited from a political deal with Henry Clay, one of the five nominees, who threw his support in the House to Adams in return for being named Secretary of State. This unfortunate combination of events discredited King Caucus as a means of nominating a presidential candidate.

After 1824, presidential nominations swung briefly to the state level as legislatures and conventions chose "favorite sons" as candidates. But if the legislative caucus had proved to be too centralized for the political necessities of the day, selection by individual states was too decentralized for selecting a nationwide official. Some device was needed that would represent party elements in various parts of the country and at the same time facilitate the nomination of a common candidate by these diverse groups.

The Convention

The nomination method that emerged to meet these needs was a **national party convention** composed of delegates from various states. It was not a major party but a minor one, the anti-Masonic party, that pioneered the way in 1831. The National Republicans (who, like the anti-Masons, had no appreciable representation in Congress and thus could not have used the legislative caucus effectively even if they had wanted to) called a similar convention the following year. So did the Democratic Republicans under President Jackson, who saw a convention as an ideal means for getting his handpicked candidate, Martin Van Buren, chosen by the delegates as vice president.

For a number of years the convention became the dominant means of nominating candidates at both the state and the national level. Delegates to state conventions were chosen either directly by party members in their localities (towns, cities, or counties) or, more often, by county conventions whose delegates themselves had been selected by party members in smaller local units. The state convention in turn selected candidates for statewide office and chose the state's delegates to the national presidential convention. The system thus allowed rank-and-file members of the party to participate in the choosing of delegates but left the nomination process in the hands of the delegates. Viewed in the way we analyzed political parties in the last chapter, actual candidate selection lay with the party organization, that is, those who were most active in party affairs.

In time, however, disillusionment with the convention set in. Critics charged that instead of representing various elements of the party, the convention was the instrument by which a small clique controlled the nomination process for private purposes. These critics pointed out that the convention system lent itself to manipulation at various stages of the process: ad hoc meetings to choose delegates were frequently called without proper notice to all interested parties, and such meetings could be packed by ineligible participants; contests between rival delegations from a particular area were common, and the convention that ultimately ruled on the disputes frequently did so unfairly or without full knowledge of the facts; finally, the convention proceedings themselves placed great powers in the hands of the presiding officers over such key matters as the recognition of speakers, ruling on motions, and the calling for votes. Rather than eliminate the injustices of convention rules, however, foes of the convention chose instead to develop an entirely new means for nominating officials that would give the general public a greater role in the process—the *direct primary.*

The Direct Primary

The **direct primary** permits voters themselves to decide who will be nominated for public office. In contrast to the convention system, whereby the voters indirectly decide who will be nominated by choosing delegates who actually make the nomination decision, in the primary the voters select the nominees themselves.

The direct primary in the United States is chiefly the product of this century. Although it was actually used before the Civil War in some localities and was adopted voluntarily by the Democratic party in several Southern states in the post-Reconstruction period when it became apparent that the nomination process there was in effect the election, the movement to make the primary mandatory developed in the early 1900s. It became a part of the general Progressive movement that called for taking government out of the control of the political bosses of the day and placing it where it belonged—in the hands of the people.* Under the leadership of Robert LaFollette, Wisconsin passed the first law for a statewide, direct primary in 1903. Other states soon followed suit, and by 1917 all except a few used it for most party selections. Today the direct primary is utilized by all 50 states for some, if not all, nominations.

Nominations in the United States have thus become progressively democratized as the selection of candidates has passed legally from the party in the government to the party organization and, ultimately, to the party in the electorate. Even so, as the rest of this chapter will indicate, the process differs from one office to another. Presidential candidates, for instance, continue to be nominated by national conventions rather than by a popular primary. In addition, primary laws themselves vary, so that candidates chosen by this general method do not all face the same rules of the game. Finally, aside from the legalities of the nomination process, political forces shape the particulars of various electoral contests.

NOMINATING THE PRESIDENT

No other political candidate faces the range of obstacles that confront a person with presidential ambitions. The rules that govern the nomination process for the presidential candidate are infinitely more complex than those for congressional aspirants or state and local politicians. But even more important, presidential-nomination campaigns place demands of time, energy, resources, and planning on candidates and their staffs that dwarf the efforts of any other office-seeker.

The Nature and Impact of Current Nomination Rules

The rules that govern any political contest are important. On one hand, they shape the process, determining the strategies and tactics that participants follow in order to maximize their chances of winning. On the other hand, rules become the focus of struggles for changes as people seek to have them favor their particular interests. The pre-

* In addition to the primary, other "direct democracy" devices proposed by the Progressives included the initiative, referendum, and recall procedures referred to in the last chapter.

vailing rules are seldom neutral: they inevitably give an advantage to certain individuals and interests over others, even though it is sometimes difficult to predict specific consequences of changing rules. Thus, rules both prescribe behavior in political contests and help determine their outcomes.

In recent years the rules of the presidential nomination contest have become especially important. They are highly complicated, since they come from a variety of sources, including actions of 100 separate state political parties and 50 legislatures, the national political parties, and the Congress. (Sometimes individuals also turn to the courts to interpret provisions of these regulations and to reconcile conflicts among them.) In addition, the rules have been changed so drastically and so often, particularly in the Democratic party, that it is difficult for candidates and their supporters to keep up with the changes. The results have created confusion and uncertainty for many participants and have favored those who somehow manage to puzzle their way through the welter of rules. Indeed, some persons attribute part of George McGovern's winning the 1972 Democratic nomination to his close association with the changes made in the nomination rules of that year.*

A variety of rules govern various stages of the nomination process. We will next examine three important aspects of such rules: the apportionment of convention votes among the various states, the methods states use in selecting their delegates, and the provisions that apply to the financing of candidates' campaigns. Later in this chapter we will discuss the regulations that govern the proceedings of the national convention.

The Allocation of National Convention Delegates. A presidential candidate starts out with a well-defined goal in mind: to win a majority of the votes at the party's national convention in order to be nominated for the presidency. In 1984, 1118 votes out of 2235 were required at the Republican convention; for the Democrats the figures were 1967 out of 3933.

Although the numbers of their convention votes differ, both parties use the same general principles to decide how many votes each state is allowed. They generally take into account the size of a state's congressional delegation or its population as well as its record in supporting the party's candidates in recent years. The Republicans are concerned with voting not only for the presidential nominee but also for governors, senators, and candidates for the House of Representatives; however, they generally do not take into account the *size* of the popular vote for these officials. In contrast, the Democrats focus primarily on the voting in recent presidential elections but are concerned with the total number of popular votes cast for their candidates.

The formulas used by the two major parties tend to benefit different types of states and therefore have an impact on the fortunes of particular candidates seeking the presidential nomination. The smaller states, especially those in which the Republican party dominates the nonpresidential elections, have a disproportionate influence in the GOP convention. In recent years these have been primarily the Western states, which generally backed Ronald Reagan in the 1976 and 1980 nomination contests. In contrast, the most populous states (which cast the most votes in presidential elections) have an advantage in

* As will be explained later in this chapter, Senator McGovern originally chaired a commission that helped bring about major changes in the rules for the 1972 Democratic contest.

the Democratic convention, a factor that benefited Edward Kennedy in 1980 (the Massachusetts senator prevailed in six of the ten states with the greatest number of convention votes, including the top three—California, New York, and Pennsylvania).

The Selection of Delegates. State delegates to the national conventions of both parties are chosen by three major methods. One is selection by *party leaders*, such as members of the state central committee, the party chairperson, or the governor (if the party controls that office). The second is choice by a *state convention* composed of individuals elected at caucuses and conventions held at lower geographical levels, such as precincts, wards, counties, and congressional districts. The third is direct election by the voters themselves in *presidential primaries*. Often states combine methods, using a primary to elect district delegates but allowing their state committees to choose "at-large" delegates (those representing the whole state).

Traditionally, the selection of delegates has been dominated by persons active in party affairs, the so-called "professionals." This was only natural under the first method, which uses party officials to formally appoint the delegates; however, they also dominated under the second system because professionals manipulated the caucuses and conventions to get themselves and their loyal supporters chosen as delegates. Moreover, the same kind of persons ran successfully as delegates in presidential primaries, and since many states did not require them to vote at the national convention for the candidate favored by those participating in the primary, they were free to vote their own preferences.

In the period from 1968 through 1980 there was a definite trend away from control by party professionals and towards increased participation by rank-and-file voters. In 1968 only 16 states chose delegates by a presidential primary; by 1980, 35 states did. However, between 1980 and 1984, the process reversed itself. In 1984 there were only 25 primaries (including the District of Columbia and Puerto Rico), while 27 states used the caucus system to choose their delegates.

Many of the new primary laws passed between 1968 and 1980 also increased the influence of rank-and-file voters over their party's ultimate choice for president. States encouraged delegates chosen in such primaries to indicate which candidate they personally supported for president so that voters would know how such delegates might be expected to vote at the national convention. Some states also permitted voters themselves to indicate their personal preferences for president and legally bound delegates to support the preferred candidates for one or more ballots at the convention. Moreover, under many of the new state laws a person's name was placed on the ballot if his or her presidential candidacy was generally advocated or recognized by the national news media, and a candidate who wanted to be removed from the race had to file an affidavit swearing that he or she was not a candidate in any state that presidential year. Such a system prevented candidates from choosing on their own which state primaries they wanted to enter, thus allowing voters to pass judgment on a broader range of potential nominees than might otherwise be available to them.

Along with the passage of new primary laws by state legislatures have come actions by the national political parties themselves designed to reform the selection of delegates to the national conventions.

The vast changes the *Democratic party* made in its procedures after 1968 can be traced to that year's convention in

Chicago. It was an assembly marked by acrimonious debates within the convention hall over the Vietnam War and by bloody battles outside the convention arena between war protestors and the police. The 1968 delegates were concerned that much of the chaos of that convention occurred because the regular party organization was impervious to the will of rank-and-file Democrats (Senator Hubert Humphrey won the nomination without entering a single presidential primary, because party leaders favoring him dominated the delegations of the caucus-convention states), so they adopted a resolution requiring state parties to give "... all Democrats a full, meaningful, and timely opportunity to participate ..." in the selection of delegates. Not long after, the Democratic National Committee established a commission chaired by Senator George McGovern of South Dakota to assist state parties in meeting that requirement. This action established a pattern that was to persist: following the 1972 convention a new commission, this time under the leadership of Baltimore councilwoman Barbara Mikulski, continued the effort to change the delegate selection process, as did still a third commission, under the chairmanship of Morley Winograd (the state chairman of the Michigan Democratic party), appointed after the 1976 national convention. In each case the commission recommended changes in rules affecting the selection of convention delegates for the next convention; most of these were adopted by the Democratic National Committee and ultimately by the Democratic national convention. Following the 1980 convention, the Democratic National Committee created another commission and in March 1982 approved its proposals for further changes in the 1984 nomination contest. Those proposals were subject to approval by the 1984 Democratic national convention.

For the most part, the battle lines in this series of rules changes were drawn between party professionals and political "amateurs," persons who were not traditionally active in party affairs but who became involved because of an interest in a particular candidate or issue. The amateurs won the struggle to open up the selection process when the McGovern Commission recommended that states remove restrictive voter registration laws so that non-Democrats and unaffiliated voters could become party members. At the same time, the traditional influence of party leaders was reduced by regulations that forbade them to serve automatically as *ex officio* delegates and by requirements of written party rules, adequate public notice of meetings, and the elimination of proxy voting—all designed to prevent the professionals from controlling caucuses and conventions as they had traditionally done.

A second issue that plagued all three party commissions involves the representation of particular groups within state delegations to the national convention. The amateurs scored an initial victory when the McGovern Commission recommended that minority groups, women, and young people (those between 18 and 30) be represented in state delegations "... in reasonable relationship to the groups' presence in the state." This recommendation led many states to adopt a quota system when they chose their delegates to the 1972 convention. However, other minority groups such as Italian and Polish Americans, who had traditionally supported the party, questioned why *they* had not been included in such quotas; other Democrats opposed the idea of quotas altogether because the quotas determined the *results* of the political process, rather than merely the *opportunity to participate* in it, the traditional American concept of political equality. The Mikulski Commission did adopt this latter

Over the top for McGovern.

concept of equality by eliminating the quotas in favor of more inclusive "affirmative-action plans," whereby each state party undertook to encourage ". . . minorities, Native Americans, women, and other traditionally under-represented groups to participate and to be represented in the delegate selection process and all party affairs." However, the idea of quotas surfaced again as professionals and amateurs battled over representation for the 1980 convention. This time each won a victory, the former with the decision to increase the size of state delegations by 10 percent to permit selection of state party and elected officials, and the latter with the adoption of a rule to require that state delegations be equally divided between men and women.

A third major problem with which all three party commissions struggled concerns the division of state delegation votes among the various contending candidates. The McGovern Commission recommended that states abolish the "winner-take-all" primaries—whereby all delegates were awarded to the candidate who simply received a plurality of the popular vote—in favor of a provision for ". . . the fair representation of minority views on presidential candidates." However, California refused to follow this recommendation (the commission only "urged" rather than "required" such an action), and McGovern himself received all 271 delegate votes of that state at the 1972 convention, despite the fact that in the California primary he edged Senator Hubert Humphrey by only a 45 to 39 percent popular-vote margin. The irony of that development led the Democrats to abolish statewide "winner-take-all" contests in 1976, with candidates gathering at least 15 percent of the votes in presidential primaries and caucus-convention meetings being entitled to receive their proportional share of a state's delegate votes. Finally, for the 1980 nomination, Democrats extended the proportional representation principle to district contests; the minimum cutoff figure for candidates entitled to receive delegate votes there was determined by dividing the number of district delegates by 100 (in a district with five delegates the cutoff would be thus 20 percent); however, in no case was the cutoff figure to be higher than 25 percent, regardless of the number of delegates elected in a district.

As previously indicated, after the 1980 presidential election the Democratic National Committee once again appointed a Democratic Commission on Presidential Nominations—this one under the chairmanship of Governor James B. Hunt, Jr., of North Carolina—to develop rules for the 1984 nomination contest. This time the party professionals clearly prevailed over the political amateurs in the changes proposed by the commission and later adopted by the National Committee. Most important was the creation of a bloc of "superdelegates" composed of party and elected officials to go to the convention uncommitted. This bloc, which held some 14 percent of the convention votes, was chosen by Democratic members of the House and Senate and the state parties. These state parties, particularly those of the more populous states, were also favored by another change that allowed states to once again use the winner-take-all principle at the district level and thereby reward a front-runner with a large bloc of delegate votes. Finally, these proposed changes in the 1984 rules abolished the provision that had bound all delegates to the 1980 national convention to vote on the first ballot for the candidate with whom they were linked in their state's delegate-selection process. (The vital part this 1980 provision played in that year's convention is discussed later in the chapter.)

The *Republican party* has also made some changes in delegate selection even though its leaders did not face the pressures for reform that the Democratic leaders did. A committee chaired by Missouri National Committeewoman Rosemary Ginn recommended some proposals that were implemented in choosing delegates to the 1976 convention. Included were provisions similar to those of the McGovern Commission reducing the traditional influence of party leaders by eliminating them as *ex officio* delegates, regularizing the nomination process by informing citizens how to participate in it, and maximizing participation by opening primary and convention systems to all qualified citizens.

At the same time, the Republican party has not attempted to regulate selection of national convention delegates nearly as extensively as the Democratic party. The 1972 Republican national convention turned down recommendations of the Ginn Committee to include in future conventions persons under 25 years of age in " . . . numerical equity to their voting strength in a state . . ." and to have one man, one woman, one person under 25, and one member of a minority group on each of the convention's major committees. In 1975 the Republican National Committee refused to adopt the recommendation of a new committee chaired by Representative William Steiger of Wisconsin that all states be required to have their affirmative-action plans approved by the National Committee. Nor have the Republicans moved to abolish California-type winner-take-all primaries. Thus the national Republican party has been much less willing than its Democratic counterpart to intervene in state decisions involving the selection of delegates to the national convention.

The rules changes made in the period from 1968 to 1980 had a profound effect on the choice of presidential nominees. The proliferation of primaries, plus the deliberate lessening of the influence of party leaders in caucus-convention states, made these leaders far less influential in the nomination process. Such professionals, who traditionally used their skills to select persons considered electable and loyal to the party (such as Hubert Humphrey), were largely replaced by political amateurs who supported "issue-oriented" and "anti-establishment" candidates (such as George McGovern and Jimmy Carter) for the presidency.

Democratic rules designed to increase the representation of traditionally disadvantaged groups in the nomination process also brought the intended results. Women in particular benefited. In 1968, before the Democratic reforms, they constituted just 13 percent of the delegates of the Democratic convention. In 1972 that figure tripled to 38 percent and, after a slight decline to 33 percent in 1976, rose to 50 percent in 1980 as a consequence of the party's decision to require that both sexes be equally represented at the Democratic national convention.

Democratic rules changes ending the winner-take-all contest in favor of a proportional division of states' convention votes made victories in states like California less important than before. While George McGovern owed his convention victory in 1972 to the 271 votes he won from that state, Jimmy Carter won his party's nomination both in 1976 and 1980 without winning California. (Governor Brown carried the state in 1976 and Senator Kennedy did in 1980.) The proportional rule also encouraged candidates to contest in states they did not expect to win, since they had a chance to receive some convention votes instead of being shut out completely, as had occurred in the past under the winner-take-all contests.

The subsequent rules developed by the Hunt Commission had a somewhat different effect on the 1984 Democratic contest. Walter Mondale won the nomination in large part because he was supported by a major proportion of party professionals who served as "super-delegates," and because he benefited from winner-take-all contests at the district level, especially in a number of populous states.*

Rules for Financing Presidential Nomination Campaigns. Historically, restrictions on contributions to presidential campaigns have been ineffective. Federal legislation passed in 1907 forbidding corporations to contribute money to presidential nominations (and elections) was easily circumvented by paying executives extra compensations and having them and members of their families make contributions of the bonuses in their own names. Similar prohibitions on contributions by labor unions passed in the 1947 Taft–Hartley Act were also evaded by the formation of "political action committees" to solicit voluntary donations from members and to spend the funds in the committee's name. Finally, the Hatch Act of 1940, which limited individual contributions to a federal candidate to $5,000, and a federal tax law that imposed progressive tax rates on contributions of more than $3,000 to a single committee, were both ineffective because numerous committees were formed for a single candidate, with each committee entitled to accept a $5,000 contribution.

The move for campaign reform began with President Kennedy, who was sensitive to the advantages wealth gave a candidate. He appointed the Commission on Campaign Costs, which issued a report in 1962 proposing such possibilities as public reporting of campaign expenditures, tax incentives for contributors, and matching public funds for presidential candidates. Nothing came

---

* One major exception to that tendency was the California primary in which the winner-take-all provision at the district level disproportionately favored Senator Hart.

of the proposals during the 1960s but they laid the groundwork for the wave of reform that swept the country in the 1970s. In 1971 and again in 1974 Congress passed legislation affecting campaign financing. However, in January 1976 in the case of *Buckley* v. *Valeo*, the Supreme Court ruled certain provisions of such legislation unconstitutional; later that year Congress responded by enacting still further regulations governing the use of money in federal elections. Finally, in 1979 Congress added more amendments to campaign finance legislation.

As a result of the above actions, a variety of regulations govern the financial conduct of presidential campaigns. The major ones affecting the nomination process* are discussed below.

Presidential candidates and committees are required to *provide full information* on the financing of their campaigns, including the names of all contributors who give $200 or more; they must also itemize expenses of a similar amount. Such information is filed with the Federal Election Commission, which is responsible for administering the campaign legislation; this bipartisan body consists of six members who are nominated by the president and confirmed by the Senate.

Individuals are *limited to making contributions* of $1,000 to a presidential candidate for each election (the nomination and general election are considered separate contests), $5,000 to a political action committee (one that contributes to more than one candidate), and $20,000 to the national committee of a political party, with an aggregate contribution of no more than $25,000 a year per individual contributor. Political action committees themselves organized by corporations, labor unions, professional, agrarian, ideological, or issue groups can contribute $5,000 per candidate per election, providing they have been registered with the Federal Election Commission for at least six months, have more than 50 contributors, and have supported five or more candidates for federal office. Presidential candidates are free to spend an unlimited amount of their own and immediate family money on their campaigns, but if they accept public financing (see below), their contributions to their own campaign are limited to $50,000 per election.

Candidates may *spend* as much as they wish on presidential campaigns unless they accept public financing, in which case limitations apply. For the 1984 presidential campaign, these limits for the nomination process included a national ceiling of $20.2 million plus an additional 20 percent for fund-raising costs—a total of $24.4 million. There were also limitations on spending in each state based on its population. In 1984 California had the highest spending limit—$5.4 million; the lowest figure, which applied to a number of small states, was $404,000.

There is no limitation on *independent campaign expenditures;* that is, those that are made by individuals or political committees advocating the defeat or election of a candidate but that are not made in conjunction with the candidate's campaign. However, individuals or committees making such expenditures in amounts of more than $250 must file a report with the Federal Election Commission and must state, under penalty of perjury, that the expenditure was not made in collusion with the candidate.

Candidates for the presidential nomination who are able to raise $100,000 in individual contributions, with at least $5,000 collected in twenty different states, receive *federal matching funds** for

* Some of the provisions also apply to general election campaigns, which are treated in Chapter 8.

contributions of $250 or less. In 1984 the total amount of federal matching funds available to each candidate for the nomination process was $10.1 million. The Democratic and Republican parties were also provided federal funds of up to $6 million to finance their nominating conventions.

Like the alteration in delegate selection rules, campaign finance legislation has had a major impact on presidential nominations. The sources and techniques for raising funds have been radically changed. Instead of depending on a few "fat cats" to bankroll their campaigns (in 1968 insurance executive W. Clement Stone gave $2.8 million to Richard Nixon's campaign), candidates now raise funds from a large number of small individual contributors,† primarily through direct mail solicitation. The public funds also make it possible for persons who formerly could not afford to mount a nomination campaign to do so. Senator Fred Harris had to abandon a presidential bid in 1972 because he could not raise funds from large contributors, but with federal matching moneys available, he was a candidate in 1976. Moreover, even single-issue anti-abortion candidate Ellen McCormack was able to qualify for federal funds. At the same time, the new method of raising funds from a large number of individuals and thereby qualifying for federal matching moneys means that candidates tend to start their campaigns earlier than formerly. Finally, as political scientist Herbert Alexander suggests, public funding also helps " . . . free each candidate's personal organization from the party hierarchy."

Thus a variety of rules help shape the nature of the nomination contest. The remainder of this section, focuses on the nomination campaign of presidential aspirants.

The Nomination Campaign

Early Maneuvering. Although the formal nomination process does not start until the beginning of the election year (since 1976 with the Iowa caucuses), political maneuvering takes place long before that time. A few days after the 1972 presidential election, Jimmy Carter's staff laid out a plan for winning the 1976 Democratic nomination. Shortly after vice-presidential candidate Walter Mondale lost the 1980 election, he began his quest for the 1984 Democratic presidential nomination.

Journalist Arthur Hadley calls this political interval between the election of one president and the start of the first primary to determine the next presidential candidates "the invisible primary." By this he means that a political contest occurs during this time that has many features characterizing the contests that eventually take place in the actual state primaries. The major difference between the two types of primary is that the "invisible" one takes place behind the scenes as far as the general public is concerned, whereas American voters are very conscious of the regular primaries.

* The subsidy is funded by taxpayers who on their federal income tax form indicate their willingness to have $1 of their tax payment set aside for that subsidy.

† While political action committees can help finance nomination campaigns, their contributions are not matched by federal funds. Also, some presidential candidates as a matter of principle choose not to accept contributions from political action committees. In 1984 political action committees with labor backing contributed money to some candidates running as Mondale delegates. Hart objected and even though Mondale took the position that such contributions were legal, he said that for ethical reasons he was ordering them to be returned. Hart at one point charged that the affected delegates were "tainted" but ultimately decided not to contest their seating at the convention because he was concerned that doing so would split the party.

The invisible primary is a testing ground for the would-be president to determine whether the person's candidacy is viable. One factor that Hadley emphasizes is a "psychological" one. Is the candidate willing to undergo the grueling process needed to win, characterized by extended absences from home, long hours on the campaign trail, and short, sometimes sleepless nights? Former Vice President Walter Mondale withdrew from the 1976 race in November 1974 with the following statement: "I found that I did not have the overwhelming desire to be president which is essential for the kind of campaign that is required. I don't think anyone should be president who is not willing to go through the fire."*

An important task for the presidential candidate at this stage is the assembling of a *staff* to plan the strategy of a campaign and what Hadley calls a "constituency," a larger group of workers who are willing to do the advance work necessary to organize states for the upcoming primary and caucus-convention contests. Recent Democratic party nominees benefited from having dedicated supporters who began their organizational activities very early. A full one and one-half years before the Wisconsin primary in April 1972, a young McGovern staff member, Eugene Pokorny, began to build a base of operation there; in early 1975 a Carter staffer, Tim Kraft, was assigned the task of putting together a Carter organization for the Iowa precinct caucuses to be held in January 1976; in 1979 Terry Turner was made director of Carter's field operations in the Hawkeye State.

Another major factor in this early phase—and perhaps the most important—is how would-be candidates fare with the *media.* As columnist Russell Baker notes, the members of the media are the "great mentioner," the source of name recognition and publicity. Candidates who are ignored because reporters and commentators do not regard them as serious candidates find it almost impossible to emerge as viable presidential possibilities. Adverse comments can also seriously damage a candidacy: in his quest for the 1980 Democratic nomination, Jerry Brown was portrayed by the media as a "spacey," "far-out" politician whose ideas, rhetoric, and lifestyle disqualified him for the presidency. In that same contest, Edward Kennedy's 1979 interview with CBS commentator Roger Mudd turned out to be a disaster as the senator seemed unable to give an adequate explanation of his role in the 1969 accidental drowning of a young woman, Mary Jo Kopechne; his strained relationship with his wife, Joan, and his alleged affairs with other women; why he wanted to be president and how his policies and political views differed from those of President Carter. Many observers concluded that the Massachusetts senator never recovered from that interview, which occurred before his official presidential campaign ever began.

On the other hand, candidates who tend to do well in the invisible primary exploit the advantages provided by the media. Early in his 1976 campaign Carter's staff recommended that he compile a list of important political columnists and editors (such as *New York Times* columnist Tim Wicker and *Washington Post* editor Katherine Graham) and cultivate them by making favorable comments on their articles and columns and, if possible, by scheduling visits with them. Some candidates may also appear in the print media with magazine articles or

* In late 1982 and early 1983, three potential Democratic candidates, Senator Edward Kennedy of Massachusetts, Representative Morris Udall of Arizona, and Senator Dale Bumpers of Arkansas, all publicly announced that they would not be candidates for the 1984 presidential contest. Kennedy gave family obligations as his major reason for not running this time while Udall and Bumpers emphasized the lack of money.

books, such as Kennedy's *Profiles in Courage*, Nixon's *Six Crises*, Carter's *Why Not the Best?*, and Hart's *A New Democracy*. They also use television and radio, appearing regularly on shows such as "This Week with David Brinkley," and "Face the Nation." They may even use a syndicated radio program or news column of their own, as Ronald Reagan did to advance his political views and, indirectly his candidacy.

People with presidential ambitions typically take additional steps to enhance their prospects with leaders of their party as well as the public. Edmund Muskie, who was nominated for vice president by the Democrats in 1968, began accepting speaking engagements outside his home state of Maine soon after he and Hubert Humphrey were defeated. Jimmy Carter assumed the position of Coordinator of the 1974 Democratic Congressional Campaign, a job that took him to 30 states, where he had the opportunity to become acquainted with Democratic leaders. A trip abroad may also keep candidates in the news and, if they have not had much experience in foreign affairs, help to counteract the charge that they are not knowledgeable in this vital area.

Another key aspect of the invisible primary is the raising of *funds* necessary for the nomination campaign. As previously explained, the new finance legislation that favors raising money in small amounts from many individuals requires candidates to get an early start in soliciting funds. In fact, financial maneuvering may precede the candidate's own personal campaign. In January 1977, with $1 million he had left over from his 1976 campaign, Ronald Reagan established a political action committee called the Citizens for the Republic. The organization contributed over $600,000 to 400 Republican candidates at the federal, state, and local levels in the 1978 elections, but the remainder of its total expenditure of $4.5 million went to pay operating expenses and traveling costs for Reagan, who served as the principal speaker at political gatherings held for the GOP candidates. Thus Reagan himself was the major beneficiary of the Citizens for the Republic: he ingratiated himself with the Republican candidates who received contributions from the organization, and at the same time gained valuable contacts with Republican party supporters as well as the list of political contributors to the Citizens for the Republic, who were natural targets for his own fund-raising for the 1980 presidential campaign. Candidates in the party out of power pursued a similar strategy in the next presidential contest. Walter Mondale established a PAC, Committee for the Future of America, in February 1981 that raised $2.4 million and contributed to more than 200 House, Senate, and gubernatorial candidates in 1982; John Glenn's PAC, National Council on Public Policy, involved a much more modest effort (it raised $38,500 in October and November 1982) to underwrite the senator's travels and speech-making on behalf of 1982 Democratic candidates.*

As the presidential election year approaches, campaign fund-raising moves into high gear. During the last three months of 1979 seven candidates each raised more than $1 million, including Republicans Connally, Reagan, Bush, and Dole and Democrats Kennedy, Carter, and Brown. (Ultimately six of the seven received federal matching funds—Connally chose to finance his campaign from private sources alone—as did Republican candidates John Anderson, Howard Baker, and Philip

* Senator Edward Kennedy of Massachusetts also formed a PAC, Committee for the Future of America, that distributed money to a wide variety of Democratic candidates at all levels of government in 1982.

Crane, and Democratic long-shot Lyndon LaRouche.) Financing for the 1984 contest got off to an earlier start: during the first three months of 1983, Mondale raised over $2 million, Askew, $800,000, Hart, $465,000, Cranston, $440,000, and Hollings, almost $250,000.

In recent years presidential candidates have also found it wise to enter *prenomination "popularity" contests* held in some states, even though such contests have no legal effect on the composition of the state delegation to the national convention. The Carter forces packed a Jefferson–Jackson Day fund-raising dinner held in Iowa in October 1975 and, as a result, won the straw poll taken there. Four years later members of then President Carter's staff worked hard to get his supporters elected as delegates to the Florida Democratic state convention held in November 1979; as a result, he clearly defeated Senator Kennedy in a straw vote taken at the convention. At the same time, Ronald Reagan was scoring a triumph over his Republican opponents in a comparable poll taken at the Republican state convention. Such popularity contests started earlier for the 1984 race: in January 1983, native-son Cranston won a preferential poll at a Democratic party state convention in California; in April of that same year, Mondale came out first in a similar poll conducted at a party convention held in Kennedy's home state of Massachusetts. The following June, Cranston also scored victories in straw polls in Wisconsin and Alabama, while Mondale won in Maine the following October.

The early phase of the 1984 contest took on a new dimension when, as previously discussed, both the 14-million-member AFL–CIO organization with its 98 affiliated unions and the 1.7-million-member National Education Association, the nation's largest individual labor union, endorsed Mondale as the Democratic candidate prior to the holding of the official state contests. Shortly thereafter, so did the National Organization of Women (NOW).

This early phase of the nomination campaign, which political scientist Donald Matthews refers to as "... the emergence of presidential possibilities," serves as a testing period for would-be candidates, especially those in the out party.* As previously indicated, some drop out before the official campaign begins. Others establish themselves as leaders in the public-opinion polls taken at the beginning of the year and go on to win their party's nomination. As Table 7.1 shows, this normally occurred from 1936 through 1968. However, in two recent instances the front-runner was ultimately replaced by a dark horse—McGovern, who was preferred by only 3 percent of the Democrats in January 1972, and Carter, the choice of only 4 percent in the same month of 1976. Thus poll leaders cannot afford to relax their efforts on the basis of their early popularity: the final decision on the nominee depends upon presidential primaries as well as caucus-convention contests.

Targeting the Nomination Campaign. Recent developments have served to expand the number of state contests in which candidates become involved. State primary laws that automatically place nationally recognized candidates on the ballot make them candidates in some contests they might prefer to bypass. The proportional representation feature of some state contests encourage candidates to enter races they do not expect to win since they did receive some delegate votes in a losing cause. Moreover, the electorate expects candidates to demonstrate political support in all parts of the country. As a result, in 1980 both Jimmy Carter and Edward

* In the party in power, the incumbent president is typically the frontrunning candidate to succeed himself.

Table 7.1
Continuity and Change in Presidential Nominating Politics (1936–1984)

Year	*Leading Candidate at Beginning of Election Year*	*Nominee*
Party in Power		
1936 (D)	Roosevelt	Roosevelt
1940 (D)	Roosevelt	Roosevelt
1944 (D)	Roosevelt	Roosevelt
1948 (D)	Truman	Truman
1952 (D)	Truman	Stevenson
1956 (R)	Eisenhower	Eisenhower
1960 (R)	Nixon	Nixon
1964 (D)	Johnson	Johnson
1968 (D)	Johnson	Humphrey
1972 (R)	Nixon	Nixon
1976 (R)	Ford[a]	Ford
1980 (D)	Carter[b]	Carter
1984 (R)	Reagan[c]	Reagan
Party out of Power		
1936 (R)	Landon	Landon
1940 (R)	?	Willkie
1944 (R)	Dewey	Dewey
1948 (R)	Dewey–Taft	Dewey
1952 (R)	Eisenhower–Taft	Eisenhower
1956 (D)	Stevenson	Stevenson
1960 (D)	Kennedy	Kennedy
1964 (R)	?	Goldwater
1968 (R)	Nixon	Nixon
1972 (D)	Muskie	McGovern
1976 (D)	Humphrey[a]	Carter
1980 (R)	?[b]	Reagan
1984 (D)	Mondale[c]	Mondale

[a] The 1976 information was taken from the January Gallup poll.

[b] Carter led Kennedy in all Gallup polls conducted after the seizure of the hostages by Iran in November 1979. In a February 1980 Gallup poll listing eight candidates, 34 percent of Republican voters named Reagan as their first choice and 32 percent chose Ford; however, when the choice was narrowed to those two candidates, 56 percent preferred Ford and 40 percent, Reagan.

[c] Since President Reagan was unopposed for the Republican nomination, there was no preferential poll taken; however, a mid-February Gallup poll showed that 86 percent of Republicans approved the President's performance in office. The Gallup poll indicating Mondale to be the leading candidate among Democrats was taken in mid-November 1983.

SOURCE: Matthews, Donald, "Presidential Nominations: Process and Outcomes," in James Barber (ed.), *Choosing The President* (Englewood Cliffs, N.J.: Prentice-Hall, 1974), p. 54. The question mark shows that no single candidate led in the polls.

Kennedy were on the ballot in 34 of the 35 Democratic preference primaries (ignoring only Michigan, where the primary results were not binding and delegates were chosen in separate caucuses.) On the Republican side, George Bush was entered in all 34 of the GOP preference primaries and Ronald Reagan in 32 (he was not on the ballot in Puerto Rico and the District of Columbia). In 1984, Mondale and Hart entered all 25 primaries and Jackson 24 (he was not on the ballot in Puerto Rico).

Of course, having a candidate's name appear on a state ballot does not mean he or she will wage an all-out campaign there. Limitations of time and energy prevent campaigning actively in each state. Moreover, the allocation of money becomes a major problem. Not only is there an overall restriction on spending (a total of $24.4 million in 1984 for those accepting public financing), but spending limits also apply in each state. Such considerations require presidential candidates to establish priorities among the large number of primaries and caucus-convention contests. The primaries, in particular, are important since about three-fourths of the delegates to national conventions are chosen in such primaries. Moreover, candidates are much more likely to campaign personally in primary states than in caucus-convention ones, and expenditures in the former are much greater than in the latter.

Candidates take a number of factors into account when deciding which primaries they should emphasize in their nomination campaigns. One is the time the primary is held. The earliest contest, traditionally New Hampshire, usually attracts most of the major contenders because it is the first test of popular sentiment. Although its number of delegates is small (22 of the 3933 at the 1984 Democratic national convention, 22 of the 2235 at the Republican one), it focuses immediate attention on the winner, as it did on John Kennedy in 1960, Carter in 1976, and Hart in 1984. Moreover, even if a candidate loses in New Hampshire but draws a greater percentage of the vote than expected, the media may interpret the results as a "moral" victory, a judgment that benefited Eugene McCarthy in 1968 and George McGovern in 1972.*

New Hampshire appeals to presidential candidates for another reason: its small area and population make campaigning there a manageable operation. Only about 20,000 Democrats were registered in 1976, and the Carter organization claimed to have contacted about 95 percent of them. Thus, the state was ideal for the former governor in the early stages of the nomination contest before he acquired substantial financial resources for media expenditures and his contingent of Georgia volunteers could conduct an effective door-to-door campaign.

Other primaries provide a late indication of voter preference. The California primary, for example, traditionally occurs near the end of the primary season. If the earlier primaries have not produced a clear favorite, the Golden State can determine the party's nominee. Both Goldwater in 1964 and McGovern in 1972 owed their ultimate selection to their primary victories in California, which projected them as "winners," as delegates throughout the country looked toward the upcoming national convention. Moreover, the rules of the nomination contest also make California an attractive target for presidential candidates. It has the largest number of state delegates at each of the party conventions and, for Republicans, a winner-take-all provision that delivers those delegates in a solid bloc to the winner of the primary.

* It should be pointed out, however, that the media has not followed that practice since the 1972 contest.

Other factors besides timing and delegate strength affect candidates' decisions about where to concentrate campaign efforts. Naturally, they try to choose states where they think they have the best chance of winning. In 1976 and again in 1980 the Carter forces concentrated major efforts in his native South. In 1976 Henry Jackson chose Massachusetts and New York as special targets because both states contained many Catholics, Jews, and labor-union members, with whom the Washington senator felt he had close ties. In 1984 Mondale selected Illinois, New York, and Pennsylvania because of similar ties with the same constituencies. Morris Udall in 1976 and John Anderson in 1980 zeroed in on Massachusetts and Wisconsin because they expected to do well in the liberal academic communities concentrated in those states, while Gary Hart pursued a parallel strategy in 1984 in several New England states. The two Republican contenders in 1976, Gerald Ford and Ronald Reagan, worked hard in their home states of Michigan and California to advance their candidacies, as did 1980 Democratic candidates Jimmy Carter in Georgia and Edward Kennedy in Massachusetts.

At times, however, candidates may deliberately choose to contest primaries that are not considered advantageous to them to demonstrate that they have a broader appeal than is generally recognized. John Kennedy went into the West Virginia primary in 1960 to prove that a Catholic could win in a state in which the population was 95 percent Protestant. In 1976 Jimmy Carter chose the Pennsylvania primary to show that a Southern Baptist could do well in a northern industrial state with a large Catholic population. Both risks proved to be good ones that greatly advanced the Kennedy and Carter candidacies.

A major problem for candidates is how to handle a primary that they clearly expect to lose. The most successful tactic in that case is to convince the public and particularly the media that one is not contesting the primary, so that a loss is not considered a genuine defeat. George McGovern successfully pursued that ploy in the Florida primary in 1972, as did Ronald Reagan in Wisconsin in 1976. Another advantage of such a tactic is that it enables candidates to save their resources for more favorable primaries.

What is most important for candidates to avoid is raising false expectations. In 1976, shortly before the New Hampshire primary, the Reagan staff released the results of a public-opinion poll showing him to be ahead of Ford; the California governor's losing that primary by a single percentage point was interpreted by the media to be a serious defeat for him and a major victory for President Ford. In 1980 John Connally decided to zero in on the South Carolina primary as the one that would establish his candidacy; when he lost to Reagan there, the Texas governor was forced to withdraw from the race altogether.

Although, as was previously suggested, in recent years primaries have become more crucial in nomination campaigns than caucus-convention contests, in some instances the latter may become very important. Recently, Iowa has taken on major importance because its caucuses are the first test of political strength of the various candidates, and therefore the media attach great significance to a victory there. Jimmy Carter's successful campaign in Iowa in 1976 established him as the Democratic pack leader that year; four years later his defeat of Senator Kennedy in the Hawkeye State gave him a psychological edge a month later in the New Hampshire primary.

Caucus-convention states also become important if no clear victor emerges in the presidential primaries. In 1976 both Gerald Ford and Ronald

Reagan diligently pursued delegates chosen in Republican party caucuses and conventions, especially in the period immediately preceding the Republican convention. In the end, Ford owed his nomination to the fact that previously uncommitted delegations such as Mississippi cast their ballots at the national convention in his favor. In 1984 Mondale owed his victory over Hart to the fact that he won more delegates in caucus states, particularly large ones such as Texas and Michigan.

Ronald Reagan and Campaign Manager, Edwin Meese.

Recent Trends in Preconvention Politics. Presidential nomination campaigns are highly complex operations that call for a variety of specialists. Included are *pollsters*, who help candidates assess their nomination prospects and provide vital feedback on the reactions of voters to the candidates and their campaigns, on the issues that people are thinking about, and on attitudes of various social and economic groups about such issues. Also involved are *media consultants*, who help candidates develop a favorable image, write their speeches, and plan their television appearances. Another important group is *direct-mail specialists*, who help with the raising of money and getting out the vote. Organizing these various operations, developing strategy, and managing the overall campaign are *political managers* to whom candidates have turned since the 1952 presidential contest. Since that time presidential campaigns have become increasingly professional in nature.

Along with the professionalization of the nomination process has come its popularization, as control over the fate of presidential candidates has passed from a relatively few party professionals to rank-and-file voters. The attitudes of such voters, in turn, evolve during the course of the nomination contest. In the early stages of the contest the media help determine who the viable candidates are; then once the state primaries and caucuses begin, they assess who the "winners" and "losers" are, often thereby influencing the results of future state contests as voters tend to gravitate toward the "winners" and desert the "losers." Periodic public-opinion polls also reflect the presidential preferences of the American voters, as do the results of various state primaries and caucuses.

Moreover, these various forces affect one another. Candidates who receive favorable treatment from the media tend to do well in the primaries, and their showing there, in turn, raises their standings in the polls. Favorable polls also impress representatives of the media as well as political activists and many rank-and-file voters, resulting in more victories for the poll leaders in both nonprimary and primary contests. The end result of this reinforcement process is that by the time the delegates gather for their party's national convention, generally one candidate has emerged who has been most extensively and favorably carried by the media, who leads in the polls, and who also has clearly won more primary and caucus-conven-

The pollsters: George Gallup and Louis Harris.

* There have been some recent exceptions to that trend, with two candidates ending the preconvention period virtually even in those respects: Republicans Gerald Ford and Ronald Reagan in 1976, and Democrats George McGovern and Hubert Humphrey in 1972 and Walter Mondale and Gary Hart in 1984.

1952 Democratic Convention Keynoter and Nominee, Adali Stevenson.

tion contests than any rival.* However, one more hurdle remains for the front-runner—the party's national convention.

The National Convention. The national convention is important to presidential candidates for two major reasons. First, whatever may have happened before, the actual nomination occurs at the convention. Second, the convention provides opportunities for candidates to strengthen their chances to win the general election the following November.

A number of decisions that precede the balloting on presidential nominations can have significant effects. Sometimes the location of the convention is important. (This decision is officially made by the National Committee: for the out party, the chairman of the National Committee has the greatest say in the matter; for the in party, the president does.) Illinois governor Adlai Stevenson's welcoming speech to the Democratic delegates assembled in Chicago in 1952 is credited with influencing their decision to nominate him that year. In 1968 the events that grew out of the confrontation between protestors and Mayor Daley's police in the same city contributed to Hubert Humphrey's defeat in the general election.

Contests between rival slates of delegates from states where there have been disputes in the selection process are also important. At the 1952 Republican convention, the Credentials Committee awarded Robert Taft a majority of the delegates in several southern states, but this decision was overturned on the floor of the convention in favor of the ultimate nominee, Dwight Eisenhower. There were 82 separate challenges involving 30 states and over 40 percent of the delegates at the 1972 Democratic convention; most of them stemmed from alleged violations of the McGovern–Fraser guidelines. Eventually, all but two were settled by the Credentials Committee: the fight over the California delegation and another dispute that led to a convention decision not to seat the Illinois delegation linked with Mayor Daley of Chicago on the grounds that it did not contain an adequate representation of youth, women, and minorities and was chosen through closed slate-making processes.

Fights over rules of convention proceedings sometime take on great significance. One of these battles occurred at the 1976 Republican convention when the Reagan forces moved to amend the rules so as to acquire candidates to name their vice-presidential choice in advance of the balloting on presidential candidates, hoping thereby to force Ford to name a running mate and thus risk the loss of supporters who would be disappointed with his decision. (Before the convention Reagan had chosen liberal-to-moderate Pennsylvania Senator Richard Schweiker as his vice president, a move calculated to bring him needed support from uncommitted delegates in large eastern states such as New York and Pennsylvania.) The defeat of that amendment helped pave the way for President Ford's victory on the first ballot that year. Four years later Edward Kennedy's forces attempted to get the 1980 Democratic convention to vote down a rule, first proposed by the Winograd Commission and later adopted by the Democratic National Committee, that required convention delegates to vote on the first ballot for a presidential candidate with whom they were linked in their home state's primary or caucus-convention. When the convention upheld the rule, the Massachusetts senator knew he had no chance of winning the Democratic nomination (Carter had more than a majority of the delegates pledged to him) and immediately withdrew his candidacy on the very first night of the convention.

Writing and adopting the party platform is another major convention decision. Although these documents have traditionally been ridiculed as containing promises the party does not intend to keep, the fact is that many delegates and political leaders take them seriously.* In 1948 some southern delegations walked out of the Democratic convention because they felt that the platform was too liberal on the issue of civil rights; 20 years later the delegates of the same party carried on a bitter debate over the Vietnam plank of the platform. Republicans have also experienced major conflicts over their party platform: in 1964 the conservative Goldwater forces, which controlled that convention, refused to make any concessions to party moderates such as governors Nelson Rockefeller of New York and George Romney of Michigan on the issues of civil rights and political extremism.

One of the problems of platform fights is that the intraparty conflict may influence the general election campaign. Some Southerners formed a third party in 1948 (the States' Rights party headed by South Carolina Governor J. Strom Thurmond), which actually carried four southern states—Alabama, Louisiana, Mississippi, and South Carolina. Republican governors Rockefeller and Romney did little to help Goldwater in 1964, and many Democrats opposed to the pro-administration plank on Vietnam in the party's 1968 platform did not rouse themselves in the general election campaign that year.

Because of the possibility of splitting the party in the fall campaign, presidential candidates and their supporters sometimes decide not to fight their major rivals over the platform. After defeating Ronald Reagan for the 1976 Republican nomination, President Ford allowed the views of the California governor to prevail on several major provisions of the platform, including advocating a "moral" foreign policy (contrasted to the détente policy with the Soviet Union previously pursued by the Ford administration). In 1980 President Carter followed a similar procedure in permitting the Kennedy forces to insert into the Democratic platform provision for a $12 billion anti-recession job program.

Credential contests, adoption of rules of procedure, and the writing of the party platform are tests of strength for the various candidates and often determine who will prevail in the most important decision of the convention—the balloting for president that typically takes place on the third day of the proceedings. In the interim, preparations are made for the roll-call vote. Presidential hopefuls frequently call on caucuses of state delegations, and sometimes individual delegates are contacted for their support. Polls are taken of delegates so that candidates know how many votes they can count on and from whom they may pick up additional support. In 1960 Edward Kennedy retained contacts with the Wyoming delegates he had worked with the previous spring and was in their midst when his brother won the nomination on the first ballot. Also in 1960, Richard Nixon arranged to have his picture taken with each delegate at the Republican convention.

The kind of strategy a candidate employs in the balloting depends on the amount of his delegate support. If he is the frontrunner, as President Ford claimed he was in 1976, he concentrates on holding the votes he has been promised and on picking up any additional votes needed to win a majority on the initial ballot. The candidate and his workers use the bandwagon technique to achieve this goal, that is, they argue that since he is going to win the nomi-

* Political scientist Gerald Pomper has found that presidents of both parties work with considerable success to get platform pledges enacted into law.

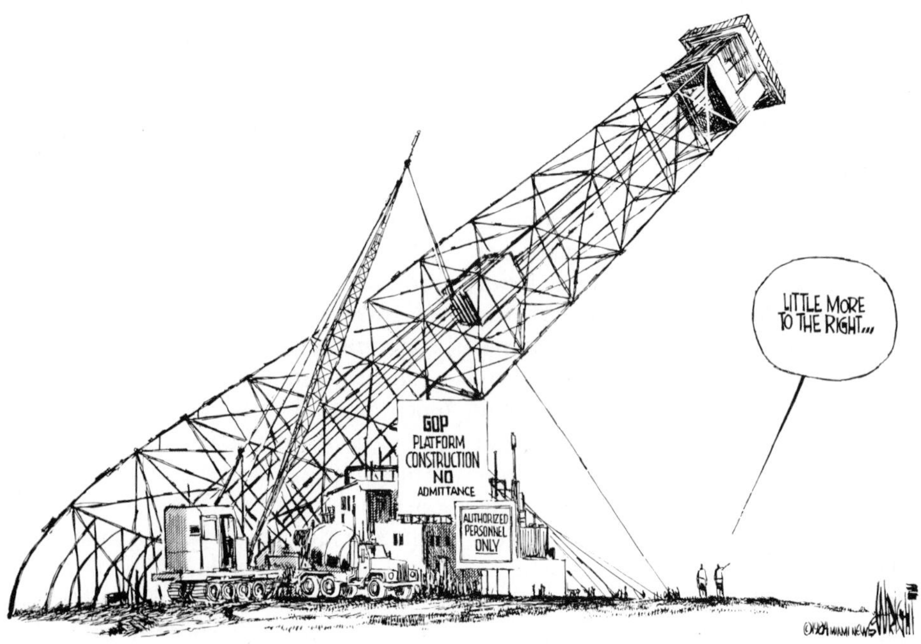

nation anyway, delegation chairpersons or individual members who are politically smart will come out now for his candidacy and not wait until the matter has already been settled. The candidate, it is suggested, will remember early support in the future when he is in a position to do political favors. Franklin Roosevelt did so quite specifically after he was elected in 1932: he determined whether a person seeking a political position had backed him "before Chicago" (where the convention had been held).

Candidates with less delegate support attempt to counter the bandwagon technique with their own strategies. They try to create the impression that the nomination is still uncertain, as the Reagan forces did at the 1976 Republican convention. At times, they may encourage delegates who do not support them to cast their ballots for favorite sons or other minor candidates. The important thing is to hold down the vote for the frontrunner on the first ballot. Candidates also attempt to forge alliances to stop the leader. For example, they may agree that at some time during the balloting those who fall behind in the voting will throw their support to others. The difficulty with making such an arrangement is that minor candidates may frequently have greater differences among themselves than with the leader. The only alliance that might conceivably have stopped Richard Nixon at the 1968 Republican convention would have been one between Nelson Rockefeller and Ronald Reagan. However, given their divergent views on vital issues of the day plus Rockefeller's failure to support Goldwater in 1964 (Reagan had made the best speech of that campaign on Goldwater's behalf), the two governors were hardly a compatible political combination.

The leader, along with other candidates, offers various enticements in bargaining with possible political supporters. Some people are interested in getting the party to take a particular stand on the platform. Others have more tangible concerns: senators or governors may seek the candidate's support in their own campaigns; other political leaders may be looking toward a Cabinet post. Although a presidential candidate himself may refuse to make such commitments so that he can go before his party and the electorate as a "free" man beholden to no one, his supporters do not hesitate to make promises. One delegate in the 1960 convention claimed to be the 19th person to whom the Kennedy forces had offered the vice-presidency.

A definite trend at recent conventions is an early victory for the candidate who arrives at the convention with the greatest number of pledged delegates. In the 18 conventions that the two major parties have held since World War II, only two nominees—Thomas Dewey in 1948 and Adlai Stevenson in 1952—failed to win a majority of the convention votes on the first ballot. Thus, the convention has become a body that typically *legitimizes* the decision on the presidential nominee that has already been made by the time the delegates gather to choose a candidate officially.

The selection of the vice-presidential nominee is the final decision of the convention. Although in theory the delegates make the choice, as a matter of political custom they allow presidential nominees to pick their own running mates. On rare occasions nominees may decide against expressing their own preferences and permit the convention to make an open choice, as Adlai Stevenson did in 1956. However, the typical presidential nominee confers with leaders whose judgment he trusts and, when he makes the decision, the word is passed on to the delegates. Even though some delegates may resist a particular vice-presidential candidate, nominees generally get their way. In 1940 Franklin Roosevelt threatened to refuse the presidential nomination unless Henry Wallace was chosen as his vice president. In 1960 John Kennedy insisted on Lyndon Johnson as his running-mate over the objections of some liberal elements of the party, including his brother Robert. In effect, the vice president is the winning presidential candidate's first political appointment.

Various considerations underlie the choice of a vice-presidential candidate. Traditionally there has been an attempt to balance the ticket, that is, to select a person who differs in certain ways from the presidential nominee. For example, the two candidates may come from separate parts of the country. Over the years, the Democratic party has often chosen Southerners to run with presidential nominees who were typically from other two-party areas; the Kennedy–Johnson ticket in 1960 was such a combination. In 1976, when a Southerner, Jimmy Carter, won the Democratic presidential contest for the first time since before the Civil War, the process worked in reverse; he chose Senator Walter Mondale from the northern state of Minnesota as his running-mate. In 1972 Senator Thomas Eagleton was originally chosen by George McGovern to run with him (as we will see, Eagleton was ultimately forced off the ticket), because the Missourian possessed certain characteristics the South Dakotan lacked: affiliation with the Roman Catholic church, ties to organized labor, and previous residence in a large city (St. Louis). In 1980 Ronald Reagan chose George Bush (whom he reportedly did not much admire personally) in order to win support of moderate elements of the Republican party. The ticket is balanced in these ways to broaden its appeal and to strengthen the party's chances in the general election.

There are indications, however, that some presidential candidates are at least considering how the vice-presidential candidate will perform in office. The trend toward assigning the second in command important responsibilities has led some candidates to choose as their running-mates people with whom they

The Reagan Bush Ticket.

feel they can work effectively. This was the reason why Carter chose Walter Mondale over a number of other Northern liberal senators he had interviewed for the position, including Edmund Muskie of Maine, Frank Church of Idaho, John Glenn of Ohio, and Adlai Stevenson III of Illinois. The possibility of succession to the highest office has also led presidents to choose running-mates who they felt would best be able to step into the presidency if anything should happen to them. There is some evidence that John Kennedy not only chose Lyndon Johnson to help balance the Democratic ticket in 1960 but that he also considered the Texan as the most capable leader among his rivals for the presidential nomination in 1960.

Whatever the considerations are that prompt a presidential nominee to choose a running mate, there is no doubt that the decision is often made too quickly, and frequently without complete knowledge of the candidate's background. A classic case occurred in 1972, when McGovern and his staff met the morning after his nomination (many of them having had only two or three hours' sleep) and by five o'clock that afternoon finally settled on Senator Thomas Eagleton. The Missourian accepted the nomination after several other people had either turned it down, could not be contacted, or were vetoed by key McGovern supporters. During that time no one turned up the information on Eagleton's past experiences with mental illness that ultimately led McGovern to force him off the ticket.

After this last major decision of the national convention, the final night of the proceedings is given over to acceptance speeches. It is a time for attempting to bring back together the various candidates and party elements that have confronted each other during the long preconvention campaign and the hectic days of the convention. Major party figures are usually expected to come to the convention stage to pledge their support for the winner in the upcoming campaign. At times, however, personal feelings run too high and wounds fail to heal sufficiently for a show of party unity. Important members of the liberal wing of the Republican party in 1964 did not support the GOP standard-bearer, Barry Goldwater, and many McCarthyites among Democrats in 1968 (including the candidate) refused to endorse the chosen nominee, Hubert Humphrey, at least immediately. In 1972 prominent Democratic leaders, including George Meany of the AFL–CIO, did not support McGovern. Senator Kennedy and many of his followers did not enthusiastically endorse President Carter on the final night of the 1980 Democratic convention. Thus the convention does not always achieve one of its main objectives: to rally the party faithful for the general election battle, a subject we will discuss in the next chapter. First, however, we need to analyze the factors affecting the nomination of candidates for the Senate and House of Representatives.

THE NOMINATION OF MEMBERS OF CONGRESS

Although senators and members of the House of Representatives are national officials in the sense that they enact laws that govern the entire nation, they are more commonly considered representatives of smaller geographical units. This being so, their method of selection is left, under the Constitution, to the individual states. How a representative or senator gains his or her party's nomination, therefore, depends on state law.

Primary Laws

Most states nominate both senators and members of the House by means of a direct primary. There are, however, differences among primaries, which span the months from late winter to early fall. Most are **"closed"**—that is, restricted to voters who are affiliated with a party as evidenced by declaration of their affiliation when they register to vote or by pledging that they have supported the party's candidates in the past or that they will in the future. Some states, however, have **"open"** primaries that allow a voter to choose which party's primary he or she wants to vote in, and a few use a **"wide-open"** primary that permits a person to vote in one party's primary for some officials and in another's for different officials. In most states the *plurality* candidate—the one receiving the largest number of votes—wins the nomination. In the remaining states (primarily in the South and Border regions) a *majority* vote is needed to win; if no candidate receives a majority on the first ballot, a run-off election is held between the top two vote-getters.*

While most states let the party in the electorate choose congressional candidates, a few grant that right to party activists by using state conventions to nominate senators or members of the House of Representatives. Other states use a combination of the party organization and the party in the electorate to nominate candidates. In some of these states official endorsement of candidates by the state central committee or state party convention precedes the primary; in others the process is reversed: the convention is used to choose a candidate in the event that the top vote-getter in the primary does not receive the requisite proportion of votes (usually 35 percent).

The congressional aspirant thus faces a variety of legal requirements in seeking his or her party's nomination. The political factors affecting candidacy, however, are even more diverse and complex.

The Politics of Choosing Congressional Candidates

It is far more difficult to discuss the naming of congressional candidates than the nomination of the president. For one thing, students of politics have focused more attention on the presidency. Moreover, even the researcher who has data on the politics of some individual congressional nominations cannot properly conclude that these are necessarily typical of 535 races for the national legislature (100 Senate and 435 House). Nonetheless the limited information that we have on the subject reveals certain basic political patterns in congressional nominations.

Senatorial candidates have generally been drawn from major pools: state governors and members of the House of Representatives. State legislators constitute a third, but less frequent source of senatorial aspirants. The national executive branch has also become a good recruiting ground for senators: former Vice-President Hubert Humphrey returned to a Senate seat, and Abraham Ribicoff, one-time Secretary of Health, Education, and Welfare, went to the Senate after serving in the post; John F.

* Presidential candidate Jesse Jackson severely criticized such primaries and demanded that the Democratic party abolish them. Under his reasoning, a black candidate can win the plurality of votes in the first primary, but loses out in the runoff because white voters join forces to choose the first-ballot runner-up.

Bill Bradley: From basketball court to Senate chamber.

Kennedy's presidential assistants Pierre Salinger and Theodore Sorensen also ran for the upper chamber, although unsuccessfully. Of late, celebrities like basketball star Bill Bradley and pioneer astronaut John Glenn have become Senators. The position of United States senator is so highly prestigious that it attracts persons from all areas of public life.

The same cannot be said of the House of Representatives. Few governors or officials of the national executive branch are likely to consider a postion there as a move up the political ladder. Sitting senators naturally have no interest in the less prestigious House, and even those that are defeated for reelection are more likely to seek some other position—a governorship, a place in the national executive branch, or employment as a lobbyist—than to run for the more parochial lower chamber of Congress. So where do members of the House come from? Primarily from state legislatures and county or city posts. Indeed, some House aspirants have no previous political experience at all.

Congressional candidates are recruited in various ways. Some are self-starters who take the initiative on their own. At other times party leaders, other senators or representatives, interest-group representatives, or personal friends stimulate a candidacy. However the process is initiated, it usually involves those groups eventually. In other words, a person who first decides to seek congressional office on his or her own will try to determine how much support can be rallied from these various sources. For without help from at least some of them, a would-be candidate is unlikely to have the resources necessary for the nomination and election contests that lie ahead.

The extent to which state and local party organizations become involved in congressional nominations varies. In states that use a party convention either to officially nominate or screen congressional candidates, an aspirant must generally win the support of party leaders in order to have a chance for the nomination, especially for the Senate. This is also true of nonconvention states where strong party organizations make a practice of committing resources (mainly workers and money) in the primary. Thus most potential Democratic senatorial aspirants in Illinois simply did not run if they could not win the support of Chicago's late mayor Richard Daley. Although few states in the nation have such a potent party organization,* the support of political activists is essential for a congressional nomination in some other urban areas as well.

In some instances, however, the support of party organizations is not crucial for congressional nominations. Some state laws prevent official party organizations from endorsing candidates in the primary. Even where no such legal restrictions exist, party organizations or individual party leaders may think it wise to remain neutral in intraparty contests in order to avoid antagonizing

* The situation continued after Daley's death. When Illinois congressman John Fary (who had been picked to run by Daley in 1975) ignored the local party's request that he retire in 1982, he was overwhelmingly defeated in the Democratic primary by its hand-picked candidate, William Lipinski.

unendorsed candidates, some of whom may eventually win despite the lack of organizational support. Finally, party support in contests for the House of Representatives is hampered because in many states there are no official party organizations for congressional districts, only for counties and the state. All these circumstances force congressional candidates to build their own personal organizations of workers and financial contributors for primary campaigns.

If assistance in many congressional primaries is minimal from state and local party groups, it is almost nonexistent from national party officials and leaders. As a matter of political custom, congressional nominations are considered state and local concerns into which national leaders should not intrude. Even as popular a political leader as Franklin Roosevelt was unsuccessful in his attempt in 1938 to purge certain Southern congressmen in the Democratic primaries because they had voted against his liberal legislative proposals. Most presidents consider it politically unwise to try to unseat congressional incumbents of their party. Not only do defeats in those primaries result in a loss of presidential prestige; they also make political enemies of the victors, on whom the chief executive may have to depend for support of his legislative program.

About the only congressional primaries in which national leaders are likely to intervene are in those areas where the other party controls the seat or where the incumbent in their own party is not running for re-election. In such circumstances the president or other national officials may encourage a person to enter the primary and even go so far as to offer the candidate financial assistance. Even in these cases, national officials are wary of intraparty squabbles and generally support only candidates who are acceptable to most, if not all, important party leaders. Most instances of national party intervention involve contests for the Senate rather than the House, because individual senators are more important politically to the president than the more numerous members of the lower chamber.

One final fact of political life is that most congressional primaries are not competitive, in part because most congressional elections, particularly for the House of Representatives, are not competitive. Candidates of the minority party in an area do not ordinarily battle vigorously for the honor of going down to defeat in the general election. On the other hand, candidates of the majority party might be expected to be more plentiful; however if the incumbent is seeking re-election, challengers in his or her own party generally have little chance of success. Previous campaign experience, close relationships with voters, greater knowledge of issues, and superior financial resources give the veteran legislator almost insurmountable advantages over his or her opponents. Recent estimates indicate that on the average only 1 percent of incumbent representatives are defeated for renomination.

Senatorial nominations are now much more competitive than those for the House. The prestigious nature of the position draws multiple candidacies even in the state's minority party, and the majority party naturally has a good share of contested nominations. In 1978, 3 of 25 incumbent senators were defeated in the primaries, but only 5 of 382 incumbent representatives were.

Even though congressional nominations are generally noncompetitive, spirited battles do occur at times, particularly when the incumbent is not seeking re-election or when he is considered politically vulnerable for some reason. The reasons may include his age, his status as a one-term congressman with comparatively little seniority and campaign experience, or a change in the district he has been representing, so that a new constituency with a different electorate is created.*

For the presidential or congressional candidate, the nomination process constitutes the first of the two hurdles to be cleared if he or she is to hold public office. For a nominee in a competitive situation with the candidate of the opposition party, the general election campaign ahead may be even more trying than the one the nominee has just completed. It is to that subject that we turn in the next chapter.

* The apportionment of congressional districts is discussed in the next chapter.

ASSESSMENT

The current system of choosing presidential nominees is highly pluralistic. It draws on the diverse experiences and perspectives of party professionals, political amateurs, and journalists who help to screen the various candidates. At the same time, it ensures that the preference of rank-and-file voters will help to determine the final choice of the nominee. It therefore represents a variety of interests that have a legitimate concern in the selection of the nation's highest public official.

However, the system became imbalanced in the 1970s. Representatives of the media were substituted for party professionals as the major screeners of candidates, the group from whom the general public takes its cues concerning their respective merits. The media representatives have definite biases in evaluating these candidates. They are preoccupied with matters of political style, in particular how charismatic candidates are and how they come across on television. Journalists also are disposed toward newcomers who, as "new faces," not only create more public attention than established politicians, but who also tend to attack the "establishment," creating the kind of conflict that benefits the media. However, once such a candidate is elected president, he is now a part of that establishment, and media representatives go about their regular business of attacking him, rather than supporting him as they did during the period in which he was a newcomer.

On the other hand, party professionals have different perspectives on presidential candidates. Rather than assessing how charismatic or "anti-establishment" they are, professionals are more likely to evaluate how successful nominees might be in helping to mitigate and compromise the many demands made by increasingly assertive groups in our complex society and how effective such nominees will be in working with other public officials on the nation's problems. Party professionals also have a stake in ensuring that those persons nominated and elected as president will reflect well on their party. Moreover, if their presidential candidate is elected, they continue to take an interest in how that person is doing. Those who hold public office themselves work with the president on the nation's problems, and so are a potential source of political support, as well as restraint, on the chief executive.

The recent decision of the Democratic party to provide a bloc of super-delegates composed of public and party officials chosen by such officials themselves, has helped to restore a balance in the nomination process. It allows political "peers" of candidates, persons with an appreciation of the art of *governing* (what the candidate has to do if he or she is elected), to inject that perspective into the decision as to who should represent the party in the general election. At the same time, the retention of presidential primaries to select most of the convention delegates not only requires that candidates pass muster with rank-and-file voters but also ensures that the healthy concern of political amateurs with the issues and the media's focus on the personality and communication skills of presidential candidates (important attributes of persons holding the nation's highest office), will also be reflected in the nomination process.

There are still serious problems with the present system, which allows states like Iowa and New Hampshire to hold their delegate-selection process earlier than other states. Too much campaigning, media attention, and money are concentrated on these small and not necessarily representative jurisdictions. As a result, candidates who win in these states have an unfair advantage in the remainder of the contest because the media tend to single them out as the ultimate victors, a prediction that contains the features of a self-fulfilling prophecy. States should be grouped by geographical regions or time zones, and the times of delegate-selection processes (particularly primaries) should be set on four or five specific dates over a period from early March to early June of the presidential year. Such an arrangement would force candidates to demonstrate their appeal and vote-getting abilities in broader and more representative political arenas than those that exist under the present system.

SELECTED READINGS

For an excellent treatment of candidate selection in democratic political systems, see Leon Epstein, *Political Parties in Western Democracies* (New York: Praeger Publishers, 1967). A very helpful treatment of the nomination process in the United States is contained in Frank Sorauf, *Party Politics in America* (Boston: Little, Brown, 5th ed., 1984). A major criticism of primaries is V. O. Key Jr., *An Introduction to State Politics* (New York: Alfred A. Knopf, 1956).

There are a number of very good general treatments of presidential nominations and elections. One that first appeared in 1964 and is now in its sixth edition is Nelson Polsby and Aaron Wildavsky, *Presidential Elections* (New York: Charles Scribner's Sons, 1984). Three recent similar studies are John Kessel, *Presidential Campaign Politics* (Homewood, Ill.: Dorsey Press, 2nd ed., 1984), Richard Watson, *The Presidential Contest* (New York: John Wiley & Sons, 2nd ed., 1984), and Stephen Wayne, *The Road to the White House* (New York: St. Martin's Press, 2nd ed., 1984).

There are also excellent in-depth studies of individual presidential campaigns. Theodore White's four classic studies of *The Making of the President (1960, 1964, 1968, and 1972)* (New York: Atheneum Publishers) are highly readable accounts of the nomination and election campaigns in those four election years. Another journalistic and exhaustive analysis of the 1968 race by three reporters of the *London Sunday Times*, Lewis Chester, Godfrey Hodgson, and Bruce Page, is *The American Melodrama: The Presidential Campaign in 1968* (New York: The Viking Press, 1969). Two excellent analyses of the 1976 campaign are Martin Schram, *Running for President: The Carter Campaign* (New York: Stein and Day, 1977) and Jules Witcover, *Marathon: The Pursuit of the Presidency, 1972–1976*

(New York: The Viking Press, 1977). An excellent analysis of the 1980 campaign is Austin Ranney, (ed., *The American Elections of 1980* (Washington, D.C.: American Enterprise Institute, 1981).

A number of recent studies focus on the role that the media assume in presidential contests. For an analysis of the part that the press plays in presidential campaigns, see David Broder, "Political Reporters in Presidential Politics," in Charles Peters and Timothy J. Adams, eds., *Inside the System* (New York: Praeger Publishers, 1970) and Timothy Crouse, *The Boys on the Bus* (New York: Random House, 1970). The role of the mass media and public relations firms is treated in Joe McGinniss's journalistic best-seller, *The Selling of the President, 1968* (New York: Trident Press, 1968), and in Dan Nimmo's scholarly analysis, *The Political Persuaders: The Techniques of Modern Political Campaigns* (Englewood Cliffs, N.J.: Prentice-Hall, 1970). For an excellent analysis of the role of television in the 1976 campaign, see Thomas Patterson, *The Mass Media Election: How Americans Chose Their President* (New York: Praeger, 1980).

Studies of congressional nominations are limited. An excellent comparative study of 10 congressional campaigns in 1962 in the Bay Area of California is David Leuthold, *Electioneering in a Democracy: Campaigns for Congress* (New York: John Wiley & Sons, 1968). A more recent study of the 1978 congressional primaries is Louis Mandel, *From Obscurity to Oblivion: Running in the Congressional Primary* (Knoxville: University of Tennessee Press, 1982).

1984 PRESIDENTIAL DEBATES
LEAGUE OF WOMEN VOTERS

CHAPTER 8

The Election of Candidates

As the quest for the presidency or a seat in Congress shifts from the nomination to the election phase, candidates face a new series of political problems. The rules change from those that prevail for the nomination process to those relating to general elections. New political appeals must be developed to take account of the fact that the campaign is now essentially a one-on-one contest, pitting the nominees of the two major parties against one another (although, on occasion, particularly in presidential elections, a strong third-party candidate may complicate the situation). The audience of the campaign increases greatly (generally about twice as many persons vote in the general election as participate in the nomination process), and therefore candidates and staff members must decide how they can win the support of those new voters, as well as appeal to persons of the other party who backed losing candidates in the nomination process. Complicating the entire situation is the fact that this new expanded phase of the fall campaign is compressed into about 10 weeks. In this chapter we analyze each of these factors, first for presidential campaigns and then for congressional ones.

ELECTING THE PRESIDENT

The Rules of the Election Contest

The Electoral College. One of the supreme ironies of the American political system is that the **electoral college**, which now governs the contest in which most Americans vote, was not designed as a popular election system. In fact, it was distrust of the ability of the common man to choose the nation's highest political official (Constitutional Convention delegate George Mason suggested that to allow the people such a choice made no more sense than "... to refer a trial of colors to a blind man . . .") that led the Founders to create the electoral college in the first place. The college provided that each state legislature choose, by whatever means it desired, a number of electors (none of whom could be members of Congress or hold other national office) equal to its total number of senators and representatives in Congress. The individual electors would assemble, at a fixed time, in their respective state capitals and cast two votes for president. These votes were then transmitted to the nation's capital, to be opened and counted in a joint session of Congress. The person receiving the largest number of electoral votes would be declared president, provided he received a majority; if no candidate received a majority, then the House of Representatives, voting by states (one state delegation, one vote), would choose the president from among the five candidates receiving the highest number of electoral votes. After the choice of president was made, the person with the next highest number of electoral votes would be declared vice president. If two or more contenders received an equal number of electoral votes, then the Senate would choose the vice president from among them.

The electoral college was based on the assumption made by many of the Founders that since the average person did not have the ability to make sound judgments about the qualifications of the various presidential candidates, this crucial decision should be left to a small group of electors—a political elite who would have both the information and the wisdom necessary to choose the best persons for the nation's two highest offices. However, the formation and organization of political parties in the 1790s proceeded at such a rapid pace that by the election of 1800 the electors no longer served as independent persons exercising their own personal judgment on candidates' capabilities; rather they acted as agents of political parties and the general public. In fact, party discipline was so complete that all Republican electors in 1800 cast their two votes for Thomas Jefferson and Aaron Burr. Although it was generally understood that the former was the Republican candidate for president and the latter for vice president, the Constitution provided no means for the electors to make that distinction on their ballots. The result was a tie in electoral votes between Jefferson and Burr; neither won a majority (one over half), and the matter was thrown into the House of Representatives for a final decision.

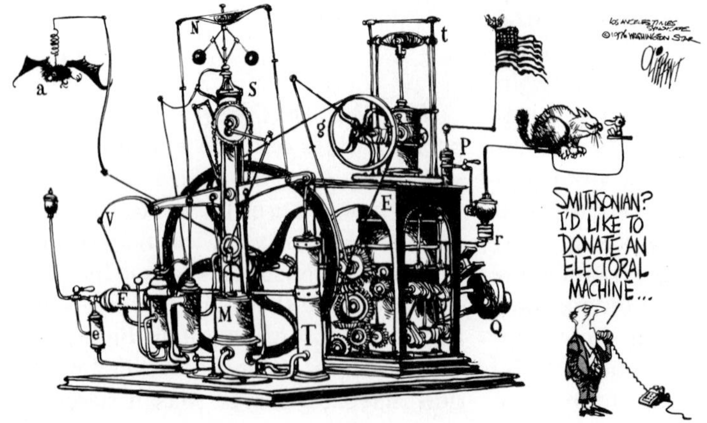

Ironically, the Federalists, despite their major defeat in the congressional elections of 1800, still controlled the **lame-duck** Congress (which did not expire until March 1801) and therefore were in a position to help decide which Republican would serve as president and which as vice president. At the urging of Alexander Hamilton, who disagreed with Jefferson on policy matters but distrusted Burr personally, some of the Federalist representatives eventually cast blank ballots, which permitted the Republican legislators to choose Jefferson as president.

One result of this bizarre chain of events was the ratification in 1804 of the Twelfth Amendment stipulating that electors cast separate ballots for president and vice president. The amendment also provides that if no presidential candidate receives a majority of the electoral votes, the House of Representatives, balloting by states, will select the president by majority vote from among the three (rather than the five) candidates receiving the highest number of electoral votes; if no vice-presidential candidate receives a majority of electoral votes, similar procedures are to be used by the Senate in choosing between the two persons with the highest number of electoral ballots.

Over the years a number of other major changes have affected the operation of the electoral college. By 1804 a majority of states had taken the selection of electors from their legislatures and vested this right in the general electorate. By 1836 most states had abandoned the "district" system—under which the candidate receiving the plurality of the popular votes in a congressional district received its electoral vote, with the statewide popular vote winner capturing the two electoral votes representing the state's two senators—in favor of the **"unit"** or **"general ticket"** system, whereby all the state's electoral votes were awarded to the statewide winner. Finally, as we shall see in the next chapter, over the years various barriers to voting based on such factors as property ownership, race, sex, and being 21 years of age, have been removed by individual states or by action of the national government.

Thus the increasing democratization of American political life is reflected in the procedure for choosing our most important public official. The system originally conceived by the Founders as one in which members of the political elite from the various states would select the president has given way to a national plebiscite in which most Americans are eligible to participate. Yet the formal provisions of the electoral college remain the same as they were in 1804, when the Twelfth Amendment was adopted.

Today these formal provisions provide a strange system for choosing the chief executive. Although most Americans view the system as a popular election, it really is not. When we mark our ballots for a presidential candidate, the vote is actually cast for the electors who are linked with that candidate. In mid-December the state electors associated with the winning candidate (party faithfuls who are chosen in primaries, conventions, or by state committees) meet in their state capitals to vote. (About one-third of the states attempt by law to bind the electors to vote for the winner, but there is some question whether such laws are constitutional.) The results of the electoral balloting are transmitted to Washington, D. C. and, on the following 6 January, they are counted and the outcome is announced before a joint session of the Congress by the presiding officer of the Senate—the incumbent vice president. If, as usually happens, one candidate receives a majority of the electoral votes, the vice president officially declares that candidate to be president, a procedure that has occasionally resulted in some ironical moments. In

The 1800 deadlock—Thomas Jefferson and Aaron Burr.

January 1961 Richard Nixon declared his opponent, John Kennedy, to be president; eight years later another vice president, Hubert Humphrey, declared his political opponent, again Richard Nixon, as the chief executive!

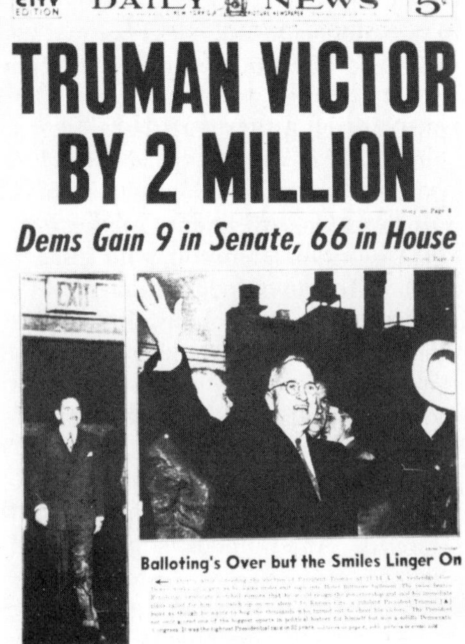

CITY EDITION DAILY NEWS 5¢

TRUMAN VICTOR BY 2 MILLION

Dems Gain 9 in Senate, 66 in House

Balloting's Over but the Smiles Linger On

The electoral college as it operates today violates some of the major tenets of political equality. Not every person's vote really counts the same: the influence one has in the election of the president depends on the political situation in one's particular state. For many Americans who support a losing candidate in their state, it is as though they had not voted at all, since under the general-ticket system all the electoral votes of a state go to the candidate who wins a plurality of its popular votes. Other citizens who live in populous, politically competitive states have a premium placed on their vote because they are in a position to affect how large blocks of electoral votes are cast. Nor does the electoral college ensure that the candidate who receives the most popular votes will win the presidency: John Quincy Adams in 1824, Rutherford B. Hayes in 1876, and Benjamin Harrison in 1888 went to the White House even though they trailed their political opponents, Andrew Jackson, Samuel Tilden, and Grover Cleveland. In 1976 Jimmy Carter almost suffered the same fate: if some 9000 voters in Hawaii and Ohio had shifted their ballots to President Ford, the latter would have edged out Carter in the electoral college, 270–268.

The requirement that a candidate win a majority of the electoral votes or have the election decided by the House of Representatives also violates the idea of political equality. In 1948 Harry Truman defeated Thomas Dewey by over 2,000,000 popular votes, but if some 12,000 people in California and Ohio had voted for Dewey rather than the president, the election would have been thrown into the House of Representatives for a decision. The same thing could have happened in 1960 if some 9000 persons in Illinois and Missouri had voted for Nixon instead of Kennedy, and again in 1968 if about 42,000 persons in Missouri, New Jersey, and Alaska had cast their ballots for Hubert Humphrey rather than President Nixon.* Permitting the House of Representatives, voting by states, to select the president of the United States is not consistent with the "one person, one vote" principle.

The 1968 election also illustrates another danger of the electoral college system: an elector need not cast his or her ballot for the candidate who wins the plurality of votes in the elector's state. Had Nixon failed to win a majority of the electoral votes, third-party candi-

* In all these elections, persons other than the two major party candidates received electoral votes; therefore Dewey, Nixon, and Humphrey could have carried the above states and still not have had a majority of the electoral votes.

date George Wallace would have been in a position to bargain with him. Wallace could have asked his electors (45)* to cast their ballots for Nixon, which would have given the latter enough electoral votes so that the election would not go into the House. While Wallace's 45 electoral votes would not have been enough to give Humphrey a majority of the electoral votes (even if the latter had carried Missouri, New Jersey, and Alaska), the Alabama governor could have tried to bargain with Humphrey by offering to use his influence with Southern representatives to get them to choose him over Nixon.

These problems have created a great deal of dissatisfaction with the electoral college over the years. The sentiment for changing it has increased recently, particularly in the wake of the 1948, 1960, 1968, and 1976 elections, in which a switch in votes of a relatively few persons in key states would have sent the selection of the president into the House or immediately changed the result. Yet while there is widespread agreement on the necessity for changing the electoral college, there is marked disagreement over what form that change should take. Five basic plans have been suggested as substitutes for the present system.

The first, known as the **automatic plan,** which would make the least change in the present system, would eliminate the possibility of "faithless electors" by abolishing the office and automatically casting a state's electoral votes for the popular-vote winner in that state. If no candidate received a majority of the electoral votes, a joint session of Congress would choose the winner with each representative and senator having one vote.

The second, known as the **district plan,** proposes that we return to the method the states used early in our history (and recently reinstated by Maine), under which the presidential candidate who received the plurality vote in each House district would receive its electoral vote, with the remaining two electoral votes going to the statewide popular winner. If no candidate receives a majority of the electoral votes, senators and representatives, sitting jointly and voting as individuals, would choose the president from the three candidates having the highest number of electoral votes. This plan's major supporters have been members of Congress and private groups from rural areas, such as the American Farm Bureau. If the plan were adopted, the crucial areas would be the politically competitive congressional districts where the two major parties traditionally divide the vote 55 to 45 percent.

A third proposal, known as the **proportional plan,** would divide each state's electoral votes in proportion to the division of the popular vote: a candidate receiving 60 percent of the popular vote in a state would receive 60 percent of its electoral votes. A plan of this nature was introduced by Republican Senator Henry Cabot Lodge of Massachusetts and Democratic Representative Ed Gosset of Texas and passed the Senate in 1950 but failed to be enacted by the House. The plan would eliminate the present advantage of the large states in being able to throw all their electoral votes to one candidate and has, therefore, been opposed by many of their legislators, including John Kennedy when he was a senator from Massachusetts. One possible consequence of a proportional division of the electoral

* Although Wallace actually earned 45 electoral votes, he received 46 because one elector in North Carolina (which went for Nixon) cast his vote for the Alabama governor. In 1960, 1972, and 1976, single electors in Oklahoma, Virginia, and Washington also did not cast their ballots for the candidates receiving the popular vote plurality in their states.

Senator Birch Bayh, sponsor of the direct election of the president.

votes would be a fairly even split between the two major candidates so that neither received a majority; hence there would be a greater likelihood of elections being thrown into Congress for decision.*

The fourth plan, **direct popular election** of the president, has picked up major support in recent years, especially since its recommendation in 1967 by a special commission of the American Bar Association. In addition, it has been endorsed by such politically disparate groups as the Chamber of Commerce of the United States and the AFL–CIO. In 1969 the House passed a constitutional amendment providing that the president (and vice president) be elected by a minimum of 40 percent of the popular vote and, if no candidate received so large a vote, that a runoff be held between the two frontrunners. The Senate failed to pass the amendment, however, despite the efforts of its major sponsor, Birch Bayh, Democrat of Indiana. After Carter's narrow electoral college victory in 1976, Bayh introduced the same measure, but it has yet to clear the Congress.

A fifth proposal, recently advanced by a research group, The Twentieth Century Fund, is known as the **national bonus plan.** It would award the nationwide popular winner 102 "bonus" votes (2 for each state plus 2 for the District of Columbia), these extra votes to be added to the electoral votes received under the present state-by-state system. To win the election a candidate would still have to receive a majority of the new total number of electoral votes, 640 (538 + 102) or 321 votes; if no one did, a runoff would be held between the two frontrunners. Thus the proposal retains the electoral college system but makes the total electoral vote better reflect the nationwide popular vote. It also allows the voters rather than the House of Representatives to make the final choice of the president if no candidate receives a majority of the electoral votes.

We will evaluate the merits of these plans, along with the present system, in the Assessment section at the end of the chapter. We next examine the rules governing campaign finance in the presidential election.

Campaign Finance. The legal provisions for financing the general election differ considerably from those governing presidential nominations. Complete public financing is provided to nominees of the major parties (those who received 25 percent or more of the popular vote in the last presidential election) for the general election—in the 1984 presidential election that figure amounted to $40.4 million†—but to receive that money, nominees must agree not to accept other contributions to their campaign. Candidates of minor parties (those receiving between 5 and 25 percent of the vote in the previous election) receive partial public financing. Finally, candidates of parties ineligible to receive public financing on the basis of votes received in previous elections can be at least partially reimbursed after the current election if they receive at least 5 percent of the vote in that current election.

There are, however, two provisions of the campaign finance law that permit the major party candidates to benefit from campaign expenditures besides

* Most of the proportional plans have suggested lowering the winning electoral-vote requirement from a majority to 40 or even 35 percent to avoid the possibility of having the election go to the House. They have also proposed that, if no candidate receives the requisite proportion of electoral votes, the two houses, meeting jointly and voting as individuals, choose the president.

†In addition, that year the national committees of the two major parties were authorized to spend $6.8 million on behalf of their nominees.

those they make themselves from public funds. As is true of the nomination process, there is no limitation on independent campaign expenditures, that is, those made by individuals or political committees that advocate the defeat or election of a presidential candidate but that are not made in conjunction with the candidate's own campaign. (Again, however, such individuals and committees must file reports with the Federal Election Commission and must state under penalty of perjury that the expenditure was not made in collusion with the candidate.) In addition, an amendment to the campaign finance law enacted in 1979 permits state and local party organizations to spend money for any purpose except campaign advertising and hiring outside personnel; this means that they can engage in such grass-roots activities as distributing campaign buttons, stickers, and yard signs, and getting people registered and to the polls to vote.

Thus, like the provisions for financing presidential nomination campaigns, those governing the general election have brought major changes in the funding of fall presidential campaigns. The two major party candidates no longer need depend on wealthy fat cats and other private sources to finance their campaigns (although they may benefit from independent expenditures made by such sources as well as from grass-roots activities by state and local parties). The law also has the effect of limiting and equalizing the expenditures made by the two major party candidates, which is a distinct advantage for the Democrats because historically Republican presidential candidates have spent more than their opponents.* (See Table 8.1, which shows that except for 1948, the Republican presidential candidate outspent his Democratic opponent from 1940 through 1972, the last contest prior to the enactment of the campaign finance law providing public funding.) Finally, the law benefits the candidates of the two major parties, who receive full public financing of their general election compared to minor

* Presidential candidates, of course, are free to refuse public funds for the general election that have been available since 1976. However, to date none of them has done so, perhaps because of the difficulty of raising money under the previously discussed limitations on contributions from individuals and political committees; candidates may also feel that the American public favors the use of the public rather than private funds in the general election.

Table 8.1
Costs of Presidential General Elections (1940–1972)

Year	Republican		Democratic	
1940	$ 3,451,310	Willkie	$ 2,783,654	F. Roosevelt[a]
1944	2,828,652	Dewey	2,169,077	F. Roosevelt[a]
1948	2,127,296	Dewey	2,736,334	Truman[a]
1952	6,608,623	Eisenhower[a]	5,032,926	Stevenson
1956	7,778,702	Eisenhower[a]	5,106,651	Stevenson
1960	10,128,000	Nixon	9,797,000	Kennedy[a]
1964	16,026,000	Goldwater	8,757,000	Johnson[a]
1968	25,402,000	Nixon[a]	11,594,000	Humphrey
1972	61,400,000	Nixon[a]	30,000,000	McGovern

[a] Indicates winner.

SOURCE: Excerpted from Herbert E. Alexander, *Financing Politics: Money, Elections and Political Reform* (Washington, D.C.: Congressional Quarterly Press, 1976), Table 2.1, p. 28, reprinted by permission of Congressional Quarterly, Inc.

party candidates, who are entitled to only partial financing or none at all if they represent a party that did not receive at least 5 percent of the popular vote in the previous presidential election and who fail to reach that figure in the current election.

The General Election Campaign

Traditionally American presidential campaigns have been inaugurated on Labor Day, but individual candidates are free to choose other times, depending on the political circumstances. Gerald Ford, seeking to reorganize his forces after a bruising battle with challenger Ronald Reagan at the Republican national convention held in August 1976, waited until a week after Labor Day to launch his fall campaign. In contrast, in 1980 Ronald Reagan, with the Republican nomination locked up the previous May and conferred officially on him at the party's July national convention, actually started to campaign the last week in August. He did so in order to try to counteract the favorable publicity the Democratic convention held earlier that month had provided the incumbent president, Jimmy Carter. Thus the conditions under which candidates themselves win their party's nominations, plus the circumstances surrounding their opponent's choice, shape decisions on the beginning of the fall campaign.

Close attention is also paid to the locality of the first speech of the official campaign. Democratic candidates have traditionally delivered theirs in Cadillac Square in Detroit to symbolize the party's close ties with organized labor on that group's special event, Labor Day. However, Jimmy Carter chose other sites for his two presidential campaigns. In 1976 it was Warm Springs, Georgia, a city in his home state closely associated with President Franklin Roosevelt; Roosevelt visited there many times seeking comfort for his paralytic condition and it was there that he died. Four years later President Carter chose Tuscumbia, Alabama, also located in his native South. Two recent Republican candidates, Gerald Ford in 1976 and Ronald Reagan in 1980, also chose symbolic sites to launch their respective campaigns: the former, Ann Arbor, Michigan, the scene of Ford's college football triumphs, and the latter, Ellis Island in New York City harbor, the port of arrival for millions of immigrants seeking a new life in the United States.

Targeting the Campaign. As with the nomination process, presidential candidates must decide the particular states where they will concentrate their efforts in the fall campaign.* Complicating the situation is the fact that the latter contest takes place simultaneously in all 50 states rather than in stages and must be concentrated in a much shorter period of time than the nomination campaign. Moreover, unlike the nomination process, there are no legal limits on the amount of money presidential candidates can spend in the individual states in the general election; thus they have a freer hand in their choices but those choices become more difficult.

By far the most important factor in targeting the fall campaign is the electoral college. The candidate's goal is clear: to win the presidency, he or she must win a majority of the 538 electoral votes or 270 votes. This fact places a premium on carrying those states with the largest number of electoral votes. In presidential elections held in the 1970s and in 1980, the 11 largest states—California, New York, Pennsylvania, Texas, Illinois, Ohio, Michigan, New Jersey,

* Although campaign activities are, of course, carried in the national media, local media give special publicity to the candidate and thus affect the immediate audience. Moreover, some voters are flattered by the fact that a candidate takes the time and effort to come to their locality to campaign.

Florida, North Carolina, and Indiana—together had a total of 271 votes, enough to elect even a candidate who lost the other 39 states. (In 1984, these states totalled 266 electoral votes—just short of the necessary majority.) Naturally, candidates from both major political parties tend to concentrate on such states as prime targets for personal visits. Another element that affects candidates' decisions on where to campaign is the competitive situation in a particular state, that is, whether the state generally goes to one party's candidate or whether it swings back and forth from one election to the next. Distinctly one-party states are likely to be slighted by both of the major party candidates: the party in control does not think it is necessary to waste time there (in 1968 Nixon did not visit or spend money in Kansas; as one campaign aide put it, "If you have to worry about Kansas, you don't have a campaign anyway"); in contrast, the opposition party is likely to think it futile to exert much effort in such obvious enemy territory.* The "swing" states naturally draw the major portion of attention from presidential candidates of both parties.

Recently, both our major political parties have developed areas where their presidential candidates are generally successful. The Republicans have been strongest in the West; Democratic strength has been concentrated in the Northeast. The situation in the once-solid Democratic South has varied with individual elections. It was vital in the Democratic electoral strategies of Kennedy in 1960 and Carter in 1976 and helped to put both men in the White House. On the other hand, Humphrey in 1968 and McGovern in 1972 wrote off the region, and the election results reflected this decision: Humphrey carried only Texas (considered by some political observers to be a western rather than a truly southern state), and McGovern did not win any of them.† On the other hand, since 1968 the Republican candidates have thought it worthwhile to contest the southern states and Reagan even managed to defeat native son Jimmy Carter there in 1980. (The President carried only his home state of Georgia and two border states, Maryland and West Virginia.)

The regions that have been most crucial in recent presidential contests are the Middle Atlantic states—New York, Pennsylvania, and New Jersey—and the Middle West states of Ohio, Michigan, Indiana, and Illinois. Together this tier of seven highly industrial states controlled 170 electoral votes in the 1970s and the 1980 election. (In 1984, the total votes declined to 156.) They also tended to be highly competitive, which meant that campaign efforts there could be very important in deciding which candidate prevailed.

The most systematic plan in targeting a presidential campaign was developed for Jimmy Carter in 1976 by Hamilton Jordan. He assigned points to each state, using three criteria. The first was its number of electoral votes. The second was its Democratic potential based on how many Democratic office-holders there were, as well as how well McGovern had done there in 1972. The third was how much of a campaign was needed in a particular state, taking into account factors such as how well Carter

* However, presidential candidates sometimes venture into states thought to belong politically to their opponents. In 1976 Jimmy Carter made some trips into normally Republican areas in order to put President Ford on the defensive and to make him spend time and money in states he would normally carry; four years later Carter also visited California in hopes of requiring Ronald Reagan to use some resources to protect his home state.

† Political scientist John Kessel reports the comment made during the 1972 campaign that ". . . McGovern could not carry the South with Robert E. Lee as his running mate and Bear Bryant as his campaign manager."

had done in the preconvention period, how much time or resources he had previously expended in the state, and how close to Ford he was in the polls. The various campaigners were allocated points—for example, one day of Carter's time was worth seven points, Mondale's, five points, and a Carter child, one point—and then assigned states so that scheduling points matched those developed under the political-importance formula.*

Manipulating Political Appeals. *Political party labels*, unimportant in the nomination process, become a major factor in general election campaigns. Given the Democrats' status as the majority party since the days of Franklin Roosevelt, it is natural that over the years their candidates have emphasized their party affiliation and linked their opponents with the minority Republican party. Thus in 1960 John Kennedy stressed that he stood "... where Woodrow Wilson stood, and Franklin Roosevelt stood, and Harry Truman stood," whereas "... his opponent [Richard Nixon] stood with McKinley, Taft, Harding, Landon, and Dewey." (Significantly, Kennedy did not mention such popular Republican presidents as Lincoln, Theodore Roosevelt, or Dwight Eisenhower.) Twenty years later Jimmy Carter pursued a similar strategy, playing up the fact that he represented the party of Franklin Roosevelt, Harry Truman, John Kennedy, and Lyndon Johnson (leading Ronald Reagan to quip that the only Democratic president that Carter was not talking about was himself). In fact, Carter went a step further that year by appealing to the memory of unsuccessful presidential candidate Hubert Humphrey, pointing out that if a few more Democrats in each precinct had voted in 1968 for Humphrey, he, rather than Richard Nixon, would have been elected president that year.

* This carefully thought out plan is to be contrasted with the pledge Richard Nixon made at the 1960 Republican National Convention to visit all 50 states personally. In the closing days of the campaign Nixon took precious time to fly to Alaska, which he had not previously visited, while his opponent, John Kennedy, was barnstorming through heavily populated Illinois, New Jersey, New York, and the New England states.

Over the years, Republican presidential candidates have devised various tactics to counteract the partisan advantage enjoyed by their Democratic opponents. One is to advise the voters to ignore party labels and vote for the "best man." Richard Nixon used this approach in his 1960 campaign, urging Americans to cast their ballots for the person who had experience in foreign affairs, who had stood up to Soviet leader Nikita Khrushchev and bested him in a "kitchen debate."* Another tactic is to suggest that the Democratic presidential candidate does not represent the views of the rank-and-file members of the party. In 1972 Nixon charged that the Democratic convention had rejected the historic principles of that party and implored, "To those millions who have been driven out of their home in the Democratic party, we say come home." Another ploy open to Republican presidential candidates is to associate themselves with past Democratic presidents: in 1976 Gerald Ford tied his candidacy to that of former Democratic chief executive Harry Truman, who, as an underdog incumbent, struggled successfully for the same goal as Ford's: election to the office in his own right, not merely by succession. Four years later Ronald Reagan linked his own desire for major changes in American society with the "New Deal," "Fair Deal," and "New Frontier" administrations of Roosevelt, Truman, and Kennedy. (Car-

* The informal exchange between Khrushchev and Nixon over the comparative worth of communist and capitalist economic systems took place at a kitchen display at a fair in Moscow while Nixon was visiting there as vice president during the Eisenhower administration.

"Kitchen Debaters" Nikita Khruschev and Richard Nixon.

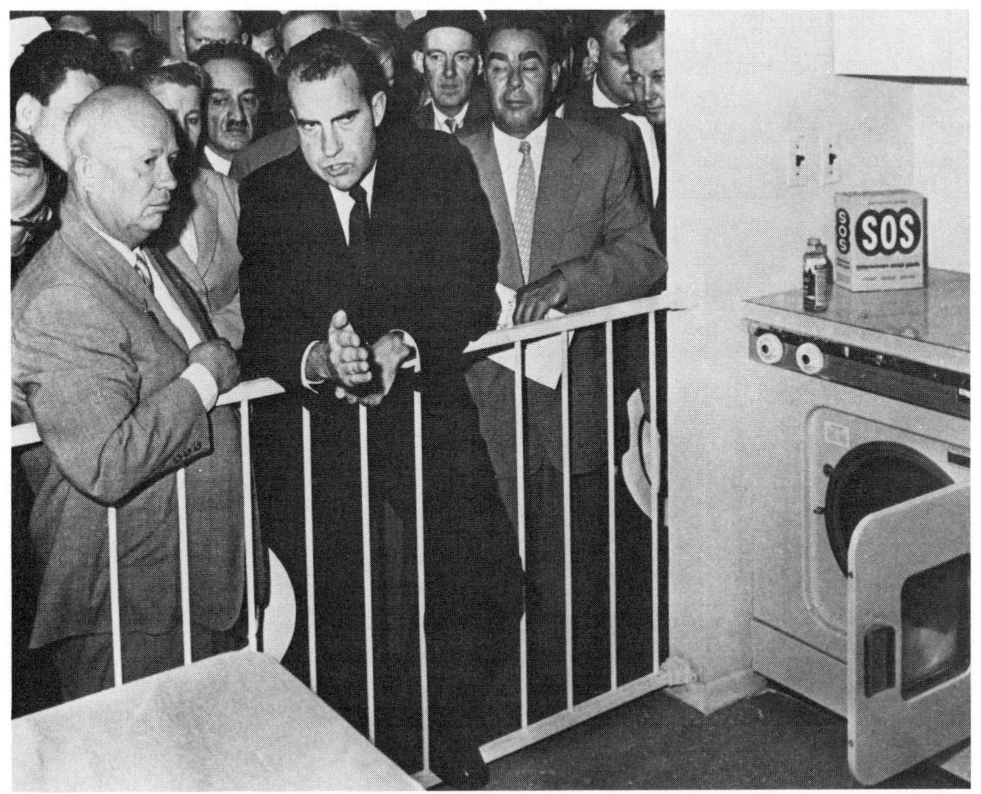

ter retorted that it was standard Republican practice to run for the presidency by ignoring former GOP chief executives* and embracing presidents of the opposite party.)

Whether a candidate represents the majority or the minority party, it is important that prominent political figures in it support his campaign. In 1964 Goldwater's candidacy suffered (although it is unlikely that he could have won the presidency in any event) from the fact that some leading Republicans dissociated themselves from the party's presidential nominee and conducted independent campaigns of their own. Senator Eugene McCarthy's lukewarm and belated endorsement of Hubert Humphrey in the last stages of the 1968 campaign did little to help the latter avert his narrow defeat that year. In 1972 large numbers of Democratic candidates for Congress and state offices deliberately dissociated themselves from the McGovern–Shriver ticket.

Incumbent presidents who are running for re-election start out with certain advantages in the electoral contest. They are typically better known to the voters than their opponents, who must strive to narrow the recognition gap between the two candidates. The incumbent president frequently assumes the role of statesman, too busy with the affairs of the nation to participate in a demeaning, partisan campaign. As journalist Timothy Crouse describes the 1972 campaign, "Around the White House, it bordered on treason to call Nixon a candidate." In 1976 Gerald Ford followed his advisers' recommendation by conducting the early stages of the campaign from the White House "Rose Garden," gathering presidential publicity by receiving visitors, signing or vetoing bills, and calling press conferences to make announcements.

While the incumbent is operating above the partisan fray, others are free to make political attacks on the opposition. Frequently, the vice-presidential candidates assume that role, as Hubert Humphrey did for the Democrats in 1964 and Robert Dole did for the Republicans in 1976.† Or the president's supporters may develop an entire team to carry on the effort. In 1972 the Committee to Re-elect the President (note that Nixon's name did not even appear in the title of the committee) organized a special surrogate's office to schedule campaign appearances of 35 White House aides, cabinet members, senators, representatives, mayors, and Republican party officials.

The incumbent president is also in a position to use the prerogatives of his office to good advantage during the election campaign. In 1976 President Ford suddenly recommended legislation to expand the national park system and to reduce the amount of down payments for mortgages guaranteed by the Federal Housing Administration. The president can disburse forms of political "patronage" available to the nation's chief executive. In 1980 President Carter announced his support for water projects in Kentucky and Tennessee that he had previously opposed, offered the steel industry protection against foreign imports, approved financial aid to enable residents of Love Canal (the polluted area near Niagara Falls, New York) to move away from that region, and announced federally subsidized loans for drought-stricken farms. Even

* Carter's allegation was true: neither Gerald Ford nor Ronald Reagan did much to invoke the memory of the popular Dwight Eisenhower, perhaps because they felt that most voters did not think of Eisenhower as a typical Republican.

† One of the interesting features of the 1980 campaign was the fact that President Carter did *not* use Vice President Mondale much in that way; instead, the president himself launched frequent personal attacks on Ronald Reagan while for the most part Mondale played the role of the "happy warrior" in the campaign.

Chicago—whose mayor, Jane Byrne, supported Edward Kennedy in the primary fight—received its share of national government "goodies," which prompted her honor to declare that while diamonds are still a girl's best friend, federal grants are the next best. Nor was President Carter insensitive to ethnic considerations: he awarded the Medal of Honor to an Italian–American veteran of World War II who had sought it for years, and he went on television to announce the provision of $670 million in credit guarantees for Poland and to praise the dignity of that nation's valiant people at a time of internal crisis.

Incumbent presidents can also utilize their office to publicize important events in foreign and military policy. During 1972 President Nixon visited both Communist China and the Soviet Union, gathering extensive media coverage in the process. In the 1980 campaign Jimmy Carter was accused of allowing statements on military policy considered beneficial to the president to be first "leaked" to the press and then ultimately confirmed by administration officials. One involved Presidential Directive 59, supposedly changing our nuclear strategy to target Soviet military installations rather than cities and industrial complexes. Another related to the development of a "stealth" aircraft that is said to be virtually invisible to enemy detection devices and thus capable of penetrating its defenses. (Critics of Carter charged that both disclosures were designed to counter attacks by Reagan that the president had allowed our military capabilities to decline compared with those of the Soviet Union.)

Challengers of incumbent presidents are faced with the problem of countering advantages possessed by the sitting president. One tactic open to them is to charge the president with abusing the powers of his office—as the Reagan people did with respect to Directive 59 and the "stealth aircraft" incidents. Another possibility open to challengers who have occupied important offices themselves is to cite the importance of their previous governmental experience. Thus during the 1980 campaign Ronald Reagan made much of the fact that he had served two terms as governor of the nation's most populous state, one whose budget was the seventh largest in the world, exceeded only by those of the six largest nations.

Because so much public attention in a presidential campaign focuses on the candidates themselves, the *personality and character* that the aspirants project are particularly important. Each campaign organization strives to create a composite image of the most attractive attributes of its candidate. Although the image necessarily deviates from reality, it must still reflect enough of the essential characteristics of the candidate to be believable. One effective tactic is to take a potential flaw and convert it into an asset. Thus, the somewhat elderly Dwight Eisenhower (he was 66 at the time of his second campaign in 1956) was pictured as a benevolent "father" (or even "grandfather") whose mature judgment was needed to lead the nation in times of stress.* In contrast, the youthful John Kennedy, who was 43 when he ran for the presidency in 1960, was characterized as a man of "vigor" who would make America "feel young again" after the Eisenhower years.

Presidential candidates frequently take their opponents' images into account when shaping their own. In 1976

* In 1980 the Republicans handled the potential problem of an even older Ronald Reagan (he was almost 70 at the time of the fall campaign) in a very different way: he was painted as an unusually vigorous man for one his age. This image was helped considerably by Reagan's full head of hair, as contrasted to Ike's bald pate.

Gerald Ford portrayed himself as a man of maturity and experience to counteract Jimmy Carter's emphasis on being a "new face" and an outsider to the Washington scene. Four years later as the incumbent president, Carter tried to come across as a deliberate and moderate person who could be trusted to maintain his calm in a crisis, as contrasted to his supposedly impetuous and irresponsible opponent, Ronald Reagan. The latter, in turn, pictured himself as a decisive leader who could overcome the nation's problems, as opposed to Carter, painted as an uncertain, vascillating person overwhelmed by the burdens of the presidency and inclined to blame the "spirit of malaise" of the American people for the country's difficulties.

Besides molding their own images to take account of their opponents', candidates can directly attack the images of their opposition to put them in a bad light. Accordingly, in 1976 Gerald Ford described Jimmy Carter as follows: "He wavers, he wanders, he wiggles, he waffles"; he also charged that his opponent had a strange way of changing his accent: "In California he tried to sound like Cesar Chavez; in Chicago, like Mayor Daley; in New York, like Ralph Nader; in Washington, like George Meany; then he comes to the farm belt and he becomes a little old peanut farmer." During the second debate, after Ford claimed that Eastern Europe was not under Soviet domination, Carter countered that the president must have been "brainwashed" when he went to Poland. (Carter was thereby comparing Ford to George Romney, the former Michigan governor whose nomination campaign collapsed in 1968 after he said he had been brainwashed by the military in the course of a trip to Vietnam.) The Georgian also said that during the second debate Ford had "... showed very vividly the absence of good judgment, good sense, and knowledge ..." expected of a president. Four years later Carter suggested that a Reagan presidency would divide Americans "... black from white, Jew from Christian, North from South, rural from urban ..." and could "... well lead our nation to war." Reagan, in turn, impugned Carter's honesty, saying that the president's promise that he would never lie to us reminded him of a quote from Ralph Waldo Emerson, "The more he talked of his honor, the more we counted our spoons."

More often, however, presidential candidates try to project a favorable image of themselves rather than cast an unfavorable light on their opponents. Thus in 1968 Nixon focused his attention on refurbishing his own former portrait as a humorless and overly aggressive political infighter. In touching up the picture, he strove to present a "new Nixon" who could laugh at himself (referring to his 1960 loss to Kennedy and his performance in the presidential debates that year, he acknowledged being "an electoral college 'dropout' who had flunked debating") and had somehow matured and become more humane over the eight years since he had last run for the presidency.

Fairly early in life many Americans begin to think of themselves as members of *ethnic, geographic, or religious groups.* As they get older, they also begin to identify with groups associated with their occupations and to consider themselves as businesspeople or farmers or members of labor unions. Sometimes people relate politically to groups to which they do *not* belong. For example, a well-to-do white liberal who sympathizes with the underdog in society may favor programs that benefit poor blacks. Moreover, such reference groups can also be negative: a self-made businessperson may have an unfavorable image of labor unions or social welfare organizations.

Presidential candidates take these group attitudes into account in devising campaign appeals. Since the days of Franklin Roosevelt, the Democratic party has aimed its campaigns at certain groups thought to be particularly susceptible to its political overtures. Included have been Southerners, blacks, members of ethnic groups, organized labor, Catholics, Jews, intellectuals, and big-city "bosses" and their political supporters. (Hence the quip that the Democratic party has more wings than a boardinghouse chicken!) At the same time, the Democrats have usually tried to depict the Republicans as the party of "big business" and the rich.

Republican candidates have been less likely to use explicit group appeals in their presidential campaigns. In fact, in 1964 Senator Goldwater conducted an antigroup campaign. The Republican candidate seemed to go out of his way to antagonize particular blocs, speaking against the Tennessee Valley Authority (TVA) in Knoxville; against Social Security financing in retirement communities like St. Petersburg, Florida; and against the "War on Poverty" in Charleston, West Virginia, near the heart of Appalachia. (In writing off such groups as "minorities," Goldwater ignored the fact that an aggregation of minorities makes up a majority.) In 1968 Richard Nixon tried a different approach, aiming his campaign at the "Forgotten Americans who did not break the law, but did pay taxes, go to work, school, church, and love their country." He thereby sought to associate the Democrats with negative reference groups such as welfare recipients, atheists, and war protestors. However, in 1972, hoping to captialize on George McGovern's unpopularity with many traditional Democratic groups, the Committee to Re-elect the President turned out campaign buttons and bumper stickers for almost 30 nationalities, provided copy for ethnic newspapers and radio stations, and made special appeals to Catholics, Jews, blacks, and Hispanics.

The 1980 presidential election involved a wide variety of group appeals by both major-party candidates. With assistance from vice-presidential candidate, Walter Mondale, and Carter's former rival, Edward Kennedy, President Carter implored union workers, members of ethnic groups, blacks, and Hispanics to stay with their traditional party. He also made a special appeal to Southerners to help re-elect a native son.

Ronald Reagan, in turn, targeted many of these same groups in his campaign. He toured a General Electric plant he had visited 26 years before when he was host of the television series "GE Theatre," appealing to union workers by pointing out that he himself had been the president of a labor union for six terms, the only presidential candidate who could make that claim. The Republican nominee also courted the Polish vote, meeting on Labor Day with Stanislaw Walesa, father of the leader of the strike against the Polish government. Reagan also wooed blacks with the argument that their high unemployment rate was attributable to the sluggish state of the economy. (Some black leaders, including the Reverend Ralph

Candidate Ronald Reagan meets with Stanislaw Walesa, father of Polish strike leader, Lech Walesa.

Abernathy and Hosea Williams—close associates of the late Martin Luther King, Jr.—unexpectedly endorsed the Republican candidate.) Reagan also used vice-presidential candidate George Bush's ties with Texas (and the fact that his son, Jeb, is married to a Mexican) to make appeals to the Hispanic population. Finally, Reagan took his campaign to the South to challenge President Carter in his home area.

Other groups took on special significance in the 1980 election. One was women, who according to polls were disproportionately in the Carter camp because they feared that Reagan might be "trigger-happy" in time of international crisis and because of his failure to support the Equal Rights Amendment. During the campaign the Republican nominee devoted a special half-hour television broadcast to an address in which he tried to assure Americans in general and women in particular that he is a man of peace.

Another group that became important in 1980 was evangelical Christians, those who believe in the literal interpretation of the Bible and its corresponding application to everyday living, many of whom report having been "born again." Conservative on both economic and social issues, they organized themselves into a variety of groups, the most famous being the Moral Majority, which as noted in Chapter 5, is associated with television preacher Jerry Falwell of Lynchburg, Virginia. Overwhelmingly in support of Jimmy Carter in 1976, many of them (including Falwell himself) in 1980 personally favored Ronald Reagan, who told a religious gathering in Dallas early in the campaign, "I know you can't endorse me. But . . . I want you to know that I endorse you!"*

Traditionally both major political parties have been associated with certain broad *issues and events* in American life. Democratic presidential candidates have generally emphasized economic issues because this gives them the chance to link the Great Depression to the Republican president, Herbert Hoover, who was in office at the time, and the chance to benefit from the fact that over the years the voters have tended to trust Democrats to handle the economy better than the Republicans. In contrast, Republican candidates have focused more on foreign policy issues because Democratic presidents were in power at the time of World Wars I and II, as well as the Korean and Vietnamese conflicts, a factor that has led many voters to conclude that Republicans are better able to keep the peace than Democrats.

However, the circumstances surrounding a particular election can lead to changes in the above pattern. In 1980 the poor economic record of the Carter administration led Ronald Reagan to focus the campaign on that issue. Meanwhile, President Carter concentrated on foreign policy so that he could raise fears about Reagan's reliability in keeping the nation out of a nuclear war.

While candidates focus on major issues in American society, they often do so only in very general terms. A catchy slogan is often used by the out party to link the one in power with unfortunate political events; thus the "Korea, corruption, and communism" brand was stamped on the Democrats by Republicans in 1952. The party in power responds in the same way, as when the Democrats defended their record that same year by telling the voters, "You never had it so good." In 1976 the situation was reversed: Democrats talked

* A poll taken by the *Los Angeles Times* during the campaign indicated that black evangelicals overwhelmingly favored Carter but that whites were divided in their preferences: those who reported that they regularly watched television preachers and/or sent them money were for Reagan, whereas the white evangelicals who did not were for Carter.

about Watergate, inflation, unemployment, and President Ford's pardon of Richard Nixon (Carter refused to attack Ford on the issue, but his vice-presidential candidate, Walter Mondale, did), whereas President Ford claimed that his administration had cut inflation in half, brought peace to the nation ("Not a single American is fighting or dying"), and restored faith, confidence, and trust in the presidency. In 1980 the 1952 pattern was repeated: Ronald Reagan blamed President Carter for the nation's mounting economic problems and for allowing us to fall far behind the Russians in military preparedness; at the same time the Democratic president pointed with pride to the signing of the Egyptian–Israeli accord, the ratification of the Panama Canal Treaty, and the development of an energy program.

This sort of general attack and defense characterizes most presidential campaigns. The party out of power has the advantage of associating all the ills of American life with the administration; the party in power is in the position of claiming that all of the nation's blessings have resulted from its leadership. The candidate who is in the most difficult situation is the nonincumbent nominee of the party in power, such as Nixon in 1960 and Humphrey in 1968. Both served as vice president in administrations whose politics they did not fully endorse. Nixon, for instance, did not believe Eisenhower was doing enough in space exploration and national defense. Humphrey opposed the bombing of North Vietnam when it was first initiated in 1965. Yet each hesitated to criticize an administration in which he had served. Humphrey's inability to disassociate himself from the Johnson administration's approach to Vietnam is considered one of the major reasons for his defeat in 1968.

While framing political issues in only very general terms, presidential candidates also typically made few concrete proposals for dealing with such issues.* Thus, in 1960 Kennedy urged that he be given the chance to "... get the nation moving again," but he was very vague about what he would specifically do to move the nation forward. Nixon was even more indefinite in 1968; he refused to spell out his plans for dealing with the major American political issue, Vietnam. His excuse was that if he did so, he might jeopardize the Paris peace talks.

There have been some presidential campaigns, however, when candidates have made specific suggestions for dealing with issues. In 1972 George McGovern proposed that the defense budget be cut by 30 percent, and early in his campaign he advocated that all persons regardless of need be given a $1,000 grant by the government. In 1980 President Reagan advocated the passage of the Kemp–Roth tax plan, which called for reducing taxes 10 percent each year over a period of three years.

In manipulating political appeals, candidates usually attempt to develop *a general theme* that will incorporate a wide variety of matters and leave the voters with an overall impression of the campaign. Sometimes the theme focuses on the candidates themselves, as did Humphrey's slogan, "He's a man you can trust," and as did the Carter–Mondale phrase, "tested and trustworthy." Or it may be essentially an appeal to a broad group, such as Nixon's "Forgotten Americans," who did not break the law but did pay their taxes, go to work, school, and church, and love their coun-

* Political scientist Donald Stokes calls "position issues" those that "... involve advocacy of governmental action from a set of alternatives ..." contrasted to "valence issues," which "... merely involve linking of the parties with some condition that is positively or negatively valued by the electorate."

try. At other times the theme is directed at issues and political events ("Korea, corruption, and communism" or "peace and prosperity") or takes the form of Kennedy's general call for action, "We've got to get the nation moving again," or McGovern's plea, "Come home, America," or Carter's promise to make the government as "... truthful, capable, and filled with love as the American people," or Reagan's invitation to a "new beginning." Once the theme is established, candidates try, by constant repetition, to get the electorate to respond emotionally to it. Their success in doing so, however, depends on another important aspect of presidential campaigns: how political appeals are communicated to the American voter.

"Fellow Reaganites, Reaganians, Reaganizers, Reaganists, Reaganologists, Reaganonomists, Reaganicians, Reaganettes, Reaganolians, Reaganuks, Reaganiks, Reaganauts, Reaganuts, Reaganheads, Reaganophiles, and Reagan-o-Rooters . . ."

Communicating Political Appeals. With a voter audience twice the size of the "*selectorate*"* and a much shorter campaign period to reach the electorate, it is natural that presidential candidates place even more emphasis on the use of the mass media during the election campaign than they did during the nomination process. One measure of that emphasis is the fact that in the 1980 campaign Jimmy Carter and Ronald Reagan each spent some $18 million of the $29.4-million subsidy from the federal government on television, radio, and print advertisements, with the heaviest concentration of such ads appearing in the last few days of the campaign. Of the three types of media, television is by far the most important. It takes much less effort to watch than to read, particularly since viewing can be combined with other activities but reading cannot. In addition, people are more inclined to believe what they see on television than what they read in the newspapers or hear on the radio. As a result, since 1952, television has been the chief source of campaign information for most Americans.

Over the years presidential candidates have employed a number of television formats. Richard Nixon's 1968 campaign used 60-second spot announcements during popular programs such as Rowan and Martin's "Laugh-in" and appearances before panels of citizens who asked questions that Nixon could answer in a seemingly spontaneous fashion. The makeup of both the panels and the questions were carefully screened by Nixon's advisers in order to avoid possible embarrassment or surprise. To make the show even more interesting, former football coach and television personality Bud Wilkinson intercepted the questions and lateraled them to the candidate.

In 1972 the use of television for political communication underwent additional change. Although spot commercials continued to be used (one, for example, symbolized McGovern's proposed cuts in defense spending with a hand sweeping away toy soldiers and miniature ships and planes), five-minute commercial advertisements became more common. There were also longer programs, consisting of a series of addresses by McGovern on Vietnam and

* Political scientist Hugh Heclo uses this term to describe persons who help to choose presidential nominees as contrasted to the "electorate," which casts its vote in the general election.

"LET'S FACE IT—IF HE USES ALL THE EQUAL TIME HE'S ENTITLED TO, HE'S BOUND TO MAKE A FOOL OF HIMSELF IN PUBLIC."

the issue of corruption. Semi-documentary formats such as a candidate's discussing issues with the "man in the street" were used as well. McGovern was filmed interacting with workers and small businessmen, and Nixon's trips to China and the Soviet Union were dramatized for television viewers.

In 1976 Ford utilized the medium somewhat more imaginatively than Carter. The president held an informal television interview with television personality and former baseball player Joe Garagiola, who tossed him some "gopher-ball" questions: "How many foreign leaders have you met with, Mr. President?" to which Ford modestly replied, "124, Joe." In the last stages of the campaign the Ford forces also broadcast short television interviews with voters in Georgia, who described Carter as "wishy-washy." Carter's use of television concentrated on short commercials in which he looked directly into the camera and talked about various issues, aimed at counteracting Ford's version of him and representing himself as a strong, positive leader with specific programs.

During the 1980 campaign the television ads varied in length from 30 seconds to 30 minutes, but most were short spot messages designed to reach peak audiences. The Carter television ads appeared in three separate stages: the first showed the candidate being presidential, that is, meeting with foreign dignitaries and working late at night in the Oval Office; the second consisted of interviews with people "in the street" saying that Reagan "scared" them; the third had Carter being praised by party figures such as Lady Bird Johnson and Ted Kennedy and by rank-and-file Democrats—a farmer, a steelworker, and a rubberworker. Most of the Reagan TV ads featured the candidate himself, whom the Republicans considered to be a superb communicator, looking straight into the camera. They stressed three themes: Reagan's record as governor of California; his stand on issues, especially the economy; and a recitation of the record of President Carter, illustrated the graphs of rising consumer prices.

On three occasions in recent years debates between presidential candidates became the most important communication source of the campaign.* The first occurred in 1960 between then Vice President Richard Nixon and Senator John Kennedy. In the first debate Nixon's somewhat uncertain manner and his physical appearance (he had not fully recovered from a recent illness and

* A problem in holding presidential debates is a provision of the Federal Communications Act of 1934 requiring the networks to provide equal time to *all* candidates, including those of minor parties. In 1960 Congress temporarily suspended the provisions of the Act to allow the Nixon–Kennedy debates. In 1976 and again in 1980 the debates were sponsored and paid for by the League of Women Voters. The networks supposedly covered them as "news events," a legal fiction that was exposed when the first Carter–Ford debate was interrupted for 28 minutes until an audio failure could be repaired.

the television accentuated his heavy beard) were contrasted with Kennedy's confident demeanor and bright, alert image (he wore a blue shirt and dark suit that contrasted with the television studio background rather than fading into it as did Nixon's light-colored clothes). Also, unlike Nixon, Kennedy had prepared thoroughly for the debates. The result was a perceived victory for the young Massachusetts senator.* Also contributing to that perception was the fact that people had not expected Kennedy to best Nixon, who had come into political prominence in part because of his debating skills in previous campaigns. From that point on Kennedy's campaign took on more enthusiasm and the senator himself credited the debate for his eventual close victory over the vice president.

In 1976 debates again played a major part in the campaign. In this case it was the second encounter between President Ford and Jimmy Carter that was crucial. In that debate, Ford made a statement that he did not consider countries of Eastern Europe (in particular, Yugoslavia, Romania, and Poland) to be under Soviet domination. To make matters worse, the President refused to change his answer even after the startled questioner (a newspaperman) gave him the opportunity to do

* This was especially true of people who watched the first Nixon–Kennedy debate on television. However, those who heard that same debate on the radio thought the two candidates came out about equally.

John Kennedy makes a point in 1960 debate with Richard Nixon.

so; in fact, it was not until several days after the debate that the President's staff finally convinced him to retract his statement. Many observers of the campaign considered that gaffe to be the crucial event of the campaign—one that ended the dramatic decline in public support for Carter (and the increased support for Ford) that had characterized the previous month of the campaign.

In 1980 the debate situation became more complicated. The sponsors of the debate, the League of Women Voters, originally extended an invitation to debate not only to President Carter and Ronald Reagan but also to independent candidate John Anderson; the latter's presence was based on the fact that his standing in the public-opinion polls exceeded the 15 percent level the League established as a cutoff point. Carter refused to participate on the grounds that the debate would serve to legitimize the Anderson candidacy, which he claimed was strictly a "creation of the media"; in contrast, Reagan, who perceived that Anderson would draw more votes away from Carter than from himself, accepted the League's invitation and criticized Carter for refusing to debate. Ultimately, just a week before election day (when Anderson's public support had fallen below 15 percent) a single debate was held between the two major-party candidates. Although both men looked and handled themselves well and neither made a serious mistake, most observers considered that Reagan won the debate on style rather than substance. Although Carter aides congratulated themselves that the president had kept the focus of the debate on Reagan rather than his own presidential record, the tactic apparently backfired. On the one hand, many viewers thought the president was too aggressive in his accusations; on the other hand, they felt reassured by Reagan's responses and were convinced that he would not be a trigger-happy president if he were elected to the office. *

A third source of communication in presidential campaigns is the coverage provided by representatives of the mass media themselves, both the broadcast (television and radio) and print (newspapers and magazines) media. However, these representatives are not nearly as important in general election campaigns as they are in the nomination stage. By the time of the fall election, the situation is much more structured. The contest is essentially down to two candidates, who by then are fairly well known to the electorate; in addition, the voters are in a position to associate the candidates with the respective parties they represent and to evaluate them on that basis.† Moreover, the candidates themselves have more money to spend on campaign communications than they did in the nomination process and if debates are held, they are more focused (typically involving only two candidates) and reach a wider audience than any in the nomination campaign.

The type of campaign coverage by the media is similar to that in the nomination stage. Great attention is paid to the election "game," that is, which party candidate is leading in the public-opinion polls and by how much, and the "hoopla"—campaign rallies and the like.

---

* In addition, journalist Albert Hunt suggests that Reagan convinced many viewers of the debate that he was sufficiently smart to go head-to-head with the president and not crumble. On the other hand, the president did not meet the great expectations the viewers had of his debate performance, namely, that he explain why things had not gone very well in the previous four years and why he would do better in a second term.

† Political scientist Michael Robinson also argues that the media have less of an effect in elections when the candidates take very different stands on the issues, as was the case in the Reagan–Carter contest in 1980.

The media also tend to focus on "campaign issues" (rather than policy ones) such as Jimmy Carter's remark in the 1976 campaign that he " . . . lusted after women in his heart . . . " and Ford's previously mentioned comment on Eastern Europe. The same focus continued in 1980: the media played up Jimmy Carter's attacks on Ronald Reagan and the latter's advocating the teaching of the literal interpretation of the biblical account of creation on an equal basis with the theory of evolution.

Political scientist Thomas Patterson's study of the 1976 election contest does indicate, however, that the voters became more aware of the candidates' positions on policy issues as the campaign progressed. He attributes some of that increase to their familiarity with the policy tendencies of the Democratic and Republican parties. However, his analysis also shows that newspaper coverage of policy issues increased voters' awareness of them, particularly those voters who had previously not been highly interested in policy issues. In contrast, the short, superficial coverage of the issues by network news did not raise voters' awareness of the issues.

Thus despite the dominance of television in recent presidential contests, the other media continue to play a role in such campaigns. Newspapers not only cover the issues in more detail than television but are free to endorse candidates. (Over the years such endorsements have clearly favored the Republican candidates, except in 1964, when the press favored Johnson over Goldwater.) The print media are also available for advertisements stressing visual effects. In 1960 the Democrats used pictures of John Kennedy and his attractive wife, Jackie, in many of their ads. In 1976 the Republicans printed full-page ads comparing the cover of *Newsweek* magazine, which featured President Ford, with the cover of *Playboy* magazine, which carried its controversial interview with Carter in which he confessed that he " . . . lusted after women in his heart."

Radio also plays a role in presidential campaigns. It is less expensive to use than television and can be used in ways that television cannot, such as broadcasting to commuting drivers, as President Ford did in a series of early morning chats during the 1976 campaign. There is also the distinct possibility that a particular candidate will come across better on radio, a reason suggested for President Nixon's using the medium for more speeches than he delivered on television during the 1972 campaign. Moreover, in some cases, as with National Public Radio, presidential campaigns are carried in much more depth than they are on television.

Thus the formats available in the various media make it possible to emphasize different types of appeals and to reach disparate groups. Political scientist Dan Nimmo distinguishes between two major types of audiences. The first consists of the politically concerned and interested, who use the print media as well as television and radio to obtain information on presidential campaigns. The second contains less politically involved persons who must be reached through television and sometimes radio, particularly by means of spot announcements, such as those used by Richard Nixon during his 1968 campaign.

Campaign Organization and Workers. Although the mass media reach more people in the general election campaign than in the nomination contest (there is more money spent in a shorter period of time and some voters become politically interested only after the parties nominate their respective candidates), nonetheless not everyone personally follows the election campaign, particularly in print and on radio. They are dependent on those who do to pass along information on such matters as the candidates' stands on the issues. (Of course, the transmitters often alter the messages in keeping with their own views and biases.) Beyond that, personal contacts are particularly important in getting many people to make the most basic political decision: whether or not to vote at all. Sometimes the only thing that will overcome the apathy of citizens is the dogged determination of someone to see that they register to vote and then to take them to the polls.

Presidential candidates typically start the general election campaign with a core of individuals who, in effect, constitute their own personal organization. If there has been a spirited nomination battle, the major organizers of the campaign shift their attention to the general election. Thus John Kennedy put his brother Robert in charge of his 1960 campaign against Richard Nixon, and Hamilton Jordan continued as the head of Jimmy Carter's 1976 fall campaign. Other persons who worked for the candidate in the primary and caucus-convention states are also generally available for the election campaign.* Moreover, incumbent presidents frequently shift key members of their administration to work on the fall campaign. In 1972 Richard Nixon initially put his attorney general, John Mitchell, in charge of the Committee to Re-elect the President and transferred other persons in the White House office to assignments on the committee. Three key figures in the Carter administration, Robert Strauss, Hamilton Jordan, and Gerald Rafshoon, played crucial roles in the 1980 campaign.

However, because the electorate for the general campaign is so much broader than the selectorate that participates in the nomination phase, presidential candidates must expand their fall supporters to include people who have not been involved previously. One potential source of new recruits is political rivals who sought the nomination themselves. In 1972 George McGovern asked Hubert Humphrey to campaign for him; Humphrey did so out of personal friendship and party loyalty. Candidates may seek to co-opt not only the personal support of their rivals, but also the latter's campaign workers. In 1976 in many states the Ford and Reagan people co-chaired the general election campaign. However, in many instances personal loyalties and commitments to issues are so strong that it is not possible to recruit such workers. In 1968 the Humphrey organization was unsuccessful in getting many of Eugene McCarthy's supporters to work in the general election campaign after McCarthy lost the presidential nomination. In 1980 many persons who backed Edward Kennedy's unsuccessful bid for the Democratic nomination did not work for President Carter in the fall campaign.

Individuals associated with the regular party organization are another potential source of campaign workers. Termed "organizational loyalists" by political scientist John Kessel, these are the individuals who owe their allegiance to the party instead of a particular presidential candidate or a set of political issues. Because of such loyalties, they are often willing to work in the fall campaign for whichever candidate wins their party's nomination, no matter what their personal feelings about that person. At the same time, because they are pragmatic and not ideological, party loyalists may not work hard for a presidential candidate who they think is a loser and will hurt the party ticket. Many Republicans took this attitude to-

* Some may not be. In 1972, after George McGovern forced his initial vice-presidential candidate, Senator Thomas Eagleton of Missouri, off the ticket because of revelations that the senator had been treated for past mental illness, some of McGovern's youthful supporters became disillusioned and did not work for him in the fall campaign.

ward Goldwater in 1964, as did some Democratic leaders toward Humphrey in 1968 and McGovern in 1972.

Another potential source of workers in presidential general-election campaigns is state and local political parties. Traditionally there have been problems getting such organizations involved in presidential campaigns. For one thing, races at the leaders' own level are more important to their interests (particularly in patronage positions) than the presidency. Moreover, the national, state, and local organizations are rivals for the same resources, such as visits by candidates and financial donations. Finally, the campaign finance legislation passed in the early 1970s providing public funds for presidential campaigns prohibited state and local parties from spending money on such campaigns.

However, as previously suggested, this latter situation changed with the passage of the 1979 amendment to the campaign finance legislation, permitting state and local organizations to spend money in presidential campaigns for any purpose except campaign advertising and hiring outside personnel. This legislation enabled both parties in 1980 to develop grass-roots support for their presidential campaigns. However, the Republicans clearly outdid the Democrats that year: early in the fall campaign Reagan met with Republican members of Congress on the steps of the Capitol to symbolize cooperation among all elements of the party to elect Republicans to public office. As election day approached, the GOP claimed to have half a million Reagan volunteers ringing doorbells and another 400,000 manning telephone banks on his behalf.

However, Democratic presidential candidates have generally benefited from another major source of campaign workers: those provided by organized labor. According to journalist Theodore White, in 1968 the AFL–CIO claimed to have registered 4.6-million voters, printed and distributed over 100-million pamphlets, operated telephone banks in 638 localities, sent out 70,000 house-to-house canvassers, and provided almost 100,000 volunteers on election day to get people to the polls. Of course, this effort was extended on Hubert Humphrey's behalf and is credited with eventually helping to swing into line a large number of workers who initially planned to vote for George Wallace.

In contrast, the antipathy of George Meany and other AFL–CIO leaders toward George McGovern caused the organization to remain neutral in the 1972 presidential race; its efforts were concentrated on helping elect Democratic congressmen and state and local officials. In 1976 the AFL–CIO returned to its traditional policy of supporting Democratic presidential candidates and played an important role in getting its members and their families registered and to the polls to vote for Jimmy Carter on election day. Moreover, despite the fact that some of its major leaders backed Senator Kennedy in the Democratic nomination struggle, labor generally did support President Carter in the 1980 election, with the National Education Association especially active on his behalf.

Campaign Finance. The campaign reform legislation previously described has had a major impact on recent general election campaigns. In 1976 both Ford and Carter accepted federal matching funds ($21.8-million each that year) and were therefore restricted to that figure (plus another $3.2-million that each national committee could spend on behalf of its presidential candidate) for the entire campaign. As a result, both sides had to conduct more restricted campaigns than they did in 1972, when the Republicans spent $61 million and the Democrats $30 million. The public subsidy provided equally to both candidates meant that Ford had to forego the traditional Republican advantage in campaign funds. However, as the incumbent president, he received a great deal of free publicity, and his "Rose Garden" strategy enabled him to harbor his financial resources for the last 10 days of the campaign, in which he spent $4 million on TV and radio broadcasting, primarily in airing television commercials with Joe Garagiola. All told, both candidates spent about half of their total campaign outlay on the mass media, particularly television, so they had limited funds available for organizing the campaign at the grass-roots level. Buttons, bumper stickers, and yard signs, which had been used extensively in former campaigns, were largely missing (recall that under the law then in effect state and local parties could not assist the presidential campaign by spending money for such purposes), as were the fund-raising activities of previous elections.

The 1980 campaign brought new developments in campaign finance. The two major-party candidates accepted public financing and, as was previously indicated, each spent about $18 million of the $29.4 million provided by the federal government on the mass media, which again meant that they had limited funds available for grass-roots activities. However, this time the law permitted state and local parties to make expenditures for such activities. Preliminary figures provided by the Federal Election Commission indicate that Republican state and local committees spent $15 million on grass-roots efforts on Reagan's behalf compared with $5 million expended by Democratic organizations for Carter.

Also of increased importance in the 1980 campaign were the actions of independent groups in support of Reagan. In the summer of 1980 several organizations announced plans to spend up to $70 million on media efforts for the Republican candidate. A citizen's interest group, Common Cause, together with the Federal Election Commission and the Carter–Mondale Presidential Committee, legally challenged such expenditures on the grounds that such groups were not truly autonomous since some of their leaders had been closely associated with Reagan in past political campaigns. Although such challenges were unsuccessful, they did impede the fund-raising efforts of the independent groups and forced them to cut back on their original plans. Eventually it was estimated that independent organizations spent $10 million on Reagan's behalf. While such expenditures were much smaller than originally anticipated, they were nonetheless significant: independent groups were estimated to have spent only $100,000 for President Carter, 1 percent of that expended for Reagan.*

Thus both the rules of the game and campaign strategies and resources developed by the opposing candidates shape the nature of presidential campaigns. As indicated by the following

"According to our estimates, a campaign budget around six point two million is needed to successfully sing your praises."

Drawing by Bernard Schoenbaum. © 1984 The New Yorker Magazine, Inc.

* Carter, however, did better than Reagan with labor unions: estimates indicate that they spent $15 million for the Democratic president compared to $1 million for the Republican nominee.

section, the same is true of congressional campaigns.

ELECTING MEMBERS OF CONGRESS

The Rules of the Election Contest

Apportionment and Drawing of District Lines. Unlike presidential aspirants, congressional candidates do not face complex electoral college rules governing how special types of votes are determined and counted; they do not need a majority of votes to be elected; nor do they have to contend with contingency procedures in the event they fail to receive some proportion of the vote. All that congressional aspirants need to do is win a plurality of the popular votes. Moreover, senatorial aspirants, as well as House candidates in states that have only one representative, have an easily defined constituency—the whole state population. But those who seek a seat in the House from the other kind of states face a very real problem: how are the geographical limits of their constituency determined? What rules of the game govern that decision?

The Constitution provides that members of the House of Representatives be apportioned among the states according to population. In order to keep the allocation of House seats current with changes in state populations, an enumeration of national population every 10 years was prescribed, a practice that has been followed each decade since 1790.

The Constitution does not establish a permanent size for the House of Representatives, leaving the matter to Congress. Beginning with 65 members, the House gradually expanded over the years until it reached the size of 435 in 1912 after New Mexico and Arizona came into the Union. Congress has generally maintained the membership at that figure since then.*

Holding the size of the House of Representatives constant in the face of national population growth has resulted in an increase in the average number of persons represented by each legislator. In 1912 the figure was just over 200,000; today it is over 500,000. Apportioning the permanent House membership among the various states means that after each census, each state gains, loses, or stays even depending on how its population changed in relation to the national average in the preceding decade.†

Thus the provisions of the Constitution pertaining to apportionment and the laws of Congress establishing the size of the House of Representatives together provide the means for determining how many representatives each state is allowed. For the congressional candidate, however, an even more salient issue remains: what method will be used to distribute congressional seats within a state?

For the first half-century of the nation's existence, each state was free to determine how congressional seats were to be apportioned internally. Many states elected their representatives at large, much as they allocated electoral votes for presidential candidates. Congress itself, however, reacted differently

* When Alaska and Hawaii were admitted into the Union in the 1950s, two representatives (one for each) were temporarily added to the House membership. After the 1960 census, the membership was again reduced to 435.

† As a result of reapportionment required by the 1980 census, 17 seats in the House of Representatives had to be moved from one state to another. States in the Northeast and Midwest generally lost seats while those in the West and South won them. Most affected were New York, whose House delegation declined from 39 to 34, and Florida, whose delegation increased from 15 to 19.

to the two situations: it permitted states to make their own decisions on electoral college matters but in 1842 intervened in legislative apportionment by requiring that members of the House of Representatives be chosen in separate, "single-member" districts.

Although single-member districts have the virtue of making individual legislators responsible to a limited number of constitutents, they are also subject to the vice of having their boundaries drawn to favor certain groups over others, typically by distributing voters so as to maximize the political influence of a state's majority party. (A state legislature draws the boundaries of its own legislative districts as well as those of the state's congressional districts.) This feat is accomplished by concentrating voters who support the minority party in a few legislative districts, allowing their candidates to carry those constituencies by wide margins, or by spreading them fairly evenly and seeing to it that they are outnumbered by the majority party's supporters in the districts concerned. The purpose of both techniques is to minimize the minority party's (hence, maximize the majority party's) number of district victories.

The common result is strangely shaped legislative districts. Some are *noncontiguous;* others, while contiguous, are long, thin strips, *not compact* entities. In fact, one state legislative district in Massachusetts that resembled a salamander was responsible for the coining of a word, **gerrymander** (the Democratic governor at the time was Elbridge Gerry), that is used to describe the technique by which legislative district boundaries are manipulated politically.

Gerrymandering can benefit not only the majority party but other kinds of political interests. Incumbent legislators manipulate boundaries of districts to protect themselves against electoral challengers from within their own party.

Sitting state legislators as well as congressional representatives avoid political battles against one another by maintaining the boundaries of their districts in the face of population shifts within the state that call for redistributing. This latter technique, known as the **"silent" gerrymander,** leads to the third abuse of legislative districts: *different-sized constituencies.* Areas that lose population are overrepresented in that their state legislators and members of Congress represent relatively few people; regions that gain residents are underrepresented since their representatives have extra-large constituencies. Thus the silent gerrymander generally tends to benefit rural areas with dwindling numbers and to work to the disadvantage of urban localities with burgeoning populations.

As the nation became urbanized, the silent gerrymander produced more and more unequal legislative districts. The disparities were particularly pronounced at the state level, where constitutional provisions granted local units (such as towns and counties) representation in the state legislature, frequently without regard to their size. In 1960 the most populous district of the California state Senate had 422 times as many people as the smallest one. At the national level, the differences were less marked; even so, the ratio between the largest and smallest congressional districts in Texas in 1960 was four to one. Yet neither state legislatures nor successive Congresses were disposed to change the situation. It was asking too much to expect representatives, many of whom came from malapportioned and gerrymandered districts, to commit possible political suicide by changing the system. Faced with the unwillingness of legislative bodies to remedy the situation, aggrieved parties turned to the courts for assistance.

For a number of years the courts refused to deal with the abuses of gerrymandering, taking the position that legislative apportionment is a "political" problem whose remedy lies not with the judiciary but with state legislatures and Congress. However, in a 1962 case, *Baker* v. *Carr,* the Supreme Court held that legislative reapportionment was not a "political" question and, therefore, federal courts could hear such matters. Several landmark cases followed. In *Wesberry* v. *Sanders* (1964) the court invalidated unequal congressional districts in Georgia; citing the language in the Constitution providing that representatives be apportioned among the states according to population and that they be chosen by the people of the states, the justices ruled that ". . . as nearly as practicable, one man's vote in a congressional election is to be worth as much as another's." (The opinion was popularly condensed to **"one man, one vote."**) The same year, in *Reynolds* v. *Sims*, the court held that the "equal protection of the laws" clause of the Fourteenth Amendment requires that state legislative districts be substantially equal and that seats in both houses of a bicameral state legislature must be apportioned on the basis of population.

For a period thereafter it appeared that the Supreme Court would use the same approach to deal with there districting of both state legislatures and the House of Representatives. However, in the 1972 case of *White* v. *Weiser* the Court invalidated a Texas plan for congressional districts that provided for a maximum population disparity of only 4 percent between districts on the grounds that the plan did not meet the requirement of a good-faith effort to make the districts equal. By way of contrast, in *Mahan* v. *Howell,* decided that same year, the court upheld are districting plan for the Virginia House of Delegates with a disparity of over 16 percent between districts under the reasoning that the state legislature was following a rational state policy, in this case of protecting political subdivisions (cities and counties) in order to provide representation for local governmental units. Thus the court continues to seek precise mathematical equality among congressional districts at the same time that it remains satisfied with eliminating gross malapportionment for state legislative districts.*

Few decisions of the Supreme Court have had more immediate repercussions than those dealing with legislative apportionment. State legislatures throughout the country were forced to reapportion themselves, as well as draw new congressional districts. Hundreds of lawsuits were filed challenging the validity of both old and new legislative districts. Congress and the state legislatures sought ways to avoid some of the effects of the reapportionment decisions. Most objectionable to state lawmakers has been the requirement that both houses of the state legislature be

* In a 1983 case, *Karcher v. Daggart*, the Supreme Court invalidated a New Jersey legislative redistricting plan in which the congressional districts varied in population by a maximum of 0.69 of one percent.

based on population. The late Senator Everett Dirksen of Illinois sought to initiate a constitutional amendment to allow one house to be based on some other criterion (such as geographical units), but it failed to pass the Senate. Later attempts to initiate such an amendment through actions of the state legislatures have also been unsuccessful.

To date, the decisions have been generally successful in rectifying the disparities in population of both state–legislative and congressional districts. But they have scarcely touched the other abuses of gerrymandering: drawing noncontiguous and noncompact districts with strange shapes to benefit particular groups. Thus it is possible for a state legislature to distribute residents equally among districts but still benefit the majority party or an incumbent legislator.* A recent practice is to add suburban dwellers to an essentially rural or big-city constituency but to keep their number sufficiently small so that the rural or city residents still dominate the district. Candidates still have to contend with this situation in running for state legislatures and the House of Representatives.

Despite these efforts of legislators to preserve the status quo, the reapportionment decisions have nonetheless brought about changes in the character of both state–legislative and congressional districts. However, the fear of many persons that conservative Republican legislators from rural areas would be replaced by liberal Democratic legislators from large, central cities has generally been unfounded. What has happened is that fast-growing suburbs (particularly those on the outer fringes of metropolitan areas), many of them populated by Republicans and conservative Democrats, have experienced the greatest increase in representation. Thus in many instances—particularly in the North, Midwest, and West—it is conservative, suburban Republicans and Democrats (not liberal, big-city Democrats) that have replaced conservative rural Republicans both in state legislatures and the House of Representatives.

Congressional Campaigns

Congressional campaigns are similar to presidential ones in several ways. The congressional candidate makes the same basic political appeals involving his personal image, his party label, pleas for group support, general positions on issues, and the development of a campaign theme. He also seeks the best means to communicate his appeals and the best use of money and manpower to do so. To that end, he acquires and allocates scarce political resources for conversion into votes.

There are, however, important differences between the two types of campaigns. Perhaps most basic is the great advantage a congressional incumbent enjoys over a challenger. First of all, the incumbent is more likely to be running in a relatively homogeneous one-party state or district, whereas a candidate for the presidency has to compete for a more diverse and competitive nationwide constituency. Second, even if the general party competition in a state or congressional district is close, advantages accrue to the incumbent simply because as a senator or House member he or she has contacts with many constituents and frequently does favors even for those who normally identify with the opposite party. Due to gratitude for such services, plus a belief that an incumbent may be unbeatable anyway, social and economic groups that generally support the other party often yield to his or her appeal.

As political scientist David Mayhew

Senator Everett Dirksen of Illinois.

* When partisan difficulties develop over legislative redistricting, federal judicial panels are often appointed to make such decisions. Frequently, however, their decisions also reflect the partisan backgrounds of the judges.

suggests, an incumbent senator or member of Congress can use his or her office to make various kinds of appeals to constituents. One type of activity is *"advertising"*—getting his or her name before the electorate to create a favorable image through making frequent visits to constituents, addressing high-school commencements, and sending out infant-care booklets. A second activity is *"credit-claiming"*—creating the impression that he or she is responsible for the building of a new dam in the district or the awarding of a grant to a local government or university; the incumbent can also emphasize "casework" for individual constituents—seeing that older persons get their social security benefits, students the information needed to write term papers. The legislator can also engage in *"position-taking"*—making public statements or taking action such as cosponsoring legislation that will appeal to particular constituents. (In 1973, 76 senators supported a provision to block trade benefits to the Soviet Union until it allowed Jews to emigrate without paying high fees to leave the country.) As Mayhew suggests, the emphasis that legislators give to their various activities varies: senators participate more in position-taking than House members, who tend to favor credit-claiming.

As we shall see in Chapter 10, incumbent legislators enjoy a variety of privileges that enable them to carry on the above activities. Included are travel allowances for frequent trips home, the franking privilege that permits them to distribute a broad variety of literature to their constituents without mailing charges,* the opportunity to appear on local television and radio programs, and money to hire staff members to handle casework in their states or districts.

The incumbent also enjoys another advantage over the challenger: access to campaign workers. Unlike the presidential candidate, someone running for Congress has no pool of regular party workers to which he or she can automatically turn. Since many states do not have any party organization for congressional districts, individual candidates must build their own following. An incumbent can call on those who have helped in past races, but a challenger who is seeking a congressional seat for the first time must start from scratch. In addition, incumbent legislators can assign campaign duties to regular members of their staff situated in Washington or their home state or district.

The advantages of incumbency are especially marked in elections for the House of Representatives. Congressional districts are often drawn to benefit incumbents; moreover, the longer members of Congress are in office, the better known they become to the voters. As political scientist Richard Fenno points out, House members develop a "home style" by which they seek to inspire "trust" from the voters, emphasizing their personal qualifications and moral character rather than issues, policy, or even partisanship. In contrast, their challengers typically suffer from major disadvantages: lack of political experience,† an unrealistic assessment of their chances of winning, limited coverage from the media, and a shortage of money with which to conduct their campaign. As a result, incumbents tend

* However, under existing law, mass mailings at public expense cannot be made less than 60 days before a primary or general election in which the incumbent is a candidate.

† When an incumbent is thought to be vulnerable for reasons such as running in a newly created congressional district, newness to office (such as a first termer), advanced age, and the like, he or she is more likely to draw a challenge from a person with considerable political experience.

"Well, it's a new approach."

Drawing by Whitney Darrow. © 1976 The New Yorker Magazine, Inc.

to be victorious, even when national political tides are running against their party. In 1980 when Ronald Reagan was defeating Jimmy Carter handily for the presidency and the Republicans succeeded in recapturing the Senate for the first time since 1955, 89 percent of Democrats in the House of Representatives defeated Republican challengers in the fall congressional elections.

While incumbency is also a factor in Senate elections, it is not nearly as important as it is in races for the House. Senators represent entire states, which are not as likely to be as heavily partisan or tailored to their particular political interests as are individual House districts. Senators do not generally have as close personal relationships with their constituents as House members do with their smaller constituencies; moreover, senators are more clearly associated with national political issues, many of which are highly controversial, than members of the lower chamber. Senators also face more potential challengers, many of whom have considerable political experience and are better able to raise money than opponents of incumbents in House races. The media also cover Senate campaigns more extensively than those of the House and, in the process, give more publicity and resulting visibility to opponents of Senate incumbents than to House challengers. All these factors make the results of Senate races much more competitive than those of the House: only 54 percent of the Democratic incumbent senators won in 1980 compared to the previously noted 89 percent of House Democrats who survived a general election challenge that year.

The campaign finance situation for members of Congress also differs from that of presidential contenders. As we have seen, the latter now enjoy partial public financing for presidential primaries and full financing for the general election; but congressional candidates must raise all their funds from private sources. Moreover, for candidates who accept financing, there are spending limitations in presidential elections, which are equalized between the candidates of the two major parties; in contrast, the limits set by the 1974 legislation on congressional spending in the general election ($150,000 each for senatorial candidates and $70,000 for House candidates) no longer apply since they were invalidated by *Buckley* v. *Valeo*. As a result, incumbents have an advantage: they find it easier to raise money than challengers (people are not moved to give money to probable losers) and usually outspend their rivals by a ratio of 2:1.* Even more difficult for challengers is the fact that the Supreme Court upheld the legislative limits on contributions ($1000 for individuals, $5000 for political committees), which means that money must come from a wide variety of sources.

A source that has become increasingly important in financing congressional campaigns in recent years is special-interest groups that channel their contributions through political action committees (PAC'S). Figure 8.1 indicates that PAC contributions increased almost six times between 1974 and 1984, growing from $12.5 million to $83.1 million. In 1974, 608 PAC's were in operation; their total contributions constituted 14 percent of all moneys received by House candidates and 12 percent of those raised by Senate candidates. In 1982, 3,371 PAC's participated in the congressional elections; their total contributions amounted to 31 percent of moneys raised by House candidates and 19 percent of those received by Senate candidates.

A variety of groups utilize PAC's to channel their contributions in congressional contests. Traditionally labor has been the major user of PAC's but in recent years corporate and business-related trade associations have increased their use of PAC's the fastest. Generally speaking, labor PAC's have given most of their contributions to Democratic candidates, corporate ones to Republican ones, and trade associations have split their funds, with Republican can-

* In addition, political scientists Roger Davidson and Walter Oleszek have recently estimated that salary, travel, office, staff, and communication allowances are worth more than $1 million over a two-year House term and between $4 million and $7 million over a six-year Senate term.

Figure 8.1 Growth of Special-Interest Contributions to Federal Candidates (1974–1982)
(SOURCE: Federal Election Commission)

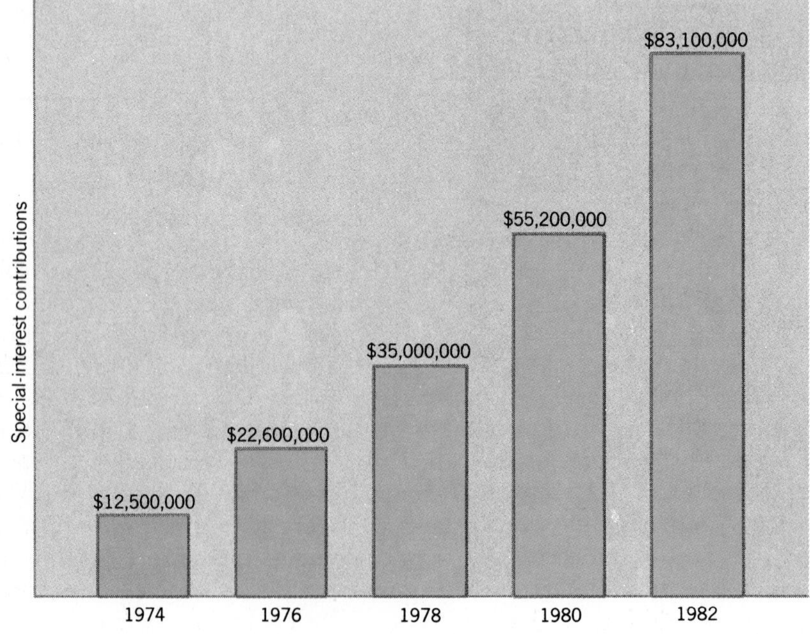

didates receiving somewhat more than Democratic ones. These PAC's have all tended to support incumbents but in 1980 corporate PAC's backed a number of Republican challengers, and in 1982, labor PAC's followed suit by channeling more funds to Democratic challengers.

Also growing in importance in recent years in congressional campaigns have been independent or "unconnected" PAC's. Unlike labor, corporate, and trade PAC's, these organizations are not limited by law to contributions of $5,000 per candidate per election; rather, as in presidential elections, they can spend unlimited amounts of money to advocate the election or defeat of a congressional candidate, provided such expenditures are not made in conjunction with a candidate's own campaign. In 1980 independent conservative groups spent $2.3 million, about $1 million of that directed by the National Conservative Political Action Committee against liberal Democratic senators; when several senators such as George McGovern of South Dakota, Frank Church of Idaho, Birch Bayh of Indiana, John Culver of Iowa, and Warren Magnuson of Washington were defeated, NCPAC claimed credit for their political demise. However, things went differently in 1982: some Democratic senators such as Paul Sarbanes of Maryland and Daniel Moynihan of New York utilized the negative advertising to win the electoral and financial support of voters who resented such tactics. Moreover, new liberal independent groups such as Independent Action (started by Democratic Arizona Representative Morris Udall) and Harriman's Democrats (named for longtime Democratic political leader and former New York governor Averill Harriman) entered the electoral fray on behalf of Democratic candidates.

Increased attention to PAC's (particularly by the media) has tended to obscure another major source of campaign funds for congressional candidates—political party committees, including the national committee, as well as campaign committees in the House and Senate. Under the law, such committees can together make *direct* contributions of $5,000 per election to House candidates and $17,500 to Senate aspirants, in addition to "coordinated expenditures" with state committees for "in-kind" assistance, such as polling and media production. Republican congressional candidates have benefited far more from such sources than Democrats: in 1981–1982, the three national Republican party committees gave $18.6 million in direct contributions to their congressional candidates compared with $3.3 million by comparable Democratic committees.

There are two other sources of financing for congressional candidates. Despite the $1,000 limit on contributions by private individuals, such contributions remain the single most important source of campaign funds (in recent years about 60 percent of total funds in House elections and 70 percent in Senate contests). Also available is money from candidates themselves: in 1976 Republican Senator John Heinz III of Pennsylvania, heir to his family's pickle and catsup fortune, spent almost $2.5 million of his own money to finance his successful campaign.

Thus both the rules of the game and the campaign strategies and resources developed by the opposing candidates shape the outcome of presidential and congressional campaigns. Yet we know relatively little about the effect such activities actually have on the electorate. Winners tend to congratulate themselves on having conducted an effective campaign; losers are inclined to blame their defeat on circumstances they could not control, such as their minority party status or the superior resources of their opponent, which even their best campaign efforts could not overcome.

The presidential or congressional campaign, however, is only one of the factors that shape how persons decide to vote. Others include long-term political predispositions of individuals, which they acquire in the socialization process described in Chapter 4, together with their reactions to short-term forces, such as particular candidates and issues in specific elections. Such matters are explained in-depth in the next chapter, which deals with voting behavior in both presidential and congressional contests.

ASSESSMENT

The general election rules for choosing our nation's highest political figure are archaic and should be changed as soon as possible. As indicated earlier, the electoral college makes little or no sense in the present situation in which the president is expected to be chosen in a nationwide popular election: retaining it means playing a game of electoral roulette which the nation almost lost in four recent elections and can ill afford to lose at any time. A major argument for its retention that John Kennedy used in the 1950s—that its bias in favor of large urban states compensates for the rural bias in the House of Representatives—no longer applies with as much force since the congressional redistricting that has taken place to meet the one-person, one-vote principle.

The direct popular election of the president is superior to the district, proportional, and national bonus proposals. The first would incorporate into the selection of the president the gerrymandering abuses that still remain despite the reapportionment decisions—manipulating House district boundaries (including noncompact, noncontiguous ones) to favor particular political interests. Although the proportional and national bonus systems are superior to the present general-ticket system, they still do not guarantee what should be guaranteed: that the president is the person who receives the most popular votes.

The major objection to the popular election of the president is that it violates the principles of federalism since it substitutes the mass of individual voters for states as the determinant of the outcome of the election. Yet the principles of federalism, which we examined in Chapter 3, do not include favoring state interests in the choice of the national executive; states are already given special protection in the composition of the Senate. States should not have special consideration in the selection of the president; he or she should represent all the American people, no matter where they live.

The public financing of presidential contests has served to equalize the resources available to the two candidates and spared both major parties the problems and dangers associated with raising funds from private sources. These two advantages should also be extended to congressional contests. The advantages of incumbency, which have been overwhelming in recent years, should be mitigated by government subsidies to provide challengers with sufficient funds to mount a serious campaign against sitting members of Congress. At the same time, congressional candidates should be freed of the political obligations created by the acceptance of moneys from special-interest groups that are increasingly channeled through political action committees. Public financing would also have the advantage of making limits on campaign spending and the size of personal contributions once again effective: despite the fact that the Supreme Court ruled in *Buckley* v. *Valeo* that such restrictions are unconstitutional when applied to private funds, they would be binding on incumbents or challengers who accept public funding of their campaigns.

SELECTED READINGS

An excellent recent analysis of the electoral college is Neal Pierce and Lawrence Longley, *The People's President: The Electoral College in American History and The Direct Vote Alternative* (New Haven: Yale University Press, rev. ed., 1981). The studies of presidential nomination campaigns cited in the Selected Readings for the previous chapter also cover the general election campaign. These include general treatments of the subject, in-depth studies of individual campaigns, and the role of the media in presidential campaigns.

Good references on reapportionment are *Representation and Apportionment* (1966) and *Congressional Districts in the 1970's* (1973), both published by Congressional Quarterly Press of Washington, D. C. An excellent recent analysis of developments following the 1980 census is Alan Ehrenhalt, "Reapportionment and Redistricting," which appears in Thomas Mann and Norman Ornstein (eds.), *The American Elections of 1982* (Washington, D. C.: American Enterprise Institute, 1983).

Very good recent analyses of congressional campaigns and elections include Eddie Goldenberg and Michael Traugott, *Campaigning for Congress* (Washington, D. C.: Congressional Quarterly Press, 1984); Barbara Hinckley, *Congressional Elections* (Washington, D. C.: Congressional Quarterly Press, 1981); Gary Jacobson, *The Politics of Congressional Elections* (Boston: Little, Brown, and Company, 1983); and the Mann–Ornstein study cited above. Insightful analyses of how members of Congress deal with problems of re-election include Richard Fenno, *Home Style: House Members in Their Districts* (Boston: Little, Brown, and Company, 1978) and David Mayhew, *Congress: The Electoral Connection* (New Haven: Yale University Press, 1980).

Two excellent recent studies of campaign finance are Herbert Alexander, *Financing Politics: Money, Elections, and Political Reform* (Washington, D. C.: Congressional Quarterly Press, 3rd ed., 1983) and Gary Jacobson, *Money in Congressional Elections* (New Haven: Yale University Press, 1980).

FIRST
VOTE
COMMITTEE
VOTERREGISTRATIONVOTERREGISTRATION

CHAPTER 9

Voting Behavior

As we saw in Chapter 1, voting is the process by which those "outside" government pass judgment on those "inside." If citizens in a democracy are unhappy with what those in public office are doing about the major problems facing society, the remedy is to replace them. Thus democracies provide their people with competing leaders and enable them to choose between them.

Not all persons, however, actually participate in choosing their leaders. As we shall see, some do not possess the legal right to vote. Others possess that right but for one reason or another do not choose to exercise it.

VOTING PARTICIPATION

One of the hallmarks of a democratic society is that instead of breaking heads, it counts them. According to democratic theory, each person is the best judge of his or her own interests. Accordingly, one must be able to vote for leaders who pursue policies that favor one's interests and against those who do not. Everyone, then, should have the right to vote unless for some reason one is incapable of making judgments about one's own self-interest.

The **franchise** in the United States has had a history of expansion, as a series of reasons for withholding the ballot from various groups have been eliminated over the years, either by the states or the national government. Property qualifications (based on the assumption that the votes of the poor could be bought) disappeared at the state level by the end of the Civil War.* Almost immediately the battle to enfranchise the blacks (who traditionally were considered unable to think for

* The exception to this development is the requirement in some jurisdictions that voters be property owners in order to participate in referendums on bond issues.

Women get the vote: 1920.

themselves) began. As described in Chapter 15, this struggle persisted into the 1960s.

The twentieth century has seen the vindication of the voting rights of two other major groups—women and young people. As we shall see in Chapter 15, the former ultimately defeated the legal notion that a woman's place is in the home (not in politics) when the Nineteenth Amendment, ratified in 1920, denied the United States or any of the states the right to discriminate in voting rights on the basis of sex. Youth won its major victory in the early 1970s: Congress first passed a statute granting 18-year-olds the right to vote in national, state, and local elections, but when the Supreme Court ruled that a national law could only affect voting in national elections, the Twenty-sixth Amendment was enacted to extend that right to state (and local) elections as well.

Two other voting restrictions were removed in the early 1960s with the passage of the Twenty-third and Twenty-fourth Amendments. The former granted the residents of the District of Columbia the right to vote in presidential elections, a privilege they had been denied since the nation's capital was located there at the beginning of the nineteenth century. The latter eliminated the payment of poll taxes (in use in five Southern states at the time) as a requisite for voting in primaries and general election contests for the president, vice president, senators, and members of the House of Representatives. (In a 1966 decision, *Harper* v. *Virginia,* the Supreme Court eliminated the poll tax as a requirement for voting in state elections by ruling that it violated the equal-protection clause of the Fourteenth Amendment.)

Several other voting restrictions are still retained by most states. Some relate to special groups that are presumed not to have the intelligence or moral character necessary to cast a ballot. These

Eighteen-year olds win the vote.

include prisoners and the mentally incompetent, for example. Persons who are convicted of a crime are denied the right to vote in most states, a practice that was recently upheld as constitutional by the Supreme Court, even after the person has served his sentence.*

One voting qualification that has come under attack in recent years is the requirement of lengthy residence in a state, county, or precinct. While residency requirements make sense in relation to elections of state and local officials of whom a newcomer might have little knowledge, they are less justified in presidential elections. In the 1970 act that lowered the voting age to 18, Congress provided that persons can vote in an election for these officials if they have lived in the place concerned for at least 30 days.

Another major voting qualification

* Another type of disability is alien status; all states today require voters to be citizens.

imposed by some states is *literacy*. The states differ, however, in the way they measure literacy. Some require minimal efforts such as writing one's name or filling out an application form to vote. Others, like New York, require voters to demonstrate their ability to comprehend certain reading passages. Some Southern states have administered literacy tests that favor whites over blacks. To obviate the use of literacy tests for that purpose, Congress passed a law in 1965 suspending literacy tests in areas where less than 50 percent of the voting-age population was registered or voted in November 1964. The act was subsequently amended in 1970 to cover areas where a similar situation existed in November 1968. In 1975 the act was extended for seven more years and its provisions expanded to cover the voting rights of persons of Spanish heritage, American Indians, Asian Americans, and Alaskan natives. In 1982, the act was extended for 25 years with provisions requiring certain areas of the country to provide bilingual election materials until 1992.

Thus the trend in the United States has been toward counting more and more heads. As the following sections show, however, the right to vote and the actual exercise of that right are two separate matters.

General Trends in Voting Turnout

One of the ironies of American elections is that more and more of our citizens have acquired the right to vote in recent years, but there has been a trend toward a smaller and smaller proportion of them actually exercising that right. As Table 9.1 indicates, the estimated number of persons of voting age has more than doubled since Franklin Roosevelt was first elected to office in 1932, but after reaching a high point in 1960, the percentage of such persons who actually went to the polls has declined in the last five presidential elections. The most marked drop—over 5 percent—occurred between the 1968 and 1972 elections.

Table 9.1
Participation in Presidential Elections (1932–1980)

Year	Estimated Population of Voting Age (Millions)	Number of Votes Cast (Millions)	Percentage of Vote Cast
1932	75.8	39.7	52.4
1936	80.2	45.6	56.0
1940	84.7	49.9	58.9
1944	85.7	48.0	56.0
1948	95.6	48.8	51.1
1952	99.9	61.6	61.6
1956	104.5	62.0	59.3
1960	109.7	68.8	62.8
1964	114.1	70.6	61.9
1968	120.3	73.2	60.9
1972[a]	140.8	77.7	55.2
1976[a]	152.3	81.6	53.5
1980[a]	164.4	86.6	52.6

[a] Elections in which persons 18 to 20 years old were eligible to vote in all states.

SOURCE: *Statistical Abstract of the United States*, 1982–83, Table No. 801.

This recent decline in voter participation runs counter to some of the traditional theories that attempt to explain why people do not vote. Frequently, restrictive laws, particularly those relating to registration and voting, are said to prevent citizens from going to the polls. Yet many states have eased these restrictions in recent years and, as just mentioned, Congress has facilitated voting in presidential elections for new residents, so that it was generally easier for a person to register and vote for a president in 1980 than 1960. Nonvoting is also often attributed to a person's lack of education; however, the level of education of American citizens was higher in 1980 than 1960. The failure to vote is frequently linked to a lack of political information. However, because of increased use of the mass media, and particularly, because of the televising of the Carter–Reagan debate in 1980, more Americans than ever (over 100 million tuned in on the debate) were aware of the candidates and their views on public issues. Finally, close political races are supposed to stimulate people to get out and vote because they think their ballot might conceivably make a difference in the outcome. All the pollsters forecast that the 1964 and 1972 elections would be landslides and the 1968, 1976, and 1980 elections would be close contests,* but a smaller percentage of persons voted in 1968 than 1964, and participation also declined after 1972.

The televised Carter-Reagan debate.

It is possible to attribute some of the decline in voter turnout in recent years to the extension of the right to vote to 18-year-olds, which first took effect in the 1972 presidential election. Analyses of participation in that election by age group (see Table 9.2) showed that 18- to 20-year-olds did not vote as much (proportionately to their number) as persons 21 and over. Therefore, some of the overall 5 percent decline in voter turnout between 1968 and 1972 was caused by the addition of persons to the potential electorate in the latter year who were less inclined to vote. However, this factor does not help to explain the decline in participation between 1964 and 1968 and again after 1972. Moreover, analyses of the 1972 election indicate that persons 21 and over did not participate as much proportionately as in 1968.

It is difficult to determine why voting has declined in presidential elections in recent years. Political scientists Paul Abramson, John Aldrich, and David Rohde, who analyze this decline in *reported* turnout in all presidential elections since 1952, link it to two major factors. The first is an erosion in the strength of political party identification of many Americans (the next section contains a discussion of that matter), which they feel results in less psychological involvement in politics. The second factor is a decline in a sense of political efficacy: over the years, fewer and fewer people have thought public officials cared about their opinions and/or have

* While Reagan defeated Carter by almost 10 percentage points (51–41), it was not until the last weekend before the election that the polls showed Reagan outdistancing the incumbent president.

Table 9.2
Voting Participation of Various Groups (by Percentage)[a] in Presidential Elections of 1972, 1976, and 1980

	Year		
Group Characteristic	*1972*	*1976*	*1980*
Male	64.1	59.6	59.1
Female	62.0	58.8	59.4
White	64.5	60.9	60.9
Black	52.1	48.7	50.5
Age			
18–20 years old	48.3	38.0	35.7
21–24 years old	50.7	45.6	43.1
25–44 years old	62.7	58.7	58.7
45–64 years old	70.8	68.7	69.3
65 and over	63.5	62.2	65.1
Residence			
Metropolitan	64.3	59.2	58.8
Nonmetropolitan	59.4	59.1	60.2
North and West	66.4	61.2	61.0
South	55.4	54.9	55.6
School year completed			
Grade 8 or less	47.4	44.1	42.6
Grade 9 to 12	52.0	47.2	45.6
Grade 12	65.4	59.4	58.9
More than 12	78.8	73.5	NA[b]

[a] Based on estimated population of voting age. The percentage is based on those *reporting* that they voted and is higher than those who actually voted.

[b] The information reported is not comparable to that for the 1972 and 1976 elections.

SOURCE: *The Statistical Abstract of the United States*, 1977, Table 814; *ibid*, 1982–83, Tables 805, 806.

felt that as citizens they have any say about what the government does. These latter attitudes, in turn, relate to public disaffection with our government's policies on issues such as race relations, Vietnam, and the Watergate scandals, as well as a general feeling that government has failed to solve our economic and social problems.

Political Factors in Voting Turnout

Among the factors that affect voting turnout in the United States are the general political circumstances of an election. As shown by Figure 9.1, there has been some variation in both presidential and congressional voting over the years: both generally rose between 1948 and 1960 (with the exception of the 1956 election); from 1960 through 1978, however, participation in congressional contests, like that in presidential races, generally declined, particularly in 1974 after the Watergate revelations. Moreover, there is a difference in the turnout rate in the two types of elections. In a typical presidential election year some 5 percent of those who cast their ballot for the chief executive fail to mark a ballot for a member of Congress; moreover, in the midterm congressional elections when there is no presidential contest to attract voters to the polls, voting in general is about 10 to 15 percent less than the presidential turnout figure.

A similar pattern prevails in elections for state and local officers. Governors draw more voters to the polls than state legislators. The further one goes down the levels of government, the smaller the voting turnout becomes: fewer persons vote for a mayoralty candidate than a gubernatorial one. Thus a common argument in praise of grass-roots democracy—that the people have more interest in political officers of smaller geographical units—is simply not true, at least as judged by votes.

Why do voters take more interest in certain elections than others? They may feel that a particular official can have more effect on their lives than others. (Presidents can affect whether a son is sent off to war; the city council can improve the condition of the streets.) Moreover, contests for higher political positions attract wide public attention simply because candidates use the mass media (particularly television) so much. The networks give more extensive coverage to what they view to be the more significant elections. It may even be that, generally speaking, more attractive can-

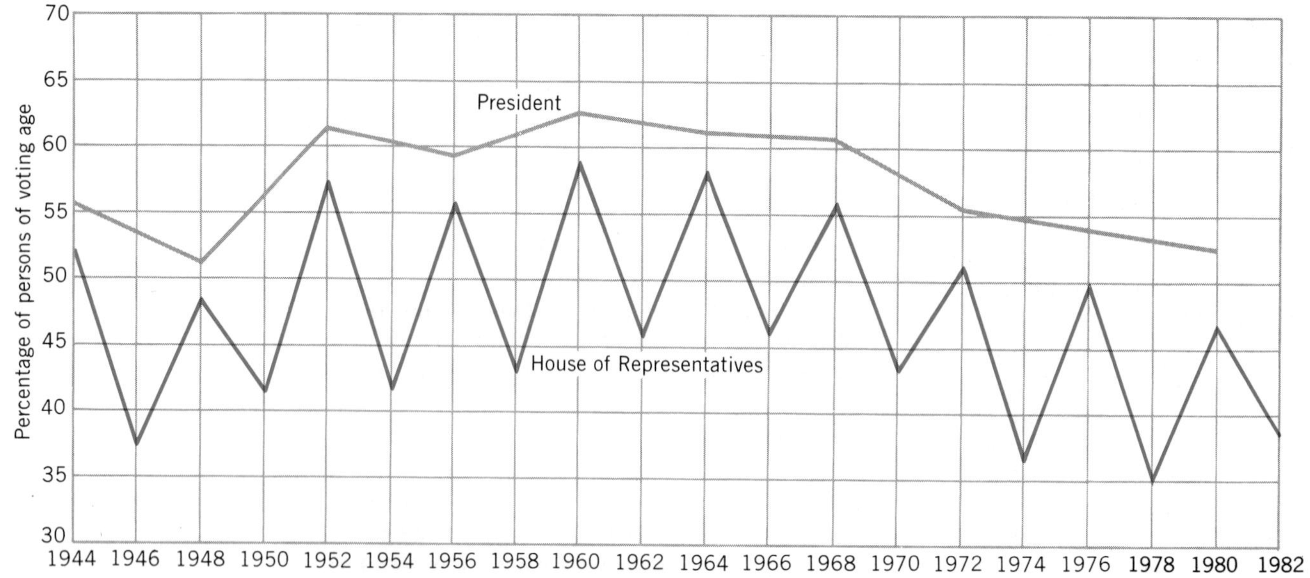

Figure 9.1 Voter Turnout in Elections for the Presidency and the House of Representatives (1944–1982)
(SOURCE: Statistical Abstract of the United States, 1977, Table 813; *ibid.*, 1984 Table 439.)

didates run for higher offices and thus stimulate voters' interests in their campaigns.

Group Differences in Voting Turnout

As indicated by Table 9.2, there are variations among groups as to their participation in presidential elections. Two of the least-participating groups—blacks and young people—were formerly denied the franchise. One possible reason for this pattern is that some of the "newly" enfranchised may still be affected by public attitudes that originally denied them the right to vote. Nonwhites, especially older people who grew up in the South where they were formerly denied the franchise, may feel that they are not able to make good choices. Some 18- to 20-year-olds may also feel that they are too immature to intelligently exercise the right to vote. In all probability, however, the voting patterns of these two groups are also related to other factors. Many blacks still have a limited education, which as Table 9.2 shows, is linked to low voting participation. Many 18- to 20-year-olds have not yet settled down and become involved in community affairs, another factor related to voting turnout. It is significant to note that women, another group that has traditionally had a comparatively low rate of participation, now vote as much as men, a development that is probably linked to their increased level of education. (In recent years, women have begun to outnumber men among college students.)

Group differences in voter turnout are rooted in psychological feelings that affect all kinds of political participation, including voting. Well-educated people are more likely to be aware of political developments and their significance than poorly educated people. In addition, well-educated persons tend to feel politically efficacious. That is, they have a sense of confidence about the value of their opinions and believe that people in public office will listen to them; therefore, they think that what they do has an important effect on the political process. Poorly educated persons, however, are likely to feel that political officials do not care about them or their opinions. General attitudes about other people also affect voting behavior; those who trust people are more likely to cast their ballots than those whose cynicism and hostility toward others make them feel alienated.

Political scientists Raymond Wolfinger and Steven Rosenstone conclude that generally speaking, occupation is not nearly as closely related to voting participation as education. However, they find that persons in two occupations in particular—farmers and government employees—have an especially high voting turnout. They attribute this tendency to the fact that both groups are closely related to the activities of government. Farmers are dependent upon various public programs giving and loaning money, limiting production, buying crops, guaranteeing prices, and the like. Government employees, in turn, deal with many matters on a daily basis that become campaign issues; in addition, those in patronage positions have a vital stake in the outcome of elections.

The influence of a social group to which a person belongs is frequently important to his or her voting participation. Thus if one belongs to a business organization or labor union whose members talk much about political affairs, one is apt to develop an interest of one's own in such matters. If so, one's political interest will lead one to make the effort to vote. Moreover, even if a person is not interested in politics, he or she may feel that it is nevertheless a citizen's duty to vote. Such an attitude is much more likely to exist in the upper and middle classes than in the lower class.

If the reasons that prompt certain persons to vote and influence others to remain at home on election day are varied, the factors that shape preferences between competing groups of candidates are even more complex.

VOTING PREFERENCES

The reasons underlying voting decisions have long been of interest to students of democratic politics. Some political philosophers created the model of the rational citizen who carefully studies the major issues that his or her society faces, decides what public policies are needed to deal with them, and then chooses the candidate whose views on such matters are closest to his or her own. Viewed in this context, the results of elections turn on the "issues" and the candidates' stand on them. Historians, journalists, and other political observers writing on individual campaigns have similarly tended to focus on issues, along with dramatic events and personalities, as the key factors in election outcomes. They have also been inclined to attribute victory or defeat to campaign strategies.

Survey techniques developed in the United States in the 1930s have made it possible to interview a carefully selected sample of persons on some matter and, on the basis of their responses, to generalize how a much larger group feels about it. These techniques became highly useful for eliciting the reasons behind electoral decisions. Instead of relying on what other persons *thought* the reasons were, it was now possible to get the actual reasons from the voters themselves. Moreover, rather than focusing on what the voters *should* consider in making voting decisions, the emphasis now turned to what they actually *did* take into account.

In-depth studies of voters' attitudes began in the 1940 presidential campaign with a single county (Erie) in Ohio; another followed of the 1948 campaign in a single city (Elmira, N. Y.).

These early studies, which were originally conducted to analyze the ways in which media coverage during the campaign changed voters' attitudes and behavior, demonstrated instead that voting behavior was more closely linked to long-term factors such as affiliation with social groups (churches, unions, political parties) and social-class differences in income, occupation, and education. Thus the major approach of these studies was *sociological* in nature since they related voting behavior to group membership and social status.

In the immediate postwar period another group of specialists on consumer behavior at the Survey Research Center of the University of Michigan at Ann Arbor began to study voting in the 1948 election. Rather than concentrating on a single community, however, they interviewed a nationwide sample of Americans on how they voted in that election and why they voted as they did. Moreover, their general approach to voting was a *psychological* rather than a *sociological* one; instead of emphasizing the group affiliations and social status of persons, the Michigan group concentrated on the psychological motives that prompted individuals to vote as they did, including such major factors as their **partisan identification** or **affiliation** and their attitude toward the *candidates* and the *issues* of a particular election.

The 1948 venture was a pioneering, experimental project, but beginning with the 1952 election, the Michigan group provided a comprehensive and systematic analysis of each presidential election. In 1960, four of the scholars at the Survey Research Center, Angus Campbell, Philip Converse, Warren Miller, and Donald Stokes, published a classic study, *The American Voter,* based on data gathered for the 1952 and 1956 elections; for many years this study constituted *the* authority for students of voting behavior in the United States. Later the Michigan group established the Inter-University Consortium on Political Research, through which scholars from all over the United States and abroad share the election data gathered each four years. Ultimately this arrangement has borne fruit with the publication of a number of studies analyzing presidential voting since 1952. As we shall see, these studies indicate that there has been a substantial change in the voting behavior of Americans over the course of the two decades, particularly since the 1964 presidential election.

Voting Preferences in Presidential Elections

Party Affiliation. Analyses of presidential elections in the 1950s by Campbell and associates indicated that the single most important determinant of voting at that time was the party affiliation of the voter. This general psychological attachment, shaped by family and social groups, tended to intensify with age. For the average person looking for some guidance on how to cast his or her vote amid the complexities of personalities, issues, and events of that time, the party label of the candidates was the most important reference point. In this era (voting specialist Philip Converse refers to it as the "Steady State" period), partisanship was also fairly constant: when asked, an average of about 45 percent of Americans in 1952 and 1956 said they thought of themselves as Democrats and about 28 percent as Republicans. When further asked to classify themselves as "strong" or "weak" partisans, identifiers in both parties tended to divide equally between those two categories. Independents in both years averaged about 23 percent of the electorate.

As Table 9.3 indicates, however, partisan affiliation began to change in the mid-to-late 1960s. In 1964 affiliation with the Democratic party rose about 5 percent and fell about 3 percent for the

Table 9.3
Party Identification (1952–1980)

	1952	1956	1960	1964	1968	1972	1976	1980
Strong Democrat	22	21	21	26	20	15	15	17
Weak Democrat	25	23	25	25	25	25	25	23
Subtotal	47	44	46	51	45	40	40	40
Strong Republican	14	14	13	13	14	13	9	9
Weak Republican	13	15	14	11	10	10	14	14
Subtotal	27	29	27	24	24	23	23	23
Independent	22	24	25	23	30	35	36	34

SOURCE: The University of Michigan Center for Political Studies.

Republican party, with the independents' share of the electorate also declining slightly. However, beginning with the 1968 election this latter group began to increase, primarily at the expense of the Democrats, until it constituted one-third of the electorate in 1972. (Also noteworthy is the fact that even those persons who stayed with the Democrats were more inclined than formerly to say that they were weak rather than strong Democrats.) Moreover, after 1968 more persons considered themselves independents than identified with the Republican party.

Another indication of the declining importance of political party identification in presidential elections is the increase in recent years in the number of "switchers," that is, persons who vote for one party's candidate in one presidential election and for another party's candidate in the following one. Political scientist V. O. Key's analysis of presidential voting from 1940 to 1960 showed that on the average one-eighth to one-fifth switched; recent information from the Center for Political Studies indicates that from 1968 to 1976 the proportion ranged from one-fifth to one-third. A similar phenomenon has occurred in split-ticket voting, that is, casting a ballot for candidates of more than one party for different offices at the same election. In 1952 some 13 percent of Americans voted a split ticket in presidential-House races; by 1972 that figure had risen to 30 percent. After declining to 26 percent in 1976, it rose to 35 percent in 1980. What is even more significant is the fact that recently even persons who claim to identify with one of the major parties have increasingly displayed partisan disloyalty by switching and ticket-splitting.

Thus independence of political parties, whether measured by voters' subjective attitudes toward the parties themselves or reports of their actual behavior in the voting booth, has increased in recent years in the United States. However, as has been explained by election analysts Norman Nie, Sidney Verba, and John Petrocik, this rise in independents is not spread evenly across the voting population. It has occurred primarily among young people, particularly those who entered the electorate in 1964 or later. New voters who came of age since that time are much more likely to be political independents than those who belong to previous political generations.

Recent analyses of independents in the United States indicate that not only have they grown dramatically in numbers but they have also changed in character. The Michigan group found that independents in the 1950s tended to be less knowledgeable about political issues and candidates and to participate less in the political process than partisans. However, political scientist Gerald Pomper's analysis of the behavior of independents in recent elections indicated that they are just as knowledgeable about political matters as partisans. Furthermore, while not as likely to vote as partisans, independents participate as much or more than partisans in other political activities, such as writing to political officials and voting on referendums. Thus nonpartisanship, rather than general political disinterest, characterizes many of the younger independents, particularly those with a college education. What seems to have happened is that a new type of independent has been added to the ranks of the kind prevalent in the 1950s.

It is difficult to determine the particular reasons for the decline in partisanship among American voters. One factor has been a decreased transfer of partisanship from one generation to another. As Nie, Verba, and Petrocik point out, beginning in the late 1960s younger voters became less likely than earlier generations to retain their family partisan affiliation. Converse also identifies two "shock" periods that weakened partisan loyalties. The first, beginning in 1965 and stemming from the Vietnam War and racial unrest, affected persons of all ages, Democrats somewhat more than Republicans. The second, beginning in 1972, which Converse associates with the Watergate revelations and the disclosure that precipitated the resignation of Vice President Spiro Agnew, had a distinct impact on older Republicans.

However, it should be noted from Table 9.3 that the decline in partisanship reached its peak in 1972. The proportion of independents did not change significantly in the two presidential elections after that. Thus the trend away from party affiliation appears to have stopped and may be in the process of reversing itself.*

Presidential adviser John Erlichman ponders question from Senate Watergate Committee.

Social Groups and Social Class. The early voting studies of presidential elections in the 1940s showed that a fairly close association existed between social group membership and social status on the one hand, and support for one of the two major parties on the other. Democrats received most of their support from Southerners, blacks, Catholics, and persons with limited education and income and a working-class background. Republican candidates were supported by Northerners, whites, Protestants, and persons with higher levels of education and income and a professional or business background.

Table 9.4 shows how various groups voted in presidential elections from 1952 through 1980. There was a general decline in the level of support that many of these groups gave their traditional party's candidates over the 28-year period. Especially noticeable for

* In a Gallup poll taken in late April 1982, 27 percent of the respondents declared themselves to be Independents, compared to the 34 percent figure in 1980.

the Republicans was their loss of votes from white-collar workers and Protestants. The most significant drop for the Democrats came from the Southern vote in the 1968 and 1972 elections. However, this vote was regained in 1976 by the Democratic candidate from Georgia, Jimmy Carter (and then lost again in 1980). The only group that significantly increased its support for its traditional party candidate over the 28-year period was nonwhites, who were more firmly in the Democratic camp in 1980 than 1952.

Table 9.4 also shows that the circumstances of particular elections can greatly alter group voting tendencies. In 1964, when the very conservative Barry Goldwater was the Republican standard-bearer, all the groups—including those that typically support the GOP, such as the college-educated, professionals, and businesspeople, along with Protestants and Westerners—voted for the Democratic candidate, Lyndon Johnson. In 1972, when the very liberal George McGovern ran on the Democratic ticket, all the groups that traditionally sympathize with that party, with the exception of nonwhites, voted for the Republican candidate, Richard Nixon.

Thus party identification and group affiliation have not meant as much in recent presidential voting as they once did. As the following discussion indicates, other forces, such as candidates and issues, are now more important in the political world of the American voter.

Table 9.4
Vote by Groups in Presidential Elections since 1952 (Based on Gallup Poll Survey Data; Expressed in Percentages)

	1952		*1956*		*1960*		*1964*		*1968*			*1972*		*1976*		*1980*		
	Stev.	*Ike*	*Stev.*	*Ike*	*JFK*	*Nixon*	*LBJ*	*Gold.*	*HHH*	*Nixon*	*Wallace*	*McG.*	*Nixon*	*Carter*	*Ford*	*Carter*	*Reagan*	*And.*
National	44.6	55.4	42.2	57.8	50.1	49.9	61.3	38.7	43.0	43.4	13.6	38	62	50	48	41	51	7
Race																		
White	43	57	41	59	49	51	59	41	38	47	15	32	68	46	52	36	56	7
Nonwhite	79	21	61	39	68	32	94	6	85	12	3	87	13	85	15	86	10	2
Education																		
College	34	66	31	69	39	61	52	48	37	54	9	37	63	42	55	35	53	10
High School	45	55	42	58	52	48	62	38	42	43	15	34	66	54	46	43	51	5
Grade School	52	48	50	50	55	45	66	34	52	33	15	49	51	58	41	54	42	3
Occupation																		
Prof. and Business	36	64	32	68	42	58	54	46	34	56	10	31	69	42	56	33	55	10
White Collar	40	60	37	63	48	52	57	43	41	47	12	36	64	50	48	40	51	9
Manual	55	45	50	50	60	40	71	29	50	35	15	43	57	58	41	48	46	5
Religion																		
Protestants	37	63	37	63	38	62	55	45	35	49	16	30	70	46	53	39	54	6
Catholics	56	44	51	49	78	22	76	24	59	33	8	48	52	57	42	46	47	6
Section																		
East	45	55	40	60	53	47	68	32	50	43	7	42	58	51	47	43	47	9
Midwest	42	58	41	59	48	52	61	39	44	47	9	40	60	48	50	41	51	7
South	51	49	49	51	51	49	52	48	31	36	33	29	71	54	45	44	52	3
West	42	58	43	57	49	51	60	40	44	49	7	41	59	46	51	35	54	9
Members of Labor Union Families	61	39	57	43	65	35	73	27	56	29	15	46	54	63	36	50	43	5

SOURCE: Excerpted from *The Gallup Opinion Index*, December 1980, pp. 6, 7.

Candidates. The influence of candidates on the outcome of elections is difficult to determine. As political scientists Warren Miller and Teresa Levitin suggest, it is much easier to focus on the specific qualities of a particular candidate, such as Eisenhower's personal warmth, Kennedy's youth and Catholicism, and Johnson's expansive style, than it is to compare candidates systematically over a series of elections.

Recognizing these limitations, it is nonetheless possible to make some overall comparisons of how voters reacted to candidates from 1952 to 1980. Each presidential year the Michigan Center for Political Studies asked people whether there was anything about each of the major candidates that would make them want to vote for or against that candidate. The total number of favorable and unfavorable comments were then tabulated for each candidate; the more favorable (compared to unfavorable) comments a candidate received, the more positive the score. The overall scores, positive and negative, of the two major-party candidates were compared with one another to determine the relative appeal of the two candidates in any given election year. Figure 9.2 shows the appeal evoked by different candidates from 1952 through 1980.

Two major findings are revealed in Figure 9.2. One is the variability in the reactions that voters demonstrated toward the candidates over the course of the eight presidential elections. The differences in candidate appeal were much less pronounced in 1952, 1960, 1968, 1976, and 1980 than they were in 1956, 1964, and 1972. The second finding is that except for two instances, 1964 and 1976, the Republican candidate was more favorably evaluated by voters than the Democratic candidate. Although it is not noteworthy that Dwight Eisenhower was more popular than Adlai Stevenson in 1956 and that Richard Nixon received a more favorable rating from the voters than George McGovern in 1972, it is somewhat surprising to find that Nixon was evaluated higher by the voters than John Kennedy in 1960.

It is difficult to determine why Republican candidates have generally been more popular lately than their Democratic opponents, but political scientist Herbert Asher has suggested some possibilities. One is that the Democratic party draws support from a broader variety of divergent groups than the Republican party, and this fact makes it more difficult to please all elements of the Democratic party. Another possible explanation is that since Republicans are clearly the minority party, they have to be particularly concerned with nominating very attractive candidates. Finally, the nature of the times has favored Republican candidates. In 1952 and 1968 the incumbent Democratic party was faced with defending the Korean and Vietnam wars; such hostilities were either over or virtually over when the Republicans were the incumbent party in 1956 and 1972.

Voters' attitudes on candidates stem from numerous sources, including the associations voters make between candidates and their partisan affiliations, candidates' stands on issues, voters' perceptions on how candidates have managed or would manage the government, and candidates' personal qualities such as background and experience, personality and character traits, personal and political "style," and competence and trustworthiness. Political scientists Arthur Miller and Warren Miller's 1977 analysis of voters' reactions to the two presidential candidates in 1976 indicates that evaluations of President Ford were based primarily on his past performance in office and his trustworthiness. Carter was judged for the most part on the basis of his party identification and a partisan ideology that combined future expectations of which

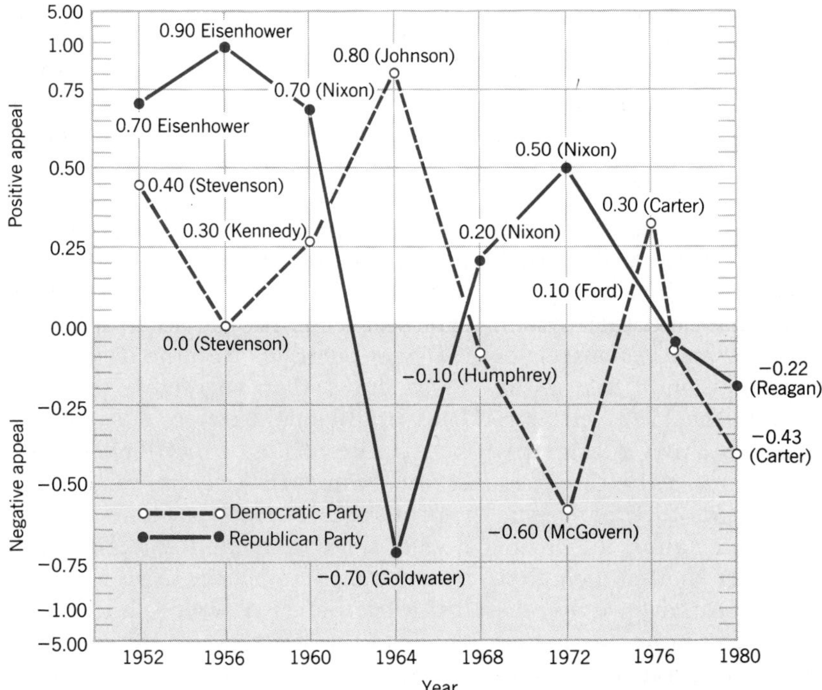

Figure 9.2 Appeal Evoked by Democratic and Republican Candidates for President (1952–1980)
[SOURCE: Arthur Miller and Warren Miller (1977). "Partisanship and Performance. Rational Choice in the 1976 Presidential Election." Paper delivered at the Annual Meeting of the American Political Science Association, p. 90. The 1980 data are from Arthur Miller (1981). "Policy and Performance Voting in the 1980 Election." Paper delivered at the Annual Meeting of the American Political Science Association, Figure 1. (Data are from the American National Election Studies conducted by the Center for Political Studies, University of Michigan.)]

party and candidate would do a better job, particularly in dealing with economic problems. As the authors stated, the results of the 1976 election ultimately turned on "incumbent performance versus partisan ideology."

It should be noted that 1980 was the first election in which both major-party candidates were evaluated negatively. Arthur Miller describes the electorate as being forced to choose between "the lesser of two evils." Jimmy Carter was perceived as doing a poor job as president. Moreover, the percentage of persons who said he made them feel angry rose from 39 percent in interviews conducted in January and February of 1980 to 63 percent just before the election. Over the same period of time the percentage of individuals who said Reagan made them feel "uneasy" (primarily over his being able to develop good relations with other countries) increased from 24 to 44 percent.

Political Issues and Ideology. Campbell and his associates, who analyzed the voting behavior of Americans in the 1950s, suggested that as a matter of logic, issues are potentially important in determining how an individual casts his or her ballot only if three conditions are present. First, the person must be aware that an issue or a number of issues exist. Second, the issues must be of some personal concern to the individual. Third, the voter must perceive that one party better represents his or her own thinking on the issues than the other party.

When Campbell and his associates applied these three conditions to the American voters in the 1952 and 1956 presidential elections, they found that relatively few voters met the three criteria. About one-third of the persons in their survey were not aware of *any* of the 16 major issues about which they were questioned. Moreover, even the two-thirds who were aware of one or more issues frequently were not personally concerned about the matter. Finally, a number of those who were aware and concerned about issues were not able to perceive differences on them between the two parties. The result of the analysis was that at the most, only about one-third of the electorate *potentially* voted on the basis of issues. (The proportion who *actually* voted as they did because of issues could have been, and probably was, even lower than that.)

More recent studies of political attitudes in the 1960s and early 1970s by Pomper and Nie, Verba, and Petrocik show a rise in the potential for voting on the basis of issues. First, there has been an increase in the number and types of issues of which voters are aware. Whereas the Eisenhower years were characterized by some voter concern for traditional domestic issues (welfare, labor–management relationships) and foreign policy matters (the threat of communism, the atomic bomb), beginning with the 1964 election the scope of such concerns broadened to include issues like civil rights and Vietnam. The latter issue in particular continued to concern voters in the 1968 and 1972 contests and was joined by such new matters as crime, disorder, and juvenile delinquency (sometimes referred to collectively along with race problems as the "social issue").

Moreover, the connection between voters' own attitudes on issues and their perceptions of where the parties stand on such matters has grown closer in recent years. Pomper's analysis of voters' attitudes on issues from 1956 through 1972 shows that beginning with the 1964 presidential election, attitudes became more related to partisan identification. Democrats were more likely to express the "liberal" position on economic, civil rights, and foreign policy issues than Republicans. Also voters in the 1960s perceived more clearly than voters in the 1950s that differences existed between the general approaches the two parties took on such issues. Moreover, there has been an increasing consensus among such voters that the Democratic party takes a liberal approach on such issues and Republicans a conservative one. With these developments, the potential for voting on the basis of issues has increased in recent years. Correlations of voters' attitudes on issues with the way they voted in presidential elections in the 1960s compared to the 1950s also show that this potential for issue voting was converted into actuality.

Recent analyses also indicate a change in the way the American people think about politics. When voters in the 1950s were asked by Campbell and his associates to indicate what they liked or disliked about the candidates and the parties, only about one in ten responded in ideological terms by linking his or her attitudes on such matters to political issues or utilizing such general concepts as "liberal" or "conservative" to describe differences between candidates and parties. Far more people made references to *group benefits*—such as Democrats helping the working man and Republicans, business—or to *the nature of the times,* linking Democrats to foreign wars and Republicans to economic downturns and depressions. Moreover, over one-fifth of the voters in the 1950s gave replies that had no issue content at all, such as "I just like Democrats better than Republicans," or "Ike's my man." However, more recent studies by Nie, Verba, and Petrocik have shown that the number of "ideologues" increased considerably, to as much as one-third of the electorate in 1964, for example. What is particularly noticeable is a movement away from conceiving of politics primarily from the vantage point of group benefits and toward viewing it in broader terms of issues and general political ideas.

Related to this broadening of the conceptualization of politics is the increased ability of the voters to be able to relate political issues to one another on the basis of a general liberal–conservative dimension. Studies of the electorate in the 1950s by Philip Converse showed that voters displayed what he called a lack of "constraint," that is, a low level of consistency, in attitudes on political issues. For example, persons who took the "liberal" position that government should take an active role in providing welfare for the needy did not necessarily think it should assume a similar role in encouraging racial integration in the schools; nor were voters' attitudes on either of these domestic matters related to their opinions on the foreign policy issue of what stand our government should take toward the threat of communism in the world. However, as election analysts Norman Nie and Kristi Andersen pointed out, beginning with the 1964 election there was an increase in the correlation of attitudes on the various issues; voters' positions on domestic issues were more likely to correlate with one another as well as with their attitudes on foreign policy issues.

Many persons assumed that the decline in social unrest growing out of the U. S. involvement in Vietnam and the racial tensions that gripped America in the late 1960s and early 1970s would mean a return to a less ideological and issue-related presidential election in 1976. However, Miller and Miller's analysis of that election indicates that this did not occur. Using the same criteria that were used to discern the development of ideological thinking in the earlier period—voters' liberal and conservative attitudes on issues, their perceptions of party differences on such matters, and a correlation among their attitudes on various issues—led Miller and Miller to conclude that there was only a slight decline in such thinking between 1972 and 1976. As far as issues were concerned, they found that economic matters were much more important to the electorate in 1976 than social or cultural issues; Democrats were particularly concerned over the rise in unemployment prior to the election. The fact that many voters believed that the Democratic party would do a better job than the Republicans in dealing with unemployment, and the fact that Carter placed particular emphasis on economic compared to noneconomic issues in his campaign, prompted many voters to distinguish between the two parties and their respective candidates on that basis. The outcome that year was that the voting decision was much more closely linked to attitudes on economic issues than to social and cultural attitudes.

Analysis of the 1980 election shows that economic issues were again more important to the electorate that year than social and cultural issues, with inflation being the most important concern for many voters. Arthur Miller attributes President Carter's defeat primarily to voter dissatisfaction with his performance in office, particularly his inability to deal with the economy and, to a lesser extent, with a perceived de-

RATIFY
EQUAL RIGHTS
AMENDMENT
ERA
N.O.W

UNITE AGAINST CUTBACKS!!!
New American Movement
IBEW
OUR MANDATE
MORE HOUSING
AFL-CIO SOLIDARITY DAY
FEED THE PEOP
NOT
THE PENTAGO
Don't Cut Social Security
AFSCME
A CLEAN

cline in our nation's prestige in the world. Warren Miller (1981) also sees dissatisfaction with the incumbent's performance in office as an important element in his defeat but believes that many persons voted for Reagan because they were in agreement with his conservative policies. Abramson, Aldrich, and Rohde view both dissatisfaction with Carter's performance in office and evaluations of the policy stands of the two major candidates as factors in Reagan's victory but feel that the former was somewhat more important than the latter.

Thus voting in presidential elections is influenced by many forces. Over the years candidates of the two major parties have generally been associated with different sets of factors. Democrats have been favorably regarded for their party affiliation, their attitudes toward social groups, and their stands on domestic issues. In contrast, Republicans have benefited from their stance on foreign policy issues, their party philosophy, their perceived ability to manage the government, and a generally favorable assessment of them as candidates.

We will subsequently examine how various clusters of electoral factors result in different types of presidential elections, which, in turn, affect the operation of the American political system. First, however, we need to examine voting in congressional elections.

Voting Preferences in Congressional Elections

Only recently have studies of voting behavior in Congressional elections appeared that are at all comparable to those of presidential elections. Moreover, it is difficult to generalize about congressional elections since they occur in 435 separate House districts and 50 senatorial districts. However, analyses do reveal certain broad patterns of voting behavior in such elections.

In contests for the House of Representatives, the most important factor in voting decisions is an evaluation of the opposing *candidates*. This evaluation is based primarily on their *personal characteristics and qualifications*. Such assessments rebound overwhelmingly to the benefit of the *incumbent* member of Congress because voters are much more likely to be able to *recall,* or if not to recall, *recognize* the name of the incumbent than his or her opponent. Moreover, studies show that voters not only tend to know who the incumbent is but also have a *high personal regard* for that person. As noted in the previous chapter, both between elections and in campaigns themselves, House members stress their personal qualifications rather than their party affiliation or stand on the issues. This fact helps to explain voting behavior in House elections: constituents respond favorably to the kinds of appeals that incumbent candidates make. *Challengers* to House incumbents thus face an uphill battle: they must somehow manage to convince the voters that the incumbent is not serving their personal needs, or that he or she is not a likeable person, or that they (the challengers) are more likeable or would better serve constituents' needs. In some instances, House challengers who have sufficient funds may be able to focus voters' attention on party and policy differences between themselves and their incumbent opponents but that is not an easy task.

The latter possibility is much more likely to occur in U. S. Senate elections. *Party affiliation* becomes a much more important factor in voting for that office than it is for the House of Representatives. Since senators have a much broader constituency than House members, voters are less likely to know about senators' personal qualities; this being the case, voters judge them more on the basis of their party ties, their experi-

John Rotenberg of Brookline, Massachusetts campaigning for Congress.

ence, or their general stands on issues. Moreover, as discussed in the previous chapter, incumbent senators face much more formidable opposition from candidates who have the financing necessary to focus attention on party and policy differences between themselves and the incumbent. In addition, greater media coverage of senatorial races provides voters with more information on such matters than they obtain on House elections.

While *issues* do become important on occasion, particularly in Senate elections, they are not nearly as important in congressional voting as assessments of candidates and party affiliation. Nor do issues play as much of a role in congressional elections as in presidential ones. Relatively few voters are aware of the voting records of incumbents (particularly members of the House) or the differences in the respective policy stands of the opposing candidates.

Even though this is the case, issues and events sometimes play an *indirect* role in congressional elections. For example, studies show that in midterm elections, the fate of incumbents representing the president's party turns at least in part on the popularity of the Chief Executive and the general state of the economy. If these factors are unfavorable, the president's party may lose a large number of congressional seats (particularly in the House of Representatives) as incumbents are ousted from office. As political scientist Gary Jacobson suggests, that development occurs not primarily because individual voters take those factors into account when deciding how to cast their ballot, but rather because these generally unfavorable conditions stimulate opposition from more able and experienced candidates. As evidence for this argument, Jacobson points to the fact that the state of the economy and presidential popularity have their strongest impact on midterm congressional elections when they are measured *not* at election time but in *the first quarter of the year* (when potential candidates are trying to make up their minds whether or not they should take on the incumbent).

The end result of the above developments is a tendency for presidential, senatorial, and House elections to involve different considerations and to bring about disparate results. Presidential contests increasingly turn on voter evaluations of both major-party candidates, together with a concern with salient issues and events; Senate races are decided on the basis of party affiliation, along with candidate evaluations and to a lesser extent, issues, but those evaluations and issues do not necessarily correspond to those involved in presidential voting; and the incumbency factor makes most Representatives virtually immune from the influence of national political trends or the influence of presidential and senatorial contests. Thus the electoral process is increasingly segmented, with voters casting ballots for different reasons for president, the Senate, and the House of Representatives.

VOTING BEHAVIOR AND THE OPERATION OF THE AMERICAN POLITICAL SYSTEM

The collective decisions of individual voters determine not only the results of the elections but also the operation of the political system. Elections that turn on long-term forces such as traditional party loyalties build stability into the system because representatives of the majority party remain in power over a considerable period of time. Other short-term factors such as individual candidates or dramatic political events produce change as the party is turned out of office. Thus our political system contains elements that are conducive to both stability and change, desirable characteristics of any human institution.

In fact, students of American presidential elections have categorized them according to different clusters of electoral factors. An election in which the long-term partisan orientation of the electorate results in keeping the traditional majority party in power is a **maintaining election.** The majority-party candidate wins primarily because the voters choose him or her on the basis of their traditional party loyalties. Short-term forces, such as candidates and issues, are present, but rather than determining which party wins, they contribute to the size of the majority party's victory. When they favor that party, as they did in 1964 when the Goldwater candidacy benefited the Democrats, the vote margin separating the two major candidates is larger than usual. If short-term forces are in balance, as they were in 1948, the vote division approximates the proportion of voters who identify generally with the two parties.

While maintaining elections provide general continuity in governance, others result in change. A **deviating election** occurs when short-term forces sufficiently benefit the minority party that they override the long-term partisan preferences of the electorate. A particularly appealing candidate or some salient issue or event allows the minority-party candidate to win with the support of some majority-party members, independents, and a good share of new voters. The electorate does not, however, change its basic party preferences. Examples of deviating elections are 1952, 1956, 1968, and 1972: they were won by the Republican candidates, Eisenhower and Nixon, but the commitment of many persons to the major party—the Democrats—was unaltered.*

The election that brings about major political change is referred to as a **critical,** or **realigning election.** Such elections involve a major realignment of electoral support among blocs of voters who switch their traditional party affiliation. An unusual number of new voters may also enter the electoral arena and cast their ballots disproportionately for one party's candidate. Unlike the deviating election, the effects of the realigning one tend to persist in the form of durable loyalties to the advantaged party. Political historians usually include five elections in the realigning category: 1800, 1828, 1860, 1896, and 1932.

The realignment of partisan forces is associated with changes in social and economic conditions that have not been accommodated within existing arrangements. In the case just cited, the majority Republican party did not concern itself sufficiently with the needs of immigrant and low-income groups from urban areas. The increased movement of these groups into the Democratic camp, plus the economic depression of 1929 that affected a wide variety of citizens, triggered a massive swing to the minority Democratic party by old and new voters alike and ushered in a long period of Democratic rule.

---

* Analysts of the Survey Research Center refer to an election following a deviating period as a **reinstating** one, because it reinstates the usual majority party in power. Examples are the 1960 and 1976 elections, when the Democrats returned to power after the two Eisenhower and Nixon victories. Thus a reinstating election is like a maintaining one in that long-term partisan factors determine the result.

An indication that the parties are not meeting the needs of certain groups is the fact that a significant third-party movement often precedes the realignment. The rise of the Free Soil party and the Republican party itself, which began as a third party, eventually culminated in the realignment of 1860; the Populist party played a role in the critical election of 1896; and La Follette's Progressives contributed to the reorganization of American politics that occurred in the late 1920s and early 1930s. The rise of the American Independent party in 1968 led some observers to predict that 1972 would be a realigning election. However, it did not occur: while the Republican presidential candidate, Richard Nixon, did win an overwhelming victory over the Democratic standard-bearer, George McGovern, the Democrats retained control over both houses of Congress, and recaptured the presidency four years later.

Immediately after the 1980 election there was again comment that the decisive Reagan victory (51 percent of the popular vote to 41 percent for Carter), plus the unexpected Republican capture of the Senate, 33 additional seats in the House of Representatives, four governorships, and over 200 state legislative seats, meant that 1980 was a realigning election. The fact that a number of major social groups that traditionally have voted Democratic—including Catholics, blue-collar workers, and persons with no college education—cast their ballots for the Republican nominee gave further credence to the contention that the liberal New Deal era in American politics was over and a new Republican majority along the lines first proclaimed by Kevin Phillips in 1969 had finally been formed. When President Reagan then proceeded to embark on a succession of major policy changes, and when by mid-1981 the percentage of persons declaring themselves to be Republicans equalled that of the Democratic party, some observers became even more convinced that a party realignment had taken place.

However, even at the time of the election, there were some reasons for caution in accepting that contention. If the 1980 elections are compared with our five previous realigning elections (1800, 1828, 1860, 1896, and 1932), some major differences appear. For one thing, the new majority party that emerged in each of those cases captured not only the presidency but *both* houses of Congress, not just the Senate as in 1980. For another, in each of those cases the emerging party controlled the House of Representatives in the session *preceding* the key presidential election, whereas Republicans had 117 fewer House seats than the Democrats in the 1979–1981 congressional session. Moreover, there was generally an increase in voting participation in previous realigning elections, but as previously indicated, participation in the 1980 election actually declined slightly.

Subsequent events called further into question the contention that the 1980 election was a realigning one. As Reagan's problems with the Congress and the economy developed in late 1981 and continued in 1982, the percentage of persons declaring themselves to be Republicans declined and the Democrats once again emerged as the party fa-

vored by more voters. In the 1982 elections the Democrats picked up 26 seats in the House of Representatives, a net gain of 7 governorships, and some 160 additional state legislative seats, indicating that many Democrats had not permanently deserted their traditional party.

Thus the predictions that the 1972 and 1980 elections would be realigning ones proved to be untrue. At the same time, the fact that the Democrats lost both the presidency and the Senate in 1980, and failed to gain any seats in the latter body in the 1982 Congressional elections (at a time when economic conditions were *not* favorable for the Republican administration), indicates that the nation has not returned to the normal Democratic-majority-party situation that has generally prevailed since the 1930s. The electoral situation in the United States thus remains in a highly uncertain state.

ASSESSMENT

As we have already observed, one of the hallmarks of a democratic society is that a large number of people enjoy the right to have some influence over important decisions that affect their lives. To a considerable degree that influence is exercised through the ballot that enables persons to vote for leaders who they believe will protect their interests and against those who they believe will not. The progressive extension of the franchise in the United States has meant that more and more citizens have acquired the right to vote because they have been considered rational enough to make judgments about their own self-interest.

It is also encouraging that the voting decision appears to have become more rational in recent elections. Beginning with the 1964 presidential contest, the American electorate has become more aware of issues and the candidates' stand on them; moreover, these factors are now playing a larger role in its presidential choice. This is an improvement over the past situation, in which most Americans voted as they did because of their emotional predisposition toward a political party rather than on the basis of what the respective candidates proposed to do about the nation's major problems.

There is also some indication that voters are learning to distinguish between relevant and irrelevant issues in presidential campaigns. It is a healthy sign that the voters concerned themselves primarily with the state of the American economy in 1976 and, despite the publicity given the *Playboy* and Butz incidents (the former involved an interview printed in the magazine in which Carter confessed that he "lusted" after women in his "heart"; the latter, a racial slur made by Secretary of Agriculture Earl Butz which led to his resignation), Carter's religious views, and the abortion controversy, apparently largely ignored those matters when they made their voting decision. The same development was true in 1980 when the electorate focused on the state of the economy and foreign affairs and appeared to pay little attention to the candidates' attacks on each other [President Carter warned that a Reagan presidency would seriously divide Americans from each other, and the challenger linked (mistakenly) the President's initial campaign appearance with the birthplace of the Ku Klux Klan], as well as highly emotional issues such as abortion and prayer in public schools.

There is, however, one discouraging aspect of recent elections: the decline in voter participation in both presidential and congressional elections in the period from 1960 to 1980. While it is possible that this decline might be attributable to a general public satisfaction with the current situation in the United States (if things are going well, why bother to vote?), the evidence presented in Chapter 4 and earlier in this chapter is to the contrary: people have been increasingly discouraged about the state of the nation and the unresponsiveness of political leaders to the needs of ordinary citizens. It seems much more likely, therefore, that many people have been choosing not to vote because they perceive that their vote has little effect on how the nation's affairs are governed.

However, the situation seems to have changed in the last few years. Voting participation in midterm congressional elections increased somewhat between 1978 and 1982 and rose in many mayoralty and gubernatorial elections in the early 1980s. In 1984, several groups, including blacks, women, Hispanics, poor people, and some southern whites who have traditionally had low rates of electoral participation, were targeted for special registration-to-vote drives. It may well be that people are once again beginning to feel that their vote makes a difference in the governance of the nation (President Reagan's impact on the direction of public policy is recognized by both his admirers and detractors) and therefore are making a special effort to participate in the electorial process.

SELECTED READINGS

For an excellent recent analysis of voting in the United States, see Raymond Wolfinger and Steven Rosenstone, *Who Votes?* (New Haven: Yale University Press, 1980).

A classic study of voting behavior in presidential elections in the 1950s is Angus Campbell, Philip Converse, Warren Miller, and Donald Stokes, *The American Voter* (New York: John Wiley and Sons, 1960). More recent general studies of the same subject are Warren Miller and Teresa Levitin, *Leadership and Change: The New Politics and The American Electorate* (Cambridge, Mass.: Winthrop Publishers, 1976); Norman Nie, Sidney Verba, and John Petrocik, *The Changing American Voter* (Cambridge, Mass.: Harvard University Press, enlarged ed., 1979); and Gerald Pomper, *Voter's Choice: Varieties of American Electoral Behavior* (New York: Dodd, Mead, 1975). Analyses of voting in the 1980 presidential election include Paul Abramson, John Aldrich, and David Rohde, *Change and Continuity in the 1980 Elections* (Washington, D. C.: Congressional Quarterly Press, 1982); Arthur Miller, "Policy and Performance Voting in the 1980 Election," Paper delivered at the 1981 Annual Meeting of the American Political Science Association; and another paper delivered at that same meeting by Warren Miller, "Policy Directions and Presidential Leadership: Alternative Interpretations of the 1980 Presidential Election."

Two recent very good studies of voting in congresssional elections are the Hinckley and Jacobson books cited in the Selected Readings at the end of the last chapter.

Two excellent studies of party realignment are Walter Burnham, *Critical Elections and the Mainsprings of American Politics* (New York: W. W. Norton, 1970) and James Sundquist, *Dynamics of the Party System: Alignment and Realignment of Political Parties in the United States* (Washington, D.C.: The Brookings Institution, rev. ed., 1983).

Studies that link voting behavior to the operation of the American party system, the general political system, and democratic theory are William Chambers and Walter Burnham, eds. *The American Party System: Stages of Political Development* (New York: Oxford University Press, 2nd ed., 1975); Angus Campbell, Philip Converse, Warren Miller, and Donald Stokes, *Elections and the Political Order* (New York: John Wiley and Sons, 1966); and Gerald Pomper and Susan Lederman, *Elections in America: Control and Influence in Democratic Politics* (New York: Longman, 2nd ed., 1980).

PART 3

Official Decision-Making

CHAPTER 10

Congress

On March 26, 1984 a group of New York Democratic Congressman Ed Towns' supporters anxiously awaited the arrival of Texan Jim Wright, the House Majority Leader, who was scheduled to speak at a fund-raising dinner for the legislator from Brooklyn. Having just seen Wright on television from El Salvador where he was heading the U.S. delegation observing the Salvadoran elections, some of Towns' friends told the Congressman that there was no way Wright could possibly keep his speaking commitment. Towns' assurance to contributors that Wright would be there was vindicated when the tired Texan walked into the Brooklyn restaurant rendezvous just four hours after getting off a flight from El Salvador and two hours after briefing President Reagan on the elections. Wright explained that the White House had arranged a special Air Force plane to get him to the fund-raiser on time. "You had the whole White House standing on its head for Ed Towns," he told the delighted citizens of Flatbush.

This incident epitomizes the realities and complexities of the world in which members of Congress must operate. Ed Towns, the black freshman congressman from the newly created 11th District of New York which contains a heavy concentration of both blacks and Hispanics, managed to prevail in the 1982 Democratic congressional primary because two of his opponents split the Hispanic vote between them. Wright's appearance at the fund-raiser was therefore a "must" if Towns hoped to hold his seat against future challengers when the electoral situation might not be so fortunate. Wright's coming to his district meant a lot to Towns; as he later told a group of contributors, "For people here in my area, seeing the Majority Leader coming in for a freshman member of Congress is very impressive." Towns hoped that such a political coup, plus his service on the Public Works and Transportation Committee (an important decision-making body for deciding where federal projects would be located), would enable him to retain his seat in the 1984 congressional elections when the opposition party's popular leader, President Reagan, would also be up for re-election.

For Jim Wright, the situation was quite different. First elected to Congress in 1946, he carefully cultivated his constituents over the years, using his seat on the Public Works Committee to obtain water projects and highways for his district; he was also a strong supporter of defense spending, some of which went to General Dynamics, his district's leading employer and producer of the TFX fighter plane. Although he was firmly ensconced in his district (he easily turned aside a 1980 Republican well-financed challenge from a former mayor *pro tempore* of Fort Worth), Wright continued to keep his political fences mended with his constituents and lunched each Wednesday with the Texas congressional delegation.

In 1977, when his seniority on the Public Works Committee put him in line for the chairmanship, Wright decided to abandon his essentially local constituency orientation to politics and enter the national arena by seeking the position of Majority Leader of the House of Representatives. To the surprise of many, he won (although it was a close election that went to three ballots) over two other much better-known figures in the House, Congressmen Richard Bolling of Missouri and Phillip Burton of California. Unlike his two controversial opponents, Wright had few political enemies; in addition, his post on the Public Works Committee had enabled him to do favors for congressmen from all over the nation who benefited from the location of dams and federal buildings in their districts.

Although Wright was initially viewed with suspicion by many liberal Democrats who considered him too pro-military, he proved to be a loyal lieutenant of liberal House Speaker "Tip" O'Neill of Massachusetts, helping him to plan strategy and tactics for the scheduling of legislation. Wright's special talents as an orator (he was frequently referred to as Congress's "Wizard of Ooze") enabled him to become the spokesman for the Democratic party in debates with the Republicans. When Ronald Reagan captured the White House in 1980, Wright along with O'Neill, became the president's chief antagonists on economic policy. In response to pressure from young Democrats in the House, Wright also became more liberal in his voting record, coming out against the MX missile. At the same time, he supported the President on El Salvador, and thus was chosen to lead the U.S. delegation there in March 1984.

When Tip O'Neill announced he would run one more time and then retire from office in 1986, Wright began to put himself in line for the top post in the House. Anointed by the Speaker himself, lacking any major liberal opponent for the position, and benefiting from a stack of IOU's he gathered in the process of visiting districts of Democratic members of Congress in all parts of the country, Wright was expected to have little trouble winning the Speakership. Asked whether Wright would have his vote, the grateful Towns replied, "You can bet on that."

As the Wright–Towns relationship illustrates, congressional service involves a peculiar blend of local and national politics. In this chapter we will analyze how such considerations are reflected in a variety of congressional activities, including the major functions performed by the nation's legislative body.

FUNCTIONS OF CONGRESS

Congress carries out a variety of functions in the American political system. Its major tasks are those that are performed on a continuous basis and that consume the greatest share of its members' time. Other responsibilities are minor ones in the sense that they are handled on a sporadic basis and constitute a relatively small proportion of the legislator's heavy workload.

Major Functions of Congress

Legislating. One of the major responsibilities of Congress is to enact legislation to deal with the major problems of American society. For example, a number of years ago Congress passed a law requiring manufacturers of automobiles to install safety equipment (such as seat belts and head rests). The law stipulated that if the auto manufacturers failed to comply with its provisions, they could be fined or prevented from selling vehicles. As a result of the action of Congress, individuals and groups can be forced under pain of legal penalties to do what they otherwise would postpone or never do at all: despite the contentions of the automobile manufacturers that they would develop safety devices and install them in all their motor vehicles, they did not do so until Congress forced them to take such actions.

There is, of course, nothing inevitable about Congress's recognition of a problem and decision to take action to meet it. Americans had been killing and injuring each other on the highways for almost a half-century before the first congressional law was enacted in 1966 to require safety equipment on motor vehicles. Until that time it was assumed that the problem of vehicular accidents should be approached in other ways, such as constructing well-designed highways and regulating licenses to drive.

Contributing to the change in congressional thinking on the issue was Ralph Nader, a young lawyer whose bestselling *Unsafe at Any Speed* condemned the automobile industry for its failure to develop means of cushioning what he called the "second impact" (the one that occurs when drivers and passengers are thrown about inside the car after the initial impact with the other vehicle). Joining Nader were doctors who were on duty in emergency rooms when accident victims were brought in; lawyers who represented injured persons in automobile accidents; and an important governmentally, Senator Abraham Ribicoff, who led a vigorous campaign for highway safety when he was governor of Connecticut. When the administration of President Johnson added its support to the idea by proposing legislation for federal automobile safety standards, Congress ultimately responded with the passage of the National Traffic and Motor Vehicle Safety Act of 1966.

In making its decisions on needed legislation, then, Congress responds to pressures from a variety of sources.

Seen as Curb on Teen-Age Traffic Deaths

House Panel Approves U.S. Drinking Age of 21

By STEVE FARNSWORTH, *Times Staff Writer*

WASHINGTON—The House Energy and Commerce Committee Tuesday approved a bill that would effectively establish a nationwide drinking age of 21, a move supporters said would save "thousands of lives" by decreasing alcohol-related teen-age traffic deaths.

The measure now goes to the full House.

Critics of the bill contend that a higher drinking age would not stop young people from driving when intoxicated and that the bill might unconstitutionally infringe on states' regulatory powers.

The Presidential Commission on Drunk Driving

Some are private groups and individuals who have a particular concern or interest in a problem and develop ideas about what should be done about it. A political party or candidate may propose legislative action to deal with a particular issue. Frequently the initiative comes from the executive branch. Indeed, it has been estimated that about 80 percent of all laws passed by Congress are originally proposed by the president or some administrative agency. Finally, members of Congress themselves develop an interest in particular matters and become advocates of legislation designed to meet a major societal problem.

Although passing laws to meet societal problems continues to constitute an important function of Congress, it is no longer as influential in legislation as it was earlier in the nation's history. Not only does Congress now tend to allow and even to *expect* the president to take the initiative in major legislative proposals (we will examine this matter in Chapter 11), but it also is less inclined to make major changes in the content of those proposals.

In fact, Congress increasingly turns over to executive agencies the job of formulating precise rules and regulations for handling particular problems. Thus in the case of automobile safety standards, what Congress did was to recognize that standards were necessary, but it relinquished the responsibility of devising them. The language of the National Traffic and Motor Vehicle Safety Act of 1966 merely stated that the standards developed by executive officials should be "appropriate" and "practicable," "meet the need for motor vehicle safety," and "be stated in objective terms." Within these broad guidelines, the Federal Highway Safety Bureau (renamed the National Highway Traffic Safety Administration when the 1966 act was amended in 1970), which was entrusted with the responsibility of administering the law, was granted authority to develop standards that it feels are necessary to make motor vehicles safe.

Congress takes this approach to public problems for two major reasons. One is that its members do not have either the time or the expertise to deal with the intricacies of the broad variety of issues with which they must be concerned. They can only hope to identify some major problems and suggest general approaches for dealing with them, leaving particular policies to specialized agencies in the executive branch. Thus legislators as generalists could determine that developing safety standards for automobiles was desirable without having special knowledge of what these standards should be.

The second reason is that lawmakers often decide to leave the development of specific policies to executive officials for political considerations. Although all agreed on the need for safety devices on automobiles, they disagreed on which particular devices or on how long manufacturers should be given to install them. Thus officials in the Federal Highway Safety Bureau were caught in the crossfire between the automakers, who wanted them to act cautiously in devising and implementing safety standards in order to allow the industry time to adjust to the new requirements, and critics like Nader and Senator Ribicoff, who demanded that they act quickly to develop strict regulations.* Quite naturally, members of Congress typically prefer to allow others besides themselves to be exposed to such political pressures.

Controlling the Administration of Governmental Activities. The above devel-

* The dispute continued for many years: in 1984 regulations were issued to phase in the installation of airbags between 1986 and 1989 unless states representing two-thirds of the U.S. population pass mandatory seat-belt laws prior to April 1, 1989.

opments reflect a shift in the major functions performed by the American Congress. Today it is less a body that develops specific rules regulating the actions of private individuals and groups than it is one that delegates to the executive branch the authority to develop rules under the supervision of Congress. In other words, Congress is not so much involved in directly controlling the activities of citizens through its own actions as in indirectly affecting the public through determining how administrative officials shall carry on that function. In the process, Congress has become less a body that legislates and more an institution that *controls the administration of governmental activities* performed by executive officials.

Besides establishing broad legislative guidelines for carrying out the programs it authorizes, Congress has a variety of other means of controlling the administration. These include such powers as creating the organization of the executive branch in which governmental programs are administered, providing (or *not* providing) moneys to carry on such programs, as well as confirming (or *not* confirming) presidential appointment of those who occupy the major administrative positions entrusted with carrying out such programs. We will examine these powers in detail in Chapter 12, which deals with the federal bureaucracy.

Informing and Educating the Public. A third function of Congress is what Woodrow Wilson, in his classic study *Congressional Government* (written in 1885), referred to as the *informing* function.* By this he meant that the national legislative body has the obligation of ed-

*Before going into public life Wilson was a professor of government. His study of Congress remains one of the most perceptive analyses of that institution ever written.

Health and Human Services Secretary Margaret Heckler explains a point to Senator William Armstrong of Colorado.

Chairman Sam Ervin and his Watergate Committee in action.

ucating the general public on the major issues and on some of the basic approaches that can be taken to alleviate them. Thus when Congress holds hearings on automobile safety, pollution, or the control of drugs, it is trying to inform the American people (as well as its own members) about these problems and the steps that might conceivably be taken to deal with them.

The major vehicle for the informing function of the Congress is an investigating committee, which typically operates under either the House or the Senate, although in some instances both chambers create a joint committee to look into a matter. At times one of the regular committees or subcommittees conducts the investigation: the Senate Operations Subcommittee on Executive Reorganization, chaired by Senator Ribicoff, looked into the issue of auto safety. On other occasions a special committee is created to investigate a problem: in early 1973 the Senate established the Select Committee on Presidential Campaign Activities under the chairmanship of Senator Sam Ervin to inquire into Watergate and related issues.

The size of the public affected by a congressional investigation depends on the innate interest created by the subject of the inquiry, the extent to which the hearings are covered by the media, and the skills of the committee members, particularly the chairman. All three of these factors converged to make the Watergate hearings one of the most dramatic incidents of recent years: the break-in and related scandals were intensely interesting to most Americans, particularly when leading administration figures like H. R. Haldeman, John Ehrlichman, and John Mitchell came to testify before the committee; the three television networks took turns covering the proceedings live in the daytime, and public television rebroadcast them at night; and chairman Sam Ervin with his droll humor and biblical quotations became a folk hero to many Americans.

While few congressional investigations are as dramatic or reach as broad a public as the Watergate hearings, they all have two potential practical effects. One is that an aroused public will induce individuals and groups to change their behavior. One of the purposes behind congressional inquiries into automobile safety was the hope that manufacturers would voluntarily inaugurate safety programs to protect the public against needless deaths and injuries. The hearings of the Ervin Committee were also designed to influence candidates for public office, as well as those serving in high government posts, to conduct themselves more ethically than those associated with Watergate.

Generally speaking, however, voluntary actions alone are not sufficient to deal with major problems under investigation, and it is necessary to force persons to change their behavior under pain of legal sanctions. In this case the informing function serves another purpose: laying the groundwork for appropriate legislation. Concerned legislators hope that when enough groups are made aware of an issue and what might be done about it, they will put pressure on Congress to take action. When Senator Ribicoff conducted hearings on automobile safety, he was seeking to build public support for mandatory safety equipment for automobiles. Senator Ervin hoped that the Watergate hearings would lead to the passage of the kinds of remedial legislation recommended by his committee, including major changes in the financing of presidential campaigns, the establishment of a new Office of Public Attorney to investigate

"Its a television first. Two committees are investigating each other."

A LETTER TO NEW JERSEYANS ON:
- LOCATING MISSING CHILDREN
- IMPROVING OUR SCHOOLS
- CLEANING UP TOXIC WASTES
- IMPROVING THE COLLECTION OF CHILD SUPPORT PAYMENTS
- GATHERING SUPPORT FOR THE FAIR TAX

FROM **Bill Bradley**
U.S. SENATOR

JULY, 1984

NEW HOPE TO FIND MISSING CHILDREN

Perhaps you watched the recent television movie, "Adam," the true story of the kidnapping and murder of 6-year-old Adam Walsh. This movie graphically showed the anguish, frustration and courage of Adam's parents in trying to locate their missing child.

Yet, even out of the tragedy of Adam Walsh came the opportunity to press forward for a more comprehensive solution to prevent thousands of additional children from suffering the same fate. A nationwide grassroots organization dedicated to finding missing children reports that there are 150,000 children reported missing each year. Almost 100,000 of them are abducted by a parent; of the other 50,000 who run away or are abducted, 5,000 return unharmed, 5,000 are found dead and the rest remain missing.

In 1982, Congress responded to this problem by enacting the Missing Children Act, a law I cosponsored, which directed the FBI to include data on missing children in their computer. Before this bill was passed, parents had to rely strictly on the aid of state and local police. This made the job of enlisting the help of police in neighboring states nearly impossible. The FBI would not become officially involved in a case unless it had proof of a kidnapping in the form of a ransom demand or evidence that the child had been taken out of the state. The Missing Children Act was a good first step, but it does not go far enough.

That is why I am cosponsoring the Missing Children's Assistance Act of 1983,

During a recent "New Jersey Now" show, Sen. Bradley discusses missing children issue with John Walsh, father of 6-yr. old Florida boy whose abduction and murder received national attention after airing of T.V. docu-drama "Adam".

S. 2014, which will establish a national toll-free telephone line to link parents with their missing children and a clearinghouse to help state and local governments in locating and recovering missing children. On February 21, I testified on this bill before the Senate Subcommittee on Juvenile Justice. The Judiciary Committee approved the bill on May 25.

Most recently I have helped a concerned group of New Jerseyans who will not only assist parents in their search for missing children, but also help educate parents and children on ways to prevent abductions.

I have also been working closely with all of the major education associations in the state to help launch a program in the schools to educate children about the problem.

wrongdoing in the executive branch, and greater congressional review of federal intelligence and law-enforcement agencies.

In addition to educating the public in general on issues, many members of Congress try to keep their constituents informed on a variety of problems, including those of special local interest. Such information typically goes out in the form of mass-produced newsletters, television broadcasts, and government publications. Although the primary motive behind such communications is often personal promotion of the legislator, nonetheless they do help to keep private citizens informed on matters of public concern.

Servicing Constituents. A final major function of Congress pertains to relationships with constituents, namely, the *service* task that legislators perform for people in their state or congressional district who request assistance in dealing with practical problems involving the federal government. For instance, an elderly woman may inquire about her Social Security benefits or a father may seek help in clarifying his son's or daughter's eligibility for a college loan. In performing this function, members of Congress act as intermediaries between private individuals and the administrative agencies in the executive branch. They help to get people in touch with the proper person to handle the problem, put in a good word on their behalf, and see to it that their constituents are well treated and receive benefits to which they are entitled. Indeed, much of the time of the average legislator is taken up with personal casework for the folks back home.

The legislative, administrative-control, informing, and service functions together constitute the major responsibilities of Congress. Of course, they are not entirely separable, and one frequently has important consequences for another. Overseeing the executive branch, for example, helps to make members of Congress aware of additional legislation needed to make government more effective. Handling cases of constituents alerts legislators to de-

No gender gap here.

fects in the procedures of executive agencies that require legislation or stricter administrative control by Congress.

The performance of these functions also has important byproducts for society. By serving the needs of constituents, lawmakers "represent" their interests and help develop the loyalty and allegiance of people to the political system. The give-and-take of the legislative process accommodates and compromises competing demands, and serves to help make the final decision acceptable to the concerned parties. This, in turn, helps to legitimize the political system so that citizens in general are willing to abide by the rules and regulations developed by Congress and executive agencies.

Minor Functions of Congress

In addition to its major responsibilities the Congress performs other tasks on an irregular basis. Although not as vital to the overall functioning of the legislative body, on occasion they can become highly important to the operation of our political system.

In some instances Congress acts like a *judicial* (rather than a legislative) body by resolving disputes involving individuals. An example of this type of function is the power to *remove executive and judicial officials of the national government from their positions.* The persons subject to removal include "The President, the Vice-President and all civil officers of the United States . . ."; the grounds for removal include ". . . treason, bribery or other high crimes and misdemeanors." The removal procedure involves the voting of an impeachment resolution by a majority of the members of the House of Representatives followed by a trial and a vote of conviction by two-thirds of the members of the Senate.

It is sufficent to note for the moment that the general impeachment process has been rarely used. Impeachment proceedings have in fact been initiated 50 times in the House, but only 12 of these cases managed to reach the Senate for a trial; of these 12, only 4 resulted in convictions. All of the convictions involved federal judges (not officials of the executive branch); the last case occurred in 1936.

Each chamber also has power over the *seating and disciplining of its own members.* Thus both the House and the Senate have jurisdiction over disputed elections; they can also refuse to seat a person for failure to meet their qualifications for membership. While Congress has been asked often to determine the winner in contested elections, it has rejected the clear choice of the voters for lack of requisite qualifications in fewer than 20 cases since 1789. Both chambers have also been loath to discipline sitting members: 7 senators and 22 representatives have been formally censured by their colleagues for misconduct;* 15 senators and 4 House members have actually been expelled from their respective chambers.

The two houses of Congress are also involved on occasion in matters of *leadership selection for the executive branch.* As we saw in Chapter 8, if no candidate for president or vice president receives a majority of the electoral votes, these matters are referred, respectively, to the House of Representatives and Senate for an ultimate decision. Both of these houses may also become involved if the president should prove to be unable to carry on the duties of his office or if there should occur a vacancy in the vice presidency. Congress also determines by legislation who will succeed to the nation's highest office if something hap-

* Two recent cases (1983) involved Representative Daniel Crane (R-Illinois) and Gerry Studds (D-Massachusetts) who were censured for sexual misconduct with teenage congressional pages.

pens to both the president and the vice president.

Congress also becomes involved on occasion in *specialized areas of public policy making.* As we have seen in Chapter 2, both houses join in initiating constitutional amendments; they also have special powers in foreign and military policy. Finally, Congress has the constitutional power "... to exercise exclusive legislation in all cases whatsoever ..." for the nation's capital. Thus residents of the District of Columbia find not only national policies but also their local concerns determined by the United States Congress.

Congress, then, performs a variety of specific functions in the political system that have important side effects for individuals, groups, and the larger society. The following section focuses on the individuals who perform those functions—the members of the American Congress.

MEMBERS OF CONGRESS AND THEIR WORLD

Over the years our national legislators have ranked low in the estimation of many observers. They are common objects of derision for contemporary political cartoonists who picture them as bumbling, loquacious people of meager talent. Commentators in the past were often no kinder in their estimations. Alexis de Tocqueville, that perceptive French analyst of the Jacksonian period, referred to the "... vulgar demeanor of that great assembly." He went on to describe its members as "... almost all obscure individuals, village lawyers, men in trades, or even persons belonging to the lower class." To what extent do Tocqueville's comments accurately picture members in Congress today?

Backgrounds of National Legislators

Contemporary members of Congress resemble those described by Tocqueville in at least one important respect: they do tend to come disproportionately from the legal profession. Although *lawyers* constitute less than 1 percent of the adult population in the United States, almost half of the members of the Ninety-Eighth Congress (1983–1985) were attorneys.

There are a number of reasons why attorneys have traditionally dominated Congress. For one thing, the tools of the lawyer's trade—the ability to analyze statutes and administrative regulations, verbal and argumentative facility, and skills in negotiations—are precisely those needed by the persons who perform the major functions of the Congress—legislating, controlling the administration, informing the public, and representing constituents. As a professional, a lawyer enjoys prestige in the community. Moreover, the lawyer's role is to provide help in various kinds of personal problems. People, then, regard lawyers as natural legislators.

Members of the legal profession themselves also seek legislative positions. In fact, some people go to law school in the first place not just to practice but to prepare themselves for a political career. The law is also a "dispensable" profession—that is, it can be fitted in well with service in public life. Should a lawyer–legislator be defeated for re-election or decide to retire from Congress, he or she can return to the legal profession fairly easily, since law does not change as much as fields like medicine and engineering.

If by "men in trades" Tocqueville means those in *business,* then this characterization also applies today. Next to lawyers, people in business and bankers constitute the most numerous group in both the House and Senate: they account for about 30 percent of the members of the Ninety-Eighth Congress.

The third most prevalent occupational group in today's Congress was not even mentioned by Tocqueville: *teachers.*

"And close with the usual—'I neither condemn nor condone it, but suspend judgment pending further study.'"

This group has been increasing in recent years and presently constitutes about one-eighth of the national legislature. In recent times, lawmakers have included a number of former college professors, such as senators George McGovern of South Dakota, Mark Hatfield of Oregon, Daniel Patrick Moynihan of New York, and S. I. Hayakawa of California.

Tocqueville's description of persons belonging to the lower class has limited application to the Congress today. In 1977 a **Blue-Collar Caucus** was formed of House members who worked with their hands before going to Congress, but only fourteen members—some 3 percent of the body's membership—could qualify on the basis of their previous occupation. Included among the group were a former professional heavyweight boxer, a one-time bartender, and a former riverboat captain.

In social backgrounds, members of Congress generally fit the stereotype of the male, white Protestant. Although more than half the population is female, only about 4 percent of the members of the Ninety-Eighth Congress (1983–1985), including only two senators (Nancy Kassebaum, R-Kansas and Paula Hawkins, R-Florida), were women. Although blacks make up 11 percent of the American people, they also constituted only 4 percent of that Congress

Senator Nancy Kassebaum of Kansas.

Senator Moynihan of New York—from classroom to Senate.

and have no members in the Senate at all. A nation that is just over one-half Protestant is represented by a Congress that is two-thirds Protestant.

But while these characteristics continue to hold true of members of Congress, important changes are occurring in the composition of that body. In the Ninety-Sixth Congress, for the first time in 30 years lawyers made up less than half of the membership of the House of Representatives. Moreover, the 21 female members who were elected to serve in the lower chamber for the 1983–1985 term represented an all-time high for women. Finally, there has been a marked increase in the number of Roman Catholic, Jewish, and Hispanic members of the Congress in recent years. Members have also become younger: in 1983 the average age was 47, compared with 53 in the early 1950s.

Tenure and Career Patterns of Members of Congress

As we saw in Chapters 7 and 8, incumbent members of Congress have great advantages in political campaigns. Those advantages (assuming their desire to remain in office) are reflected in increasing tenure over the years. In the early years of this century members of the House of Representatives averaged about six years in office; by the late 1960s the average tenure was some eleven years. The tenure of senators has also increased over the years since they became directly elected in 1914; by the latter part of the 1960s over three-fourths were beyond their first term in office.

As political scientist Samuel Huntington pointed out at that time, service in the national legislature had become increasingly professionalized and permanent over the years as more and more persons spent their entire working life in their congressional position. (The major exceptions were senators seeking the presidency and House members running for the Senate or the governorship of their own states.) Huntington emphasized in particular the decline in the movement of persons from Congress to a major executive position in the national government. From 1897 to 1940, one-fifth of Cabinet members had previously served in Congress; between 1941 and 1963 that ratio fell to one-seventh; and in the Johnson and Nixon administrations, only one Cabinet member in 15 had served in Congress.

However, the situation described above changed greatly in the 1970s. A combination of early retirements and defeats of incumbents in congressional primaries and general elections (many of which occurred after the Watergate revelations) has resulted in a rapid infusion of new members into both houses of Congress. For example, by the Ninety-Sixth Congress (1979–1981), over half the members of the House had served four years or less and 55 senators had served six years or less. Moreover, there was some trend toward the selection of more former members of Congress to Cabinet posts by presidents Ford and Carter: two of the nine appointments by the former and the same number of appointees among Carter's initial eleven choices for his Cabinet had previously served in Congress.*

Members of Congress as "Locals"

Another important aspect of the national legislator's life is the basic orientation to local community and state. In a society in which more and more young people never return home after college and workers and executives move around the country frequently as job opportunities dictate, Senate and House members retain deep roots in their home soil. Most of them return to their

* Only one of President Reagan's initial cabinet appointees, Richard Schweiker, Secretary of Health and Human Services, served in the Congress.

hometowns—or at least their native states—after they finish their education and become immersed in political life.† Of course, once elected, they remain residents as long as they stay in Congress.

In fact, members of Congress are creatures of two worlds. One—Washington, D. C.—is the locale for two of their major functions, legislating and supervising the executive agencies of the national government. The other—their home area—is the focus of informing and servicing-their-constituent's functions.

Members of Congress retain close ties with their home areas in order to get re-elected. To this end, senators and representatives find it wise to spend as much time "back home" as possible, particularly in an election year. For those who live in the East, not far from the nation's capital, extended weekends at home are the rule: many belong to what is known as the "Tuesday–Thursday Club"—that is, they are in Washington the middle three days of the week when the Congress customarily transacts its business and return to their local constituencies during the other four days. But even those from areas more remote from the District of Columbia find it advisable to make it home at least one weekend a month, and in those short periods when Congress is not in session, many of its members are on the road visiting various parts of their constituency.

Living in these two worlds is not an easy task for legislators. It frequently means separation from their families to avoid taking children out of school in their home areas. They face problems of allocating their time and that of their staff members between Washington and their home base. Increasing numbers of lawmakers have home offices manned by permanent staff members to service the needs of their constituents. The double life of members of Congress also calls for adjustment in interests and personal lifestyles. Back home they are expected to be "folksy," to demonstrate an avid interest in local events, and the progress of their constituents' children and grandchildren; in Washington they are called upon to demonstrate a capacity to deal with domestic and foreign problems in a complex and sophisticated world.

The lifestyle of our national legislators and the way they spend their time reflect the demands of these two worlds. A typical day, drawn from an account by the late representative Clem Miller of California, goes as follows:

6:45 A.M.	Rise, read *Washington Post.*
8:00 A.M.	Breakfast with the British ambassador.
8:30 A.M.	Look over mail and dictate replies to inquiries.
9:00 A.M.	Office appointment with business lobbyist to discuss trade legislation.
10:00 A.M.	Subcommittee hearings on depressed-area bill.
12:00 NOON	Attend debate on House floor.
1:00 P.M.	Lunch in office. Read state and local newspapers.
2:00 P.M.	Meeting with Harvard economist John Kenneth Galbraith to discuss tight money and economic policy.
2:45 P.M.	Listen to debate on floor of Congress.
3:30 P.M.	Meeting with a member of the House Appropriations Committee on public works in home district.
5:00 P.M.	Sign letters dictated in morning. Go over afternoon mail. Meet with constituents.

† The Constitution requires that senators and House members be inhabitants of the state they represent. By custom the latter are also inhabitants of the district they serve.

6:15 P.M. Leave for home.
7:15 P.M. Eat dinner.
8:00 P.M. Read another newspaper from home district. Go through reports, speeches, and magazines. File material for future speeches.
11:00 P.M. Read chapter from book.
11:45 P.M. To sleep.

Thus the life of a member of Congress is not an easy one. Neither is it boring, however. Moreover, as the following section indicates, a position in Congress is not without its privileges as well.

Congressional Pay and Perquisites

As of January 1, 1984, both House members and Senators had basic salaries amounting to $69,800 a year. They were also entitled to earn up to $20,940 in honoraria (fees for speaking engagements and consultations). Thus they were entitled to receive a total of $90,740 from those two sources, a figure that placed their earnings in the top 1 percent that year.*

Another major perquisite ("perk") enjoyed by a member of Congress is allowance for a *staff*. In 1982 members of the House were entitled to an allowance of $352,536 to have 18 full-time persons to work in Washington and their home district offices. For senators, the amount of money permitted for staff depended on the population of the state they represented, ranging from $621,054 for those from states with fewer than 2 million residents to $1,247,879 for those with more than 21 million residents. In addition, in 1975 junior senators won the right to appoint additional staff with salaries totaling just over $100,000 to help them with their committee assignments.†

In addition to staff, members of Congress also receive *special allowances* for a variety of other expenses, including trips home. There are also allowances for other expenses connected with communicating with constituents, including stationery, postage, telephone, telegraph, newsletters, and inexpensive use of television and radio studios. There is also free office space, and an allowance for office equipment.

Another privilege, that of the *frank*, enables members of Congress to mail letters and packages under their signatures without being charged for postage. Besides providing a major means for communication with their constituents on a variety of matters, the privi-

* Many members of Congress enjoy additional income from other sources such as investments in stocks or bonds or profits from family businesses.

† Two of the major problems with respect to congressional staffs are preventing members from placing relatives in such positions and from using committee staff to do their personal work.

My feet are killing me!

A Senator (D'Amato of New York) lives a hectic life.

Checking the election results.

Stealing a moment with the family.

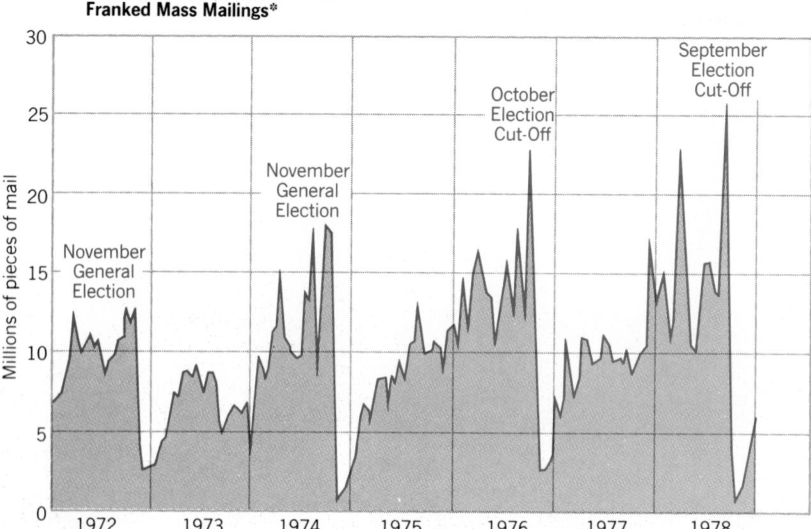

Figure 10.1 House of representatives—franked mass mailings.*

* "Mass mail" is defined as a mailing of more than 500 pieces of mail of which the content is "substantially identical." Exempted from the definition are letters sent out in response to incoming mail and mailings to the news media, to fellow members of Congress, or to state, local, or federal government officials.

SOURCE: *Common Cause, et al., plaintiff v. William F. Bolger, et al. defendants.* Memorandum in Support of Plaintiffs' Motion for Summary Judgment, May 22, 1981. Reprinted in Mary McNeil (ed.), *How Congress Works* (Washington, D. C.: Congressional Quarterly Inc., 1983, p. 142.)

lege can also be used to mend political fences just prior to elections. However, the Congress in the 1970s began to place restrictions on the use of the frank immediately prior to elections (see Figure 10.1 for the effect of such restrictions on use by members of the House), and in 1981 permanently banned any franked mass mailings within sixty days of a primary or general election in which an incumbent is a candidate.

Finally there are a number of other valuable "perks" enjoyed by legislators. Included are traveling abroad at the taxpayer's expense, free medical care and parking while at work, use of recreational facilities, low-cost food, haircuts and gifts at government-subsidized establishments, and even plants and pictures with which to decorate their offices.

At the same time it should be realized that our national legislators have special demands placed on them. The cost of maintaining two homes (as many of them do),* plus the expense of entertaining constituents while they are in Washington (lunch in the Senate dining room is not free but goes on the legislator's bill), adds up to a heavy drain on the personal resources of members of Congress. Thus while they live a busy and good life, it is not one that permits most to build up even a modest fortune.†

* It should also be noted that the Washington, D.C. area has one of the highest costs of living in the nation, especially for housing.

† It should be noted, however, that Congressional pensions are very generous. A 1984 study by the National Taxpayers Union showed that the average retired Congressman draws a pension of 35,386 a year; 138 of them collected more than they earned while in office.

Weekend in Paris: There Are Junkets and Junkets

By E. J. DIONNE Jr.
Special to The New York Times

PARIS, May 30 — On this Memorial Day, there were probably more members of the United States Congress in France than in Washington.

That often happens this time of year because this is the weekend of the Paris International Air Show. According to the official lists, there were at least 33 Senators and House members in France for this, the 35th show, at which aircraft manufacturers try to sell their wares, and often entertain lawmakers and prospective customers.

In addition, five members of Congress took a ride to Le Creusot, a leafy industrial town in the middle of east central France, to check out France's fast train, the TGV, which stands for the Train à Grande Vitesse.

The word that comes to mind for all this, the one used by some of the lawmakers themselves, is junket. For some of them, the word strikes real fear: It is the kind of word an electoral opponent might use with some effect. Other members of Congress do not worry so much, either because they come from safe districts or because they think their travels can easily be justified.

BICAMERALISM IN THE AMERICAN CONGRESS

One basic and distinctive feature of the American Congress is that it has two separate and independent chambers. A number of factors contributed to the decision of the Constitutional Convention to divide it so. One was the British legacy; the English Parliament was divided into two chambers: the House of Lords and the House of Commons. A second was the bicameralism of many of the colonial legislatures, where the upper chamber was composed of emissaries of the crown appointed by the king or his representatives and the lower consisted of individuals elected by the colonists themselves.

But these traditions were not determinative; after all, the legislature under the Articles of Confederation has been unicameral. Rather, the two-house legislature grew out of the conflicts described in Chapters 2 and 3: the political struggle between large and small states and the legal battle over the issue of whether national legislators were to represent sovereign states or individuals. The "Connecticut Compromise" settled both arguments.

Bicameralism continues to have an effect on the workings of the American Congress. Most nations in the world today have two legislative chambers (two unicameral exceptions are Denmark and New Zealand), but they are equally important in only a few places. Rather, upper houses in nations like Great Britain and Italy are relics of the days of aristocracy; they are composed of persons who hold life tenure but who have little influence over the legislative process, which is controlled in reality by the popular lower body. Only in countries like Australia and the United States does the upper house act as a coordinate legislative chamber. Of these few, the United States Senate is preeminent, the most influential upper legislative chamber in the world.

The Founders had distinct purposes in mind for the Senate compared to the House of Representatives. They created it to protect the interests of sovereign states, a function also served by upper legislative chambers in other federal systems, such as Australia, Switzerland, and West Germany. Beyond this, the Senate was expected to safeguard property interests: the prestigious nature of a Senate seat, it was thought, would attract an aristocratic elite, insulated from popular control by both indirect selection and a long term in office. In contrast, the directly elected House members with two-year terms were to reflect the interests of the many, those with little in the nature of worldly goods.

Linked to the protection of states'

rights and property interests was the intention of using the Senate to check on hasty legislation passed by the House of Representatives. (As Washington explained the Convention's decision to the absent Jefferson, delegates provided for two houses to act on legislation for the same reason that they poured their coffee into a saucer—to let it "cool.") Thus the bicameral legislature was meant to serve two major purposes: the representation of different interests and deliberative, careful lawmaking.

The Founders also had separate special functions in mind for the Senate and House. The Senate was to pass on the qualifications of the president's nominees to major positions in the national government, and it was to play a major role in foreign policy through the power to "advise and consent" on treaties negotiated by the president with other countries. The House was entrusted with the special and traditional prerogative of lower chambers: originating bills to raise revenue.

Having examined the reasons behind the Founders' adoption of a two-house legislature, we now turn to the ways in which the Senate and House carry on their business.

THE NATURE OF POWER IN CONGRESS

One of the most intriguing and controversial questions about any organization is, who controls it? Americans today seem preoccupied with this basic issue as it pertains to both private and public groups—universities, churches, and corporations, as well as all levels and branches of government. The standard answer, particularly with those who are unhappy with our basic institutions, is that the "establishment"—an inner clique—determines the decisions of all of them.

The political scientist examining the issue of organizational control tries to discover *who* has "power." By power a political scientist means the ability of one person (A) to get another (B) to do his or her (A's) bidding. The political scientist asks who can get others to do what he or she wants them to do even though they personally would prefer not to? Who are the leaders and who are the followers?

A related issue is the question of *how* power is exercised—whether through coercion or persuasion. Another question is what is the *source* of power? Does an individual have it because he or she occupies a particular position in an organization or because he or she has special skills in interpersonal relationships?

In Congress power involves the ability to shape major decisions. Thus legislators exercise power who successfully initiate, block, or make changes in legislative proposals through their ability to get other members to go along with their desires. Power can be exerted in other functions of the legislature too. The senators who took the leadership in successfully defeating President Nixon's nominations of Clement Haynsworth and G. Harrold Carswell to the Supreme Court were exercising power.

Who exercises power in the American Congress? As political scientist Randall Ripley suggests, there are various possibilities. It may be the persons who hold *elected positions* in the two chambers, such as the presiding officers of the two houses and the party officials chosen by the Democratic and Republican members. If so, we say that power is *centralized.*

Another possibility is that congressional power is primarily exercised by chairmen of the various committees and subcommittees of the Senate and House. In such circumstances, power is *decentralized.*

Power might not reside in those who hold official positions in the Congress, whether presiding officers, party officials, or committee and subcommittee chairmen. Rather, the organization may be controlled behind the scenes by an inner clique, some of whose members may not occupy any official post at all. Power in that situation is *informal.*

Finally there is the possibility that neither the official leadership of the Congress, nor any informal group controls decisions but that rank-and-file members are to a great degree their own persons. That power is *individualized.*

With these general considerations in mind, in the following sections we will analyze the exercise of power in the American Congress. Because the situation differs somewhat in the two chambers, the Senate and the House will be examined separately. Attention will also be focused on the major changes that have taken place in the power structures of both bodies in recent years.

POWER WITHIN THE SENATE

There are two kinds of central leaders in the Senate. One is composed of those who preside over the body and exercise essentially ceremonial duties in that chamber. Included in this group are the vice president of the United States and the Senate ***president pro tempore.*** The other type of central leader occupies a party position, such as a **Majority Leader, Minority Leader,** and party **Whip.** There are great differences in the amount and type of power that these two types of leaders exercise in the Senate.

Presiding Officers—Vice President and President *Pro Tempore*

Under the Constitution the vice president of the United States is the president of the Senate. As such, the vice president is entitled to preside over it and exercise such duties as recognizing speakers and ruling on points of procedure. The vice president has no vote, however, unless there is a tie among the senators, in which case he or she can cast a ballot to break it. The vice president can also assign bills to committee, a decision that can be important if a measure can be referred to more than one committee. One, for example, might speed it on its way to passage, while another might pigeonhole it or bury it, a matter that we shall examine subsequently in this chapter.

The vice president is not an important figure in the Senate. Because the vice president is not chosen by the senators themselves, they regard him or her as an outsider, especially when he or she belongs to the opposite political party from the one that controls the upper chamber—the fate of Republicans Richard Nixon, Spiro Agnew, Gerald Ford and Nelson Rockefeller in Democratic Senates. Yet even when the vice president is from the party in control, he or she is still an outsider to some degree. Lyndon Johnson did not try to run the Senate when he was vice president from 1961 to 1963 as he had done as Majority Leader in the previous six years. Senate Democrats would have considered the attempt highly improper, even though he was an esteemed colleague whose leadership they had accepted in the preceding period.

The president *pro tempore,* who presides over the Senate in the absence of the vice president, is not a powerful figure in the Senate either, even though selected by the members themselves. The choice is distinctly ritualistic: the party that controls the Senate nominates the person with the most seniority and in a straight-line party vote the majority nominee defeats the candidate of the minority party.

Since presiding over the Senate is generally unimportant, frequently none of the above officials does so. The role is assumed instead by freshman senators of the majority party who take a turn at exercising the responsibility.

"I don't feel like it, that's why. Why don't you exercise your power?"

Majority and Minority Leaders

The single most powerful person in the United States Senate is the *Majority Leader,* who is chosen by the members of the party in control. Although experience in the Senate is an important asset for a would-be leader, it is by no means determinative. Lyndon Johnson, considered by some observers to be the most influential Majority Leader (1955–1961) in the history of the Senate, came to that position after only one term in office. Democrat Mike Mansfield, Johnson's successor, and William Knowland, the Republican leader from 1953 to 1955, were both in the early years of their second term when chosen.

The Majority Leader has a number of rewards with which to affect the behavior of fellow senators. The Leader can use his or her influence with the committee that makes assignments to Senate standing committees. Lyndon Johnson's decision to allow freshmen senators to sit on one important committee (previously they had been placed only on obscure ones) helped build a base of political support on which he drew for a number of years. The Leader can also see to it that favored senators get appointed to select committees that take foreign "junkets," that they receive favorable office space, that some governmental installations (post offices, dams, federal buildings, air bases, and the like) are placed in their states, that grants are awarded to universities and local governments in their area, and that private bills they favor (such as allowing a relative of a constituent to come into the country under a special act of Congress) are given favorable consideration.

Even more crucial to the influence of the Majority Leader is his or her position in the center of the Senate's communications network. As the person responsible for legislative scheduling, the Leader is in a position to know the status of bills: to which committee they have been assigned; what their chances are of being favorably reported out; which senators are for and against them; and when and under what conditions they will be ready for debate and voting on the floor of the chamber. In a confusing system of specialized committees and complex legislative procedures, the Majority Leader is the one person who sees the overall workings of the Senate. The Leader thus possesses more information on more matters than any other senator and can use it to further his or her influence. Moreover, it is to the Leader that the rank-and-file member must turn for knowledge and advice about particular concerns.

The Majority Leader also acts as the chamber's communication link with the president.* The relationship is particularly close if, as is usual, both persons are from the same party. Then the Leader is regularly briefed by the president on the administration's programs and is expected to use his or her influence to get favorable Senate action on them. The Majority Leader thus becomes a source of intelligence on what the president wants, how keenly the president wants it, and what compromises the president is willing to accept to get some measure enacted. Information on presidential attitudes is sometimes important even when the president and the Majority Leader are not from the same party. In developing Democratic legislative proposals in the late 1950s, Lyndon Johnson took into account what President Eisenhower would and would not accept (for example, how many units of public housing at what cost) and scaled down his party's bills to avoid a presidential veto.

The Majority Leader not only conveys presidential wishes to senators, but he or she also informs the chief executive of their attitudes. The Leader's colleagues thus expect him or her to be not just the president's person but theirs as well. Playing both these roles satisfactorily is not an easy matter, but the Majority Leader who does so can do much to cement good relationships between the legislative and executive branches of the national government.

In many respects the *Minority Leader* parallels the majority counterpart: he or she is elected by colleagues; the Minority Leader tends to have experience, but seniority alone is not determinative (Everett Dirksen of Illinois and his son-in-law, Howard Baker Jr. of Tennessee, both came to the post during their second term in the Senate); and the Minority Leader serves as the focal point of communication among senators of the minority party. Because the Minority Leader works closely with the Majority Leader in legislative scheduling, he or she too is a source of information on the status of bills and their likelihood of being enacted into law.

The Minority Leader also has certain prerogatives that allow political influence over his or her colleagues—the Minority Leader can influence committee assignments to some degree—but the rewards he or she can bestow are not as plentiful as those of the Majority Leader. For example, the Minority Leader has less to say about where governmental installations are to be located. The Minority Leader is also less likely to have the president's legislative program as a focal point for rallying colleagues. Even when the Minority

Two highly skilled legislators.

Democratic Senate Majority Leader Lyndon Johnson.

Republican Senate Majority Leader Howard Baker.

* The Leader also confers regularly with his party counterpart in the House of Representatives.

Leader does (Republican senators Robert Taft and William Knowland were Minority Leaders during the Eisenhower administration; Everett Dirksen held the post during the earlier Nixon years; Hugh Scott was Minority Leader in the later years of Nixon's presidency and during the Ford administration), he or she has difficulty influencing a body controlled by the opposition party. The president may indeed find it politically more profitable to work with the opposition Majority Leader, particularly if the president's own party has relatively few senators compared to the majority party.

Whips

Both the Majority and Minority Leaders have assistants commonly referred to as *Whips.* The term came from the British Parliament, which borrowed it from foxhunting: the whip, or "whipper-in," was responsible for keeping the hounds from leaving the pack during the chase of the fox. By analogy, the Whip keeps the rank-and-file members from straying from the party fold; he or she sees to it that they are present to vote on key legislative measures and to cast their ballot as party leaders desire.

According to Edward Kennedy, who served as Democratic Whip from 1969 to 1971, the name is a misnomer, for the Whip does not have the ability to bring colleagues into line. The Whip serves as a potential communication link between his or her **Floor Leader** (this is the term applied to either the Majority or Minority Leader) and the rank-and-file members of the Whip's party, letting each know what the other is thinking so that legislative strategy can be planned accordingly. (For example, the legislative leaders will not want to bring a bill to a vote until they have the support necessary for passage.)

Even that function is not indispensable to the two Floor Leaders, since they can personally contact the limited number of senators from their parties without too much difficulty. When Lyndon Johnson was Majority Leader, he was reputed to have talked daily with every Democratic senator.

To a considerable extent the situation of a Whip under his Floor Leader is like that of a vice president under the president: frequently the two who are supposedly serving as a team come from the opposing factions of the party—Democratic Whip Alan Cranston of California, for instance, is much more liberal than the Majority Leader, Robert Byrd, with whom he serves. Personal relationships between the two may also be strained, as they were between former Democratic Whip Russell Long of Louisiana and his leader, Mike Mansfield of Montana. If so, the Floor Leader may simply work around his Whip, as Mansfield did when he appointed four assistant Whips to aid him in the Senate. Like the vice president's, the Whip's job is what his or her superior wants it to be: when Edward Kennedy replaced Long in 1969, Mansfield not only used the young senator (whom he admired) to gather information and get Democratic senators to the floor for crucial votes, but permitted Kennedy to share legislative scheduling and other leadership responsibilities. Mansfield also turned over many of the details of handling the legislative business of the Senate to his subsequent Whip, Robert Byrd.

The post of Whip also resembles the vice presidency in that it may constitute a stepping-stone upward. Since 1949, four Democrats—Scott Lucas, Lyndon Johnson, Mike Mansfield, and Robert Byrd—and three Republicans—Kenneth Wherry, Everett Dirksen, and Hugh Scott—have been promoted to the Floor Leader's position by their party colleagues. Thus the position of Whip has recently become a training ground for the top party post in the Senate.

Party Committees

There are three major groups in each party. One is concerned with the assignment of members to standing committees (the Democrats call theirs the **Steering Committee**; the Republicans, the **Committee on Committees**). The second, the **Policy Committee**, is responsible for discussing the issues and helping to establish legislative agendas. The third, known as the **Conference**, to which all members of each party belong, serves as the major organizing body for each party. However, as we shall see, the parties differ in how they choose members of the first two committees as well as in the role the three groups play in party affairs. In addition, the particular style of the Floor Leader affects how the various groups operate.

The Democratic Steering Committee is chaired by their Floor Leader, who also nominates all its members; such nominations are typically approved by the Democratic Conference. Its membership usually includes the Whip and many chairmen of standing committees as well. Although seniority in the Senate is a major factor in assignments and transfers, the Floor Leader can influence these decisions. As we have seen, Lyndon Johnson initiated a rule that guaranteed even the most junior senator a major committee assignment, a tradition that was continued by his successor, Mike Mansfield. However, the operating styles and political preferences of the two majority leaders differed considerably. Johnson told the Steering Committee whom he wanted to see placed on various committees, while Mansfield generally permitted the committee members to make their own decisions on such matters. Also, under Johnson the more conservative senators dominated the most important committees; in contrast, Mansfield used his influence with the Steering Committee to see to it that new, liberal senators were assigned to such committees.

The Republican Committee on Committees is chaired not by the Floor Leader but by some other senior senator with good standing among party colleagues. Except for the chairman, its members rotate every two years. The influence of the Floor Leader on the committee has also been lessened by the Republicans' tendency in assignments and transfers to standing committees to follow the seniority principle fairly strictly.

The Legislative Reorganization Act of 1946, which created the Senate Policy committees, intended that they would be executive groups entrusted with the planning, development, and implementation of party programs. Under Lyndon Johnson the seven-member Democratic group, composed largely of senior conservative senators from the South, was used to schedule legislation, with Johnson largely dictating its decisions. Under Mansfield the committee's size was expanded, junior liberal senators were added to the body, and the Majority Leader let the committee members play a larger role in determining which legislation should be brought to the floor and when it would be considered. The Republican Policy Committee is more independent of the party leadership, because it is chaired by someone other than the Floor Leader and its members are nominated by the chairman of the Republican Conference and approved by the members of the Conference. It has also been of considerable service to rank-and-file Republicans in doing research, reporting on legislation, and providing them with material for use in their campaigns.*

Finally, the Conferences of the two parties have also varied in recent years.

* Both the Republican and Democratic Policy Commitees tend to be more important when their party does not control the White House and therefore needs some guidance on policy matters.

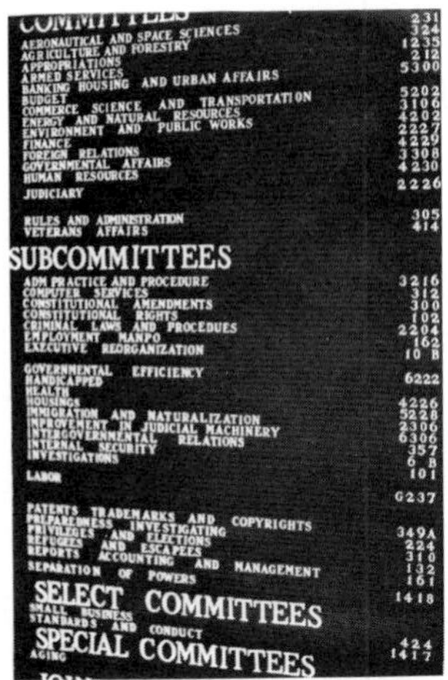

Again the Floor Leader chairs the Democratic one, but how the Conference operates depends on the inclinations of individual leaders. Under Johnson, the Conference met only at the beginning of the legislative session for the limited purpose of organizing itself for the next two years; in contrast, with Mansfield at its head, the Conference met frequently and initiated many of the reforms discussed below dealing with the selection and staffing of committees as well as the procedures used in committees and on the floor of the Senate. The Republicans choose some senator besides their Floor Leader to chair the Conference; they meet frequently; and they occasionally even pass a resolution favoring a particular piece of legislation. Even so, like members of the Democratic Conference, they shy away from passing binding resolutions on controversial bills for fear that they will antagonize dissenting Republican senators and thereby jeopardize party unity.

Standing-Committee Chairmen

A second major source of power within the Senate lies with the chairmen of the permanent standing committees to which bills are referred for consideration prior to floor action. Over 90 years ago Woodrow Wilson referred to them as "little legislatures" in which the real work of Congress is accomplished. The greater volume of legislation that the Congress considers, plus the need for specialization in a more complex and technical society, has made the Senate—and the House as well—even more dependent on the committees today than they were in Wilson's time. Both chambers are inclined to accept the action (or inaction) of standing committees on most legislation.

The jurisdictions of committees are determined by the Senate itself. In 1946 the Senate and the House passed the Legislative Reorganization Act, reducing the number of committees from 33 to 15. Over the years that number increased, and in early 1977 the Senate once again overhauled its committee structure, this time paring the number from 31 to 25. By 1983 the chamber had 16 regular permanent committees. In the process, similar activities undertaken by separate committees were consolidated, including the concentration of energy legislation in one committee, which also deals with natural resources.

The standing committees of the Senate deal with a variety of subjects, including such divergent matters as agriculture, banking and currency, the armed services, and foreign relations. Three are concerned with money matters: the Finance Committee, which deals with raising it, Appropriations, which decides how it shall be spent, and Budget, that tries to relate the two activities.

Not all standing committees, however, are of equal importance. The special role that the Senate plays in foreign affairs makes the Foreign Relations and Armed Services committees particularly crucial to the Senate's work. Appropriations is a particularly important committee because the level of expenditures allotted for various governmental programs reflect senatorial priorities and helps to determine how well each program operates. The Finance Committee is significant because it makes decisions about how the tax burden will be distributed among the population. The Budget Committee is key because it sets an overall spending figure for the Senate.

The committees' pecking order is reflected in their membership. Senior senators with high status among their colleagues are most likely to populate the key committees. Some freshmen senators manage to get on such committees early in their careers: one example is Harry Byrd Jr. of Virginia who sat on both the Armed Services and Finance

Committees in his first term in office. More commonly, if a seat is open, a senior member is transferred to it from another committee; sometimes a senator gives up one committee chair to accept another one, as Senator John Sparkman of Alabama did when he resigned the chair of the Banking, Housing, and Urban Affairs Committee to become chairman of the Foreign Relations Committee.*

Traditionally both parties have followed a **seniority custom** of choosing the member with the longest continuous service on a committee as its chairman or ranking minority member. However, recently both parties have made it possible for members to overturn that custom: Republican committee members choose their own chairman, subject to the approval of the Republican Conference; Democratic members vote by secret ballot on a committee chairman if one-fifth of the Democratic senators request it. However, to date, neither party has used these new rules to deny the chair to an individual entitled to it under the seniority custom.

As a result of the seniority system, senators from "safe," one-party states (which return them to office again and again) who choose to stay with a particular committee assignment move automatically up the ladder to the chair when their party controls the chamber. When the Democrats exercise control (they have failed to control the upper chamber only eight years since 1933), the chairmen of committees—particularly the important ones like Appropriations, Finance, Armed Services, and Foreign Relations—have traditionally come from the South. The traditional ranking minority members of such committees, ready to take over the chairmanships when the Republicans gain control of the Senate (as they did in 1981 and continued in 1983), have tended to come from the area where the GOP has traditionally been strong—the Midwest. This situation is changing, however, for both Democrats and Republicans. †

The power of the standing-committee chairman in the Senate stems from two main sources. One is the preferments at his or her disposal vis-à-vis other committee members. The chairman can favor a colleague, for example, by helping him or her become the chairman of an important subcommittee. The chairman can also see to it that a member gets to go on trips the committee makes in connection with its work. Moreover, he can allow a member to become the sponsor of an important piece of legislation, to lead the fight on the floor for its adoption, and to be included as a member of the conference committee assigned to work out any differences between the Senate and House over the measure.

These activities also relate to the other major power base of a committee chairman: the ability to utilize the procedures of his or her own committee and the floor action of the entire chamber on legislation referred to it. As we shall see later in this chapter, the standing-committee chairman looms large in the legislative process.

An Inner Club or Establishment

Observers of the Senate in the 1950s like political scientist Donald Matthews

* Minority party members also have choices: In 1983 Senator John Stennis (D-Miss.) decided to become the ranking member of Appropriations and to give up a comparable position on Foreign Affairs to which he was also entitled.

† For example, the Republican chairman of the powerful Armed Services Committee prior to his recent retirement was a southerner (John Tower of Texas), while its ranking Democratic member prior to his recent death was a westerner (Henry Jackson of Washington).

and journalist William White contended that the body was controlled behind the scenes by a clique known as the **"Inner Club"** or **"Establishment."** Supposedly centered on senior Southern Democrats like Richard Russell of Georgia, Robert Kerr of Oklahoma, and Lyndon Johnson of Texas, the group was also thought to include Republicans like Everett Dirksen and liberal Democrats like Hubert Humphrey who followed certain "folkways" or customs required of "Club" types. Included were such norms as serving an *apprenticeship* before becoming actively involved in Senate affairs; *specializing* so as to become an expert in a particular area of public policy; carrying one's share of the *legislative workload*; being *courteous* to other senators and avoiding personal attacks on political opponents; practicing *reciprocity* by honoring one's agreements and understanding other senators' problems and points of view; and remaining *loyal to the Senate* by not using it as a steppingstone to the presidency or vice presidency.

Not all students of the Senate of the 1950s agreed with Matthews's and White's assessment of its power structure. Difficulties in agreeing on who precisely was included in the "Inner Club" raised questions about its actual existence; some doubted whether a group composed of persons with such divergent political views as Russell and Humphrey could ever have worked together on vital legislation involving controversial issues of public policy. In any event, there is general agreement that even if such a group did control the Senate a quarter century or so ago, it no longer does. Principal figures like Russell, Kerr, Johnson, and Dirksen are gone, and a new breed of legislators have come into prominence.

The Power of Individual Senators

Attitudes of many senators towards the folkways that prevailed in the 1950s have changed greatly in recent years. They no longer consider it disloyal to the Senate to seek the presidency; since 1960 that body has become the major recruiting ground for the nation's highest office, particularly for the party out of power. (In 1980, Senators Howard Baker of Tennessee and Robert Dole of Kansas sought the Republican nomination; in 1984, Senators Alan Cranston of California, John Glenn of Ohio, Gary Hart of Colorado, and Ernest Hollings of South Carolina tried for the Democratic one.) Senators today are less likely to specialize in a particular area of public policy than formerly: frequently members of their professional staff are the real experts on the substance of legislation. Many senators today also concentrate more on providing services for their constituents (and on raising money for election campaigns) than on carrying their share of the legislative workload. There is also less civility and reciprocity accorded to fellow senators: unpleasant confrontations are more frequent, as are obstructionist tactics such as attaching numerous amendments to pending bills and engaging in filibusters (this tactic will be discussed in the next section). Finally, new senators no longer feel that they must serve an apprenticeship before becoming actively involved in promoting legislation on important issues of public policy. Thus while some senators still respect the old folkways, an increasing number do not, and as a result, we have a much more individualistic Senate today than in the 1950s.

In addition, recent developments in the structuring and staffing of committees have significantly increased the power of individual senators, including those without much seniority in that body. The Legislative Reorganization Act of 1946 limited the number of standing Senate committees to 15, but over the years that number was increased; even more significant has been the proliferation of subcommittees—smaller units into which parent committees subdivide to handle their ever-increasing workload. Even though the major committee reorganization in 1977 reduced the number of Senate committees and subcommittees, they still stood at 16 regular committees operating through 102 subcommittees at the beginning of the Ninety-Eighth Congress (1983–1985). Thus there are a large number of committee and subcommittee positions to be filled by the 100 members of the Senate.

Moreover, in recent years the Senate has acted to limit the number of committee and subcommittee positions that an individual senator can occupy. Under the terms of the 1977 reorganization, for example, each senator is limited to membership on three committees and a total of eight subcommittees. Beginning in 1979, senators were also restricted to chairing one full committee and two subcommittees. The end result of these limitations is that committee and subcommittee posts and chairs are distributed widely among members of the Senate, including very junior members of that body.

Unlike the situation in the 1950s, a new senator today can begin to exercise influence in the Senate very early in his or her career. By becoming a member—and even more importantly, a chairman of a subcommittee—he or she can exert power that is felt up the line, for parent committees are inclined to accept the actions of their subcommittees, and the entire chamber often respects the decisions of the standing committees, although floor challenges to committee recommendations have become more frequent in recent years. Also contributing to the junior member's effectiveness is a 1975 Senate resolution that permits the new senator to have additional staff to help with his or her legislative duties.

Thus individual senators can today play a meaningful legislative role after a relatively short period of service. The newness of many of our national programs, the willingness of young legislators to educate themselves so that they become known as Senate "experts" on vital issues, and the availability both of the chance to become a subcommittee chairman and of staff with which to operate, all contribute to the legislative effectiveness of junior members of the Senate.

One other feature of the Senate allows individual members to be influential in the affairs of that chamber: toleration of, and even respect for, the critic or dissenter. Among senators who have played that role in recent years are Wayne Morse of Oregon, Ernest Gruening of Alaska, William Fulbright of Arkansas, Eugene McCarthy of Minnesota, and William Proxmire of Wisconsin. The Senate's tolerance of deviant views, plus the natural interest that unpopular views engender among the media, ensure that persons who disagree with their colleagues on major matters of public policy will find a ready outlet for their criticisms as indicated by the publicity given criticisms of the Vietnam war by Morse, Fulbright, and McCarthy. Moreover, the eventual change that took place in our nation's handling of that tragic war attests to the fact that critics of traditional policies can ultimately be effective in determining public policy.

Power in the United States Senate is thus distributed broadly among a variety of persons. (Persons occupying major leadership positions are listed in Table 10.1.) Before we analyze the major patterns of influence that prevail there, it would be instructive to compare and contrast the situation just described with that of the lower chamber of the United States Congress, the House of Representatives.

Senate dissenters: William Fulbright, William Proxmire and Eugene McCarthy.

Table 10.1
Major Leaders of the U. S. Senate, 98th Congress (1983–1985)

Ceremonial Offices		
Vice President of the United States		**George Bush (Texas)**
President *Pro Tem* of the Senate		**Strom Thurmond (South Carolina)**
Party Leaders	*Majority Party (Republicans)*	*Minority Party (Democrats)*
Floor Leader	Howard Baker (Tennessee)	Robert Byrd (West Virginia)
Whip	Ted Stevens (Alaska)	Alan Cranston (California)
Chairman of the Conference	James McClure (Idaho)	Robert Byrd (West Virginia)
Secretary of the Conference	Jake Garn (Utah)	Daniel Inouye (Hawaii)
		[Steering Committee]
Committee on Committee Chairman	Nancy Kassebaum (Kansas)	Robert Byrd (West Virginia)
Policy Committee Chairman	John Tower (Texas)	Robert Byrd (West Virginia)
Important Standing Committees	*Chairman (Republicans)*	*Ranking Minority Members (Democrats)*
Appropriations	Mark Hatfield (Oregon)	John Stennis (Mississippi)
Armed Services	John Tower (Texas)	Henry Jackson* (Washington)
Budget	Pete Domenici (New Mexico)	Lawton Chiles (Florida)
Finance	Robert Dole (Kansas)	Russell Long (Louisiana)
Foreign Relations	Charles Percy (Illinois)	Claiborne Pell (Rhode Island)

* Died September 1, 1983. Place taken by Sam Nunn (Georgia).

POWER WITHIN THE HOUSE OF REPRESENTATIVES

In some respects the sources and distribution of power within the House and the Senate are quite similar. Yet, as indicated below, there are also some differences in the power structure of the two chambers.

House Speaker Tip O'Neil.

Party Leaders

Unlike the Senate, the House has no purely ceremonial figure to preside over its deliberations. This function is handled by the body's most powerful figure—the *Speaker of the House of Representatives.* Theoretically chosen as an officer of the entire chamber, the Speaker is, in essence, selected by the caucus of the majority party, since this group nominates and then votes for the Speaker over the opposing party's candidate. Thus the Speaker is both a House and a party official.

Because this is so, the ceremonial duties of the vice president and the political powers of the Senate Majority Leader are combined in the office of Speaker, who has the power of recognition, rules on procedural questions, and refers bills to committees. But unlike the vice president, the Speaker is not a neutral figure with no vote except in a tie: not only can the Speaker vote, but he or she also can and does leave the chair to lead and participate in debate. Like the Senate Majority Leader, the Speaker is the floor captain of his or her party, plans strategy, and schedules measures for consideration and action.

The Speaker has generally the same rewards to dispense in exercising influence over colleagues as his or her Senate counterpart: assistance in obtaining a favorable committee assignment, appointment to select committees, help with favored private bills, invitations to serve as floor leader for a measure or to preside over the House, and help with a tough political campaign. Like the Senate Majority Leader, the Speaker is in the center of the internal communication network of the House as well as being its link with the White House and Senate.

In recent years the power of a Democratic Speaker has increased considerably. As indicated below, a new Democratic **Steering and Policy Committee** was created in 1973 with the responsibility of nominating persons for committee assignments as well as helping to devise and direct the party's legislative program. These added responsibilities redounded to the benefit of the Democratic Speaker, who was made chairman of the Democratic Steering and Policy Committee and given a dominant role in choosing members of the committee. Furthermore, the Speaker was granted additional powers to affect the procedures of the House that are described in more detail later in this chapter: the Speaker is now empowered to refer bills to standing committees and to nominate the chairman and Democratic members of the **House Rules Committee** which plays a critical role in determining the scheduling and consideration of legislation on the floor of the House. Also redounding to the benefit of the Democratic Speaker is the recent increase in the number of Assistant Whips as well as the financial and staff resources of the Whip's office.

Working with the Speaker of the House is the *Majority Leader.* Officially chosen by the majority party caucus, the Majority Leader is often the favorite of the Speaker. In any event, the Majority Leader's influence in the House will be what the Speaker permits it to be. Generally the Majority Leader assists the Speaker in scheduling legislation, distributing and collecting information of concern to the majority-party members, and attempting to persuade the rank-and-file legislators to go along with the wishes of the legislative party leaders and the president, if the president is from their party. As a subordinate, however, the Majority Leader frequently has a higher goal in mind: selection as Speaker when the incumbent dies or retires. For Democratic Majority Leaders of late this aspiration has been realized: five in a row—William Bankhead of Alabama, Sam Rayburn of Texas, John McCormack of Massachusetts, Carl Albert of Oklahoma, and Thomas O'Neill Jr. of Massachusetts—were all promoted to the top position in the House.*

The nominee of the minority party caucus who loses out in the election for the speakership becomes the *Minority Leader* of the House. This role is essentially the same as it is in the Senate: to work with the Majority Leader in scheduling legislation and to lead the opposition party. The Minority Leader has some influence over committee assignments and the like but suffers from the same frustrations as his or her Senate counterpart: fewer preferments than the majority party can offer and, except when the Minority Leader's party controls the presidency, lack of an external program around which to muster the support of House colleagues.

The *Majority* and *Minority Whips* have the same general function as in the Senate: to serve as a communications link between the party leadership and rank-and-file members and to see to it that the latter are there when crucial votes are taken. This function takes on far

* Should the Democrats retain control of the House in 1986 when Speaker O'Neill is planning to retire and then select Majority Leader Jim Wright to replace him, the tradition would be continued.

more importance in the House than it does in the Senate, however, because the greater number of members in the lower chamber makes it almost impossible for the party leaders themselves to reach them. (Whereas Lyndon Johnson could be in touch with all members of his party in the Senate in the 1950s, Sam Rayburn, serving as the Speaker of the House at the same time, could not.) Both parties have elaborate organizations composed of representatives (called *Assistant Whips*) from various areas of the nation who serve as liaison with colleagues from their regions.

There are, however, some differences in the parties' approach to the Whips. The Democratic Whip is appointed by their Floor Leader with the concurrence of the Speaker (when he is a Democrat), while the Republican Conference (a body to which all House Republicans belong) chooses that party's Whip. As a consequence, the Democratic Whip is always part of the party team, a result that does not always occur in the G. O. P. (For instance, when Gerald Ford was chosen Minority Leader in 1965, he backed another candidate against the long-time incumbent Leslie Arends—who had served since 1943—but the Republican Conference continued Arends in office.) This difference in selection policy affects the pattern of succession to higher party offices in the House. Democratic Speakers John McCormack, Carl Albert, and Thomas O'Neill previously served as Whips (as well as Majority Leaders), but no Republican Whip in this century has been similarly promoted.

Party Committees

The functions of party committees in the House of Representatives parallel those in the Senate: assigning members to committees, taking the leadership in developing a legislative program, and establishing an overall group for party decision-making in the House. However, as indicated below, the parties differ in how they handle such responsibilities; moreover, the Democratic party has made major changes in recent years with respect to such matters.

Traditionally, the Democratic party used its members on the House **Ways and Means Committee** (this committee is described in the next section) to serve as its Committee on Committees, which also included the Speaker, Majority Leader, and the chairman of the Democratic Caucus (a body composed of all Democrats in the House). This group not only assigned members to standing committees but also followed the seniority custom in nominating the committee chairmen. While its nominees for chairmen had to be approved by the Democratic Caucus, there was no effective way for the **Caucus** to register its disapproval of a particular chairman because the nominees were all presented in a single slate. Moreover, if the entire slate were voted down, the Committee on Committees could submit a second slate also containing the objectionable chairman, but with the names of some favored chairmen removed. Faced with this situation, the Democratic Caucus automatically approved the recommendations of the Committee on Committees.

Beginning in 1971, however, the Democrats began to change their system to give the Caucus a more meaningful role in choosing committee chairmen. Initially the Committee on Committees was required to present its nominees for chairmen one committee at a time, and upon demand of 10 or more Democratic members of the House, any nomination could be debated and voted on. Later the system was changed so that all individual chairmen were voted on automatically and, if 20 percent of the members demanded it, the vote was by secret ballot. Ultimately, as we have seen, in 1973 House Democrats took the responsibility of nominating committee chairmen away from the Committee on Committees altogether and placed it in the newly created Steering and Policy Committee. New rules also provide for nominations to be made from the floor of the Caucus meetings in the event that an initial nomination of the Steering and Policy Committee is voted down.

The new system soon had an effect on the choosing of chairmen of standing committees. In 1975 three standing committee chairmen—Bob Poage (Texas) of the Agriculture Committee, F. Edward Hebert (Louisiana) of the Armed Services Committee, and Wright Patman (Texas) of the Banking, Currency, and Housing Committee—lost their positions as a result of action by the Democratic Caucus. In addition, Wayne Hays (Ohio), chairman of the Administration Committee, barely survived when the late Phillip Burton (California), chairman of the Caucus, convinced its members to retain Hays in office even though the Steering and Policy Committee had not approved his nomination. However, Hays did lose his chairmanship in 1976 when he became involved in a scandal (a secretary on the staff of the Administration Committee accused him of keeping her on the payroll to serve as his mistress) and, under pressure from the Caucus, resigned his position to avoid being voted out of it.

In addition to their new role in choosing chairmen of the standing committees of the House, both the Democratic Steering and Policy Committee and the Democratic Caucus have recently begun to play a more meaningful role in other business of the House. The committee has taken the leadership in helping the Speaker of the House develop and implement the party's legislative program, thus serving as an executive committee for the party's policies and practices. The Caucus, which used to restrict itself to a short meeting at the beginning of a congressional session to choose its leadership and ratify committee assignments, now conducts its organizational meeting prior to the opening of the session and meets more regularly during the session on matters of public policy. An impressive demonstration of power was a vote taken in 1975 binding the Democratic members of the powerful Rules Committee (described below) to allow amendments to a tax bill to be made on the floor of the House removing special concessions for oil and gas interests.

The above events have thus made a substantial difference in the role that Democratic party committees play in House affairs. While not commanding the attention of recent activities of the majority party, House Republicans have also made some changes in the way they handle the choosing of ranking members of standing committees. In 1971 they changed their procedure so that all members of the House Conference (the counterpart of the Democratic Caucus) can vote by secret ballot on each nomination made by their Committee on Committees. The Republican Policy Committee (which, unlike the Democratic one, dates not from 1973 but back to 1949) has been active since its creation in helping to develop a consensus of rank-and-file members on legislation and in communicating their attitudes to the party leadership. Recently, however, this function has been increasingly assumed by the Republican Conference.

Standing-Committee Chairmen

Traditionally, standing-committee chairmen have held a powerful position in the House. Protected by selection through the automatic system of seniority, they dominated the consideration of legislation by their committees, including the decision whether or not to utilize subcommittees, and if so, how these subcommittees should be staffed and financed. However, a number of recent reforms have drastically reduced the powers of committee chairmen in the House of Representatives.

As we have already seen, one major difference in the situation of House committee chairmen is that their tenure is no longer secure. Instead of automatic nomination by the Committee on Committees on the basis of seniority, followed by rubber-stamp approval by the party rank-and file, chairmen and ranking minority members must now pass muster with the Democratic Steering and Policy Committee or its counterpart, the Republican Committee on Committees, and be individually approved by the members of the Democratic Caucus or the Republican Conference. The recent action of House Democrats in deposing three committee chairmen serves as a reminder that aspirants for that position must keep their fences mended both with party leaders in the House and rank-and-file members.

The 1970 Legislative Reorganization Act passed by a coalition of Republicans and liberal Democrats also makes it much more difficult for chairmen to dominate the proceedings of committees. Included among the provisions of the act are the requirements that members be given advance notice of committee meetings, that all its roll-call votes be made public, that committee members be given three days to file minority or supplementary reports on committee legislation, and that they be empowered to call up for floor action a bill being withheld by the chairman. In addition, the act encouraged the holding of "open" meetings. In 1973 the House went further by providing that normal committee meetings be open to the public unless a majority of the committee members vote by roll call to close a particular meeting.

Finally, as a result of recent Democratic reforms, their committee chairmen have lost control over the operations of subcommittees. Chairmen no longer can decide unilaterally whether or not to have subcommittees, make discretionary decisions on which legislative matters to refer to them, and control their membership, staff, and budget. Now most regular standing committees are divided into subcommittees, and legislative hearings increasingly begin at the subcommittee level. Moreover, the choice of subcommittee chairmen now lies not with the standing-committee chairmen but with the Democratic members of the committee,* and each subcommittee chairman and ranking minority member is guaranteed staff and a budget rather than having to depend on the committee chairmen for such matters.

Thus the days of the arbitrary House committee chairmen are past. This does not mean that chairmen are no longer influential figures in the House of Representatives. It means rather that they must now be more sensitive to the needs and desires of their committee colleagues and win their respect and support, rather than depending on an unresponsive system to perpetuate and justify their existence and actions.

Some of the same committees that are important in the Senate are also crucial to the operation of the House of Representatives. Appropriations is as important, if not more so, in the House (compared to the Senate) because of the political custom that spending measures originate in the lower chamber. Similarly, Ways and Means (the counterpart of the Senate Finance Committee) is vital because revenue measures *must* by constitutional edict originate in this chamber. In addition, the committee has jurisdiction over such vital subjects as social security, health care, welfare, and foreign trade. As in the Senate, the

* The exceptions are chairmen of subcommittees of the House Appropriations Committee, who are chosen by the Democratic Caucus.

House Ways and Means Committee conducts a hearing on taxes.

Budget Committee is important as a potential source of fiscal control.

There are, however, differences in the committee pecking order in the two chambers. Neither the Foreign Affairs, nor the Armed Services Committee is as important in the House as its Senate counterpart. Yet the House Rules Committee is a key body because of the crucial role it plays in procedures for scheduling legislation;† in contrast, the Senate Rules and Administration Committee (which concerns itself with such matters as supervising the Senate library and restaurant) is almost at the bottom of the priority list in the upper chamber.

Informal Leadership in the House

Observers of the House have been less likely than students of the Senate to impute influence to an inner "club" or "establishment." The most prominently mentioned clique of this type was Speaker Sam Rayburn's "board of education," an informal group of changing membership that is reputed to have made major decisions at certain times during the late Speaker's tenure in office. Little has been written about the actual composition of the "board," however, and no such group has existed under other party leaders.

One possible reason for the absence of a House "club" is that the sheer size of the body makes it difficult for a small group to control it from behind the scenes. While the formal and informal leaders of a small group may be different people, the more members an organization has, the more difficult contact between them becomes. As a result, only those in formal positions of authority have the visibility and communication ties with the general membership necessary to control the organization. These facts of organizational life may help to explain why party leaders and committee chairmen generally exercise influence in the House. Re-

† It should be noted, however, that in 1983, the membership of the Rules Committee was reduced because the House leadership was unable to persuade senior members to take vacant seats on the Committee, presumably because membership on the Committee does not attract money or media attention that are important for re-election.

cently newer types of informal groups have been organized in the House such as the **Black Caucus,** the **Women's Caucus,** and the previously mentioned Blue-Collar Caucus. However, the relatively small size of these groups (typically less than 20) has limited their influence in the chamber.

Informal patterns of influence have not been totally lacking in the House. In the past, large state delegations frequently constituted important blocs of power that were often controlled by strong leaders like William Green of Pennsylvania and Charles Buckley of New York. However, the demise of local party organizations has eroded the political base of such individuals and broken up the bloc voting of states in the House.

The most significant unofficial organization in the House in recent years has been the **Democratic Study Group.** Established in 1959 by a relatively small bloc of liberal Northern and Western Democrats to research problems, to rally members to be present for crucial votes, and to help to finance liberal Democratic candidates, the group now numbers over half the membership and has taken the leadership in House reforms involving the seniority rule and establishment of the party's Steering and Policy Committee. The group was also instrumental in getting the Democratic Caucus to set a date for withdrawal from Vietnam and opposing a constitutional amendment against busing to achieve racial balance in the schools. One indication of the group's growing influence in the House is that one of its members, Thomas O'Neill, recently became Majority Leader of the House, then its Speaker.

In the early 1980s, a group of Southern Democrats, the Conservative Democratic Forum (also known as the "Boll Weevils"), became an important force in the House. It was this group that provided vital support for President Reagan's 1981 program of tax and budget cuts.

The Power of Individual Representatives

The rank-and-file member of the House has less influence in the chamber than an individual senator. Many representatives experience a real shock when they leave state and local political circles, where they have been influential figures, and are swallowed up in the anonymity of national politics. Typically in the early stages of a House member's career, he or she is an unknown, not only to the general and "attentive" publics but also to most colleagues.

Several factors help explain this situation. One is the difference in the size of the two chambers. As one of 435 persons, the rank-and-file House member is simply less visible than a senator, who is one of 100. Consider particularly the representatives from a populous state like California, with a congressional delegation of over 40 members, compared to two senators. It is also more difficult for the average representative to gain notoriety as a maverick or dissenter than a senator. Few, if any, become "household names" in the same sense as a Fulbright, a Morse, or a Proxmire.

Faced with these handicaps, the rank-and-file representative has traditionally had to struggle to gain some visibility and influence in the chamber. Writing in the 1960s, one close student of the subject, political scientist Richard Fenno, suggested that the best way a young member of the House could do that was to ingratiate himself or herself with some senior party leader or committee chairman in order to become the chairman's protégé. The senior lawmaker would then see to it that the protégé got a good committee assignment, a subcommittee chair, the opportunity to preside over the House, or other privileges. In turn, the dutiful protégé would serve an apprenticeship by specializing, doing committee work, speaking only in areas of his or her speciality, and cooperating with party and committee leaders. If these chores were performed satisfactorily over a long period of time (and if the junior legislator kept getting re-elected), the principle of seniority would yield him or her the eventual reward: a place in the power structure of the House.

Both parties in the House, however, have recently begun to vest more power and responsibility in their junior members. Republicans were the first to do so by giving better committee assignments to freshmen and bringing them more into the decision-making process of the Republican Conference. Contributing to this development was the contest in 1965 in which Representative Gerald Ford utilized the support of younger Republicans in defeating the incumbent Charles Halleck for the minority leadership and then subsequently rewarded his supporters with more influence in party affairs. Democratic leaders have not had to resort to such tactics because there have been no genuine contests for party posts in many years; however, recent Majority Leaders like Albert and O'Neill have seen to it that junior Democrats get better committee assignments and play a role in the expanded activities of the Democratic Caucus.

Another institutional development in the House has also contributed to the increased influence of junior House members, especially Democrats: the greater use of subcommittees to conduct legislative business. As in the Senate, the increase in the scope and complexity of legislative matters has forced the House to create more and more specialized subcommittees; in the Ninety-Eighth Congress (1983–1985) there were 141 of them operating within 22 permanent standing committees. Moreover, recent actions of House Democrats in restricting the number of subcommittees on which an individual can sit and allowing each committee member to choose one subcommittee assignment before permitting any member to choose a second one have served to distribute posts to a large number of members, including many freshmen. Possessed of such a subcommittee position, and with control over staff and budget for its operation, young members of the House no longer need to depend so heavily on the apprentice–protégé system to win visibility and influence in the lower House of the Congress.

The Distribution of Power: A Summary

This analysis indicates that power is not highly concentrated in either chamber of Congress. Although majority party officials such as the Speaker of the House and Majority Leaders in both chambers have important means of influencing their colleagues, persuasion is generally more effective than coercion (as Everett Dirksen put it some years ago, ". . . the oil can is mightier than the sword. . ."), particularly in dealings with individuals who have seniority and power sources of their own. However, House Democrats have recently begun to vest more authority in the Speaker: as chairman of the recently created Steering and Policy Committee, the Speaker now has more influence over committee assignments, and the additional authority to name the Democratic members of the Rules Committee and to refer bills to committees strengthens the Speaker's ability to affect legislation.

While committee chairmen remain influential persons in both the House and Senate, they are not as powerful as they once were. Their selection is no longer automatic, as the deposing of three Democratic House chairmen reveals. In addition, more and more legislative activity is being decentralized in increasingly autonomous subcommittees.

Individual members of the Senate are more powerful than the members of the House of Representatives. Their small number plus the greater attention that the mass media focus on members of the upper chamber makes rank-and-file senators much more visible than their counterparts in the House. However, recent attempts of both parties to award junior members of the House more important committee assignments—together with the proliferation of subcommittees, many of which are chaired by such members—makes rank-and-file members of the House more important today than they were in the past.

Finally, the patterns of leadership differ between the two parties. As indicated in Table 10.2, House Democrats concentrate almost all power in the hands of their Floor Leader, who uses other party officials and committees to further his purposes.* The Republicans distribute influence among party officials more widely. It is difficult to determine the reason for this distinction. It may reflect the Republicans' general distrust of political power. It may also be related to a pragmatic feature of politics: the Democrats have controlled both houses of Congress for most of the period since 1933 and may have found it necessary to concentrate authority in their Floor Leaders in order to get legislative proposals enacted into law.

Closely related to the distribution of power in the American Congress is the question of how this power is actually exercised in the course of the legislative process. The following section explores the basic procedures of both the House and the Senate for considering legislation.

CONGRESSIONAL PROCEDURE: RUNNING THE LEGISLATIVE OBSTACLE COURSE

One outstanding characteristic of Congress is the tortuous process through

* The same practice is true of Senate Democrats.

Table 10.2
Major Leaders of the U. S. House of Representatives, 98th Congress (1983–1985)

	Party Leaders	
	Majority Party (Democrats)	
Speaker	Thomas O'Neill Jr. (Massachusetts)	
Floor Leader	Jim Wright (Texas)	
Whip	Thomas Foley (Washington)	
Chairman of the Caucus	Gillis Long (Louisiana)	
Secretary of the Caucus	Geraldine Ferraro (New York)	
Chairman, Steering and Policy Committee	Thomas O'Neill Jr. (Massachusetts)	
	Minority Party (Republicans)	
Floor Leader	Robert Michel (Illinois)	
Whip	Trent Lott (Mississippi)	
Chairman of the Conference	Jack Kemp (New York)	
Vice Chairman of the Conference	Jack Edwards (Alabama)	
Secretary of the Conference	Robert Lagomarsino (California)	
Chairman, Committee on Committees	Robert Michel (Illinois)	
Chairman, Policy Committee	Dick Cheney (Wyoming)	
	Important Standing Committees	
Chairman (Democrats)		*Ranking Minority Members (Republicans)*
Appropriations	Jamie Whitten (Mississippi)	Silvio Conte (Massachusetts)
Budget	James Jones (Oklahoma)	Delbert Latta (Ohio)
Rules	Claude Pepper (Florida)	James Quillen (Tennessee)
Ways and Means	Dan Rostenkowski (Illinois)	Barber Conable Jr. (New York)

which most proposals must pass. In a typical session only about one in 100 proposed measures is finally enacted into law. The other 99 fail to surmount some obstacle along the way.

The procedures of Congress are so complex and technical that only the parliamentarians of the two chambers plus a few veteran members grasp their intricacies. Nonetheless it is possible to outline in general terms the process through which legislative proposals are screened and the kinds of political, as well as legal, considerations that affect their ultimate disposition. There are some differences in detail between the Senate and the House, but the general stages are similar.

Introduction of Bills and Referral to Committees

The introduction of bills in either chamber is a simple matter: a member merely has a proposal drawn in proper form (a legislative counsel offers assistance with this chore) and introduces it in his or her name (the actual source of the bill may be the president, an administrative agency, or even an interest group). Since both chambers now permit cosponsors, a measure frequently bears the signature of a number of senators or representatives to indicate that it has considerable support. (Often members from both political parties, different regions of the country, or even different political philosophies—liberal, moderate, conservative—join together as sponsors for that reason.) Similar measures can be introduced simultaneously in the two chambers with the exception that revenue and appropriation bills originate in the House.

Naturally some bills are more important and have a greater chance of passage than others; particularly successful are those that are suggested by or have the backing of the president or some executive agency (known as **"administration" bills**). Also, a major measure often bears the name of the chairman of the standing committee to which it is referred because its backers calculate that this will ensure sympathetic handling both in committee and on the floor.

Generally speaking, deciding which committee a bill should be referred to presents no great difficulty for the presiding officers of the Senate and the House. Even when a measure can be sent to several committees, the sponsor can have it drafted so that it is appropriate to one in particular. Previous decisions on similar bills provide precedents, so that only new types of legislation present any real problem.* In such circumstances the discretion of the presiding officer is crucial and may help determine the ultimate fate of the bill.

Committee Consideration

One student has suggested that the standing committees are the kilns in which legislation is baked, where proposals are sorted, mixed, and molded into form. For most bills, however, they are more like Woodrow Wilson's description of them: "... dim dungeons of silence ..." from which most measures never emerge. (Recent estimates indicate that, on the average, of 10 bills referred to committee, only one is reported out favorably.)

In fact, standing committees do not even hold hearings on most of the bills referred to them. A chairman may simply not schedule any, a practice that used to effectively end the matter; however, recent reforms now make it possible for a majority of the committee members to force a chairman to hold hearings on a bill if they want to consider it. Even then, however, the hearings may be so delayed or dragged out that there is little chance of concluding them in time to get the bill reported out and passed before the end of the congressional session.

Bills that the chairman and most committee members favor are scheduled for early hearings by the committee or, even more often, a subcommittee. A variety of witnesses appear at such hearings to give their views on a bill. Typically these include: officials of the executive branch who have an interest in the legislative proposal (the Secretary of State or Defense will normally kick off hearings on matters of foreign policy); members of Congress from both houses; and private citizens, particularly spokespersons for concerned interest groups. Both supporters and opponents are provided an opportunity to appear, although the chairman's own attitude on a bill often determines which side is favored in the scheduling of witnesses.

Witnesses generally read a prepared statement setting forth their views and supporting evidence for them, and then face interrogation from the committee members. The kind of treatment a per-

* Both houses have a way around this problem, however, since a bill can be referred to more than one committee in either chamber. In addition, the Speaker, with the approval of the House, may create *ad hoc* committees to consider measures that overlap the jurisdictions of several committees.

Hearing the witness.

son receives often depends on how his or her attitudes on the bill in question compares with those of the committee chairman. Sometimes, however, other committee members will come to the defense of a beleaguered witness, particularly if they are sympathetic with that witness's stand on a matter.

Most analysts of congressional hearings agree that they reveal little factual information to determine how committee members vote. Indeed, most members have pronounced views on the matter before the hearings even begin. Why, then, are they held? Because they do serve other purposes. One relates to the informing function of Congress: media coverage of testimony given in hearings alerts citizens to the bill and the stands of various groups and individuals. Hearings thus widen the public concerned with the issue.* Hearings also act as safety valves for the losers. Legislative defeat is easier to accept if one has been given the opportunity to state one's views, that is, to feel that one has had one's day in court.

At the conclusion of the hearings the subcommittee or committee involved goes into executive session to reach a decision about the bill. (These sessions used to be held in private but in recent years are generally open to the public unless their disclosures would "endanger national security" or violate chamber rules.) The members may give it a favorable or unfavorable recommendation, suggest that it be tabled, or, more typically, amend it in any way they desire. The amendment process is usually referred to as the **mark-up** of the bill, since the committee members go over the measure line by line to rewrite it. When a subcommittee has completed the initial consideration of a bill, the parent committee is free to make changes. Generally, however, it tends to go along with the decisions of the subgroup. Bills that are favorably reported are often accompanied by a report describing their purpose and scope; those on which there is a disagreement may also contain dissenting, minority views.

Scheduling Bills for Floor Action

Senate. There is generally no problem in scheduling for floor action any bills reported by standing committees of the Senate. If a bill is noncontroversial, the chairman of the standing committee may ask for unanimous consent to hear the bill at once, and, if no one objects, floor action follows. If a bill is controversial, scheduling is left to the Majority Leader, who works it out with the Minority Leader and, if the Democrats control the chamber, with their Policy Committee as well. The Majority Leader also generally discusses the scheduling of administration bills with the president or executive agency officials.

In the Senate there are even ways to

* Not all hearings are public, however. If testimony covers confidential matters (such as national defense) or may injure the reputations of third parties, it may be taken in private.

97TH CONGRESS
1ST SESSION

H. R. 1

To make regulations more cost-effective, to ensure periodic review of old rules, to improve regulatory planning and management, to eliminate needless formality and delay, to enhance public participation in the regulatory process, to establish a select committee of the House of Representatives to conduct investigations of Federal agency rules, to establish procedures for congressional review of agency rules, and for other purposes.

IN THE HOUSE OF REPRESENTATIVES

JANUARY 5, 1981

Mr. MOAKLEY introduced the following bill; which was divided and referred as follows: Titles I, II, and III to the Committee on the Judiciary and title IV to the Committee on Rules

---

A BILL

To make regulations more cost-effective, to ensure periodic review of old rules, to improve regulatory planning and management, to eliminate needless formality and delay, to enhance public participation in the regulatory process, to establish a select committee of the House of Representatives to conduct investigations of Federal agency rules, to establish procedures for congressional review of agency rules, and for other purposes.

get bills to the floor that have not been reported out of a standing committee. The most prevalent tactic is to move the bill as an amendment to a measure that is already on the floor for action. Since amendments need not be germane to the general measure to which they are attached (one exception is policy amendments to appropriations measures), almost any bill can be rescued from a standing committee. Liberals interested in civil rights legislation, for instance, sometimes used this technique to bypass the Senate Judiciary Committee chaired by Senator Eastland of Mississippi; an early civil rights measure was also attached as an amendment to a bill authorizing foreign aid.

Another tactic is to place a House-passed measure on the Senate calendar for action without sending it to a standing committee, a maneuver that can be accomplished if a single senator objects to committee referral. It has been used frequently to get civil rights bills already passed by the House to the Senate floor for action without the necessity for having them considered by the Judiciary Committee.

Two other possibilities exist for bypassing Senate standing committees and bringing matters directly to the floor for action. One is suspension of rules, a method that is used primarily for amendments to appropriations bills to which the rule of germaneness does apply. The other is a motion to discharge the standing committee from consideration of a bill already referred to it. Both motions, however, can be defeated fairly easily by a filibuster, a matter that we will explore below.

In fact, the possibility of a filibuster acts as a restraint on all four tactics, as does the informal courtesy of reciprocity among senators that standing commitees should not generally be bypassed in the legislative process. Nonetheless, the availability of the nongermane amendment, consideration of a House-passed measure, and motions to suspend the rules and discharge a committee of a bill make it likely that a measure favored by a majority of the Senate membership will not be blocked by a standing committee.

House. A variety of methods are available to get bills to the floor of the lower chamber for action. Private bills—such as those waiving immigration requirements for individuals—and noncontroversial public bills of minor importance are placed on special calendars. Certain types of legislation are also treated in a special way. Six standing committees—Appropriations, Budget, House Administration, Rules, Standards of Official Conduct, and Ways and Means—have direct privileged access to the House floor for particular measures.

Another means of getting proposed legislation to the floor is to suspend the House rules, a motion that requires a two-thirds vote. If adopted, the suspension procedure limits debate to 40 minutes and prohibits amendments from being attached to the bill. Traditionally used only for minor measures, in the mid-1970s it began to be utilized for major legislation as well. (For example, the Emergency Natural Gas Act of 1977 was approved by a large majority of the House under a suspension of the rules, even though it was subjected to only one day of committee hearings.) As the number of measures considered under suspension of the rules mushroomed—449 in the Ninety-Fifth Congress (1977–1979)—many members of both parties began to resent what they considered an abuse of this special procedure. In January 1979 the House approved guidelines that prohibit any bill with an estimated cost of over $100 million from being considered under the suspension procedure unless a special request from the Speaker of the House to waive the guidelines is granted.

Despite these special procedures, however, most major legislation does not go directly to the floor of the House; rather, it must clear the House Rules Committee. This potent group has the power to issue vital "rules" on the scheduling of a measure for floor action. It can determine whether or not it should be sent to the floor at all and, if so, *when* the debate should take place and *how long* it should last. Moreover, the committee has a lot to say about whether the bill can be amended on the floor and under what conditions such amendments can take place. An "open" rule permits germane amendments to be proposed on the floor. A "closed" rule prohibits such amendments altogether or allows amendments to be proposed only by the committee that reported the bill. A "modified" rule may specify what parts of a bill may be amended, when such amendments may be offered, the order in which they may be proposed, and who may offer them. It should be noted, however, that the Democratic Caucus is now empowered to discuss amendments and instruct Democrats on the Rules Committee to make those amendments "in order" for House debates.

Because it makes such crucial decisions affecting floor action on bills, the Rules Committee is in a strong position. It can kill a bill altogether by deciding not to hold a hearing on a rule for it. Or even if the committee does hold hearings on a bill, it can delay action on a measure by preventing a committee quorum from developing or by lining up a series of witnesses to testify against issuing a rule for the bill. The committee can also insist that changes be made in the content of a measure as the price for scheduling it for floor debate.

In the period from the late 1930s to the early 1960s the Rules Committee was controlled, under the chairmanship of Howard Smith of Virginia, by a coalition of Southern Democrats and Northern Republicans who used it to kill, delay, and emasculate much liberal legislation. In 1961, at the urging of President Kennedy, Speaker Sam Rayburn succeeded in getting the House to change the size of the committee from 12 to 15; the appointment of two new carefully selected Democrats then gave the liberals a majority on the committee. This change, the defeat of Smith in a primary fight in 1966, the appointment of other liberals to the committee, the adoption of rules denying the chairman the right to set meeting dates, requiring the consent of the majority of the committee to table a bill, and setting limits on proxy voting by members—all have served to diminish the committee's role in frustrating liberal legislative proposals. The fact that the Speaker now has the power to nominate the chairperson and Democratic members of the Rules Committee also ties the body closely to the Speaker rather than allowing it to operate as an independent committee, as it once did.

As in the Senate, there are ways that House members can circumvent a standing committee as well as the Rules Committee. For one, a bill can be discharged from a standing committee after 30 days if there is no report on it and from the Rules Committee after only seven days of consideration without action. To rescue a bill under the **discharge rule,** a majority of the House members merely has to sign a petition. However, members are reluctant to use this device to enact legislation: from 1937 through 1982, the House passed only 15 bills through the use of the discharge petition and only two of those eventually became law. Discharge is much more effective as a threat. If the Rules Committee sees that a petition will probably be successful, it is inclined to release the bill in question. By doing so, the committee can exercise some control over the conditions of debate on the floor, whereas if a bill is discharged, no such control is possible.*

Another procedure, known as **Calendar Wednesday,** can be utilized to free legislative proposals from the Rules Committee. Each Wednesday, under House regulations, standing committee names are read in alphabetical order; members can call up a bill that has been reported to the Rules Committee but has not been given a rule for floor action. This tactic, however, is generally ineffective and is used very infrequently. Indeed Calendar Wednesday is usually dispensed with by unanimous consent of the House, and even if it is not, it is difficult to dispose of a measure within a single legislative day as required. Since the rule was adopted in 1909, it has been successfully used on only two occasions.

Clearly, in the House—unlike the Senate—committees are generally formidable roadblocks to legislative action. In some instances, however, House members appreciate these barriers. Pressures may build up from powerful interest groups to pass legislative proposals the representatives do not actually favor; the chairmen of the standing and Rules committees (most of whom come from "safe" districts and hence are fairly invulnerable to such pressures) can then be blamed if the measures never come to the floor for a vote.

Floor Action

Senate. Debate on the Senate floor tends to be informal, and members are not inclined to adhere closely to even the limited number of rules that govern debates. For example, rules requiring that remarks be germane to the discussion are seldom enforced. Senators are not inclined to challenge a colleague who is speaking off the subject, and if the senator acknowledges that he or she is doing so, they will usually grant unanimous consent to continue.

This tolerance for discussion makes the Senate a unique legislative body. It is the only one in the world that generally has the right of unlimited debate, whereby a senator can speak for as long as he or she wants on a measure. On most occasions, however, members do not exercise that right, and debate terminates simply because senators voluntarily stop talking on a bill and proceed to vote on it.

There are ways, however, that debate may be closed involuntarily in the Senate. One is by a unanimous-consent agreement to terminate discussion. Even senators who oppose a bill may be willing to stop debating it because they concede that the majority should be able to work its will on the matter.

In some instances, however, feelings are so high against a particular bill (as on a highly emotional issue such as civil rights) that the minority is willing to use extraordinary means to prevent its passage. In this event members join together to **filibuster** it—that is, to keep discussing it so long that no vote can be taken on the measure. The participation of a number of senators is required since one or a few cannot talk continuously for a long period. The technique is usually most effective at the end of a legislative session, when time is short and members have other business that they need to transact.

There are measures that can be taken to defeat a filibuster. One is to keep the Senate in continuous session so as to wear down the filibusterers. That tactic, however, is often subject to a counter-

* The Rules Committee also has a power of "extraction," whereby it can introduce rules for bills that standing committees do not want to report; however, it has invoked that power only four times in the last three decades.

ploy: some years ago when Lyndon Johnson attempted to use this technique to break a filibuster against a civil rights bill, the minority retaliated by constantly calling for a quorum (the Constitution requires a majority of body membership to be present to do business), which necessitated many of those favoring the bill to get to the chamber at all hours of the night to keep the Senate in session. Meanwhile, only one of the minority's valiant band—the one talking—had to be there at any one time.

If such tactics fail, a filibuster can be stopped by a **cloture** motion, which terminates debate. This method, which traditionally required a two-thirds vote for passage, was changed in 1975 so that three-fifths of the total membership of the Senate (60 if there are no vacancies in the 100-member body) can invoke cloture. If the motion is passed by that margin, each senator may speak for one hour on any one previously proposed amendment, after which time the bill must come to a vote.

The use of cloture has varied over the years since it was first adopted by the Senate in 1917. From then until 1960 cloture was successfully invoked on only four occasions; however from 1960 to 1982 the motion was passed 49 times. The kind of senators affected by cloture has also changed. Traditionally the motion has been used to stop filibusters by conservative southerners on civil rights legislation. In contrast, during the 1970s cloture was often used against liberal northerners who employed filibusters against the Vietnam War, military spending, and the extension of the draft.

In recent years a new tactic has emerged to delay final action on legislation: the **post-cloture filibuster.** The technique involves using roll calls, quorum calls, and the reading of germane amendments offered prior to the invoking of cloture—none of which counts against the one-hour speaking limitation allotted to each senator after the invoking of cloture. Senators James Abourezk (D-South Dakota) and Howard Metzenbaum (D-Ohio) used the technique in 1977 to delay a vote on a controversial natural gas deregulation bill for two weeks. Ultimately this post-cloture delay was terminated when Majority Leader Robert Byrd (D-West Virginia), got Vice President Walter Mondale to rule certain amendments as being "out of order," and the two senators, feeling betrayed by the Carter administration, ended their filibuster. In 1979 the Senate approved a resolution providing that after cloture is invoked, a final vote must be taken after no more than 100 hours of debate—with time spent on quorum calls, roll-call votes, and other parliamentary procedures counted against the 100-hour limit. (The resolution permits the Senate to extend the 100-hour time limit by a three-fifths vote).

After debate terminates in the Senate, whether voluntarily or by unanimous consent or through a cloture motion, the chamber moves to a vote on the bill. Prior to final passage, votes are taken on any amendments to the bill, some of which are designed to clarify a measure, others to defeat it. In addition, opponents move that the bill be sent back to committee, a tactic designed to kill it. In voting on motions as well as on the final amended bill, there are three possibilities: a voice vote, a division (standing) vote, or, if one-fifth of the members request it, a roll-call vote. The latter, which is reserved for controversial measures, requires each senator to answer yea or nay when his or her name is called; since the votes are recorded, the public can determine how each member voted.

House. The first step in bringing a bill to the floor of the House is the adoption of the "rule" for its consideration issued by the Rules Committee. When that is accomplished (members seldom vote down a rule since in the future they will need one for their own legislation from the committee), the House resolves itself into the Committee of the Whole to consider the bill.

The Committee of the Whole House device was borrowed from the seventeenth-century British practice of getting the Speaker (who was the king's man) out of the chair so that members of the House of Commons could act independently of his scrutiny. Although the original purpose is not applicable (the Speaker does, however, as a matter of custom vacate his or her place as presiding officer), the device is useful today for other reasons. When members are meeting as the Whole House, a quorum of 100 rather than 218 (the majority of the entire membership) is sufficient to do business; moreover, amendments are debated under a five-minute rather than an hour limitation rule. In addition, before 1970 actions of members while in the Committee of the Whole were protected from public scrutiny: no roll-call votes were possible and other votes—voice, division, and teller (under the teller arrangement, members favoring and opposing a bill pass through separate aisles)—were not recorded. As a result of a change in the House rules in 1970, however, one-fifth of the Committee quorum (20) can ask that clerks record how (as well as whether) members vote on teller tallies. Thus a relatively small number of House members can now force their colleagues to make their votes on measures a matter of public record. Some congressional observers credit this new procedure with contributing to the defeat of the funding of the supersonic transport plane (SST) because members had to make their vote known on a measure that was unpopular with many of their constituents.

When the voting is concluded, the Committee of the Whole dissolves and reports back to the House, which must then act on the Committee's decisions. Negative actions taken by the Committee of the Whole are final; affirmative decisions on bills and amendments to them are subject to overruling by the House. A motion is also in order to recommit a bill to the committee that reported it. The voting procedures of the House (contrasted to the Committee of the Whole) are the same as those of the Senate, with the exception that yea and nay votes are now recorded electronically, which eliminates the need for time-consuming roll calls.

Resolving Differences Between Senate- and House-Passed Bills

Even if a measure has been able to get by the many roadblocks outlined above, unless it passes both chambers in identical form it still has one major obstacle to surmount: getting the two houses to agree on its content. For most bills this is no great problem. The differences are resolved by informal consultation between the two chambers or by one house accepting the amendments of the other.

On controversial measures, however, it is usually necessary to iron out the differences between Senate and House bills through the use of a **Conference Committee** composed of representatives from each chamber. Typically, the presiding officers of the two houses both appoint from three to nine members*—generally the chairman of the standing committee that considered the measure, the ranking minority member, and other prominent committee and subcommittee members, with the committee generally reflecting the partisan composition of the House and Senate. These individuals meet (such meetings were formerly held in private but since

* There has been a trend in recent years to increase the size of conference delegations. To deal with the natural gas portion of President Carter's 1977 energy bill, the Senate appointed 28 conferees and the House, 25.

Measure to Raise $50 Billion in Revenue Is Approved by House-Senate Conferees

Bill Includes Tax Changes; Other Panel Agrees to Cut Spending by $11 Billion

By JEFFREY H. BIRNBAUM
Staff Reporter of THE WALL STREET JOURNAL

WASHINGTON—House-Senate conferees approved a complex and voluminous tax bill that would raise about $50 billion in revenue through fiscal 1987. But the modest revenue increase seemed almost an afterthought.

The bill is a potpourri of tax changes. Some of its most significant provisions are tax cuts that are likely to have a major effect on financial markets.

In addition, a sister panel to the tax conference has agreed to cut Medicare, limit increases in Medicaid and make other changes that would trim spending by $11 billion during the period.

The surprise of the all-night drafting session that concluded at about 5:30 (EDT) Saturday morning came when the House accepted a tax provision that has long been [illegible]

1975 they have generally been open to the public) to resolve their differences and recommend a report on a common bill. When agreement is reached (a majority of each chamber's representatives must approve it), it is sent to the respective houses for approval along with an explanatory statement. Neither house can change the Conference Committee version; both houses must accept it as it is, send it to the Conference Committee for further negotiations, or vote it down completely, which kills the bill. As a rule, agreement is ultimately reached, and the report (and hence the bill) is ready for presidential action, a matter that we will examine in the next chapter. (See Figure 10.2 for the complete procedure for enacting legislation.) First, however, we need to assess the operation of Congress.

ASSESSMENT

Traditionally Congress has been an undemocratic body. It has been controlled primarily by committee chairmen from "safe" districts, chosen on the basis of seniority, who were to a great degree immune from pressure by either the party leaders in Congress or, the rank-and-file members. Moreover, the closed nature of committee meetings and secrecy of voting in committee and the House made it difficult for members of the public to know what their legislators were doing on important issues and to hold them accountable for their actions. Also contributing to this latter problem was the lack of information about contributions of private individuals and groups to campaigns and other activities of lawmakers.

The 1970s have brought a number of reforms designed to rectify the above abuses. As we saw in Chapter 8, the campaign-spending legislation passed in recent years has done much to illuminate the financial situation with

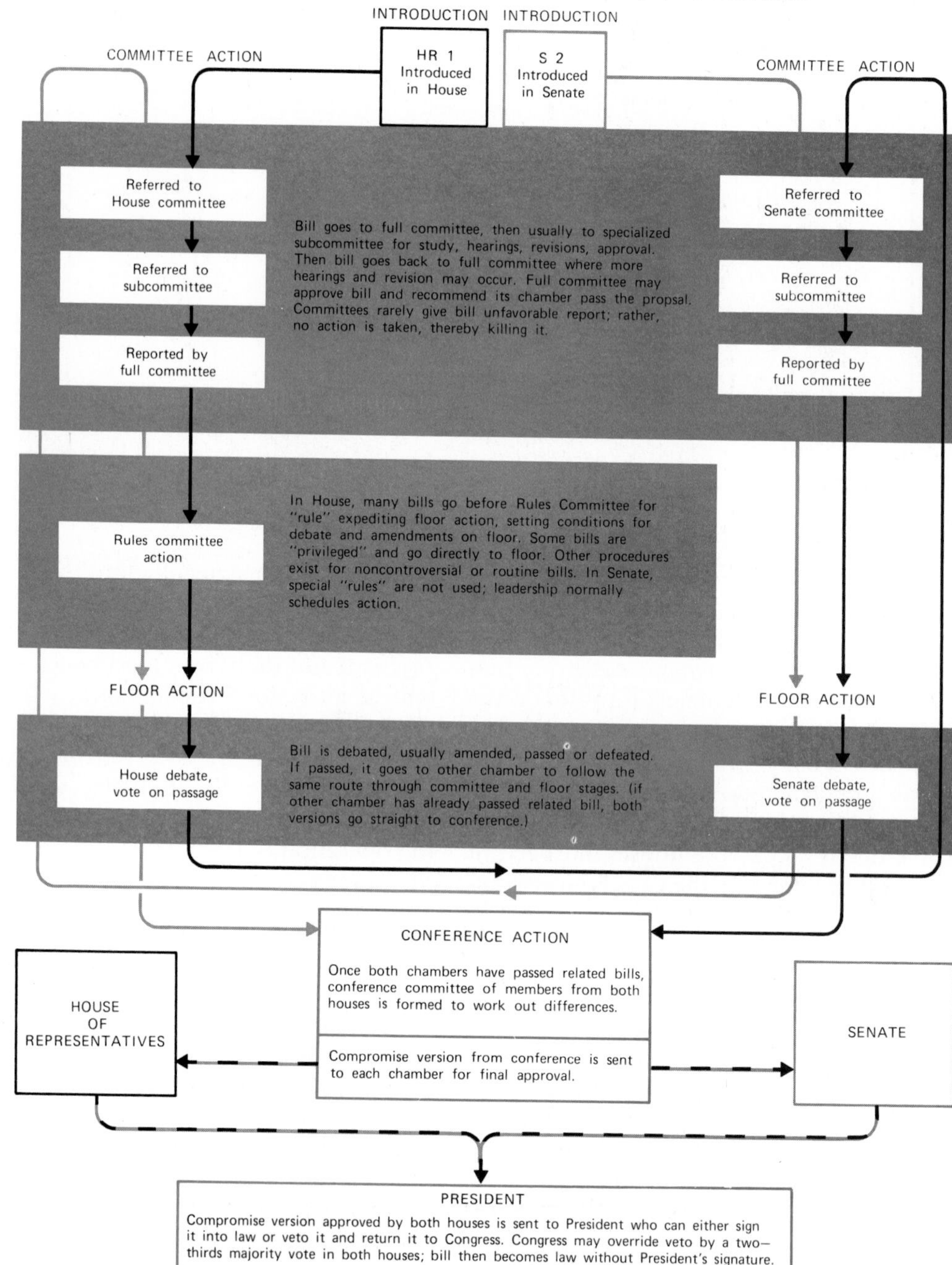

Figure 10.2 How a bill becomes law.

SOURCE: *Congressional Quarterly Almanac, 1976*, Washington, D. C.: Congressional Quarterly Inc., p. xxv.

respect to elections. Also, the newly enacted regulations affecting Members of Congress—providing for full disclosure of lawmakers' personal finances and for certain restrictions on their outside income—make it more difficult for some individuals and groups to put members of Congress in their debt than formerly.

The procedures of both houses and Congress have also been opened up in the 1970s. Committee proceedings, including those used to "mark up" bills as well as meetings of conference committees, are increasingly conducted in open session. Moreover, roll-call votes of standing committees are more readily available for inspection and the secrecy of teller voting in the House has been eliminated. Thus "sunshine" rather than shadow has come to characterize many of the procedures of Congress.

Individual legislators, including rank-and-file members of the House of Representatives, have also gained more influence in recent years. The creation of additional subcommittees plus rules limiting the number of such chairmanships and memberships an individual member can hold has served to distribute more posts to junior members; rule changes providing more staff and budget and greater autonomy for subcommittees from the chairman of the parent committee have also redounded to the benefit of rank-and-file members of Congress.

Finally, the situation of Democratic party leaders and committees in the House of Representatives has also been strengthened considerably in recent years. Additional powers granted to the Speaker of the House—including referring bills to committee, chairing and naming many of the members of the newly created Steering and Policy Committee, and choosing Democratic members of the Rules Committee—have added to the potential influence of the majority party's leader in the House. The role of the Steering and Policy Committee in helping to place legislators on committees and in planning and steering the party program through Congress has added to the potential of congressional party government, as have the recent activities of the Democratic Caucus in making committee assignments and in playing a more significant part in the development of public policy.

While on balance these reforms are healthy for democratic government, they are not an unmixed blessing. There has been a marked increase in the number of early retirements of members of Congress, prompted at least in part by their unhappiness over some of the newly adopted financial restrictions (especially those pertaining to outside income), as well as by the fact that seniority is not longer as important in determining the influence members can exert, particularly in the House. Moreover, it is difficult to reconcile some of the recent reforms with each other. For example, the development of "subcommittee government" decentralizes power in the House of Representatives, and it is by no means certain that the additional powers granted to the Speaker and party committees is sufficient to bring these subcommittees under centralized control. Thus Congress will have to balance two perennial aspects of democratic government: maximizing the role of individuals and (at the same time) permitting the majority to work its will.

SELECTED READINGS

A classic study of Congress is Woodrow Wilson's *Congressional Government:A Study in American Politics* (Boston:Houghton, Mifflin, 1891). Excellent recent general treatments of Congress include Roger Davidson and Walter Oleszek, *Congress and Its Members* (Washington, D. C.:Congressional Quarterly Inc., 1981); Lawrence Dodd and Bruce Oppenheimer (eds.), *Congress Reconsidered* (Washington, D. C. Congressional Quarterly Inc., 2nd ed., 1981); and Mary McNeil (ed.), *How Congress Works* (Washington, D. C.: Congressional Quarterly Inc., 1983). A short, perceptive analysis of recent trends affecting Congress is Morris Fiorina, *Congress:Keystone of the Washington Establishment* (New Haven:Yale University Press, 1977).

The world of a senator in the 1950s is graphically portrayed in Donald Matthews, *U. S. Senators and Their World* (Chapel Hill:University of North Carolina Press, 1960). Two excellent treatments of the life of a member of the House in the same era are Charles Clapp, *The Congressman:His Work as He Sees It* (Washington, D. C.:The Brookings Institution, 1963), and Clem Miller (John Baker (ed.)), *Letters of a Congressman* (New York:Charles Scribner and Sons, 1962). For a recent study providing insight into the world of seven members who came to the House in 1978, see John Bibby (ed.), *Congress Off the Record* (Washington, D. C.:American Enterprise Institute, 1983).

An excellent comparative study of six House standing committees is Richard Fenno, *Congressmen in Committees* (Boston:Little, Brown, 1973). A recent study of changes occurring in congressional committees in the 1970s and early 1980s is Steven Smith and Christopher Deering, *Committees in Congress* (Washington, D. C: Congressional Quarterly Inc., 1984).

For an excellent analysis of congressional procedure, see Walter Oleszek, *Congressional Procedures and the Policy Process* (Washington, D. C: Congressional Quarterly Inc., 2nd ed., 1984).

CHAPTER 11

The Presidency

For many Americans, the presidency conjures up mixed reactions and emotions. Some persons—particularly those who lived through the Great Depression and World War II—think of the office as "*heroic.*" They associate it with Franklin Roosevelt's inaugural address in 1933, which counseled a desperate people that ". . . the only thing we have to fear is fear itself," followed by the enactment of programs that put people back to work and restored their dignity. They also remember the role that FDR played in leading the nation through the dark days of World War II, which culminated in victory over the Axis powers and the ultimate establishment of the United Nations. They marvel that plain, ordinary Harry Truman—the Missouri haberdasher—could follow in FDR's footsteps by helping to restore the war-torn economies of Western European nations and forging military alliances to contain aggression from one of our wartime allies, the Soviet Union.

However, many of these same people—as well as their sons and daughters—have a far less favorable image of the American presidency of the late 1960s and early 1970s. They associate the presidency with the tragic, undeclared war in Vietnam, begun on a small scale with military advisers sent by John Kennedy and then escalated under Lyndon Johnson into a major conflict that continued for five more years under Richard Nixon—the longest war in the nation's history, costing almost 50,000 American lives. They also link the presidency with a second tragedy, this time a domestic one—the Watergate affair involving burglary, wiretapping, and sabotage of political opponents, improper solicitation and expenditure of campaign funds, and the compiling of an "enemies" list of persons inimical to the Nixon administration—persons on whom the FBI and other executive agencies were to take revenge. This presidency—termed an *imperial* one by historian Arthur Schlesinger Jr. because

Harry Truman.

it arrogated powers to itself not provided for by the Constitution—was as feared as the Roosevelt presidency was admired.

In the latter part of the 1970s, a third image of the office began to emerge—that of an *imperiled* or *impossible* presidency. Cast in these terms, Gerald Ford and Jimmy Carter were not powerful, heroic, or imperial, but rather impotent, overwhelmed by forces they could not control. These forces included increasingly assertive interest groups, each demanding that its concerns be satisfied *now;* a weakened party system that prevented their rallying political support for their programs; aggressive members of the media who employed investigative and adversarial journalism to probe the personal weaknesses and exaggerate the mistakes of both Ford and Carter; and a hostile Congress, all too willing and able to confront both presidents and vote down their proposals.

There are no easy answers as to which of these discrepant images of the presidency best fits the realities of the office in the 1980s. However, we explore a number of matters that bear on the issue in this chapter. We first examine the kind of office the Founders contemplated when it was originally established. This is followed by an analysis of how the institution has changed over the years, with particular emphasis on the influence that individual presidents have had in molding the nature of the office. We then shift to the contemporary presidency and focus on three of its more demanding roles—party chief, influencer of public opinion, and leader of the Congress.

THE ESTABLISHMENT OF THE PRESIDENCY

As we saw in Chapter 2, the experiences under the Articles of Confederation demonstrated vividly that the national government could not carry on executive activities through legislative committees. Therefore those who gathered in Philadelphia were convinced that the new government required some kind of separate executive branch. They did not agree by any means, however, about what the nature and powers of the executive should be.

There was even some question of establishing monarchy: as John Jay put it in a letter to George Washington, "Shall we have a king?" Of the 55 delegates at the Constitutional Convention, however, only Hamilton seemed willing to seriously consider the British model, which he considered the "best in the world." Others either opposed it on principle or recognized, as John Dickinson of Delaware put it, that a monarchy was "out of the question." The American experience under George III and the colonial governors had created a climate of opinion that excluded any kind of monarchy, however limited.

There were, however, other American models to consider: the state governorships of the day. For the most part these were weak offices overshadowed by state legislatures, but there were two exceptions: New York and Massachusetts both provided for independent governors vested with important political powers. That the governors of these two states served effectively without endangering political freedom convinced many of the delegates that a strong chief executive accountable to the people was not to be equated with a tyrannical king or colonial governor.

Two disparate concepts concerning the nature and powers of the national executive emerged. One was the idea of a "weak" executive whose primary function would be to put the will of the legislature into effect. To this end, a plural executive would be established, or even if only one person headed the branch, a powerful council would share his powers and hold him in check. The Congress would choose the chief executive for a limited term; moreover, he could not be reappointed immediately and would even be subject to removal by the legislative body during his term of office. The powers of the executive would be limited and in essence delegated to him by Congress, which would also make appointments to the executive branch and exercise the treaty- and war-making powers. This concept of the office provided no executive veto of laws passed by the Congress.

At the other extreme was the idea of a "strong" executive, independent of the Congress, and exercising important functions in the new government. Under this concept a single chief executive, chosen by some means other than legislative appointment, would have no limit placed on his tenure. If he were to be removed at all, it would be only for certain definite, enumerated reasons, and then only after impeachment and conviction by a judicial body or the legislature. His powers would be derived from the Constitution and not be subject to legislative interference. He would appoint judicial and diplomatic officials and participate in the execution of foreign affairs, including the making of treaties. He would have a veto over legislation passed by Congress, a power that he would exercise either alone or in conjunction with the judiciary. Finally, either there would be no executive council at all, or, if one did exist, it would be merely an advisory body whose actions would not bind the chief executive.

In the initial stages of the Convention, it appeared that the delegates would adopt the "weak" executive model. However, an early decision to provide for a single executive was a major victory for the friends of a strong presidency, which included such influential figures as Pennsylvanians James Wilson and Gouverneur Morris, Rufus King and Elbridge Gerry of Massachusetts, Charles Pinckney and John Rutledge of South Carolina, and Alexander Hamilton of New York. The assumption that George Washington would be the first president also meant that the delegates were willing to create a strong office, since they felt that he would not abuse its powers. Moreover, having greatly increased the powers of the Congress over those of the former Confederation legislature, some delegates believed that a strong chief executive was needed to counterbalance the new legislative body.

The Inauguration of George Washington.

As a result of these factors, the presidency ultimately created by the Convention is much closer to the strong-executive model described above. He is chosen by some method other than legislative appointment (electoral college), is eligible to succeed himself, and can be removed only for specific causes (treason, bribery, high crimes and misdemeanors), and then only upon the bringing of an impeachment charge by the House of Representatives and conviction by the vote of two-thirds of the members of the Senate. He is not dependent on the Congress for his authority; rather, specific powers are granted to him by the Constitution. In addition, as a result of the efforts of Gouverneur Morris, he is given broad undefined authority by the opening sentence of Article II: "The executive power shall be vested in a President of the United States of America."

At the same time, the president does not enjoy all the prerogatives of the strong-executive model. Although he has the veto power, it is not absolute, since his action can be overridden by a two-thirds vote in each of the two houses of Congress. Moreover, his appointment power is subject to the approval of the Senate, as is his authority to negotiate treaties. Thus although the Founders did not create a council that shares all the chief executive's powers with him, they did grant the upper chamber of the national legislature a check on certain presidential actions.

Certain amendments to the Constitution change the executive articles somewhat: the Twelfth, on the choosing of the president and vice president; the Twentieth, pertaining to the beginning of their term, the Twenty-Second, which limits the tenure of the chief executive; the Twenty-Fifth, about presidential disability and succession. Yet the essential constitutional framework of the presidential office remains as it was created almost two centuries ago. Most of the vast changes in the presidency since that time have arisen not from formal legal alterations in its structure but from informal political customs and precedents.

THE DEVELOPMENT OF THE PRESIDENCY

One of the dominant trends in American political life has been the growth of the presidency. The legislative and judicial branches of the national government have also increased in power and influence over the years, but not at the same pace. Thus the separation of powers is similar to the division of powers described in Chapter 3: all branches (like all levels of government) have augmented their political authority, but some have done so more than others.

Although the overall trend has been in the direction of a more powerful presidency, growth has not been constant. The office occupied by Grant was not as potent as that of Lincoln. Conditions in American society, the people's reaction to them, and the personal qualities of particular incumbents have affected the functions and influence of the presidency.

Conditions and Factors Affecting the Development of the Presidency

In defending a single chief executive in the Federalist papers, Alexander Hamilton emphasized what he termed *energy* as a desirable characteristic of good government. He went on to suggest that energy was particularly associated with the executive compared to a legislative body. As he put it, "Decision, activity, secrecy and despatch will generally characterize the proceedings of one man in a much more eminent degree than the proceedings of any greater number; and in proportion as the number is increased, these qualities will be diminished."

More than any other single factor this axiom of human behavior so clearly put by Hamilton explains the growth of presidential power and influence. The need for ". . . decision, activity, secrecy and despatch . . ." has become increasingly necessary to a leading power in an interdependent world. If military action is contemplated, the president as commander-in-chief of the armed forces has a crucial role to play in decisions on committing American troops. As historian Arthur Schlesinger Jr. suggests, it is the capture of ". . . the most vital of decisions, the decision to go to war," that had led to the **"Imperial Presidency,"** an office that has appropriated powers reserved by the Constitution and historical practice to Congress.

Even without military action, the president generally plays a dominant part in foreign affairs. He has a number of powers—such as the negotiation of treaties that require senatorial approval and executive agreements that do not, the initiation as well as the breaking off of diplomatic relationships with foreign governments, and the choosing of representatives abroad—that make his voice the crucial one in foreign affairs. Moreover, as in military matters, diplomacy requires a certain amount of secrecy. As the late British scholar Harold Laski expressed it, "Diplomatic negotiations are like a proposal of marriage; they must be made in private even if the engagement is later discussed in public."

The president's role in crises, however, is not confined to military and foreign affairs. To an increasing extent the American people have demanded that the national government "do something" about economic depressions, social problems such as race relations, the plight of the cities, and other pressing concerns. Once again such expectations have enhanced the influence of the presidency, because a president can move swiftly and forcefully to help counteract mass unemployment, send troops to assist in integrating the schools, or deal with major riots, such as those that occurred in some of our nation's cities in the late 1960s. Thus the presidency has grown in power and influence as the American people have accepted the concept of the **positive state,** that is, one in which the government—particularly the national one—plays a major role in meeting (and, it is hoped, on occasion even preventing) the many crises of our troubled society.

Hamilton's conviction that a large assembly has trouble taking decisive action has been borne out by the experience of the American Congress. As he suggested, the problem becomes greater as the number of members is increased; this is precisely what happened as the number of senators and representatives grew from 26 and 65, respectively, in the first Congress to 100 and 435 today. The present American political system makes it especially difficult for legislators to move quickly on problems. The variety of viewpoints represented by legislators from different constituencies in a large and diverse country prevents the national legislature from making the rapid decisions called for in a crisis. Also contributing to congressional sluggishness has been the way power has generally been distributed within the two chambers and the traditional predominance in positions of authority (especially the chairmanships of standing committees and, increasingly, subcommittees as well) of legislators who are inclined to support the status quo rather than to respond to demands for change in society. Because the Congress often cannot, or will not, act decisively when the occasion demands, people turn to the president to do so.

Hamilton may not have foreseen another development that has led to the expansion of presidential power and influence: the democratization of the selection process for chief executive. (Given his distrust of the common man, he certainly would have disapproved the development.) The shift from choice by elites in the various states to a national popularity contest has given the president a nationwide constituency that no other officeholder (except his political inferior, the vice president) can claim. As a result, he is the most visible figure in American politics and the one official from whom the public expects action and leadership. Because the president is accountable at the ballot box to

Abraham Lincoln.

the American people as a whole, he can claim them as his following and as support for his policies.

All these conditions have contributed to the natural growth of the presidency, uninhibited by the constitutional provisions relating to the office. The indefinite phraseology of the opening sentence of Article II of the Constitution—"The executive power shall be vested in a President of the United States"—has been, in effect, a grant of broad authority for bold and innovative ventures. Supplementing this general grant of presidential power are other clauses—for instance, ". . . he shall take care that the laws be faithfully executed . . ."—on which presidents can draw for legal justification of their actions. Woodrow Wilson may have exaggerated the situation somewhat when he claimed in 1908 (five years before he occupied the presidency himself) that the chief executive ". . . has the right in law and conscience to be as big a man as he can," but few students of the presidency would deny the great potential of the office.

Wilson's observation points up still another major factor in the development of the presidency: the important part that individual presidents have played in the process. Neither the natural conditions conducive to the increase in presidential power and influence, nor the legal potentialities of the office in themselves guarantee decisive actions. The crisis that both James Buchanan and Abraham Lincoln faced were virtually identical. Buchanan, however, took the position that he was powerless to prevent secession, whereas Lincoln took bold steps to try to counter it.

Individual Presidents and the Development of the Office

How a particular president handles the powers and duties of the office naturally depends upon his own personality and character. His family background as well as the experiences he had as a young adult have a major effect on his sense or lack of self-confidence, his psychological needs, the kind of values he acquires, and the perceptions he has of himself and the world around him. They also shape his political philosophy and his view of how he should conduct himself as president. His performance in that role will also depend upon his verbal abilities, how effectively he works and interacts with others, and how much time and effort he is willing to put into the job.

Students of the subject like Erwin Hargrove and James Barber distinguish between presidents "of action," or **"active" presidents** on the one hand, and those of "restraint," or **"passive" presidents** on the other. The former are persons who invest a great deal of energy in the presidency and whose personal needs and skills are translated effectively into political leadership; the latter are inclined to devote less time and effort to being president and have neither the inclination, nor the ability to exercise political power effectively. Active presidents exert leadership over Congress, chart new directions in public policy, and take actions that stretch the powers of the presidential office; passive presidents respond to congressional initiatives, support the status quo, and do not use the full authority of their office.

Barber also makes another general distinction among presidents that he refers to as the "positive-negative" dimension of their performance. **Positive presidents** enjoy political life and derive a great deal of personal satisfaction from serving in the office. **Negative presidents** do not experience pleasure from being president, but serve because of compulsion or out of a sense of duty to their country.

Barber suggests a typology of four types of president with varying motivations and purposes. **Active-positive presidents** want to accomplish results, particularly changes in governmental institutions, procedures, and policies. **Active-negative presidents** are preoccupied with acquiring and maintaining power for its own sake. The **passive-positive presidents** want most to be popular, to be loved and admired by others. **Passive-negative presidents** have a deep sense of civic virtue and rectitude.

There are, of course, major problems in attempting to analyze presidents in this way. It is very difficult to establish complex relationships between particular events and influences in persons' lives and their subsequent behavior, especially when the data consist of general biographical accounts rather than intensive personal interviews that psychologists use to explore specific matters. Therefore what has come to be known as **psychohistory** must be accepted with considerable caution. Moreover, individuals do not fit neatly into cubbyholes; it should be understood that in attempting to categorize presidents, scholars must assess the overall tendencies of their character and behavior to determine which pure type they most closely exemplify.

With these reservations in mind, we shall examine four individual presidents that Barber uses to illustrate each of the types of president. These include Franklin Delano Roosevelt, Woodrow Wilson, William Howard Taft, and Dwight Eisenhower.*

* It would be tempting to use Richard Nixon rather than Wilson to exemplify the active-negative president; however, we do not yet have the excellent scholarly studies of the perspective of history on Nixon that we do on Wilson. It also seemed better to use Taft rather than Warren Harding to illustrate the passive-positive president because the latter's extremely poor performance in office (he is generally rated as our worst president) might create the impression that all passive-positive presidents are doomed to such abject failure.

Active-Positive. Franklin Delano Roosevelt exemplifies the active-positive president. Born in 1882, the only child of wealthy parents of Dutch background, he grew up on the family estate in the Hudson River Valley in New York state, not going to school until he was 14. Doted over by a mother who kept him in dresses until he was five years old, and by a father much older than his wife who introduced him to the joys of ice-boating and sailing, his childhood could only be characterized as serene and secure. He was the object of great affection from his family and friends and responded with a trust and love for others.

Franklin's education was what one would expect of a family with a patrician tradition. He went to a prep school (Groton) whose headmaster, Endicott Peabody, instilled in him "manly Christian character" and an upper-class sense of social responsibility for the less advantaged in society. Then on to Harvard, where he was editor-in-chief of the school newspaper, the *Harvard Crimson,* to Columbia law school, and, upon graduation, to a conservative New York law firm in 1907.

Bored with the law, Roosevelt announced to his fellow law clerks that he intended to go into politics, following a career ladder similar to that of another Roosevelt—his much-admired cousin, Theodore; the steps would be New York legislator, Assistant Secretary of the Navy, governor of New York, and, if luck shone on him, president of the United States. By 1910 he had reached the first office, and at age 31 he accepted Teddy's old job as Assistant Secretary of the Navy, in which capacity he served for seven years. After an unsuccessful race as the Democratic vice-presidential candidate in 1920 and a tragic bout with polio in 1921, he eventually followed his political schedule, becoming governor of New York in 1929 and president in 1933.

Roosevelt's political life was one of action, but he had no consistent political philosophy beyond that of the patrician's sense of social responsibility for the disadvantaged, which he had acquired at Groton. He was pragmatic, willing to experiment, and, if a particular course of action was not productive, to try another. His view of public office paralleled that of his cousin Teddie: it is preeminently a place of moral leadership.

Roosevelt left a legacy of action and innovation unmatched by any other chief executive. When he came into office in March 1933, business failures were legion, 12 million of his countrymen were unemployed, banks all over the country were closed or doing business under restrictions, and the American people had lost confidence in their leaders as well as in themselves. Following his "nothing to fear" inaugural address, the new chief executive moved into action: a four-day bank holiday was declared, and an emergency banking bill was prepared within a day's time. During his first 100 days in office the nation was to witness a social and economic revolution (Roosevelt's "New Deal") as Congress adopted a series of far-reaching government programs insuring bank deposits, providing crop payments for farmers, establishing codes of fair competition for industry, granting labor the right to organize, providing relief and jobs for the unemployed, and creating the Tennessee Valley Authority (a government corporation) to develop that region. With these measures and other programs that followed (Social Security, public housing, unemployment compensation, and the like), Roosevelt was to establish the concept of the "positive state" in America—a government that had the obligation to take the leadership in providing for the welfare of all the people.

Roosevelt did not ignore relations with other countries. Soon after he took office he recognized the Soviet Union diplomatically, embarked on a "Good Neighbor policy" toward South Americans, and pushed through a Reciprocal Trade Program lowering tariffs with other nations. In his second term FDR began the slow and difficult task of preparing the nation for its eventual entry into World War II by funneling aid to the Allies, trading 50 "over-age" destroyers to Britain for defense bases in this hemisphere, and obtaining the passage of the nation's first peace-time draft. As FDR himself put it, after Pearl Harbor "Old Dr. New Deal" became "Dr. Win-the-War," taking over the economic control of the war effort granted him by Congress and establishing the victorious strategy of concentrating on defeating Germany first (rather than Japan). While the hostilities were still going on, he took the leadership in setting up the United Nations. (Unfortunately, he died before the organization was established in 1945.)

Roosevelt was also an innovator whose actions left a major impact on the presidential office itself. Not only was he an effective legislative leader, but he was also responsible for a major reorganization of the executive branch, including the creation of the Executive Office of the President, which we will examine in the next chapter. Most important of all, FDR was the most effective molder of public opinion that the nation has ever known. It was he who pioneered the use of **"fireside chats"** over radio to explain his actions to the people. In addition, he raised the presidential press conference to new heights as a tool of public persuasion. As a man who could take idealistic goals, reduce them to manageable and practical programs, and then sell them to the Congress and the American people, Roosevelt had no peer.

Despite this record of achievement, however, Roosevelt made some mistakes, particularly after his smashing

FDR addresses the nation.

electoral victory in 1936. As we saw in Chapter 7, he was unsuccessful in purging certain Southern congressmen in the Democratic primaries in 1938. When he tried to expand the size of the Supreme Court in order to add persons who shared his views, the public and Congress reacted against his **"court-packing" plan.** Thus active-positive presidents in their zeal to accomplish results sometimes underestimate the force of custom and expectations as to what is proper and improper in American politics.

Active-Negative. Thomas Woodrow Wilson epitomizes Barber's active-negative type of president. Born in Staunton, Virginia the son of a Presbyterian minister with a large congregation, Tommy had the benefit of a rich intellectual background. However, he was slow to learn: he was 9 years old before he learned his alphabet and 11 before he could read. He was also frail and wore glasses in marked contrast to his father, a tall handsome man with a commanding physical presence. Tommy was loved; but he was also dominated by a father who expected much of him and ridiculed him when he did not live up to the expectations. Surrounded early in life by girls and intimidated by the rough play of boys, Tommy retreated to the protection provided by his mother, a quiet, gentle woman.

At 16, young Wilson went off to Davidson College, a small Presbyterian school in North Carolina. He experienced homesickness, his health failed, and he came home where he stayed for over a year until he entered Princeton at 18. There his shyness initially prevented him from acquiring many friends, but by his sophomore year he found a niche for himself: he organized the Liberal Debating Club, wrote its constitution, and became its most prominent member. Eventually, like Roosevelt, he went on to become the editor of his school paper, the *Princetonian.* He also wrote an outstanding paper on cabinet government in the United States, which was published by the *International Review,* then edited by his enemy-to-be, Henry Cabot Lodge.

Later Wilson attended the University of Virginia Law School but withdrew and, after practicing for only one year in Atlanta, returned to school to attend Johns Hopkins University, where he received a doctorate in political science. Continuing his scholarly career, he taught at Bryn Mawr College in Pennsylvania and at Wesleyan College in Connecticut, where he was also a successful football coach. He then returned to Princeton, where he became one of the outstanding lecturers on the campus. Eventually he became president of his alma mater.

Wilson made an auspicious start as president of Princeton by taking the leadership in developing a new curriculum, reorganizing academic departments, and modifying its tutorial system, However, he met his first defeat when he tried to abolish the traditional undergraduate eating clubs and replace them with residential quadrangles. Subsequently he got into a bitter struggle with Andrew West, the dean of the graduate school, over the development of a graduate center; when Wilson refused to compromise on that issue, he lost it as well. At this point he decided to abandon academic life for a public one by running for and winning the governorship of New Jersey in 1908: he went to the presidency five years later.

Unlike Roosevelt, Wilson suffered from insecurity, which biographers Alexander and Juliette George attribute primarily to the overwhelming domination of his father, whom he could not please but would not oppose. The result was a displacement of his hostility on male figures like West and Lodge, who became his mortal enemies. Character traits associated with Wilson's sense of personal inadequacy included an unwillingness to compromise and a compulsion to work, coupled with a lack of satisfaction with his considerable achievements.

Wilson's values and world view reflected his Calvinistic background. He believed that God ordained him to be president of the United States and that his own causes were those of the Almighty. His political philosophy was a kind of Jeffersonian faith in smallness (the government should regulate large corporations) and the innate wisdom of the common people. As we have seen, Wilson's concept of the presidency was one of unlimited potential (the president has ". . . the right in law and conscience to be as big a man as he can . . ."), coupled with a desire to convert it into a kind of prime ministership similar to that of the British, whose political and social institutions he so much admired.

Wilson used various techniques to implement his prime-minister concept of the presidency. A skilled public speaker, he was the first president since John Adams to go before the Congress in person to give his State of the Union message. He held frequent meetings with legislative leaders, both at the White House and in a previously seldom-used President's Room in the Capitol. Like Jefferson, he was a powerful party chief who worked through congressional leaders and the Democratic Caucus to influence legislative decisions. He also did not hesitate to take his case to the people: on one occasion when special-interest spokespersons made concerted efforts to defeat a low-tariff bill he favored, Wilson made a public statement decrying the fact that ". . . the people at large should have no lobby and be voiceless in these matters, while great bodies of astute men seek to create an artificial opinion and to overcome the interests of the public for their private profit."

These techniques were highly successful as Wilson took the leadership in both domestic and foreign affairs. In his first term in office he pushed through a vast program of economic reform, which included major measures lowering tariffs, raising taxes for the well-to-do, creating a central banking system, regulating unfair trade practices, providing cheap loans to farmers, and establishing an eight-hour day for railroad employees. When the United States became involved in World War I during his second term, rather than prosecute it through unilateral executive action as Lincoln did, Wilson went to the Congress and obtained authority to control the economic, as well as the military, aspect of the war. He was thus granted the power to allocate food and fuel, to license trade with the enemy, to censor the mail, to regulate the foreign language press of the country, and to operate railroads, water transportation systems, and telegraph and telephone facilities. At the end of the war, he made a triumphant trip to Europe, where he assumed the leading role in the writing of the Versailles peace treaty.

Eventually, however, Wilson's sense of moral righteousness and his unwillingness to compromise proved to be his downfall. Conceiving the League of Nations as his contribution to a practical implementation of the teachings of Jesus Christ, he adamantly refused to accept any reservations proposed by the

Woodrow Wilson departing for Versailles Peace Conference.

Senate for the League of Nations Covenant of the Versailles treaty. In the process he played into the hands of his archenemy, Henry Cabot Lodge, who calculated that Wilson's intransigence and personal hatred of him would be so intense that the president would reject all compromises. In the end Lodge proved to be right: spurning the advice of close friends like Colonel House as well as his wife's pleas, Wilson claimed it ". . . better a thousand times to go down fighting than to dip your colors to dishonorable compromise." A trip to win popular support for the League ended in failure, and as a result the country whose leader proposed the League of Nations ended up not belonging to the organization at all.

Passive-Positive. An example of the passive-positive president is William Howard Taft. Like Roosevelt and Wilson, he had a doting mother who showered him with love. His father, 17 years older than his mother, was a lawyer who was given to preachments on discipline but not inclined to follow his own advice as far as Willie was concerned. Taft's boyhood was a pleasant one; unlike Wilson, he liked physical combat and was not a stranger to an occasional fight. But most of all he was a friendly lad with a perennial smile and sunny disposition.

Taft's romance with life continued when he left home to attend Yale University. There he was taken into the exclusive Skull and Bones Club and was considered the most popular boy in the entire school. While his extensive social life seemed to his father to be inconsistent with high scholarship, Taft graduated second in a class of 132. Following that, he attended the University of Cincinnati Law School.

Back home in southern Ohio, Taft served a short stint as a reporter covering the courts and then began a career in law and politics that eventually resulted in his being appointed a state—and later, a federal—judge. He enjoyed the role of referee rather than advocate in legal proceedings and set a goal for himself of an appointment to the

William Howard Taft and Wife, Nellie.

United States Supreme Court. But his ambitious wife, Nellie, whom he dearly loved, steered his career away from the judiciary toward the active political arena.

In 1900 Taft complied with President McKinley's request to head a commission to govern the Philippines. Ultimately McKinley's successor, Theodore Roosevelt, called him home to be his Secretary of War, where he served as a diplomatic trouble-shooter and domestic peacemaker. Taft fell under the President's spell and at his urging allowed himself to be nominated for the presidency in 1908, when Roosevelt retired from the office.

Taft had an engaging personality and found it difficult to say no to anyone, including his ambitious wife and a wide host of friends. Most of all in life he wanted approval and to be loved. While he flirted with the Progressive ideas of his hero, Roosevelt, at heart Taft was a conservative with a great admiration for existing institutions and a fear of radicals and militants. He needed order and reason in his life and found them in the law. In contrast to his predecessor, who argued that he could take any action not expressly forbidden by the Constitution or the laws, Taft held that the president possessed only those powers specifically delegated to him from those two sources.

When Roosevelt left for a trip to Africa in 1909, all was well between him and the new president. However, Taft soon began to disappoint his mentor. After making tariff reductions his first objective, he finally signed a bill giving generous concessions to domestic producers. He also was unable to arbitrate a fight between Gifford Pinchot, the conservation-minded chief of the Forest Service, and his boss, Richard Ballinger, Secretary of the Interior, whom Pinchot accused of giving away public lands to private profiteers. Respecting the authority of the superior officer, Taft ultimately accepted Pinchot's resignation.

These and other incidents led the Progressive wing of the Republican party and Roosevelt to conclude that Taft was not the man to whom they could entrust their leadership. He, in turn, was horrified when Roosevelt proposed that the voters had the right to overturn judicial decisions. Ultimately Roosevelt opposed Taft for the Republican nomination in 1912 and, when he failed, ran on the Progressive ticket. The resulting split in the Republican party helped put Woodrow Wilson into the White House.

After he left the presidency Taft was appointed to the post he had wanted all along: the chief justice of the United States. He worked harder and longer in that position than he ever did as president. In the structured judicial environment removed from the pressures of the political arena, Taft found peace with his first love, the law.

Passive-Negative. Dwight Eisenhower typifies the passive-negative president. Unlike Roosevelt, Wilson, or Taft, Ike was not born of a rich or prominent family; his father was a mechanic in a creamery who moved his family from Texas to Abilene, Kansas when Ike was six. The family of eight was jammed into a house with only 800 square feet. Ike enjoyed physical activities, particularly sports, and seems to have been influenced primarily by his mother, a woman with a fundamentalist religious background who managed with some success to calm Ike's considerable temper.

Naturally the family's meager resources would not permit Ike to go off to an Ivy League college like Harvard, Princeton, or Yale. He managed to get into West Point (after being turned down at Annapolis because he was too old) with the primary aim of continuing the athletic career he had begun in high school. Unfortunately he injured his knee badly in a football game and was forced to give up not only football but baseball, track, and boxing as well. Following that incident he fell into despondency and his grades suffered. He graduated from the Point 61st in a class of 164, hardly a promising prospect for playing a leading role in the nation's military establishment.

Subsequently, Ike redeemed himself in the army, graduating first in a class of 275 from the Command and General Staff school, served on General Douglas MacArthur's staff in the Philippines, and shortly after the attack on Pearl Harbor was assigned to the War Plans Division with the job of preparing a blueprint for the cross-channel invasion of Europe. In that capacity he came to the attention of Army Chief of Staff George Marshall, and at Marshall's suggestion he was placed by President Franklin Roosevelt in command of the invasion of Africa and eventually of the victorious Allied forces in Europe.

As the nation's number-one war hero, Ike was subjected to pressures to run for president in 1948 by many persons, including some Democrats who were disillusioned with Harry Truman. He declared that he had no interest in a political career and instead became army chief of staff and then president of Columbia University, a position for which he was ill suited. Subsequently, and against his wishes, he accepted President Truman's request in 1950 to become Supreme Commander of the North Atlantic Treaty Organization. Persuaded by Republican politicians to

Ike meets troops bound for European invasion.

run for president in 1952, he won easily over the Democratic candidate, Adlai Stevenson.

Eisenhower's major personal assets were an extremely pleasant personality that radiated optimism, unusual organizational abilities, and a happy facility for getting people with differing viewpoints to work together. He had little political ambition and accepted positions not for his own personal aggrandizement but out of a deep sense of duty to his country. His primary values were a belief in individualism and voluntary action and a marked dislike for the coercion of big government. His conception of himself as president was that of a nonpartisan leader bringing unity to the nation.

Eisenhower's performance in office reflected his background and values. He refused to play the role of party leader, assigning that task to his vice president, Richard Nixon. He sought both to make Congress a coequal branch of government rather than the inferior institution that he felt it had become under Roosevelt and Truman, and to return powers to the states that the national government had assumed. As an administrator of the executive branch, Eisenhower implemented methods that he had learned in the military: an extensive delegation of authority to others and a rigid chain of command.

In keeping with his conservative political philosophy and passive conception of the presidency, Eisenhower did not attempt new ventures in public policy. On the other hand, he made no effort to turn back the clock by eliminating the major features of the Democratic rule of the previous 20 years. He moved rather cautiously within the established framework, proposing an increase of social security benefits, eliminating segregation in the nation's capital, and adding to the country's military commitments around the world.

These then are examples of the different types of president who have served in the nation's highest office in this century. As Barber suggests, there is a connection between the climate of public expectations and the kind of person that is chosen as president. In times of crisis, the American people turn to an activist like Roosevelt or Wilson to do something about their mounting problems; when the public tires of effort and sacrifice, it prefers a passive type such as Taft or Eisenhower to restore a sense of national unity and calm. There is also a cyclical pattern to presidential types: activists inherit problems that passive executives ignore; the latter slow down the excesses of the former.

Thus a variety of influences have contributed to the development of the American presidency: the press of foreign and domestic events, the inability and unwillingness of Congress to assume leadership, and the actions of strong chief executives that established precedents for their successors to draw on. Increasingly, however, the public has come to expect all chief executives to exhibit the initiatives of presidents of "action." In the process, the office has become more and more complex and demanding. The kinds of varied responsibilities that contemporary presidents face, as well as the methods they utilize to discharge those responsibilities, are examined below.

In a very real sense the American president stands at the center of the American political system. As the prime elected official, he is the head of his political party. At the same time he is expected to be the president of all the people, including those who voted against him. As such, he acts as the ceremonial head of the government; in addition, as a leader of a democratic nation, he both reflects and molds public opinion. Moreover, he must not only head the executive branch but also provide legislative leadership and nominate judges that populate the federal courts.

Finally, he plays a dominant part in policy-making in both domestic and foreign affairs.

In this chapter we will examine some of these aspects of the contemporary presidency. We first analyze the chief executive's relationships with two major forces outside the government—his own political party and the general public. We then focus on his connection with the Congress. (We defer until later chapters the president's involvement with executive and judicial officials and the role he plays in the making of public policy.)

THE PRESIDENT AND HIS PARTY

Of the various activities of the president, that of party leader would have been least appreciated by the Founders, who visualized him as a neutral figure standing above conflict and promoting unity and justice in society. Yet it is expected today that the chief executive will be the avowed chief of the party that put him in the White House. It was, indeed, while President Kennedy was conducting party business—trying to restore some semblance of unity to the Texas Democratic organization—that he was struck by an assassin's bullet.

The president's role as partisan leader involves him in all the major political activities of his party. He is expected to play some part in the election contests for various offices in our political system. As party chief, he also has the responsibility for identifying problems and formulating programs to deal with them. Finally, the president has a major role in organizing and managing the government as a means of implementing his programs.

The President and Electoral Activities

Naturally the president's part in electoral activities is most pronounced as far as his own office is concerned. If a president decides to seek re-election, the renomination is normally his for the asking; he dominates every aspect of the convention—location, choice of major officers, party platform, and selection of his running mate—and makes strategic decisions regarding the general election campaign. The chief executive may choose, for example, to have little to do with congressional candidates of his own party running in a presidential year, a strategy that Nixon followed in 1972 in his quest for traditionally Democratic voters. Or he may deliberately associate himself with such candidates as Reagan did in 1980 by posing with them on the steps of the U. S. capitol.

American presidents have also come to play an important part in midterm congressional elections. Even Dwight Eisenhower, who did not enjoy playing the role of partisan leader, gave some 40 speeches in the 1954 campaign. President Kennedy took an active part in the 1962 congressional elections until the Cuban missile crisis forced him to cancel speaking engagements and return to Washington. Although Lyndon Johnson did not go on the campaign trail in the latter stages of the 1966 campaign (in part because he felt the Vietnam War had made him so unpopular that many congressional candidates would prefer that he stay away), the pattern of presidential involvement was restored (in fact, expanded) by Richard Nixon in 1970 when he traveled to more than 20 states on behalf of Republican candidates. His successor, Gerald Ford, visited a similar number of states in 1974 to try to help members of Congress and governors running on the Republican ticket. In 1978 Jimmy Carter—along with Vice President Mondale, the First Lady, and members of the Carter family—took to the campaign trail, particularly in states with competitive Senate contests. In 1982 Ronald Reagan launched a highly partisan campaign to make the midterm elections a referendum on his economic policies.

President Reagan on the stump for New Jersey gubernatorial candidate Tom Kean.

A popular president who decides to campaign in the midterm elections has the difficult decision of determining which candidates he will support. Should he concentrate on crucial competitive contests, or should he also assist close political friends who seem to be in no appreciable danger of being defeated but who seek his assistance anyway? Should he campaign in favor of important party figures even though they voted against him on a number of major legislative measures? If the president does not, and an ignored person wins anyway, the latter may retaliate with even less support in the future; moreover, if his party's candidate loses, the opposition replacement may be even more opposed to the president's programs.

Because of such unattractive possibilities, a president may be tempted to try to pick his party's nominees for Senate and House seats. As we saw in Chapter 7, however, this course of action violates the political custom of local determination. If there is local opposition, the president who gambles on intervention, only to have his protégé lose in a primary fight, risks a decline in political prestige and the enmity of the winning candidate. Franklin Roosevelt's failure to purge certain Southern congressmen in the 1938 midterm elections has deterred other chief executives from becoming involved in spirited nomination contests.

If the battle lines in a congressional nomination have not been drawn, however, a president can influence the selection of congressional candidates by taking early action in support of certain persons. President Kennedy, for example, encouraged certain people, such as Joseph Tydings Jr. of Maryland, to seek a seat in Congress, and President Nixon persuaded 10 Republican members of the House to give up their seats to run for the Senate, where they would be more important politically to him. Thus chief executives attempt to build a base of support in Congress by personally recruiting men and women who share their general views on public affairs. Presidents also work discretetly behind the scenes through sympathetic state political leaders to interest certain people in running. They may also use their influence to funnel needed funds to candidates they favor.

A president's ability to affect the persons who are selected for Congress is limited, however. The large number of elections for the House of Representatives (435 every two years) precludes any significant presidential involvement in them. Even presidents as popular as Dwight Eisenhower find it difficult to transfer popularity to others, especially in a nonpresidential election. As previously indicated, an incumbent member of Congress is in a very strong electoral position: as long as the legislator keeps his or her political fences mended with state and local party leaders and constituents, he or she has little to fear from presidential opposition. The difficulties that a president faces in midterm elections are reflected in Richard Nixon's experience in 1970: of the 21 Republican senatorial candidates that he campaigned for in the general election, only 8 won. Gerald Ford's record was even more discouraging in 1974: of the 33 candidates he tried to help in Senate, House, and gubernatorial races, there were 5 Senate winners, 2 governors, and no winners in the House of Representatives.

Yet it would be a mistake to write off the president's role in congressional campaigns as meaningless. In competitive states (as well as some congressional districts), a visit by the chief executive, a special endorsement, a letter, a photograph taken with the candidate, or a channeling of funds to the candidate may provide the margin of victory. Moreover, as we have seen in Chapter 8, the president can now help raise money for congressional candidates in presidential election years since he receives public funds for his own general campaign. Furthermore there is some evidence that national issues (particularly the state of the economy) are becoming more important, even in midterm elections, and that the fate of both Senate and House aspirants in many areas may turn on the level of public support for the current administration. Thus even if the president does not become directly involved in a congressional race, his conduct in office may indirectly affect its outcome.*

Despite the potentialities of the president's role as party leader, however, there are considerations that deter him from playing it on all occasions. President Eisenhower was dependent on votes from Democratic members of Congress for many of his programs, particularly in foreign policy. Presidents Kennedy and Johnson also received crucial Republican support on civil rights legislation as a result of the efforts of the Republican Floor Leader in the Senate, Everett Dirksen. The Minority Leader also defended Johnson's Vietnam policies more vigorously than many Democrats. In such circumstances, it was hardly surprising that neither Democratic president expended any genuine effort to get Dirksen defeated in Illinois. Richard Nixon treated some of his Democratic supporters the same way: his Attorney General, Richard Kleindienst, told Mississippians in the 1972 campaign that if he lived there, he would vote for Senator James Eastland. When many Southern Democrats voted in 1981 for Ronald Reagan's program of budget and tax cuts, the Republican president said publicly that he didn't see how he could oppose them in the 1982 congressional elections.

Other factors also prompt some presidents to play down their activities in midterm elections. If their party's can-

* As previously indicated in Chapter 8, if in the first quarter of the congressional election year, the president stands low in the polls or the economy is doing poorly, such conditions may encourage able and experienced candidates from the opposite party to run; eventually such candidates may oust incumbents from the president's party.

didates do not do well, the election may be interpreted as a repudiation of their administration. Campaign rhetoric can also be taken personally by members of the opposition party, making it more difficult for the president to get their future support for his legislative program. The chief executive may also be concerned that too much time spent on the campaign trail will create the impression in people's minds that he is not exerting enough effort on the more important duties of his office; it may also detract from his image as the leader of all the American people.

Presidents resort to certain tactics to offset these disadvantages. One is to schedule foreign visits (which emphasize the chief executive's nonpartisan role as the entire nation's representative) to coincide with congressional elections: Richard Nixon visited the Middle East and Mediterranean areas in early October 1970. Another is to make use of the vice president: Spiro Agnew campaigned longer and in more states that year than Nixon, and it was he, rather than the president, who attacked the opposition candidates in personal terms.* This practice allowed Nixon to take the "high road" in the campaign by stressing issues rather than personalities.

Developing Party Programs

One area of partisan activity that the president clearly dominates is the preparation of party programs for dealing with major national problems. An incumbent president has the biggest hand in the writing of the party platform at the national convention. He also has the opportunity to identify party issues and programs during the course of the campaign. He may choose to emphasize certain parts of the platform, ignore others, or even take stands at variance with those contained in the document.

Traditionally, students of American politics have concluded that party platforms and presidential campaign speeches are not to be taken seriously. (The former are for candidates to "run" on, not to "stand" on; the latter are merely rhetoric and do not involve commitments on the candidate's part.) However, recent studies by two political scientists have called into question these somewhat cynical views. As noted in Chapter 7, Gerald Pomper and Susan Lederman's analyses of the party platforms of the Republican and Democratic parties over the period from 1944 through 1978 revealed that pledges made in such platforms were taken seriously by presidents who worked with the Congress, as well as by means of their own executive orders, to get most of them enacted into law. Similarly, Fred Grogan found that both Lyndon Johnson and Richard Nixon acted on more than half of the promises they made in campaign speeches in 1964 and 1968, respectively. The former, whose party controlled the Congress, acted more fully on campaign promises requiring legislative action; the latter, facing an opposition-dominated Congress, was more inclined to carry out those pledges that required executive action alone.

Partisan Influences in Organizing and Managing the Government

The extent to which presidential programs actually get implemented depends to a considerable degree on the president's influence over the party within the government. This group is composed of officials in the legislative

* Nixon also let the Vice President handle the sticky job of criticizing Republican Senator Charles Goodell of New York, who voted against the president on a number of key issues such as Vietnam. Agnew even helped raise money for the victorious Conservative party candidate, James Buckley.

and executive branches who are either elected under a partisan label or appointed primarily because of their party activities or because it is expected that they will implement party views on public-policy matters.

The president's control over his party in the legislature is distinctly limited. He has little to do with its composition, since most senators and representatives are elected independently. Moreover, he has comparatively little influence over the organization of his party in Congress. Although some presidents have played a major role in determining their party's legislative leadership (Thomas Jefferson did, for example), for the most part American chief executives have been chary of interfering with the right of Congress to choose its own leaders. Dwight Eisenhower was forced to work with Senate Republican Leader William Knowland, whose views on foreign policy were quite different from his own. During part of John F. Kennedy's administration the Democratic Speaker of the House was John McCormack, a political rival from Kennedy's home state.

The president has more influence over the party in the executive branch, a matter that we will examine in detail in the next chapter. The only other elected official, the vice president, is his person, to be used or not as the president sees fit. In addition, the president can make appointments to policy-making posts that both reward individuals for their service to the party and permit him to influence the administration of government programs. In particular, his closest political advisers on the White House staff constitute what is, in effect, the president's personal party: persons who have labored in his presidential campaign continue to protect his interests and promote his policies after they assume top governmental posts in his administration.

THE PRESIDENT AS HEAD OF STATE AND LEADER OF PUBLIC OPINION

As we saw in Chapter 4, private citizens have general attitudes about the nation, its form of government, and major public officials, as well as particular views of specific political matters, such as social problems and policies for dealing with them.

To a considerable extent, the American president is the major focus of each of these public attitudes. Like the British monarch, our chief executive is the symbol and the personification of the nation and the state. It is the president who inspires feelings of loyalty and patriotism, particularly in times of crises, when he becomes the rallying point for national efforts. Thus both political friends and foes of Franklin Roosevelt turned to him for leadership when the Japanese attacked Pearl Harbor in December 1941.

Even though this is a democratic nation, the presidency is surrounded with the trappings of ceremony and pomp. The inauguration of a president bears certain resemblances to the coronation of a king, complete with the taking of an oath in the midst of notables and the multitude. Ceremonial aspects of the office have generally included the display of the presidential seal and the playing of "Hail to the Chief" when the president arrives at an event, along with a round of traditional duties: visiting other nations and entertaining foreign heads of state when they visit Washington, D. C., lighting the giant Christmas tree on the White House lawn, throwing out the first ball at the opening of the baseball season, proclaiming a variety of "weeks" devoted to a host of good causes, and the like. All such activities emphasize the role that the chief executive plays in embodying the nation, its government, and its ideals.

Unlike the British monarch, however, the American president not only "reigns" but "rules." As the nation's leading political figure, he is expected to develop and put into effect controversial policies that are binding on the entire populace. In doing so, he must lead public opinion on vital public issues; at the same time he must respect the broad limits that public attitudes (particularly those of interest groups) place on his actions.

The size and composition of the president's "public" varies with circumstances. He may have almost the entire nation as an audience for his inauguration or a major speech in time of crisis. But his target may be much smaller, as for an address on a current issue to the annual meeting of a major interest group such as the NAM`or the AFL–CIO. The president must even take into account the attitudes of foreign publics on certain matters: one of the considerations that led President Kennedy to stop the shipment of Russian missiles into Cuba by blockade rather than invasion was his assessment of foreign reactions, particularly in Latin America.

As the most visible political figure in the nation, the president is constantly in the public spotlight. Almost everything about him—including his golf or tennis game, favorite foods and songs, health, and reading habits—becomes a matter of intense interest. In fact public attention focuses on his entire family. Yet a president cannot depend on public curiosity alone (much of which is trivial) for success in wielding political power. He must establish close ties with a variety of publics in order to convert personal popularity into political effectiveness. Such ties enable him to help mold public opinion while informing himself about the attitudes of citizens.

Personal Trips

One of the earliest means developed for communicating with the American pub-

A President Does Many Things: Handing out diplomas at West Point.

Visiting with Iowa Farmers.

Confering with Prime Minister Ghandi.

Attending an international conference.

lic was the "Grand Tour," first used by George Washington in a two-month trip through the South in 1791. Enduring both the rigors of travel and a surfeit of wining and dining by citizens eager to please the new chief executive, Washington found the trip valuable. According to his own account of the venture, it both reassured him that the new Federalist government was popular in the

Tipping an elbow at an Irish Pub.

Relaxing at the Ranch.

South as well as New England and enabled him to learn with more accuracy than he could have gained by any other means the "disposition" of the people.

Modern presidents have continued the Washington tradition. Johnson and Nixon both spoke of the invigorating feeling they experienced in getting away from Washington, D. C. and establishing contacts with the people in other parts of the country; Jimmy Carter took a trip by paddleboat down the Mississippi. (Smarting from the political infighting in the nation's capital, presidents find the adulation of crowds a good tonic; it also reassures them that the popularity they enjoyed on the campaign trail has not disappeared.) Many presidents today find it helpful to extend their travels abroad as evidenced by Eisenhower's trip to 11 nations, Kennedy's tour of Europe with his wife, and Nixon's visits to China, the Soviet Union, and the Middle East. In his early months in office, Jimmy Carter went to Great Britain to meet with leaders of the major Western industrial nations. Ronald Reagan continued the globe-trotting tradition, attending economic summits, visiting China, the Normandy beaches on which the 1944 Allied invasion began, and his family's ancestral home in Ireland. Such ventures capture the attention of a variety of publics, including the people of the countries visited, ethnic groups at home (Irish-Americans, Italian-Americans, English-Americans, and the like), and the general American populace.

Not all presidential trips, however, turn out to be triumphant. The most notable failure was Woodrow Wilson's ill-starred attempt in 1919 to take his case for the Versailles peace treaty and the League of Nations to the American people when these proposals ran into political difficulties in the Senate. He collapsed near the end of the tour and was disabled for a long period. He was particularly discouraged because his efforts went completely for naught: the American people failed to respond to his pleas, and some historians have concluded that not a single senator's vote was changed by this difficult journey.

Presidents contemplating trips, for whatever purpose, face the possibility not only of failure but also, even when successful, of draining away valuable time from other facets of their demanding job. Because of these hazards presidents in recent years have commissioned vice presidents to make journeys for them both at home and abroad. Moreover, leading cabinet members are also frequently dispatched to explain administration policies to interested publics and to get their reactions to such policies. Jimmy Carter sent his wife, Rosalynn, on a series of trips in this country and abroad for the same purposes.

White House Visits, Mail, and Public Opinion Polls

In most personal contacts between a president and other citizens, they come to him. Along with meeting public officials, a chief executive spends much of his day in the White House receiving individuals and group representatives in connection with a variety of matters. (Harry Truman, for example, averaged about 100 such visits a week.) The activities include holding sessions with interest-group representatives pertaining to public-policy concerns, welcoming delegations of young people visiting the capital, and honoring persons receiving the Congressional Medal of Honor as well as those singled out for achievement in letters, the arts, or sports. Such visits enable the president to create a favorable impression upon his flattered guests, and they also provide him or her with clues to what is on the minds of a variety of Americans.

Another source of information is the letters, telegrams, and telephone calls that pour into the White House from the American people. The volume has varied with the incumbent: after Jimmy Carter initiated his program to encourage citizen involvement in government, the White House was flooded with 70,000 letters a week; Ronald Reagan received 100,000 letters and telegrams in the two weeks following the presentation of his economic program in February 1981. Particular events, such as the "incursion" into Cambodia in 1970, swell the flood. Although the views expressed give the chief executive some idea of public reactions to vital issues

"Hi! We're the Clark family, from Paducah, Kentucky, and we thought we'd just drop in and see the President to tell him what we're thinking."

(his staff compiles the number registering pro and con attitudes and analyzes the major reasons behind them), letter-writers, telegram-senders, and long-distance callers do not necessarily constitute a cross-section of the American people. Typically, they have intense feelings one way or the other on an issue, and they come disproportionately from the more educated and/or articulate segment of the citizenry.

A more reliable barometer of attitudes of the general population is provided by public-opinion polls taken by private firms such as the Gallup, Harris, and Roper organizations. Since the days of Franklin Roosevelt, presidents have had an avid interest in such polls because they provide various kinds of useful basic information. One is the attitude of the public toward specific issues of public policy, such as the pace of school integration or the percentage of unemployed people. Another is the degree of approval or disapproval of his handling of a particular situation, such as the war in Vietnam. Still another is the public estimate of his overall handling of his job, a question that is periodically put to the American people by the pollsters. Recent presidents have even hired their own personal pollsters (such as Patrick Caddell for Jimmy Carter and Richard Wirthlin for Ronald Reagan) to probe public attitudes more deeply on issues in which the chief executive is particularly interested.

A close student of public-opinion polls, John Mueller, analyzed the polls taken on presidential performances from the beginning of the Truman administration in 1945 to the end of the Johnson administration in early 1969 and concluded that certain basic factors affect the popularity chief executives enjoy with the American public. One general pattern is for that popularity to decline over a period of time. Presidents typically start with a high standing in the polls, but as they undertake various actions, they antagonize more and more groups. Mueller labels this the "coalition of minorities" factor, that is, different minorities react unfavorably to specific presidential decisions, as businessmen did when President Kennedy forced them to roll back a steel price rise in 1962 and as Southerners did when chief executives enforced the Supreme Court decision on school desegregation. These different groups become unhappy with the president for different reasons, but the end result is a progressive decline in presidential popularity.*

In addition to this overall downward trend, Mueller determined that public opinion on the presidency reacted to certain kinds of events. A downturn in the economy, particularly as reflected in an increase in the rate of unemployment,† harmed presidential popularity. International events cut both ways. At the time of a dramatic event involving national and presidential prestige, a **"rally-round-the flag"** phenomenon results, with Americans supporting their chief executive. This occurs even if things turn out badly, as they did, for example, at the Bay of Pigs in 1961 when the United States effort to help ex-Cuban forces invade the island and overthrow Fidel Castro ended in a fiasco. On the other hand, wars that drag on such as those in Korea and Vietnam ultimately harm the president's popularity.

* One exception to this principle was Dwight Eisenhower, whose popularity continued to remain high during his stay in office. One possible explanation (among others) that Mueller suggests for this phenomenon is that Eisenhower did not do much in domestic policy and so did not antagonize groups as much as other presidents.

† Some studies also show that growth in the rate of inflation also hurts the president's popularity, particularly among more affluent citizens.

Contacts with Interest Groups

Presidents attempt to influence the attitudes of not only the general public but special publics as well. They give major addresses on business to the convention of the National Association of Manufacturers or the United States Chamber of Commerce or speak on labor relations to a similar meeting of the AFL–CIO. Of course, it is impossible for a person as busy as the president to personally address all the major groups in our society, so they typically dispatch emissaries, such as concerned cabinet officers, to speak on behalf of them and their programs.

Beyond a concern with current matters of public policy, however, presidents also attempt to convince members of social groups that they are sympathetic to their problems. Often chief executives pay particular attention to those groups that helped to get them elected. (They thus attempt to convert their electoral coalition into one that helps them govern.) Democratic presidents tend to focus on labor unions and black organizations, while Republicans concentrate on business and professional organizations. At the same time, the president knows that as the leader of the nation, he is supposed to represent all the people. Tradition provides that chief executives appear before major interest groups, even those that are politically opposed to them. Thus Richard Nixon addressed the annual convention of the AFL–CIO and Ronald Reagan spoke before a similar assembly of the NAACP.

Presidential concern with winning the political support of particular groups is reflected in the recent development of having members of the White House staff serve as liaisons with such groups; often these liaisons are members of the groups themselves. First initiated in the administration of Lyndon Johnson, this practice has been continued in subsequent administrations. For example, Louis Martin, a black newspaper publisher, served as

Testing a Union reception.

the major liaison with minorities for Jimmy Carter, while Edward Anders, a corporation lawyer, performed a similar role with the Jewish community.

Recent presidents have gone a step further by establishing an official Public Liaison Office to handle relationships with special-interest groups in general. First officially initiated in the Ford administration when William Baroody, Jr. was made public liaison chief, it was continued by Jimmy Carter, who appointed Margaret "Midge" Costanza, an early campaign supporter. When she fell out of favor, he subsequently replaced her with Anne Wexler.* When Ronald Reagan became president, Elizabeth Dole took over the official responsibility of establishing liaison with outside interest groups until she became Secretary of Transportation and was replaced by Faith Whittlesey. The official representation of interest groups in the White House has become an institution in the administrations of both major political parties.

In some instances, however, presidents attack special-interest groups. John Kennedy publicly castigated the steel companies when, contrary to what he conceived to be an understanding with them, they raised steel prices in 1962. During his presidency Jimmy Carter publicly criticized oil companies, doctors, and lawyers for being unduly concerned with their own financial interests rather than society in general. Such actions generally reflect a president's unhappiness with the attitudes of such groups toward his policies but also may be calculated to curry favor with the general public, who themselves resent the attitudes of groups they feel are too rich and powerful.

Thus presidents attempt to shape the attitudes of the general public as well as those of special publics in order to win their favor and support. To a considerable extent, their success depends upon their ability to communicate their appeals through the media, a subject to which we now turn.

The Press

Historically, the most important medium linking the president to the American public has been the press. In the early years of the republic there was a partisan press similar to what prevails in many European countries today. The Federalists had their party organ, the *Gazette of the United States,* while the *National Gazette* spoke for the Republicans. The partisan press reached its apogee during the presidency of Andrew Jackson when federal officeholders were expected to subscribe to the administration organ, which was financed in part from revenues derived from printing official government notices.

In the latter part of the nineteenth century, however, the partisan press began to disappear in the United States, largly because of two developments. One was the invention of the telegraph, which led to the formation of wire services that distributed news to all parts of the country; the information transmitted tended to be standardized and politically fairly neutral to avoid antagonizing the diverse readerships of the various newspapers in the country. The other factor was the increased use of the press for advertising by business concerns; this innovation provided newspapers with a secure financial base and lessened their dependence on official notices and other types of party largesse.

* This development illustrates the difficulties that may arise from the fact that the liaison person may conceive of the role as one of articulating the demands of interest groups. Ms. Costanza got in trouble, at least in part, because she was an ardent feminist who supported the provision of federal funds for abortion and publicly criticized President Carter for his contrary position on that issue. Ms. Wexler conceived her role more as one of soliciting interest-group support for Carter's programs.

The Press and The Cuban Missile Crisis.

The modern press in the United States is nonpartisan in the sense that newspapers are not overtly affiliated with particular parties. There is little question, however, that most of today's newspapers have distinct partisan preferences that they disguise thinly, if at all. The *Chicago Tribune* speaks distinctly for the more conservative elements of the Republican party, while the *St. Louis Post Dispatch* clearly represents the views of the liberal Democrats.

It is important, however, to distinguish between the owners and editors of newspapers on the one hand and the members of the working press—reporters and commentators—on the other. Most of the former, representing the interests of management and business in general (on whom they depend for advertising revenue), tend to defend the status quo and favor the Republican party. The latter, interested in the world of ideas, are more inclined to want change in American life and are more often attuned to the general philosophy of the Democratic party.

A president must take these realities into account when he utilizes the press to further his influence over public opinion. Each has sought to establish useful relationships with reporters who can help or hinder his efforts. Theodore Roosevelt initiated the practice of providing working quarters in the White House for reporters and granting personal interviews. Woodrow Wilson later established the regular press conference to which all Washington correspondents were invited.

Over the years the press conference* has become a major tool used by presidents both to influence public opinion and to gauge the public mind. Each president has used the institution in his own way. Some, like Harding, Coolidge, and Hoover, have required that questions be submitted in advance. (This practice began when Harding was unprepared for a question involving a treaty and gave an erroneous and damaging interpretation of it.) Others, like Franklin Roosevelt, have permitted spontaneous questioning. The frequency of press conferences has also varied widely among presidents; FDR held as many in his first three months in office (28) as Richard Nixon did in his first four years. Moreover, in times of crisis chief executives have tended to hold few press conferences, in part because they have little time for them, in part because they wish to avoid divulging sensitive information.

The success of a press conference depends on the skills of the president. Harry Truman, who enjoyed the give-and-take of exchanges with the reporters, nonetheless performed poorly in formal encounters: he tended to answer questions quickly rather than thoughtfully, and was unable to envision just how his words would look in print or how they might be interpreted. Dwight Eisenhower also came across badly. Not only did he have trouble expressing himself clearly and grammatically, but he also displayed meager knowledge about many vital issues of the day.† In contrast, Franklin Roosevelt and John Kennedy were masters of the press conference. The former had a keen sense of what was newsworthy and even suggested reporters' headlines for them. He also prepared members of the press for actions he took on controversial problems by educating them initially with confidential background information; consequently reporters tended to support Roosevelt's ultimate decisions because they understood the reasons behind his actions. Kennedy, who served a brief stint as a newspaper man and enjoyed the company of reporters, used his press conferences to great advantage; his ability to field difficult questions impressed not only the members of the press involved, but also the American public who viewed the proceedings on live television. Jimmy Carter's overall performance in press conferences was generally considered successful: he came across as calm, well-prepared, frank, and articulate.

Presidential contacts with the working press have thus changed over time. Today, it is expected that the chief executive will conduct some formal press conferences attended by hundreds of Washington reporters and watched simultaneously by millions on television. Not all presidents feel at ease in that situation, however. President Johnson, who preferred to converse with small groups of reporters, also experimented with informal, hastily called conferences held in a variety of settings; at times he led the assembled press on a brisk walk around the White House. Even Kennedy did not confine his meetings with reporters to formal press conferences; he also gave exclusive stories to special reporter friends, a practice that was naturally resented by many other members of the working press. Jimmy Carter granted his first press interview three days after he took office; he met with four reporters of the Associated Press and the United Press International. Later on in his administration he also invited major news media figures to the

* It is of course, a misnomer to call the meeting today a "press" conference since members of the broadcast media (television and radio) also participate in the proceedings.

† Political Scientist Fred Greenstein has suggested that on some occasions Eisenhower deliberately utilized such tactics in order to obscure or avoid discussing delicate matters.

"You there in the first row."

White House for informal dinners.

Presidents also attempt to work through other elements of the press besides the Washington reporters and correspondents. President Kennedy invited newspaper editors and owners to White House conferences at which he discussed major public issues. President Nixon, wary of the Washington press corps, chose to experiment with a number of approaches for establishing contacts with sympathetic elements of the medium, for example, holding briefings before selected editors and executives of news organizations around the country with key officials like Henry Kissinger on hand to discuss foreign policy problems and decisions, and furnishing editorial writers around the nation with transcripts of his speeches and comments on issues.

Other Mass Media

Television and radio are, of course, available to a president who wants to address the American people directly without having his remarks filtered through reporters or editorial writers. While holding relatively few press conferences, Richard Nixon appeared on prime-time television more often during his first 18 months in office than Presidents Eisenhower, Kennedy, and Johnson combined during comparable periods. Franklin Roosevelt made effective use of radio for his famous "fireside chats." His resonant voice and effective timing were the envy of professional broadcasters; his facility for discussing complicated social problems in understandable terms won the confidence of the American people in difficult times. He made the first of his chats at the end of his first week in office and continued to utilize them effectively during his 12 years in the White House. At the same time he was careful not to overuse the technique because, as he put it, " . . . individual psychology cannot, because of human weakness, be attuned for long periods of time to a constant repetition of the highest note in the scale."

Television required new techniques and formats. Dwight Eisenhower hired movie and television star Robert Montgomery to coach him on methods of projecting a favorable image. On one occasion he appeared with cabinet members to convey the idea that his administration was a "team" in which individual specialists joined efforts in the common cause of "good government." Nixon announced the appointment of his cabinet on television as a means of dramatizing the event and introducing the appointees. John Kennedy, searching for an equivalent of FDR's fireside chat, had major television commentators come to the White House for personal interviews in which he fielded questions from the informal comfort of his favorite rocking chair. In his first address to the nation, Jimmy Carter used Roosevelt's format; seated in a chair before an open hearth and wearing a cardigan sweater, the new president sought to project an image of informality and also to underscore his concern with the nation's energy crisis.

Today's president can utilize a variety of media to shape public opinion. How effectively he does so will depend on his own communication skills as well as his ability to gauge when and how far he should go in trying to alter public sentiments on controversial matters. To some extent there is a built-in conflict between the president and the media representatives. The former often wants to suppress information that he feels will endanger the nation's security or put his administration in a bad light; the latter, in turn, are eager for news, however sensitive it may be, and have an interest in criticizing the president and his associates as a means of stimulating public interest and thereby creating a demand for their services. Almost every president has complained of unfair treatment by the media, while newsmen have often charged that the president and his team are "managing" the news to further their own political purposes. The situation became exacerbated during Richard Nixon's presidency: convinced that media representatives were personally prejudiced against him, the administration responded with presidential denunciations of television commentators, attacks by Vice President Agnew against the liberal bias of the Eastern press, threats not to renew licenses of stations that carried "ideological payola" and failed to provide a "balanced" treatment of public affairs, and the wire-tapping of telephones of some newsmen considered to be hostile to the administration.

Recent Developments in Presidential Public Relations

While all presidents have tried to win the support of the American people, none has approached the task more systematically and imaginatively than Jimmy Carter. Even before he took office, his political pollster, Patrick Caddell, prepared a 51-page memorandum suggesting public relations goals for the new president and means for accomplishing these goals. Emphasizing that ". . . governing with public approval requires a continuing political campaign," Caddell suggested a number of actions be taken to demonstrate that Carter is an "open man," and "different from other politicians."

Some of Carter's early moves were designed to show that he was a "people's president" who had no use for the trappings of the Nixon "imperial presidency." At the swearing-in ceremony at the Capitol, the president wore a dark blue business suit rather than the traditional formal morning coat, then walked down Pennsylvania Avenue to the White House rather than riding at the head of the inaugural parade as his predecessors had done. In the days that followed, the new president continued to cut down on presidential pomp, abandoning the playing of "Hail to the Chief" by the Marine Corps band when he arrived at ceremonies, eliminating the use of chauffeured limousines by members of the White House staff, and reducing drastically the number of television sets in the White House. He also enrolled his 9-year-old daughter, Amy, in a public school rather than private school, as all presidents since Theodore Roosevelt had done.

During his early days in office, President Carter also initiated a number of new approaches to the American people. He participated in a telephone call-in show and visited a New England community for a mock town-meeting, staying overnight with a family that had supported his presidential campaign. Later he visited Los Angeles, where he fielded questions from a public audience. He even had his energy adviser, James Schlesinger, send letters to 450,000 citizens, soliciting their views on ways to handle the energy problem. Thus President Carter sought to sensitize himself to the views of his fellow citizens and to convince ordinary Americans that he cared about them and their problems.

A year and a half after he took office, Carter brought Gerald Rafshoon—who had managed the political advertising for his 1970 gubernatorial and 1976 presidential campaigns—into the White House to handle public relations. Rafshoon's major responsibility was to help the president present his public policies to the American people more effectively. He also was placed in charge of speech-writing as well as scheduling administration spokespersons for television talk shows, conventions, and other forums. Rafshoon was also credited with persuading President Carter to change his image to that of a more forceful leader—by vetoing legislation, for example, to show Congress that he had the courage of his convictions.*

The Reagan administration carefully adapted its use of the media to the strengths of the chief executive. Tabbed the "Great Communicator," Reagan benefited greatly from his previous professional experience in radio, films, and television. He rivaled Franklin Roosevelt in his skill at delivering a prepared speech. To take advantage of those skills, the president frequently addressed the nation on prime-time television and, as previously indicated, used a series of Saturday morning radio broadcasts to justify his administration and its policies.

The administration also avoided or restricted its use of other types of media formats that President Reagan did not handle as well as prepared speeches. These involved ones that required the president to give spontaneous answers to questions. Thus the President did not participate in call-in shows or invite reporters to the White House for informal, on-the-record question-and-answer sessions. Also, President Reagan would not answer impromptu questions from reporters at photo sessions. He participated in fewer press conferences than President Carter or many of his predecessors; moreover, a number were aired during the daytime rather than during the prime-time hours in the evening when a larger audience would have had the opportunity to observe a presidential press conference.

A president's relations with his party colleagues and the American people create the potential for the public support required of the leader of a democratic nation. However, the decisions he

* Rafshoon later returned to his own advertising agency so that he could manage political advertising for Carter's 1980 presidential campaign.

makes either on his own or in conjunction with other public officials depend on the legal powers of the presidency and his ability to convince other officeholders to act as he desires. (Political scientist Richard Neustadt suggests that the essence of presidential leadership is persuading others that what he wants them to do is not only in the president's interest but in theirs as well.) Among such officeholders are the members of the United States Congress.

THE PRESIDENT AND CONGRESS

Although the primary responsibility for making the laws is vested in Congress, the Founders clearly intended the president to play a vital role in influencing legislation. To that end they granted him certain powers through which he might affect legislative decisions, among them giving messages and recommendations to Congress, calling it into special session, and vetoing bills. In some instances the use of these powers is mandatory: as discussed in detail below, even President Eisenhower, who was not inclined to exercise strong leadership over Congress, remarked that " . . . the Constitution puts the president right square into the legislative business."

Beyond the legal powers vested in the president, however, certain practices have developed over the years that have increased his influence over the making of the laws. These practices were initiated by individual presidents who wanted to exercise strong leadership over legislation. But over the years Congress and the American people have come to expect that all presidents will follow them as part of the political, if not legal, duties of the office.

Messages and Recommendations

Article II, Section 3 of the Constitution is specific in its language that the president " . . . shall from time to time give to the Congress information on the **State of the Union** and recommend to their Consideration such Measures as he shall judge necessary and expedient." Chief executives since Washington have generally followed his practice of presenting an annual message to the Congress at the beginning of each regular session, but the method of delivery has changed over time. Washington and Adams gave their messages in person, but Jefferson (a notoriously poor public speaker) dispatched a written message, giving as his reason that such a speech intruded on the privacy of the legislature and that the practice smacked too much of the royal prerogative from which it developed.* This practice continued until Woodrow Wilson surprised Congress and the nation by delivering a message in person shortly after he was inaugurated. Since Wilson's time all presidents (no matter how meager their speaking skills) have appeared before Congress to deliver the annual State of the Union Message.

Although the assembled senators and representatives are the immediate target of the speech, the president has other audiences in mind as well. In a sense the message is addressed to all the American people, who today can watch the proceedings on television. In fact, the State of the Union Message is beamed to nations around the world via satellite and becomes a matter of interest to political friends and enemies alike. For through this general pronouncement the president indicates the problems that he feels are of concern to American society and suggests policies to mitigate them.

Typically the State of the Union Mes-

* The message followed the British tradition whereby the king delivered a "speech from the throne" to Parliament. This custom was carried to the New World in the form of pronouncements by colonial governors to the legislatures of the day.

sage contains far more concerns and proposals than the president expects Congress to review; 25 or 30 separate matters may be treated in the speech. (Covering such a wide variety of topics is designed to appeal politically to a broad range of interest groups.) Moreover, the president seldom attempts to distinguish among the problems on the basis of their relative importance. Finally, the policy proposals made in the message are usually couched in very vague terms. Thus the State of the Union Message is somewhat like a party platform in its comprehensiveness and generality, yet it does represent some screening of policy proposals made in the platform.

Modern presidents, however, do not restrict their recommendations to Congress to those contained in this message. Instead they adopt the practice, initiated by Woodrow Wilson, of following up this general pronouncement with a series of specially written messages focusing on specific problems and outlining in detail proposals for dealing with them. In 1973 Richard Nixon abandoned the idea of a single message altogether by giving an initial "overview" statement and then following it with five other messages devoted to natural resources and the environment, the economy, human resources, community development, and law enforcement.

A final presidential step in spelling out precisely what should be done about a particular issue is the development of a specific bill. Even though Congress may (and usually does) make changes in the "administration" proposal, the bill enables the chief executive to affect ultimate legislative actions by forcing senators and representatives to focus on what the president thinks should be done about a given problem.

Congress itself has come to realize that large assemblies cannot establish a legislative program that reflects an overall system of priorities. The program must come from an outside source—the president. (This is true even when different parties control the presidency and the Congress: rival legislative leaders made it clear to Presidents Truman, Eisenhower, Nixon, and Ford that they expected them to propose specific programs, including administration bills.) When Congress passed the Budget and Accounting Act of 1921, requiring the chief executive to present a comprehensive plan of suggested expenditures by the various executive agencies (we will examine this matter in the following chapter), it indirectly placed in his hands the job of establishing priorities among governmental programs, since success depends on financing. In recommending expenditures, the president is forced to express his preferences among programs. Thus the annual **Budget Message** is a much better indication of which policies and programs in particular the president favors, and how much so, than is the annual State of the Union Message. (Unlike the latter, the Budget Message forces him, as the saying has it, ". . . to put his money where his mouth is.") As a result of the passage of the Full Employment Act of 1946, the president must also give an annual **Economic Message** to the nation in which he estimates, among other matters, how much money the government may expect to take in from existing revenue measures and how additional moneys might be raised should they be needed.

Today's presidents are thus expected to develop both a comprehensive legislative program reflecting overall priorities and concrete proposals for dealing with specific problems. Following a practice first developed in the Truman administration, presidents now have departments include, with their estimates of financial expenditures, information on legislative matters of interest to them. Such information contains actual drafts of bills and the names of other executive agencies interested in the matter. With this systematic inventory of proposals at his disposal, a president can better screen and coordinate the legislative concerns of the many agencies of the executive branch.

Calling Congress into Special Session

The president has the constitutional prerogative to convene the Congress—both houses or either one—on "extraordinary occasions." (For example, the president might want to bring only senators together to confirm an executive appointment or approve a treaty.) Unlike many state governors, however, he has no power to restrict the agenda of the **special session.** He thus runs the risk not only that legislators may ignore what he wants them to do but also that they may decide to take actions that he considers peripheral or even opposes.

The use of the power to call Congress into special session has varied. The practice became particularly prominent in the first third of this century, as presidents (beginning with Taft) called special sessions shortly after they took office in March of the year in order to get the Congress busy immediately rather than waiting for the then-appointed time of December. The highly productive congressional session held during the first year of the Wilson administration (1913–1914) and the famous "Hundred Days" under Franklin Roosevelt were both specially convened by the chief executives.

Since the passage of the Twentieth Amendment in 1933, the president's power to call the Congress into special session has become less important as a tool of legislative leadership. He is inaugurated on 20 January, but the two houses assemble on 3 January; therefore, there is no necessity for convening them as Wilson and FDR did when they first took office. Since Congress begins each annual session on 3 January, it is ready to receive the president's various messages later in the month. Beyond this, Congress now meets almost year-round (exceptions are holiday recesses, breaks for national conventions, election-year campaigns, and the immediate postelection period in November and December), so there is relatively little time when the lawmakers are not available for hearing presidential legislative requests.*

Even so, the power to call Congress into special session is still potentially useful as an electoral tactic when one party controls the presidency and another the Congress. Harry Truman used it effectively in the summer of 1948, when he convened the Republican-controlled Congress after the party's national convention was held and a platform adopted; in so doing, he challenged the GOP legislature to enact the platform's policy proposals into law. He used its failure to do so to great effect in his fall campaign.

The Veto Power

More important than the authority to call Congress into special session is the president's **veto power,** which gives him three options with respect to a measure passed by Congress: (1) he may sign it, thereby making it a law; (2) he may veto the measure by withholding his signature, in which case it (together with an explanatory message) is returned to the chamber in which the measure originated; this nullifies the measure unless each house, by a two-thirds vote, repasses it over his veto; (3) he may take no action, so that it becomes a law within 10 days unless Congress has adjourned; if that is the case, the measure is said to have been **"pocket vetoed."**

Conceived originally by the Founders

"They can't say I'm not doing anything"

* The president's discretion *not* to convene Congress is also less important than it once was. Lincoln's tactic of acting on his own in the early months of the Civil War would not be available today.

as a defensive weapon for the president to protect himself against encroachments into his domain by a powerful legislature, the veto developed into a tool that can be used to shape public policy. Franklin Roosevelt vetoed over 600 measures—a record—partly because he was in office longer than any other president, partly because he had strong views on public policy and was willing to use the prerogative to demonstrate his political power. He was known to tell his aides, "Give me a bill I can veto," in order to let members of Congress know that they had to deal with a president.

The most important single factor affecting the use of the veto has been political conflict between the Congress and the chief executive. The control of the presidency and the Congress by opposite political parties tends to create the kind of conflict that gives rise to frequent vetoes, as evidenced by the number of times Harry Truman (250) and Dwight Eisenhower (181) exercised the prerogative.†

Actual use is not the only gauge of the veto power's value, for the mere *threat* to use it can be a valuable weapon for a president who wishes to shape pending legislation. By passing the word on which features of a particular bill he finds objectionable and what must be done in order to make it acceptable to him, the president can affect the content of any measure that is sent to him. This tactic does not always work, however. Legislators may not be willing to scale down measures that they favor; moreover, if the Congress is controlled by the opposite political party, its leadership may accept the presidential challenge and force him to veto what they believe is a popular measure. The Democrats in Congress in 1970 sent President Nixon a bill for hospital construction that he vetoed for economy reasons. Not only did they successfully override his veto, but they also charged in the congressional campaign that year that his veto indicated his lack of concern for the health needs of the citizens.

The mere possession of these several legal powers does not, of course, ensure presidential success with Congress. Political factors play a major part in determining how effective the president's use of his powers will be.

Conditions Limiting Presidential Influence with Congress

Every president faces certain basic conflicts with Congress that were built into the constitutional system by the Founders. Operating on Madison's advice that ". . . ambition must be made to counteract ambition," they deliberately created rivalry between the executive and the legislature by assigning important constitutional powers to each, thus inviting them to compete for political leadership. By granting the rivals independent bases of political power, they ensured that each would be capable of protecting its interests.

Their expectations have proved to be very accurate. Since the days when some members of the first Congress began to withstand the attempts of Alexander Hamilton (and indirectly of Washington) to push an economic program, senators and House members have resisted presidential efforts to dominate their affairs as well as those of the nation.

Of course, the conflict between the presidency and the Congress is likely to be even more pronounced if the two are controlled by opposite political parties:

† While Congress can override a presidential veto, over the years only about one in 25 vetoes have met that fate. This tendency even prevailed during Nixon's difficult year of 1973, when Congress overrode only one of his 9 vetoes. However his successor, Gerald Ford, was overridden 12 times in a total of 66 bills he vetoed, which made him the most overridden president since Andrew Johnson. (Truman also was overridden 12 times, but he vetoed 250 bills.)

added to the natural rivalry between the branches of government is the competition between parties for political leadership. Still, members of Congress from a president's own political party frequently engage him in political battle. In fact, as the late British scholar Harold Laski suggested, some members, particularly those in the House of Representatives, have a vested interest in doing this as a means of gaining publicity. As long as the press plays up conflict because it is more newsworthy than cooperation, a legislator who opposes a president will find public attention focused on him or her. The lawmaker can then appeal to constituents by claiming not to be a rubber stamp for the president, and that he or she is battling to protect their interests. Of course, a legislator takes into account the popularity of the president: few Republican senators or representatives picked a fight with Dwight Eisenhower or Ronald Reagan.

Conflicts also reflect differences in constituencies. Since the president receives a nationwide vote, he tends to look at public-policy issues from a national perspective. A senator or member of the House of Representatives is necessarily concerned with how a matter affects residents, particularly the "attentive publics," of his or her state or district. The careers of John Kennedy and Lyndon Johnson gave vivid evidence of the different attitudes appropriate to different offices. As a representative and then a senator from Massachusetts, Kennedy voted to protect principal industries in that state (watchmaking, textiles, and the like) from the economic effects of foreign competition. When he became president, the first important piece of domestic legislation that he helped steer through Congress was a Reciprocal Trade Act designed to promote commerce between the United States and other countries. Similarly, when Lyndon Johnson represented Texas in the House and Senate, he was not a strong advocate of civil rights; when he assumed the presidency, however, he sucessfully promoted several major statutes protecting minority rights and appointed blacks to major governmental positions, including Thurgood Marshall, the first black to sit on the United States Supreme Court.*

President Johnson's increased concern with the problems of the blacks stemmed not only from the national perspective of his office but also from a keen appreciation of the number of blacks in the populous states with many electoral votes. The large-state bias built into the election of the president tends to make Democratic candidates solicitous of groups (blacks, "ethnics," labor-union members) concentrated in urban areas. But this concern produces political conflicts between presidents and Southern legislators whose constituencies contain fewer voting members of those groups.

Constituency differences also result in conflicts between Republican presidents and members of Congress. Even though Eisenhower's popularity enabled the Republican party to capture the presidency in 1952, he immediately ran into political difficulties with Daniel Reed and John Tabor (representing rural areas in New York and Illinois, respectively), who, as chairmen of the House Ways and Means and Appropriations committees, respectively, sought to cut taxes and reduce his budget requests for mutual security. Richard Nixon, who pursued a "Southern" strategy in his quest for votes in 1968, saw his nominations of South Carolinian Clement Haynsworth and Floridian G. Harrold Carswell to the Supreme Court opposed by a number of Republican

* When Johnson was the Majority Leader of the Senate, he did assist with the passage of the Civil Rights Act of 1957, but it was a conservative measure compared to the legislation of the 1960s.

senators from the North, who differed with them over racial matters.

The separate electoral cycles under which presidents and members of Congress operate also leads to differences between the two. In the fall of 1982 in the midst of a major recession, President Reagan urged the electorate to "stay the course," that is, to stick with his economic policies that he claimed were only beginning to take effect and would soon bring about prosperity. However, many Republican legislators who were up for re-election that year were concerned about their immediate electoral fate and preferred to run on state and local issues rather than the president's economic program.

Informal Methods of Influencing Legislation

Such political realities make it difficult for a president to make effective use of his constitutional tools (messages, special sessions, and vetoes), but there are informal methods for influencing Congress. Two sources have already been discussed: party loyalty and public opinion. A president can appeal to his colleagues in Congress to follow the party program and, with senators and representatives who are vulnerable politically, he can threaten to withhold political backing. He can also cultivate the support of the people—particularly "attentive publics"—for his legislative programs and depend on them to exert pressure on members of Congress to enact those programs into law.

Personal persuasion is another valuable technique, one with a variety of manifestations: wooing individual legislators with personal flattery and invitations to social affairs at the White House,* making phone calls to important senators and representatives (particularly those who are not publicly committed on an issue) immediately preceding a crucial roll call; and for the president whose party also controls the Congress, holding periodic conferences with the leadership of the House and Senate as well as with major standing-committee chairmen. At times chief executives even meet with members of the opposition party, as President Ford did with the freshmen Democrats who took office in January 1975. Although personal contacts do not necessarily bring a president all the results he desires, they often win some immediate congressional support for his programs and may also create a reservoir of goodwill on which he can draw in future attempts at legislative leadership.

Beyond personal persuasion, a president has a certain amount of patronage to use as a bargaining point with recalcitrant legislators. Franklin Roosevelt deliberately postponed filling government positions in which lawmakers were interested until major portions of his legislative program were enacted into law. Even though fewer public jobs are at the disposal of presidents today (over the years more and more have come under Civil Service regulations, requiring competitive examinations), modern patronage exists in the form of government contracts, grants, and defense installations. Recent presidents have seen to it that major military bases have been located and retained in the home states of principal congressional leaders and committee chairmen, particularly those from southern states like Texas, Georgia, Alabama, and Florida. Chief executives have also seen to it that legislators from their party are given advance notice of these government contracts, grants, and defense installations and the opportunity to publicly announce such awards through their congressional offices.

Beginning with the Eisenhower ad-

* Personal favors may also be bestowed on important constituents of legislators; examples include invitations to social functions, remembrances of birthdays and anniversaries, memorabilia, and White House mess privileges.

ministration, presidents have also used systematic lobbying efforts on behalf of their legislative programs. Included in such efforts are persons handling legislative liaison from various executive departments, a central liaison unit within the White House Office, and, in some instances, the vice president (Lyndon Johnson used Hubert Humphrey—and Jimmy Carter, Walter Mondale—in that capacity). Such individuals typically divide their responsibilities so that some concentrate on the Senate and others on the House: in addition, they are assigned to legislators from certain geographical areas, and they also specialize in particular subject-matter legislation. They also work closely with party leaders in both houses.

These executive-branch lobbyists use the same general techniques as representatives from private-interest groups. They are thus involved not only in direct contacts with senators and representatives but also employ indirect lobbying to reach legislators through intermediaries, such as congressional staff, campaign contributors, defense contractors, newspaper editors, state and local party leaders, and other politically important persons from legislators' constituencies. The executive-branch lobbyists also join forces with private-interest groups to work on legislation of common interest to both kinds of organizations.

Presidents who want to exercise strong legislative leadership and are skillful in utilizing the tools to do so can often persuade members of Congress to enact their programs into law. Particularly successful legislative leaders in this century are Woodrow Wilson, Franklin Roosevelt, Lyndon Johnson, and Ronald Reagan. Yet each of them benefited from particular conditions that favored their efforts. In Wilson's case there existed a sentiment for progressive domestic legislation among political leaders and "attentive publics" alike when he came to office; moreover, he had a large Democratic majority in the House and a number of liberal Republicans supported his social and economic legislative programs in the Senate. Roosevelt was elected in a time of crisis, when the nation and the Congress turned instinctively to the president for leadership; he also enjoyed large congressional majorities. When Johnson took office, major social and economic legislation delayed for a quarter-century was ripe for enactment; to get it passed he asked Congress to honor John Kennedy's memory by acting speedily on measures that the late president had initiated, and he counted on the bumper crop of freshman legislators elected in 1964 to support his (Johnson's) proposals. Reagan benefited from a conservative mood in the country that called for doing something about what were considered to be the liberal excesses of recent Democratic administrations; he also was favored by the Republicans recapturing the Senate and by votes from a group of southern Democrats in the House who supported his program of tax and budget cuts. Thus the general political climate of the times and the specific situation in Congress constitute major factors in a president's legislative success.

Of course, other presidents besides those who have unusual success with Congress also play a part in the development of public policy. As political scientist Erwin Hargrove suggests, there is a cyclical pattern to such activity. Some presidents such as Theodore Roosevelt and John F. Kennedy, who were not able to get Congress to enact many of their legislative proposals, nonetheless helped *prepare the way* for the legislative achievements of their successors (here, Wilson and Johnson). Others, such as Hoover and Eisenhower, were primarily interested in *consolidating* past legislative gains by means of effective administration rather than new legislative ven-

SWEEPING CHANGES MARK CROWDED ROOSEVELT YEAR

President Has Shaped Vital Policies, Revised Some, Reversed Others and High Associates Have Been Replaced.

EMERGENCY SITUATIONS MET

With Steady Eyes on Road Ahead, the Executive Is Ready to Develop, as Needed, New Strategy to Overcome Obstacles.

By ARTHUR KROCK.

WASHINGTON, Nov. 11.—It was a year ago this week that Franklin D. Roosevelt was elected President of the United States. Nine months of this period he has been in office. What have been the changes in his outlook, his policies, his associates and in himself?

Last November most everybody was happy. Even among the fifteen millions who had voted for Herbert Hoover hope sprang eternal. For three years the country had labored under depression. Whatever else might be said and disputed about Mr. Hoover's administrative ability, he had been an unlucky President.

Now the new deal was to come. No, one was quite certain what it would be. although the political economists who had

tures. In ignoring the need for legislation to meet new problems in American society, such presidents in turn lay the groundwork for the eventual preparation and *achievement* phases of policy-making.There is also a time dimension to legislative accomplishments of individual presidents. Generally speaking, these accomplishments come early in a president's first term. Wilson's major legislative victories occurred in 1913–1914; Franklin Roosevelt's particularly in his first 100 days* (but throughout his first term in office); Lyndon Johnson's in the 1964–1966 period, following his succession to the office and election in his own right; Ronald Reagan's

* While it was unusual for legislation to be passed in such a short period of time, a study by political scientist Paul Light of various presidents' legislative proposals from Kennedy through Carter shows that those *initiated* in the January–March period have by far the best chance of being enacted into law.

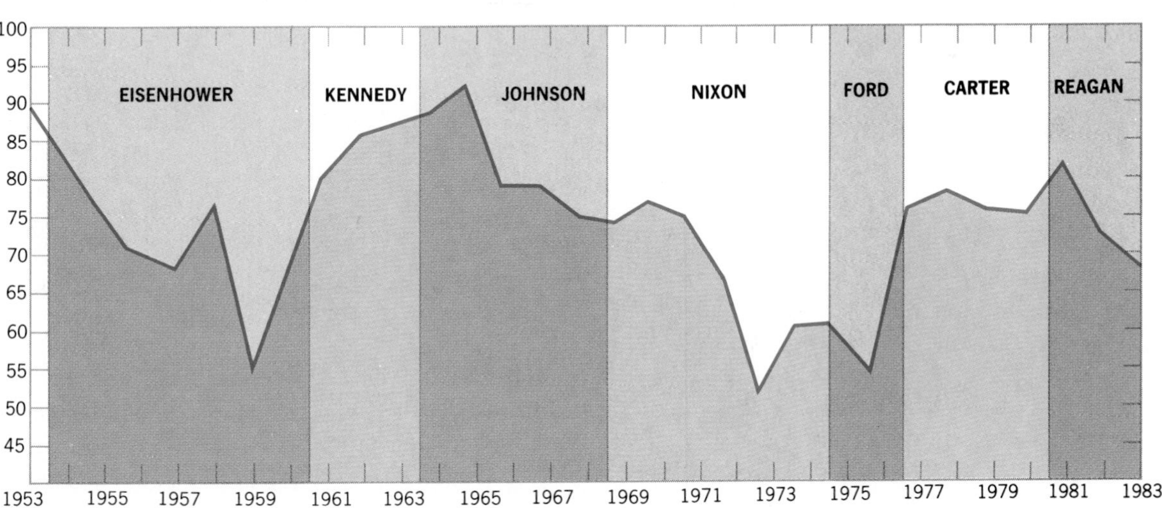

Figure 11.1 Presidential success on congressional votes (1953–1983). Percentages based on votes on which presidents took a position.

SOURCE: *Congressional Quarterly Almanac, 1983*, Washington, D. C.: Congressional Quarterly Inc., 1984, p. 20–C.

during the first eight months of 1981. By February of most president's second year in office, what political scientist John Kessel calls the "Midterm Election" stage begins, that is, members of Congress are preoccupied with re-election and hence avoid politically difficult proposals. Figure 11.1 illustrates the highs and lows in the legislative accomplishments of recent presidents.

Thus the president's role as legislative leader is one of great importance in the American political system, as is the responsibility of chief administrator, a topic we consider in the next chapter.

ASSESSMENT

It is wrong to characterize the American presidency as either an heroic, imperial, or imperiled office. Such characterizations view the presidency at a particular point in time and suggest that the condition is permanent—they mistake a snapshot for a portrait. The presidency changes over time, depending upon the kind of individual who occupies the office, the extent to which that person can handle the particular problems he or she faces, and the action (or inaction) of other political actors.

One major area of change for our chief executive is public politics. As previously indicated in Chapter 4, not so many years ago individual incumbents benefited from the generally positive attitude most Americans had toward our nation, its constitutional system, and its chief political officer, the president. However, two major debacles in the 1960s and 1970s—the Vietnam War and the Watergate scandals that threatened the domestic underpinnings of our constitutional order—combined to make our people increasingly skeptical of the national government and the presidency as an institution. As a result, unlike many of their predecessors, recent American presidents have not been able to draw so readily upon the innate trust and confidence of the American people to support and sustain them in difficult times. Some of that trust and confidence may have returned in the early 1980s but skepticism is still much higher than it has been traditionally.

Although Vietnam and Watergate sensitized the American people to the potential abuse of presidential power, there has not been a permanent major scaling down of the presidency. Presidents Ford and Carter did consciously reduce the dimensions of the office in response to the apparent demand of the public, but by 1980 an electoral majority clearly indicated through its choice of Ronald Reagan that the United States is inescapably dependent on vigorous presidential leadership to cope with complex and often intractable problems. President Reagan has not restored the imperial presidency, but he has moved forcefully to establish a predominant leadership role for himself in domestic and international affairs.

The relationship between the president and the mass media has also changed. It is doubtful whether even presidents as skillful in handling their representatives as Franklin Roosevelt and John Kennedy would fare as well with today's assertive members of the press, television, and radio fraternity, who employ the tenets of investigative and adversary journalism. It is significant that whereas John Kennedy, first as a presidential candidate and then as an incumbent of the office, was able to charm and deflect the criticisms of most members of the media, his younger brother, Ted—no less personally appealing and in some ways a more skillful legislator and politician than JFK—was the subject of vigorous questioning from generally sympathetic reporters like Roger Mudd, out to prove that the media were not soft on political liberals in general and the Kennedys in particular. There is some recent indication, however, that the American people are beginning to resent too much negative reporting by the media, which sometimes inclines them to side with the president. This occurred in late 1983 when the Reagan administration refused to allow media representatives to observe the early stages of the invasion of Grenada, and, when they complained, the public generally supported the president's decision.

Presidents have found the media to be both a means of building support for themselves and their programs and a potential threat to their popularity. On the one hand, the media, especially television, afford presidents the opportunity to preempt the political stage and make direct appeals to millions of citizens. Presidents with the ability to communicate effectively via television, such as Ronald Reagan, enjoy an enormous advantage over their political opponents. On the other hand, presidents who do not have such skills, such as Lyndon Johnson, may project a negative image on television that undercuts their support.

Presidential dealings with other informal groups linking the American people to their government have also become very difficult. As was previously suggested, the decline in the influence of our political parties means that the president cannot count on his own party to help him rally majorities to support his administration and policies. Instead, he must face an increasingly broad array of assertive interest groups—economic, social, and cultural—that pressure him to support their particular issue concerns and, particularly in the case of single-issue groups, that judge his performance in office almost entirely on that basis.

However, recent presidents have tried to overcome these difficulties. President Reagan has made a concerted effort to be a strong leader of his party and has had considerable success in drawing together the disparate elements of the Republican party, including those serving in and campaigning for Congress, as well as state and local offices. Recent chief executives of both political parties have organized a special unit to work with interest groups and have used them with some effect to support presidential policies.

Presidential leadership has also been hindered by the recent developments within Congress that were discussed in the previous chapter. The devolution of power within that body from senior chamber leaders and committee chairpersons down to subcommittees chaired and populated by very junior members means that the president must garner support for his legislative programs from a broad range of independent members of Congress who can no longer be counted on to follow the lead of their more experienced elders. Chief executives have tried to cope with these difficulties by employing their own legislative liaison to work with individual members of Congress, an arrangement that worked out very well in the early stages of the Reagan administration.

SELECTED READINGS

Classic studies of the presidency include Edward Corwin's public-law treatment of the office, *The President:Office and Powers, 1787–1948* (New York:New York University Press, rev. ed., 1948); Clinton Rossiter's political analysis, *The American Presidency* (New York:Harcourt, Brace, and Jovanovich, 1960); and Richard Neustadt's political power approach, *Presidential Power:The Politics of Leadership from FDR to Carter* (New York:John Wiley and Sons, 1980). Good recent general treatments of the presidency include Thomas Cronin, *The State of the Presidency* (Boston, Little, Brown, 2nd ed., 1980); Michael Nelson (ed.), *The Presidency and the American Political System* (Washington, D. C.: Congressional Quarterly, Inc., 1984); and Richard Watson and Norman Thomas, *The Politics of the Presidency* (New York:John Wiley and Sons, 1983).

Very good studies of the psychological aspects of presidential performance are James Barber, *The Presidential Character:Predicting Performance in the White House* (Englewood Cliffs, N. J.:Prentice-Hall, 2nd ed., 1977); Bruce Buchanan, *The Presidential Experience:What the Office Does to the Man* (Englewood Cliffs, N. J.:Prentice-Hall, 1978): and Erwin Hargrove, *Presidential Leadership:Personality and Political Style* (New York:MacMillan, 1966). Excellent psychological treatments of individual presidents are Alexander and Juliette George, *Woodrow Wilson and Colonel House* (New York:John Day, 1956) and Doris Kearns, *Lyndon Johnson and The American Dream* (New York:Harper and Row, 1976).

A basic study analyzing the problems that presidents have historically faced as party leaders is James Burns' *Deadlock of Democracy:Four-Party Politics in America* (Englewood Cliffs, N. J.:Prentice-Hall, 1963). Two good recent studies treating the subject from a variety of perspectives are Robert Harmel (ed.), *Presidents and Their Parties:Leadership or Neglect?* (New York:Praeger, 1984) and John Kessel, *Presidential Parties* (Homewood, Ill.:Dorsey Press, 1984).

A basic analysis of the president's role as leader of public opinion is Elmer Cornwell, *Presidential Leadership of Public Opinion* (Bloomington, Ind.:Indiana University Press, 1965). A good recent treatment of the subject is George Edwards, *The Public Presidency:The Pursuit of Popular Support* (New York:St. Martin's Press, 1983). An excellent study of the president's relationship with the media is Michael Grossman and Martha Kumar, *Portraying the President:The White House and the News Media* (Baltimore: Johns Hopkins University Press, 1981).

An excellent legally oriented study of presidential–congressional relations is Louis Fisher, *The Constitution Between Friends* (New York:St. Martin's Press, 1978). Two very good analyses emphasizing the president's political relations with Congress are George Edwards, *Presidential Influence in Congress* (San Francisco:W.H. Freeman, 1980) and Stephen Wayne, *The Legislative Presidency* (New York:Harper and Row, 1978). Erwin Hargrove explains his concept of the cyclical nature of policy-making in Chapter 6 of his *The Power of the Modern Presidency* (New York:Alfred A. Knopf, 1974). For a recent analysis of many of the aspects of presidential–congressional relations, see Anthony King (ed.), *Both Ends of the Avenue:The Presidency, The Executive Branch, and Congress in the 1980s* (Washington, D. C.: American Enterprise Institute, 1983).

CHAPTER 12

The Bureaucracy

While elected officials in recent years have battled over a host of controversial issues—inflation, energy, unemployment, abortion, and school prayer—they have taken aim at a common foe: the federal **bureaucracy.** Members of Congress regularly commiserate with their constituents over the evils perpetrated by "nonelected bureaucrats" and the miles of red tape that ensnare helpless citizens who have to do business with Washington. Presidential candidates have also lashed out at appointed federal officials. Alabama governor George Wallace referred to them as ". . . pointy headed intellectuals and theoreticians who can't park their bicycles right."

Nor are attacks on bureaucracy limited to its natural enemies—politicians from the party out of power. (At the 1952 Democratic convention, Vice-President Alben Barkley referred to a "bureaucrat" as a ". . . Democrat with a job that some Republican wants.") Also joining in the criticism in recent years are the very officials that theoretically head up the bureaucracy—incumbent presidents. Richard Nixon referred to the bureaucratic colossus in Washington as a "fearless machine." Gerald Ford cautioned that ". . . a government big enough to give you everything you want is a government big enough to take from you everything you have." Jimmy Carter declared in his 1977 inaugural address that "small is beautiful" and vowed to cut back the number of workers on the government payroll and to simplify federal regulations. Four years later Ronald Reagan echoed the same sentiments: in his inaugural address he declared his ". . . intention to curb the size and influence of the federal establishment"; two weeks later in a broadcast to the nation on the economy he reported that he had ". . . already placed a freeze on hiring replacements for those who retire or leave government service."

What accounts for this great animosity toward the federal bureaucracy? How justified are the criticisms leveled against it? How realistic are proposals for reforming it? To try to answer such basic questions we must first understand what the federal bureaucracy *is* and what it *does;* how it is *organized* and *operates;* the kinds of *persons* who staff the bureaucracy and how they are chosen; what *means* exist to check its possible abuses and to make it responsive to popularly elected officials and the general public.

THE NATURE OF BUREAUCRACY

The scorn for the federal bureaucracy expressed by recent officeholders is not a new or unique reaction to the activities of the government and its officials. According to a leading scholar of the subject, Reinhard Bendix, the word **bureaucracy** can be traced to eighteenth-century France: the term *bureau,* referring to a cloth covering the desk of a public official, was combined with *cracy* (rule) to suggest an autocratic type of government. During the following century this unflattering word spread to other European countries where critics of absolutist governments employed it to describe the complex procedures and high-handed manner of autocratic public officials. Today the term retains its unfavorable meaning. It summons up the image of a blundering petty official—called a *bureaucrat*—who spends his or her time developing meaningless forms with which to torment innocent citizens and applying rules and regulations rigidly with no concern for the specifics of a case. The bureaucrat is also seen as building a personal empire composed of ever-increasing numbers of subordinate employees, all at the expense of the government treasury and the tax-paying citizenry.

While this hostile use of the term *bureaucracy* remains a popular one, political scientists and sociologists employ the term in a more neutral sense to describe a large-scale organization with certain common features.* Prominent among

* Several of these features apply to private organizations as well as public ones. A bureaucracy exists in General Motors just as in the federal government. However, this discussion concentrates on public bureaucracies.

these is the handling of complex tasks through a *division of labor* that allows persons with various kinds of skills to concentrate on different aspects of the total operation. Another feature is a *hierarchical* form of organization in which authority flows downward from superiors to subordinates. Modern-day bureaucracies recruit persons for their *technical expertise* and expect them to be *politically neutral,* that is, to make decisions based only upon their expertise, not on partisan or personal considerations. For a bureaucrat to meet these expectations, he or she is protected from arbitrary dismissal and given incentives to remain a permanent employee of the bureaucracy.

It is precisely these characteristics of bureaucracy that explain its prominence today at all levels of government, including the federal. As we saw in Chapter 10, Congress has neither the expertise, nor the time to deal with the intricacies of all the various issues facing the nation. At best, it can *identify* a problem such as pollution, *suggest* some basic approaches for dealing with the problem, and *leave it to the experts* in a specialized agency to grapple with the issue on a day-to-day basis. (Meanwhile Congress moves on to other matters.)

As the federal government has intervened more and more in the economic and social life of the nation, the federal bureaucracy has become increasingly important as nonelected officials make decisions that vitally affect the lives of citizens. For example, agencies help to determine who is entitled to certain *benefits.* Recently, the Department of Agriculture issued new regulations concerning food stamps that had the effect of removing several million persons from the program, but at the same time increased the amount of stamps to which

Explaining the Reagan Administration's initial Social Security reforms.

Arguing for social security benefits.

eligible persons were entitled. Federal agencies also *regulate* economic activities. Thus all mobile homes must meet federal construction safety standards set by the secretary of the Department of Housing and Urban Development.

In determining the distribution of benefits and regulations, the federal bureaucracy acts in various capacities. Some of these are primarily *executive* or managerial in nature, such as in the hiring of qualified personnel and the allocation of funds so that an agency does not run out of money before the end of the fiscal year. In other instances, the bureaucracy's functions are more *legislative* in nature, such as when it develops general rules and regulations that govern, for example, the kinds of safety equipment that must be installed in automobiles or aircraft. Moreover, in some instances, agencies undertake *judicial* functions, for instance, deciding which applicant for a television franchise should receive it or whether a given person is entitled to a veteran's disability pension.

It would be a mistake to think of the federal bureaucracy as performing essentially routine clerical tasks. While some of them are—as when an agency simply enforces a provision of a law that is clear-cut and has a specific application—many of the activities involve great discretion. Congress may provide only broad guidelines in stating that freight rates set by the Interstate Commerce Commission must be "just" and "reasonable," or that in assigning radio frequencies and television channels, the Federal Communications Commission must take into account the "public interest, convenience, and necessity." Thus federal agencies deal frequently with vague and essentially unfinished laws that they must interpret, supplement, and apply to a variety of individuals, groups, and circumstances.

The federal bureaucracy has thus become a major force in our national government, making not only executive decisions but those of a discretionary nature more typically associated with legislatures and courts. Moreover, its activities dwarf those of the older, more traditional bodies. As a former commissioner of the Federal Communications Commission put it: "While the courts handle thousands of cases a year and Congress produces hundreds of laws each year, the administrative agencies handle hundreds of thousands of matters annually." Another measure of comparative activity demonstrates that fact even more clearly. Currently some 2.9 million persons are employed in the federal bureaucracy compared to 39,000 employed by Congress and 16,000 by the federal courts.

While the bureaucracy is an increasingly important component of our national government, it is by no means an autonomous body. Rather, as the following section demonstrates, it is the *legal creature* of two traditional branches—the president and the Congress. Together they determine *what* the bureaucracy does, *how* it goes about its work, and *who* is in charge of its operations.

THE PRESIDENT, CONGRESS, AND THE BUREAUCRACY

Since the bureaucracy is entrusted with administration of the laws, it is natural to expect that the president, vested by broad constitutional language (Article II, Section 1) with the "Executive Power," should play a major role in its functioning. Indeed, language in Section 3 of that same Article charges the chief executive with the duty to ". . . take care that the laws be faithfully executed." At the same time, however, Article I, Section 8 grants Congress the authority to make all laws "necessary and proper" not only for implementing its own delegated powers, but for carrying out ". . . all other powers vested by this Constitution in the Government of the United States, or in any department or officer thereof." Thus the Founders intended that the president and Congress should share the responsibility for the functioning of the bureaucracy.

This joint responsibility is implemented by specific powers shared by the president and Congress that affect the operation of the bureaucracy. As the following discussion indicates, the *structure* for carrying out the activities of the bureaucracy is today created by action of both the chief executive and the Congress. Together they also determine the amount and allocation of *moneys* that are expended by the bureaucracy. Finally, both the president and the Congress influence the *appointment and removal* of the men and women who occupy the major positions in the federal bureaucracy.

The Structure of the Bureaucracy

While one might expect that the president possessed the power to determine the organization and internal operation of the executive branch, as a matter of fact it is the Congress that is granted this constitutional authority. Since 1789, when the national legislature first created the departments of State, War (and Navy), and Treasury, along with the Office of the Attorney General and the Post Office, the executive structure that has evolved has been primarily a product of congressional action. Such action has determined not only the general nature and scope of government programs, but the specific organizations in which they are administered. In some instances Congress has placed new programs within existing organizations; in other cases it has created new entities to handle them. It has also shifted programs from one unit to another.

Congressional control over the organization of the executive branch goes beyond its general structure. National legislators can also determine the internal operation of executive agencies by deciding the subunits into which they are to be divided as well as the different ranks of officials who carry out various aspects of the programs. Congress has also legislated on even more detailed internal matters, such as determining how executive agencies shall enter into contracts, issue publications, purchase supplies, or use the mails and means of travel.

The development of a broad variety of New Deal programs in the 1930s created a burgeoning bureaucracy. In 1936 President Roosevelt appointed a Committee on Administrative Management chaired by Louis Brownlow, a distinguished former city manager, to analyze and make suggestions concerning the management of the executive branch. The major recommendation of the group was that the president "needs help" in administering the bureaucracy and that some of this help should be provided by presidential assistants with a "passion for anonymity." In 1939 Congress granted President Roosevelt the authority to reorganize the executive branch subject to some restrictions (for example, certain agencies were exempted from being reorganized), and he responded that same year with an executive order creating the Executive Office of the President, a highly important unit that we will examine in detail later in this chapter.

This pattern of joint executive–legislative involvement in executive reorganization has persisted over the years since 1939. Congress has periodically granted the president the power to reorganize the executive branch but has kept for itself the right to veto the **reorganization plans.** Beginning in 1949 that veto took the form of a resolution passed by either house within 60 days of the issuance of a presidential **reorganization plan;** if neither chamber took any action to nullify such a plan within that period, it automatically went into effect.* (Since 1964 the authorizing legislation has also prohibited the creation of cabinet-level departments by executive order, reserving to Congress alone the power to take that action by statute.) In response to a request by President Carter, Congress once again enacted such a statute granting the chief executive the authority to reorganize the federal bureaucracy. That authority expired on April 7, 1981 and has not been renewed.

Armed with this statutory authority to reorganize the executive branch, and frequently fortified with suggestions by outside commissions composed of prestigious private citizens,† chief executives have taken the leadership in making some major changes in the bureaucracy. These include the addition of the Department of Health, Education, and Welfare during the Eisenhower administration, and two additional cabinet-level departments during Lyndon Johnson's presidency—the Department of Housing and Urban Development and the Department of Transportation. President Nixon reorganized the Bureau of the Budget during his first term, giving it the title of the Office of Management and Budget, and created the Domestic Council to help coordinate the various domestic programs of the federal government. In the Carter admin-

* As discussed later in this chapter, this type of legislative veto has now been declared unconstitutional; future presidential reorganization plans will have to be approved by both houses of Congress and subsequently signed by the president.

†In the late 1940s and early 1950s two separate bodies chaired by former President Herbert Hoover reported their recommendations to Presidents Truman and Eisenhower.

istration, two new* departments—Energy and Education—were added to the executive branch.

However, a number of major presidential reorganization proposals have *not* been approved by Congress. President Truman was unsuccessful in upgrading the Federal Security Agency (in charge of the Social Security programs) to departmental status, and President Kennedy met defeat in his effort to create a Department of Urban Affairs. Congress refused to approve Lyndon Johnson's proposal for merging the Commerce and Labor departments; it also declined President Nixon's bid to combine seven existing departments (Agriculture; Commerce; Health, Education, and Welfare; Housing and Urban Development; Interior; Labor; and Transportation) into four (Community Development; Economic Affairs; Human Resources; and Natural Resources). President Reagan originally proposed that the Energy and Education departments be abolished but congressional reaction was so cool that the administration did not push the legislation to do so.

Typically, presidential reorganization plans are proposed on the grounds that they will prevent duplication of work, group agencies with similar functions together, and save the taxpayers money. However, there is little evidence that they actually accomplish these managerial goals; for example, only 4 of the 92 reorganization plans submitted to the Congress from 1949 through 1973 were supported by precise dollar estimates of savings. Rather, as one veteran observer of the Washington scene, Harold Seidman suggests, such plans are highly *political* in nature. The method of organization determines priorities among governmental programs (a new program may be placed in a specially created unit to prevent its being slighted by an existing agency with other ongoing programs). The organization in which a program is administered also affects the kind of access that interest groups have to the bureaucracy. Thus President Johnson's proposed merger of the Departments of Commerce and Labor was opposed by both business and labor because each feared a loss of the influence it had enjoyed in the department with which it was most familiar.

One other major factor greatly impedes executive reorganization: the committee structure of Congress. Under the Legislative Reorganization Act of 1946, each standing committee of the Congress exercises legislative oversight over certain executive agencies. Therefore if such agencies are reorganized, that action affects the activities of the corresponding congressional committees. As Seidman puts it, "The key to rationalizing executive branch structure lies in the reorganization of Congress, not the reverse." As we saw in Chapter 10, traditionally the national legislature has shown little inclination to fundamentally change its committee organization for *any* purpose, let alone for accommodating its major constitutional rival, the president.

Secretary of Transportation, Elizabeth Dole.

Money

Like the creation of the structure of the bureaucracy, the provision of money for its operations is a joint responsibility of both the president and Congress. The process involves three basic steps: (1) the requesting of funds for the operation of the executive branch—a procedure that is today controlled by the president, (2) the authorization of government programs and the appropriation of funds for them—two separate procedures, both of which are carried

* When the new Department of Education was created, the name of the Department of Health, Education, and Welfare was changed to Health and Human Services.

out by the Congress, and (3) the actual spending of the money—a decision in which both the president and the Congress share.

Requests for Funds. Initially, Congress granted the first Secretary of the Treasury, Alexander Hamilton, the authority to ". . . prepare and report estimates of the public revenues and the public expenditures." In this way it provided for some executive control over agency requests for funds. However, this practice was later abandoned in favor of a process in which the Secretary of the Treasury simply passed on to the Congress the departments' own estimates of expenditures without making any changes. The end result of this lack of executive authority to examine and revise department estimates—and to relate them to revenues—was a growth of government spending and the incurring of large deficits. Eventually Congress became concerned with these deficits and passed the Budget and Accounting Act of 1921, placing responsibility for the preparation of a budget on the president. To assist him in this responsibility, the Bureau of the Budget was created and placed in the Department of the Treasury. When the Executive Office of the President was established by executive order in 1939, the Bureau was transferred from the Treasury Department to the Office; since 1970 it has been known as the Office of Management and Budget (OMB).

The preparation of the presidential budget today is a lengthy and complicated process. In the spring (some 10 months before the president's budget is presented to Congress the following January), the Treasury, the OMB, and the Council of Economic Advisers (this body will be discussed in the next section) develop the administration's economic projections of overall spending and tax policies for the next fiscal year. At the same time, executive agencies are requested to submit estimates of their financial needs for the next year.

During the summer months the annual budget battle shifts to the departmental level. The head of a bureau (or other subunit of a department) proposes estimates of needs for the coming year. The departmental budget staff screens these requests and makes recommendations to the departmental secretary concerning them. That fall, after the departmental secretary makes a decision on the total department figure to propose for the coming year, the process moves upward again. The OMB examines each departmental budget and holds hearings at which agency heads are required to justify their estimates. Following this procedure the OMB makes recommendations to the president on expenditures, and each agency is later notified of the amount the president allows it. If an agency feels that the chief executive has trimmed its budget too much, it can appeal its case—if the departmental secretary is willing to do so. Ultimately the president makes the final decision on all requests, and all budget materials are combined in a single document and submitted to Congress. In his Budget Message that same month the president presents this information to the national legislators in summary form.

Authorizing Programs and Appropriating Funds. Traditionally, this exclusively congressional phase of the total money-providing process has been highly decentralized as agency heads knock on the doors of a variety of groups in presenting their case for funds. Initially they must receive **congressional authorization** for their programs from the appropriate substantive committees (Agriculture, Armed Services, Labor, and the like) of both the House and Senate. These authorizations may provide a maximum dollar figure that can be expended for such programs, but as political scientist Aaron Wildavsky, a close student of the budgetary process, explains, these are only "hunting licenses" which the two congressional Appropriations committees (House and Senate) are under no obligation to recognize or honor. For it is these latter committees, operating through subcommittees (each of which has jurisdiction over one or more executive agencies) that have traditionally made the final decisions on how much money is actually **appropriated** for the various executive agencies. The recommendations of these subcommittees are generally adopted by their parent Appropriation Committee and the entire chamber (House or Senate), with a conference committee ultimately settling House–Senate differences on appropriations.

This highly fragmented process has proved over the years to be most unsatisfactory. There has been no way to ensure that the funds Congress appropriates for expenditures are related to the amount of money it raises through revenue measures. Nor has the legislature been willing to set an overall figure for expenditures in a given fiscal year and to see to it that its appropriations for various programs stay within that total figure. Finally, Congress has often failed to complete the appropriation process before the end of the fiscal year on June 30, with the result that it has had to pass supplemental appropriations to permit government agencies to carry on activities at previous levels of expenditures until the legislators can reassess their needs.

Faced with these problems, Congress passed a major budget reform act in 1974 providing for a Congressional Budget Office as well as new budget committees in each chamber to study and recommend charges in the president's budget. New procedures have also been established that require Congress to develop an alternative congressional budget relating appropriations and spending to taxes and the federal debt and under a "reconciliation" procedure, requiring that appropriations stay within an overall spending figure authorized by the two chambers. The reform measure also seeks to remedy Congress's failure to complete its appropriation process on time by establishing a new fiscal year (running from 1 October to 30 September, rather than 1 July to 30 June) that gives the legislators three extra months to act upon budget proposals made by the president the previous January.

After several unsuccessful attempts to use the reconciliation procedure in the 1970s, Congress utilized it for the first time in 1980 when it ordered certain committees to cut various programs by $8.2 billion. However, the new procedure really came into its own in 1981, the first year of the Reagan administration. In March the president sent Congress a package of budget cuts calling for a reduction in domestic spending of $48.6 billion for fiscal 1982 (beginning October 1, 1981). Working closely with the Director of OMB, David Stockman (a former Republican congressman from Michigan), the Senate Budget Committee sent reconciliation instructions to 14 committees requiring them to alter programs to cut $36.4 billion in fiscal 1982 spending. The Democratically controlled House Budget Committee called for only $15.8 billion cuts in its comparable instructions to House committees. However, the whole House, with the support of all Republican members and 63 Democrats, adopted a substitute resolution cosponsored by conservative Democratic congressman Phil Gramm of Texas and Republican congressman Delbert Latta of Ohio, providing $37.3 billion in reductions for fiscal 1982.* Eventually conferees of the two chambers agreed on a final reconciliation package of $35.2 billion in cuts for fiscal 1982, and total reductions of $130.6 billion in fiscal years 1981–1984, which President Reagan signed into law in August 1981.

This bold use of the reconciliation procedure set off a storm of criticism from many members of Congress, as well as long-time observers of the legislative process. They were concerned that the process short-circuited the use of authorization and appropriations committees that had traditionally examined the merits of individual programs, and that it subordinated such committees to the centralized authority of the Budget Committees of the two houses. Many also were unhappy that the 1974 legislation that was designed to provide Congress with greater fiscal independence of the White House had actually become the means by which President Reagan usurped Congress' traditional power-of-the-purse. Defenders of the reconciliation procedure argued that it enabled Congress to exercise overall control of spending, a basic function that it failed to fulfill when it allowed authorization and appropriation committees to decide how much should be spent on individual programs without regard to total expenditures.

It is difficult at this point to assess the long-range effects of the Budget Reform Act of 1974. If Congress continues to discipline itself to actually use the reconciliation procedure, the Budget Committees of the two chambers will gain power at the expense of individual authorization and appropriation committees. It is less clear, however, that the reconciliation procedure will also serve to shift the balance of fiscal power between Congress and the president. The 1981 experience appears to have been shaped by President Reagan's general control of the Congress that year. In subsequent sessions he has been forced to compromise on fiscal matters with the leadership of his own party in the Senate and the Democrats who control the House. Both congressional groups have changed the president's priorities so as to provide fewer cuts in domestic programs and more restraint in military spending; they have also forced President Reagan to accept some tax increases.

One traditional fiscal problem that persists is the failure of Congress to pass appropriation bills by the end of the fiscal year. Despite the fact that the Budget Reform Act of 1974 extended that year from June 30 to September 30, members of Congress continue to miss the deadline and have to resort to *continuing resolutions* that maintain funding for agencies at last year's level. Such stopgap measures fail to reflect shifts in policy priorities provided for in budget resolutions passed earlier in the congressional session.

* House Democrats later denied Gramm his seat on the Budget Committee for his role in this dispute. However, he resigned his House seat, ran successfully for it as a Republican, and became a Republican member of the Committee. In 1984, he became the Republican nominee for the Senate.

"Even if we cut spending in half, both halves would continue to grow."

Spending. Most moneys appropriated by the Congress are spent by the executive branch without question. However, in some instances, presidents have **impounded** funds—that is, refused to spend them—for various reasons. In some instances, chief executives have merely deferred spending because of changing circumstances; Jefferson did this when the settlement of differences with the French concerning the Mississippi River made the moneys appropriated for gunboats unnecessary. In some cases Congress itself authorizes the withholding of funds, as happened in 1967, when Congress directed a spending cut in which the president was expected to participate. A number of recent chief executives, including Truman, Eisenhower, Kennedy, and Johnson, have invoked their authority as commander in chief to justify refusing to spend moneys for military forces and weapons that they did not think were necessary for the nation's defense.

The most dramatic use of impoundment, however, was practiced by Richard Nixon. Not only did he refuse to spend large sums of money appropriated by Congress (some $40 billion in his first four years in office alone), but his impoundments were directed at a broad range of domestic, not national defense programs. (Singled out as particular targets were programs in agriculture, housing, and water-pollution control.) Moreover, the reasons Nixon invoked for his actions—that he had the constitutional right to impound funds when spending of moneys would cause inflation or require an increase in taxes—involved major financial issues that have traditionally been left to the Congress. The fact that the president directed many of his impoundments at legislation he personally disapproved (and had unsuccessfully vetoed) also indicated that he was utilizing this weapon to affect particular public policies rather than to impose financial control over the total level of government spending.

Nixon's use of impoundment was soon challenged on two fronts. Some impoundments were struck down by the federal courts, including a $9-billion impoundment of federal water-pollution control money that was nullified by the Supreme Court. In addition, when Congress passed the law reforming its budgeting procedures, it also included provisions limiting presidential impoundments. The act, known as the Congressional Budget and Impoundment Control Act of 1974, stipulates that if the president *defers* the expenditure of funds, either house can pass a resolution forcing him to release them. If he believes certain moneys should not be spent at all, he may propose a *rescission* of them; however, both houses must approve this rescission within 45 days and have it signed by the president, or he must release the funds at the end of that period.

Since the passage of the 1974 legislation, Congress and presidents have been trying to adjust to the new impoundment procedure. Congress has generally been more willing to allow deferrals of expenditures to stand—by not passing resolutions against them—than it has been to approve of rescissions within the 45-day period and have that action signed by the president. However, as discussed in the last section of this chapter, the type of legislative veto used to nullify presidential deferments of expenditures was declared to be unconstitutional by the Supreme Court in 1983. It remains to be seen how that decision will affect the deferral of expenditures; some students of the subject point out that Congress can get around the Court's decision by including in an appropriations act a stipulation that any proposal to defer spending for certain specified programs would be treated as a rescission. Thus the money would be released for spending unless both chambers approved the rescission within 45 days and the president signed it.

Thus the provision of money for the activities of the bureaucracy is a process shared by both Congress and the president. While one may think of budgets, appropriations, and expenditures as dull, bookkeeping kinds of operations, in reality they are the stuff of which public policy is made. For the allocation of money reflects decisions involving priorities, preferences, and values; as political scientist James Davis Jr. suggests, it ". . . converts hopes and symbols into reality."

This being the case, the process by which funds are allocated to various governmental programs is a highly *political* one. As Aaron Wildavsky describes the process, it involves a number of persons who assume different roles and employ various calculations and strategies. Department heads generally serve as *advocates* for their agencies and programs, calculating the amount of their requests on the basis of how much the OMB and the Congress are likely to cut from their budget; the OMB acts *to protect the president* against an overweening budget but at the same time attempts to increase spending for the chief executive's favorite programs; the House Appropriations Committee traditionally adopts the role of *guardian of the Treasury* against raids by overambitious bureaucrats and selfish interest groups; its Senate counterpart typically conceives of itself as a *court of appeals* for groups whose essential programs have been emasculated by the niggardly House; and finally, the chief executive generally strives to *protect the financial stability* of the nation while also supporting the favored programs of a variety of groups that helped to put him in office.

Personnel

As we have already seen, Congress has the ultimate authority in determining the structure of the executive branch, including the major positions in the departments and subunits, through which a broad range of government programs are administered. The Constitution also grants the national legislature broad authority over appointments to such positions. Article II, Section 2 does provide that the president shall appoint, *with the "advice and consent of the Senate,"* ambassadors, consuls, other public ministers, and Supreme Court justices, as well as ". . . all other Officers of the United States whose appointments are not herein otherwise provided for, and which shall be established by law." However, that same section also empowers Congress by law to vest the appointment of ". . . such inferior Officers as they think proper in the President alone, in the Courts of Law, or in the heads of departments."

Thus Congress generally controls how appointments in the bureaucracy are made. Only major diplomatic and judicial appointments specifically require presidential nomination and senatorial confirmation; otherwise it is up to Congress to decide whether the appointment to a particular position it creates (or allows the president to create with its approval) must follow the same nomination–confirmation procedure, or whether the president or some department head can make the appointment alone.

The general pattern is for Congress to allow the president to appoint persons with whom he works most closely on a personal basis, such as those in the White House Office. (We will examine this unit in the next section.) Other major officials in policy-making positions must be approved by the Senate. Finally, those in lesser or "inferior" positions are appointed by department heads rather than the president.

Within this broad legal framework, political aspects of appointments to the bureaucracy have evolved over the years. The custom of **"senatorial courtesy,"** which has been in effect since the Washington Administration, means that the chief executive must clear appointments to federal positions within a particular state with the senators of his own party from that state.* If the senator or senators involved do not approve the person nominated or have nominees of their own, as a matter of courtesy the entire Senate will refuse to confirm the appointment.

Senators are inclined to allow the president to have his way, however, in appointing officials whose offices have "national" jurisdiction or scope. For example, the Senate has refused to confirm a president's nominee for a cabinet post only eight times in the nation's history. The most recent occurrence of this was during the Eisenhower administration: the Senate voted against confirming Lewis Strauss as Secretary of Commerce, primarily because while serving as head of the Atomic Energy Commission he incurred the wrath of Clinton Anderson of New Mexico, a powerful and respected member of the Senate. However, sometimes the president or the nominee himself will withdraw his name from consideration for a post, as Theodore Sorensen (a close presidential aide of President Kennedy) did when his nomination by Jimmy Carter as director of the Central Intelligence Agency (CIA) ran into difficulties with many conservative senators in early 1977.

The Senate has been less deferential to the chief executive in appointments to the **independent regulatory commissions** which are considered less close to the president than cabinet-level departments and more aligned with Congress. The Senate has also been more inclined to look into the particular qualifications of persons serving on such commissions and to be less tolerant of the use of such appointments for strictly political purposes. When President Ford nominated Warren Radman, former attorney general of New Hampshire, as chairman of the Interstate Commerce Commission just 20 days before the 1976 presidential primary in that state, the appointment was attacked by both Democrats *and* Republicans as a tactic to boost the president's chances in that primary; ultimately, because of this opposition, the nominee asked that his name be withdrawn.

In some instances, individual senators can be very influential in appointments to the bureaucracy. Several of the officials on independent regulatory commissions owed their appointments to the support of the late Senator Dirksen of Illinois, who, as Minority Leader, forced President Nixon to withdraw the nomination of Dr. John Knowles as assistant Secretary of Health, Education, and Welfare, even though he was the first choice of the departmental secretary, Robert Finch.

The other major power affecting the staffing of the bureaucracy, namely, the ability to *remove* persons from office who are not performing satisfactorily, is not provided for at all by the Constitution. Three of the Founders had differing views on the subject. James Madison took the position that removal was part of the executive power, while Thomas Jefferson said it was a matter that Congress had the authority to determine. Alexander Hamilton took an intermediate position, arguing that removal was linked to appointment: the same person or persons who were involved in the process of choosing an appointee

* Woodrow Wilson even consulted with senators of the opposite party (Republican). However, more typically, if there are no senators of the president's party from a state, he will consult with members of the state congressional delegation from his party or the chairman of the state party organization or other persons prominent in state-party affairs.

should also be entitled to participate in the appointee's removal. If the person was appointed by the president alone, the chief executive could remove the appointee from office; if the appointee had been confirmed by the Senate, then that body would have to consent to the person's removal.

Generally speaking, the Congress has been willing to allow the president to remove officials from office. The Tenure of Office Act of 1867 forbade the removal of officers appointed with the consent of the Senate, unless the Senate also agreed to the removal, and President Andrew Johnson's defiance of the act in removing Secretary of War Stanton was made a major ground of the impeachment action initiated against him. The failure of the Senate to convict the president left the issue unresolved, as no case challenging the act was brought before the Supreme Court.

Ultimately, however, the Court became involved in the issue. President Wilson removed a postmaster general from office, and some years later, in *United States* v. *Meyer* (1926), the Court—speaking through Chief Justice Taft, himself a former president—upheld Wilson's action as an executive prerogative, thus supporting the view of Madison on removal. However, when Franklin Roosevelt later removed a member of the Federal Trade Commission for the reasons not set forth in the governing statute ("malfeasance" and "misfeasance" in office) but because his political philosophy regarding the governmental regulation of business differed from Roosevelt's own, the Court struck down FDR's action as unconstitutional in *Humphrey's Executor* v. *United States* (1935). The Court distinguished the latter case from the former one on two grounds: (1) unlike the Post Office Department, the FTC "occupies no place in the executive department" (the justices did not say, however, what "place" the commission *did* occupy), and (2) the commission exercises not only executive but quasi-legislative and quasi-judicial functions. Thus officials of regulatory commissions and other agencies involved in such activities* can be removed from office only for the reasons set forth by Congress.

"G" Man supreme—J. Edgar Hoover.

It should be understood, however, that the removal of government officials involves not only *legal* but highly *political* considerations as well. Even when chief executives possess the power to remove a person from office, they may be reluctant to do so because of the person's political popularity. Thus a number of presidents of both political parties tolerated a variety of independent actions by the former head of the Federal Bureau of Investigation J. Edgar Hoover, primarily because they feared that his dismissal would hurt them politically. Conversely, a number of years ago a member of the Federal Communications Commission, accused of favoring the awarding of a television franchise to a station in which he had a financial interest, resigned voluntarily in order to save President Eisenhower (who had appointed him) from political embarrassment.

Frequently it is the Congress rather than the president that is actually responsible for officials leaving office. While the national legislature does not generally have the *direct authority* to remove such officials (the exception being the extraordinary process of impeachment), congressional investigations can have the *indirect effect* of accomplishing that purpose. Thus both Dwight Eisenhower and Richard Nixon had their closest political associates (the former, Sherman Adams; the latter, H. R.

* In a 1958 case, *Weiner* v. *U. S.*, the Supreme Court invalidated President Eisenhower's removal of a member of the War Claims Commission (he wanted to appoint a person of his own choice) on the grounds that the agency was one of "intrinsic judicial character."

Haldeman and John Ehrlichman) driven from office against their will because of the heat generated against them by congressional committees. The first administrator of the Environmental Protection Agency in the Reagan administration, Anne Gorsuch Burford, resigned for the same reason. Congress can also financially starve agencies headed by officials whom they disapprove of or have the officials' functions transferred to another unit. Such actions led Harold Seidman, a veteran of the Washington bureaucracy for almost a quarter-century, to conclude that ". . . probably more executive-branch officials have been fired or reassigned as a result of pressure from Congress than by the President."

Thus the president and Congress jointly determine the operation of the bureaucracy, providing it with the structure, the funds, and the staff needed to carry out a wide variety of government programs. The following section focuses on the first aspect of that operation—the organization of the bureaucracy.

THE ORGANIZATION OF THE EXECUTIVE BRANCH

We have already seen that one of the hallmarks of bureaucracy is a division of labor that facilitates specialization by function or task. Nowhere is that principle more evident than in the organization of the executive branch as represented in Figure 12.1. As the figure shows, a great variety of units dealing with different types of matters are included within the executive arm of the national government. It is possible, however, to place these units into several broad categories based on the essential functions and tasks they perform, as well as on the legal and political relationships that they enjoy with the president, the Congress, and interests outside the government itself.

The White House Office

Closest to the president are the members of the **White House Office,** a part of the larger Executive Office of the President. They are, in the phrase of Patrick Anderson, "the president's men": he appoints them without the necessity of senatorial approval, assigns them whatever duties he deems appropriate, and removes them when they no longer serve his purposes. (The election of a new chief executive generally means a complete turnover in the composition of the White House Office.) Moreover, as the president's men, they are not subject to interrogation by congressional committees.

The White House Office is organized to assist the president in his numerous tasks. Included are those assistants who write his speeches, arrange his appointments, plan his trips, facilitate his relationships with the press and other media, and smooth his way in dealings with Congress, with other executive branch officials, with political-party officials, and with interest-group representatives. Others advise him on matters of public policy, such as national security and economic and domestic affairs. Although their tasks vary, they share a common concern: the welfare of the president. As Theodore Sorensen, a former aide to President Kennedy, described their responsibilities: "We were appointed for our ability to fulfill the President's needs and talk the President's language. We represented no man but John Kennedy."

The White House staff is populated with people whom the president knows well personally and in whom he has great trust and confidence. During the Kennedy administration, men like Sorensen (who was formerly on Kennedy's Senate staff), were much in evidence, along with Arthur Schlesinger Jr., with whom the president had close intellectual ties. Also represented were political campaign associates like Lawrence O'-

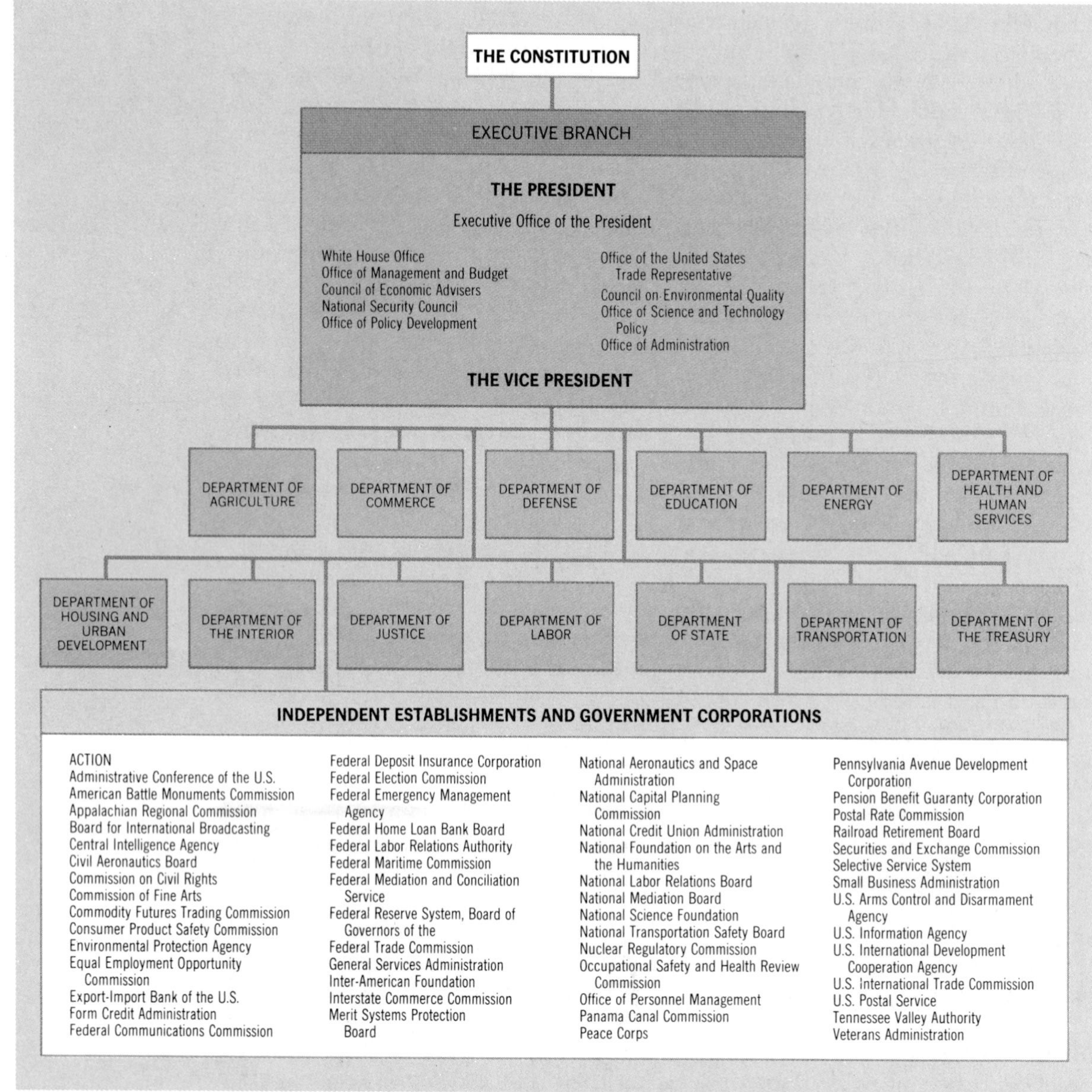

Figure 12.1 The Executive Branch of the U. S. Government.
SOURCE: The National Archives and Records Services, General Services Administration.

Brien. Nixon also appointed to his White House Office people he knew intimately, including Robert Finch and H. R. Haldeman, long-time friends from California politics; Bryce Harlow, who served in the Eisenhower White House Office while Nixon was vice president; and Leonard Garment, a former New York law partner, who was also a major figure in the 1968 presidential campaign. Gerald Ford's White House staff included Philip Buchan and William Seidman from his home state of Michigan; Donald Rumsfeld and Rogers Morton, former associates in the House of Representatives; and Robert Hartman, who served as his chief of staff when he was vice president. Of the seven highest-level aides of Jimmy Carter when he first took office, six were Georgians, including Presidential Assistant Hamilton Jordan, director of his 1976 presidential campaign, and Press Secretary Jody Powell, who had worked with Carter since his 1970 gubernatorial campaign. Two of the three major figures in the Reagan administration, Edwin Meese and Michael Deaver, were Californians who had long been associated with Reagan's political career.*

* The third member of what was referred to as the "troika," was James Baker, a Texan, who had previously been associated politically with two of Reagan's political rivals, Gerald Ford and George Bush.

Flexibility is the major characteristic of the White House Office organization. Presidents Kennedy and Truman had relatively few persons in major positions in the Office—on the average, about 15; Eisenhower and Nixon generally used more than twice that number.† Positions also change. For the one traditional press secretary, Nixon substituted two: Ronald Ziegler was made special assis-

† The White House Office staff mushroomed during the first Nixon administration: the total number of employees was 311 in 1970; one year later it was 600. It remained close to that level after Gerald Ford assumed the presidency and actually increased during the early months of the Carter administration despite the president's vow to reduce its size. In March 1984 the Reagan White House Office staff numbered 366.

President Reagan and his White House Aides ponder a problem.

tant for press relations, and Herbert Klein, who was made director of communications for the executive branch, was responsible for supervising and coordinating public statements made by units throughout the branch.

Frequently one individual emerges as the most important figure in the White House Office. This person may perform a variety of tasks for the president. Theodore Sorensen was a jack-of-all-trades for John Kennedy (who referred to him as his "intellectual blood bank"): he wrote the president's speeches, helped formulate his legislative program, and acted as his troubleshooter on a variety of public-policy issues. William Moyers performed a similarly broad array of duties for Lyndon Johnson, including a short stint as his press secretary. Or the president may place such a person in charge of the White House Office; although originally opposed to the idea, in the third year of his administration, Jimmy Carter made Hamilton Jordan his chief of staff in order to centralize authority in the Office. In making decisions about the internal organization and operation of the White House Office, the president applies a single criterion: "What is likely to serve my personal political interests most effectively?"

Other Units in the Executive Office of the President

The other units shown in Figure 12.1 that are also located in the **Executive Office of the President** have close relationships with the president, but their personnel are not so much "the president's men." For example, their appointments must be confirmed by the Senate. Moreover, while the top officials in these units leave with a change in administration, many lower-level employees remain. Persons who serve in these posts tend to be specialists in their particular areas of responsibility, not generalists who occupy the positions in the White House Office. (Members of the Council of Economic Advisers are unlikely to be switched to another position in the Executive Office as are White House aides.) The president is less likely to be personally familiar with them and frequently accepts recommendations from others about who would, for example, make a good chairman of the Council of Economic Advisers. Symbolically, White House staff people are generally located in the White House itself while others in the Executive Office are housed in a separate building across the street.

Most important of the units located in the Executive Office of the President is the **Office of Management and Budget.** Known as the Bureau of the Budget prior to its reorganization by President Nixon in 1970, the agency concentrated its efforts on helping the chief executive prepare his budget and legislative recommendations. It also assisted him in making decisions on whether or not to veto a bill: the agency's procedure was to get the reaction of executive-branch units to the bill in question and then to give its own recommendation on the matter. Nixon extended the organization's responsibilities to include other aspects of executive management, including the evaluation and coordination of existing government programs, improvement of executive-branch organization, the devising of information and management systems, and the development of executive talent.

Three other units in the Executive Office are especially important in providing advice and helping the president coordinate a wide variety of governmental activities. The **Council of Economic Advisers** is composed of three professional economists who advise the chief executive on his annual Economic Report to the nation and the economic policies that his administration should pursue. The **National Security Council** advises the president on foreign, military, and domestic policy aspects of the nation's security. A comparable group, the **Office of Policy Development** (formerly known as the Domestic Policy Staff), composed of officials concerned with the country's internal problems, performs a similar integrating function for the president. Thus the Executive Office includes agencies responsible for initiating and coordinating programs in three broad areas of public policy with which the president is concerned—the economy, national security, and domestic affairs.

Also included in the Executive Office of the President are agencies to deal with problems that are thought to require special presidential attention. Thus the Office of Economic Opportunity was originally located in the Office, reflecting President Johnson's particular concern with his major Great Society programs. During the Nixon administration, special units were created to concentrate on environmental quality, consumer affairs, telecommunications policy, and drug-abuse prevention. Gerald Ford added a Council on Wage and Price Stability and another on Presidential Clemency. Frequently, however, such specialized agencies are favorites of a particular chief executive and may not be so highly regarded by his successor: President Nixon first transferred some operations of the OEO—an agency he inherited—to other units in the bureaucracy and then tried to kill the OEO altogether; in turn, Nixon's own agencies on drug-abuse prevention and telecommunications policy were deemphasized by Gerald Ford and eliminated altogether in the Carter administration.

The Cabinet Departments

The next general category of units in terms of closeness to the president is the 13 departments granted **cabinet** rank by Congress. The heads of these departments (called *secretaries*) are appointed by the president with the consent of the Senate. As previously suggested, however, only rarely does the Senate refuse to confirm a president's nominee for a cabinet post; it is his right to choose cabinet officers and to remove them if he is dissatisfied with the way they are performing. When a new president comes into office, an entirely new cabinet team generally comes in with him.*

Although Congress does not generally interfere with the president's selections for the cabinet, other factors place some real limitations on his choices. For one thing, some cabinet posts require special experience and expertise: the Secretary of the Treasury, for example, must have a broad knowledge of financial affairs. The president is also expected to introduce some partisan balance into the makeup of the cabinet. The losing faction at the previous national convention is often permitted to name some cabinet officials: several "Taft men," for instance, were included in Eisenhower's initial cabinet. Similarly, both liberal and conservative elements of a party are usually represented. If a national crisis exists or an election is close, the president may even include members of the opposition party in his cabinet: Franklin Roosevelt's wartime cabinet included two Republicans; John Kennedy, and eventually Richard Nixon, chose persons of the opposite party for cabinet posts, as did Ronald Reagan, who picked Jeane Kirkpatrick, a Democrat, as Ambassador to the United Nations, a post that carries cabinet rank.

A former member of Congress is usually included, presumably to help

* A vice president who succeeds to the office of president is likely to keep the same team for the transition period, as Lyndon Johnson did after John Kennedy's assassination and as Gerald Ford did after Richard Nixon's resignation.

President Reagan's top team.

the president establish good relationships with that body. Most chief executives, have considered it politic to include a southerner in the cabinet; traditionally the Secretary of Interior comes from the western part of the United States, where most of the vast public lands under the department's jurisdiction are located. In fact, many of the departments have a "clientele" that is, particular groups that they serve:* thus the Commerce Department caters to business and the Department of Labor to the working person. In making appointments to these cabinet positions, the president takes into account the attitudes of interest groups toward the person who is to head the department: he would not, for example, appoint a Secretary of Agriculture who is unacceptable to the farmers of the country.†

Four of the 13 departments, however—State, Defense, Treasury, and Justice—do not have as specialized a clientele as the other nine departments. The first departments to be established in the federal government, their func-

* The composition of the cabinet reflects the political power of various interest groups: one sign that a group has arrived politically is the establishment of a cabinet-level department to serve its needs.

† There has also been a tendency in recent years to appoint persons from certain groups to the cabinet, even though they do not constitute clientele of particular departments. Thus Reagan's cabinet included in addition to Ambassador Kirkpatrick, two other women, Elizabeth Dole, Secretary of Transportation, and Margaret Hecker, Secretary of Health and Human Services, as well as a black, Samuel Pierce, Secretary of Housing and Urban Development.

tions relate to general problems of governance rather than the needs of a particular segment of our society. Because their activities are so basic, presidents typically pay more attention to these four departments and are inclined to place "strong" persons in such positions. Thus the two most prominent persons in the Eisenhower cabinet were Secretary of State John Foster Dulles and George Humphrey, the Secretary of the Treasury; Robert McNamara, the Secretary of Defense, and Attorney General Robert Kennedy were the most powerful members of the Kennedy administration; and Attorney General John Mitchell and Secretary of State Henry Kissinger were the leading figures in the Nixon administration.

One close student of the subject, political scientist Thomas Cronin, suggests that the Secretaries of State, Defense, Treasury, and the Attorney General constitute an **"inner" cabinet** in contrast to the **"outer" cabinet** (i.e., the heads of the other nine departments). The former are closer to the presidential orbit in terms of sharing his general perspective on problems; because of this, they have a "counseling" role with the chief executive. In contrast, the latter represent special interests that the president would like to subordinate to general concerns of his administration; as a result of this basic conflict, members of the outer cabinet are more likely to adopt an "advocate's" (rather than a "counseling") role with the president.

The Independent Agencies

The independent offices and establishments listed in Figure 12.1 are all "independent" in the sense that they are not part of any cabinet department, but their degree of independence from the president and the Congress varies. There are four major types of these **independent agencies.**

One type performs a specific function and is headed by *one administrator;* examples are the National Aeronautics and Space Administration and the Veterans Administration. Their relationships with the president parallel those of cabinet departments.* Major administrators are appointed by the chief executive with the consent of the Senate and are removable by his action alone. Even so, the heads of these independent agencies frequently stay in office after a new president takes over; the late General Lewis Hershey, for example, served as head of the Selective Service System for a succession of presidents of both political parties until he retired because of age. Seidman describes the administrations of such agencies as occupying a "no-man's land" between the "President's men" and "agencies of the Congress."

Included in the latter type by Seidman are the six *independent regulatory agencies,* which are administered through boards rather than single administrative heads.† This general group of agencies includes the Civil Aeronautics Board (CAB), Federal Communications Commission (FCC), Federal Maritime Commission (FMC), Federal Trade Commission (FTC), Interstate Commerce Commission (ICC), and the Securities and Exchange Commission (SEC). The members of these boards are less subject to presidential control because they have fixed terms (five to seven years) and cannot be removed by the president except for causes set forth in the statute creating each agency. Moreover, the commissioners' terms are usually "staggered" (that is, overlapping) so that few (if any) expire simul-

* Some cabinet departments were originally independent agencies that acquired cabinet status when they became more important politically.

† It is considered to be easier for a president to influence the thinking of a single administrator than to affect the attitudes of a multimember board.

taneously. This combination of lengthy, staggered terms and removal only for cause makes board members relatively free from presidential control and influence.

The rationale for insulating these commissions from presidential control is that they are concerned with regulating activities of major private industries and so should be free of partisan politics that might interfere with their objectivity and fairness. (Most boards are required to be composed of members of both major parties.) The result of this policy, however, is to create a political vacuum into which other forces rush, including not only members of Congress, but also groups supposedly regulated by the agencies. Thus the railroads take a great interest in the Interstate Commerce Commission, which regulates the fares that they charge and the routes that they follow, and television-station owners exert influence over the Federal Communications Commission, which determines the conditions that they must meet to obtain and retain their licenses. As a result, the special interests that are supposedly regulated by government agencies frequently end up controlling the regulators.

Included in the third major category of independent agencies are the **government corporations,** exemplified by the Tennessee Valley Authority and the United States Postal Service, agencies that are relatively free of control by either the president or the Congress. Because these agencies perform commercial functions (the TVA builds dams and channels, and produces and sells electrical power, while the Postal Service distributes mail), they are organized along the lines of a private corporation, with a governing board that makes policy for the unit. Like the commissioners of the independent regulatory agencies, the board members of government corporations are appointed by the president with the consent of the Senate and serve long, staggered terms to prevent any one president from controlling the activities of those units. Furthermore the corporations are less subject to financial control by the president or the Congress than are other executive departments and agencies because they are not dependent on annual appropriations for their operations. Rather, long-term appropriations are provided (Congress, for example, committed itself to a 15-year funding program for the Postal Service); in addition, corporations furnish some of their own financing (the Postal Service uses revenues that it generates from its own activities and is also empowered to borrow money by issuing bonds). Government corporations are therefore free of the usual process of defending their estimates for the coming fiscal year before the Office of Management and Budget, the president, and the Congress. Although their operations are reviewed annually by all three, since the corporations are not requesting funds, the scrutiny tends to be less severe than it is for other executive units.

The final type of independent agency includes those providing *central services and controls* such as the Office of Personnel Management and the General Services Administration. The former establishes overall policies and guidelines governing such matters as the recruitment, classification, evaluation, promotion, and termination of all employees covered by the merit system described in the following section. The latter controls buildings, supplies, transportation and communications facilities, and records utilized by all agencies. The OPM and the GSA provide services to and regulate the activities of other governmental units rather than the private individuals and groups with which most public agencies are concerned.

Thus as political scientist Stephen Bailey has suggested, the executive branch is a "many-splintered" thing, comprising a variety of organizations with different functions and different legal and political relationships with the president, Congress, and outside groups. The employees of these organizations collectively constitute the executive-branch personnel, the bureaucrats.

THE BUREAUCRATS

As we have seen, federal bureaucrats have become an inviting target of criticism for politicians and citizens alike. For one thing, their numbers are thought to rise dramatically every year. For another, a popular stereotype exists of the federal bureaucrat as a petty clerk employed by the Department of Health and Human Services and who is located in Washington, D. C.

As a matter of fact, the realities of public employment contradict both of the above assumptions. Rather than swelling in numbers, the size of the federal bureaucracy has been comparatively stable in recent years. In 1955 some 2.4 million civilians worked for the national government; by 1969 that figure had grown to 3 million; in 1984 it was 2.9 million.* Measured as a proportion of the total U. S. work force (which grew considerably over the period of two decades), the percentage of federal employees actually declined from 4 percent in 1955 to 3 percent in 1982.

Nor does the stereotype of the clerk square with the great variety of occupations in the federal service. Employees of the national government represent a great variety of skills, similar to those possessed by persons who work in private enterprise. White-collar employees run the gamut from professionally trained doctors, lawyers, and engineers to persons involved in more traditional clerical and general office duties. Moreover, 450,000 federal employees (about one-sixth of the total) are blue-collar workers who operate mobile industrial equipment, do manual labor, repair aircraft, and engage in other trades.

As indicated by Table 12.1, it is *not* Health and Human Services that harbors the most federal employees; it is Defense. The latter, with over 1 million *civilian* employees, has more than seven times as many persons working for it as does HHS, which does not even have as many employees as two of the major independent agencies, the Postal Service and the Veterans Administration. These three largest units of the federal government (Defense, Postal Service, and the Veterans Administration) together employed over 1.9 million of the 2.9 million civilians that worked for the national government in 1984.

Nor are federal civilian workers concentrated in the area of Washington, D. C. as is commonly supposed; 352,000 (or one in nine) lived there in 1984. The rest were located in every state in the country. Almost as many resided in California as in the nation's capital; over 139,000 lived outside the United States.

Thus the federal bureaucracy is composed of persons with a wide variety of occupational skills who work in diverse agencies (see Figure 12.1) and are located in every state of the Union as well as abroad. The compensation they receive for their services also varies greatly: cabinet members in 1983 received $80,100 a year, while persons at the lowest levels of the pay scale earned only about $9000. Despite this broad range of persons with different occupational, educational, and social backgrounds, it is possible to place these various types in two broad categories. One is composed of those who dedicate themselves to public service (career ser-

* This situation is contrasted with the rapid growth of public employees at the state and local level from 43.5 million in 1955 to over 13 million in 1982.l

Table 12.1
Number of Civilians Employed by Cabinet Departments and Selected Independent Agencies (March 1984)

Unit	Employees
Cabinet Departments	
Agriculture	113,661
Commerce	34,837
Defense	1,045,710
Education	5,261
Energy	17,197
Health and Human Services	145,906
Housing and Urban Development	12,584
Interior	74,240
Justice	60,179
Labor	19,143
State	24,180
Transportation	62,243
Treasury	134,544
Independent Agencies	
U. S. Postal Service	673,214
Veterans Administration	239,956

SOURCE: U. S. Office of Personnel Management, Monthly Release of Federal Civilian Workforce Statistics, pp. 10, 11, 13.

vice) and enjoy security of tenure in their job. The other comprises persons in political posts in the bureaucracy who typically come into office for a limited period and then generally move on to positions in private enterprise or other jobs in public life.

The Career Service

The principle that federal employees should hold positions on the basis of merit rather than as a reward for their political activities first became established as a matter of law with the passage of the Pendleton Act in 1883. Over the years this principle has become so accepted that today almost all employees of the executive branch are under one or another kind of merit system for selection and tenure. Over 2 million are governed by the rules of the Office of Personnel Management regulating entrance requirements and general working conditions. In addition, some federal agencies, because of their special needs, have their own merit systems. Included in this group are such well-known organizations as the Federal Bureau of Investigation, the Central Intelligence Agency, the Nuclear Regulatory Commission, the Tennessee Valley Authority, the U. S. Postal Service, and the Foreign Service.

These various merit systems operate on similar principles. Persons are hired on the basis of their abilities. Generally this means performing well on a competitive examination: agencies are typically authorized to fill a vacancy from among the three candidates scoring highest on the test. Not all examinations are competitive, however; if a job calls for professional or technical skills that are in relatively short supply, it may be filled by someone who gets a minimum score on the examination. Some posi-

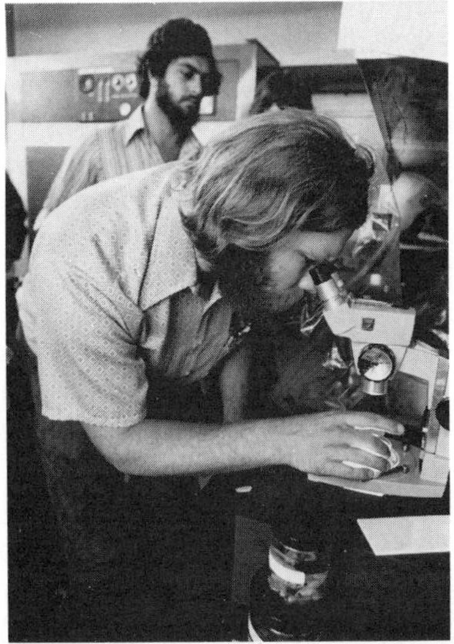

Who says government workers are all paper pushers?

tions that involve policy-making or confidential relationships with high government officials may require no examination at all.

Working conditions are governed by definite rules and procedures. Positions and pay are ranked on the basis of difficulty as reflected in the **General Schedule** (G. S. 1 through G. S. 6 constitute lower-grade positions; G. S. 7–G. S. 12, middle-grade; G. S. 13–G. S. 18, higher-grade) that governs all organizations coming under the jurisdiction of the Office of Personnel Management. (Agencies with their own merit systems use similar methods for classifying positions.) In-service training is provided for employees,* and promotions are based on performance on the job. A career employee can be dismissed only for "cause" after procedural safeguards (hearings and the like) have been satisfied.

Critics of the merit system charge that it is essentially a negative one that rewards docile functionaries who carefully fulfill its numerous requirements (including filling out countless forms and reports) rather than imaginative persons who relish innovation and experimentation in the public's business. While such a blanket charge against all public servants is undoubtedly exaggerated, the fact remains that the civil service system does seem to appeal to persons concerned with job tenure and security. The turnover rate for federal employees is much lower than it is for private industry. Moreover, there is a tendency for employees to stay in the same agency and to rise in its hierarchy through seniority rather than transferring to better positions in another organization in the executive branch.

In 1978, at the urging of President Carter, Congress passed a civil service reform bill providing the most extensive revision of federal employment since the civil service system was established in 1883. It assigned the former responsibilities of the Civil Service Commission to two new agencies, the Office of Personnel Management, which now handles matters such as examinations, training and the administration of salary and other benefits, and the Merit Systems Protection Board, which hears most appeals and complaints from federal employees or applicants. The new law also created a Senior Executive Service of top federal managers and policymakers who receive cash bonuses for high-level performance (rather than automatic pay raises for longevity of service), have less secure tenure than civil-service employees, and who are more subject to transfer from one agency to another. Middle-level employees (G. S.–13 through G. S.–15) are also now entitled to receive merit pay on top of their automatic raises based on length of service. Finally, the 1978 law grants federal managers somewhat more flexibility in firing incompetent employees.

Traditionally, federal employees have been expected to give up certain liberties enjoyed by persons working in the private sector, particularly the right to engage in political activities. In recent years, however, federal employees (like their counterparts at the state and local levels) have become much less willing to accept such restrictions and have made concerted efforts to get them lifted.

Restrictions on political activities of federal career employees have been imposed under the rationale that such restrictions are necessary to preserve a neutral civil service, free from partisan influences. Regulations of the Office of Personnel Management, together with the Hatch Act passed by Congress in 1939, protect federal employees from being coerced into making financial contributions or working in a partisan campaign. They also prohibit employees from voluntarily participating in many political activities. At the same time, federal employees do retain certain rights, including that of voting and expressing their opinions on political matters.

In recent years some **career service** employees have taken the position that limitations on their political rights interfere with their First Amendment freedoms. However, their attempt to have existing restrictions declared unconstitutional on that ground was rejected by

* One notable example is the Federal Executive Institute, which conducts intensive eight-week sessions led by academic and career professionals for upper-level executives (those in G. S. 16–G. S. 18 positions).

the Supreme Court in *U. S. Civil Service Commission* v. *National Association of Letter Carriers* (1973), upholding the Hatch Act. Subsequently they turned to the legislative arena to accomplish their purposes. In 1976 the Democratic Congress passed legislation that would have allowed public employees to participate in partisan campaigns and run for office, but President Ford successfully vetoed the bill. Since that time, Congress has been unwilling to reenact such legislation.

Political Executives

"Political Executives" are those who hold policy-making positions, among them officials of the Executive Office of the President, secretaries of cabinet departments, and the heads of independent offices and establishments. They also include second- and third-level officials, such as assistant and under-secretaries of departments and heads of certain subsidiary bureaus, administrations, divisions, and services. All told, only about 700 persons serve as federal political executives.

Recruiting and retaining capable persons for these positions constitutes one of the major personnel problems faced by the federal service. Typically, a newly elected president chooses some knowledgeable person to lead a talent search for able men and women in private industry, state and local government, or academe to fill the top posts in the bureaucracy. While many are flattered by such requests, they must obtain leaves of absence from their present positions and, if they are persons employed by industry, generally take a cut in salary as well. Moreover, even if such persons agree to come to Washington, they often leave shortly,* sometimes, for financial reasons to accept better-paying positions in private industry or even, in some cases, in state or local governments.

Such losses have severe consequences because while political executives are relatively few in number, they are vital to the functioning of the government. They bear the responsibility of converting political goals into concrete programs and results. Because of their role, they are seldom technicians or specialists; rather they are "politicians" who spend most of their time dealing with individuals and groups, both inside and outside government, that can help or impede their mission.

The single most important official to a political executive is, of course, the *president,* to whom in most instances the political executive ultimately owes his or her appointment. In turn, the executive's own power to appoint and remove major subordinate political officials is dependent on support from the president. How his or her unit stands within the executive branch also frequently depends on the actions taken by the president under a reorganization statute authorized by Congress. The executive also depends on the president's recommendations for financing and legislative proposals.

Given the vast responsibilities of the president, it is natural that a political executive has relatively few, if any, direct contacts with the chief executive. Accordingly, he or she must spend time cultivating the persons around the president, particularly those on the *White House staff* and in the *Office of Management and Budget.* Political executives also have some contact with their counterparts in other agencies. However, as political scientist Hugh Heclo notes, they seldom are around long enough or trust each other enough to really get to know each other. Heclo refers to this as a "government of strangers."

As we have seen, *Congress* shares all the major powers that affect the bu-

* The average tenure of under-secretaries or assistant secretaries is less than two years.

Drawing by Gerberg; © 1980. The New Yorker Magazine, Inc.

reaucracy with the president. Senators can block presidential appointments and, in some instances, themselves determine who will be placed in charge of government agencies. Members of Congress can also force executive officials out of office through investigations. While the chief executive can propose the budget for each agency, the Congress ultimately determines the moneys that will actually be appropriated for its operations. Under the Congressional Budget and Impoundment Control Act of 1974, Congress can force the president to spend those moneys. Finally, the Congress has the final say over which agency will administer a particular program as well as over the internal operation of that agency.

While the entire Congress ultimately affects how an agency fares, a political executive is most concerned with the *committees* and *subcommittees* that have special power over his or her organization. Included are those that deal with the substantive policy area in which the agency operates, pass on its budget requests, and oversee its administration. A political executive must establish good relations with particular committee and subcommittee chairmen as well as with important members of congressional staffs, on whom the chairmen depend heavily for information and advice.

Thus political executives are subject to the actions of both the president and the Congress. In a very real sense they must serve two political masters. Further, they find themselves competing with their counterparts in other executive agencies over scarce funds and jurisdiction. Thus for many years the Forest Service in the Department of Agriculture and the National Park Service in the Department of the Interior have vied for the control of vacant lands, particularly in the western part of the United States. Similarly, the Defense Department's Army Corps of Engineers and the Interior Department's Bureau of Reclamation have battled for the right to develop the waterways of the nation.

Under such circumstances, a political executive finds it necessary to secure political allies outside as well as inside the formal structure of government. One natural outside source is his or her *"clientele."* Thus the Veterans Administration establishes close relationships with the American Legion and the Veterans of Foreign Wars, and the Department of Education does the same with the National Educational Association, the American Federation of Teachers, and other professional educators. The support of such interest groups can prove to be very useful in the political process.

Many political executives also seek to build a broader basis of outside support than that provided by special-interest groups; they look to the *general public* as well. Perhaps best known for its activities in this regard is the Federal Bureau of Investigation. As many visitors to Washington, D. C. know, one of the most interesting tours of governmental agencies is provided by the Bureau. It has also succeeded in making itself the subject of many magazine articles, books, movies, and even television series, which extol the virtues of the "G-men." In the process its former director, J. Edgar Hoover, became a Washington legend, virtually immune from control not only by the attorney general of the United States, of whose office the bureau is a part (witness the difficulties between Hoover and attorneys general Robert Kennedy and Ramsey Clark), but by the president of the United States.

While political executives spend most of their time courting outside individuals and groups, they have another important constituency they must also cultivate: *the employees of their own agencies.* Particularly important are senior civil servants who generally have served a long time. With their superior knowledge of their agencies' internal operations—as well as of the personnel and procedures of other executive agencies, key congressional committees and subcommittees, and concerned interest groups—these permanent employees are in a position either to facilitate or impede the policies and desires of the political executives. Lower-level employees also look to the political executives for leadership and expect them to protect the agencies' interests in perennial battles involving adequate funding for and jurisdiction over important government programs.

Maintaining good relations with all these individuals and groups is a difficult and delicate task for political executives. In many instances they are subject to competing demands. The president may cut an agency's budget, while the chairman of a key congressional committee or subcommittee may advise the political executive to work behind the scenes with him to help get the cut restored. The chief executive may advise the executive to tone down efforts to enforce rules and regulations against business concerns, while senior civil servants and other employees of the agency urge increased enforcement as necessary to preserve the essential mission of their organization.

Political executives placed under such cross pressures must decide how to deal with the situation. With skillful maneuvering they may be able to steer a compromise course of action that will satisfy the contending parties. However, in some cases compromise is not possible, and they must favor one side over another. An executive's loyalty to or shared political philosophy with the president—or ambition for other more important assignments in the executive branch—may be reason for throwing his or her lot in with the chief executive. Conversely, a calculation that a powerful committee or subcommittee chairman will be around longer than the president—or an executive's conversion to the values and mission of the agency as seen by its permanent employees—may result in a decision to go against the wishes of the president who appointed him or her.

The political executive who chooses the latter course of action will generally find ready allies outside his or her own agency. One source of support is the congressional committees and subcommittees that tend to favor the programs of the political executive's agency. Another is the interest groups that stand to benefit from such programs.

These three-way alliances of executive units, congressional committees and subcommittees, and interest groups are called **"iron triangles"** and **"policy subgovernments"** operating within the larger political system. However described, they point to the existence of enduring political relationships that advance common interests. For example, expanding and improving the services provided by the Veterans Administration increases the prestige and influence of its director and raises the morale of the agency's permanent employees; a program of better benefits for veterans also naturally pleases the American Legion and the Veterans of Foreign Wars. By the same token, such a program is usually favorably regarded by congressional committees and subcommittees involved with veterans' affairs, since senators and representatives generally seek assignments to committees that deal with matters in which they have a personal interest and to which they are sympathetic.

One of the major problems in controlling the bureaucracy is to prevent these triangles or subgovernments from dominating the making of public policy. The following section analyzes some of the major techniques that have been utilized to try to exercise control over these alliances and over other aspects of bureaucratic activities as well.

ATTEMPTS TO CONTROL THE BUREAUCRACY

We have seen that both the president and the Congress possess constitutional powers over the structure, financing, and personnel of the executive branch. By using these weapons judiciously and with an appreciation of the complexity of bureaucratic politics, both branches are in a position to exercise some control over the bureaucracy.

Presidential Attempts to Control the Bureaucracy

Although the president is the chief executive and administrator under our constitutional system, he can experience great difficulties in making members of the bureaucracy responsive to his wishes. Franklin Roosevelt, the epitome of a strong president, experienced great frustration in influencing administrators. Bemoaning his inability to get action and results from the Treasury and State departments, he went on to exclaim:

> *But the Treasury and State Departments put together are nothing compared with the Na-a-vy. The admirals are really something to cope with—and I should know. To change anything in the Na-a-vy is like punching a feather bed. You punch it with your right and you punch it with your left until you are finally exhausted, and then you find the damn bed just as it was before you started punching.*

A generation later another ambitious chief executive experienced similar difficulties. Arthur Schlesinger Jr. reports in his biography of John Kennedy that the resistance Kennedy encountered from executive officials was almost as great as the opposition he received from the members of Congress.

A number of factors contribute to the president's inability to control the bureaucracy. He can hardly be expected to supervise the activities of the almost 3 million persons on the executive-branch payroll in recent years. Moreover, he has no say at all in the appointment or the removal of the overwhelming number of them who come under one or more of the merit systems utilized for permanent civil servants. And while in theory he exercises such prerogatives over political executives, in reality his lack of first-hand knowledge of personnel matters is such that he must depend upon others for recommendations for appointments to high posts and for removing individuals who do not perform well in their jobs.

Adding to the problem of presidential control over the bureaucracy is the fact that the Congress shares all his major powers over the bureaucracy. The national legislators are in a position to thwart his reorganization plans, starve his favorite programs while taking good care of their own, investigate an agency he supports, and even to have some influence on who occupies the major policy-making posts in the executive branch.

Finally, and perhaps most important, is the conflict that exists between the values and perspectives of the president compared to those of what Schlesinger calls the "**permanent government.**" The chief executive typically takes a broad view of the nation's needs and is interested in fitting the activities of individual executive organizations into his overall political program. In doing so, he must establish a system of priorities that gives precedence to some governmental programs and agencies over others and that limits total governmental expenditures. His time frame is also shaped by the realities of electoral and congressional politics: he wants to implement his campaign promises before the next presidential election, when the voters will pass judgment on his performance in office, and he also knows that his best chance for success with Congress is during the honeymoon period just after he is inaugurated.

Members of the "permanent government" typically look at matters very differently from the president: their world is smaller than his. They are interested in their own agency and its programs and are unwilling to see them cut back in the interest of the president's overall system of priorities, economy, and efficiency. They are also less sensitive to political constraints and realities than the president and operate on a different calendar. While the chief executive thinks in terms of presidential terms and congressional sessions, they look at more long-range considerations, such as the past history and long-term future of a program, or the political lifespan of an agency head or congressional chairman.

All presidents face these same basic problems in controlling the bureaucracy. However, they react differently to such problems and develop diverse techniques to deal with them. The following discussion focuses on the methods employed by two presidents—one Democrat and one Republican—in attempting to tame the bureaucracy and convert it to their own purposes and goals.

Franklin Roosevelt. While Roosevelt is normally remembered as a powerful legislative leader and masterful manipulator of the press and public opinion, he was also an innovative administrator. He handled bureaucratic leaders essentially by playing them off against each other. FDR created overlapping responsibilities among different administrative units: work-relief programs came under the joint jurisdiction of Harry Hopkins, head of the Works Progress Administration, and Harold Ickes of the Public Works Administration. Termed the **competitive theory of administration,** his policy was deliberately designed to create rivalries between individuals, a practice that he justified on the basis that each person would therefore try to do a better job than his counterpart. (This technique also provided FDR with more information than he would have gained from any one person alone and so enabled him to stay on top of situations.) Roosevelt also frequently bypassed the chain of administrative command by dealing directly with assistant secretaries and bureau chiefs without

Secretary of Labor, Frances Perkins.

Harry Hopkins, Head of Works Progress Administration.

informing cabinet officials (their superiors) of such actions.

Roosevelt's use of his cabinet reflected his general philosophy of administration. His cabinet was made up of persons representing a broad spectrum of political persuasions, from the conservative Secretary of the Treasury, Will Wooden, to the liberal Frances Perkins (the first woman ever appointed to the cabinet), who served as Secretary of Labor. Given this diversity of political views, Roosevelt made no effort to utilize the cabinet as a policy-making or coordinating body. Rather he used it as a sounding board to test how actions he considered taking would be received by the various clientele groups represented by department heads sitting in the cabinet.

During the early years of World War II, FDR tried to do what no previous president had ever done: give important administrative responsibilities to his vice president. Henry Wallace was made chairman of a succession of economic boards entrusted with overseeing the production of war materiel. However, Wallace soon became embroiled in a series of battles with Secretary of State Cordell Hull and Secretary of Commerce Jesse Jones; Roosevelt ended the conflict within his administration by abolishing a key Wallace-headed board and transferring its responsibilities to a new agency under another chairman. So ended a noble experiment in making a vice president a highly important administrator, a practice that neither Roosevelt nor his successors would repeat.

A more successful tactic that FDR used to control the bureaucracy was to develop *his own counterbureaucracy.* Included in that latter category were heads of newly created agencies operating outside traditional departments, such as the Securities and Exchange commission (SEC) and the National Labor Relations Board (NLRB), which regulated the stock exchange and labor–management relations, respectively. Roosevelt also utilized free-wheeling "troubleshooters" like Thomas Corcoran and Harry Hopkins who, as the president's personal representatives, were given ad hoc assignments to cut red tape and overcome obstacles to the settlement of disputes in both domestic and foreign policy. As previously indicated, in 1939 with the creation of the Executive Office of the President, another form of FDR's personal bureaucracy became institutionalized.

Ronald Reagan. The Reagan administration that took office in 1981 took a number of actions designed to control the federal bureaucracy. One was to cut back on the unwieldy size of the White House Office staff. At the same time, responsibilities were centralized and divided to avoid internal conflicts. Edwin Meese was placed in charge of developing policy through his control of the Office of Policy Development. James Baker was named Chief of Staff with the responsibility of carrying out policy. Michael Deaver was assigned the task of scheduling the president's time and being his major adviser on political matters involving long-time presidential associates. Thus the troika of Meese, Baker, and Deaver became the nerve center of the White House Office and the Reagan administrative presidency.

The Reagan administration also devised a strategy for relating the activities of the White House Office to those of the cabinet. The mechanism for this purpose was *cabinet councils* for functional areas such as economic affairs, commerce and trade, human resources, natural resources and environment, and food and agriculture. Each such council was chaired by a staff member from the Office of Policy Development, who worked with members of the council in developing policy papers for handling matters of concern to the group. The designated cabinet secretary for each council chaired sessions to refine issues raised by such policy papers. Final policy decisions made by councils took place in sessions that were often chaired by President Reagan himself. Thus cabinet councils were designed to relate activities of individual executive departments to each other and to the general policies of the president and his White House Office staff.

The Reagan administration also took particular care in appointing political executives to choose persons who shared the ideology of the president, who would be loyal to him, and who would be willing to change traditional bureaucratic ways of doing things. All top-level appointments were cleared by the president's chief aide in charge of personnel and the White House troika of Meese, Baker, and Deaver. Cabinet members were also consulted on subcabinet appointments, and when they differed with the White House group on a particular appointment, the president himself was personally involved in discussions of the matter. The order in which appointments were made also reflected administration priorities: those for regulatory positions that were important to business were filled quickly, while appointments to agencies concerned with the rights of minorities, consumers, union members, and workers were filled much later or left vacant.

Finally, the Reagan administration was able to maintain the loyalty of committed political executives who resisted capture by the "permanent government" much better than executives in previous administrations. Breakfast meetings for large groups of subcabinet appointees were held, with the president and his top advisers serving as main speakers. (Such events were designed to mitigate the problems of a "government of strangers" referred to earlier.) Building on their ideological compatibility and better knowledge of each other, Reagan political executives behaved much differently than their predecessors: many proposed cuts in their agency's budget and transferred and removed employees they felt were not completely loyal to the President and his policy objectives. Some also made major policy changes in their departments: James Watt, Secretary of Interior, opened federal lands to coal and timber exploration and increased contracting for offshore oil drilling; Ann Gorsuch Burford, administrator of the Environmental Protection Agency, cut back enforcement actions and changed some federal regulations relating to air and water pollution.

Congressional Efforts to Control the Bureaucracy

Congress experiences some of the same difficulties in controlling the bureaucracy as the president. One of these problems is the sheer size of the establishment. For the national legislators, this fact of life is most graphically reflected in the difficult task of assessing the relative needs of hundreds of agencies with combined annual budgets of several hundred billion dollars. The fact that the appropriation for each agency is made each year results in legislators being overwhelmed by a task that is constantly with them.

Moreover, as previously suggested, Congress must share its powers over the bureaucracy with the president. Just as it may thwart his efforts, so too he may frustrate congressional attempts to control the executive branch through its authority over the structure, funding, and the personnel of the bureaucracy. This sharing of powers by the Congress and the president enables members of the bureaucracy to play off the constitutional rivals against one another.

Finally, Congress, like the president, faces the problem of controlling the iron triangles of government agencies, interest groups, and congressional committees and subcommittees. Although these last units are created by and subject to the authority of the entire body, the decentralized nature of congressional decision-making is such that the committees are granted considerable autonomy. As Herbert Kaufman, a student of legislative–executive relations suggests, the substantive and appropriations committees and their staffs typically develop "possessive and protective attitudes" toward government agencies with which they are associated. In return for the protection they provide such agencies, lawmakers receive reciprocal benefits: the location of facilities and programs in states and congressional districts of committee members; considerate treatment of their constituents who have business with the agencies; and influence over the hiring of job applicants by the bureaucracy.

Recently, however, the entire Congress has begun to make some efforts to establish better control over the bureaucracy and its interest group and committee allies. One important move in that direction was taken with the passage of the budget reform legislation of 1974. If Congress continues to discipline itself to stay within its overall budget limit and to require its authorization and appropriations committees to respect that total figure, this procedure should serve to restrict the budgets of individual agencies.

Another mechanism increasingly used by Congress in recent years to check the bureaucracy is the use of the **legislative veto.** This control tool has taken various forms, including the power of *both houses* of Congress to check executive actions by concurrent resolution (one *not* requiring the approval of the president), vesting that authority in *either chamber* by a simple resolution; or granting the power to do so to *certain committees* of either house. Such vetoes typically have granted the above groups a specified period of time (usually 60 or 90 days) to reverse an executive decision either by requiring that the legislators act *positively* to do so (as in dealing with presidential *deferments* of expenditures) or by specifying that the executive decision is ineffective after the designated time unless the legislators specifically approve that decision (as with presidential *rescissions* of expenditures). In use since 1932 (such vetoes typically appeared in executive branch reorganization legislation), nearly half of the approximately 200 provisions for congressional review of executive action have been placed in legislation passed since 1970. Moreover, such provisions have been aimed not only at presidential actions but also at decisions made by lower-level administrators.

In 1983 the Supreme Court seriously undercut Congress's use of the legislative veto. In *Immigration and Naturalization Service* v. *Chadha* the Court invalidated a veto by the House of Representatives of an action by the Service suspending the deportation of a Kenyan East Indian who had overstayed his student visa. In an opinion written by Chief Justice Warren Burger, the Court ruled that such a legislative veto was unconstitutional because it violated a procedure that requires that regular actions of Congress be approved by both houses and then be presented to the president for his signature or veto. Some students of the subject interpreted the decision narrowly to mean that one-house vetoes could not be used to nullify actions affecting one individual as was true in the *Chadha* case. However, one month later the Court in a brief statement affirmed two lower court decisions holding as unconstitutional legislative vetoes of actions affecting a broad range of persons taken by two independent regulatory commissions—the Federal Energy Regulatory Commission (FERC) and the Federal Trade Commission (FTC). (The FERC case involved an agency plan for deregulating natural gas prices; the FTC case grew out of a proposed rule requiring used car dealers to disclose information on auto defects before a sale takes place.) The fact that the legislative veto of the FTC regulations required action by *both* houses of Congress laid to rest the theory that the Court was only concerned about one-house legislative vetoes.

These judicial decisions set off a wave of reaction from members of Congress who debated what steps should be taken to deal with the Court's invalidating traditional forms of the legislative veto. Some advocated repealing all statutes containing unconstitutional legislative vetoes and rewriting them to limit power delegated to the executive branch. Others suggested that legislative vetoes be cast in a form that the Supreme Court would approve of, namely, a joint resolution passed by both houses of Congress that had to be signed by the president. Still others advocated adding amendments to appropriations bills to bar spending to carry out an agency regulation that Congress disliked, or the passage of a constitutional amendment overturning the Supreme Court decisions on legislative vetoes. As of mid-1984, Congress had not decided how to handle the situation raised by judicial decisions affecting the legislative veto.

In recent years Congress has also given consideration to still other controls over the bureaucracy. One is the establishment of **zero-based budgeting**—a system under which executive agencies would be required to justify all expenditures for the next fiscal year rather than simply to apply for an increase over the previous year's appropriation, the procedure presently followed. Tried experimentally in individual agencies, zero-based budgeting has yet to be adopted on a broad basis. A second type of control is **sunset legislation** which would place government programs on a definite schedule of congressional consideration: unless the Congress specifically authorized a program at the end of the designated period of time, it would automatically be terminated.* (The Senate recently passed such legislation providing for a comprehensive review of most federal spending programs every 10 years, but as yet the House has been unwilling to follow suit.) Patterned after similar laws already in effect in several states, zero-based budgeting and sunset provisions represent new approaches to the perennial congressional problem of taming the bureaucracy.

---

* A recent study by Herbert Kaufman showed that of a sample of 175 federal executive organizations in existence in 1923, 148 (85%) were still in operation in 1973. Moreover, in most cases the activities of the 27 units that did not survive were taken over by other agencies.

ASSESSMENT

As we saw at the outset of this chapter, the federal bureaucracy has recently become the favorite target of politician and citizen alike: both blame it for almost all the nation's ills. Yet ironically it is these same persons who have been primarily responsible for the development of the bureaucracy. The former have passed the laws authorizing governmental programs, providing the funds, and creating the organizations to carry them out. The latter have used their political influence, typically organized through interest groups, to see to it that federal programs are created to meet their needs.

In fact, a good case can be made for the fact that our diverse and "many-splintered" bureaucracy is not a catastrophe but a generally healthy development. Given the pluralistic nature of an American society composed of a broad variety of social and economic groups, it is natural that the bureaucracy should reflect and be receptive to such diverse interests. The growth in the number of government agencies and programs over the years has occurred because formerly disadvantaged groups have developed the political influence to have their interests represented in the executive branch of government along with more powerful economic interests that have traditionally been well-represented there.

There is, of course, a danger that special interests will become so well ensconced in the bureaucracy that they will be almost immune from effective control. There are, however, two major types of safeguards that serve to lessen that possibility. One is the fact that executive agencies and their congressional and interest-group allies are typically opposed by rival alliances, and the competition prevents any of them from becoming all-powerful. In Madison's terms, ". . . ambition is made to counteract ambition."

The other major control over the bureaucracy is the legal powers that elected officials possess over its activities. If disposed to exercise it, both the president and the Congress can utilize their authority over executive-branch organization, funding, and staffing to rein in a too-powerful bureaucracy. Moreover, recent developments indicate that both the chief executive and the national legislature have begun to exert concerted efforts to accomplish that purpose. Not all these efforts, however, have been salutary, and this is particularly true of recent presidential actions. Centralizing policy-making in the White House staff at the expense of the regular departments has some obvious disadvantages. One is the fact that members of that staff are often appointed for their contribution to presidential electoral politics and are inexperienced and lack knowledge about substantive policy issues as well as about the governmental process in general. They may also mistakenly interpret presidential election results as creating a "mandate" to undertake actions they personally favor but which the voters do not—the Reagan administration cut back on environmental protection and education programs at a time when polls showed strong public support for them. There is also the simple problem of manageability: trying to run the government almost entirely from the White House overloads the system at the center and strains the capacities of even the most able individuals. Finally, excessive centralization in the executive branch means that the advice of experienced and knowledgeable senior civil servants who are familiar with the day-to-day operation of government programs is ignored or discounted when important public-policy decisions are made.

Recent congressional attempts to establish better overall control of the executive budget are generally encouraging. It remains to be seen, however, whether legislators can handle this task effectively, along with their new responsibilities reviewing presidential impoundments. Even more questionable are proposals for zero-based budgeting and the periodic reauthorization of all government programs under the provisions of sunset laws. While certainly commendable in theory, they call for a kind of exhaustive scrutiny of the bureaucracy that may well be beyond the capacity of Congress. It would, indeed, be ironical if Congress in its zeal to control the executive-branch bureaucracy ended up creating its own unwieldy counterbureaucracy.

SELECTED READINGS

Reinhard Bendix's general treatment of the concept of bureaucracy appears under that title in the *International Encyclopedia of the Social Sciences,* 2d ed., vol. 2, pp. 206–19. An analysis of bureaucracy emphasizing technical expertise is Francis Rourke, *Bureaucracy, Politics, and Public Policy* (Boston: Little, Brown, 2d ed., 1976). Peter Woll, *American Bureaucracy* (New York: W. W. Norton, 1963), focuses on the legal aspects of bureaucracy. Emmette Redford approaches the subject from the standpoint of democratic theory in *Democracy in the Administrative State* (New York: Oxford University Press, 1969); and Harold Seidman concentrates on the political aspects of the bureaucracy in *Politics Position, and Power* (New York: Oxford University Press, 3d ed., 1980).

Louis Fisher, *Presidential Spending Power* (Princeton: Princeton University Press, 1975), emphasizes the historical development of that power. A political analysis of budget-making is Aaron Wildavsky, *The Politics of the Budgetary Process* (Boston: Little, Brown, 3d ed., 1979).

A classic study of the cabinet is Richard Fenno, *The President's Cabinet* (Cambridge: Harvard University Press, 1959). For an historical analysis of Senate action on presidential nominations, see Joseph Harris, *The Advice and Consent of the Senate* (Berkeley: University of California Press, 1952). An excellent recent study of the subject is G. Calvin Mackenzie, *The Politics of Presidential Appointments* (New York: The Free Press, 1981). Very good studies of close presidential advisers are Louis Koenig, *The Invisible Presidency* (New York: Holt, Rinehart, and Winston, 1960) and Patrick Anderson, *The President's Men* (Garden City, N. Y.: Anchor, 1969).

Very good studies of high-level civil servants and political executives include John Carson and R. Shael Paul, *Men Near the Top* (Baltimore: Johns Hopkins University Press, 1966); Dean Mann, *The Assistant Secretaries* (Washington, D. C.: The Brookings Institution, 1965); and Hugh Heclo, *A Government of Strangers: Executive Politics in Washington* (Washington, D. C.: The Brookings Institution, 1977).

Three excellent studies of the president's relationship to the bureaucracy are Thomas Cronin, *The State of The Presidency* (Boston: Little, Brown, 2d ed., 1980); Stephen Hess, *Organizing the Presidency* (Washington, D. C.: The Brookings Institution, 1976); and Richard Nathan, *The Administrative Presidency* (New York: John Wiley & Sons, Inc., 1983).

CHAPTER 13

The Courts

During the 1980 presidential campaign, both major party candidates—Democratic incumbent Jimmy Carter and Republican challenger Ronald Reagan—came under the scrutiny of women's groups that wanted more females appointed to federal judgeships. Because of that pressure, Reagan promised that ". . . one of the first Supreme Court vacancies in my administration will be filled by the most qualified woman I can find." Just six months after taking office the new president nominated Sandra Day O'Connor, an Arizona state judge, to fill the vacancy created by the retirement of Supreme Court Justice Potter Stewart, a 23-year veteran of the nation's highest tribunal.

O'Connor, then 51 years old, seemed to fit the president's description of "the most qualified woman I can find." Graduated *magna cum laude* from Stanford University with a degree in economics, she went on to Stanford Law School where she was third in her 1952 class, two places behind William Rehnquist, a sitting member of the Supreme Court. (Despite that record, when she applied to the law firm in which Reagan's Attorney General, William French Smith, was a partner, she was offered a job as a legal secretary.) For a few years, O'Connor held minor public legal offices and engaged in private practice, but curtailed her career after the birth of her second of three sons in order to spend time with her family. In 1965 she resumed her career by taking a position as assistant attorney general for Arizona and then went into politics. She served in the state senate, and eventually was elected majority leader, the first woman in the nation to hold such a post. She subsequently was elected judge of the Maricopa County Superior Court and in 1979 was appointed to the Arizona Court of Appeals by Democratic governor, Bruce Babbitt. She was holding this position when President Reagan nominated her for the High Court.

In addition to her general legal and political qualifications, O'Connor had some special attributes that recommended her to the President. She shared his general philosophy that judges should defer to the actions of legislative and executive officials, and like the President, favored shifting more responsibilities from the federal to the state courts. O'Connor also had some influential persons urging her nomination, including Arizona's senior Senator Barry Goldwater, Justice Rehnquist, and Attorney General Smith.

As might be expected, her nomination brought praise from liberals and moderates who were not accustomed to applauding President Reagan's actions. Democratic Representative Morris Udall of Arizona said that O'Connor "... is about as moderate a Republican as you'll ever find appointed by Reagan." Democratic Senator Edward Kennedy of Massachusetts also praised the nomination, and Eleanor Smeal, president of the National Organization for Women (NOW), called it "... a major victory for women's rights."

However, despite her generally conservative record as a state judge and enthusiastic support from Senator Goldwater, O'Connor's nomination ran into vocal opposition from some elements of the New Right who charged that she favored abortion and criticized her support of the Equal Rights Amendment. Senator Jesse Helms of North Carolina said he was "skeptical" about the choice, and Reverend Jerry Falwell, head of the Moral Majority, declared it a "disaster." J. C. Willkie, president of the National Right-to-Life Committee, said O'Connor's appointment represented a repudiation of the 1980 Republican platform pledge to appoint judges "... who respect traditional family values and the sanctity of human life."

In confirmation hearings before the Senate Judiciary Committee, O'Connor was asked her views on a number of controversial issues. She refused to discuss recent Supreme Court decisions or issues that might come before the Court. O'Connor did say, however, that while she was personally opposed to abortion, she thought her personal views and beliefs should have no place in resolving legal issues pertaining to the matter. In response to questioning by Senator Kennedy, she said that she had always been concerned about discrimination against women. At the same time, O'Connor told Senator Joseph Biden of Delaware that she thought it would be "inappropriate" for her as a Justice of the Supreme Court to be involved in efforts to promote the Equal Rights Amendment.

In the end, O'Connor's nomination prevailed. In mid-September 1981, the Senate Judiciary Committee voted 17–0 to approve her nomination, with Senator Jeremiah Denton of Alabama abstaining on the grounds that he was not satisfied with her responses to his questions on abortion. A week later the entire Senate voted 99–0 to approve her nomination.

Thus ended a major event in the nation's judicial history—the nomination and confirmation of the first woman to the U. S. Supreme Court. Later in this chapter we will examine the selection and backgrounds of judges to all the federal courts, including the question of how women and minorities have done in appointments to such tribunals. First, however, we need to explore the general nature of the various federal courts and the role they play in our judicial system.

THE JURISDICTION OF FEDERAL COURTS

The general jurisdiction of the federal courts is set forth succinctly in Article

Chief Justice Burger swears in Sandra Day O'Connor in presence of her husband, John.

III, Section 2 of the Constitution. Two words used there, **cases and controversies,** have been construed by the federal courts to mean that the litigation they hear must involve an actual dispute. Two parties cannot trump up a lawsuit merely to have the Supreme Court interpret a federal statute or determine its constitutionality. Nor will federal judges render **advisory opinions** about how or whether a particular law should be enforced. Only a party that has actually been adversely affected by the provisions of a law can obtain an interpretation or a test of its constitutionality.

Assuming an actual case brought by a legitimate plaintiff, it can be heard by federal courts only if it falls within one of two broad categories. One concerns the *subject matter* of the suit, which is limited to litigation involving the federal Constitution, a federal law, a treaty, or admiralty and maritime matters.

The other category relates to the *particular parties* to the suit. If an official of the United States is suing or being sued, the federal courts can hear the case. They have jurisdiction over cases affecting ambassadors and other agents of foreign governments, disputes between a state or one of its citizens and a foreign government or one of its citizens. Interstate conflicts can also come to the federal courts. These include litigation between states, between citizens of different states, between citizens of the same state who claim lands under grants of different states, and between a state and a citizen of another state (but only if the state is bringing suit).

The jurisdiction of federal courts is established by the Constitution, but the way it is exercised is for the most part determined by Congress. The only constitutional provision that restricts its discretion is the stipulation in Article III, Section 2 that in cases involving ambassadors, other public ministers, and consuls, and those in which a state is a party, the Supreme Court has **original jurisdiction** (the power to hear the case for the first time).

With this exception, Congress can make what rules it wishes. For example, it may forbid the federal courts to handle a particular kind of case. Indeed, a suit between citizens of different states must involve $10,000 or more before a federal court will hear it; Congress has turned over to the state courts controversies involving lesser amounts of money. Or Congress may allow both federal and state courts to hear a particular type of case—in other words, to exercise **concurrent jurisdiction.** Suits between citizens of different states involving more than $10,000 are in that category: if both parties desire, they can litigate the matter in a state court. Finally, Congress has the power to assign **exclusive federal jurisdiction;** for instance, cases involving alleged violations of a federal criminal statute must be heard in a federal court, not a state one.

In addition to its power to allocate cases between federal and state courts, Congress can also decide at which level in the federal judiciary a matter will be heard. The only judicial tribunal specifically mentioned in the Constitution is the Supreme Court; Article II, Section 1 empowers Congress to create **"inferior"** (that is, lower) **courts** to assist with the processing of federal litigation. The following section of that same article also empowers Congress to regulate the appellate jurisdiction of the Supreme Court, determining what matters it will review that have initially been tried in lower courts. The federal judicial system today, as developed through statutes passed by Congress over the years since the initial Judiciary Act of 1789, includes, in addition to the United States Supreme Court, the United States district courts and the United States courts of appeals.*

MAJOR FEDERAL COURTS

The District Courts

The **United States district courts** are primarily courts of original jurisdiction. Although they get some cases from state courts and review some actions of federal administrative agencies, for the most part the district courts are the trial tribunals of the federal judiciary. It is here that the spirited battles occur, involving opposing attorneys, witnesses, a jury (though often, particularly in civil cases, the parties waive a jury trial), and a single presiding judge (however, in reapportionment cases, and those in which Congress specifically authorizes the convening of a panel, three judges sit as a group to hear the case). The overwhelming proportion of federal cases—90 percent—begin and end in the district courts.

District courts concern themselves with a wide variety of matters. It is here that the federal government brings antitrust suits and prosecutes persons who steal automobiles and take them across a state line. Cases involving citizens of different states are much like those that fill the dockets of state courts: automobile accidents, breaches of contract, and labor cases. In 1982, 238,000 cases were initiated in the federal district courts; of these 21,000 actually went to trial.

* In addition to the federal courts of general jurisdiction authorized by Article III, there are special federal courts that handle disputes arising from particular functions of Congress under powers granted by Article I. Included are the U. S. Court of Appeals for the Federal Judicial Districts, the U. S. Court of Military Appeals, territorial courts, the United States Claims Court, which hears claims brought against the national government, the U. S. Court of International Trade and the U. S. Tax Court.

This flood of cases led Congress in 1978 to enact the Omnibus Judgeship Act, increasing the number of federal district judges from 398 to 515.* They are national courts, but they are oriented to a considerable degree to states and localities. Each state has at least one federal district court, and no court jurisdiction crosses state lines. Although district court judges occasionally are assigned to hear cases in other districts (for example, a visiting North Dakota district court judge issued the famous injunction in 1957 prohibiting Governor Faubus and other Arkansas officials from interfering with the integration of the Little Rock schools), for the most part they preside over disputes in their own area.

"IT'S NOTHING PERSONAL, PRESCOTT. IT'S JUST THAT A HIGHER COURT GETS A KICK OUT OF OVERRULING A LOWER COURT."

The United States Courts of Appeals

The **United States courts of appeals** (also referred to as circuit courts) serve as the major appellate tribunals in the federal court system. They principally review the decisions in cases initially heard in federal district courts and the orders and decisions of federal administrative units, particularly the independent regulatory agencies. In 1982 approximately 28,000 cases were initiated by the courts of appeals, most of which ended right there; only a small proportion went to the United States Supreme Court for final disposition.

As Figure 13.1 shows, there are 11 regional courts of appeals located in various parts of the United States, plus one in the District of Columbia.† The size of the courts varies from four judges in the First Circuit in the New England area to 23 in the Ninth Circuit in the West. In some instances judges sit in different cities located within a court's jurisdiction.

To expedite their considerable case load, courts of appeals are divided into panels of three judges. The chief judge of each court determines the composition of the various panels, which are changed from time to time so that a judge does not always have the same colleagues. On application of the parties or the judges themselves, a case can be heard **en banc,** that is, by the entire court. The procedure is fairly rare; it is restricted to legal questions of exceptional importance or cases in which the court feels that a full tribunal is necessary to secure uniformity in its decisions or compliance with a controversial decision.

Courts of appeals judges tend to be less closely tied to particular states and localities than their counterparts in district courts. Thus Fifth Circuit judges have been more likely to vote in favor

* The 117 new federal district judgeships, plus 35 additional ones for the U. S. courts of appeals (to be discussed later in the chapter), is the largest number of judgeships ever created by a single act of Congress.

† In addition to the regional courts, there is a United States Court of Appeals for the Federal Judicial Districts whose jurisdiction is nationwide and which hears appeals on specialized matters, particularly patent, trade mark, and copyright cases.

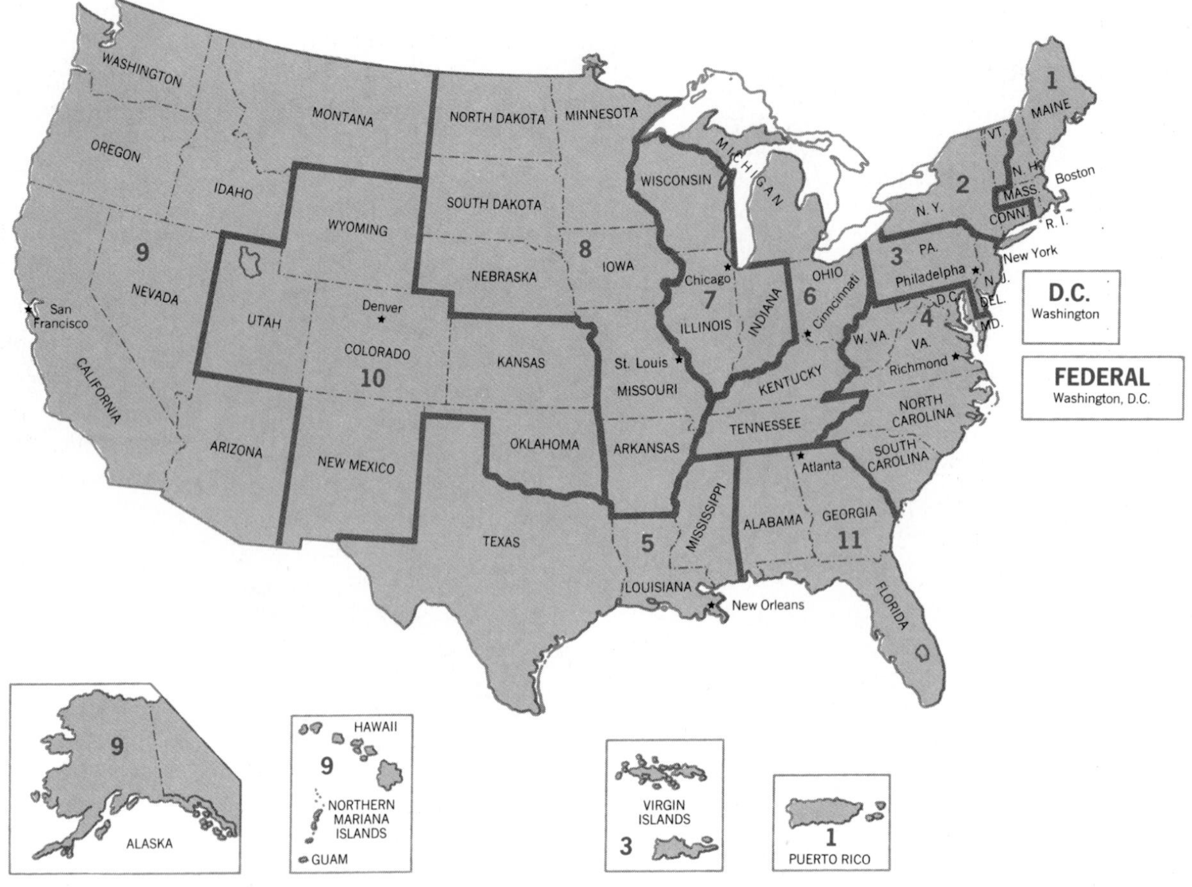

Figure 13.1 U.S. Courts of Appeals.
* U.S. Court of Appeals for the Federal Judicial Districts
SOURCE: Administrative Office of the U.S. Courts.

of blacks in civil rights cases than their brethren in the southern federal trial courts and have overruled a number of lower court decisions that originally favored white litigants.

The United States Supreme Court

Attorneys frequently assure clients who have lost cases in state or lower federal courts that they will take the matter to the **United States Supreme Court** where it will be settled in their favor. Designed as a tactic to console clients and convince them that their attorneys will stand by them, the promise is seldom realized. For one thing, most people lack the financial resources needed to carry legal battles to the highest tribunal. Costs naturally vary with the nature of the suit and the court level at which it is first tried, but at a minimum, tens of thousands of dollars will be involved in court and attorneys' fees, and in many instances the figure will be in the hundreds of thousands.* For another, even

* It has been estimated that the litigation that eventually resulted in the 1954 school desegregation decision *Brown* v. *Board of Education* (this case is discussed in Chapter 15) cost the National Association for the Advancement of Colored People over $200,000.

if one has the money to fight a case to that level, one may not be willing to take one's chances on the decision.

Besides, there is a great difference between taking a case to the United States Supreme Court and getting the justices to hear it. In 1982 over 5,000 cases were reviewed, but the court heard only about 200.

The Supreme Court has almost complete discretion over the cases it will hear. Litigation that comes within the *original jurisdiction* of the court (cases involving foreign ambassadors, ministers, and consuls, and those in which a state is a party) may come to it for initial consideration. But even here there is some leeway since Congress has granted district courts *concurrent jurisdiction* over controversies pertaining to foreign diplomatic personnel and some involving a state. As a result, most cases heard for the first time before the Supreme Court involve two states. In any event, cases of original jurisdiction constitute a very minor part of the case load of the Supreme Court, typically amounting to only a few cases each year. For all practical purposes, the Supreme Court is an appellate body.

Congress, which regulates the appellate jurisdiction of the Supreme Court, has established two major sources of cases: the United States courts of appeals and the highest courts of the various states.* Yet the court is granted discretion over which cases it will actually review. Typically, it chooses only those that involve a "substantial federal question" or that for "special and important reasons" the court feels it should hear. In other instances the court may choose a case because it involves the interpretation of an important federal statute or because it raises a legal issue on which various district courts or courts of appeals have ruled differently. It is not enough that members of the Supreme Court believe that the wrong party won in the lower court or that a legal injustice has been done. Before they accept a case (four justices must agree to do so), they must also feel that it raises important issues transcending the particular parties and case involved, and have important consequences for the American political system or society in general.

The most important factor affecting decision-making by the Supreme Court is that it is a *collegial* body. Unlike the courts of appeals, it does not divide itself into separate panels to hear different cases. Members have taken the position that the Constitution refers to one Supreme Court, not several, and therefore all judges should normally participate in each case. (The fact that the court has almost complete discretion over the cases it will hear enables it to concentrate its attention on relatively few; otherwise the court could never employ collective decision-making.)†

The annual session of the Supreme Court is spread over a 36-week period from October to June, although on occasion the court issues decisions after that time. During this period the court sets aside about four days a week during two weeks of each month to hear oral arguments of opposing counsel on cases that the court has chosen for a full hearing. Typically, the time is divided between the two sides, with each attorney having a half-hour to an hour to present

The Supreme Court Building.

* Certain cases come directly to the Supreme Court from the federal district courts, as do some from special federal courts or territorial courts. The Court also allows major cases for which there are compelling reasons for an immediate decision, to be heard without going through a court of appeals.

† Several years ago a suggestion was made by a group appointed by Chief Justice Burger that a National Court of Appeals be created to screen cases for the Supreme Court to hear. However, the proposal drew opposition from other justices.

Members of the United States Supreme Court.

and defend his case. The justices feel free to interrupt attorneys for questions at any point: interrogation by Justice Frankfurter was considered a harrowing experience, not unlike a searching oral examination of a graduate student. Contributing to the tension for many, if not most, attorneys is the fact that this may be their first and last appearance before the court. Only the Solicitor General, who presents cases in which the United States is a party (about half of all those argued before the court), gets extensive experience in the nation's highest court.

The overwhelming proportion of the work of the Supreme Court, however, takes place behind the scenes or the **"purple curtain"** (which forms the backdrop for the public appearances of the court). The justices spend most of their time individually reading and studying cases and discussing them with their law clerks (recently graduated students of the nation's top law schools) as well as with some of their colleagues. However, they come together as a single group for **conferences,** held on Friday (increasingly supplemented by post–3:00 P.M. Wednesday meetings) to make joint decisions on certain matters.

One major matter settled in conference is the choice of cases that the Court will hear that term. Another is the way cases already heard by the Court should be decided. In both matters the Chief justice gives his views first, then the associate justice with the longest service on the Court speaks, and so on to the most junior person. The voting on both issues proceeds in reverse order, with the chief justice voting last.

After the case is decided, it must be determined who will write the opinion setting forth the decision of the Court and the reasons behind that decision. If the chief justice votes with the majority, he decides who should write the opinion. If the case is a major one, he will probably assume the responsibility himself, as Chief Justice Warren did in *Brown* v. *Board of Education* in 1954. If the chief justice is not on the prevailing side, the most senior justice on that side writes the opinion himself or assigns it to one of his colleagues.

These procedures allow for a great deal of maneuvering. For example, Chief Justice Burger has been charged with deliberately holding back in voting in some cases until he could see how they would come out—and then voting with the majority. The reason given for the tactic is that he then could retain the right to determine who would be assigned the writing of the opinion, including himself if he was so inclined.

Whether or not this charge is true, the fact remains that the power to assign the writing of opinions is an important one. An opinion is often assigned to the justice whose views are closest to those of the minority, the idea being that he may perhaps be able to win some of the justices initially disposed toward the minority view over to the majority's side. This tactic is often pursued when a premium is placed on getting a unanimous or nearly unanimous opinion by the Court, a particularly desirable goal in controversial decisions when the justices want maximum public acceptance, as they did in the *Brown* case. For the same reason, an opinion may be assigned to a justice with personal or background characteristics that help to make the result more palatable: Chief Justice Warren assigned the controversial opinion in the *Schempp* decision outlawing the reading of the Bible and the recitation of the Lord's Prayer in the public schools to Justice Tom Clark, a deeply religious southern conservative.*

While the chief justice is thus in a key position to affect the writing of opinions, the other justices also play an important role in the process. Warren Burger's name alone appeared on the opinion rendered in *United States v. Nixon* (holding that the President had to turn over tapes of conversations with his aides relating to the Watergate break-

* This case is examined in Chapter 14.

"All the News That's Fit to Print"

The New York Times.

LATE CITY EDITION

Copyright, 1954, by The New York Times Company.

VOL. CIII...No. 35,178. NEW YORK, TUESDAY, MAY 18, 1954. FIVE CENTS

HIGH COURT BANS SCHOOL SEGREGATION; 9-TO-0 DECISION GRANTS TIME TO COMPLY

McCarthy Hearing Off a Week as Eisenhower Bars Report

SENATOR IS IRATE

President Orders Aides Not to Disclose Details of Top-Level Meeting

President's letter and excerpts from transcript, Pages 24, 25, 26.

By W. H. LAWRENCE

Special to The New York Times.

WASHINGTON, May 17—A secrecy directive by President Eisenhower resulted today in an abrupt recess for at least a week of the Senate's Army-McCarthy hearings.

Democratic and Republican Senators, some publicly and some privately, predicted that the in-

Communist Arms Unloaded in Guatemala By Vessel From Polish Port, U. S. Learns

State Department Views News Gravely Because of Red Infiltration

Special to The New York Times.

WASHINGTON, May 17—The State Department said today that it had reliable information that "an important shipment of arms" had been sent from Communist-controlled territory to Guatemala.

It said the arms, now being unloaded at Puerto Barrios, Guatemala, had been shipped from Stettin, a former German Baltic seaport, which has been occupied by Communist Poland since World War II. The Guatemalan regime has been frequently accused of being influenced by Communists.

The New York Times May 18, 1954

Site of arms arrival (cross)

quantity of arms involved, the Department of State considers

Embassy Says Nation of Central America May Buy Munitions Anywhere

Barrios last Saturday, the State Department reported, carrying a large shipment of armament consigned to the Guatemalan Government.

The State Department did not divulge the exact quantity of the arms, their nature or where they had been manufactured.

Reliable sources told The New York Times, however, that ten freight car loads of goods listed in the manifest as "hardware" had been unloaded from this ship and sent to the city of Guatemala since Sunday. Guatemala is 150

REACTION OF SOUTH

'Breathing Spell' for Adjustment Tempers Region's Feelings

By JOHN N. POPHAM

Special to The New York Times.

CHATTANOOGA, Tenn., May 17—The South's reaction to the Supreme Court's decision outlawing racial segregation in public schools appeared to be tempered considerably today.

The time lag allowed for carrying out the required transitions seemed to be the major factor in that reaction.

Southern leaders of both races in political, educational and community service fields expressed comment that covered a wide

1896 RULING UPSET

'Separate but Equal' Doctrine Held Out of Place in Education

Text of Supreme Court decision is printed on Page 15.

By LUTHER A. HUSTON

Special to The New York Times.

WASHINGTON, May 17—The Supreme Court unanimously outlawed today racial segregation in public schools.

Chief Justice Earl Warren read two opinions that put the stamp of unconstitutionality on school systems in twenty-one states and the District of Columbia where segregation is permissive or mandatory.

in), but in actuality it was a collective one, with various justices reputed to have written different portions of the opinion, including the statement of the facts (Blackmun), the authority of the judiciary (Stewart), presidential confidentiality (Powell), the extent of the subpoena power (White), the special prosecutor's standing to sue for the tapes (Brennan), and the nature of executive privilege (Burger himself after extensive changes in his original wording).

Thus the collegial process does not end with the assignment of an opinion to a justice. Negotiation (walking the Supreme Court corridors as some Court observers put it) continues as the writer strives to word the opinion so that a maximum number of justices join in it. A justice may even adopt suggestions and reasonings of other justices in order to dissuade them from writing opinions of their own. (Separate opinions may be either *concurring* ones, in which the writer agrees with the result reached by the majority opinion, but not for the same reasons, or *dissenting* opinions—those reaching the opposite result.) The threat to write such a separate opinion—especially in controversial cases in which the court particularly wants to give the image of a united tribunal—is a source of leverage for justices who wish to see opinions written in a way that reflects their particular thinking. The process can also work in reverse: Justice Stanley Reed was originally against the majority view in *Brown* v. *Board of Education* but ultimately voted with the majority because he was concerned that a dissenting opinion from a southerner like himself might encourage some people not to accept the decision. Thus he put aside his own personal views for what he conceived to be the good of the country.

Getting nine persons with strong, diverse views to work together well as a group is not an easy feat. One close student of the subject, political scientist David Danelski, has pointed out that it calls for both "task" leadership or expediting the work of the court, and "social" leadership or helping establish good interpersonal relationships among the justices. The key part that the Chief Justice plays in conference discussions and in the assignment of opinions furnishes him with the opportunity to provide both types of leadership. How well a given Chief Justice performs, however, depends on his personality and skills in interpersonal relationships. Danelski feels that Chief Justice Hughes was successful in providing the court with both task and social leadership. Chief Justice Taft performed the social role effectively but let his good friend Justice Van Devanter become the task leader during his tenure. Moreover, some chief justices are unsuccessful in either role: Danelski puts Harlan Stone in that category and journalists Bob Woodward and Scott Armstrong suggest that the same is true of the present chief justice, Warren Burger.

The final stage in the decision-making process of the Supreme Court is the announcement of its decisions and the reasons for them in open session on **"opinion day,"** typically held on two or three Mondays each month while the Court is in session.* The justices present their opinions orally: some read them verbatim, others merely summarize their major points. These sessions are frequently enlivened by caustic comments and even verbal exchanges between justices who differ strongly on cases under discussion.

The operation of the federal courts,

* By delivering all its opinions on Monday, the court creates problems for the mass media, which frequently must report and comment on a variety of cases at one time. Former Chief Justice Warren initiated a practice of releasing some opinions on other days, but most are still delivered on Monday.

"I'm afraid there's been some mistake."

Drawing by Richter; © 1979 The New Yorker Magazine, Inc.

of course, depends not only on their jurisdiction and their customs but also on the individual judges. The following section explains how judges are chosen and describes the kinds of persons who become judges at all three levels of the federal judiciary.

THE SELECTION AND BACKGROUNDS OF FEDERAL JUDGES

Unlike most state judges, who are elected by the people, federal jurists are appointed. The Constitution specifically states that the president shall nominate and, by and with the advice and consent of the Senate, appoint Supreme Court judges. Congress provides for the same process to be used for staffing the lower federal courts, so the president and the Senate are partners in the appointment process for all federal judges.

The Politics of Selection

Traditionally, both the president and the Senate have sought the assistance of other officials to help them carry out their responsibilities of appointment. The attorney general's office recommends judicial candidates to the president. The Senate Judiciary Committee considers the nominees and votes as a group, recommending confirmation or rejection. Although neither the president, nor the entire Senate is obliged to accept the advice of the attorney general's office or the Senate Judiciary Committee, both are generally inclined to do so.

In recent years additional groups have begun to make their influence felt in federal judicial selection. Since the Eisenhower administration, the Committee on the Federal Judiciary of the American Bar Association has evaluated persons being considered for the federal bench. It has customarily used the ratings "exceptionally well-qualified," "well-qualified," "qualified," and "not qualified." Although presidents are not required to refer prospective nominees to the Committee for consideration, they have generally done so.

Even more significant in the selection of federal judges were new elements introduced by the Carter administration. During the 1976 presidential campaign, the Democratic candidate stated that as president he would select all federal judges ". . . strictly on the basis of merit without any consideration of political aspects or influence." After he took office he negotiated an agreement with James Eastland (D., Miss.), chairman of the Senate Judiciary Committee, under which the president would appoint merit panels to help him choose circuit court judges. In return, he agreed to leave the selection of district judges to senators.

In February 1977 President Carter issued an executive order creating the United States Circuit Judge Nominating Commission; the Department of Justice subsequently issued supplemental instructions to guide its operation. The entire commission, whose members were appointed by the president, was divided into 13 panels—one for each federal circuit, with two for the then extra-large Fifth and Ninth circuits. Each panel had 11 members, which included lawyers, laypersons, women, and minorities, and at least one resident from each state within the circuit. When a vacancy occurred because of the retirement of a sitting judge or the creation of a new judgeship (recall that the 1978 Omnibus Judgeship Act added 35 additional circuit judgeships), the appropriate panel was convened to interview applicants and within 60 days recommended to the president the names of three to five persons for the circuit judgeship. The president then selected from that list the individual he nominates for the judgeship.

As suggested above, senators retained the right to suggest persons to the president for federal district judgeships. However, a number of them chose to follow the president's request that they also use merit commissions to help them with such recommendations. There was, however, variation in the way that members of such commissions were selected and in how their recommendations were handled. Some senators chose all the commissioners themselves, while others permitted members of Congress and state bar associations to name some of the commissioners. Some senators instructed merit commissioners to transmit their recommendations for district judges directly to the Justice Department and the president without the senators' endorsement; others asked that the commissioners send them the list of recommended persons and then narrowed the field to the exact number of judicial vacancies and submitted only those names to President Carter.

The Reagan administration took the position that the nominating commissions developed under President Carter to help select circuit court judges were unnecessary and abolished them. At the same time, Republican senators were encouraged to use screening mechanisms, including but not restricted to advisory groups or commissions, in submitting a list of three to five names for a district judgeship.

Whatever means is used to recommend names for federal judgeships to the president, he does the actual nominating; the person's name is then transmitted to the Senate, which confirms or rejects it. The Senate Judiciary Committee, operating through subcommittees, conducts hearings and invites testimony. Interest groups, including bar associations, as well as nonlegal groups that have been unable to prevent the president from nominating a person they do not favor may carry the fight against the nominee to the committee. The Senate committee has also traditionally sent a blue slip of paper to each of the two senators—regardless of party—from the state where the appointment is to be made and given them the chance to register disapproval by not returning the slip.* In addition, senators of the state concerned who are from the president's own party can invoke the informal rule of "senatorial courtesy," declaring the nominee "personally obnoxious." This merely means that the senator opposes the nominee for political reasons or prefers someone else to the president's candidate. When this occurs—rarely of late—the Senate may refuse to confirm the nomination as a matter of political custom. Unless the nomination is withdrawn by the president, the Judiciary Committee makes a recommendation on the nomination, but the final decision is up to the entire Senate.

Patterns and Trends in the Selection of Federal Judges

The variety of persons and groups that participate in the selection of federal judges makes the process a complex one. Those who are especially influential in the choice of one judge may not be nearly so important in the selection of another. The eventual outcome depends on a number of factors: the level of federal court involved, the attitudes and political skills of the president and particular senators involved, the characteristics of the candidate, and the general political tenor of the times. Nonetheless it is possible to discern certain basic patterns and trends in the selection of federal judges.

Although the Constitution clearly provides that the president is to nominate and, by and with the advice and consent of the Senate, to appoint all federal judges, the process for the district courts typically works in reverse. The initiative comes from the Senate, or more precisely the senator or senators of the president's party from the state concerned. (This remains generally so even for senators who now use screening commissions since they can decide who to appoint to them.) The president has a veto power over those who are offensive to him politically or who fail to meet the minimum qualification standards of the organized bar, but the rule of senatorial courtesy, which has been in effect since the Washington administration, is a powerful weapon against the president. Moreover, few chief executives are willing to risk the loss of political support in the Senate over a district court judgeship, since the work of such a tribunal is seldom crucial to his own political goals or programs.

The president is generally more influential in the selection of judges to the United States courts of appeals. He takes more of a personal interest in them than in district court appointments for two reasons. First, the courts of appeals handle matters of more importance to him. For example, their review of actions of the independent reg-

* When Edward Kennedy assumed the chairmanship of the Judiciary Committee in 1979, he announced plans to change the blue slip procedure so that failure to return a slip would not automatically kill a nomination. When Republican Senator Strom Thurmond became committee chairman in 1981, he announced his intention to follow the practice developed by Kennedy.

ulatory commissions can affect his overall economic program. Second, courts of appeals judgeships are less numerous and more prestigious, which invites the interest of his major political supporters.

The president clearly dominates the selection process for the Supreme Court. He is, of course, vitally interested in the decisions reached by that tribunal since they affect the operation of the entire political system and the functioning of American society in general. Since a Supreme Court judgeship is so prestigious, few, if any, lawyers would be inclined to turn down the post. With the entire nation as the court's geographical jurisdiction, no senator or even group of senators has a special say over the allocation of judgeships. Only the entire Senate can thwart the president's wishes.

The historical record of Supreme Court appointments is that about one in five presidential nominations has either been rejected outright or not acted on by the Senate, a far higher proportion of failure to confirm than for any other federal office. There has been considerable variation in the fate of nominees at different times. Bitter political battles led to a number of failures to confirm in the period from 1829, when Andrew Jackson took office, until Grant left the presidency in 1877. At the other extreme, from 1894 (when two of President Cleveland's nominees were rejected) until 1968, when the Senate failed to act on Lyndon Johnson's nomination of Associate Justice Abe Fortas to the chief justiceship and on the nomination of Homer Thornberry to take Fortas's place, only one nominee—a southern court of appeals judge, John J. Parker—failed to be confirmed. The Fortas matter was soon followed by the outright rejection of two of President Nixon's nominees, Clement Haynsworth and G. Harrold Carswell, courts of appeals judges from South Carolina and Florida, respectively, within a few months' time in late 1969 and early 1970.

An analysis of the circumstances surrounding the above incidents in this century reveals the factors that contribute to the Senate's failure to confirm presidential nominees. Perhaps the most basic is the presence of major political differences between key senators and the president. Democrats joined with progressive Republicans of the day to defeat the nomination of Judge Parker by Republican President Herbert Hoover. The same type of coalition of Northern Democrats and liberal Republicans was formed to defeat Haynsworth and Carswell. On the other hand, prominent Senate Republicans allied themselves with conservative Democrats from the South to filibuster successfully against Justice Fortas.

These four failures to confirm also reflected broader political divisions in the nation. All three of the rejected Republican nominees—Parker, Haynsworth, and Carswell—were southerners who were bitterly opposed by black and liberal interest groups for their rulings on civil rights cases. The former two were also considered antilabor. Fortas, in turn, had incurred the enmity of a number of conservative groups through his liberal decisions in obscenity cases and suits involving the rights of the accused in criminal proceedings.

Other issues have played a role in the three most recent incidents. Several senators who had originally supported Fortas's elevation subsequently joined with others in urging that he resign from the Court when his acceptance of a fee from a family foundation became known. Some senators were also opposed to Fortas's continuing to advise President Johnson on political matters while he was serving on the Court. Judge Haynsworth was criticized for ruling on cases involving companies in which he had a financial interest, while Judge Carswell's role in helping incorporate a segregated social club in his hometown in Florida contributed to the defeat of his nomination. While the political infighting in these three nomination battles was particularly vicious, and although these issues represented outward manifestations of deeper partisan and philosophical differences between the contending parties, it is very possible that the financial affairs of Supreme Court nominees, as well as their offbench activities in general, may in the future come under closer scrutiny.

The opposition to Judge Carswell's nomination by members of the bar, particularly law professors who claimed that his opinions were mediocre, may indicate that the legal qualifications of Supreme Court nominees will also be analyzed more carefully in the future. This development would suggest an increased role for the American Bar Association's Committee on the Federal Judiciary in future appointments.* The fact that the Committee found Carswell qualified for the position may lead it to analyze candidates more thoroughly in the future and to check their legal credentials with both the academic segment of the bar and practicing attorneys.

Characteristics of Federal Judges

The characteristics of federal judges reflect a number of the considerations that bear on their appointment. The most basic qualification is membership in the *legal profession.* Although this is not a legal requirement, it is an informal custom: no nonlawyer has ever been appointed to a federal judgeship. Moreover, in keeping with contemporary preparation of lawyers, almost every judge appointed to the federal bench since the end of World War II has been a graduate of a law school.

Another common attribute of federal judges is *public experience.* All except one of the 102 judges who have served on the Supreme Court were previously engaged in public service at some level of government or participated in political activities. Lower federal court judges also have political backgrounds; in fact they are frequently described as "lawyers who knew a United States senator," particularly those on district benches. Attorneys who refrain from any type of participation in public affairs are not likely to be as visible to senators or presidents or their advisers as lawyers who are active in public life.

As might be expected, the most prevalent kind of previous public office is one connected with the *courts.* Judges have often been city, county, or state prosecutors or district attorneys. Some have also served as United States attor-

Judge G. Harold Carswell.

* Republican presidents have been more inclined than Democratic ones to pay heed to the Committee's ratings; it has also played a more important role in the selection of lower federal judges than of Supreme Court justices.

neys or their associates, while a few have been solicitor general or attorney general of the United States.

Previous *judicial experience* is also common among federal judges, although not as common as might be supposed. A recent analysis revealed that about one-third of the district judges had previously been state judges; two in five judges on courts of appeals had been on the bench previously, most ot them as federal district judges. The Supreme Court draws its appointees from both pools: of the 102 justices in the nation's history, 22 came from an inferior federal court and the same number from a state bench.*

There has been increased attention given in recent years to recruiting to the federal courts members of politically disadvantaged groups, particularly women, blacks, and Hispanics. As indicated by Table 13.1, the Carter administration had far more success than any of the other recent administrations in placing members of those groups on both the district and courts of appeals benches. The fact that President Carter had a clear policy of affirmatively seeking persons from those groups, and that the Circuit Judge Nominating Commission that operated in his administration included many women and minority members, undoubtedly contributed to that result.

Federal district and courts of appeals judges tend to be affiliated with the *same political party* as the president who appoints them. Chief executives typically choose 90 percent or more of their appointees from their own party. Presidents also tend to stay within party ranks when making appointments to the Supreme Court: only 13 of the 102 justices have been named by a president of another party.

When a president does cross party lines, particularly for a Supreme Court appointment, it is likely to be because he has a high regard for the person concerned and a conviction that the nominee, while affiliated with the opposition, shares the president's *general political philosophy* and views on public policy issues. A vivid statement of this consideration is contained in a letter Republican President Theodore Roosevelt once sent to his good friend Senator Henry Cabot Lodge of Massachusetts explaining a nomination:

> . . . *the* nominal *politics of the man* [Horace H. Lurton, a Democrat] *has nothing to do with his actions on the bench. His real politics are all important. . . . He is right on the Negro question; he is right on the Insular business; he is right about corporations; and he is right about labor. On every question that would come before the bench, he has so far shown himself to be in much closer touch with the policies in which you and I believe.*†

Although presidents attempt to choose people for the Supreme Court who share their general political views, they are not always successful in doing so. Justices often behave in ways not anticipated by their benefactors. Immediately after he was appointed to the Court by Theodore Roosevelt, Oliver Wendell Holmes Jr. voted on the side of

* Extensive judicial experience among Supreme Court justices is not common: of the 102 justices, only 24 had 10 or more years' experience on some court. Although the lack of such experience has been criticized, some of the most eminent jurists, including John Marshall, Roger Taney, Louis Brandeis, Felix Frankfurter, and Earl Warren, had no prior judicial experience at all.

† Lodge replied that a Republican with similar views could be obtained and persuaded Roosevelt to nominate William Moody, the attorney general of Massachusetts. Lurton was subsequently appointed by Roosevelt's successor, another Republican, President William Howard Taft.

Table 13.1
Judicial Appointments of Women and Minorities to the Lower Federal Courts (1963–1983) (in percentages)

Administration	U. S. District Courts Women	Blacks	Hispanics
Johnson	1.6	3.3	2.5
Nixon	0.6	2.8	1.1
Ford	1.9	5.8	1.9
Carter	14.4	13.9	6.9
Reagan*	9.3	0	5.1

Administration	U. S. Courts of Appeal Women	Blacks	Hispanics
Johnson	2.5	5.0	0
Nixon	0	0	0
Ford	0	0	0
Carter	19.6	16.1	3.6
Reagan*	0	4.3	0

* Based on the first three years of his administration.

SOURCE: Data on the Johnson, Nixon, Ford, and Carter administrations are from Sheldon Goldman, "Carter's Judicial Appointments: A Lasting Legacy," *Judicature*, Vol. 64, No. 8 (March 1981) pp. 348, 350. Information on the first three years of the Reagan administration comes from *Congressional Quarterly Almanac* (Washington, D. C.: Congressional Quarterly, Inc., 1983), pp. 302–304.

private enterprise and against the administration in a famous antitrust case, *Northern Securities* v. *United States* (1904). President Eisenhower had little reason to suspect that his nominee for chief justice, Earl Warren, would become one of the most liberal jurists in the history of the Supreme Court. Yet once the chief executive has placed a man on the court, there is little he can do about his appointee's decisions since for all practical purposes, he is there for life.*

A Supreme Court appointment is so important because many social, economic, and political issues of the day become involved in litigation that comes to the Court for a decision. Most of these decisions require the Court to interpret major congressional statutes. Some, however, involve the justices of the Supreme Court in an even more demanding and controversial task: interpreting the Constitution itself.

* All federal judges hold office during "good behavior" or until they die or choose to retire voluntarily. They can also be impeached, but only four have been removed in that manner, and none of them was a Supreme Court justice.

Chief Justice Earl Warren.

JUDICIAL REVIEW

Although the expression **judicial review** might conceivably be applied to a court's re-examination of any matter already handled by a lower tribunal, it has a much more precise meaning. It refers to the power of a court to review the actions of all public officials—legislative, executive, and judicial—to see whether they are inconsistent with the governing constitution and, if the court finds that they are, to declare them unconstitutional and hence unenforceable.

In exercising judicial review, a court thus regards a constitution as being superior to ordinary laws or executive and judicial decrees. In determining that an official action is unconstitutional and therefore invalid, the court must find that a legislator, an executive, or a judicial official has done something that he or she has no authority to do under the constitution or that he or she has taken some action that is forbidden by the constitution.

Judicial review exists at various levels of our political system. For example, state courts have the power to determine whether actions of state legislators, executives, or judicial officials violate the state constitution and to render invalid those that do. On such matters the decision of the highest state court is final. State courts also have the power to interpret the national constitution as it applies to state actions. It can also decide whether a federal law or treaty is in violation of the national constitution. But the rulings of state courts are not final on these issues; they may be appealed to the federal courts for final disposition. On the other hand, the federal judiciary has the final say on whether actions of state or national officials violate the national constitution.

Some aspects of judicial review are more controversial than others. The right of a court to set aside actions of political officials—that is, legislators and executives—has been of more concern to students of the democratic process than its power to invalidate what other judges have done. The power of the federal courts to review the actions of national officials has been more seriously questioned than their authority to render unenforceable the activities of state officials. It is the combination of these two most criticized aspects of judicial review—the power of federal courts to invalidate actions of legislative and executive officials of the national government—that has provoked the greatest controversy.

Very few nations grant courts the power of judicial review as it is exercised in the United States. Typically, in countries with a federal form of government the power is granted to judicial tribunals, as in Australia, Canada, India, and West Germany. Even in these nations, however, the role of the courts in invalidating actions of political officials has never taken on the significance that it has in the United States. It would therefore be instructive to examine how our courts acquired the power of judicial review and the ways in which they have used it over the years.

The Establishment of Judicial Review in the United States

Ironically, judicial review is not specifically provided for in the Constitution. Nowhere does it expressly grant federal courts the right to nullify actions of public officials. The power has been derived by implication from certain wording in the Constitution and interpretation of the intentions of the Founders. Article V, Section 2, which provides that the *national* constitution, law, or treaties shall be "supreme" over state constitutions or laws, has been used to justify the power of federal courts to invalidate state actions. The clause itself, however, does not state that national courts should pass on such conflicts; in fact it specifically mentions state judges and provides that they shall be bound by the supremacy clause, which might be construed to mean that state rather than federal judges should have the power of judicial review. The argument for federal courts' invalidating actions of the other two branches of the national government is even less supported by the wording of the Constitution.

Nonetheless most historians agree that the Founders favored judicial review and expected the federal courts to exercise it over both state and national actions. Why, then, did they not provide for it specifically in the Constitution? One theory is that everyone took the power for granted anyway, since most of the state courts of the time were exercising judicial review over the actions of state officials. Another is that the delegates were aware that owing to the secrecy of the Convention and constitutional provisions for a Senate and a president that the people did not elect, many citizens would view the new government as too elitist. Specifically granting to appointed judges with life tenure the power to overrule actions of popularly elected officials would make matters even worse and almost ensure that the Constitution would not be ratified. Therefore for reasons of political expediency the delegates may have deliberately omitted any reference to judicial review.

Hamilton, however, was not so cautious or discrete. In *Federalist* 78 he specifically stated that the federal courts possess the power of judicial review and gave justifications for it, some of which are legalistic. He held that a constitution is a type of law and that, since it is the province of the courts to interpret laws, they necessarily interpret the Constitution. He pointed out that the Constitution is a fundamental law, which means that if judges find ordinary legislation in conflict with it, the Constitution prevails and the legislation is invalid.

Hamilton also drew on his views of human nature to justify judicial review. Legislators cannot be trusted always to respect the limitations placed on them by the Constitution; when they do not, the courts must intervene to protect the rights of the people. Nor are the people themselves to be entirely trusted; they too will suffer "the effects of ill humor" on some occasions and threaten the minority party or the rights of particular classes of citizens. Again it is the judges, trained in settling controversies growing out of "the folly and wickedness of mankind," who can be counted on to protect the rights of minorities.

Although Hamilton's views were thus set forth in a frank and bold fashion, they were simply his own and not binding on anyone else. The issue could only be settled ultimately by public officials. It remained for the Supreme Court itself to establish its power of judicial review through actual exercise of that prerogative. This it did in the famous case of *Marbury v. Madison,* decided by Chief Justice John Marshall in 1803.

Whereas Hamilton based his case for judicial review on legalistic arguments, the circumstances of the *Marbury* decision could hardly have been more political. After the Federalists were defeated in the election of 1800, they labored—in the interval until the Republicans assumed control of the presidency and the Congress in the following year—to retain a Federalist foothold in the one remaining branch still open to them: the judiciary. The lameduck Congress passed legislation creating a number of new circuit judgeships along with justiceships of the peace in the District of Columbia. In the waning days of his administration, President John Adams appointed Federalists to these new judicial posts (they became known as **"midnight" appointments** because they were accomplished shortly before that hour on 3 March 1801). In the last-minute rush, however, John Marshall, who was then Secretary of State (and at the same time also serving as Chief Justice of the Supreme Court) did not get all the necessary commissions of office signed; included among them was one making William Marbury a justice of the peace in the District of Columbia. The new Republican Secretary of State, James Madison, who, along with the new president, Thomas Jefferson, resented the Federalists' attempt to pack the bench, refused to deliver the commission to Marbury or otherwise honor his appointment.

Chief Justice John Marshall.

Frustrated in his attempts to obtain his commission, Marbury turned for help to the Supreme Court, over which John Marshall presided as a result of his appointment by President Adams. Marbury asked that the court issue a **writ of mandamus** (an order requiring a public official to perform an official duty over which he has no discretion) compelling Madison to deliver the commission. As his authority for the suit, he invoked a provision in the Judiciary Act of 1789 granting the Court the power to issue such writs.

Marbury's case placed Chief Justice Marshall (who should have disqualified himself from hearing it, since he was the one who failed to deliver the commission while he was still Secretary of State) on the horns of a dilemma. If he (and the rest of the Federalist judges on the court) ruled that Marbury was entitled to the commission, his political enemy, President Jefferson, could simply order Madison not to deliver it, which would serve to demonstrate that the judiciary could not enforce its mandates. On the other hand, to rule that Marbury had no right to the commission would seem to justify Jefferson's and Madison's claim that the midnight appointments were improper in the first place.

But the chief justice was up to the challenge. He slipped off the horns of the dilemma by ruling that, while Marbury had the right to the commission and a writ of mandamus was the proper remedy to obtain it, the Supreme Court was not the tribunal to issue it. In reaching this result, he reasoned that the original jurisdiction of the Supreme Court is provided for in the Constitution, and Congress cannot add to that jurisdiction. Therefore the section of the Judiciary Act of 1789 granting the Supreme Court the power to issue writs of mandamus in cases it hears for the first time is unconstitutional and hence unenforceable.

The ruling extricated Marshall from an immediate difficulty; it had other effects as well. It created the possibility that the Federalists could use this newfound power to check actions of the Republican Congress and president. Most crucial of all from a long-term standpoint, it established the power of the courts to declare acts of public officials invalid.

Crucial as the *Marbury* v. *Madison* ruling was, it did not settle all the aspects of judicial review. For one thing, it applied only to the actions of the national government. Not until seven years later, in the case of *Fletcher* v. *Peck* (1810), did the Court invalidate a state law on the grounds that it violated the national constitution. Moreover, the *Marbury* case did not define the scope of judicial review. As some persons, like Jefferson, reasoned, the ruling merely meant that the Court could strike down laws that affected the judiciary itself (as the Judiciary Act of 1789 did), but that it had no power over matters pertaining to the other two branches of government because each was the judge of the constitutionality of matters within its own province. Not until the *Dred Scott* case (1857), in which the Court invalidated Congress's attempt to abolish slavery in the territories, did the Court lay that theory to rest by striking down a law that had nothing to do with the courts.

The Supreme Court's Use of Judicial Review

Although judicial review puts a powerful weapon in the hands of the Supreme Court, for the most part the power has been used with considerable restraint, particularly with respect to federal laws. In the some 180 years since *Marbury*, the Court has invalidated all or part of 110 national laws, an average of less than one a year. (In the same period of time, it has declared over 800 state laws unconstitutional, or about four per year.)

The court's use of judicial review has not been uniform over the years, however. After all, 54 years transpired between the *Marbury* v. *Madison* decision at the beginning of the nineteenth century and the *Dred Scott* case on the eve of the Civil War. In contrast, the Court declared unconstitutional no fewer than 13 New Deal laws during the period from 1934 to 1936.

The types of issues of concern to the Supreme Court have changed over the years. Subject matter has naturally varied from case to case, but different basic themes have dominated the court's attention in different eras of our constitutional history. The issues have reflected both the major problems of American society at the time and the justices' own conceptions of the values that they should protect through the power of judicial review.

The major issue facing the court from 1789 until the Civil War was *nation–state relationships.* As we saw in Chapter 3, Chief Justice Marshall took the leadership in providing support for a strong national government. The constitutional basis for its expansion came in the form of a broad interpretation of both the interstate commerce power and the "necessary and proper" clause. At the same time, state activities that affected the powers of the national government were invalidated. Toward the end of the era, when Marshall died and was replaced by Roger Taney, the court moderated its stand on nation–state relationships. For example, it ruled that states could regulate interstate commerce, provided that the regulation concerned local matters and did not affect a subject requiring uniform treatment throughout the United States. As a whole, however, the era was clearly a time of general support for the nation over the states in constitutional conflicts.

The pre-Civil War period was also characterized by judicial protection of *private property.* In fact, there was a connection between the nation–state and property-rights issues: for the most part, the federal government was promoting business and commercial interests, while the states were more involved in trying to regulate them. Thus judicial support for a strong national government dominant over the states favored commercial interests. Furthermore, Chief Justice Taney's decision in the *Dred Scott* case invalidating Congress's attempt to abolish slavery in the territories showed the court's solicitude for another type of property holder: the large landowner in the South.

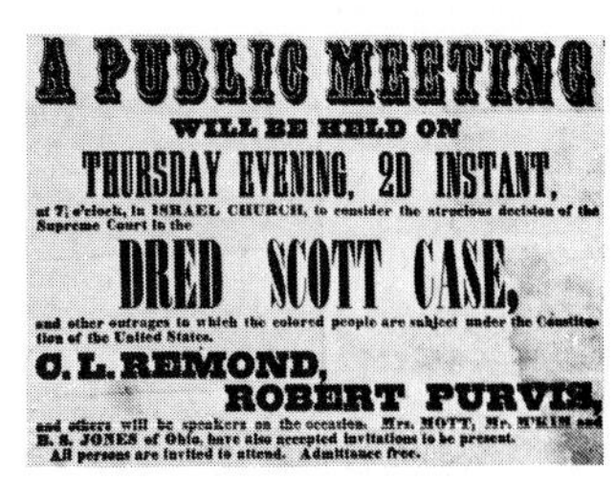

The Civil War settled the nation–state problem, and the courts became preoccupied with one overriding issue in the period that followed: *business–government relations.* Unlike the earlier era, however, both the national government and the states were involved in regulating burgeoning industrial empires along with smaller commercial enterprises. Therefore favoring one level of government over the other would not accomplish the goal of many justices of the day: protecting business against what they conceived to be improper governmental interference.

The Court thus embarked upon a two-pronged judicial attack on government regulation of business by the two political levels. It frustrated the national government's control of industry by limiting the scope of the interstate commerce power to cover only businesses that were actually involved in interstate commerce (such as railroads, shipping companies, and the like) and those that directly affected that commerce; this approach freed concerns involved in agriculture, mining, and production from control by the federal government. Similarly, the taxing power of the national government was contracted through judicial rulings inquiring into congressional motives behind the use of that power: for instance, a special tax on businesses using child labor was invalidated on the grounds that the purpose of the tax was not to raise money but to discourage the use of child labor. State regulation of business was also thwarted through a novel interpretation of the due process clause of the Fourteenth Amendment. Although, as we will see in the next chapter, historically that clause had always referred to *procedures* used by public officials, the Supreme Court now gave it a *substantive* meaning by holding that what the justices considered to be unreasonable regulation of private interests denied persons their property without due process of law.*

This dual approach served to protect business against regulation by government, both national and state. It dominated the Court's thinking in the early part of this century, continuing into the 1930s when it was utilized to strike down many New Deal laws. President Roosevelt, following his re-election in 1936, sought to curb the Court's power over his programs by introducing legislation permitting him to appoint additional justices equal to the number sitting on the Court who had reached the age of 70 and had not retired. This proposal provoked a storm of protest from critics who charged that FDR was trying to pack the Court, and it ended in a congressional defeat for the president on the issue. Although FDR lost the battle in the Congress, he won the war in the courtroom: Justice Owen Roberts, who had, to that point, generally been aligned with the four justices on the court invalidating social and economic legislation, began in 1937 to vote with the four on the other side. With this change (a satirical description was "a switch in time saves nine"), the era of the court's preoccupation with property rights came to an end.

Justice Owen Roberts.

* Another tactic that the court used to protect business was to interpret the word *person,* which appears in the Fourteenth Amendment, to include *corporations.* Thus the court utilized an amendment that was designed to safeguard the civil liberties of individuals to protect the property rights of business interests.

Since 1937 the Supreme Court has focused almost all its attention on protecting the *personal liberties of individuals* against infringement by either the national government or the states. The Court has been very active in the last 45 years, voiding 44 federal laws from 1938 to 1983. (This compares with 66 federal laws invalidated in the century and a half from 1789 to 1937.) As we shall see in the next chapter, included in the Court's concerns have been violations of First Amendment freedoms, along with procedural rights of the accused spelled out in the Fourth, Fifth, Sixth, and Eighth amendments. In addition, the due process clause of the Fifth Amendment has been utilized to invalidate federal criminal statutes for the vagueness of their language and to outlaw the segregation of the schools in the District of Columbia, a matter that is considered in Chapter 15. The Court has also been vigilant against infringements of personal liberties at the state level, relying on the due process and equal protection clauses of the Fourteenth Amendment to protect individuals against actions violating freedom of expression and religion, denials of procedural safeguards in criminal cases, and racial discrimination.

This brief review of the uses to which the Court has put judicial review over the years raises the issue of how individual judges conceive of the power of judicial review. What is the nature of the process? That is, what specifically does a judge do when he goes about deciding whether a law or executive or court order is unconstitutional? What role does he think judicial review should play in the political process?

Concepts of Judicial Review

Justice Owen Roberts was closely associated with the legalistic concept of judicial review. He once described the process as a rather simple one: all a judge does is to lay the constitutional provision involved beside the statute being challenged and decide whether the latter squares with the former. According to Justice Roberts, judges do not "make" law; they "find" it.

Another associate justice of the Supreme Court, Felix Frankfurter, had a much different concept of judicial review. Acccording to him many of the key words and phrases that appear in the Constitution, such as "due process of law" and "equal protection of the law," are so vague and undefined that they compel a judge to read his own views into them. Those views, in turn, depend on the judge's own personal philosophy and scheme of values, which he acquires from his particular background and experiences. Since matters of discretion are involved, judges, in Frankfurter's view, *do* "make" law rather than simply "find" it.

Few students of the judicial process, including judges themselves, would agree with Justice Roberts's simplistic concept of judicial review. If deciding whether a law is constitutional or not is as simple as he claims, why is there so much disagreement among justices hearing the same case? Or why does the Court overrule its former decisions, as it has done on many occasions over the years? Frankfurter's concept of the process of judicial review is much more realistic.

But even if a judge concedes that values play a part in his thinking, he still has the problem of deciding the extent to which he will allow his values to affect his rulings on constitutional issues. Perhaps because Frankfurter was so sensitive to how an individual's background and experiences shape his personal values, he is generally identified as a **"nonactivist"** judge, one who was hesitant to substitute his constitutional values for those of legislators and executives. For example, in a 1940 decision, *Minersville School District* v. *Gobitis,* Frankfurter, in upholding the right of a school board to expel students who refused to salute the flag as required by Pennsylvania state law, took the position that the courts have no competence to tell political authorities that they are wrong to use this method of instilling patriotism in children.

The **"activist"** attitude concerning the role that judges feel they should play in constitutional issues is exemplified by Justice Robert Jackson's opinion in *West Virginia State Board of Education* v. *Barnette,* decided three years later, which specifically overruled the *Gobitis* case. In declaring a similar West Virginia flag-salute law unconstitutional, Jackson reasoned that the law interfered with a child's freedom of speech because he had the right to be silent and not be obliged to utter what was not in his mind. The justice went on to assert that the right of legislative discretion to which Frankfurter referred should be more restricted when it affects civil liberties than when property rights are involved.

This last comment of Justice Jackson points up another important aspect of the concept of judicial review: how activist or nonactivist a judge is may well depend on the particular value that is at stake in a given case. Thus Justice Jackson was less willing to defer to the judgment of political authorities on civil liberties than he was on those affecting property rights. Other judges, like Frankfurter, may be unwilling to permit freedom of speech or racial tolerance to occupy a higher place in their scheme of values than property interests.

Analysis of Supreme Court decisions over the years reveals the attitudes of individual justices that underlie the positions they take in a series of cases reaching the Supreme Court. Some, for example, consistently vote on the side of the individual in civil liberties cases; others tend to favor economic have-nots in litigation against affluent interests; still others generally prefer one side in litigation between certain kinds of individuals; federalism is also an issue that some justices respond to in a fairly consistent manner.

However, personal values do not always control a case. A judge sometimes puts other considerations ahead of them. He may, for example, respect the views of an influential colleague on a case or decide to go along with his fellow judges in order to present a unanimous decision to the public. He may also hesitate to overrule a former case; nonactivist judges also hesitate to invalidate actions of other public officials.

There is little question, however, that in exercising the right of judicial review, Supreme Court justices have considerable discretion in deciding cases on the basis of their own value systems. (As Max Lerner commented some years ago, "Judicial decisions are not babies brought by constitutional storks.") Unlike many cases at the lower level of our judicial system, those that reach the Supreme Court do not typically involve technical legal issues but rather broad philosophical questions for which there are no easy or automatic answers. In passing on such matters, justices of the Supreme Court, then, like legislative and executive officials, make public policy.

Judicial review is certainly an important feature of American democracy, but its role in public-policy making must be kept in perspective. For one thing, most of the work of the Supreme Court consists of the interpretation of statutes passed by Congress, not in determining whether they are constitutional. Moreover, as the following section indicates, even when the Supreme Court does decide a constitutional issue, the controversy is not necessarily ended.

THE SUPREME COURT IN THE POLITICAL PROCESS

Even though the life tenure of Supreme Court justices protects them from the kinds of pressures that elected officials face, they are not totally insulated from the political process. In particular, the two coordinate branches of the national government are in a position to check the Court's actions in a number of significant ways. Included are direct checks involving specific judicial decisions and indirect methods designed to affect the general activities of the Supreme Court.

The Court and Congress

Congress has the power to affect Supreme Court decisions by passing laws that reverse or modify what the Court has previously done on an issue. Examples of this technique, already referred to in Chapter 3, are the enactment of legislation deeding tideland oil properties to the states after the Court had ruled that the national government, not the states, owned such lands, and the passage of legislation permitting states to regulate insurance companies following a Court decision holding that they fell under the control of the national government through its interstate commerce power.

Some reversals of Supreme Court decisions cannot be accomplished through ordinary legislation, and Congress must initiate constitutional amendments to achieve its purposes. When the court ruled in *Chisholm* v. *Georgia* (1793) that a state could be sued in a federal court by a citizen of another state, the Eleventh Amendment was enacted to deny jurisdiction in such cases. The *Pollock* v. *Farmers' Loan and Trust Company* decision (1895), which invalidated a national income tax, was ultimately reversed through the passage of the Sixteenth Amendment granting Congress the power to enact such a tax without apportioning it among the various states. More recently, when the Supreme Court ruled in 1970 that Congress could not grant 18-year-olds the right to vote in state and local elections, the Twenty-sixth Amendment was enacted in 1971 to achieve that result.

In addition to reversing specific judicial decisions, the national legislature can affect the Court's consideration of particular kinds of issues through its power to determine the Court's appellate jurisdiction. A famous example of the use of this power is the passage in the immediate post–Civil War period of legislation that had the effect of denying the Court appellate jurisdiction over certain cases in which the constitutionality of the Reconstruction acts was at issue. The tactic was particularly effective in that instance because the Court bowed to Congress's will by dismissing a case on which it had already heard arguments but had not yet ruled.

Taking away the Court's jurisdiction over a case it has already heard is rare; trying to prevent the justices from deciding certain issues in future litigation is much more common. This was the approach used by Senator William Jenner of Indiana in the late 1950s when he introduced legislation that would have denied the Court appellate jurisdiction over a number of issues on which he felt that the Court had unduly favored the rights of individuals at the expense of internal security. Included in the statute's coverage were the rights of witnesses before congressional committees, the removal of federal employees for reasons of national security, state antisubversion laws and regulations regarding the activities of school teachers, and state statutes pertaining to admission to the bar. More recently, attempts have been made to deny the Supreme Court appellate jurisdiction over other controversial issues such as reapportionment, abortion, busing, and school prayer. Like the Jenner bill, all failed to be passed by Congress.

Control over court personnel is still another power whereby Congress can affect the actions of the tribunal. Thus the number of justices is determined by legislation, and this number has varied from five to ten over the years since 1789. An example of the use of this power for political purposes was the enlargement of the Court by the Radical Republicans in 1869 after President Johnson left office so that President Grant (whom they controlled) could appoint an additional justice. Franklin Roosevelt tried a similar technique in 1937 with his Court-packing bill. The number of justices has remained at nine since 1869, however, which may mean that manipulating the size of the Court is now considered improper and will be, as in Roosevelt's case, unsuccessful.

The concern of Congress with Court personnel can also be directed at particular persons. As we have already seen, the Senate can interject constitutional issues into its consideration of nominees to the Court. In recent years nominees have frequently been questioned by the Senate Judiciary Committee about their judicial philosophy and "activist" or "nonactivist" views; at the time of his nomination for the chief justiceship, Associate Justice Fortas was criticized by Senators Eastland and McClellan for his rulings in obscenity cases. Nor do attacks on judges necessarily cease once they are confirmed. Justice William Douglas, who joined the court in 1939, was on two occasions—the first in 1953 and the second in 1970—the object of impeachment resolutions in the House of Representatives. Neither attempt was successful.

Thus the Congress has a number of

Justice William O. Douglas.

weapons that it can use to affect the activities of the Supreme Court. For the most part it has used the less drastic of these measures, such as reversals or revisions of Supreme Court decisions and the failure to confirm nominees, rather than more severe anticourt actions, such as altering the appellate jurisdiction of the Court, tampering with its size, or impeaching sitting judges.*

The Court and The Presidency

Like the Congress, the president has several powers at his disposal that can effect the actions of the Supreme Court. One such power has already been discussed: the appointment of justices. As Robert Dahl has pointed out, over the years one new justice has been appointed on the average of every two years; a president, then, can expect to appoint two judges for each term he has in office. Thus a chief executive can, through a judicious choice of persons with policy views similar to his own, influence the general direction of the court's thinking, as Franklin Roosevelt did through his nine appointments. If the Court is divided, even a smaller number of appointments can be crucial: immediately after President Nixon chose Chief Justice Burger and Associate Justice Blackmun, the court began to modify the general tenor of its rulings, particularly with respect to procedural rights of the accused in criminal proceedings. Subsequent appointments by Nixon (Powell and Rehnquist), Ford (Stevens), and Reagan (O'Connor) eventually brought about changes in the Court's general attitude on a range of civil liberties and civil rights issues we will examine in Chapters 14 and 15.†

The president also shares with Congress the power to enact legislation affecting the court. In fact, the initiative for such legislation may come from the chief executive, as it did in the Court-packing plan of 1937. Even when this is not the case, however, the president's veto power means that legislation affecting the Court will probably not be successful unless it meets with his approval.

Finally, the president has the ability to affect Supreme Court decisions that require his action for implementation. Recall one of Chief Justice Marshall's problems in the *Marbury* v. *Madison* decision: if he ruled that the former had a right to his justice-of-the-peace commission, President Jefferson might tell Madison not to deliver it to him. Just such an eventuality occurred when Marshall ruled in two separate decisions, *Cherokee Indian* v. *Georgia* (1831) and *Worcester* v. *Georgia* (1832), that the state had no legal authority over land occupied by the Cherokee Indian tribe, and President Jackson refused to take steps to implement either ruling. On the other hand, the positive effect that a chief executive can have on a Supreme Court ruling is demonstrated by President Truman's order to Secretary of Commerce Charles Sawyer to return the steel mills to their private owners after the Court's decision in *Youngstown Sheet and Tube Company* v. *Sawyer* (1952) that

* There are other potential weapons that Congress could use against the Court, but past experience demonstrates that they have little chance of passage. Included are requirements that Court decisions invalidating national laws be either unanimous or by extra-majorities, that Congress be empowered to overrule Supreme Court decisions by extra-majority votes, and that the electorate be given the power to overturn such decisions. Attempts to require that Supreme Court justices have previous judicial experience have also failed to gather sufficient congressional support to pass.

† Ironically, while Jimmy Carter appointed more persons to the lower federal courts than any president in history, he made no appointments to the Supreme Court. He became the first full-term chief executive in history to be denied the opportunity to name at least one member to the Court.

the chief executive had no authority to seize them. Further evidence of the key role that the president plays in implementing Court rulings is provided by the actions of Presidents Eisenhower and Kennedy in sending federal troops and marshals to enforce school desegregation decisions. President Nixon's compliance with the Court's decision that he turn over tapes subpoenaed by the special prosecutor led to disclosures of the President's involvement in the Watergate cover-up that ultimately forced him to resign his office.

The combination of powers of the Congress and the president with respect to the Supreme Court means that they can have a major effect on its actions. Robert Dahl, who some years ago analyzed the ultimate outcome of Court decisions declaring acts of Congress unconstitutional, concludes that legislation reversing and revising such decisions and new presidential appointees to the court who vote to overrule them, mean that if the two political branches are agreed on a matter of public policy, they will eventually get their way. Dahl contended that the most the Court can do is delay the application of a policy for a number of years, as occurred, for example, between the 1895 ruling in the Pollock case and the passage of the Sixteenth Amendment in 1913.

While members of Congress and the president have positive powers that they can use to check the Supreme Court, other public officials are frequently able to have a negative effect on its actions through delaying or even avoiding the execution of its orders. For just as some Supreme Court decisions require the president to enforce them, others depend for their ultimate effectiveness on what individuals in other political positions do about implementing them.

Lower Courts and Supreme Court Decisions

Typically, a Supreme Court decision does not end a legal controversy; rather, it remands the case to a lower court which is entrusted with proceeding further on the matter in light of the Court's opinion. One might assume that inferior tribunals would promptly carry out the orders of the highest court; as a matter of practice, lower courts frequently delay or modify the upper court's wishes in significant ways.

The possibilities of lower courts' altering the intentions of the Supreme Court are particularly promising when the highest court's order itself is uncer-

"All the News That's Fit to Print"

The New York Times

LATE CITY EDITION

Weather: Mild, rain early today; partly cloudy tonight, tomorrow. Temp. range: today 60-76; Wed. 60-68. Highest Temp.-Hum Index yesterday: 66. Details on Page 66.

VOL. CXXIII . . No. 42,551 — © 1974 The New York Times Company — NEW YORK, THURSDAY, JULY 25, 1974 — 15 CENTS

NIXON MUST SURRENDER TAPES, SUPREME COURT RULES, 8 TO 0; HE PLEDGES FULL COMPLIANCE

tain and vague. The classic instance was the Supreme Court's directive following the 1954 desegregation decision to the federal district courts to supervise the integration of the public schools in their areas so that it occurred with **"all deliberate speed."** The exceedingly slow pace of integration in parts of the South led some critics to charge that many judges emphasized the "deliberativeness" of the process to the exclusion of its "speed."

But even when the Court does not grant the lower federal tribunals such broad discretion in implementing its decisions, judges are frequently able to avoid the Court's rulings by distinguishing them in subsequent cases. In doing so, they draw distinctions between the facts of the cases in which these rulings were originally made and those present in the litigation before them.

State tribunals, like lower federal courts, can also obstruct Supreme Court decisions. After the court ruled in 1958 that Alabama could not require the National Association for the Advancement of Colored People to furnish copies of its membership lists as a condition for operating in the state, a prolonged legal battle was carried on at the state level. Through a combination of delays and avoidances with respect to the upper court's rulings, Alabama was able to keep the NAACP from operating in the state for over six years after the 1958 decision was handed down.

State and Local Officials and Supreme Court Rulings

The dramatic events following the 1954 school desegregation decision attest to the role that state officials can also play in obstructing rulings of the Supreme Court. As will be indicated in Chapter 15, Governor Orval Faubus intervened after a federal district court approved the decision of the school board in Little Rock, Arkansas to integrate the schools of that area in the fall of 1957, and it became necessary for President Eisenhower to send federal troops to enforce the district court's order. As we shall also see in Chapter 15, the legislature of Virginia tried to void the integration of the public schools by repealing compulsory school attendance laws and permitting students to attend private schools subsidized by the state. (As with the Faubus incident, however, the Supreme Court's will eventually prevailed as it invalidated Virginia's attempt to circumvent its rulings in this way.)

In many instances the effectiveness of Supreme Court rulings depends on local officials. Studies have indicated, for example, that despite decisions outlawing Bible reading and prayers in the public schools (we will examine these decisions in the next chapter), boards of education still permit such practices in some communities, particularly in rural areas. Similarly, the effect of cases involving the rights of the accused (also discussed in the following chapter) turn on the actual interrogation practices of local law-enforcement officials, while book and magazine dealers determine the consequences of the host of obscenity cases with which the Court has dealt in recent years.

Even though the Supreme Court must depend on others to effect compliance with its rulings, for the most part compliance does occur. Attempts to delay and avoid its edicts are reserved to the more controversial areas of public policy in which the Court's opinions run counter to traditional practices and beliefs. Even then, however, the Court's will eventually prevails in most cases. Despite the unpopularity of school desegregation decisions in the South, the general opposition to the outlawing of prayers and Bible reading in the schools, and the natural reluctance of legislatures to reapportion themselves along the lines required by the Court, the fact of the matter is that many schools did become integrated, religious exercises did disappear from most schools, and state legislatures all over the nation have redistricted themselves as well as the House of Representatives. Such sharp departures from former practices in controversial areas of public policy testify to the major influence that the Court continues to exercise on American life.

ASSESSMENT

It is difficult to reconcile judicial review with some of the major principles and assumptions of democracy. Granting nine persons (or, more precisely, five, since that constitutes a majority of the Court), who are appointed and serve for life, the power to overturn the actions of elected legislative and executive officials violates the idea of majority rule. It also is at variance with the democratic assumption that there are no elites who are intelligent or unselfish enough to make decisions that vitally affect the interests of the remaining members of society.

As indicated in Chapter 1, however, democracy does not always trust the majority; it also seeks to protect certain fundamental rights of minorities. In deciding on constitutional questions, the Supreme Court is in a position to safeguard the fundamental rights of democracy: freedom of speech, the press, and religion, equality, procedural due process in criminal proceedings, and private property.

But assuming that such minority rights should be safeguarded, there still remains the question why Supreme Court justices should be granted that power: what is special about their training and/or position in the political system that qualifies them rather than legislative or executive officials to protect the rights of minorities?

If the major issues that came to the Supreme Court for decision were narrow legal ones, it could be argued that the training of the justices gave them a special expertise to pass judgment on such matters. But as previously suggested, this is not so: the issues that are resolved are mostly broad philosophical ones involving basic values such as racial equality, the separation of church and state, and freedom of speech and the press. There is nothing in a law school education that specifically prepares a judge to deal with such matters; indeed, students of sociology, religion, and communication are probably better qualified than jurists to deal with these three issues. (One area where Supreme Court justices do have special training and sometimes experience as well is in dealing with the procedural rights of accused persons, but even then they are not necessarily familiar with the practical consequences their rulings have on the work of policemen, prosecutors, defense counsels, and trial judges.)

A more valid argument for the Court's prerogative in protecting the rights of minorities is the rather unique political situation that justices enjoy compared to elected legislative and executive officials. It is unrealistic to expect the latter to fully protect the rights of minorities when they are elected by majorities, particularly in times of emergency and stress when the general public is likely to show little concern for the rights of unpopular minorities. A classic example is the "law and order" issue, which has led many members of Congress and executive officials to advocate stricter policies toward persons accused of crime. Only officials who enjoy life tenure can afford to take the position that some Supreme Court judges have taken with respect to the procedural rights of the accused.

Whether judicial review is consistent with democracy or not, it will in all probability continue to be a part of our governing process. It has some 180 years of tradition behind it. Moreover, persons of all different political persuasions support judicial review when it favors values they cherish. Thus conservatives in the 1930s applauded the Court's role in protecting property interests from the incursions of Franklin Roosevelt's New Deal; in recent decades liberals have praised Supreme Court judges for their role in the desegregation of public schools, the reapportionment of state legislatures, and the provision of additional procedural safeguards for those accused of crime.

Judicial review will also survive because it is not an absolute power. Judges are sensitive to public attitudes, as indicated by Justice Roberts's switch in voting on New Deal issues after the 1936 presidential election that Franklin Roosevelt won by a landslide. Furthermore, the Congress and the president have important powers that affect decision-making by the Supreme Court. That body is very much a part of the democratic process.

SELECTED READINGS

An analysis of the lower federal courts written from a political rather than a legal standpoint is Richard J. Richardson and Kenneth N. Vines, *The Politics of Federal Courts* (Boston: Little, Brown, 1970). A similar approach to all the federal courts, including the Supreme Court, as well as to the judicial process in general is Herbert Jacob, *Justice in America* (Boston: Little, Brown 3d ed., 1978). Two good general treatments of the Supreme Court are John R. Schmidhauser, *The Supreme Court* (New York: Holt, Rinehart and Winston, 1960), and Glendon A. Schubert, *Constitutional Politics* (New York: Holt, Rinehart and Winston, 1964). A major reference work is *Guide to the U. S. Supreme Court* (Washington, D. C.: Congressional Quarterly Inc., 1979). A more recent work by the same publisher is *The Supreme Court: Justice and the Law,* 3d ed., 1983. For a controversial inside look at personal relationships among members of the Burger Court, see Bob Woodward and Scott Armstrong, *The Brethren: Inside the Supreme Court* (New York: Simon and Schuster, 1979).

An historical account of the Senate's role in the selection of federal judges (as well as executive officials) is Joseph P. Harris, *The Advice and Consent of the Senate* (Berkeley: University of California Press, 1953). For an excellent analysis of the role that the Federal Judiciary Committee of the American Bar Association plays in the selection of federal judges, see Joel B. Grossman, *Lawyers and Judges: The ABA and the Politics of Judicial Selection* (New York: John Wiley and Sons, 1965).

A general treatment of judicial review is Robert K. Carr, *The Supreme Court and Judicial Review* (New York: Farrar and Rinehart, 1942). An historical analysis of the subject is Robert G. McCloskey, *The American Supreme Court* (Chicago: University of Chicago Press, 1960). For an analysis of judicial review from the standpoint of democratic theory, see Howard E. Dean, *Judicial Review and Democracy* (New York: Random House, 1967).

For a book favoring judicial activism, see Charles L. Black Jr., *The People and the Court: Judicial Review in a Democracy* (New York: The Macmillan Co., 1960). Another, counseling judicial restraint, is Alexander M. Bickel, *The Least Dangerous Branch: The Supreme Court at the Bar of Politics* (Indianapolis: Bobbs–Merrill, 1962). Two early studies of attitudes of Supreme Court justices are C. Herman Pritchett, *The Roosevelt Court* (New York: The Macmillan Co., 1948), and his subsequent *Civil Liberties and the Vinson Court* (Chicago: University of Chicago Press, 1954). A more sophisticated analysis of the same subject is Glendon A. Schubert, *The Judicial Mind* (Evanston: Northwestern University Press, 1965).

An early study urging that the courts be viewed within a political framework is Jack Peltason, *The Federal Courts in the Political Process* (New York: Doubleday and Co., 1953). Two books analyzing the consequences of Supreme Court decisions are Theodore Becker, ed., *The Impact of Supreme Court Decisions* (New York: Oxford University Press, 1969), and Stephen Wasby, *The Impact of the United States Supreme Court: Some Perspectives* (Homewood, Ill.: Dorsey Press, 1970). Two good studies of conflicts between the Supreme Court and the Congress are Walter F. Murphy, *Congress and the Court* (Chicago: University of Chicago Press, 1962), and C. Herman Pritchett, *Congress versus the Supreme Court* (Minneapolis: University of Minnesota Press, 1961). Chapter 6 of Robert Dahl, *Pluralist Democracy in the United States* (Chicago: Rand McNally, 1967), analyzes the extent to which the Court has been able to check actions of the Congress and the president over the years.

PART 4

Individual Freedoms

I read banned books.
AMERICAN SOCIETY OF JOURNALISTS & AUTHORS

CHAPTER 14

Civil Liberties

For 40 years city officials of Pawtucket, Rhode Island have constructed a Christmas display near the downtown shopping district. It incorporates a variety of elements, including reindeer, Santa Claus' sleigh and house, a Christmas tree, colored lights, and a nativity scene or crèche. In 1980 several residents of the city in conjunction with the state chapter of the American Civil Liberties Union filed a suit challenging the inclusion of the crèche in the display on the grounds that it violated the First Amendment's prohibition against an "establishment" of religion. Both the federal district court and the federal court of appeals upheld the claim. The city appealed to the Supreme Court, asking it to reverse the lower court rulings so that the city could continue to use the nativity scene in the Christmas display. Filing an *amicus curiae* brief* with the High Court on the side of the city was Rex Lee, the Solicitor General of the United States, who represented the view of the Reagan administration on the issue.

The Supreme Court in a 5–4 decision ruled in favor of the city. The majority opinion written by Chief Justice Warren Burger declared that the Constitution does not require complete separation of church and state; it " . . . affirmatively mandates accommodation, not merely tolerance, of all religions, and forbids hostility towards any. Anything less would require a 'callous indifference' that was never intended by the Establishment Clause." Applying a three-part test to this particular case, the Chief Justice and his assenting colleagues found that the city had a secular (not sectarian) purpose for including the crèche in its display, that the primary effect of the display did not impermissibly advance religion, and that the city display did not create an "excessive entanglement" between religion and government.

* An *amicus curiae* brief is a brief filed by an individual or group who is not a direct party to the lawsuit but who has an interest in its outcome.

Speaking for the minority justices (Brennan, Marshall, Blackmun, and Stevens) Justice Brennan held that Pawtucket's action amounted to an "impermissible governmental endorsement of a particular faith." He then went on to say that regarding the crèche as merely a traditional symbol, no different from Santa's house or reindeer, ". . . is not only offensive to those for whom it has profound significance but also insulting to those who insist, for religious or personal reasons, that the story of Christ is in no sense a part of 'history,' nor an unavoidable element of our national 'heritage.' " In a separate dissenting opinion in which Justice Stevens joined, Justice Blackmun declared, "Surely, this is a misuse of a sacred symbol."

The decision brought a mixed response, generally being favored by Roman Catholics bishops and fundamentalist Christians but criticized by Jewish, Islamic, and some Christian groups. As we shall see, this was just one of a series of recent controversial cases in which the Court has had to rule on church–state relationships. Before explaining them in detail, however, we need to explore the broad issue of civil liberties in the United States.

LIBERTY AND AUTHORITY

Civil liberties are freedoms enjoyed by individuals in a democratic society. However, as indicated in Chapter 1, such liberties are never absolute; society, acting through the authority of government, imposes restrictions on those liberties. In fact, there is an inevitable conflict between liberty and authority in a free society. Both concepts exerted powerful and divergent influences on our own nation's development. Many of the early settlers came to America for religious liberty—the right to worship God as they saw fit rather than as prescribed by the dictates of an established church. At the time of the Revolutionary War, Patrick Henry proclaimed, "Give me liberty or give me death," and a century later the country fought a bloody civil war over the liberty of the black man. Yet the place of authority in the American political tradition is reflected in the colonists' initial reluctance to use violence to overthrow British rule and in our people's continuing attachment to law and order and the attendant legal system inherited from the mother country.

Indeed, the classic problem of all democratic societies is how to reconcile liberty and authority. Madison grasped the essential nature of the issue for constitution builders when he stated in *Federalist* 51, "In framing a government which is to be administered by men over men, the great difficulty lies in this: you must first enable the government to control the governed; and in the next place, to control itself." Lincoln pointed up the same problem for those seeking to preserve constitutional order. Calling on Congress in July 1861 to support a series of measures he deemed necessary for the nation's survival, he posed the rhetorical question. "Must the government, of necessity, be too strong for the liberties of its own people, or too weak to maintain its own existence?"

Democratic governments must somehow preserve political authority at the same time that they promote the liberties of their people. The issue becomes not a matter of liberty *or* authority but liberty *and* authority. For without the minimum conditions of order, individual liberties are meaningless; concomitantly, *perfect* order is present only in the deadening security of a prison. The crux of the issue is, how much liberty and how much authority? How can a free and secure society achieve a balance between these two values?

Even if a democracy manages to strike a delicate balance between individual liberty on the one hand and governmental authority on the other, another knotty problem remains: how can it resolve conflicts that arise because the exercise of certain liberties by some persons impinges on different rights claimed by others? A classic case is the newspaper editor who, in the course of enjoying freedom of the press, publishes information relating to a crime that jeopardizes the right of the accused to a fair trial.

THE GENERAL NATURE OF CIVIL LIBERTIES

It is helpful to distinguish between two major types of liberties protected by the American Constitution, those "in" government and those "from" government. The former relate to *participation in the political process.* The most obvious such liberty is voting; however, Americans can affect what the government does in other ways as well. For example, the First Amendment freedoms of speech, press, assembly, and petition permit individuals to communicate their ideas on public issues to government officials as well as to their fellow citizens.

Liberties "in" government may properly be viewed from the standpoint not only of the individual who enjoys them but also of the government, which is their ultimate beneficiary. As we noted previously, democratic societies assume that there is no discoverable political truth and that the closest we can come to this ideal is to adopt what emerges as the political choice from the marketplace of ideas. Thus the exercise of the franchise together with the ancillary rights of speech, press, assembly, and petition are essential to the operation of a democratic form of government because they become the means for achieving one of the major aims of constitutionalism: holding the rulers *responsible* to the ruled.

The other major aim of constitutionalism is *limiting* the scope of government, that is, walling off areas of human activity from governmental interference. Liberties "from" government, then, relate to *the private preserves that individuals enjoy against the state.* A primary example is freedom of religion, which is safeguarded by the First Amendment. Another is the sanctity of an individual's house (a reflection of the traditional British concept that "a man's home is his castle"), as well as his or her person, papers, and effects against unreasonable searches and seizures. Amendments Two through Eight of the Constitution all serve to protect an individual's property, freedom of movement, and life by providing that no person may be deprived of those by the government except under carefully prescribed conditions. For example, one's property may be taken by the government for public use only if one receives just compensation. A person may be fined, imprisoned, or even put to death for committing a crime, but only after the government has followed definite procedures designed to safeguard that person's interests.

Liberties "from" government are thus related to a basic democratic value, *privacy,* which was considered in Chapter 1. This concern with privacy has been reflected in some major Supreme Court cases in recent years dealing with such controversial issues as the right of a woman to have an abortion, a subject we will examine later in this chapter.

The American Constitution thus provides a variety of liberties designed to keep the government both responsible to the people and limited in its intrusion into their personal affairs. We have already examined those liberties relating to participation in the electoral process, such as making financial contributions to political campaigns, voting, and having one's vote count equally in congressional elections. In this chapter we focus on several other basic liberties, including freedom of religion, freedom of expression, privacy, and the protections offered persons accused of committing a crime.

It should be noted that the liberties described above relate to everyone in American society. In the next chapter we will examine a related but somewhat different issue: the struggle for equality waged by members of particular groups in society, such as blacks, women, and Hispanics. The term that has been used in recent years to designate that particular issue is civil *rights* rather than civil *liberties,* and that distinction has been observed by separating the two matters into separate chapters. It should be understood, however, that traditionally no distinction has been made between the terms *liberties* and *rights* (the first 10 amendments of the Constitution are referred to as the Bill of Rights, and none of them deals with the issue of equality); in this chapter the term *right* is used interchangeably with *liberty* in order to avoid the awkwardness of having constantly to repeat the latter word.

Finally, it should be noted that our federal system provides safeguards against improper actions by either the national government or the states. However, as we shall see, the sources of these protections are different.

CONSTITUTIONAL RESTRICTIONS ON THE NATIONAL GOVERNMENT: THE BILL OF RIGHTS

Those who took the initiative in calling the Constitutional Convention were primarily concerned with protecting property rights from state governments. In contrast, they gave almost no consideration to safeguarding civil liberties from actions of national authorities. When George Mason (a major author of the Virginia Declaration of Rights) proposed toward the end of the Convention that a committee be appointed to prepare a Bill of Rights for the document, Roger Sherman replied briefly that the various states already had bills of rights and, therefore, one for the national government was unnecessary. The delegates quickly sided with Sherman on the issue, and Mason's motion failed to draw support from a single state. With the exception of the idealistic (and nonbinding) language of the Preamble referring to "Justice" and "the Blessings of Liberty" and the few restrictions on Congress in Article I, Section 9, the original Constitution emerged from the Convention with few safeguards for civil liberties.

In the ratification campaign the absence of a Bill of Rights became one of the major targets for those opposed to the Constitution. Even Adams and Jefferson, who favored its adoption, were unhappy that the framers had not included a statement of rights. Hamilton said that none was necessary since the national government possessed certain enumerated powers only and thus had no authority to invade individual liberties; Wilson argued that enumerating rights would be dangerous because any not expressly listed would be presumed to have been purposely omitted. Randolph held that listing rights was futile—"You may cover whole skins of parchment with limitations, but power alone can limit power."

The proponents of a Bill of Rights eventually had their way, however: several of the states ratified the Constitution with the express understanding that the first order of business for the first Congress would be the drawing up of a Bill of Rights to be submitted as amendments to the Constitution. Acting under a moral rather than legal obligation, Washington in his first inaugural address asked Congress to give careful attention to the demands for such amendments, and Madison took the leadership in coordinating the suggestions of state-ratifying conventions and introducing them into the House. Congress pared down the list of proposals; 10 were eventually ratified. Both anti-Federalists and Federalists gained from the process: the former saw their initial support for a Bill of Rights vindicated while the latter gained additional popular support for the Constitution they authored.

Thus the struggle over the protection of civil liberties against the national government took place within political arenas: the Constitutional Convention, the Congress, and the ratifying state legislatures. But we shall see that a similar battle against encroachments of state officials came primarily through the

CONSTITUTIONAL RESTRICTIONS ON STATE VIOLATIONS OF CIVIL LIBERTIES

Early in our constitutional history the states rather than the national government showed greater concern for civil liberties. Jefferson and Mason drafted Virginia's Declaration of Rights shortly before the Declaration of Independence was signed. In it they set forth the same general tenets that were later echoed in the more famous document: men are entitled to certain inherent rights of life, liberty, property, and the pursuit of happiness. Moreover, the Virginia Declaration spelled out in much greater detail than the national one the basic freedoms of the press and religion and the right to a jury trial that were safeguarded against action by Virginia officials. Other jurisdictions followed suit, with the result that all the early state constitutions either contained a separate bill of rights or incorporated similar provisions as part of the basic document.

When the first Congress turned to the development of a Bill of Rights, its primary attention was focused on the national authorities for obvious reasons: this was the level of government that persons concerned with civil liberties feared, and in any event state officials were restricted by their own constitutions. At one point the House proposed an amendment prohibiting states from infringing on the right to trial by jury in criminal cases or on rights of conscience, speech, and the press, but the measure was defeated by the Senate. Although the first 10 amendments nowhere stated specifically that they applied to the national government but not the states (the First Amendment does read, however, "Congress shall make no law," and presumably this phrase is read into the amendments that follow), this was undoubtedly the intention of those who drafted them in the early 1790s, and four decades later the Supreme Court so ruled in *Barron* v. *Baltimore* (1833).

What the Senate and the Court initially refused to do—that is, to utilize the first 10 amendments to restrict state as well as national authorities—has largely come to pass today as a result of a number of decisions of the Supreme Court. In 1925 the Court held in *Gitlow* v. *New York* that freedom of speech and the press are such fundamental rights that they should be construed as "liberties" protected by the Fourteenth Amendment from impairment by states. Subsequently, by similar judicial reasoning, all the other First Amendment freedoms and some others as well (such as the right to privacy) have been added to the liberties so protected. To date the Court has been unwilling to say that the Bill of Rights applies *in toto* to the states, but, as we will see later in this chapter, almost all the procedural safeguards set forth in Amendments Four through Eight, which federal authorities must respect in criminal cases, have now also been held to bind state officials in proceedings against persons accused of violating state laws. So the afterthought of the national Constitution—the first 10 amendments—has become a major source of rights "in" and "from" government at the state level, while state constitutions—which served as inspirations for the Bill of Rights—have proved to be less effective in protecting civil liberties.

FREEDOM OF RELIGION

Americans, who enjoy freedom from government interference in religious matters, frequently assume that this right has been traditional ever since the Puritans fled England in the early 1620s and came to Massachusetts to escape the dictates of the official Anglican church. The facts of the matter, however, are that the Puritans proceeded to establish a church of their own—the Congregational—and forced all inhabitants to follow its religious precepts. Other colonies followed a similar practice, and as late as the Revolutionary War most of them had established churches.

The established churches that prevailed before the Revolution did not survive long in the postwar period. The Virginia Declaration of Rights of 1776 contained an article on religious freedom drafted by Patrick Henry, and three years later the Anglican church was disestablished there. A proposal favored by Patrick Henry and George Washington to make all Christian churches state religions of equal standing and to support them by taxation was rejected in favor of the preference of Madison, Jefferson, and Mason for the separation of religious and civil affairs. As this policy was enunciated in the famous Virginia Statute of Religious Liberty of 1786, ". . . no man shall be compelled to frequent or support any religious worship, place, or ministry whatsoever." This general attitude towards church–state relations also became dominant in other states as the proliferation of religious sects made it the only practical course of action to pursue.

Religious freedom also became a national policy. It was written into the Northwest Ordinance of 1787 and that same year was implemented in the constitutional clause prohibiting the use of a religious test as a requirement for public office (Article VI). Finally, religious freedom was guaranteed in the First Amendment's provision that ". . . Congress shall make no law respecting an establishment of religion, or prohibiting the free exercise thereof."

Historically the Bill of Rights served as a check on the national government only, and therefore actions of state and local officials on religious matters were not affected by the provisions of the national Constitution. In 1940, however, in the case of *Cantwell* v. *Connecticut,* the Supreme Court extended the principle of its previously mentioned 1925 decision on free speech (i.e., it is so fundamental that it should be construed as a "liberty" safeguarded by the Fourteenth Amendment) to make it applicable to the states. With this decision, the First Amendment protection of free choice in religion, which had been of little constitutional importance up to that time (few activities of national authorities touched on religious matters), became a matter of great concern as state and local actions affecting religious freedom began to be challenged in the federal courts.

It should be noted that the relevant First Amendment provisions contain two separate concepts: (1) the government cannot by law establish religion; (2) the government cannot prohibit the free exercise of religion. Thus public authorities cannot take either positive or negative action with respect to religious matters. Although these two concepts are somewhat related, for the most part they convey distinct ideas and have been so treated by the courts. For these reasons, we will examine them separately.

Prohibition Against the Establishment of Religion

The first major case in which the Supreme Court directly articulated the concept of separation of church and state was *Everson* v. *Board of Education,* decided in 1947. The case arose in New Jersey, where, pursuant to state law, a local school board reimbursed parents for costs they incurred in transporting their children to parochial schools. Since the Court by this time had ruled that religious liberty was protected against state action by the Fourteenth Amendment, the issue in the case was whether such expenditure of funds constituted the establishment of religion.

The majority opinion, written by Justice Hugo L. Black, interpreted the principle of the separation of church and state to mean that neither the federal, nor a state government can pass laws that ". . .aid one religion, aid all religions, or prefer one religion over another." Nor can either levy a tax to support any religious activity. He went on to adopt Jefferson's thesis that there must be a "wall of separation" between church and state, even though no such language appears in the First Amendment itself. (Jefferson used the famous phrase in 1802 in a letter to a religious group explaining his interpretation of the First Amendment.)

But having enunciated what appeared to be a strict interpretation of church–state relations, Justice Black and the majority of the Court nevertheless held that the reimbursement of parents did not violate the wall-of-separation principle and hence was constitutional. They took the position that the use of public funds for transportation did not aid religion or the church, but benefited the children by contributing to their safety. Four justices dissented from the majority opinion. Justice Jackson said that the majority view reminded him of Byron's heroine, Julia, who ". . .whispering 'I will ne'er consent'—consented." Another contended that the child-benefit theory employed by the majority could be employed with equal justification for other expenditures for parochial schools, including teachers' salaries, buildings, equipment, school lunches, textbooks, and so forth, since all ultimately benefit the child who attends the school.

Over the years the Supreme Court has had to draw fine lines on this difficult issue. In the past it has tended to strike down financial support for parochial primary and secondary schools on the grounds that aid for such items as teachers' salaries, instructional materials, or reimbursement of tuition or tuition tax credits for parents who send their children to nonpublic schools—all advance the religious activities of such schools or ". . .foster excessive governmental entanglement. . ." with religion. On the other hand, the court has generally approved expenditures of both federal and state grant moneys to church-related colleges and universities. In doing so, the justices have emphasized not the specific form of the aid, but the character of such institutions of higher learning, finding them not to be so "pervasively sectarian" that aid would have the primary effect of advancing religion. The distinction the Court seems to be drawing is one between aid to parochial schools that have a self-professed purpose of instilling religious values in children and which are subject to church control, and aid to church-related colleges and universities in which religion plays a minor role in the school curriculum and where the institutions themselves are largely independent of church authorities.

Behind the dispute over the application of the child-benefit theory to expenditures for parochial schools lies a

Justice Hugo Black.

SUPREME COURT OUTLAWS OFFICIAL SCHOOL PRAYERS IN REGENTS CASE DECISION

RULING IS 6 TO 1

Suit Was Brought by 5 L. I. Parents Against Education Board

Majority opinions and dissent will be found on Page 16.

By ANTHONY LEWIS
Special to The New York Times.

WASHINGTON, June 25—The Supreme Court held today that the reading of an official prayer in New York public schools violated the Constitution.

The prayer was drafted by the New York Board of Regents and recommended in 1951 for recital aloud [illegible] teachers and [illegible]

more fundamental difference in attitude concerning the role that such schools can and should play in a democratic society. Those who support expenditures for parochial schools take the position that they are important for the education of a large number of students in our society, and that without them the public schools would be forced to absorb more students, with a consequent rise in educational costs. They also point out that, as the Supreme Court held in a 1925 case, *Pierce v. Society of Sisters,* parents have a legal right to send their children to parochial schools, and if this right is to become meaningful, then some assistance for those schools is needed to relieve the double financial burden of parents who now must pay taxes for public schools that their children do not attend. Finally, the parochial schools are not viewed as raising serious religious problems in American society because they devote most of their activities to educating students in secular rather then sectarian subjects.

Those who oppose public expenditures for parochial schools take the general position that public schools have had an important democratizing influence by bringing together children of various religious backgrounds in their formative years. They regard the separation of children in the schools on the basis of religion as undesirable, particularly since religious differences are often related to ethnic, social, and economic distinctions among individuals. They therefore do not want to see the government take any action that may foster parochial schools at the expense of public ones. They feel that if parents want to send their children to church-supported rather than to public schools, they should bear the financial burden of that choice themselves and not expect the rest of society to assist them. Finally, they believe that it is not possible in the educational process to draw clear distinctions between sectarian and secular matters and that religious points of view have an effect on how nonreligious subjects are taught.

The Supreme Court has been faced in recent years with another issue relating to the establishment of religion: whether public schools themselves may foster religious exercises in any way. In a 1948 case, *McCollum* v. *Board of Education,* the Court held that school officials in Illinois violated the establishment clause by permitting religious leaders to come to the school during the regular hours to conduct religious classes for students whose parents desired that they receive such instruction. (Other students were given a study period during that time.) Subsequently, however, in *Zorach* v. *Clauson* (1952) the Court held that a similar practice in New York was constitutional because the instruction took place off school property. Dissenting justices argued that where the instruction took place was unimportant and that the use of New York's compulsory school-attendance law to promote religious instruction during regular school hours constituted an establishment of religion.

Recent cases indicate that, while the Court will tolerate religious instruction held off school property during the school day, it will not permit school authorities to conduct religious exercises. In *Engel* v. *Vitale* (1962) the justices declared unconstitutional a practice in New York State of reciting during the regular school period a prayer composed by state officials. That the prayer was religiously neutral, favoring no sect or creed ("Almighty God, we acknowledge our dependence upon thee and we beg thy blessings upon us, our parents, our teachers, and our country"), and that the prayer was voluntary, so students who objected to it did not have to participate in the ceremony, made no difference to the justices. The following year, the Court, in *Abington Township School District* v. *Schempp,* outlawed the reading of the Bible or the recitation of the Lord's Prayer in the public schools. In both cases there was only one dissenter, Justice Potter Stewart, who declared that none of these practices constituted the establishment of religion.

As with the issue of financial aid to the parochial schools, important policy differences exist between those who favor and those who oppose religious exercises in public schools. The former argue that majorities as well as minorities have rights, and it is no great burden on the students who do not want to participate to remain quiet during the ceremonies. The opposition takes the position that the failure to participate in such exercises tends to brand the individuals involved as "oddballs" in the eyes of their fellow students, and that, in any event, religious instruction should be left to other institutions in society—the family and the church—that are better able to offer it than the public schools, which are designed to provide secular education.

Beyond differences about whether a particular practice is wise or unwise for good church–state relationships in a free society, there is also fundamental disagreement over exactly what the Founders meant to prohibit concerning the establishment of religion. One general line of thinking is that they merely wanted to prevent government officials from preferring one religion to another. Under this interpretation the national government (and now state or local ones) can financially support religious activities or foster them in other ways as long as they do not discriminate among various sects and churches in the process. A stricter interpretation of the establishment clause is that those who wrote it into the First Amendment desired to prohibit public officials from undertaking activities that would promote any or all religious groups. Under this reasoning the clause is designed to prevent discrimination not only among religious groups but between religious and nonreligious ones. Thus atheists, who do not believe in a Supreme Being, and agnostics, who have doubts about the existence of one, are also meant to be protected by the establishment clause.

Whatever the historical merits of these two interpretations may be, we do not have a complete separation of church and state in the United States. Financial support for religion exists in the form of salaries paid to chaplains that serve the spritual needs of members of Congress, the service academies, and military forces. Indirect financial assistance is also provided to churches in the form of an exemption from the payment of taxes on property used for religious purposes, a practice that has recently been declared constitutional by the Court. Nor have we removed all vestiges of religion from our public life. Even though the Supreme Court has banned prayers from the public schools, they are still used to open sessions of Congress and the Supreme Court, and each year since 1952, under congressional authority, the president has declared a National Day of Prayer. Finally, the phrase "in God we trust" appears on our currency, and during the Eisenhower administration the words "under God" were added to the Pledge of Allegiance to the Flag.

In recent years the Supreme Court has adopted a less absolutist view on the separation of church and state. In *Widmer* v. *Vincent* (1981), it held that a state university that allows administratively recognized groups to use its facilities for meetings cannot deny such a group this right just because it wants to hold religious meetings.* In 1983 the Court upheld Minnesota's state income tax credit for tuition, textbooks, and transportation expenses for parents who send their children to private parochial schools as well as those whose children attend public schools (*Mueller* v. *Allen*); that same year it also validated the practice of the Nebraska state legislature of opening each session with a prayer given by a chaplain paid by the state (*Marsh* v. *Chambers*). Finally, in the 1984 crèche decision, the Court construed the establishment clause liberally to accommodate the use of a nativity scene in a city Christmas display.

The Free Exercise of Religion

Cases involving the free exercise of religion reached the Supreme Court prior to those relating to the establishment of

* In 1984 Congress enacted legislation granting groups the right to hold religious meetings in the facilities of primary and secondary schools during non-school hours.

religion. The first major case, *Reynolds* v. *United States,* arose in the late 1870s over the Mormon practice of plural marriages. Congress passed a law against polygamy in the territories, and the issue posed by its action was whether this law violated the First Amendment clause prohibiting the national government from interfering with the free exercise of religion. In its decision the Court made a clear distinction between religious beliefs and actions stemming from those beliefs. Thus, the justices reasoned, Mormons could hold the belief that God permits men to have as many wives as possible, but they had no right to implement their belief, because it violates social duty and order.

In other instances, however, the Court has permitted religious groups to act on their beliefs, even though they affect the rights of others. A classic series of cases arose in the 1930s and 1940s as a result of activities of members of the Jehovah's Witnesses sect. Acting on the belief that each member of the group is a minister and has the duty to spread the gospel, Witnesses distributed and sold religious literature in the public streets without complying with state and local laws relating to permits, fees, or taxes. The Court upheld their activities and sustained their right to pass out religious tracts door to door in residential areas. In sustaining such actions the Court balanced the religious liberty of Jehovah's Witnesses to propagate their faith against the right of individuals to privacy—that is, the freedom of individuals not to be bothered by persons seeking to convert them to religious beliefs—and found the former to be more important.*

* Groups can be required, however, to observe reasonable restrictions on proselytizing on public property. In *Heffron* v. *International Society for Krishna Consciousness* (1981) the Court upheld requirements of the state of Minnesota that persons distributing literature or soliciting funds at a state fair must do so from a fixed booth.

Another line of cases relating to the free exercise of religion turns on the issue of whether public authorities can force persons to take actions that run counter to their religious beliefs. As indicated in the previous chapter, two landmark cases in the early 1940s put to constitutional test the practice in some states of requiring students as a part of daily exercises to salute the flag under penalty of being expelled from school. In the first one, *Minersville School District* v. *Gobitis* (1940), the Supreme Court upheld the statute on the grounds that if the legislature felt that the ritual instilled patriotism in children and thus promoted national unity, the Court ought not to interfere with that judgment. Just three years later, however, in *West Virginia State Board of Education* v. *Barnette,* the Court overruled the earlier decision under the reasoning that public officials could not compel students to utter words that they did not believe. In so ruling, Justice Jackson held that under our Constitution, no official can prescribe what is orthodox in politics, nationalism, or religion and force others to confess to such beliefs. In *Wisconsin* v. *Yoder* (1972), the Court upheld the right of Amish parents to refuse to send their children to public schools beyond the eighth grade. Speaking for the majority, Chief Justice Burger held that the worldly values such schools teach are in marked contrast with those inculcated by the Amish way of life, which he characterized as resting on a religious, not merely a philosophical basis.

Amish first grader.

Still another related issue is the observance of days of rest. In a 1961 case, *McGowan* v. *Maryland,* the Supreme Court upheld the constitutionality of Sunday closing laws against attacks that they denied freedom of religion to individuals who closed their stores on Saturday in keeping with their beliefs. In so doing, the Court held that, although Sunday was originally celebrated as a day of rest for religious reasons, it is now a secular holiday, set aside for recreation and family activities. Thus closing laws are no longer related to religious beliefs. The Court also pointed out that persons who celebrate Saturday as a religious holiday are free to close their stores on that day. While recognizing the potential economic burden (their stores would then be closed on both Saturday and Sunday), the justices held that this is merely the indirect effect, not the purpose, of a law regulating secular activity.

Thus the Supreme Court has tried to balance the religious rights of individuals against the interests of other individuals and society generally. As the following section indicates, the justices have struggled to achieve a similar equilibrium with respect to other vital First Amendment freedoms.

FREEDOM OF EXPRESSION

In addition to freedom of religion, the First Amendment spells out a number of other liberties with which Congress may not interfere: freedom of speech and the press, the right of peaceful assembly, and the right to petition the government for a redress of grievances. Together they constitute means by which individuals or groups express their views and communicate them to one another, as well as to their public officials. Insofar as such expressions relate to public issues, they are liberties "in" government, enabling citizens to try to influence public decisions. When they pertain to nonpublic affairs and concerns, however, they are liberties "from" government, for they protect the freedom to communicate views on private matters.

The Supreme Court has recognized another related freedom, that of association, even though no such right appears in the language of the First Amendment itself. In protecting a Southern chapter of the National Association for the Advancement of Colored People from a state law requiring it publicly to divulge its membership, the Court ruled, in *NAACP* v. *Alabama* (1958), that " . . . freedom to engage in association for the advancement of beliefs and ideas is an inseparable aspect of the 'liberty' assured by . . . the Fourteenth Amendment which embraces freedom of speech." The Court did not restrict this freedom of association for public issues only; it rather said that ". . . it is immaterial whether the beliefs sought to be advanced by associations

pertain to political, economic, religious, or cultural affairs." Thus freedom of association is added to other First Amendment rights. (Because the case involved not only the right to associate but also the right to keep group membership lists confidential, the decision also indicates the Supreme Court's concern with the issue of privacy.)

Like religious freedom, those First Amendment liberties relating to expression did not become a matter of major concern for the Supreme Court until relatively recent times. It was not until 1919 that the highest tribunal first directly faced an issue of free speech, in *Schenck* v. *United States,* a case (to be discussed below) concerned with antiwar activities during World War I. In the 1960s civil rights and Vietnam protests presented the Court with still other vital issues involving First Amendment liberties.

Before discussing decisions in these areas, it will be helpful to analyze the general approaches the Court has adopted in seeking to reconcile the right of personal expression with society's concern for order and authority. With these approaches in mind, we will then examine how the Court has applied them to specific situations.

General Approaches to the Issue

Of the various approaches to the issue of freedom of expression, the one advocated by the late Supreme Court Justice Hugo Black is the most *absolute.* Black argued that the Founders wanted the words of the First Amendment to be taken literally; the phrase that Congress shall make "no law" abridging the freedom of speech or the press means just that—national authorities (and presumably state ones as well) cannot take any action that interferes with the free expression of views. Justice Black even went so far as to suggest that the First Amendment means that libel and slander actions (suits brought by private individuals against others who have defamed their character or reputation through written or oral statements) cannot be brought in federal courts. He was also unwilling to have restrictions placed on newspaper comments on criminal cases, even though these comments may jeopardize the right of the accused persons to a fair trial.

While Justice Black held absolutist views regarding the constitutional sanctity of the oral and printed word, he did not extend this attitude to conduct or action. For example, he did not recognize picketing as an absolute right, even though the Supreme Court ruled in *Thornhill* v. *Alabama* (1940) that it is a form of symbolic speech and is thus entitled to the protection of the First Amendment. Moreover, Justice Black took a rather conservative position on the methods by which speech can be implemented. He stated that freedom of speech does not mean that one can express oneself whenever, wherever, and however one pleases. In line with this reasoning, he contended that one person cannot use another person's private property to exercise freedom of expression and that there are even limits on the utilization of public property for such a purpose. Thus Justice Black believed the First Amendment protects absolutely the *content* of speech but not the *manner* by which it is expressed.

A similar general view on freedom of expression was advocated by the late philosopher Alexander Meiklejohn. His attitudes, however, derived not from the historical meaning of the First Amendment itself but from the logic of *self-government.* He argued that freedom of expression is important not only for the individual but also for society; it is not just one's right to speak that is involved but also society's obligation to hear what one has to say. The only way to ensure that a free society will arrive at good decisions is to see to it that all viewpoints are considered, no matter how wrong or dangerous we may consider some of them to be. Meiklejohn suggested that it is not a question of balancing intellectual freedom against public safety; rather, freedom is the bulwark of public safety.

The major difference between Black's and Meiklejohn's views is that Black would apply his absolutist approach to expressions relating to both public and private concerns, while Meiklejohn would restrict his to public affairs. Thus the philosopher, unlike the justice, would not bar private libel and slander suits and would tolerate other reasonable restraints on utterances not relating to "community thinking" or "self-government." Like Black, Meiklejohn would allow restrictions to be placed on the manner in which speech is expressed. For example, the government may suspend utterances until order is established, so that all views may be heard. As he himself expressed it, "When the roof falls in, the moderator may, without violating the First Amendment, declare the meeting adjourned."

Two other general approaches to freedom of expression concern the posture the Supreme Court should take in passing on speech and allied rights. As indicated in the previous chapter, judges differ on the extent to which they feel they should interfere with the actions of legislators and executives on the grounds that they are unconstitutional. Some argue for an "activist" role for the Court, requiring judges to scrutinize carefully the activities of other public officials and to invalidate those that violate what they conceive to be constitutional principles; others feel that Supreme Court justices should assume a "nonactivist" role by presuming the actions of legislators and executives to be constitutional and seldom substituting their constitutional judgments for judgments of those officials.

Those who adopt a **preferred-position** approach to the expression issue (the position is generally associated with Supreme Court Justices Harlan Stone and Wiley Rutledge, but other judges have also followed it) believe that when speech and allied rights become involved in litigation, the Court should take an activist role in reviewing the actions of legislators and executives. The reason is that the First Amendment freedoms are so basic to maintaining the openness of our political system and society that they deserve special or preferred treatment by the courts over other issues. Thus the Court should carefully scrutinize actions of public officials relating to freedom of expression at the same time that it presumes that their activities regulating economic affairs are constitutional. The basis for this special solicitude for rights of free expression is that these rights are particularly important for unpopular minority groups that frequently cannot protect their interests in the political processes of the legislative and executive branches. The special phrasing of the First Amendment (the Congress "shall make no law" respecting religion and expression) further justifies the Court's looking carefully at governmental regulation of such matters rather than presuming them to be constitutional.

The difference between the preferred-position approach and the views advocated by Black and Meiklejohn is thus one of degree. The latter two argue that political authorities cannot place *any* restrictions on the content of political expressions, while those who adopt the preferred-position approach are willing to permit some restrictions, but only under very special circumstances. All three approaches evidence a special solicitude for First Amendment freedoms and require that they be granted a special place in our constitutional order of values.

The man most critical of all the above

approaches was Supreme Court Justice Felix Frankfurter. He was a "nonactivist" who felt that judges should be very reluctant to substitute their constitutional judgments for those of legislative and executive officials on all kinds of issues, including those pertaining to expression. He attacked the preferred-position approach to the problem as a "mischievous phrase" that ". . . attempts to express a complex process of adjudication by a deceptive formula"; he also rejected the absolutist positions of Black and Meiklejohn as doctrinaire. In place of such approaches Frankfurter called for a pragmatic **"balancing,"** that is, a case-by-case weighing of competing values and the exercise of judgment in deciding when restrictions on freedom of expression are warranted in order to protect society's interest in order and authority, or the rights of other individuals or groups. Thus Frankfurter rejected the idea that freedom of expression is either an absolute value or one that is to be necessarily preferred over other legitimate interests.

Although these general approaches to freedom of expression reflect important basic attitudes towards this vital issue, they have not proved to be very helpful in dealing with the wide variety of pertinent cases that have come to the Supreme Court in the last half-century. Although Justice Douglas moved closer to Black's position in his last years on the bench, no other justices have been willing to adopt an absolutist approach. The preferred-position and balancing approaches have been expressed in opinions from time to time, but both reflect a general mood rather than a usable guideline. Thus the former merely suggests that restrictions on freedom of expression are constitutional only under unusual circumstances without indicating what those circumstances are; the latter calls for a balancing of interests without determining the specific interests to be balanced and the weights to be assigned to each.

In attempting to develop more usable guidelines, the Supreme Court has turned to another type of attack on the problem. Rather than look at the issue from the standpoint of the historical meaning of the First Amendment, the logic of self-government, or a general philosophy concerning the role of the Supreme Court vis-à-vis legislators and executives in the protection of free speech, some judges have placed the issue on an *empirical* basis. In doing so, they have utilized certain basic tests relating to the actual *consequences* of given expressions.

Tests of the Consequences of Expression

The judge most prominently identified with analyzing freedom of expression on the basis of consequences was Justice Oliver Wendell Holmes Jr. In the *Schenck* case of 1919 referred to earlier, which involved the indictment of a Socialist for violating the World War I Espionage Act by circulating antiwar leaflets to members of the armed forces, the celebrated jurist spelled out the test to be applied in free-speech cases. Rejecting an absolutist approach by suggesting that no man had the constitutional right to falsely shout fire in a theater, Holmes stated:

> *The question in every case is whether the words are used in such circumstances and are of such a nature as to create a clear and present danger that they will bring about the substantive evils that Congress has a right to prevent. It is a question of proximity and degree.*

In this particular case Justice Holmes upheld the conviction on the basis that the antiwar actions did create a **clear and present danger** to the prosecution of the war, an evil that Congress had the right to prevent. Later that same year, however, in a dissenting opinion in *Abrams* v. *United States,* Holmes held that restrictions on the publication of pam-

Felix Frankfurter.

Oliver Wendell Holmes, Jr.

phlets that attacked the sending of an American expeditionary force to Russia were unconstitutional because the circumstances failed to fulfill the requirements of the test.

The key to the test proposed by Holmes is the meaning of the words *clear* and *present* as they are used in conjunction with danger. Some construe the former to mean "obvious"; Holmes himself never defined *clear* with any exactitude, but he seems to have had in mind the *probable effect* of the speech. Equally crucial to the application of the test is the interpretation of the word *present.* Holmes stated his meaning with considerable precision in the *Abrams* case, in which he said it was a danger that ". . . imminently threatens immediate interference with the lawful and pressing purposes of the law." In any event, the test is considered favorable to freedom of expression, since it places the burden on those that seek to limit expression to demonstrate that restrictions are necessary to prevent the imminent occurrence of an evil that will probably result from the utterance involved.

In contrast with the "clear and present danger" test is the **bad tendency** rule, first utilized by the Supreme Court in *Pierce* v. *United States,* decided just one year after the *Schenck* opinion. Again, Socialists were convicted for distributing antiwar pamphlets, but in this instance there was no indication that any of this literature reached members of the armed forces or had an immediate effect on the war. Even so, the Court upheld the conviction on the ground that the action might eventually have a tendency to cause insubordination and disloyalty among the troops. In so ruling, the Court lifted from those doing the restricting the burden of proving that the speech in question would probably result in an immediate evil and substituted the less onerous requirement of demonstrating that the utterances *might tend* to bring about an evil sometime in the future.

Finally, in 1950 the Supreme Court developed a third empirical standard for evaluating the constitutionality of restrictions on freedom of expression; this standard has come to be known as the **gravity of the evil** or **sliding scale test.** In the 1950 *Dennis* case involving major officers of the American Communist Party charged with conspiracy to overthrow the government by force, Chief Justice Fred M. Vinson ruled that ". . . the Court must ask whether the gravity of the evil, discounted by its improbability, justifies such invasion of free speech as is necessary to avoid the evil." Thus the decision added a new dimension to the issue: the nature of the evil to be avoided. If the evil is grave enough—such as the violent overthrow of the government by force—then one need not demonstrate that the expression to be regulated will probably result in the immediate occurrence of the evil. However if the evil to be represented is not so grave—such as a local disturbance—then those seeking to regulate expression must show that it will probably and imminently bring about the disturbance. Although the Court did not say so, it seemed to be suggesting that if the evil is serious enough, the "bad tendency" test is to be employed; if the evil is not so serious, the "clear and present danger" standard is applicable.

Although the empirical tests provide more definite guidelines for analyzing freedom-of-expression issues than the preferred-position and balancing approaches, they leave unanswered a number of major questions. For example, in the "clear and present danger" test, *to whom* is the occurrence of the evil to be "clear"—the Congress, the president, or the jury that tries the case? What is meant by "present"—tomorrow, next month, next year? In the "gravity of the evil" test, how grave is "grave," and what criteria does one take into account in deciding that question?

The plain fact of the matter is that verbal formulas cannot capture all the complexities of social situations, and judges must ultimately exercise considerable discretion in deciding freedom-of-expression issues. They look at the total circumstances of the particular case before them. Thus it may make a difference *who* made the statement in question—a college freshman or a major official of the Communist party? *When* the statement is made may well be the crucial factor in the Court's thinking—in the midst of a war or threat of war, or during a period of relative calm in international affairs? *Where* the words were said may well be determinative—in a university graduate seminar or at a mass meeting containing militant groups opposed to the speaker's point of view?

Therefore we need to look at the broad environment and the events associated with particular freedom-of-expression issues if we are to understand the nature of such issues and the considerations that are taken into account in dealing with them. In the following sections of this chapter we will focus on some of the major areas in which the important problems of free speech have arisen in recent years.

Political Protests

The dominant domestic political problem in the United States in recent decades was the civil rights revolution, a topic that we will examine in the next chapter. During the last half of the 1960s the war in Vietnam emerged as the major issue in foreign policy. Political protest was an important part of both developments. In the civil rights movement, protests were leveled against the entire structure of segregation and discrimination in the United States; the antiwar protest's main targets were the military, Congress, and the executive branch, as epitomized by the many demonstrations that took place in Washington, D. C.

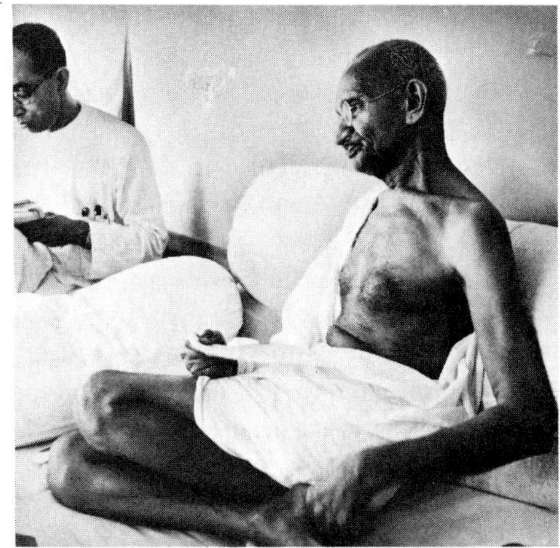

Mahatma Gandhi.

The protests over civil rights and the war in Vietnam involved different purposes and methods. In some instances protesters sought to stay within the law, as did most of those involved in the various demonstrations in the nation's capital; however, others, such as those who tried to occupy the Pentagon in a major protest in 1967, deliberately chose to violate regulations, knowing full well that they would be arrested for doing so.

This latter type of protest, known generally as **civil disobedience,** has been most prominently identified in the United States with Martin Luther King and the antisegregation movement. Borrowed from Mahatma Gandhi, who used civil disobedience successfully against the British in India (Gandhi had borrowed the technique from an American protester, Henry Thoreau, who refused to pay taxes used to prosecute the Mexican War), it is based on the philosophy that individuals need not obey laws that they consider unconstitutional or immoral. Rather, as a matter of conscience and in order to communicate their disapproval of such laws, they are obliged to disobey them. At the same time, if persons follow the doctrine of civil disobedience as taught by leaders like King and Gandhi, they are expected to use passive resistance, not violence, as a tactic and to be willing to accept the legal consequences of punishment for violating laws if their validity is upheld by the courts.

Civil disobedience in the United States in recent decades has taken two major forms. In some instances, protesters have deliberately broken a specific law; thus blacks sat in at Southern lunch counters in violation of segregation statutes in order to show their disapproval of those laws. On other occasions dissenters have violated laws to which they did not specifically object in the course of registering their displeasure with other concerns. An example of this method is the attempt of some protesters to interfere with the flow of traffic into Washington, D. C. in the spring of 1971 in order to publicize their views on the war in Vietnam.

The Supreme Court has never specifically condoned civil disobedience as a means of registering dissent, yet its use by political protesters has raised fundamental constitutional issues for the Court. For example, the infraction of segregation statutes brought into question the constitutionality of such laws, a matter we will examine in the next chapter. In addition, deliberate violations by protesters of regulations regarding the use of public property, along with innocent infractions by others not committed to the idea of civil disobedience, have forced the Supreme Court to determine how far political officials can go in restricting the actions of demonstrators without interfering with their constitutional right of free expression. We examine this latter issue next.

Civil Rights Demonstrations. The most fundamental freedom-of-expression issue raised by civil rights demonstration cases concerns the kinds of limits that may constitutionally be imposed on the place of and how political protests are conducted. A 1963 case, *Edwards* v. *South Carolina,* involved a demonstration held on the grounds of the state capitol by blacks protesting discriminatory practices. Police ordered the crowd of 200 protesters to disperse and, when they failed to do so, arrested them for breach of the peace. The Supreme Court reversed their convictions, emphasizing that the demonstrators were peaceful, that their protest had not interfered with pedestrian or vehicular traffic into the capitol area, and that it had not resulted in a threat of violence either from the demonstrators themselves or the crowd of onlookers. The Court further held that a state may not make criminal the peaceful expression of unpopular views, even though such views may anger some persons who hear them.

Political protest, civil disobedience style.

Other cases have sustained the use of public property for demonstrations, provided they are peaceful and do not interfere with the operation of the facility. In a 1966 case, *Brown* v. *Louisiana,* the Supreme Court upheld a sit-in at a public library by five black adults protesting segregation of this public service. The majority opinion, written by Justice Abe Fortas, stressed that the defendants had the right to protest the segregation of public facilities by "silent and reproachful" presence in a place ". . . where the protestant has every right to be." Four judges dissented in an opinion written by Justice Black, arguing that the blacks were expressing their protest in an inappropriate and unauthorized place, since they had no right to be there after they completed their business.

Although Justice Black's views did not prevail in that instance, they did in the 1966 case of *Adderly* v. *Florida,* which concerned a demonstration of 200 college students outside a county jail. Their convictions for violating a trespass law were upheld by Justice Black and four of his colleagues on the grounds that the students had no right to be on a part of the jail grounds that was set apart for security purposes and not open to the public. In so ruling, Black held that the state, like a private individual, has ". . . the power to preserve the property under its control for the use to which it is properly dedicated." The opinion also contained the statement, typical of Justice Black, that people who engage in protest do not have the right to do so ". . . whenever, however, and wherever they please." Three other judges joined Justice Douglas in dissent, arguing that a county jail housing political prisoners is an obvious center for protest and that the students had not upset the jailhouse routine.

Antiwar Protests. Cases concerning the Vietnam war that reached the Supreme Court did not involve demonstrations by large numbers of people but, rather, protests by individuals. Typically they arose from acts of disobedience and defiance directed against the war and the military, such as the burning of draft cards and the wearing of black armbands in schools. The major legal issue raised by these cases is what constitutes permissible **symbolic speech,** since political views are expressed through conduct rather than words.

In the first major case of this nature, *United States* v. *O'Brien* (1968), four young men were convicted for burning their draft cards in violation of a federal statute making such destruction or mutilation a crime. Chief Justice Warren, speaking for the majority of the Court, sustained their convictions on the grounds that not all conduct can be labeled speech simply because the person engaging in it intends to express an idea, and that the use of draft cards contributed to the administration of the Selective Service System. He held that acts of dissent can be punished if the government has ". . . a substantial and constitutional interest in forbidding them, the incidental restriction of ex-

pression is no greater than necessary, and the government's real interest is not to squelch dissent."

The Supreme Court held, however, in a 1969 case—*Tinker* v. *Des Moines Independent Community School District*—that local school officials could not punish students for violating regulations against wearing black armbands to protest the war in Vietnam. Justice Fortas held this conduct to be ". . . closely akin to pure speech . . ." and pointed out that it had not resulted in any substantial disruption of or material interference with school activities. Justice Black in dissent expressed his usual sentiment that a person does not have the constitutional right to express himself whenever, wherever, and however he or she pleases and objected to transferring the power to regulate pupils from school officials to the Supreme Court.

The Court has thus exhibited a high tolerance for protests against established authority. Other types of actions upheld by the justices have included denouncing the United States flag (*Smith* v. *Goguen*, 1971), wearing a military uniform in a play that was unfavorable to

(1982), it upheld nonviolent boycotts as a collective form of free speech. In *U. S.* v. *Grace* (1983), the Court struck down as unconstitutional a federal law that barred all demonstrations on sidewalks in front of the Supreme Court Building.

Obscenity

No civil liberties issue in recent years has given the Supreme Court more difficulty than obscenity. Most of its members have agreed on the fundamental constitutional question enunciated in the rulings in two key 1957 cases, *Roth* v. *United States* and *Alberts* v. *California*, that obscenity is *not* protected under the freedom-of-speech principle; however, the justices have frequently disagreed over what materials are in fact obscene and the kinds of regulations that can be placed on the distribution and use of such materials.

One major issue has been the development of a satisfactory standard by which to judge obscenity. The test developed in the *Roth* and *Alberts* cases was ". . . whether to the average person, applying contemporary community standards, the dominant theme of the material taken as a whole appeals to prurient interest." In other words, it is not sufficient that the material appeal to the lewd interest of a person especially sensitive to such matters or fail to appeal to a particularly insensitive person; rather, the attitudes and tastes of the *average* person are taken into account. Another important requirement of the *Roth–Alberts* standard is that one cannot focus on isolated passages of a film or piece of literary work to judge its obscenity; instead it is necessary to look at the dominant theme of the entire work.

Another major issue in the area of obscenity concerns the value of the material in question. In a 1966 ruling, *Memoirs* v. *Massachusetts*, a plurality of the Court added a requirement to the *Roth–Alberts* standard: the work must be

". . . utterly without redeeming social value . . ." in order to be declared obscene. This naturally had a liberalizing effect on the obscenity problem, since it is very difficult to prove that material has no social value whatever. Speaking for the Court in *Miller* v. *California* (1973), Chief Justice Burger specifically rejected that standard, substituting in its stead whether a work has ". . . no serious literary, artistic, political, or scientific value." While this latter test takes a variety of considerations into account, it is easier to demonstrate that material has no serious value than it is to establish that it is entirely without value.

Another change in the law of obscenity enunciated in the *Miller* v. *California* decision (1973) involves an interpretation of the word *community* in the phrase "contemporary community standards." For a number of years *community* was construed to mean the nation as a whole, but Chief Justice Burger changed that interpretation in the Miller case to mean a smaller geographical area; however, the opinion is not clear whether the area is to be a state or

HIGH COURT RULES ADS CAN BE PROOF OF OBSCENE WORK

Backs Ginzburg Conviction and 5-Year Term—Cites 'Titillating' Promotion

'FANNY HILL' PLEA WINS

Bench Also Upholds Verdict Against Yonkers Producer of 'Sadistic' Material

Excerpts from court opinions will be found on Page 24.

By FRED P. GRAHAM
Special to The New York Times

WASHINGTON, March 21—By a vote of 5 to 4, the Supreme Court upheld today the obscenity conviction of Ralph Ginzburg, publisher of "Eros" and other erotic literature, and decided that "titillating" advertising could be proof that the advertised material was obscene.

The Court also affirmed, by a 6-to-3 vote, the conviction of

a locality. In *Jenkins* v. *Georgia* (1974), the Court seems to leave the area up to the trial court: the judge can instruct the jury to apply a statewide standard, but such an instruction is not mandatory, and hence *community* can be construed to mean the home community of the jurors.

Despite the *Miller* decision, however, the decision of a jury is not necessarily determinative of what material is in fact obscene. In the *Jenkins* case, which involved the conviction of a Georgia theatre-owner who had shown the film *Carnal Knowledge,* the Court ruled that juries do not have ". . . unbridled discretion in determining what is patently offensive." Justice Rehnquist went on to explain that despite the fact that there are suggestive scenes of sexual acts in the film, ". . . there is no exhibition of the actors' genitals, lewd or otherwise"; he also stated that ". . . nudity alone is not enough to make material legally obscene." The Court took a similar position in a 1975 case, *Esznoznik* v. *City of Jacksonville,* in overturning a city ordinance banning drive-ins from showing movies containing nudity.

Some of the key cases indicate that the Court is willing to go beyond the above tests and look at the total situation in determining whether certain materials are obscene. In *Ginzburg* v. *United States* (1966) the Court not only examined the three works in question (the magazine *Eros,* the newsletter "Liaison," and a book, *The Housewife's Handbook on Selective Promiscuity*), but also determined that the ". . . leer of the sensualist . . ." permeated the advertising for them, a practice the court termed "pandering—the business of purveying textual or graphic matter openly advertised to appeal to the erotic interest of their customers." Two years later in *Ginsburg* v. *New York* (1968), the Court also indicated that the *audience* makes a difference in the obscenity issue: authorities can regulate the sale of materials to minors that would not be constitutionally permissible in dealing with adults.

One of the more puzzling aspects of recent obscenity cases has to do with the possession and distribution of obscene materials. In *Stanley* v. *Georgia* (1969), the Court held that authorities cannot prohibit a person from viewing obscene materials (in this case it was films) shown in the privacy of his or her own home. As the Court put it: "If the First Amendment means anything, it means that a State has no business telling a man sitting alone in his own home, what books he may read or what films he may watch." Yet in two 1971 cases decided the same day, *United States* v. *Reidel* and *United States* v. *Thirty-seven Photographs,* the Court ruled that Congress may constitutionally prevent the mails from being used for distributing obscene materials and it may also prohibit an individual from importing such materials from abroad even for private use. Thus the Court recognizes the right of a person to read or view obscene works in his or her own home but denies that person a major means of obtaining them.

A basic controversy also exists over the reasons for attempting to establish controls over obscene materials. A 1970 Report of the Commission on Obscenity and Pornography (a group of private citizens appointed by President Lyndon Johnson to look into the matter) concluded that there was no empirical evidence that exposure to explicit sexual materials plays a significant role in the causation of social or individual harms such as crime, delinquency, sexual or nonsexual deviancy, or severe emotional disturbances. For these (and other reasons) the Commission held that ". . . there is no warrant for continued governmental interference with the full freedom of adults to read, obtain or view whatever such material they wish." However, President Nixon (who was in office when the Commission's report was issued) repudiated the report and its recommendations as "morally bankrupt" and called on states to enact anti-obscenity laws. Moreover, in a 1973 case, *Paris Adult Theater* v. *Slaton,* Chief Justice Burger also expressly rejected the Commission's reasoning in holding that ". . . a sensitive key relationship of human existence, central to family life, community welfare, and the development of human personality, can be debased and distorted by the crass commercial exploitation of sex"; he went on to suggest that ". . . nothing in the Constitution prohibits a state from reaching such a conclusion and acting on it legislatively simply because there is no conclusive evidence or empirical data." Nor did the Chief Justice think it important that the theater had prevented juveniles from seeing the films involved and given adequate notice to adults concerning the nature of the films.*

There is little question that the obscenity area constitutes a judicial thicket. Justice Burger himself has asserted that it is ". . . an area where there are no eternal verities." Others have gone further: the Justice Hugo Black once complained that "I can imagine no task for which this Court of lifetime judges is less equipped to deal," and in his dissent in the *Miller* case Justice William O. Douglas opined: "There are no guidelines for deciding what is and what is not 'obscene.' The Court is at large because we deal with tastes and standards of literature." It remains to be seen how successful the court will be in dealing with what Justice John Harlan referred to as ". . . the intractible obscenity problem."

* In dealing with cases involving pornography, the Court has placed children in a separate category from adults. In *New York* v. *Ferber* (1982), it upheld state laws prohibiting the promotion of sexual performances by children under 16, reasoning that such depictions are beyond the protection of the First Amendment.

THE RIGHT TO PRIVACY

Of course, there is nothing new about the right to privacy. Justice Felix Frankfurter once referred to it as ". . . the right to be left alone—the most comprehensive of rights and the right most valued by civilized man." Alan Westin, a close student of the subject, associates it with a number of elements in American political philosophy—individualism, limited government, and the link between private property and liberty that Madison borrowed from John Locke. Moreover, the right to privacy underlies some of the basic Bill of Rights amendments protecting an individual's thoughts and religious beliefs, home, other property, and his or her person itself from arbitrary imprisonment or even death at the hands of law-enforcement officials.

Rather, what is new is the Supreme Court's expanding the right of privacy beyond its link with such traditional protections and granting it an independent status of its own. The leading case

HERBLOCK'S CARTOON

in which the Supreme Court indicated its willingness to take this approach to the right of privacy is *Griswold* v. *Connecticut* (1965). In ruling that the state of Connecticut could not prohibit the use of contraceptives by married couples, the majority of the Court enumerated a right of marital privacy, even though it conceded that none was specifically provided for in the Constitution. Justice Douglas spoke of "zones of privacy" created by various guarantees of the First, Third, Fourth, Fifth, and Ninth amendments that help give such guarantees "life and substance"; included is that of marital privacy, which he claimed was older than the Bill of Rights. Justice Goldberg preferred to locate this right in the due process clause of the Fourteenth Amendment as one ". . . so rooted in the traditions and conscience of our people as to be ranked as fundamental"; he also noted that the Ninth Amendment provides that ". . . the enumeration in the Constitution, of certain rights, shall not be construed to deny or disparage others retained by the people." Speaking in dissent, Justice Black voiced his usual sentiment for a literal interpretation of the Constitution: "I like my privacy as well as the next one, but I am nevertheless compelled to admit that government has a right to invade it unless prohibited by some specific constitutional provision."

The Court has since indicated its willingness to extend the reasoning of *Griswold* to the decision whether or not to have children. In *Eisenstadt* v. *Baird* (1972) the Court held that it was also unconstitutional to try to forbid the dissemination of birth control information and devices to unmarried persons. Speaking for the majority, Justice Brennan stated: "If the right of privacy means anything, it is the right of the individual, married or single, to be free from unwarranted governmental intrusion into matters so fundamentally affecting a person as the decision whether to bear or beget a child." A further extension of this same principle came in two 1973 decisions, *Roe* v. *Wade* and *Doe* v. *Bolton,* which invalidated Texan and Georgian statutes regulating abortions. In these decisions the Court reaffirmed the personal right of privacy enumerated in *Griswold* and *Eisenstadt* in ruling that during the first trimester of pregnancy the abortion decision is up to the woman and her attending physician. (The Court did say, however, that during the second trimester of the pregnancy, a state can regulate abortion to protect the mother's health, and in the stage after viability—when the fetus is potentially able to live outside the mother's womb—it can prohibit abortion because of the potential of human life.)

Since 1973 the Court has ruled on the constitutionality of a number of restrictions enacted by state and municipalities on the right of abortion. It has invalidated those requiring the consent of the father, that the abortion be performed only in a hospital, and that there be a waiting period of 24 hours between the signing of an "informed consent" form and the performance of the abortion. The Court has also generally struck down requirements that a minor woman receive parental or judicial consent for an abortion. However, it did uphold a Missouri law that provided a procedure through which the Court might decide whether a minor was mature enough to make the decision for herself (*Planned Parenthood Association of Kansas City, Mo.* v. *Ashcroft, Ashcroft* v. *Planned Parenthood of Kansas City, Mo.*, 1983).

While the Court has been reluctant to interfere with the right of a woman (in consultation with her physician) to decide on whether to have an abortion, it has upheld as constitutional provisions that bar the use of public funds for abortions of poor women. Included are such provisions enacted by the federal government (*Harris* v. *McRae,*

Providence, Rhode Island Abortion Rights Rally.

1980); states (*Williams* v. *Zbaraz, Miller* v. *Zbaraz, United States* v. *Zbaraz,* 1980) and municipalities (*Poelker* v. *Doe,* 1977).

However, while the Court was extending the right to privacy to cover some highly personal areas of an individual's life, it was ruling that others lay outside the scope of that right. For example, it has struck down a Georgia law allowing newspaper reporters to be sued for publishing or broadcasting the name of a rape victim, ruling that states may not impose sanctions for the publication of truthful information contained in official court records open to public inspection (*Cox Broadcasting* v. *Cohn,* 1975). It has also refused to exempt from disclosure under the Freedom of Information Act summaries of honor-code cases of the Air Force Academy from which the names of cadets have been deleted (*Department of the Air Force* v. *Rose,* 1976). In *Landmark Communications Inc.* v. *Virginia* (1978) the Court ruled that a state could not sue a newspaper for printing a true report of confidential proceedings of a state commission considering disciplinary action against a sitting state judge. In *Smith* v. *Daily Mail Publishing Co.* (1979), it held that a state may not make it a crime for a newspaper to violate a requirement that it obtain prior judicial approval before publishing the name of a child involved in juvenile court proceedings. In such cases the right of privacy has given way to freedom of expression and information. The right of privacy and confidentiality of individual bank accounts was also denied by a Supreme Court decision (*U. S.* v. *Miller,* 1976), ruling that the government has the right to obtain records of checks and other transactions relating to such accounts.

The next section analyzes another broad area of civil liberties—that involving the rights of the accused in criminal proceedings.

CRIMINAL PROCEDURE

It has long been a central feature of the Anglo-American legal systems that the serious sanctions available in criminal procedures cannot be invoked against an accused person arbitrarily. As early as the fourteenth century, English courts provided that no man could be imprisoned or put to death except by **"due process of law."** English settlers in America brought with them a concern for the rights of the accused and a determination to protect those rights in criminal procedures. This solicitude for the rights of the accused in criminal cases has continued to be a hallmark of the American legal system. Supreme Court Justice Felix Frankfurter once observed that ". . . the history of liberty has largely been the history of the observance of procedural safeguards."

This concern derives from a number of fundamental beliefs. The rights of a person to privacy and freedom from arbitrary governmental action are basic values in democracies in general and the American society in particular. Justice, or giving every person his or her due, is also a major purpose of the law. Finally, democracy attempts to protect the citizen from the state. Government is a powerful institution, and in a criminal case the parties are seldom of equal strength. The state can marshal its vast resources against a single person, who must struggle to defend him- or herself against charges of having committed a wrong against society.

These considerations are reflected in the American system of criminal justice. The government is forbidden to violate the privacy of the individual through unreasonable searches and seizures of home or person. Nor may it arrest a person for arbitrary reasons. In the trial, the state must prove its charge "beyond a reasonable doubt." Such prohibitions and requirements are deliberately designed to favor the accused by making it difficult for the government to succeed in its attempt to deny him or her, property, freedom of movement, or the very right to life itself.

Sources of Criminal Procedure and Rights of the Accused

The dual legal system in the United States has resulted in separate lists of criminal offenses and trial procedures for the nation as a whole and the 50 separate states. The overwhelming proportion of criminal acts violate state rather than federal laws and are tried in the state courts. Included are such major crimes as auto theft, burglary, rape, and murder. There are criminal offenses against the national government, however: for example, assassination of the president and taking a stolen automobile across state lines violate federal criminal laws and are subject to prosecution by federal officials in federal courts.*

There are several sources for rules governing criminal procedure and the rights of the accused in federal cases. The principal source is the United States Constitution, particularly the Fourth, Fifth, Sixth, and Eighth amendments, which spell out certain prohibitions and procedural methods that must be respected. Specifically, the Fourth Amendment protects an individual against **unreasonable searches and seizures** of person or property; the next two amendments detail how a person must be charged and tried for a federal offense; the Eighth Amendment re-

* Since a single act can violate both state and national criminal laws, the accused can be prosecuted by both jurisdictions. Such dual prosecutions do not violate the **double jeopardy** prohibition of the Fifth Amendment because under our federal system two separate levels of government are involved.

stricts the severity of sanctions that can be imposed upon a person as well as the amount of the bail that must be posted in order to gain release from custody pending trial.

In addition to the specific procedural protections spelled out in these four amendments, the Fifth Amendment contains the historic English guarantee that a person cannot be denied life, liberty, or property without due process of law. The federal courts have interpreted that broad clause to mean that a person is entitled to a hearing before a fair and impartial tribunal. In the process, they have held that a person is entitled to other protections besides those specifically spelled out in the Fourth, Fifth, Sixth, and Eighth amendments—for example, that a plea of guilty or not guilty must be made before a trial proceeds and that the defendant must be personally present at every stage of the trial where his or her substantive rights may be affected.*

In addition to national constitutional provisions, acts of Congress also govern the rules of the federal criminal process. As we shall see below, the Omnibus Crime Control and Safe Streets Act of 1968 spells out the conditions under which confessions can be introduced in federal courts. Moreover, the federal courts themselves also issue certain rules pertaining to their handling of criminal matters. Each of the 50 states has its own constitution, and state legislatures and courts develop rules for criminal procedures. Federal and state criminal processes are thus based on separate and distinct sources, but there is one provision of the national Constitution that has served to link them, namely, the provision of the Fourteenth Amendment that declares that a state cannot ". . . deprive any person of life, liberty, or property, without due process of law. . ."—an extension to the states of the restriction on the national government in the Fifth Amendment.

The due process clause of the Fourteenth Amendment is open to various interpretations. One is to equate it with the same clause in the Fifth Amendment. Under this interpretation the accused in a state criminal procedure, as in a federal court, is entitled to a hearing before a fair and impartial tribunal with the protection of specific safeguards (such as the right to be present at every stage of the trial). This is an interpretation of minimal procedural protection.

The interpretation of maximum procedural protection would construe the clause to include all the specific prohibitions and procedural methods spelled out in the Fourth, Fifth, Sixth, and Eighth amendments. This is the interpretation favored by the late Supreme Court Justice Hugo Black: the clause **incorporates** every safeguard mentioned in these four amendments.† By this reasoning, the accused in a state criminal case should enjoy all the procedural rights that he or she has in federal proceedings (plus any other protections granted by a particular state's constitution or laws).

The Supreme Court has followed a middle ground in its interpretation of the matter by including within the coverage of the clause the general concept of a hearing before a fair and impartial tribunal, along with certain of the specific procedural matters spelled out in

* Although this is the general rule, the courts have been faced with the problem of how to deal with defendants who deliberately try to disrupt their trial. In *Illinois* v. *Allen* (1969) the Supreme Court upheld the right of a judge to remove a defendant from the courtroom who used vile and abusive language.

† Black's incorporation theory covers not only the procedural safeguards spelled out in these four amendments but also other rights included in the first 10 amendments. It would have the effect of making all such rights a person enjoys vis-à-vis the federal government also available in relation to the states.

the four earlier amendments. In choosing among such safeguards the Court has applied a general test first enunciated by Justice Benjamin Cardozo in a 1937 case, *Palko* v. *Connecticut:* is the particular procedural right at issue "... of the very essence of a scheme of ordered liberty"? Is it "... so rooted in the traditions and conscience of our people as to be ranked as fundamental"?

For a number of years the Supreme Court was rather selective about the procedural safeguards it was willing to bring under the due process clause of the Fourteenth Amendment. For example, in the *Palko* case it refused to consider the double jeopardy prohibition of the Fifth Amendment as "fundamental" so as to prevent the state of Connecticut from appealing cases in which an accused person was acquitted in a lower court as a result of errors of law. Subsequently, the Court refused to transfer other federal procedural rights to the states, including the right to a jury trial and the right to counsel in all criminal cases.

In so refusing, the Court took the position that under the federal system of government, states ought to be free to experiment with different criminal procedures as long as they do not violate the nation's fundamental traditions or "... a scheme of ordered liberty." Just because the Founders reacted to particular circumstances of their time and provided specific safeguards in federal criminal cases, the justices held, it does not follow that identical procedures need to be followed by all the individual state governments 200 years later.

Gradually, however, the Supreme Court has read more and more of the specific provisions of the Fourth, Fifth, Sixth, and Eighth amendments into the due process clause of the Fourteenth Amendment. In *Benton* v. *Maryland* (1969) the same right at issue in the *Palko* case was extended to the states: the Fifth Amendment prohibition against double jeopardy. In the decision specifically overruling that earlier case, Justice Thurgood Marshall stated that the prohibition "... represents a fundamental idea in our constitutional heritage." Today as a result of a series of such decisions, of all the safeguards spelled out in the four amendments, only the ones requiring grand jury indictment* and prohibiting excessive fines and bail remain outside the coverage of the due process clause of the Fourteenth Amendment.

What has happened is that the Supreme Court has maintained the same test first developed in the *Palko* case; however, it has come to regard more and more procedural rights as "traditional," "fundamental," or as "of the very essence of a scheme of ordered liberty." Although the test applied is still Cardozo's, the results now approach Black's preference for the wholesale application of federal rights in criminal cases to the states.

A byproduct of this trend in the Court's attitude has been the convergence of the rights of the accused and of court procedures in federal and state criminal actions. As a result, today there is a substantial similarity in the criminal procedures of both types of jurisdiction.

Recent Trends and Controversies in Criminal Procedure

The Supreme Court has been very much concerned in recent years with the protection of the accused in criminal cases. Not only has it extended more and more procedural rights from federal courts to state tribunals, but it has also liberalized its interpretation of a number of basic rights so as to benefit accused persons. The Court's aim has been to extend the concept of equal justice under the law to the poor and uned-

* A grand jury is a group of citizens that hears the evidence against the accused and decides whether it is sufficient to warrant further proceedings.

ucated, who so often get into difficulty with legal authorities.

The Right to Counsel. The Sixth Amendment stipulates that "... in all criminal prosecutions, the accused shall enjoy the right... to have the assistance of counsel for his defense." In 1790 Congress passed a law providing legal counsel for all persons charged with federal capital crimes, that is, those punishable by death. However, it was not until 1938 in the case of *Johnson* v. *Zerbst* that the Supreme Court held that such counsel had to be provided to persons accused of *any* federal criminal offense.

The right of defendants to the assistance of counsel in state criminal cases has been even more restricted. It was not until 1932 that the Court held in *Powell* v. *Alabama* that persons charged with a capital offense were entitled to have a lawyer represent them. This first of the "Scottsboro" cases involved nine young illiterate black men (aged 13 to 21) who were accused of raping two white girls on a freight train. The Court ruled that the particular circumstances of the case—the ignorance and illiteracy of the defendants, their youth, public hostility toward them, and the fact that they stood in deadly peril of their lives—meant that the failure of the trial court to make an effective appointment of counsel (initially the judge appointed all members of the local bar and when none appeared, appointed a local attorney the very day of the trial) constituted a denial of due process under the Fourteenth Amendment.

While the *Powell* ruling extended the right to counsel to all persons charged with capital state crimes, the Court continued to look at the particular circumstances of each case to determine whether defendants accused of lesser crimes were entitled to the services of an attorney. In 1942 in *Betts* v. *Brady* the Court held that the failure to provide an attorney to a 43-year-old man of ordinary intelligence and ability in a noncapital case did not violate the fundamental fairness provided for by the due process clause of the Fourteenth Amendment. In the two decades that followed, the Supreme Court reviewed noncapital state criminal cases to determine whether "special circumstances" prevailed that required the appointment of an attorney, such as the defendant's illiteracy, ignorance, youth, or mental incapacity, or whether the charge was complex, or whether there was community hostility, or whether the conduct of the prosecutor or the judge at the trial was improper.

In a 1963 case, *Gideon* v. *Wainwright*, however, the Court overruled the *Betts* decision, ruling that the right to counsel is so fundamental to a fair system of criminal justice that it should be extended to *any* state **felony** case.* (Gideon was convicted of breaking and entering a pool hall and stealing coins from a cigarette machine). Writing for the majority, Justice Black (who had dissented in the *Betts* case) contended that in our adversary system of justice no person can be assured a fair trial unless provided with counsel; lawyers in criminal courts are thus necessities, not luxuries.

Gideon was a landmark case in that it opened the door to a series of specific questions involving the right to counsel. One concerns the kind of criminal cases to which it applies. Initially it was thought that the right to counsel might be restricted to felony cases, but in *Argersinger* v. *Hamlin* (1972) the Supreme Court ruled that any deprivation of liberty is a serious matter, and therefore the right also applies to misdemeanor offenses that carry a potential prison or

---

* A *felony* is a serious crime; a minor one is a **misdemeanor.** A felony ordinarily has a potential penalty of imprisonment for at least a year and a day.

ALABAMA APPROVES SCOTTSBORO RULING

But People Are Angry at Red Disturbances Which Have Attended Case.

SCOUT 'INTIMIDATION' PLEA

Feeling in State Is Against the Communist Attempts to Arouse Racial Hatred.

HOPE FOR FULL JUSTICE

Change of Venue Urged as Means of Assuring Fair New Trial for Condemned Negroes.

By JOHN TEMPLE GRAVES 2d.
Editorial Correspondence, THE NEW YORK TIMES.

BIRMINGHAM, Nov. 10.—On the same day that the United States Supreme Court ordered a new trial for the seven Negroes sentenced to death at Scottsboro for criminal assault on two white girls a crowd of 2,000 unemployed men and women assembled in front of the City Hall in Birmingham to hear radical speeches and to demand food and money from the City Commission. The assemblage, composed principally of Negroes and said to have been called by a local Communist organization, was dispersed by the police after pamphlets had been circulated from an undisclosed source threatening those participating in the demonstration with action by the Ku Klux Klan. Subsequently, the City Commission received a committee representing the assemblage and promised attention to individual cases of distress.

jail sentence. However, in *Scott* v. *Illinois* (1979), the Court limited the *Argersinger* ruling by holding that the right of counsel does not apply to cases involving such offenses where no jail sentence is imposed, even though such a sentence could have been imposed.

Another question involves the particular stages of the criminal process to which the right to counsel applies. The Supreme Court has extended the right to proceedings before and after the actual trial. It thus ruled in an important 1964 case, *Escobedo* v. *Illinois,* that the accused is entitled to the assistance of an attorney when an investigation is no longer a general inquiry into an unsolved crime but has begun to focus on a particular suspect, taken into custody, whose statements under interrogation will be used at his or her trial. At the same time the court ruled in *Kirby* v. *Illinois* (1972) that the right to counsel does *not* apply to persons in police lineups who have not yet been indicted. A year later in *United States* v. *Ash* (1973) the Court held that the constitution does not require that an attorney be present at a pretrial photographic lineup. At the other end of the process, the Court ruled in *Estelle* v. *Smith* (1981) that a defendant was entitled to have an attorney present at an interview with a psychiatrist whose testimony was taken into account in the imposition of a sentence of death. In a 1963 case, *Douglas* v. *United States,* the Court held that defendants are entitled to an attorney when their lower court conviction is appealed to a higher court; however, it has denied such a right in a prison disciplinary hearing (*Wolff* v. *McDonnell,* 1974) and in a parole violation hearing (*Morrissey* v. *Brewer,* 1972).

Since the *Gideon* case, the federal government and the states have wrestled with the problems of who should act as attorneys for the accused and how they should be compensated for their services. In 1966 the national government passed legislation providing funds for attorneys appointed by federal courts to assist defendants in criminal proceedings. States have handled the matter in different ways. Some have provided **public defenders,** attorneys paid by public funds who concentrate on providing a legal defense in criminal cases for all persons who cannot afford an attorney of their own. Others have provided funds to compensate attorneys appointed in individual cases. Still others have refused to face up to the problem at all, with the result that lawyers have had to provide their services free of charge.

Confessions. The Supreme Court has also been concerned about *confessions.* It has utilized its powers to supervise the administration of justice in federal cases by imposing strict limitations on the interrogation of suspects by federal agents. For example in a 1957 case—*Mallory* v. *United States*—the Court ruled that a confession obtained during a ten-hour questioning of the accused between arrest and arraignment was inadmissible at the defendant's trial because the delay gave the opportunity for the extraction of the confession.*

The Supreme Court has also become increasingly vigilant about the use of confessions in state proceedings. Not only has it invalidated those involving physical force or the threat of such force; it has also shown increased concern about the use of psychological pressures. In this connection the Court has looked at the "totality of the circumstances" surrounding a confession to determine whether it was voluntary or involuntary. Under that test the Court has balanced the pressures exerted against the ability of the defendant to

* As indicated later in this chapter, the Court has recently begun to alter the rule that evidence that is improperly obtained cannot be used at a trial to establish the guilt of the defendant.

resist them, taking into account such factors as the kind and duration of the interrogation, and the age, intelligence, and literacy of the accused.

The Supreme Court has also changed its rationale for excluding involuntary confessions. Formerly they were excluded because they were likely to be unreliable. In a 1961 decision, *Rogers* v. *Richmond,* the Court suggested another reason: that because ours is an **accusatory**—not an **inquisitorial—system,** the state should be required to prove the guilt of the defendant by evidence other than that which it obtains by coercion out of his or her own mouth. Since the Supreme Court subsequently held in a 1964 decision—*Mallory* v. *Hogan*—that the Fifth Amendment privilege against self-incrimination expressly applies to state proceedings, confessions extracted by state officials can also be invalidated on that basis rather than merely on the grounds that they may be unreliable.

Thus the Supreme Court has increasingly expanded the right to counsel and prohibitions against incriminating confessions so as to protect accused persons. Moreover, it has linked the two in a way that provides even further safeguards. The classic instance with respect to state proceedings was a 1966 case, *Miranda* v. *State of Arizona,* the crux of which was that after a two-hour questioning by police officers the accused had confessed to kidnapping and rape. In overturning his conviction the Court ruled that once he had been taken into custody or deprived of his freedom of action in any significant way, law enforcement officials should have informed him that he had the right to remain silent and that anything he said could later be used against him. They had the additional obligation to tell him that he had the right to an attorney at the questioning and that if he lacked funds to hire one, he would be provided one by the state. Since officials had not complied with these procedural requirements, the Court ruled that the defendant's confession was illegally introduced into evidence and his conviction was invalid.

Few Supreme Court cases have evoked the storm of protest that followed the announcement of the *Miranda* decision. Law-enforcement officials complained that it would handcuff their efforts to deal with criminals, and that in its zeal to protect the rights of the accused the Court had forgotten that the real victim was the person against whom the offense was directed, not the one who committed it. Some critics even went as far as to link the nation's mounting crime rate with the permissive attitude of the Supreme Court.

Eventually this sentiment was found in many members of Congress, and when that body passed the Omnibus Crime Control and Safe Streets Act of 1968, it included a provision that sought to prevent the application of the *Miranda* ruling in federal criminal proceedings. The act stated that if a judge, after looking at all the circumstances surrounding a particular confession, found it to have been given voluntarily, then it would be admissible in evidence, even though each procedural requirement established in the *Miranda* decision had not been met. In addition, the law sought to alter the effect of the *Mallory* decision by providing that delay in bringing a person before a federal magistrate would not invalidate a confession if it were found to be voluntary and were given within six hours after the arrest of the accused.

In recent years, the Court has had to deal with a number of cases raising issues relating to the *Miranda* decision. Some of its subsequent rulings have qualified the broad principles set forth in that opinion. Thus the Court held in *Harris* v. *New York* (1971) that an unwarned defendant's confession can be admitted for the purpose of discrediting the defendant's testimony if he or she takes the witness stand (but it cannot be used as *evidence* in the prosecution's case). In *Michigan* v. *Tucker* (1974)—a case in which an unnotified defendant named a friend who later incriminated him—the Court ruled that the friend's testimony could be used in the trial because *Miranda* only bars the defendant's own statements, not those of other persons. The Court also held in *Michigan* v. *Mosley* (1975) that if a defendant exercises the right to be silent when questioned about a crime, but at a second interrogation voluntarily makes statements about a different crime, the latter statement is not protected by the original decision to remain silent and can be used as evidence against him or her. The Court also refused in a 1976 decision, *United States* v. *Mandujano*, to extend the principle of the *Miranda* case to witnesses who appear before grand juries, and, in a 1979 case—*Fare* v. *Michael C.*—to juveniles who request to see their probation officers.

While some of the recent Supreme Court decisions have thus restricted the application of the *Miranda* decision, others have extended its principles. In *Doyle* v. *Ohio* and *Wood* v. *Ohio* (1975), the Court ruled that a defendant's remaining silent after being advised of the right to remain so during interrogation could not be used against him or her in a trial. Moreover, in a highly controversial 1977 decision, *Brewer* v. *Williams*, the Court ruled that a police officer's statement to a defendant accused of the rape and murder of a 10-year-old-child that it would be hard to find her body after more snow had fallen and that the girl's parents deserved to be able to give her a "Christian burial," constituted an interrogation, even though the officer did not actually ask the defendant where the body was. When the defendant responded by showing the officers the location of the body and that evidence was introduced at the trial, the defendant's lawyer objected on the grounds that the evidence was obtained on a trip on which the attorney was not permitted to accompany the defendant and against the attorney's explicit instructions that the defendant not be questioned during the trip. The Supreme Court ruled that the trial court's admission of the evidence violated the defendant's right to counsel and ordered the defendant to be retried, a result that Chief Justice Burger called ". . . intolerable in any society which purports to call itself an organized society."

The Death Penalty. Another subject of controversy in criminal law is the *death penalty*. In a 1972 case, *Furman* v. *Georgia*, the Supreme Court ruled against the death penalty as it was currently applied by the states. Two justices, Brennan and Marshall, felt that it is inherently unconstitutional because it violates the "cruel and unusual punishments" clause of the Eighth Amendment; but others who joined in the opinion placed emphasis on the fact that it is applied so rarely, "so wantonly and freakishly," particularly against disadvantaged persons in society, that it serves no valid purpose. The decision thus left open the possibility that states could pass new death penalty statutes that would avoid the imposition of that severe sentence in a capricious way. Between 1972 and 1975 some 30 states did enact new death penalty laws containing various provisions such as making the penalty mandatory for certain offenses (such as the murder of a police officer) or establishing separate procedures for determining the guilt of the defendant and deciding what sentence he or she should receive.

In 1976 the Court heard five related cases involving the constitutionality of the death penalty laws of Georgia, Texas, Florida, North Carolina, and Louisiana.* It upheld the laws of the

"All the News That's Fit to Print"

The New York Times

LATE CITY EDITION

Weather: Rain today; showers likely tonight. Fair and milder tomorrow. Temp. range: today 68-74; Thursday 66-76. Temp.-Hum. Index yesterday 71. Full U.S. report on Page 70.

VOL. CXXI . No. 41,796 © 1972 The New York Times Company NEW YORK, FRIDAY, JUNE 30, 1972 15 CENTS

SUPREME COURT, 5-4, BARS DEATH PENALTY AS IT IS IMPOSED UNDER PRESENT STATUTES

first three states and invalidated those of the latter two. While there were a number of differences among the five death penalty laws, all three of those that were upheld contained the two-part procedure providing for the separate determination of guilt and sentencing, and required those making decisions (on whether to impose the sentence of death) to take into consideration the character and record of the defendant and the circumstances of the particular offense. In contrast, the invalidated North Carolina and Louisiana statutes provided for a mandatory death sentence for first-degree murder, departing from what the judges regarded as standards of contemporary society that consider such a mandatory sentence as unduly harsh and rigid.

Since the 1976 rulings, the Court has continued to invalidate provisions of state capital punishment laws, including a Georgia law involving the crime of rape (*Coker* v. *Georgia,* 1977) and an Ohio statute relating to murder (because it limited too strictly the mitigating factors that could be considered in deciding whether to impose the death penalty—*Lockett* v. *Ohio,* 1978; *Bell* v. *Ohio,* 1978). In *Beck* v. *Alabama* (1980), the Court struck down an Alabama law that limited a jury's discretion in a capital case to choosing between a mandatory death sentence and acquittal, rather than allowing it to find the defendant guilty of a lesser crime. It also set aside a death penalty sentence for a driver of a getaway car who did not kill or witness the killing of victims involved in the robbery (*Enmund* v. *Florida,* 1982).

Wiretapping and Other Electronic Surveillance. Perhaps no area of law enforcement has been more controversial and confusing than that involving the use of wiretaps and electronic devices to gather evidence on suspected criminals. An early judicial decision, *Olmstead* v. *United States* (1928), approached the matter on the basis of the literal language of the Fourth Amendment protecting "... the right of the people to be secure in their persons, houses, papers, and effects against *unreasonable searches* and *seizures.*" Under this approach the Court held that wiretapping of telephones was not unconstitutional because the device used did not involve a physical intrusion into the suspect's premises, nor was any material thing seized. Filing dissents in the *Olmstead* case were Justice Holmes, who called wiretapping a "dirty business," and Justice Brandeis, who made his famous statement that the Constitution grants individuals "... the right to be left alone—the most comprehensive of rights and the right most valued by civilized man."

The Court later abandoned the literal approach to the issue, ruling in a 1967 decision—*Katz* v. *United States*—that the Fourth Amendment "... protects people, not places," and that therefore whether a physical intrusion of the premises takes place or whether any material thing is seized is irrelevant. At

Justice Louis Brandeis.

* The five cases were *Gregg* v. *Georgia, Jurek* v. *Texas, Proffitt* v. *Florida, Woodson* v. *North Carolina,* and *Roberts* v. *Louisiana.*

the same time, the Court held in that decision that the Constitution does not forbid electronic surveillance provided authorities obtain a valid warrant authorizing the eavesdropping, as required by the Fourth Amendment for searches and seizures. (In that case, however, the justices actually extended the protection of the amendment by holding that police officers must obtain a warrant to eavesdrop on persons in a semipublic place, such as a telephone booth.)

With the *Katz* decision as its guide, Congress enacted Title III of the Omnibus Crime Control and Safe Streets Act of 1968, which permits *court-approved* wiretaps and electronic surveillance in the investigation of a number of crimes. The statute also provides certain exceptions to the necessity of obtaining a court order in order to eavesdrop, for example, in the case of conspiratorial activities threatening the national security or those conspiratorial activities characteristic of organized crime. If an activity is so classified by the Attorney General of the United States or the principal prosecuting attorney of any state or its subdivisions, the surveillance can proceed *without* a court order, provided an application for an order is obtained within 48 hours after the surveillance has occurred or begins to occur. In additon, the 1968 statute also states that its provisions do not ". . . limit the constitutional power of the president to take such measures as he deems necessary to protect the nation against actual or potential attack or other hostile acts of a foreign power . . ."

In recent years the Court has been faced with a series of cases involving the interpretation of the 1968 statute, as well as the general provisions of the Fourth Amendment to the Constitution. In a 1972 decision, *United States* v. *United States District Court for the Eastern District of Michigan,* the Court ruled that the wiretapping of radical domestic groups without prior judicial approval was unauthorized under the 1968 statute as well as being a violation of the Fourth Amendment to the Constitution. Two years later in *United States* v. *Giordano* and *United States* v. *Chavez,* the justices invalidated the evidence obtained from the intercepted conversations of two accused criminals on the grounds that the approval of wiretaps relating to their activities came not from Attorney General John Mitchell or one of his assistants specially designated for that purpose, but from a minor aide and sometimes from the latter's secretary. In a 1977 decision, *United States* v. *Donovan,* the Court interpreted the 1968 statute to require that applications for court orders for wiretaps or electronic surveillance identify all individuals who are suspected of criminal activity under investigation and who are expected to be overheard rather than just the principal target of the surveillance. The justices also stated that the 1968 law requires that after the surveillance is completed, the judge who issued the order be furnished with a list of all persons overheard so that he can decide who, in addition to those named as targets in the order, should be informed that they were overheard.

In two recent cases the Court appeared to adopt a somewhat more lenient attitude towards the use of electronic equipment. In *Dalia* v. *United States* (1979), it held that since Congress must have understood that most electronic "bugs" can be installed only by persons who secretly enter a premises, warrants authorizing such surveillance need not explicitly authorize covert entry. In *United States* v. *Knotts* (1983) the Court held that monitoring signals from a beeper placed inside a container sold to a suspected drug dealer (the signals enabled the police to follow the suspect's car to a cabin where, with the aid of a search warrant, they found a drug laboratory) did not violate the suspect's privacy and so did not constitute either a "search" or "seizure."

The Exclusionary Rule. One of the most controversial policies developed by the Supreme Court is known as the *exclusionary rule.* First adopted by the Court in *Weeks* v. *United States* (1914), it provided that evidence improperly acquired through an unreasonable search and seizure cannot be used in federal courts. Subsequently, the principle was extended to evidence unconstitutionally acquired through incriminating confessions or without the proper protection of an attorney.

Initially, the exclusionary rule applied only to federal law-enforcement officials. In fact, the *Weeks* case announced what became known as the "silver platter" doctrine, whereby federal prosecutors could use evidence in federal courts that was obtained by state agents through an unreasonable search and seizure. The reasoning behind this doctrine was that the Fourth Amendment applied only to the federal government, not the states.

However, in a 1949 case, *Wolf* v. *Colorado,* the Court held that the Fourth Amendment protection against unreasonable searches and seizures also applied to state officials. But the Court refused to apply the exclusionary rule to enforce this guarantee against such officials. In making that decision, Justice Felix Frankfurter reasoned, "When we find that in fact most of the English-speaking world does not regard as vital to such protection the exclusion of evidence thus obtained, we must hesitate to treat this remedy as an essential ingredient of that right."

Eventually, however, the Supreme Court required that state practice be brought into line with the federal. In *Elkins* v. *U.S.* (1960), the Court reversed the "silver platter" doctrine, stating, ". . . to the victim it matters not whether his constitutional right has been invaded by a federal agent or by a state officer." A year later in *Mapp* v. *Ohio* the Court overruled the *Wolf* case in holding that evidence improperly acquired by state officials cannot be used in state courts.

Despite this general trend in the expansion of the exclusionary rule, not everyone has been happy with it. Before coming to the Supreme Court, Justice Benjamin Cardozo (then a New York state judge) stated in a 1926 opinion, "The criminal is to go free because the constable has blundered." Many years later Chief Justice Warren Burger suggested that the rule be replaced by some other remedy that would not force society to free criminals just because technical mistakes were made in the process of gathering evidence. He suggested that persons whose constitutional rights are violated be empowered to sue the offending official for monetary damages.

In the 1970s the Court began to chip away at the exclusionary rule through a series of decisions that narrowed its scope. In *United States* v. *Calandra* (1974), the Court held that the rule should not be used to prevent the use of illegally acquired evidence in questioning witnesses before a grand jury. Two years later in *United States* v. *Janis,* the Court decided that the rule does not apply in civil proceedings. In *United States* v. *Havens* (1980) the Court held that prosecutors could use illegally obtained evidence to impeach the credibility of a witness by showing that the answers he gives on cross-examination are contradicted by evidence in the hands of the state. Thus the Court restricted the exclusionary rule to barring the use of illegally obtained evidence to establish the guilt of the defendant in a criminal trial.

In 1984 the Court made more frontal attacks on the exclusionary rule. In *Nix* v. *Williams* it announced an "inevitable discovery" exception to the rule that permits the use of illegally acquired evidence that would have been eventually discovered through legal means. In so ruling the Court held that the "inevitable discovery" exception applied, even though there was no indication that the police misconduct in acquiring the evidence illegally was inadvertent, that is, there was no necessity of showing that the police acted in "good faith."

In a landmark case, *United States* v. *Leon* (1984), the Court made its most important exception to the exclusionary rule to date in holding that if local police act in "good faith" in gathering evidence through the use of a search warrant that turns out to be invalid, that the evidence gathered can be used in state court against the defendants. Writing for the majority, Justice Byron White emphasized the fact that it was a judge, not a police officer, who issued the invalid search warrant and that the rule was designed to deter police illegality, not that of judicial officers who have no stake in the outcome of particular criminal prosecutions. The dissenters (Justices Brennan, Marshall, and Stevens) adopted a broader view of the purpose of the exclusionary rule, arguing that the use of illegally gathered evidence inflicts a second constitutional injury upon a defendant and destroys the integrity of the judicial system that allows the use of such evidence.

The relationship of the rights of persons accused of crimes and the rights of society in protecting its members against dangerous individuals remains a major issue in a democracy. Drawing the line between these competing values is a difficult and perennial test in a free but orderly society.

ASSESSMENT

For the most part, basic constitutional guarantees are in a healthy state in the United States today. The Supreme Court has tolerated some breaches in the strict wall of separation between church and state, but it has refused to allow the expenditure of public funds for salaries of instructors in parochial schools. Moreover, it has taken a definite stand against religious exercises in the public schools. The Court has also adopted a very liberal position on the rights of religious minorities to proselytize for their beliefs and to refuse to take actions contrary to their beliefs, such as saluting the flag or sending their children to public schools beyond the eighth grade.

Some areas of freedom of expression have also been characterized by a considerable degree of forbearance on the part of the Court. For example, it has shown considerable toleration of political protests, including those conducted on sidewalks outside the Supreme Court Building.

However, the Court appears to have embarked on a questionable course of action as far as obscenity is concerned. While one can certainly make a good argument that obscene materials should not be accorded as important a place as political expression in a free society, it seems futile as a practical matter for judges to try to determine what is or is not obscene; moreover, interpreting community standards to mean those of states or localities presents enormous problems in a society in which books and films are produced for and distributed to a national audience. Rather than trying to outlaw allegedly obscene material altogether, it would be better for the Court to allow communities to regulate them through such measures as restricting the materials to certain geographical areas where consenting adults would have to go to view them and where impressionable juveniles would not be exposed to them.

The issues raised by cases involving the right to counsel, confessions, the death penalty, the use of wiretapping and electronic surveillance and the exclusionary rule pose difficult dilemmas for American society. With our crime rate increasing several times faster than our population growth, it is easy to see merit in Justice Cardozo's observation that ". . . justice is due the accused, but also the accuser" as well as in Justice Stanley Reed's statement that the ". . . purpose of due process is not to protect an accused against a proper conviction, but against an improper conviction." Permitting potentially dangerous persons to go free because of mistakes made by well-meaning but harried police officers operating under extreme pressures raises the distinct possibility that we have overemphasized the rights of the accused at the expense of his victim and society in general.

On the other hand, it is difficult to argue that the end justifies the means in a free society, that police officers should be able to violate the law in order to enforce it. As Justice Brandeis put it so well a number of years ago: "Crime is contagious. If the government becomes a lawbreaker, it breeds contempt for the law; it invites every man to become a law unto himself; it invites anarchy." This being the case, it would be best to restrict the exception to the exclusionary rule to mistakes made by judges and not to extend it to activities of police officers.

There are some possibilities for helping to deal with the problem. One is to make a major investment in more and better-trained police officers, prosecutors, public defenders, and judges. The other is to help the victims of crime by providing them with financial assistance and services designed to mitigate the trauma and difficulties they encounter as a result of their unfortunate experience.

SELECTED READINGS

One of the better histories of constitutional developments in the United States, including civil liberties issues, is Alfred H. Kelly and Winifred A. Harbison, *The American Constitution: Its Origins and Development* (New York: W. W. Norton, 5th ed., 1976). The classic legal study of freedom of speech during the period from 1920 to 1940 is Zechariah Chafee, *Free Speech in the United States* (Cambridge: Harvard University Press, 1942). A broad social and political analysis of human rights in America from World War I until the early 1960s is found in John Roche, *The Quest for the Dream* (New York: The Macmillan Co., 1963). *The Supreme Court and Individual Rights* (Washington, D. C.: Congressional Quarterly Inc., 1979) is an excellent comprehensive analysis of Supreme Court decisions relating to civil liberties.

The historical evolution of church–state relations in the United States is treated in Alan Grimes, *Equality in America* (New York: Oxford University Press, 1964). Philip Kurland, *Religion and The Law* (Chicago: Aldine Publishing Co., 1962), analyzes Supreme Court cases pertaining to religion.

Two very good analyses of the role of the Supreme Court in free-speech cases and the approaches used to resolve such issues are Martin Shapiro, *Freedom of Speech: The Supreme Court and Judicial Review* (Englewood Cliffs, N. J.: Prentice-Hall, 1966), and Samuel Krislov, *The Supreme Court and Political Freedom* (New York: Free Press, 1968). Justice

Black's views on free speech are contained in a compilation of his statements edited by Irving Dilliard under the title, *One Man's Stand for Freedom: Mr. Justice Black and the Bill of Rights* (New York: Alfred A. Knopf, 1963). Alexander Meiklejohn sets forth his opinion of freedom of expression in *Political Freedom: The Constitutional Powers of the People* (New York: Oxford University Press, 1965).

Paul Kauper discusses judicial trends in such areas as church and state, obscenity and censorship, and freedom of association in *Civil Liberties and the Constitution* (Ann Arbor: University of Michigan Press, 1962). Milton Konvitz treats these same First Amendment issues in his study, *Expanding Liberties: Freedom's Gains in Postwar America* (New York: The Viking Press, 1966). A brief analysis of the problems posed by protests and demonstrations is contained in a book by former Supreme Court Justice Abe Fortas, *Concerning Dissent and Civil Disobedience* (New York: New American Library, 1968).

An excellent general analysis of the right to privacy is Alan Westin, *Privacy and Freedom* (New York: Atherton, 1967).

Henry Abraham's excellent book, *Freedom and the Court: Civil Rights and Liberties in the United States* (New York: Oxford University Press, 4th ed., 1982) treats basic aspects of the criminal process. A general analysis of the subject is contained in David Fellman, *The Defendant's Rights* (New York: Holt, Rinehart and Winston, 1958). A highly readable account of the legal battle over the right to counsel is Anthony Lewis, *Gideon's Trumpet* (New York: Random House, 1964). An interesting attack on the *Miranda* decision is Fred Graham, *The Self-Inflicted Wound* (New York: The MacMillan Co., 1970).

CHAPTER 15

Civil Rights

During 1983 a number of black activists debated whether they should run a black candidate in the 1984 Democratic nomination contest for the presidency. Buoyed by recent victories of black mayoral candidates such as Harold Washington of Chicago and Wilson Goode of Philadelphia, some leaders argued that a presidential candidacy would serve notice to the white community that their (black's) time had come. They also felt that such a candidacy would draw increased attention to the particular political concerns of blacks and would stimulate a high turnout of young blacks who had not voted previously. Other leaders, however, opposed a black presidential candidacy on the grounds that it would draw votes away from liberal white candidates sympathetic to black needs such as Walter Mondale and allow a more conservative candidate to win the Democratic nomination. Some also reasoned that a black presidential candidate could not possibly win the nomination and that a defeat would only serve to disillusion young blacks.

There was also disagreement over who would be the best person to run as a black presidential candidate. Some favored a traditional black officeholder such as Maynard Jackson, a former mayor of Atlanta. Others preferred another Jackson—Jesse, the charismatic leader of People United to Serve Humanity (PUSH) who had never held public office but had labored all his life in the civil rights movement. However, Jesse Jackson's candidacy was opposed by many black leaders for a number of reasons: perceptions that he had attempted to exaggerate his ties with the late Martin Luther King Jr. in order to promote himself; charges of major administrative and money management problems in his organizations; and his outspoken support for Palestinian nationalism and criticism of Israeli policy in the Middle East. Detroit mayor Cole-

Jesse Jackson argues his case.

Nation of Islam Minister Louis Farrakhan.

man Young (a Mondale supporter) summarized the practical case against Jackson's candidacy: "Jesse, first of all, has no experience. And he has no platform. And he has no chance."

By fall 1983, it had become apparent that if any black was going to make a serious bid for the presidency,* it would be Jesse Jackson. In late September he made a "fact-finding mission" to Western Europe (a step often taken by American politicians prior to making a presidential announcement) accompanied by a leading congressional supporter, Representative Ronald Dellums of California. Jackson told a group of black GI's in West Germany that they should vote for congressmen, senators, and their own commander-in-chief; at least one-third of the audience registered to vote on the spot amid chants of "run, Jesse, run!" In early November 1983, Jackson ended the suspense by officially announcing his candidacy for the Democratic nomination for president.

As previously indicated in Chapter 7, the Jackson candidacy surpassed the expectations of even his most optimistic supporters. He won primaries in the District of Columbia and Louisiana, drew well in several southern-state caucuses, and showed impressive strength in urban areas with a large black population. While his famed "Rainbow Coalition" of blacks, women, Hispanics, and poor people did not materialize as much as was hoped, Jackson's candidacy nonetheless extended beyond the black community as evidenced by his obtaining over 20 percent of the total votes cast in the 25 states that held presidential primaries. Almost 400 delegates went to the Democratic national convention pledged to Jackson, twice the figure predicted at the beginning of the contest.

Some of the concerns of those blacks who opposed Jackson's candidacy also turned out to be true. He did drain away many votes that would have otherwise gone to Mondale, enough so that Mondale failed to score the decisive victory over Senator Hart that he would have achieved in a two-person race. Jackson's controversial views on the Middle East, his unfortunate reference to New York Jews as "Hymies," and the anti-Semitic bombast of a major supporter, Black Muslim leader Louis Farrakhan,† alienated many members of the Jewish community. Moreover, Jackson's insistence on changing the Democratic nomination rules (although he won over 20 percent of the primary vote, he garnered less than 10 percent of the delegates) and on having the Democratic party abolish run-off primaries threatened to divide the party and destroy the unity of the Democratic national convention.‡

Immediately after lining up the necessary delegate votes to assure his presidential nomination (see Chapter 7), Walter Mondale put his old friend and trusted aide, John Reilley, in charge of the process of selecting his running mate. A variety of possibilities were considered for adding political strength to the Democratic ticket. One strategy was to shore up needed support in the South by choosing some senator from that region, such as Lloyd Bentsen of Texas or Dale Bumpers of Arkansas. Another strategy suggested that he join with his major nomination contest rival, Gary Hart, in order to pick up needed

* New York Congresswoman Shirley Chisholm was an official candidate for the Democratic presidential nomination in 1972, but her effort was only a "token" one.

† The Black Muslims are discussed later in this chapter.

‡ For an analysis of Jackson's role in that convention, as well as the election campaign, see Appendix A.

support from *Yumpies* (Young Upwardly Mobile Professionals). Mondale himself flew East to talk with Governor Mario Cuomo of New York and Governor Michael Dukakus of Massachusetts, feeding rumors that they were his personal choices for the second spot on the ticket.

Eventually Mondale employed the same selection process that Jimmy Carter used to choose Mondale eight years before—a series of personal visits to the home of the candidate for one-on-one discussions. Seven people were invited to North Oaks, Minnesota. Included were two blacks, Mayor Tom Bradley of Los Angeles and Mayor Wilson Goode of Philadelphia. Also making the trek were three women: Kentucky Governor Martha Layne Collins, New York Congresswoman Geraldine Ferraro, and Mayor Dianne Feinstein of San Francisco, host city of the convention. Also on the guest list were two Texans, Henry Cisneros, the young Hispanic mayor of San Antonio, and Senator Bentsen.

The selection process came in for a great deal of criticism from a variety of sources, including Mondale's two major rivals for the Democratic nomination. Senator Hart criticized the former vice-president for pandering to women and minorities; Jackson claimed it was a form of tokenism because Mondale had no intention of actually choosing any of those persons.

Eventually, however, in early July, two weeks before the Democratic convention, Mondale confounded his critics and cast aside the label of being an overly cautious politician by choosing Geraldine Ferraro, the New York Congresswoman, as his running mate. (Cisneros and Feinstein were said to be the other major finalists.) In the process he turned his back on the "old politics" condemned by Senator Hart, in favor of a major political gamble that a third-term congresswoman and former prosecutor from Archie Bunker's district in Queens, New York with a very liberal voting record could galvanize his campaign and help him forge a political coalition that would oust Ronald Reagan and George Bush from office.

Thus Democratic presidential politics in 1984 gave clear testimony to how far blacks, women, and Hispanics had come in their quest for equality. In this chapter we analyze the long battles these groups waged to achieve their present status in American life. Each analysis follows a similar pattern: the general nature of the group, an historical account of how its members have been treated over the years, recent group activities designed to improve its situation, and current policies developed to deal with the issue. This chapter concludes with a brief analysis of other groups attempting to assert their rights.

BLACKS

In 1980 there were 26.6 million blacks in our nation's total population of 226 million. Thus almost one in eight Americans was a member of its largest minority group. While considerable numbers of blacks continue to live in the South—particularly Mississippi, South Carolina, Louisiana, Georgia, and Alabama, where they constitute between one-third and one-fourth of the population—blacks also populate other areas of the nation, especially our large central cities. In fact, over 70 percent of the inhabitants of the nation's capital, the District of Columbia, are black. Also significant is the fact that the growth rate of black Americans is more than twice that of the white population.

Despite gains made by blacks in recent years, they are still second-class citizens in many respects. In 1981 the average per capita income of households headed by whites was almost \$8500; for comparable black households, it was about \$4500. The unemployment rate

Mayor Wilson Goode of Philadelphia.

of blacks in 1982 was more than twice that of whites—almost 19 percent compared to about 8.6 percent. A similar pattern prevailed in education—less than 9 percent of black Americans finished four years of college compared to over 18 percent of white Americans. In the early 1980s blacks served as mayors of some of our largest cities (e.g., Thomas Bradley of Los Angeles, Andrew Young of Atlanta, Coleman Young of Detroit, Harold Washington of Chicago, and Wilson Goode of Philadelphia), and they were also well represented in county governments and state legislatures in those areas of both the North and the South where the black population was concentrated. However, there were no black state governors, and when Edward Brooke of Massachusetts lost his Senate seat in 1978, the nation's most prestigious legislative body was left without a single black member.

With this brief look at the situation of black Americans today, we now shift to trace the historical background of race relations in the United States. In doing so, we focus on major events, leaders, groups, and government actions that shaped those relations in the 90-year period from the end of the Civil War until the mid-1950s, when the modern phase of the struggle of American blacks began.

Race Relations in America (1865–1955)

During Reconstruction, Northern churches and the federal government embarked on a program of bringing liberated slaves into the mainstream of American life. Public schools were created for them, and a number of major black universities, including Howard, Atlanta, and Fisk, along with the Hampton Institute for Industrial Education, were founded. Congress passed legislation granting blacks the right to sue, to give evidence in court, and to buy, sell, and inherit property; Congress also outlawed segregation in transportation, schools, and public accommodations. Southern state constitutions were redrawn to extend suffrage to all adult male citizens, and the Fifteenth Amendment specifically prohibited states denying the right to vote on the basis of race, color, or previous condition of servitude. Benefiting from their newfound political rights, blacks were elected to the United States Senate, the House of Representatives, and state and local offices as well. But the halcyon days of Southern blacks ended when a political deal was struck between Northern Republicans and Southern Democrats in the disputed presidential election of 1876*: the latter acquiesced in the choice of the GOP standard-bearer, Rutherford B. Hayes, over the Democratic candidate, Samuel J. Tilden, in return for Hayes's agreement to withdraw Northern troops from the South when he came to office. When President Hayes fulfilled that promise in 1877, the decade of Reconstruction came to a close.

* The dispute arose over competing groups of electors in certain states. An electoral commission chosen to resolve the issue settled it in the Republicans' favor.

Next followed the systematic exclusion of blacks from various facets of Southern life. This segregation was initially based on custom, but in time state laws were passed providing for segregation in public schools, transportation, and accommodations. White Southerners proceeded to disenfranchise blacks through a series of legal techniques, including poll taxes, literacy tests, and the exclusion of blacks from participation in the Democratic party primaries. However, not all Southerners restricted their efforts to subordinate blacks to legal means: during the 1880s and 1890s there were an average of 100 lynchings a year. By the early years of the twentieth century, the process of segregation, disenfranchisement, and intimidation was complete.

At about this same time the locus of race problems began to shift away from the rural South, where the overwhelming proportion of blacks lived, to the urban North and West, to which they migrated in increasing numbers after the turn of the century. While many blacks bettered themselves economically by moving to the North, they found it far from the promised land they sought. Typically, they settled in the low-rent areas of the city, forming black ghettoes in the process. Those who wanted to move to white neighborhoods and could afford to do so found themselves thwarted by residential segregation ordinances, restrictive covenants in deeds forbidding the sale of property to non-Caucasians, and, in many cases, violence in the form of personal beatings and the stoning and bombing of their homes. Residential segregation, in turn, resulted in the separation of blacks from whites in the neighborhood school system. Blacks seeking employment found their way barred by their limited education and skills, white workers who feared the loss of their own jobs, and labor unions that discriminated against them. Thus, while blacks found life in the Northern ghetto better than that on the Southern plantation, discrimination and segregation were part of their everyday lives.

Blacks reacted in a variety of ways to the conditions they faced in both the rural South and the urban North. The leader most associated with accommodation to the situation, particularly in the South, was Booker T. Washington. Born a slave and educated at Hampton Institute, he urged blacks to prepare themselves for jobs that whites would permit them to hold: those involving manual skills. The program he developed at Tuskegee Institute stressed farming and handicrafts. Washington also urged blacks to develop their own businesses as a means of advancing their race economically. At the same time Washington urged blacks to accept segregation and political disenfranchisement. In a famous speech in 1895 that brought him world fame, he stated: "In all things that are purely social, we can be as separate as the fingers, yet one as the hand in all matters essential to natural progress."

Although Washington was the major black political figure at the turn of the twentieth century, he came under increasing criticism from a small group of Northern intellectuals—editors, lawyers, ministers, and teachers. The most prominent of these critics was W. E. B. Du Bois, a Harvard-educated black social scientist who taught at Atlanta University. He agreed with Washington's support for black businessmen but was opposed to his emphasis on vocational education. Du Bois felt that the race could best be improved by providing a liberal education to its ". . . talented tenth," who would eventually lift their less gifted brethren. In 1909 he joined a group of well-known white leaders—including the philosopher and educator John Dewey; the founder of Hull

Booker T. Washington.

W.E. DuBois.

House, Jane Addams; the eminent lawyer Clarence Darrow—to form the National Association for the Advancement of Colored People (NAACP). The association, which soon became the major group fighting for black rights, later led the way in the court battles to end segregation and disenfranchisement.

The migration of blacks to the cities led to the establishment in 1914 of another important organization, the National Urban League. Founded by conservative blacks, white philanthropists, and social workers, it concentrated its efforts on finding employment opportunities for blacks and helping them adjust to urban life. It adopted a conciliatory approach in persuading employers that blacks were good workers. Like the NAACP, the organization was strongly middle-class in its orientation.

Soon after its founding the NAACP embarked on a series of successful test cases on several legal fronts. It won its initial victory in *Guinn* v. *United States* (1915) when the Supreme Court invalidated the "grandfather clause" of the Oklahoma constitution exempting persons from having to take a literacy test to vote if their ancestors were entitled to vote in 1866 (a right enjoyed exclusively by whites). The NAACP subsequently waged a battle against the white primary (a legal device excluding blacks from participating in the choice of Democratic nominees in Southern states), culminating in *Smith* v. *Allwright* (1944) in which the Court held that such primaries violated the provisions of the Fifteenth Amendment against denying citizens the right to vote on account of ". . . race, color or previous condition of servitude." The NAACP also succeeded in getting the Supreme Court to outlaw public ordinances providing residential segregation, as well as restricted covenants in private deeds forbidding the sale of property to nonwhites (*Shelley* v. *Kraemer,* 1948). Subsequently, the Court struck down segregation in railroads and buses as constituting interference with interstate commerce.

Most significant, however, of all the legal battles for blacks has been that to achieve equal treatment in the public schools. Faced with an 1896 Supreme Court decision, *Plessy* v. *Ferguson,* that separate public facilities for persons of different races are constitutional provided they are equal, NAACP lawyers first attacked the **"separate but equal" doctrine** on a case-by-case basis. Its initial victory came in *Missouri ex rel. Gaines* v. *Canada* (1938), in which the Supreme Court ruled that a state did not meet its constitutional responsibilities by refusing to admit a black to its law school and then offering to pay his expenses to a school in a neighboring state that admitted blacks: the "separate but equal" doctrine meant separate but equal within the state. Subsequently, the Court began to examine whether facilities and practices in higher education were actually equal, ruling that a special Texas law school established for blacks did not have the faculty, library, and reputation of its regular law school, and that Oklahoma could not force a black graduate student to sit in separate sections of classrooms, libraries, and dining facilities.

In the early 1950s the NAACP lawyers decided to abandon their policy of chipping away at the "separate but equal" doctrine and to make the legal argument that separate facilities for different races *in and of themselves* violate the "equal protection of the laws" clause of the Fourteenth Amendment. Their strategy was vindicated when the Chief Justice of the Supreme Court, Earl Warren, ruled in an historic unanimous decision—*Brown* v. *Board of Education of Topeka* (1954)—that separate educational facilities are inherently unequal because segregation creates a feeling of inferiority in black children that may affect their hearts and minds in a way unlikely ever to be undone. The following year

"All the News That's Fit to Print"

The New York Times.

LATE CITY EDITION
Fair and cool today. Mostly sunny, continued cool tomorrow.

Copyright, 1954, by The New York Times Company.

VOL. CIII ... No. 35,178. NEW YORK, TUESDAY, MAY 18, 1954. FIVE CENTS

HIGH COURT BANS SCHOOL SEGREGATION; 9-TO-0 DECISION GRANTS TIME TO COMPLY

McCarthy Hearing Off a Week as Eisenhower Bars Report

SENATOR IS IRATE

President Orders Aides Not to Disclose Details of Top-Level Meeting

President's letter and excerpts from transcript, Pages 24, 25, 26.

By W. H. LAWRENCE
Special to The New York Times.

WASHINGTON, May 17—A secrecy directive by President Eisenhower resulted today in an abrupt recess for at least a week of the Senate's Army-McCarthy hearings.

Democratic and Republican Senators, some publicly and some privately, predicted that the investigation might never resume in earnest. However, there were other Senators who insisted that the investigation would go on to completion.

The recess was voted after Herbert Brownell Jr., the Attorney General, disclosed formally that criminal prosecutions might be instituted against those involved in the "preparation and dissemination" of an altered, condensed but still confidential Federal Bureau of Investigation report. This was offered in evidence last week by Senator Joseph R. McCarthy, Republican of

Communist Arms Unloaded in Guatemala By Vessel From Polish Port, U. S. Learns

State Department Views News Gravely Because of Red Infiltration

Special to The New York Times.

WASHINGTON, May 17—The State Department said today that it had reliable information that "an important shipment of arms" had been sent from Communist-controlled territory to Guatemala.

It said the arms, now being unloaded at Puerto Barrios, Guatemala, had been shipped from Stettin, a former German Baltic seaport, which has been occupied by Communist Poland since World War II. The Guatemalan regime has been frequently accused of being influenced by Communists.

"Because of the origin of these arms, the point of their embarkation, their destination and the quantity of arms involved, the Department of State considers that this is a development of gravity," the announcement said.

A freighter arrived at Puerto

The New York Times May 18, 1954
Site of arms arrival (cross)

Embassy Says Nation of Central America May Buy Munitions Anywhere

Barrios last Saturday, the State Department reported, carrying a large shipment of armament consigned to the Guatemalan Government.

The State Department did not divulge the exact quantity of the arms, their nature or where they had been manufactured.

Reliable sources told The New York Times, however, that ten freight car loads of goods listed in the manifest as "hardware" had been unloaded from this ship and sent to the city of Guatemala since Sunday. Guatemala is 150 miles from Puerto Barrios. The

Continued on Page 10, Column 5

REACTION OF SOUTH

'Breathing Spell' for Adjustment Tempers Region's Feelings

By JOHN N. POPHAM
Special to The New York Times.

CHATTANOOGA, Tenn., May 17—The South's reaction to the Supreme Court's decision outlawing racial segregation in public schools appeared to be tempered considerably today.

The time lag allowed for carrying out the required transitions seemed to be the major factor in that reaction.

Southern leaders of both races in political, educational and community service fields expressed comment that covered a wide range. Some spoke bitter words that verged on defiance. Others ranged from sharp disagreement to predictions of peaceful and successful adjustment in accord with the ruling.

But underneath the surface of much of the comment, it was evident that many Southerners recognized that the decision had laid down the legal principle rejecting segregation in public education facilities.

They also noted that it had left open a challenge to the region

Associated Press Wirephoto

LEADERS IN SEGREGATION FIGHT: Lawyers who led battle before U. S. Supreme Court for abolition of segregation in public schools congratulate one another as they leave court after announcement of decision. Left to right: George E. C. Hayes, Thurgood Marshall and James M. Nabrit.

1896 RULING UPSET

'Separate but Equal' Doctrine Held Out of Place in Education

Text of Supreme Court decision is printed on Page 15.

By LUTHER A. HUSTON
Special to The New York Times.

WASHINGTON, May 17—The Supreme Court unanimously outlawed today racial segregation in public schools.

Chief Justice Earl Warren read two opinions that put the stamp of unconstitutionality on school systems in twenty-one states and the District of Columbia where segregation is permissive or mandatory.

The court, taking cognizance of the problems involved in the integration of the school systems concerned, put over until the next term, beginning in October, the formulation of decrees to effectuate its 9-to-0 decision.

The opinions set aside the "separate but equal" doctrine laid down by the Supreme Court in 1896.

"In the field of public education," Chief Justice Warren said, "the doctrine of 'separate but equal' has no place. Separate ed-

SOVIET BIDS VIENNA CEASE 'INTRIGUES'

Envoy Warns Austrian Chief on Inciting East Zone—Raab Denies Charges

City Colleges' Board Can't Pick Chairman

The Board of Higher Education was unable to elect a chairman at its annual meeting last night at Hunter College.

A spokesman said it was the first time "within memory of board officials" that such a

2 TAX PROJECTS DIE IN ESTIMATE BOARD

Beer Levy and More Parking Collections Killed—Payroll Impost Still Weighed

the Court entrusted the federal district courts with requiring local school boards to make ". . . a prompt and reasonable start toward full compliance . . ." with the 1954 ruling and with seeing to it that desegregation proceeded ". . . with all deliberate speed."

In contrast to the judiciary, the other two branches of government did little to ensure the rights of blacks. Despite the lobbying efforts of the NAACP, the Senate even refused to enact antilynching legislation, as Southern senators used the filibuster successfully against it. Nor were many liberal presidents of this century committed to civil rights: Theodore Roosevelt arbitrarily discharged three black companies of soldiers on unproven charges of rioting in Brownsville, Texas; Virginian Woodrow Wilson did not permit blacks in the Marines in World War I; and Franklin Roosevelt introduced no major civil rights legislation and only issued an executive order establishing a Committee on Fair Employment practices in 1941 after A. Philip Randolph threatened to lead a march on Washington to secure job opportunities for blacks. It remained for a border-state politician, Missourian Harry Truman, to take the first significant steps for racial equality by outlawing segregation in the armed services and civilian jobs in the national government, ordering firms doing business with the federal government not to discriminate in hiring, proposing a broad civil rights program to the Congress, and appointing a committee to study race relations in the United States. Republican Dwight Eisenhower continued the process of desegregating the armed forces and took the leadership in ending segregation in the District of Columbia as well.

Thus by the mid-1950s the judicial and executive branches of the national government had begun to respond to black demands. As the next section indicates, however, these demands increased in the following period.

The Race Revolution

What we term the **race revolution** is the sharp break from the past that occurred in the civil rights movement in the post-

World-War-II period. An event that epitomized this development was the arrest in December 1955 in Montgomery, Alabama of Rosa Parks, a black seamstress, who refused to move to the back of the bus. The bus boycott by blacks that followed led by a young black minister, Dr. Martin Luther King Jr., ultimately led to a Supreme Court ruling outlawing segregated seating on municipal buses.

A central feature of this event and others that followed was the increased determination of blacks not to accept the status quo in race relations any longer. For the first time a large segment of the black community refused to accommodate itself to its inferior position in American society and decided to take action to change that position. What had been a battle in which a relatively few well-educated middle-class blacks participated, became a movement that involved a large number of working- and lower-middle-class blacks as well.

The revolution was not only against the system of race relations that blacks had tolerated over the years but also against black leadership. A new breed of black leaders expressed dissatisfaction with the approaches of the NAACP and the National Urban League to the race problem, namely, pursuing the battle for black rights in courtrooms and legislative chambers or behind the scenes in conciliatory conversations with white government leaders and private employers. What was needed, according to the new leaders like King, was to have masses of blacks take direct action in the form of boycotts, sit-ins, marches, and the like to win rights for themselves.* There was also a new sense of urgency in the civil rights movement. Blacks were not willing to wait until legal cases eventually won rights for their children; they wanted these rights for themselves now.

Of course, this new direction and sense of urgency in the civil rights movement did not occur overnight; it developed over a period of time and involved a number of events and factors. World War II contributed to the eventual revolution in a number of ways. Many black men had the novel experience of being treated well by whites. Those who served overseas received respect and social acceptance from citizens in France, Great Britain, and elsewhere that they had never enjoyed in the United States. When they returned home, the reversion to an inferior position was naturally resented by many former black GI's, who then determined to do something about it. Moreover, the irony of the nation's fighting a war against Nazi Germany with its racist philosophy and at the same time practicing a brand of racism of its own (not only were our troops generally segregated, but we also kept separate supplies of blood for blacks and whites) was not lost on black soldiers.

Events in the post-World-War-II era contributed to the development of the race revolution. The end of colonialism in Africa and the emergence of new free nations under the leadership of blacks gave American blacks a new sense of pride in their race and a desire to enjoy the same freedom as their brethren. Also helping the blacks' cause with our political leaders was the fact that our rivals in the Cold War, the communists, held up American pretentions of equality to the uncommitted nations of the world.

The attitudes and actions of whites in the United States on the race issue also affected how blacks themselves viewed

* As indicated later in this chapter, these tactics were used prior to King's arrival on the civil-rights scene; however, he gave them wider notoriety, and in the eyes of most Americans he came to symbolize their use.

World War II. Black tank unit.

the situation. Many began to perceive that whites were growing more sympathetic towards their cause. Particularly influential were Supreme Court cases and executive actions invalidating voting restrictions and segregation in education, transportation, and the armed services. Thus, as blacks gained additional rights, they came to want even more as a natural rise in expectations set in.

Early Directions in the Race Revolution. The initial phase of the race revolution was dominated by the Reverend Martin Luther King Jr., who worked to achieve full integration of blacks in all aspects of American life. His approach was nonviolence or passive resistance, a technique borrowed from Mahatma Gandhi, who used it successfully against the British in India. In 1957 King founded the Southern Christian Leadership Conference (SCLC), a loose organization of southern clergymen who joined together to fight against segregation and for blacks' voting rights, particularly in the South. King's dominant role in the civil rights struggle, however, stemmed not from his position with that organization but from the symbolic leadership he provided for blacks generally, many of whom were affiliated with other organizations.

One such group that came to prominence in the early 1960s was the Student Nonviolent Coordinating Committee (SNCC). Composed of black college students who initially protested against segregation at Southern lunch counters early in 1960, it was officially founded in April of that year at a meeting attended by King and other civil rights leaders. SCLC provided SNCC with financial and other assistance, as did other black organizations such as the NAACP. In time Northern college students also helped with the group's primary activities: sponsoring sit-ins and freedom rides to protest segregation in public accommodations and transportation, and registering Southern blacks to vote. Under the leadership of John Lewis, SNCC, as its name stated, was also committed to the principle of nonviolence.

A third group, which also assisted SNCC and joined the civil rights effort in the South, was the Congress of Racial Equality (CORE). Established in Chicago in 1942, the organization carried out a successful sit-in the following year to protest segregation in restaurants in that city. This interracial group, composed of students of the Federated Theological Seminary of the University of Chicago and college graduates engaged in white-collar occupations, attracted little attention during the remainder of that decade or in the one that followed; but in the spring of 1961, shortly after James Farmer became its national director, the organization launched freedom rides through the South to test whether nondiscrimination policies were actually being observed in interstate transportation.

These three organizations formed the nucleus of the movement to achieve integration and secure black political rights through direct-action techniques designed to bring quick results. Sympathetic whites from the North contributed financially to the movement, and many of them, particularly college students, went to the South to assist with the integration of public facilities and the registration of blacks to vote. The

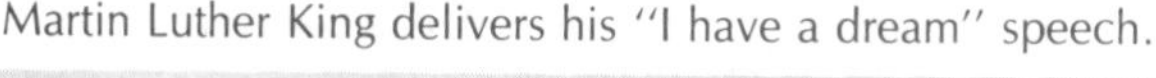

Martin Luther King delivers his "I have a dream" speech.

coalition of blacks and white liberals reached a high point in August 1963 when some 200,000 persons responded to the call of A. Philip Randolph and the pacifist socialist Bayard Rustin (who had first experimented with personal sit-ins in the 1940s) to join a march on Washington as a means of persuading Congress to enact civil rights legislation. It was at this gathering (remarkable for its orderliness, given the number of people that participated) that Dr. King delivered his famous "I have a dream" speech ("I have a dream that my four little children will one day live in a nation where they will not be judged by the color of their skin but by the content of their character . . .").

Just as the civil rights movement seemed to reach new heights, however, it began to develop frustrations. Direct-action techniques failed to bring results in desegregating facilities in Mississippi and Alabama; the black Mississippi political party, the Freedom Democratic party, which came to the Democratic presidential convention in the summer of 1964 to challenge the seating of the regular Democratic delegation on the grounds of black disenfranchisement, was granted only token representation: two at-large seats. In the North direct action proved ineffective both against de facto segregation of the schools occasioned by residential segregation of the races and against job discrimination by employers and labor unions alike. Violence broke out in some of the nation's major cities: Harlem experienced difficulties in the summer of 1964, and the nation was shocked the following summer when the Watts section of Los Angeles exploded in the worst riot in the nation's history.

In the period from 1964 to 1966 more and more blacks became dissatisfied with nonviolent, direct action as a means of achieving their goals. Contrariwise, many white liberals became alarmed at the incidents of violence and began to withdraw their support (particularly financial) from the civil rights movement. Martin Luther King Jr. experienced increased difficulty in bridging the gaps between black factions and between the two races. The stage was thus set for a new phase in the civil rights battle.

The Shift to Black Power. In the summer of 1966 another major event occurred that changed the course of the civil rights struggle. James Meredith (whose enrollment at the University of Mississippi in 1962 had touched off a riot that led to the intervention of federal troops) began a Freedom March through that state to interest blacks in registering to vote. The march had barely begun when Meredith was shot and wounded. King rushed to the scene to resume the march, cautioning the participants to remain nonviolent. In contrast, however, a young Howard University graduate, Stokely Carmichael, Chairman of the Student Nonviolent Coordinating Committee, urged Mississippi blacks to follow a new approach in the civil rights battle: "Black Power."

Carmichael never defined the term Black Power. It has remained vague, partly because it represents a general mood or call for action rather than a specific program with concrete goals, and partly because it means different things to different people. Nonetheless it is possible to spell out certain ideas that have come to be identified with black power.

Black power for some of its advocates has meant primarily *economic power* in the form of more black businesses (black capitalism) as well as getting white firms to do business with such companies and to hire more black workers. Others have emphasized *political power,* electing blacks to public office, particularly in the rural South and urban areas of the North, where the black population in

Black Power leader Stokely Carmichael.

the United States tends to be concentrated. Still others interpret black power to mean the idea of *black consciousness,* a feeling of pride in the race that is reflected in the establishment of Black Studies programs in colleges and universities to acquaint members of the race with their cultural heritage, and in moves to have blacks gain control of primary and secondary schools in areas where they live, substituting black teachers for whites and tailoring the curriculum to fit the special needs of their children.

Malcom X.

Carried to its extreme, black power means separation of the races rather than the integration of them. Such a goal has been strongly opposed by the NAACP and the National Urban League and has drawn little sympathy from the SCLC. However, the leadership of both CORE and SNCC moved in the direction of separation in the mid-1960s when Floyd McKissick and Stokely Carmichael, respectively, replaced moderates James Farmer and John Lewis, who formerly headed those organizations. Moreover, two other interest groups explicitly embraced an extreme policy of segregation by advocating that separate geographical areas be set aside for blacks.

The Black Muslims, founded in 1930, have wanted to establish an exclusive black state in the United States where no whites are to be allowed. Believing that blacks originally lived in a high state of civilization in Mecca but were conquered by whites and made to worship the white Jesus, the Black Muslims believe in the superiority of the black race and hence the desirability of separation. One of the former leaders of the organization, Malcolm X (who was slain in 1965 by another Black Muslim), likened blacks in the United States to a colonized people such as those in Africa who must win freedom from their white oppressors.*

---

* As indicated at the beginning of the chapter, the present leader of the organization, Louis Farrakhan, made some anti-Semitic remarks during the 1984 nomination race; some persons accused him of referring to Judaism as a "gutter religion."

The second separatist group with beliefs similar to those of Malcolm X is the Black Panthers, who have wanted the central cities to be controlled by blacks. Marxist in orientation, Black Panther leaders like Eldridge Cleaver sought ties with the ex-colonial Third World as well as with white revolutionaries in the United States in order to overthrow the capitalist system, which they feel enslaves both blacks and whites.* Founded in Oakland, California in 1966 to protect blacks there against alleged police brutality, the Panthers were involved in periodic shoot-outs with police (however, some of these were not entirely of the Panthers' making), whom they consider agents of the white society that holds them in colonial bondage.

It has never been very clear whether the use of violence is considered part of Black Power and, if so, under what circumstances such use is permissible. Carmichael himself vacillated on the issue, and the leaders of CORE sanction it only in self-defense. Only the Black Panthers overtly advocated it as a weapon of guerrilla warfare to be used against white oppressors such as the police. Moreover, much of the violence associated with urban riots in Los Angeles, Detroit, Washington, and other major cities in the mid-to-late 1960s appears to have resulted from spontaneous reactions by masses of blacks to specific events (such as alleged police brutality and the assassination of black leaders like Martin Luther King Jr.) rather than demonstrations planned and executed by organized interest groups and their leaders.

Recent Developments in the Race Revolution. Like the 1950s and 1960s, the

The young militant—Eldridge Cleaver.

* Cleaver, at one time Minister of Information for the Black Panthers, abandoned his anti-U. S. stand and commitment to violence and voluntarily returned to the United States in 1975, after seven years abroad, to face charges of attempted murder and assault stemming from a 1968 shoot-out with the Oakland police. He subsequently served nine months in prison.

Black Nationalists.

NAACP leader Benjamin Hooks.

1970s and early 1980s were characterized by changes in group activity on behalf of blacks. Some organizations like SNCC have disappeared from the scene altogether in recent years, while others like the Black Panthers in Oakland seem to have abandoned the rhetoric of revolution in favor of such community-action programs as providing free meals to hungry ghetto children and escort service to protect the elderly against muggings. At the leadership level of the National Urban League, Vernon Jordan replaced the deceased Whitney Young and then John Jacob succeeded Jordan; Benjamin Hooks has become Executive Director of the NAACP, succeeding the long-time holder of that post, Roy Wilkins.

The leaders of the national interest groups referred to above no longer dominate the civil rights struggle as they did in the past. No individual comparable to Martin Luther King Jr. exists today in whom the overwhelming proportion of blacks have faith. Jesse Jackson comes the closest to being a national leader with a particular appeal to young blacks, but as previously indicated, many black leaders do not support Jackson. A kind of "generation gap" exists in the black community between Jackson and his supporters, who feel it is sometimes necessary to confront the political establishment in order to achieve more influence, and more traditional leaders like mayors Bradley, Goode, and Young who prefer to work within the establishment to achieve results.

The absence of one dominant figure means that black leadership is fragmented, with individuals having their political base in their own community. The general civil rights movement also has tended to focus more at the local level in recent years. As Julian Bond, at the time a black member of the Georgia legislature, expressed the situation: "Black people aren't so much interested now in marching from Selma to Montgomery as they are in doing something right there in Selma."

Another recent development is the redirection of black demands into traditional political channels. The protests of the early 1960s in Selma and Birmingham in the South and the urban riots in Watts, Detroit, and other northern centers in the latter part of the decade have been replaced by blacks seeking and obtaining political office. Organizations of black officeholders have also emerged, exemplified by the Congressional Black Caucus as well as the National Political Convention of Elected Officials and Political Activists, both of which propose programs of interest to blacks and lobby white officeholders to enact them into law. So blacks have begun to pressure the political system from within as well as from without.

Thus political activity on behalf of blacks has undergone substantial change. As one close student of the movement, political scientist Charles Hamilton, describes it, the civil rights struggle has moved from ". . . court to street to politics." However, two events occurring in May 1980 vividly demonstrated that the potential for violence remains a part of our racial situation. When an all-white jury acquitted four white policemen charged with having beaten to death a black insurance man in Miami, a black ghetto in that city exploded in three days of rage that claimed 16 lives, injured 400, and resulted in property damage estimated at $100 million. Vernon Jordan, then director of the National Urban League, commented that ". . . the ingredients that caused the explosion in Miami are present in every city in this country"; the following week Jordan himself was gunned down in Fort Wayne, Indiana; fortunately, he recovered. Such incidents raise the question whether the public policies described in the next section will be sufficient to meet the nation's current and future racial problems.

Racial violence in Miami, Florida.

Recent Governmental Policies on Race Relations

Unlike the pre-1955 era, the recent period has been one in which all three branches of the national government have played a major role in developing public policies to deal with the race issue. The following discussion focuses initially on the arm that historically has been the least receptive to black interests—the Congress—and then discusses the part that the executive branch and the courts have assumed in decision-making that affects race relations in the United States.

Congress. Because President Eisenhower wanted to retain the political support of Southern Democrats (which Truman lost after he presented his civil rights program to Congress), and because Eisenhower felt that laws had little effect in changing racial attitudes (such changes could occur only in the "hearts of men"), he asked for no civil rights legislation during his first three years in office. However, in the late fall of 1955 NAACP lobbyist Clarence Mitchell initiated a meeting with congressmen from both political parties sympathetic to civil rights, and it was decided that they should push for the enactment of legislation protecting the right of blacks to vote. Meanwhile Herbert Brownell, attorney general under President Eisenhower, convinced the reluctant chief executive to submit a bill giving the attorney general the right to seek judicial relief against persons violating any kind of civil rights of blacks, including voting. The bill passed the House, and a major battle loomed in the Senate between the legislation's supporters and Southerners who were ready to use their favorite weapon, the filibuster, to block its passage. Ultimately, however, the Senate majority leader, Lyndon Johnson, used his influence in favor of a compromise: the Southerners agreed to forego a filibuster if the bill were restricted to the protection of the right to vote only, not other civil rights as well. Following the outbreak of racial violence and difficulties in enforcing school desegregation and the right to vote in some southern states, in 1960 Congress passed additional legislation strengthening somewhat the enforcement of voting rights and providing limited criminal penalties for bombings and the obstruction of federal court orders on school desegregation. Thus, the initial congressional response to black demands was essentially a moderate one.

The next stage in the legislative battle over civil rights was of a far different character. The Conference on Civil Rights, representing 50 organizations, pushed in 1963 for comprehensive legislation: equality of access to public accommodations, fair employment, stipulations for cutting off federal funds to state and local programs practicing discrimination, and the provision of the original 1957 bill empowering the attorney general to seek judicial relief for the violation of *any* civil right, not just voting. President Kennedy moved in that direction prior to his assassination; ultimately—with the help of the new chief executive, Lyndon Johnson (who urged that the legislation be enacted in the slain president's memory), with outside pressure from churches, organized labor, and other liberal groups, joined by a bipartisan coalition in Congress—the comprehensive Civil Rights Act was made law in the summer of 1964. The next year, President Johnson supported new legislation to eliminate barriers to voting. Following violence growing out of voting-rights demonstrations led by Martin Luther King Jr. in Selma and a nationwide television speech by Lyndon Johnson in which he linked Selma with Lexington, Concord, and Appomattox as places that shaped a "... turning point in man's unending search for freedom," Congress responded with the Voting Rights Act of 1965. It suspended literacy tests and authorized the appointment of federal examiners to supervise electoral procedures in areas using such tests where less than one-half the voting population was registered or voted in November 1964.

One major area remained outside the legislative accomplishments of the 1950s and 1960s: housing. (President Kennedy's executive order of 1962, described below, excluded existing homes, and its restriction to housing insured or guaranteed by federal agencies left about 80 percent of new housing unaffected.) In early 1966 President Johnson asked the Congress to enact broad housing legislation, but the political situation was greatly different from the early 1960s: the legislation aimed not only at discrimination in the South but also at all-white suburbs in the North; churches that had been so active on behalf of previous legislation did not come to its support; in place of peaceful demonstrations, there were riots in Chicago and Cleveland, and cries of "Black Power!" As a result, the housing bill failed to come to a vote in either house of Congress in 1966 and 1967. The next year, however, prodded by President Johnson and the Leadership Conference (that now included 100 organizations), and shocked by the assassination of Martin Luther King Jr., the Congress finally enacted into law a housing bill that also included protection for civil rights participants. Thus the last major piece of civil rights legislation came into effect during the final year of the administration of Lyndon Johnson, the Southerner who, ironically, had done the most for racial equality in the United States.*

The Executive Branch. Presidents possess a number of powers that can be used positively to affect the interests of blacks. One is to ask Congress to pass helpful legislation and then to use presidential influence with the legislators to

* As indicated in Chapter 9, the Voting Rights Act of 1965 was subsequently extended in 1970, 1975, and 1982.

see that proposals receive favorable action by them; another is to issue executive orders, without the concurrence of Congress, that have the binding effect of law. Presidents can also appoint blacks or persons sympathetic to their needs to high executive or judicial positions and see to it that executive agencies use their powers to benefit black citizens.

Republican Dwight Eisenhower had a mixed record on race relations. As we have seen, he did continue the desegregation of the armed forces that Truman had begun and took the leadership in ending segregation in the District of Columbia as well. However, he refused to speak out personally in favor of school desegregation and only belatedly sent federal troops to enforce a court order ordering integration of schools in Little Rock, Arkansas. Moreover, only reluctantly and under pressure from liberal Republicans did he propose any civil rights legislation to Congress.

John Kennedy was more sympathetic to black demands than Eisenhower. The young president spoke out against the moral evil of discrimination, appointed blacks to high public office, dispatched troops to Mississippi and Alabama to protect blacks entering state universities, and signed an order forbidding discrimination in federally assisted housing. But such bold executive actions were not matched by Kennedy's record as legislative leader. Not until spring 1963, after Americans had viewed police brutality against Martin Luther King Jr. and his followers in Birmingham on nationwide television and the country's churches rallied to the cause of blacks, did Kennedy finally send a broad civil rights bill to Congress for action.

When JFK was assassinated in November 1963, his successor, Lyndon Johnson, used his great political skills to get Congress to pass the Kennedy proposals in 1964 and, as previously indicated, continued to push for further legislation that was ultimately enacted into law in 1965 and 1968. Moreover, the Southerner from Texas also used executive powers extensively on behalf of blacks, appointing Thurgood Marshall to the Supreme Court and Robert Weaver to his cabinet (the first blacks to serve in these bodies) and establishing a President's Commission on Equal Opportunity under the chairmanship of Vice President Hubert Humphrey to coordinate the activities of various executive agencies on behalf of blacks.

Blacks found a much less sympathetic chief executive in Richard Nixon. Honoring a campaign pledge to Southerners to take their interests into account in his presidency, the new Republican president slowed administrative efforts to achieve school desegregation by threatening to withhold federal funds from recalcitrant school boards, came out strongly in opposition to the busing of children to provide greater racial balance in the schools, and, as discussed in Chapter 13, unsuccessfully tried to place Clement Haynsworth of South Carolina and G. Harrold Carswell of Florida on the United States Supreme Court. On the other hand, the Nixon administration provided financial assistance to black business entrepreneurs, stepped up **"affirmative action"** programs to increase minority hiring by organizations having contracts with the federal government, and initiated the Philadelphia Plan (named after the city in which the plan was begun) whereby contractors on construction projects financed by federal funds set "goals" or "quotas" for the employment of additional blacks.

Nixon's successor, Gerald Ford, showed more political sensitivity to blacks, meeting early in his administration with leaders of the Congressional Black Caucus. He also appointed a black, William Coleman, as Secretary of the Department of Transportation.

Justice Thurgood Marshall.

Patricia Harris.

However, he continued Nixon's general racial policies, emphasizing the economic rather than the social aspects of the civil rights struggle. Thus, the Ford administation backed "affirmative action" programs but strongly opposed busing.

Blacks had high hopes when Jimmy Carter came to the presidency: he had pursued a moderate racial policy while serving as governor of Georgia, and blacks had played a prominent role in both his nomination and his election as president in 1976. Carter did appoint both Andrew Young, a member of Congress from Georgia and a protégé of Martin Luther King Jr., as our ambassador to the United Nations, and Patricia Harris, a black lawyer active in Democratic party politics, first as Secretary of Housing and Urban Affairs, and then subsequently as Secretary of Health, Education and Welfare (later changed to Health and Human Services). However, many blacks subsequently became disillusioned with Carter when Young was forced to resign after making a series of public statements that got him into trouble with the State Department (he said, among other things, that the presence of Cuban troops in Angola brought ". . . a certain stability and order . . ." to that country) and for holding an unauthorized meeting with the representatives of the Palestine Liberation Organization. Also, Carter's economic policy of trying to fight inflation by balancing the budget and curbing credit cut into the funding of social programs benefiting blacks and set back the automobile industry, which employed many members of the nation's largest minority.

Blacks have had several major difficulties with the Reagan administration. It initially did not push for the extension of the Voting Rights Act, and took the position that violations of the Act should require actual proof of the "intent" to discriminate, in contrast to the policy favored by most civil rights groups that it be sufficient to show that an election law or procedure merely "results" in discrimination. Eventually President Reagan signed a compromise bill worked out by Republican Senator Robert Dole of Kansas that was closer to the position asserted by the civil rights groups. The Reagan administration also proposed ending an 11-year-old policy of the Internal Revenue Service (I.R.S.) of denying tax exemptions to private, racially segregated schools on the grounds that Congress never granted the I.R.S. the authority to make such a policy. The announcement set off a wave of protest in Congress (including some Republican legislators) and the administration backed off the matter, which was ultimately settled by the Supreme Court decision, *Bob Jones University* v. *U. S., Goldsboro Christian Schools* v. *U. S.* (1983), holding that in light of the clear national policy against racial discrimination in education, the I.R.S. was correct in deciding in 1970 that it would no longer grant tax-exempt status to discriminatory private schools. Finally, many blacks were angered by President Reagan's attempt to summarily dismiss three members of the U. S. Civil Rights Commission (an independent, bipartisan body originally established in 1957 to act as a "watchdog" on racial discrimination) and to replace them with commissioners who shared his opposition to busing and affirmative-action quotas. Eventually, a compromise was worked out, expanding the Commission from six to eight members, with the president having four appointments and the Senate and House having two each. However, civil rights' groups claimed that the Republicans went back on an agreement to have two liberal Republican members of the Commission (Mary Louise Smith and Jill Ruckelshaus) reappointed, and instead gained control of the Commission by appointing three Democrats (Morris Abram, John Bunzel and Robert Destro) who agreed with President Reagan's views against busing and quotas.

The Courts. While the judiciary has not dominated the making of racial policy in the recent period as it did in the pre-1955 era, the courts continue to be an important arena in the civil rights struggle. The Supreme Court has struck down discrimination in public transportation and recreational facilities. It has also upheld congressional statutes forbidding discrimination by private persons in employment, public accommodations, and housing. While private clubs have generally been held to be beyond the scope of antidiscrimination provisions, the courts have forbidden discrimination in private organizations that use public facilities, ruling that a community swim club could not deny membership to a black man leasing a home in the community served by the club (*Tillman* v. *Wheaton–Haven Recreational Association,* 1973).

Two important policy areas have proved to be the most controversial and difficult for the courts in the civil rights struggle: one has to do with the desegregation of the public schools; the other involves affirmative action programs relating to education and employment.

As we have already seen, *Brown* v. *Board of Education* (1954) outlawed segregation in the public schools, and the following year the Supreme Court assigned federal district courts the dual responsibility of requiring local school boards to make a ". . . prompt and reasonable start toward full compliance . . ." with the 1954 ruling and of seeing to it that desegregation proceed ". . . with all deliberate speed." In the fall of 1957 a federal district court ordered the desegregation of the schools of Little Rock, Arkansas; despite the fact that only nine black children were involved, Governor Orval Faubus called out the National Guard to prevent the enforcement of the order. Ultimately President Eisenhower had to send federal troops

Little Rock High School, Fall 1957.

into the area to enforce the court decree. Subsequently, President Kennedy was forced to dispatch federal troops to Oxford, Mississippi and Tuscaloosa, Alabama to overcome the resistance of Governor Ross Barnett and Governor George Wallace, respectively, to the attendance of black students at the two state universities.

Southern states and communities also resorted to legal maneuvering to try to avoid integrating their schools. Prince Edward County in Virginia closed its public schools and with state assistance provided tuition money for students to attend private nonsectarian schools. Other communities devised "freedom of choice" laws, permitting children to choose the school that they wanted to attend, and manipulated pupil placement to avoid the effects of desegregation. The Supreme Court voided such actions as interfering with the elimination of segregated "dual" school systems in favor of integrated "unitary" ones mandated by the *Brown* decision. Some 15 years after that decision, the Court held in *Alexander* v. *Holmes County Board of Education* (1969) that " 'All deliberate speed' for desegregation is no longer constitutionally permissible . . . The obligation of every school district is to terminate dual school systems at once."

At the beginning of the 1970s the problems of desegregating the nation's schools became more complex. The major issue shifted from how to deal with obstructive tactics designed to perpetuate dual schools to the question of what positive steps should be required to bring about a greater degree of racial integration in the classroom. The nature of the problem also changed from segregation in Southern schools caused by legal discrimination **(de jure segregation)** to separation of the races in schools in all parts of the country, including the North, brought about by residential living patterns **(de facto segregation).**

In a 1971 case, *Swann* v. *Charlotte–Mecklenburg Board of Education,* the Supreme Court approved a variety of measures ordered by the federal district court to bring about a greater degree of integration in the schools of Charlotte,

Busing Black students to South Boston High.

North Carolina. Included were the use of racial quotas, the pairing or grouping of noncontiguous attendance zones, and even the busing of children beyond their immediate neighborhoods. (As Chief Justice Burger put it, "Desegregation plans cannot be limited to the walk-in school.") At the same time, the Court was careful to point out that it was dealing with *de jure*, not *de facto*, segregation and that it was not requiring the total elimination of all-black or all-white schools or expecting each school to reflect the racial composition of the school system as a whole.

The first Supreme Court case involving a large non-Southern city was *Keyes* v. *School District No. 1, Denver, Colorado,* decided in 1973. While there was no evidence of statutorily authorized segregation in the city's schools, the Court found that the Denver school board had brought about segregation in some areas of the city through the creation of school attendance zones and the location of school sites. According to the justices, this *de jure* segregation in one part of the district established a presumption of intentional segregation in all of Denver's core-city schools, which could only be rebutted by direct evidence to the contrary. In the absence of such proof, the court held that the Denver school board had a duty to desegregate the entire school system "root and branch."

The Denver case, however, involved only a single school district. In 1974 the Court was faced with a case involving *de facto* segregation in the Detroit metropolitan area that affected not only the central-city school district but also suburban school districts. The federal district court there decided that the problem of racial imbalance in the schools of that large northern community could not be met by simply desegregating the central-city schools, and ordered that 53 of the 85 suburban school districts be included within the area designated for desegregation. However, the majority of the Court, speaking through Chief Justice Burger, held that since none of the 53 suburban school districts operated segregated schools or contributed to the discrimination that was found to exist in the Detroit city school district, it was improper to include them in the desegregation plan. The Chief Justice stressed the fact that substantial local control of public education is a deeply rooted tradition in this nation, and therefore concluded that school district lines may not be treated as mere administrative conveniences that can be casually ignored.

In two 1979 cases, *Columbus Board of Education* v. *Penick* and *Dayton Board of Education* v. *Brinkman,* involving public schools in these Ohio communities, the Supreme Court upheld lower federal court findings that both areas had largely segregated schools in 1954 at the time of the *Brown* decision and that their school boards had an affirmative constitutional responsibility to end that segregation. The Court also ruled that the two boards had taken recent actions—approving optional attendance zones and assigning teachers and students to them—that resulted in the creation of racially identifiable schools. The Court concluded that such actions had a "... foreseeable and anticipated disparate (racial) impact ..." that constituted "... relevant evidence to prove the forbidden purpose ..." of perpetuating a dual school system. The Court also reasoned that such actions had a current systemwide impact in segregating the public schools of the two communities, and therefore massive school busing affecting those school districts was justified.*

* In *Washington* v. *Seattle School District No. 1* (1982), the Court ruled that a voter-initiated state law prohibiting school boards from voluntarily using busing and pupil reassignment to desegregate public schools violated the "equal protection of the laws" clause of the Fourteenth Amendment.

Thus, the Supreme Court has been struggling with the problems both of determining what kind of evidence is necessary to show that public authorities have deliberately fostered segregation policies, and the proper *scope* of judicial remedies—that is, how much of a geographical area should be included within a given desegregation plan. As we are about to see, the Court has also been faced with drawing difficult lines in the policy area of "affirmative action."

Affirmative-action programs involve the development of means to compensate blacks (and other minorities) for past discrimination. Operating primarily in the fields of education and employment, the programs seek to increase the representation of minorities in those fields through the assignment of "quotas"—that is, determining that a certain proportion of persons admitted to an academic program or hired for a position be from minority groups. The constitutional question involved is whether such programs indirectly result in "reverse discrimination" against persons not included in the favored minority groups, thereby violating antidiscrimination provisions of recent civil rights legislation and/or the "equal protection of the laws" clause of the Fourteenth Amendment.

A landmark case, *University of California Regents* v. *Bakke,* involving the use of affirmative action in higher education, reached the Supreme Court in 1978. Bakke, a 38-year-old white engineer, was twice denied admission to the medical school at the University of California at Davis, which set aside 16 places in each 100-member medical class for minority applicants. Bakke contended that this procedure was improper because he had been denied admission while minority applicants less qualified than he had been admitted to the medical school. The majority of the Court

"QUOTAS IN SCHOOLS DON'T BOTHER ME, QUOTAS IN UNIONS DON'T BOTHER ME, QUOTAS IN INDUSTRY DON'T BOTHER ME. BUT A QUOTA HERE ON THE BENCH— THAT WOULD BOTHER ME."

ruled that such a fixed quota system violated Title VI of the Civil Rights Act of 1964 (forbidding discrimination in any program receiving federal financial assistance) and/or the "equal protection clause" of the Fourteenth Amendment. However, a majority of the court held that it is permissible for admissions officers to consider race as one of the complex of factors that determine which applicants will be admitted or rejected.

Two 1979 cases, *Steelworkers of America* v. *Weber* and *Kaiser Aluminum and Chemical Corp.* v. *Weber,* which the Supreme Court consolidated for argument and decision, raised the issue whether a private company could implement an affirmative-action plan that set aside 50 percent of all plant training positions in order to increase the number of minority persons holding skilled jobs in the aluminum industry. The majority of the Court decided the case strictly on statutory grounds, ruling that such a voluntary plan did not violate Title VII of the Civil Rights Act of 1964 barring discrimination in employment. In doing so, the Court stressed the difference between this situation, which involved voluntary action by a private company, and a situation involving alleged discrimination in the use of public funds.

In *Follilove* v. *Klutznick* (1980), the Court upheld a 1977 public works act that required that 10 percent of a $4 billion federal building program be awarded to businesses owned by minorities. The Court stressed the fact that once the Congress finds that past discrimination existed in a particular area, it is not necessary that Congress act in a ". . . wholly 'color-blind' fashion." At the same time, the opinion, written by Chief Justice Burger, cautioned that any congressional program that employs racial or ethnic criteria to accomplish the objective of remedying the present effects of past discrimination must be "narrowly tailored" to the achievement of that goal.

In two 1984 cases, the Court continued to struggle with the affirmative-action issue. In *Bratton* v. *Detroit* the Court refused to review a Court of Appeals decision upholding a Detroit plan of promoting one black police sergeant to lieutenant for every white so promoted until half the city's lieutenants are black. However, in *Firefighters Local Union 1784* v. *Stotts,* the Court held that a federal judge erred when he directed the Memphis fire department to ignore its seniority system in order to save the jobs of black officers that were to be lost because of layoffs dictated by budget cuts. The Court, speaking through Justice Byron White, said that the 1964 Civil Rights Act intended to provide relief only to persons who were actual victims of discrimination, not to those who were simply members of an entire class of people who had suffered from discrimination in the past. Thus, the Court seemed to be disposed favorably towards affirmative-action programs designed to favor blacks in the *promotion* process but not towards plans that gave them special treatment in deciding who should be *fired* when jobs were eliminated for budgetary purposes.

We see, then, that the battle for the rights of blacks has been waged by various groups and has involved policies formulated by all three branches of the national government. We shall further see, in the following section, that the same has been true of the struggle for the rights of American women.

WOMEN

Of the various groups discussed in this chapter, only women are not in fact a minority. In 1982 over 51 percent of the United States population was female. Nonetheless women are a minority group–not from the standpoint of mere numbers but in terms of their share of the good things in life. For example, in 1977 (the latest year for which figures

Alan Bakke arrives at his first day of medical school.

are available) women owned less than 7.1 percent of the business firms in the United States, and receipts from such female businesses constituted 6.6 percent of those from all businesses. In 1981 the median income of women was $5458 compared to $13,478 for men. In 1982, 21.9 percent of men had four years or more of college, compared to only 14.0 percent for women. There were also distinct occupational differences between the two sexes: while 93 percent of registered nurses in 1978 were women, only about 11 percent of *all* persons in health-related professions were female.

On the other hand, women posted some major gains in the 1970s. In 1972 women received less than 44 percent of all the undergraduate degrees conferred that year; in the fall of 1979 women for the first time outnumbered men as students on the nation's campuses—5.9 million compared to 5.7 million. Advancement for women in professional schools was even more dramatic. In 1972 women received about 7 percent of the law degrees conferred in the United States; only eight years later that percentage rose to 40. In business and management the comparable figures were 10 percent (1972) and 31 percent (1980); in engineering 1 percent/8 percent. Thus, women are clearly preparing themselves to assume a much more vital role in major professions in our society.* But as the following sections indicate, the struggle for women's rights has been a long and difficult one.

REPORT

OF THE

WOMAN'S RIGHTS

CONVENTION,

Held at SENECA FALLS, N. Y., July 19th and 20th, 1848.

ROCHESTER:
PRINTED BY JOHN DICK,
AT THE NORTH STAR OFFICE.

The Historical Background

One of the interesting features of the struggle for the rights of women in the United States is the fact that it has often been clearly tied to the cause of blacks. Women were a part of the antislavery movement in the United States from its beginning. The reasons for their taking up the battle for the rights of blacks varied. Many women came from families that opposed slavery, while others undoubtedly identified with the slave. As one close student of the subject, Catherine Stimpson, put it, "Recognizing the severe oppression of the black, they saw, perhaps for the first time, an image of themselves." But whatever the reason, women joined male abolitionists in attempting to ban slavery in the United States.

Ironically, however, women soon found that many of the men who were battling for the cause of slaves did not welcome them as equal participants in the struggle. When women showed up at a convention held in Philadelphia in 1833 to form the American Anti-Slavery Society, the convention refused to seat them as delegates. Five days later, the women (both black and white) met to found a separate Female Anti-Slavery Society. Nor was prejudice against women in the antislavery movement restricted to the United States. The expanding abolitionist movement resulted in the holding of a World Anti-Slavery Convention in London in 1840; the women delegates were relegated to the galleries and not permitted to participate in any of the proceedings. Among those women delegates were a group of Americans, including Lucretia Mott and Elizabeth Cady Stanton. These two women decided to hold a women's rights convention when they returned to America. Eight years later in 1848 some 300 persons assembled at Seneca Falls, New York and approved a Declaration of Sentiments modeled after the Declaration of Independence—"We hold these truths to be self-evident: that all men *and women* are created equal." From 1848 until the beginning of the

* In 1980 the first women were graduated from the nation's service academies. Of some 2500 West Point, Annapolis, and Air Force Academy graduates that year, approximately 200 (8 percent) were women.

Civil War similar conventions were held nearly every year in different cities in the East and Midwest. Thus, women's rights activities in the United States can be traced directly to the participation of many women in the cause of blacks.

When the Civil War began in 1861, women's rights advocates were urged to forego their cause and throw their full support behind the war effort. While some like Stanton and Susan B. Anthony continued to argue that the struggles for the rights of blacks and women were inseparable, the movement for women's rights essentially stopped during the war. However, when the hostilities were over, a battle developed over the suffrage issue. The more militant feminists wanted to add "sex" to the ". . . race, color, or previous condition of servitude . . ." language of the Fifteenth Amendment as a reason for which the right to vote could not be denied. However, black leaders like Frederick Douglass opposed linking women and black suffrage on the grounds that it would make it easier to defeat the Amendment. Some women's rights advocates agreed with Douglass and reasoned that if black men were enfranchised first, it would ultimately make their gaining the vote for women easier. Ultimately, the view of Douglass and his allies prevailed, and the women's rights movement separated itself from the cause of racial equality.

The feminists were agreed on the need for female suffrage, but the movement split into two factions based on differences over goals and tactics. In 1869, Anthony and Stanton organized the National Suffrage Association; six months later, Lucy Stone and others formed the American Women Suffrage Association. The former organization advocated the broad cause of women's rights and regarded the vote as the means to achieve the general improvement of women's situation in the United States; the latter concentrated on the suffrage issue alone and, for the sake of appearing "respectable," deliberately avoided taking stands on controversial issues involving marriage and the church. The National group also pushed for an amendment to the federal constitution, while the American association sought change on a state-by-state basis. In time more and more women threw their lot in with the more conservative American association, and the Anthony–Stanton group ultimately shifted its focus towards the suffrage issue alone. In 1890 the two organizations merged as the National American Women Suffrage Association, which subsequently became increasingly conservative and a single-issue organization.

In time, however, a new generation of women suffragists came to the forefront. Particularly important was Alice Paul, a young, militant woman who in 1913 formed a small radical group known as the Congressional Union (later to be reorganized as the National Women's Party). The purpose of the organization was to work exclusively for an amendment to the federal constitution (some gains in women's suffrage had been made at the state level, but these were limited primarily to western jurisdictions) and to use unorthodox means if necessary to win the right to vote, including organized parades, mass demonstrations, and hunger strikes; moreover, some of the members of the National Women's Party were willing to allow themselves to be arrested and put in jail in order to dramatize the issue. Eventually in 1920, 72 years after the Seneca Falls Convention and a half-century after blacks had won the right to vote, women were finally enfranchised by the Nineteenth Amendment.

Having won its major battle for the right to vote, the women's movement virtually collapsed. Only a few groups continued to work for their cause. In 1923 the National Women's Party

Early battlers for women's rights: Susan B. Anthony and Elizabeth Cady Stanton.

Young feminist Alice Paul.

drafted an Equal Rights Amendment and had it introduced into Congress every year, lobbying vigorously for its passage, but without success. The National Federation of Business and Professional Women's Clubs (BPW), founded in 1919, urged that Civil Service examinations of the federal government be opened to women as well as men, lobbied for an equal pay bill, and in 1937 went on record in favor of the Equal Rights Amendment. However, the two organizations generally labored in vain, victims of the absence of political allies, a dramatic issue, or public support. It was not until the 1960s, 40 years after the passage of the Nineteenth Amendment, that the women's rights movement began once again to come into its own.

The Reemergence of Women's Rights—Reform from Within the Government

The struggle for women's rights reemerged in American life in the 1960s, not because of pressure from interest groups operating outside the political system, but as a result of initiatives taken by individuals within the federal government. When President Kennedy took office in 1961, he appointed as head of the Women's Bureau in the Department of Labor, Esther Peterson, a long-time labor lobbyist who had been a member of Kennedy's staff during the 1960 campaign. She suggested that the new president establish a commission to investigate the status of women in the United States and to recommend measures to improve that status. Following that suggestion, Kennedy issued an executive order in December 1961 creating a President's Commission on the Status of Women, a body composed of 13 women and 11 men from public and private life, headed by Eleanor Roosevelt.

In October 1962 the commission issued a report, *American Women,* composed primarily of factual information on the status of women in employment and education, together with some recommendations for governmental action. The recommendations were generally moderate in tone; for example, the commission opposed the passage of the Equal Rights Amendment, favoring instead the judicial interpretation of the Fifth and Fourteenth Amendments as a means of equalizing opportunities of women with those of men. It also did not favor adding "sex" to an existing executive order barring racial discrimination by federal contractors; it was felt that sexual and racial discrimination involved different considerations. However, two of its moderate recommendations did bring about concrete results: in 1962 President Kennedy, at the urging of his brother Robert, issued a directive revising the interpretation of an 1870 law that barred women from high-level federal employment; the following year the Congress passed the Equal Pay Act, amending the Fair Labor Standards Act of 1938 to require that men and women receive equal pay for equal work performed under equal conditions.

One other major piece of legislation affecting women's rights was also passed by Congress in 1964: Title VII of the Civil Rights Act. This legislation included "sex" as well as ". . . race, color, religion, and national origin . . ." as reasons for which private companies could not discriminate in hiring. However, the act contained some important exceptions. It did not cover either employees of federal, state, and local governments or teachers and administrators of educational institutions. Moreover, the Equal Employment Opportunity Commission (EEOC), the executive agency entrusted with the enforcement of the act, had to depend primarily on employers' voluntary compliance with its findings since it was given no authority to sue them for discriminatory practices.

Thus, this early phase in the reemergence of the women's rights movement was essentially a moderate one. Some feminists had serious doubts about the purposes behind some of these developments. For example, they regarded the appointment of the Commission on the Status of Women as an easy way for President Kennedy to pay off his political obligations to the women who were active in his 1960 campaign and as a way of currying their support for the 1964 election; some also charged that it was a means of heading off a move for the Equal Rights Amendment. (Recall that the commission opposed the passage of such an amendment in its final report.) They also questioned motivations behind the passage of the 1963 Equal Pay Act and Title VII of the 1964 Civil Rights Act. The former was explained as a way of increasing the job security of men by preventing their replacement with lower-paid women, the latter as the unforeseen result of an attempt to kill the Civil Rights Bill of 1964 by burdening it with prohibition of sex as well as racial discrimination.*

For all this, the fact remains that these actions in the early 1960s were important initial steps in the reemergence of the women's rights movement after 40 years of dormancy; further, they led to the events that followed. The 1961 Commission on the Status of Women left some important legacies: similar commissions were established in state after state across the nation, and when the federal commission went out of existence, it was succeeded by a Citizen's Advisory Council on the Status of Women. Moreover, as we shall see, the increased publicity given the issue of women's rights and the desire to expand the gains made in the early 1960s stimulated the emergence of a variety of new feminist interest groups.

New Feminist Interest Groups

In the mid-1960s a series of events converged to stimulate the formation of a new type of interest group to press for women's rights. Betty Friedan, whose book *The Feminine Mystique* (1963) had stimulated many women to question their general situation in society, began commuting to Washington to gather material for a second book. While there she discussed her ideas with a number of women working in Congress, the executive branch, and the Citizen's Advisory Council. Many of these women were concerned with getting the Equal Employment Opportunity Commission (EEOC) to take sex discrimination in private employment as seriously as it did racial discrimination. When the two largest politically oriented organizations—the National Federation of Business and Professional Women's Clubs and the League of Women Voters—refused to launch an anti-sex-discrimination campaign for fear of being labeled "feminist" or "militant," some of the women working inside the government suggested privately that what was needed was the formation of a group that would speak on behalf of women and pressure the government for action in the same way that civil rights groups had done for blacks.

Within that general atmosphere, a specific issue and a particular event combined to set off the movement for a feminist interest group. The issue was the failure of the EEOC to prevent newspapers from running want-ads with separate listings of jobs for men and women. The event was the third annual conference of State Commissions on the Status of Women that met in Washington in late June 1966. The

The Friedan mystique.

* The fact that Representative Howard K. Smith of Virginia, an avowed opponent of the Civil Rights Act, offered the amendment to add "sex" to its language naturally aroused the suspicion of many persons. However, most feminists, including those in Congress, supported the amendment.

women agreed that the conference should pass a strongly worded resolution condemning sex discrimination in employment but were told that the conference was not allowed to pass resolutions or take action. This convinced the women that a new organization had to be set up at once. A group, including Friedan, met and, acting on her spur-of-the-moment suggestion, decided to call the group NOW (National Organization for Women). They also sent telegrams to the EEOC urging that it issue guidelines prohibiting "Help Wanted—Male" and "Help Wanted—Female" columns in newspapers.

From these beginnings NOW soon moved into the forefront of the women's rights movement. In late October 1966 its incorporation was announced at a press conference in Washington, Betty Friedan was elected the first president, and the group adopted a resolution calling for action ". . . to bring women into full participation in the mainstream of American society *now*, exercising all the privileges and responsibilities thereof in truly equal partnership with men." It later became involved in almost every area of feminist activity, pressuring the EEOC for favorable rulings, opposing the nomination of G. Harrold Carswell to the Supreme Court for his antifeminist positions, filing suits against the nation's 1300 largest corporations for sex discrimination, lobbying for federal and local funds for child-care centers, and picketing "all-male" bars.

In time, however, the women's movement became too broad to be accommodated within one interest group. Major differences developed regarding the goals of women as well as the best means of securing these goals. A variety of organizations were formed in the late 1960s, which students of the women's movement generally divide into two major groupings: the first is referred to as the **"women's rights"** branch, the second as the **"women's liberation"** branch.

Persons active in the women's-rights wing of the movement were typically middle-class in background, professionally oriented, and employed by private industry, the government, or the academic world. Their major purpose was to achieve equality for women and to do it through traditional political and legal channels. Such a group was the Women's Equity Action League (WEAL). Formed in 1968 by persons who felt NOW's controversial call for the repeal of antiabortion laws would damage the organization's image, it focused its efforts on removing discrimination against women in employment, education, and tax policies. Two other similarly oriented organizations also established in 1968 were the Federally Employed Women (FEW), a group that sought to remove sex discrimination within the national government, and Human Rights for Women, Inc. (HRW), which provided free legal assistance for women seeking legal redress to remedy sex inequities practiced against them. While such groups had different emphases and memberships, they had the common approach of seeking to improve the situation of women by working within the existing political system and utilizing traditional means to change its practices.

In sharp contrast to the women's-rights branch of the movement was that of women's-liberation, which also developed in the late 1960s. Participants in this branch were also middle-class in background but typically had participated in three areas of protest activities in the early and middle 1960s: civil rights, the peace movement, and the "New Left"—an indistinct collection of persons who sought to bring about radical change in American society through "participatory democracy" and confrontation with the existing "establishment."* While differing on their political goals, all three of these protest movements had one thing in common: a refusal to take the aspirations of women seriously. (When a woman tried to present a paper entitled "The Position of Women in SNCC," Stokely Carmichael countered, "The only position for women in SNCC is prone"; those who tried to get a plank on women's liberation adopted at an SDS convention were pelted with tomatoes and thrown out of the meeting.) Enraged at such treatment, women withdrew from these organizations and established groups in major metropolitan areas to fight for women's liberation. In keeping with their origins, such groups excluded men, unlike women's-rights organizations, which welcomed sympathetic males to their ranks.

Both the goals and operating methods of the women's-liberation organizations differed radically from the women's-rights branch of the movement. Instead of seeking to equalize the economic and educational opportunities of men and women as the latter did, the liberationists attacked more fundamental aspects of the male–female relationship in society, including traditional roles of women in raising children, doing housework, and cooking. Instead of "purposive" undertakings such as lobbying for executive, judicial, and legislative actions to change sex discrimination, the women's-liberation groups were interested in "solidarity" activities, the holding of "rap sessions," and practicing "consciousness-raising" techniques designed to educate themselves to the fact that what many of them had previously conceived as *individual* problems in their lives were actually experiences *common to all women*. Moreover, the participants in women's-liberation activities condemned the large national organizations and tightly structured associations of the women's-rights branch and deliberately created small, local groups without formal offices, which operated under the principle of participatory democracy.

Unlike the women's-rights groups that were well-structured and permanent, the women's-liberation groups were amorphous and temporary. The fact that the latter's goals were remote (radically changing basic male–female relationships in society) and their operating principles vague and structureless (consciousness-raising through group sessions with no formal leaders) made them less purposive and well-organized than the women's-rights organizations. There was also a serious cleavage within the liberation movement between the "politicos," who blamed women's plight on capitalism and sought a socialist society as a means of remedying such ills, and the "feminists," who attributed women's problems to men in general rather than to a particular economic system. Moreover, extremists from both groups tried to take over the movement, the former through the Socialist Workers Party (SWP) and/or its youth affiliate, the Young Socialist Alliance (YSA), which sought to co-opt liberation members for their own Marxist purposes, and the latter by means of a lesbian clique, which argued that the best way to fight a male-dominated world was to have no sexual association with men. This combination of remote goals, structurelessness, and bitter infighting within the liberation branch of the movement, together with

* The best-known "New Left" organization was Students For a Democratic Society (SDS), established in 1962 by a group of college students. Active primarily on college campuses, its particular targets were racism, militarism, and "impersonal" institutions—corporations, universities, churches, and the like. The organization split into warring factions in 1969 and soon disappeared from the political scene.

the intense, emotional demands placed on women to prove their commitment to the cause, resulted in a high turnover in its membership.

The struggle for sexual equality has undergone significant changes in the United States in recent years. While the women's-rights/women's-liberation elements of the movement are still present, the schism between them is less significant today than it was in the late 1960s. The consciousness-raising techniques of the movement are no longer lodged in radical organizations; instead they have become a part of the activities of women's centers situated on college campuses and in local communities throughout the nation. Moreover, national organizations such as the Women's Action Alliance (WAA), conceived by Gloria Steinem at about the same time as *MS* magazine, act as clearinghouses of information for consciousness-raising groups across the country.

NOW has also expanded its activities to include concerns of the liberation branch. While it once considered lesbians a threat to the survival of the organization, it has sinced established a Task Force on Sexuality and Lesbianism. Meanwhile, WEAL, FEW, HRW, and other similar groups continue to seek legal changes in the status of women in American society. There is an increased awareness among women that a variety of organizations are required to meet their needs (the 1985 edition of the *Encyclopedia of Associations* lists over 100 separate feminist organizations) and that they must join forces to accomplish their purposes. They have also come to appreciate the importance of politics as a means of accomplishing their goals, as evidenced by the establishment of the National Women's Political Caucus (NWPC) to encourage the election and appointment of women to political office and to raise women's issues during and between elections. We shall see below that such activities have begun to generate a response from the national government.

Recent Governmental Policies Affecting Women

All three branches of the federal government have developed policies affecting women. As indicated below, the executive has been most receptive to feminist interests, but Congress and the courts have also become important arenas in the struggle for women's rights.

The Executive Branch. In the latter part of the 1960s, the national government began to respond more affirmatively to the increased demands for women's rights. Much of the initial activity came from the executive branch. The Equal Employment Opportunity Commission, entrusted by Title VII of the Civil Rights Act of 1964 with preventing sex discrimination in private employment, issued new guidelines in 1968 prohibiting newspapers from publishing separate want-ad columns for men's and women's jobs. The following year the same commission ruled that state "protective" legislation (laws passed in the early part of the twentieth century restricting the employment of women to certain occupations and establishing maximum hours, minimum wages, maximum weights to be lifted, and the like) were no longer relevant to the expanding role of the female worker in the American economy and had been superseded by Title VII of the 1964 Civil Rights Act, which prohibits discrimination in employment on the basis of sex. In 1965 President Johnson issued an executive order preventing those with federal contracts from discriminating in their employment on the basis of ". . . race, color, religion, and national origin . . ."; two years later, following extensive lobbying by women's groups, the word *sex* was added to the executive order. That same order, as amended, also prohibited discrimination in employment by the federal government itself. Thus, women began to achieve what had earlier been denied them: getting executive agencies to pay as much attention to discrimination against them as was directed to the situation of blacks.

Congress. Women also began to turn to the Congress for help in their battle against sex discrimination. Both the Comprehensive Health Manpower Training Act and the Nurses' Training Act enacted in 1971 contained anti-sex-discrimination provisions; that same year Congress also passed the Child Development Act providing free daycare for children of families of limited income, but this was successfully vetoed by President Nixon.* Important congressional victories for women in the 1970s included the Equal Opportunity Act of 1972, which extends the coverage of the anti-discrimination provisions of the 1964 civil rights law to educational institutions and state and local governments; the Education Amendments Act of that same year, which prohibits sex discrimination in all federally aided education programs; and a 1974 law that extends the jurisdiction of the U. S. Commission on Civil Rights (an independent bipartisan group originally set up to study problems of minorities) to include sex discrimination.

However, for the advocates of women's rights, by far the most dramatic congressional victory in the 1970s was the passage of the Equal Rights Amendment. Originally introduced in Congress in 1923, and first endorsed by both Republican and Democratic parties in their platforms in the 1940s, the amendment passed the Senate in 1950 and 1953 but failed to clear the House of Representatives both years. In the early 1970s the pressures for its enactment became overwhelming. With ERA backed by the Citizens Advisory Council

* In 1977 parents were granted a tax credit of up to $400 for annual child-care costs per child, not to exceed $800 per family.

Fighting the good cause.

on the Status of Women, the Women's Bureau, and President Nixon himself, Democratic Congresswoman Martha Griffith of Michigan took over the task of helping to steer ERA through the national legislature, while a National Ad Hoc Committee for ERA, composed of almost every women's interest group and such allies as Common Cause and the liberal Americans for Democratic Action, kept up pressure for its passage. Finally in March 1972, almost a half-century after it was first introduced in Congress by the National Women's Party, the Equal Rights Amendment received the needed two-thirds vote of both the House and the Senate and was ready for ratification by three-fourths of the state legislatures.

Initially, ERA had easy sailing at the state level as 28 legislatures ratified it during the first year. However, in January 1973 a national "Stop ERA" campaign surfaced led by Phyllis Schlafly, an articulate woman from Illinois who was noted for her leadership in conservative causes. Rightist organizations, including the John Birch Society, the Christian Crusade, and Young Americans for Freedom, joined the opposition effort, claiming that ERA would result in the drafting of women, deny wives the support of their husbands, and remove children from the custody of their mothers. State legislatures soon felt the same kind of outside pressure to oppose ERA that members of Congress had experienced earlier for its passage. As a result, the momentum went out of the pro-ERA movement in the latter part of the 1970s. In 1979, when the ratification period for the amendment was about to expire, women's groups persuaded the Congress to extend it until 1982.

Anti-ERA leader Phyllis Schlafly.

The early 1980s brought mixed policy results for the women's movement. The Equal Rights Amendment failed to be ratified by 1982 by the necessary 38 states, as legislatures in 15 states (primarily in the South) failed to adopt it. Moreover, attempts to have the ratification period extended once more failed. Thus, one of the major policy goals of women's groups was not achieved.

On the other hand, the women's movement did make important progress on the congressional front in "economic equity" legislation. An emergency jobs bill passed in 1982 contained provisions for $1 billion for jobs and services of particular benefit to women. In mid-1984 Congress passed the Retirement Equity Act expanding pension coverage for employees who leave work (for example, to have a child) and then subsequently go back to the job; this legislation also ensures the pension rights of homemakers whose working spouses die before reaching retirement age. Congress also enacted legislation strengthening the means of collecting child-support payments, including requiring the withholding of money from the paychecks of parents.

The Courts. While the judiciary has not played as vital a role in the battle for women's rights as it has in that for blacks' (particularly the early stages of that latter struggle), in the 1970s the courts did develop favorable policies in a variety of matters of great concern to women. Included were the abortion decisions described in the previous chapter and decisions supporting equal pay for equal work, equal opportunities in education and sports, and the receipt of credit. Other Supreme Court decisions held that companies may not compel pregnant women to take leave from their jobs at a single specified time in their pregnancy, nor can they divest women of their accumulated seniority simply because they take maternity leave. The Court has also set aside a state law establishing minimum height and weight requirements for prison guards and ruled that a municipality cannot require its female employees to make higher contributions to a pension fund than male employees earning the same salary. The Court also invalidated state laws giving preference to men over women in administering estates of the deceased.

While women prevailed in the 1970s in most cases involving sex equality, they also suffered some judicial losses. The Supreme Court, for example, ruled that a state can require a married woman to adopt her husband's last name before receiving a driver's license and that divorced women are not entitled to all the Social Security benefits that go to married women; it also upheld a state law giving preference in public employment to veterans (most of whom, of course, are men). The court also ruled that private companies could exclude pregnancy from a disability-benefits plan and refuse to grant sick pay to women employees absent from work because of pregnancy and childbirth. (However, women turned to Congress to nullify these latter two rulings: in 1978 Congress amended Title VII of the Civil Rights Act of 1964 to prohibit discrimination against pregnant women in any area of employment and to require employers to offer health insurance and temporary disability plans to provide coverage to women for pregnancy, childbirth, and related medical problems.)

Women continued to experience both judicial wins and losses in the 1980s. In a major case, *Arizona Governing Committee for Tax Deferred Annuity and Deferred Compensation Plans* v. *Norris* (1983), the Supreme Court held that despite the fact that women as a group live longer than men, an employer's retirement plans cannot include an annuity option that provides a smaller monthly retirement payment for women than for men who have contributed the same amount to the plan. In so ruling, the Court held that Title VII of the 1964 Civil Rights Act requires that employees be treated by their employers as individuals, not as members of groups, in determining pay and other conditions of employment. However, in a 1984 case, *Grove City College* v. *Bell,* the Court held that Title IX of the 1972 Education Amendments that provides for cutting off federal assistance to educational institutions that discriminate does not apply to all programs at an institution receiving federal assistance, but only to the particular program receiving the aid. Therefore, the fact that college officials refused to sign forms certifying that the College had complied with Title IX of the 1972 Act does not prevent the granting of federal assistance to students involved in the College's financial aid program.

Thus, women have made significant gains in recent years. As political scientists, Joyce Gelb and Marian Palley, suggest, women are more likely to be successful when an issue is perceived as one affecting *role equity* (treating men and women in similar situations equally*), rather than one involving *role change* (requiring a change in the traditional roles played by men and women in society).

HISPANICS

Hispanics, also known as Spanish-Americans, are persons who come from Spanish-speaking nations. Our 1980 population included 8.7 million people from Mexico, 2 million from Puerto

* A current, controversial issue that will test the idea of "similar situations" is that of "comparative worth." This notion suggests that persons holding not only the same job but also ones that are similar in value should receive the same pay. Thus, maids (most of whom are women) who now earn about half the pay of janitors (who are mostly men) should be paid the same as janitors. In June 1984, the House of Representatives voted in favor of a study to determine whether sex bias plays a role in determining the pay level of employees of the federal government.

Rico, some 800 thousand from Cuba, and the remaining 3 million from countries in Central or South America or elsewhere. Together they totalled 14.6 million, 6.5 percent of the U. S. population.

The situation of Hispanics epitomizes that of a disadvantaged minority. In 1982, the median family income of all Americans was $20,171 but for Hispanics it was $15,178; about twice as many Hispanic families—29.9 percent—were below the poverty line as Americans in general (15.0 percent). In 1983, the unemployment rate of Hispanics was 14 percent compared to 10 percent of our general population. In 1982, 37.9 percent of the U. S. population completed four years of high school but only 27.2 percent of Hispanics had. The disparity was even greater in higher education: 17.7 percent of Americans graduated from college but less than half of that proportion—7.8 percent—of Hispanics had done so.

As indicated above, by far the most dominant group among Hispanics are Mexican-Americans, who constitute 60 percent of our total Hispanic population. Mexican-Americans are also known by other names: many younger members of the group prefer to be called Chicanos; political leaders frequently use the term *La Raza* ("the race"). Mexican-Americans also are called by other names, depending upon where they live. In New Mexico, they are generally referred to as Spanish-Americans, in Texas as Latin-Americans, and in Colorado often simply as Mexicans.

Mexican-Americans are more important politically than other Hispanics, not only because of their greater numbers but because of their concentration in particular states where they constitute an important political force. The concentation in the Southwestern part of the United States is frequently referred to as the "Tamale Belt." It includes primarily five states—New Mexico, Texas, Arizona, California, and Colorado—where Mexican-Americans all together comprise about one out of every five residents. (The concentration is particularly heavy in New Mexico, where about one-in-three residents are Mexican-Americans; they constitute one-in-seven of the population in Texas; and about one-in-ten in the other three states).* Moreover, the Mexican-American population is a young one—over 40 percent is under 18 years of age compared to about 30 percent of our total population. Some demographers predict that Los Angeles—which, after Mexico City, is already the second largest Mexican metropolitan area in the world—will have a Chicano majority in 20 years. The fact that more than 80 percent of Mexican-Americans live in metropolitan areas (compared to about 66 percent of the nation at large) is likely to affect the future composition of other large cities as well.

The Hispanic population is growing so fast (a result of both increased immigration and a high birth rate among persons who are already here) that some demographers predict that by the turn of the twenty-first century, Hispanics will be more numerous than blacks and will constitute the nation's largest minority. In the following sections, we analyze its most numerous and politically important nationality group—Mexican-Americans.

Historical Background of Mexican-Americans

The initial experience of Mexican-Americans with American society was as

* The next two states in terms of the concentration of Hispanics are New York, where they constitute 6.5 percent of the population (mostly Puerto Ricans who live in New York City), and Florida, where they amount to 5 percent (composed mostly of Cubans in the Miami area).

Bilingual class.

a conquered people. Following the conclusion of the Mexican-American War in 1848, the Treaty of Guadalupe Hidalgo ceded Mexican lands in part of what is now seven southwestern and western states to the United States in return for $15 million. The treaty guaranteed traditional land grants to individual Mexicans along with some parcels for the whole community. However, the Mexican-American lands were subsequently seized by both legal and illegal means as the conquered people lost their property to cotton plantation owners, cattle and sheep men, miners, and farmers. Some Mexican-Americans (the treaty granted them citizenship) struck back by conducting raids against the Americans who took their lands; there were also clashes between Mexican-American laborers and the management of the railroads. Faced with exclusion from politics in all states except New Mexico, Mexican-Americans turned inward, forming mutual aid societies to protect themselves and to preserve Mexican culture and traditions. This early period, which Mexican scholar Alfredo Cuellar terms one of "conflict and apolitics," came to a close about 1920.

The second period, lasting from 1920 until World War II, was of a far different character. Rather than attempting to retain ties to their home country, Mexican-Americans sought to assimilate to American life. Faced with mass deportation back to Mexico (which wanted its former citizens as laborers to fulfill the goals of its revolution, while many Americans wanted to export those who were on the public "dole" during the Depression), Mexican-Americans formed interest groups to fight deportation, provide entertainment and social activities for their people, and to help prepare themselves for an active role as American citizens. The most important group, The League of United Latin American Citizens (LULAC), used English as its official language and excluded noncitizens. Referred to as the Kiwanis Club of Mexican-Americans, LULAC members were willing to accept second-class citizenship—at least for a while—as a precondition to entering the mainstream of American life.

World War II helped usher in the third general period in the political development of Mexican-Americans. Almost a million of them went off to fight, and Mexican-American units were among the most decorated in combat. Also, the wartime industrial effort drew hundreds of thousands of them to urban communities, where for the first time they entered high-paying, skilled jobs. After the war, the G.I. Bill of Rights enabled Mexican-American veterans to go to college and to receive other benefits, such as housing and expanded economic opportunities. As a result, Mexican-Americans experienced a new sense of self-esteem and, like blacks, refused to accept second-class citizenship. Instead, they began to demand equality.

This new mood of Mexican-Americans was reflected in their politicization into American political life. In California community organizers, following the tactics of Saul Alinsky (who first helped organize white ethnics in Chicago), formed Community Service Organizations (CSO) that engaged in grass-roots politics (getting Mexican-Americans registered and to the polls) resulting in the election of the first chicano, Edward Roybal, to the Los Angeles city council. When Roybal and Manual López failed to win election to statewide office in California, many activists abandoned the policy of working only within the Democratic party and formed the Mexican American Political Association (MAPA) to encourage chicano candidacies in either major party. In Texas the refusal of a funeral home in the town of Three Rivers to conduct services for a Mexican-American soldier who died in the Battle of the Philippines* led in 1948 to the establishment of the American G.I. Forum, an interest group that joined the NAACP in bringing civil rights suits and lobbying government officials to eliminate inequities facing Mexican-Americans in health, education, employment, and the use of public facilities. Also joining the effort to outlaw school desegregation was LULAC, which came to be known as the chicano counterpart of the NAACP. While all these activities brought many more Mexican-Americans into the political mainstream, for the most part the people involved were middle-class. Not until the modern period described below did many Mexican-Americans from the lower classes become involved in politics.

* Lyndon Johnson, then a member of Congress, intervened in the incident with the result that the soldier received a hero's burial in Arlington National Cemetery.

Recent Chicano Politics

As with blacks, the civil rights struggle of Mexican-Americans in the 1960s evolved from the developments of previous periods but underwent a radical change. Rather than merely seeking integration into American society, the chicano movement emphasizes the unique culture of Mexican-Americans and seeks to retain that culture by instilling a sense of pride in being a chicano. (This parallels the similar development in black consciousness.) Also the tactics of chicanos differ from those of previous Mexican-American leaders; the new leadership has been willing to work through third parties and to use boycotts, sit-ins, and confrontations to defend and advance the rights of their members. Finally, the chicano movement has moved beyond the middle-class base of former Mexican-American politics to enlist lower-class chicanos, particularly young ones, in its civil rights fight.

One of the major features of the recent chicano movement is its diversity and fragmentation among different political leaders and groups. Reies López Tijerina, the leader of the People's Constitutional Party, has operated in New Mexico, focusing primarily on getting back land grants originally provided for by the Treaty of Guadalupe Hidalgo, and using tactics such as taking over disputed areas and making a citizen's arrest of the state attorney general. Another party, the Raza Unida Party (LRAP) headed by José Angel Gutierrez, has entered into electoral politics in Texas and succeeded in placing chicanos in local and county offices in the Lone Star state. In Colorado, Rodolfo "Corky" Gonzales's "Crusade for Justice" has concentrated on civic action to help alleviate the problems of urban chicanos, particularly those living in the Mexican-American ghettos (called barrios) of Denver. César Chávez has helped to organize the United Farm

Chicano leader Cesar Chavez.

Workers in California in their battle against both owners and labor unions like the Teamsters. In addition to the activities of the "Big Four" (leaders) of chicano politics, student groups have also been involved in trying to improve the situation of Mexican-Americans in the public schools, and "Brown" and "Black Berets" (the former operate in California, the latter in New Mexico) have acted as shock troops in chicano protests, seeking to protect the participants from possible abuse by the police. Some chicano church groups (overwhelmingly Catholic) have also associated themselves with the National Social-Activist Industrial Areas Foundation (founded by Alinsky in 1940) in mobilizing Mexican-Americans from the depressed lower Rio Grande Valley of South Texas to the streets of Los Angeles.

Mexican-Americans have begun to win major political offices in recent years. First Jerry Apodaca, then Toney Anaya were elected governor of New Mexico, while Raul Castro captured the Arizona statehouse. Two Chicanos have also been elected mayors of large cities—Henry Cisneros of San Antonio and Federico Pena of Denver. As indicated at the beginning of the chapter, Cisneros was one of the finalists for the Democratic vice-presidential nomination in 1984.*

Jerry Apodaca and wife, Carla, celebrate victory in New Mexico Democratic gubernatorial primary.

Recent Public Policies Affecting Mexican-Americans

Mexican-Americans have benefited considerably from the civil rights policies described earlier in the section on blacks. Legislation and executive orders pertaining to such matters as public accommodations, employment, voting, housing, and education typically contain language forbidding discrimination based on "national origin" as well as race. Moreover, court cases involving discrimination against both blacks and Mexican-Americans turn on the same considerations—statutory violations as well as those relating to the "equal protection of the laws" clause of the Fourteenth Amendment. Thus for the most part it has not been necessary for Mexican-Americans to seek special governmental policies to meet their particular needs.

However, one major exception to that general rule is the use of the Spanish language, which is of particular concern to Mexican-Americans (as well as to other Hispanics). Thus, Mexican-Americans have sought to have Spanish taught and used as a second language

* Many persons also credit Mexican-Americans in Texas with playing a decisive role in the 1982 gubernatorial race in which Democratic candidate Mark White defeated incumbent Republican William Clements, and in Walter Mondale's victory over Gary Hart in the 1984 Democratic presidential caucus in Texas.

TEXAS BAR TO ALIENS IN PUBLIC SCHOOLS VOIDED BY U.S. JUDGE

1975 Law Ruled Unconstitutional Violation of Due Process and Equal Rights Protection

Special to The New York Times

HOUSTON, April 21 — A Federal judge today declared unconstitutional a 1975 Texas law that effectively bars illegal alien children from attending the public schools.

In a long-awaited opinion that affects thousands of such children, Federal District Judge Woodrow Seals wrote here that by excluding the childr school, "we public

in the public schools. Also, public officials have increasingly begun to use Spanish in government buildings, publications, and surveys (e.g., in the 1980 census).

A second major public-policy issue of special concern to Mexican-Americans is what should be done about the massive influx into the United States of illegal Mexican aliens, or "undocumented workers," as many chicano leaders prefer to call them. After struggling with this explosive issue for a number of years, in mid-1984 both the Senate and the House passed legislation designed to deal with it. Both measures—the Senate bill sponsored by Senator Alan Simpson (R-Wy.) and the House bill by Representative Romano Mazzoli (D-Ky.)—granted legal status or amnesty to millions of illegal aliens already in this country but provided penalties for employers who knowingly hire illegal aliens. The House version of the legislation also included a provision for a new "guest-worker" program that could bring in thousands of foreign workers every year to harvest perishable crops.

The Simpson–Mazzoli proposal drew political opposition from a variety of groups. Chicano leaders feared that the employer penalty provision would result in discrimination against their people because employers would be afraid to hire anyone—including legal residents—who looked foreign, spoke with a foreign accent, or had a foreign-sounding name. On the other hand, many representatives from the Southwest felt that the provisions for granting amnesty to illegal aliens were too generous and rewarded persons who violated the law to come here. Many leaders of organized labor were concerned that the guest-worker program would take jobs away from Americans. The Reagan administration objected to what it conceived to be a costly provision of the House bill that granted 100 percent reimbursement to states for expenses associated with the amnesty program. As of this writing (late August 1984), House members of a conference committee designed to iron out differences between the versions of the two chambers had not yet been appointed and the future of the legislation is very uncertain.*

Thus, Mexican-Americans, like blacks and women, have made significant gains in recent years and promise to become an even more important force in American politics in the future. The final section of this chapter briefly describes the struggles of other groups to assert their rights.

CIVIL RIGHTS OF OTHER GROUPS

Another group, American Indians, also known as Native Americans, has also made some progress in recent years in winning rights that have been denied them. As was true of blacks, they have turned to the courts to gain redress of their grievances. Native Americans have won a number of lawsuits involving violations of treaties; rulings have granted them hunting and fishing rights and substantial financial awards as compensation for past wrongs. Congress has also passed legislation guaranteeing First Amendment rights and criminal-due-process protection to Native Americans living under the jurisdiction of tribal governments. Tribes have also been granted the authority to administer federally-supported housing, welfare, education, and food-stamp programs, and to receive community-development grants and federal funds for tribally controlled community colleges.

Homosexuals, also known as "gays,"

* Also presenting difficulties was the fact that the Democratic presidential nominee, Walter Mondale, promised Mexican-American leaders that he would do whatever he could to kill the measure.

Native Americans demonstrating on treaty rights.

Sioux Lose Court Round In Their Bid for Black Hills

OMAHA, Sept. 11 (AP) — A Federal district judge today dismissed a suit in which the Oglala Sioux sought to block the Government from paying more than $117 million to nine Sioux tribes for the Black Hills of South Dakota.

The Indians would prefer the land.

have also made major progress in recent years. A number of city and county councils have enacted ordinances prohibiting discrimination against gays in jobs, housing, and public accommodations. State legislatures have passed laws eliminating the imposition of criminal penalties for sexual activities conducted in private between consenting adults of the same sex. The executive branch of the national government has issued guidelines providing that individuals cannot be denied employment with most federal agencies solely because of homosexuality. The Gay Rights National Lobby currently lobbies in Congress on revising the Civil Rights Act of 1964 to cover homosexuals, and seeks to protect their interests in immigration laws, legal services, and providing federal funds for research on Acquired Immune Deficiency Syndrome (AIDS).

In 1973, Congress passed the Rehabilitation Act, which prohibits discrimination against handicapped persons in federally assisted programs. The act obliges any company or organization with a federal contract over a certain amount to take affirmative action to employ and promote the handicapped. All buildings financed with federal funds must also be designed, constructed, or remodeled in order to be accessible to the physically handicapped. In 1975, Congress enacted the Education for Handicapped Children Act, which requires that all school-age children in the United States who have physical, mental, emotional, or learning handicaps be provided a public education to meet their special needs at no cost to their parents. Such special education must be given in the "least restricted" environment possible, which means in some cases that they must be educated with nonhandicapped children—a process known as *mainstreaming*.

The rights of persons at both ends of the age spectrum have also been at issue in recent years. As we saw in Chapter 9, persons 18 to 20 years of age have won the right to vote in recent years. Legal battles are being waged to grant juveniles the same rights as adults in crimi-

"Freedom Trail" March in Boston.

"Mainstreaming" the retarded in school cafeteria.

nal proceedings and to recognize the special rights of children to adequate nutrition, a healthy environment, loving care, and intellectual and emotional stimulation. The elderly are also successfully asserting their rights. In 1978, Congress enacted legislation raising the mandatory age for retirement from 65 to 70 in private industry and removed it altogether for federal employees.

The battle for civil rights is currently being waged on many fronts. Nonsmokers seek to ban smoking in public places, the terminally ill want the right to die with dignity, and welfare recipients assert their rights, including the ability to make more of the decisions over how they will live their lives. Thus the quest for greater freedom and equality continues in American society.

ASSESSMENT

The race revolution has resulted in major advances for blacks. Progress has been especially notable in the ending of legal discrimination in education, employment, and the use of public accommodations, and in the enfranchisement of many blacks. The latter, in turn, has resulted in increased political power of blacks as reflected in the increased numbers of them elected to public office, especially at the local level, as well as those who have been appointed to high positions in the federal government. The race revolution has also brought major improvements in the social and economic status of many blacks. They increasingly enjoy the benefits of higher education and find professional opportunities open to them through affirmative-action programs and the desire of many whites to demonstrate their racial tolerance. As a result of these developments, many blacks have now become a part of the American middle class.

On the other hand, the race revolution has had almost no impact on the lives of lower-class blacks. Without education, skills, or income, it means little to the ghetto- or poor-rural black to know that members of his race are entitled to dine at the finest restaurant or are eligible for the executive-training program of a major corporation. In fact, racial progress has tended to create divisions between blacks who have made it into the middle-class society and those left behind on the lowest rungs of the socioeconomic ladder. Our society has been able to remove barriers to blacks in their ambition and drive to improve their situation, but it has failed to instill that ambition in those blacks who feel trapped in a life of despair and devoid of hope.

American women have also made significant gains in recent years. The women's rights aspect of the movement has been particularly effective in reducing discrimination against women in education, jobs, sports, the receipt of credit, and retirement, and in opening opportunities to women that were formerly denied them. (The rapid increase in the number of women attending college and professional schools in recent years bodes well for the future advancement of women in managerial and professional positions.)

Women have been less successful in convincing our society to restructure the institutions of home and work. Despite the fact that more than half of American wives now work outside the home, our nation still has not provided child-care centers subsidized by the federal government as almost every other industrialized country in the world does. Nor has American industry done much to develop "flextime," a system of tailoring work schedules so that working mothers and fathers can share in the care of children. Also, the contributions that housewives make to the family are not reflected in our Social Security retirement system.

The situation of Mexican-Americans in the United States generally parallels that of blacks. They have benefited from the same legal battles against discrimination, enabling some of their members to move up the socioeconomic ladder, assisted by affirmative-action programs in education and employment. Also, some Mexican-Americans have been elected to political office at the state and local level and have increasingly occupied appointive positions in the federal government as well. The rapid growth of this minority group means that in the future it will exercise increased influence in the American political system.

Thus a variety of minority groups have made major gains in American society in recent years. The civil rights movement has to some degree been contagious: disadvantaged persons of various backgrounds have had their own sense both of grievance and of efficacy heightened by observing how others have fought for and won greater rights. On the other hand, the various battles over civil rights have sometimes pitted disadvantaged groups against each other as they compete for admission to institutions of higher education, for jobs, and for political positions and access to government benefits. There is also some indication that many Americans who are not members of disadvantaged minority groups are beginning to feel that such groups have benefited too much from special considerations—particularly affirmative-action programs—and that they themselves have become subjected to "reverse discrimination." The future of the civil rights struggle in the United States remains an uncertain one.

SELECTED READINGS

The classic historical study of race relations in the United States is John Hope Franklin, *From Slavery to Freedom* (New York: Alfred A. Knopf, 3rd ed., 1967). An excellent short treatment covering the entire historical period is August Meier and Elliott Rudwick, *From Plantation to Ghetto* (New York: Hill and Wang, rev. ed., 1970). A very good study of the Reconstruction period and its aftermath is C. Vann Woodward, *The Strange Career of Jim Crow* (New York: Oxford University Press, 3rd ed., 1966). A study of the race revolution is contained in Louis Lomax, *The Negro Revolt* (New York: New American Library, 1962), and the concept of Black Power is analyzed in Stokely Carmichael and Charles Hamilton, *Black Power* (New York: Random House, 1967). Good recent studies of the political activities of blacks are Milton Morris, *The Politics of Black America* (New York: Harper and Row, 1975), Lucius Barker and Jesse McCorry Jr., *Black Americans and the Political System* (Cambridge: Winthrop Publishing Co., 1976), and Lewis Killian, *The Impossible Revolution, Phase 2: Black Power and the American Dream* (New York: Random House, 2nd ed., 1975).

A provocative historical analysis of the relationship between the struggles of blacks and those of women in the United States is Catherine Stimpson's "Thy Neighbor's Wife, Thy Neighbor's Servants: Women's Liberation and Black Civil Rights," which appears in Vivian Gornick and Barbara K. Moran, *Women in Sexist Society* (New York: New American Library, 1971). Excellent general treatments of the women's movement are Jo Freeman, *The Politics of Women's Liberation* (New York: David McKay, 1975), Judith Hole and Ellen Levine, *Rebirth of Feminism* (New York: New York Times Book Co., 1971), and Joyce Gelb and Marian Palley, *Women and Public Policies* (Princeton, N. J.: Princeton University Press, 1982). An influential book written by one of the leaders of the women's movement is Betty Friedan, *The Feminine Mystique* (New York: W. W. Norton, 2nd ed., 1974).

An excellent historical account of the treatment of Mexican-Americans in the United States is Alfredo Cuellar, "The Political Development of the Mexican American People," which appears in Joan Moore and Harry Panchon, *Mexican Americans* (Englewood Cliffs,

N. J.: Prentice-Hall, 1971). Equally good as an overview of the political activities of Mexican-Americans is Maurilio Vigil, *Chicano Politics* (Washington, D. C., University Press of America, 1977). "Brown Power" is treated in Part Two of James Mencarelli and Steve Severin, *Protest: Red, Black, Brown Experience in America* (Grand Rapids, Mich.: William B. Eerdmans, 1975). Short accounts of recent developments among Mexican-Americans include "Chicano on the Move," *Newsweek* (January 1, 1979), pp. 20–27, and "Arriba! The Rapid Rise of Hispanic Voting Power," *The Washington Post National Weekly Edition,* April 9, 1984, pp 6, 7.

PART 5

Public Policies

CHAPTER 16

Fundamentals of Public Policy

So far we have viewed the American political system from a variety of perspectives. One of these was the way our *formal institutions*—including the Constitution, the Congress, the presidency, the bureaucracy, and the courts—function in the conduct of public affairs. We have also focused attention on the role that *informal associations*, such as interest groups and political parties, play in conveying public attitudes and demands to leaders in public office. Sometimes we have concentrated on the *behavior of individuals*—voters, representatives, presidents, judges—and the kinds of psychological and social factors that influence their behavior. By combining these perspectives, we can begin to understand the general process by which decisions are made by our national government.

However, limited attention has been given to *what* our national government *does* and the *policies* it adopts to meet various problems in American society. The only policy areas that have been singled out for examination so far are those dealing with civil liberties and civil rights. These are, however, special cases since they concern basic constitutional rights and are decided, to a greater degree than most public problems, by one branch of government—the courts.

This chapter will systematically analyze the general nature of public policy and how it is formulated and implemented in the United States. It will be concerned with a number of basic questions. What causes public officials to decide that a particular problem merits their attention? Once they try to deal with a problem, who actually gets involved and how do they go about deciding what to do? After a law has been passed, what happens? Is the issue resolved, or does the political struggle continue? What impact does a government policy actually have on the problem it is designed to meet? Before turning to these questions, however, we need

President Reagan and Chinese Premier Zhao Ziyang sign an exchange agreement.

to discuss the general nature of public policy and the types of policy with which public officials are involved.

THE GENERAL NATURE OF PUBLIC POLICY

Public policy is a *course of action that public officials take to try to deal with a particular area of concern,* such as national defense, inflation, or health care. By *course of action* we mean a series of decisions bearing on a common problem. Following the seizure of American hostages by the Iranians, President Carter's decision to freeze that country's assets in the United States was not of itself a "public policy." However, when that choice was coupled with others—such as his refusal to extradite the Shah, on the one hand, or to launch a full-scale invasion or naval blockade of Iran on the other—these decisions and actions taken together constituted executive policy on certain aspects of our relations with revolutionary Iran.

Note too that *course of action* means what public officials *actually do* about a particular problem rather than what they merely *say they will do.* Early in his administration, President Carter announced that the state of "human rights" in other countries would be a central concern of American foreign policy. However, in time it became apparent that our ability to affect the treatment of the world's oppressed, including political prisoners, was distinctly limited and would take second place to other priorities—such as signing the Strategic Arms Limitation Talks (SALT) agreement with the Soviets and obtaining vital oil supplies from Middle Eastern nations, including Iran, then controlled by the Shah. Thus our *actual* policy on human rights deviated significantly from the president's version of it.

The same situation occurred with respect to President Reagan's statements and actions concerning the federal budget. When he took office in 1981, he said he would balance the budget by 1984. In fact, the president never sent a balanced budget to Congress, and during that time the nation experienced by far the greatest deficits in its entire history. Thus, President Reagan's expressed policy of balancing the budget fell victim to other policies that were more important to him—massive tax cuts (that resulted in greatly decreased revenues) and a major military buildup (that greatly increased defense expenditures).

The above examples point up another feature of public policy. When government officials decide *not to pursue some course of action* (in these cases, to push the issue of human rights and so possibly jeopardize our relations with the Soviet Union and the Shah of Iran, or to insist that government revenues equal expenditures), that also constitutes a form of policy. Political scientist Thomas Dye suggests that public policy is ". . . whatever governments choose to do or not to do."

Some students of public policy identify still another requirement of public policy: that it *be directed toward some pur-*

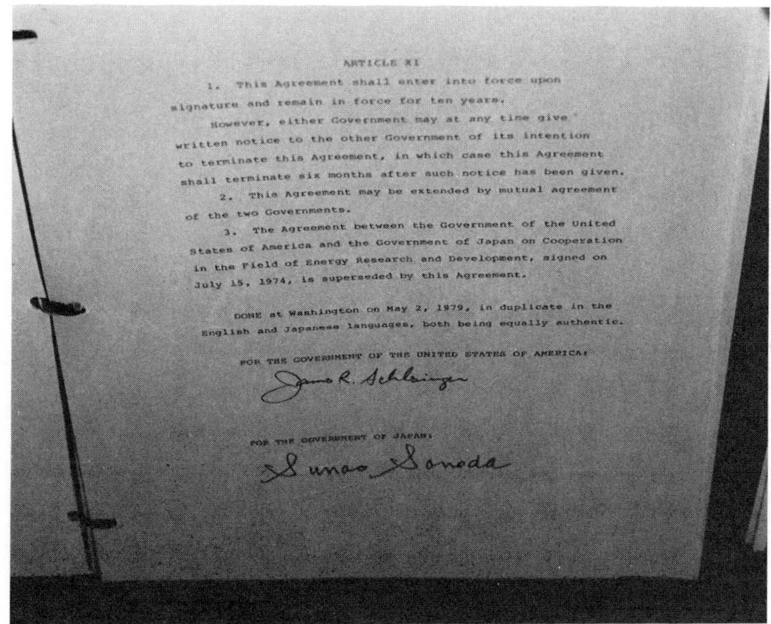

ARTICLE XI

1. This Agreement shall enter into force upon signature and remain in force for ten years. However, either Government may at any time give written notice to the other Government of its intention to terminate this Agreement, in which case this Agreement shall terminate six months after such notice has been given.

2. This Agreement may be extended by mutual agreement of the two Governments.

3. The Agreement between the Government of the United States of America and the Government of Japan on Cooperation in the Field of Energy Research and Development, signed on July 15, 1974, is superseded by this Agreement.

DONE at Washington on May 2, 1979, in duplicate in the English and Japanese languages, both being equally authentic.

FOR THE GOVERNMENT OF THE UNITED STATES OF AMERICA:

James R. Schlesinger

FOR THE GOVERNMENT OF JAPAN:

Sunao Sonoda

pose or goal. However, it is not always easy to determine the specific goal of a policy, especially if the goal is vague and changeable, being primarily an attempt to improve in a general way some undesirable situation. As one close student of the subject, Charles Lindblom, puts it, public policy is ". . . better described as moving *away* from known social ills rather than as moving *toward* a known and relatively stable goal."

Finally, public policy is to be distinguished from a policy pursued by a private organization. For one thing, public policy typically affects far more people and is supported by the authority of the government. Also, people are inclined to follow policies adopted by public officials because they consider the latter's authority and directives legitimate as well as enforceable by the government's monopoly of the legitimate use of force. Owing to these special characteristics, public policy closely affects the lives of all of us; it is, as we shall see later in this chapter, a subject in which many—both individuals and groups—are interested and attempt to influence.

TYPES OF PUBLIC POLICY

Public policy may be categorized in a number of ways. One principal distinction is between *foreign and military policy,* on the one hand, and *domestic policy* on the other. The former shapes our external relationships—economic, political, and military—with other nations. Domestic policy governs the nation's internal affairs, including the overall operation of its economy, in addition to regulating major sectors of society—such as business, labor, and agriculture—and important issues, such as social security. While the distinction between foreign and domestic spheres is significant, we should recognize that these two areas are not sealed compartments in which discrete policies are developed. Government policies concerning major agricultural crops (e.g., wheat) may affect our relationships with importing nations such as the Soviet Union; in turn, our policies regarding the Middle East may affect the volume and price of imported oil and the condition of our economy.

Air traffic controllers strike.

Another major differentiation is between policy that confers *benefits* on individuals or groups and policy that *regulates* their activities. Included in the first are direct payments of cash to persons, the allocation of food stamps to the poor, and subsidies of various kinds to private business (such as helping to finance the construction and operation of our merchant marine, or providing credit to farmers or veterans at lower interest rates than private financial institutions charge). The second type of policy involves activities such as preventing public employees from engaging in strikes. However, these two types of policy are not entirely separate; frequently public policy on a particular matter involves both kinds of activities. For example, farmers may receive government price supports for a certain crop—but only if they agree to limit the number of acres of it that they plant.

For many students of the political process, the most helpful categorization of public policy is based on *scope,* that is, on the range of individuals and groups affected by a policy. as well as those who participate in its formation. Political scientist Emmette Redford uses the term **micropolitics** to describe the most limited range of policy-making; one of his colleagues, Theodore Lowi, labels it the **"distributive" policy** area. Such politics involves distributing benefits to individuals, small groups, and communities. This can include legislation to allow a specific individual to immigrate to this country, to grant a business firm a tax break, or to build a new government facility in a particular community. Policies of this kind are characteristically worked out in congressional subcommittees (or committees) and executive bureaus, although final approval will be given by Congress itself or higher executive officials. Quite often there is little conflict in such policy-making because participants engage in *logrolling,* that is, supporting each other's pet projects. Typically, much of this activity occurs behind the scenes: partici-

U.S. Orders GM To Recall Cars For Air Pollution

Goal Is for Maker to Replace Valve Free; Plan Affects 550,000 of 1980 Models

By Andy Pasztor
Staff Reporter of The Wall Street Journal

WASHINGTON—The U.S. ordered General Motors Corp. to recall 550,000 of its 1980-model cars after federal environmental officials found that as many as 40% of the recalled vehicles exceed air-pollution standards.

Environmental Protection Agency officials said they took the unusual step of ordering a recall to make sure that all of the pants do not particularly want the public to know about special favors, and the media tend to ignore the activity because of its limited effect on society.

The next most inclusive type of policy range Redford refers to as *subsystem politics* (Lowi calls it **regulatory**). This involves policies relating to an entire functional area, such as transportation (airlines, railroads), communication (radio, television), or public utilities (electricity, gas, water). Because broad interests are involved (an entire industry rather than an individual business firm), policy tends to be made at a higher level of the political system, its formulation involving executive agencies, trade associations, consumer groups, and congressional committees. (These are the "iron triangles," or "policy subgovernments," referred to in Chapter 12.) There is more competition among the participants in subsystem politics than in micropolitics because the government is deciding whether it wants to regulate an entire industry and, if so, how it should go about doing it. For this reason, and because of the greater range of interests concerned, the media are much more likely to cover subsystem than micropolitics, making the regulatory process more politically visible.

Finally, there is what Redford calls **macropolitics.** (Lowi has a similar policy area, which he terms **redistributive.**) This type of policy range involves the allocation of costs and benefits affecting broad social groups and classes, such as industry, labor, and agriculture, or the affluent and the disadvantaged. Included are taxing and spending policies affecting the overall economy, as well as other major issues, such as social programs. Coalitions of "liberal" and "conservative" interest groups engage each other in ideological conflict over such policies, and in many instances so do the two major political parties. The president and congressional leaders are also major participants; media coverage of macropolitics is extensive. Thus, this type of policy-making takes place at the highest level of the political system and is the most politically visible kind of government activity.

Helpful as this method of classification is, it does not mean that a particular issue always remains in the same policy area. At times the media may report on micropolitical matters, such as favoritism for a particular company or industry (e.g., the national government's helping to "bail out" the Chrysler Corporation from bankruptcy). Such a revelation makes the issue more politically visible and raises it to a higher level in the political system. Also, presidents may on occasion make a major issue of what is ordinarily considered micropolitics, as Jimmy Carter did when he tried to prevent the development of certain water projects (typical "pork barrel" legislation). Also, individuals and groups that feel they are losing out in subsystem politics may seek to raise an issue to the macro level by interesting others in the matter, including the media and major public officials. Individuals and groups concerned with findings that associate health hazards with cigarette smoking

Judge Signs Pact That Splits Bell

By ERNEST HOLSENDOLPH

Special to The New York Times

WASHINGTON, Aug. 24 — Federal Judge Harold H. Greene today signed a consent agreement between the Justice Department and the American Telephone and Telegraph Company, setting into motion a plan to separate A.T. & T. from its 22 fully owned telephone companies in 18 months.

Officials at A.T. & T. said the company expects to present to the Justice Department complete, detailed plans for the divestiture well before the six months allowed under the terms of today's agreement.

Today's action by Judge Greene marked the end of an eight-year antitrust battle between the Government and Bell, a confrontation that reached its climax in January when the two

'What a novel idea. Applying it to the poor, too.'

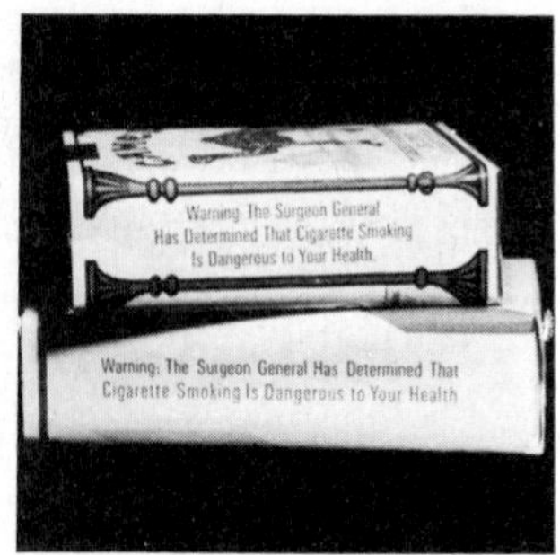

failed to make progress on the issue as long as it was perceived to be controlled by the tobacco interests dominant in congressional committees and the Department of Agriculture. Only after the mass media, President Kennedy, and other executive officials became involved with the issue did the health interests succeed in having warnings on the dangers of smoking placed on packages of cigarettes.

Thus, a variety of public policies affect our lives. The following section analyzes how such policies are developed.

STAGES IN PUBLIC POLICY-MAKING

While not all public policies are made in exactly the same way, students of the subject generally recognize four chronological stages or phases through which policies typically proceed. The first involves *getting an issue on the policy agenda* so that public officials may consider what, if anything, to do about it. The second stage is the consideration process itself, with officials *formulating various approaches* for dealing with the matter and then *adopting* (or choosing not to adopt) *a particular policy.* Stage three involves *implementing the policy,* carrying through on the details of its operation. Finally, there is the process of *determining the impact of the policy,* that is, *evaluating* whether or not it accomplishes what it was designed to do.

Issues and the Policy Agenda

Traditionally, students of government have focused on how public officials debate issues and decide what to do about them. Important as such decision-making is, it fails to take into account the fact that some issues never reach these officials in the first place. As political scientist E. E. Schatteschneider has suggested, political organizations tend to have a "bias" in favor of exploiting some kinds of conflicts and suppressing others. "Some issues are organized into politics while others are organized out."

Organizing an issue into politics means getting it on the policy agenda. Two close students of public policy, Roger Cobb and Charles Elder, identify two distinct kinds of agendas. One they call the **systemic agenda,** the other the **institutional agenda.**

The systemic agenda is informal; it is established by persons outside the government. Cobb and Elder suggest that it ". . . consists of all issues that are commonly perceived by members of the political community as meriting public attention and as involving matters within the legitimate jurisdiction of existing governmental authority." These issues are usually expressed in general, abstract terms (e.g., ending racial discrimination), and are not arranged in any clear order of priority. The systemic agenda is essentially a *discussion* agenda.

The institutional agenda (also called *governmental* or *formal*) is established by public officials. Cobb and Elder define it as ". . . that set of items explicitly set up for the active and serious consideration of authoritative decision makers." The phase "active and serious" is used to exclude pseudo-agenda items, those issues that decision-makers acknowledge in order to placate their supporters but do not seriously consider. (A legislator might introduce a bill to please a constituent but arrange to have it assigned to a committee that will never report it out.) Issues on the institutional agenda are typically defined in much more specific terms (such as the high unemployment rate among blacks) than those on the systemic agenda.

It is fairly easy to identify the issues that appear on the institutional agenda. They include items of business for all three branches of government, such as legislative calendars or the formal dockets of executive agencies and the courts.

Moreover, there are separate institutional agendas for governments at all political levels, whether national, state, county, or municipal.

It is much more difficult to spell out with precision the issues that are included on the systemic agenda. One possible source is those items mentioned in public-opinion polls reporting what Americans think are the most important issues facing the country. Issues receiving prominent comment in the mass media can be another indication of which matters most concern important groups outside the formal government. Also, the platforms of the two major political parties reflect the issues that party activists—many of whom do not hold government positions—believe merit public attention and possible action by officials. Candidates for office may also help place issues on the systemic agenda.

In a democratic society like the United States, a fairly close relationship should exist between issues on the two types of policy agendas. If public officials are responsive to citizen attitudes (even anticipating them in many instances), then public concerns requiring government attention should receive serious consideration almost as soon as they surface. Thus, the lag time between the appearance of an issue on the systemic agenda and its incorporation in the institutional agenda should be relatively short.*

Factors Affecting the Placement of Issues on the Policy Agenda. In a society as large and complex as the United States, there is no scarcity of issues of potential concern to public officials. Yet limitations of time and public resources prevent their dealing with all of them. Certain factors help determine which issues make it onto the policy agenda and which are left off.

One important determinant is the *kind of individual(s) or group* that is trying to interest the public and official decision-makers in a particular issue. Political systems tend to favor persons and groups that enjoy the social prestige, occupy the crucial positions in the economic structure, and possess the political resources necessary to have their demands considered. Thus, those from the professions and the business and financial worlds have traditionally been able to make their influence felt in the development of policy agendas.

The particular *nature of the issue* also affects whether it is given serious consideration by decision-makers. As Cobb and Elder point out, "old" issues—that is, those that have been on the policy agenda in the past—tend to crowd out "new" issues. Some items, such as the size of social security increases and the hourly rate to be paid under the minimum wage law, come up periodically for review by public officials, so that no special effort is required to get them onto the formal agenda.

On the other hand, what John King calls a "focusing event," such as a disaster or crisis, can trigger concern about a previously ignored or unsettled issue. The oil spill that occurred off Santa Barbara in 1969 stimulated the environmental protection movement that had begun to come into its own in the early 1960s. Ten years later, the near-disaster at the Three Mile Island nuclear plant at Harrisburg, Pennsylvania dramatically reopened the whole issue of the control of nuclear energy. Events can also act to *displace* one kind of issue with another. After many oil-producing nations began to greatly raise the price and limit the volume of oil sold to the United States in the 1970s, environmental is-

* In some instances, the agenda order is reversed: in the early 1960s when President Kennedy first decided to develop a broad program to combat poverty, there was no indication that either the general public or the mass media were concerned about the issue.

Santa Barbara beaches after 1969 oil spill.

Mother and child on first anniversary of near disaster at Three Mile Island.

sues involved in the adoption of automobile antipollution devices (which industry asserted were costly and a drain on fuel efficiency) became much less salient to many Americans.

As Robert Eyestone suggests, the *public mind* also affects the kinds of issues that get on the policy agenda. This is particularly true of general attitudes toward government. If the public becomes disillusioned with government's attempts to wage a successful war on poverty or crime, it will be less likely to demand that officials deal with other problems, such as health care or welfare. A general "taxpayers' revolt" like that associated with Proposition 13 in California may also make it difficult to get public officials to address even the most serious issues. In time, however, such general attitudes may change as citizens see major societal needs go unmet or the quality of public services seriously decline; if this occurs, these changes may well facilitate a broadening of the policy agenda.

Strategies and Techniques for Expanding the Policy Agenda. While some groups enjoy the deference, resources, and organization that permit them to get issues on the policy agenda without too much difficulty, most must exert a major effort to have their demands heard by public officials. This is especially true of new organizations, as well as those that have not traditionally enjoyed much influence in the political arena. That such groups typically try to persuade persons inside and outside the government to consider issues with which these persons have not previously been involved, makes the task of agenda-building a particularly difficult one. Nevertheless, there are a number of basic strategies and techniques that can be employed to try to overcome adversity of this kind.

One basic strategy is to *rally the full weight of a group's own resources* behind the issue in question. In Chapter 5 it was noted that the rank-and-file membership of an organization may be only marginally interested in and knowledgeable about the goals of their own association. In this case the group's leadership must persuade its own members of the importance of the issue and solicit their assistance in convincing public officials of the intensity of their feelings about it.

Another basic strategy is to *broaden the scope of the issue* to gain the support of persons and groups not immediately involved. (This is important in convincing government officials that the matter is of broad public concern rather than of limited importance.) A technique frequently employed to accomplish this purpose is to *define an issue* so that it appeals to a broad audience; this is typically done by invoking basic beliefs and

In the spirit of Proposition 13: The campaign for Proposition 4.

values in American life. Thus, homosexuals seeking to have restrictions on their teaching in public schools lifted couch the issue in terms of basic civil rights or "freedom of choice" rather than associating it with their particular sexual preferences or lifestyle.

A fundamental technique used to broaden public concern with an issue is to *get the mass media involved in the matter.* Leading media personalities (e.g., Dan Rather, Tom Brokaw, or Peter Jennings) who enter millions of American homes every weeknight are in a unique position to arouse public interest in an issue. Groups also use the media to gain public sympathy for their cause: television coverage of police using dogs and cattle prods against blacks in Birmingham, Alabama in the early sixties did much to make civil rights more salient to many Americans and rendered the entire issue much more politically *visible.*

In some instances, traditional techniques are unsuccessful and groups resort to *protest* as a tactic to gain the attention of both the general public and official decision-makers. This approach almost always ensures good media coverage, particularly on television, which favors dramatic events that are visually exciting. If a group can bring about a confrontation with the police—as war protesters at the 1968 Democratic National Convention deliberately did—the media can do much to portray them as martyrs and increase the chances of having their policy interests taken into account by concerned persons.

However, protest is not considered a legitimate political technique by many Americans, and its use may be counter-

Israeli Foreign Minister Yitzak Shamir appears on NBC's "Today" show with Tom Brokaw.

productive. The caravan of tractors that descended on Washington in the winter of 1979 to demand higher price supports for wheat and corn appeared to do little to get their grievances placed on the national policy agenda. On the other hand, the actions of independent truckers that same summer—refusing to move goods and interfering with fuel and food deliveries—dramatized the is-

Media cover use of police dogs on civil rights demonstrators.

Farmers' demonstration.

Truckers' demonstration.

sue of scarce and high-priced diesel fuel and brought quick action from public officials, including President Carter. That the general public itself was frustrated with fuel problems undoubtedly made Americans more receptive to the truckers' concern than the plight of the farmers.

Methods of Restricting the Policy Agenda. While many groups are trying to expand the policy agenda to include their issues, others are working to restrict its content. This is particularly true of interests that are doing well in the private sector or that have already received what they need in the way of government assistance. One of their principal goals is to resist the politicization of new issue disputes and to keep them in the private sphere. As Cobb and Elder suggest, there are a number of means by which they are able to achieve this goal.

One way to keep issues off the policy agenda is to *discredit* the individuals and groups supporting them. Thus, groups like Americans for Democratic Action or the American Civil Liberties Union can be branded as "socialist" or "radical" or "un-American." Another possibility is to zero in on a group's leaders. They can be denounced as "dictatorial" or "power-hungry" or as not having the interests of the rank-and-file members at heart. Or the leaders can be "coopted"—that is, given publicity and honorific positions in return for their not working vigorously to advance issues of concern to members of their organization.

Another technique is to deal with the issues themselves. One strategy is to agree that a grievance exists but to suggest that it be handled in another way. Thus, racial discrimination should be attacked—but in the home or the pulpit, not by public officials; or, if by public officials, then by local authorities rather than federal bureaucrats. Groups seeking to keep issues off the public agenda also use basic symbols and values to accomplish their purposes. They extol "the American way" as the voluntary way that prevents government from encroaching on the lives of private citizens. Or they suggest that problems cannot be solved by "throwing money at them." Or they bespeak the virtues of private property and individual initiative over the compulsion of an all-powerful central government.

Thus conflicts over the policy agenda are continuous as groups vie to expand and restrict its issue content. We shall see in the following section that battles over public policy continue after items reach the institutional agenda as public officials grapple with what, if anything, should be done about them.

Formulating and Adopting Public Policy

The process of official consideration of an issue on the formal agenda involves two major steps. One is the formulation of alternative ways to handle the issue. The other is the selection from among these alternatives (including no action at all) of the one that should be enacted into law. Note, however, that while the two steps are distinct in theory, in practice they often blend together: persons formulating proposals may well take into account the chances of adoption by decision-makers and frame them accordingly.

Policy proposals come to public officials from a variety of sources in the American political system. Many originate *outside the government.* Traditional interest groups attempt to influence government decisions that affect their members; quite naturally, they themselves originate many ideas of what should be done about issues on the policy agenda. In recent years, public-interest groups such as Common Cause and Public Citizen Inc. have also developed policy proposals that they feel will be beneficial to the general public. Scholars in universities, whose research is often supported by private organizations such as the Ford and Rockefeller foundations, often make policy recommendations based on their findings. Private policy-planning groups such as The Brookings Institution and the American Enterprise Institute (typically staffed by academics) also study issues and draw up ideas for handling them. Political parties are a source of policy proposals, many of which are included in their platforms. In some instances, a private citizen, such as a Ralph Nader, can propose a new approach to an issue, for

Pass the word.

Give your doctor a shot.

Give your waitress a tip.

Needle your tailor.

Fill in your dentist.

Give your lawyer some advice.

Do your neighbor a favor.

A lot of people you know may feel left out.

Your friends, relatives, neighbors and business associates may not yet be a part of Common Cause, "an uncommonly successful lobby," according to *The Christian Science Monitor*. *The Monitor* says "there has never been a reform movement so active and with such a record of accomplishment" as Common Cause.

You can help the people you know become a part of the effort to fight the power of wealthy special interests, uphold high standards of ethics in government, put an end to the nuclear arms race and achieve equal rights for all citizens.

We can use their help to build on the strength of the 250,000 who have already *acted* on their beliefs by joining Common Cause.

Here are some ways you can pass the word:

- Give someone a gift membership in Common Cause by filling out the form on page 56 and returning it to us in the postage-paid envelope provided in this magazine.
- Give this issue of *Common Cause Magazine* to someone you think should know about us and urge him or her to use the enclosed envelope to join Common Cause.
- Send us the names and addresses of two, three, 10 or more people who you think might want to know more about us, and we'll send each of them a package of information about Common Cause. (Feel free to use the envelope in this magazine to forward those names to us.)

Common Cause

example, providing safety equipment on automobiles rather than depending on driver education to deal with the problem of highway crashes.

Decision-makers can also turn to sources *within the government* for policy ideas. Executive agencies that deal daily with a wide variety of problems become very familiar with how existing policies operate and what can be done to improve them. White House advisers assist the president in developing proposals, especially those dealing with macro or redistributive policies. Some chief executives also appoint "task forces" and commissions, which include prestigious private citizens as well as public officials, to focus on a particular problem and recommend policies for dealing with it. Finally, Congress is a major source of policy proposals. Members of regular standing committees, together with their staff, become experts on matters that they deal with on a continuous basis and, like experts in the executive branch, develop recommendations for handling them.

Decision-makers thus suffer from no shortage of ideas about what to do about issues on the policy agenda. They also have a variety of options for handling them. One is to do nothing—at least for the present. Many issues are *postponed* while decision-makers gather more information or wait for additional public pressure that eventually forces them to take action. They may also deal only *symbolically* with an issue, expressing concern but suggesting that the cost of resolving the matter is excessive. Or they make a *token response,* committing far too few funds to deal with the issue adequately.

In some instances, of course, decision-makers do adopt significant policies for dealing with issues on the institutional agenda. Even then, however, they are likely to build on decisions made in the past, that is, to amend or revise previously adopted policies. Thus, policy-making in the United States tends to be *incremental;* only rarely, in times of a crisis, and/or sometimes when a new president such as a Franklin Roosevelt or Ronald Reagan takes office, are decision-makers likely to develop genuinely innovative approaches to political issues.

The legislative process through which many public policies are originally adopted contributes to their incremental nature. As Chapter 10 revealed, congressional procedure can be complex and tortuous. It requires that separate majorities supporting a bill be developed at several stages—in subcommittees, committees, and on the floor of both the House and the Senate. Moreover, extra majorities are sometimes required, as when a Senate filibuster is cut off or a presidential veto is overridden. Further complicating matters is the need, after policies are authorized, to appropriate funds for them as this involves a whole new process.

Public policies, particularly innovative ones, are adopted after a long period of consideration; as Nelson Polsby has observed, most take many years between initiation and adoption. During that time, they go through an "incubation" process: members of Congress propose bills that they know will not pass at the present time, make speeches on their behalf, and line up support for them from interest groups. These steps keep proposals alive while the problems they address become worse; committee hearings on the subject also continue to focus public attention on the issue. Eventually they may become politically ripe for adoption and be enacted into law.

Even then, however, the policy-making process is not complete. As the following section indicates, the process merely moves into another phase: *implementation.*

Implementing Public Policy

After policy goals and objectives have been adopted by the legislative body and funds appropriated to help achieve them, the actual **implementation** phase of policy-making begins.* By this is meant the carrying out or administration of a policy. We have previously considered many aspects of this process, particularly in the chapters on the bureaucracy and the courts; its consideration here will be brief, designed only to review some of the major points involved in carrying out a governmental activity or policy.

Recall that Congress typically passes laws that contain broad, general words and phrases, such as *just* or *reasonable* or *public interest, convenience, and necessity*. There are two reasons for this: members of Congress do not have the time or expertise to deal with the intricacies of a wide variety of issues; also, the political buck is passed to others to determine precisely what those phrases shall mean. As a result, executive agencies and the courts deal with essentially unfinished laws, which they must interpret, supplement, and apply to a variety of individuals, groups, and circumstances.

Of these two branches, the executive is more deeply involved in implementation. The administrative agencies handle hundreds of thousands of cases a year, laying down rules that determine how government benefits will be distributed and regulations enforced. They are also engaged in adjudication, deciding whether a benefit or regulation applies to a particular individual or group.

Although less heavily engaged than administrative agencies, the federal courts also play an important role in implementing public policy. Sometimes they directly administer policies, such as those pertaining to the naturalization of citizens or business bankruptcies. More often, the courts become involved only after administrative agencies have acted on a policy matter, deciding whether an agency had legal jurisdiction over the issue, or whether its proceedings were conducted properly and its findings supported by the evidence, or whether its interpretations of pertinent statutes were valid. Courts also occasionally affect the implementation of laws by passing on their constitutionality.

Other public officials also participate in the implementation of public policy. The president is involved through his power of appointment of executive and judicial personnel, his authority to reorganize the executive branch, and his decisions regarding the expenditures of funds. Members of Congress investigate the activities of executive agencies, ultimately decide which organizational unit will administer a policy, and play a part in the choice of persons that occupy administrative and judicial positions. Moreover, in our federal system, much of the implementation of federal policies occurs at the state and local level, which means that governors and state legislators (as well as mayors and city council members) affect how these policies are carried out.

Finally, private individuals and groups play a vital role in the implementation of public policy. Administrative agencies frequently appoint representatives of interest groups affected by public policies to provide advice on how they should be administered. Such groups also help to rally support for policies favored by the administrators. Moreover, many federal grants and contracts go to private individuals, groups, and businesses whose activities deter-

* It should be understood, however, that in some instances executive and judicial officials adopt policies to deal with issues that have not previously been considered by a legislative body.

mine whether the objectives of the federal funds are achieved.

Implementation thus constitutes one more phase in the policy-making process. The fact that so many government agencies and private groups are generally involved makes successful implementation of policies exceedingly difficult. Also complicating the process is the necessity of obtaining agreement at a number of crucial decision points along the way between the initiation and completion of a project. The tendency of individuals to view matters from the perspective of their particular vantagepoint, and the fact that there is often a high turnover of personnel in key positions, are also factors that can contribute to the difficulty of implementation.

George Edwards suggests that successful implementation depends on four major factors. Policies must be clearly *communicated* to the appropriate persons who are in a position to carry them out. Such persons must have the *resources* (staff, expertise, information) and *disposition,* that is, desire to do so. Finally, the *bureaucratic structure* involved in implementation must facilitate coordination among the various persons involved in carrying out policies.

Evaluating Public Policy

Evaluation is the final stage in the making of public policy; evaluation means making a judgment on the merits of a policy. Such a judgment is important in helping to decide whether a particular policy should be continued in its present form, changed or amended in some way, or discontinued altogether.

There are various ways of judging the merits of a public policy. Elected officials may be expected to view it from a *political* standpoint. Is their identification with a particular policy—such as federal aid to education or local law enforcement—likely to win or lose them votes in the next election? Or policies can be assessed on the basis of their *implementation.* Is an administration's particular program efficiently operated—has it resulted in training more teachers or police officers, or has it provided better classrooms or equipment with which to capture lawbreakers?

More recently, however, evaluation has taken on a more precise meaning, one that has to do with assessing the *impact of a policy on the social or economic problem it was designed to address.* Evaluation is thus concerned *not* with policy *outputs* but with policy *outcomes.* Instead of judging federal assistance policies by the size of the teaching staffs or police departments they produce, one should look at whether students learn more or crime diminishes as a result of such policies.

A number of groups inside and outside the government are involved in evaluating public policy. In the process of overseeing executive agencies, congressional committees inquire not only into implementation but also into the kinds of *results* produced. In recent years the General Accounting Office, an arm of Congress, has been heavily involved in the evaluation of government programs. Administrative agencies and specially-appointed presidential commissions also conduct studies of the effectiveness of government programs. Moreover, the same kinds of private groups and individuals that formulate policy proposals also analyze their results. Examples include traditional interest groups and "watchdog" ones (such as Common Cause and Ralph Nader's groups), private research organizations (e.g., The Brookings Institution and the American Enterprise Institute), and persons associated with the academic world.

Evaluation research is the assessment of how well public policies achieve their objectives. The first step is to spell out as precisely as possible what are these objectives. Then one must determine what are the actual consequences of the policy. A third step is to judge how close the consequences come to the objectives. If there is a significant difference between the two, then other matters must be explored—the reasons for the disparity, and what, if anything, can be done to close the gap between the objectives and the consequences of a policy.

There are many difficulties involved in evaluation research. Policy objectives are frequently vague and abstract (e.g., helping disadvantaged persons to adjust to urban life). Goals can sometimes be potentially contradictory, as when disadvantged persons are involved in the actual administration of a poverty program while at the same time it is insisted that the administration be highly efficient and not entail risks of the taxpayer's money. Nor is it always easy to measure consequences. A program to improve the reading skills of ghetto children might not bring that particular result; yet it could have the effect of making both children and parents feel that public officials are concerned with their welfare. Although the intended consequence is lacking, an unforeseen (and favorable) one arises in its place. Under those circumstances, should the program be continued or not?

Evaluation of public policies is, finally, a *political process* in which complete objectivity may be impossible. Persons operating a program tend to have a vested interest in its continuance and to regard its evaluation as a means of justifying the policies that they have been administering. A clientele that benefits from a government program may be suspicious of evaluations that could result in changes in the administration of a program or in its discontinuance altogether. So may be presidents and legislators who feel that particular policies are popular with the voters, even though they do not accomplish all that had been hoped for them.

Despite these problems, the evaluation of public policies continues as researchers learn better how to deal with such problems. The magnitude of the problems our society faces and the limited resources we have to deal with them make it imperative that we determine as accurately as possible which policies work and which do not. If political decision-makers profitably use the results of evaluation research, they can formulate and implement new or changed policies to meet society's needs.

ASSESSMENT

There is no question that policy-making in the United States is a long, complex, and tortuous process. The fact that it involves so many separate stages and that proposals for dealing with issues may be amended or defeated altogether at a variety of decision points means that it is difficult to bring about major changes in American society. Changes tend to occur slowly and incrementally rather than rapidly and innovatively.

Some observers of American politics have suggested that these characteristics of our policy-making process result in the control of our political system by elites. Further, it is contended that these elites are interested in protecting the status quo, that is, the existing distribution of wealth and privileges in society from which they personally benefit. Finally, it is argued that the particular technique that elites employ to protect their interests is to keep issues that threaten the status quo off the political agenda so that they never receive serious consideration by public officials.

While there is little question that elites are influential in our policy-making process, it is simply not true that they control the political agenda. Dramatic events can force consideration of issues that economic elites would have our public officials ignore. Two incidents—the oil spill off the coast of Santa Barbara and the incident at Three Mile Island—led to the adoption of policies involving the protection of the environment and the cessation of licensing new nuclear facilities that the oil companies and the nuclear industry were unable to prevent.

In fact, it is possible for the disadvantaged to *create* events that draw public attention to their problems; in recent years it has been particularly effective for groups to stage political *protests*. Contributing to the effectiveness of this technique is the coverage of such protests by the *mass media,* which thrive on conflicts in American society, especially those that can be presented in a visually exciting manner. The disadvantaged groups examined in the last chapter—blacks, women, and Hispanics—have all utilized political protests covered by the media to draw attention to their grievances.

Once an issue gets on the political agenda, there is no shortage of suggestions for dealing with the matter. This stage of the policy process is particularly *pluralistic* as individuals and groups inside and outside the government try to convince public officials that their particular proposals will help to meet the problem and that it is in the political interest of the officials to adopt their proposals. The end result of the formulation and adoption stage of the policy-making process is usually a compromise "solution" that does not satisfy any group completely but that is nevertheless acceptable to all or most of them.

In recent years, disadvantaged groups have increasingly turned to a particular political arena to get their demands considered—the *courts*. When political pressures from established groups deter legislators and executives from dealing with an issue, concerned parties are able to use lawsuits to seek redress for their grievances. Decisions handed down by federal courts in the last quarter-century have benefited a number of formerly disadvantaged groups: residents of urban areas, consumers, and environmentalists, as well as the groups examined in the last chapter. The fact that federal judges enjoy life tenure enables them to follow their own consciences on the rights of minorities. Moreover, such decisions indicate that individuals are capable of transcending their own selfish interests; for example, Supreme Court rulings advancing the rights of blacks, women, and Hispanics have been made primarily by white males of Northern European background.

While the policy-making process in the United States has brought about major changes in our society in recent years, it also contains elements that tend to perpetuate the status quo. The same type of *public mind* or *mood* that fostered rapid social change in the 1960s and early 1970s gave way to an increasing conservatism in the late 1970s and early 1980s, as epitomized by the adoption of Proposition 13 in California and decisions to cut federal domestic spending primarily at the expense of government programs for the disadvantaged. Moreover, the *implementation* stage of the policy-making process favors those interests that are resisting change. It is much easier to get legislation passed that is designed to clean up the environment or to end discrimination in housing than it is to develop administrative regulations backed by enforcement powers that actually accomplish those purposes. Finally, changes that occur in American society do so within the broad parameters of our *prevailing value system,* one that emphasizes such basic elements as private property and free enterprise.

SELECTED READINGS

There are a number of good general discussions of public policy in the United States. Two particularly helpful ones are James Anderson, *Public Policy-Making* (New York: Praeger Publishers, 1975), and Charles Jones, *An Introduction to the Study of Public Policy* (North Scituate, Mass.: Duxbury Press, 2nd ed., 1977).

Emmette Redford's categorization of public policies appears in his *American Government and the Economy* (New York: The Macmillan Co., 1965), and Theodore Lowi's is contained in "American Business, Public Policy, Case Studies and Political Theory," *World Politics* 16 (July 1964); 677–715. A. Lee Fritschler's *Smoking and Politics* (Englewood Cliffs, N. J.: Prentice-Hall, 3rd ed., 1983) is an excellent illustration of how an issue moved from the "subsystem" to the "macropolitics" level.

E. E., Schatteschneider, *The Semi-Sovereign People* (New York: Holt, Rinehart, and Winston, 1960), analyzes the bias in the American political system and how conflicts change when they are expanded to include new groups and political arenas. Three books dealing with how issues get on the public agenda are Roger Cobb and Charles Elder, *Participation in American Politics: The Dynamics of Agenda-Building* (Baltimore: The Johns Hopkins Press, 2nd ed., 1983), Robert Eyestone, *From Social Issues to Public Policy* (New York: John Wiley and Sons, 1978), and John Kingdom, *Agendas, Alternatives and Public Policies* (Boston: Little, Brown and Company, 1984). Part Three of Carol Greenwald, *Group Power: Lobbying and Public Power* (New York: Praeger Publishers, 1977), analyzes how interest groups utilize successive stages of the policy-making process to try to accomplish their goals. Nelson Polsby's concept of the "incubation" process for the development of public policy appears in "Strengthening Congress in National Policymaking," The *Yale Review,* Vol. 59 (Summer, 1970), pp. 481–497.

An excellent case study of the problems involved in implementing public policy is Jeffrey Pressman and Aaron Wildavsky, *Implementation* (Berkeley: University of California Press, 1973). For a very good general discussion of the matter, see George Edwards, *Implementing Public Policy* (Washington, D. C.: Congressional Quarterly Press, 1980). For a good analysis of the problems involved in evaluating public policy, see Carol Weiss, *Evaluation Research* (Englewood Cliffs, N. J.: Prentice-Hall, 1972).

CHAPTER 17

Economic Policies

With the election of Ronald Reagan in 1980, the country witnessed a radical change in the nation's political agenda. The one-time liberal Democrat turned conservative Republican called for a "new beginning," that is, the rescue of the country from the "failed" policies of the past. Reagan believed that the nation's economic ills, especially inflation, high-interest rates, and budget deficits, were caused by a bloated federal government. ("Government is not the *solution* to our problem; rather, the government *is* the problem.") To remedy the situation, it was necessary to take more of the major responsibility for economic and social problems from the federal government and to assign it to the states, the localities, and the private sector.

On February 18, 1981, the administration announced its economic program designed to help shrink "Big Government." One major aspect of the program was a cut of over $40 billion in the projected rate of domestic spending, particularly in the burgeoning social programs. At the same time, the president proposed a major reduction in individual income taxes—30 percent over three years. To counteract inflation, he supported a policy that called for the Federal Reserve Board to provide a controlled growth in the nation's money supply. Finally, the president embraced the concept of deregulation, that is, cutting back on government regulations that he felt were stifling business and interfering with the resurgence of the private sector of the economy.

In the months that followed, the new president achieved major political successes, particularly with his program of budget and tax cuts. Cajoling members of Congress and using prime-time television to rally the American public to put pressure on their representatives, he managed to push through measures reducing previously projected domestic expenditures by $33 billion. He also persuaded Congress to cut taxes by 25 percent over the next three years and to begin a policy of "indexing" taxes in 1985, so that increases in income resulting from inflation would be counteracted by larger deductions and exemptions, thus holding taxes constant. Supporting the new president was a virtually united Republican party in both chambers of Congress and a group of Southern "Boll-Weevil" Democrats that gave Reagan a working majority in the Democrat-controlled House of Representatives.

The president's other economic policies also were generally implemented. Chairman Paul Volcker of the Federal Reserve Board continued to keep a firm hand on the growth of the money supply. (He had actually begun such a policy back in the latter days of the Carter administration.) At the same time, the administration moved its program of regulatory relief forward. The president assigned Vice-President George Bush the task of overseeing the withdrawal and revision of proposed and existing administrative regulations. He also appointed administrative officials such as James Watt (Interior) and Ann Gorsuch Burford (Environmental Protection Agency) who were sympathetic with his goals of cutting back government regulation of the private sector.

Despite these initial political successes, however, the economy soon went into a deep recession. Between early August 1981, when the president's tax bill was signed into law, and Labor Day the stock market fell precipitously and bond rates moved up. In the latter part of the year, the unemployment rate began to rise significantly; by the end of 1982, more than one-in-ten Americans looking for work could not find it. Business bankruptcies rose to record highs. The policies of the Federal Reserve Board did succeed in drastically reducing the inflation rate but interest rates remained high, making it difficult for Americans to purchase automobiles and homes. Moreover, instead of presenting a balanced budget for fiscal 1984 as he had promised in his campaign, President Reagan proposed the highest deficits in the nation's history.

In time, however, the economy began to turn around. In August 1982 the stock market experienced a major rally, and during 1983 unemployment fell significantly. The automobile and housing industries reported major increases in sales as did industrial corporations and retailers. Meanwhile, inflation remained low (about 4 percent) and consumers expressed a growing confidence in the economy.

As Americans looked forward to the 1984 presidential election, the economic picture was mixed. The president could point with pride to the continued decrease in unemployment and the low rate of inflation. However, interest rates remained high and so did the federal budget deficit—$180 billion projected for fiscal 1985 alone. Moreover, neither the Republican president, nor his Democratic opponents in Congress could agree on a program to significantly reduce the deficit. The former refused to consider a major increase in taxes or a significant decrease in the rate of spending for national defense (defense expenditures rose by $83 billion from fiscal 1981, the last year of the Carter administration, to fiscal 1984, the third year of the Reagan administration); the latter were opposed to further cuts in domestic social programs that they claimed had already been pared to the bone.

In this chapter we will explore all the developments outlined above. It begins with a discussion of the most basic issue raised by President Reagan: the general role the government should play in the nation's economy. It then moves to an analysis of *microeconomics*, activities relating to key sectors of the economy, for example, business, labor, and agriculture. The latter sections of the chapter focus on *macroeconomics,* the management of the entire American economy, including our taxing and spending policies.

THE GENERAL ROLE OF GOVERNMENT IN THE ECONOMY

Every society has some system for allocating material goods among its members; this allocation involves both the production and the distribution of such goods. The key issues are *what* goods are to be produced and distributed. Also important are *who* will make these decisions and *what process* will be used to make them.

There are, of course, many possible arrangements for making such important decisions on the allocation of material goods. Here we will examine two extreme examples of economic systems and the justifications advanced for each of them. As we shall see, however, no society, including our own, has adopted one system to the complete exclusion of the other. Moreover, these two examples do not exhaust the possibilities for allocating material goods; there are a variety of other arrangements for doing so.

Laissez-Faire Capitalism

What has come to be known as **laissez-faire capitalism** is essentially an economic system that allows private individuals and groups rather than government officials to make the key decisions on the production and distribution of goods. The figure most often associated with this system is *Adam Smith,* sometime professor of logic and moral philosophy at the University of Glasgow in the late eighteenth century. Smith set forth and defended this economic system in an influential book, *The Wealth of the Nations* (its full title was *An Inquiry Into the Nature and Causes of the Wealth of Nations*) published in 1776, the year of the American Declaration of Independence from Great Britain.

"Laissez-Faire" Capitalist, Adam Smith.

Smith argued in his treatise that there is a "natural liberty" of every person to pursue his economic self-interest. Thus an individual is capable of making his own decisions both on how he will use his talents to produce goods and on which goods, in turn, he will purchase from others. Moreover, these decisions benefit not only the individual but society as a whole. As Smith viewed the situation, there is an "invisible hand" that leads people to promote the public interest, even though that is not their intention. As he put it, "It is not from the benevolence of the butcher, the brewer, or the baker that we expect our dinner, but their regard to their own self-interest. We address ourselves not to their humanity but to their self-love . . ."

Translating this general philosophy into an economic system, Smith argued that a "natural order" operates in the form of a balance between the demand and supply of goods. When the supply of a good exceeds the demand for it, the market price falls and people will produce less of it. In the opposite situation—that is, when the supply of a good falls below the demand for it—the market price rises, stimulating people to produce more of it. Thus ". . . the quantity of every commodity brought to market naturally suits itself to the effectual demand."

These assumptions led Smith to conclude that the government should generally stay out of the economic sphere (*laissez-faire* means essentially "hands off"; literally, "let do"). To restrict a person in the use of his labor or the employment of his capital encroaches on his liberty; moreover, private individuals are better judges of such matters because public officials do not have the wisdom or knowledge for ". . . superintending the industry of private people and of directing it towards the employments most suitable to the interest of society." Smith also felt that governments themselves should not engage in economic activities because they are ". . . always, and without exception, the greatest spendthrifts in society."

It should be pointed out, however, that Smith did recognize some exceptions to an economic system based on private enterprise alone. Government, he thought, has the obligation not only to protect individuals from both external enemies and internal disorder but to develop "public works" that would prove unprofitable for private individuals or groups to undertake. In addition, Smith justified government regulation of banking, currency, and interest rates; the provision of a tariff to protect a domestic industry necessary for national defense; and a legal system to enforce contracts and the payment of debts.

"Collectivist" Karl Marx.

Das Kapital.

Kritik der politischen Oekonomie.

Karl Marx.

Erster Band.

Buch I: Der Produktionsprocess des Kapitals.

Hamburg

Verlag von Otto Meissner.

1867.

Despite these exceptions, however, Smith's economic system is basically one in which private individuals and groups undertake the major economic activities of society and a free market determines both the goods that will be produced and the prices that will be charged for them. Competition among producers ensures that the most efficient of them will prevail and the consumer's interests will be protected. Today such a system is referred to by names such as **free** or **private enterprise,** or as one operating on the basis of a **free** or **private market.**

Collectivism

Collectivism is the exact opposite of laissez-faire capitalism; in it, the allocation of resources lies not with private individuals and groups but with the government. Thus public officials decide what goods will be produced, how they will be produced, and the method by which they will be distributed. An underlying justification for this type of economic system is that since the production and distribution of material goods is a collective enterprise in which many people and groups participate, control over the economic system should be vested in the only institution that represents all these diverse interests—the government or state.

While many figures have espoused the principles of collectivism, the person most often associated with this economic system is *Karl Marx.* A freelance journalist who left his native Germany when the radical newspaper that he worked for was shut down by the government, Marx lived for a time in France and Belgium before being forced to leave the continent altogether for England in 1848. That same year saw publication of the *Communist Manifesto,* in which Marx collaborated with his friend Friedrich Engels; some 20 years later Marx's own *Das Kapital,* based on his research on the British Museum Library, appeared. In these two works—the first an inflammatory call for workers of the world to revolt against their capitalist masters, the second a scholarly study of the historical evolution of the capitalistic system—Marx set forth the reasons for his opposition to capitalism and proposed total state control of the economy, a system he called **communism.**

Unlike Smith, Marx viewed society not in terms of individuals or small groups but in broad social classes. The basic class distinction is between those who own the means of production and those who do not. Thus under the agricultural economy of feudalism there were the lords and the serfs; under industrial capitalism there are the owners—whom he called the **bourgeoisie**—and the workers, the **proletariat.** However, while the basic means of production changed as factories replaced land as the most important feature of the economy, the relationship between the owners and workers remained the same. The former, whether they were lords or factory-owners, were seen as exploiting the latter, the serfs or industrial workers.

Marx, even more than Smith and for different reasons, viewed the government of a capitalist nation as a social danger. While the latter considered such a government incompetent to oversee private economic activities or to undertake such activities itself, Marx regarded the state or government as the oppressive instrument of the dominant class, used to help exploit the propertyless masses. By enforcing the laws that favor the property-owning class, government becomes what Marx called the "executive committee" of the dominant class.

Marx saw two stages in the movement from a capitalist to a communist economy. First, it would be necessary for industrial workers to overthrow the bourgeois regime and replace it with a "dictatorship of the proletariat." During the period of dictatorship, the bureaucracy of the displaced capitalist state would be destroyed, the means of production converted from private to public property, and any efforts of the bourgeoisie to stage a counterrevolution repressed.

Upon the accomplishment of these goals, a second-stage communist economic system would develop under which people would contribute according to their individual abilities and receive material goods according to their needs. In this classless society—since, with property owned in common, no basis would exist for class distinctions—there would be no need for a government of people. Such a government would, to use Engels' own words, simply "wither away," to be replaced by ". . . the administration of things and the direction of the process of production."

Communist theories about the withering away of the state have proved to be utopian; it has not occurred in any nation that has adopted a collectivist economic system. Rather, such countries have remained in the initial Marxian stage, in which most of the means of production are owned by an all-powerful state. (The usual reason given for why the movement from the first to the second communist stage has not yet occurred is that the danger of a capitalist counterrevolution remains.) While Marx himself would have thoroughly disapproved the continued presence of such an all-powerful state, it is common for people today to identify nations like the Soviet Union and the People's Republic of China as *Marxist.*

Despite these qualifications about true Marxism, however, the fact remains that collectivism represents the major theoretical alternative to laissez-faire capitalism. Collectivism emphasizes not our individualism but our social nature. It acknowledges no invisible hand guiding the use of private property so that it operates in the public interest; rather, collectivism believes that private ownership perverts one's original cooperative nature and results in a society in which members of one class exploit those of another. In place of a "market" or "free" economy, there is to be a collectivist or **command economy,** in which the government determines the production and allocation of goods (and services) among members of society.

The "Mixed" Economy

An analysis of the actual economies of nations around the world would indicate that they are generally **"mixed,"** that is, they combine elements of both private and public ownership of economic goods. Among major nations, the Soviet Union and the People's Republic of China come closest to the collectivist model, although each allows some ownership of personal goods and in some cases the use of small plots of land. Much more common, however, is **socialism,** a system in which major economic activities—particularly basic means of production, distribution, and commerce—are owned and administered by the government. Examples include iron and steel industries, railroads and airlines, and banks. The remaining economic activities stay in private hands. Such systems, adopted voluntarily by democratic governments rather than occurring as a result of revolution (as Marx thought would be necessary in most countries—a possible exception he noted being England), are prominent in Western Europe and many of the new nations that were formerly part of the British Empire.

Our own nation also has a mixed economy. We have less ownership of basic industries by the national government than most countries, the major exceptions being roads, the post office, and the Tennessee Valley Authority, which manufactures and distributes electrical power wholesale to local governments and private companies. Most of our "socialism" is at the local level in the form of utilities (water, gas, and electricity) and transportation systems (buses and subways). Moreover, such enterprises fit even Adam Smith's exception to private enterprise, that is, they constitute "public works."*

However, the simple division of economic activities in the United States into those that are publicly and privately owned does not capture the variety of our mixed economy. Between these polar extremes are other arrangements that are more or less public or private in nature. For example, instead of owning and operating an enterprise entirely by itself, the government may allow private companies to hold joint stock in it (such as in the communications satellite) or to contract for its use (as with atomic energy). Or private companies may carry on an activity but have the price they charge for their services set by government (as with public utilities that are considered to be "natural" monopolies in which competition between companies would be wasteful). Government may heavily subsidize private companies that are engaged in a vital activity (e.g., shipbuilding for our merchant fleet). On the other hand, it may also closely superintend a business in order to protect the general public (e.g., regulating the food and drug industry).

Over the years our government has become increasingly involved in the American economy. As the following sections indicate, the tight web of relationships that exist between the public and the private sectors in the United States applies to three major economic areas—business, labor, and agriculture.

GOVERNMENT AND BUSINESS

While businessmen are typically the most fervent advocates of the principles of free enterprise and laissez-faire, they have not hesitated to seek approval for government policies running counter to such principles when to do so has served their own interests. Such policies include a wide range of programs that *promote* business interests and involve *regulatory* policies that fail to allow adequate competition in the American economy.

Promoting Business Interests

The earliest actions of our national government that can be seen as promoting business fall within the area of exception to laissez-faire principles that Smith recognized. These include, in addition to a provision for an army and navy, the establishment of a banking and currency system as well as courts to enforce contracts and the payment of debts. Alexander Hamilton's early call for the enactment of a tariff to protect American business against foreign competition was also a policy specifically con-

* Public expenditures for the armed services, law enforcement, and education would also have met with Smith's approval.

"The public sector be damned!"

doned by Smith, although the Scotsman confined such protection to industries necessary for the national defense—a restriction not met by Hamilton's request for a *general* duty on imported goods.

Over the years, however, government has provided a series of benefits for business that Smith probably would have found it difficult to justify under laissez-faire principles. These include direct *subsidies,* such as the cash and lands deeded to the railroads, and payments made to airlines to carry the mail and to firms that build and operate American merchant ships. There are also indirect subsidies in the form of low-cost postal rates to publishers of newspapers and magazines, or in the mere fact that some motor carriers fail to pay the full cost of the damage they do to our highways.

Major provisions for credit have also benefited American businesses over the years. In 1930, during the Great Depression, the Reconstruction Finance Corporation was established to make loans to businesses. By the time the agency was liquidated in 1954 (long after the depression), it had lent over $50 billion to American firms, including some of the very largest ones. At the insistence of small businesses, a new agency—the Small Business Administration—was created in 1953 to take the RFC's place. The new organization, operating as an independent agency, continues to provide credit to American entrepreneurs.

Even more extensive has been the government's willingness to *guarantee* the payment of loans made to private business. Particularly prominent have been guarantees involving the repayment of mortgage loans for private housing—a program that has benefited not only many homeowners (especially veterans) but the housing industry, for example, builders, realtors, and mortgage-lenders. Loan guarantees have also been extended to railroads and in recent years to the Lockheed Aircraft

Chrysler Chairman, Lee Iacocca.

Corporation and the Chrysler Corporation. In fact, a recent government study indicated that by the end of 1978, government guarantees totalled $254 billion—$1 of every $12 of supposedly private loans.

Finally, business benefits from two other kinds of government assistance. One is the gathering and publication of information valuable to businessmen in general—such as decennial census data on economic activities—or of concern to specific industries, such as the weather bureau's forecasts (benefiting those involved in aviation, shipping, or recreational activities). The other is the use of facilities paid for by public funds. The beneficiaries include shipping companies that utilize harbors, canals, and lighthouses, and airlines that use terminals, runways, and traffic control equipment.

Maintaining Competition in the American Economy

It will be recalled that one of the major assumptions behind Adam Smith's system of laissez-faire was that competition among producers of a good would operate to hold down its price and maintain its quality. Such competition was achieved without great difficulty in Smith's day (the latter half of the eighteenth century) when economic activities were in the hands of individuals and small business concerns. However, the Industrial Revolution brought specialization and the concentration of capital and labor in fewer and larger firms. Moreover, the development of the corporate form of business organization, with its provision for the limited liability of shareholders and the legal perpetuity of the unit,* facilitated this development. Also contributing to the increased concentration of economic wealth were actions taken by businessmen to reduce competition: agreements to limit production, fix prices, allocate markets, and share profits; in addition there were purchases of and mergers with rival firms. By the latter part of the nineteenth century, combinations or "trusts" dominated a number of key industries in the American economy, such as sugar, tobacco, steel, and meat-packing.

In time these developments touched off a major political reaction from a number of aggrieved groups, including small entrepreneurs who lost out to the trusts in dog-eat-dog competition, workers who found their livelihood increasingly dependent on a few giant firms, and farmers plagued with high costs for storing their produce and exorbitant rates for hauling it to market. Joining these groups were political liberals concerned with the trusts' domination of American economic and political life and advocates of laissez-faire who longed for the days of genuine economic competition.†

In 1890, Congress passed the Sherman Antitrust Act, which was designed to curb the trusts and restore competition to the American marketplace. Section 1 of the act outlawed contracts, combinations, or conspiracies in restraint of trade and made those involved in them guilty of a misdemeanor. Section 2 provided a similar sanction for those who monopolize or attempt to monopolize or combine or conspire with others to monopolize trade or commerce. This legislation laid the groundwork for a legal assault on the abuses of an increasingly concentrated economy.

However, as the national government began to use the Sherman Act to move

* This situation is in contrast to single proprietorships and general partnerships, in which all the owners' assets (not just their financial investment in the particular company) are subject to levy for payment of the debts of the business, and where the company is terminated when the owners die.

† It should be noted, however, that some historians, such as Gabriel Kolko, contend that some business concerns actually favored government regulation as a means of avoiding the effects of cutthroat competition.

"ISN'T IT JUST POSSIBLE THAT I'M OVERDOING THIS BUSINESS?"

against the trusts, it found its efforts thwarted by the courts. When a suit was brought against the American Sugar Refining Company, which controlled 98 percent of the sugar-refining industry, the Supreme Court ruled in 1895 that although the company was a monopoly, it was involved in "manufacturing," not "commerce"; hence, it was not subject to the national government's power over interstate commerce. A few years later the Court reversed itself, holding that the Sherman Act applied to manufacturing activities that "affected" commerce (as contrasted to just activities that were "in" commerce). However, the Court later created another roadblock to the enforcement of the act by ruling that it was not meant to prohibit *all* restraints of trade, only "unreasonable" ones. It was not enough to show that a company's size enabled it to dominate an industry; the government also had to show that the firm reached that position by pursuing predatory practices against its competitors.

In 1914 Congress enacted two new pieces of legislation to facilitate antitrust actions. The first, the Clayton Act, spelled out specific kinds of predatory practices that businesses were forbidden to engage in. Included were establishing discriminatory prices (selling goods cheaper to one purchaser than to another), entering into arrangements in which a purchaser agreed not to handle any goods of the seller's competitors or else agreed to buy other products of the seller as a condition for receiving the goods in which it was interested, acquiring stock in rival companies or other assets in order to lessen competition or create a monopoly, and establishing "interlocking directorates" (those in which people serve simultaneously on the boards of directors of two or more corporations and who are thus in a position to interrelate their business activities). The second major piece of legislation, the Federal Trade Commission Act, also generally prohibited "unfair methods of competition" and created an administrative commission to conduct studies of business organizations, to investigate alleged violations of antitrust laws, and to assist the courts in developing antitrust decrees. The FTC was also granted joint jurisdiction with the Justice Department to enforce the Clayton Act.

Over the years the antitrust division of the Justice Department and the Federal Trade Commission have used a variety of legal sanctions to try to maintain competition in the American economy.

These have included bringing both civil and criminal suits* in the federal courts by the Justice Department and the issuance of *cease and desist orders* by the FTC, which require companies to stop engaging in unfair methods of competition. Historically, criminal convictions have been relatively rare, although 29 companies manufacturing electrical equipment were found guilty of price fixing in 1960 and some of their executives were sentenced to jail for a year. In the last few years there has been an increased use of criminal prosecutions for illegal activities such as price-fixing and bid-rigging by cartels. Civil proceedings have also been utilized, most of them ending in a *consent agreement* whereby the government agrees to drop the suit if the company agrees to take some action, such as stopping some practice that tends to impede competition or divesting itself of another company's stock.*

The battle to maintain competition in the American economy has been difficult to sustain. Its success depends on the willingness of individual presidents, attorneys general, and commissioners of the FTC to pursue aggressive antitrust actions against offending companies, as well as provision by Congress of adequate funds for the executive agencies to carry on these activities. The fact that the alleged violators of antitrust laws are wealthy corporations, with huge financial resources and legal talent often exceeding that available to the government contributes to the difficulties of dealing with antitrust matters.

Judicial attitudes have also affected the struggle to foster economic competition. As we have seen, the Supreme Court initially required that charges of predatory practices be proved before it would find a company in restraint of trade or commerce. However, it has subsequently ruled that the ability of a firm to control a substantial percentage of a market constitutes an illegal monopoly, even though it cannot be shown that the company used improper means to achieve that control. Nor is it necessary that a firm actually raise its prices or exclude its competitors from a market; it is sufficient that it have the *power* to do so.

Over the years the national government generally has been able to act successfully against various kinds of combinations. One such combination grows out of **horizontal mergers,** that is, mergers of companies engaged in the same stage of industrial production. The Supreme Court thus required Bethlehem Steel Company to divest itself of assets of Youngstown Sheet and Tube Company. The court also ruled that antitrust legislation covers combinations resulting from **vertical mergers**—those that occur between companies that do not compete with each other but are involved in different stages of production. As a result, the DuPont Corporation was required to divest itself of General Motors stock (it owned 23 percent of the shares) because it could use that ownership to gain an advantage over its competitors in the sale of automotive fabrics and finishes to General Motors.

Nevertheless, antitrust legislation has failed to curb a new type of corporate merger—the **conglomerate.** Such mergers do not involve competing firms or those with supplier–purchaser relation-

* The purpose of a civil suit is to enforce the rights of an individual or group through financial compensation for past wrongs or the prevention of future ones; criminal suits involve the rights of society as a whole against law violators, with enforcement taking the form of a fine, imprisonment, or death.

† In addition to civil suits brought by the government, the Sherman Act authorizes private parties to sue and recover triple damages from violators of the law. In the 1960 case cited above, more than 2000 such suits were filed by utility companies against the electrical equipment firms involved.

ships; instead, they occur when a company acquires another concern in order to penetrate a new geographical market, to handle a related product, or to involve itself in an entirely new type of venture as when the Mobil Oil Company took over Montgomery Ward, the giant retail store.

It is not clear whether existing antitrust laws cover conglomerates; recent administrations have shown little inclination to act against them to the same extent that they have against horizontal and vertical mergers. Table 17.1 shows that, since 1960, conglomerate mergers have exceeded the two older forms combined both in number and the size of the assets of the involved businesses.

The Reagan administration adopted a more lenient attitude towards the concentration of industry in the United States. Invoking guidelines reputedly based on economic efficiency rather than abstract legal considerations, administration officials approved a vertical merger involving DuPont's $7.8-billion purchase of the Continental Oil Company. It also sanctioned a number of major horizontal mergers in the oil industry, including Texaco's $10.1-billion takeover of Getty Oil and Standard Oil of California's $13.3-billion merger with Gulf Oil, the largest merger in U. S. history.* The Justice Department also dropped a 13-year-old antitrust suit against the International Business Machine Corporation.

While the Reagan administration

* Such actions brought a threatened moratorium (which failed to materialize) on mergers of the nation's largest oil companies by some congressmen who were concerned not only with increased concentration in the industry but with the fact that moneys used to pay for such takeovers were diverted from exploration for additional domestic oil supplies.

Table 17.1
Mergers and Acquisitions—Manufacturing and Mining Concerns Acquired (1960–1979)

		Large Concerns (Assets of $10 Million or more) Acquired					
		Number of mergers			*Assets acquired (mil. dol.)*		
Year	*All concerns acquired, total*	*Horizontal and vertical*	*Conglomerate*	*Total*	*Horizontal and vertical*	*Conglomerate*	*Total*
1960	844	14	37	51	453	1,082	1,535
1965	1008	16	48	64	573	2,631	3,254
1970	1351	12	79	91	1,174	4,730	5,904
1971	1011	8	51	59	578	1,882	2,460
1972	911	24	36	60	773	1,112	1,885
1973	874	25	39	64	1,093	2,056	3,149
1974	602	24	38	62	1,417	3,049	4,466
1975	439	7	52	59	267	4,683	4,950
1976	559	18	63	81	1,031	5,248	6,279
1977	590	30	69	99	1,937	6,733	8,670
1978	610	35	76	111	4,675	6,050	10,724
1979	519	10	87	97	1,231	11,637	12,867

SOURCE: U. S. Bureau of the Census; data from The Federal Trade Commission.

thus generally preferred a "hands-off" attitude towards business, it did move on some fronts to foster greater competition in the economy. It refused to approve a merger involving U. S. Steel and National Steel. In 1982, the Justice Department won a settlement with American Telephone and Telegraph Company involving a $140-billion break-up of the nation's largest trust into a number of regional companies. Finally, an investigation of price-fixing by highway contractors led to a series of cases resulting in fines totaling $47 million and the jailing of 127 businessmen.

Thus antitrust policy has generally been most effective in preventing predatory practices by businesses and curbing horizontal and vertical mergers. It has been far less effective in actually breaking up existing trusts and moving against proposed conglomerates. Today American industries are generally not controlled by a single huge firm; **oligopolies** are much more common, that is, dominance by a few giant concerns, such as the "Big Three" of automobiles—General Motors, Ford, and Chrysler.

Regulating Business

Public Utilities. While public policy in the United States is generally directed at maintaining competition among private companies, an exception exists for industries providing such basic commodities and services as energy (electricity), resources for home and business (water, gas), transportation (buses, trains, airlines), and communications (telephone). Designated as **public utilities,** such concerns are usually treated in one of two ways. We have already noted that in some instances they are placed under public ownership and operation; the Tennessee Valley Authority and local utilities are cases in point. The other approach is to leave such activities in private hands but to have the government regulate them extensively.

Public utilities have certain characteristics in common that justify their being treated differently from competitive industries. For one thing, they typically provide services not easily dispensed with or for which it is hard to find a substitute. Such utilities are also thought to be "natural" monopolies, since a single concern can render a service more

Boston Edison power plant.

efficiently and competition between firms would probably involve a costly duplication of services. Public utility companies tend to require major capital investments and business conducted on a large enough scale to provide low unit costs, thus keeping costs within the range of the average consumer.

Since there is no competition between public utilities, the government must protect the interests of consumers. This protection takes several forms. Most common is control over both the rates charged and the quality of service provided; this includes ensuring that a utility does not discriminate in the treatment of its customers. Other kinds of regulation involve control over the entry of new firms into the field (preventing costly duplication of services) and close supervision of a utility's financial structure and accounting methods.

Government encounters some of the same difficulties in regulating public utilities as it does in trying to maintain competition among private firms. To make such regulation effective, it is necessary that the president and the members of the independent regulatory agencies (e.g., the Interstate Commerce Commission, the Federal Communications Commission, the Federal Energy Regulatory Commission) vigorously pursue policies designed to protect the interests of consumers and that Congress provide them with adequate funds for the purpose. (The same is true of governors, public utility commissions, and legislatures at the state level.) Making the task particularly difficult is the fact that the regulated industries typically have financial and legal resources superior to those of the government agencies entrusted with the responsibility of regulating them. Moreover, government agencies must often obtain guidance in matters affecting policy from the very companies that the agencies are supposed to be regulating. In addition, members of regulatory bodies frequently come from the affected industries or leave government employment to work for such industries because of higher salaries.

The Carter and Reagan administrations have moved to deregulate certain basic industries. Viewed as a means of cutting back on government red tape and fostering more competition in the American economy, deregulation efforts have been concentrated in the field of transportation. Airlines and toll roads have been given greater freedom to set fares and to offer new services and routes. Similar developments have occurred with respect to bus lines and to a lesser extent with truck lines. The effects of deregulation have been mixed: the entry of new companies into these fields has increased competition and led to a discounting of some fares but it has also resulted in bankruptcies and an increase in fares on noncompetitive routes.

The Reagan administration also focused on deregulating other basic industries. Financial services were particularly affected. Banks and savings and loan companies were given broader authority to set interest rates paid on various types of savings accounts and certificates. Deregulation also led to a lessening of specialization between types of financial institutions. Banks and savings and loans were authorized to compete with security companies in selling money-market instruments; the latter, in turn, began to offer their customers traditional banking services such as loans to individuals.

While deregulation of basic industries accelerated in the late 1970s and early 1980s, the movement eventually began to meet some resistance in Congress. The national legislature refused to follow the Reagan administration's recommendation that the price of natural gas be decontrolled. Members of Congress also opposed an administration plan to allow banks to sponsor and

Let's see our competitors top those rates!

manage mutual funds (broad portfolios of stocks and bonds) and to sell insurance and real estate. Deregulation of the broadcast and cable-television industries also met resistance in Congress.

Other Types of Businesses. Over the years, government has regulated not only public utilities but other industries vital to the nation's health, safety, and welfare. Since the early days of this century, food and drug products have come under the scrutiny of the federal government. In recent years, government has also enacted programs to clean up the environment, protect consumers from defective and unsafe products, and establish safer conditions in the workplace.

As with public utilities, in the late 1970s public officials began to move towards some relief from the effects of regulation. President Carter issued an executive order requiring federal agencies to analyze the economic effects of proposed and final rules. A Regulatory Analysis Review Group was established to review such analyses but it lacked the power to bring recalcitrant agencies into line.

President Reagan came into office even more committed to a broad program of regulatory relief. As previously indicated, shortly after he was inaugurated, he established a Task Force for Regulatory Relief under Vice-President Bush to review existing regulations with the purpose of eliminating as many as possible. On February 17, 1981 (the same day the president announced his general economic program), he issued an executive order granting the Office of Management and Budget (OMB) the power to review all federal rules and to reject any that did not demonstrate that the social benefits exceeded the economic costs. The president also placed people sympathetic to business in charge of major regulatory agencies.

Initially, the move towards deregulation had some success. The number of pages in the Federal Register declined significantly, particularly in the first year of the Reagan administration. The OMB forced the Environmental Protection Agency (EPA) to suspend several provisions of a regulation requiring industry to clean toxic chemicals from waste before sending it to municipal sewage-treatment plants. EPA officials let up on enforcement actions against affected industries in favor of a more conciliatory approach in order to obtain voluntary compliance with regulations. They also went along with the budget cuts proposed by the Reagan administration, which resulted in fewer personnel for the enforcement of existing rules and regulations.

However, in time, the deregulation movement ran into difficulties. Disclosures of lethal amounts of toxic waste in water supplies in communities such as

Times Beach, Missouri shocked the American public. Disclosures that officials of the EPA were making decisions to clean up waste sites based on politics (i.e., targeting sites in areas thought to be favorable to Republican candidates) and were meeting privately with company officials to arrange easy settlements of possible legal violations led to the replacement of Ann Gorsuch Burford as head of the EPA and the criminal conviction of Assistant Administrator Rita Lavelle for lying to a congressional committee investigating the agency. Eventually more than 20 of the EPA's top officials resigned or were fired amid charges that politics and industry favoritism had prevented their enforcing the agency's rules. Subsequently, President Reagan appointed William Ruckelshaus, a respected public official who served as the first administrator of the EPA from 1970 to 1973, to take over the agency and restore its mandate and prestige.

These developments, along with a general failure of the Reagan administration to recognize the extent of the public's commitment to a safe environment and consumer protection, resulted in a slowdown of the deregulation movement. The president failed to convince Congress to enact several basic statutes designed to mitigate what he considered to be the overregulation of American business. Included were efforts to rewrite the Clean Air Act (the administration's highest priority among environmental laws), another involving air pollution, a uniform federal statute on product liability, and other health-and-safety laws. As a result, President Reagan failed to accomplish permanent statutory reform of government regulation of business and ran the risk that program changes stemming from

Checking for dangerous dioxin in Times Beach, Missouri.

Beleagered E.P.A. official Rita Lavelle faces Congressional committee.

budget cuts and policy shifts by executive officials would be reversed by subsequent administrations with a different attitude towards the deregulation of business.

GOVERNMENT AND LABOR

Public policy on labor has generally been to allow conditions of employment to develop primarily from collective bargaining between employers and employees. However, government has intervened in the bargaining process in three distinct ways. Its most prominent role has been establishing the *procedural rules* of bargaining; this includes determining which tactics the two sides are allowed to use against each other in any struggle over employment conditions. Beyond that, government has enacted policies that directly affect the *substance* of agreements between employers and employees, for example, when it fixes minimum wages and maximum hours. Finally, government has developed policies for dealing with *major labor disputes* that threaten the public interest.

Establishing the Rules that Govern Collective Bargaining

In the process of bargaining over conditions of employment, both employers and employees have developed certain tactics designed to work to their advantage (and to the disadvantage of the other side). With the rise of the large corporation, employees found that as individuals they did not have much bargaining power with their employers. If, for example, a person threatened to quit his or her job because the pay was too low or the hours too long, the company could simply hire someone else to take his or her place. However, if many employees joined together to organize a union and then threatened to go on **strike** unless working conditions were improved, the consequences for the employer were much more serious.

While the strike has been the major

tactic of labor in its disputes, employees have developed other strategies. One of these is **picketing,** that is, surrounding a place of employment with people protesting their grievances with management, a tactic designed to discourage workers and customers from entering the premises or having any business relationship with the company. Another strategy is a **boycott** against an employer—a refusal to handle or purchase his goods. A boycott directed against the actual employer is called a **primary boycott.** One directed against another party with whom employees really have no grievance but who does business with their employer is known as a **secondary boycott.**

Employers in turn have developed their own tactics. Over the years, a major tactic has been to try to prevent employees from joining unions. Employees were sometimes required to sign **yellow-dog contracts,** under which they agreed not to join a union as a condition of employment. Another tactic was to fire those who did join, and, in some instances, to place their names on a **blacklist** sent to other employers in an effort to prevent their employment elsewhere. Employers also undermined unions by fostering the establishment of **company unions** dominated and controlled by the employer rather than the employees. Finally, employers developed a weapon of their own to counteract a strike—the **lockout;** they closed their business or discharged large numbers of striking workers.

In addition to using their respective tactics and weapons, employers and employees have also turned to the government for assistance in their disputes. In this, both sides have sought the same general goals. On the one hand, they have tried to get the government to declare their opponents' tactics illegal. On the other, they have sought to have their own tactics upheld as legitimate.

In this country's early years, government was clearly on the side of the employer. Beginning in 1806 the courts

Boston University faculty and staff press their demands.

held in a series of decisions that the formation of unions was a criminal conspiracy because it constituted an illegal restraint of trade. The rationale behind such decisions was based on Adam Smith's laissez-faire economics; by organizing to obtain a raise in pay, employees were interfering with the natural law of supply and demand, which established the proper level of wages.

Eventually the Supreme Court ruled in *Commonwealth* v. *Hunt* (1842) that union activities were not illegal per se, but depended on the *objectives* of the unions and the *means* used to accomplish those objectives. However, this decision did not usher in a new era of prolabor policy. Employers were free to use the tactics described above (yellow-dog contracts, discharges, blacklists, lockouts) to combat unions and to engage labor spies and strikebreakers. Police were often used to prevent unions from meeting and to help drive union organizers out of town. On some occasions federal troops intervened in labor disputes, usually on the grounds that violence was threatened; such intervention typically resulted in the suppression of a strike and victory for the employers.

In time, employers developed a much more sophisticated weapon to use in labor disputes: the **injunction.** When threatened with a strike or other type of concerted activity, an employer went to court and obtained a writ ordering employees to cease those actions on the grounds that they threatened to do irreparable damage to the employer's business. Injunction proceedings were often held without any notice to the employees. Judges, whose legal training emphasized property rights and whose social backgrounds were much closer to employers than working-class people, were inclined to issue injunctions readily and punish violaters with fines or imprisonment.

THE AMERICAN TWINS.
"United we stand, Divided we fall."

Since the courts so clearly favored employers, labor turned to Congress to redress the proemployer bias in labor policy. Early in this century, Congress passed a series of acts designed to provide that redress, but they were either declared unconstitutional or interpreted by the Supreme Court as still permitting the courts to determine whether particular labor activities were "lawful," "legitimate," and "peaceful." It was not until 1932 and the passage of the **Norris–La Guardia Act** that the general labor movement achieved a notable victory in its struggle with management.*

The Norris–La Guardia Act was aimed precisely at abuses arising from the indiscriminate use of injunctions in labor disputes. Federal courts were prohibited from issuing injunctions against particular activities, such as strikes, peaceful picketing, or membership in a labor union. Injunctions were to be used only to prevent irreparable damage to property or to preserve public order, and to provide adequate notice to employees as well as protection of their

* In 1926 Congress passed the Railway Labor Act (examined below), which contained provisions favorable to employees but which is restricted to that industry alone.

rights. Further, the act prohibited the enforcement of yellow-dog contracts by federal courts.

Three years later, in the midst of the New Deal, Congress passed the National Labor Relations Act of 1935 (also known as the Wagner Act), the most prolabor legislation in American history. It declared that employees have the right to join labor organizations, to bargain collectively through representatives of their own choosing, and to engage in concerted activities to further their interests. To facilitate that process, the law designated certain activities of employers (*not* employees) as "unfair labor practices." Included were restraining, coercing, or interfering with employees in the exercise of rights guaranteed by the act; establishing company unions; discriminating against employees because of union membership; discharging or discriminating against employees who file charges under the act. This new legislation also made it an unfair labor practice for an employer to refuse to bargain collectively with a union representing his employees.

The Wagner Act also established legal machinery and an agency to enforce its provisions. Charges of unfair labor practices by employers are filed with the National Labor Relations Board, an independent regulatory commission headed by a three-person board empowered to investigate complaints, hold hearings, reinstate dismissed employees, and issue cease and desist orders (enforceable in the federal courts) against employers found guilty of unfair labor practices. In addition, the board is empowered to determine the appropriate bargaining unit (craft, plant, company) for elections to decide whether employees want to organize a union and which union they want to have represent them. Such elections are decided by a majority vote. A vote for a particular union obliges all future employees in the bargaining unit to join the union, either before they are hired **(a closed shop)** or within a designated period of time afterwards **(a union shop).**

The Wagner Act ushered in the "Golden Age" of organized labor in the United States. In the 12-year period following its passage in 1935, union membership rose from 4 million to over 15 million, with much of the growth in the industrial unions (CIO) compared to the craft unions (AFL). Strikes arising from disputes over the recognition of unions also declined in this period.

However, strikes growing out of labor–management differences over wages, hours, and other conditions of employment (which lay beyond the scope of the Wagner Act) did not decline, except during World War II, when both the AFL and the CIO gave the government no-strike pledges. In 1946, shortly after the war, major strikes broke out in the automobile, steel, and meat-packing industries; the United Mine Workers, under the leadership of John L. Lewis, refused to obey a court order to return to the coal mines. In addition, jurisdictional disputes occurred between the AFL and CIO over which union had the right to organize particular industries. These developments helped to create a feeling among many Americans that labor had grown too powerful and arrogant and that the relationship between employers and employees had become unbalanced in favor of the employees. When the Republican party recaptured control of the Congress in 1946, the stage was set for the enactment of new legislation designed to correct the reputed imbalance in labor–management relationships.

Congress then enacted the Labor–Management Relations Act of 1947 (also known as the Taft–Hartley Act), which placed limitations on certain activities of organized labor. The unfair labor practices that under the Wagner Act had been restricted to actions of employers, were expanded to include those of employees as well. Included were union attempts to restrain or coerce employees in the exercise of their right to join or *not* to join a union, excessive or discriminatory initiation fees, exaction of payment from an employer for services not rendered (known as **featherbedding**), and secondary boycotts or jurisdictional strikes. In addition, the act declared it to be an unfair labor practice for employees to refuse to bargain in good faith with their employer.

The new legislation contained other features designed to counteract what was thought to be the prolabor bias of the Wagner Act. The membership of the NLRB was expanded from three to five,* and a separate office of general counsel was created to screen cases before they were taken to the board. The act also outlawed the closed shop and, while retaining provisions for a union shop, made it possible for labor contracts to provide for an **open shop** (individual employees do not have to join the union in their bargaining unit) in those states passing open-shop legislation.

Finally, the Taft–Hartley Act provided for increased supervision of internal union affairs. Unions are required to file annual reports on their finances, including the compensation of their major officers, their rules and procedures, and initiation fees and dues. Unions failing to comply with these provisions are not permitted to use the NLRB machinery to conduct union elections or to handle unfair labor complaints against employers.

The regulation of internal union affairs continued to be a major feature of labor policy under the Labor–Management Reporting and Disclosure Act of 1959 (Landrum–Griffin Act). Stimulated by Senate testimony of corruption and abuse of power by some union officials, this new legislation expanded the financial reporting required by the Taft–Hartley Act to include information on loans made to union officers, members, or employees. The law also regulates the administration of trusteeships, the legal device used when a national union organization takes over the administration of a local union thought to be in difficulties. In addition, the act contains a "bill of rights" for rank-and-file members that provides for democratic procedures in the internal affairs of unions. These guarantees include the right to participate in meetings and vote in union elections, to sue the union, and to be free of arbitrary disciplinary actions. Landrum–Griffin also stipulates that elections for national union officials be held at least every five years (and every three years for local officials).

No major legislation affecting collective bargaining was enacted in the 1960s and 1970s despite efforts by organized labor to change existing policy in several ways. Most irksome to labor has been Section 14(b) of the Taft–Hartley Act, which has enabled 20 states (mostly in the South) to enact legislation permitting open-shop contracts. Referred to as **right-to-work laws** by their supporters, they are viewed by labor as allowing "free riders" to get all the benefits of union membership without having to devote their time or dues money to the organization.† But while Section 14(b) has been a constant target for repeal, labor has so far been unsuccessful in getting repeal legislation passed.

Several other changes in policy have also eluded labor leaders in recent

* Undoubtedly, many congressmen who supported the Taft–Hartley Act looked forward to the election of a Republican president in 1948 and calculated that he would appoint probusiness people to the board. That strategy backfired when the Democratic incumbent, Harry Truman, retained his office in an upset victory.

† Under the terms of the Taft–Hartley law, a union is required to serve all people in the bargaining unit that it represents, regardless of whether they are union members.

years. One of these would permit **common-site picketing,** that is, picketing of an entire construction project rather than merely one or two entrances to the project as provided for under existing law. Other changes sought but not achieved include reforming procedures of the NLRB, expanding the size of its membership, speeding up the holding of elections to choose union representatives for employees, and debarring companies that violate labor legislation from obtaining government contracts. Labor unions have also tried to get Congress to reverse a 1984 case, *National Labor Relations Board* v. *Bildisco & Bildisco,* that permits companies to void labor contracts by filing for bankruptcy.*

Establishing the Conditions of Employment

While government has generally been content with allowing conditions of employment to be determined by collective bargaining between employers and employees, it has also intervened on occasion to pass laws prescribing what those conditions shall be. One reason given for this kind of intervention is that certain individuals are not capable of protecting their interests and so government should do it for them. Another is that certain minimum standards of employment should exist for all of society.

Children and women have traditionally been objects of special labor legislation. Today laws regulating the minimum age at which children can be employed, their maximum hours of work, and hazardous and unhealthy jobs from which they must be excluded are in effect in all states; in addition, the national government provides similar protection for children employed by firms engaged in interstate commerce. Similar legislation for women (together with the establishment of minimum wages for them) was also passed by many states in the early part of this century. However, as Chapter 14 indicates, such protective legislation has been superseded by Title VII of the 1964 Civil Rights Act, which prohibits discrimination in employment on the basis of sex.

In recent years, government policy on conditions of employment has tended to shift from a concern with certain types of people towards prescribing standards for all employees. Particularly prominent has been regulation prescribing minimum wages and maximum hours of employment, with provision of overtime pay for work beyond the prescribed number of hours. Since 1938 the national government has regulated these matters for people working in interstate businesses.

Another type of government policy affecting working conditions concerns various kinds of *insurance* to protect workers' interests. One of these, **workmen's compensation,** provides for employees injured in the course of their employment; compensation is paid by employers from insurance they must purchase to protect themselves against such claims. Another is **unemployment insurance,** which provides weekly payments for a prescribed period to workers who are thrown out of work through no fault of their own. (This latter program, together with ones providing benefits for disabled and retired workers, are analyzed in depth in the following chapter.)

A final area of government legislation on working conditions is *standards of safety and health.* The development and enforcement of these standards has traditionally been a concern of state governments, but the national government has become increasingly involved. That involvement became more pro-

* In 1983 Continental Airlines used that tactic to renege on a labor contract; within a few days of filing for bankruptcy, it resumed operation with its pilots and other employees carrying on their former jobs at greatly reduced pay.

nounced with the passage of the Occupational Safety and Health Act of 1970. Under its provisions, the Occupational Safety and Health Administration (within the Department of Labor) has the authority to issue and enforce health and safety rules, to conduct inspections of work places, and to issue citations for violations. One of the most controversial agencies in the federal government, OSHA has become a symbol of overregulation and a target of small business—which claims that its regulations are arbitrary and that they needlessly drive up costs—while its supporters defend it as providing workers with the protection they have needed for so long.*

Procedures for Settling Major Strikes

For the most part, government in the United States has adopted a "hands-off" policy on strikes, regarding them as a natural part of the collective bargaining process. (They are, after all, labor's major tactic in most disputes with management.) There are, of course, some exceptions to this rule. Some states have laws preventing strikes by people working in vital fields, such as hospitals, public utilities, and police and fire protection. Under the Taft–Hartley Act, employees of the federal government are forbidden to strike.

Legal prohibitions of strikes are rare and other means have been developed for dealing with them. Most common is **mediation,** in which neutral agents (mediators) serve as go-betweens to the contending parties. (The National Mediation Board has jurisdiction over railroad and airline disputes and the Federal Mediation and Conciliation Service assists parties in other industries.) Mediation and conciliation is a voluntary approach to the problem, since the mediators cannot force a settlement on the disputants. However, as experienced practitioners of the art of negotiation, they may be able to suggest a compromise or new solution that the parties had not considered themselves.

Another approach to dealing with a strike is to require that it be *postponed* for a period while a special procedure is employed to try to settle it. This is the means employed for "national emergencies" that ". . . imperil the national health and safety." Under the terms of the Taft–Hartley Act, when the president believes that a strike fits this category, he appoints a fact-finding board to investigate and report to him on the matter. He may then direct the attorney general to seek an injunction delaying the strike for an 80-day period. During this time the Federal Mediation and Conciliation Service is brought in to work with the disputing parties, and the NLRB polls the employees to determine whether they will accept the employer's last offer. If no settlement is reached by the end of the 80-day period, the injunction becomes inoperative and the strike may be renewed.

A final means of dealing with strikes is **arbitration,** under which the terms of final settlement of the dispute are decided by a third party and the settlement ends the strike. Such arbitration can be *voluntary,* which means that the parties to the dispute decide to submit it to the third party, or *compulsory,* in which case they are required by law to do so. Most of the arbitration employed in the United States has been voluntary; the Railway Labor Act of 1926, for example, provides for its use if the parties so desire. However, on several occasions since 1963, Congress has passed special legislation *requiring* the use of arbitration in nationwide railway strikes.

As Table 17.2 shows, the number of

* Recently, OSHA has shifted its emphasis more in the direction of preventing health hazards, such as those associated with harmful chemicals.

Table 17.2
Work Stoppages (1950–1981)

	Work Stoppages		*Workers Involved*	
	Number Beginning in Year	*Average Duration (Calendar Days)*	*Number (× 1,000)*	*Percentage of Total Employed*
1950	4843	19.2	2410	5.1
1955	4320	18.5	2650	5.2
1960	3333	23.4	1320	2.4
1965	3963	25.0	1550	2.5
1967	4595	22.8	2870	4.3
1968	5045	24.5	2649	3.8
1969	5700	22.5	2481	3.5
1970	5716	25.0	3305	4.7
1971	5138	27.0	3280	4.6
1972	5010	24.0	1714	2.3
1973	5353	24.0	2251	2.9
1974	6074	27.1	2778	3.5
1975	5031	26.8	1746	2.2
1976	5648	28.0	2420	3.0
1977	5506	29.3	2040	2.4
1978	4230	33.2	1623	1.9
1979	4827	32.1	1727	1.9
1980	3885	35.4	1366	1.5
1981	2568	(NA)	1081	1.2

Source: U. S. Bureau of the Census; data from the U. S. Bureau of Labor Statistics.

strikes occurring between 1950 and 1981 fluctuated from a high of some 6100 in 1974 to a low of some 2600 in 1981. Between 1968 and 1977 strikes ranged between 5000 and 6000 a year but declined significantly after 1977. The average duration of strikes was also relatively stable but began to rise in 1978. However, that same year the number of workers involved in work stoppages declined and it continued to do so. Since 1960 the percentage of employed people on strike has never reached 5 percent and after 1978 fell below 2 percent. Thus strikes fluctuated over the 30-year period; recently, however, they have declined both in number and in workers involved but their average duration has increased.

GOVERNMENT AND AGRICULTURE

The farmer has traditionally been considered a rugged individual who by hard work and diligence can supply the necessities of life for himself and his family without depending on others. Whatever the romance, in reality vast changes in agriculture have increasingly made it a commercial venture. The farmer is dependent on a number of other groups: manufacturers of agricultural machinery, railroads, truckers and ships that transport produce to distant markets, firms that provide storage facilities, and a variety of "middlemen"—millers, grain operators, wholesalers, and retailers. Having to deal with these forces—and the vagaries of the weather—farmers have turned to the government to provide various kinds of financial relief. This relief has taken three major forms: regulation of the groups that the farmer depends on for his livelihood, a variety of programs that promote agriculture, and price supports that provide farmers with a "fair price" for their products.

Regulating Other Groups to Protect the Farmer

In the period following the Civil War, the farmer found his economic fortune in the hands of two groups: those who stored his crops (primarily grain) until they were ready for the market and those who transported his goods to the market. Agricultural politics in this era were aimed primarily at curbing what the farmer considered the exorbitant rates charged by these two groups. The Granger Movement of the 1870s resulted in the establishment of state commissions to regulate rates charged by grain elevators. Railroads also became subject to state regulation—and national control as well, when the Interstate Commerce Commission was established in 1887.

In time the national government began to regulate other middlemen.In 1921 Congress passed the Packers and Stockyards Act, which governs the markets that sell livestock, meat, and poultry and their products to the public. The act aims at ensuring honest and fair practices in livestock care. It further seeks to prevent packers from discriminating in their treatment of farmers and monopolizing the market through the apportionment of territories, purchases, or sales. In 1927 the national government extended additional protection to the farmer with the passage of the Producer Agency Act, which controls the activities of firms handling perishable commodities, such as fresh fruits and vegetables.

Another group that has come under government regulation is the dealers and brokers who trade in agricultural commodities. In 1922 the national government enacted legislation designed to control unfair speculation and price manipulation in the grain market. That control was extended in 1936 to a broader range of agricultural products—butter, eggs, and potatoes to name a few—traded on the commodity markets.

Promoting Agriculture

Farmers have long benefited from government programs designed to promote agriculture and increase its productivity. In 1862 the Homestead Act was enacted, providing 160 acres of public land free to families that would live on the plot and cultivate it for a period of five years. That same year saw the establishment of the Department of Agriculture and the passage of the Morrill Act, which granted sections of public land to states to help them establish colleges offering instruction in agriculture and the mechanical arts. (Hence, the origin of A & M colleges and universities, so prominent in the midwestern and western parts of the United States.) In 1914 the federal government established an extension division in the Department of Agriculture staffed with county agents to demonstrate new agricultural techniques to farmers. In 1935 the Soil Conservation Service was organized to provide technical advice to farmers; in addition, the Rural Environmental Assistance Program provided financial assistance to farmers to develop soil conservation techniques and projects.

The government also enacted a number of other programs to assist the nation's farmers. Legislation passed in 1916 created a system of federal land banks to grant long-term agricultural loans, and farmers to this day benefit from special credit arrangements handled through the Farm Credit Administration. Other farm credit agencies include the Farmers Home Administration and the Rural Electrification Administration. The Department of Agriculture aids farmers in marketing their products by providing them with information on the supply and demand, together with the price and quality of agricultural commodities. The government also facilitates the marketing of farm products by permitting farmers to form **cooperatives,** a special legal device through which they can join forces to purchase supplies and sell their products without being subject to antitrust suits.

Supporting Farm Prices

The programs promoting agriculture described above are based on the assumption that increased production of farm products is a desirable policy because it benefits farmers and consumers alike. However, this is not so if the supply of farm goods exceeds the demand for them. In such circumstances, under the natural laws of the marketplace, prices fall—a development that is good for the consumer but not for the farmer. Much of farm policy in recent years has focused on the problem of keeping the income of farmers up in the face of agricultural surpluses that tend to depress the prices paid for crops.

Demands for governmental programs supporting farm prices first arose at the end of World War I, when food prices fell as a result of the loss of wartime markets. A tariff was enacted to protect American farmers from foreign competition, but domestic production continued to exceed domestic consumption, which served to keep the price of food low. A "two-price" plan was then devised: the government would purchase agricultural products, which would cause the domestic price to rise; these same goods would then be sold at the (lower) world market price, the deficit to be paid for with a tax on domestic sales. However, bills providing for the two-price approach were either defeated in Congress or vetoed by the president (Coolidge). When Franklin Roosevelt became president in 1932, the stage was set for a new approach to the problem of low farm prices.

During the 1930s Congress passed legislation whose principal concern was providing **parity** to farmers, that is, establishing agricultural prices that would give farmers' commodities a purchasing power equal to that during the period 1909–1914. (If the proceeds from the sale of a bushel of wheat would buy a commodity such as a shirt then and if the price of a shirt had doubled since that time, then the price of wheat should also double.) Farmers who agreed to limit the acreage they planted in certain basic crops—wheat, cotton, corn, tobacco, rice, and peanuts—would receive loans or cash payments equal to a certain percentage of the parity price. (The percentage fluctuated over the years, depending upon congressional and administrative action.) Also, to reduce an excess supply, mandatory quotas were established on the marketing of such crops, provided that two-thirds of the farmers involved voted in favor of such quotas in a referendum. This same legislation also permitted the government to dispose of surpluses of such crops in ways that would not affect the domestic market (e.g., by distributing them to needy families or through school lunch programs).

In the period following World War II, the two major political parties battled over the farm program. Democratic congressmen and President Truman favored high, rigid price supports (such as 90 percent of parity), and their Republican counterparts and President Eisenhower were committed to lower, flexible price supports geared to the market. Policy thus vacillated depending on the administration in power.

In the 1960s and 1970s agricultural programs were in a period of flux as additional crops became eligible for price supports. At the same time, however, there has been a trend towards loosening controls on the amount of acreage a farmer can plant or market. In 1973 "target prices" were substituted for traditional price supports, with farmers receiving deficiency payments equal to the difference between the target and the market price, providing they set aside some of their productive land. Recent legislation has also established limits on the amount of support payments an individual farmer can receive from commodity programs, but as shown by Table 17.3, the highest average payments go to persons owning the larger, more productive farms. The table also shows that government payments increased greatly between 1980 and 1982. (See the following discussion for information on how payments grew even faster in 1983.)

As might be expected, the Reagan administration initially said that it would follow a general "hands-off" policy towards agriculture. However, burgeoning surpluses occasioned by good weather and improved productivity, coupled with a decline in both domestic demand and the volume of farm exports, forced the administration to deal with these surpluses. By executive order in 1983, it instituted a Payment-in-Kind (called PIK) program, whereby the government provided grain and cotton from its stockpiles to farmers who agreed to take a certain number of acres devoted to such crops out of production. (The idea was to reduce storage costs associated with federal stockpiles and at the same time to cut crop production through a reduction in planted acreage.) However, the plan ran into difficulties. Participation exceeded expectations. Many participating farmers retired their least fertile land and improved production on the remaining acreage. In some instances, the government did not have ample supplies stored in some geographical areas and had to pay handsome fees to major grain companies with available crops. Moreover, the government waived the usual $50,000 limitation in payments to individuals since it involved an in-kind rather than cash transaction; as a result, substantial transfers were made to large farm operators, including absentee corporate operators such as Prudential Insurance Company and major petroleum corporations. Finally, the costs of the program (some $9 to 10 billion) far exceeded administration projections. Except for wheat, the PIK program was discontinued in 1984.

Later in 1983, President Reagan reluctantly signed legislation that ran counter to his general "hands-off" attitude towards agriculture. Faced with the necessity of the federal government's spending $3 billion to buy surplus dry milk, butter, and cheese, he approved a new dairy price-support bill

Table 17.3
Government Payments to Farms by Program, and Value of Farm Sales (1970–1982)

Item	Unit	1970	1975	1976	1977	1978	1979	1980	1981	1982
Total	Mil dol	3717	807	734	1819	3030	1375	1286	1932	3492
Feed grain	Mil dol	1504	279	196	187	1172	494	382	243	713
Wheat	Mil dol	871	77	135	887	963	114	211	625	652
Cotton	Mil dol	919	138	108	89	127	185	172	222	600
Conservation	Mil dol	208	181	195	197	194	179	198	186	165
Sugar Act	Mil dol	88	61	—	65	—	—	—	—	—
Wool	Mil dol	49	—	—	—	—	—	—	35	46
Payments to farms with sales of:										
Less than $2,500	Mil dol	355	37	26	55	63	22	18	27	46
$2,500–$4,999	Mil dol	227	38	27	53	65	27	25	37	65
$5,000–$9,999	Mil dol	400	54	43	96	136	57	52	77	138
$10,000–$19,999	Mil dol	671	82	60	126	159	64	56	83	147
$20,000–$39,999	Mil dol	826	140	117	279	397	157	138	205	360
$40,000–$99,999	Mil dol	708	230	231	618	1059	466	431	646	1161
$100,000–$199,999	Mil dol	266	105	113	305	601	298	288	436	798
$200,000–$499,999	Mil dol	140	64	69	184	377	195	191	289	533
$500,000 and over	Mil dol	124	57	48	103	173	89	87	132	244
Avg. payment per farm	**Dollar**	**1260**	**320**	**294**	**741**	**1244**	**566**	**530**	**794**	**1455**
Farms with sales of:										
Less than $2,500	Dollar	251	46	34	74	96	39	35	52	93
$2,500–$4,999	Dollar	631	123	86	172	205	84	75	111	199
$5,000–$9,999	Dollar	1074	174	137	311	430	175	156	232	416
$10,000–$19,999	Dollar	1855	260	195	415	539	219	196	291	522
$20,000–$39,999	Dollar	2734	445	380	923	1360	553	494	735	1317
$40,000–$99,999	Dollar	4305	729	712	1914	3053	1243	1109	1650	2958
$100,000–$199,999	Dollar	7331	1091	1051	2800	4439	1806	1612	2399	4300
$200,000–$499,999	Dollar	10555	1665	1553	4043	6299	2564	2288	3404	6102
$500,000 and over	Dollar	29795	5193	3807	7944	10051	4091	3651	5432	9737

Source: U. S. Bureau of the Census; data from the U. S. Department of Agriculture.

that provides payments to farmers for not producing milk. In early 1984, the president won a legislative victory when Congress passed a law freezing "target prices" on wheat, corn, cotton, and rice. However, the legislation provided early cash payments in 1984 for farmers who agreed not to grow these crops in 1985.

Thus the federal government continues to play a major role in promoting and regulating the activities of the three major elements of our economy—business, labor, and agriculture. The following sections focus on the part the government has assumed in the overall management of the economy.

"That's the price we pay, sir, for living in a free society."
Drawing by Dana Fradon © 1981 The New Yorker Magazine, Inc.

THE OVERALL MANAGEMENT OF THE AMERICAN ECONOMY

American political leaders traditionally subscribed to the laissez-faire principle that a "natural order" governed the overall performance of the economy. Just as natural forces governed the supply and demand for individual goods, they also operated to keep the total supply and demand of all goods within society in balance. When imbalances occurred—resulting in a rapid rise or fall in overall prices and gains or losses in the nationwide rate of employment and wages—they were considered temporary in nature. In time, built-in forces in the economy would right the imbalance between overall supply and demand without the need for government interference in the process. In any event, upturns and downturns in the economy (referred to as "business cycles") were the price one paid for the other virtues of a free economy.

The nation's plunge, in 1929, into its worst depression—one whose effects were felt around the world—brought some government action. As economist Herbert Stein suggests, the president, Herbert Hoover, was not irrevocably committed to the principles of laissez-faire. However, he did want state and local governments and the private sector to play a major role in fighting the depression rather than placing an excessive reliance on the federal government. Moreover, by the end of 1931, when the embattled president did decide to substantially involve the national government in trying to counteract the depression, he pursued a policy of balancing the federal budget as a means of restoring the faith of businessmen in the government's soundness. This meant cutting back on federal expenditures and raising revenues through increased taxes. As we shall see, many of today's economists would agree that these were precisely *not* the policies to be pursued.

In the presidential campaign of 1932, Hoover's opponent, Franklin D. Roosevelt, also advocated balancing the budget. When he took office in 1933, Roosevelt pursued that policy for a short period, asking Congress for emergency powers to cut expenditures, especially government payrolls and veterans' benefits for nonservice-connected disabilities. However, with no relief from the depression in sight, Roosevelt soon reversed course, advocating a policy that Hoover had rejected: a national public works program to put the unemployed back on a payroll. Still, Roosevelt continued to cling to the policy of a balanced budget; in 1937 his pursuit of it cut short the nation's recovery and yielded an economic downturn the following year.

Meanwhile on the other side of the Atlantic, British economist John Maynard Keynes published his influential *General Theory of Employment, Interest, and Money* (1936), in which he attacked the laissez-faire theory of a self-correcting balance in the economy and argued that in time of depression the government should pursue a policy exactly opposite to balancing the budget. Instead it should embark on a program of increased government spending to compensate for the decline in the total demand for goods and services in the private sector. Thus Keynes advocated what is called **"deficit spending"** (government outlays exceed its tax revenues) as a means of counteracting an economic downturn.

Although Roosevelt and Keynes even met on one occasion, there are indications that neither really understood the other. Roosevelt continued to try to balance the federal budget; it was not until the 1938 downturn in the economy that Keynes's theory of deficit spending was officially endorsed as a legitimate method of dealing with an economic relapse. Even then the amount of deficit spending was limited and remained so until World War II, when the huge expenditures necessitated by the war effort greatly exceeded tax revenues. It was then that the nation witnessed the kind of deficit spending that Keynes had in mind. Moreover, for the first time since the Great Depression, the economy underwent a major expansion.

These experiences with the depression and the war, together with concern for the prospects of a postwar economy (serious dislocations had occurred after World War I), led to the passage of the Employment Act of 1946. This legislation declared it to be official policy that the federal government—along with industry, labor, agriculture, and state and local governments—would cooperate to provide ". . . maximum employment, production, and purchasing power." The act provided for the Council of Economic Advisers, composed of three professional economists, to assist the president in developing a program to implement those policies; the Joint Economic Committee of Congress, to consider the president's proposals and advise the two houses on his recommendations; and the President's Economic Report, which annually provides an account of the economic trends.

Thus over a period of little more than a decade, there occurred a major change in attitudes towards the role of government in managing the economy. Political officials, drawing upon the expertise and advice of economists, are now expected to promote a high level of employment, stability in prices of goods and services, and growth in the output of the American economy.* When employment and output fall, leading to a recession† (or, if deep and long enough, a depression), the government will act to try to rectify these conditions; or, if prices rise too rapidly, leading to inflation, public officials will intervene in the economy to deal with that situation as well.

John Maynard Keynes.

* Another feature of this economic policy, namely, a favorable balance of payments with other nations, falls in the area of international trade and finance and is beyond the scope of this discussion.

† A recession is usually considered to characterize the economy when the gross national product (the total value of all goods and services) falls for two consecutive quarters.

Treasury Secretary Donald Regan points to a chart at a hearing to discuss the fiscal 1985 Federal Budget.

Policy Instruments for Managing the Economy

Political officials have a variety of policy instruments or tools for trying to manage the economy. Such policy instruments can be conveniently placed into four major categories: fiscal policy, monetary policy, wage–price guidelines, and mandatory controls over wages and prices.

Fiscal Policy. **Fiscal policy** involves an attempt by the government to manage the economy by manipulating the level of government spending and taxation. However, economists disagree on the nature of that manipulation. There are three major theories on how fiscal policy should best be handled in order to foster a healthy, stable economy.

The first macroeconomic theory might be termed *traditional economic conservatism.* Its major goal is the balancing of the budget so that government expenditures do not exceed its revenues. A balanced budget is thought to be necessary to assure the private financial community—major banks, Wall Street investment houses, and the like—that the nation's economy is "sound." Moreover, if the economy goes into a decline, which results in shrinking tax revenues because of lessened economic activity, the remedy is to increase taxes and decrease public expenditures in order to bring the nation's budget back into balance. This course of action is designed to *prevent borrowing* by the federal government, which economic conservatives believe drains off a portion of funds available for private investment and depresses the asset values of private financial institutions.

Traditional economic conservatism also has a kind of "moral" component to it. Balancing the nation's budget is similar to balancing one's individual or family budget—it requires discipline. Economist Herbert Stein thus refers to it as the "old-time religion."

As was previously suggested, Herbert Hoover turned to traditional economic conservatism—increasing taxes and holding down government expenditures—in order to try to bring the nation out of a deep depression. Its failure to do so did much to discredit the theory—at least in time of economic depression. However, it continues to hold an attraction to many people, particularly those in the financial community. Moreover, Republican presidents Dwight Eisenhower and Gerald Ford frequently spoke of "balancing the budget."

The second major fiscal theory is *Keynesianism,* named for its proponent, John Maynard Keynes, the British economist referred to above. The essence of Keynesianism is that one manages the economy by managing *the aggregate demand for goods and services.* If a decline develops in demand in the private sector, then steps must be taken to compensate for that decline. One way to do that is to increase public expenditures, which puts money in the hands of those who sell goods or services to the government. The other is to lower taxes, which keeps more money in the hands of those who can then *spend* that money, thus creating more demand for goods and services.

Thus, unlike traditional economic conservatism, Keynesianism is *not* concerned with *always* balancing the budget. As previously indicated, deficit spending is favored in an economic downturn. The government can then borrow money and pay it back when recovery occurs and the economy is flourishing. Moreover, if *demand* becomes *too great* for the amount of goods and services being provided, a situation that brings on inflation, then the government is expected to pursue opposite taxing and spending policies. In that instance, taxes are to be increased and public expenditures decreased, the former for siphoning off a portion of money left in private hands (and thus cutting back on private demand), the latter for reducing the flow of money to those who sell goods or services to the government (which also reduces private demand). Thus the underlying assumption of Keynesianism is that the economy can be managed through the control of *aggregate demand.*

Keynesianism was first associated

"I'm an Episcopalian on my mother's side and a supply-sider on my father's."

with the administration of Franklin Roosevelt, who, as indicated above, reluctantly utilized its policies during the latter part of the 1930s, and by necessity, during World War II when huge military expenditures greatly exceeded tax revenues. It became the dominant macroeconomic theory in the postwar period and was pursued most vigorously by the Kennedy and Johnson administrations, both of which sought full employment and rapid economic growth. Moreover, in January 1971, when Republican President Richard Nixon presented his budget, even he announced that he was now a "Keynesian." However, later in the 1970s, the theory began to lose favor, primarily because of increased dissatisfaction with the nation's high rate of inflation to which Keynesianism was thought to be contributing. (Public officials found it much easier politically to fight unemployment by cutting taxes and increasing public expenditures than to raise taxes and cut government expenditures, the Keynesian prescription for dealing with inflation.)

The third major fiscal theory is referred to as *"supply-side" economics,* a term first used in 1976 by economist Herbert Stein. The essence of supply-side economics is that instead of focusing on *demand* as the crucial factor in economic activity (which Keynesians do), emphasis should be placed on increasing the *supply* of goods and services. The best way to accomplish that goal is to cut the tax rate. When individuals and businesses find that they can keep more of their earnings, they will be willing to work harder and to produce, save, and invest more. Increased savings will then be available to finance economic investment by business or for government borrowing necessitated by a temporary loss of revenues due to the cut in rates of taxation. Eventually the increased level of economic activity will expand the taxable income base so that total tax revenues will be as great as they were when higher rates were in effect.

Senator Warren Roth (R-Del.) and Representative Jack Kemp, cosponsors of Kemp-Roth tax-cut plan.

While many economists have subscribed to the general proposition that a cut in the tax rate on the production or sale of goods will act as an incentive to produce more of them, supply-side economics in its purest and most recent form developed in the latter part of the 1970s. Arthur Laffer, an economist at the University of Southern California (drawing upon earlier ideas of Columbia University economist, Robert Mundell), promoted the theory and explained it to Jude Wanniski, an editorial writer for the *Wall Street Journal* who, in turn, sold it to the editors of that influential newspaper. Wanniski later convinced Jack Kemp, a Republican congressman from Buffalo, of its virtues, and Kemp, along with Republican senator William Roth of Delaware, incorporated the theory in a bill calling for a 10 percent across-the-board individual income tax cut each year for three years. The Republican National Committee endorsed the bill in 1977, and the following year, Ronald Reagan became the first major presidential candidate to subscribe to it. Although Reagan later seemed to cool to the idea, in early 1980, after losing the Iowa caucuses to George Bush, Reagan went on to emphasize the theory in his primary campaign in New Hampshire where he bested Bush (who later referred to some of the more optimistic assumptions of the theory as "Voodoo Economics"). As indicated at the beginning of this chapter, the newly elected Ronald Reagan made the Kemp–Roth bill a cornerstone of his economic program.

Monetary Policy. **Monetary policy** is used to manage the economy through regulating the supply of money, credit, and interest rates. When the nation is threatened with a recession, the economy is stimulated by enlarging the supply of money, which makes it easier for individuals and business firms to obtain credit, and lowering the interest rate to encourage them to borrow money for the purchase of goods and services or investment. Such measures are collectively referred to as an **"easy money" policy.** On the other hand, a threat of inflation calls for a "cooling down" of the economy by limiting the money supply, making it more difficult for individ-

"Would you mind coming back Tuesday? Money's a bit tight today."

uals and firms to get credit, and discouraging them from borrowing by raising interest rates. These policies together are known as a **"tight money" policy.**

Monetary policy in the United States is for the most part carried out through the Federal Reserve System. First created by legislation passed in 1913 in response to the economic panic of 1907, the system has been described by political scientist Michael Reagan as ". . . a pyramid having a private base, a mixed middle, and a public apex." At the top is the Federal Reserve Board, composed of seven members appointed by the president with the consent of the Senate to fourteen-year overlapping terms. The middle level is the Federal Open Market Committee, made up of the seven board members and the presidents of five of the twelve Federal Reserve banks. At the bottom of the pyramid are the nation's 12 district Federal Reserve banks (known as "bankers' banks"), which are formally owned by the "member" banks in each of the districts. (All national banks are member banks, as are state banks that want to belong to the system and meet certain requirements.) Formal power over various aspects of monetary policy is vested in different levels of the system, but in fact the Federal Reserve Board controls the entire operation. Moreover, the chairman of the board tends to dominate the other members so that he becomes by far the principal figure in determining monetary policy in the United States. (Witness the attention focused on FRB Chairman Paul Volcker in recent years.)

The most important monetary policy instrument is control over the nation's money supply through buying and selling government securities in the open market, that is, where the securities are bought and sold (usually New York City). When the board buys such securities, the payments it makes for them become deposits in the Reserve banks;

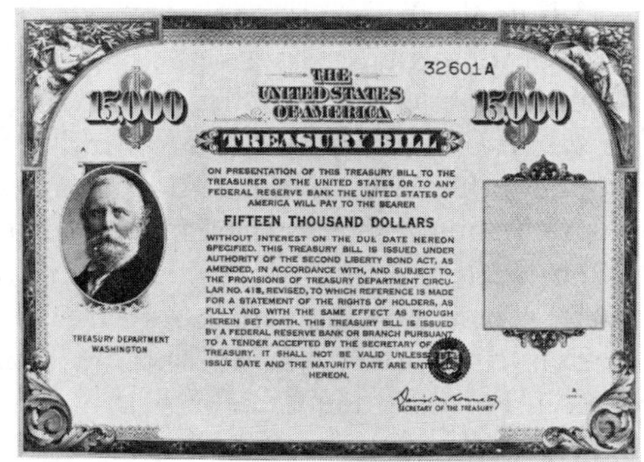

these deposits then constitute reserves that can be used for loans to member banks, which in turn grant loans to individuals and business firms. When the board sells securities, the process works in reverse; the payment it receives for such securities from the Reserve banks decreases their reserves and hence their loan-making capacity. Thus the board can increase or decrease the money supply available for use in the economy and thereby affect aggregate demand.

The Federal Reserve Board controls two other types of policy instruments that affect the overall economy. It can raise or lower the **discount rate**—the interest rate that member banks must pay for money borrowed from the Federal Reserve banks. (The higher the discount rate, the less likely member banks are to borrow money, and the greater the interest rates they then charge for loans to individuals and firms.) Also the board sets the **reserve requirements**—the ratios of reserves to loans—for member banks. If the reserve requirement is 10 percent, these banks can make \$10 in loans for every \$1 of reserves; if the ratio is raised to 20 percent, they can make only \$5 in loans for every \$1 of reserves.*

* In addition to this overall regulation of bank credit, the board can exercise control over particular kinds of financial transactions. For example, it is empowered to establish margin requirements for the purchase of stock. If the

While the Federal Reserve Board exercises these three types of controls, an additional monetary policy instrument is available to another government agency, the Department of the Treasury, through its *management of the national debt.* The national debt is constantly being refinanced, and the way this is done affects interest rates and credit. For example, if the Treasury Department decides to refinance the debt by issuing long-term securities, this will raise the interest rate paid to purchasers (and affect private interest rates), since such securities carry higher rates than short-term ones. Also, if short-term government securities are sold to commercial banks, this raises the amount of their reserves and thereby increases the amount of money they can lend individuals and business firms.

While economists generally acknowledge the value of monetary policy in managing the economy some, of them place major emphasis on a policy instrument known as *monetarism.* While there are a number of monetarists, particularly prominent is the "Chicago School," so named because its major proponents, particularly Milton Friedman, teach at the University of Chicago. They are most concerned with *preventing inflation* and contend that the way to do this is to limit the growth of the money supply to no more than the actual growth rate of the economy. On occasion, when the economy is heating up, it may be necessary to actually contract the money supply. This will serve to keep interest rates high and discourage borrowing, which will tend to slow down economic activity and right the imbalance in the economy. Strict monetarists feel that if such policies are followed, one need not worry about fiscal policy or the size of the budget deficit.

Thus traditional economic conservatism, Keynesianism, supply-side economics, and monetarism constitute four distinct theories on the policies that should be followed in managing the economy. However, it should be recognized that economic policies pursued by public officials often contain elements of more than one such theory. For example, Reaganomics combines three of them. Its provisions for major tax cuts represents supply-side economics. Its stress on holding down domestic spending in order to balance the budget reflects the basic principles of traditional economic conservatism. Its emphasis on restricting the growth in the money supply incorporates the ideas of monetarism.

It should be noted that despite their differences, the four major macroeconomic theories have one feature in common. They represent *indirect* approaches to managing the economy. That is, they attempt to manipulate levels of production, aggregate demand, taxation and expenditures, as well as the money supply, credit, and interest rates, because these factors are thought to shape fundamental goals of economic activity—the level of prices, employment, wages, and economic growth. However, as the following sections reveal, direct controls can also be used to regulate such matters.

Wage–Price Guidelines. **Wage–price guidelines** represent an attempt by the national government to counter the threat of inflation directly by holding down increases in wages and prices. In the early 1960s the Kennedy administration developed guidelines to hold wage increases to the rate of growth in labor productivity, which was then 3.2 percent annually. However, by 1967 when increased government spending for the Vietnam War and the Great So-

---

margin figure is set at 90 percent, only 10 percent of the purchase price can be borrowed. By lowering and raising this figure, the board can encourage or discourage investment in the stock market.

ciety programs brought about an inflation rate exceeding 3.2 percent, that particular guideline was abandoned by the Johnson administration. Subsequently, the guidelines were officially terminated during the Nixon administration. Similar guidelines were reinstituted by President Carter in 1978. Wage increases were set at 7 percent annually (with special rules for fringe benefits and other types of compensation). Price increases were to be held to one-half of 1 percent below those that prevailed in the base period 1976–1977.

Since wage and price guidelines are voluntary, their implementation depends primarily on moral suasion and the influence of public opinion. Presidents and other public officials resort to "jawboning"—exhorting those who seek to exceed the limits that it is their patriotic duty to help avoid inflation. President Kennedy lashed out at steel companies that sought to raise prices in 1962, after which they decided to rescind the price increase. However, the failure of some companies to go along with the increase may have influenced that decision more than the president's action.

Government has still other means at its disposal to get parties to respect its guidelines. In some instances it has threatened to sell its own stockpile of a particular product as a means of increasing the supply and lowering the price. President Johnson used this tactic with both aluminum and copper. President Carter threatened to deny government contracts to companies that exceeded his administration's guidelines—an action that was held by the courts to be legal.

Mandatory Controls over Wages and Prices. It might be expected that a nation that prided itself on having a "free economy" would not resort to **mandatory controls** over wages and prices except in times of emergency. This has been the general situation in the United States. During World War I, World War II, and the Korean War, such controls were imposed. They were most extensive during World War II, when they were extended to wages, rents, and wholesale and retail prices and were coupled with the rationing of scarce items like gasoline and some kinds of food.

Ironically, the only time that similar controls have been exercised in recent years was during the administration of Republican Richard Nixon. Nixon, whose experiences with the Office of Price Administration (OPA) during World War II soured him on such controls, nonetheless instituted them in August 1971 after fiscal and monetary policy failed to stem inflation. (A Democratic Congress granted Nixon the right to impose the controls in the Economic Stabilization Act of 1970.) Over the next three years, the program went through four distinct phases. The first phase froze most prices, wages, and rents for a 90-day period. The second replaced the temporary freeze with mandatory limitations of a 5.5 percent wage increase and 2.5 percent price increase. The third lifted such controls with the exception of food prices and costs in the health field and the construction industry. When inflation returned, a fourth and final phase involved a 60-day freeze on prices. In early 1974 all controls were lifted except those on oil prices, which soared following the actions of the Organization of Petroleum Exporting Countries (OPEC). Thus the nation ended its experience with mandatory controls with most public officials (including President Nixon) and the general public far from satisfied with their operation.

Difficulties in Managing the Economy

Writing in the middle 1960s Walter Heller, former chairman of the Council of Economic Advisers, confidently proclaimed in his book, *New Dimensions of Political Economy* that the economist had "arrived" on the New Frontier with John Kennedy and was "firmly entrenched" in the Great Society of Lyndon Johnson. As justification of his announcement, he pointed to the economic record from 1960 to 1965, during which period consumer prices rose at an annual rate of 1.3 percent and unit labor costs were even more stable, rising 0.6 of 1 percent per year. Meanwhile the unemployment rate declined from 7 percent to 4 percent, corporate profits doubled, and the gross national product advanced by one-third over the five-year period. Thus the goals of the Employment Act of 1946—price and cost stability, a high level of employment, and growth in the output of the American economy—were clearly met in what Heller referred to as "the age of the economist."

Unfortunately, the 1970s did not live up to Heller's confident predictions. When Gerald Ford took office as president in August 1974, prices were rising at an annual rate of nearly 12 percent, and by May 1975 unemployment stood at over 9 percent. Nor did Ford's Democratic successor, Jimmy Carter, fare any better. At the end of the decade, consumer prices were rising at a rate of 13 percent, and unemployment had reached almost 6 percent. No matter how one might describe the 1970s, it was definitely *not* the age of the economist.

The Reagan administration succeeded in bringing down the rate of inflation but at the cost of high unemployment during its first two years in office. In the third year, the unemployment rate began to decline but interest rates remained fairly high. Most disappointing was the failure to balance the budget by 1984 as the president had promised to do: instead, the nation experienced the largest deficits in its history.

Thus major difficulties exist for decision-makers who seek to use the policy instruments described above to manage the economy. Some of these difficulties are *economic* in nature. Others may be attributed to *political* factors.

Economic. One of the major economic difficulties in managing the economy is the fact that economic theories do not always work out as they are supposed to. Economists frequently speak of the "trade-off" between inflation and unemployment, or what they refer to as the **Phillips curve:** as one rises, the other falls. Thus if fiscal and monetary policies are used to curb inflation, the result is a rise in unemployment. Conversely, if such policies are used to bring down the unemployment rate, this will cause prices to rise. However, at times in the 1970s, the Phillips curve was "inoperative": both prices and unemployment were rising simultaneously. Moreover, the rate of economic growth was declining. Thus the American economy was experiencing what is frequently referred to as **"stagflation,"** the worst of all possible worlds. As economist Arthur Okun put it, inflation and unemployment were ". . . intertwined and combined in a way that is historically unprecedented, and by the verdict of many economic textbooks, theoretically impossible."

Other elements of macroeconomic theory also became suspect in the 1970s. Prices and wages continued to rise even when the supply of goods like automobiles exceeded the demand for them—contrary to what Adam Smith had predicted. This led some economists to charge that prices and wages were being "administered" by business and labor. Management gave in to labor's demands for major wage increases, hiked prices to accommodate the increased labor costs, added more profit for itself, and passed on both kinds of costs to the consumer, in the form of higher prices.* Also, when fiscal and monetary policies designed to stimulate the economy failed to bring the unemployment rate down to the level predicted, economists explained that such macroeconomic policies could not deal with **"structural unemployment,"** that is, unemployment concentrated in specific industries, geographical areas, or particular segments of the work force, such as teenagers, blacks, poor whites, or chicanos that lack basic educational and vocational skills.

Another problem attendant in using fiscal and monetary policies to manage the economy is the fact that those whose economic behavior they are designed to affect may not react or behave in the predicted manner. For example, if one lowers the tax rate as favored by supply-side economics, it may *not* necessarily result in people choosing to work more because it is worthwhile to do so. They may instead decide that since their after-tax income has increased, they can affort to work *less* and still retain the same amount of money. Or even if they decide to work more, they may not work so much more that the tax revenues generated from that increased activity compensate for the revenue losses incurred because of a decline in the tax rate.

Finally, even when fiscal and monetary policies operate as intended, it is difficult to use them effectively. For one thing, they depend on the ability of economists to predict in advance the direction that the economy will move in; yet, given the changeable character of the American economy, it is difficult to make such predictions with the necessary degree of accuracy. There is also the danger that using fiscal and monetary policies to deal with one economic problem may bring on another of equal or greater severity. If a tight-money policy is used to counteract inflation, it may send the economy into a recession; on the other hand, stimulating the economy to fight high unemployment may result in inflation. The ability of economists to "fine-tune" the economy is thus far from proved.

Nor are direct controls free from difficulties. It is somewhat easier to impose voluntary or mandatory controls on wages than to impose them on prices because of the ability of manufacturers to cut back on the quality and/or quantity of products to meet price limits. Moreover, it is relatively easy to avoid or violate direct controls; their enforcement depends on a vast and often inefficient bureaucracy.

Political. Even if the economic difficulties discussed above can be overcome, there are major political considerations that affect the management of the economy. For one thing, some of the macroeconomic theories discussed above are much more painful to apply than others. Both traditional economic conservatism and monetarism call for sacrifices from some elements of the public. Raising taxes and cutting back on expenditures in order to balance the budget takes money out of the hands of taxpayers and some of those who sold goods or services to the federal government. Keeping a firm hand on the money supply or contracting it on occasion raises interest rates for businesses and individuals who want to borrow money to invest or spend. A slowed-down economy typically results in people being thrown out of work or not being rehired. These consequences lead some economists to refer to such painful policies as "castor-oil" economics.

Applying other economic theories brings much more pleasant consequences—at least for a time. Cutting

* This pattern changed somewhat during the recession of the early 1980s. Many labor unions accepted cuts in wages and fringe benefits; however, there were no comparable cutbacks in the prices of many goods.

taxes and increasing government expenditures, as Keynesians advocate during economic downturns, puts more money in the hands of taxpayers and those who sell goods or services to the federal government. Massive tax cuts as advocated by supply-siders are also popular with both individuals and businesses; moreover, the idea that this can be accomplished without bringing on deficits is comforting to people who are concerned with that problem. Such a feeling leads economist Herbert Stein to label supply-side economics and other elements of Reaganomics as the "economics of joy."*

Further complicating the political problems of managing the economy is the fact that economic policy-making is highly fragmented in our political system. Not only are both the executive and legislative branches intimately involved in the process, but within each branch there are major units that frequently represent different perspectives. This is true of the "troika" or "triad" that advises the president on economic matters—the chairman of the Council of Economic Advisers, the director of the Office of Management and Budget, and the Secretary of the Treasury. In 1984 Martin Feldstein, Chairman of the CEA, constantly warned the president and the nation that the large budget deficits were endangering the health of the economy and that taxes should be raised immediately to cut back on the deficits. In contrast, Secretary of the Treasury Donald Regan was concerned that raising taxes in the early stages of the economic upturn would cut short the recovery. At one point the feuding between the two became especially fierce: Regan specifically disavowed the annual report of the CEA, declaring that Congress should "throw it away."

The situation becomes even more complex if the fourth member of the executive branch's economic "quadriad"—the Chairman of the Federal Reserve Board—is added to the picture. While the president can remove members of the triad if he is displeased with them,† he cannot take such action against the Chairman of the Federal Reserve Board, who, for example, can pursue a "tight-money" monetary policy at the same time the president wants to see the economy expand. Presidents can attempt to persuade the chairman of the "Fed" to pursue policies his administration favors (over the years, chairmen have tended to try to accommodate the wishes of the chief executive), but the president has no legal method of forcing him to do so.‡

Differences also occur within Congress over economic policy. Some of them reflect partisan attitudes—over the years Democrats have tended to favor higher levels of domestic expenditures than Republicans. Some differences, however, transcend party and are institutional in nature. As Chapter 12 indicates, the House Appropriations Committee generally favors lower levels

Economist Herbert Stein testifies before Republican Platform Committee.

* In addition to the tax revenues argument, Stein identifies two other optimistic assumptions of Reaganism: (1) that inflation can be reduced without a transitional period of increased unemployment; (2) that government domestic expenditures can be reduced without harming anyone except bureaucrats because the budget is full of waste, fraud, and counterproductive programs.

† In mid-1984, Chairman Feldstein resigned his position in order to resume teaching economics at Harvard University. Secretary Regan and several other key figures in the Reagan administration were not distressed with his departure.

‡ Presidents are also generally reluctant to openly criticize the chairman of the "Fed" because of the "independence" the latter is supposed to enjoy. At times other members of the president's economic team may take on that role: in mid-1984, when Chairman Volcker was trying to hold down the growth of the money supply, Secretary Regan complained that such action was causing interest rates to rise.

of expenditures than its senatorial counterpart. Moreover, the Budget committees of both chambers tend to prefer lower expenditures than their Appropriations committees.

Finally, as political scientist Edward Tufte has demonstrated, the electoral cycle has a definite effect on economic policy. Both the president and the Congress generally act to stimulate the economy in an election year. This takes the form of increases and advances in social security and veterans' benefits (typically accompanied with a notice mentioning the name of the incumbent president) or tax cuts or rebates. Tax increases, on the other hand, are scheduled for nonelection years. These actions generally have the desired effect: disposable income and employment rise in even-numbered years (when presidential and congressional elections are held) and fall in odd-numbered years. Administrations that fail to tailor their economic policies to take account of political factors may pay the consequences: many observers attribute Richard Nixon's defeat in 1960 to the failure of President Eisenhower to try to stimulate the economy when it took a downturn at the end of his administration.* Thus, public officials who must make decisions on the overall management of the economy frequently allow political considerations to override economic ones.

TAXING AND SPENDING IN THE AMERICAN ECONOMY

So far we have been concerned with taxing and spending as fiscal policy instruments to be used in the overall management of the American economy. In this section we focus on the actual record of taxation and expenditure by the national government in recent years. We also examine in more detail the sources from which the national government raises its tax resources and the kinds of functions for which it spends its money.

Level of Governmental Expenditures and Receipts

It comes as no surprise that expenditures by the national government have risen dramatically in recent years. Table 17.4 shows that they increased from under $10 billion in 1940, before our entry into World War II, to almost $93 billion in 1945, the end of hostilities. They then declined in the post-war years, not approaching the 1945 figure until 1960. Since that time, expenditures have increased greatly, more than doubling between 1960 and 1970, and almost tripling between 1970 and 1980. Moreover, they rose almost 40 percent in the period between 1980 and 1983.

Table 17.4 also shows that federal government expenditures generally exceeded receipts in the analyzed years. In only one of the 12 years shown (1960) did the national government take in more money than it spent; the difference was only very small, about $300 million.† In all the other analyzed years it incurred a debt. However, not until 1975 did the annual deficit begin to approach the one incurred during the wartime year of 1945. It should be noted that the annual deficits in 1982 and 1983 were particularly high, $111 and $208 billion, respectively, because the tax cuts passed in 1981 began to take effect and government expenditures continued to increase markedly. The cumulative effect of these annual deficits

* Nixon learned the political lesson well; when he was up for re-election in 1972, he pursued a stimulative policy for the economy. While other matters undoubtedly influenced the outcome of the election, the relatively healthy state of the American economy at the time was a major factor in Nixon's landslide victory.

† In one other recent year not shown in the table (1969), government receipts ($187.8 billion) exceeded expenditures ($184.5 billion), which produced a surplus of $3.3 billion.

Table 17.4
Federal Receipts, Expenditures, and Debts: Selected Years (1940–1983)
(In billions of dollars)

					Percentage of GNP	
	Receipts	Expenditures	Surplus or Deficit (−)	Outstanding Gross Debt	Expenditures	Outstanding Gross Debt
1940	6.4	9.5	−3.1	50.7	10.0	53.4
1945	45.2	92.7	−47.5	260.1	42.7	119.9
1950	39.5	42.6	−3.1	256.9	16.1	96.9
1955	65.5	68.5	−3.0	274.4	18.0	72.1
1960	92.5	92.2	.3	290.9	18.5	58.4
1965	116.8	118.4	−1.6	323.2	18.0	49.0
1970	192.8	195.7	−2.8	382.6	20.2	39.5
1975	279.1	324.2	−45.2	544.1	21.9	36.8
1980	517.1	576.7	−59.6	914.3	22.4	35.5
1981	599.3	657.2	−57.9	1003.9	22.9	35.0
1982	617.8	728.4	−110.6	1147.0	24.0	37.8
1983 (est)	597.5	805.2	−207.7	1383.7	25.2	43.3

SOURCE: U. S. Bureau of The Census; data from the U. S. Office of Management and Budget.

is also dramatic; the nation's outstanding debt grew from $51 billion in 1940 to almost $1.4 trillion estimated in 1983.

Of course, government expenditure and debt must take into account the size of the federal government's economic base. In 1940 we had a gross national product (the total value of all goods and services) of $100 billion; in 1982 it was over $3 trillion. As Table 17.4 shows, 1945 still represents the high point for both expenditures and outstanding debt as a percentage of the nation's gross national product (GNP): the former constituted over 40 percent and the latter, 120 percent of the GNP. In the 1970s expenditures represented about one-fifth of the GNP and the outstanding debt about one-third to close to two-fifths of that figure. However, both figures rose significantly in the early 1980s, the former reaching one-quarter of the GNP in 1983 and the latter over three-fifths of it.

Types of Governmental Expenditures

Our national government spends money for a wide variety of functions. However, these expenditures may be conveniently divided into several major categories. The first is *national defense*—the costs of weapons and the salaries of men and women serving in the armed services. The second is *income security*, which includes items such as social security, unemployment benefits, Civil Service and military retirement benefits, and food stamps. Remaining major categories include *health*, *veterans' benefits*, and *interest* on the national debt. "Other" expenditures (see Fig. 17.1) cover a number of governmental functions, such as education, international affairs, transportation, national resources, the environment, energy, agriculture, and community and regional development.

Figure 17.1 shows how the federal expenditure dollar changed over the period from 1960 (the last year of the Eisenhower administration) to 1980 (the last year of the Carter administration) and the early years of the Reagan administration. In 1960 almost one-half of

Jim Morin
The Miami Herald

all expenditures went for national defense; in 1980 about one-fourth was devoted to that purpose. In contrast, over the same 20-year period, income security payments rose from one-fifth of the federal expenditure dollar to one-third of it. Expenditures for health rose dramatically from 1 percent of total government outlays in 1960 to 10 percent in 1980. The share of federal expenditures for paying interest on the national debt and other nondefense expendi-

Figure 17.1 Federal Expenditures: 1960, 1980, and 1983
(SOURCE: U.S. Bureau of the Census; data from the U.S. Office of Management and Budget)

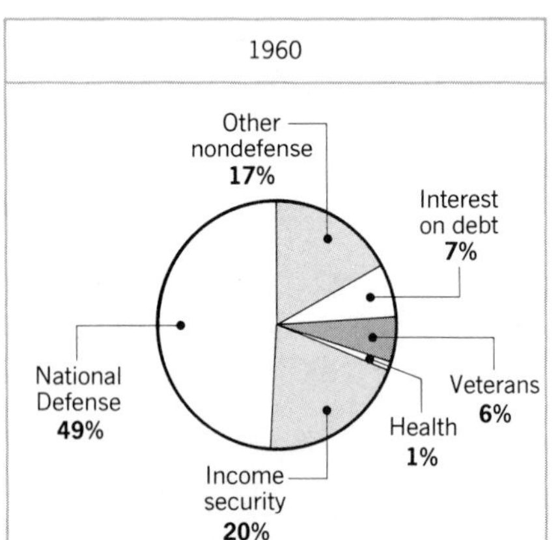

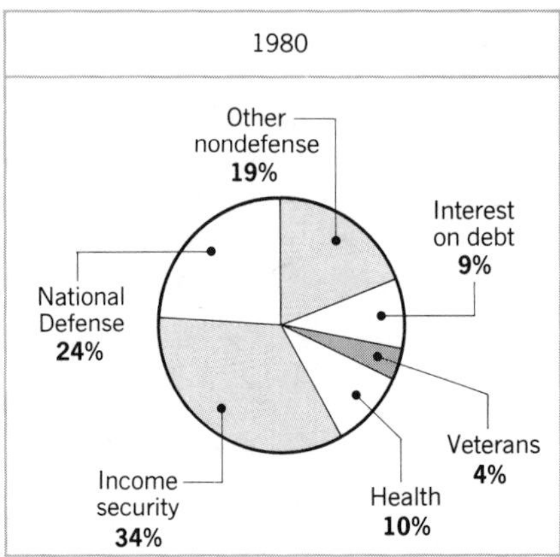

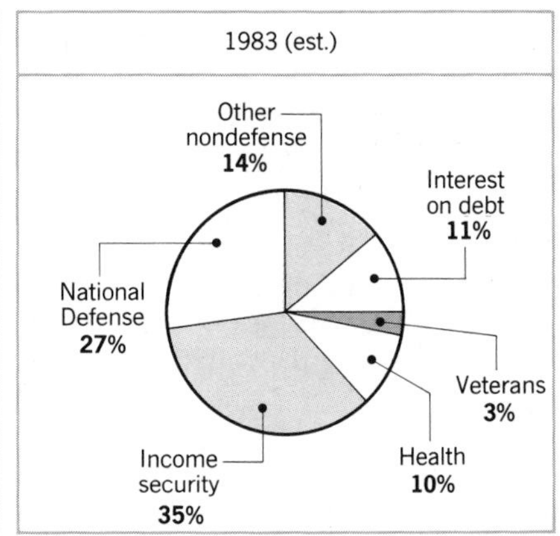

tures rose 2 percent over the 20-year period while outlays for veterans benefits declined by a similar percentage.

Figure 17.1 also reveals changes made in the federal expenditure dollar in the three-year period from 1980 to 1983. Outlays for national defense, interest on the debt, and income security rose to some degree. Other nondefense and veterans expenditures declined by comparable amounts. Outlays for health care remained constant.

Sources of Government Revenues

The overwhelming proportion of the revenues raised by the national government—over 98 percent—comes from some type of tax levied on individuals or businesses. (The remainder comes from resources derived from government enterprises such as the post office and from fees such as those paid for the use of federal parks.) The issue thus becomes one of determining what kinds of taxes will be levied and upon whom the tax burden will fall.

In recent years the federal government has depended heavily on the *income tax* to raise revenues. Levied on both individuals and corporations, this tax has the advantage of being based on the "ability to pay," since the rate of taxation increases as income rises. Moreover, its collection can be facilitated by withholding moneys from income received during the course of the year. Of increasing importance in recent years are proceeds from *social insurance taxes* and *contributions* associated with income security programs. Both of these possess the dual virtues of being paid in part by those who benefit from them and of being collectible through periodic deductions from income.

A third major source of federal revenues is the *excise tax,* levied on the purchase of selected goods, such as gasoline, liquor, cigarettes, furs, and jewelry. Although they are supposedly levied on "luxuries" that people can supposedly do without, there is a serious question whether some of these items, such as gasoline are really luxuries (e.g., many lower-income people must drive their cars to work). Moreover, excise taxes tend to consume a larger share of lower-class than upper-class income. They also single out particular industries for a special tax burden.

Finally, a small share of federal receipts comes from *customs* charged on goods imported into this country as well as from *gift* and *estate* taxes.

Figure 17.2 shows how the proportion of federal receipts changed from 1960 to 1980 and the first three years of the Reagan administration. Two of the major revenue sources—the individ-

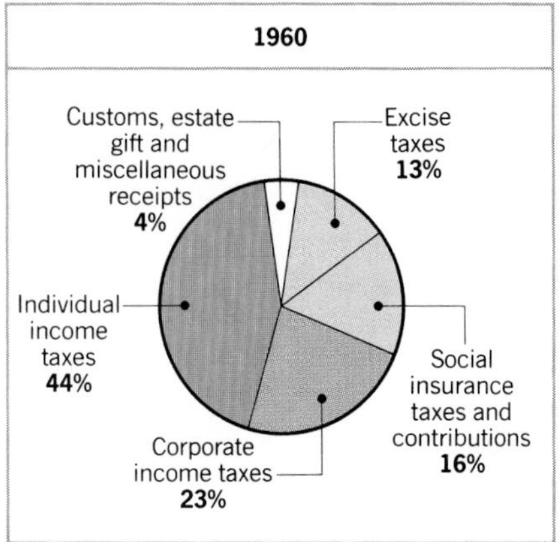

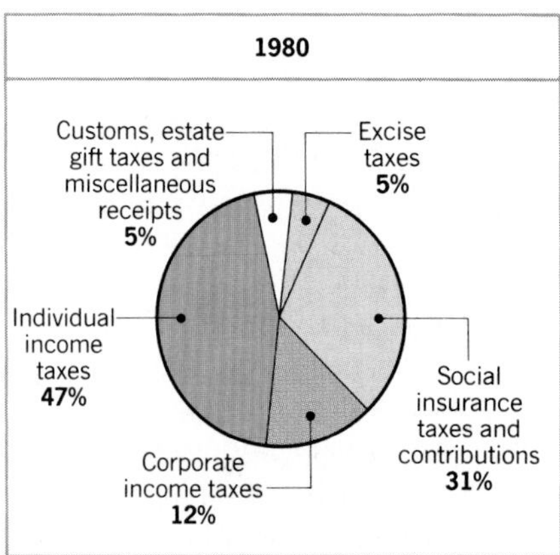

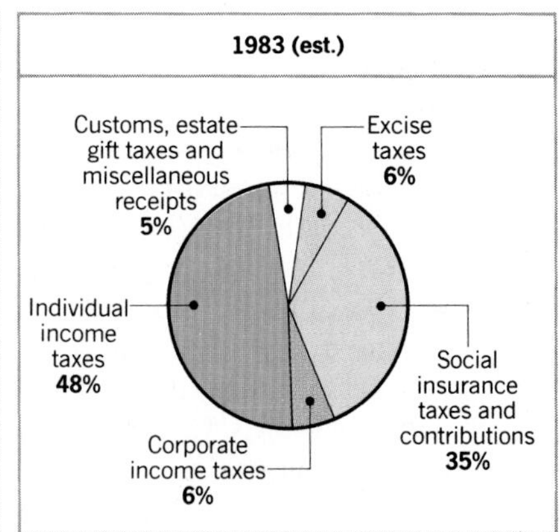

Figure 17.2 Federal Receipts: 1960, 1980, and 1983
(SOURCE: U.S. Bureau of the Census; data from the U.S. Office of Management and Budget)

ual income tax and the combination of customs, gift, and estate taxes (included in the figure with "miscellaneous receipts," that is, revenues from government enterprises and fees) remained fairly constant. However, the relative contribution of the other three kinds of taxation changed greatly over the 20-year period. Both the corporate income and excise taxes became substantially less important in 1980 than they were in 1960, while social insurance taxes and contributions made up the difference. In fact, the latter's contribution to the federal tax dollar almost doubled over the two decades from 1960 to 1980.

Some of these same general trends continued in the early years of the Reagan administration. Individual income taxes continued to provide almost half of the federal receipts and the share of total revenues from social insurance taxes and contributions rose to over one-third. Meanwhile, the proportion of receipts from the corporate-income tax fell from 12 to 6 percent in the three-year period from 1980 to 1983. Proceeds from excise taxes and customs, estate, and gift taxes remained fairly constant.

When one compares the changes in the expenditure and revenue situation over the years, one trend becomes very clear: public officials became increasingly concerned with the income security of our citizens. But while they were willing to spend more money to help provide that security, they also expected the recipients of such benefits (as well as their employers) to help pay for the growing costs of such programs. The next chapter analyzes the nature of major social programs designed to provide financial security for our citizens and shows how such programs have changed over the years, including new developments under the Reagan administration.

ASSESSMENT

For the most part, the American economy has been a success story. Over the years it has provided more and more Americans with a very good standard of living. American technical know-how and our high level of productivity have been the envy of people around the world.

A great deal of this success is undoubtedly due to the abundance of natural resources with which our country has been blessed. However, we have also been innovative in developing those resources. The relationship between the government and the economy has been a pragmatic one. Our political officials have not been slaves either to laissez-faire capitalism or collectivism; instead, they have used a variety of approaches to promote and regulate economic activity in both the private and the public sector. Moreover, all three major areas of the American economic society—business, labor, and agriculture—have benefited from government programs.

As a nation we were relatively slow to use the government to manage the overall operation of the economy. Not until the Great Depression of the 1930s did national officials begin to use fiscal policy to stimulate the economy. Not until 1946 did we develop an explicit national policy calling for maximum employment, production, and purchasing power, and the creation of executive and congressional agencies to help achieve those goals.

The use of policy instruments to successfully manage the overall economy reached its zenith in the first half of the 1960s when all the right things happened: prices held remarkably steady, unemployment declined, and the output of the American economy grew dramatically. However, since then the record has been far less impressive. The major expenditures occasioned by waging two wars simultaneously—one against poverty and the other against the North Vietnamese—drove up both wages and prices and set off a spiral of inflation. Moreover, at times, particularly in the 1970s, relatively high unemployment accompanied that inflation.

The case is still out on the ultimate effects of "Reaganomics," or what Republican Senator Howard Baker of Tennessee, the Senate Majority Leader, called a "riverboat gamble" when it was inaugurated in 1981. Inflation has been brought down but interest rates remain relatively high. To date (mid-1984), neither of the major assumptions of supply-side economics has turned out to be true. The percentage of personal income devoted to savings has not risen; in fact, it has actually fallen. Moreover, the taxable income base has not expanded to nearly compensate for the loss of revenues occasioned by the substantial cut in tax rates. (As a result, we are experiencing the largest deficits in the nation's history.) The economy is improving but in ways that typically occur in the early stages of a recovery as the pent-up demand for goods and services asserts itself and businesses begin to replace their inventories. Ironically, the recovery to date is best explained by *Keynesianism* (tax cuts have helped to generate additional demand), the one economic theory that is not incorporated in Reaganomics.

SELECTED READINGS

A well-written book explaining major economic concepts and theories in nontechnical terms is Leonard Silk, *Economics in Plain English* (New York: Simon and Schuster, 1978). An historical account of the relationship between the public and private sectors in the United States is contained in Emmette Redford, *The Role of Government in the American Economy* (New York: The Macmillan Co., 1966). A provocative book on the American economy is John Kenneth Galbraith's *The Affluent Society* (Boston: Houghton Mifflin, 1957). A follow-up study by Galbraith is *The New Industrial State* (New York: New American Library, 1968).

A number of books treat the government's role in various areas of the economy, including business, labor, and agriculture. The two most helpful are James Anderson, David Brady, and Charles Bullock III, *Public Policy and Politics in America* (Monterey, Cal.: Brooks/Cole, 2nd ed., 1984) and Emmette Redford, *American Government and the Economy* (New York: The Macmillan Co., 1965). A provocative study that argues that many businesses favored regulation as a means of avoiding competition is Gabriel Kolko, *The Triumph of Conservatism* (New York: Free Press, 1963).

An excellent discussion of macroeconomic policies is contained in Chapter 2, "Economic Stability Policies," which appears in Charles Bullock III, James Anderson, and David Brady, *Public Policies in the Eighties* (Monterey, Cal., Brooks/Cole Publishing Company, 1983). The two best histories of macroeconomic policies since the 1920s and early 1930s are written by Herbert Stein, *The Fiscal Revolution in America* (Chicago: University of Chicago Press, 1969), and *Presidential Economics: The Making of Economic Policy from Roosevelt to Reagan and Beyond* (New York: Simon and Schuster, 1984). For an account of the management of the economy in the Kennedy administration, see Walter Heller, *New Dimensions of Political Economy* (New York: W. W. Norton, 1966). A very good analysis of the formation of fiscal policy in the United States is Lawrence Pierce, *The Politics of Fiscal Policy Formation* (Pacific Palisades, Cal., Goodyear Publishing Company, 1971). For an insightful analysis of the manipulation of the economy for political purposes, see Edward Tufte, *Political Control of the Economy* (Princeton, N. J.: Princeton University Press, 1978). Economic and political developments of the early 1980s are treated in Chapter 2, "Fiscal and Political Strategy in the Reagan Administration," by Hugh Heclo and Rudolph Penner, which appears in Fred Greenstein (ed.), *The Reagan Presidency: An Early Assessment* (Baltimore: The Johns Hopkins University Press, 1983).

U.S. DEPARTMENT OF AGRICULTURE
FOOD COUPON
DO NOT FOLD
OR SPINDLE
DEPARTMENT OF AGRICULTURE
FOOD COUPON
ONE DOLLAR
THE UNITED STATES OF AMERICA

CHAPTER 18

Social Policies

Along with Ronald Reagan's general dislike of "Big Government," came a particular concern with social programs. In his maiden political speech on behalf of Barry Goldwater during the 1964 presidential campaign (the one that drew Reagan to the attention of prominent conservative businessmen who convinced him to run for the governorship of California two years later), Reagan said of the Social Security system: "Can't we introduce voluntary features so that those who can make better provision for themselves are allowed to do so? Incidentally, we might allow participants in Social Security to name their own beneficiaries, which they cannot do in the present program. These are not insurmountable problems."

When Reagan was elected governor of California in 1966, he made welfare-system reform one of his major priorities. During his first term he got nowhere with the California legislature. However, early Reagan's second term, Bob Moretti, the Democratic speaker of the Assembly and the second most powerful man in the California state government approached Reagan and offered a truce. After extensive negotiations, Reagan Republican conservatives and Moretti Democratic liberals worked out a political compromise. The governor got reforms tightening eligibility requirements for welfare recipients, while the liberal Democratic legislators obtained higher benefits and automatic cost-of-living increases for those who remained on welfare.

In September 1975, shortly before he announced his campaign for the Republican presidential nomination, Reagan proposed that major federal social programs totalling $90 billion be transferred to the states. In the campaign in New Hampshire the following January, the Ford opposition team confronted the Reagan forces with facts and figures showing how the cost of replacing federal social programs would require low-tax states like New Hampshire to enact an income or sales tax or both in order to pay for such programs. Although Reagan thought his bold proposal helped his presidential campaign, most political observers disagreed; they contended that it placed him in a defensive position and contributed to his very close loss in that first presidential primary of the 1976 campaign.

By the 1980 presidential campaign, Reagan had grown more circumspect on the matter of social programs. In an interview with the *Detroit News* on January 13, 1980, he distinguished between those who should and should not receive welfare assistance. On the subject of reducing welfare rolls, he explained:

> *Now remember . . . we're not talking about those people who are invalid and through no fault of their own cannot provide for themselves. We have always taken care of those people—and always will. We're talking about those people who are able-bodied and who for whatever reason—it may be lack of skill or whatever—have not been able to make their way out there in the competitive world. So the idea of welfare should be to put those people back on their feet, make them self-supporting and independent.*

In his acceptance speech at the 1980 Republican national convention, Reagan again stated his philosophy on social programs: "We Republicans believe it is essential that we maintain both the forward momentum of economic growth and the strength of the safety net beneath those in society who need help." In his debate in Detroit with President Carter just one week before the 1980 election, Reagan was very protective of the Social Security program. While calling for a task force to look into the financial problems of that program, with recommendations on how to reform it and make it actuarily sound, the Republican candidate also assured the live and television audience ". . . that no one presently dependent on Social Security is going to have the rug pulled out from under them and not get their check."

In his major economic speech to a joint session of Congress on February 18, 1981, the newly-elected president echoed the sentiments he had expressed during the campaign. He assured Social Security recipients that their checks were not going to be taken away from them, and they would continue to receive cost-of-living benefits. He also pledged that Medicare and supplemental income for the blind, aged, and the disabled would not be cut. The president explained that all those with "true need" could rest assured that "the social safety net" of programs would be exempt from any budget cuts. At the same time, the president stated that while the Food Stamp program would continue to serve the deserving, those *not* in "real need" or who were "abusing the program" would be removed from it. He also pledged to tighten welfare eligibility and pay more attention to outside sources of income in determining the amount of welfare an individual is allowed.

In this chapter we focus on what some have termed President Reagan's "attack on the welfare state." The chapter begins with a short historical account of the development of social programs in the United States, and then explains the essential differences among such programs. It then analyzes separately six of the most important social programs, their establishment, how they have changed over the years, what President Reagan has proposed in terms of reforming them, and what has come of his proposals.

DEVELOPMENT

While the federal government has traditionally played a major role in promoting and regulating fields such as business and agriculture, it was much more reluctant to help members of the general populace with special economic needs. Early American attitudes towards the poor (derived largely from British practices) placed the major responsibility for caring for them on their immediate families, their relatives, and private charities. If help from these sources was not available, public assistance then became the duty of local government units (typically the township or county), which financed aid through a poor tax. Needy people who could work were sent to workhouses; those who could not were placed in poorhouses. (Frequently, both were located in separate sections of the same building.) In some instances, payments in cash, food, or clothing were made in lieu of institutionalization. In any event, the provisions for the poor were woefully inadequate: the poorhouses were dilapidated, and they frequently harbored petty criminals and the mentally handicapped along with the indigent; the cash payments, designed only for emergencies, were kept below the income received by the lowest-paid worker. This inhumane treatment pricked few consciences because poverty was regarded as a reflection of moral deficiencies: to be poor was sinful.

In fact, some contended that public assistance for the poor interfered with the operation of natural economic laws. One prominent spokesman for this viewpoint was a nineteenth-century English economist, Thomas Malthus, who developed the theory that population

Immigrant lodgers at New York City Police Station in the early 1890's.

rises at a faster rate than the food supply, which results in a shortage of the latter; feeding the poor thus only keeps them alive and worsens the situation. A similar view was espoused by Herbert Spencer, an English sociologist prominent in the latter half of the century, who contended that the laws of natural selection allow only the fittest to survive; providing help for the poor enables the unfit to continue to exist, thus weakening the human race.

Although Malthus and Spencer had some impact on attitudes in the United States (the "robber barons" who dominated industries such as oil, railroads, and steel in the latter part of the nineteenth century naturally seized on the Englishmen's philosophies to justify their own exploitation of the poor), the idea gradually became accepted that certain people simply could not care for themselves and therefore the general public had an obligation to assist them. More of the responsibility for aid began to be assumed by states (rather than counties), which developed specialized institutions for the blind, the deaf, the delinquent, and the insane. Cash payments to the handicapped were increasingly provided by the states: by 1930, 20 states had programs for the blind, 45 gave aid to mothers with dependent children, and 12 provided assistance to the aged.

Another institution of the late nineteenth and early twentieth centuries also assumed some responsibility for the poor: the urban political machine. As previously indicated in Chapter 6, the precinct captain was ready to dispense aid in the form of food, clothing, and the like to the needy who in turn were expected to vote for the machine's political candidates. It was particularly appealing to the poor because the assistance provided by the political boss was dispensed without the long forms and embarrassing questions that typically accompanied public-assistance programs.

The national government was not considered responsible for the needy, with the exception of certain special groups such as Indians, merchant seamen, and veterans. The Depression, however, suddenly changed that. By 1932, when about one of four workers was unemployed, poverty had changed from the condition of a relatively few "unworthy" Americans to the plight of millions, most of whom had previously been employed as "worthy" citizens. Moreover, the existing system for handling the problems of the poor collapsed as local governments and states ran into financial difficulties. Only the national government remained as a potential provider for the poor, but President Hoover clung to the traditional belief that relief should be handled by local governments. He eventually approved a limited federal relief program, but it remained for the new President, Franklin D. Roosevelt, to persuade the nation to assume a new attitude toward the role of the national government in providing for the needy.

In the early stages of Roosevelt's New Deal, efforts were directed toward the recovery of the economy. The measures passed to meet that problem were the Federal Emergency Relief Act and work programs such as the Civilian Conservation Corps (CCC) and the Works Progress Administration (WPA). These programs were temporary in nature and designed to get money quickly into the hands of the vast number of people who had been thrown out of work by the Depression.

Subsequently, the Roosevelt administration turned its attention to providing permanent assistance to particular groups that needed special help. The President appointed a special Committee on Economic Security to look into the matter and then endorsed its recommendations in a congressional message. Congress responded with the passage of the Social Security Act of 1935, the most important social program ever enacted.

The Social Security Act provided various types of financial assistance to people with special needs. For the elderly, assistance came in the form of retirement benefits. For the unemployed, it meant weekly payments for a specified period to those thrown out of work because of conditions beyond their control. The act also targeted financial assistance to three other groups that were thought to be incapable of earning a living for themselves: the aged poor, the blind, and children deprived of normal parental support by the death, incapacity, or absence of a parent.

In time the federal government added other major programs for people with special needs. In the 1950s, *disabled persons* became recipients of financial assistance. In 1965 Congress passed a *medicare* program to help meet the health care needs of senior citizens in general and a separate *medicaid* program for poor people, many of whom were receiving other types of government assistance as well. Finally, in the 1960s it also instituted a major *food stamp* program to help meet the nutritional needs of poor people.

We thus have a broad range of social programs that have been adopted by the federal government in the last 50 years.* Before examining those programs in detail, however, it would be helpful to explain the major differences that exist among them.

CHARACTERISTICS

The most basic difference between the various social programs outlined above is that some are based on an *insurance* principle as contrasted to those financed from *general revenues.* The primary example of the former is the Social Security program, which provides retirement benefits drawn from a special trust fund. (That fund, in turn, is financed through monthly payroll deductions taken from persons' salaries, supplemented by similar contributions from their employers.) A primary example of the latter is the program of Aid-to-Families-with-Dependent-Children (AFDC).

It should be noted that the distinctions between these two general types of social programs also extend to matters besides how they are financed. Benefits from the social security program go to *all those* who are retired, whether or not they are in actual financial need of these benefits. Thus middle and even upper-income people receive retirement money. In contrast, social programs financed from general revenue go only to those who have an *actual need* for such benefits. (They typically must meet some kind of "test" to determine whether their particular situation satisfies the requirements of actual need.) This latter type of program is considered a "welfare" or "relief" program and its general clientele are poor people from the lowest social class in our society.

Other basic differences also exist among major social programs in the United States. Some provide *cash* assistance and allow recipients to decide how they will use the money to meet their various needs. Others focus on meeting *specific needs,* such as health care and food, and pay moneys to the provider of the care or goods rather than the person being helped. Major social programs also are financed and administered by different levels of government. Some, such as the social-security retirement program, are financially supported entirely by the federal government which also administers it. In contrast, the AFDC program is financed

* There are, of course, many, many government programs designed to assist people with special needs. The programs selected for discussion in this chapter are the most expensive and most controversial ones.

jointly by federal and state governments and is administered primarily by the latter with some supervision by the former.

Despite these basic differences among major social programs, they have one characteristic in common: they are known as "entitlement" programs. This means that people automatically qualify for benefits if they meet the required conditions, such as age or income. Unlike other public programs, the government by law *must appropriate* the moneys necessary to finance them. The only way to alter their costs is to change the eligibility and benefit standards associated with them. This basic characteristic makes it particularly difficult for the government to control the costs of major social programs. As the following discussion indicates, however, the federal government has been much less willing to change the conditions associated with some social programs than with others.

OLD AGE AND SURVIVORS INSURANCE

Background

The Old Age and Survivors Insurance program was established in 1935 to help supplement the income of older Americans who depended on sources such as private savings and pensions. The initial law provided for a one-percent tax on both employees and their employers on the first $3,000 of wages. The amount of retirement benefits were keyed to the wages earned by workers, with such benefits to go to those 65 years or older.

From this modest beginning, the program gradually expanded its coverage and benefits; and payroll taxes were levied to finance such benefits. In 1939, supplemental benefits were provided for dependents and survivors of covered workers. In 1950, new people were added to the program, including the self-employed and regularly employed domestic and farm workers; in addition, coverage was made optional for employees of state and local governments and nonprofit private organizations. In 1956, the retirement age for women was lowered to age 62 and five years later, for men as well. (In both cases, benefits were set at 80 percent of those available at age 65.) Meanwhile both the benefits and payroll taxes levied to finance them were increased: by 1970, the average monthly benefit was over $100 a month and the payroll tax of both employers and employees was four percent on the first $7,000 of a workers' wages.

Until 1970, the Old Age and Survivors Insurance (OASI) program was considered the most successful social program in our nation's history. Not only did it provide increasing benefits for covered workers, but it also possessed major political assets that made it appealing to both major political parties and those with different political philosophies. Liberals supported the program because it provided increasingly generous benefits for older people, making them more financially secure and independent. Conservatives liked the program because it was based on an "insurance" principle that tied benefits to contributions and was very compatible with the traditional value of individualism.

Developing Problems

In 1972, Congress embarked on a major change in the OASI program. Future benefits were pegged to the Cost-of-Living Index in order to guarantee that recipients would not lose purchasing power because of an increase in inflation. (Changes in the amount of benefits were referred to as COLA's—cost-of-living adjustments.) At the time, the idea made a certain amount of economic sense because wages (upon which payroll taxes were levied) were increasing faster than prices (upon which benefits were calculated). It also had some political advantages since changes in benefits were automatic rather than subject to political pressures for periodic increases. At the time it was also thought that indexing would provide smaller increases in benefits than periodic action by Congress.

However, the 1970s brought major social and economic changes that undermined the financial soundness of the OASI program. Lower birth rates shrank the size of the future work force supporting the retirement system at the same time as greater longevity of retirees increased the total amount of benefits received prior to death. While such developments affected the long-term financial status of the program, other factors had more immediate economic effects. Growing inflation rates increased the benefits that were tied to the Cost-of-Living Index. At the same time, higher levels of unemployment and slow growth in the wages of the employed limited the payroll tax contributions that supported the insurance system.

As the financial status of the OASI program deteriorated, government officials searched for ways to deal with the situation. In 1977, President Carter convinced Congress of the necessity of passing a major payroll tax increase, which at the time constituted the largest peacetime tax increase in the nation's history. Supposedly this legislation was to put the program on a sound financial basis for the remainder of the century. However, within a year's time a combination of rampant inflation and high unemployment destroyed that assumption, and the Carter administration was forced to go back to Congress to ask for other changes in the OASI program, including phasing out benefits to postsecondary school children; tying minimum benefits for new retirees to previous earnings; gradually raising the minimum age for retirement from 62 to 65 and that for normal retirement from 65 to 68; and allowing the Old Age Assistance program to borrow money from two other Social Security trust funds, those used to finance the disability and Medicare programs. (Both these programs are discussed below.) However, Congress was unwilling to adopt any of these proposals, and so the OASI program was in deep financial trouble when the Reagan administration came into office in 1981.

Proposals by the Reagan Administration

The Reagan administration lost no time in proposing major changes in the OASI program. On February 18, 1981, the president recommended abolishment of the minimum monthly benefit, the phasing out of benefits for older students, and the elimination of the lump-sum death benefits when a retiree left no surviving beneficiary. On May 18, 1981, he proposed much more fundamental changes in the retirement system, including a significant reduction in benefits for early retirees and delaying for three months the COLA's scheduled to take effect in July 1982.

The latter proposals in particular set off a storm of criticism: within a week's time, the Senate passed a resolution condemning reductions in retirement benefits by a 96–0 vote. The President beat a hasty retreat and in an attempt to politically defuse the issue, in December 1981, he established a bipartisan commission on social security reform that was to report back to Congress one year later (after the 1982 congressional elections were over).

In early 1983, the bipartisan commission presented a series of recommendations that became the basis for major changes in the OASI program. Congress enacted these changes into law in March 1983. The coverage of the system was extended to future federal civilian employees; in addition, all employees of nonprofit organizations were required to come under the retirement system; state and local governments are prohibited from withdrawing from it; a portion of the social-security benefits of people with retirement income of over a certain amount is taxed; the effective date of scheduled payroll tax increases was advanced; and automatic adjustments of cost-of-living adjustments were delayed from mid to the end of the year. Finally, beginning in 2015, the early retirement age is increased from 62 to 66.

It remains to be seen whether these recent changes have placed the OASI program on a sound financial basis or whether further adjustments will be required in the near future. Today it has become by far the nation's most expensive social program, one that paid out benefits totaling some $170 billion in 1983. As Figure 18.1 indicates, the average monthly payment to retired persons quadrupled in the period from 1970 to 1982; moreover, even when inflation is taken into account, such benefits increased by over $100 a month during that period. In 1973, the average benefit constituted about 39 percent of the final wage the retiree was earning while still working; by 1981, that benefit had risen to 55 percent of that wage.

UNEMPLOYMENT INSURANCE

Established the same year as the Old Age and Survivors Insurance program (1935), this program provides compensation in cash for workers who become unemployed. Like OASI, it is based on an insurance principle. In this case, benefits are paid from a special trust fund, into which proceeds from a payroll tax are paid. The tax is collected by the federal government—but determined (within federal regulations) by each state, with some establishing a higher

AFL-CIO rally in Boston.

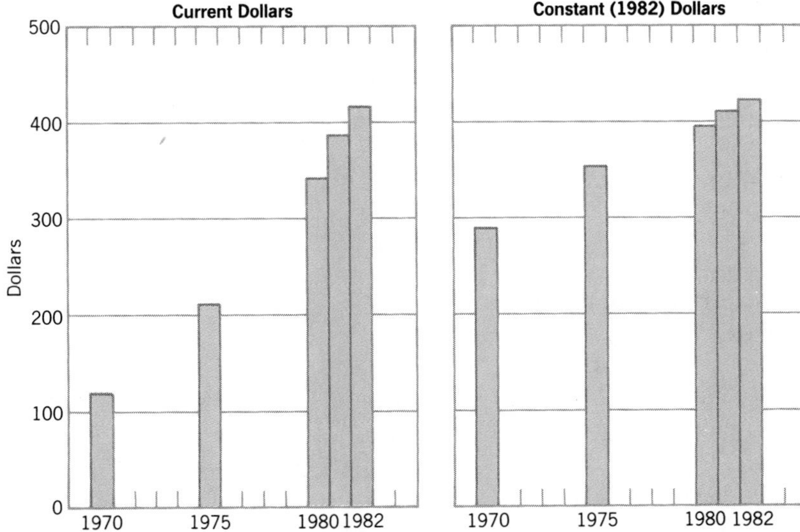

Figure 18.1 Social Security—Average Monthly Benefit Payments to Retired Workers (1970–1982)
(SOURCE: U.S. Bureau of the Census)

rate than others. States also differ on who has to pay the payroll tax: most levy it entirely on employers, but a few also require employees to make payments.

Individual states also establish conditions affecting the receipt of unemployment benefits. To become insured, a worker must typically work for from six to nine months on a job covered under the program. Thus new entrants, as well as re-entrants, to the work force are not eligible for benefits. Those who are eligible receive a weekly payment averaging 35–40 percent of their previous wages, with such payments normally being available for a period of 26 weeks. There is considerable variation in benefits paid by individual states.

Legislation also provides *extended unemployment benefits* (EB) when insured unemployment rises above some "trigger" level in the state in which the worker is employed. This EB program is financed jointly by federal and state payroll taxes, and the duration of extended benefits is established by individual states. Such benefits are typically for a maximum duration of 13 weeks, making 39 total weeks of benefits available under the regular and extended program. In 1981, President Reagan proposed and Congress accepted an increase in the state trigger rate,* which reduced the coverage of the EB program. By the end of 1982 (a recession year), only 14 states with very high unemployment rates were providing extended benefits.

During the 1975 recession and again in the early 1980s, temporary legislation was passed by Congress extending unemployment benefits beyond 39 weeks (or 26 in states not qualifying for EB). The 1975 recession legislation lengthened benefits by 26 weeks, giving a potential duration of 65 weeks (39 plus 26) of unemployment benefits. The early

* Prior to 1981, there was a trigger rate for the entire country, which made extended benefits available in all states. However, the president recommended the complete elimination of the national trigger rate in favor of one for individual states; the lawmakers went along with his recommendation.

1980s legislation generally provided for more modest extensions of benefits; the number of weeks varied according to the history and level of insured unemployment in a particular state. Typically these temporary laws (two were enacted in the early 1980s) provided extensions of from 8 to 16 weeks.

Unemployment insurance thus provided less support for the unemployed in the recession of the early 1980s than in the mid-1970s. In an average week in 1976, two-thirds of unemployed people received regular, extended, or supplemental benefits; in late 1982 at the height of that depression, only one-half did. Moreover, despite the fact that the 1980s recession lasted longer than the 1970s one, the duration of 1980s benefits was shorter because the applicable legislation was not as generous as that in the 1970s. Nonetheless, in 1983, benefits under all federal and state unemployment insurance programs cost some $35 billion.

AID TO THE ELDERLY POOR, BLIND, AND DISABLED

Background

Cash assistance to the elderly poor and the blind (*not* the disabled) was part of the Social Security Act of 1935. Such people were thought to have special needs that required public assistance. As previously indicated, some states had laws providing such aid, but the Social Security Act constituted a recognition that the federal government also had a responsibility to help the elderly poor and the blind.

Unlike the Social Security retirement and unemployment insurance programs, the ones enacted for these two categorical groups were financed from general revenues; moreover, recipients had to meet a "means" test to receive the benefits. Both programs were financed jointly by the federal and state governments, and the latter played a major role in determining the eligibility

Unemployment claims line in Providence, Rhode Island.

of potential recipients and the amount of their benefits. Thus assistance to the aged poor and the blind were "welfare" or "relief" programs administered as categorical grant-in-aid programs.

Assistance for the disabled developed somewhat differently. It was not until the 1950s that the federal government undertook responsibility for such people. And then the responsibility took two separate forms. In 1950, Congress passed legislation of a welfare nature for permanently and totally disabled people who could demonstrate a need for financial assistance. Six years later it enacted an insurance program financed by a payroll tax to provide cash benefits for disabled persons, similar to those received by retired people under the 1935 Social Security Act.

These two distinct types of programs for the disabled have now been joined with similar social programs. In 1974, the Congress combined the categorical welfare programs for the aged poor, the blind, and the disabled into the Supplemental Security Income (SSI) Program. At the same time, its primary funding was taken over by the federal government which now provides uniform minimum benefits throughout the country. (Most states also provide an additional cash payment to recipients but this is not required under the federal law.) In turn, the disability insurance program was incorporated into the Old Age and Survivors Insurance Program, with the combination being designated as Old Age, Survivors, and Disability Insurance (OASDI). Thus present-day social-security payroll taxes are allocated between the retirement and disability programs, with proceeds going into two separate trust funds to finance the two types of benefits.

Recent Developments

Welfare and insurance programs have developed major differences in recent years. Unlike other social programs, the SSI one has not experienced major increases. In fact, the number of recipients of assistance to the aged poor, blind, and permanently and totally disabled declined from 4.3 million in 1975 to 3.9 million in 1982. In that latter year the average monthly payment for the aged poor was only $146 and for the permanently and totally disabled, $229. As a result, the SSI program is not currently a controversial one.

The experience with the disability insurance program has been quite different. People who have been employed for a certain period of time and who are unable to engage in any substantial gainful activity because of physical or medical impairment that may result in death or disability for at least 12 continuous months are eligible to receive benefits. Eligibility thus turns on both medical and vocational factors. The initial determination of disability is made by a state Disability Determination Service (DDS), with a provision for appealing disallowances to an Administrative Law Judge (ALJ) employed by the Social Security Administration (SSA). Denials of claims at that level are appealable to the Appeals Council within the SSA.

After remaining fairly constant for a number of years, as indicated by Table 18.1, disability insurance awards increased by almost 200,000 (some 55 percent) from 1969 to 1974. (This was a period of high unemployment and one in which legal services for the poor improved, conditions that may have affected the increase in claims.) In addition, the cost of benefits burgeoned dramatically in the latter part of the 1970s as a result of Congress' action in 1972 in raising such benefits by 20 percent and tieing future benefits to the Cost-of-Living Index. As Table 18.1 indicates, although the number of awards actually declined by over 100,000 between 1974 and 1979, payments almost doubled from $6.9 billion to $13.7 billion during that five-year period.

This dramatic increase in costs led Congress in 1980 to enact legislation to deal with the situation. The new law increased the proportion of state-agency allowances of initial claims that were to be reviewed by the Social Security Administration. In addition, the legislation required state agencies to review at least every three years existing grants of benefits to be sure that people who were once found to be disabled were still unable to work.

Proposals by the Reagan Administration

When the Reagan administration took office in January 1981, it sought even more drastic changes in the disability insurance program. The president recommended to Congress that the period of disablement necessary to make one eligible for benefits be raised from 12 to 24 months, and that the period of employment required for eligility in the program also be lengthened. Congress refused to go along with these proposals. However, the battle was then waged on the administrative front as the Social Security Administration accelerated the more extensive review process begun during the Carter administration, concentrating particularly on continuing investigations of existing grants of benefits. As a result, the number of people removed annually from the disability rolls increased from some 34,000 in 1976 to 107,000 in 1981. (Table 18.1 also shows a major decline in the number of awards and the allowance rate of new applications in the period from 1977 through 1982.)

A storm of protest soon developed over the wholesale terminations of disability benefits. Critics charged that the

Table 18.1
Disability Insurance Applications, Awards, Allowance Rates, and Benefits (1969–1982)

Calendar Year	Number of Applications (thousands)	Number of Awards (thousands)	Allowance Rate (percent)	Amount Paid (millions)
1969	725.1	344.7	48	$ 2,542
1970	868.2	350.8	40	3,067
1971	924.4	415.9	45	3,758
1972	947.8	455.4	48	4,473
1973	1,066.9	491.6	46	5,718
1974	1,330.2	536.0	40	6,903
1975	1,267.2	592.0	47	8,414
1976	1,232.2	551.5	45	9,966
1977	1,235.2	569.0	46	11,463
1978	1,184.7	464.4	39	12,513
1979	1,222.6	408.7	33	13,708
1980	1,390.0	389.2	28	15,437
1981	1,234.8	345.3	28	17,200
1982	1,120.0	298.5	27	17,337

SOURCE: Anthony Champagne and Edward Harpham (eds.), *The Attack on the Welfare State* (Prospect Heights, Ill.: Wayland Press, Inc., 1984), Table 2, p. 47. Compiled from figures prepared by Social Security Administration, Office of Research and Statistics. Reprinted in U. S. Congress, House of Representatives, Committee on Ways and Means, *Background Material and Data on Major Programs Within the Jurisdiction of the Committee on Ways and Means*, 98th Cong., 1st sess. (February 8, 1983), pp. 43, 85.

Rally of disabled in Washington, D.C.

mentally impaired were particularly affected; many were forced out on to the streets and were without the ability to assert their right to appeal. Claims were also made that many of the terminations resulted from hasty decisions based on inadequate information, as well as a conservative political climate. In 1983, with the support of many Republicans, Congress passed legislation continuing disability payments during the termination proceedings, providing affected people with the opportunity to have face-to-face contact with those making the decisions on their benefits, and requiring that the results of continuing disability investigations be reported to Congress twice a year.

AID-TO-FAMILIES-WITH-DEPENDENT-CHILDREN

Background

By 1930, cash assistance to mothers with dependent children was provided by 45 states. When the Social Security Act was passed in 1935, the federal government assumed part of the responsibility for assisting needy children under a program known as Aid-To-Dependent-Children (ADC). Like cash assistance to the elderly poor and the blind, this was a welfare program, with individual states assuming a portion of the costs and making major decisions on the eligibility of recipients and the level of their benefits. However, unlike the program for the elderly poor and the blind, the ADC program subjected applicants to tests of moral fitness; moreover, recipients were considered by many as "undeserving" (they could work but preferred to live on welfare) recipients of the public "dole."

Some liberalization of the program did occur in the 1950s and early 1960s. The Social Security Act was amended in 1950 to allow coverage of not only dependent children but also their mothers or other adults with whom they were living. As a result, the name of the program was changed from Aid-to-Dependent-Children (ADC) to Aid-to-Families-with-Dependent-Children (AFDC). The Act was amended again in 1956 to require states to provide social services to families to assist them in planning the use of their finances. In 1962, funds were also made available to states to assist families with unemployed fathers (prior to that time, such fathers had to absent themselves from the home in order to allow their wives and children to qualify for benefits), but only half of the states took advantage of that provision in the federal law.

Rapid Growth in the Program

The 1960s brought great increases in the number of AFDC recipients and the costs of the program. In 1960, some 800,000 families received payments; by 1970 that number had grown to 2.6 million. Expenditures rose even more dramatically—from $1.1 billion in the former year to $4.9 billion in the latter. A number of factors contributed to the rapid growth in the AFDC program, including the migration of blacks and poor whites from the rural South to the urban North (many of whose states had more liberal programs than those in the South), civil-rights organizers who helped the poor to demand and receive payments, and the establishment of a "poverty" line by the Deprtment of Labor that allowed many previously ineligible persons to receive benefits.

This rapid growth in a traditionally unpopular program brought public demands for a reform of AFDC. In 1967, Congress passed the Work Incentive Program (later known as WIN), permitting states to require recipients to work in order to receive benefits, and allowing states to determine which people were employable and what jobs were suitable for them. The 1967 law also provided financial incentives to encourage members of AFDC families to work. Instead of deducting net earnings in excess of the allowable income limit set by states for AFDC recipients from their payments, the first $30 they earned each month plus one-third of the remainder of their earnings were excluded from calculations of payment.

The 1970s brought further attempts to change the AFDC program. President Nixon proposed replacing it altogether by substituting a federal Family Assistance Program (FAP) that would have taken the administrative and financial responsibility from the states and provided direct federal payments to all families with needy children. However, the Congress refused to adopt this bold new plan; in 1974 when it combined categorical assistance programs for the elderly poor, the blind, and the disabled into the federal Supplemental Security Program (SSI), Congress did *not* include AFDC, which was retained as a separate program administered primarily by the states. The Carter administration's attempt to replace AFDC with a Program for Better Jobs and Income (PBJI), similar to the Nixon FAP met a similar fate at the hands of Congress.

Proposals by the Reagan Administration

President Reagan came into office determined to reduce the scope and costs of the AFDC program. However, unlike the Nixon and Carter proposals, his changes met with success. Allowable family assets for eligible recipients have been reduced from $2,000 to $1,000 and all earnings above permissible state-income levels are now deducted from payments. States have also been given the option of counting food stamps and housing subsidies as a part of that state-income level. Coverage of 18–21-year-olds attending school is no longer allowed, and assistance for pregnant women does not begin until the sixth month of pregnancy.

These changes brought the intended

results. Federal funds for the program were cut by $1 billion in 1982 and another $1 billion the following year. Substantial further savings are projected for the future. However, as previously indicated in Chapter 3, President Reagan did not succeed in getting Congress to adopt his boldest proposal: to transfer the entire AFDC program back to the states.

Today the AFDC program serves a special clientele. Its major recipients are single-parent families headed by a female who has never been married or who is divorced or separated from her former husband.* The women are generally very poorly educated with limited job skills. Most of the families have one or two children, who typically are of preschool or elementary school age. Almost half of the recipients are black, and in recent years there has been an increase in Hispanic and Asian recipients. In 1982, 10.5 million people were receiving benefits totalling about $14 billion from federal and state governments.

HEALTH CARE

Background

What to do about the medical needs of our people has long been an issue in American politics. When the Social Security bill was originally proposed in 1935, there was some sentiment for including a health-insurance provision. However, opposition from the American Medical Association convinced President Roosevelt that including health insurance would jeopardize the rest of the bill, so that provision was left out of the bill. In 1949, President Harry Truman recommended that Congress pass a comprehensive federal health program. The AMA again moved into action to oppose the program. The organization assessed each of its members a $25 fee to finance a major lobbying campaign against the administration's health bill and hired a public-relations firm, Whitaker and Baxter, to orchestrate the effort. The AMA also participated in the 1950 congressional elections and claimed credit for defeating some of the major supporters of compulsory health insurance.

Defeated in efforts to provide health care for all Americans, the Truman administration proposed a more limited coverage for beneficiaries of Old Age and Survivors Insurance (OASI). A special Presidential Commission on Health Needs recommended in 1952 that Social Security contributions be used to finance the purchase of personal health benefits for the aged from private companies. However, even that proposal to restrict health-care protection to the elderly and to work through the private rather than the public sector drew opposition from the AMA, which viewed compulsory national health insurance as "a foot in the door" towards "socialized medicine." To counter the insurance approach, the AMA proposed a traditional welfare program operated through the states that would be restricted to those aged who were in actual financial need of assistance. Subsequently, the AMA approach won out when the Congress passed the Kerr–Mills Bill in the last year of the Eisenhower administration, providing for a limited state-run program for the elderly poor whose eligibility was determined by means tests that differed from one jurisdiction to another.

The Passage of Major Health-Care Legislation

The battle over health care continued

* Since the change in the Social Security law was made in 1939 to cover survivors and dependents of deceased workers, widows and their children receive retirement benefits under that program and do not normally qualify for AFDC assistance.

in the 1960s. President Kennedy's proposal for a health-insurance program for the aged to be financed through social-security taxes failed to pass the Congress despite the president's taking his case to the American people in a nationally televised broadcast. However, favorable developments during the Johnson administration, including an expanding economy and political support from a number of new liberal Democratic congressmen who came into office on the president's 1964 coattails finally resulted in the enactment of a comprehensive health-care program in 1965, some 30 years after the first proposals of the New Deal era.

The 1965 legislation passed by Congress incorporates both the insurance and the welfare approaches to health care. The first program, known as *Medicare,* provides hospital and nursing-home care for aged and disabled persons (since 1973 it also covers end-stage kidney disease), with the government paying for most of the cost of care for the first 100 days and the patient being responsible for a greater share of the cost of extended treatment. The program, known as Hospital Insurance (HI), is funded from payroll taxes, which like those for retirement and disability benefits, go into a special trust fund. In addition, people over 65 can voluntarily participate in a separate program known as Supplemental Medical Coverage (SMI), which pays for a portion of doctors' bills. SMI is financed through premiums paid by individuals to the federal government or on their behalf from general revenues.

In addition to these insurance programs, in 1965 Congress also enacted a *Medicaid* program. Based on need, it pays for acute and long-term care for AFDC recipients, the aged and disabled poor, and in some 30 states, the "medically indigent," people with low incomes who do not qualify for welfare but for whom special medical costs would cause an economic burden. This program, funded jointly by the federal and state governments, is administered by the states (Arizona, however, does not participate in it), which determine the level and conditions associated with the receipt of benefits.

Thus there are two distinct health-care programs operating in the United States. Medicare is an insurance program for all Americans regardless of their economic situation, most of whom are aged. Medicaid is a welfare program for the poor of all ages. Table 18.2 shows the differences in the people served by the two programs. Most of the 27 million people covered by Medicare in 1981 were above the poverty line and over 65 years of age. White recipients outnumbered blacks ones by almost a 10–1 margin, and people of Spanish origin by a 36–1 margin. In contrast, most of the 19 million Medicaid beneficiaries

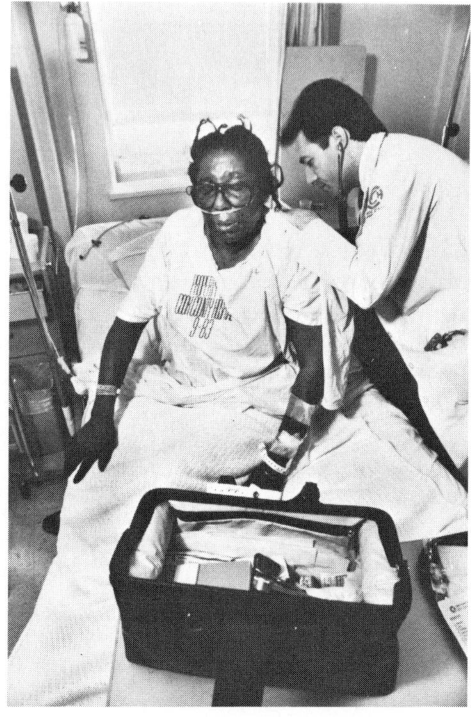

Doctor at Cook County Hospital, Chicago examines Medicare patient.

Table 18.2
Medicare and Medicaid—Selected Characteristics of People Covered in 1981 (In Thousands)

Poverty Status	Total	Male	Female	White	Black	Spanish Origin	Under 15 Yrs. Old	15–44 Yrs. Old	45–64 Yrs. Old	65 Yrs. and Over
Medicare										
People covered, total	27,308	11,433	15,775	24,324	2,511	679	*	723	2,213	24,271
Below poverty level	4,454	1,394	3,060	3,341	1,028	193	*	224	513	3,716
Above poverty level	22,754	10,039	12,715	20,983	1,483	486	*	499	1,700	20,555
Percent of total population	15.4	13.6	17.1	15.9	13.1	7.1	*	.7	5.0	96.3
Medicaid										
People covered, total	19,407	7,531	11,876	12,134	6,607	2,179	6,891	7,337	2,098	3,081
Below poverty level	11,687	4,352	7,335	6,432	4,827	1,507	4,927	4,308	1,178	1,274
Above poverty level	7,720	3,179	4,541	5,702	1,780	672	1,964	3,029	920	1,807
Percent of total population	8.6	6.9	10.1	6.2	24.7	16.9	13.5	6.9	4.8	12.2

* Not applicable.
SOURCE: U. S. Bureau of the Census.

were below the poverty line and included people of all ages, including some 7 million children under 15 years of age. In that program, whites outnumbered blacks by less than 2–1 and people of Spanish origin by less than 6–1.

Growth in Costs of Health Care

The enactment of both the Medicare and Medicaid programs resulted in major increases in government expenditures for health care. Several factors contributed to these increases. People covered by the two programs, primarily the aged and the poor, began to use medical facilities much more than when they had to pay their own medical expenses and could not afford care. Hospital and doctors' bills grew much faster than the overall rate of inflation; some of this growth was attributable to high costs associated with new expensive equipment and the increased utilization of various tests to determine causes of medical problems that are difficult to diagnose. In many instances, however, outright fraud was involved, with some doctors and laboratories submitting bills for services and tests that were not actually performed. The basic problem underlying all these developments was the fact that neither the consumers, nor the providers of health care, had to concern themselves with the costs associated with the rapid expansion of medical service, since such costs were simply passed on to the federal or state governments.*

The cumulative effect of these factors is reflected in the rapid growth of health-care expenditures in the United States in recent years. In 1967, Medicare payments for both the regular hospital and voluntary medical insurance plans totalled over $4 billion: by 1981, these costs had grown to over $43 billion. Meanwhile, in the same period,

* The same factor operated to increase costs associated with private health-insurance plans such as those provided by Blue Cross and Blue Shield.

Medicaid expenditures increased from $3 billion to over $27 billion. In the process, the total Medicare–Medicaid expenditures of over $70 billion a year became the nation's second most costly social program (only Social Security retirement benefits were greater.)*

By the early 1970s it had become apparent to public officials that something would have to be done to slow the rapid growth in health-care costs. In 1972, Congress authorized the establishment of Professional Standards Review Organizations (PSROs), groups of physicians charged with reviewing hospital stays for Medicare and Medicaid patients and empowered to disallow payments for unnecessary medical services. The same law granted Medicare administrators the right to limit hospital payments. Some states also required health-care officials to obtain approval before undertaking major investments in new hospitals and expensive equipment, thereby attempting to eliminate duplicate facilities. In 1974, Congress passed legislation mandating that all states require providers of health care to obtain a certificate of need for new investments and stating that payments provided under federal legislation would be denied if states failed to comply.

Attempts to curb medical expenditures continued in the Ford and Carter administrations. The former proposed placing limits on the rates of increase of reimbursement of Medicare expenses for both hospitals and doctors and charging patients 10 percent of hospitalization costs (with improved federal coverage of very large bills). Congress never seriously considered either proposal. President Carter asked Congress to limit the growth of hospital expenditures in general, including those made by the private sector. Intense lobbying by hospital and business interests, together with supposed voluntary efforts to contain hospital costs, resulted in a 1979 defeat for the proposed cost-containment legislation. By 1981, however, hospital expenditures were rising 8 percentage points faster than other prices.

Proposals of the Reagan Administration

President Reagan came into office determined to do something about skyrocketing health-care costs. In his first budget, he sought larger cutbacks in Medicaid than in Medicare expenditures. Ironically, the former—a welfare program for the poor—was not included in the administration's social "safety net," while the latter—an insurance program for the nonpoor as well as the poor—was a protected program and as such, was spared budget cuts.

The Reagan administration recommended a broad range of proposals designed to cut federal expenditures by transferring more of the costs to the states, to individuals receiving health-

"My policy covers a couple of aspirin, some Band Aids and a hot water bottle. It's called 'Minor Medical'."

* Total national health-care expenditures for all purposes and from all sources grew from $42 billion, (constituting 6 percent of the Gross National Product) in 1965 to $287 billion (some 10 percent of the GNP) in 1981.

care service, as well as to the providers of such services. A few of the recommendations were enacted into law by Congress.* These include reductions in the amount of federal matching funds provided to the states for the Medicaid program. Deductible hospital expenses were raised for all Medicare patients and insurance premiums were increased for those voluntarily participating in the Supplemental Medical Insurance (SMI) plan. The tax code was changed to eliminate the separate deduction for health-care insurance premiums; the cost of such premiums are now included with other medical and dental expenses, and the allowable deduction for such expenses raised from those exceeding 3 to those exceeding 5 percent of a taxpayer's adjusted gross income. In 1983 Congress passed legislation providing for a Prospective Payment Plan whereby hospitals and nursing homes are paid a flat Medicare fee (fixed in advance) for each of over 400 various types of illnesses (called diagnosis-related groups—DRG'S—) requiring hospital care. This approach is designed to encourage hospital officials to hold down costs by eliminating unnecessary tests and extended patient stays, problems that developed when they were permitted to bill retrospectively on the basis of actual costs incurred in individual cases. In 1984 Congress also passed legislation placing a temporary freeze (effective until October, 1985) on Medicare payments to physicians.

FOOD STAMPS

Background

As is true for most social programs in the United States, the one providing food stamps to the needy traces its roots back to the administration of Franklin D. Roosevelt. In 1939, a program was implemented whereby people could purchase some food stamps and in the process, receive others free of charge. The former could be used for any food purchases, while the latter could be utilized only for foods that were designated as surplus commodities by the Secretary of Agriculture. The program, which ended in 1943, established two important precedents: (1) food was not free but required the recipient to pay for a portion of its value; (2) the program benefited not only the needy recipients but the farmers who were able to dispose of surplus commodities and receive compensation.

In the two decades that followed, the Department of Agriculture distributed surplus commodities directly to the

* It will be recalled from Chapter 3 that in 1983 President Reagan proposed transferring the Medicaid program entirely to the federal government.

Distribution of surplus cheese in New Bedford, Massachussetts.

needy but they were limited to such basic ones as cornmeal, cheese, dried milk, and the like. In addition, the amounts distributed were large (usually a month's supply), which created problems for recipients who did not have adequate refrigeration. While helpful to some of the needy, this surplus commodities program failed to provide a balanced diet of safe food.

Sensitized to the problem of inadequate nutrition of the poor during his campaigning in 1960 in depressed areas of West Virginia, President Kennedy in his first executive order established a pilot food-stamp program in six states. The program was extended in 1962 to 18 additional states, with provision for further expansion through 1963. Areas were chosen that would test the workability of the food-stamp program in a variety of situations. (It is interesting to note, however, that not until March 1963 was a pilot project placed in a congressional district represented by a *Republican.*)

The food-stamp program developed in the executive branch during the Kennedy administration received legislative sanction in 1964 when Congress enacted a major food-stamp program as part of President Johnson's War on Poverty. The expanded program was set up on a community basis in 41 states and the District of Columbia that chose to terminate their participation in the established surplus-commodities-distribution program. States set the eligibility criteria, subject to approval by the Department of Agriculture, with recipients given the right to purchase stamps necessary to provide a low-cost, nutritionally adequate diet that was established by the Department of Agriculture. Alcoholic beverages, tobacco, and certain imported foods could not be purchased with food stamps.

The food-stamp program was continued—and in some instances, liberalized—by Republican administrations. In 1970, Congress adopted President Nixon's proposal that stamps be provided free for families of four whose income was less than $30 a month, and that families with income above that level who qualified for the program, not be required to spend more than 30 percent of their income for food stamps. The same legislation, however, required able-bodied adults who received benefits to register and accept available employment. A 1973 law required all counties that had not done so to switch from surplus food distribution to the food-stamp program. President Ford proposed that recipients pay a greater share of the cost of food stamps but Congress refused to go along; his attempts to tighten eligibility standards and increase costs to recipients through administrative requirements were blocked by the courts.

Responding to a General Accounting Office report that the government was losing half a billion dollars annually through fraud and error in the food-stamp program, President Carter proposed changes in the program. Congress adopted his recommendation for eliminating the purchase-of-food-stamp requirement for all participants in the program, who were to receive free coupons worth the cost of a "Thrifty Food Plan" (a revised version of the previous low-cost nutritionally adequate diet), minus 30 percent of the family's net income. In turn, the 1977 law tightened the eligibility requirements for recipients, especially for students and aliens. Despite such tightening, however, the costs of the food-stamp program ballooned, a consequence of high unemployment rates (which increased participation in the program) and rapid inflation that brought higher food prices (which increased the cost of allotments to recipients).

Table 18.3 shows how the food-stamp program grew over the period from its establishment until the end of the Carter administration. As indicated, there were some 600,000 participants in 1965; by 1980, it covered over 22 million people. Meanwhile, the cost of the federal program grew from $33 million to some $8.7 billion.

The Reagan administration was determined not only to reform the food-stamp program but to reduce its costs. Greater efforts were made to discover fraud in the administration of the program and states were made financially liable for losses of food stamps. Provisions were added to permit communities to require participants to work and be paid in food stamps at the minimum-wage rate. Eligibility requirements were tightened, and striking workers were excluded from eligibility unless they had been receiving stamps prior to going on strike. In 1982, for the first time in the history of the food-stamp program, the number of participants declined, in this case by almost one-million people.

Table 18.3
Federal Food Stamp Program (1965–1981)

			Value of Stamps Issued				
					Federal Government Contribution		
Year	Partici-pants (1,000)	Average monthly partici-pation (1,000)	Total coupon value (mil. dol.)	Cost to partici-pants (mil. dol.)	Total (mil. dol.)	Percent of total coupon value	Average monthly per par-ticipant
1965	633	425	85	53	33	38.0	$ 6.38
1970	6,457	4,340	1,090	540	550	50.4	10.55
1971	10,549	9,368	2,713	1,190	1,523	56.1	13.55
1972	11,594	11,109	3,309	1,512	1,797	54.3	13.48
1973	12,107	12,166	3,884	1,753	2,131	54.9	14.60
1974	13,524	12,862	4,727	2,009	2,718	57.5	17.61
1975	19,197	17,064	7,266	2,880	4,386	60.4	21.41
1976	17,982	18,549	8,700	3,373	5,327	61.2	23.93
1977	16,134	17,077	8,351	3,284	5,067	60.7	24.73
1978	16,000	15,248	8,280	3,141	5,139	62.0	24.73
1979	19,309	17,652	* 7,225	747	6,478		30.59
1980	21,989	20,077	* 8,686		8,686		34.35
1981	22,158	21,976	*10,633		10,633		39.99

* As of Jan. 1, 1979, participants were no longer required to pay for a portion of total coupon value.

SOURCE: U. S. Bureau of the Census; data from the Department of Agriculture.

Food protest in New York City.

ASSESSMENT

Since the 1930s our nation has been committed to the general proposition that all individuals are entitled to certain basic needs—food, shelter, health care, and the like—and that if they are unable to meet such needs themselves, the government has the responsibility to provide them. Thus, even Ronald Reagan—considered among recent political leaders to be the most antagonistic towards the "welfare state"—promised to create a "social safety net" of programs for the "truly needy."

However, rapid increases in costs associated with major social programs have caused public officials to take a hard look at such programs in order to determine what might be done to reduce, or at least slow, their growth and expense. As one analyzes their attempts to do so, it becomes clear that the social safety net under some of these programs is stronger than it is under others. Despite the fact that the Social Security retirement and Medicare programs are by far the most expensive, they have been left comparatively untouched by recent changes.

One possible reason for the solicitude of public officials for these particular programs is the fact that they are based on "insurance" rather than "welfare." Thus recipients are considered to be "entitled" to such benefits because they have "earned" them through their payroll deductions over the years. The fact of the matter, however, is that today most people who live any length of time draw far greater benefits than they contribute to the retirement system. The financial transfer that takes place in such programs is not one between the affluent and the "truly needy," but one between younger wage-earners and older retirees, both of whom come from all social classes.

A better explanation of the solicitude of public officials for the Social Security retirement and Medicare programs is the fact that they both have a common constituency: older Americans from all economic stations in life, together with their children and other relatives who do not want the financial burden of taking care of them. Any attempt to change in any significant way the major benefits of these two programs brings threats of political retaliation from that large and vocal constituency.

Other programs have also been spared major cuts. These include particularly those for the aged poor and the blind. Such groups clearly fit the category of people who most public officials and citizens agree suffer from special conditions. In the terms of the Reagan administration, they are the "truly needy."

This leaves other groups traditionally served by social programs that must be deemed to be "*untruly* needy" (if indeed such terms are not contradictory). Of late, this has included the temporarily disabled, families with dependent children, and many individuals who have been traditionally served by Medicaid and food-stamp programs. There is a great suspicion by many public officials, including President Reagan, that many such people are "undeserving" and do not belong on the public "dole." Particularly hard-hit by recent budget cuts have been individuals who are able to work but do not earn enough income to provide themselves or members of their families with a decent standard of living. Ironically, recent changes actually penalize the "working poor" by counting all their outside income in determining their eligibility for various types of social programs. Faced with the prospect of losing major benefits such as Medicaid or food stamps, it makes more economic sense for some individuals *not* to be employed, which is directly contrary to fostering a "work ethic."

There are also political realities behind the differential treatment of various social programs. Those that have been most affected in recent years lack the powerful constituencies possessed by the Social Security retirement and Medicare programs. There are far fewer people served by the affected welfare programs (as well as disabled persons receiving insurance benefits); in addition, these people lack the social and political skills and organization to make their influence felt in the public arena.

Few people would quarrel with the idea of removing the "undeserving" from public-assistance rolls. The problem is determining who these people are. The stricter one makes eligibility requirements, the more likely it is that the "undeserving" will not receive such benefits. On the other hand, such requirements also increase the possibility that the "truly needy" will be denied such benefits. Such a tradeoff raises a serious moral and political problem: if 500,000 "undeserving" people are eliminated from a social program but another 500,000 "deserving" persons are also eliminated in the process, is that a good policy decision in a democratic society? My personal view is that it is *not*.

SELECTED READINGS

Two excellent general studies treating basic issues in social programs are Martha Derthick, *Policymaking for Social Security* (Washington, D. C.: The Brookings Institution, 1979) and Gilbert Steiner, *The State of Welfare* (Washington, D. C.: The Brookings Institution, 1971). Chapters 5 and 6 in Charles Bullock, James Anderson, and David Brady, *Public Policy in The Eighties* (Monterey, California: Brooks/Cole Publishing Company, 1983) distinguish between welfare kinds of social programs and those for the "many," such as Social Security retirement benefits.

The best overall analysis of recent attempts to reform social programs in the United States is Anthony Champagne and Edward J. Harpham (eds.), *The Attack on the Welfare State* (Prospect Heights, Ill.: Waveland Press Inc., 1984). It is valuable not only for the breadth of its coverage but also for its excellent historical treatment of the various social programs and how recent reforms have sought to change them. A recent in-depth analysis of both Social Security retirement and health-care programs is *Social Security and Retirement: Private Goals, Public Policy* (Washington, D. C.: Congressional Quarterly Inc., 1983). Recent developments in the same programs are also analyzed in chapters by Alicia Munnell and Louise Russell in Joseph Pechman (ed.), *Setting National Priorities: The 1984 Budget* (Washington, D. C.: The Brookings Institution, 1983). Richard Nathan's chapter, "The Reagan Presidency in Domestic Affairs," which appears in Fred Greenstein (ed.), *The Reagan Presidency: An Early Assessment* (Baltimore: The Johns Hopkins University Press, 1983), also treats recent changes in social programs.

CHAPTER 19

Foreign and Military Policies

In April 1981, President Ronald Reagan announced that his administration intended to sell five advanced AWACS (Airborne Warning and Control System) aircraft and certain other aircraft and air-to-air missiles to Saudi Arabia. Formal notification was transmitted on October 1 to Congress, which under the terms of the Arms Export Control Act, had 30 days to disapprove, that is, veto the sale.* The Reagan administration cited a number of *advantages* to the sale: (1) it would help maintain our nation's access to Middle East oil (Saudi Arabia was the largest producer); (2) it would deter Soviet influence in the area; (3) it would enhance the security of nations friendly to the United States, including Israel; and (4) it would demonstrate our nation's resolve to protect the security of countries bordering the Persian Gulf. In testimony before the Senate Foreign Relations Committee, Secretary of State Alexander Haig warned that if Congress vetoed the sale, Saudi Arabia's confidence in our nation's ability to conduct a coherent, effective foreign policy would be diminished.

Israel, however, saw the situation quite differently. Prime Minister Menachem Begin informed our State Department that providing AWACS to Saudi Arabia would present a very serious threat to his nation's security. A number of arguments were advanced *against* the sale: (1) given the political instability of the region, the aircraft might fall into the hands of hostile governments; (2) Saudi Arabia's limited armed forces did not need sophisticated weapons such as the AWACS to protect that nation; (3) such weapons might add to the political instability of Saudi Arabia and encourage the type of internal

* It will be recalled from Chapter 12 that this form of legislative veto was later invalidated by the Supreme Court in *Immigration and Naturalization Service* v. *Chadha* (1983).

First AWACS aircraft takes off on test flight.

opposition that helped to topple the Shah of Iran; and (4) to counter the enhanced Saudi defense, Israel would have to increase its military spending and thereby damage its economy.

Both sides soon began to mount major lobbying efforts on the issue. Led by the American–Israeli Public Affairs Committee (AIPAC), the traditionally potent Israeli lobby launched a grassroots campaign to rally American public opinion against the sale and to direct that sentiment to members of Congress. Although it sought to block the sale altogether, the Israeli lobby had a fallback position that called for imposing major conditions and restrictions on the sale; it also called for a public pledge from President Reagan that the military superiority of Israel would be preserved.

While Israel was used to winning battles for the hearts and minds of the American people, it faced a formidable opponent this time. Several Arab governments retained former congressmen as lobbyists, such as Senator J. William Fulbright of Arkansas; Saudi Arabia was represented by Frederick Dutton, a State Department official during the Kennedy administration. The Arab lobby also launched a public relations and media campaign stressing the defensive nature of the AWACS and the role that a well-equipped Saudi military establishment could play in protecting the security of the Persian Gulf area. Aiding the Arab effort was a growing concern among many Americans that Israel was becoming too aggressive (it launched a preemptive strike against a nuclear installation in Iraq in the summer of 1981, and several weeks later intensively bombed Beirut, Lebanon), and that a moderate Arab state such as Saudi Arabia had a legitimate defensive need for the AWACS and other military equipment.

The political battle over the AWACS had different results in the House and the Senate. On October 14, 1981, the former body passed a resolution by a 301–111 vote disapproving the sale. The struggle then shifted to the Senate, since under the terms of the Arms Export Control Act *both* houses had to disapprove the sale in order to veto it. On October 15, the Senate Foreign Relations Committee voted 9–8 against the sale, but that same day the Senate Armed Services Committee approved the sale by a 10–5 vote. Before the issue reached the Senate floor for debate, however, the Reagan administration launched a concerted lobbying campaign to get it to approve the sale. The President promised to provide Israel with radar-jamming equipment that would supposedly prevent the AWACS from jeopardizing Israel's security; he pledged that following the provision of the AWACS, there would be no large-scale military build-up in the Persian Gulf area; and he lined up former presidents Nixon, Ford, and Carter, to endorse the AWACS sale. The administration's efforts were successful: seven new Republican senators were persuaded to come over to the President's side and the motion to disapprove the sale failed by a 48–52 vote. Thus, President Reagan ultimately was granted authority to provide 8.5 billion dollars worth of military equipment to Saudi Arabia.

This incident points up a number of factors in foreign and military policy-making in the United States today, such as an increased emphasis on the Middle East as an area of vital concern, the Reagan administration's reliance on a strong military establishment to protect the interests of the United States and its allies, conflicts between the President and many members of Congress over the conduct of our foreign and military policies, and the ways that domestic politics helps to shape the nature of those policies. Before exploring these matters, however, we need to analyze the essential nature of foreign policy and the role that military matters play in such a policy.

THE GENERAL NATURE OF FOREIGN POLICY

Foreign policy is frequently defined as the official acts of government taken in relation to other countries. Although such official *acts* constitute the essence of foreign policy, *anything* that affects our relationship with other nations bears on foreign policy. *Statements* as well as actions by government officials often influence how other countries view their intentions. In the 1950s and 1960s the United States often seemed to judge Communist China more by Mao Tse-tung's boasts of Chinese power than by his nation's relatively cautious policies—for example, the failure to invade Taiwan, which was (and is) still occupied by the Nationalist Chinese.

Although domestic and foreign policy are interrelated (consider the effect of the Vietnam War on the domestic programs of President Lyndon Johnson), the two take place within essentially different settings. The government responds in the one case to demands of groups that are active in internal politics and in the other to initiatives taken by other nations. At the same time, of course, the United States originates actions of its own in the international arena. The essential problem of governance in both foreign and domestic policy is the same: working out accommodations among competing interests. Almost entirely absent from the international arena, however, is the ultimate means available in domestic politics for controlling conflict: laws that can be enforced through the government's monopoly on the use of legitimate force. Although international law does exist, it is binding on nations only to the extent that they are willing to subject themselves to it. History demonstrates that when a nation's vital interests are at stake, it is seldom willing to do so. Political scientist Stanley Hoffmann has stressed the fact that while procedures for cooperation exist in both domestic and world politics, the "... permanent possibility of free and legitimate recourse to violence remains the mark of international relations." As evidence of the relative importance of violence in international affairs, consider that we typically link military and foreign policy but do not link police and domestic policy. In fact, foreign and military policy are so closely related that they are frequently referred to under the singular term, *national security policy.*

Like domestic policy, however, American foreign policy is broad in scope. The time has long passed when our foreign affairs were the concern of a relatively small number of professional diplomats who concentrated their efforts on major European powers and countries in this hemisphere; currently a wide range of people in many departments of the government, as well as private life, play a role in our relationships with over 150 nations around the globe.

Our foreign policy is pursued through a variety of means. *Political* channels include membership in international organizations like the United Nations, as well as the exchange of diplomatic representatives and the signing of bilateral agreements with individual nations. *Economic* aspects of foreign policy involve reciprocal trade agreements and financial assistance to other nations. The important *military* component to which reference has already been made is reflected in forming mutual defense alliances, sending arms to friendly nations, negotiating agreements such as the one banning the testing of nuclear weapons, and actually resorting to force, as in Korea and Vietnam. Of increasing importance is the *cultural* side of foreign policy as represented by broadcasts to foreign countries, overseas libraries, student-exchange programs, and goodwill tours of popular entertainers like the late Louis Armstrong. Together, these activities shape foreign policy, or what Arthur Schlesinger Jr. calls the ". . . face a nation wears to the world."

This range of activities involves various individuals and groups both inside and outside the government. The following section discusses the major participants in foreign and military policy and their comparative importance.

THE POLICY-MAKING PROCESS

The President

Harry Truman once told a group of Jewish War Veterans that he "made" American foreign policy. Although this statement is a bit exaggerated, it is fair to say that the chief executive dominates foreign policy in a way that he does not dominate domestic policy. As political scientist Aaron Wildavsky puts it, we have one president but "two presidencies," one for domestic affairs and the other for foreign and military affairs.

The great influence of the chief executive in foreign affairs stems in part from certain broad legal powers. He has a number of constitutional prerogatives that enable him to play the role of the nation's *chief diplomat.* He can, for example, negotiate agreements with foreign countries, either by a formal treaty—for which he must receive Senate approval by a two-thirds vote (and usually does)*—or by an **executive agreement,** a written or oral agreement with a foreign head of state that does not require Senate approval. Of the latter, some he negotiates under legislative authority (for instance, reciprocal trade agreements adjusting tariffs within limits set by Congress), and some he can exercise entirely on his own (for a notable example, the Yalta agreements Franklin Roosevelt entered into in 1945 with the Soviet Union affecting developments in Central Europe and the Far

* The Senate has turned down or refused to act on only about 10 percent of the treaties negotiated over the years. It can, however, indirectly defeat a treaty through attaching reservations to it that are unacceptable to the chief executive or foreign country involved. President Wilson's opponents used this technique to defeat the Treaty of Versailles.

Churchill, Roosevelt and Stalin at Yalta.

East). The president can also terminate a treaty without the consent of the Senate, as Jimmy Carter did with respect to the 1954 Mutual Defense Treaty with Taiwan.

Aside from his agreement-making authority, the president determines formal diplomatic relationships with other nations. He has the prerogative to recognize foreign countries diplomatically. When rival groups purport to represent a nation, the president's decision regarding the diplomats he receives determines which government we regard as the legitimate one. (Not until 1979 did the United States recognize the government of mainland China, a recognition granted by President Carter.) The chief executive can also break off relationships with a nation by asking that its representatives be withdrawn as President Wilson did a few weeks before the declaration of war against Germany in 1917. When President Carter granted diplomatic recognition to mainland China, he also withdrew it from Taiwan, effective one year later.

The president also chooses and can dismiss as well the major officials involved in the making of foreign policy. Although he must seek Senate approval for his nominees for cabinet positions, such as the Secretary of State, and diplomatic representatives abroad, he is seldom turned down.* Moreover, the chief

* In 1981, however, the Senate Foreign Relations Committee recommended *against* the nomination of Ernest Lefever for Assistant Secretary of State for Human Rights and Humanitarian Affairs (the first time since 1925 that the Committee had turned down a presidential nomination). Lefever decided to withdraw his nomination rather than face a floor fight on the issue.

Senior Deputy Prime Minister Deng and President Carter sign accord.

Sadat, Begin and Carter celebrate the signing of the Camp David agreement.

executive can avoid this possibility altogether by appointing personal envoys to conduct diplomatic activities. Thus, Franklin Roosevelt used Harry Hopkins to handle delicate matters with our allies in World War II, although the latter held no official diplomatic post in FDR's administration.

Finally, the president can employ **"personal" diplomacy.** Woodrow Wilson, for example, attended the Paris Peace Conference as the head of the United States delegation. Richard Nixon's dramatic visits to China and the Soviet Union, and Jimmy Carter's efforts on behalf of a peace treaty between Egypt and Israel, are other examples of personal diplomacy, a technique generally employed by presidents since World War I.

If anything, the powers that the president exercises over *military matters* are even more awesome than those that he wields over diplomacy. Many chief executives have claimed the authority to send American troops anywhere in the world, including into actual combat. Recent major commitments of American troops to battle were made by executive action alone, for example, President Truman's decision to order American forces into Korea in 1950, along with presidential actions with respect to Vietnam. These fairly recent examples have many precedents. According to some counts American troops have been involved in military action overseas on more than 150 occasions, but Congress has declared war on only five occasions: the War of 1812, the Mexican War, the Spanish–American War, and World Wars I and II.

As commander-in-chief of the armed forces, the chief executive possesses major powers that enable him to dominate military policy. He chooses, with Senate approval, the major functionaries, both civilian and military, such as the Secretary of Defense, the Joint Chiefs of Staff, and other high-ranking officials. He can also remove them. Thus, Abraham Lincoln went through a series of commanders of the Northern forces in the Civil War until he found a man to his liking, Ulysses S. Grant. President Truman eventually decided to relieve General Douglas MacArthur from his command in Korea when the general persisted in publicly advocating policies (such as bombing China) that Truman did not favor. President Carter relieved Army Major General John Singlaub from his command in South Korea for suggesting that Carter's plan to withdraw American troops from that country would lead to war.

The Truman–MacArthur incident points up another prerogative of the president as commander-in-chief: determining major *strategic decisions* governing the conduct of hostilities. Truman decided to fight a "limited" war in Korea because he was concerned about drawing the Soviet Union into the war on the side of mainland China (the two at that time were partners in a defense pact) and because he did not want to involve the United States in an all-out war in Asia at a time when it had major military commitments in Europe. Franklin Roosevelt also made a number of strategic decisions that affected how World War II was fought, including giving the war in Europe initial priority over the one in Asia. President Carter made a major strategic decision to give priority to nuclear attacks on military targets in the Soviet Union rather than cities and industrial complexes.

Basic decisions involving *weapons* are also up to the president. Thus, Truman proceeded with Roosevelt's initial commitment to the development of the atomic bomb and then made the awesome decision to use it against the Japanese in the closing days of World War II. He also decided later to go ahead with the manufacture of the hydrogen bomb, even though some of his advisers opposed this course of action. President Carter proceeded with the development of the MX missile system; on the other hand, he terminated the B-l bomber. President Reagan, in turn, revived the production of the B-1 bomber and decided to change the basing mode of the MX from rotation from one site to another (a plan designed to hide its location), to a stationary site (a far less complex and expensive system but one presumably more vulnerable to Soviet attack).

As commander-in-chief, the president even has the authority to make *tactical military decisions*. Although they generally leave such matters to professional officers, chief executives have been known to enter into the details of military operations. At the time of the Cuban missile crisis in 1962, President Kennedy insisted on planning the position of American ships off Cuba. Lyndon Johnson not only decided to bomb North Vietnam in 1965 but also chose the targets. Richard Nixon determined that the harbors of key ports of North Vietnam should be mined and ordered the resumption of bombing at Christmas in 1972 after peace negotiations appeared to be breaking down.

In the final analysis, the president has great influence over the most basic decisions regarding foreign and military policies. When he assumed office, President Reagan decided not to continue President Carter's policy of *limiting* nuclear arms as reflected in the Strategic Arms Limitation Talks (SALT). Instead, Reagan pursued a policy of *reducing* arms that both sides already had in their arsenals as reflected in his call for Strategic Arms Reduction Talks (START) with the Soviet Union. President Reagan also recommended a rapid military build-up that would increase defense spending by 50 percent (in constant dollars) within a five-year period; the program called for military spending of

Andre Gromyko and President Reagan leave White House after conference.

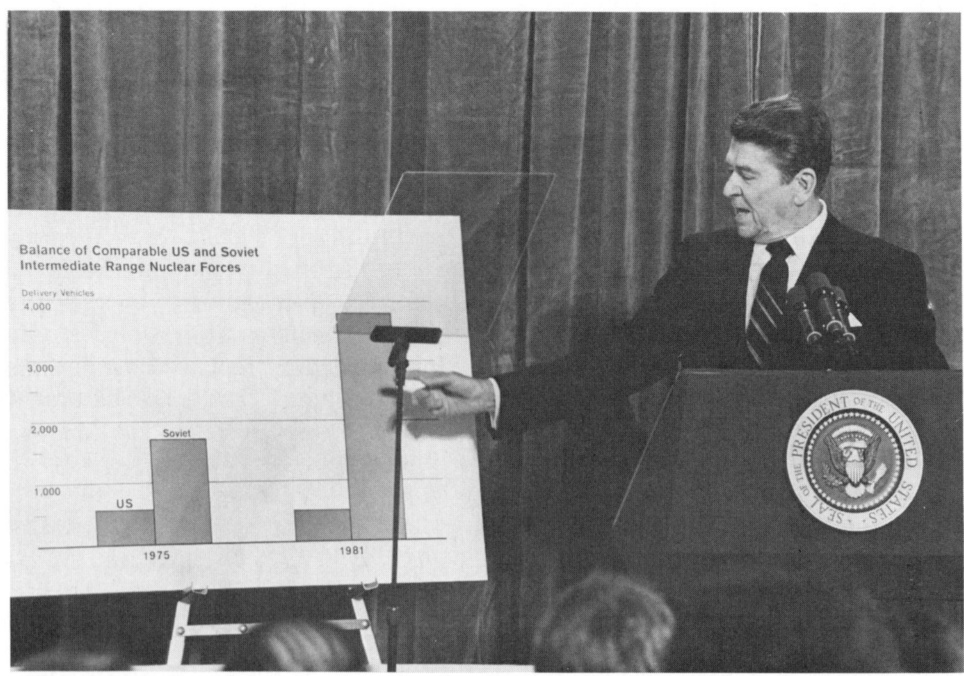

President Reagan explains U.S.-Soviet nuclear situation.

$1.6 trillion in fiscal years 1983 through 1987, which would raise the defense budget to more than $365 billion annually by the latter year. Both decisions have had a major impact on American foreign and military policies: to date (mid-1984), we have been unable to convince the Soviets to continue participating in the START negotiations, and our defense expenditures rose from $160 billion in fiscal 1981 (the last year of the Carter administration) to $247 billion in fiscal 1984.

Thus, the president has a wide range of powers affecting foreign and military affairs that he can exercise in the manner contemplated by Hamilton in the Federalist papers—with "... decision, activity, secrecy and despatch." His preeminence in these areas of public policy stems both from the breadth of his prerogatives and his ability to take decisive initiatives that others find it difficult to counter or reverse. Although the Congress has the power to refuse to appropriate funds for military ventures such as those in Korea and Vietnam, it is reluctant to exercise this authority when the lives of Americans fighting there depend on supplies and equipment. Another advantage that the president enjoys over Congress (and over other participants in foreign policy-making) is superior information about international developments that the executive-branch members located here and abroad provide him.

Major Executive-Branch Personnel

The wealth of resources available to the president in foreign affairs is reflected in the size of the two major departments involved: Defense and State. As of March 1984, the former had over 1 million *civilian* employees, the latter just under 25,000. In addition, other departments, such as Treasury, Commerce, Labor, and Agriculture, have people assigned to international affairs.

The three top presidential advisers in

foreign affairs are the Secretary of State, the Secretary of Defense, and a member of the White House staff, currently designated as the Assistant to the President for National Security Affairs. (At times, a single individual may hold two positions simultaneously: from 1973 to 1975 Henry Kissinger served as Assistant to the President for National Security Affairs and Secretary of State.)

The first official is expected to bring a political perspective for foreign policy, the second offers a military view, and the third presumably takes both these interests into account in counseling the chief executive. Of course, the division between the Secretaries of State and Defense is by no means complete: each is expected to appreciate the perspective of the other. At times, persons holding these positions have appeared to reverse roles. Secretary of State Dean Rusk was considered by many observers to have adopted an essentially military stance towards the problems of the Vietnam war, while Secretary of Defense Robert McNamara (particularly towards the end of his term) and his successor, Clark Clifford, were supposedly convinced that the conflict there was essentially political and could not be won on the military battlefield.*

The relative influence that each of these three exercises in foreign policymaking depends on the relationship he enjoys with the president. Dwight Eisenhower had great admiration for and confidence in Secretary of State John Foster Dulles and gave him broad discretion in handling a variety of matters: conducting high-level negotiations with foreign leaders, representing the American position on issues before the United Nations, and the like.

The importance of Dulles in the Eisenhower administration is contrasted with the part assigned to the Secretary of State in the administration of John Kennedy and during Richard Nixon's first term. Kennedy chose Dean Rusk, a low-key figure from a private foundation with no political support of consequence, and so limited Rusk's role in foreign affairs that the chief executive, in effect, became his own Secretary of

* This assessment is by no means unanimous: some analysts believe that it was Rusk, rather than Clifford, who convinced Lyndon Johnson to stop the bombing of the North in the spring of 1968.

Henry Kissinger.

The Weather

Today—Variable cloudiness, windy, chance of precipitation near zero through tonight; high from 45 to 50, low in the 20s. Wednesday — Fair, colder. Temperature range: Today, 25-50; Yesterday, 20-45. Details C5.

The Washington Post

Times Herald

Index — 60 Pages, 4 Sections

Amusements	B 6	Metro	C 1
Classified	C 7	Obituaries	C 6
Comics	B 8	Outdoors	D 7
Crossword	B 4	Sports	D 1
Editorials	A16	Style	B 1
Financial	D 8	TV-Radio	B 5

95th Year No. 79 © 1972, The Washington Post Co. TUESDAY, FEBRUARY 22, 1972 Phone 223-6000 Circulation 223-6100 Classified 223-6200 15c Beyond Washington, Maryland and Virginia 10c

President Nixon meets with Chinese Communist Party Chairman Mao Tse-tung. Others, from left, are Premier Chou En-lai, interpreter Tang Weng-shen and Presidential adviser Henry Kissinger.

Nixon Sees Mao, Chou in Day of Cordiality

State. Richard Nixon followed a similar course of action by initially appointing William Rogers, a close personal friend with very limited experience in foreign affairs. Secretary Rogers seems not to have been briefed ahead of time on the Cambodian invasion and to have played no role in helping to work out the arrangements for the most dramatic diplomatic event of the Nixon administration: the President's announcement of his trip to Communist China.

The man who did play a major part in both of these decisions was Henry Kissinger, who served initially only as Assistant to President Nixon for National Security Affairs. The fact that McGeorge Bundy, who held that same post under Kennedy (as well as under Johnson for a period), and Zbigniew Brzezinski under Carter, were also important figures suggests that some presidents (especially those who want to take a major leadership role themselves) want the advice of strong persons who are knowledgeable about foreign affairs. At the same time, there are advantages in having such advisers on the White House staff, where they can be controlled and where they are also generally free from questioning by congressional committees and members of the press that might lead to disclosures of vital information.*

The role of the Secretary of Defense in foreign policy also varies with the incumbent and his relationship with the president. Robert McNamara, a highly competent, forceful figure who advised both Kennedy and Johnson, had a major impact on policies during his six years in office. In contrast, of the three secretaries who served in that post in the eight years of the Eisenhower administration (Charles Wilson, Neil McElroy, and Thomas Gates), only the

* When Kissinger eventually was nominated as Secretary of State, some senators expressed concern that he would use his other position as Assistant to the President for National Security Affairs to shield himself from the questioning that a departmental secretary would have to face.

National Security Advisor Zbigniew Brezinski confers with President Carter.

first appears to have had much say in major foreign-policy decisions. President Nixon also appeared to pay relatively little attention to the advice of James Schlesinger compared to Kissinger. President Ford followed the same practice until he ultimately removed Schlesinger from office because of his inability to get along with Kissinger. On the other hand, Harold Brown and Caspar Weinberger were major figures in the Carter and Reagan administrations, respectively.

Although the Secretaries of Defense and State and the president's Assistant for National Security Affairs are generally the key figures in foreign policy-making,* the chief executive depends on other top-ranking officials for advice and recommendations. He may, for example, look to other members of the White House staff for general advice as President Reagan did to Edwin Meese or for assistance in special areas of concern as Kennedy did to Arthur Schlesinger Jr. on Latin-American affairs. The president may also seek the counsel of second- or third-level officials in executive departments. Thus, Franklin Roosevelt completely bypassed his Secretary of State, Cordell Hull, and dealt with Under-Secretary of State Sumner Welles on a range of foreign-policy issues. Assistant Secretaries of State with expertise in a certain region (Europe, Africa, East Asia and the Pacific, and so on) and the director assigned to a specific country are also important sources that chief executives can tap for information and advice. Thus, John Kennedy placed great faith in the counsel of G. Mennen Williams, Assistant Secretary of State for African Affairs.

As a result of experiences in World War II, a number of official organizations have been created through statute (primarily by the National Security Act of 1947) to assist the president in foreign and military affairs. One is the National Security Council (composed of the President, the Vice-President, and the Secretaries of State and Defense), which operates as a kind of miniature cabinet to advise the president on the integration of domestic, foreign, and military policies relating to national security. But like the larger cabinet, it operates at the sufferance of the president. Truman and Eisenhower convened it regularly, whereas Kennedy preferred to utilize ad hoc groups such as the one he assembled at the time of the Cuban missile crisis, and Johnson met regularly with the "Tuesday Lunch" group (composed of top foreign and military advisers but also his press secretary and *not* the vice-president) to advise him particularly on the Vietnam War. Even if a president presents a problem to the NSC, he need not accept its recommendations: Eisenhower declined to do so when that body recommended intervention in Indochina in 1954 on the side of the French against the Vietnamese forces.

Reporting to the NSC is another body of considerable significance in foreign and military policy: the Central Intelligence Agency. Developed from the Office of Strategic Services (OSS) during World War II, in 1947 this agency was entrusted with coordinating the intelligence work (gathering and interpreting information about other nations) carried on by units operating under the Army, Navy, Air Force, and State Department. The CIA was also given a monopoly on espionage and other covert activities undertaken in foreign countries. Over the years, the agency has reportedly undertaken a

* Frequently, there are rivalries between these officials; President Carter's Secretary of State Cyrus Vance and his National Security Adviser, Brzezinski, differed over the general approach we should take to relations with the Soviet Union; President Reagan's Secretary of State George Shultz and his Secretary of Defense, Weinberger, disagreed over the role our troops should play in the Middle East.

Cyrus Vance.

Casper Weinberger.

George Schultz.

wide variety of activities, including successful ventures—such as helping rebels to overthrow the leftist Arbenz government in Guatemala in 1954—and fiascos, such as training Cuban exiles to invade their island in 1961 at the Bay of Pigs, where they were slaughtered by Castro's forces. Despite the imposing nature of the CIA (its exact budget is secret) and the scope of its operations (it has sometimes had closer diplomatic relations with foreign governments than the State Department), like all agencies in the executive branch its influence ultimately depends on the president. After the CIA mistakenly assured Kennedy that if we helped the Cuban exiles invade the island there would be internal uprisings against Castro, the President had all overseas operations placed under the ambassadors concerned. He also ordered the entire range of intelligence activities to be re-examined by a special board and asked the director of the CIA, Allen Dulles, to resign. The CIA ran into difficulties again in the 1970s for its alleged role in helping to overthrow the Marxist government of President Allende of Chile and for spying on Vietnam War protesters; as a result, director William Colby was forced to resign. On the other hand, President Carter granted the director of the agency, Stansfield Turner, unprecedented authority over all intelligence agencies of the federal government.*

The president's major professional military advisers are the Joint Chiefs of Staff. Created by Franklin Roosevelt in World War II and placed on a permanent statutory basis by the National Security Act of 1947, the Joint Chiefs presently include a chairman and the military chiefs of the three services (Army, Navy, and Air Force). Their expertise puts them in a position to exercise a major influence on military policy. Like other executive agencies, however, they are under the president's control. Almost as soon as he took office, Dwight Eisenhower inaugurated a "new look" in military policy, which emphasized nuclear "massive retaliation" (as provided by the Air Force) over conventional warfare (as favored by the Army). The president, who placed great stress on obtaining unanimous recommendations from the Joint Chiefs, maneuvered the then-Army chief-of-staff, Matthew Ridgeway (who naturally opposed the new policy), into appearing publicly to endorse it. President Kennedy also used his power effectively over the Joint Chiefs. Angered by the bad advice he got from them on the Bay of Pigs operation, the chief executive replaced the chairman, General Lyman Lemnitzer, with a military man more to his liking—General Maxwell Taylor.

These, then, are the major agencies of the executive branch that are involved in foreign and military policy.† Of course, as we have already noted, others such as the Department of Commerce, Agriculture, and Labor, which are primarily concerned with domestic matters, engage in some activities relating to foreign affairs. Moreover, those agencies concerned with the financial and budgetary control of government operations (such as the Treasury and the Office of Management and Budget) play a role in establishing limits on, as well as the direction of, the activities undertaken in international affairs. Both these agencies, for example, had

* While public attention is focused on the CIA, far more personnel involved in intelligence operations are attached to the Department of Defense; in addition, both the State and Treasury departments conduct important foreign intelligence activities.

† Other units that play a part in the day-to-day operation of our foreign policy include the Foreign Service, the U. S. International Development Cooperation Agency, the Arms Control and Disarmament Agency, and the U. S. Information Agency.

an important part in developing and implementing the "new-look" military policy of the Eisenhower administration based on our nuclear power, which was designed to produce "more bang for the buck" than conventional weaponry.

Congress

Congress has traditionally had much less influence in foreign and military affairs than in domestic matters. As we have seen, concern for the attributes of ". . .decision, activity, secrecy and despatch. . ." prompted the Founders to grant the president, rather than Congress, the more important constitutional powers in the field of national security. For example, he can officially recognize a foreign government diplomatically; Congress can only pass resolutions in favor or opposition. Even where the national legislators do have prerogatives, they are often placed in a position of having to react to presidential initiatives. He officially negotiates the treaties and makes the diplomatic and military appointments that senators must then consider. Although Congress alone has the formal power to declare war, the president can render that power almost meaningless by committing troops to battle on his own, as was done in both Korea and Vietnam.

In the period from the end of World War II until the late 1960s, Congress was not disposed to use its traditional powers effectively in dealing with matters of national security. While it exercised its power-of-the-purse prerogative vigorously in cutting domestic programs proposed by the president, for much of the post-World-War-II period it gave the chief executive all he requested in the way of military funds—usually more, in fact. Major conflicts between Congress and the president in the 1950s and most of the 1960s occurred because the legislators wanted to spend more money and maintain higher levels of military force than the president did. While this situation began to change, especially in the Senate, in the late 1960s, the House (which traditionally is more tightfisted with money than the upper chamber) was more reluctant to use its power of the purse to reduce military expenditures or even to alter the conduct of the war in Vietnam.

Nor has the congressional power of investigation traditionally been as potent in foreign and military affairs as in domestic policy. Such investigations suffer because they often occur considerably after major executive actions have taken place. The inquiry into the events at Pearl Harbor in 1941 took place five years later after the war was over.

Studies point up the inferior part that the legislative branch played in foreign and military affairs in the postwar period compared to the executive. Aaron Wildavsky's analysis of congressional voting on executive proposals from 1948 through 1964 indicates that, excluding refugee and immigration bills, presidents prevailed about 70 percent of the time on defense and foreign policy, compared to 40 percent in the domestic sphere. Similarly, James Robinson's study of foreign and military policy issues from the late 1930s to the early 1960s showed that the executive rather than the Congress had more to do with almost all the major decisions reached during that period. Congress was a very junior partner to the executive in the making of foreign and military policy during that period.

As the Vietnam War began to wind down in the late 1960s and early 1970s, Congress reasserted itself in the field of foreign and military policy. This reassertion became even more pronounced after the war was over. In the process, Congress influenced our nation's role in international affairs by exercising the traditional powers that it had permitted to atrophy in the immediate post-World-War-II period.

The *power of the purse* became a major

instrument by which Congress affected our foreign and military policy. In the early 1970s, Congress significantly cut presidential requests for military expenditures rather than adding to them as it had done in the preceding period. The national legislators also refused to go along with presidential wishes for particular military ventures. In 1973 they barred all past and future appropriations from being used to carry on military activities in or over Cambodia and Laos; in 1976 they also refused to grant President Ford's plea for financial assistance to anticommunist forces engaged in a civil war in Angola. Congress also refused Ford's request for additional military aid to Cambodia and South Vietnam when the two countries were on the brink of collapse, and for a while Congress cut off aid to Turkey in retaliation for that country's invasion of Cyprus in a dispute with the Greek residents of that island.

Congress also used its power over the purse to force the executive branch to *inform and consult* with national legislators on major foreign and military issues. It passed a provision of an appropriation bill that stated that no American troops should be withdrawn from South Korea without consultation with Congress. The national legislators also used their authority over foreign aid to require the State Department to issue an annual report on the human-rights record of over 100 countries, with the understanding that assistance levels for individual countries would reflect how well or how poorly they treated their citizens.

This same concern of Congress with being informed and consulted on major foreign and military matters was also reflected in the area of *international agreements.* In 1969 the Senate passed a sense-of-the-body resolution (without the binding force of law) that no future commitments be made without the approval of Congress; in 1972 both houses enacted legislation requiring the executive to submit to Congress all international agreements (executive agreements as well as treaties) within 60 days of their execution. National legislators have also recently played a much greater role in the formulation of treaties. Almost half of the senators visited and talked to General Torrejos and other Panamanian officials in connection with the Senate's approval of the Panama Canal Treaty. Moreover, the treaty that was ultimately approved contained important "conditions" attached by the Senate providing for the future rights of the United States, particularly the right of defending the canal's neutrality and securing for our ships priority of passage in time of emergency.

In the 1970s, Congress also reasserted its traditional *war powers.* In 1970 it repealed the Gulf of Tonkin Resolution of 1964, which granted the president broad authority to undertake actions to deal with threatened enemy aggression in Vietnam, and which the administration asserted was the "functional equivalent" of a declaration of war. Then in 1973 Congress passed over President Nixon's veto of the War Powers Act. This legislation requires that before introducing our armed forces into actual or imminent hostilities the president has to *consult* with Congress ". . . in every possible instance . . ."; in any event, he is to *report* to Congress within 48 hours of actually committing such forces. Moreover, unless Congress approves the president's actions, the forces must be withdrawn within 60 days (30 additional days if they are in danger); Congress can also terminate the commitment of our forces prior to the 60-day deadline through the passage of a concurrent resolution (not subject to a presidential veto).*

Finally, in the 1970s, Congress began to exercise its powers of *investigation* and **oversight** over foreign and military affairs. After major investigations into the

Signing of Panama Canal Treaty.

activities of our intelligence agencies, both houses created permanent committees to oversee their activities. Legislation was also passed requiring covert actions (secret activities designed to influence and sometimes to subvert or overthrow foreign governments) conducted by or on behalf of the CIA to be reported in "timely fashion" to appropriate committees of Congress. The national legislators have also provided for supervision of arms sales and the export of nuclear materials to other countries.

The Reagan administration obtained some major presidential successes in influencing Congress on foreign and military policies. On the recommendation of the President, the lawmakers did substantially increase defense expenditures. As indicated at the beginning of the chapter, the Senate also approved the sale of AWACS to Saudi Arabia. Congress ultimately supported the development of the B-1 bomber and the MX missile, and provided economic and military aid to El Salvador. Finally, acting under the terms of the War Powers Act, both houses passed a resolution signed by the President on October 12, 1983, granting for a period of 18 months (until April 12, 1985) the authority for our armed forces to participate in a multinational force designed to help keep the peace in Lebanon. (On February 7, 1984, President Reagan withdrew the troops to ships offshore after American casualties included 264 deaths and 134 wounded.)

However, the Congress was by no means a rubber stamp for the Reagan administration on foreign and military policy matters. It did not give the President all he wanted for military expenditures: in 1982, the lawmakers reduced the President's defense budget by $17.6 billion—the largest cut in recent memory. The same was true of the aid for El Salvador, which did not reach the level proposed by the Reagan administration. Moreover, committees in the House and Senate investigated foreign-policy activities carried out by executive officials in

U.S. "peace keeping" forces in Lebanon.

El Salvador and intelligence operations against the Marxist government of Nicaragua. Congress was also reluctant to go along with the administration's request to provide assistance to forces opposing the Nicaraguan regime (called the Contras). Lawmakers also tried to get the President to renew the effort to get an arms-control agreement with the Soviet Union, and in May 1983 the House passed a resolution calling for a nuclear freeze. (However, it contained a provision suspending the freeze if progress was not made in achieving arms-control between the United States and the Soviet Union by a specified date.) Thus, Congress in the early 1980s occupied an intermediate position on foreign and military policies: it was not as assertive in dealing with the executive branch as it was in the 1970s, but it did not return to the subservient position it assumed in the postwar period.

The Courts

If Congress has traditionally been a junior partner to the executive in foreign and military policy, the Supreme Court for all practical purposes has not been a member of the firm at all. Throughout American history the Court has declined to intervene in international affairs on the grounds that they constitute "political" matters that are better left to the popular branches of government. Judges are also reluctant to substitute their judgment for that of the president on foreign and military affairs because they do not have the same sources of information and expertise on such matters. Thus, a number of legal challenges were lodged against actions taken by public officials during the Vietnamese hostilities on the grounds that Congress had not officially declared war, but none of these challenges was ever heard by the Supreme Court.*

* The Court in a 1952 decision, *Youngstown Sheet and Tube Company* v. *Sawyer,* did invalidate President Truman's seizure of the steel industry (where a strike was, in the President's judgment, imperiling our situation in Korea), but that action occurred after a cease-fire had been declared. The Court also heard cases involving military matters after the conclusion of the Civil War and World War II. Thus, judges are inclined to intervene in such matters only after military crises are past.

Popular Control

Generally speaking, Americans are not as well informed about foreign-policy issues as domestic concerns. (As one close student of the subject, Bernard Cohen, suggests, most of the time the real problem is finding more than a handful of people who know what the foreign-policy issues *are*—much less what they are *about.*) For one thing, such issues usually have less *immediacy* for them. If the president recommends a tax increase or cut, the average citizen can appreciate the impact that the policy has on his or her own life. It is much less clear how he or she is affected by a change in the government of El Salvador. Moreover, a great deal of *secrecy* necessarily surrounds our relationships with other countries, and thus the public is not privy to information that would enable it to make informed judgments about international developments. Furthermore, foreign and military affairs are often so *complex* and *technical* that the average citizen would have trouble comprehending them, even if he had the necessary information.

To compound the problem for the average citizen, the ordinary reference groups that help to guide his opinions on domestic concerns are not as meaningful for foreign-policy issues. A person who is not conversant with the advantages and disadvantages of a national health insurance program, for example, may get some clues from how business or labor leaders feel about it. His party affiliation, too, may help him make up his mind on the matter if one candidate favors the plan and another opposes it. However, because different social and economic groups, as well as political parties and candidates, have been less likely in recent years to be lined up on one side or the other on foreign and military concerns, helpful clues are missing.

Lacking guidelines to judge foreign-policy matters, most Americans in the period after World War II adopted a rather permissive attitude toward the actions that our government took in international affairs. When presidents involved the nation in the world's problems (as all of them did since World War II), the public was generally willing to support their efforts. As previously suggested, in time of crisis Americans "rally round the flag" (and thus their leader), as evidenced by the increased ratings President Kennedy received in public-opinion polls even at the time of the Bay of Pigs fiasco and those that President Carter got after the failure of the hostage rescue mission in Iran. The same reaction occurred when President Truman first sent American troops into Korea in 1950 and President Johnson extended commitments in Vietnam in 1965.

At the same time, however, public support for particular military ventures (as contrasted to a general policy of involvement in world affairs) erodes when they run into difficulties. As John Mueller has pointed out, after the Chinese entered the Korean war in late 1950 and our casualties began to mount and hopes for a short war were dashed, support for the war dropped significantly. The same thing began to occur (though at a slower rate) in Vietnam in mid-1966 after the Buddhist crisis, increased casualties, and a public perception developed that we were in for a long, bloody war. Moreover, public disenchantment with this war continued even after casualties declined: in May 1971 a Gallup poll showed that 61 percent of the public thought that we had made a mistake in sending our troops to Vietnam.

While public opinion is thus slow to react to international affairs (as political scientist Gabriel Almond suggests, public attitudes on such matters reflect a "mood" that is general and emotional rather than specific and rational), once formed, it establishes an outer limit on presidential actions. The isolationist

Vietnam War protest on Boston Commons.

mood of the country growing out of the experiences of World War I was such that Franklin Roosevelt had to carefully bring the American public around to supporting his goal of involving the nation in the Allies' struggle against the Axis powers, a policy that ultimately succeeded only after the Japanese attack on Pearl Harbor. The public reaction to the Vietnamese war has acted in recent years as a similar restraint on presidential attempts to involve our nation in ventures abroad.

Although the general public's interest in foreign affairs is sporadic, responding mostly to dramatic events (such as military encounters), there is an "attentive public" (estimated to be about 15 percent of the population) that follows a range of international developments with some regularity. These are the persons who pride themselves on having a cosmopolitan outlook on the world. They keep informed on what happens in world politics by reading books, articles, and editorials on the subject, attending lectures and debates dealing with such matters, and discussing current events with one another. Composed primarily of professionals such as academics, lawyers, bankers, newspaper editors, and schoolteachers, this group also constitutes an important source of information on foreign developments for members of the general public who may look to them for advice and clues.

Joining this group from time to time are those with a particular interest in a specific issue. Thus, American Jews are likely to be concerned about events in the Middle East that affect Israel and the fate of Soviet Jews. Economic considerations also play a part in stimulating interest in certain issues: businessmen who are threatened by competition from Japanese imports respond to actions the government takes affecting foreign trade.

In many instances these attentive

New York City rally for Soviet Jews.

publics organize themselves into *interest groups* to try to influence foreign policy. They may take the form of a general-purpose organization (such as the Foreign Policy Association) or they may adopt a particular approach or point of view (like the Committee for Nuclear Responsibility). They may reflect ethnic (Zionist Organization of America) or economic (Trade Reform Action Coalition) concerns. Also active in trying to influence American foreign policy are other governments, such as Taiwan's trying over the years to prevent our diplomatic recognition of Communist China or Saudi Arabia's attempting to influence our policy in the Middle East.

Another general type of lobby that has been given great attention in recent years is the so-called **military–industrial complex.** This is the general name given to the combination of professional military men, defense contractors, and their congressional allies (who want military installations and defense industries in their districts), who are said to exert tremendous pressures to keep military spending at a high level and to further a "hard-line" policy with communist nations. Although there is no overall formal organization that speaks for all these groups, they coordinate their efforts through interest groups such as the American Security Council.

It is difficult to determine just how much influence attentive publics and organized interest groups actually have on foreign and military policy because of the secrecy and complexity of the decisions involved. Those decisions that are made in a short period of time, which affect all the members of American society fairly equally, and about which private groups have no presumed expertise (for example, what to do about the Cuban missile crisis), are unlikely to be much influenced by interest groups. On the other hand, long-term policies that have a particular impact on certain segments of the population and concern matters about which such groups are considered to possess special knowledge (such as businessmen are thought to have about foreign trade) presumably reflect a higher degree of group influence. In any event, most students of interest groups attribute less influence to them in foreign affairs than domestic affairs.

The same generalization applies to *political parties.* The necessity for presenting a united front to the world and the desire to achieve continuity in our policies toward other nations means that party leaders and candidates are less likely to take opposite stands on foreign than domestic affairs. Even when they do (as when the Republican party in the 1952 presidential campaign called for the "liberation" of Eastern European countries behind the Iron Curtain), the policies that the new administration actually follows when it comes to political office tend to parallel those of the former party in power. Thus, partisan factors that characterize so much of domestic policy-making are much less important in foreign and military affairs.

One final group that plays a role in foreign affairs is made up of the representatives of the *mass media*. Reporters and commentators of the press, radio, and television act as potential *intelligence-gathering* and *communication links* for the various participants in the policy process. Thus, executive officials and members of Congress learn of each other's attitudes on international developments from the media. The media also furnish the electorate with information on the activities of public officials and, at the same time, provide the officials with feedback on how their actions are (or are likely to be) received by the American public and other nations as well. Finally, representatives of foreign governments look to the media for clues on the attitudes and intentions of American officials.

But the media do more than transmit information on the actions and attitudes of other individuals and groups that are involved in policy-making in foreign affairs. The media themselves become active *participants* in the process. They are in a position to *interpret* international developments for the public, and frequently their version of developments differs markedly from the impressions that public officials are trying to create. Thus, the Johnson administration tried to picture the Tet offensive in Vietnam in early 1968 as a last-ditch military effort of the Communists that failed; large elements of the media construed it, rather, as evidence that major cities in the South were still vulnerable to enemy attack. At times the media, especially commentators and editorial writers, even become *advocates* of certain courses of action that may run counter to the policies being pursued by public officials: the late prominent journalist Walter Lippmann, for one, was long a critic of our involvement in land wars in Asia.

As evidenced by the "Pentagon papers" incident in 1971, when the government tried unsuccessfully to prevent the publication of an official study of our involvement in Vietnam, a natural conflict exists in a democratic society between media representatives and officials involved in foreign and military affairs. The former believe in maximum disclosure of official actions, in the people's "right to know" what their public servants are doing in any area of public concern (including that of national security), and in the soundness of the media's analyses of international developments. On the other hand, public officials are concerned lest such disclosures interfere with the delicate operations involved in protecting the nation's security, and they are highly suspicious

Pentagon Papers go on sale.

that the media are more particularly interested in producing their own version of official actions and intentions in order to create conflict so that they can better sell their services.

Thus, the process by which American foreign and military policy is made is highly complex and involves basic issues of decision-making in a democratic society. The following section takes up an equally difficult problem: what goals and approaches does a democratic society like the United States pursue in international affairs?

GENERAL GOALS AND APPROACHES

The United States, like other nations, naturally pursues a variety of goals in foreign affairs. Like individuals, the nation has been motivated in international relations by two general purposes: *ideals* and *self-interest.* The former has led us to seek moral goals that transcend national boundaries. The latter source of action has caused us to pursue our own selfish concerns or what is generally referred to in foreign affairs as the **"national interest."**

The ideals involved in the conduct of foreign policy are the same values that any democratic nation seeks in domestic politics: liberty, equality, justice, goodwill, peace, and the like. The important consideration is that as a nation we have not been satisfied with merely implementing these ideals in the United States; we have sought to extend them to other nations as well. The person most associated with this doctrine in foreign affairs is Woodrow Wilson: in his speech to Congress on April 2, 1917, asking for a declaration of war on Germany, he explained that the nation was fighting ". . . for the rights of nations great and small, and the privilege of men everywhere to choose their way of life and of obedience. The world must be made safe for democracy." At the same time, the chief executive assured the legislators: "We have no selfish ends to serve. We desire no conquest, no dominion. We seek no indemnities for ourselves, no material compensation for the sacrifices we shall freely make." While perhaps not aspiring to as lofty goals as Wilson, Jimmy Carter's concern with the state of "human rights," not just in this country but abroad, reflects a similar idealistic approach to foreign policy.

It is somewhat more difficult to define precisely what is included in the national interest. At a minimum it means self-preservation for a nation. Survival involves maintaining territorial integrity, basic governmental institutions, and political independence. Closely akin to the latter is a nation's political self-sufficiency, that is, the ability to conduct its affairs without depending on other countries. One aspect of that self-sufficiency is reflected in the general withdrawal of the United States from international involvement when it pursued a policy of isolationism during the nineteenth and the early part of the twentieth centuries.

The national interest can be constued, however, to cover additional concerns, such as the protection of citizens and property beyond the country's territorial boundaries or the right of access of businessmen to foreign markets. Some persons would also include the nation's honor, prestige, and its "way of life" as part of the national interest. At times, the nation has also been willing to embark on imperialistic ventures (as in Texas, Cuba, and the Philippines) in order to *increase* national honor or prestige.

A varied array of persons have advocated the national-interest approach to international affairs. Theologian Reinhold Niebuhr, journalist Walter Lippmann, professional diplomat George Kennan, and political scientist Hans Morgenthau have all advocated

President Wilson asking Congress for a declaration of war on Germany.

that the United States stop trying to pursue universal idealistic goals (such as bringing liberty and justice or democratic institutions to other countries) and concentrate on protecting and advancing our own national interest. Similarly, Secretary of State Henry Kissinger and the two presidents under whom he served—Nixon and Ford—placed emphasis on protecting the national interest by maintaining a balance of power among the nations of the world, including such traditional ideological foes as the Soviet Union and China. While expressing concern over human rights in countries such as the Soviet Union, they felt that there are practical limits on our nation's ability to press its moral values on other countries. This approach is generally referred to as a "realistic"—as compared to an "idealistic"—one in foreign affairs.

Although the "idealism–self-interest" dichotomy is helpful in assessing what a nation's goals are (or should be) in international affairs, it is deficient in some other respects. For one thing, nations do not pursue one appraoch exclusively to the complete detriment of the other. Few people advocate pursuing idealistic goals if they seem to threaten national survival: there has been little disposition to bring democracy to nations behind the Iron Curtain at the risk of a major war with the Soviet Union. On the other hand, there are moral limits to what realists propose to further the national interest: none of those notables mentioned above, for example, has advocated a preventive war to protect the national interest. Thus, a democratic nation's foreign policy involves reconciling both ideals and self-interest.

It is even difficult in some instances to separate the two types of goals, especially when the national interest is defined broadly. Thus, Walt Rostow, an economic historian who served in major foreign policy posts in the 1960s, conceives of the American national interest as including our basic societal values and what he terms our "... still developing way of life." To protect these interests Rostow suggests that we *maintain a world environment* in which the societies of the area he terms Eurasia (Europe, Asia, the Middle East, and Africa) develop along lines consistent with our own values and way of life. These include societies with a solicitude for the "... dignity of the individual as against the claims of the state ..." and societies that may not necessarily be democratic at the present time but "... accept as a goal a version of the democratic value judgments consonant with their culture and their history." Thus, Woodrow Wilson's idealistic goal of making the world safe for democracy and Rostow's conception that the American national interest requires a world environment composed of nations with democratic values and aspirations turn out to be quite similar.

Conflicts over the goals of American policy often turn, not on the "idealism–self-interest" dichotomy, but on what is to be included within the definition of national interest and, perhaps even more importantly, the kind of world environment deemed necessary to protect such interests. Rostow's statement that "... under modern conditions, it is difficult to envisage the survival of a democratic society as an island in a totalitarian sea ..." reveals his assessment that the internal political order of a country determines its relationships with other nations. As he views the situation, totalitarian societies are inherently dangerous to democratic ones. Not everyone, however, believes this to be the case. Realists generally believe that what counts is the specific relationship that exist between nations: Yugoslavia, long a nondemocratic society, is not hostile to the United States. This reasoning suggests that our national interest is not necessarily jeopardized by the presence of totalitarian societies in the world.

Another consideration that plays a part in determining the goals and approaches a nation pursues in foreign policy is an assessment of the *power* it is able to wield in the international arena. Realists have been critical of the many commitments that the United States has made in recent years on the grounds that they exceed our resources. In their view we have failed to maintain a balance between our goals and the means we possess for accomplishing those goals. Specifically, the realists charge that the nation has pursued a general policy of *globalism,* of trying to affect international relations on all kinds of matters in all parts of the world, rather than practicing a doctrine of *limitation,* of restricting our activities to vital concerns in particular areas where we have the actual power to make our policies effective.

Thus, views concerning the policies that the government should follow in international affairs turn on different conceptions of goals, the kind of world environment needed to protect and foster such goals, and the means we have to make those goals effective. The following section utilizes these frames of reference to analyze the major policies that the nation has followed in the post-World War II period.

AMERICAN FOREIGN POLICY SINCE WORLD WAR II

World conditions at the end of the war in 1945 were radically different from those at the beginning of hostilities in 1939. When the war began, there were seven great powers in the world—Germany, Italy, Japan, Great Britain, France, the Soviet Union, and the United States. The fighting resulted in the defeat of the first three and the complete exhaustion of the next two, leaving only the Soviet Union and the United States as significant powers in international affairs. Of these two, the United States was by far the more powerful: unlike the Soviets, we had not been invaded; we also possessed the atomic bomb while the Soviets did not. Thus, the United States stood at the pinnacle of world power and influence at the end of the war. Moreover, unlike the situation after World War I, we were determined not to retreat to a policy of isolationism but to involve ourselves actively in international affairs.

American foreign policy after the end of the war was indeed characterized by active involvement on a global basis. The following analysis focuses first on three geographical areas in which the United States has made major economic and military commitments that greatly affect international relations and our role in them. The concluding section of this chapter analyzes recent developments in American foreign policy.

Europe: 1945–1950

Even while the United States and the Soviet Union were allies during World War II, difficulties arose that eventually led to conflicts between the two major powers in the postwar period. Soviet Premier Joseph Stalin never forgot that American, British, and Japanese forces tried unsuccessfully to put down the Bolshevik revolution following World War I. He also resented the Allies' decision to wait until 1944 to launch a second front against Germany, meanwhile leaving the Soviet Union with the major burden of fighting Hitler's armies. To these suspicions and resentments was added a major conflict on the future of Eastern Europe. The Soviets (who regarded this area, across which armies had marched in successive invasions of Russia, as vital to their security interests) wanted control over the countries of Eastern Europe when the war was over. While Churchill acceded to Stalin's wishes in this regard (the Soviet Union, in turn, was to give Britain a free hand in Greece), the policy was not acceptable to the United States. Scholars differ about the reasons: Arthur Schlesinger Jr. attributes our attitude to the acceptance of a general "universalist" view that national security could be assured only by international organization (as compared to a balance of power in Europe) and to a refusal of liberals to accept the spread of police states in the area. Willian A. Williams suggests that the United States' position was consistent with our historic policy of seeking open access to economic markets. In any event, allowing Eastern European countries to be controlled by the Soviets, it was felt, would constitute a recognition of political and economic spheres of influence.

The postwar future of Germany also created conflicts with the Soviets. During the war the United States considered the possibility of weakening Germany economically by making it a "pastoral" nation, but subsequently it became our purpose (after destroying its war-making capabilities) to restore Germany economically and politically so that it could serve as a counterweight to Soviet influence in Central Europe. These policies intensified Soviet fears of the re-emergence of a powerful Germany, an eventuality that they hoped to prevent by keeping the conquered nation economically weak and politically divided. Moreover, the Soviet Union's desire to exact reparations (for damages suffered during war) by stripping German industries was also at odds with our policy of keeping the plants intact.

The war had barely ended before both sides began to engage each other in verbal battle. In late October 1945 President Truman announced that the United States would ". . . refuse to recognize any government imposed upon any nation by the force of any foreign power." Within a week, Soviet foreign minister Vyacheslav Molotov responded that peace could not be reconciled with an armaments race "... preached abroad by certain especially zealous partisans of the imperialist policy.... In this connection we should mention the discovery of atomic energy and the atomic bomb." In February 1946, Stalin predicted that the capitalist world would once again split into hostile camps leading to war, and suggested that the Soviet Union prepare itself for that development by increasing its industrial capacity at the expense of consumer goods. One month later Churchill gave his famous speech at Westminster College in Fulton, Missouri charging that "From Stettin in the Baltic to Trieste in the Adriatic, an iron curtain has descended across the continent, allowing police governments to rule Eastern Europe."

Meanwhile, along with words, actions taken by the American and Russian governments began to contribute to what soon became known as the **Cold War.** When the Soviet Union applied for a loan from the United States in the fall of 1946, our government claimed to have "lost" the application until the following March, when it suddenly turned up, to the great suspicion of the Soviets. In May 1947, we prohibited the Soviets from taking any more reparations from the parts of Germany we occupied. In turn, the Soviets refused to evacuate troops from Iran and demanded that they be granted oil concessions there. Russia also put pressure on Turkey to allow it to share control over the Dardanelles between the Black Sea and the Mediterranean. (American.demands for the withdrawal of the troops in Iran and the movement of a carrier into the Mediterranean eventually caused Stalin to back down on both fronts.) The two nations also failed to agree on the control of atomic energy: the Soviets turned down an American proposal for international control because they were unwilling to allow inspection of the natural resources and interior of their country and because they felt that the proposed plan served to guarantee an American monopoly of the bomb.

Most important of all the factors heightening the tensions of the Cold War was the Soviet Union's treatment of the countries of Eastern Europe. In the Yalta agreements signed in February 1945 it was agreed that "free elections" would be held in those nations at "the earliest possible time." Initially, some contests were held (for example, in November 1945 the non-Communists won the elections in Hungary), but in late 1946 and early 1947 police actions removed opposition candidates in Rumania and Poland, and the Soviets began to subvert the government of Hungary. Thus, American hopes for self-determination and democracy for these countries, together with economic markets for American products, came to a bitter end.

In this atmosphere, in February 1947 the British ambassador informed the U. S. State Department that despite his nation's traditional commitments, it could not provide the economic and military aid needed by Turkey and Greece. The following month President Truman asked Congress to provide $400 million of American-controlled military and economic aid to stop communist-supported rebellions in those two countries. The late Dean Acheson, then an Under-Secretary of State, told leading members of Congress that the aid was needed to control the expansion of the Soviets in the Middle East and other areas, an expansion that was part of a Communist plan to "... encircle and capture the ultimate objective of Germany." Two months later Congress met the President's request, which came to be known as the Truman Doctrine.

Soon the Doctrine evolved into an even more ambitious venture: the Marshall Plan. In June 1947, at a commencement address at Harvard University, Secretary of State George C. Marshall explained the plan's aims: to

The Berlin airlift.

restore the nations of Europe economically by providing credits to buy American goods to help them rebuild their industries. Although Marshall invited the Soviet-bloc countries to participate in the plan, Stalin refused to let them do so because of the requirement that the economic records of each country be opened for scrutiny and because he wanted each country to be able to draw up its own plans for assistance rather than have to participate in a general European proposal. (The Soviets then responded with a plan of their own to integrate the economies of Eastern European countries with that of the Soviet Union.) President Truman sold Congress both on the economic advantages of the Marshall Plan for American business and on its value as a means of preventing the spread of communism in Western European countries weakened economically by the war (the Communist coup overthrowing the democratic government of Czechoslovakia in February 1948 provided evidence of recent subversion); the President saw the plan become a reality in June 1948, when he signed a bill creating more than $5 billion in aid.

George C. Marshall.

One more major program remained to make Western Europe safe from feared Russian expansion and subversion: the formation in 1949 of the North Atlantic Treaty Organization (NATO), in which the United States joined other nations in pledging joint action in the event that any of them was attacked. That same year the Soviet blockade of access to West Berlin (located within the Soviet Zone of Germany) came to an end after the United States successfully airlifted food and other essentials to the city for over 11 months. Although the latter days of the decade thus looked generally favorable to America and our Western European allies, the explosion of an atomic bomb by the Soviets in September 1949 meant that the days of our nuclear monopoly were at an end.

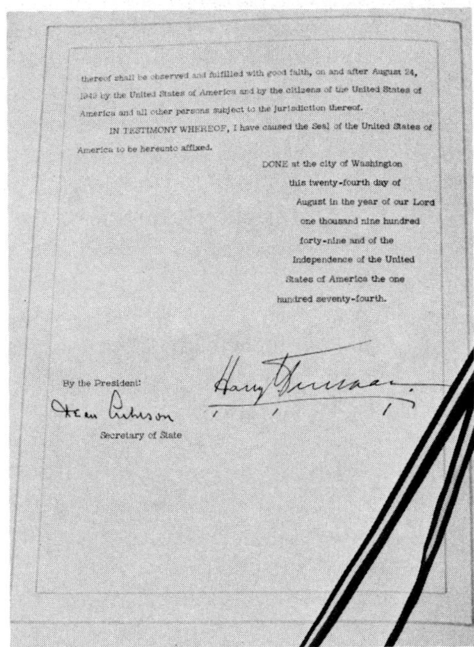

thereof shall be observed and fulfilled with good faith, on and after August 24, 1949 by the United States of America and by the citizens of the United States of America and all other persons subject to the jurisdiction thereof.

IN TESTIMONY WHEREOF, I have caused the Seal of the United States of America to be hereunto affixed.

DONE at the city of Washington this twenty-fourth day of August in the year of our Lord one thousand nine hundred forty-nine and of the Independence of the United States of America the one hundred seventy-fourth.

By the President:

Secretary of State

Signatures on NATO pact.

Thus, American foreign policy in Europe in the immediate postwar period reflected major conflicts with the Soviet Union. Its overall assumptions and objectives were best articulated in an article written by George Kennan under the pseudonym "Mr. X.," which appeared in *Foreign Affairs* magazine in July 1947. In it Kennan attributed Soviet conduct to what he termed a ". . . traditional and instinctive Russian sense of insecurity . . ."; a Communist ideology that advocates revolution to defeat capitalist forces in the outside world; and Stalin's determination to use the perceived threat of "capitalist encirclement" to regiment his people and consolidate his own political power. Kennan suggested that Soviet aggression be ". . . contained by the adroit and vigilant application of counterforce at a series of constantly shifting geographical and political points," a policy that he predicted would eventually lead to ". . . either the break-up or gradual mellowing of Soviet power." As we shall see below, **"containment"** became the basis of our policy not only in Europe but in Asia as well.

Korea

Another area of controversy between the United States and the Soviet Union in the postwar period was Korea, a country that had been occupied by Japan since 1910. As early as 1943 President Roosevelt expressed his preference for the eventual independence of the country. He felt, however, that an apprenticeship period would be necessary to prepare the Koreans to rule themselves and that during that interval (Roosevelt had in mind 20 years or longer) the country should be placed under the trusteeship of the United States, the Soviet Union, and one or two other countries. Stalin informally agreed to his proposal but nothing definite concerning Korea's future was planned either at Yalta in February 1945 or at Potsdam the following July. The Potsdam meeting did, however, provide for the entry of the Soviet Union into the war in the Far East. When it did so, after the United States dropped two atomic bombs on Japan in early August 1945, the two major powers made a hasty decision to divide Korea at the thirty-eighth parallel so that the Japanese could surrender to Russian troops north of that line and to American forces below it.

During the months following the end of the war, two separate Korean regimes emerged to lead their countrymen. In the North a Communist-dominated government set up a People's Republic that had Soviet support. In the South right-wing groups under the leadership of Syngman Rhee emerged victorious in elections held under the auspices of the American military government.

The development of the two rival regimes backed by the two major powers contributed to the difficulties that followed. A five-year trusteeship approved by the United States and the Soviets in late 1945 met violent opposition from Koreans, especially Rhee, who wanted immediate independence. Proposals for free elections to be held throughout the country made first by the United States and later by the United Nations were not acceptable to the People's Republic or the Soviets, who feared that the North would lose the elections since twice as many Koreans lived south of the thirty-eighth parallel. As a result, the two zones continued their separate governments. In 1948 the Soviets withdrew their troops and we followed suit the next year. However, while the Soviet Union provided the North with extensive equipment and training for their troops, American military assistance for the South was extremely limited.

Nor did the United States give any indication that it would send its own troops to help defend South Korea if it were attacked. In March 1949, General Douglas MacArthur, Supreme Commander of the occupation forces in Japan, told a British journalist that America's line of defense ran through a chain of islands from the Philippines to the Aleutians through the Ryukyus (this line lay east of Korea); he was also quoted as saying that ". . . anyone who commits the American army on the mainland of Asia ought to have his head examined." In January 1950, Secretary of State Acheson defined essentially the same defense perimeter in a speech before the National Press Club, saying that if South Korea were attacked, it would be the responsibility of the United Nations to come to its assistance.

When the North Koreans attacked across the thirty-eighth parallel on June 25, 1950, however, President Truman responded by committing air and naval forces and, when that aid did not stem the tide, American ground troops as well. The United Nations also asked its members to come to the aid of the Republic of Korea. Ultimately, 16 nations contributed to the United Nations forces fighting in Korea, but the United States provided the overwhelming share of the air and naval power and, with South Korea, most of the ground forces also.

It is not entirely clear why North Korea decided to attack, but it appears that the Soviet Union was concerned about our unilateral action in negotiating a peace treaty with Japan without Soviet participation and hoped to bring all of Korea under Communist control in order to counteract the threat posed by a strongly anti-Communist Japan. It is also possible that Stalin wanted to divert Western pressure from Europe to the Far East or to test American resistance to an armed attack. In any event, the Soviet Union apparently took the United States at its word about its defense perimeter, and assumed that the South could be taken militarily without risking direct confrontation with us.

Why the United States decided to resist the aggression after previously stating that Korea lay outside its defense perimeter is also not completely certain. However, President Truman reveals in his memoirs that he viewed the invasion as the same kind of aggression that Japan, Italy, and Germany engaged in during the 1930s and concluded that this time the aggressors must be taught that force would meet with resistance. The President also explained to MacArthur that ". . . we are fighting in Korea . . . to carry out our commitment of honor to the South Koreans and to demonstrate to the world that the friendship of the United States is of inestimable value in time of adversity." Dean Acheson, by then Secretary of State, told a congressional committee that the aggression was ". . . a challenge to the whole system of collective security, not only in the East, but everywhere in the world." Korea was also considered important to the security of Japan.

Whatever the reasons, the commitment of American forces soon began to turn the war around. In mid-September United Nations troops under MacArthur conducted a landing behind the enemy lines at Inchon and within two weeks linked up with forces from the South to cut off large numbers of North Korean troops. Although President Truman had announced in June that our objective was to restore the division of the country at the thirty-eighth parallel, in September he declared that Koreans had a right to be "... free, independent and united." Late that month he ordered MacArthur north of the parallel, and on October 7 the United Nations General Assembly endorsed the President's order as the first troops moved into the North.

The war, however, soon took another dramatic turn. Communist leader Chou En-lai told the Indian ambassador to mainland China that if the UN troops crossed the thirty-eighth parallel and included South Koreans within their forces, China would send troops in to help the North Koreans. This message was relayed through the Indian government (the main link to China since Washington at that time had no direct diplomatic contacts with Peking), but the American government discounted the threat as Communist propaganda passed on by the ambassador, who was considered friendly to Communist China. In mid-October MacArthur assured President Truman that the Chinese had no air force and that if their troops tried to move into Korea without air cover, they would be slaughtered. In late October, however, the first Chinese prisoner was captured, and on November 25 Chinese "volunteers" crossed the Yalu River in force, trapping and destroying large numbers of UN troops. Within three weeks the UN forces were pushed back across the thirty-eighth parallel, and it looked for a time as if they might be driven from the peninsula altogether.

Reinforcements, however, enabled MacArthur once again to turn the tide, and in January 1951 UN troops moved back towards the parallel. Here the fighting stabilized, while a conflict arose within the United States government over how the war should now be waged. MacArthur urged instituting a naval blockade of China, bombing its military

General Douglas MacArthur at Inchon.

and industrial installations, and utilizing Chinese Nationalist troops, perhaps on the Chinese mainland itself. Truman, however, concerned lest Soviet troops should come to the aid of the Chinese and apprehensive about the possibility of tying the United States down in a major war in Asia at a time when Europe was still threatened by the Soviets, chose instead to fight a limited war and to seek negotiations with Peking. When MacArthur refused to follow orders and his actions threatened to hamper the negotiations, the President relieved him of his command in April 1951.

Truman's policy soon brought results. In late June 1951 the Soviets suggested an armistice and a withdrawal of both forces from a neutral zone across the thirty-eighth parallel. The following month negotiations began, but not until July 1953—after Dwight Eisenhower had come into office and a group of new leaders had replaced Stalin—was an armistice signed. More than 30 years later no final peace settlement had yet been agreed to and the nation was still partitioned. The United States has a mutual defense treaty with South Korea, and over 40,000 American troops remain stationed there. Thus, the containment policy, originally intended for Europe, was applied in Asia as well, under the assumption that China and the Soviet Union were allies and that together they constituted a major Communist threat to America and the Free World. As we shall see, developments in Korea had a major influence on still another area of American concern: Vietnam.

Vietnam

As with Korea, President Roosevelt's initial preference for Vietnam in the postwar period (the Japanese occupied it in 1940 after a period of French rule) was a multination trusteeship, with eventual independence to be granted in 20 years or more. However, concern about the Communist background of Ho Chi-Minh, the strongest local figure, and the desire to favor France, a wartime ally, led to a decision at the end of the war to permit France to reoccupy Vietnam prior to the granting of independence. In early 1946 Ho's forces (called the Vietminh) occupied the northern part of the country and the French the South. Tentative plans called for an eventual referendum in the South to see if its people wished to have the authority of the Vietminh extended there, and for the inclusion of Vietnam in the French Union. Tensions increased between the French and the Vietminh, however, and in December 1946 hostilities broke out.

In the early stages of the fighting the United States did not commit itself to either side. We were torn between our fears of Ho's Communist connections and a distaste for supporting French colonialism. Gradually, however, the former took precedence over the latter. After the Chinese Communists defeated the Nationalists in 1949, we became concerned that Vietnam would come under Chinese control. That fear intensified after the Chinese entered the Korean War, a development that we viewed as a prelude to their expansion throughout East Asia. At the same time, the United States became increasingly concerned with obtaining French support for containing the Soviet Union in Europe. One means of accomplishing this objective was to relieve France of the burden it was carrying waging the war in Vietnam.

American policy in Vietnam from 1950 to 1954 was to assist the French economically to fight that war. After the termination of the hostilities in Korea, we stepped up this assistance, absorbing more and more of the costs of the war. Despite these efforts, however, the Vietminh became increasingly successful in the fighting. By early 1954 it became obvious that economic assistance alone would not defeat Ho Chi-Minh's forces; outside military assistance would have to be provided. We tried to interest the British in joining us in sending troops to Vietnam. They felt, however, that the Communist movement there was indigenous rather than Chinese- (or Soviet-) inspired and that a settlement should be reached that would reflect the realities of the power situation there. When President Eisenhower determined not to commit American troops alone, France pursued the course of action advocated by the British.

The settlement of the war came as a result of a conference held in Geneva from May to July 1954. Participants in the conference included Britain and the Soviet Union (as joint chairmen), France, the United States, Communist China, Cambodia, Laos, the French-sponsored state of (South) Vietnam, and the Democratic Republic of (North) Vietnam. One document signed by France and North Vietnam provided for the temporary division of Vietnam at the seventeenth parallel into two zones pending reunification; the withdrawal of French and Vietminh troops to their respective zones; the movement of Vietnamese to the North or South as they chose during a 300-day period; a ban on receiving military materiel or personnel in either zone; and the appointment of an International Control Commission to supervise the carrying out of the terms of the agreement. A second document, a Final Declaration, expressing approval of the first agreement and, fixing July 1956 for the holding of general elections throughout the country for the purposes of reunification, was signed by no one but was verbally supported by all the conference participants except South Vietnam and the United States. We stated that we were not "... prepared to join ..." in the declaration, but would "... refrain from the threat or use of force to disturb ..." the agreements reached, and we warned that we viewed with grave concern "... any renewal of aggression in violation ..." of them.

The reason why the Geneva settlement was not acceptable to the United States was that we did not want to be associated with any agreement that consigned territory to Communist rule. (Secretary of State John Foster Dulles considered any such action "appeasement.") The South Vietnamese opposed the Geneva agreement because they felt that they would lose to the Communists in the elections for two reasons: more people lived in the North than the South, and there was no non-Communist leader with the popular appeal of Ho Chi-Minh.

Our subsequent actions and those of the South Vietnamese reflected these attitudes. In September 1954, the United States entered into a treaty with Britain, France, Australia, New Zealand, the Philippines, Thailand, and Pakistan to create the South East Asia Treaty Organization (SEATO) to provide security against aggression in the area. South Vietnam was specifically included in the territory covered by the treaty. At the same time we backed a native leader, Ngo Dinh Diem, against the French puppet, Bao Dai, for the leadership of South Vietnam. Bao Dai was deposed and Diem came to power pledged to give Vietnam genuine national independence. We supported Diem's regime economically and backed his decision to call elections for South Vietnam alone and to refuse to consult with the North Vietnamese about the national elections to be held in 1956. As justification for this course of action, Diem argued that honest elections could not be held in the North and that South Vietnam had refused to endorse the Geneva agreements and, hence, was not bound by them.

In the years that followed, Diem tried with American assistance to consolidate his regime in the South. His political base, however, was narrow: he was a Catholic and enjoyed his greatest strength among the educated class liv-

Secretary of State John Foster Dulles confers with Premier Ngo Dinh Diem of South Vietnam.

ing in the cities; he had almost no support from the largest religious group, the Buddhists, or the lower classes, especially the peasants who lived in villages outside the major population centers. Diem also alienated many South Vietnamese by jailing his political opponents. When the Communists in the South (called the Viet Cong) saw their hopes for a unified Vietnam under Communist control dashed by the failure to hold the 1956 elections, they began a program to detach the rural population from the Diem administration. To accomplish that end, they began a terrorist campaign against government officials and interfered with the collection of taxes by the central government. The Viet Cong won the support of large sections of the village population through political appeals calling for land redistribution and the end of unfair taxation. This village population became an important source of recruits, food, and information on the movement of enemy forces in the guerrilla warfare that the Viet Cong launched against the South Vietnamese government. By the end of the 1950s large sections of rural South Vietnam were under the control of the Communists.

In the early 1960s, the war entered a new phase. The military operations of the Viet Cong stepped up as they penetrated more and more areas of the South and began to mount larger-scale attacks on the South Vietnamese army. Along with these developments, those fighting to overthrow Diem began to receive more assistance from the North in the form of equipment, military advisers, and even some troops. The Viet Cong also established a political arm—the National Liberation Front—which included non-Communists, such as the Social Democrats. The religious intolerance of Diem's family alienated more and more South Vietnamese, including the Buddhists, who mounted demonstrations against his regime.

The United States responded to these challenges with changes in its policies. Soon after President Kennedy took office in 1961, he decided to increase aid to Diem and send American military men to serve as advisers to the South Vietnamese troops. The American government also inaugurated programs designed to break the hold of the Viet Cong on the villages and put pressure on Diem to initiate social and economic reforms. None of these efforts met with much success: the military situation worsened; we made little headway with the pacification of the villages; and the corruption and nepotism of the South Vietnamese government persisted. In November 1963, the Diem regime was overthrown by a military coup that American officials were apparently aware of and did nothing to prevent.

The problems of South Vietnam did not end, however, with the demise of Diem. A succession of governments headed by generals-of-fortune followed, which resulted in increasing instability in the South. As the military situation grew worse, the United States increased its commitment of American troops; by 1964 they numbered 25,000. In August 1964, following torpedo attacks on American warships in the Gulf of Tonkin, President Johnson sent retaliatory strikes against North Vietnamese torpedo-boat facilities. He also used the incident to obtain a congressional resolution authorizing the chief executive ". . . to take all necessary measures to repel any armed attack against the forces of the United States and to prevent further aggression."

In 1965 the moment of truth arrived. The United States would have to take over the war or see South Vietnam fall to the Communists. President Johnson chose the former course of action. In February, the United States began the systematic bombing of the North; that same spring American forces abandoned the role of "advisers" and were openly committed to combat in the South. That June, Air Vice-Marshal Ky became premier. With our prodding, elections were held the next year to choose delegates to write a constitution, and in balloting held in 1967 a government was chosen with Nguyen Van Thieu as president and Marshal Ky as vice president. Meanwhile, the commitment of American troops accelerated; by early 1967 they numbered 400,000.

The massive commitment of American troops halted the Communist tide and in the words of one observer made the war "unlosable." At the same time, the North Vietnamese stepped up their infiltration of supplies and troops to the South. A stalemate in the fighting occurred as President Johnson came under competing advice: the military wanted him to commit still more troops to the fray, while Secretary of Defense

U.S. paratroopers in Vietnam.

Robert McNamara proposed an end to the escalation and the consideration of a political solution to the war.

In 1968 President Johnson decided upon the latter course of action. Following the Tet offensive in late January, in which the Communists demonstrated their ability to attack urban areas in force, the military asked for an additional 206,000 men (at the time the United States had over a half-million men in Vietnam), a request that would have necessitated calling up the reserves. The President refused and in a dramatic announcement to a nationwide television audience on March 30, 1968 ordered a halt to the bombing of the North, called for a convening of peace talks to end the war, and took himself out of contention for the presidential contest in November. As that election was being held, peace talks convened in Paris involving representatives of North Vietnam, the National Liberation Front, South Vietnam, and the United States.

When Richard Nixon took office in January 1969, he embarked on a program of what he called "Vietnamization," which involved turning over more and more of the fighting to the South Vietnamese and the systematic withdrawal of American troops. At the same time, he intensified the bombing of North Vietnam and mined its harbors (a bold step that his predecessors were unwilling to take). Nixon also continued to use the Paris peace talks as a means of achieving a negotiated settlement with the Viet Cong and North Vietnamese. Meanwhile, the ending of the draft and the decline of American casualties as more and more of the troops came home helped to defuse much of the internal opposition to the war.

In January 1973, hostilities came to an end when representatives of the United States, South Vietnam, North Vietnam, and the Viet Cong's provisional government signed an agreement in Paris; that same day an internationally supervised cease-fire went into effect. By the end of March, American prisoners of war were released and the remaining troops were withdrawn from Vietnam. Subsequently, however, in

North Korean representatives Le Duc Tho, and Henry Kissinger at Paris peace talks.

1975 the North Vietnamese overran the South, and all of that beleaguered country came under Communist rule.

Thus, the war in Vietnam constitutes the major military commitment of the United States after World War II, a commitment that cost some 46,000 American lives. Over the years our leaders justified their actions there on a number of grounds. In some instances they emphasized "idealistic" goals, such as permitting the Vietnamese to choose their own form of government and fulfilling promises made to them. At other times the reasons given for our fighting there related to American's own interests: the loss of valuable raw materials (tin, rubber, and rice) or the damage to American prestige, honor, and credibility that would accompany a defeat or a failure to keep our commitments. Our involvement there also reflected a view of the conditions in the world environment that threatened our freedom and that of other nations. (We thus subscribed to the "domino" theory—if Vietnam were lost to the Communists, then one by one other nations in Asia would fall—and to the even more inclusive assumption that if the Communists won a war of "national liberation" in Vietnam, then Communists in underdeveloped countries all over the world, particularly South America and Africa, would be encouraged to launch similar wars.) As the following section indicates, recent changes in that world environment, and our assessment of how those changes affect the United States, continue to shape American foreign policy.

Recent Developments

Just as world conditions at the end of World War II shaped the nature of American foreign policy in the immediate postwar period, so changes in the international environment since that time have influenced the course of American foreign policy in recent years. The following discussion provides basic background information on major alterations that have occurred in the world since the end of World War II. It then analyzes the kinds of issues such changes pose for current American foreign and military policies.

Changes in the International Environment. The single most important factor affecting American foreign policy in recent years is that we no longer dominate the world *militarily* as we did in 1945. In 1949, the Soviets broke our monopoly on the atomic bomb and in 1953 exploded a hydrogen device just a year after we did. In 1957, they placed a satellite in orbit, demonstrating that they were capable of delivering a nuclear warhead. In the early 1970s, the Soviets achieved nuclear parity with the United States, a fact recognized by the signing of the SALT I agreement in 1972. By the 1980s some military experts were claiming that the Soviet nuclear arsenal was superior to that of the United States.

Nor does the United States dominate the world *economically* as it did in 1945, when we alone accounted for 50 percent of the world's gross national product. By the early 1970s the combined output of the economies of Western Europe and Japan had become greater than ours. Japan and West Germany became the third and fourth most economically powerful nations in the world (after the United States and the Soviet Union) and competed effectively with us, not only in the world market, but even in the domestic market of the United States (especially in the automobile industry).

Another development shaping recent American foreign policy has been the emergence of a large number of new independent nations, a consequence of the disbanding of former colonial empires, particularly those of Great Britain and France. (When the United Nations was founded in 1945 it had 51 members; by mid-1983, that membership had expanded to 157). Most of these

Japanese imports invade American automobile market.

new nations are poor, a situation exacerbated by the fact that their economic growth has not kept pace with their rapidly expanding populations.* As a result, those nations whose economies are least able to accommodate an expanded population are the very ones that are generally experiencing that phenomenon.

The relationships among the nations of the world have also become much more fluid in recent years. In the immediate postwar period two major blocs emerged—the United States, Western Europe, the British Commonwealth, and Japan arrayed against the Soviet Union, Eastern Europe, and Communist China—with each side cementing its ties through military alliances. However, in the late 1950s a split began to occur in Sino–Soviet relations, and in the mid-1960s France withdrew from the integrated NATO command. Moreover, even those countries that remain generally allied with the two respective superpowers have become much more independent: Western European nations no longer automatically follow the American lead, and countries in Eastern Europe such as Rumania deviate from the wishes of the Soviets on some foreign-policy issues.

Finally, there have been basic economic developments in recent years that vitally affect American foreign policy. One is the emergence of OPEC—the international cartel that has a major effect on the price and volume of *oil,* on which our economy, as well as those of developed and developing nations alike, depends.† Another is the vital impor-

* Expanding population is a joint product of a lowered incidence of *death,* due to medical and nutritional improvements successfully introduced into developing countries, and a high number of *births* resulting from a failure of many of those same nations to accept modern birth control methods.

† At this date (mid-1984) there is no shortage of oil in the world but many students of the subject believe that this is a temporary situation.

OPEC officials confer.

tance of *food* to many of the nations of the world (including the Soviet Union, which has made major purchases of wheat in recent years), a factor that particularly benefits the United States and Canada, which together account for 75 percent of commercial wheat exports. Also of increasing importance to our foreign policy is the growth of American-based multinational corporations: in 1976 the economic activities of Exxon and General Motors exceeded the gross national product of all but 22 nations of the world.

These, then, are the major changes that have occurred in the world environment in recent years. As indicated below, they provide our decision-makers with new challenges and opportunities in vital areas of American foreign policy.

Current Policy Issues. The major issue in American foreign policy remains today what it has been since the end of World War II: how to deal with the world's other superpower, the Soviet Union. Making the situation more difficult for the United States is the fact that we no longer enjoy the military superiority that contributed to Soviet decisions to avoid confrontations with us by withdrawing from Iran at the end of World War II and removing the missiles it placed in Cuba in the early 1960s. Perhaps emboldened by its own improved nuclear capability and a perception that the American experience in Vietnam makes it less likely that we will continue to play an active international role, the Soviet Union (along with its ally, Cuba) has recently become involved in supporting Communist forces in several African countries, such as Angola, Ethiopia, and Mozambique, and reportedly in Central American countries such as Nicaragua and El Salvador as well. Moreover, the Soviet invasion of Af-

© Jeff MacNelly/Tribune Media Service

ghanistan in December 1979 represents a departure from the former Soviet policy of accepting that country's status as an independent, neutral nation. The fact that Afghanistan borders Iran also raises a potential Soviet threat to our vital interests in the Persian Gulf.

These new developments confront American decision-makers with some major policy questions. Should we build up an American military presence in the Persian Gulf, even if our European allies are unwilling to contribute to the build-up? Or is such a move beyond our capabilities and likely either to be ignored by the Soviets or to lead us into a confrontation with the Soviets in an area where they have overwhelming military superiority? Should we try to develop a closer alliance with the Chinese as a means of countering the possible Soviet threat, or is that policy likely to involve us unnecessarily in Sino–Soviet conflicts and to contribute to Soviet fears that the United States and China are planning a joint attack against her?

The new power status of our Western European and Japanese allies also presents new problems in American foreign policy. One is to convince them that their vital interests are as much affected by recent Soviet actions as our own and that they—especially Japan—should assume a greater share of the burden of defense expenditures necessary to counter the (perceived) Soviet threat. Another is to have them contribute to a lessening of unfair economic competition with the United States by no longer either "dumping" goods on the American market (selling them cheaper here than in their own country) or subsidizing export industries to enable them to sell goods here at an artificially low price. Other possible policies designed to relieve our recent very unfavorable international balance of payments (resulting from importing goods worth more than those we export) is to persuade countries like Japan to accept (or continue to accept) a voluntary quota on the export of such major items as textiles, steel, and automobiles to the United States and/or to reduce tariffs they have erected against our agricultural products.

The United States is also confronted with a number of policy issues in the area of our relations with developing nations. Particularly important are those with Middle Eastern countries from which we have imported much oil in recent years. We have a vital interest in seeing that a settlement is reached between our traditional ally, Israel, and her Arab neighbors, but despite the progress made with the signing of the recent peace treaty between Israel and Egypt, the problem of the status of the Palestinians in areas of the West Bank presently occupied by Israel has yet to be resolved. (The Palestinian Liberation Organization [PLO] wants the creation of a separate independent state but is unwilling to recognize the legitimacy of Israel as a nation; the latter, in turn, refuses even to consider the creation of such a state until Israel receives that recognition.)

Another area of increased concern for the United States is Central America. The Reagan administration has embarked on a policy of providing economic and military assistance to friendly regimes in countries such as El Salvador to assist them in their struggle with rebel troops reportedly supplied by out side forces hostile to the United States.* The question remains, however, whether these regimes have genuine popular support, and whether the nations involved have the kind of economic resources and social institutions necessary to develop viable democratic governments.

Aside from our relations with particular nations, the United States faces some basic foreign policy issues. One has to do with the sale of arms to other countries. Despite a 1976 campaign pledge by Jimmy Carter to cut back on the sale of such arms, we remain the premier exporter of weapons in the world, with the Middle Eastern countries being the major purchasers. These arms sales seem inconsistent with our general policy of promoting world peace; they also raise the distinct possibility that the very same weapons may be used by Israel and the Arab states against each other. On the other hand, cutting back on the sales of such weapons will hurt the American economy

* As previously indicated, the Reagan administration has also sought assistance for the Contras (groups fighting against the Marxist government of Nicaragua), but the Congress has been reluctant to provide that assistance.

U.S. military advisors in El Salvador.

(the Department of Labor recently estimated that every $1 billion worth of U. S. arms delivered overseas provides some 52,000 American jobs) and denies us a major source of income from Middle Eastern nations to help offset our disbursements to them for oil. Moreover, if we refuse to sell such arms, it may be expected that other countries (the Soviet Union, France, and Great Britain are other major exporters) will do so.

Current American foreign policy also involves other moral issues. Should we, for example, use food as a weapon as we did recently when shipments of grain were cut off to the Soviet Union in retaliation for its invasion of Afghanistan? Should we also withhold food from other countries with which we have major differences (such as Cuba)? How far should we pursue our human-rights policy? Has this policy not been rather selectively applied, that is, used primarily against countries that are poor and friendly enough to qualify for U. S. aid (particularly those in Latin America), but *not* against those that are economically and strategically important to the United States (such as South Korea)?

There are also a number of major issues that relate to our nation's military forces. The most basic is how much military personnel and weaponry is sufficient to deter enemy attacks on the one hand, and on the other, how do we avoid squandering economic resources and risking a nuclear confrontation in an ever-escalating arms race? How can we maintain a balance between nuclear and conventional arms, as well as between highly complex and costly weapons and smaller, more easily maintained ones? Finally, there is the matter of how we should recruit members of the military—can we continue to rely on all-volunteer forces at a time when personnel requirements are expanding while the size of the population of service age is shrinking? Moreover, is it fair in a democratic society that a disproportionate share of those who serve their country come from economically and socially disadvantaged groups?

These are some of the major foreign- and military-policy issues with which our society has been primarily concerned in recent years and with which it will continue to struggle in the years ahead. Defending our nation's vital interests in a dangerous world, and at the same time maintaining its domestic economy and internal political and social institutions, will remain a major challenge for American democracy.

ASSESSMENT

The checks and balances that exist among the three branches of government and the influence of public opinion, political parties, and interest groups—all of which characterize the making of domestic policy—were generally absent from decision-making in our foreign and military affairs for a considerable period after World War II. In the 1970s Congress reasserted itself in such affairs, primarily by exercising its traditional powers over the purse, international agreements, and the commitment of armed forces. It also used its powers of investigation and supervision to scrutinize the intelligence community more carefully. (Some of these trends continued in the early 1980s.) Such developments placed a sound brake on the previous tendency of the executive branch to overcommit the nation militarily; they also made foreign policy-making more open and democratic.

However, such experiences

graphically demonstrated the limitations of some of these congressional actions. Presidents continued to use our armed forces in crisis situations—for example, to rescue the ship *Mayaguez* from its Cambodian captors and the abortive attempt to rescue our hostages in Iran—without consulting Congress. Moreover, in response to Soviet actions in Africa and Afghanistan, and its assistance to leftist forces in Central America, Congress began to loosen the purse strings over military expenditures, and pressure mounted for Congress to relax its controls over the covert activities of the Central Intelligence Agency. Even more, the floor debate over the Panama Canal treaty showed the awkwardness of trying to involve a large number of rank-and-file senators in the formulation of an international agreement. Such instances indicate that considerations of secrecy, dispatch, and expertise are such that one may expect most decisions involving foreign and military affairs to continue to be made primarily by the president and his advisers in the executive branch.

Given these facts of life, it is particularly important that vital checks and balances be built into the system by which the chief executive reaches the awesome decisions regarding foreign and military policies. As this process operates, the presidential advisers structure the situation and shape the options from which he chooses; the prize in the political struggles thus becomes not the public's mind, but the president's. Each participant has the goal of convincing the chief executive that his or her concept of political reality (the intentions of other nations, our own capacities, the significance of a particular event) is the *true* one. If the process is to operate as it should, the president must be exposed to as wide a range of views and proposals as possible so that he can choose intelligently from among them.

One possibility for effecting better executive policy-making in foreign affairs is to employ what political scientist Alexander George refers to as a system of "multiple advocacy." This system would use the Special Assistant to the President for National Security Affairs as a **"custodian"** to organize competing information, views, and options on how to handle particular matters from a variety of presidential advisers; the president would serve as the **"magistrate"** of the process, making the final decision on the course of action to be pursued. These procedures might well broaden (as well as refine) the advice and options that a president receives on foreign-policy matters. As George suggests, such a system would not guarantee "good" decisions in every instance, but it might help prevent some very "bad" decisions. Given our experience in Vietnam, that in itself would be no small accomplishment.

The record of our government in protecting and furthering our national interest in the international arena in the postwar period is a mixed one. Although some "revisionist" historians have suggested that the United States overestimated the Soviet threat of expansion in Europe after the war and underestimated the Soviet Union's concern with its own security, their evidence for such allegations is not convincing, particularly from the standpoint of what was known about possible Soviet intentions *at that time,* not from the vantage-point of hindsight. We can never know for sure what Stalin might have done had the United States not inaugurated the Truman Doctrine, the Marshall Plan, and NATO to protect Europe. Given our cultural ties with Western Europe, its industrial potential, and the importance of preserving these historic Western democracies, the policies instituted to prevent their possible fall to the Soviets were clearly in the American national interest. Certainly few persons would quarrel with the results achieved: the economic and political re-emergence of these countries within a short period of time. At the same time, we avoided a direct confrontation with the Soviet Union in Eastern Europe, its primary area of concern.

The justifications for American policies in Korea are less clear-cut. If the United States intended to provide South Korea with protection in the postwar period, our government clearly erred in indicating that it was not within our defense perimeter. On the other hand, there were good reasons for our going to its aid. It was the South Koreans who asked for free elections, which the North refused; moreover, a United Nations commission confirmed that the North was the aggressor. The geographical location of Korea *did* affect the security of Japan, in which we had a vital interest. In addition, the attack on June 25, 1950 came soon after the coup in Czechoslovakia, the blockade of Berlin, the first Soviet explosion of an atomic device, and the coming to power of the Communist government in China (which soon developed close relationships with the Soviet Union); all these events gave the appearance of an increasing Communist offensive against the Free World. Once the commitment was made, the most serious mistake in Korea was to change the goal of the intervention from restoring the division of the country at the thirty-eighth parallel to trying to occupy the North, a decision that brought about Chinese intervention.

With the exception of the decision not to intervene in Vietnam on the side of the French in 1954, our policy with respect to that country suffered from questionable goals and dubious assumptions. We badly underestimated the ability and popular appeal of Ho Chi-Minh as the outstanding nationalist leader of Vietnam; on the other hand, we overestimated the amount of support Diem enjoyed, as well as his commitment to establishing a democratic regime. We interpreted the enemy as international Communism, with close connections among the Soviets, Chinese, North Vietnamese, and Viet Cong; in actuality, the Soviets and Chinese have been at odds with each other since the late 1950s, and North Vietnam has tried to avoid domination by China, a nation that has occupied Vietnam in the past. We were also overly optimistic about our ability to crack the will of the Viet Cong and the North Vietnamese and our own capacity to fight a guerrilla war in the jungles of Vietnam with weapons better suited for conventional warfare across definite battle lines (as occurred in Korea, for example). Most of all, we failed to understand that the conflict in Vietnam was primarily a political, not a military, struggle for the allegiance of the South Vietnamese people.

In the period following the Vietnam War, American foreign policy became more restrained. We no longer depended so much on a network of worldwide alliances to protect our interests; we rather tried to ease tensions with traditional foes like the Soviet Union and Communist China, at the same time taking into account that their rivalry might enable us to keep their power balanced and therefore less threatening to us. We were also less willing to provide arms and technical assistance to factions involved in civil wars in developing nations (in Africa, for example) like that which occurred in Vietnam.

With the Soviet invasion of Afghanistan and the advent of the

Reagan administration, however, American foreign and military policy seems to have entered a new phase. Some observers have suggested that what is termed **"the Vietnam syndrome"** (meaning a too-cautious response to international developments) is now a thing of the past. Whether that assessment is true or not, it remains to be seen how well our policy-makers fare at avoiding an overextension of our military commitments on the one hand, and failing to protect our nation's vital security interests on the other.

SELECTED READINGS

Daedalus, the journal of the American Academy of Arts and Sciences, devoted its Fall 1962 issue to a broad analysis of American foreign policy. Two selections in that issue that are particularly helpful in conveying the essentials of foreign policy are Ernest May, "The Nature of Foreign Policy: The Calculated Versus the Axiomatic," and Stanley Hoffmann, "Restraints and Choices in American Foreign Policy."

The president's role in foreign affairs is treated by Sidney Warren, *The President as World Leader* (Philadelphia: J. B. Lippincott, 1964), and in military affairs by Ernest May, ed., *The Ultimate Decision: The President as Commander-in-Chief* (New York: George Braziller, 1960). Arthur Schlesinger Jr.'s *The Imperial Presidency* (Boston: Houghton Mifflin, 1973) analyzes changes in the presidency brought about by recent developments in foreign and military affairs. Aaron Wildavsky compares the president's role in foreign and domestic affairs in "The Two Presidencies," *Transaction* (Dec. 1966): 7–14. An excellent study of the role of the bureaucracy in foreign affairs is Morton Halperin, *Bureaucratic Politics and Foreign Policy* (Washington, D. C.: The Brookings Institution, 1974).

For a treatment of the role of Congress in foreign policy from the late 1930s to the early 1960s, see James Robinson, *Congress and Foreign Policy-Making* (Homewood, Ill.: Dorsey, 1962). Two very good recent studies of Congress's reassertion of its role in such policy are Cecil Crabb, Jr. and Pat M. Holt, *Invitation to Struggle: Congress, The President, and Foreign Policy* (Washington, D. C.: Congressional Quarterly Press, 2nd ed., 1984), and Thomas Franck and Edward Weisband, *Foreign Policy by Congress* (New York: Oxford University Press, 1979).

An insightful discussion of the role of public opinion in foreign policy is Gabriel Almond, *The American People and Foreign Policy* (New York: Harcourt, Brace, 1950). An historical analysis of the subject is Frank Klingberg, "The Historical Alteration of Moods in Foreign Policy," *World Politics* (Jan. 1952): 239–73. An excellent study of the attitudes of the American people on recent wars is John Mueller, *War, Presidents and Public Opinion* (New York: Wiley, 1973). Bernard Cohen's *The Public's Impact on Foreign Policy* (Boston: Little, Brown, 1973) provides needed clarity in relating public opinion to decisions involving foreign affairs.

The role that interest groups play in the making of foreign policy is anlayzed in Bernard Cohen, *The Role of Non-Governmental Groups in Foreign Policy Making* (Boston: World Peace Foundation, 1959) and Raymond Bauer et al., *American Business and Public Policy* (New York: Atherton, 1963). Bernard Cohen, *The Press and Foreign Policy* (Princeton: Princeton University Press, 1963), is the best treatment of the subject.

For an analysis of the goals of American foreign policy, see Robert Osgood, *Ideals and Self-Interest in America's Foreign Relations* (Chicago: University of Chicago Press, 1953). Walt Rostow gives his definition of the national interest in Appendix A of his book *The United*

States in the World Arena (New York: Harper and Row, 1960). Two excellent statements of the "realist" point of view on the goals and approaches of foreign policy are George Kennan, *American Diplomacy, 1900–1950* (Chicago: University of Chicago Press, 1951), and Hans Morgenthau, *Scientific Man Versus Power Politics* (Chicago: University of Chicago Press, 1946).

A traditional view of the Cold War is Arthur Schlesinger Jr., "Origins of the Cold War," *Foreign Affairs* (Oct. 1967): 22–53. Two of the better "revisionist" treatments of the subject are William A. Williams, *The Tragedy of American Diplomacy* (New York: Dell Publishing Co., 2nd rev. ed. 1972), and Walter La Feber, *America, Russia, and The Cold War, 1945–1980* (New York: John Wiley and Sons, 4th ed., 1980). The best account of the events leading up to the Korean War is Soon Sung Cho, *Korea in World Politics, 1940–1950* (Berkeley: University of California Press, 1967).

A very good analysis of American foreign policy in the postwar years is Robert Osgood et al., *America and the World from the Truman Doctrine to Vietnam* (Baltimore: The Johns Hopkins Press, 1970). Three excellent analyses of the Vietnam experience are James C. Thomson Jr., "How Could Vietnam Happen?" *The Atlantic Monthly* (Apr. 1968): 47–54, Frances Fitzgerald, *Fire in the Lake: The Vietnamese and the Americans in Vietnam* (Boston: Little, Brown, 1972), and Leslie Gelb, *The Irony of Vietnam: The System Worked* (Washington, D.C.: The Brookings Institution, 1979). David Halberstam analyzes the role of the nation's foreign policy elite in recent developments, particularly in Vietnam, in *The Best and the Brightest* (New York: Random House, 1972). Two books that are highly critical of American foreign policy are William Fulbright, *The Arrogance of Power* (New York: Vintage Books, 1966), and Gabriel Kolko, *The Roots of American Foreign Policy* (Boston: Beacon Press, 1969). An interesting in-depth study of the most influential man in American foreign policy during the early 1970s is Marvin and Bernard Kalb, *Kissinger* (Boston: Little, Brown, 1974).

An excellent analysis of the major changes that have occurred in the world in recent years is contained in Chapters 5 and 6 of Charles Kegley Jr. and Eugene Wittkopf, *American Foreign Policy: Pattern and Process* (New York: St. Martin's Press, 2nd ed., 1982). Two good recent studies of national security are James Fallows, *National Defense* (New York: Random House, 1981) and Harold Brown, *Thinking About National Security: Defense and Foreign Policy in a Dangerous World* (Boulder, Colorado: Westview Press, 1983).

COMPLETE RESULTS OF *ALL* THE RACES

TONIGHT
Clear, mid 30s

TOMORROW
Mostly sunny, upper 50s

Details, Page 2

NEW YORK POST

FINAL
WALL STREET EXTRA

TV listings: P. 79

WEDNESDAY, NOVEMBER 7, 1984 35 CENTS

Vol. 183, No. 307

AMERICA'S FASTEST-GROWING NEWSPAPER

ABC AVERAGE SALES EXCEED 930,000

TRIUMPH & CRISIS

Reagan romps in historic landslide as Russian arms ship docks in Nicaragua

HOW SWEEP IT IS! Triumphant President Reagan celebrates last night with (from left) daughter Maureen, First Lady Nancy, son Ron and daughter-in-law Doria. Complete coverage starts on Pages 2 and 3.

Appendix

The Presidential Contest of 1984

THE NOMINATION PROCESS

(For an account of the presidential nomination process through the early June primaries, see Chapter 7, pp. 201–205; for the selection of the Democratic vice-presidential candidate, see Chapter 15, pp. 510–511.)

The Democrats

Walter Mondale used the period after the close of the primaries to help secure his nomination. As soon as the final results of the June 5th state contests became known, he called on people such as Andrew Young and Gillis Long to help him round up the 1967 delegate votes necessary for nomination. In the following weeks he continued to line up additional support in order to assure his nomination on the first ballot.

Mondale also used the time between the end of the primaries and the national convention to decide on his running-mate. After investigating a number of possibilities and interviewing seven candidates at his home in North Oaks, Minnesota, he selected Geraldine Ferraro. While the ultimate effect of his selection on the general election is difficult to assess, most observers agree that the choice of the first woman candidate for such a high office killed Senator Hart's chances of gaining the nomination. (Hart announced at the convention that he too would have selected Ferraro as his vice-presidential candidate and only regretted that he had not picked her first.) The choice silenced Jesse Jackson's criticism that Mondale's interviews of women, blacks, and Hispanics for the vice-presidential nomination were only "token."

Two days later, Mondale made another announcement—he was recommending that Bert Lance, chairman of the Georgia State Democratic Committee, replace Charles Manatt, chairman of the Democratic National Committee. Reports suggested that Mondale made this move for several reasons: to demonstrate that his choice of Ferraro—a member of Congress from New York City—did not mean he was writing off the South in the presidential campaign; to gain Jackson's support, with whom Lance got along well; and to reward Lance for his role in the narrow victory in the Georgia primary on "Super" Tuesday, when Mondale desperately needed a victory to halt the Hart bandwagon. However, the announcement set off a firestorm of objections: the timing was bad—Mondale should have waited until *after* he had the convention's nomination; Lance's resignation as director of the Office of Management and Budget because of alleged questionable banking practices during the Carter administration; and the lack of appreciation shown for Manatt's contribution to the Democratic party. Faced with these criticisms, Mondale quickly moved to repair the damage by announcing that Manatt would be retained as National Committee Chairman with a special fund-raising role, while Lance was to be general chairman of the presidential campaign. (A few weeks later Lance resigned, stating that he did not want to divert public attention from the substantive issues of the campaign.)

Thus, as the Democrats gathered for their national convention in San Francisco, Mondale's situation was still uncertain. He had apparently received enough pledged votes for the nomination and had chosen a popular running mate. However, the Manatt–Lance affair raised questions about his political judgment and that of his close aides. It also remained to be seen whether Mondale could rally the support of his chief challengers, Hart and Jackson, as well as the Democratic party in general for the fall campaign.

The National Convention. The Democratic convention turned out even better than the most optimistic party leaders had predicted. Fears that radical and homosexual groups in San Francisco would stage confrontations with the police similar to those at the 1968 convention in Chicago failed to materialize. Protests representing a variety of causes did occur but they were peaceful and did not engage the interest of the media.

Nor were there the divisive fights over rules that had characterized the Democratic conventions in 1972 and 1980. For example, Senator Hart decided *not* to contest the selection of some Mondale delegates he claimed were chosen with the improper use of labor PAC funds, and the report of the Credentials Committee was adopted by a voice vote. An agreement on future party rules was worked out before the convention (it provided for the appointment of a review commission to consider changes such as diminishing the role of party officials in future conventions), and the report of the Rules Committee also won a voice-vote adoption.

The Democratic platform was a product of compromise. While the Platform Committee was controlled by Mondale forces, it did provide some concessions to Senator Hart (a plank that delineated the conditions under which a Democratic president would use American forces abroad) and Reverend Jackson (the use of ". . . affirmative action goals and timetables and other verifiable measurements.") Three other provisions favored by Jackson—outlawing the "first use" of nuclear weapons, calling for major reductions in military spending, and opposing the use of "run off" primaries—were voted down on the convention floor. Significantly, while the Democratic platform was more liberal than previously on social issues such as the support for homosexual rights, it was economically more conservative; it did not support major new jobs or welfare programs.

The nominations of both the presidential and vice-presidential candidates also went well. Mondale, Hart, and

Jackson were all placed in nomination (as was George McGovern, who withdrew in favor of Mondale). After New Jersey gave Mondale the necessary majority, Hart addressed the convention and moved that Mondale's nomination be made unanimous by acclamation. Ferraro had an even easier time. The role-call vote had barely begun when Arkansas passed in favor of New York, which moved that the nomination be passed by acclamation (which it was).

Thus, the Democrats avoided any major dissensions. (A threatened major boycott by Hispanic delegates in protest over immigration legislation also failed to materialize.) Equally important were a series of speeches that served to unify and galvanize the party for the fall campaign. Leading the way was an electrifying keynote address by Governor Mario Cuomo of New York (rated by many observers as one of the best of all time), which noted that many Americans did not share in President Reagan's "... shining city on the hill ..." and that government should be like "family," "... sharing benefits and burdens for the good of all." In a dramatic speech Jackson pledged his support to the eventual Democratic nominee and asked forgiveness from anyone (especially Jews) whom he had discomforted or pained during the campaign. Hart also called for Democratic unity against the Reagan administration and a blueprint for a new democracy "... of expanded economic opportunity and a safer world." In her acceptance speech, Ferraro, like Cuomo, stressed family values and the importance of living by "fair" rules. Introduced by Senator Kennedy, Mondale in his acceptance speech acknowledged the mistakes of the Carter administration and stressed the fact that the party platform contained "... no defense cuts that weaken our security; no business taxes that weaken our economy; no laundry lists that raid our Treasury." He zeroed in on the nation's huge budget deficits and told the American people, "Let's tell the truth ... Mr. Reagan will raise taxes and so will I. He won't tell you. I just did." Unlike the 1980 Democratic convention, when Senator Kennedy failed to give enthusiastic support to President Carter, most of the 1984 Democratic candidates (Senator Hollings was *not* there) came to the platform in a display of unity as the convention closed amid the delegates' flagwaving and swaying to rock tunes, such as "Celebration" and "Beat It."

Democratic keynote speaker Mario Cuomo.

The Republicans

Unlike Walter Mondale, President Reagan had no important political decisions to make before his party's national convention. With no opposition candidates and a united party, the incumbent President only had to think of the general election campaign. To counter the political momentum following the close of the Democratic national convention (a Gallup Poll conducted July 19 and 20 for *Newsweek* found 48 percent of the respondents for Mondale–Ferraro compared to 46 percent for Reagan–Bush), the President held a press conference on July 24 in which he denied the charge Mondale made in his acceptance speech that he (Reagan) had a secret plan to raise taxes (Reagan did admit, however, that under certain circumstances, it might be necessary). The next day the President hit the campaign trail, appearing first in Austin, Texas, where he charged the Democrats with "... going so far left, they've left America," and then, after stopping off in Georgia, heading north to Hoboken, New Jersey for a festival at St. Ann's Roman Catholic Church (St. Ann is the patron saint of women).

Unforeseen events played a role just prior to the Republican convention. Ann Gorsuch Burford, the deposed head of the Environmental Protection Agency, who in a classic case of bad timing (similar to the Manatt–Lance incident) was nominated as the chairperson of an advisory group on the environment the day after the President spoke to a group of environmentalists, resigned after describing the advisory committee as a "nothing-burger." The President also inadvertently "joked" into an open microphone just before one of his radio broadcasts that we were going to "bomb" the Russians in five minutes. Countering those Republican gaffes were the financial troubles of Geraldine Ferraro, which slowed the campaign momentum of the Democratic ticket. As the Republicans gathered in Dallas for their national convention, they were in a fairly strong political position, one they hoped to strengthen further during the four-day proceedings.

The National Convention. As expected, the Republicans assembled in Dallas not as a decision-making body but to "coronate" Ronald Reagan and to prepare the party for the fall campaign. Persons who gathered to protest policies of the Reagan administration were effectively kept away from the convention hall, which, coupled with the 100-degree heat, caused many of them to leave the city in despair. There were, of course, no fights over rules. The platform proceedings held the week before were dominated by the most conservative elements of the Republican party, who went beyond the wishes of the White House and gave the President little, if any, "wiggle" room on future tax increases, its criticism of the monetary policies of the Federal Reserve Board, and its suggestion that a return to the gold standard might be a "useful mechanism" for achieving price stabilization. (The platform also was extremely conservative on social issues, failing to even mention the Equal Rights Amendment and reiterating the language of the 1980 platform in favor of the appointment of judges who oppose abortion.) Finally, the voting for president and vice-president was conducted on the same roll-call ballot. Reagan received 2223 votes with two abstentions, Bush received 2221 votes with two abstentions, and both Jeane Kirkpatrick, the United Nations Ambassador and Congressman Jack Kemp of New York State received one vote.

The convention, however, did serve to position the Republicans for the fall campaign as they made concerted efforts to win the support of certain groups. Women, in particular, were singled out for special attention. The opening night, which was referred to as "Ladies Night," included featured speakers such as Jeane Kirkpatrick; Katherine Ortega, an Hispanic woman serving as Treasurer of the U.S.; Margaret Heckler, Secretary of Health and Human Services; and Dr. Virginia Boyack, who gave a salute to senior citizens. Later in the proceedings the delegates heard from other prominent women such as Elizabeth Dole, Secretary of Transportation. (However, Senator Nancy Kassebaum of Kansas, although given the title of deputy chair of the convention, spent only a day-and-a-half in Dallas, saying she did not want to be "window-dressing.")

Another group targeted for particular attention were Democrats. Ms. Kirkpatrick (who, as a woman and a Democrat, was a "twofer") began by saying that she was ". . . grateful that you would invite me, a lifelong Democrat" to the convention and then commented that ". . . I realize that you are inviting many lifelong Democrats to join our common cause." Also prominently on display was former professional football player, Roosevelt Grier, a close associate of the late Robert Kennedy, who pledged his support for "four more years" of Ronald Reagan. The President himself in his acceptance speech pointed out that he too was a Democrat; he explained that he had not left the party, the party had left him, and welcomed Democrats to "our" side. Underscoring the theme was a frequent rendition of "Happy Days are Here Again," the song most often associated with Franklin D. Roosevelt.

Another group that received special treatment from the Republicans was fundamentalist ministers. The President at a prayer breakfast stated that ". . . religion and politics are necessarily related," and that persons who opposed voluntary prayer in the public schools ". . . are intolerant of religion." The Republican platform not only endorsed voluntary prayer in the public schools but also tuition tax credits and vouchers to facilitate parents' sending their children to private (including religious) schools. Finally, Reverend Jerry Falwell delivered the benediction the night the President was nominated, television evangelist James Robinson, opened another convention session, and the closing benediction was given by Dr. W. A. Criswell, the conservative pastor of the First Baptist Church of Dallas.

Another major element of the Republican convention was what might best be referred to as "Democrat-bashing." A series of speakers mounted the podium to excoriate the opposition party—at least the one associated with Jimmy Carter and Walter Mondale. Ambassador Kirkpatrick praised the party of Truman, Kennedy, and Johnson, but went on to charge the "San Francisco" Democrats with treating foreign policy as an "afterthought," and with acting like an "ostrich," that is, shutting out the world by ". . . hiding its head in the sand." The keynote speaker, Ms. Ortega, echoed the same theme, inviting "mainstream Democrats" shut out of their traditional party home, to join the GOP. Former President Gerald Ford charged Mondale with "peddling fear" and ridiculed his "New Realism" as something you get ". . . by crossing Jimmy Carter's innocence with George McGovern's 'pie in the sky' ". Senator Barry Goldwater repeated the major theme of his 1964 presidential acceptance speech, "Let me remind you, extremism in the defense of liberty is no vice," and charged that "Every war in this century began and was fought under Democratic administrations." In his acceptance speech, Vice-President George Bush claimed that "For over half a century, the liberal Democrats have pursued a philosophy of tax and spend, tax and spend," and announced the verdict of history, "Your time has passed." Even the President, who many expected to give an upbeat speech, spent much of it castigating the Democratic-controlled House of Representatives, and charged that "If our opponents were as vigorous in supporting our voluntary prayer amendment as they are in raising taxes, maybe we could get the Lord back in the schoolrooms and the drugs and violence out."

Despite the dominant negative tone, there were some positive moments in the Republican convention, mostly provided by film presentations. Former Dallas Cowboys' quarterback Roger Staubach introduced a short film on Nancy Reagan, and a similar one on Bush preceded his acceptance speech. The same procedure was used for the President: an 18-minute film on his accomplishments—including shots of his trips to China and the Normandy invasion beaches—preceded Reagan's acceptance speech. Moreover, the President ended that speech on a positive note, referring to the Statue of Liberty, the passing of the Olympic torch, ". . . a shining city on the hill . . ." and a ". . . springtime of hope." Singer–pianist Ray Charles closed the proceedings by leading the delegates in "America the Beautiful," as they swayed back and forth, waving their flags.

Republican keynote speaker Katherine Ortega.

THE GENERAL ELECTION CAMPAIGN

While the two national conventions naturally attracted a great deal of political attention, other events also had a potential impact on the fall campaign. The media zeroed in on the Ferraro–Zaccaro family finances until the vice-presidential candidate released both her tax returns and those of her husband, and faced a two-hour grilling on nationwide television from assembled reporters. Some questions remained unanswered after the press conference (particularly whether Ferraro should have divulged information on family companies in which she was an officer and stockholder, on financial forms filed with Congress) but most observers concluded that she handled herself very well under fire (at the conclusion of the press conference, reporters gave her a standing ovation). Meanwhile, after some confusion over whether the Reagan administration would or would not recommend a tax increase after the election (the President maintained it would not; Vice-President Bush in a separate interview hedged on the issue), the Republicans settled on a common answer: taxes would be raised only as a "last resort."

The week before Labor Day, the traditional beginning of the fall campaign, the Democratic ticket got a double boost when it received the endorsement of John Anderson (a former moderate Republican who ran as an independent candidate in 1980), as well as a commitment from former-rival Reverend Jesse Jackson that his support of Mondale would be ". . . wide-based, deep, and intense." It was hoped that Anderson's endorsement would help Mondale with young, professional, moderate Republicans and independents who had voted for the former Illinois congressman in 1980 and backed Senator Hart in the 1984 Democratic nomination campaign. Jackson's commitment was expected to assist Mondale with young blacks and other members of the Rainbow Coalition. Along with the Jackson endorsement came an announcement that one of his supporters, former Atlanta Mayor Maynard Jackson, would serve as a "senior policy adviser," while Detroit Mayor Coleman Young, a Mondale supporter, was designated the director of voter registration. (Mondale had previously named another of his black supporters, Congressman Charles Rangel of New York, national co-chairman of the Democratic campaign.)

The Republican team—which was already leading by some 10–15 percentage points in the polls—got off to a much better start in the Labor Day opening of the fall campaign. Reagan spoke to a large enthusiastic crowd in his original political base of Orange County, California, while Bush did well before a smaller group in Illinois. In contrast, the Mondale–Ferraro joint team effort fell victim to overambitious scheduling. Their campaign opened at the Labor Day parade in New York City, they then flew to Merrill, Wisconsin (population 9500) for a noonday rally, and ended up that evening in Long Beach, California. The early morning (8:45 A.M.) parade in New York drew a sparse crowd, which dampened the spirits of the two candidates during the long day. Despite a warm greeting in California from Los Angeles Mayor Tom Bradley and two nomination rivals, Senators Cranston and Hart, things did not go well in Long Beach. The sound system mysteriously went out in the middle of Mondale's speech.

Targeting the Campaign

The major regional battlegrounds of the 1984 campaign were the same as in other recent presidential elections—the Middle Atlantic states of New York, Pennsylvania, and New Jersey, and the Midwest states of Ohio, Michigan, Illinois, and Missouri. They received major attention because of their number of electoral votes and general political competitiveness; also some of them had "rust-belt" economies that had not fully recovered from the recession and were therefore considered opportunities for the Democrats. Also of importance were three upper Midwest states: Mondale's home state of Minnesota and the two surrounding states, Iowa and Wisconsin, in which Mondale was well-known and which had sizeable farm economies that were not doing well. President Reagan responded to the Mondale forays in these states, concentrating particularly on Ohio and Michigan but paying a last-minute visit to Minnesota in the hope of achieving a 50-state sweep that would include his opponent's political home base.

In other regions, Mondale and Ferraro targeted particular states. While conceding most states west of the Mississippi to Reagan and Bush (the Republicans have controlled that region in presidential elections since 1968), the Democratic candidates spent a considerable amount of time in the three West Coast states of California, Oregon, and Washington. Even though California was the President's home state, its large number of electoral votes (47) and the fact that Ferraro appeared to be popular there made it an attractive target. While campaigning in California, it made sense to go to Oregon and Washington, two politically moderate states thought to present an opportunity for the Democrats. The President and Vice President also spent sometime in the Far West, although few Republicans thought they would lose in Reagan's home territory.

Early in the campaign, both sides spent a considerable amount of time in the South. The Mondale–Ferraro team calculated that they had to win some of the states in the region in order to collect the 270 electoral votes needed for election. They hoped that Jesse Jackson could turn out a large black vote there. Major targets included Texas with its 29 electoral votes and large Hispanic population; Georgia, Carter's home state; and Alabama with its large union population. However, the Bert Lance affair hurt Mondale in Georgia, as well as the southern states in general. As the campaign progressed, it also became apparent that the presence of two northern liberals on the Democratic ticket, plus President Reagan's close ties with southern white ministers, constituted major political handicaps for the Democrats that even a large black vote could not overcome. As a result, with the exception of Texas, Mondale and Ferraro spent relatively little time in the region in the latter stages of the fall contest, and the Reagan–Bush team also shifted its campaign to other areas where the race was perceived to be closer.

These latter areas were border states such as Maryland and West Virginia that the Democrats had carried in 1980 and Kentucky which was also considered to be fairly competitive. Finally, two traditionally Democratic New England states, Massachusetts (the only state carried by McGovern in 1972) and Rhode Island, were targeted for some campaigning by the candidates of both parties.

Manipulating Political Appeals

Political Party Labels. As might be expected of representatives of the majority party, the Democratic candidates invoked the memories of popular Democratic presidents of the past—Franklin Roosevelt, Harry Truman, and John Kennedy. In particular, Mondale pointed out that Truman was counted out in 1948 by the pollsters in his race against Republican candidate Thomas Dewey. In one campaign appearance, Mondale held up the famous erroneous headline of the *Chicago Tribune,* "Dewey Defeats Truman."

As in 1980, Ronald Reagan also paid homage to the same presidential heroes, pointing out that he too was once a Democrat. The President said that he switched parties when he found that the leadership of the Democratic party no longer stood for America's responsibilities in the world and failed to protect the working people of the country.

Mondale responded in the first presidential debate in Louisville that in 1960, while he was supporting Kennedy, Reagan was heading up Democrats for Nixon. (In the debate, Reagan volunteered the information that he had voted for Eisenhower.) Later on in the campaign, Mondale released a copy of a letter written by Reagan in July 1960 to Nixon in which he compared Kennedy's policies to those of Karl Marx and Adolf Hitler. Reagan responded by acknowledging the accuracy of the letter, but said he was ". . . pleasantly surprised to find the difference between Kennedy the candidate and Kennedy the president;" he praised the late President for his "toughness" during the Cuban missile crisis and his economic program. (Kennedy initiated a major tax cut, for example.)

President Reagan also awarded a Congressional Gold Medal in honor of the late Hubert Humphrey to Muriel Humphrey, his wife, in a Rose Garden ceremony (Joan Mondale also attended) in which the President praised the spirit of the great "Happy Warrior." (Ironically, Reagan and Humphrey differed on virtually all the major political issues of the day.) First Lady Nancy Reagan also gave a luncheon to commemorate the 100th anniversary of the birth of Eleanor Roosevelt, wife of President Franklin Roosevelt, a major political figure in her own right.

Thus, the Republicans continued the appeal first begun at their national convention for the votes of Democrats (they hoped to draw support from about 25 percent of them). Significantly, the candidates avoided references to recent chief executives of both political parties—Reagan for obvious reasons did nothing to invoke the memory of Richard Nixon, but also ignored Gerald Ford and even Dwight Eisenhower; Mondale naturally played down his association with Jimmy Carter, but also avoided mention of Lyndon Johnson. Thus, the only political figures that were used in the campaigns of both major party candidates were the Democratic presidents of at least a generation ago.

Incumbency. Throughout the presidential election year, President Reagan used the powers of incumbency to good advantage. In the spring, he traveled to China on a trip that was very well covered by the media. In June, he journeyed to the Normandy beaches of France to lead the commemoration of the fortieth anniversary of the invasion of Europe by Allied forces, an occasion attended by veterans and their families (one daughter whose story was featured in the media came in place of her father who had just died), and watched by hundreds of millions of people around the world. The President also laid a wreath at the grave of an unknown soldier of the Vietnamese War.

During the fall campaign, President Reagan continued to reap the advantages of incumbency. He announced that Soviet Deputy Premier and Foreign Minister Andrei Gromyko would visit the White House to discuss the possibility of resuming talks on nuclear arms reduction (Walter Mondale also met with Gromyko.) The President managed to provide double-barreled assistance to beleaguered American farmers: the Russians would be permitted to buy an extra 10 million metric tons of grain, and credit arrangements would be changed to provide greater relief for farmers who were heavily in debt. While rejecting the idea of formal quotas on the importation of foreign steel, the President announced a decision to negotiate such quotas on a "voluntary" basis for up to five years. (We had previously negotiated such quotas on Japanese automobiles.) Finally, the President announced, just three days before Mondale was scheduled to campaign in Times Beach, Missouri, that the federal government would be cleaning up the toxic wastes there.[7] (Mondale claimed that the same development occurred at other waste sites and that, if he just had enough time, his campaign visits to hundreds of sites could eliminate the toxic-waste problem in the United States.)

Candidate Image. The President sought to project the same image he used throughout his political career: a direct, likeable person with a common-sense, no-nonsense approach to solving problems. He also emphasized his leadership qualities and the fact that he had helped turn the country around after years of drift and confusion. He tried to identify himself with the basic American values of love of country and freedom and an optimistic view of the future.

Mondale, in turn, sought to come across as a compassionate person, concerned with the problems of the disadvantaged and equity and fairness in American society. He also stressed his years of political experience and his knowledge of what it takes to make government work.

At times, the candidates attacked each other. Both Reagan and Bush sought to picture Mondale as a "big-spender" and to associate him with the "malaise" of the Carter years. He was accused of being gloomy about the country and its prospects—"whine on harvest moon," as Vice-President Bush liked to put it. The Mondale–Ferraro team, in turn, attacked the President for not "being in charge," for being the most "disengaged" president in recent history, that is, one who lacked the knowledge necessary to govern the nation. They also accused him of being a "rich person's president," uninformed and unconcerned about the problems of the poor and disabled.

Ethnic, Geographical, or Religious Groups. As in past elections, the Democratic candidates made specific appeals to some of the major groups that have traditionally been associated with the New Deal coalition—blacks, ethnics, Catholics, Jews, and blue-collar workers. Much was made of Geraldine Ferraro's Italian-American background—the first person with those ethnic roots to run for such a high political office. However, as in 1980, with the exception of blacks, the Republicans did not concede these groups to the Democrats. An "ethnic week" was set aside in which the GOP candidates specifically courted groups such as Italian-Americans and Polish-Americans. Appeals were made to Catholics on the basis of opposition to abortion (aided by a statement by Archbishop John J. O'Connor of New York who publicly criticized Ferraro for her opposition to a constitutional amendment to outlaw it) and in favor of a tax credit for parents who send their children to private (including parochial) schools. The Republicans tried to appeal to Jews by criticizing Mondale for not repudiating Jesse Jackson's anti-Semitic remarks and (Jackson's) association with Louis Farrakhan, the Black Muslim leader.

Some of the social groups that first emerged as key groups in the 1980 presidential election continued to be targets for both major-party candidates. Mondale and Ferraro zeroed in on Hispanics, especially in Texas and California, while Reagan and Bush sought to make inroads with these voters and Cuban-Americans in Florida (who could be appealed to because of their strong anti-Communism). Women were specifically courted by the Democrats because of the perceived gender-gap, based on the positive appeal of the Ferraro candidacy, women's supposed dislike of the President's views on a strong military establishment, and his opposition to social programs and the Equal Rights Amendment. The Republicans, in turn, made specific appeals to fundamentalist Christians, especially in the South. Assisting the Republican cause was the fact that many of these appeals came through conservative Protestant ministers who focused their congregations' attention on issues such as abortion and prayer in the public schools.

Another group of voters emerged in 1984 as a particular target for both political parties—young voters. Traditionally Democratic in their sympathies, college-age youth were wooed by Republican appeals of job opportunities in an expanding economy and love of country. The Democrats responded by trying to appeal to the idealism of young people to help those less fortunate than themselves and their concern about the dangers of nuclear war. As a result, many of the campaign appearances of both parties' candidates took place on college campuses (Mondale gave one of his best speeches at George Washington University), with both supporters and hecklers typically in attendance.

Issues and Political Events. Without question, by far the most important issue in the 1984 campaign was the economy. Benefiting from a general upswing that began in early 1983, Republicans asked voters the same question that Reagan posed in his 1980 debate with Jimmy Carter, "Are you better off today that you were four years ago?" The implication was that this time they were, that lower taxes, inflation, and interest rates were all redounding to the benefit of the average American. As to the huge federal deficit, the President assured voters that a reduction in government expenditures along the lines recommended by the Grace Commission (a panel of top corporate executives headed by J. Peter Grace, chief executive officer of W. R. Grace and Co., appointed to look into ways of reducing government costs), plus growth in the economy that raise additional revenues, would reduce the deficit in the years ahead. The President reiterated his traditional opposition to taxes and vowed that he would only raise them as a "last resort." Both Reagan and Bush painted a rosy picture of an "opportunity" society and warned voters of the dangers of going back to where we were before the Reagan administration took office.

The Democrats naturally portrayed a far different economic situation. They stressed the fact that although President Reagan had promised to balance the budget, during his administration we still have the largest deficits in the nation's history. Those deficits would in the near future choke off the recovery and set off a new round of inflation or another recession. To meet the problem, Mondale unveiled a plan that would by 1989 reduce the budget deficit by two-thirds. It called for cuts in defense spending and health and agriculture programs, and for an increase in taxes for those in the upper-income brackets and corporations. The Democrats warned voters that taxes would go up no matter who was elected president, but that the Republicans would do this by increasing those of modest means and leaving wealthy individuals and corporations alone.

The 1984 campaign also focused on foreign-policy issues. The President and Vice-President claimed that as a result of increased defense expenditures, the United States was again "standing tall," pointing to the fact that during the Reagan administration the Soviets had not taken over an inch of foreign soil. They also reminded voters that in 1983 American forces had, at the request of surrounding countries, liberated Grenada from a Marxist dictatorship and saved American medical students. The Republicans also contended that now that we had become strong again through rebuilding our defenses, the Soviets would soon be inclined to negotiate a nuclear arms agreement with us, which would be a major goal of the second Reagan–Bush administration.

The Democrats attacked the foreign policy record of the Reagan administration as unsuccessful. They pointed out that the President was the first American chief executive in the atomic era not to have met with a foreign chief of state;

Mondale promised to make such a meeting the first order of his administration so that something could be done about these "God-awful" weapons that threatened to destroy the world. Both Mondale and Ferraro focused on the terrorist bombings in Lebanon that on three separate occasions resulted in the deaths of American military and civilian personnel. They pointed out the administration's failure to properly fortify our embassy against such attacks and to protect the marines participating in a so-called peace mission there. Finally, the Democrats criticized the increasing American role in Central America, the CIA's mining of the Nicaraguan harbors, and the provision of manuals to the Contras on the use of illegal terrorist tactics against the Nicaraguan regime.

Religion took on an increased importance in the 1984 campaign. President Reagan's statement at a prayer breakfast in Dallas at the time of the Republican convention that ". . . religion and politics are necessarily related," set off a spirited debate on the proper relationship between church and state, especially with respect to prayer in the classroom. The President claimed that those who opposed such use of voluntary prayers were ". . . intolerant of religion"; Mondale countered that as a "preacher's kid," he was taught that ". . . religion is a personal and family matter in which the state has no place." Another related "moral" issue was abortion. The President argued that such a procedure violated the human rights of the unborn and in effect constituted murder; the Democrats responded that no matter what one's personal views were on the issue, one should not attempt to use the state to dictate to a woman what she should do on such a private matter as carrying a child to term.

The Mondale–Ferraro team also tried to inject a number of other issues into the campaign. They focused attention on the administration's very poor record on the environment, that is, "They would rather take a pollutor to lunch than to court." The Democrats also pointed to the fact that five of the present Supreme Court Justices are over 75 years of age, which means that the next president may well be able to shape the composition of the Court for the next generation. Noting that the 1984 Republican party platform calls for the appointment of judges ". . . who respect family values and the sanctity of human life . . ." (translation—anti-abortion), Mondale charged that Jerry Falwell would be picking judges of the Supreme Court. Finally, particularly after the first debate (see below), the Democrats tried to raise the matter of Reagan's age; rather than attack the issue directly, they focused instead on the question of his "competence" and whether he really is "in-charge."

The general *theme* of the Republicans was that Americans were "better off" in 1984 than they were four years ago and that we should not return to the failed policies of the past. This state of well-being included not only the economic situation of our individual citizens but the condition of the nation as a whole: America is "standing tall." Moreover, the future of our "opportunity" society will be even better.

The Democratic theme turned on "what kind of people are we?" Do we really want to think only of our own economic self-interest or should we be unconcerned about the persons less fortunate than ourselves? (As Mondale put it, "I would rather lose a race about decency than win one about self-interest.") They also asked Americans to think *not* about whether they are better off *today* in 1984 but whether they will be better off *tomorrow* (with a huge deficit, an escalating arms race, and a more polluted environment). While conceding that America is in relatively good shape at the moment, the Democrats argued that under their administration, it would be even better.

Communicating with the Public

As in other recent campaigns, the candidates spent over half their public funds (over 40 million) on the media, with the lion's share being spent on television commercials. The Republicans aired a half-hour nostalgic film (an expanded version of the 18-minute one shown at the Republican national convention) showing the president riding his horse, walking on a hilltop with Nancy, speaking at the Normandy beaches, and taking the oath of the office. Most of the Republican commercials, however, were 30-second ones. The most famous, "It's morning again in America," depicted the sun shining on San Francisco Bay, people hurrying to work, and a bride and groom kissing at a wedding, while a mellifluous voice (in all probability the same one as is heard in the ads for Gallo wine) asked, "Why would we ever want to go back to where we were less than four short years ago?" Most of the other spot commercials also sought to tap the "feel-good" mood of the country, but later on in the campaign some negative ones appeared. One features a series of persons shown toiling at their jobs, while a voice warned, "Walter Mondale thinks you can work harder to pay his taxes."

The Democrats aired no extended political commercials; instead they relied entirely on 30-second spot commercials. Early in the campaign they ran primarily negative ads attacking the Reagan–Bush record. One showed a roller coaster climbing its tracks, (depicting the temporary upswing in the economy), then plunging downward (reflecting what will happen tomorrow as a result of record Reagan deficits), with a voice intoning, "If you're thinking of voting for Ronald Reagan in 1984, think of what will happen in 1985." Towards the end of the campaign, more positive Democratic commercials appeared. One pictured a warm, dynamic Walter Mondale, talking to a group of students, urging them to "stretch their minds," and to live their dreams, telling them he wanted to help them to be what they wanted to be.

As in the 1976 and 1980 campaigns, debates played a prominent part in the 1984 campaign. Initially, the Democrats requested six separate presidential debates, and a format that called for a moderator and the candidates' being able to ask each other questions. However, the Republicans refused that request, arguing that six debates would be boring and insisting that the format follow previous presidential debates. Eventually the parties compromised on two presidential debates, along with one between the vice-presidential candidates, with the format of all three debates utilizing members of the media asking the candidates questions.

The first presidential debate, held in Louisville, Kentucky in early October, began with considerable controversy as both sides turned down 100 journalists before settling on four questioners. The debate itself turned out to be a clear victory for the challenger, Mr. Mondale, who projected himself as calm, bright, and confident, while the President appeared confused, inarticulate, and in his summation, to have lost his train of thought altogether. Mondale also got the better of the debate on the merits. When the President at one point repeated the line of his 1980 debate with Carter, ". . . there you go again . . ." Mr. Mondale turned pointedly to Mr. Reagan and asked, "Remember the last time you said that?," and then answered the question himself: "You said it when President Carter said you were going to cut Medicare" . . . and what did you do right after the election? You went out and tried to cut $20 billion out of Medicare." The challenger managed to attack the President's policies without attacking him personally, saying at one point, "I like President Reagan."

The debate sent shock waves through the Republican camp which was not used to seeing Reagan lose a debate, let alone so badly (as even Reagan supporters agreed was the case). Even more alarming was the fact that the debate raised the issue of whether the President's age had slowed him down and made him incapable of handling the demands of the office for the next four years. Meanwhile, the media declared Mondale to be the clear winner, and Democratic campaign workers took renewed hope from the encounter as crowds at Mondale–Ferraro rallies burgeoned.

This set the stage for the debate between Vice-President George Bush and Geraldine Ferraro. Republicans counted on Bush to slow the Democratic momentum, while Democrats hoped that Ferraro cold add to the momentum by showing that she could stand up to an opponent with much more experience. This debate was much closer, with observers giving the slight nod to the Vice President, who started poorly (he was almost frenetic in his opening remarks aimed at demonstrating his dynamism) but seemed to better Ms. Ferraro when the debate got around to foreign-policy matters. Still, the challenger came across as calm and thoughtful, and demonstrated tht she had learned a lot in the short period in which she had become a national political figure.

Concerned that President Reagan's advisors had put him through too rigorous preparation for the first debate (trying to fill his head with too many facts and figures), they cut back that preparation and held a pep rally prior to (instead of *after*) the second debate. This time, the debate, held in Kansas City, Missouri, was close, with general agreement that while Mr. Mondale probably won on the merits (effectively attacking the President on Lebanon, arms control, and Central America) the President prevailed on style, appearing much more relaxed and coherent (although he did again ramble in his closing remarks.) Most important, the President defused the age issue when in response to a question on the matter, he replied that he was not going "... to exploit my opponent's youth and inexperience," a clever retort that drew a broad smile even from Mondale.

The media coverage of the campaign, especially by television, paralleled that of other recent presidential campaigns. Much attention was paid to the "horse race" aspect, with virtually daily announcements of the results of myriad polls showing how far the challenger trailed the incumbent. The media also focused on "campaign" (not substantive) issues, such as George Bush's remarks to a group of longshoremen that he had tried to "kick a little ass" in his debate with Geraldine Ferraro. The media also played up the "hoopla" of the campaign—the bands, the balloons, how many people attended a rally, the presence of hecklers, and the like—rather than what the candidates actually said. Moreover, the Reagan team masterfully managed the campaign, issuing short statements or "themes" for the day designed to be carried on 90 second clips on prime-time television and spinning a "cocoon" around the President, scheduling no news conferences, and not even allowing him to answer questions from reporters. (A favorite ploy was to rev up the helicopter engines so Reagan could not hear reporters' questions as he headed to or from Camp David or a campaign appearance.)

Campaign Organization and Finance

Despite the fact that the Democratic nomination contest was heated at times, both Gary Hart and Jesse Jackson worked hard on Mondale's behalf in the fall campaign. Hart was particularly active on college campuses where he had drawn major support and in California where he captured the presidential primary. Jackson focused his attention on the black community where he was particularly popular among young voters.

One distinctive feature of the 1984 campaign was the extent to which both political parties sought to register new voters. Initially, it was thought that the Democrats would benefit most from this effort by registering such traditionally low-voting groups as blacks, Hispanics, women, and poor people. However, their registration effort ran into a number of difficulties: rivalries among organizations attempting to register some of the same people; the reluctance of some political organizations to add new voters who would then share in decisions made in Democratic primary contests for various offices; the failure to take the legal steps necessary to qualify for moneys provided for registration drives by foundations; and the fact that the Democratic National Committee provided state parties with too little money too late for effective planning. Moreover, the Republican party launched an all-out registration drive of its own to counteract the rival party's effort, registering a large number of white Southerners with the assistance of fundamentalist ministers, and selecting key states such as California, Texas, and Florida for special drives. They also employed sophisticated methods, for example, targeting persons with Hispanic surnames who are well-off financially through the use of lists of those who own their own homes, drive expensive automobiles, or subscribe to the *Wall Street Journal* or other business publications. The Republican National Committee also ran a highly organized, efficient operation that distributed large sums of money to state parties in time for them to use the money effectively.

Both sides spent a considerable portion of their federal funds—$40.4 million for each candidate plus $6.9 million for each National Committee—on registration efforts. (More, of course, was expended on the media.) Early in the campaign each announced plans to raise an additional $20 million in "soft-money" (cash from corporate and union treasuries, and individuals who had already given their $25,000 maximum contribution), which could be channeled to state parties for voter registration under the law.

THE RESULTS OF THE PRESIDENTIAL ELECTION

The election was a resounding victory for Ronald Reagan. He outdrew Walter Mondale 59–41 percent in the popular vote and by 525–13 in the electoral count. The former Vice President carried only his home state of Minnesota (even there he won by only a few thousand votes) and the District of Columbia. The incumbent President swept all major regions of the country by large margins: in the South he drew 63 percent of the vote compared to 37 percent for Mondale; in the East where the race was the closest, Reagan won by a 10 percent popular margin—55 to 45.

The Reagan landslide cut across virtually every group in America. He carried both the male and female vote despite the presence of Ferraro on the Democratic ticket, whites backed him by a 2–1 margin, as did independents and college graduates, while both young and elderly voters preferred him over Mondale by a 60–40 percent margin. The incumbent President won the majority of the votes of virtually every ethnic group, including Italians, Poles, Slavs, Germans, and Scandinavians. He also carried the Protestant vote by 2–1 margin and the Catholic vote by 3–2.

Walter Mondale did prevail with a few major groups. Blacks were his major supporters, backing him by a 9–1 margin. Jewish voters and those living in large cities also supported him by a substantial margin, as did those earning less than $10,000 a year. Mondale also won the majority of the votes of Hispanics, Orientals, and labor-union members, but his margin among these groups (averaging 55–45) was much smaller than expected.

However, the Reagan landslide did not extend to other political offices in the American political system. Republicans picked up only 14 seats in the House of Representatives (after having lost 26 seats in the 1982 congressional elections) and had a net loss of two seats in the Senate, which left them with a 53–47 seat margin. Moreover, they had a net gain of only one governorship, which left them in control of 16 governorships compared to 34 for the Democrats. The GOP added over 300 state legislative seats, but controlled both chambers in only 11 states compared to 28 for the Democrats, with 10 states having divided party control of their legislature. (The fiftieth state, Nebraska, has a nonpartisan, unicameral legislature.)

ANALYSIS OF THE 1984 PRESIDENTIAL CONTEST

It is difficult at best to determine the precise reasons for developments as complex as presidential nominations and elections, especially immediately after the events. Only when full information is available from in-depth surveys can one analyze the motivations of voters. Nevertheless, the results of public-opinion polls, gross election data, statements of candidates and their supporters, as well as general trends in American politics provide helpful clues to the major factors that affected the 1984 presidential contest.

The Nomination

The situation in the party-out-of-power, in this case, the Democrats, resembled that of other recent presidential nominations contests. Initially, there were a considerable number of aspirants—eight originally entered the 1984 contest—but that number rapidly declined in the face of embarrassing defeats in early caucuses and primaries. After the second state contest (New Hampshire), Askew, Cranston, and Hollings dropped out, while the third round of contests on Super Tuesday ended the nomination quest of Glenn and McGovern. That left three candidates, Mondale, Hart and Jackson, who continued to battle until the convention itself.

Each of the three Democratic contenders had a definite political base. Mondale represented the traditional New Deal coalition of union members, some ethnic minorities, Jews, older more established black leaders and their supporters, and some white Southerners; he also won the endorsement of the NEA and NOW; and was the overwhelming favorite of most Democratic party and public officials. The former Vice President's regional base consisted particularly of the Middle Atlantic and Midwest states of the industrial "Frost Belt," along with some support from farm and Southern states. Hart represented in particular the Yumpies (Young Upwardly Mobile Professionals) and political amateurs in general who were disillusioned with Mondale and what they considered to be the "old" politics of catering to special-interest groups, especially organized labor. The Colorado senator ran especially well in the West and Northeast. Finally, Jesse Jackson claimed to speak for the Rainbow Coalition (blacks, Hispanics, women, and the poor), but in reality drew most of his support from one part of that rainbow—blacks. Jackson's regional base was primarily the District of Columbia and some Southern states, but he also did well in urban areas with a large black population in all parts of the nation.

A major problem for the Democrats was that none of these major candidates was able to significantly expand his support beyond his particular political base. The two with the greatest overlapping support were Mondale and Jackson, but Jackson's decision to stay in the race, even though he had no chance of winning it, denied Mondale the chance to capture the nomination as early as he would have been able to do in a two-man race with Hart. The result was a long and, at times, bitter campaign that provided the Republicans with ammunition against the Democratic candidate in the fall campaign (for example, Hart's charges that Mondale was the captive of organized labor).

Finally, the early withdrawal of Askew, Hollings, and Glenn left some Democrats essentially unrepresented in the nomination contest, for example, political conservatives and some moderates. This included white Southerners, some members of the business community, and middle and working-class Americans who did not share the liberal views espoused by all three major candidates on such issues as support of welfare programs, affirmative action, and abortion. As a result, this group of traditional Democrats represented a golden opportunity for the Republicans in the fall campaign.

The General Election

Presidential elections are essentially referendums on the incumbent and his record in office and that was certainly true in 1984. President Reagan's landslide victory reflected the electorate's impression of him as a likeable person who is a strong leader; he also benefited from the perception of most voters that they were better off financially than they were four years ago, and that they would continue to be better off economically under a Reagan second term than under a Mondale presidency. Contributing greatly to that perception was the upswing in the economy that began in 1983; most voters assumed that the upswing was brought about by the policies of the Reagan administration and that such policies would continue to keep the nation prosperous in the years ahead.

President Reagan benefited from the fact that the voters were generally satisfied not only with their own individual situation but with the condition of the nation. After two decades of social unrest over racial problems, the Vietnamese war, the Watergate scandals, and the energy crisis, Americans *wanted* to feel good about themselves and their country. The upbeat spirit of the Olympics and a nation at peace continued to characterize the dominant mood of the nation during the fall campaign. President Reagan, himself an incorrigible optimist, both tapped into and shaped that mood.

There is some indication that many voters were seeking *political stability* in the nation as well. With an entire generation having passed since a president served two full terms (Eisenhower in the 1950s), Americans appeared to be looking for a chance to permit another incumbent to have the opportunity that was denied for one reason or another to five previous presidents: Democrats Kennedy, Johnson, and Carter, and Republicans Nixon and Ford.

It is also clear that the electorate in the 1980s has moved away from the liberal views that characterized the New Deal era and much of the 1960s. Many working-class people, as well as members of ethnic groups, no longer view the federal government as providing benefits that enable them to climb the social and economic ladder; they see government as the instrument that takes their hard-earned money through taxes and distributes it to persons on welfare, many, if not most, of whom are lazy and do not deserve such help.* Many of the Yumpies who supported Hart for the Democratic nomination, as well as young college voters, shared the same concern with an "opportunity" society that would allow them to advance their own careers rather than worrying about the problems of those less well-off than themselves.

* One notable exception to that general sentiment was expressed by an Italian-American, Joseph Giordano, who gave President Reagan emergency treatment when he was shot by John

Thus, the voters in 1984 were primarily preoccupied with their own personal financial well-being. Some were concerned with issues such as arms control, "fairness," and the environment, but polls indicated that most of those persons subordinated those matters to their basic emphasis on economic considerations. Some also expressed concern about the size of the deficit but were generally opposed to paying higher taxes in order to help reduce that deficit.

While President Reagan won the election primarily because of his personality, record in office, and general political philosophy, some negative characteristics of the Mondale–Ferraro ticket also contributed to the general election results. Walter Mondale suffered from his association with President Carter and did not have the *communications skills* of President Reagan; the *content of his message* on the necessity of raising taxes was unpleasant compared to the President's assurances that budget deficits would come down without raising taxes. More over, Geraldine Ferraro's candidacy as not the asset that had originally been anticipated; while some said her presence on the ticket made them more likely to vote Democratic than otherwise, more voters expressed the opposite sentiment.* While all these factors undoubtedly contributed to the size of the Mondale–Ferraro defeat, it is highly doubtful that any Democratic ticket could have defeated Reagan at a time of an economic upturn, an America at peace, and a generally optimistic mood.

Hinckley in March 1981. Reagan identified Giordano at a speech before the Italian-American Foundation, using him as an example of how a milkman's son through hard work and the sacrifice of his family, could become a prominent surgeon and save a president's life. Giordano issued a public statement pointing out that his medical education was supported by low-interest government loans and that the medical profession benefited greatly from federally-funded research. He said that, unlike the President, he did not view such programs as causing people to become so dependent that they lose initiative but rather as enabling people with few resources to reach their full potential.

Party Realignment

As in 1980, there was some talk of a major-party realignment triggered by Reagan's and Bush's convincing popular-vote victory and even more one-sided win in the electoral college. However, the results of the congressional races were quite different. Republicans picked up only 14 seats in the House of Representatives (compared to the 33 they won in 1980 and 26 they lost in 1982). Moreover, while retaining control of the Senate, they had a net loss of two seats (as compared to the 12 they won in 1980 and their break-even record in 1982). Thus 1984 did not resemble previous realigning elections in which the victorious party won both houses of the Congress, as well as the presidency.

There were some signs, however, that although 1984 was not a realigning election, it may have helped to lay the groundwork for a future party realignment. Young people (18–24) and others voting for the first time clearly favored President Reagan, providing a potential base for future Republican victories. Public-opinion polls also showed that the traditional gap between persons identifying themselves as Democrats and Republicans narrowed considerably, and that a majority of the American people (including many Democrats) believe that the Republican party is better able to lead the nation and handle the economy. Moreover, while the Republicans picked up only 14 House seats, they captured a majority of the

* The reasons for that sentiment are not certain, that is, whether they related primarily to general attitudes on women as candidates for high office or were more closely connected to specific features of Ferraro's particular situation, such as her financial disclosure difficulties, lack of experience in foreign affairs, and liberal political views.

vote in hotly contested congressional races and gained four House seats from Texas and three from North Carolina. Finally, the Republicans added 338 state legislative seats in 1984, picking up 58 in the 400-member House in New Hampshire, 16 House seats in Texas, and making substantial gains in the legislatures of North Carolina, South Carolina, and Florida.

While the Republican party is still generally regarded as the *minority* party in the United States, the fact of the matter is that it has been the *majority* party in *presidential elections* for over a generation. In the nine elections held since 1952, the GOP has won six (Eisenhower, Nixon, and Reagan each twice), and the Democrats have only won three (Kennedy, Johnson, and Carter). Moreover, five of the six Republican wins have been by substantial margins, the single exception being Nixon's narrow victory over Humphrey in 1968. In contrast, only one of the Democratic victories, Johnson over Goldwater in 1964, was decisive; Kennedy edged out Nixon in 1960 by just over 100,000 votes, while Carter won over Ford by only two percentage points in the popular vote in 1976. (Johnson's victory was the only one in which the Democratic presidential candidate won a majority of the popular vote.) Finally, no Democratic president since 1952 has won re-election, whereas three Republicans—Eisenhower, Nixon, and Reagan—have been elected to a second term.

Over this 32-year period (1952–1984), the Roosevelt New Deal coalition of white Southerners, organized labor, blacks, ethnic groups, Jews, Catholics, big-city residents, and liberal intellectuals has found it increasingly difficult to remain united. The overriding purpose that held that coalition together in the 1930s and 1940s—the desire to see the federal government develop domestic economic programs to help each of the constituent groups—has changed. Some of these groups no longer feel the national government is benefiting them; rather they view it as taxing them to provide benefits to others who do not necessarily desire them. Moreover, the expansion of the national governmental agenda beyond domestic economic concerns to foreign policy, social, and cultural issues has created more bases of disagreement among the various groups. The civil-rights revolution pitted Southern whites against blacks; affirmative-action programs brought similar cleavages between Jews and blacks. The expansion of America's military role in Vietnam brought disagreements between "hawkish" ethnics and working-class people and "dovish" liberal intellectuals. Issues such as abortion created tensions between Catholics and fundamentalist Protestant Southerners on the one hand, and a new group in the Democratic coalition, feminists, on the other. Thus, as more and more matters that once were handled privately became issues on the national political agenda, conflict among groups in the Democratic party increased.

This internal conflict within the Democratic party has been felt primarily in presidential contests. The reason is that in such contests all the groups must agree on a *common presidential candidate* (and a vice-presidential candidate as well). Given the variety of issues involved in presidential politics, it is difficult to nominate a candidate whose views do not offend some group or groups in the coalition. Exacerbating the situation is the nomination process itself, a lengthy series of state primaries and caucuses, made especially difficult by the confrontational style and emphasis of political amateurs and media representatives. The typical result is an exhausted Democratic candidate and squabbling, alienated groups that are prime targets for defection to the Republican candidate in the fall campaign.

The internal divisions in the Democratic party do not present the same problems in congressional races, especially for the House of Representatives. The constituencies are more homogeneous and each can nominate its own kind of Democrat. Liberals in San Francisco can choose Ron Dellums; conservatives in Tulsa can select Jim Jones. Thus the broad variety of Democratic groups that presents such a problem in presidential contests is actually an advantage in congressional races.

Democrats benefit from other major factors in congressional contests. One is that since they still control most of the state legislature, they are the party that draws most of the congressional district lines, an advantage that has accrued to Democratic congressional candidates for many years. The other electoral advantage the Democrats possess is incumbency. In most House races the officeholder runs an essentially nonpartisan campaign that stresses his or her personal trustworthiness and helpfulness to constituents rather than controversial political issues. Moreover, greater political experience and constant exposure to the district voters between elections provides the incumbent with clear advantages over his or her challenger. As a result, few sitting congressmen are defeated even when their party's presidential candidate is going down to a resounding defeat.

Thus our two-party system is essentially a layered one, with the Republicans in the majority in presidential elections and the Democrats in House races as well as most state legislature contests. The Senate tends to be more competitive: state constituencies are not as diverse as a national one, which benefits the Democrats, there is no chance of manipulating constituency boundaries, and incumbency advantages based on personal services provided to constituents are not as pronounced as in the House, which benefits the Republicans. Both parties are also capable of fielding able, experienced, well-financed challengers against incumbents, which also makes Senate contests more competitive and the body itself more subject to partisan turn-overs.

Both parties face difficulties in changing the existing political situation. The Democrats must somehow develop programs and candidates that appeal to (or at least do not alienate) a broad variety of groups in presidential contests. They must also change their presidential nomination process so that it fosters less confrontation and more deliberation and compromise. The Republicans in turn, must build on their recent gains in state legislative contests so that after the 1990 census they can draw more of the congressional district lines in those bodies, as well as the lines for congressional contests. Republicans must also field especially attractive, well-financed congressional candidates and provide them with electoral advice and services sufficient to overcome the natural advantages of incumbency possessed by Democratic members of the House of Representatives. Should both parties succeed in accomplishing these changes, the American political party system would become more competitive for all kinds of offices, rather than just for the Senate.

Implications of the 1984 Election for Future Governing

As in 1980, the resounding Reagan victory raised the issue of whether it constituted a "mandate," that is, a set of instructions from the electorate on how he should govern the nation in his second term. The problem with that interpretation of the election is that the incumbent President made few specific promises about what he would do about the major issue of the economy if he were elected other than to suggest that he would seek some sort of tax reform that would make the system simpler but revenue "neutral" (that is, not raise additional revenues), and seek spending cuts along the lines suggested in the report of the Grace Commission. Perhaps even more important is what the President insisted he would *not* do: attempt to reduce the budget deficit by raising taxes (except as a "last resort") or cut Social Security benefits.

Immediately following the election, the President was confronted with some unfavorable economic news—the economy slowed down considerably in the third quarter of the year, causing the projected deficit to rise from some $180 billion to $210 billion. Some Republican advisors (including the Director of the OMB, David Stockman) told Reagan that it would not be possible to grow ourselves out of the deficit, that the Grace Commission recommendations were not politically feasible, and that domestic programs for the poor had been so drastically cut in the past that future cuts in domestic spending would have to come from programs benefiting the middle-class. The Secretary of the Treasury, Donald Regan, presented the President with a tax simplification plan that would cut tax rates but eliminate many previous loopholes and subsidies, primarily those benefiting upper-class individuals and corporations (who could be expected to fight the adoption of the plan).

Thus, the election provided the President with little guidance on how to handle the major economic problems with which he was immediately faced. As Reagan himself conceded the day after the election, there was no electoral mandate except that the people wanted him to keep on doing what he had been doing, the assumption being that his administration's policies were working. But if these policies appeared no longer to be working, he himself would have to determine *when* that point occurred (for example, a "last resort" situation that would require an increase in taxes) and *what particular changes* should be made to meet the new conditions (for example, what type of new tax program should be enacted).

The post-election political situation also complicated problems for President Reagan. The Republican gains in the House were insufficient to allow him to resurrect the Republican–"Boll-Weevil" Democratic coalition that had passed his major program of budget and tax cuts back in 1981. Moreover, there were fewer Republicans in the Senate than during his first term in office, and the new Republican leadership (individuals such as Majority Leader Robert Dole and Finance Chairman Robert Packwood) were independent persons with economic views that differed considerably from those of the President. Moreover, the President was faced with deciding whether to accept the advice of traditional economic conservatives like Stockman and Dole, who felt that taxes must be raised in order to reduce the budget deficits, or that of Regan and Congressman Jack Kemp who argued that such deficits could be handled through "supply-side" policies promoting economic growth. Finally, President Reagan faced a hostile Speaker of the House, Tip O'Neill, along with other Democratic congressmen who resented the Republican campaign charges that they were "wild" spenders and tax raisers, and who vowed to make the President take the leadership in proposing budget cuts and tax increases.

ASSESSMENT

This year's Democratic nomination contest continued, and in some respects, augmented many of the undersirable developments of recent years. It lasted far too long and exhausted the participants in the process. It was unfavorably affected by the media, which once again emphasized the "horse race" aspect (who's in front and by how many lengths), and concluded at the very onset of the campaign that Mondale had it all wrapped up, and then after his loss to Hart in one unrepresentative state, New Hampshire, that the former Vice-President's candidacy was at an end. They also continued to emphasize the trivial (was Hart 46 or 47, and whose idea was it to drop his true name, "Hartpence"?), and at times labeled persons in highly inappropriate ways, for example, referring to Mondale as a "wimp," which said far more about the sophomoric views of the commentator than the actual character of the candidate.

There were, however, some improvements in the nomination process. The holding of a series of debates in which the Democratic candidates were able to ask each other questions did much to educate the public on their views and their ability to articulate them in the face of opposing views. Moreover, the increase in the number of state caucuses (compared to primaries), together with the presence of "super delegates" at the national convention, allowed officeholders and party officials to play a greater role in the selection of the party's presidential candidate; this development introduced a healthy element of "peer" review into the selection process.

The general election campaign did little to foster a meaningful dialogue between the candidates and the American people. President Reagan held no press conferences after July 24 so that members of the media had no opportunity to ask him questions about a number of important matters, such as developments in El Salvador, Lebanon, the Phillipines, and the domestic economy. Administration officials shielded the President from inquiries on other occasions (at one point he said that "they" wouldn't let him answer any questions), presumably because they feared what his answers would be, or that the inquiries would detract from the canned "message" the administration was trying to convey that particular day. However, not only the administration was at fault: as previously indicated, the media themselves played up the "hoopla" of campaign rallies rather than the substance of what the candidates said, and concentrated on who said what about Geraldine Ferraro's alleged "bitchiness" rather than examining in-depth her views on foreign policy or her record in the Congress.

The two debates provided the *only* real information on the candidates, their abilities, and their views; they were especially helpful for Mondale about whom the American people knew precious little (except that he was trailing badly in the polls). The debates would have been improved, however, had the two candidates been able to ask each other questions.

The ultimate irresponsibility of the media came with the commercial networks' decisions to project a presidential winner before the polls had closed in all parts of the country. The reason given—that if they failed to do so, they would lose "credibility" with the public—was believed by no one but media executives themselves. It ignored the fact that their Canadian counterparts broadcast returns into regions only when their polls have closed, and that every day of the week, the American networks themselves delay the broadcast of news to the West Coast to accommodate the later time there. They should be willing to make similar adjustments to prevent affecting the voting of residents of Western states not only in the presidential election, but in simultaneous congressional and state contests as well.

Glossary

"Access" The opportunity of private persons and groups to present their views on political matters to government officials with the understanding that such views will be considered.

Accusatory System A criminal law system in which the government is required to prove the guilt of the defendant by evidence other than that provided by the defendant.

"Active–Negative" Presidents Those who invest a great deal of energy in the office but who do not derive personal satisfaction from serving, and who are preoccupied with acquiring and maintaining power for its own sake.

"Active–Positive" Presidents Those who invest a great deal of energy in the office, derive personal satisfaction from serving, and who want to accomplish results, particularly changes in governmental institutions, procedures, and policies.

"Active" Presidents Those who invest a great deal of energy in the office, exerting leadership over Congress, charting new directions in public policy, and stretching the powers of the presidential office.

"Activist" Judge A judge who closely scrutinizes the actions of legislative or executive officials and who is willing to invalidate those actions which he or she believes violate constitutional principles.

Administration Bill Bills introduced into Congress that have the backing of the president or some executive agency.

Advisory Opinion Legal opinion given by a court to a government official advising in advance of actual litigation how or whether a particular law should be enforced.

Advocacy Advertising Advertisements that carry essentially a political viewpoint rather than just a commercial message.

"Advocate's" Role The term used to describe the role certain cabinet members assume in seeking to advance the interests of persons and groups especially affected by their departments.

Affirmative Action Plans Plans that attempt to encourage organizations (such as political parties and public and private employers) to take positive action to involve and hire members of traditionally disadvantaged groups, such as blacks, women, and chicanos.

"All Deliberate Speed" The phrase used by the Supreme Court in its 1955 order implementing its 1954 school desegregation ruling. The order entrusted the federal district courts with requiring local school boards to make ". . . a prompt and reasonable start toward full compliance . . ." with the 1954 ruling and seeing to it that desegregation proceed ". . . with all deliberate speed."

"Amateurs" Persons who participate in party activities primarily out of a concern for the public interest and the desire to see basic principles and values they espouse implemented in public programs and policies.

***Amicus Curiae* Brief** A brief filed by an individual or group that is not a direct party to a lawsuit but has an interest in its outcome.

"Anti-Federalists" Subsistence farmers, small businesspeople, artisans, mechanics, and debtors who were generally satisfied with the economic and political conditions during the Articles of Confederation period. This group, which had few national leaders, unsuccessfully opposed the ratification of the Constitution.

Apportionment or Reapportionment (Legislative) The process of allocating or reallocating seats in the House of Representatives among the various states on the basis of population.

Appropriation The actual amount of money that Congress authorizes for a given purpose.

Arbitration The process under which the terms of a final settlement of a labor dispute are decided by a third party.

Articles of Confederation The framework that determined the governance of the United States in the period following American independence from Great Britain and prior to the adoption of the present Constitution. The Articles vested most important powers in the states rather than in the national government. Under the Articles the legislature was the preeminent branch of the national government.

Automatic Plan Plan proposed for changing the present Electoral College system that would eliminate the presidential electors and automatically cast a state's electoral votes for the popular-vote winner in that state.

Automatic Stabilizers Changes in the economy such as an increase in unemployment compensation payments and a decrease in tax revenues during an economic downturn (during an inflation the opposite occurs) that tend to mitigate fluctuations in the economy and serve the general purposes of a deliberate fiscal policy.

"Bad Tendency" Test The judicial test that permits restrictions on freedom of expression if it can be demonstrated that the utterance involved might tend to bring about an evil sometime in the future.

"Balancing" Approach The concept associated with Justice Felix Frankfurter that calls for a case-by-case weighing of values in deciding when restrictions on freedom of individual expression are warranted in order to protect society's interest in order and authority.

Bicameral Legislature A legislature divided into two separate chambers—usually called the House of Representatives and the Senate. Of the American states, only Nebraska does not have a two-house legislature.

Black Caucus Unofficial organization of black members of the House of Representatives who confer and plan political strategy on matters of common concern.

Blacklist A list of persons who have been discharged for participating in union activities that is sent to other employers with the purpose of discouraging them from hiring those persons.

"Black Power" A vague term associated with greater economic and political power for blacks along with the idea of black consciousness.

"Block" Grants Grants by the national government (usually funneled through state governments) for general purposes such as health, education, and welfare, rather than specific, limited programs. (See Special Revenue Sharing.)

Blue-Collar Caucus A recently formed unofficial organization of members of the House of Representatives who prior to becoming members of Congress were in occupations in which they worked with their hands.

"Boll Weevils" A group of Southern Democracts (officially called the Conservative Democratic Forum) formed in the early 1980s in the House of Representatives. They generally gave support to President Reagan's economic program, particularly in 1981.

Bourgeoisie A term used by Karl Marx to describe those members of the middle class who are the private owners of the means of production.

Boycott A refusal to handle or purchase goods—a tactic designed to dramatize grievances against management.

Budget Message Annual message required by the Budget and Accounting Act of 1921 in which the president proposes suggested expenditures for the various executive agencies during the next fiscal year.

Bureaucracy A large-scale organization subdivided into specialized units with a hierarchical chain of command that employs persons who are expected to make decisions on the basis of technical expertise rather than for partisan or personal reasons.

Cabinet A body composed of the heads of the 13 executive departments granted cabinet rank. Presidents can and do invite other officials, such as the director of the Office of Management and Budget, to join in cabinet meetings.

Cabinet Councils Groups of executive branch officials in the Reagan administration who relate the activities of the White House Office to those of the Cabinet.

"Calender Wednesday" A seldom-used procedure in the House of Representatives under which members can bring to the floor for action bills that have been reported by standing committees to the Rules Committee but that have received no rule from that committee.

"Campaigners" The term used by Verba and Nie to describe the persons in their study who concentrated their efforts on participating in political campaigns but who had little to do with "communal" activities. (See "Communalist.")

Career Service The category of public service that employs persons on a merit rather than a political basis and provides them with security of tenure.

"Case and Controversy" Litigation involving an actual dispute that is required to give a federal court jurisdiction over a case.

CategoricalGrants Grant programs restricted to specific, limited purposes such as Aid to Dependent Children.

Caucus Body consisting of all the members of the Democratic party in the House of Representatives that performs its organizing function and is its ultimate decision-making group.

Certiorari A writ issued by a higher court calling up a record of a proceeding in a lower court for review.

"Check and Balance" The theory that by giving each of the other branches of the government the right to participate in a process that is the primary responsibility of one of them (such as the president's power to veto laws passed by Congress), each branch can assert and protect its own rights by withholding its support for the essential activities of a coordinate arm of the government.

Civil Disobedience The deliberate violation of a law to protest its immorality or the immorality of other laws, coupled with the willingness to accept the consequences of one's disobedience.

Civil Liberties The freedoms that individuals enjoy in such diverse matters as religion, speech, press, assembly, and petition; the rights of the accused in criminal cases; the protection of private property and other forms of privacy; the right to vote.

Civil Rights The rights or liberties of minority groups in general or of blacks in particular.

"Clear and Present" Danger Test The test proposed by Justice Oliver Wendell Holmes under which restrictions on freedom of expression are invalid unless they are necessary to prevent the imminent occurrence of an evil that will probably result from the utterance in question.

"Closed" Primaries Those in which only persons affiliated with a political party can participate, such affiliation to be evidenced by a declaration when they register to vote, or by pledging that they have supported the party's candidates in the past or that they will do so in the future.

Closed Shop An arrangement under which employees must join a union before they can be hired to work for an employer.

Cloture A method of terminating debate in the Senate under which 60 percent of the total membership can bring a bill to a vote.

"Coincident" Issues Issues such as social programs for the poor that run parallel to traditional New Deal economic issues.

Cold War The term used to describe the rivalry and tensions that developed between the United States and the Soviet Union in the period after World War II.

Collectivism An economic system in which the government controls production and other economic activities.

"Command" Economy An economic system in which government officials make all the major decisions with respect to the production and allocation of goods, rather than having the private market determine those matters.

Committee of the Whole House A device under which the House of Representatives goes into a special procedure for initially discussing and debating legislation that has different rules (such as a quorum of 100 instead of 218) from those that apply when it is meeting as a regular chamber.

Committee on Committees The committee used by Republicans in both the Senate and the House of Representatives to assign their members to standing committees.

Common-Site Picketing Picketing of an entire project rather than just one or two entrances to the project.

"Communalists" The term used by Verba and Nie to describe persons in their study who were active in cooperative ventures in community affairs but who avoided the conflict of political campaigns.

Communism An economic system associated with the theories of Karl Marx in which the government totally controls the economy.

Comparative Worth The idea that persons holding different jobs but ones similar in value should receive the same pay.

Company Unions Unions dominated and controlled by an employer rather than by employees.

"Competitive Theory of Administration" Term applied to Franklin D. Roosevelt's idea of creating overlapping responsibilities among different administrative units so as to deliberately create rivalries that made each administrator try harder and provided FDR with more information than one administrator alone would provide.

"Complete Activists" The term used by Verba and Nie to describe persons in their study who participated in all types of political activity with great frequency.

Concurrent Jurisdiction The power of two courts (such as federal and state) to hear the same kind of case.

Concurrent Powers Powers possessed jointly by the national and the state governments, such as the power to tax.

Concurring Opinion An opinion written by a justice who agrees with the result reached by the justice writing the majority opinion, but who does not agree with the reasons for that result.

Confederation or Confederative System A political system in which the people grant broad power over certain matters to the governments of the component parts of the system, and those governments, in turn, grant power over a narrow range of those matters to the central government.

Conference (Supreme Court) The meetings at which the members of the Supreme Court collectively make decisions on which cases to hear and how those cases they have already heard should be decided.

Conference Committee A committee consisting of members of both the Senate and House of Representatives that is appointed by the presiding officers of the two chambers to iron out differences between bills passed by the two houses on a common subject matter.

Conferences The bodies, consisting of all Democrats and Republicans (separate bodies) in the Senate, and Republicans only in the House of Representatives, that perform the organizing function for the party and are its ultimate decision-making group.

Conglomerate Mergers Mergers that do not involve competing firms or those with supplier–purchaser relationships; instead they occur when a company acquires another concern in order to penetrate a new geographical market, to handle a related product, or to involve itself in an entirely new type of venture.

Congressional Authorization Congressional approval of a proposed governmental program, together with a maximum expenditure for that program.

"Connecticut Compromise" The plan favored by the delegates at the Constitutional Convention from that medium-sized state that resolved the conflict between the "large-state" Virginia Plan, which based representation in the national legislature on state populations or financial contributions to the national government, and the "small-state" New Jersey Plan, which provided for equality of the state representation. The compromise provided for a House of Representatives based on the size of state populations and a Senate in which each state has two members.

Constituency The persons to whom a public official is politically responsible because such persons choose that official or because he or she is chosen by someone else to look after those persons' interests.

Constituent Service An important function of legislatures at the state and national level, in which individual legislators provide citizens with assistance in dealing with problems they may have with the government.

Constitution The basic framework that determines the functions, procedures, and structure of the government. In a democratic system, the constitution both grants and restricts the exercise of political power.

Constitutional Democracy A system of democracy that emphasizes placing limits on government through legal means.

Constitutionalism The concept that those in positions of political authority should be responsible to the mass of the people for their actions, and that government, even when acting with the support of the majority, should not interfere with the rights of minorities in such matters as religion, the ownership of private property, freedom of speech, and the like.

"Constraint" (Lack of) The term used to describe a low level of consistency on political issues such that a person is inclined to take a "liberal" position on one issue and a "conservative" position on another.

"Containment" The policy proposed by George Kennan and adopted by our political leaders during the period following World War II whereby the United States would apply counterforce against the actions of the Soviet Union at a series of constantly shifting geographical and political points.

"Continuing" Resolution A resolution passed by Congress that provides funding for government agencies at last year's level.

"Cooperative" Federalism Sometimes referred to as the "new" federalism, the term suggests that the national, state, and local governments are "partners" that do not operate independently of one another but cooperate in carrying out various public functions.

Cooperatives A special legal device through which groups such as farmers can join forces to purchase supplies and sell their products without being subject to antitrust suits.

Council of Economic Advisers A group of three professional economists, located in the Executive Office of the President, that advises the president on his annual Economic Report to the nation and on the economic policies that his administration should pursue.

"Court-Packing" Plan A term given to Franklin Roosevelt's proposal that if sitting justices of the Supreme Court reached age 70 and did not retire, he, as president, be authorized to nominate additional justices to the court.

Critical or Realigning Election An election in which there is a major realignment of blocs of voters who switch their traditional party affiliation, and/or a significant number of new voters who cast their votes disproportionately for one party's candidate, the end result being a permanent change in the social support provided the respective parties.

"Cross-Cutting" Issues Issues such as race, law and order, and Vietnam, that do not divide the electorate along the same lines as the traditional New Deal economic issues.

"Custodian" Role proposed by Alexander George for an official such as the Special Assistant to the President for National Security Affairs, who would organize, for the chief executive's consideration, competing information, views, and options on how to handle particular matters in foreign and military policy.

Decomposition of Party (also Party Decomposition) The idea that the two major American political parties are losing their traditional ability to serve as rallying points for majorities of individually powerless citizens.

***"De Facto"* Segregation** Segregation caused by residential living patterns rather than intentionally discriminatory legal action or inaction.

Deficit Spending A situation under which government outlays exceed tax revenues, a policy advocated by British economist John Maynard Keynes in order to create more demand in the economy in the time of an economic downturn.

***"De Jure"* Segregation** Segregation caused by intentionally discriminatory legal action or inaction.

"Demands" Claims that individuals or groups place on political leaders.

Democracy A system of government in which a large number of people enjoy the right to have some voice in important decisions that seriously affect their lives.

"Democratic Study Group" An unofficial organization of Democratic members of the House of Representatives that has recently taken a major role in reforming the practices of the Democratic party in that chamber.

Deviating Election One in which a short-term force such as an appealing candidate or some salient issue or event sufficiently benefits the minority party that it overrides the long-term preferences of the electorate.

Direct Democracy A system of government in which citizens personally participate in the making of governmental decisions.

Direct Lobbying Communicating directly with political decision-makers to try to influence what they do about a political matter.

Direct Popular Election A proposal for abolishing the Electoral College system in favor of one under which the presidential candidate receiving the largest popular vote nationwide would be declared the winner, provided he or she received a minimum percentage of the vote (such as 40 percent). If no candidate did, there would be a runoff election between the two top candidates, or Congress would choose from the front-runners.

Direct Primary A system under which the voters themselves nominate their party's candidates for elective office.

Discharge Rule A rule permitting a majority of the members of the House of Representatives to discharge a bill from a standing committee or the Rules Committee.

Discount Rate The interest rate that member banks must pay for money borrowed from the Federal Reserve Banks.

Dissenting Opinion An opinion written by a justice who disagrees with the result of a decision reached by the majority of the justices of a court.

Distributive Policy The most limited range of policy-making involving distributing benefits to individuals, small groups, and communities. Such policy is made by congressional subcommittees and executive bureaus.

District Plan Plan proposed for changing the Electoral College so that the presidential candidate receiving the plurality of popular votes in a congressional district would receive its electoral vote, with the winner of a plurality of the statewide popular vote receiving the remaining two electoral votes of the state.

Division of Powers The allocation of powers between the national government and the governments of the states (or other subunits of the national government).

Double Jeopardy A constitutional provision prohibiting the federal government (and by judicial interpretation also the states) from trying a person more than once for the same criminal offense.

"Due Process of Law" A term that has traditionally meant that the government cannot deprive a person of his or her life, liberty, or property without observing certain procedural safeguards designed to protect such interests.

"Easy-Money" Policy The policy of trying to counteract a recession by making it easy to borrow money.

Economic Equality A concept subject to different interpretations. A literal interpretation would hold that all persons should receive the same amount of worldly goods regardless of their individual contributions to society. Western democracies, however, while favoring a fairly wide distribution of wealth, emphasize equality of opportunity, not results.

Economic Message Annual message required by the Full Employment Act of 1946 in which the president reports to the Congress on general economic conditions in the nation, including, among other matters, how much money the government may expect to take in from existing revenue measures and how additional moneys might be raised, should they be needed.

Electoral College The system whereby electors chosen in the various states (and equal in number to the senators and representatives from that state) choose the president and the vice-president.

Elite Political Culture or Opinion Basic political beliefs of political leaders compared to ordinary citizens. (See Political Culture and Public Opinion.)

Elitist Political System A system in which political, economic, and social resources are concentrated in the hands of a relatively few individuals and groups.

En Banc A court sitting with all its members rather than only a portion of them.

Entitlement Programs Programs for which persons automatically qualify if they meet the required conditions (such as age or income); the government by law must appropriate the moneys necessary to finance them.

Equality Equality has several meanings. See Economic Equality, Equality of Opportunity, Social Equality, and Equality under the Law.

Equality of Opportunity The right of all persons to develop themselves to the fullest extent of their capabilities. Some persons believe that government only has the obligation to guarantee that formal opportunities are open to all persons, while others contend that government should equalize actual opportunities by providing basic services (health care, education, and the like) that are vital to individual self-development.

Equality under the Law The concept that the law is applied to persons impartially without regard to the identity or status of the individual involved.

"Equal Protection of the Laws" Clause A provision of the Fourteenth Amendment that forbids states from denying equal protection of the laws to any person within their jurisdiction. In recent years courts have utilized this clause to protect blacks and women from discrimination by state or local governments and to prevent malapportionment of legislative bodies.

Evaluation Assessing the merits of a public policy, particularly its impact on the social or economic problem it is designed to address.

Exclusionary Rule Rule relating to the exclusion from a criminal trial of evidence that has been improperly obtained.

Exclusive Federal Jurisdiction The power that only federal, not state, courts have to hear a particular type of case.

Executive Agreement An oral or written agreement entered into by the president with a foreign nation or nations either under the authority and within limitations established by Congress, or by the president acting on his own.

Executive Office of the President An executive branch unit consisting of a variety of agencies (such as the Council of Economic Advisers, the National Security Council, and the Domestic Policy Staff) that assist the president on major problems in public policy.

Executive Oversight A major function of legislatures at both the state and national level, in which the representative assembly checks on how executive agencies are interpreting and applying public policy.

"Expressed" Powers Those specific, enumerated powers set forth in Article I, Section 8 of the Constitution that are granted to the Congress.

"Expressive" Motives Psychological motives for political participation based on an individual's personal satisfaction in doing the "right" thing, even though he or she sees no real chance that a favorite candidate will be elected or a favored bill enacted.

"Faction" A term used by James Madison in *Federalist Paper* No. 10 to describe ". . . a number of citizens, whether amounting to a majority or minority of the whole, who are united and actuated by some common impulse of passion or of interest, adverse to the rights of other citizens, or to the permanent and aggregate interests of the community." Madison considered the most common and durable source of factions to be the uneven distribution of property. Today the term is used to designate groups that are part of a larger body, such as the conservative faction of the Republican party, or the southern faction of the national Democratic party.

Featherbedding Exaction of payment by an employer to an employee for services that are not rendered.

Federalism or Federal System A political system in which political power is divided between the central government of a country and the governments of its component parts so that each level is legally independent of the other within its own sphere of activity.

Federalist Papers A series of newspaper articles authored by Alexander Hamilton, James Madison, and John Jay that explained and defended the Constitution. They appeared during the battle over the ratification of the Constitution and are credited with influencing persons in key states like New York to vote in favor of ratification.

"Federalists" Persons in commerce and finance, as well as the professions, who felt aggrieved by the economic conditions during the Articles of Confederation period and favored a strong national government with power over commerce and taxation. The group, which contained most of the national leaders of the day, successfully campaigned for the ratification of the Constitution.

Felony A serious crime usually carrying a potential penalty of imprisonment for at least a year and a day.

Filibuster The technique of discussing a bill so long in the Senate that no vote can be taken on it.

"Fireside" Chats Radio talks addressed to the American people by Franklin Roosevelt in an informal, intimate tone, designed to acquaint them with problems facing the nation and to explain his actions in dealing with them.

Fiscal Policy A policy under which government officials attempt to manage the economy by manipulating the level of government spending and taxation.

Floor Leader Either the majority or minority party leader in the Senate or House of Representatives.

Franchise The right to vote that in the United States has been extended to more and more groups over the years (non-property-owners, blacks, women, 18-year-olds).

"Free" or "Private" Enterprise An economic system in which private individuals and groups undertake the major economic activities of society.

"Free" or "Private" Market Economy An economic system in which the goods that are produced and the prices that are charged for them are determined by the private market rather than by government officials.

General Jurisdiction (Courts) The second level of the state court hierarchy, in which the majority of serious criminal and important civil suits are heard. These are the major trial courts in the states.

General Revenue Sharing The distribution of a portion of the resources of the national government to states and localities with few or no restrictions on how the money should be spent.

General Schedule A system developed by the Office of Personnel and Management for classifying all merit positions in the federal service.

Gerrymander The drawing of legislative district lines in order to favor certain political interests such as the majority party or incumbent legislators.

Government Corporations Government agencies that undertake commercial enterprises (such as the Tennessee Valley Authority) and that are governed by boards of directors who serve long, staggered terms and are less subject to annual financial control by the president and Congress than other public agencies.

Grants-in-Aid Grants by the national government to the states, usually of cash, but in some instances involving things such as agricultural commodities.

"Gravity of the Evil" or "Sliding Scale" Test The judicial test under which the type of restriction permitted on freedom of expression depends on the seriousness of the evil to be prevented. If the evil is grave enough, then one need not demonstrate that the expression to be regulated will probably result in the immediate occurrence of the evil. But if the evil is not so grave, then one must demonstrate the probability of its immediate occurrence.

Gross National Product The total value of all goods and services in a national economy.

"Heroic" Presidency A "strong" presidency, epitomized by Franklin D. Roosevelt, that is "good" for the nation.

Horizontal Mergers Mergers of companies involved in the same stage of industrial production.

House Rules Committee Committee of the House of Representatives that possesses the power to issue "rules" on the scheduling and terms of debate of legislation on the floor of the chamber.

House Wednesday Group A group of liberal Republicans in the House of Representatives that has a staff to help its members formulate public policies.

Impeachment The bringing of a charge by a majority of the House of Representatives against the president, vice president, or any U. S. civil officer (such as a judge), accusing him or her of treason, bribery, or "high crimes and misdemeanors" justifying his or her removal from office.

"Imperial" Presidency A presidency, epitomized by Richard M. Nixon, that is "bad" for the country because it arrogates powers not provided for by the Constitution.

"Imperiled" Presidency A weak presidency, represented by Jimmy Carter, that is "bad" for the country because it cannot cope with the needs of our society.

Implementation The carrying out or administration of public policies by the executive branch and the courts.

"Implied" Powers All those powers that are "necessary and proper" for carrying into effect the expressed powers of the national government.

Impoundment The temporary or permanent refusal of the president to spend moneys appropriated by the Congress.

"Inactives" The term used by Verba and Nie to describe persons in their study who did not participate in any form of political activity.

Incorporation Theory The idea that the due process clause of the Fourteenth Amendment that applies to the states includes all the procedural safeguards spelled out in the Fourth, Fifth, Sixth, and Eighth Amendments that apply to the national government.

Independent Agency One not part of any cabinet-level department. Included are agencies headed by one administrator, such as the Veterans Administration, independent regulatory commissions, government corporations, and those providing central services and controls such as the Office of Personnel Management and the General Services Administration.

Independent Regulatory Commission An executive unit headed by a bipartisan, multimember board that regulates activities of major private industries and whose members serve long, staggered terms and can be removed only for cause.

Independents Persons who do not identify with a particular political party.

Indirect Lobbying Working through intermediaries to try to influence political decision-makers on a political matter.

"Inferior" Federal Court All federal courts below the U. S. Supreme Court.

A system that permits citizens (not legislators) to propose that certain laws be enacted.

Injunction (Labor) A court order forbidding workers to strike or participate in other concerted activities against their employer on the grounds that such actions threaten to do irreparable damage to the employer's business.

"Inner" Cabinet The Secretaries of State, Defense, and Treasury, and the Attorney General, all of whom share the broad perspectives of the president and have a "counseling" role.

"Inner Club" or "Establishment" A term used to describe the informal group of senators—mostly southern Democrats—who supposedly controlled the Senate in the 1950s from behind the scenes.

Inquisitorial System A criminal law system in which the government depends on evidence obtained from the defendant him- or herself in establishing his or her guilt.

Institutional Agenda A governmental or formal agenda established by public officials consisting of that set of items explicitly set up for their active and serious consideration.

"Instrumental" Motives Psychological motives for political participation based on a specific goal such as a victory for a particular candidate or the passage of a certain bill.

Interest Group Any group of persons, having a shared attitude on a matter, that makes claims or demands on others in society with respect to that matter.

"Iron Triangles" Three-way alliances of executive agencies, congressional committees and subcommittees, and interest groups that combine efforts in various areas of public policy in order to advance their common interests.

Judicial Review The power of a court to review the actions of all public officials—legislative, executive, and judicial—to see whether they are inconsistent with the governing constitution, and, if the court finds that they are, to declare them unconstitutional and, hence, unenforceable.

Jury (Petit Jury) The body of citizens that hears the evidence and decides on the facts in a civil or criminal proceeding.

Justice The traditional idea that each person should receive what is "due" him or her in life.

Keynesianism Macroeconomic theory favoring managing the economy by managing the aggregate demand for goods and services.

"Kickback" A political contribution to a political party by a government contractor consisting of a portion of the money paid to the contractor by the government.

"Laissez-Faire" Capitalism An economic system associated with the theories of Adam Smith that allows private individuals and groups, rather than government officials, to make key decisions on the production and distribution of goods.

"Lame Duck" Congress The term used to designate the former Congresses (since changed by the Twentieth Amendment) in which members defeated in November of even-numbered years remained in office until the following March.

Law Rules and regulations issued by national, state, or local governments that can be enforced through the legitimate use of force.

Legislative Caucus A system used early in our history in which party members in the state legislature and the House of Representatives nominated candidates for statewide office and for president and vice president, respectively.

Legislative Veto The power of legislators to reverse decisions of executive officials.

Liberal Democracy A system of democracy that is concerned primarily with the liberty of the individual.

Liberty The right of individuals to select their own purposes in life together with the means to accomplish those purposes provided those choices do not unduly interfere with the rights of other persons.

Life Cycle The various stages of one's life—early family relations, school, college, work—through which an individual passes and that have separate kinds of influence on his or her political attitudes.

Lobbying Communicating with political decision-makers to try to influence them on a political matter.

Lockout A tactic used by employers involved in a labor dispute whereby they close their business or discharge large numbers of workers.

Logrolling A process whereby legislators or interest group representatives exchange support for measures in which they are separately concerned.

"Lug" A financial contribution by a public employee to a political party, usually based on a certain percentage of his or her salary.

"Machine" A party organization, run by a "Boss," that provides material and social benefits for persons in return for their vote.

Macroeconomics Activities involving the overall economy.

Macropolitics The broadest range of policy-making, involving the allocation of costs and benefits affecting broad social groups and classes such as industry, labor, and agriculture, or the affluent and the disadvantaged. Such policy is made at the highest level of the political system by the president and Congress and is covered extensively by the media.

"Magistrate" Role proposed by Alexander George for the president in weighing various information, views, and options provided him on foreign and military matters on which he makes the final decision.

Maintaining Election An election in which the long-term partisan orientation of the electorate results in keeping the traditional majority party in power.

Majority Leader The leader of the majority party in both the Senate and the House of Representatives.

Mandatory Controls Government controls over such matters as wages and prices that are enforceable by law.

"Mark Up" The procedure under which legislative committees or subcommittees go over a bill (often line by line) to amend and at times almost rewrite it.

Material Benefits Tangible rewards, often monetary, that persons seek to gain through membership in an organization.

Mediation A process involving the use of neutral persons to try to settle labor disputes between contending parties.

Medicaid A social welfare program for acute and long-term medical care based on the "need" of recipients such as the aged and disabled poor.

Medicare A social insurance program that provides hospital and nursing-home care for aged and disabled persons.

Microeconomics Activities pertaining to key sectors of the economy such as business, labor, and agriculture.

Micropolitics See distributive policy.

"Midnight" Appointments Appointments made by Federalist President John Adams to judicial posts, just prior to his leaving office, that were designed to give his party, defeated in the presidential and congressional elections of 1800, a foothold in the judicial branch of the national government.

Military–Industrial Complex Name given to the combination of professional military men, defense contractors, and congressional members (who want military installations and defense industries in their districts) who are said to exert tremendous pressures to keep military spending at a high level and to further a "hard-line" policy with Communist nations.

Minority Leader The leader of the minority party in the Senate or the House of Representatives.

Misdemeanor A minor crime usually carrying a penalty of a fine or imprisonment of a year or less.

"Mixed" Economy An economic system that combines elements of both private and public control of economic activities.

"Mixed" Government A system of government favored by John Adams that provides for representation of both property and numbers of people in the political structure. Thus, the Founders expected the Senate to represent primarily persons of economic substance from the upper social classes while the House of Representatives would represent the interests of the many in society, the common people who owned no private property of any consequence.

Monetarism Macroeconomic theory that is primarily concerned with preventing inflation by controlling the growth of the money supply.

Monetary Policy The management of the economy through regulating the supply of money, the availability of credit, and interest rates.

National Bonus Plan A proposal for changing the electoral college system to award 102 "bonus" votes to the winner of the nationwide popular vote, these electoral votes to be added to electoral votes received under the present state-by-state system.

"National Interest" The self-interest of a nation, including such matters as maintaining its territorial integrity, basic governmental institutions, access to foreign markets, honor, prestige, and "way of life."

National Party Convention The system that developed in the 1830s and that still exists today under which citizens from the various states choose delegates to the national convention who, in turn, nominate the party's candidates for president and vice president.

"Necessary and Proper" Clause The clause in Article I, Section 8 of the Constitution that grants Congress the power to make laws "necessary and proper" for carrying into execution its specific, enumerated powers previously set forth in that section. This clause is the basis of the "implied" powers of the national government.

"Negative" Presidents Those who do not experience pleasure from being president but who serve because of compulsion or out of a sense of duty to their country.

New Christian Right A conservative force composed of fundamentalist Protestant ministers and "evangelicals"—persons who believe in the literal interpretation of the Bible and its application to everyday living, many of whom report to having been "born again"—who have become increasingly active politically in recent years on behalf of moral standards, traditional family values, and "Americanism."

New Deal Coalition The blacks, southerners, members of organized labor, ethnic groups, intellectuals, and urban political bosses that supported Franklin Roosevelt.

New Jersey Plan The plan introduced at the Constitutional Convention favored by the small states that provided for a one-house national legislature with each state having the same number of representatives.

"Nonactivist" Judge A judge who presumes that actions of legislative or executive officials are constitutional and who seldom substitutes his or her constitutional judgment for that of such officials.

Office of Policy Development A group of officials located in the Executive Office of the President who advise the chief executive on the nation's internal problems.

Office of Management and Budget A unit in the Executive Office of the President that provides the chief executive with advice on budgetary and legislative matters, the coordination of government programs, executive branch organization, information and management systems, and the development of executive talent.

Oligarchy A system of government in which political authority is vested in a few persons who are not accountable or responsible to the mass of people.

Oligopoly An industry dominated by a few giant firms.

"One Man–One Vote" The phrase used to summarize the Supreme Court ruling in *Wesbury* v. *Sanders* (1964) that House members must represent approximately equal numbers of people because "one man's vote in a congressional election is to be worth as much as another's."

"Open Diplomacy" The term applied to conducting diplomatic relations in public view rather than secretly behind the scenes.

"Open" Primaries Those primaries in which a voter may choose to participate in whichever political party's primary he or she chooses regardless of his or her own affiliation.

Open Shop An arrangement whereby an employee does not have to join a union as a condition of employment.

"Opinion" Day The day (usually Monday) on which the Supreme Court announces in open session its decisions on various cases and the reasons for them.

Original Jurisdiction The power of a court to hear a case for the first time.

"Outer Cabinet" Secretaries of the nine departments that have a special clientele (such as Agriculture and Labor) and who have an "advocatory" role with the president.

Oversight Congressional control over the executive branch through requiring agencies to report on their activities and to receive congressional approval of them.

Parity The price to be charged for certain agricultural crops that would give farmers producing them a purchasing power equal to that which they enjoyed in a prosperous era, such as 1909–1914.

"Parochial" Participants The term used by Verba and Nie to describe the persons in their study who participated in political activities by initiating particularized contacts with government officials on matters that affected their personal lives, but who did not engage in "campaign" or "communal" activities. (See "Campaigners" and "Communalists.")

"Participatory" Democracy The concept that ordinary persons should play a greater part in making decisions that vitally affect their lives and that democracy's major purpose should be the full development of an individual's personality and character through participation in the political life of the community.

Partisan Identification or Affiliation A favorable psychological attitude that a person develops towards a particular political party, which inclines him or her to vote for that party's candidates.

Party in the Electorate Those persons who are supporters of, voters for, and identifiers with a political party.

Party in the Government Those persons who hold official positions in the legislative or executive branch and are either elected under a party label or appointed to a position primarily because of their relationship to a particular party. Moreover, in the discharge of their official duties they are expected to reflect the views of their party.

Party Organization Those persons active in party affairs whether they hold an official party post or not.

"Passive–Negative" Presidents Those who do not have the inclination or ability to exercise political power effectively, do not experience pleasure from being president, and who serve out of a sense of civic duty and rectitude.

"Passive–Positive" Presidents Those who do not have the inclination and ability to exercise political power effectively, but who do enjoy serving in the office, primarily because they want to be popular, or to be loved and admired by others.

"Passive" Presidents Those who do not have the inclination or the ability to exercise political power effectively and who tend to respond to congressional initiatives and support the status quo, and who do not use the full authority of their office.

Payment-in-Kind (PIK) Program A program instituted by the Reagan administration whereby the federal government provides grain and cotton from its stockpiles to farmers who agree to take a certain number of acres devoted to such crops out of production.

Peers Contemporaries of an individual contrasted to authority figures such as parents, teachers, and the like.

Period Effects Salient political events that have a similar impact on the political attitudes of persons of all ages.

"Permanent Government" The term applied to members of the federal bureaucracy who remain in their positions rather than change from one presidential administration to another and who are primarily concerned with the activities of their own agency rather than an overall presidential program.

"Personal" Diplomacy The carrying on of diplomacy, particularly handling major treaties and agreements, by the president rather than lower-level officials.

Phillips Curve The trade-off between inflation and unemployment so that as one rises, the other is supposed to fall.

"Picket Fence" Federalism The symbol of present-day federalism, with the "pickets" representing the close relationships that exist among officials of national, state, and local governments engaged in the same functions (highways, welfare, and the like), and the crossrails depicting the horizontal relationships among legislators and chief executives who as generalists try to regulate and integrate the activities of the specialists engaged in the various functions.

Picketing Surrounding a place of employment with persons dramatizing their grievances with management—a tactic designed to discourage workers and customers from entering the premises or having any business relationship with the company.

Pluralistic Political System A system in which political, economic, and social resources are distributed widely among a large number of individuals and groups.

"Pocket" Veto A veto that occurs when the president takes no action on a bill when Congress is no longer in session at the end of the 10-day period after he receives the measure.

"Police Power" The power granted to the states to pass laws for the "health, safety, and morals" of the people.

Policy Committee The committee used by both parties in the Senate and the Republicans in the House of Representatives to plan and develop party programs.

"Policy Subgovernments" See "Iron Triangles."

Political Culture The fundamental beliefs of citizens concerning the ends or purposes of political activity; the general nature of the political process; the part that individual citizens play in the process.

Political Equality The equal right of persons to participate in the political process through voting, joining interest groups, serving in political office, and the like.

"Political Executives" Persons who hold top policy-making positions in the executive branch, including officials of the Executive Office of the President, secretaries of cabinet departments, heads of independent offices and establishments, as well as second- and third-level officials in such agencies.

"Political Generation" A group of age cohorts who share salient political experiences during pre- and early adulthood as exemplified by the "Depression generation," who were 17–25 years old in the period 1929–1935.

Political Generation Influences The salient political events that a person experiences during his or her pre- and young-adult years (17–25) that help to shape his or her political attitudes.

Political Party An organization that runs candidates for public office under its label.

Political Setting The general political environment of an area—relating to such matters as whether politics has traditionally been an important activity or whether political contests are close—which affects the general level of political participation by residents of the area.

Political Socialization The process by which persons acquire political attitudes over the course of their lifetime.

Political "Subculture" The distinctive political beliefs of members of certain social groups such as blacks, chicanos, southerners, easterners, and the like.

"Position" Issues Issues that involve advocacy of governmental action from a set of alternatives.

"Positive" Presidents Those who enjoy political life and who derive a great deal of satisfaction from serving in the office.

"Positive" State The concept that government, and particularly the national government, should play a major role in dealing with major economic and social problems of society.

"Preferred Position" Approach The concept that First Amendment freedoms enjoy a special status in our constitutional system and that therefore judges should carefully scrutinize the actions of legislative or executive officials that relate to such freedoms, even though they presume that such officials' actions in other matters (such as regulating economic affairs) are constitutional.

Presidential Primary A system under which voters choose delegates from their state to represent them at the national presidential nominating convention.

President Pro Tempore The chief ceremonial officer of the Senate who presides over the chamber in the absence of the vice president.

Pressure Group The older term for interest group that implies that the group is selfish and that it uses improper means—force, bribery, and threats—to achieve its purposes.

Primary Boycott A boycott directed against the employer with whom persons have a grievance.

"Private-Regarding" Groups Groups that hold values placing their short-term benefit before the welfare of the city as a whole. Such groups view city politics as another means of group advancement, in contrast to "public-regarding" groups, which are willing to forego immediate group advantage for the benefit of the entire city.

"Professionals" Persons who are active in party affairs because they want some tangible, material benefit, or enjoy the "game" of politics for its own sake.

"Project" Grant-in-Aid Grants that require the specific approval of the national government (such as moneys for municipal waste-treatment plants) rather than being automatically provided to all communities that apply for them.

Proletariat The term used by Karl Marx to describe the workers in an industrial society who are exploited by those members of the middle class who are the private owners of the means of production.

Proportional Plan A plan proposed for changing the present Electoral College system so that a state's electoral votes would be divided in proportion to the division of the popular vote in that state for presidential candidates.

Proportional Representation A system of allocating delegates to a convention, or seats in a legislative body, that takes into account the proportion of the popular vote cast for the various candidates.

Psychohistory The use of psychological factors in explaining the behavior of individuals and the way such behavior affects events.

Public Defender An attorney paid by public funds who concentrates on providing a legal defense in criminal cases for all persons who cannot afford an attorney of their own.

"Public-Interest" Groups Interest groups with the goal of bringing improvements in society as a whole rather than for just their own membership.

Public Opinion Attitudes of citizens toward matters that affect the day-to-day operation of the political system, such as important issues facing the nation, policies to be followed in dealing with such issues, and candidates and persons who hold public office.

Public Policies Decisions made by public officials that affect the distribution of benefits and the incidence of burdens among individuals and groups in society.

"Publics" Separate groups of persons with distinctive views on different political matters.

Public Utilities Concerns providing vital services (such as natural resources, transportation, communication) that are treated as "natural" monopolies and that are owned or extensively regulated by the government.

"Purple Curtain" The curtain that forms the backdrop for public appearances of the justices of the Supreme Court. Most of the work of the court occurs behind the scenes (hence, behind the "Purple Curtain").

"Purposive" Benefits Benefits that transcend one's own personal interests and are associated with other individuals or groups or with society as a whole.

"Quadriad" The term used to describe the four major officials who advise the president on economic policy: the chairman of the Federal Reserve Board (and the three other executive officials—the chairman of the Council of Economic Advisers, the director of the Office of Management and Budget, and the Secretary of the Treasury—who are known as the "troika").

Quota System The system developed by the Democratic Party in 1972 under which some states selected as delegates to the national convention members of minority groups, women, and young people, in proportion to their numerical presence in the state population.

"Rally-'Round-the-Flag" The tendency of the American people to initially come to the president's support at a time of international crisis.

Random Sampling A technique of eliciting information from a small number of persons (the sample) that is representative of the views of a larger group (the population) from which the sample is drawn. The important statistical principle involved is that each person in the population must have an equal chance of being chosen in the sample.

Recall A system that permits citizens to oust officeholders between elections.

"Reconciliation" Procedure A procedure requiring congressional appropriations to stay within overall spending figures authorized by the two chambers.

Redistributive Policy See Macropolitics.

Reference Groups or Symbols Groups or symbols that a person identifies with, either affirmatively or negatively, even though he or she is not personally associated with them.

Referendum A procedure for referring proposed laws to the voters for an ultimate decision.

Regulatory Policy Policy relating to an entire functional area (such as transportation) involving executive agencies, interest groups, and congressional committees.

Reinstating Election Following a deviating election, an election in which long-term partisan factors operate so that the traditional majority party is returned to office.

Reorganization Plans Plans proposed by presidents to the Congress for changing the organization of the executive branch of the government.

Representative Democracy A system of government in which ordinary citizens do not make governmental decisions themselves but instead choose public officials (usually through elections) to make decisions for them. This system is used in political units that are too large to employ direct democracy.

Reserve Requirements The ratio of reserves to loans that member banks are required to maintain by the Federal Reserve Board.

Revenue-Sharing The distribution of a portion of the resources of the national government to states and localities. (See General Revenue Sharing and Special Revenue Sharing.)

"Right-to-Work" Laws Legislation permitting open-shop contracts.

Role Change An issue requiring a change in the traditional roles played by men and women in society.

Role Equity An issue that focuses on whether men and women in similar situations are being treated equally.

"Run-off" Primary A type of primary that provides that if no candidate wins a majority of the votes on the first ballot, a "run-off" is held between the two top vote-getters. Used primarily by the Democratic party in the South, it has been severely criticized by the Reverend Jesse Jackson, who argues that a black candidate can win the plurality of the vote in the first primary but loses out in the run-off because white voters join forces to choose the first-ballot runnerup.

Secondary Boycott A boycott directed not against the employer with whom persons have a grievance, but against one who does business with that employer.

"Selective Benefits" Benefits that accrue only to members of an organization, such as low-cost insurance, health benefits, malpractice insurance, and the like.

"Selectorate" Term used to describe the persons who help to choose presidential nominees, contrasted to the "electorate," which casts its vote in the general election.

"Senatorial Courtesy" The custom that senators will refuse to confirm presidential nominations to executive or judicial positions if a senator from the state concerned opposes the nomination.

Seniority Custom The custom typically followed by both parties in the Senate and House of Representatives of choosing the member with the longest continuous service on a standing committee as its chairman or ranking minority member.

"Separate But Equal" Doctrine The doctrine enunciated in *Plessy* v. *Ferguson* (1896) that separate public facilities for persons of different races are constitutional provided they are equal.

Separation of Powers (Processes) The concept borrowed by the Founders from the French political thinker Montesquieu, that the liberties of the people are best protected by a system in which political power is distributed among the three branches of the government so that the legislature has the primary responsibility for making the laws, the executive for putting them in effect, and the judiciary for interpreting them.

"Shuttle Diplomacy" The type of procedure used in international negotiations (particularly associated with former Secretary of State Henry Kissinger) in which separate, secret conferences are held with all parties to a dispute and public statements on such matters are withheld until negotiations are completed.

"Silent" Gerrymander The technique of failing to redraw legislative districts to reflect changes in population within a state.

Social Class Status The social position one enjoys as a result of educational, occupational, or economic background.

Social Equality The concept that persons should be free of class or social barriers and means of discrimination. Disagreement exists on the role (if any) that government should play in trying to ensure social equality.

Social Insurance Programs Programs financed from special trust funds (such as Social Security retirement benefits) that generally go to persons whether or not they demonstrate an actual need for them.

Socialism An economic system in which major economic activities—particularly the basic means of production, distribution, and communication—are owned and administered by the government.

"Social Issue" The collective term used to describe issues other than traditional economic and foreign policy matters, and including such matters as race, crime, and disorder.

"Social" Lobby Trying to keep communication channels open to political decision-makers by entertaining them socially.

Social Welfare Programs Programs financed from general revenues that go to persons who can demonstrate an actual need for the benefits. Also known as "relief" programs.

"Solidary Benefits" Intangible benefits such as friendship and fellowship that people seek from belonging to an organization.

Speaker The major officer of the House of Representatives, who is theoretically chosen by the entire membership of the House, but who in reality is selected by the members of the majority party in that chamber.

Special Revenue Sharing The distribution of a portion of the resources of the national government to states and localities, with the latter authorized to spend the moneys for certain broad purposes. (See Block Grants.)

"Special Session" Power The power of the president to call one or both Houses of Congress into special session at times other than when they are in session.

Split-Ticket Voting Voting for candidates of more than one party for different offices at the same election.

Stagflation The simultaneous increase in both unemployment and inflation together with a decline in the rate of economic growth.

Standard Metropolitan (Statistical) Area A central city with a population of 50,000 or more, together with the county in which that city is situated and other counties that are economically and socially integrated with the county in which the central city is situated.

State Convention Choice of Delegates A system under which delegates to the national presidential nominating convention are chosen by state convention delegates who themselves are elected at lower geographical levels, such as precincts, wards, counties, and congressional districts.

"State of the Union" Message The annual message mandated by the Constitution in which the president reports to the Congress on conditions in the nation and recommends measures that he thinks are necessary and expedient for dealing with such conditions.

Steering and Policy Committee Party committee of Democrats in the House of Representatives that nominates members for assignments to standing committees, and devises and directs the party's legislative program.

Steering Committee The party committee used by Senate Democrats to nominate persons to be assigned to standing committees.

Strike The withholding of their labor by workers as a means of forcing management to provide them with better wages, fringe benefits, or working conditions.

Structural Unemployment Unemployment that is concentrated in specific industries, geographical areas, or particular segments of the work force, such as teenagers, blacks, poor whites, or chicanos, that lack basic educational and vocational skills.

Subsystem Politics See Regulatory Policy.

"Sunset" Law A law that would place all government programs on a limited schedule (such as five years) of legislative consideration and that would have programs terminate automatically at the end of that period unless the legislature specifically reauthorized them.

"Super Delegates" National and state elected and party officials chosen by such officials themselves who served as legally "unpledged" delegates to the 1984 Democratic National Convention, most of whom voted for Walter Mondale.

"Supply-side" Economics Macroeconomic theory that emphasizes the importance of increasing the supply of goods and services that are produced in society.

"Supports" The cooperation and assistance that individuals—and particularly interest groups—provide to political leaders.

"Switchers" A term for persons who vote for one party's candidate for an office (such as the presidency) one year and for another party's candidate for that office in the following election.

Symbolic Speech Political views expressed through conduct rather than words.

Systemic Agenda An informal agenda established by persons outside the government and consisting of all those issues that are commonly perceived by members of the political community as meriting public attention and as involving matters within the legitimate jurisdiction of existing governmental authority.

Traditional Economic Conservatism Macroeconomic theory emphasizing the necessity of balancing the budget.

Third Parties The term applied to all minor parties in the United States, that is, all parties except the Democrats and Republicans.

"Tight-Money" Policy The policy of trying to counteract inflation by making it difficult to borrow money.

"Troika" The term used to describe the three major executive branch officials that advise the president on economic policy—the chairman of the Council of Economic Advisers, the director of the Office of Management and Budget, and the Secretary of the Treasury.

Unemployment Insurance Insurance that provides weekly payments for a prescribed period to workers who are thrown out of work through no fault of their own.

Unicameral Legislature A legislature in which the entire membership is contained in a single house. Nebraska is the only state at present with a one-house legislative assembly.

Union Shop An arrangement under which employees must join a union within a designated period after they are hired by an employer.

"Unit" or "General Ticket" System The system, presently used by all states except Maine, of awarding all the state's electoral votes to the presidential candidate who wins a plurality of the popular votes in the state.

Unitary System A political system in which the people grant broad power over their activities to the central government, which, in turn, delegates authority over a limited number of those activities to the governments of the component parts.

United States Court of Appeals The major appellate courts of the federal judicial system that principally handle cases that begin in the U. S. District Courts as well as appeals from orders and decisions of federal administrative units, particularly the independent regulatory agencies.

United States District Court A trial court in the federal judicial system that hears such matters as bankruptcy cases, antitrust prosecutions, and suits involving the interstate theft of automobiles.

United States Supreme Court The highest court in our federal system, consisting of nine justices who have original jurisdiction over cases involving foreign ambassadors, ministers and consuls, and those in which a state is a party, but who hear most cases on appeal from lower courts.

Unreasonable Searches and Seizures Invasions of privacy of one's person or property forbidden by the Fourth and—through judicial interpretation—the Fourteenth Amendment of the Constitution.

"Valence" Issues Issues that merely involve the linking of the parties with some condition that is positively or negatively valued by the electorate but that do not involve advocation of some sort of governmental action to deal with that condition. (See "Position" Issues.)

Vertical Mergers Mergers between companies that do not compete with each other but are involved in different stages of production.

Veto Power The power of the president to nullify an act passed by Congress, which accomplishes that purpose unless both Houses repass the measure over his veto by a two-thirds vote.

Virginia Plan Authored by James Madison, the first plan considered by the Constitutional Convention called for a radical break from the Articles of Confederation. The plan, which was favored by large, wealthy states, provided for a strong national government and a two-house legislature based on state populations or financial contributions to the national government.

"Voting Specialists" The term used by Verba and Nie to describe the persons in their study who voted in presidential elections and always or almost always in local elections, but who did not participate in other forms of political activity.

Wage-Price Guidelines General levels of wages and prices established by government officials, which they try to implement through moral persuasion and the influence of public opinion rather than the force of law.

Ways and Means Committee A standing committee of the House of Representatives in which revenue measures originate and which also has jurisdiction over other vital matters such as health care, welfare, and foreign aid.

Western Democracy The form of democracy developed in Western nations like Great Britain, Switzerland, and the United States.

Western Representative Democracy See Representative Democracy and Western Democracy.

Whips Assistants to the majority and minority leaders in the Senate and House of Representatives who serve as communication links between the party leaders and rank-and-file members of the party.

White House Office A unit within the broader structure of the Executive Office of the President that is populated with the closest aides of the president—those who write his speeches, arrange his appointments, and facilitate his relationships with the media, Congress, other executive officials, and political parties and interest groups.

"Wide-Open" Primary A system that permits a voter to participate in one party's primary for some officials and in another's for different officials.

"Windfall Profits" Tax A tax levied on profits that are not expected or deserved. A recent example is the tax levied on the profits of oil companies that they made as a result of having oil prices rise from the levels previously set by the government to that established by the world market manipulated by the Organization of Petroleum Exporting Countries (OPEC).

Women's Caucus An unofficial organization of women members of the House of Representatives who confer and plan political strategy on matters of common concern.

"Women's Liberation" Branch of the Feminist Movement That part of the women's movement that has sought to alter basic elements of male–female relationships in society, using such methods as "consciousness-raising" through local groups.

"Women's Rights" Branch of the Feminist Movement That part of the women's movement that has sought primarily economic and educational equality for women through traditional political and legal channels.

Workmen's Compensation Compensation paid to employees injured in the course of their employment.

Writ of Mandamus A court order requiring a public official to perform an official duty over which he or she has no discretion.

Yellow-Dog Contract An agreement between an employer and an employee under which the latter agrees as a condition of employment that he or she will not join a union.

"Zero-Based" Budgeting A system under which agencies would be required to justify every dollar they plan to spend during the next fiscal year rather than simply to apply for an increase over their previous year's appropriation, as is presently done.

The Constitution of the United States of America

We the People of the United States, in Order to form a more perfect Union, establish Justice, insure domestic Tranquility, provide for the common defence, promote the general Welfare, and secure the Blessings of Liberty to ourselves and our Posterity, do ordain and establish this Constitution for the United States of America.

Article I

Section 1. All legislative Powers herein granted shall be vested in a Congress of the United States, which shall consist of a Senate and House of Representatives.

Section 2. The House of Representatives shall be composed of Members chosen every second Year by the People of the several States, and the Electors in each State shall have the Qualifications requisite for Electors of the most numerous Branch of the State Legislature.

No Person shall be a Representative who shall not have attained to the age of twenty five Years, and been seven Years a Citizen of the United States, and who shall not, when elected, be an Inhabitant of that State in which he shall be chosen.

Representatives and direct Taxes shall be apportioned among the several States which may be included within this Union, according to their respective Numbers, which shall be determined by adding to the whole Number of free Persons, including those bound to Service for a Term of Years, and excluding Indians not taxed, *three fifths of all other persons.** The actual Enumeration shall be made within three Years after the first Meeting of the Congress of the United States, and within every subsequent Term of ten Years, in such Manner as they shall by Law direct. The Number of Representatives shall not exceed one for every thirty thousand, but each State shall have at Least one Representative; and until

* Italics indicate passages altered by subsequent amendments. This was revised by the Sixteenth (apportionment of taxes) and Fourteenth (determination of persons) amendments.

such enumeration shall be made, the State of New Hampshire shall be entitled to chuse three, Massachusetts eight, Rhode-Island and Providence Plantations one, Connecticut five, New-York six, New Jersey four, Pennsylvania eight, Delaware one, Maryland six, Virginia ten, North Carolina five, South Carolina five, and Georgia three.

When vacancies happen in the Representation from any State, the Executive Authority thereof shall issue Writs of Election to fill such Vacancies.

The House of Representatives shall chuse their Speaker and other Officers; and shall have the sole Power of Impeachment.

Section 3. The Senate of the United States shall be composed of two Senators from each State, *chosen by the Legislature thereof,** for six Years; and each Senator shall have one Vote.

Immediately after they shall be assembled in Consequence of the first Election, they shall be divided as equally as may be into three Classes. The Seats of the Senators of the first Class shall be vacated at the Expiration of the second Year, of the Second class at the Expiration of the fourth Year, and of the third Class at the Expiration of the sixth Year, so that one third may be chosen every second Year; *and if Vacancies happen by Resignation, or otherwise, during the Recess of the Legislature of any State, the Executive thereof may make temporary Appointments until the next Meeting of the Legislature, which shall then fill such Vacancies.†*

No Person shall be a Senator who shall not have attained to the Age of thirty Years, and been nine Years a Citizen of the United States, and who shall not, when elected, be an Inhabitant of the State for which he shall be chosen.

The Vice President of the United States shall be President of the Senate, but shall have no Vote, unless they be equally divided.

The Senate shall chuse their other Officers, and also a President pro tempore, in the Absence of the Vice President or when he shall exercise the Office of President of the United States.

The Senate shall have the sole Power to try all Impeachments. When sitting for that Purpose, they shall be on Oath or Affirmation. When the President of the United States is tried, the Chief Justice shall preside: And no Person shall be convicted without the Concurrence of two thirds of the Members present.

Judgment in Cases of Impeachment shall not extend further than to removal from Office, and disqualification to hold and enjoy any Office of honor, Trust or Profit under the United States: but the Party convicted shall nevertheless be liable and subject to Indictment, Trial, Judgment and Punishment, according to Law.

Section 4. The Times, Places and Manner of holding Elections for Senators and Representatives, shall be prescribed in each State by the Legislature thereof; but the Congress may at any time by Law make or alter such Regulations, except as to the Places of chusing Senators.

The Congress shall assemble at least once in every Year, and such Meeting shall be *on the first Monday in December,** unless they shall by Law appoint a different Day.

Section 5. Each House shall be the Judge of the Elections, Returns and Qualifications of its own Members, and a Majority of each shall constitute a Quorum to do Business; but a smaller Number may adjourn from day to day, and may be authorized to compel the Attendance of absent Members, in such Manner, and under such Penalties as each House may provide.

Each House may determine the Rules of its Proceedings, punish its Members for disorderly Behavior, and, with the Concurrence of two thirds, expel a Member.

Each House shall keep a Journal of its Proceedings, and from time to time publish the same, excepting such Parts as may in their Judgment require Secrecy; and the Yeas and Nays of the Members of either

* Revised by Seventeenth Amendment.

† Revised by Seventeenth Amendment.

* Revised by Twentieth Amendment.

House on any question shall, at the Desire of one fifth of those Present, be entered on the Journal.

Neither House, during the Session of Congress, shall, without the Consent of the other, adjourn for more than three days, nor to any other Place than that in which the two Houses shall be sitting.

Section 6. The Senators and Representatives shall receive a Compensation for their Services, to be ascertained by Law, and paid out of the Treasury of the United States. They shall in all Cases, except Treason, Felony and Breach of the Peace, be privileged from Arrest during their Attendance at the Session of their respective Houses, and in going to and returning from the same; and for any Speech or Debate in either House, they shall not be questioned in any other Place.

No Senator or Representative shall, during the Time for which he was elected, be appointed to any civil Office under the Authority of the United States, which shall have been created, or the Emoluments whereof shall have been encreased during such time; and no Person holding any Office under the United States, shall be a Member of either House during his Continuance in Office.

Section 7. All Bills for raising Revenue shall originate in the house of Representatives; but the Senate may propose or concur with Amendments as on other Bills.

Every Bill which shall have passed the House of Representatives and the Senate, shall, before it become a Law, be presented to the President of the United States; if he approve he shall sign it, but if not he shall return it, with his Objections to that House in which it shall have originated, who shall enter the Objections at large on their Journal, and proceed to reconsider it. If after such Reconsideration two thirds of that House shall agree to pass the Bill, it shall be sent, together with the Objections, to the other House, by which it shall likewise be reconsidered, and if approved by two thirds of that House, it shall become a Law. But in all such Cases the Votes of both Houses shall be determined by Yeas and Nays, and the Names of the Persons voting for and against the Bill shall be entered on the Journal of each House respectively. If any Bill shall not be returned by the President within ten Days (Sundays excepted) after it shall have been presented to him, the Same shall be a Law, in like Manner as if he had signed it, unless the Congress by their Adjournment prevent its Return, in which Case it shall not be a Law.

Every Order, Resolution, or Vote to which the Concurrence of the Senate and House of Representatives may be necessary (except on a question of Adjournment) shall be presented to the President of the United States; and before the Same shall take Effect, shall be approved by him, or being disapproved by him, shall be repassed by two thirds of the Senate and House of Representatives, according to the Rules and Limitations prescribed in the Case of a Bill.

Section 8. The Congress shall have Power To lay and collect Taxes, Duties, Imposts and Excises, to pay the Debts and provide for the common Defence and general Welfare of the United States; but all Duties, Imposts and Excises shall be uniform throughout the United States;

To borrow Money on the credit of the United States;

To regulate Commerce with foreign Nations, and among the several States, and with the Indian Tribes;

To establish an uniform Rule of Naturalization, and uniform Laws on the subject of Bankruptcies throughout the United States;

To coin Money, regulate the Value thereof, and of foreign Coin, and fix the Standard of Weights and Measures;

To provide for the Punishment of counterfeiting the Securities and current Coin of the United States;

To establish Post Offices and post Roads;

To promote the Progress of Science and useful Arts, by securing for limited Times to Authors and Inventors the exclusive Right to their respective Writings and Discoveries;

To constitute Tribunals inferior to the Supreme Court;

To define and punish piracies and Felonies committed on the high Seas, and Offences against the Law of Nations;

To declare War, grant Letters of Marque and Reprisal, and make Rules concerning Captures on Land and Water;

To raise and support Armies, but no Appropriation of Money to that Use shall be for a longer Term than two Years;

To provide and maintain a Navy;

To make Rules for the Government and Regulation of the land and naval Forces;

To provide for calling forth the Militia to execute the Laws of the Union, suppress Insurrections and repel Invasions;

To provide for organizing, arming, and disciplining, the Militia, and for governing such Part of them as may be employed in the Service of the United States, reserving to the States respectively, the Appointment of the Officers, and the Authority of training the Militia according to the discipline prescribed by Congress;

To exercise exclusive Legislation in all Cases whatsoever, over such District (not exceeding ten Miles square) as may, by Cession of particular States, and the Acceptance of Congress, become the Seat of the Government of the United States, and to exercise like Authority over all Places purchased by the Consent of the Legislature of the State in which the Same shall be, for the Erection of Forts, Magazines, Arsenals, dock-Yards, and other needful Buildings;

—And

To make all Laws which shall be necessary and proper for carrying into Execution the foregoing Powers, and all other Powers vested by this Constitution in the Government of the United States, or in any Department or Officer thereof.

Section 9. The Migration or Importation of such Persons as any of the States now existing shall think proper to admit, shall not be prohibited by the Congress prior to the Year one thousand eight hundred and eight, but a Tax or duty may be imposed on such Importation, not exceeding ten dollars for each Person.

The Privilege of the Writ of Habeas Corpus shall not be suspended, unless when in Cases of Rebellion or Invasion the public Safety may require it.

No Bill of Attainder or ex post facto Law shall be passed.

*No Capitation, or other direct, Tax shall be laid, unless in Proportion to the Census or Enumeration herein before directed to be taken.**

No Tax or Duty shall be laid on Articles exported from any State.

No Preference shall be given by any Regulation of Commerce or Revenue to the Ports of one State over those of another: nor shall Vessels bound to, or from, one State, be obliged to enter, clear, or pay Duties in another.

No Money shall be drawn from the Treasury, but in Consequence of Appropriations made by Law; and a regular Statement and Account of the Receipts and Expenditures of all public Money shall be published from time to time.

No title of Nobility shall be granted by the United States: And no Person holding any Office of Profit or Trust under them, shall, without the Consent of the Congress, accept of any present, Emolument, Office, or Title, of any kind whatever, from any King, Prince, or foreign State.

Section 10. No State shall enter into any Treaty, Alliance, or Confederation; grant Letters of Marque and Reprisal; coin Money; emit Bills of Credit; make any Thing but gold and silver coin a Tender in Payment of Debts; pass any Bill of Attainder, ex post facto Law, or Law impairing the Obligation of Contracts, or Grant any Title of Nobility.

No State shall, without the Consent of the Congress, lay any Imposts or Duties on Imports or Exports, except what may be absolutely necessary for executing its inspection Laws: and the net Produce of all Duties and Imposts, laid by any State on Imports or

* Revised by Sixteenth Amendment.

Exports, shall be for the Use of the Treasury of the United States; and all such Laws shall be subject to the Revision and Controul of the Congress.

No State shall, without the Consent of Congress, lay any Duty of Tonnage, keep Troops, or Ships of War in time of Peace, enter into any Agreement or Compact with another State, or with a foreign Power, or engage in War, unless actually invaded, or in such imminent Danger as will not admit of delay.

Article II

Section 1. The executive Power shall be vested in a President of the United States of America. *He shall hold his Office during the Term of four Years,** and, together with the Vice President, chosen for the same Term be elected as follows:

Each State shall appoint, in such Manner as the Legislature thereof may direct, a Number of Electors, equal to the whole Number of Senators and Representatives to which the State may be entitled in the Congress but no Senator or Representative, or Person holding an Office of Trust or Profit under the United States, shall be appointed an Elector.

The Electors shall meet in their respective States, and vote by Ballot for two Persons, of whom one at least shall not be an Inhabitant of the same State with themselves. And they shall make a List of all the Persons voted for, and of the Number of Votes for each; which List they shall sign and certify, and transmit sealed to the seat of the Government of the United States, directed to the President of the Senate. The President of the Senate shall, in the Presence of the Senate and House of Representatives, open all the Certificates, and the Votes shall then be counted. The Person having the greatest Number of Votes shall be the President, if such Number be a Majority of the whole Number of Electors appointed; and if there be more than one who have such Majority, and have an equal Number of Votes, then the House of Representatives shall immediately chuse by Ballot one of them for President; and if no Person have a Majority, then from the five highest on the List the said House shall in like Manner chuse the President. But in chusing the President, the Votes shall be taken by States, the Representation from each state having one Vote; A quorum for this purpose shall consist of a Member or Members from two thirds of the States, and a Majority of all the States shall be necessary to a Choice. In every Case, after the Choice of the President, the Person having the greatest Number of Votes of the Electors shall be the Vice President. But if there should remain two or more who have equal votes, the Senate shall chuse from them by Ballot the Vice President.†

The Congress may determine the Time of chusing the Electors, and the Day on which they shall give their Votes; which Day shall be the same throughout the United States.

No Person except a natural born Citizen, or a Citizen of the United States, at the time of the Adoption of this Constitution, shall be eligible to the Office of President; neither shall any Person be eligible to that Office who shall not have attained to the Age of thirty five Years, and been fourteen Years a Resident within the United States.

In case of the Removal of the President from Office, or of his Death, Resignation, or Inability to discharge the Powers and Duties of the said Office, the Same shall devolve on the Vice President, and the Congress may by Law provide for the Case of Removal, Death, Resignation or Inability, both of the President and Vice President, declaring what Officer shall then act as President, and such Officer shall act accordingly, until the Disability be removed, or a President shall be elected.‡

The President shall, at stated Times, receive for his Services, a Compensation which shall neither be encreased nor diminished during the Period for which he shall have been elected, and he shall not receive within that Period any other Emolument from the United States, or any of them.

Before he enter on the Execution of his

* See Twenty-second Amendment.

† Superseded by Twelfth Amendment.

‡ Revised by Twenty-fifth Amendment.

Office, he shall take the following Oath or Affirmation:—"I do solemnly swear (or affirm) that I will faithfully execute the Office of President of the United States, and will to the best of my Ability, preserve, protect and defend the Constitution of the United States."

Section 2. The President shall be Commander in Chief of the Army and Navy of the United States, and of the Militia of the several States, when called into the actual service of the United States; he may require the Opinion, in writing, of the principal Officer in each of the executive Departments, upon any Subject relating to the Duties of their respective Offices, and he shall have Power to grant Reprieves and Pardons for Offences against the United States, except in Cases of Impeachment.

He shall have Power, by and with the Advice and Consent of the Senate, to make Treaties, provided two thirds of the Senators present concur; and he shall nominate, and by and with the Advice and Consent of the Senate, shall appoint Ambassadors, and other public Ministers and Consuls, Judges of the supreme Court, and all other Officers of the United States, whose Appointments are not herein otherwise provided for, and which shall be established by Law: but the Congress may by Law vest the Appointment of such inferior Officers, as they think proper, in the President alone, in the Courts of Law, or in the Heads of Departments.

The President shall have Power to fill up all Vacancies that may happen during the Recess of the Senate, by granting Commissions which shall expire at the End of their next Session.

Section 3. He shall from time to time give to the Congress Information of the State of the Union, and recommend to their Consideration such Measures as he shall judge necessary and expedient; he may, on extraordinary Occasions, convene both Houses, or either of them, and in Case of Disagreement between them, with Respect to the Time of Adjournment, he may adjourn them to such Time as he shall think proper; he shall receive Ambassadors and other public Ministers, he shall take Care that the Laws be faithfully executed, and shall Commission all the Officers of the United States.

Section 4. The President, Vice President, and all civil Officers of the United States, shall be removed from Office on Impeachment for, and Conviction of Treason, Bribery, or other high Crimes and Misdemeanors.

Article III

Section 1. The judicial Power of the United States, shall be vested in one supreme Court and in such inferior Courts as the Congress may from time to time ordain and establish. The Judges, both of the supreme and inferior Courts, shall hold their Offices during good Behavior, and shall, at stated Times, receive for their Services, a Compensation, which shall not be diminished during their Continuance in Office.

Section 2. The judicial Power shall extend to all Cases, in Law and Equity, arising under this Constitution, the Laws of the United States, and Treaties made, or which shall be made, under their Authority;—to all Cases affecting Ambassadors, other public Ministers and Consuls;—to all Cases of admiralty and maritime Jurisdiction;—to Controversies to which the United States shall be a party;—to Controversies between two or more States;—*between a State and Citizens of another State**;—between Citizens of different States;—between Citizens of the same State claiming Lands under Grants of different States, *and between a State or the Citizens thereof, and foreign States, Citizens, or Subjects.**

In all cases affecting Ambassadors, other public Ministers and Consuls, and those in which a State shall be Party, the supreme Court shall have original Jurisdiction. In all the other Cases before mentioned, the supreme Court shall have appellate Jurisdiction, both as to Law and Fact, with such Exceptions, and under such Regulations as the Congress shall make.

---

* Revised by Eleventh Amendment.

The Trial of all Crimes, except in Cases of Impeachment, shall be by Jury; and such Trial shall be held in the State where the said Crimes shall have been committed; but when not committed within any State, the Trial shall be at such Place or Places as the Congress may by Law have directed.

Section 3. Treason against the United States, shall consist only in levying War against them, or in adhering to their Enemies, giving them Aid and Comfort. No Person shall be convicted of Treason unless on the Testimony of two Witnesses to the same overt Act, or on Confession in open Court.

The Congress shall have Power to declare the Punishment of Treason, but no Attainder of Treason shall work Corruption of Blood, or Forfeiture except during the Life of the Person attainted.

Article IV

Section 1. Full Faith and Credit shall be given in each State to the public Acts, Records, and judicial Proceedings of every other State. And the Congress may by general Laws prescribe the Manner in which such Acts, Records, and Proceedings shall be proved, and the Effect thereof.

Section 2. The Citizens of each State shall be entitled to all Privileges and Immunities of Citizens in the several States.

A Person charged in any State with Treason, Felony, or other Crime, who shall flee from Justice, and be found in another State, shall on Demand of the executive Authority of the State from which he fled, be delivered up, to be removed to the State having Jurisdiction of the Crime.

*No person held to Service or Labour in one State, under the Laws thereof, escaping into another, shall, in Consequence of any Law or Regulation therein, be discharged from such Service or Labour, but shall be delivered up on Claim of the Party to whom such Service or Labour may be due.**

Section 3. New States may be admitted by the Congress into this Union; but no new State shall be formed or erected within the Jurisdiction of any other State; nor any State be formed by the Junction of two or more States, or Parts of States, without the Consent of the Legislatures of the States concerned as well as of the Congress.

The Congress shall have Power to dispose of and make all needful Rules and Regulations respecting the Territory or other Property belonging to the United States; and nothing in this Constitution shall be so construed as to Prejudice any claims of the United States, or of any particular State.

Section 4. The United States shall guarantee to every State in this Union a Republican Form of Government, and shall protect each of them against Invasion; and on Application of the Legislature, or of the Executive (when the Legislature cannot be convened) against domestic Violence.

Article V

The Congress, whenever two thirds of both Houses shall deem it necessary, shall propose Amendments to this Constitution, or, on the Application of the Legislatures of two thirds of the several States, shall call a Convention for proposing Amendments, which, in either Case, shall be valid to all Intents and Purposes, as Part of this Constitution, when ratified by the Legislatures of three fourths of the several States, or by Conventions in three fourths thereof, as the one or the other Mode of Ratification may be proposed by the Congress; Provided that no Amendment which may be made prior to the Year One thousand eight hundred and eight shall in any Manner affect the first and fourth Clauses in the Ninth Section of the first Article; and that no State, without its Consent, shall be deprived of its equal

Article VI

All Debts contracted and Engagements entered

* Superseded by Thirteenth Amendment.

into, before the Adoption of this Constitution, shall be as valid against the United States under this Constitution, as under the Confederation.†

This Constitution, and the Laws of the United States which shall be made in Pursuance thereof; and all Treaties made, or which shall be made, under the Authority of the United States, shall be the supreme Law of the Land; and the Judges in every State shall be bound thereby, any Thing in the Constitution or Laws of any State to the Contrary notwithstanding.

The Senators and Representatives before mentioned, and the Members of the several State Legislatures, and all executive and judicial Officers, both of the United States and of the several States, shall be bound by Oath or Affirmation, to support this Constitution; but no religious Test shall ever be required as a Qualification to any Office or public Trust under the United States.

Article VII

The Ratification of the Conventions of nine States, shall be sufficient for the Establishment of this Constitution between the States so ratifying the Same.

Done in Convention by the Unanimous Consent of the States present the Seventeenth Day of September in the Year of our Lord one thousand seven hundred and eighty seven and of the Independence of the United States of America the twelfth. In witness whereof We have hereunto subscribed our Names

• • •

ARTICLES IN ADDITION TO, AND AMENDMENT OF, THE CONSTITUTION OF THE UNITED STATES OF AMERICA, PROPOSED BY CONGRESS, AND RATIFIED BY THE SEVERAL STATES, PURSUANT TO THE FIFTH ARTICLE OF THE ORIGINAL CONSTITUTION.

(Ratification of the first ten amendments was completed December 15, 1791.)

† See Fourteenth Amendment, Section 4.

Amendment I

Congress shall make no law respecting an establishment of religion, or prohibiting the free exercise thereof; or abridging the freedom of speech, or of the press; or the right of the people peaceably to assemble, and to petition the Government for a redress of grievances.

Amendment II

A well regulated Militia, being necessary to the security of a free State, the right of the people to keep and bear Arms, shall not be infringed.

Amendment III

No Soldier shall, in time of peace be quartered in any house, without the consent of the Owner, nor in time of war, but in a manner to be prescribed by law.

Amendment IV

The right of the people to be secure in their persons, houses, papers, and effects, against unreasonable searches and seizures, shall not be violated, and no Warrants shall issue, but upon probable cause, supported by Oath or affirmation, and particularly describing the place to be searched, and the persons or things to be seized.

Amendment V

No person shall be held to answer for a capital, or other infamous crime, unless on a presentment or indictment of a Grand Jury, except in cases arising in the land or naval forces, or in the Militia, when in actual service in time of War or public danger; nor shall any person be subject for the same offence to be twice put in jeopardy of life or limb; nor shall be compelled in any criminal case to be a witness against himself, nor be deprived of life, liberty, or property, without due process of law; nor shall private property be taken for public use, without just compensation.

Amendment VI

In all criminal prosecutions, the accused shall enjoy the right to a speedy and public trial, by an impartial jury of the State and district wherein the crime shall have been committed, which district shall have been previously ascertained by law, and to be informed of the nature and cause of the accusation; to be confronted with the witnesses against him; to have compulsory process for obtaining witnesses in his favor, and to have the Assistance of Counsel for his defence.

Amendment VII

In Suits at common law, where the value in controversy shall exceed twenty dollars, the right of trial by jury shall be preserved, and no fact tried by a jury, shall be otherwise reexamined in any Court of the United States, than according to the rules of the common law.

Amendment VIII

Excessive bail shall not be required, nor excessive fines imposed, nor cruel and unusual punishments inflicted.

Amendment IX

The enumeration in the Constitution, of certain rights, shall not be construed to deny or disparage others retained by the people.

Amendment X

The powers not delegated to the United States by the Constitution, nor prohibited by it to the States, are reserved to the States respectively or to the people.

Amendment XI (January 8, 1798)

The Judicial power of the United States shall not be construed to extend to any suit in law or equity, commenced or prosecuted against one of the United States by Citizens of another State, or by Citizens or Subjects of any Foreign State.

Amendment XII (September 25, 1804)

The Electors shall meet in their respective states and vote by ballot for President and Vice President, one of whom, at least, shall not be an inhabitant of the same state with themselves; they shall name in their ballots the person voted for as President, and in distinct ballots the person voted for as Vice President, and they shall make distinct lists of all persons voted for as Vice President, and of the number of votes for each, which lists they shall sign and certify, and transmit sealed to the seat of the government of the United States, directed to the President of the Senate;—The President of the Senate shall, in the presence of Senate and House of Representatives, open all the certificates and the votes shall then be counted;—The person having the greatest number of votes for President, shall be the President, if such number be a majority of the whole number of Electors appointed; and if no person have such majority, then from the person having the highest numbers not exceeding three on the list of those voted for as President, the House of Representatives shall choose immediately, by ballot, the President. But in choosing the President, the votes shall be taken by states, the representation from each state having one vote; a quorum for this purpose shall consist of a member or members from two-thirds of the states, and a majority of all the states shall be necessary to a choice. And if the House of Representatives shall not choose a President whenever the right of choice shall devolve upon them, *before the fourth day of March next following*,* then the Vice President shall act as President, as in the case of the death or other constitutional disability of the President.— The person having the greatest number of votes as Vice President shall be the Vice President, if such number be a majority of the whole number of Electors appointed, and if no person have a majority, then from the two highest numbers on the list, the Senate shall choose the Vice President; a quorum for the purpose shall consist of two-thirds of the whole number of Senators, and a majority of the whole number shall be necessary to a choice. But no person constitutionally ineligible to the office of President shall be eligible to that of Vice President of the United States.

Amendment XIII (December 18, 1865)

Section 1. Neither slavery nor involuntary servitude, except as a punishment for crime whereof the party shall have been duly convicted, shall exist within the United States, or any place subject to their jurisdiction.

Section 2. Congress shall have the power to enforce this article by appropriate legislation.

Amendment XIV (July 28, 1869)

Section 1. All persons born or naturalized in the United States, and subject to the jurisdiction thereof, are citizens of the United States and of the State wherein they reside. No State shall make or enforce any law which shall abridge the privileges or immunities of citizens of the United States; nor shall any State deprive any person of life, liberty, or property, without due process of law; nor deny to any person within its jurisdiction the *equal protection of the laws*.

Section 2. Representatives shall be apportioned among the several States according to their respective numbers, counting the whole number of persons in each State, excluding Indians not taxed. But when the right to vote at any election for the choice of electors for President and Vice President of the United States, Representatives in Congress, the Executive and Judicial officers of a State, or the members of the Legislature thereof, is denied to any of the male inhabitants of such State, being twenty-one years of age, and citizens of the United States, or in any way abridged, except for participation in rebellion, or other crime, the basis of representation therein shall be reduced in the proportion which the number of such male citizens shall bear to the whole number of male citizens twenty-one years of age in such State.

Section 3. No person shall be a Senator or Representative in Congress, or elector of President and Vice President, or hold any office, civil or military, under the United States, or under any State, who, having previously taken an oath, as a member of Congress, or as an officer of the United States, or as a member of any state legislature, or as an executive or judicial officer of any State, to support the Constitution of the United States, shall have engaged in insurrection or rebellion against the same, or given aid or comfort to the enemies thereof. But Congress may, by a vote of two thirds of each House, remove such disability.

Section 4. The validity of the public debt of the United States, authorized by law, including debts incurred for payment of pensions and bounties for services in suppressing insurrection or rebellion, shall not be questioned. But neither the United States nor any State shall assume or pay any debt or obligation incurred in aid of insurrection or rebellion against the United States, or any claim for the loss or emancipation of any slave; but all such debts, obligations, and claims shall be held illegal and void.

Section 5. The Congress shall have power to enforce, by appropriate legislation, the provisions of this article.

* Repealed by the Twenty-first Amendment.

Amendment XV (March 30, 1870)

Section 1. The right of citizens of the United States to vote shall not be denied or abridged by the United States or by any State on account of race, color, or previous conditions of servitude.

Section 2. The Congress shall have power to enforce this article by appropriate legislation.

Amendment XVI (February 25, 1913)

The Congress shall have power to lay and collect taxes on incomes, from whatever source derived, without apportionment among the several States, and without regard to any census or enumeration.

Amendment XVII (May 31, 1913)

The Senate of the United States shall be composed of two Senators from each State, elected by the people thereof, for six years; and each Senator shall have one vote. The electors in each State shall have the qualifications requisite for electors of the most numerous branch of the State legislature.

When vacancies happen in the representation of any State in the Senate, the executive authority of such State shall issue writs of election to fill such vacancies: *Provided,* That the legislature of any State may empower the executive thereof to make temporary appointments until the people fill the vacancies by election as the legislature may direct.

This amendment shall not be so construed as to affect the election or term of any Senator chosen before it becomes valid as part of the Constitution.

Amendment XVIII (January 29, 1919)

Section 1. *After one year from the ratification of this article the manufacture, sale, or transportation of intoxicating liquors within, the importation thereof into, or the exportation thereof from the United States and all territory subject to the jurisdiction thereof for beverage purposes is hereby prohibited.*

Section 2. *The Congress and the several States shall have concurrent power to enforce this article by appropriate legislation.*

Section 3. *This article shall be inoperative unless it shall have been ratified as an amendment to the Constitution by the legislatures of the several States, as provided in the Constitution within seven years from the date of the submission hereof to the States by the Congress.**

Amendment XIX (August 26, 1920)

The right of citizens of the United States to vote shall not be denied or abridged by the United States or by any State on account of sex.

Congress shall have power to enforce this article by appropriate legislation.

Amendment XX (February 6, 1933)

Section 1. The terms of the President and Vice President shall end at noon on the 20th day of January, and the terms of Senators and Representatives at noon on the 3rd day of January, of the years in which such terms would have ended if this article had not been ratified; and the terms of their successors shall then begin.

Section 2. The Congress shall assemble at least once in every year, and such meeting shall begin at noon on the 3rd day of January, unless they shall by law appoint a different day.

Section 3. If, at the time fixed for the beginning of the term of the President, the President elect shall have died, the Vice President elect shall become President. If a President shall not have been chosen before the time fixed for the beginning of his term, or if the President elect shall have failed to qualify, then the Vice President elect shall

* Revised by the Twentieth Amendment.

act as President until a President shall have qualified; and the Congress may by law provide for the case wherein neither a President elect nor a Vice President elect shall have qualified, declaring who shall then act as President, or the manner in which one who is to act shall be selected, and such person shall act accordingly until a President or Vice President shall have qualified.

Section 4. The Congress may by law provide for the case of death of any of the persons from whom the House of Representatives may choose a President whenever the right of choice shall have devolved upon them, and for the case of the death of any of the persons from whom the Senate may choose a Vice President whenever the right of choice shall have devolved upon them.

Section 5. Sections 1 and 2 shall take effect on the 15th day of October following the ratification of this article.

Section 6. This article shall be inoperative unless it shall have been ratified as an amendment to the Constitution by the legislatures of three-fourths of the several States within seven years from the date of its submission.

Amendment XXI (December 5, 1933)

Section 1. The eighteenth article of amendment to the Constitution of the United States is hereby repealed.

Section 2. The transportation or importation into any State, Territory, or possession of the United States for delivery or use therein of intoxicating liquors, in violation of the laws thereof, is hereby prohibited.

Section 3. This article shall be inoperative unless it shall have been ratified as an amendment to the Constitution by conventions in the several States, as provided in the Constitution, within seven years from the date of the submission hereof to the States by the Congress.

Amendment XXII (February 26, 1951)

Section 1. No person shall be elected to the office of the President more than twice, and no person who has held the office of President, or acted as President, for more than two years of a term to which some other person was elected President shall be elected to the office of President more than once. But this Article shall not apply to any person holding the office of President when this Article was proposed by the Congress, and shall not prevent any person who may be holding the office of President, or acting as President, during the term within which this Article becomes operative from holding the office of President or acting as President during the remainder of such term.

Section 2. This article shall be inoperative unless it shall have been ratified as an amendment to the Constitution by the legislatures of three-fourths of the several States within seven years from the date of its submission to the States by the Congress.

Amendment XXIII (March 29, 1961)

Section 1. The District constituting the seat of Government of the United States shall appoint in such manner as the Congress may direct:

A number of electors of President and Vice President equal to the whole number of Senators and Representatives in Congress to which the District would be entitled if it were a State, but in no event more than the least populous State; they shall be in addition to those appointed by the States, but they shall be considered, for the purposes of the election of President and Vice President, to be electors appointed by a State; and they shall meet in the District and perform such duties as provided by the twelfth article of amendment.

Section 2. The Congress shall have power to enforce this article by appropriate legislation.

Amendment XXIV (January 23, 1964)

Section 1. The right of citizens of the United States to vote in any primary or other election for President or Vice President, for electors for President or Vice President, or for Senator or Representative in Congress, shall not be denied or abridged by the United States or any state by reason of failure to pay any poll tax or other tax.

Section 2. The Congress shall have the power to enforce this article by appropriate legislation.

Amendment XXV (February 10, 1967)

Section 1. In case of the removal of the President from office or of his death or resignation, the Vice President shall become President.

Section 2. Whenever there is a vacancy in the office of the Vice President, the President shall nominate a Vice President who shall take office upon confirmation by a majority vote of both Houses of Congress.

Section 3. Whenever the President transmits to the President pro tempore of the Senate and the Speaker of the House of Representatives his written declaration that he is unable to discharge the powers and duties of his office, and until he transmits to them a written declaration to the contrary, such powers and duties shall be discharged by the Vice President as Acting President.

Section 4. Whenever the Vice President and a majority of either the principal officers of the executive departments or of such other body as Congress may by law provide, transmit to the President pro tempore of the Senate and the Speaker of the House of Representatives their written declaration that the President is unable to discharge the powers and duties of his office, the Vice President shall immediately assume the powers and duties of the office as Acting President.

Thereafter, when the President transmits to the President pro tempore of the Senate and the Speaker of the House of Representatives his written declaration that no inability exists, he shall resume the powers and duties of his office unless the Vice President and a majority of either the principal officers of the executive departments or of such other body as Congress may by law provide, transmit within four days to the President pro tempore of the Senate and the Speaker of the House of Representatives their written declaration that the President is unable to discharge the powers and duties of his office. Thereupon Congress shall decide the issue, assembling within forty-eight hours for that purpose if not in session. If the Congress, within twenty-one days after receipt of the latter written declaration or, if Congress is not in session, within twenty-one days after Congress is required to assemble, determines by two-thirds vote of both Houses that the President is unable to discharge the powers and duties of his office, the Vice President shall continue to discharge the same as Acting President; otherwise, the President shall resume the powers and duties of his office.

Amendment XXVI (June 30, 1971)

Section 1. The right of citizens of the United States, who are eighteen years of age or older, to vote shall not be denied or abridged by the United States or any state on account of age.

Section 2. The Congress shall have the power to enforce this article by appropriate legislation.

The Declaration of Independence

When in the course of human events, it becomes necessary for one people to dissolve the political bands which have connected them with another, and to assume among the Powers of the earth, the separate and equal station to which the Laws of Nature and of Nature's God entitle them, a decent respect of the opinions of mankind requires that they should declare the causes which impel them to the separation.

We hold these truths to be self-evident, that all men are created equal, that they are endowed by their Creator with certain unalienable Rights, that among these are Life, Liberty and the pursuit of Happiness. That to secure these rights, Governments are instituted among Men, deriving their just powers from the consent of the governed, That whenever any Form of Government becomes destructive of these ends, it is the Right of the People to alter or to abolish it, and to institute new Government, laying its foundation on such principles and organizing its powers in such form, as to them shall seem most likely to effect their Safety and Happiness. Prudence, indeed, will dictate that Governments long established should not be changed for light and transient causes; and accordingly all experience hath shown, that mankind are more disposed to suffer, while evils are sufferable, than to right themselves by abolishing the forms to which they are accustomed. When a long train of abuses and usurpations, pursuing invariably the same Object evinces a design to reduce them under absolute Despotism, it is their right, it is their duty, to throw off such Government, and to provide new Guards for their future security.—Such has been the patient sufferance of these Colonies; and such is now the necessity which constrains them to alter their former Systems of Government. The history of the present King of Great Britain is a history of repeated injuries and usurpations, all having in direct object the establishment of an absolute Tyranny over these States. To prove this, let Facts be submitted to a candid world.

He has refused his Assent to Laws, the most wholesome and necessary for the public good.

He has forbidden his Governors to pass Laws of immediate and pressing importance, unless suspended in their operation till his Assent should be obtained; and when so suspended, he has utterly neglected to attend to them.

He has refused to pass other Laws for the accommodation of large districts of people, unless those people would relinquish the right of Representation in the Legislature, a right inestimable to them and formidable to tyrants only.

He has called together legislative bodies at places unusual, uncomfortable, and distant from the depository of their Public Records, for the sole purpose of fatiguing them into compliance with his measures.

He has dissolved Representative Houses repeatedly, for opposing with manly firmness his invasions on the rights of the people.

He has refused for a long time, after such dissolutions, to cause others to be elected; whereby the Legislative Powers, incapable of Annihilation, have returned to the People at large for their exercise; the State remaining in the mean time exposed to all the dangers of invasion from without, and convulsions within.

He has endeavoured to prevent the population of these States; for that purpose obstructing the Laws of Naturalization of Foreigners; refusing to pass others to encourage their migration hither, and raising the conditions of new Appropriations of Lands.

He has obstructed the Administration of Justice, by refusing his Assent to Laws for establishing Judiciary Powers.

He has made Judges dependent on his Will alone, for the tenure of their offices, and the amount of payment of their salaries.

He has erected a multitude of New Offices, and sent hither swarms of Officers to harass our People, and eat out their substance.

He has kept among us, in times of peace, Standing Armies without the Consent of our legislature.

He has affected to render the Military independent of and superior to the Civil Power.

He has combined with others to subject us to a jurisdiction foreign to our constitution, and unacknowledged by our laws; giving his Assent to their acts of pretended legislation:

For quartering large bodies of armed troops among us:

For protecting them, by a mock Trial, from Punishment for any Murders which they should commit on the Inhabitants of these States:

For cutting off our Trade with all parts of the world:

For imposing taxes on us without our Consent:

For depriving us in many cases, of the benefits of Trial by Jury:

For transporting us beyond Seas to be tried for pretended offences:

For abolishing the free system of English Laws in a neighbouring Province, establishing therein an Arbitrary government, and enlarging its Boundaries so as to render it at once an example and fit instrument for introducing the same absolute rule into these Colonies:

For taking away our Charters, abolishing our most valuable Laws, and altering fundamentally the Forms of our Governments:

For suspending our own Legislature, and declaring themselves invested with Power to legislate for us in all cases whatsoever.

He has abdicated Government here, by declaring us out of his Protection and waging War against us.

He has plundered our seas, ravaged our Coasts, burnt our towns, and destroyed the lives of our people.

He is at this time transporting large armies of foreign mercenaries to compleat the works of death, desolation and tyranny, already begun with circumstances of Cruelty & perfidy scarcely paralleled in the most barbarous ages, and totally unworthy the Head of a civilized nation.

He has constrained our fellow Citizens taken Captive on the high Seas to bear Arms against their Country, to become the executioners of their friends and Brethren, or to fall themselves by their Hands.

He has excited domestic insurrections amongst us, and has endeavoured to bring on the inhabitants of our frontiers, the merciless Indian Savages, whose known rule of warfare, is an undistinguished destruction of all ages, sexes and conditions.

In every stage of these Oppressions We have Petitioned for Redress in the most humble terms: Our repeated Petitions have been answered only by repeated injury. A Prince, whose character is thus marked by every act which may define a Tyrant, is unfit to be the ruler of a free People.

Nor have We been wanting in attention to our British brethren. We have warned them from time to time of attempts by their legislature to extend an unwarrantable jurisdiction over us. We have reminded them of the circumstances of our emigration and settlement here. We have appealed to their native justice and magnanimity, and we have conjured them by the ties of our common kindred to disavow these usurpations, which, would inevitably interrupt our connections and correspondence. They too have been deaf to the voice of justice and of consanguinity. We must, therefore, acquiesce in the necessity, which denounces our Separation, and hold them, as we hold the rest of mankind, Enemies in War, in Peace Friends.

We, therefore, the Representatives of the United States of America, in General Congress, Assembled, appealing to the Supreme Judge of the world for the rectitude of our intentions, do, in the Name, and by Authority of the good People of these Colonies, solemnly publish and declare, That these United Colonies are, and of Right ought to be Free and Independent States; that they are Absolved from all Allegiance to the British Crown, and that all political connection between them and the State of Great Britain, is and ought to be totally dissolved; and that as Free and Independent States, they have full Power to levy War, conclude Peace, contract Alliance, establish Commerce, and to do all other Acts and Things which Independent States may of right do. And for the support of this Declaration, with a firm reliance on the Protection of Divine Providence, we mutually pledge to each other our Lives, our Fortunes and our sacred Honor.

PHOTO CREDITS

Chapter 1

Opener: R.P. Angier/Stock Boston. Page 3: Jack Knight/The White House. Page 5: Bettman Archive. Page 7: Bettman Archive. Page 10: Martha Tabor/Picture Group. Page 13: (top) Ray Ellis/Rapho-Photo Researchers, (bottom) Mitschiro Yoshikawa/Black Star. Page 15: Fredrik D. Bodin/Stock Boston. Page 19: Ellis Herwig/Stock Boston. Page 21: (top) Jerry Berndt/Stock Boston, (bottom) Peter Menzel/Stock Boston. Page 26: (top) Steve Skloot/Photo Researchers, (bottom left) Steve Kagan/Photo Researchers, (bottom right) Jim Anderson/Woodfin Camp. Page 27: UPI.

Chapter 2

Opener: Peter Menzel/Stock Boston. Page 36: (top) Historical Picture Service, (center) John Singleton Copley (1738–1815). Deposited by the City of Boston. Courtesy, Museum of Fine Arts, Boston, (bottom) Richard Frear/National Park Service. Page 37: Emmet Collection, Manuscripts and Archives Division, The New York Public Library, Astor, Lenox and Tilden Foundations. Page 39: The New York Public Library Picture Collection. Page 41: Courtesy Free Library of Philadelphia. Page 43: Courtesy Free Library of Philadelphia. Page 44: (top) Courtesy Free Library of Philadelphia, (bottom) Pennsylvania Academy of Fine Arts, Joseph & Sarah Harrison Collection. Page 49: © Sidney Harris. Page 54: Buffalo Savings Bank, Roy W. Nagle Collection. Page 55: N.Y. Daily News Photo.

Chapter 3

Opener: Mark Antman/Stock Boston. Page 62: Bill Fitz-Patrick/The White House. Page 65: Yutaka Nagata/UN Photo. Page 68: Culver Pictures. Page 69: Courtesy Canadian Consulate General. Page 72: (top) U.S. Army Engineer District Corps of Engineering, (bottom) Dennis Brack/Black Star. Page 73: (top) J.P. Laffont/Sygma, (bottom) Anestis Diakopoulos/Stock Boston. Page 74: Courtesy Free Library of Philadelphia. Page 76: Drawing by Handelsman; © The New Yorker Magazine, Inc. Page 81: Courtesy Lockheed—George Co. Page 82: (top) Santa Fe Railway, (bottom) Courtesy Texas A&M University, Office of Public Information. Page 84: Meri Houtchens-Kitchens/Picture Cube. Page 85: P. Price/Picture Cube. Page 86: Jim Anderson/Woodfin Camp. Page 91: © Sidney Harris.

Chapter 4

Opener: Alan Carey/Image Works. Page 103: Consolidated News Pictures. Page 105: Ann McQueen/Picture Cube. Page 107: Drawing by Mulligan; © 1981 The New Yorker Magazine, Inc. Page 108: Sybil Shelton/Peter Arnold. Page 109: Ellis Herwig/Stock Boston. Page 111: American Broadcasting Co., Inc. Page 114: Drawing by Stevenson; © The New Yorker Magazine, Inc. Page 121: AP/Wide World Photos. Page 122: AP/Wide World Photos. Page 125: Alan Carey/Image Works. Page 126: (top) Anestis Diakopoulos/Picture Group, (bottom) Owen Franken/Stock Boston. Page 127: Ellis Herwig/Picture Cube.

Chapter 5

Opener: Hazel Hankin. Page 134: (top) Courtesy of Citizens for Clean Air, Inc., (bottom) Courtesy Sierra Club. Page 135: Courtesy Zero Population Growth. Page 136: Drawing by Dana Fradon; © 1980 The New Yorker Magazine, Inc. Page 137: Courtesy United Auto Workers. Page 138: (top) Charles Gupton/Stock Boston, (bottom) Shepard Sherbell/Picture Group. Page 139: (top) Leif Skoogfers/Woodfin Camp, (bottom) Cradoc Bagshaw/Black Star. Page 140: (top) Courtesy Rotary Club of New York, (bottom) Courtesy League of Women Voters. Page 141: Courtesy National Association of Manufacturers. Page 145: (top) Courtesy International Ladies Garment Workers Union, (center) Arthur Grace/Sygma, (bottom) Courtesy Free Library of Philadelphia. Page 146: Jason Lurie/Woodfin Camp. Page 148: Peter Southwick/Stock Boston. Page 149: Charles Gatewood/Image Works. Page 150: (top) Jim Anderson/Woodfin Camp, (bottom) Atlan/Sygma. Page 151: Rachel Ritchie/Picture Group. Page 155: Alan Carey/Image Works. Page 156: Dennis Brack/Black Star. Page 158: Courtesy Young Americans for Freedom. Page 160: Drawing by Stevenson; © 1972 The New Yorker Magazine, Inc. Page 162: Shepard Sherbell/Picture Group. Page 163: Courtesy Alcoa.

Chapter 6

Opener: Owen Franken/Stock Boston. Page 176: (top) Paul Sequeira/Rapho-Photo Researchers, (bottom) UPI. Page 178: Jack Spratt/Picture Group. Page 179: Culver Pictures. Page 184: Alain Nogues/Sygma. Page 185: (top) Stuart Franklin/Sygma, (bottom left) Agence France-Presse, (bottom right) Courtesy Smithsonian Institute. Page 186: (top) The New York Public Library Picture Collection, (bottom) Courtesy Smithsonian Institute. Page 187: (top) The New York Public Library Picture Collection, (center) Franklin D. Roosevelt Library, (bottom) Courtesy Smithsonian Institute. Page 188: Manuscripts and University Archives, Cornell University. Page 189: Courtesy Smithsonian Institute. Page 190: (top) Drawing by Whitney Darrow; © The New Yorker Magazine, Inc., (left) Courtesy Smithsonian Institute. Page 191: (top) Courtesy Smithsonian Institute, (center) The New York Public Library Picture Collection. Page 193: (bottom) Culver Pictures. Page 194: Courtesy Smithsonian Institute. Page 195: Wide World Photos.

Chapter 7

Opener: Los Angeles Time/AP-Wide World Photos. Page 201: © The New York Times Company. Reprinted by permission. Page 202: © The New York Times Company. Reprinted by permission. Page 203: (top) Paul R. Benoit/AP-Wide World Photos, (right) © The New York Times Company. Reprinted by permission. Page 204: Drawing by Stevenson; © The New Yorker Magazine, Inc. Page 205: Historical Picture Service. Page 206: (top) James K.W. Atherton/AP-Wide World Photos, (bottom left) Rick McKay, Cox Newspapers/AP-Wide World Photos, (bottom right) Consolidated News Pictures. Page 207: (top left) Rob Kozloff/AP-Wide World Photos, (top right) AP/Wide World Photos, (bottom left) Ron Frehm/AP-Wide World Photos, (bottom right) Diego Goldberg/Sygma. Page 208: (top left) Ron Edmonds/AP-Wide World Photos, (top right) Mark Duncan/AP-Wide World Photos, (bottom left) Taylor/Sygma, (bottom right) Peter Southwick/AP-Wide World Photos. Page 209: (top left) Barry Thumma/AP-Wide World Photos, (top right) AP/Wide World Photos, (bottom) Peter Southwick/AP-Wide World Photos. Page 216: J.P. Laffont/Gamma-Liason. Page 227: AP/Wide World Photos. Page 228: AP/Wide World Photos. Page 230: Don Wright, The Miami News—Tribune Company Syndicate. Page 232: Gianfranco Gorgoni/Contact Press Images. Page 234: Owen Franken/Sygma.

Chapter 8

Opener: Sygma. Page 242: © 1976 Washington Star. Reprinted with permission. Los Angeles Times Syndicate. Page 243: (top) Courtesy New York Historical Society, (bottom) Historical Picture Service. Page 244: Copyrighted by "The News" New York Picture Newspaper. Page 246: Conrad/Sygma. Page 250: © Sidney Harris. Page 251: AP/Wide World Photos. Page 255: AP/Wide World Photos. Page 258: Drawing by D. Reilly; © The New Yorker Magazine, Inc. Page 259: © Sidney Harris. Page 260: AP/Wide World Photos. Page 265: Drawing by Bernard Schoenbaum; © 1984 The New Yorker Magazine, Inc. Page 267: Courtesy Smithsonian Institution. Page 269: AP/Wide World Photos. Page 271: Drawing by Whitney Darrow; © 1976 by the New Yorker Magazine, Inc.

Chapter 9

Opener: Charles Gatewood/Image Works. Page 278: (left) Culver Pictures, (right) Owen Franken/Sygma. Page 280: AP/Wide World Photos. Page 286: J.P. Laffont/Sygma. Page 292: (top) Charles Gatewood/Image Works, (bottom) Ellen Shub/Picture Cube. Page 293: (left) Steve Cagan/Picture Group, (right) Joel Gordon. Page 294: Elizabeth Hamlin/Stock Boston. Page 295: Anestis Diakopoulos/Picture Group. Page 297: Cliff Schiappa/Picture Group.

Chapter 10

Opener: Michael Hayman/Stock Boston. Page 305: (bottom) Reprinted by permission of the Los Angeles Times. Page 307: Ron Bennett/UPI-Bettman Archive. Page 308: J.P. Laffont/Sygma. Page 309: © Sidney Harris. Page 310: (top) Courtesy Senator Bill Bradley, (bottom) Diego Goldberg/Sygma. Page 313: (top left) Drawing by Joe Maraski: © The New Yorker Magazine, Inc., (bottom) Rodley Mims/Sygma, (top right) Shepard Sherbell/Picture Group. Page 316: Diego Goldberg/Sygma. Page 317: Diego Goldberg/Sygma. Page 319: © The New York Times Company. Reprinted by permission. Page 322: Drawing by Richter; © 1978 The New Yorker Magazine, Inc. Page 323: (center) AP/Wide World Photos, (bottom) AP/Wide World Photos. Page 329: (top) UPI, (center) Paul Conklin, (bottom) UPI. Page 330: Arnold Sachs/Consolidated News Pictures. Page 335: John Duricka/AP-Wide World Photos. Page 336: Jean-Louis Atlan/Sygma. Page 341: P. Price/Picture Cube. Page 342: AP/Wide World Photos. Page 347: The Wall Street Journal.

Chapter 11

Opener: Bohdan Hrynewych/Stock Boston. Page 353: Dennis Brack/Black Star. Page 355: Culver Pictures. Page 361: UPI. Page 363: Culver Pictures. Page 364: Culver Pictures. Page 365: Culver Pictures. Page 368: UPI/Bettman Archive. Page 370: The New York Public Library Picture Collection. Page 372: Steiner/Sygma. Page 373: (top left) Atlan/Sygma, (top right) Bill Fitz-Patrick/The White House, (bottom) Atlan/Sygma; Page 374: (left) Sygma, (right) Tom Zimberoff/Sygma. Page 375: Drawing by Dana Fradon; © 1979 The New Yorker Magazine, Inc. Page 377: Randy Taylor/Sygma. Page 379: AP/Wide World Photos. Page 381: Steiner/Sygma. Page 386: © 1975 by Herblock in The Washington Post. Page 391: © The New York Times Company. Reprinted by permission.

Chapter 12

Opener: Jean-Claude LeJeune/Stock Boston. Page 398: © Sidney Harris. Page 399: AP/Wide World Photos. Page 400: (top) Arthur Grace/Stock Boston, (top left) AP/Wide World Photos. Page 401: Paul Conklin. Page 403: Ron Edmonds/AP-Wide World Photos. Page 406: The Wall Street Journal. Page 410: Culver Pictures. Page 413: Michael Evans/The White House. Page 416: Michael Evans/The White House. Page 417: NASA. Page 418: (top) Robert Stiles, (bottom) Courtesy U.S. Department of the Interior, Geological Survey. Page 421: (top left) Ian G. MacIntyre, Smithsonian Institution, Museum of Natural History, (top right) Courtesy Smithsonian Institution, (left center) Paul Dix-Refleno/Woodfin Camp, (right center) Richard Frear/National Park Service, (bottom) U.S. Postal Service. Page 424: Drawing by Gerberg. © 1980 The New Yorker Magazine, Inc. Page 428: (top) Wide World Photos, (bottom) UPI.

Chapter 13

Opener: Alan Decker/Picture Group. Page 437: AP/Wide World Photos. Page 439: © Sidney Harris. Page 441: J.P. Laffont/Sygma. Page 442: Courtesy Supreme Court Historical Society. Page 443: © The New York Times Company. Reprinted by permission. Page 445: Drawing by Richter; © 1979 The New Yorker Magazine, Inc. Page 449: (top) AP/Wide World Photos, (bottom) © Sidney Harris. Page 451: AP/Wide World Photos. Page 453: Historical Picture Service. Page 455: Historical Picture Service. Page 456: Historical Picture Service. Page 459: AP/Wide World Photos. Page 461: © The New York Times Company. Reprinted by permission.

Chapter 14

Opener: Jim Anderson/Stock Boston. Page 475: Noel Clark/Black Star. Page 476: © The New York Times Company. Reprinted by permission. Page 479: Susie Fitzhugh/Stock Boston. Page 480: Cliff Schiappa/Picture Cube. Page 483: (top) UPI, (bottom) New York Public Library Picture Collection. Page 485: Culver Pictures. Page 486: Leonard Freed/Magnum. Page 487: Paul Conklin. Page 489: © Sidney Harris. Page 490: © 1966 The New York Times Company. Reprinted by Permission. Page 491: © 1977 Herblock, from *Herblock on All Fronts* (New American Library, 1980). Page 493: Jack Spratt/Picture Group. Page 497: © The New York Times Company. Reprinted by permission. Page 501: (top) © The New York Times Company. Reprinted by permission, (bottom) Historical Picture Service.

Chapter 15

Opener: Al Stephenson/Picture Group. Page 509: Joe Polimeni/UPI. Page 510: AP/Wide World Photos. Page 512: Ingraham/AP-Wide World Photos. Page 513: Library of Congress. Page 515: © The New York Times Company. Reprinted by permission. Page 517: U.S. Army. Page 518: New York Daily News Photo. Page 520: (top) AP/Wide World Photos, (bottom) John Laverois/Black Star. Page 521: (top) Steven Frisch/Photo Researchers, (bottom) Nicholas Sapieha/Stock Boston. Page 522: Suzanne Vlamis/AP-Wide World Photos. Page 523: Michele Bogre/Sygma. Page 525: AP/Wide World Photos. Page 526: AP/Wide World Photos. Page 527: Bern Keating/Black Star. Page 528: Ellis Herwig/Stock Boston. Page 530: © Sidney Harris. Page 531: AP/Wide World Photos. Page 532: Seneca Falls Historical Society. Page 533: (top) Historical Picture Service, (center) Brown Brothers, (bottom) Culver Pictures. Page 535: Vicky Lawrence/Stock Boston. Page 539: John Chao/Woodfin Camp. Page 540: Bethye Lane. Page 543: Bohdan Hrynewych/Southern Light. Page 545: (left) Jason Laure/Woodfin Camp, (right) Wide World

Photos. Page 546: © 1980 The New York Times Company. Reprinted by permission. Page 547: (left) Leif Skoogfors/Woodfin Camp, (right) © The New York Times Company. Reprinted by permission. Page 548: (top) Peter Taylor/Picture Group, (bottom) Alan Carey/Image Works.

Chapter 16
Opener: Lionel Delevingne/Stock Boston. Page 556: AP/Wide World Photos. Page 557: Schwars/AP-Wide World Photos. Page 558: (top) Rose Lewis/Picture Group, (bottom) The Wall Street Journal. Page 559: (top) © 1982 The New York Times Company. Reprinted by permission, (bottom) Bill Sanders, The Milwaukee Journal. All rights reserved. Page 560: Lorinda Morris. Page 562: (top) AP/Wide World Photos, (left) Lionel Delevingne/Picture Group. Page 563: Tom McHugh/Photo Researchers. Page 564: (top) AP/Wide World Photos, (bottom) Charles Moore/Black Star. Page 565: (top) Arthur Grace/Sygma, (bottom) Taylor/AP-Wide World Photos. Page 567: Courtesy Common Cause.

Chapter 17
Opener: Owen Franken/Stock Boston. Page 577: Culver Pictures. Page 578: Culver Pictures. Page 581: Drawing by Dana Fradon; © 1981 The New Yorker Magazine, Inc. Page 582: J.P. Laffont/Sygma. Page 583: Culver Pictures. Page 586: John Coletti/Picture Group. Page 588: Hazel Hankin/Stock Boston. Page 589: Owen Franken/Sygma. Page 590: Whitehead/Sygma. Page 591: Ellis Herwig/Picture Cube. Page 592: Culver Pictures. Page 598: The New York Public Library Picture Collection. Page 602: Drawing by Dana Fradon; © 1981 The New Yorker Magazine, Inc. Page 603: Bettmann Archive; page 604: AP/Wide World Photos. Page 605: Drawing By Dana Fradon; © The New Yorker Magazine, Inc. Page 606: Harrity/AP-Wide World Photos. Page 607: Drawing by Levin; © 1981 The New Yorker Magazine, Inc. Page 608: AP/Wide World Photos. Page 613: Harrity/AP-Wide World Photos. Page 616: Jim Morin/Miami Herald. Page 617: Drawing by Stuart Leeds; © 1984 The New Yorker Magazine, Inc.

Chapter 18
Opener: Bryce Flynn/Picture Group. Page 626: Photograph by Jacob A. Riis, Jacob A. Riis Collection, Museum of the City of New York. Page 627: Mark Antman/Stock Boston. Page 630: Sandra Johnson/Picture Cube. Page 632: Bryce Flynn/Picture Group. Page 635: Jaques Charles/Stock Boston. Page 638: (top) Mark Antman/Image Works, (bottom) Steve Leonard/Time Magazine. Page 640: © Sidney Harris. Page 641: Jerry Bernt/Stock Boston. Page 642: Mike Valeri/Picture Group. Page 643: Owen Franken/Stock Boston.

Chapter 19
Opener: Walt Johnson/Picture Group. Page 650: AP. Page 653: Library of Congress. Page 654: (top) Arthur Grace/Sygma, (bottom) Owen Franken/Sygma. Page 655: Jean-Louis Atlan/Sygma. Page 656: Jean-Louis Atlan/Sygma. Page 657: (top) Michael Evans/Sygma, (bottom) The Washington Post. Page 658: D.B. Owen/Black Star. Page 660: (top) Diego Goldberg/Sygma, (center) Rodney Mims/Sygma, (bottom) Jean Louis Atlan/Sygma. Page 663: Halstead/Sygma. Page 664: Alain Keler/Sygma. Page 666: AP/Wide World Photos. Page 667: Michael Tapper/AP-Wide World Photos. Page 668: AP/Wide World Photos. Page 670: Library of Congress. Page 674: (top) Walter Sanders/Life Magazine, (bottom) AP/Wide World Photos. Page 675: AP/Wide World Photos. Page 677: U.S. Army/AP-Wide World Photos. Page 680: Howard Sochurek/Life Magazine. Page 681: AP/Wide World Photos. Page 682: Sygma. Page 684: Jean-Pierre Laffont/Sygma. Page 685: Green/Sygma. Page 687: Michel J. Philippot/Sygma. Page 688: © Jeff MacNelly/Tribune Media Services.

Appendix
Opener: The New York Post. Page A7: Arnold Sachs/Consolidated News Pictures. Page A8: AP/Wide World Photos.

Index